ELEVENTH EDITION

ACCOUNTANTS' HANDBOOK

VOLUME ONE:

FINANCIAL ACCOUNTING AND GENERAL TOPICS

Subscriber Update Service

BECOME A SUBSCRIBER!

Did you purchase this product from a bookstore?

If you did, it's important for you to become a subscriber. John Wiley & Sons, Inc., may publish, on a periodic basis, supplements and new editions to reflect the latest changes in the subject matter that you **need to know** in order to stay competitive in this ever-changing industry. By contacting the Wiley office nearest you, you'll receive any current update at no additional charge. In addition, you'll receive future updates and revised or related volumes on a 30-day examination review.

If you purchased this product directly from John Wiley & Sons, Inc., we have already recorded your subscription for this update service.

To become a subscriber, please call **1-800-225-5945** or send your name, company name (if applicable), address, and the title of the product to:

mailing address: **Supplement Department**
John Wiley & Sons, Inc.
One Wiley Drive
Somerset, NJ 08875

e-mail: **subscriber@wiley.com**
fax: **1-732-302-2300**
online: **www.wiley.com**

For customers outside the United States, please contact the Wiley office nearest you:

Professional & Reference Division
John Wiley & Sons Canada, Ltd.
22 Worcester Road
Rexdale, Ontario M9W 1L1
CANADA
(416) 675-3580
Phone: 1-800-567-4797
Fax: 1-800-565-6802
canada@jwiley.com

Jacaranda Wiley Ltd.
PRT Division
P.O. Box 174
North Ryde, NSW 2113
AUSTRALIA
Phone: (02) 805-1100
Fax: (02) 805-1597
headoffice@jacwiley.com.au

John Wiley & Sons, Ltd.
Baffins Lane
Chichester
West Sussex, PO19 1UD
ENGLAND
Phone: (44) 1243 779777
Fax: (44) 1243 770638
cs-books@wiley.co.uk

John Wiley & Sons (SEA) Pte., Ltd.
2 Clementi Loop #02-01
SINGAPORE 129809
Phone: 65 463 2400
Fax: 65 463 4605; 65 463 4604
wiley@singnet.com.sg

For updates to the chapters prior to the availability of the supplements, please go to www.wiley.com/go/accountantshandbook11E.

ELEVENTH EDITION

ACCOUNTANTS' HANDBOOK

VOLUME ONE:

FINANCIAL ACCOUNTING AND GENERAL TOPICS

D. R. CARMICHAEL
O. RAY WHITTINGTON
LYNFORD GRAHAM

BICENTENNIAL
1807
WILEY
2007
BICENTENNIAL

JOHN WILEY & SONS, INC.

Library of Congress Cataloging-in-Publication Data:

ISBN 978-0-471-79038-9

Printed in the United States of America.

10 9 8 7 6 5 4 3 2 1

ABOUT THE EDITORS

Ray Whittington, PhD, CPA, CMA, CIA, is the Dean of the College of Commerce at DePaul University. Prior to joining the faculty at DePaul, Professor Whittington was the Director of Accountancy at San Diego State University. From 1989 through 1991, he was the Director of Auditing Research for the American Institute of Certified Public Accountants (AICPA), and he previously was on the audit staff of KPMG. He was a member of the Auditing Standards Board of the AICPA and has previously served as a member of the Accounting and Review Services Committee and the Board of Regents of the Institute of International Auditors. Professor Whittington has published numerous textbooks, articles, monographs, and continuing education courses.

Lynford Graham, CPA, PhD, CFE is a Certified Public Accountant with more than 25 years of public accounting experience in audit practice and national policy development groups. He was a Partner and the Director of Audit Policy for BDO Seidman, LLP, and was a National Accounting & SEC Consulting Partner for Coopers & Lybrand, responsible for the technical issues research function and database, auditing research, audit automation and audit sampling techniques. Prior to joining BDO Seidman LLP, Dr. Graham was an Associate Professor of Accounting and Information Systems and a Graduate Faculty Fellow at Rutgers University in Newark, New Jersey, where he taught primarily financial accounting courses. Dr. Graham is a member of the American Institute of Certified Public Accountants, and a recent past member of the AICPA Auditing Standards Board. He is a Certified Fraud Examiner and a member of the Association of Certified Fraud Examiners. Throughout his career he has maintained an active profile in the academic as well as the business community. In 2002 he received the Distinguished Service Award of the Auditing Section of the AAA. His numerous academic and business publications span a variety of topical areas including information systems, internal controls, expert systems, audit risk, audit planning, fraud, sampling, analytical procedures, audit judgment, and international accounting and auditing. Dr. Graham holds an MBA in Industrial Management and PhD in Business and Applied Economics from the University of Pennsylvania (Wharton School).

ABOUT THE CONTRIBUTORS

James R. Adler, PhD, CPA, CFE, is founder of Adler Consulting Ltd., which specializes in forensic accounting. He has over 40 years of public accounting and academic experience working with generally accepted accounting principles (GAAP) and generally accepted auditing standards (GAAS). He has had a diversified clientele, including public and private entities as well as governmental bodies such as the SEC, the U.S. Department of Justice, and the FDIC. He has written and lectured extensively on the professional standards and other accounting and economic issues.

Juan Aguerrebere, Jr., CPA, is a founding member of Perez-Abreu, Aguerrebere, Sueiro LLC in Coral Gables, Florida. He has served on numerous AICPA and FICPA committees, including the AICPA Technical Issues Committee, Group of 100, AICPA Joint Trial Board, and FICPA Accounting and Auditing Committee. He has over 13 years of experience in public accounting and auditing and over 20 years of experience in accounting for financial institutions. He has lectured on numerous accounting and auditing issues. He is a member of the AICPA, FICPA, a Diplomat of the American Board of Forensic Accounting, and a Neutral/Arbitrator for the American Arbitration Association.

Vincent Amoroso, FSA, is a principal in the employee benefits section of Deloitte & Touche LLP's Washington National Office. He has published and spoken frequently in the employee benefits accounting area, both on pensions and retiree medical care.

Ian J. Benjamin, CPA, is a managing director in the Not-for-Profit Services Group of American Express Tax and Business Services, Inc. Prior to joining American Express, Mr. Benjamin was a partner at Deloitte & Touche in their Tri-State Not-for-Profit and Higher Education Services Group. He is currently a member of the FASB working group on not-for-profit organizations and the Professional Ethics Committee of the New York State Society of CPAs. He is a former member of the International Accounting Committee and the Not-for-Profit Organizations Committee of the New York State Society of CPAs.

Martin Benis, PhD, CPA, is a professor and former chairman of The Stan Ross Department of Accountancy at the Zicklin School of Business, Bernard M. Baruch College, CUNY. He is currently a consultant on accounting and auditing matters to more than 50 accounting firms and organizations throughout the United States. His articles have appeared in major accounting and auditing journals.

Andrew J. Blossom, CPA, is a senior manager in the Public Services line of business of KPMG Peat Marwick LLP. He is assigned to KPMG's Department of Professional Practice, where he is responsible for handling technical inquiries related to governmental accounting, auditing, and reporting. Mr. Blossom is a member of the AICPA Government Accounting and Auditing Committee. He received his BS degree from the University of Kansas.

William B. Boles, CPA/ABV, ASA, CFP, is a shareholder in the Harrisburg, PA Certified Public Accounting firm of Boles Metzger Brosius & Ritter, PC since it was formed in 1978. He works primarily with business valuation consulting engagements and taxation issues. Prior to 1978 he was the Director of Tax Services for the Harrisburg office of Laventhol & Horwath. His experience as a former Internal Revenue Agent along with his other client work have provided practical insight on tax, accounting, and valuation issues.

Stephen Bryan, MBA, PhD, is an associate professor of the Stan Ross Department of Accountancy at the Zicklin School of Business, Bernard M. Baruch College, CUNY. He received his doctorate in accounting from New York University.

Luis E. Cabrera, CPA, is a technical manager with the AICPA's Professional Standards and Services Team. Mr. Cabrera was previously responsible for technical research activities as a senior accountant in the national office of Pannell Kerr Forster, PC. He was also an audit senior with Coopers & Lybrand and has served as an adjunct professor of Accountancy at the Zicklin School of Business in the Stan Ross Department of Accountancy at Bernard M. Baruch College, CUNY.

Joseph V. Carcello, PhD, CPA, CMA, CIA, is a William B. Stokely Distinguished Scholar and an associate professor in the Department of Accounting and Business Law at the University of Tennessee. Dr. Carcello is the coauthor of the *2003 Miller GAAP Practice Manual.* Dr. Carcello has taught professional development courses and conducted funded research for three of the Big 4 firms. He also has taught continuing professional education courses for the AICPA, the Institute of Internal Auditors, the Institute of Management Accountants, and the Tennessee and Florida Societies of CPAs.

Peter T. Chingos, CPA, is a principal in the New York office of Mercer Human Resource Consulting and a member of the firm's Worldwide Partners Group. He is the U.S. leader for the firm's Executive Compensation Consulting Practice. For more than 25 years he has consulted with senior management, compensation committees, and boards of directors of leading global corporations on executive compensation and strategic business issues. He is a frequent keynote speaker at professional conferences, writes extensively on all aspects of executive compensation, and is often quoted in the press. He is a member of the advisory Board of the National Association of Stock Plan Professionals and currently teaches basic and advanced courses in executive compensation in the certification program for compensation professionals sponsored by Worldatwork.

Walton T. Conn, Jr., CPA, is a Partner in the Department of Professional Practice of KPMG Peat Marwick LLP, where he works in the information, communication, and entertainment practice. He has spent four years in his firm's Department of Professional Practice in New York and is a former practice fellow of the AICPA Auditing Standards Board.

John R. Deming, CPA, is a partner in the Department of Professional Practice of KPMG Peat Marwick LLP in New York. He is a former member of the AICPA Accounting Standards Executive Committee and has served on a number of FASB task forces and EITF working groups. Mr. Deming has written numerous articles on a variety of accounting issues, including leases, business combinations, pensions, and employee stock-based compensation.

Brent W. Emrick, CPA/ABV, CFP, is a shareholder in the Harrisburg, PA Certified Public Accounting firm of Boles Metzger Brosius & Ritter PC. He joined the firm in 1980 as a Staff Accountant. He works primarily with taxation issues, business valuations, financial and estate planning.

Jason Flynn, FSA, is a senior manager in the employee benefits section of Deloitte & Touche LLP's Detroit office.

Sydney Garmong, CPA, is an Executive in the Financial Institution Group at Crowe, Chizek and Company LLC. Her primary responsibility is to address accounting and regulatory issues affecting financial institutions. Ms. Garmong is a member of the AICPA's Depository Institutions Expert Panel and several other industry committees which maintain an ongoing liaison with various regulators and standard setters including the FDIC, NCUA, OCC, OTS, Federal Reserve, SEC, and the FASB. In addition to addressing technical issues, Ms. Garmong is a frequent speaker at industry and regulatory conferences. Prior to joining Crowe Chizek, she was a senior manager at the AICPA in Washington, DC. During her three years with the AICPA, she addressed financial institution and financial instrument accounting, auditing, and regulatory matters. She served as the staff liaison to the AICPA's Financial Services Expert Panel, and worked on other related projects with AcSEC, an AICPA senior technical committee.

Martha Garner, CPA, is a director in the national office of PricewaterhouseCoopers LLP, where she is the firm's industry specialist for healthcare accounting and financial reporting matters. She has served on numerous AICPA, FASB, and Healthcare Financial Management Association task forces and committees dealing with healthcare financial reporting issues. She is a contributing author on healthcare matters for *Montgomery's Auditing* and the *Financial and Accounting Guide for Not-for-Profit Organizations*, and has authored numerous healthcare articles and publications.

Frederick Gill, CPA, is senior technical manager on the Accounting Standards Team at the AICPA, where he provides broad technical support to the Accounting Standards Executive Committee. During 19 years with the AICPA, he participated in the development of numerous AICPA Statements of Position, Audit and Accounting Guides, Practice Bulletins, issues papers, journal articles, and practice aids. He was a member of the U.S. delegation to the International Accounting Standards Committee, represented the U.S. accounting profession on the United Nations Intergovernmental Working Group of Experts on International Standards of Accounting and Reporting, and was a member of the National Accounting Curriculum Task Force. Previously he held several accounting faculty positions.

Alan S. Glazer, PhD, CPA, Named to the Henry P. and Mary B. Stager Professorship, is professor of Business Administration at Franklin & Marshall College, Lancaster, Pennsylvania. He was associate director of the Independence Standards Board's conceptual framework project and has been a consultant to several AICPA committees. His articles on auditor independence, not-for-profit organizations, and other issues have been published in academic and professional journals.

Andrew F. Gottschalk, CPA, is a senior manger in the public services practice of KPMG Peat Marwick LLP. He has over 15 years of experience serving state and local governments. He is a member of the Government Finance Officers Association, the Association of Government Accountants, and the New York and Illinois Societies of CPAs.

Richard P. Graff, CPA, is CEO of The Graff Consulting Group. He serves as a financial and business adviser to the natural resources industry and has coauthored numerous publications. Prior to that, he was a partner in the international accounting firm of PricewaterhouseCoopers LLP, where he served as audit leader of the U.S. Mining Industry Group.

Dan M. Guy, PhD, CPA, is a writer and consultant. Formerly he served as a vice-president of Professional Standards and Services at the AICPA. He is a coauthor of *Practitioner's Guide to GAAS* and *Ethics for CPAs* (John Wiley & Sons); *Guide to Compilation and Review Engagements* (Practitioners Publishing Company, 1988); and has published numerous articles in professional journals, an auditing textbook (Dryden Press), and an audit sampling textbook (John Wiley & Sons).

Wendy Hambleton, CPA, is an audit partner working in the National SEC Department in BDO Seidman LLP's Chicago office. Prior to joining the SEC Department, Ms. Hambleton worked in the firm's Washington, DC, practice office. She works extensively with clients and engagement teams to prepare SEC filings and resolve related accounting and reporting issues. Ms. Hambleton coauthors a number of internal and external publications, including the AICPA's *Guide to SEC Reporting* and Warren Gorham & Lamont's *Controller's Handbook* chapter on public offering requirements.

Philip M. Herr, JD, CPA, is the director of Advanced Planning of Kingsbridge Financial Group, Inc., Point Pleasant Beach, New Jersey, and is an adjunct professor at Fairleigh Dickinson University, School of Continuing Education, Certified Employee Benefits Specialist Program and Certified Financial Planner Program. He is admitted to the New York and U.S. Tax Court Bars and is a member of the New York State Bar Association, New York State Society of CPAs, New Jersey Society of CPAs, and Association for Advanced Life Underwriting. He specializes in the areas of: tax; estates and trusts; estate, business, and financial planning; ERISA issues and transactions; retirement, employee benefit, and executive compensation planning; and use of life insurance and insurance products. He also holds the NASD 7, 24, 63, and 65 securities licenses.

Karen L. Hooks, PhD, CPA, is a professor of accountancy at Florida Atlantic University (FAU). Her primary research areas are the public accounting work environment, sociology of professions, gender, ethics, and communication. She teaches undergraduate classes, as well as in the Master of Accounting, MBA, and Master of Science in International Business at FAU. Professor Hooks has been published in *Accounting Organizations and Society, Behavioral Research in Accounting, Auditing: A Journal of Practice and Theory, Accounting Horizons, Critical Perspectives on Accounting, Advances in Accounting, Advances in Public Interest Accounting, Journal of Accountancy,* among others. She received her PhD from Georgia State University.

Keith M. Housum, CPA, is a senior manager in the tax consulting practice of Ernst & Young LLP. He specializes in the Financial Services area. Mr. Housum has over six years of experience assisting financial services clients with a variety of tax issues. Clients have ranged in size from small community-based banks to large regional financial institutions. He began his career with Ernst & Young LLP upon graduation from Case Western Reserve University with a bachelor's degree in Accounting. He is a member of the Ohio Society of Certified Public Accountants.

Henry R. Jaenicke, PhD, CPA, was the C. D. Clarkson Professor of Accounting at Drexel University. He is the author of *Survey of Present Practiced in Recognizing Revenues, Expenses, Gains, and Losses* (FASB, 1981) and is the coauthor of the 12th edition of *Montgomery's Auditing* (John Wiley & Sons, 1998). He has served as a consultant to several AICPA committees, the Independence Standards Board, and the Public Oversight Board.

Richard C. Jones, PhD, CPA, is an associate professor in the Accounting/Taxation/Business Law Department of Hofstra University. Dr. Jones's teaching interests include managerial accounting and financial reporting. His research interests focus on auditing and the international self-regulatory accounting environment. Dr. Jones has also contributed extensively to AICPA publications.

Richard R. Jones, CPA, is a senior partner in the National Accounting Standards Professional Practice Group of Ernst & Young LLP, where he is responsible for assisting the firm's clients in understanding and implementing today's complex accounting requirements. Mr. Jones's particular fields of expertise are in the areas of impairments, equity accounting, real estate, leasing, and various financing arrangements.

Allyn A. Joyce has been a business appraiser for 40 years. He is principal of Allyn A. Joyce & Co., Inc., which specializes in litigation support appraisals and litigation support appraisal reviews.

Alan M. Kall is a principal in the tax consulting practice of Ernst & Young LLP specializing in the Financial Services area. Mr. Kall has over 17 years of experience assisting financial services clients with a variety of tax and accounting issues. His clients' range in size from small community-based banks to large regional financial institutions. He began his career with Ernst & Young LLP upon graduation from Cleveland State University with a BBA in Accounting. He is a CPA and a member of the Ohio Society of Certified Public Accountants.

Eric Klis, ASA, is a manager in the employee benefits section of Deloitte & Touche LLP's Minneapolis office.

Margaret R. Kolb, CPA, is a senior manager in Litigation Consulting Department of the New York office of American Express Tax and Business Services, Inc., where she provides litigation consulting, forensic accounting, and expert witness services to law firms and insurance companies. She has prepared expert reports and provided testimony in a variety of forums. Ms. Kolb is a certified public accountant in the State of New York, a member of the American Institute of Certified Public Accountants and the New York State Society of Certified Public Accountants. She recently served for two years on the Litigation Consulting Committee of the New York State Society of Certified Public Accountants.

Debra J. MacLaughlin, CPA, is a partner and the Deputy National SEC Director in BDO Seidman LLP's Chicago office. She has over 23 years of professional accounting experience and has served clients in both the public and private sectors. As Deputy National SEC Director, Ms. MacLaughlin assists the firm's clients and engagement teams in preparing SEC filings, performs prerelease reviews of registration statements and selected Form 10-Ks, and consults on related accounting and reporting issues.

Susan McElyea, CPA, is a director in PricewaterhouseCoopers Transaction Services Group. Her 22 years of industry experience includes corporations owning real estate not used in their business, commercial and industrial developers, home-builders, hotel owners, operators, syndicators, property managers, and retail clients with substantial real estate properties. Experience includes off balance sheet structuring, lease and transaction structuring, lease analysis, securitization and bulk sales transactions, cash flow modeling, due diligence services, private and public debt offerings, development of cash flow projections related to real estate syndications, and consultation regarding accounting and reporting matters with clients in structuring various real estate transactions. Additionally, she has served as an instructor for many real estate accounting and auditing continuing education courses and contributed significantly to the 1995 John Wiley & Sons technical research book entitled *Real Estate Accounting and Reporting*.

Benjamin A. McKnight III, CPA, is a retired partner at Arthur Andersen LLP in its Chicago office. He specializes in services to regulated enterprises, is a frequent speaker, and provides expert testimony on utility and telecommunication accounting and regulatory topics.

Francine Mellors, CPA, is a director in Ernst & Young's National Department of Professional Practice in New York. Her duties include consulting and writing on various accounting topics, including employee benefit issues, as well as serving as knowledge leader and publications director for the National AABS Practice. Prior to this role, Ms. Mellors served as a vice-president in the Accounting Policy Group at the Chase Manhattan Bank and as an auditor at Deloitte and Touche. She holds a BA and an MA in Hispanic Studies and an MBA in Accounting and Management.

John R. Miller, CPA, CGFM, is a partner and member of the board of directors of KPMG LLP. He is partner-in-charge of the firm's Public Services Assurance and Resource Management Services. Mr. Miller is a member of the Comptroller General's Audit Advisory Committee and a former chairman of the AICPA's Government and Auditing Committee and is a recognized authority on governmental financial management.

Lailani Moody, CPA, MBA, is a partner in Grant Thornton LLP's Professional Standards Group. Her responsibilities are primarily in the area of accounting and financial reporting, and, in particular, stock compensation, equity transactions, and newly issued accounting pronouncements from the FASB and the FASB's Emerging Issues Task Force. She was formerly a technical manager in the AICPA's Accounting Standards Division.

Richard H. Moseley, CPA, is a managing director in the Chicago Metro office of American Express Tax and Business Services, Inc. and the co-director of the Quality Assurance Department. Mr. Moseley is responsible for providing consultation services on accounting technical issues and preparing implementation guidance for new accounting standards. He was a member of the AICPA's Accounting Standards Executive Committee and a former member of the PCPS Technical Issues Committee.

Anthony J. Mottola, CPA, CFE, is president of Mottola & Associates, Inc., a consulting firm in areas such as litigation support, financial services, strategic planning, corporate oversight, transactions structuring, and systems and business evaluation. Previously he was a partner with Coopers & Lybrand, Spicer & Oppenheim, and EVP, and a member of the board of directors of Shearson Lehman. He was special assistant to New York City's Deputy Mayor of Finance during its fiscal crises and served as the first Practice Fellow at FASB.

Dennis S. Neier, CPA, is a partner in the accounting firm of Goldstein Golub Kessler LLP, a managing director in the New York office of American Express Tax and Business Services, Inc., and the associate director of the New York Litigation Consulting Department. Mr. Neier provides litigation consulting and support, expert witness, and forensic accounting services to law firms, insurance companies, and in-house counsel. He assists in all phases of the litigation process, from precomplaint through posttrial, and has testimony experience in a variety of forums. He is certified in New York and Louisiana and is a member of the American Institute of Certified Public Accountants, the New York State Society of Certified Public Accountants, the American Arbitration Association, the Association of Certified Fraud Examiners, and the American College of Forensic Examiners, and is a diplomat of the American Board of Forensic Accounting.

Grant W. Newton, PhD, CPA, CMA, is a professor of accounting at Pepperdine University. He is the author of the two-volume set *Bankruptcy and Insolvency Accounting: Practice and Procedures: Forms and Exhibits, Sixth Edition* (John Wiley & Sons, 2006), and coauthor of *Bankruptcy and Insolvency Taxation, Second Edition* (John Wiley & Sons, 1994). He is a frequent contributor to professional journals and has lectured widely to professional organizations on bankruptcy-related topics.

Paul Pacter, PhD, CPA, is director, Deloitte Touche Tohmatsu IAS Global Office, Hong Kong. His responsibilities include IAS technical questions, developing his firm's comment letters to the IASB, advising the Ministry of Finance of China on developing accounting standards, and managing the web site, *www.iasplus.com.* From 1996 to 2000 he was International Accounting Fellow at the International Accounting Standards Committee, London. In that capacity, he managed a number of IASC's agenda projects, including financial instruments recognition and measurement, interim financial reporting, segment reporting, and discontinued operations. Previously Mr. Pacter worked for the U.S. FASB from its inception in 1973 and, for seven years, as commissioner of Finance of the City of Stamford, Connecticut. He has published nearly 100 professional monographs and articles. He received his PhD from Michigan State University and has taught in several MBA programs for working business managers.

Don M. Pallais, CPA, has his own practice in Richmond, Virginia. He is a former member of the AICPA Auditing Standards Board and the AICPA Accounting and Review Services Committee. He has written a host of books, articles, and CPE courses on accounting topics.

Ronald J. Patten, PhD, CPA, is the dean emeritus of the College of Commerce and Kellstadt Graduate School at DePaul University. He was the first director of research for the FASB and a former associate in the firm of Arthur D. Little International. He is the coauthor of *CPA Review: Practice, Theory, Auditing and Law, First and Second Edition* (John Wiley & Sons, 1974, 1978).

Michael Ramos was an auditor with KPMG. Since 1991 he has worked primarily as an author, corporate trainer, and consultant, specializing in emerging accounting and auditing matters. He is now a Vice President at AuditWatch. He has published eight books including *How to Comply with the Sarbanes-Oxley Section 404, Second Edition*, and *the Sarbanes-Oxley Section 404 Toolkit.*

Ronald F. Ries, CPA, is the managing director in charge of the Not-for-Profit Services Group in the New York office of the American Express Tax and Business Services, Inc. Prior to joining American Express, Mr. Ries was controller, treasurer, and vice president of finance for Spiral Metal Company, Inc. He is an active member of the Accounting for Non-Profit Organizations Committee of the New York State Society of Certified Public Accountants and active in the AICPA. He is a contributing editor to *The Practical Accountant* and lectures and writes frequently on various business and financial matters in both the commercial and not-for-profit sectors.

Lisa A. Ritter, CPA, CFE, is a shareholder and member of the Executive Committee of Boles Metzger Brosius & Ritter PC. She joined the firm as a Supervisor of the Audit Department in 1989. She works primarily with audits, reviews, and compilations for businesses, government, and non-profit agencies, and also provides litigation support services. She is a member of the AICPA's Auditing Standards Board.

Jacob P. Roosma, CPA, is director of the New York office of Willamette Management Associates, specializing in business valuation. He was previously a partner in the New York office of Deloitte & Touche LLP and, before that, vice president of Management Planning, Inc.

Mark R. Rouchard, CPA, MBA, is a partner in Ernst & Young's financial services practice. Mr. Rouchard has spent his entire career serving financial institution clients and has provided a wide range of accounting and auditing services to some of Ernst & Young's largest banking clients. Mark currently serves on the AICPA's Regulatory Task Force. He has spoken at AICPA conferences and written for *Bank Accounting and Finance* magazine.

Robert L. Royall II, CPA, CFA, MBA, is a partner in Ernst & Young's National Professional Practices Group in New York City, specializing in accounting for derivatives and hedging activities and financial instruments. Mr. Royall has authored or edited all of his firm's technical literature related to FASB Statement No. 133, *Accounting for Derivative Instruments and Hedging Activities*. He regularly works with the FASB staff and SEC regulators to monitor emerging interpretations in this rapidly changing area. Mr. Royall is a member of the Association for Investment Management and Research.

Steven Rubin, CPA, is a firm director in the national assurance, accounting, and advisory services department of Deloitte & Touche LLP. Previously he was the director of accounting at another national firm and a principal and the director of quality control at a local firm. Prior to that he held key staff positions at the AICPA and taught accounting as an adjunct assistant professor at Brooklyn College of CUNY, his alma mater. A frequent writer and lecturer, he is active in the New York State Society of Certified Public Accountants, where he chairs its Financial Accounting Standards Committee, and is former member of its board of directors.

Warren Ruppel, CPA, was the assistant comptroller for accounting of the City of New York, where he was responsible for all aspects of the city's accounting and financial reporting. He has over 20 years of experience in governmental and not-for-profit accounting and financial reporting. He began his career at KPMG after graduating from St. John's University, New York, in 1979. His involvement with governmental accounting and auditing began with his first audit assignment—the second audit ever performed of the financial statements of the City of New York. After that he served many governmental and commercial clients until he joined Deloitte & Touche in 1989 to specialize in audits of governments and not-for-profit organizations. Mr. Ruppel has also served as the CFO of an international not-for-profit organization. Mr. Ruppel has served as instructor for many training courses, including specialized governmental and not-for-profit programs and seminars. He has also been an adjunct lecturer of accounting at the Bernard M. Baruch College, CUNY. He is the author of four books, *OMP Circular A-133 Audits, Wiley GAAP for Governments, Not-for-Profit Organization Audits*, and *Not-for-Profit Accounting Made Easy*. Mr. Ruppel is a member of the AICPA as well as the New York State Society of Certified Public Accountants, where he serves on the Governmental Accounting and Auditing and Not-for-Profit Organizations committees. He is also a member of the Institute of Management Accountants and is a past president of the New York chapter. Mr. Ruppel is a member of the Government Financial Officers Association and serves on its Special Review Committee.

Clifford H. Schwartz, CPA, is a consultant. Formerly he served as a senior technical manager at the AICPA and a manager at Price Waterhouse LLP (now PricewaterhouseCoopers LLP).

E. Raymond Simpson, CPA, was a project manager at the FASB. He served as project manager for SFAS No. 109, "Accounting for Income Taxes," and SFAS No. 52, "Foreign Currency Translation."

Gary L. Smith, CPA, is an Ernst & Young senior manager in the National Accounting Standards Professional Practice group with over 13 years of experience serving clients in a wide variety of industries and development stages. He is responsible for assisting the firm's clients in understanding and implementing today's complex accounting requirements. His particular fields of expertise are in the areas of inventories, income taxes, consolidations, financial instruments, pensions, and commitments and contingencies. Prior to joining national, he spent 10 years working in the Washington, DC area serving multinational, middle market, and entrepreneurial clients in the technology, communications, manufacturing, distribution, professional services, and real estate industries.

Ashwinpaul C. Sondi, PhD, is president of A. C. Sondi & Associates, LLC, a financial consulting firm and a member of the Accounting Standards Executive Committee (AcSEC) of the AICPA. He is a coauthor with G. I. White and Dov Fried of *The Analysis and Use of Financial Statements, Third Edition,* 2001. His consulting and research activities include the analysis of financial statements, use of accounting data in capital markets, analysis of the financial industry, and international accounting differences.

Joel O. Steinberg, CPA, is partner at Goldstein Golub Kessler LLP in New York City, where he specializes in accounting and auditing standards. He is a member of the New York State Society of CPA's Financial Accounting Standards Committee. He has authored several articles, and he provides continuing professional education in accounting and auditing.

Reva Steinberg, CPA, is a partner in the National SEC Department in BDO Seidman LLP's Chicago office. She has over 30 years of professional accounting experience and has served clients in both the public and private sectors. She works extensively with clients and engagement teams to prepare SEC filings and resolve related accounting and reporting issues.

Reed K. Storey, PhD, CPA, had more than 30 years of experience on the framework of financial accounting concepts, standards, and principles, working with both the Accounting Principles Board, as director of Accounting Research of the AICPA, and the FASB, as senior technical adviser. He was also a member of the accounting faculties of the University of California, Berkeley, the University of Washington, Seattle, and Bernard M. Baruch College, CUNY, and a consultant in the executive offices of Coopers & Lybrand (now PricewaterhouseCoopers LLP) and Haskins & Sells (now Deloitte & Touche, LLP).

Dale K. Thompson, CPA, is a senior manager in the Asset Management Services Group at Ernst & Young. He is responsible for accounting, regulatory, and business analysis of current developments effecting mutual fund, alternative products, and investment advisory organizations. He is a frequent speaker on regulatory matters at industry and firm-sponsored events. He is a member of the AICPAs and the Massachusetts Society of CPAs.

Judith Weiss, CPA, received her MS in Accounting from Long Island University, Greenvale, New York, and holds an MS in Education from Queens College, CUNY. After several years in public accounting and private industry, she became a technical manager in the AICPA's Accounting Standards Division, where she worked with industry committees in the development of Audit and

Accounting Guides and Statements of Position. As a senior manager in the national offices of Deloitte & Touche LLP and Grant Thornton LLP, she was involved in projects related to standard setting by the FASB and the AICPA. Since 1993 Ms. Weiss has contributed to several books in the area of accounting and auditing. She has coauthored articles on accounting standards for several publications, including the *Journal of Accountancy, The CPA Journal*, and *The Journal of Real Estate Accounting and Taxation*.

Gerald I. White, CFA, is the president of Grace & White, Inc., an investment counsel firm located in New York City. During the past 30 years he has engaged in numerous professional activities relating to the use of accounting information in making investment decisions. He is coauthor of *The Analysis and Use of Financial Statements, Third Edition* (John Wiley & Sons, 2003).

Jan R. Williams, PhD, CPA, is the Ernst & Young Professor and Dean, College of Business Administration, at the University of Tennessee. He is past president of the American Accounting Association and a frequent contributor to academic and professional literature on financial reporting and accounting education. Most recently he has been involved in the redesign of the CPA examination and is a frequent speaker on this and other topics of professional significance.

Alan J. Winters, PhD, CPA, is professor of the School of Accountancy and Legal Studies at Clemson University. Previously the director of auditing research at the AICPA, he has written many articles for professional and academic journals and an auditing textbook. He is a former member of the AICPA's Accounting and Review Services Committee.

Margaret M. Worthington, CPA, is a government contracts consultant. Prior to her retirement from PricewaterhouseCoopers LLP, she was a partner in the firm's Government Contract Consulting Services practice. She has over 35 years of experience in federal contracting matters. She is coauthor of *Contracting with the Federal Government, Fourth Edition* (John Wiley & Sons, 1998) and has published numerous articles on a variety of federal contracting topics. She earned her BS at UCLA.

Gerard L. Yarnall, CPA, is a partner in the New York Office Dispute Consulting and Forensic Investigations Practice of Deloitte & Touche LLP. Mr. Yarnall was previously Director of Audit and Accounting Publications at the AICPA. He has published and spoken frequently on a wide variety of accounting and auditing topics.

Michael W. Zelko, CPA/ABV, is a Manager of the Business Valuation Department of Boles Metzger Brosius & Ritter PC. He joined the firm in 1987 as a member of the Professional staff. He works primarily with business valuation engagements and taxation issues.

PREFACE

The eleventh edition of *Accountants' Handbook* continues the tradition established in the first edition over 82 years ago of providing a comprehensive single reference source for understanding current financial statement and reporting issues. It is directed to accountants, auditors, executives, bankers, lawyers, and other preparers and users of accounting information. Its presentation and format facilitates the quick comprehension of complex accounting-related subjects updated for today's rapidly changing business environment.

This edition of the *Handbook* continues the presentation of two soft-cover volumes; this edition contains a total of 49 chapters. To provide a resource with the encyclopedic coverage that has been the hallmark of this *Handbook* series, this edition again focuses on financial accounting and related topics, including those auditing standards and audit reports that are the common ground of interest for accounting and business professionals.

In the period since the last edition we have witnessed the initial wave of changes to accounting and auditing standards in response to the bankruptcies and frauds that prompted the Sarbanes-Oxley Act of 2002. Issues of earnings management, off-the-balance-sheet related business entities, unrecognized liabilities and the expensing of stock option grants are the focus of reinvigorated standard setting. Similarly, sweeping changes in the auditing environment such as the newly required audits of internal control (see Chapter 5 and the new structures for regulating public company auditors that have been put in place. This edition of the *Handbook* places those events and changes in context, and provides transition and understanding of the events that have led up to these reforms.

This edition provides expanded chapters on fraud and fraud-related issues, as these topics have become more prominent in the business literature and in practice, and management and auditors have by law and regulation, assumed, greater responsibility for preventing and detecting fraud.

In the period since the last edition, the harmonization of accounting and auditing principles has become an important element in the direction of standards setting, both for accounting and auditing. Few major accounting or auditing standards projects are undertaken without involvement or collaboration with the international counterpart standards group. While some may be concerned that this process may slow the standards setting process somewhat, the greater input from a broader cross section of business environment and the broader focus of the standards that are being set, may indeed provide a firmer foundation for promulgating more comprehensive and enduring standards.

Although the FASB continues to be the primary source of authoritative accounting guidance, other sources of guidance are important in today's practice. Pronouncements by the SEC, GASB, and EITF are important, particularly in specialized areas. It is necessary to look to the EITF and to the AICPA audit and accounting guides for guidance in industry-related or special-transaction areas. All of those sources of accounting guidance are included in the scope of this edition of the *Handbook*.

This edition of the *Handbook* is divided into two convenient volumes:
Volume One: *Financial Accounting and General Topics* includes:

- A comprehensive review of the framework of accounting guidance today and the organizations involved in its development, including the development of international standards
- A compendium of specific guidance on general aspects of financial statement presentation, disclosure, and analysis, including SEC filing regulations

- Encyclopedic coverage of each specific financial statement area from cash through shareholders' equity, including coverage of financial instruments

Volume Two: *Special Industries and Special Topics* includes:

- Comprehensive single-source coverage of the specialized environmental and accounting considerations for key industries, including a chapter on the film industry
- Coverage of accounting standards applying to pension plans, retirement plans, and employee stock compensation and other capital accumulation plans
- Diverse topics, including reporting by partnerships, estates and trusts, and valuation, bankruptcy, and forensic accounting

The specialized expertise of the individual authors remains the critical element of this edition as it was in all prior editions. The editors worked closely with the authors, reviewing and critically editing their manuscripts. However, in the final analysis, each chapter is the work and viewpoint of the individual author or authors.

Content of the chapters in this edition have been prepared and/or reviewed by professionals practicing in accounting firms, financial executives, university professors, and financial analysts and executives. Every major international accounting firm is represented among the authors. These professionals bring to bear their own and their firms' experiences in dealing with accounting practice problems. All of the authors and technical reviewers are recognized authorities in their fields and have made significant contributions to the eleventh edition of the *Handbook*.

Our greatest debt is to the authors and reviewers of this edition. We deeply appreciate the value and importance of their time and efforts. We also acknowledge our debt to the editors of and contributors to ten earlier editions of the *Handbook*. This edition draws heavily on the accumulated knowledge of those earlier editions. Finally, we wish to thank John DeRemigis and Judy Howarth at John Wiley & Sons, Inc., for handling the many details of organizing and coordinating this effort.

For convenience, the pronoun "he" is used in this book to refer nonspecifically to the accountant and the business person. We intend this pronoun to include women.

D. R. Carmichael
R. Whittington
L. Graham

CONTENTS

CHAPTER 1

FINANCIAL ACCOUNTING REGULATIONS AND ORGANIZATIONS

Joseph V. Carcello, PhD, CPA, CIA, CMA

University of Tennessee

1.1 THE SOCIAL ROLE OF FINANCIAL ACCOUNTING

This chapter provides background on the environment in which financial accountants carry on their activities, including the specific organizations that regulate or otherwise affect those activities. Although the accounting profession has historically largely been self-regulated, the collapse of Enron and WorldCom has led to the passage of the Sarbanes-Oxley Act of 2002. The Sarbanes-Oxley Act created the Public Company Accounting Oversight Board (PCAOB), which is charged with overseeing the accounting profession. No financial accountant can practice properly without understanding these organizations and how they not only constrain but also assist the performance of financial accounting and reporting services.

(a) THE OBJECTIVE OF FINANCIAL ACCOUNTING.   An important beginning point for understanding the social role and importance of financial accounting is identifying the objective that it should meet. Although there are many opinions as to what the objective should be, the most authoritative and influential is this definition provided by the Financial Accounting Standards Board (FASB) in its Conceptual Framework project, which was intended to develop a unified theory of accounting (see Subsection 1.3(a)(v)):

> Financial reporting should provide information that is useful to present and potential investors and creditors and other users in making rational investment, credit, and similar decisions.

Thus, according to this definition, the goal is to provide information that allows users to reach better decisions than they would without it. (For simplicity, the FASB uses the term *financial reporting* to encompass the activities of "financial accounting and reporting," which includes presenting both financial statements and the additional financial information that accompanies them. This chapter uses the term *financial accounting* in this broader sense.)

Usefulness may exist at the individual company level if management provides reports to investors and creditors when seeking financing or fulfilling various stewardship reporting responsibilities. Although this perspective undoubtedly explains why some aspects of accounting are regulated, it does not really provide an adequate basis for understanding the substantial governing structure. Instead, an economy-wide perspective is needed.

(b) AN ECONOMY-WIDE PERSPECTIVE.   This section addresses two key points that are helpful for understanding why financial accounting is important for the entire economy. The first section explains the connection between the well-being of society and the information that is presented in financial statements. The second section expands on the point in the first section that effective capital markets are central to an efficient economy. It also explains how effective capital markets are efficient processors of information.

(i) From Society's Well-Being to the Financial Statements.   The diagram in Exhibit 1.1 summarizes the following discussion by showing the links between a society's well-being and the availability of useful financial statements. An important ingredient in providing for the well-being of society's members is a sound economy.

Although a variety of factors contribute to a sound economy, such as an abundance of natural resources, a stable political system, and an appropriate work ethic, one of the most critical is

Exhibit 1.1   The role of financial accounting in society.

the availability of sufficient capital resources. Without adequate capital, manufactured goods and services cannot be produced or distributed to persons who want or need them.

In turn, sufficient capital resources are made available through effective capital markets in which those who need capital can obtain it from those who are ready to provide it. If these market participants can conduct their activities in an environment free from excessive mistrust or other similar uncertainties, they are able to establish fair prices for the capital in the form of expected returns. Consequently, fair prices will encourage the flow of more capital into the markets.

In order for the markets to be effective, their participants must reach good decisions about where to invest or obtain capital under appropriate terms for the risks involved. If decisions are made haphazardly, capital will not be allocated at a fair price to those who will use it most appropriately, and the economy will not contribute as much to social well-being.

A number of elements affect the ability to reach good decisions, and one of these is useful information. If capital market participants have no information or only false, misleading, or late information, then their decisions are not likely to be good. With useful information, they can assess the risks associated with alternative strategies and establish the appropriate price for the capital.

Naturally, many different kinds of information are useful to decision makers. Some may relate to a particular company, an industry, or the national and world economies. Some types of information may be rooted in past events, whereas others are predictions of future events and conditions. Of particular importance to the capital markets is financial information, which consists of monetary measures of factors related to alternative strategies.

Finally, one source of financial information is the financial statement (and other information) that users of capital resources distribute to capital market participants. Although this information by itself is insufficient for making the capital markets work well, it is generally considered to be helpful. Furthermore, the existence of a regular reporting system brings discipline to the process. Because corporate managers know that efforts to mislead the market will generally be revealed when the statements are published, they are less likely to present fabrications.

The important economic role of financial statements causes society to be concerned about the activities of financial accountants and justifies setting up controls and other regulatory devices to help ensure the availability and usefulness of the information. As should be expected, these controls are aimed at preventing irregularities in the financial reporting system.

(ii) Market Efficiency.   The word *efficiency* is used in two different ways to describe markets. In economic theory, an efficient market is capable of allocating resources quickly and without friction. These allocations are efficient because equilibrium prices (where supply and demand curves cross) are reached quickly and uniformly across the entire market. In order to be efficient in allocating resources, a market must have a number of characteristics, including competition among a large number of buyers and sellers. Perhaps most importantly, it must have large amounts of useful information about the resources that are being traded. As described, the primary social role for financial accounting is to provide this information to the capital markets.

The second meaning of *efficiency* refers to a market's ability to gather and process this information. In this sense, an *efficient market* is able to respond quickly and appropriately to new relevant and reliable information, without regard to its source. This concept has been developed and advanced over the last 30 years in finance and accounting research into the functioning of U.S. capital markets, especially the New York Stock Exchange (NYSE).

On one level, this proposition that capital markets are efficient processors of information makes a great deal of sense because there are large incentives for market participants to gather and analyze useful information and then react to it quickly before others learn about it. These incentives also encourage the participants to seek out information wherever it can be found, even (perhaps especially) if it is not in published financial statements. In fact, the most useful information is that which no one else knows.

This point does not mean that financial statements are not useful to the capital markets; however, it does suggest that financial statements play a different role than the one that has traditionally been attributed to them.

This point does mean that sophisticated market participants must clearly understand accounting principles and the impact of management's choices among the available alternative principles. Because of this understanding, the market is able to react appropriately to the signals that it receives. As a result of this sophistication, the market does not react naively to accounting choices that are intended to present favorable results. For example, a decision by management to change from last in, first out (LIFO) inventory costing to first in, first out (FIFO) in a period of rising prices will lead to higher reported earnings. It would be naive to expect the company's stock price to increase because of the higher reported earnings because, in fact, its future cash outflows have been increased by the larger income tax payments resulting from the change. In the same way, an efficient capital market would not be misled by other accounting policy choices. In addition, an efficient market would be able to understand and act on the effects of unreported revenues and expenses. For example, a major controversy was created by a 1993 proposal (eventually leading to Statement of Financial Accounting Standards No. 123, SFAS 123) that would cause companies to report compensation expense equal to the value of stock options granted to their employees. A naive view of the market would argue that recognizing this expense would produce lower stock prices because it would cause reported income to be lower. This view assumes that the market is either unaware of or oblivious to the effects of the compensation because they are not presently included in the earnings calculation. Some opponents of the proposal argued that this expense should not be reported because it is not a real cost. If they are right in the sense that the expense does not really exist, then the act of reporting it would not affect stock prices because the efficient capital market would simply ignore the reported amount and establish appropriate stock prices despite the "noise" in the financial statements.

In addition to the logical arguments in favor of the proposition that U.S. capital markets are efficient, a great deal of systematic research has generated evidence that suggests that they are generally quite efficient. Although there is evidence that the markets are not perfectly efficient, there is abundant support for the broad notion that they cannot be fooled by differences generated solely by choosing different accounting methods.

(c) THE PARTICIPANTS IN THE FINANCIAL REPORTING SYSTEM.   Financial accounting does not take place in a sterile arena; rather, the people who conduct it have very real but quite different interests in the process and its outcome.

The primary communication channel is between financial statement preparers and financial statement users. Generally, preparers are accountants who work for corporations or other entities that need capital resources or that have stewardship reporting responsibilities. Users are investors, creditors, or advisors to those who want to commit resources to an entity or who have already done so. The self-interests of preparers and users clearly are in potential conflict.

Preparers want the reporting system to provide information that will help them get low-cost capital or that will cause them to appear to have lived up to their responsibilities. Preparers are also concerned about the costs of preparing and distributing reports and thus prefer reporting less information to fewer people. However, the efficiency of the capital markets suggests that preparers (and the stockholders of their companies) are likely to be better off if more information is reported.

Users, in contrast, are looking for truthful, inexpensively obtained, and dependable information that will enable them to make new decisions or evaluate old ones. As described above, they are not well served by information that misleads them through deliberate or inadvertent bias. If users receive unreliable information, the cost of capital will rise to compensate them for the added risks. If this mistrust is widespread, the economy will suffer because the capital markets will not be as efficient. Users also tend to want readily available, abundant information. This tendency is counterbalanced by the desire to have unique information, which is key to earning higher returns (because no one else is privy to it).

To reduce the uncertainty about the dependability of the financial statements, the services of auditors partially assure users that the preparers have not abused the reporting system by providing biased, incomplete, or otherwise misleading information. In effect, the auditors increase the credibility of financial statements. However, like the other participants, auditors have self-interests. In particular, they prefer dealing with information that is objective and can be verified because they are concerned (and reasonably so) about the possibility of second guessing by users who suffer losses after using audited information that turns out to have been incorrect. The trend in financial accounting standards to use fair values in lieu of historical costs can only exacerbate their concerns.

In summary, the three main participating groups have highly conflicting interests. In general, preparers want information that can be cheaply produced and will make them look good; users want unique information that no one else has; and auditors want information that can be successfully defended. In contrast, society needs the capital market to have widely available and inexpensive decision-useful information. Because of these conflicts, financial accounting and financial accountants have been and will continue to be subject to regulation.

This need for protecting society's interest has also led to regulating the activities of users through prohibitions against trading securities on the basis of inside or other misappropriated information. These rules are designed to assure that all market participants are playing a fair game, so that they are less likely to add undeserved risk penalties to the returns that they will accept from their investments.

(d) TYPES OF REGULATIONS FOR ACCOUNTANTS.   There are three general categories of regulations for financial accounting: standards for practice, standards for competence, and standards for behavior.

(i) Standards for Practice.   One effective regulatory policy is to establish rules governing the choice of accounting practices used in preparing financial statements. When companies use uniform accounting practices, they generate more comparable information than when each company makes its own choices. Reduction or elimination of alternative practices will also reduce or eliminate discretionary choices by preparers who are trying to present more favorable pictures. In addition, a set of practice standards gives auditors a basis for questioning or defending their clients' choices.

The standards used in financial accounting are known collectively as generally accepted accounting principles (GAAP). Originally, *general acceptance* denoted a consensus among a relatively small population of accountants that one particular practice was more common than others and therefore was presumably more useful. However, as practices grew more complex and required effective regulation, *general acceptance* has come to include designation by an authoritative body that particular accounting principles are suitable for use. Principles lacking this authoritative support are considered inappropriate.

A similar need exists for the conduct of audit procedures. Correspondingly, the practices to be applied in audits are known collectively as generally accepted auditing standards (GAAS). *General acceptance* here was also originally indicative of a consensus among practitioners but has come to mean *authoritatively mandated*. However, the PCAOB dropped the term *generally accepted auditing standards* from its vocabulary. Since its Standards are not based on the same process by which AICPA auditing standards had been set, it uses the term *rules*. The AICPA continues to use the term GAAS for standards issued for audits (private company, government and not for profit audits) that are not subject to PCAOB oversight.

Although the obvious main purpose of GAAP and GAAS is to provide guidance to practitioners, the standards also provide some assurance to statement users about the quality of the information they receive. In addition, they serve as an after-the-fact basis for evaluating the decisions of preparers or auditors. If accounting policies or practices prove to have been contrary to generally accepted standards, the persons who chose to use them can be more easily held responsible for injury resulting from those choices. Knowledge of GAAP and GAAS should help users understand (1) what the statements do and do not describe and (2) how much reliance should be placed on them.

(ii) Standards for Competency.   In addition to controlling accountants' practices, society also regulates the competence of individual accountants. By distinguishing between those who are or are not competent and by empowering only the competent accountants to perform critical tasks, useful information is more likely to be delivered to the capital markets. In addition, providing unique identification of competent accountants simplifies the search for them.

In the United States, the most common competence indicator is the license to practice as a certified public accountant (CPA). This license is granted by individual states and other jurisdictions, such as the District of Columbia, through an agency often called the State Board of Accountancy. Even though each state requires a candidate to pass the Uniform CPA Examination, there is substantial diversity in the additional requirements. Most states, but not all, require 150 hours of college education for licensure. Most states, but not all, grant certificates only after a candidate completes one, two, or more years of experience in public accounting. Some states also distinguish between certification and the license to practice. Aside from a generally recognized credential indicating a skill set in accounting, auditing, taxes and related subjects, the CPA designation permits the accountant to sign audit opinions on audits of public companies and practice before the SEC. In addition to the initial hurdles, most states impose "continuing professional education" (CPE) requirements designed to maintain the quality and the most up-to-date status of the CPA's competence. Some accountants in some states carry the designations Public Accountant or Registered Accountant. These individuals hold licenses that predate the creation of existing CPA requirements, particularly those involving formal education. In effect, these individuals were "grandfathered" when new laws were passed and were allowed to continue holding this designation. (*Public accounting* has been difficult to define precisely, but it is generally recognized as the offering of accounting services for fees to the public in general as opposed to the performing of accounting services solely for a single employer, whether a business, a not-for-profit entity, or a government agency.)

The CPA designation is not lost when the individual leaves public practice and is an important credential on the resumes of many accountants who work for corporations and government agencies. Other designations have been developed to provide additional evidence of the competence (or to provide evidence for those who choose not to qualify as CPAs) of accountants who are not in public practice.

The Certified Management Accountant certificate was developed by the Institute of Management Accountants (IMA). Although there is a rigorous examination and a requirement for experience as a management accountant to hold the CMA certificate, this designation does not grant the holder any special privileges or licenses to do anything not granted to ordinary citizens. Nonetheless, it is sought after and respected. CMAs are also required to complete ongoing CPE requirements in order to maintain their competency.

The Certified Internal Auditor (CIA) certificate is similar to the CMA, and is administered by The Institute of Internal Auditors. This designation does not grant any special statutory rights or responsibilities to persons who hold it. It is proving to be an important credential for advancement in the internal auditing profession.

(iii) Standards for Behavior.   In addition to standards for practice and competence, financial accountants are also subject to standards for behavior in the form of codes of ethics or codes of conduct. These standards distinguish between good and bad actions by accountants. To be meaningful, the codes must require more of accountants than other laws or morals demand of nonaccountants.

The accountancy laws in the various states generally incorporate a set of ethical standards. If the state authority determines that a CPA has violated these standards, it may revoke or suspend the license to practice. In other situations (generally involving some technical error), the authority may merely require remedial education.

Nongovernmental professional organizations have also established ethics codes to apply to their members. Under this arrangement, membership carries a higher standard of performance than would be faced without it. It also exposes the member to another investigative and sanctioning authority. The return to the member is a higher perceived level of ethics and some protection against the misdeeds of other less ethical practitioners. The most significant of these bodies is the American Institute of Certified Public Accountants (AICPA). There are other societies (also associations and institutes) at the state level. The Institute of Management Accounting also sanctions unethical CMAs, and The Institute of Internal Auditors sanctions unethical CIAs.

(e) REGULATORY AGENCIES AND ORGANIZATIONS.   Regulations and standards concerning practices and behavior are created by various agencies and organizations, some of which have already been mentioned. They often have the power to enforce the rules that they (or other organizations) have produced. These agencies can be classified into three categories: governmental agencies, standard setting organizations, and professional societies.

(i) Governmental Agencies.   The greatest regulatory power over financial accountants is held by governmental agencies established by legislative action to protect the public interest.

The most significant of these agencies is the federal Securities and Exchange Commission (SEC), which was created by the Securities Exchange Act of 1934. Among other powers, it was granted authority to establish accounting and auditing standards, and to discipline accountants (including preparers and auditors) who do not live up to those standards or to other professional standards of conduct. Although the SEC's jurisdiction extends only to the management, accountants, and other agents of companies whose securities are registered with it (approximately 17,000 in 2002), its influence is great because these registrants include the largest corporations in the United States. Furthermore, their accountants (internal and external) compose the most influential and powerful segments of the profession. Substantial additional information about the SEC is presented in Subsection 1.2(a) of this chapter.

As mentioned previously, the Sarbanes-Oxley Act of 2002 establishes a new entity, the PCAOB, to oversee the audit of public companies. Although the PCAOB is not an agency or establishment of the U.S. government, its existence and statutory authority is codified in federal law. The PCAOB duties include: (1) accepting the registration of all accounting firms that audit one or more SEC registrants, (2) establishing or adopting auditing, quality control, ethics, independence, and other standards relating to the preparation of audit reports for SEC registrants, (3) conducting inspections of accounting firms that audit one or more SEC registrants, and (4) investigating and, if necessary, sanctioning accounting firms that audit one or more SEC registrants for substandard practice. The PCAOB will function subject to SEC oversight. Substantial additional information about the PCAOB is presented in Subsection 1.2(b).

As mentioned earlier, each CPA falls under the jurisdiction of a state board of accountancy (see Subsection 1.2(c)). A CPA must meet the ethical requirements established at this level in order to obtain or keep the license.

(ii) Accounting Standard Setting Organizations.   In a unique blend of public statutory authority and private voluntary submission, two nongovernmental, nonprofit organizations—the FASB and the Governmental Accounting Standards Board (GASB)—create financial accounting standards. Both organizations are located in Norwalk, Connecticut, and operate under the funding and management of the Financial Accounting Foundation (FAF).

The FASB has power and influence through its designation in 1973 by the SEC as the authoritative source of accounting principles to be used in financial statements filed by SEC registrants. The FASB also gains authority through other organizations' endorsements, most notably state boards of accountancy, the AICPA, and state professional societies. An additional source of influence is participation in its deliberative processes by others affected by financial accounting, most notably statement preparers and users. Despite the importance of the FASB to the SEC (and to the effectiveness of capital markets), the Board does not receive funds directly from the federal government. However, contributions to the FASB by individuals and corporations are tax deductible, with the result that the Board is essentially subsidized through reduced costs for the donors. The PCAOB has continued to support the FASB as the source of financial accounting standards.

The GASB's influence is limited to establishing accounting principles used by state and local (but not federal) government entities. Its power comes through its endorsement by a variety of professional organizations composed of governmental accountants and governmental agencies, including state legislators and state auditors. Unlike the FASB, the GASB is partially funded through amounts appropriated by a number of state legislatures. It also receives some funds from the federal government, specifically the General Accounting Office (GAO).

More details about these unique and important Boards are presented in Subsections 1.3(a) and 1.3(b).

(iii) Professional Societies.   Of the voluntary professional societies regulating the practices of accountants, the largest by far is the AICPA, with approximately 330,000 members. This size allows it to have a large permanent staff of several hundred individuals who are responsible for regulating and providing services to the membership. The AICPA also depends on an even larger number of members to carry out its tasks through various committees. Institute membership is entirely voluntary but is virtually obligatory for CPAs who wish to stay informed and to practice at the highest levels in the profession. The auditing standards of the AICPA are set by the Auditing Standards Board, a 19-member board representing large and small audit practices, academic, government, and user groups. Estimates are that over 300,000 non-public company audit reports are issued annually. In contrast, there are less than 15,000 public companies, but the capitalization of the largest 20 percent of these public companies dwarfs the value of the smaller public and private entities that are audited.

Although similar to the AICPA, state societies of CPAs are separately funded and operated entities. They are also a curious blend of regulatory authority and service providers. Individuals who want to influence the profession in their state consider membership to be essential. All states also have their own professional organizations, which are called societies, associations, or institutes, according to local preference. They duplicate and complement the activities of the AICPA by offering CPE, publishing newsletters and journals, and providing opportunities for service and leadership through committee membership. Substantial ethics enforcement activity occurs at the state level and is controlled through a cooperative agreement with the AICPA, company referred to as JEEP. Recent years have seen state organizations playing a more active part in representing the profession's interests in state legislatures.

Through the Joint Ethics Enforcement Program (JEEP), the Ethics Division of the AICPA staff works with state societies and members of Institute ethics subcommittees to conduct investigations of alleged violations or to concur with findings conducted at the state level. These investigations attempt to establish only prima facie evidence that a section of the Code of Conduct was violated without trying to determine whether the member intended to violate it. JEEP leverages the expertise of the Institute staff to improve the overall quality and efficiency of the work that would otherwise have to be separately performed at the state level. This quality control helps ensure that the investigations protect the rights of the respondents while gathering appropriate evidence. Information about possible violations comes from other CPAs, clients, enforcement agencies, and public information, such as the *Wall Street Journal*, the *Public Accounting Report*, and SEC Accounting and Auditing Enforcement Releases. Despite the large investment in ethics enforcement, the most extreme disciplinary action that the AICPA can take is to revoke membership, in which case the CPA is no longer subject to the Institute's authority. However, the embarrassment may be substantial.

Other national societies exist, including several that are fairly large. Two of these are the IMA and the Financial Executives International (FEI), both of which generally consist of individuals who are not in public practice. Indeed, they can be characterized as organizations representing the interests of statement preparers. The Institute of Management Accountants (IMA) was originally called the National Association of Cost Accountants, and still draws most of its membership from management accountants. Nonetheless, it has played a leadership role in financial accounting standards setting through its position as one of the sponsoring organizations of the FASB. The primary units of IMA are its local chapters, which operate autonomously in order to best meet the interests of their own members. The Association also has developed a set of Standards of Ethical Conduct for Management Accountants, which requires the accountant to tell the truth to all who receive financial reports, including management and external users. The IMA administers the CMA examination and awards the CMA certificate to persons meeting all the requirements.

The Financial Executives International (FEI) is smaller than the IMA because it draws its membership from only those accountants who have substantial responsibilities in the financial area of their companies, including reporting. In addition, the FEI limits the number of members from any given company. However, because FEI members occupy higher level positions in large entities, the FEI often has more influence, particularly in dealing with the FASB as another of the sponsoring organizations. Another national organization is the American Accounting Association (AAA), which was originally created as a professional society for accounting educators. Through the middle of the twentieth century, the membership was more eclectic and included not only instructors but many practitioners. However, during the 1970s and 1980s, the AAA lost a large number of its members who were practicing accountants and became more and more oriented toward academic issues and services. Apart from the influence of individual members and the AAA's participation as a "sponsoring organization" of the FASB, it does not affect financial accounting practice to any great degree. As the major organization of accounting educators, the American Accounting Association (AAA) hopes to influence the long-term development of financial and other kinds of accounting. To this end, the greatest emphasis of the Association has been on promoting and disseminating research in accounting and finance. The AAA publishes three journals, *The Accounting Review*, *Accounting Horizons*, and *Issues in Accounting Education*. *The Accounting Review* tends to include the most rigorous and highest quality research articles published by the AAA. *Accounting Horizons* tends to publish more applied research articles. The AAA is a sponsoring organization of the FASB, and one Board member seat has always been occupied by an academic accountant. However, the Association does not have substantial influence on accounting standards because its members have not had the financial or political power possessed by others, such as the AICPA, the FEI, and the Business Roundtable.

1.2 GOVERNMENTAL AGENCIES

(a) SECURITIES AND EXCHANGE COMMISSION.   Although the Securities and Exchange Commission's (SEC's) jurisdiction is limited to publicly held corporations meeting minimum size criteria (registration is required for companies having at least $10 million in assets and at least 500 stockholders), its role as the primary regulator and protector of the country's capital markets has given it substantial influence over financial accounting practice.

(i) Background of the Securities and Exchange Commission.   The Commission was established by the Securities Exchange Act of 1934 and was charged with enforcing not only that statute but also the Securities Act of 1933. Previously, the 1933 Act had been administered by the Federal Trade Commission.

The SEC's prime mission is to achieve and maintain stable and effective capital markets for securities traded in interstate commerce. The nature of today's capital markets and communications networks makes it difficult to issue a security that is *not* traded across state borders. The SEC uses a variety of methods to accomplish its mission. The most basic is regulation of the activities of those corporations that have issued or would like to issue securities.

Under the 1933 Act, securities must be "registered" before they can be issued to the public. The purpose of registration is to establish a complete and widely available public record of information about the registrant and the securities. For example, registration creates a substantial amount of public information about the officers, directors, and other agents of the corporation, including promoters and underwriters. It also publicizes the company's plans for using the capital raised by issuing the securities. In the case of a company that has existed previously, registration also requires the presentation of financial statements and other financial data.

If the company meets the reporting requirements, the securities are allowed to "go public," regardless of their inherent riskiness. Thus, the registration process is designed to accomplish disclosure about the securities rather than to evaluate their merits. Although some states conduct merit reviews for securities traded within their borders, this approach would be very difficult to accomplish on a national level. Furthermore, many individuals believe that the capital markets should be as free as possible, as long as fraud and other forms of deceit are prohibited.

The 1934 Act went beyond the initial registration to require substantial ongoing disclosures about the corporation, its officers and directors, and its financial condition and results of operations and other activities. Thus, companies that have securities registered under the 1933 Act must provide quarterly and annual reports to the Commission, as well as ad hoc reports when crucial events occur. Again, the goal is to allow the capital markets to work effectively by getting information to market participants. The Commission staff may review the filed information for its compliance with the disclosure requirements, but there is no review of the merits of the management's behavior as described in the reports. For example, nothing in the SEC's processes prevents managers from paying large salaries to themselves, as long as the amount is disclosed. The idea is that disclosure will allow the market itself to discipline those managers who abuse their fiduciary duties. Of course, the disclosure requirement may very well have been designed to deter inappropriate behavior, because management would expect to have to suffer the consequences of publishing information about their activities. Nevertheless, the excesses of corporate top executive compensation is a contemporary topic of debate in the media, and has raised the interest of regulators.

The 1934 Act also gave authority to the Commission to regulate securities exchanges (such as the NYSE and the American Stock Exchange [ASE]) and those brokers and dealers who belong to them or otherwise conduct business for buyers and sellers of securities. This authority was expanded through the Investment Advisers Act of 1940 to encompass all who offer investment counseling. The fundamental goal of this arena of regulation is to increase market participants' confidence by reducing the likelihood of incompetence, fraud, or deceit. The line of reasoning is that if these problems can be reduced, more people are likely to invest, and if more people invest, the competition will bring about a more efficient allocation of capital.

Other legislation has given the SEC additional authorities and jurisdiction in the capital markets, but their contents are generally beyond the scope of this discussion, which focuses on the effect of the SEC on financial accounting. Subsection 1.2(a)(vi) of this chapter identifies the specific categories of regulations and publications that affect financial accountants and their clients.

It is especially important to note that the 1934 Act gave the SEC specific authority to establish accounting principles to be used by registrants in filed financial statements. This authority led to the issuance of Accounting Series Release (ASR) No. 4 in 1938, which stated that the principles used in the filings would have to enjoy "substantial authoritative support." It also stated that disclosure of a departure from such supported principles would not be an acceptable substitute for applying them. The effect of ASR No. 4 on the accounting profession is described in Subsection 1.3(a)(i) of this chapter.

(ii) Structure of the Securities and Exchange Commission.   Because the SEC is an independent agency, it does not exist within any of the three traditional branches of government (executive, legislative, or judicial). All five commissioners are appointed by the President and are confirmed by the Senate. In order to help maintain balance, and thereby boost public confidence in the capital markets, no more than three commissioners can be members of the same political party. The basic term for a commissioner is five years with the possibility of unlimited reappointments. However, history shows that it is unusual for a commissioner to complete an entire term. Most commissioners are attorneys by training, although some have had other backgrounds. One commissioner is designated by the President to serve as the chairman and has special administrative responsibilities and acts as a spokesperson for the entire commission. However, the chairman has only one vote, and thus actually has no more authority than the other commissioners.

As is true with most major organizations, a large professional staff supports the work of the commissioners. The SEC has over 2,900 employees at its Washington, D.C., headquarters and its regional offices in New York, Miami, Chicago, Denver, and Los Angeles. A number of divisions and offices deal with particular regulatory activities. The three that financial accountants are most likely to come into contact with are:

- The Division of Corporation Finance (DCF)
- The Office of the Chief Accountant (OCA)
- The Division of Enforcement

In dealing with their responsibilities, all three report directly and independently to the Commission. However, they also work closely with one another to coordinate their activities and to avoid contradictions and confusion. Exhibit 1.2 is a diagram of their interrelationships and the points of usual interface with the public.

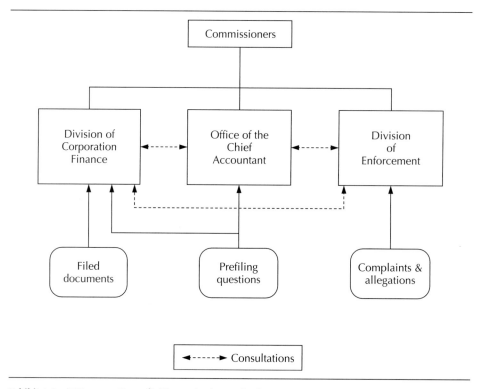

Exhibit 1.2   SEC accounting activities and suborganizations.

(iii) Division of Corporation Finance.   With a staff of several hundred people, the largest of these three sections of the SEC is the DCF, or Corp Fin. Its fundamental responsibility is to process filed documents received from registrants to determine whether they comply with the appropriate disclosure regulations. The DCF staff consists of attorneys, accountants, and financial analysts, and is organized by industry specialties. The Director is advised by a Chief Accountant for the Division, who is not the same person as the Commission's Chief Accountant.

In the process of reviewing filings, the DCF staff encounters questions about the suitability of the accounting principles applied to registrants' transactions or situations. Some registrants are careful to raise these kinds of questions before they file documents in order to determine the principles that the staff believes are applicable. In either situation, the DCF staff often resolves these questions using published GAAP or precedents established in earlier cases. In more complicated or groundbreaking situations, the DCF chief accountant consults with the Commission's OCA.

(iv) Office of the Chief Accountant.   The Commission's primary adviser on financial accounting issues and policy is the Chief Accountant, who is appointed by the Chairman and serves at his or her discretion. The OCA is supported by a professional staff, all of whom are experienced accountants, except for one attorney. As indicated in Exhibit 1.2, the OCA works with the DCF chief accountant to resolve issues raised in filings or by prefiling questions. The diagram also shows that some of these prefiling questions may come directly to the OCA.

In order to identify the accounting and auditing practices that have "substantial authoritative support," the OCA first tries to determine what the authoritative literature says about the issue, turning to its own pronouncements and interpretations only when that literature is silent or ambiguous. In conducting their research, the OCA staff members frequently consult with the FASB staff. It is also common for the registrant who raised the question to meet with the SEC staff to explain the facts and circumstances surrounding the issue and to present its point of view. When the question cannot be resolved satisfactorily from the literature, the OCA develops an answer with the goal of providing "full and fair disclosure." To present a united position on the issue, the OCA and DCF establish together what ought to be done. If the registrant does not agree with the answer, SEC procedures allow it to appeal to the full Commission. However, as a practical matter, registrants seldom make this appeal because the Commissioners virtually always support the staff.

In addition to dealing with situation-specific issues, OCA also advises the Commission on major policy matters affecting financial reporting. This role involves preparing recommendations that new SEC rules be created for registrants. It also involves overseeing standard setters, specifically the FASB. The OCA is heavily involved in overseeing the PCAOB.

(v) Division of Enforcement. The third segment of the SEC staff that commonly interfaces with financial accountants is the Division of Enforcement, which is charged with investigating violations of the statutes and regulations and recommending disciplinary action. Information about possible violations comes from a wide variety of sources, including the OCA and DCF, as well as news reports and direct complaints from individuals. When violations appear to be other than merely inadvertent or technical, the Division of Enforcement is responsible for determining whether and how to pursue a case and for discovering the facts. In some situations, the division may recommend that the Commission reach a settlement with the alleged offenders without a judicial finding. Although the findings are made public, the subjects neither admit nor deny the allegations, even though some discipline may be accepted (such as suspension or permanent disbarment from practicing before the Commission). In far fewer situations, the Commission orders cases to be turned over to a U.S. Attorney's Office for prosecution in a federal court. Naturally, the Enforcement staff cooperates fully with the U.S. attorneys in pursuing these cases.

For violations of statutes or regulations involving accountants, Commission procedures require that the Chief Accountant of Enforcement consult with the OCA to ensure that the proper facts have been uncovered and that the authoritative literature has indeed been violated. These violations typically include failure to maintain proper books and records, preparing financial statements that do not comply with GAAP, issuing an unqualified audit opinion on statements that do not comply with GAAP, or conducting an audit without complying with GAAS. Although Enforcement does not have to obtain concurrence from the OCA to go ahead with a case involving accounting or accountants, a lack of concurrence would make it difficult to persuade the Commission that a violation occurred.

(vi) Regulations and Publications. Because the SEC is a government agency, its accounting literature is structured differently from the pronouncements published by the FASB and other standards setters. This discussion provides an overall view of that structure in order to help the reader understand the SEC's regulations and publications. Those interested in more detailed descriptions of SEC financial reporting requirements will need to consult materials developed by one of several reporting services or large accounting firms. Like other agencies, the Commission publishes its pronouncements in the *Federal Register*, which are then compiled and republished by proprietary organizations for sale to practicing accountants and attorneys, as well as libraries and others.

The two main sources of the SEC's authority over accounting are the Securities Act of 1933 and the Securities Exchange Act of 1934. Five other statutes also affect accounting, but less directly. They include the Public Utility Holding Company Act of 1935, the Trust Indenture Act of 1939, the Investment Company Act of 1940, the Investment Advisor Act of 1940, and the Security Investor Protection Act of 1970. These statutes give the SEC the authority to create rules and regulations that interpret the requirements to be met by companies under its jurisdiction. (As a matter of terminology, a regulation is merely a set of related rules.)

For accountants, the most familiar regulations under the 33 and 34 Securities Acts are Regulation S-X (17 CFR 210) and Regulation S-K (17 CFR 229). Regulation S-X describes the accounting and auditing requirements that registrants must meet, including not only the financial statements but also the qualifications of (including independence) and reports filed by accountants who practice before the Commission. It consists of 13 Articles, including:

1	Application of Regulation S-X
2	Qualifications and reports of accountants
3	General instructions for financial statements
3A	Consolidated and combined financial statements

Regulation S-K includes a large number of "Items" about which a registrant must provide information (in addition to the financial statements) in registration statements, annual reports, and proxy solicitations. Some of the Items are:

101	Description of business
201	Market price of and dividends on common equity
303	Management's discussion and analysis
304	Changes in and disagreements with accountants
402	Executive compensation
404	Certain relationships and related party transactions
504	Use of proceeds
702	Indemnification of officers and directors

Some registrants are not required to comply with Regulation S-K; for example, small companies that fall under Regulation D of 17 CFR 230 are exempt, as are investment advisers.

At the next level below regulations and forms are Commission Releases, which are essentially official communications between the SEC and the public. They announce changes in the regulations and forms, interpret the regulations, describe various Commission enforcement activities, or declare general Commission policy. The SEC issues these publications only after a majority vote of the Commissioners.

Several types of releases are related to the statutes and regulations. Releases concerning matters under the 1933 Act are called *Securities Releases*. When they are published in the *Federal Register*, they are given a number with a "33-" prefix. Releases concerning the 1934 Act are called *Exchange Act Releases*, and have a "34-" prefix in the *Register*. Releases concerned with Regulations S-X and S-K fall into two categories. As might be expected, Financial Reporting Releases (FRR) announce changes and interpretations of these two Regulations. They are published with an "FR-" prefix, although they are commonly identified in the accounting literature as "FRR." It is possible for a single release to have more than one designation. In fact, it is not uncommon to find a release carrying all three.

Accounting and Auditing Enforcement Releases (AAER) announce enforcement or other disciplinary actions against individuals, firms, and registrants who have been alleged or proven to be in violation of the federal securities laws or who have otherwise fallen under the SEC's disciplinary powers. They are published under the prefix of "AAER."

Until 1982, the Commission issued ASR, concerning both financial reporting matters and enforcement actions. In that year, the separate FR and AAER series were created to avoid the confusion of dealing with the two different kinds of actions in one series. The effective portions of the ASRs were codified in FR-1.

The fourth level of literature, staff advice, is directed from the SEC staff to registrants and other interested parties with regard to its interpretation of the regulations and forms. To help avoid arbitrary or otherwise inconsistent policies, these communications are generally subjected to substantial internal review involving two or more divisions or offices, including, for example, the OCA, DCF, and the Office of the General Counsel.

Although staff advice lacks the official standing of Commission releases, a registrant faces substantial difficulty in successfully opposing it in a filing. As with every staff decision, the registrant can appeal to the Commissioners for an exception, but history has shown that few are willing to go to the expense and trouble, and fewer still succeed in overturning the staff's position.

Three categories of staff advice are of interest to accountants. Staff Accounting Bulletins (SAB) are probably the most familiar. They are issued by DCF and the OCA. A SAB is published to describe an interpretation that the staff has made either for a series of filings with similar facts and situations or for one filing that dealt with an unusual situation or that took a novel approach to the authoritative literature. The SAB assists registrants through a troubled area or lets them know that a particular approach will not pass the staff's review.

(vii) Summary. Even though the SEC has jurisdiction over only public corporations, without doubt it has exerted, and will continue to exert, a substantial influence on financial accounting by private corporations as well. The philosophy of "fair and full disclosure" permeates the practice of financial accounting for all companies, and the SEC's standards for independence and competence of auditors are fairly well established throughout the profession. The enforcement activities of the SEC are also important because they establish and defend norms of behavior expected of financial accountants.

Affiliating with a corporation registered with the SEC puts special demands on its internal and external accountants. No one should venture into this type of practice without substantial training and experience or without competent legal counsel. The requirements are extensive and complicated, and the penalties for not meeting the standards are considerable.

(b) SARBANES-OXLEY ACT OF 2002 AND THE PUBLIC COMPANY ACCOUNTING OVERSIGHT BOARD. The most far-reaching piece of federal legislation affecting the accounting profession since the securities acts of the 1930s, the Sarbanes-Oxley Act, was passed and signed into law in the summer of 2002. The Sarbanes-Oxley Act is a direct result of the allegations of financial reporting fraud at a large number of major corporations beginning in the fall of 2001 (e.g., Enron, Global Crossing, Qwest, Adelphia Communications, Tyco, and WorldCom, among others). The state of outrage in the country to these allegations of financial reporting fraud is reflected by the overwhelming votes in favor of Sarbanes-Oxley in both houses of Congress. The Sarbanes-Oxley Act passed the Senate 99 to 0, and only three votes were cast against the Act in the House of Representatives.

The Sarbanes-Oxley Act has 11 sections. These sections address: (1) the PCAOB, (2) auditor independence, (3) corporate responsibility, (4) enhanced financial disclosures, (5) analyst conflicts of interest, (6) commission resources and authority, (7) studies and reports, (8) corporate and criminal fraud accountability, (9) white-collar crime penalty enhancements, (10) corporate tax returns, and (11) corporate fraud and accountability. The first four and the last four sections are likely to be of greatest interest to practicing CPAs.

(i) Public Company Accounting Oversight Board. The Public Company Accounting Oversight Board (PCAOB) is charged with overseeing the audits of SEC registrants (hereafter public companies). All accounting firms auditing public companies must register with the PCAOB. The PCAOB is required to establish or adopt auditing, quality control, ethics, and independence standards for auditors of public companies. In addition, the PCAOB conducts inspections of registered public accounting firms. Finally, the PCAOB will investigate accounting firms for allegations of substandard performance and will have the power to discipline accounting firms and individual auditors.

The PCAOB has five full-time members, only two of whom can be licensed CPAs. Board members will be appointed by the SEC, after consulting with the Chairman of the Board of Governors of the Federal Reserve System and the Secretary of Treasury. The term of service is five years and board members are limited to two terms.

The PCAOB assesses and collect a registration fee and an annual fee from each registered public accounting firm. These fees are to be sufficient to recover the cost of both processing registrations and the required annual report that each registered accounting firm is to file with the PCAOB.

Although the PCAOB is charged with promulgating auditing standards, the Sarbanes-Oxley Act specifically requires that these standards include the following provisions:

- Registered public accounting firms must maintain work papers in sufficient detail to support their conclusions in the audit report, and these work papers must be retained for at least seven years.

- The issuance of an audit report must be approved by a concurring or second partner.
- Each audit report must describe the scope of the auditor's internal control testing. The auditor must include, either in the audit report or in a separate report, the following items: (1) the auditor's findings from the internal control testing, (2) an overall evaluation of the entity's internal control structure and procedures, and (3) a description of any material weaknesses in internal controls.
- Quality control standards related to required internal firm consultations on accounting and auditing questions.

In partial response to these requirements, the PCAOB implemented three auditing standards, effective in 2004. One on the auditor's report (AS 1), one on audits of internal control (AS 2), and one on audit documentation (AS 3).

The PCAOB inspects public accounting firms that regularly audit more than 100 public companies on an annual basis. It is intended that other public accounting firms be inspected no less often than once every three years. Inspections involve reviews of audit engagements and of the firm's quality control system. The PCAOB can report any violation of: (1) the Sarbanes-Oxley Act, (2) PCAOB and SEC rules, (3) the firm's own quality control standards, and (4) professional standards, to the SEC and to each appropriate state regulatory authority. The auditor's specific State regulations and a company's stock exchange regulations are also included in the scope of the inspections.

Registered public accounting firms and their employees are required to cooperate with PCAOB investigations. Firms that fail to cooperate in PCAOB investigations can be suspended, or disbarred, from being able to audit public companies, as can individual CPAs. Although the PCAOB does not have subpoena power (the PCAOB is specifically designated as a nongovernmental entity), there are procedures for the PCAOB to obtain needed information for an investigation via an SEC-issued subpoena. Documents and information gathered by the PCAOB in the course of an investigation are not subject to civil discovery. PCAOB sanctions include the ability to suspend or disbar firms or individual CPAs from auditing public companies, as well as monetary penalties as high as $750,000 for individuals and $15 million for firms.

The Sarbanes-Oxley Act amends the Securities Acts of 1933 and 1934 to define as GAAP those principles promulgated by a standard-setting body where the standard-setting body meets a number of requirements set out in the Act. The FASB's current structure meets the requirements set out in the Sarbanes-Oxley Act.

The PCAOB's funding, as well as the funding of the accounting standard-setting body (currently the FASB), are to be recoverable from annual accounting support fees. These annual accounting support fees are to be assessed against and recoverable from public companies, where the amount of the fee due from each issue is a function of the issuer's relative market capitalization.

(ii) Auditor Independence. The Sarbanes-Oxley Act specifically prohibits accounting firms from performing any of the following services for a public company audit client:

- Bookkeeping services
- Financial information systems design and implementation
- Appraisal or valuation services, fairness opinions, or contribution-in-kind reports
- Actuarial services
- Internal audit outsourcing services
- Management or human resources functions
- Broker or dealer, investment adviser, or investment banking services
- Legal services and expert services unrelated to the audit

The provision of any other nonaudit services for an audit client, including tax work, is allowed only if approved in advance by the audit committee. In addition, certain audit services (e.g., comfort letters for underwriters, statutory audits) must also be preapproved by the audit committee.

The Sarbanes-Oxley Act requires that audit partners on audits of public companies be rotated every five years. Also required is a timely report to the audit committee containing the following information: (1) a discussion of critical accounting policies and practices; (2) alternative accounting treatments discussed with management, the ramifications of these alternatives, and the auditor's preferred treatment; and (3) other material communications between the auditor and management (e.g., the management letter, schedule of unadjusted audit differences). Finally, a registered public accounting firm cannot perform an audit of a public company if that company's CEO, CFO, controller, chief accounting officer, or others serving in equivalent positions, were employed by the registered public accounting firm and worked on the audit engagement within one year prior to the beginning of the current year's audit.

(iii) Corporate Responsibility.   The Act specifies that the audit committee is to be directly responsible for the appointment, compensation, and oversight of the external auditor. The Act also requires that all members of the audit committee be independent. Audit committees are to establish procedures for handling complaints related to accounting, internal controls, and auditing matters, including complaints that may be submitted anonymously. Audit committees are to be given the authority to retain independent counsel and other advisers, if they deem this to be necessary. Finally, each public company must provide the funding the audit committee believes is necessary to compensate the registered public accounting firm.

The Sarbanes-Oxley Act requires the CEO and CFO of each public company to certify, in each annual and quarterly report filed with the SEC, the following conditions:

- That the CEO and CFO have reviewed the report
- To the best of the officer's knowledge, the report does not contain any material omissions or misstatements
- That the financial statements and other financial information included in the report fairly presents the entity's financial condition and results of operations[1]

---

[1] The authors of several chapters in the 11th Edition, for example, indicate in effect that some GAAP requirements cause financial statements prepared in conformity with those requirements not to fairly present results of operations or financial position. Based on those views, that places CEOs and CFOs in untenable situations. The financial statements that Sarbanes-Oxley Act of 2002 requires CEOs and CFOs to certify fairly present the company's results of operations and financial position are required to conform with GAAP, but preparing financial statements in conformity with GAAP would, based on those views, often result in financial statements that do not present fairly the company's results of operations or financial position.

Outside auditors avoid this problem by always linking the expression present fairly the financial position and results operations of the company with the expression in conformity with generally accepted accounting principles. Their message is that the financial statements fairly present only to the extent that financial statements that conform with current GAAP fairly present.

The reason the drafters of the Act omitted a reference to GAAP in the required certification apparently was to avoid the situation in U.S. v. Simon (425 F.2d 796, Fed. Sec. L. Rep P92,511). In that case, the defendants contended that the financial statements conformed with GAAP and that their audit conformed with GAAS. They asked for instructions to the jury that a defendant could be found guilty only if, according to GAAP, the financial statements as a whole did not fairly present the financial condition of the company and then only if the departure from professional standards was due to willful disregard of those standards with knowledge of the falsity and intent to deceive. The court declined and stated that the critical test was whether the financial statements as a whole were fairly presented and, if not, the basic test was whether the defendants acted in good faith. It found that an accountant is under a duty to disclose what he knows when he has reason to believe that, to a material extent, a corporation is not being operated to carry out its business in the interest of all the stockholders but for the private benefit of its president. The ultimate test is whether the auditor has told the truth as the auditor knows it.

The Act avoided that problem, but in doing so it introduced the risks of purportedly untenable situations. (This footnote was drafted with the assistance of the editors.)

- That the signing officers are responsible for the entity's internal control system, that the internal control system is appropriately designed, that the effectiveness of the internal control system has been evaluated within 90 days of the report, and that the officers' conclusions about the effectiveness of internal controls are included within the report
- That the signing officers have disclosed to their auditors and the audit committee significant deficiencies in the design or operation of the entity's internal control, and any fraud (even if immaterial) involving management or employees with a significant role in the entity's internal control structure
- Whether there have been any significant changes in internal control subsequent to the date of its evaluation

The Act makes it unlawful for any officer or director, or for any other person operating under their direction, to fraudulently influence, coerce, manipulate, or mislead the external auditor in the audit of financial statements.

The Act also requires the CEO and CFO of any issuer restating its financial statements due to material noncompliance with SEC financial reporting requirements to forfeit any bonus or incentive-based or equity-based compensation received within one year of the filing date of the financial statements that are subsequently restated. Profits realized from the sale of securities during this 12-month period also must be forfeited.

(iv) Enhanced Financial Disclosures. The Sarbanes-Oxley Act requires public companies to reflect all material adjusting entries identified by the external auditor. The Act calls for the SEC to issue final rules requiring issuers to disclose all material off-balance sheet transactions, arrangements, and obligations.

The Act specifically prohibits misleading pro forma financial information. Pro forma financial information must also be reconciled with what would be required under GAAP.

The Sarbanes-Oxley Act generally prohibits personal loans to executives. In addition, stock transactions by directors, officers, and principal stockholders must be disclosed by the close of the second business day after the date of the stock transaction.

The Act requires internal control reports in each annual report. Management must state that it is responsible for the internal control structure and also provide an assessment of the effectiveness of that structure. Moreover, the external auditor must attest to the internal control assessment made by management. Audits of internal control are the subject of a subsequent Chapter in this book.

Public companies are required to state whether they have a code of ethics for senior financial officers and, if not, why not. Also, any changes, or waivers to, the code of ethics for senior financial officers must be disclosed in a Form 8-K filing. Finally, the issuer must disclose whether the audit committee contains at least one financial expert and, if not, why not.

The Act requires the SEC to review the filings of each issuer at least once every three years. And issuers are required to disclose, in plain English, on a rapid and current basis any material changes in the issuers' financial condition and results of operations.

(v) Corporate and Criminal Fraud Accountability. The Sarbanes-Oxley Act imposes severe criminal penalties for prohibited forms of document destruction and for violations of the securities laws. Prison sentences of up to 20 years can be imposed for the destruction, alteration, or falsification of records in federal investigations and bankruptcy. The Act requires the SEC to promulgate rules relative to the retention of documents (including electronic records) by external auditors. Failure to comply with these SEC rules and regulations can lead to prison terms of up to 10 years. Finally, an individual who knowingly executes, or attempts to execute, a scheme or artifice to defraud any person relative to the securities laws faces prison sentences of up to 25 years.

The Sarbanes-Oxley Act also changes the bankruptcy laws to specify that debts incurred as a result of violations of the securities laws are not dischargeable in bankruptcy. In addition, the length of time to file a civil suit under the securities laws has been extended to two years after discovering the violation or five years after the violation occurred.

Finally, the Act provides whistleblowers certain protections against retaliation by the public company or its agents. For example, parties who knowingly retaliate against an individual for providing truthful information to a law enforcement officer relative to the commission of any federal offense can be imprisoned for up to 10 years.

(vi) White-Collar Crime Penalty Enhancements.   The Act amends the U.S. Code by increasing both the criminal penalties for mail and wire fraud from five years to 20 years. In addition, the Act imposes criminal penalties on CEOs and CFOs when they certify financial reports that do not comport with the requirements of the Sarbanes-Oxley Act. The penalties are a fine up to $1 million and imprisonment for up to 10 years for improper certifications, and a fine up to $5 million and imprisonment up to 20 years for *willfully* improper certifications.

(vii) Corporate Tax Returns.   The Sarbanes-Oxley Act contains a sense of the Senate—which is not a legal requirement—that CEOs should sign the corporate tax return.

(viii) Corporate Fraud and Accountability.   The Act imposes fines and potential prison terms of up to 20 years for tampering with a record, document, or other object or otherwise impeding an official proceeding. Also, criminal penalties available under the Securities and Exchange Act of 1934 have been increased.

In some cases, public companies attempt to make large payments to officers, directors, and others during the period of time the company is under investigation for possible violations of securities laws. The Act empowers the SEC to petition a federal district court to restrain a public company from making extraordinary payments to officers, directors, and others during the course of the investigation. The proposed payments would be placed in escrow for 45 days, and one extension of this 45-day period could be obtained. If the company is charged with a securities law violation, the contemplated extraordinary payments would continue to be held in escrow until the case was resolved.

The Act makes it easier for the SEC to suspend or permanently prohibit the ability of individuals to serve as officers or directors of public companies, if the individual has violated Section 10(b) of the 1934 Securities and Exchange Act or Section 17(a) of the 1933 Securities Act. Currently the SEC has to bring an action in federal court to bar individuals from serving as an officer or director of a public company.

(c) STATE BOARDS OF ACCOUNTANCY.   The other main category of governmental agencies affecting the practice of financial accounting comprises the 54 State Boards of Accountancy in the United States. (One board exists in each of the 50 states, the District of Columbia, Puerto Rico, the Virgin Islands, and Guam.) They have three primary regulatory missions: granting the initial license to practice public accounting, ensuring the maintenance of competency through continuing education, and disciplining licensees who fail to maintain their competency or who act in an unethical manner. States can also designate an authority to be followed for auditing (e.g., AICPA) or promulgate their own requirements. For example, New York and California adopted audit documentation regulations in advance of the new requirements in Statement on Auditing Standards No. 103, "Audit Documentation."

Because of the variety of forms (and names) for the boards, it is difficult to draw generalities. Some boards are separate freestanding agencies, whereas others are part of larger state regulatory bodies that license other professions and service providers. Funding for boards comes from general budget appropriations, dedicated credits from licensing fees, or some combination. Some boards are permanent and others are subject to periodic "sunset" reviews designed to avoid overregulation.

An accountancy board's first responsibility is to award the license to practice, which may do no more than allow the licensees to identify themselves as CPAs. In many states, the license is a legal requirement for performing the attest function (audit or review) for financial statements. The Internal Revenue Service accepts the CPA's license as sufficient qualification to practice before it by representing clients in the audit and appeals procedures.

All states require candidates to successfully complete the Uniform CPA Examination prepared, administered, and graded by the AICPA. In a few states, it is possible to pass the CPA exam and be certified without being licensed. The license is granted only after the candidate has completed an experience requirement. Other states do not differentiate between certification and licensing. Most states have an experience requirement, but some do not. Over 40 states have passed laws that do or will require the completion of an additional year's course work beyond the bachelor's degree before certification (the 150 hours requirement).

Most state boards require their licensees to participate in formal CPE. Typically, CPAs need 40 hours of class time (or its equivalent) per year to continue practicing. Some boards regulate CPE by specifying minimum hours in certain topics or by recognizing only courses offered by authorized providers, whereas others require only a report of hours completed.

A majority of state boards promulgate ethical standards of conduct through regulations interpreting the authorizing statutes; others have incorporated the ethics rules directly into their statutes. By and large, the ethics codes of state boards are the same as the AICPA's Code of Conduct, although local political factors often create differences. Because most states do not grant their boards sufficient funds to support a full-time staff for investigating allegations of unethical behavior, they must compete with other agencies for investigators' time and effort. In extreme cases, a finding of a violation will lead to revoking the individual's CPA license; however, boards do not mete out this punishment very often. Rather, they impose some rehabilitative discipline, such as a temporary suspension or the completion of additional CPE. In virtually all states, individuals automatically lose their licenses if they are convicted of a felony.

State boards are typically composed of unpaid volunteer practitioners who serve for three to five years. It is often true that at least one of the board members is not an accountant but represents the general public. This arrangement lends more credibility to the board, which may suffer from a "fox in the hen house" image caused by having only accountants regulate accountants. A difficulty in using volunteers is that the boards tend to get only part-time effort. Larger states achieve more continuity and sustained effort by having a full-time executive director and staff.

In order to gain by shared effort and to provide services efficiently, state boards have formed their own trade organization, the National Association of State Boards of Accountancy (NASBA). This group (which includes all 54 U.S. licensing authorities) provides a forum for developing unified positions on issues that can be used in individual states more effectively. For example, the NASBA directors agreed in 1989 to change the specifications for the Uniform CPA Examination. They also have developed a model code of ethics and a model accountancy law to apply in each state. These documents could be (and were) used to persuade state lawmakers to bring their statutes and regulations up to a national norm. NASBA also assists state boards faced by legislative threats of closure under sunset reviews.

Although the dispersion of certification authority across all states creates inefficiencies and inconsistencies, this arrangement is compatible with the policy of protecting states' rights against federal domination. Some professionals believe that this arrangement has outlived its usefulness, particularly for disciplining unethical accountants. Until such time as a federal agency is given a national licensing authority, however, financial accountants wanting to practice as auditors will need to be certified by one or more state boards.

1.3 STANDARD-SETTING ORGANIZATIONS

(a) FINANCIAL ACCOUNTING STANDARDS BOARD.   The Financial Accounting Standards Board (FASB) has a unique status as a private organization charged with protecting the public interest (the GASB, a related organization, is discussed in Subsection 1.3(b)). The SEC endorses it through ASR No. 150 (now codified within FR-1) as the source of "substantial authoritative support" for determining the acceptability of accounting practices for filings with the Commission. It has also been endorsed at the state level to the extent that state boards of accountancy include a requirement for complying with FASB pronouncements in their ethics codes. The FASB does not receive funds directly from either the SEC or state boards, but the tax deductibility of contributions acts as a de facto subsidy.

Although other private sector bodies, such as the AICPA and the FEI, endorse and finance the FASB, it is, by intent and design, independent of any of them. Of course, the governmental endorsements are contingent on the Board's maintaining an attitude of protecting the public interest.

(i) Brief History. Beginning in 1938 with the issuance of ASR No. 4, the SEC has given the accounting profession a loose rein to establish GAAP.

Shortly after ASR No. 4's release, the American Institute of Accountants (the forerunner of the AICPA) upgraded the level of funding, staffing, and activity of its Committee on Accounting Procedures (CAP). Over the next 20 years, it produced 51 Accounting Research Bulletins (ARB), including the all-encompassing ARB No. 43. The CAP did not survive because it suffered from two political shortcomings. First, it never was given authority by the Institute's council to establish standards that would be binding on the membership. Second, it existed within the Institute, which created at least the appearance that auditors' interests (and their clients' interests) were likely to be preferred to the public interest.

In response to criticism, the AICPA formed the Accounting Principles Board (APB) in 1958 and again increased the funding and staffing over the previous levels. During the next 15 years, the APB issued 31 Opinions and 4 Statements. In an effort to establish credibility, the APB's initial membership consisted of the top managing partners of major firms and other comparably influential accountants. Over time, the membership level slipped somewhat into lower levels of management, but highly competent technical experts continued to serve on the Board. In 1964, the AICPA Council acted to correct one of the deficiencies carried forward from the CAP by requiring members of the Institute to identify and justify their clients' departures from principles established by the APB. However, the second weakness still existed in that the Board was perceived as elevating auditors' and clients' interests above the interest of the general public in achieving full and fair disclosure for more effective capital markets.

In 1971, in response to growing sentiments and suggestions that the APB needed to be replaced by a government agency, the AICPA organized the Study Group on Establishing Financial Accounting Standards, under the chairmanship of Francis M. Wheat. During the following year, the Wheat Study Group recommended creating an autonomous standard setting body that would overcome the weaknesses of the CAP and the APB. That is, it would be granted authority to establish binding GAAP but it would not be housed within the AICPA. Thus, it would be more likely to escape the appearance of dominance by the interests of auditors and their clients. The proposal was accepted by six sponsoring organizations that provided adequate funding and other support to get the FASB established and operating in 1973. The original six sponsors were the AICPA, the FEI, the IMA, the AAA, the Securities Industry Association, and the Association for Investment Management and Research (AIMR). A critical event of the first year was the SEC's issuance of ASR No. 150.

Initially, the Board was still heavily dependent on the Institute and auditors for its funding and credibility. However, the previous concerns of dominance were raised in congressional hearings in 1975 and 1976, and the Board's bylaws were changed to make it less subject to the appearance of control by auditors and preparers.

The first chairman was a respected practitioner, Marshall Armstrong, who had been a member of the APB from 1963 through 1969. He was succeeded in 1978 by Donald J. Kirk, who had been a charter member of the FASB. Kirk served as chairman through the end of 1986, when he was replaced by Denny Beresford, who served until June 30, 1997. Edmund Jenkins, formerly of Arthur Andersen & Company, took over as the chairman on July 1, 1997. Robert Herz, formerly of PricewaterhouseCoopers, became chairman on July 1, 2002.

(ii) Structure of the Financial Accounting Standards Board. The FASB is actually only one part of a three-part organization, which also consists of the FAF and the Financial Accounting Standards Advisory Council (FASAC). The relationships among these entities, the GASB, and the Governmental Accounting Standards Advisory Council (GASAC) are diagrammed in Exhibit 1.3.

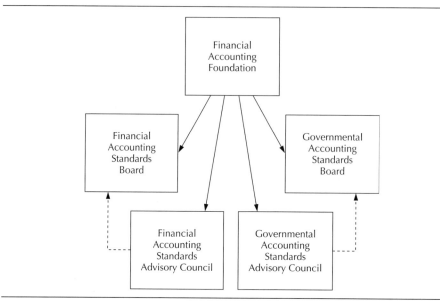

Exhibit 1.3   The structure of the Financial Accounting Foundation and the Standards Boards.

The Foundation is a nonprofit, tax-exempt Delaware corporation, managed by a 16-member Board of Trustees. They are responsible primarily for (1) raising operating funds and (2) appointing members of the two Boards and their Advisory Councils. A third unofficial function of the FAF is to shield the Board members from the kinds of pressures to compromise the public interest that shut down the CAP and the APB. Eleven trustees are appointed by the governing boards of the sponsoring organizations, and the remainder are selected by the other trustees. The creation of the GASB caused expansion of the Board to include three trustees selected by a consortium of organizations involved with local and state governments.

The Foundation bylaws strictly forbid trustees from tampering with the Boards' procedures in order to affect the standards that they issue. Of course, their control of appointments and reappointments gives the trustees substantial indirect influence. However, two of the more prominent trustees acted contrary to the spirit, if not the letter, of this restriction in 1992 through letters to the Board and other parties.[2] A major controversy arose in 1996 concerning the composition of the FAF Board after SEC chairman Arthur Levitt grew dismayed by the lack of any kind of defense by the FAF against public claims by some leaders in the FEI that the FASB was "broken and in need of substantive repair."[3] He began to privately urge the Foundation to voluntarily restructure itself to have a majority of its 16 members consist of individuals who unquestionably represent the public. (At the time, at least eight of the trustees, and possibly one other, were members of the preparer community.) When the negotiations broke down, Levitt took the issue public, first with a speech and then with a widely distributed letter that threatened to reconsider the standing of the Commission's ASR 150. As mentioned earlier, this release delegates rule-making authority to the FASB. There was no doubt that he was serious about change.

In a surprise move, the trustees engaged the services of a well-known public relations firm that specializes in fighting hostile takeovers and fired back at Levitt with a public letter that basically refused to acknowledge that the composition was a problem. Their recalcitrance provoked another public and prompt response by the SEC chairman that again threatened the Board's standing by

---

[2] Miller, Paul B. W., Redding, Rodney, J., and Bahnson, Paul R., *The FASB: The People, the Process and the Politics,* Fourth Edition. (Irwin-McGraw Hill, Burr-Ridge, IL: 1998), pp. 183–186.
[3] Id., pp. 186–192.

saying that the Commission was "required to take whatever steps [are] necessary to discharge our mandate." Private negotiations again resumed, and the FAF and SEC issued a joint press release in July 1996 that announced the appointment of four new trustees, all of whom met the chairman's criterion of being public representatives. He accomplished his goal that preparers would no longer dominate the trustees or the FASB. Levitt's sense of urgency was heightened by the fact that the trustees were about to initiate the search for a new FASB chair to succeed Dennis Beresford.

The FASAC was conceived as an experienced and informed microcosm of the Board's constituencies with the sole duty of providing feedback. It has operated that way with a membership ranging from 20 to 35 members who serve up to three one-year terms. Only the full-time chairman receives compensation. The Council has no fund-raising responsibilities and does not attempt to take a vote or reach a consensus on the issues. Rather, its job is to offer advice on projects that might be added to the agenda and on preliminary positions for existing projects.

The FASB itself has seven full-time members who must sever their relationships with their previous employers or partnerships. Each is appointed for a five-year term and can be reappointed for another. A member appointed to fill an unscheduled vacancy is eligible to serve up to two additional full terms. The FAF trustees designate the chairman, who has significant administrative responsibilities, including the leadership of Board meetings. In addition, the chairman is the Board's most visible spokesperson.

(iii) Board Publications. Although the FASB exists primarily to create financial accounting standards, it also interprets standards where they are not completely clear. In addition, it was given the assignment of developing broad theoretical concepts of financial accounting. Its position in the regulatory process and the demand from many accountants for detailed rules combine to create the need for implementation guidance. As might be expected, the FASB's publications reflect these tasks.

The main category of publications consists of Statements of Financial Accounting Standards (SFASs). They are numbered consecutively and, as of 2006, 158 SFASs had been issued. The ASR No. 150 specifically recognizes the authority of these pronouncements, and they receive similar support in state accountancy statutes and regulations. In addition, they are recognized by the Council of the AICPA as GAAP for the membership; any member not treating them as such will have violated Ethics Rule 203. Thus, financial statements must be prepared in accordance with these standards if they are to receive an unqualified audit opinion. The FASB recently adopted simple majority votes for issuance of a SFAS. Previously, five of the seven FASB members had to vote in favor of a proposed FASB standard.

Another category of publication, Interpretations (FINs), also establishes GAAP. However, relatively few have been issued since 1984, primarily because of the emphasis placed on other media for providing the kind of guidance that Interpretations were initially created to provide. Interpretations are numbered consecutively, and 48 have been issued.

A third category of Board document is the Statement of Financial Accounting Concepts (SFAC). These statements describe broader underlying concepts that the Board has determined to use in developing its standards. The statements do not constitute GAAP, and accordingly they are not identified as such by regulatory bodies or ethics codes. Nonetheless, knowledge of these statements is helpful for understanding the content of standards and for anticipating the direction of future standards. For these reasons, the Board's conceptual framework is described in Subsection 1.3(a)(v). Concepts statements are also numbered consecutively, and seven have been issued. SFAC No. 6 replaced SFAC No. 3, with the result that only six are in effect.

A fourth FASB category of publication comprises Technical Bulletins (FTBs), which are actually issued by the Board Research staff. They are narrow in scope and interpret the existing authoritative literature (i.e., ARBs, APBOs, SFASs, and FINs) to apply to situations not covered in it directly. Although Board members have the ability to prevent issuance of proposed FTBs, they do not formally vote to authorize their publication. Technical Bulletins are numbered in annual series, such as "85-3," which was the third one issued in 1985. The Board initiated FTBs in order to systematize informal advice that its staff was disseminating by telephone and letters; the use of FTBs expanded in the mid-1980s to reduce the earlier practice of issuing many highly detailed standards and interpretations. This change also allowed Board members to focus their efforts on more substantive issues.

To mitigate the need for narrow Board pronouncements while still providing quick responses to new problems (called *timely guidance* in FASB jargon), the Emerging Issues Task Force (EITF) was created in 1984. The director of the Board's research staff chairs this group, which consists of approximately 15 technical experts from major and regional accounting firms and large corporations. It meets periodically to tackle complex new problems by applying the existing literature. Transactions and events that have already transpired are the source of some issues, whereas others are based on proposed transactions. The SEC's Chief Accountant is an active participant in the discussions, despite being officially identified as only an *observer*. The Chief Accountant and the OCA staff are the prime beneficiaries of the EITF's activity because it addresses the issues that previously were brought to the OCA by registrants and their accountants.

When the EITF faces an issue, it seeks a "consensus," which is considered to exist if no more than two or three members object to a proposed solution. If more object, there is no consensus, with the consequence that the OCA is left to implement its own views. Alternatively, the Task Force may recommend that the full Board consider dealing with the issue. Prior to 1988, EITF Consensuses were not published, although minutes of the meetings were available from the Board. In 1988, the FASB began to publish highly condensed summaries of the issues and their resolutions. These summaries are presented as a public service because the outcomes are not necessarily the opinion of either a majority of the Board or the Board's staff. Under SAS No. 69, "The Meaning of Present Fairly in Conformity with Generally Accepted Accounting Principles," EITF consensus positions are considered level c pronouncements in the GAAP hierarchy. EITF consensus positions constitute GAAP if no level a or level b pronouncement exists. A consensus is acceptable for SEC filings as long as the OCA does not have a serious objection to its outcome. Like TBs, EITF issues are numbered in annual series. While adopted first by the auditing profession in SAS 69 to fill a void in the accounting literature, the implementation of a GAAP hierarchy by the FASB (currently on Exposure) will allow the AICPA auditing standards group to remove the GAAP hierarchy from its literature.

In addition to the above documents, the FASB also produces numerous other publications. The Board's staff sometimes issues implementation guides, in the form of questions and answers, on more complex financial accounting standards. These implementation guides are considered level d pronouncements in the GAAP hierarchy. Research Reports are developed in response to staff or consultant efforts to identify a problem, review the literature related to a set of issues, or propose answers. Discussion Memorandums and Invitations to Comment solicit views from the Board's constituents in early stages of deliberations. Three newsletters inform the public of the Board's activities: Action Alert, Status Report, and Highlights. Another widely distributed item is Facts about FASB, which describes the Board's mission, procedures, and membership.

Like many other organizations, the FASB has a site on the World Wide Web (*www.fasb.org*) that it uses for a variety of purposes. The site provides the public with access to press releases, major Board communications (including letters to the Board from prominent commentators and responses from the Board), and e-mail access to Board and staff members. FASB exposure drafts can be downloaded from the Board's Web site.

(iv) Due Process Procedures.   Like many other regulatory agencies, the FASB has established procedures to ensure that (1) parties affected by new regulations have an opportunity to express their views on the issues and (2) all possible positions on the issues are uncovered. Another desirable effect is that the public's participation bolsters the credibility of the output. Although the term *due process* may imply a rigid set of procedures, there is actually enough flexibility to allow the Board some freedom in determining how extensively to pursue various activities. Certain steps, however, must always be followed.

The following six basic steps take place:

1. Admission to the agenda

2. Preliminary deliberations

3. Tentative resolution

4. Further deliberations

5. Final resolution

6. Subsequent review

All six steps are public. Board meetings take place at the headquarters in Norwalk, Connecticut, and are open to all who want to attend, up to the room's capacity. Under the FASB's "sunshine" policy, Board members are not allowed to discuss the issues privately in groups consisting of more than three persons. This arrangement was adopted in the mid-1970s after criticism that the previous policy of "closed door" meetings caused some constituents to feel that their views were not being considered. The following paragraphs describe these six steps.

A project is admitted to the agenda only after substantial preliminary debate. The set of problems to be addressed in the project must meet several criteria. First, there must be diverse practice. Second, the diversity must create significant differences in financial statements, such that there is a potential for users to be misled or to incur excessive analysis costs. Third, there must be a sufficiently high probability that the issues can be resolved in a manner that justifies using Board resources. Of course, the agenda decision involves a certain amount of political activity. Ideas for problems come from the Board and staff, but more often from constituents and the SEC. The EITF deliberations have also created some projects. Apart from a Research Report, it is unusual for a publication to be issued in this phase.

The next step is to engage in early deliberations. Early during this stage, the research staff attempts to frame the issues and sound out Board members and constituents. For major projects, the staff may create a Task Force of interested experts from various constituencies to assist its inquiries. Occasionally, the Board will publish a Discussion Memorandum or an Invitation to Comment at this phase. There may be public hearings for especially significant or controversial projects in order to allow constituents to express their views and to allow Board members and staff to question persons who testify. Board meetings will generally be devoted to questions from the members to the staff and to each other. As the phase draws to a close, the staff efforts turn to helping the members find the common ground on which to build a majority vote.

The third phase is the tentative resolution. At this point in the process, a majority of the Board has voted to issue an Exposure Draft (ED), which is a proposed standard, concepts statement, or interpretation. The ED is exposed for comment for at least six weeks and occasionally for a longer period. More controversial projects may have another round of public hearings. Dissenting Board members' views are included in the ED, as well as a summary of the basis for the majority's conclusions.

During the further deliberations step of the due process, the staff and Board attempt to digest the comments received in response to the ED. Because the prior efforts have been thorough, it is very unusual for the comments to bring anything really new to the table. Many people who do not understand this situation often react negatively, particularly if they offered views that are subsequently not incorporated in the final standard. The Board's decision not to incorporate these views may be misinterpreted as failing to listen when, in fact, the presentation simply failed to persuade the Board. During this phase, Board members generally aim at fine-tuning the proposal to deal with unanticipated minor glitches. If significant changes are needed, a second ED may be necessary.

The final resolution phase is short and consists merely of taking votes from the Board members either for or against the "ballot draft" of the standard (or other pronouncement). The published document includes not only the majority's view but also the dissenters', if any. It describes the comments from the constituents and the Board's reactions to them. Many standards include an appendix illustrating the application of the requirements. Once this point is reached, the staff's efforts turn to responding to implementation problems.

In summary, the due process is molded to fit the situation. It can be prolonged to help the Board find its consensus and to gain the support of the constituency. It can also be accelerated to get an answer on the street as quickly as possible. Nonetheless, the purposes remain the same: to identify the problem, to uncover the answers, to develop a majority view, and to develop constituent support for that view. The Board specifically disavows any notion that the due process allows it to "count noses" to determine what a majority of the constituency wants. Its role is more judicial than legislative, and the Board members must reach a conclusion about what is best for the economy as a whole, even if particular groups are strongly opposed to the new accounting standard.

(v) The Conceptual Framework.   An important key to understanding the overall direction of the FASB's efforts to reform financial accounting is its project to identify a coherent theory of financial reporting, called the conceptual framework.

Because the CAP and APB were criticized for not developing a unified theoretical basis for resolving issues, the FASB's inaugural agenda included the task of identifying concepts that it could use in setting standards.

A critical initial decision in the project was to develop the framework from the "top down" by identifying the objectives of financial reporting and then working down to more specific concepts. This approach (also called *deductive*) had been tried before, most notably by Sprouse and Moonitz in the AICPA's ARS No. 3, "A Tentative Set of Broad Accounting Principles for Business Enterprises" (1962), and by the Trueblood Study Group in its report, "Objectives of Financial Statements" (AICPA, 1973). The opposite approach (called *bottom-up or inductive*) of looking at practice and identifying common threads had also been tried, most notably in APB Statement No. 4, "Basic Concepts and Accounting Principles Underlying Financial Statements of Business Enterprises" (1970). Statement No. 4 also used the "top-down" approach. Although there are several advantages and disadvantages to the two approaches, the main difference between them is that the bottom-up tends to encourage applying old solutions for new problems, whereas the top-down tends to lead to new solutions for old problems. Thus, the determination of the Board to pursue a top-down framework created a substantially greater likelihood that significant change in GAAP could be created. Accordingly, the framework project was (and has continued to be) controversial.

The SFAC No. 1, "Objectives of Financial Reporting by Business Enterprises," was issued in 1978. It presented a hierarchy of objectives, the most important being the providing of:

> ... information that is useful to present and potential investors and creditors and other users in making rational investment, credit, and other decisions.

However obvious this objective might seem on the surface, it is politically significant because it establishes that the interests of the public and financial statement users are to be ranked above the interests of auditors and preparers.

The SFAC No. 2, "Qualitative Characteristics of Accounting Information," was issued in 1980. It identifies qualities of information that make it useful for meeting the objective described in SFAC No. 1. The three primary qualities are relevance, reliability, and comparability. The important point to observe is that the Board chose qualities that reflect the users' needs instead of the needs of auditors (who prefer defensible information) and preparers (who prefer controllable and inexpensive information).

The third phase of the framework culminated in 1980 with the issuance of SFAC No. 3, "Elements of Financial Statements of Business Enterprises." It was superseded in 1985 by SFAC No. 6, "Elements of Financial Statements," which also encompasses the elements of financial statements issued by not-for-profit entities. The business elements identified by the Board included the familiar assets, liabilities, owners' equity, revenues, expenses, gains, and losses; however, its decision to make the assets and liabilities the keystone elements was enormously significant. That is, all the other elements, including "comprehensive income," were defined in terms of assets and liabilities. With this decision, the Board essentially turned away from the familiar matching concept of income that had dominated practice for decades with its emphasis on the income statement and its deemphasis of the balance sheet. Instead, under the conceptual framework, income is measured by changes in assets and liabilities because both the income statement and balance sheet are considered useful and important. There are tremendous practical implications in this choice, some of which have already been seen in SFAS No. 87 on accounting for pensions by employers, in

SFAS No. 106 on employee benefits, and in SFAS No. 109 on accounting for income taxes. In these cases, the reporting company looks to changes in assets and liabilities to determine its income instead of attempting to match costs with revenues in accordance with a predetermined or otherwise systematic or desired fashion.

SFAC No. 4, "Objectives of Financial Reporting by Nonbusiness Organizations," was also issued in 1980. (Subsequent to issuing SFAC No. 4 but before issuing SFAC No. 6, the FASB determined that the term *not-for-profit* was preferable to *nonbusiness*. In particular, the managers of a number of these entities complained that they did not like the inference that they were not "businesslike" in the way they operated.) It was the outgrowth of the FASB's decision to deal with all private entities, even though there had been no mandate from the SEC for doing so. This statement broke new ground because there had not been a significant effort to establish top-down concepts in this area. As might be expected, the main objective is similar to the one in SFAC No. 1; specifically, it says that the financial statements of not-for-profit organizations should provide:

> . . . information that is useful to present and potential resource providers and other users in making rational decisions about the allocation of resources to those organizations.

By starting with this objective, the Board again put into place the potential for substantial reform because it would be necessary to show how existing practices met this objective.

The Board encountered major roadblocks when it entered into the project's next phase, "recognition and measurement," because it was here that decisions would be reached on whether, when, and at what amount assets, liabilities, and changes in them should be reflected in the financial statements. The fundamental issue was whether there should be a movement toward including more market value information in the statements. Naturally, this phase of the project attracted much attention and created substantial controversy. In 1985, after more than three years of debate, six Board members (one dissented because he wanted to go back to the matching concept of earnings) agreed to issue SFAC No. 5, "Recognition and Measurement in Financial Statements of Business Enterprises," which was clearly a compromise. It says that things recognized in the statements should be elements and that the amount reported for them should be relevant and reliable. In effect, all that was accomplished was to affirm the contents of the preceding concepts statements. SFAC No. 5 also identified the cash flow statement as a conceptual member of the set of financial statements, and the Board eventually issued SFAS No. 95, which requires its presentation. SFAC No. 5 also identified two possible income statements, one of which would focus on earnings, whereas the other would report comprehensive income, which might include changes in current value. In 1997, after two years of deliberations, the Board issued SFAS 130, which requires companies to report the amount of comprehensive income, either at the bottom of its regular income statement or in a separate statement. This amount equals the reported net income plus and minus the changes in various unrealized changes in equity that are reported on the balance sheet. The standard addresses only the display of comprehensive income and does not introduce any new measurement requirements. However, the standard does set into place a means for reporting other components of comprehensive income, including changes in the fair market values of assets and liabilities that are currently carried at their historical costs or proceeds.

In 2000, the Board issued SFAC No. 7, "Using Cash Flow Information and Present Value in Accounting Measurements." Although accounting measurements are best determined using observable exchange transactions, sometimes measurements must be based on estimated cash flows. This concept statement provides a framework for using cash-flow based techniques for accounting measurements. SFAC No. 7 specifies that accounting measurements based on present value concepts should reflect the uncertainties associated with the underlying cash flows. SFAC No. 7 also introduces the expected cash flow approach to present value calculations. Present value calculations historically have often been based on a single set of estimated cash flows and a single discount rate, where the discount rate reflects the uncertainties associated with the cash flows. Concept Statement No. 7 states that a range of estimated cash flows should be considered and that this range of cash flows should be assigned their respective probabilities and then discounted. Measurement of the fair value of an entity's liabilities is to reflect the credit standing of the entity.

What, then, is the significance of the conceptual framework? It really needs to be interpreted from a political perspective more than from a theoretical one. First, it sets in place the possibility for significant changes in GAAP. Second, it puts users' needs (and thus the public interest) at the highest priority level. Third, it establishes that the statement of financial position should not be merely a resting place for debit and credit balances waiting to be "matched" in the future; rather, it should provide useful information about assets and liabilities. Fourth, the framework rejects matching in favor of reporting changes in assets and liabilities as income, thus raising the possibility that gains and losses from price changes could be recognized as income. Finally, it defines a number of important terms that are used in the Board's communications with its constituents and in its internal discussions. Far from being an empty academic theoretical exercise, the framework is perhaps the most significant set of pronouncements that the FASB has issued. The more that practitioners know about it, the more they will be capable of dealing with the Board and the changes that its pronouncements will bring about.

(vi) The Political Environment and the Financial Accounting Standards Board's Future. As established in the opening section of this chapter, and confirmed above, political factors very much affect financial accounting. Because accounting standards have the potential for changing the allocation of wealth among various groups and individuals in society, people are willing to spend time, effort, and money to try to establish the standards that they find advantageous. Because the interests of preparers, users, auditors, regulators, and the public can be in serious conflict, efforts to create or change standards naturally create disagreement, controversy, and dissatisfaction.

One pervasive political problem that just will not go away is standards overload. Originally, this phrase described the issuance of numerous detailed standards, but more recently it has come to encompass the issuance of complex standards that are difficult to implement, especially by smaller nonpublic companies. Exhibit 1.4 symbolizes the politics of this situation, showing that the FASB has received rule-making authority from the SEC to establish GAAP for use by public companies while, at the same time, it has received rule-making authority from state Boards and the AICPA to establish GAAP for use by private companies. It should be noted that these delegations of authority do not grant the Board any enforcement or broad policy-making powers. In fact, they have created the narrow but complex task of developing a single set of financial accounting standards that apply to both public and private companies.

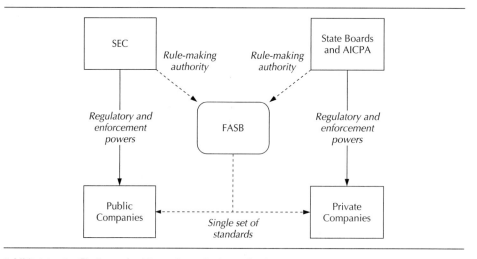

Exhibit 1.4   Conflicting authorities and standards overload.

The FASB's dilemma is that too much emphasis on SEC registrants seems to ignore the constraints affecting private companies, yet too much emphasis on private companies ignores the needs of the SEC and the public for effective capital markets. Because the SEC exerts the greatest political influence, it seems likely that FASB will continue to focus on the needs of more sophisticated users and will issue standards that may be difficult for private companies to implement. This choice leaves the state Boards and the AICPA in a difficult relationship with some of their constituents and members, but there does not appear to be any way out of this dilemma. Some have suggested applying different standards according to whether the company is private or public, but survey responses have consistently shown that a different set of GAAP for private companies would be perceived as inferior, and that users would probably demand that public company principles be applied in private companies' statements. Thus, it does not appear as if the Board will be able to change its position.

Another political problem for the FASB exists in its relationships with the SEC, Congress, and the preparer community. Beginning with ASR No. 150, the SEC has virtually always supported the FASB's efforts, with the exception of SFAS No. 19 on oil and gas accounting. The Board's existence allows the Commission to meet its own needs without appropriating public funds. It also allows the SEC to divert criticism to the FASB while a problem is being solved, or even after a standard has been issued. Thus, it seems unlikely that the SEC will seek to move standard setting authority into the federal government. Two particularly strong statements were issued by federal officials in 1988 and 1989 in support of the present arrangement. One came from SEC Chairman David Ruder when he expressed great satisfaction with the Board's efforts and results in a speech to an AICPA conference on SEC matters and in a letter to the Business Roundtable. (The Roundtable is an association of the chief executive officers of approximately 200 of the largest corporations in the United States. It is primarily a lobbying organization to help ensure the protection and promotion of the member companies' interests.) The other came from Congressman John Dingell of Michigan in a letter to Ruder, in which he fundamentally stated that he liked the existing system, and if the SEC did not protect FASB against attack, then the Congress would.

Despite this support, members of the Roundtable continued to call for fundamental reform in FASB's structure and activities on the basis that it was "too theoretical" for practice, "unresponsive to its constituents," and "out of control." In reaction to these pressures, the Groves Committee was formed by the FAF trustees to identify weaknesses and to recommend changes. In 1989, the trustees accepted a recommendation that they engage in more active supervision of the Board's activities. The specific response was to form an Oversight Subcommittee that will meet with Board members and others to assess performance of both the organization and individual members.

As briefly mentioned earlier in the chapter in the context of capital market efficiency, the FASB faced a major controversy from 1993 through 1995 in completing its project on stock-based compensation. The pivotal issue in the project was the question of whether employers would be required to report an expense for employee compensation paid with stock options. This particular controversy went to new heights when opponents of the ED took their grievances to some key members of Congress, who then drafted legislation that would instruct the SEC to reject the proposal if it was actually passed by the Board. Many other members of Congress also sent letters to the Board or otherwise expressed their deep concerns about the effect of the standard on American business. In light of the near certainty that sophisticated capital market participants were aware of the expense and were already estimating its amount, these efforts to squelch the FASB proposal were actually futile. Nonetheless, the pressure was unrelenting, and the Board announced in December 1994 that it would withdraw its proposal and substitute another alternative that would allow companies to choose between putting the expense on the income statement or disclosing its estimated amount and a pro forma measure of net income and earnings per share in a footnote to the statements. This alternative eventually was implemented in SFAS 123. The basis for conclusions section of the standard frankly proclaims that a majority of the Board voted for this compromise first because "the nature of the debate threatened the future of accounting standards setting in the private sector" and then states that the majority wanted "to bring closure to the divisive debate on this issue—not because it believes that solution is the best way to improve financial accounting and reporting." The victory for the Board's opponents was hollow because the information is there in the footnote for the market to see and use.

The failure of Enron Corporation, largely due to the disclosure of financial reporting improprieties, has resulted in fresh criticism of the FASB. Enron transferred nonperforming assets and liabilities into various special-purpose entities (SPEs). The objective of these maneuvers was to shield Enron from recognizing losses on these nonperforming assets, and to reduce Enron's perceived risk by reducing its reported debt level. Former accounting rules for SPEs did not require consolidation of assets and liabilities transferred to the SPE with the financial statements of the sponsoring entity if an outside investor made an equity contribution of 3 percent or more of the SPEs' total capitalization. Enron did not meet this requirement because some of the outside capital allegedly contributed to the SPE was not really at risk. Enron had guaranteed some of the capital investments made by outside investors using Enron's own stock as the form of guarantee.

Although Enron did not comply with the existing accounting requirements, the FASB was still subject to stinging criticism because a number of parties alleged that: (1) the current accounting rules for SPEs are too lax, and (2) the FASB's standards are too detailed and detailed standards provide incentives for preparers to design transactions that meet the letter, but not the spirit, of the standard. The FASB has issued an interpretation ("Consolidation of Variable Interest Entities"—Interpretation No. 46 to ARB No.51) to tighten the rules related to nonconsolidation of SPEs. Moreover, the Board has been criticized for failing to require companies to expense stock options, ironically by some of the same politicians who undermined the FASB's attempt to require the expensing of stock options in the 1990s. In recent years, a number of high-profile companies announced that they would voluntarily deduct the value of employee stock options in determining net income (e.g., Coca-Cola, General Electric, General Motors). Changes in the Standards require more companies to record compensation as a result of granting stock options. The implementation of the 2004 revisions to FAS 123 on Stock Compensation requires the use of the fair value method in measuring the expensing stock options.

The Sarbanes-Oxley Act includes a provision that provides funding to the FASB. This provision should serve to strengthen the FASB's independence, particularly from pressure brought to bear by issuers.

Beginning in the late 1990s and continuing with greater intensity today is a cooperative effort to converge world accounting standards. While a difficult task to accomplish in the short run, bringing accounting standards closer together facilitates international business and the comparability of financial reporting around the world. The International Accounting Standards Board and the FASB work together to narrow the differences between accounting standards, particularly on major issues.

(b) GOVERNMENTAL ACCOUNTING STANDARDS BOARD.   In response to needs expressed by various groups, a study was undertaken in the early 1980s to consider how to establish financial accounting standards for state and local governmental units. (The federal government's uniqueness has caused the application of governmental accounting standards to be limited to state and local entities.) Standards were being established through professional organizations composed of governmental accountants, but they had not been endorsed by the Council of the AICPA, with the consequence that there was some concern over whether they constituted GAAP. The study group's report recommended the creation of the Governmental Accounting Standards Board (GASB) that would be under the administration of the FAF. After several years of discussion and opposition, the trustees agreed to set up the GASB, and it began operations in 1984.

The constituencies of GASB overlap those of the FASB, but only to a limited extent. The preparers consist of elected and appointed officials who are accountable to the voting public for the use and safekeeping of funds appropriated or otherwise entrusted to them, and thus they do not coincide with the preparers regulated by the FASB. The auditor constituency is essentially the same as for the FASB, although the actual individuals are likely to be different because of specialization. Some users of the financial statements of governmental units are different from users of business statements, whereas others are the same. In effect, when governmental units go into the capital markets to obtain debt funding, they are competing with corporations for investors' attention. There is no regulatory agency comparable to the SEC with jurisdiction over governmental units, with the consequence that the GASB has no constituent like the Commission. State Boards are interested in the GASB's efforts because their licensees act as auditors for governmental units.

Without an endorsement by the SEC, the authority of GASB for setting standards is not quite as clear-cut as that of the FASB. It does have power, however, because a variety of professional societies, including the AICPA, endorse its efforts. It also has increased influence because of its affiliation with the FASB.

(i) The Structure of the Governmental Accounting Standards Board.   The GASB has five members, with only the chairman serving on a full-time basis. The other four members serve part time and commute to Connecticut as needed for meetings and consultations. In addition, the Board has a full-time director of Research and Technical Activities. The GASB's headquarters are located in the same building as the FASB and the FAF. Although the two Boards operate independently, they do share some facilities, including the Board meeting room and the library, as well as their accounting and human resource management staff.

The Governmental Accounting Standards Advisory Committee serves the same purpose as the FASAC, but it is not as large and does not have a full-time chairman.

The GASB's due process procedures are essentially the same as the FASB's and include similar steps. Some of the deliberations are more difficult to accomplish because of the geographical dispersion of the part-time members, but they nonetheless take place.

(ii) The Jurisdiction Issue.   A persistent problem in the relationship between FASB and GASB has been the overlapping of their jurisdictions in some segments of the economy. In fact, the issue of which Board should provide standards for these segments was the major stumbling block to the GASB's establishment.

Some organizations subject to the overlapping jurisdiction are utilities and providers of educational and health services. For example, some universities are operated by governments, others are private, and still others are combinations. The same situation exists for utilities, hospitals, and nursing homes. The jurisdiction issue turned first on the question of whether all these entities should be required to use the same accounting principles in order to achieve comparability. If so, the next question was which Board should establish those principles.

As long as there were no conflicts over the principles to be used, the jurisdiction dispute did not cause a practical problem. However, that situation did not exist for long because the two Boards reached opposing conclusions concerning the recognition of depreciation. Thus, the unresolved issue continued to chafe both organizations and to confuse their constituents.

It was resolved in late 1989 when the FAF's trustees first voted to implement and then shortly thereafter rejected a recommendation offered by two Special Committees that reviewed the structures of FASB and GASB. The final resolution left the jurisdiction as it had originally been defined, with GASB holding power over state and local government entities, whereas the FASB was given responsibility for all others. In addition, it was agreed that GASB would give careful consideration to the need for comparability when setting standards for public sector entities in industries that also include private companies.

1.4 PROFESSIONAL ORGANIZATIONS

(a) AMERICAN INSTITUTE OF CERTIFIED PUBLIC ACCOUNTANTS.   Of the several professional accounting organizations, the largest and most influential is the American Institute of Certified Public Accountants (AICPA). Each member must be licensed as a CPA by some jurisdiction, but need not practice as a public accountant. Less than half of the AICPA's membership is in public practice; the majority of members are in industry, government, or education.

(i) Structure. In response to assertions from congressional staff, the AICPA undertook a major restructuring in 1977 to establish a more rigorous self-regulatory system. Even though concern over alleged shortcomings was not backed up by enacted legislation, the Institute created a Division for CPA Firms, whereas previously it had only individual memberships. Members of this division commit themselves to higher standards of quality and quality control, including triennial peer reviews of their quality control systems. Subsequent to the Sarbanes-Oxley Act, the AICPA created a structure of "Centers" to improve member service. The former Securities and Exchange Commission Practice Section (SECPS) became the Center for Public Company Accounting Firms. These Centers continue to evolve in terms of member composition and organization.

As a result of a major change in policy approved by the Institute membership in 1988, all members in public practice will be subject to quality control reviews, even if they do not belong to the Division for CPA Firms. However, these reviews will not be as extensive as full peer reviews, and the AICPA will not release the results to the public.

As discussed previously, the Sarbanes-Oxley Act has replaced the AICPA's system of self-regulation and peer reviews for public companies with inspections by the newly created Public Company Accounting Oversight Board (PCAOB). The AICPA continues with its programs for audits and auditors not subject to PCAOB jurisdiction. The most significant services provided by the AICPA to its members and the public are discussed below.

(ii) Technical Standards. Despite the discontinuation of the APB and the creation of the FASB, the Institute still carries on limited accounting guidance through the Accounting Standards Executive Committee (AcSEC) and sets auditing standards for non-issuers through the Auditing Standards Board (ASB).

Prior to 2002, AcSEC examined accounting issues that had not reached the FASB's agenda, or that the FASB had decided against adding to its agenda. Accordingly, AcSEC and the FASB were in frequent contact, and FASB staff members attend AcSEC meetings. The primary form of output from AcSEC was a Statement of Position (SOP), which must be followed by Institute members. Under SAS No. 69, "The Meaning of Present Fairly in Conformity with Generally Accepted Accounting Principles," AcSEC SOPs are considered level b pronouncements in the GAAP hierarchy. SOPs constitute GAAP if no level a pronouncement exists. The Committee is composed of between 15 and 18 individuals representing various levels and segments of the profession. AcSEC issued an ED of a proposed SOP before issuing the final standard. In response to FASB concerns about the nature and authoritativeness of various standard-setting activities, AcSEC discontinued issuing SOPs. Subject to a transition plan accepted by both the FASB and the AICPA during the fall of 2002 regarding AcSEC projects in process, AcSEC and the AICPA will no longer issue general-purpose SOPs or ask the FASB to clear SOPs or practice bulletins. However, AcSEC will continue to issue Audit and Accounting Guides, which have an industry focus.

The ASB is the organization that creates authoritative GAAS. It does so by issuing Statements on Auditing Standards (SAS). This 19-member group is composed of senior auditing specialists from major and small auditing firms, as well as from industry, government, user groups and education. It uses a thorough due process, including the issuance of exposure drafts of proposed standards and its ASB meetings are open to the public. Beginning in the late 1990s, the ASB actively participated in the Standards setting activities of the International Auditing and Attest Standards Board (IAASB), and has initiated the process of converging US and International Auditing Standards. In 2006, the ASB issued a series of new pervasive standards designed to enhance the risk assessment process and to clarify numerous auditor responsibilities. A motivating factor for the standards was the increased amount of public concern over the reliability of audit reports, in the wake of the Enron and Worldcom scandals, and litigation alleging auditors' failures to protect the public against fraud and business collapses.

The Sarbanes-Oxley Act charges the PCAOB with establishing or adopting auditing standards applicable to audits of SEC registrants. The Sarbanes-Oxley Act clearly permits the PCAOB to adopt auditing standards issued by the ASB. The PCAOB adopted the AICPA authoritative literature as it stood in April 2003, and then began to write its own Standards, modifying that literature going forward. The PCAOB announced its vision of re-writing the entirety of existing auditing standards at some point. Since the PCAOB has so far not adopted any of the ASB Standards subsequent to SAS 101 on "Auditing Fair Value Measurements and Disclosures," the two bodies of auditing Standards literature are now diverging at a rapid rate. Representatives of the ASB, PCAOB and GAO meet periodically to discuss issues of mutual interest. In addition, the PCAOB regularly monitors the activities of the IAASB. Many auditors of private and public companies are concerned today about the complexity and confusion of working in the long run in an environment where there are two main bodies auditing literature.

Senior AICPA committees for specific industries provide other technical guidance. Their output is in the form of Industry Accounting and Auditing Guides. A member of the Institute is obliged to follow the provisions of these guides in auditing a client that belongs to one of the covered industries. Under SAS No. 69, "The Meaning of Present Fairly in Conformity with Generally Accepted Accounting Principles," Industry Accounting and Auditing Guides (A&A) are considered level b pronouncements in the GAAP hierarchy. These A&A Guides constitute GAAP if no level a pronouncement exists. The PCAOB has indicated that it does not have an interest in publishing its own guides at this time.

In addition to these activities, the Institute staff also provides technical assistance to members who have encountered questions in conducting their accounting, auditing, and tax practices. Specifically, members can call or write the Institute staff with their questions and receive guidance on how to resolve them. In many cases, all that is needed is to steer the member to the right portion of the authoritative literature. In other cases, the members are seeking concurrence with a position they have reached on their own. Both services are especially valuable to sole practitioners because they do not have colleagues to double check their research.

(iii) Examinations.   The AICPA produces, administers, and grades the Uniform CPA Examination under contract to individual state Boards of accountancy. This service includes writing the exam to specifications established through NASBA, maintaining security over the questions, delivering the exams to the sites, and reading and grading the exam. The Institute then sends the results to the state Board, which, in turn, notifies the candidates.

The CPA Examination is today administered as a 14 hour computerized exam. The exam is offered periodically throughout the year, rather than only in May and November as previously was the case. The CPA exam covers: Auditing and Attestation, Financial Accounting and Reporting, Regulation, and Business Environment and Concepts.

1.5 SUMMARY

This chapter has shown how financial accounting is important to society because of its contribution to the economy by helping the capital markets operate more effectively. Because of the importance of this social goal, and because history has shown that abusive accounting tends to occur as preparers attempt to gain unfair advantages, financial accounting is significantly regulated by governmental agencies, by private standard setting bodies that are endorsed and supported by governmental agencies, and by professional organizations. This regulation deals with reporting standards, competency standards, and ethical standards.

The regulation of accounting involves politics because of the conflicting interests among financial statement preparers, auditors, users, and regulators. The tension among these interests helps bring about change and improvement, but only at the risk of not fully serving the public interest. The present structure has evolved with what appears to be the central goal of protecting the public, but that mission will be attained only through careful vigilance and oversight.

1.6 SOURCES AND SUGGESTED REFERENCES

Afterman, Allan B., *SEC Regulation of Public Companies*, Prentice Hall, Englewood Cliffs, NJ, 1995.

American Institute of Certified Public Accountants, "Objectives of Financial Statements," Report of the Study Group on the Objectives of Financial Statements. AICPA, New York, 1973.

Financial Accounting Standards Board, "Objectives of Financial Reporting by Business Enterprises," Statement of Financial Accounting Concepts No. 1. FASB, Stamford, CT, 1978.

———, "Qualitative Characteristics of Accounting Information," Statement of Financial Accounting Concepts No. 2. FASB, Stamford, CT, 1980.

———, "Elements of Financial Statements of Business Enterprises," Statement of Financial Accounting Concepts No. 3. FASB, Stamford, CT, 1980.

———, "Objectives of Financial Reporting by Nonbusiness Organizations," Statement of Financial Accounting Concepts No. 4. FASB, Stamford, CT, 1980.

———, "Recognition and Measurement in Financial Statements of Business Enterprises," Statement of Financial Accounting Concepts No. 5. FASB, Stamford, CT, 1980.

———, "Elements of Financial Statements," Statement of Financial Accounting Concepts No. 6. FASB, Stamford, CT, 1985.

———, "Using Cash Flow Information and Present Value in Accounting Measurements," Statement of Financial Accounting Concepts No. 7. FASB, Norwalk, CT, 2000.

Miller, Paul B. W., Redding, Rodney J., and Bahnson, Paul R., *The FASB: The People, the Process, and the Politics* (Fourth Edition). Irwin-McGraw Hill, Burr Ridge, IL, 1998.

Sarbanes-Oxley Act of 2002. 107th Congress, 2d Session.

Skousen, Fred, *An Introduction to the SEC* (Fifth Edition). South-Western Publishing, Cincinnati, OH, 1991.

CHAPTER 2

THE FRAMEWORK OF FINANCIAL ACCOUNTING CONCEPTS AND STANDARDS

Reed K. Storey, PhD, CPA

Financial Accounting Standards Board

*Mr. Storey was a senior technical adviser at the Financial Accounting Standards Board when this chapter was written. Expressions of individual views by the members of the Financial Accounting Standards Board and its staff are encouraged. The views expressed here are those of Mr. Storey. Official positions of the FASB on accounting matters are determined only after extensive due process and deliberation.

  Mr. Storey wishes to acknowledge the assistance of Sylvia Storey, MBA, in the research for and writing of this chapter.

  This chapter was updated from the Tenth Edition by the editors.

2.1 FINANCIAL ACCOUNTING AND REPORTING

The principal role of financial accounting and reporting is to serve the public interest by providing information that is useful in making business and economic decisions. That information facilitates the efficient functioning of capital and other markets, thereby promoting the efficient and equitable allocation of scarce resources in the economy. To undertake and fulfill that role, financial accounting in the twentieth century has evolved from a profession relying almost exclusively on the experience of a handful of illustrious practitioners into one replete with a set of financial accounting standards and an underlying conceptual foundation.

An underlying structure of accounting concepts was deemed necessary to provide to the institutions entrusted with setting accounting principles or standards the requisite tools for resolving accounting problems. Financial accounting now has a foundation of fundamental concepts and objectives in the Financial Accounting Standards Board's (FASB) "Conceptual Framework for Financial Accounting and Reporting," which is intended to provide a basis for developing the financial accounting standards that are promulgated to guide accounting practice.

The FASB's conceptual framework and its antecedents constitute the major subject matter of this chapter. Some significant terms, organizations, and authoritative pronouncements need to be identified or briefly introduced. They already may be familiar to most readers or will become so in due course.

(a) **THE FINANCIAL ACCOUNTING STANDARDS BOARD AND GENERAL PURPOSE EXTERNAL FINANCIAL ACCOUNTING AND REPORTING.**   *Financial accounting and reporting* is the familiar name of the branch of accounting who's precise but somewhat imposing full proper name is *general purpose external financial accounting and reporting*. It is the branch of accounting concerned with general purpose financial statements of business enterprises and not-for-profit organizations. General purpose financial statements are possible because several groups, such as investors, creditors, and other resource providers, have common interests and common information needs. General purpose financial reporting provides information to users who are outside a business enterprise or not-for-profit organization and lack the power to require the entity to supply the accounting information they need for decision making; therefore, they must rely on information provided to them by the entity's management. Other groups, such as taxing authorities and rate regulators, have specialized information needs but also the authority to require entities to provide the information they specify.

General purpose external financial reporting is the sphere of authority of the FASB, the private-sector organization that since 1973 has established generally accepted accounting principles in the United States. General purpose external financial accounting and reporting provides information that is based on generally accepted accounting principles and is audited by independent certified public accountants (CPAs). Generally accepted accounting principles result and have resulted primarily from the authoritative pronouncements of the FASB and its predecessors.

The FASB's standards pronouncements—Statements of Financial Accounting Standards (often abbreviated FASB Statement, SFAS, or FAS) and FASB Interpretations (often abbreviated FIN)—are recognized as authoritative by both the Securities and Exchange Commission (SEC) and the American Institute of Certified Public Accountants (AICPA).

The FASB succeeded the Accounting Principles Board (APB), whose authoritative pronouncements were the APB Opinions. In 1959 the APB had succeeded the Committee on Accounting Procedure, whose authoritative pronouncements were the Accounting Research Bulletins (often abbreviated ARB), some of which were designated as Accounting Terminology Bulletins (often abbreviated ATB).

With respect to the long name "general purpose external financial reporting," this chapter does what the standards-setting bodies also have done: For convenience, it uses the shortcut term financial reporting.

(b) MANAGEMENT ACCOUNTING AND TAX ACCOUNTING.   Financial accounting and reporting is only part of the broad field of accounting. Other significant kinds of accounting include management accounting and tax accounting.

Management accounting is internal accounting designed to meet the information needs of managers. Although the same accounting system usually accumulates, processes, and disseminates both management and financial accounting information, managers' responsibilities for making decisions and planning and controlling operations at various administrative levels of a business enterprise or not-for-profit organization require more detailed information than is considered necessary or appropriate for external financial reporting. Management accounting includes information that is normally not provided outside an organization and is usually tailored to meet specific management information needs.

Tax accounting is concerned with providing appropriate information needed by individuals, corporations, and others for preparing the various returns and reports required to comply with tax laws and regulations, especially the Internal Revenue Code. It is significant in the administration of domestic tax laws, which are to a large extent self-assessing. Tax accounting is based generally on the same procedures that apply to financial reporting. There are some significant differences, however, and taxing authorities have the statutory power to prescribe the specific information they want taxpayers to submit as a basis for assessing the amount of income tax owed and do not need to rely on information provided to other groups.

2.2 WHY WE HAVE A CONCEPTUAL FRAMEWORK

"Accounting principles" has proven to be an extraordinarily elusive term. To the nonaccountant (as well as to many accountants) it connotes things basic and fundamental, of a sort which can be expressed in few words, relatively timeless in nature, and in no way dependent upon changing fashions in business or the evolving needs of the investment community.

The Wheat Report

Principle. A general law or rule adopted or professed as a guide to action; a settled ground or basis of conduct or practice.

Accounting Research Bulletin No. 7

A recurring theme in financial accounting in the United States in the twentieth century has been the call for a comprehensive, authoritative statement of basic accounting *principles*. It has reflected a widespread perception that something more fundamental than rules or descriptions of methods or procedures was needed to form a basis for, explain, or govern financial accounting and reporting practice. A number of organizations, committees, and individuals in the profession have developed or attempted to develop their own variations of what they have diversely called *principles, standards, conventions, rules, postulates*, or *concepts*. Those efforts met with varying degrees of success, but by the 1970s none of the codifications or statements had come to be accepted or relied on in practice as the definitive statement of accounting's basic principles.

The pursuit of a statement of accounting principles has reflected two distinct schools of thought: that accounting principles are generalized or drawn from practice without reference to a systematic theoretical foundation or that accounting principles are based on a few fundamental premises that together with the principles provide a framework for solving specific problems encountered in practice. Early efforts to codify or develop accounting principles were dominated by the belief that principles are essentially a "distillation of experience," a description generally attributed to George O. May, one of the most influential accountants of his time, who used it in the title of a book, *Financial Accounting: A Distillation of Experience* (1943).[1] However, as accounting has matured and its role in society has increased, momentum in developing accounting principles has shifted to those accountants who have come to understand what has been learned in many other fields: that reliance on experience alone leads only so far because environments and problems change; that until knowledge gained through experience is given purpose, direction, and internal consistency by a conceptual foundation, fundamentals will be endlessly reargued and practice blown in various directions by the winds of changing perceptions and proliferating accounting methods; and that only by studying and understanding the foundations of practices can the path of progress be discovered and the hope of improving practice be realized.

The conceptual framework project of the FASB represents the most comprehensive effort thus far to establish a structure of objectives and fundamentals to underlie financial accounting and reporting practice. To understand what it is, how it came about, and why it took the form and included the concepts that it did requires some knowledge of its antecedents, which extend back more than 60 years.

(a) SPECIAL COMMITTEE ON COOPERATION WITH STOCK EXCHANGES.   The origin of the use of *principle* in financial accounting and reporting can be traced to a special committee of the American Institute of Accountants (American Institute of Certified Public Accountants since 1957). The Special Committee on Cooperation with Stock Exchanges, chaired by George O. May, gave the word special significance in the attest function of accountants. That significance is still evident in audit reports signed by members of the Institute and most other CPAs attesting that the financial statements of their clients present fairly, or do not present fairly, the client's financial position, results of operations, and cash flows "in conformity with generally accepted accounting principles." The committee laid the foundation that has been the basis of both subsequent progress in identifying or developing and enunciating accounting principles and many of the problems that have accompanied the resulting principles.

In 1930 the Institute undertook a cooperative effort with the New York Stock Exchange aimed at improving financial disclosure by publicly held enterprises. It was widely believed that inferior accounting and reporting practices had contributed to the stock market decline and depression that began in 1929. The Exchange was concerned that its listed companies were using too many different accounting and reporting methods to reflect similar transactions and that some of those methods were questionable. The Institute wanted to make financial statements more informative and authoritative, to clarify the authority and responsibility of auditors, and to educate the public about the conventional nature of accounting and the limitations of accounting reports.

---

[1] George O. May, *Financial Accounting: A Distillation of Experience* (New York: The Macmillan Company, 1943).

The Exchange's Committee on Stock List and the Institute's Special Committee on Cooperation with Stock Exchanges exchanged correspondence between 1932 and 1934. The special committee's report, comprising a series of letters that passed between the two committees, was issued to Institute members in 1934 under the title, *Audits of Corporate Accounts* (reprinted in 1963). The key part was a letter dated September 22, 1932, from the Institute committee.

(i) "Accepted Principles of Accounting." The special committee recommended that an authoritative statement of the broad accounting principles on which "there is a fairly general agreement" be formulated in consultation with a small group of qualified persons, including accountants, lawyers, and corporate officials. Within that framework of "accepted principles of accounting," each company would be free to choose the methods and procedures most appropriate for its financial statements, subject to requirements to disclose the methods it was using and to apply them consistently. Audit certificates (reports) for listed companies would state that their financial statements were prepared in accordance with "accepted principles of accounting." The special committee anticipated that its program would improve financial reporting because disclosure would create pressure from public opinion to eliminate less-desirable practices.

The special committee did not define "principles of accounting," but it illustrated what it had in mind. It gave two explicit examples of accepted broad principles of accounting:

> It is a generally accepted principle that plant value should be charged against gross profits over the useful life of the plant....

> Again, the most commonly accepted method of stating inventories is at cost or market, whichever is lower....[2]

It also listed five principles that it presumed would be included in the contemplated statement of "broad principles of accounting which have won fairly general acceptance":

1. Unrealized profit should not be credited to income account of the corporation either directly or indirectly, through the medium of charging against such unrealized profits amounts, which would ordinarily fall to be charged against income account. Profit is deemed to be realized when a sale in the ordinary course of business is affected, unless the circumstances are such that the collection of the sale price is not reasonably assured. An exception to the general rule may be made [for industries in which trade custom is to take inventories at net selling prices, which may exceed cost].

2. Capital surplus [other paid-in capital], however created, should not be used to relieve the income account of the current or future years of charges, which would otherwise fall to be made there against. This rule might be subject to the exception that [permits use of quasi-reorganization].

3. Earned surplus [retained earnings] of a subsidiary company created prior to acquisition does not form a part of the consolidated earned surplus of the parent company and subsidiaries; nor can any dividend declared out of such surplus properly be credited to the income account of the parent company.

4. While it is perhaps in some circumstances permissible to show stock of a corporation held in its own treasury as an asset, if adequately disclosed, the dividends on stock so held should not be treated as a credit to the income account of the company.

---

[2] *Audits of Corporate Accounts: Correspondence between the Special Committee on Cooperation with Stock Exchanges of the American Institute of Accountants and the Committee on Stock List of the New York Stock Exchange, 1932–1934* (New York: American Institute of Accountants, 1934), p. 7. [Reprinted (New York: American Institute of Certified Public Accountants, 1963), and in Stephen A. Zeff, *Forging Accounting Principles in Five Countries: A History and an Analysis of Trends* (Champaign, IL: Stipes Publishing Company, 1972), pp. 237–247.]

5. Notes or accounts receivable due from officers, employees, or affiliated companies must be shown separately and not included under a general heading such as Notes Receivable or Accounts Receivable.[3]

The Institute submitted the committee's five principles for acceptance by its members in 1934, and they are now in ARB No. 43, *Restatement and Revision of Accounting Research Bulletins* (issued 1953), Chapter 1A, "Rules Adopted by Membership" (paragraphs 1–5).

The special committee's use of the word "principle" set the stage not only for the Institute's efforts to identify "accepted principles of accounting" but also for future confusion and controversy over what accountants mean when they use the word "principle."

But Were They "Principles"?   The special committee's examples of broad principles of accounting were much less fundamental, timeless, and comprehensive than what most people perceive to be principles. They had little or nothing in them that made them more basic or less concrete than conventions or rules. Moreover, the special committee itself referred to them as rules in describing exceptions to them, the Institute characterized them as rules in submitting them for approval by its members, and the chairman of the special committee later conceded that they were nothing more than rules:

> When the committee . . . undertook to lay down some of the basic principles of modern accounting, it found itself unable to suggest more than half a dozen which could be regarded as generally acceptable, and even those were rules rather than principles, and were, moreover, admittedly subject to exception.[4]

Not surprisingly, the special committee's use of the word *principles* was soon challenged. In a contest sponsored by the Institute for its fiftieth anniversary celebration in 1937, Gilbert R. Byrne's essay entitled "To What Extent Can the Practice of Accounting Be Reduced to Rules and Standards?" won first prize for the best answer to the question posed in the title. He complained about accountants' propensity to downgrade principle by equating it with terms such as *rule*, *convention*, and *procedure*.

> [R]ecent discussions have used the term "accounting principles" to cover a conglomeration of accounting practices, procedures, conventions, etc.; many, if not most, so-called principles may merely have to do with methods of presenting items on financial statements or technique of auditing, rather than matters of fundamental accounting principle.[5]

Stephen Gilman made the same point in his careful analysis of terms in five chapters of his book, *Accounting Concepts of Profit*.

> With sublime disregard of lexicography, accountants speak of "principles," "tenets," "doctrines," "rules," and "conventions" as if they were synonymous.[6]

Gilman also quoted an excerpt from the *Century Dictionary* that he thought pertinent "because of the confusion noted in some accounting writings [about] the distinction between 'principle' and 'rule'":

> There are no two words in the English language used so confusedly one for the other as the words *rule* and *principle*. You can make a *rule*; you cannot make a *principle*; you can lay down a *rule*;

---

[3] *Audits of Corporate Accounts*, p. 14. Lengthy exceptions in items 1 and 2 are summarized rather than quoted in full.

[4] George O. May, "Improvement in Financial Accounts," *The Journal of Accountancy*, May 1937, p. 335.

[5] Gilbert R.Byrne, "To What Extent Can the Practice of Accounting Be Reduced to Rules and Standards?" *The Journal of Accountancy*, November 1937, p. 366. [Reprinted in Maurice Moonitz and A. C. Littleton, eds., Significant Accounting Essays (Englewood Cliffs, NJ: Prentice-Hall, Inc., 1965), pp. 103–115.]

[6] Stephen Gilman, *Accounting Concepts of Profit* (New York: The Ronald Press Company, 1939), p. 169.

you cannot, properly speaking, lay down a *principle*. It is laid down for you. You can establish a *rule*; you cannot, properly speaking, establish a *principle*. You can only declare it. *Rules* are within your power, *principles* are not. A *principle* lies back of both *rules* and precepts; it is a general truth, needing interpretation and application to particular cases.[7]

Byrne, Gilman, and others pointed out that the form of accountant's report recommended by the special committee made accountants look foolish by requiring them to express opinions based on the existence of principles they actually could not specify. In that form of report, an accountant expressed the opinion that a client's financial statement is "fairly present, *in accordance with accepted principles of accounting consistently maintained by the company during the year under review*, its position ... and the results of its operations...." According to Byrne, that opinion presumed that accepted principles of accounting actually existed and accountants in general knew and agreed on what they were. In fact, "While there have been several attempts to enumerate [those principles], to date there has been no statement upon which there has been general agreement."[8]

That diagnosis was confirmed by Gilman as well as by Howard C. Greer:

... the entire body of precedent [the "accepted principles of accounting"] has been taken for granted.

It is as though each accountant felt that while he himself had never taken the time or the trouble to make an actual list of accounting principles, he was comfortably certain that someone else had done so....

[T]he accountants are in the unenviable position of having committed themselves in their certificates [reports] as to the existence of generally accepted accounting principles while between themselves they are quarreling as to whether there are any accounting principles and if there are how many of them should be recognized and accepted.[9]

There is something incongruous about the outpouring of thousands of accountants' certificates [reports] which refer to accepted accounting principles, and a situation in which no one can discover or state what those accepted accounting principles are. The layman cannot understand.[10]

Byrne argued that lack of agreement on what constituted accepted accounting principles resulted "in large part because there is no clear distinction, in the minds of many, between that body of fundamental truths underlying the philosophy of accounts which are properly thought of as *principles*, and the larger body of accounting rules, practices, and conventions which derive from principles, but which of themselves are not principles."[11] His prescription for accountants was to use *principle* in its most commonly understood sense of being more fundamental and enduring than rules and conventions.

If accounting, as an organized body of knowledge, has validity, it must rest upon a body of principles, in the sense defined in Webster's New International Dictionary:

"A fundamental truth; a comprehensive law or doctrine, from which others are derived, or on which others are founded; a general truth; an elementary proposition or fundamental assumption; a maxim; an axiom; a postulate."...

---

[7] Gilman, *Accounting Concepts of Profit*, p. 188.

[8] Byrne, "To What Extent Can the Practice of Accounting Be Reduced to Rules and Standards?" p. 368.

[9] Gilman, *Accounting Concepts of Profit*, pp. 169 and 171.

[10] Howard C. Greer, "What Are Accepted Principles of Accounting?" *The Accounting Review*, March 1938, p. 25.

[11] Byrne, "To What Extent Can the Practice of Accounting Be Reduced to Rules and Standards?" p. 368.

Accounting principles, then, are the fundamental concepts on which accounting, as an organized body of knowledge, rests.... [T]hey are the foundation upon which the superstructure of
accounting rules, practices and conventions is built.[12]

Gilman, in contrast, could find no principles that fit Byrne's definition. He concluded that most,
if not all, of the propositions that had been put forth as principles of accounting should be relabeled
"as doctrines, conventions, rules, or mere statements of opinion."[13] He called on accountants to
admit that there were no accounting principles in the fundamental sense and to waste no more time
and effort on attempts to identify and state them.

May's Attempts to Rectify "Considerable Misunderstanding."   In several articles and a book,
George O. May responded to those and other criticisms of "accounting principles" and explained
what the special committee, as well as several other Institute committees of which he was chairman,
had done and why. He detected, in the criticisms and elsewhere, what he described as "considerable misunderstanding" of both the nature of financial accounting and the committees' work on
accounting principles and thought it necessary to get the matter back on the right track.

Although he acknowledged that "in the correspondence the [special] Committee had used the
words 'rules,' 'methods,' 'conventions,' and 'principles' interchangeably,"[14] May considered questions such as whether the propositions should be called rules or principles not to be matters "of
any real importance." As Byrne had pointed out, if there were any principles that fit his definition,
"they must be few in number and extremely general in character (such as 'consistency' and 'conservatism')."[15] Thus, they would afford less precise guidance than the more concrete principles
illustrated by the special committee. Those who scolded the special committee for misusing "principles" had apparently forgotten that "accounting rules and principles are founded not on abstract
theories or logic, but on utility."[16]

May urged the profession and others to focus efforts to improve financial accounting, as had
the special committee, on the questions "of real importance"—the consequences of the necessarily
conventional nature of accounting and the limitations of accounting reports. He explained the philosophy underlying the recommendation of the special committee and summarized that philosophy
in the introductory pages of his book:

> In 1926, ... I decided to relinquish my administrative duties and devote a large part of my time to
> consideration of the broader aspects of accounting. As a result of that study I became convinced
> that a sound accounting structure could not be built until misconceptions had been cleared away,
> and the nature of the accounting process and the limitations on the significance of the financial
> statements which it produced were more frankly recognized.
>
> It became clear to me that general acceptance of the fact that accounting was utilitarian and based
> on conventions (some of which were necessarily of doubtful correspondence with fact) was an
> indispensable preliminary to real progress....
>
> Many accountants were reluctant to admit that accounting was based on nothing of a higher order
> of sanctity than conventions. However, it is apparent that this is necessarily true of accounting as
> it is, for instance, of business law. In these fields there are no principles, in the fundamental sense
> of that word, on which we can build; and the distinctions between laws, rules, standards, and con-
> ventions lie not in their nature but in the kind of sanctions by which they are enforced. Accounting
> procedures have in the main been the result of common agreement between accountants....[17]

---

[12] Byrne, "To What Extent Can the Practice of Accounting Be Reduced to Rules and Standards?" pp.
368 and 372.

[13] Gilman, *Accounting Concepts of Profit*, p. 257.

[14] May, *Financial Accounting*, p. 42.

[15] George O. May, "Principles of Accounting," *The Journal of Accountancy*, December 1937, p. 424.
[The article was a comment on Byrne's essay.]

[16] George O. May, "Terminology of the Balance Sheet," *The Journal of Accountancy*, January 1942,
p. 35.

[17] May, *Financial Accounting*, pp. 2 and 3.

He also reiterated and amplified a number of points the special committee had emphasized in *Audits of Corporate Accounts* concerning what the investing public already knew or should understand about financial accounting and reporting, such as, that because the value of a business depended mainly on its earning capacity, the income statement was more important than the balance sheet and should indicate to the fullest extent possible the earning capacity of the business during the period on which it reported; that because the balance sheet of a large modern corporation was to a large extent historical and conventional, largely comprising the residual amounts of expenditures or receipts after first determining a proper charge or credit to the income account for the year, it did not, and should not be expected to, represent an attempt to show the present values of the assets and liabilities of the corporation; and that because financial accounting and reporting was necessarily conventional, some variety in accounting methods was inevitable.

The Special Committee's Definition of "Principle."   May not only identified the definition of *principle* the special committee had used but also explained why it had chosen that particular meaning. In his comment on Byrne's essay, he recalled the committee's discussion and searching of dictionaries before choosing the "perhaps rather magniloquent word 'principle' . . . in preference to the humbler 'rule.'" The definition of "principle" in the Oxford English Dictionary that came closest to defining the sense in which the special committee used the word was the seventh definition:

> A general law or rule adopted or professed as a guide to action; a settled ground or basis of conduct or practice.

The time and effort spent in searching dictionaries was fruitful—the committee found exactly the definition for which it was looking:

> [The] . . . sense of the word "principle" above quoted seemed . . . to fit the case perfectly. Examination of the report as a whole will make clear what the committee contemplated; namely, that each corporation should have a code of "laws or rules, adopted or professed, as a guide to action," and that the accountants should report, first, whether this code conformed to accepted usages, and secondly, whether it had been consistently maintained and applied.[18]

Thus, the special committee opted for the lofty *principle* rather than the more precise *rule* or *convention* because the definition that best fit the committee's needs was a definition of *principle*, albeit an obscure one, not a definition of *rule* or *convention*. Moreover, *rule* and *convention* carried unfortunate baggage:

> [The] word "rules" implied the existence of a ruling body which did not exist; the word "convention" was regarded as not appropriate for popular use and in the opinion of some would not convey an adequate impression of the authority of the precepts by which the accounts were judged.[19]

Whereas *principle* conveyed desirable implications:

> It used to be not uncommon for the accountant who had been unable to persuade his client to adopt the accounting treatment that he favored, to urge as a last resort that it was called for by "accounting principles." Often he would have had difficulty in defining the "principle" and saying how, why, and when it became one. But the method was effective, especially in dealing with those (of whom there were many) who regarded accounting as an esoteric but well established body of learning and chose to bow to its authority rather than display their ignorance of its rules. Obviously, the word "principle" was an essential part of the technique; "convention" would have been quite ineffective.[20]

---

[18] May, "Principles of Accounting," pp. 423 and 424, emphasis added.

[19] May, *Financial Accounting*, p. 42.

[20] Id., p. 37.

Rules were elevated into principles because the committee thought it necessary to use a word with the force or power of *principle* to prevent the auditor's authority from being lost on the client.

(ii) The Best Laid Schemes.   The special committee's program focused on what individual listed companies and their auditors would do. Each corporation would choose from "accepted principles of accounting" its own code of "laws or rules, adopted or professed, as a guide to action" and within that framework would be free to choose the methods and procedures most appropriate for its financial statements but would disclose the methods it was using and would apply them consistently. An auditor's report would include an opinion on whether or not each corporation's code consisted of accepted principles of accounting and was applied consistently. The Stock Exchange would enforce the program by requiring each listed corporation to comply in order to keep its listing.

The Institute was to sponsor or lead an effort in which accountants, lawyers, corporate officials, and other "qualified persons" would formulate a statement of "accepted principles of accounting" to guide listed companies and auditors, but it was not to get into the business of specifying those principles. The special committee had explicitly considered and rejected "the selection by competent authority out of the body of acceptable methods in vogue today [the] detailed sets of rules which would become binding on all corporations of a given class." The special committee also had avoided using "rule" because the word implied a rule-setting body that did not exist, and it had no intention of imposing on anyone what it considered to be an unnecessary and impossible burden. "Within quite wide limits, it is relatively unimportant to the investor what precise rules or conventions are adopted by a corporation in reporting its earnings if he knows what method is being followed and is assured that it is followed consistently from year to year."[21] Moreover, the committee felt that no single body could adequately assess and allow for the varying characteristics of individual corporations, and the choice of which detailed methods best fit a corporation's circumstances thus was best left to each corporation and its auditors. Because financial accounting was essentially conventional and required estimates and allocations of costs and revenues to periods, the utility of the resulting financial statements inevitably depended significantly on the competence, judgment, and integrity of corporate management and independent auditors. Although there had been a few instances of breach of trust or abuse of investors, the committee had confidence in the trustworthiness of the great majority of those responsible for financial accounting and reporting.

In the end, the special committee's recommendations were never fully implemented. Nonaccountants were not invited to participate in developing a statement of accepted accounting principles. In fact, although the Institute submitted the special committee's five principles for acceptance by its members, it attempted no formulation of a statement of broad principles, even by accountants. Nor did the Exchange require its listed companies to disclose their accounting methods.

The Special Committee's Heritage.   The only recommendation to survive was that each company should be permitted to choose its own accounting methods within a framework of "accepted principles of accounting." The committee's definition of "principle" also survived, and "accepted principles of accounting" became "generally accepted."

The special committee's definition of "principle"—"A general law or rule adopted or professed as a guide to action; a settled ground or basis of conduct or practice"—was incorporated verbatim in Accounting Research Bulletin No. 7, *Report of the Committee on Terminology* (George O. May, chairman), in 1940, but it was attributed to the *New English Dictionary* rather than to the *Oxford English Dictionary*. When ARB 1–42 were restated and revised in 1953, the same definition of "principle," by then attributed only to "Dictionaries," was carried over to Accounting Terminology Bulletin No. 1, *Review and Résumé.*

"Generally" was added to the special committee's "accepted principles of accounting" in *Examination of Financial Statements by Independent Public Accountants*, published by the Institute in 1936 as a revision of an auditing publication, *Verification of Financial Statements* (1929). According

---

[21] *Audits of Corporate Accounts*, pp. 8 and 9.

to its chairman, Samuel J. Broad, the revision committee inserted "generally" to answer questions such as "... accepted by whom? business? professional accountants? the SEC? I heard of one accountant who claimed that if a principle was accepted by him and a few others it was 'accepted.'"[22]

In retrospect, the legacy of institutionalizing that definition of principle has been that the terms principle, rule, convention, procedure, and method have been used interchangeably, and imprecise and inconsistent usage has hampered the development and acceptance of subsequent efforts to establish accounting principles. Moreover, within the context of so broad a definition of "principle," the combination of the latitude given management in choosing accounting methods, the failure to incorporate into financial accounting and reporting the discipline that would have been imposed by the profession's adopting a few, broad, accepted accounting principles, and the failure to enforce the requirement that companies disclose their accounting methods gave refuge to the continuing use of many different methods and procedures, all justified as "generally accepted principles of accounting," and encouraged the proliferation of even more "generally accepted" accounting methods.

Finally, despite the reluctance of the Institute to become involved in setting principles or rules, it eventually assumed that responsibility after the U.S. SEC was created.

(iii) Securities Acts and the Securities and Exchange Commission—"Substantial Authoritative Support".

The Securities Exchange Act of 1934 established the SEC and gave it authority to prescribe accounting and auditing practices to be used by companies in the financial reports required of them under that Act and the Securities Act of 1933. The SEC, like the Stock Exchange before it, became increasingly concerned about the variety of accounting practices approved by auditors. Carman G. Blough, first Chief Accountant of the SEC, told a round-table session at the Institute's fiftieth anniversary celebration in 1937 that unless the profession took steps to develop a set of accounting principles and reduce the areas of difference in accounting practice, "the determination of accounting principles and methods used in reports to the Commission would devolve on the Commission itself. The message to the profession was clear and unambiguous."[23]

In April 1938, the Chief Accountant issued Accounting Series Release (ASR) No. 4, *Administrative Policy on Financial Statements*, requiring registrants to use only accounting principles having "substantial authoritative support." That made official and reinforced Blough's earlier message: If the profession wanted to retain the ability to determine accounting principles and methods, the Institute would have to issue statements of principles that could be deemed to have "substantial authoritative support." Through ASR 4, the Commission reserved the right to say what had "substantial authoritative support" but also opened the way to give that recognition to recommendations on principles issued by the Institute.

(b) COMMITTEE ON ACCOUNTING PROCEDURE, 1938–1959.

The Institute expanded significantly its Committee on Accounting Procedure (not principles) and gave it responsibility for accounting principles and authority to speak on them for the Institute—to issue pronouncements on accounting principles without the need for approval of the Institute's membership or governing Council. The committee was intended to be the principal source of the "substantial authoritative support" for accounting principles sought by the SEC.

The president of the Institute was the nominal chairman of the Committee on Accounting Procedure. Its vice chairman and guiding spirit was George O. May.

(i) No Comprehensive Statement of Principles by Institute.

The course the committee would follow for the next 20 years was set at its initial meeting in January 1939. Carman G. Blough, who had left the Commission and become a partner of Arthur Andersen & Co. and who was a

---

[22] Zeff, *Forging Accounting Principles in Five Countries*, p. 129.
[23] Id., p. 134.

member of the committee, recounted in a paper at a symposium at the University of California at Berkeley in 1967 how the committee chose its course:

> At first it was thought that a comprehensive statement of accounting principles should be developed which would serve as a guide to the solution of the practical problems of day to day practice. . . .
>
> After extended discussion it was agreed that the preparation of such a statement might take as long as five years. In view of the need to begin to reduce the areas of differences in accounting procedures before the SEC lost patience and began to make its own rules on such matters, it was concluded that the committee could not possibly wait for the development of such a broad statement of principles.[24]

The committee thus decided that the need to deal with particular problems was too pressing to permit it to spend time and effort on a comprehensive statement of principles.

Statements of Accounting Principles by Others.   Although the Institute attempted no formulation of a statement of broad accounting principles, two other organizations did. Both statements were written by professors, and each was an early representative of one of the two schools of thought about the nature and derivation of accounting principles.

AMERICAN ACCOUNTING ASSOCIATION'S THEORETICAL BASIS FOR ACCOUNTING RULES AND PROCEDURES. "A Tentative Statement of Accounting Principles Underlying Corporate Financial Statements," by the Executive Committee of the American Accounting Association (AAA) in 1936, was based on the assumption "that a corporation's periodic financial statements should be continuously in accord with a single coordinated body of accounting theory."[25] The phrase "Accounting Principles Underlying Corporate Financial Statements" emphasized that improvement in accounting practice could best be achieved by strengthening the theoretical framework that supported practice. The "Tentative Statement" was almost completely ignored by the Institute, and its effect on accounting practice at the time was minimal. However, two of its principles (one a corollary of the other) and a monograph by W. A. Paton and A. C. Littleton based on it proved to have long-lasting influence and are described shortly.

SANDERS, HATFIELD, AND MOORE'S CODIFICATION OF ACCOUNTING PRACTICES.   In contrast to the AAA's attempt to derive a coordinated body of accounting theory, *A Statement of Accounting Principles*, by Thomas Henry Sanders, Henry Rand Hatfield, and Underhill Moore, two professors of accounting and a professor of law, respectively, was a compilation through interviews, discussions, and surveys of "the current practices of accountants" and reflected no systematic theoretical foundation. It was prepared under sponsorship of the Haskins & Sells Foundation and was published in 1938 by the Institute, which distributed it to all Institute members as "a highly valuable contribution to the discussion of accounting principles."

The report was excoriated for its virtually exclusive reliance on experience and current practice as the basis for principles, its reluctance to criticize even the most dubious practices, and its implication that accountants had no greater duty than to ratify whatever management wanted to do with its accounting as long as what it did was legal and properly disclosed. Many, perhaps most, of the characteristics criticized were inherent in what the authors were asked to do—formulate a code of accounting principles based on practice and the weight of opinion and authority. Even so,

---

[24] Carman G. Blough, "Development of Accounting Principles in the United States," *Berkeley Symposium on the Foundations of Financial Accounting* (Berkeley: Schools of Business Administration, University of California, 1967), pp. 7 and 8.

[25] Page 188 of the "Tentative Statement," which was published in *The Accounting Review*, June 1936, pp. 187–191. [Reprinted in *Accounting and Reporting Standards for Corporate Financial Statements and Preceding Statements and Supplements* (Iowa City, IA: American Accounting Association, 1957), pp. 60–64.]

the report tended to strike a dubious balance between auditors' independence and duty to exercise professional judgment on the one hand and their deference to management on the other.

It was, nevertheless, "the first relatively complete statement of accounting principles and the only complete statement reflecting the school of thought that accounting principles are found in what accountants do. . . . " It was a successful attempt to codify the methods and procedures that accountants used in everyday practice and "was in fact a 'distillation of practice.'"[26] Moreover, since the Committee on Accounting Procedure adopted and pursued the same view of principles and incorporated existing practice and the weight of opinion and authority in its pronouncements, *A Statement of Accounting Principles* probably was a good approximation of what the committee would have produced had it attempted to codify existing "accepted principles of accounting."

SETS OF PRINCIPLES BY INDIVIDUALS.   Three less ambitious efforts in 1937 and 1938—eight principles in Gilbert R. Byrne's prize-winning essay,[27] nine accounting principles and conventions in D. L. Trouant's book, *Financial Audits*,[28] and six accounting principles in A. C. Littleton's "Tests for Principles"[29]—provided examples, rather than complete statements, of principles. Each described what "principles" meant and gave some propositions to illustrate the nature of principles or to show how propositions could be judged to be accepted principles. The resulting principles were substantially similar to those of the special committee. For example, all three authors included the conventions that revenue usually should be realized (recognized) at the time of sale and that cost of plant should be depreciated over its useful life. An interesting exception was Trouant's first principle—"Everything having a value has a claimant"—and the accompanying explanation: "In this axiom lies the basis of double-entry bookkeeping and from it arises the equivalence of the balance-sheet totals for assets and liabilities."[30] That proposition not only was more fundamental than most principles of the time but also was distinctive in referring to the world in which accounting takes place rather than to the accounting process.

Principles from Resolving Specific Problems.   None of those five efforts to state principles of accounting seems to have had much effect on practice, although Sanders, Hatfield, and Moore's *A Statement of Accounting Principles* may indirectly have affected the decision of the Committee on Accounting Procedure to tackle specific accounting problems first: "[A]nyone who read it could not fail to be impressed with the wide variety of procedures that were being followed in accounting for similar transactions and in that way undoubtedly it helped to point up the need for doing something to standardize practices."[31]

In any event, the Committee on Accounting Procedure decided that to formulate a statement of broad accounting principles would take too long and elected instead to use a problem-by-problem approach in which the committee would recommend one or more alternative procedures as preferable to other alternatives for resolving a particular financial accounting or reporting problem. The decision to resolve pressing and controversial matters that way was described by members of the committee as "a decision to put out the brush fires before they created a conflagration."[32]

(ii)   The Accounting Research Bulletins.   The committee's means of extinguishing the threatening fires were the ARB. From September 1939 through August 1959 it issued 51 ARBs on a variety of subjects. Among the most important or most controversial (or both) were No. 2, *Unamortized Discount and Redemption Premium on Bonds Refunded* (1939); No. 23, *Accounting for Income*

---

[26] Reed K. Storey, *The Search for Accounting Principles* (New York: American Institute of Certified Public Accountants, 1964), p. 31. [Reprinted (Houston, TX: Scholars Book Company, 1977).]

[27] Byrne, "To What Extent Can the Practice of Accounting Be Reduced to Rules and Standards?" p. 372.

[28] D. L. Trouant, *Financial Audits* (New York: American Institute Publishing Co., Inc., 1937), pp. 5–7.

[29] A. C. Littleton, "Tests for Principles," *The Accounting Review*, March 1938, pp. 16–24.

[30] Trouant, Financial Audits, p. 5.

[31] Blough, "Development of Accounting Principles in the United States," p. 7.

[32] Id., p. 8.

Taxes (1944); No. 24, *Accounting for Intangible Assets* (1944); No. 29, *Inventory Pricing* (1947); No. 32, *Income and Earned Surplus* [*Retained Earnings*] (1947); No. 33, *Depreciation and High Costs* (1947); No. 37, *Accounting for Compensation in the Form of Stock Options* (1948); No. 40 and No. 48, *Business Combinations* (1950 and 1957); No. 47, *Accounting for Costs of Pension Plans* (1956); and No. 51, *Consolidated Financial Statements* (1959).

Each ARB described one or more accounting or reporting problems that had been brought to the committee's attention and identified accepted principles (conventions, rules, methods, or procedures) to account for the item(s) or otherwise to solve the problem(s) involved, sometimes describing one or more principles as preferable. Because each Bulletin dealt with a specific practice problem, or a set of related problems, the committee developed or approved accounting principles (to use the most common descriptions) case by case, ad hoc, or piecemeal.

Piecemeal Principles Based on Practice, Experience, and General Acceptance.   As a result of the way the committee operated and the bases on which it decided issues before it, the ARB became classic examples of George O. May's dictum that "the rules of accounting, even more than those of law, are the product of experience rather than of logic."[33] Despite having "research" in the name, the ARBs, rather than being the product of research or theory, were much more the product of existing practice, the collective experience of the members of the Committee on Accounting Procedure, and the need to be generally accepted.

Since the committee had not attempted to codify a comprehensive statement of accounting principles, it had no body of theory against which to evaluate the conventions, rules, and procedures that it considered. Although individual ARBs sometimes reflected one or more theories apparently suggested or applied by individual members or agreed on by the committee, as a group they reflected no broad, internally consistent, underlying theory. On the contrary, they often were criticized for being inconsistent with each other. The committee used the word "consistency" to mean that a convention, rule, or procedure, once chosen, should continue to be used in subsequent financial statements, not to mean that a conclusion in one Bulletin did not contradict or conflict with conclusions in others.

The most influential unifying factor in the ARBs as a group was the philosophy that underlay *Audits of Corporate Accounts*, a group of propositions that May and the Special Committee on Cooperation with Stock Exchanges had described as pragmatic and realistic—not theoretical and logical. For example, the Bulletins clearly were based on the propositions that the income statement was far more important than the balance sheet; that financial accounting was primarily a process of allocating historical costs and revenues to periods rather than of valuing assets and liabilities; that the particular rules or conventions used were less significant than consistent use of whichever ones were chosen; and that some variety in accounting conventions and rules, especially in the methods and procedures for applying them to particular situations, was inevitable and desirable.

Most of the work of the Committee on Accounting Procedure, like that of most Institute committees, was done by its members and their partners or associates, and the ARBs reflected their experience. The experience of Carman G. Blough also left its mark on the Bulletins after he became the Institute's first full-time director of research in 1944. The Institute had established a small research department with a part-time director in 1939, which did some research for the committee but primarily performed the tasks of a technical staff, such as providing background and technical memoranda as bases for the Bulletins and drafting parts of proposed Bulletins. Committee members and their associates did even more of the committee's work as the research department also began to provide staff assistance to the Committee on Auditing Procedure in 1942 and then increasingly became occupied with providing staff assistance to a growing number (44 at one time) of other technical committees of the Institute.

The accounting conventions, rules, and procedures considered by the Committee on Accounting Procedure and given its stamp of approval as principles in an ARB were already used in practice, not only because the committee had decided to look for principles in what accountants did but

---

[33] May, *Financial Accounting*, p. vii.

also because only principles that were already used were likely to qualify as "generally accepted." General acceptance was conferred by use, not by vote of the committee. Each Bulletin, beginning with ARB 4 in December 1939, carried this note about its authority: "Except in cases in which formal adoption by the Institute membership has been asked and secured, the authority of the bulletins rests upon the general acceptability of opinions . . . reached."

The committee was authorized by the Institute to issue statements on accounting principles, which the Institute expected the SEC to recognize as providing "substantial authoritative support," but the committee had no authority to require compliance with the Bulletins. It could only add a warning to each Bulletin "that the burden of justifying departure from accepted procedures must be assumed by those who adopt other treatment."

The committee's reliance on general acceptability of principles developed or approved case by case, ad hoc, or piecemeal invited challenges to its authority whenever it tried either to introduce new accounting practices or to proscribe existing practices. Moreover, although the SEC also dealt with accounting principles case by case, ad hoc, or piecemeal, its power to say which accounting principles had substantial authoritative support—its own version of general acceptability—limited what the committee could do without the Commission's concurrence.

CHALLENGES TO THE COMMITTEE'S AUTHORITY.   The Committee on Accounting Procedure introduced interperiod income tax allocation in ARB No. 23, *Accounting for Income Taxes* (December 1944). The reason it gave for changing practice was that "income taxes are an expense that should be allocated, when necessary and practicable, to income and other accounts, as other expenses are allocated. What the income statement should reflect . . . is the [income tax] expense properly allocable to the income included in the income statement for the year" (page 186 [fourth page of ARB 23], carried over with some changes to ARB No. 43, *Restatement and Revision of Accounting Research Bulletins* (June 1953), Chapter 10B, "Income Taxes," paragraph 4).

A committee of the New Jersey Society of Certified Public Accountants reviewed ARB 23 soon after its issue and questioned whether the new procedures it recommended were "accepted procedures" at the date of its issue. General acceptability, the committee contended, depended on the extent to which procedures were applied in practice, which only time would tell. The committee proposed that the Institute submit a new Bulletin to a formal vote a year after issue because approval of a Bulletin by more than 90 percent of its members would demonstrate its general acceptability and authority.[34]

The Institute ignored the proposal, but the New Jersey committee had in effect challenged the authority of the Committee on Accounting Procedure to change accounting practice, raising an issue that would not go away. The Institute's Executive Committee or its governing council found it necessary to reaffirm the committee's authority a number of times in the following years,[35] and in the committee's final year its authority to change practice was challenged in court, again on a matter involving income tax allocation. Three public utilities, subsidiaries of American Electric Power, Inc., sought to enjoin the Committee on Accounting Procedure from issuing a letter dated April 15, 1959, interpreting a term in ARB No. 44 (revised), *Declining-balance Depreciation* (July 1958).

> The object of the letter was to express the Committee's view that the "deferred credit" used in tax-allocation entries was a liability and not part of stockholders' equity. The three plaintiff corporations alleged that classification of the account as a liability would cause them "irreparable injury, loss and damage." They also claimed that the letter was being issued without the Committee's customary exposure, thus not allowing interested parties to comment. The Federal District Court ruled against the plaintiffs. An appeal to the Second Circuit Court of Appeals was lost, the Court saying inter alia, "We think the courts may not dictate or control the procedures by

---

[34] "Comments on 'Accounting for Income Taxes,'" A Statement by the Committee on Accounting Principles and Practice of the New Jersey Society of Certified Public Accountants, *The Journal of Accountancy*, March 1945, pp. 235–240.

[35] Zeff, *Forging Accounting Principles in Five Countries*, pp. 160–167.

which a private organization expresses its honestly held views." Certiorari was denied by the U.S. Supreme Court, and the committee's letter was issued shortly thereafter [July 9, 1959].[36]

Neither the Institute's repeated reconfirmations of the committee's status nor its success in court corrected the weaknesses inherent in accounting principles whose authority rested on their general acceptability. The Institute did not finally face up to the problem until almost two decades later when the authority of the APB was challenged on another income tax matter—accounting for the investment credit.

INFLUENCE OF THE SECURITIES AND EXCHANGE COMMISSION.   Because accounting principles in the ARBs would be acceptable in SEC filings only if the Commission deemed them to have "substantial authoritative support," two committees of the Institute carefully cultivated a working relationship with the Commission to try to ensure that the Bulletins met that condition. The Committee on Cooperation with the SEC met regularly with the SEC's accounting staff and occasionally with the Commissioners. The Committee on Accounting Procedure and the director of research met with representatives of the SEC as needed and took great pains to keep the Chief Accountant informed about the committee's work, not only sending him copies of drafts of proposed Bulletins but also seeking his comments and criticisms and, if possible, his concurrence. Efforts to secure his agreement usually were successful.[37]

Some differences of opinion between the Committee on Accounting Procedure and the Commission were inevitable, of course, but they were the exception rather than the rule. Most disagreements were settled amicably, as was the long-running disagreement over the current operating performance and all-inclusive or clean surplus theories of income. The committee and the Commission sometimes were able to work out a compromise solution. The committee often adopted the Commission's view, at least once withdrawing a proposed Accounting Research Bulletin because of the Commission's opposition and at other times apparently being discouraged from issuing Bulletins by the Commission. The Commission occasionally adopted the committee's view or at least delayed issue of its own accounting releases pending issue of a Bulletin by the Institute.

The Commission affected accounting practice indirectly through its influence on the ARB. It also directly exercised its power to say whether or not a set of financial statements filed with it met the statutory requirements by means of rulings and orders, some published but most private.

The Commission published some formal rules, mostly on matters of disclosure rather than accounting principles. For example, the first regulations promulgated by the newly formed SEC required income statements to disclose sales and cost of goods sold, information that many managements had long considered to be confidential. Over 600 companies, about a quarter of those required to file registration statements in mid-1935, risked delisting of their securities by refusing to disclose publicly the required information. The Commission granted hearings to a significant number of them and also heard arguments of security analysts, investment bankers, and other users of financial statements that the information was necessary. The Commission then "notified all of the companies affected that the information was necessary for a fair presentation and that this need overcame any arguments that had been advanced against it."[38]

The companies had little choice but to comply, and the effect of the rule was to put reporting of sales and cost of sales in the United States decades ahead of most of the rest of the world. The controversy surrounding initial application of the rule subsided, and reporting sales and cost

---

[36] Zeff, *Forging Accounting Principles in Five Countries*, p. 166.

[37] Id., pp. 150 and 151; Blough, "Development of Accounting Principles in the United States," pp. 8 and 9. Carman G. Blough, first Chief Accountant of the SEC (1935–1938), became a charter member of the Committee on Accounting Procedure and later became the first full-time director of research of the Institute. Chief Accountants during the life (1938–1959) of the Committee on Accounting Procedure were William W. Wentz (1938–1947), Earle C. King (1947–1956), and Andrew Barr (1956–1972), whose term also included most of the life (1959–1973) of the committee's successor, the Accounting Principles Board.

[38] Blough, "Development of Accounting Principles in the United States," p. 10.

of goods sold has been common practice for so long that few people now know of its once controversial nature or of the Commission's part in promulgating it.

The Commission largely exercised its power behind the scenes through informal rulings and orders in "deficiency letters" on registrants' financial statements. The recipient of a deficiency letter could decide either to amend the financial statements to comply with the SEC's ruling or go to Washington to try to convince the staff, and anyone else at the Commission who would listen, of the merits of the accounting that the staff had challenged. If that informal conference process failed to produce agreement, a registrant could do little except comply or withdraw the registration and forgo issuing the securities. The only appeal to the Commission of a staff ruling on an accounting issue was in the form of a hearing to determine whether a stop order should be issued to prevent the registration from becoming effective because it contained misrepresentations—in effect "a hearing to determine whether or not [the registrant was] about to commit a fraud.... [Since b]usinessmen who have any reputation do not put themselves in the position of putative swindlers merely to determine matters of accounting,"[39] those private administrative rulings effectively settled most accounting questions.

The SEC's far-reaching rule that assets must never be accounted for at more than their cost was promulgated in that way. "[N]either the Securities and Exchange Commission nor the accounting profession issued rules or guidelines directly proscribing write-ups [of assets] or supplemental disclosures of current values. The change was brought about by the intervention of the SEC's staff, who 'discouraged' both practices through informal administrative procedures."[40] "[T]he SEC took a stand from the very beginning.... establish[ing] its position so early [that] we often overlook the fact that in [the basis for accounting for assets] the Commission never gave the profession a chance to even consider the matter insofar as registrants are concerned."[41]

****In the sense that the commission's role has long been forgotten or unknown, experience with the cost rule was similar to that of the rule requiring disclosure of sales and cost of sales. But the similarity ended there. The cost rule involved accounting principle rather than disclosure. And, instead of subsiding as did resistance to the disclosure rule, controversy surrounding the cost rule intensified and in the years following the Second World War led to a major and long-lasting division within the Institute.

Because of widespread concern about the effects on financial statements of the high rate of inflation during the war and the greatly increased prices of replacing assets after the war, the Institute had created the Study Group on Business Income, financed jointly with the Rockefeller Foundation. Its report concluded that financial statements could be meaningful only if expressed in units of equal purchasing power. It advocated accounting that reflected the effects of changes in the general level of prices on the cost of assets already owned and the resulting costs and expenses from their use,[42] a change in accounting considered necessary by many Institute leaders and members.

While the Study Group was still at work, the Committee on Accounting Procedure, supported by many other Institute leaders and members and by the SEC, issued ARB No. 33, *Depreciation and High Costs* (December 1947), which rejected "price-level depreciation" and suggested instead that management annually appropriate net income or retained earnings in contemplation of replacing productive facilities at higher price levels. The Bulletin effectively blocked use of depreciation in excess of that based on cost in measuring net income that had been contemplated or adopted by a few large companies but also provoked an active opposition to the committee's action.

Prominent among those who criticized the committee for in effect applying the SEC's cost rule instead of facing up to the accounting problems caused by the effects of changes in the general price

---

[39] A. A. Berle, Jr., "Accounting and the Law," *The Accounting Review*, March 1938, p. 12. [Reprinted in *The Journal of Accountancy*, May 1938, p. 372.]

[40] R. G. Walker, "The SEC's Ban on Upward Asset Revaluations and the Disclosure of Current Values," *Abacus*, March 1992, pp. 3 and 4.

[41] Blough, "Development of Accounting Principles in the United States," p. 10.

[42] *Changing Concepts of Business Income*, Report of the Study Group on Business Income (New York: The Macmillan Company, 1952), pp. 1–4, 103–109.

level was George O. May,[43] who had been instrumental in creating the Study Group on Business Income. He served as consultant to and then as a member of the group and later would be a joint author of its report. He criticized the committee's action for prejudging and undermining the Study Group's efforts, thereby foreclosing any real discussion of "... the relation between changes in the price level and the concept of business income."[44] He considered ARB 33 to be, however, only one of a number of missteps over the following decade that showed that the committee had lost its way. He also criticized the committee, among other things, for failing to cast aside outmoded conventions in favor of others more consonant with the changed conditions in the economy and for adopting public utility accounting procedures such as the Federal Power Commission's "original (or predecessor) cost"—cost to the corporate or natural person first devoting the property to the public service rather than cost to the present owner—that the committee itself earlier had held to be contrary to generally accepted accounting principles.[45]

Despite the criticisms, the committee held its course, though not without some wavering. It twice considered issuing a Bulletin approving upward revaluations of assets but each time dropped the attempt in the face of the unequivocal opposition of the SEC. Although the number of dissents to the cost rule increased each time the committee revisited the question of changing price levels, the committee "was unable to marshal a two-thirds majority in favor of a new policy"[46] and in 1958 dropped the subject from its agenda.

Whether it was influencing accounting practice directly through publishing rules or establishing them in informal rulings and private conferences with registrant companies or indirectly through the Committee on Accounting Procedure, the SEC generally seems to have had its way.

Decision to Issue Principles Piecemeal Reaffirmed.   The Committee on Accounting Procedure had to deal ad hoc with the SEC's comments on and objections to its Bulletins, issued or proposed, because it had no comprehensive statement of principles on which to base responses to the Commission's own ad hoc comments and rulings. Although the committee had decided early not to take the time required to develop a statement of broad principles on which to base solutions to practice problems (p. 2-12), the need for a comprehensive statement or codification of accounting principles continued to be raised occasionally, and the committee periodically revisited the question. Each time it decided against a project of that kind.

One of those occasions was in 1949, when the committee reconsidered its earlier decision and began work on a comprehensive statement of accounting principles. Ultimately, however, it again abandoned the project as not feasible and instead in 1953 issued ARB 43, *Restatement and Revision of Accounting Research Bulletins*. ARB 43 superseded the first 42 ARBs, except for three that were withdrawn as no longer applicable and eight that were reports of the Committee on Terminology and were reviewed and published separately in Accounting Terminology Bulletin No. 1, *Review and Résumé*. Although ARB 43 brought together the earlier Bulletins and grouped them by subject matter, "this collection retained the original flavor of the bulletins, i.e., a group of separate opinions on different subjects."[47]

Thus, the decision of the Committee on Accounting Procedure at its first meeting to put out brush fires as they flared up rather than to codify accepted accounting principles to provide a basis

---

[43] George O. May, "Should the LIFO Principle Be Considered in Depreciation Accounting When Prices Vary Widely?" *The Journal of Accountancy*, December 1947, pp. 453–456.

[44] George O. May, "Income Accounting and Social Revolution," *The Journal of Accountancy*, June 1957, p. 38.

[45] John Lawler, "A Talk with George O. May," *The Journal of Accountancy*, June 1955, pp. 41–45; George O. May, "Business Combinations: An Alternative View," *The Journal of Accountancy*, April 1957, pp. 33–36; and an unpublished memorandum dictated by May in 1958 and quoted in Paul Grady, ed., *Memoirs and Accounting Thought of George O. May* (New York: The Ronald Press Company, 1962), pp. 277–279.

[46] Zeff, *Forging Accounting Principles in Five Countries*, pp. 155–157 and 165–166.

[47] Storey, *The Search for Accounting Principles*, p. 43.

for solving financial accounting and reporting problems set the course that the committee pursued for its entire 21-year history. All 51 ARBs reflected that decision.

Influence of the American Accounting Association.   During the 21 years that the Committee on Accounting Procedure was issuing the ARBs, the AAA revised its 1936 "A Tentative Statement of Accounting Principles Underlying Corporate Financial Statements" in 1941, 1948, and 1957, including eight Supplementary Statements to the 1948 Revision. In the "Tentative Statement," as already noted, the executive committee of the AAA emphasized that improvement in accounting practice could best be achieved by strengthening the theoretical framework that supported practice and attempted to formulate a comprehensive set of concepts and standards from which to derive and by which to evaluate rules and procedures. Principles were not merely descriptions of procedures but standards against which procedures might be judged.

The executive committee of the Association, like the committees of the Institute concerned with accounting principles, regarded the principles as being derived from accounting practice, although the means of derivation differed—distillation or compilation according to the Institute and theoretical analysis according to the Association. Thus, the "Tentative Statement" set forth 20 principles, each a proposition embodying "a corollary of this fundamental axiom":

> Accounting is . . . not essentially a process of valuation, but the allocation of historical costs and revenues to the current and succeeding fiscal periods. [page 188]

Although the AAA's intent was to emphasize accounting's conceptual underpinnings, the "Tentative Statement" was substantially less conceptual and more practice oriented than might appear, not only because its principles were derived from practice but also because its "fundamental axiom" was essentially a description of existing practice. The same description of accounting was inherent in the report of the Special Committee on Cooperation with Stock Exchanges, was voiced by George O. May at the annual meeting of the Institute in October 1935,[48] and was evident in most of the ARBs.

That the principles in the Statements of the AAA were significantly like those in the ARBs should come as no surprise. "Inasmuch as both the Institute and the Association subscribed to the same basic philosophy regarding the nature of income determination, it was more or less inevitable that they should reach similar conclusions, even though they followed different paths."[49]

The AAA's 1941 and 1948 revisions generally continued in the direction set by the 1936 "Tentative Statement." Some changes began to appear in some of the Supplementary Statements to the 1948 Revision and in the 1957 Revision. They probably were too late, however, to have had much effect on the ARBs, even if the Committee on Accounting Procedure had paid much attention.

Long-lasting influence on accounting practice of the "Tentative Statement," as noted earlier, came some time after it was issued and mostly indirectly through two of its principles on "all-inclusive income" (one a corollary of the other) and a monograph by W. A. Paton and A. C. Littleton.

"All-Inclusive Income" versus "Avoiding Distortion of Periodic Income".   "A Tentative Statement of Accounting Principles Underlying Corporate Financial Statements" strongly supported what was later called the *all-inclusive income* or *clean surplus theory*. The principle (No. 8, page 189), which gave the theory one of its names, was that an income statement for a period should include all revenues, expenses, gains, and losses properly recognized during the period "regardless of whether or not they are the results of operations in that period." The corollary (No. 18, page 191), which gave the theory its other name, was that no revenues, expenses, gains, or losses should be recognized directly in earned surplus (retained earnings or undistributed profits).

---

[48] George O. May, "The Influence of Accounting on the Development of an Economy," *The Journal of Accountancy*, January 1936, p. 15.

[49] Storey, *The Search for Accounting Principles*, p. 45.

The SEC later strongly supported that accounting, and it became a bone of contention between the SEC and the Committee on Accounting Procedure. The committee generally favored the "current operating performance" theory of income, which excluded from net income extraordinary and nonrecurring gains and losses "to avoid distorting the net income for the period." The disagreement broke into the open with the issue of ARB No. 32, *Income and Earned Surplus* [Retained Earnings] (December 1947), whose publication in the January 1948 issue of *The Journal of Accountancy* was accompanied by a letter from SEC Chief Accountant Earle C. King saying that the "Commission has authorized the staff to take exception to financial statements which appear to be misleading, even though they reflect the application of Accounting Research Bulletin No. 32 (page 25)." Two more Bulletins, ARB No. 35, *Presentation of Income and Earned Surplus* (October 1948), and ARB No. 41, *Presentation of Income and Earned Surplus* (*Supplement to Bulletin No. 35*) (July 1951), followed as the committee and the SEC tried to work out a number of compromises. Each effort proved unsatisfactory to one or both parties.

Years later the APB would adopt an all-inclusive income statement in APB Opinion No. 9, *Reporting the Results of Operations* (December 1966). That accounting and reporting has since been modified by admitting some significant exceptions, primarily by FASB Statement No. 12, *Accounting for Certain Marketable Securities* (December 1975),[50] and FASB Statement No. 52, *Foreign Currency Translation* (December 1981). Thus, net income reported under current generally accepted accounting principles cannot accurately be described as all-inclusive income, but the idea of all-inclusive income is still generally highly regarded, and many still see it as a desirable goal to which to return.

"Matching of Costs and Revenues" and "Assets Are Costs".   Two members of the AAA executive committee that issued "A Tentative Statement of Accounting Principles Underlying Corporate Financial Statements" in 1936 undertook to write a monograph to explain its concepts. The result, *An Introduction to Corporate Accounting Standards*, by W. A. Paton and A. C. Littleton (1940), easily qualifies as the academic writing that has been most influential in accounting practice. Although the monograph rejected certain existing practices—such as last in, first out (LIFO) and cost or market, whichever is lower—it generally rationalized existing practice, providing it with what many saw as a theoretical basis that previously had been lacking.

The monograph accepted two of the premises that underlay the ARBs: (1) that periodic income determination was the central function of financial accounting—"the business enterprise is viewed as an organization designed to produce income"[51]—and (2) that (in the words of the "fundamental axiom" of the AAA's 1936 "Tentative Statement") accounting was "not essentially a process of valuation, but the allocation of historical costs and revenues to the current and succeeding fiscal periods."

> The fundamental problem of accounting, therefore, is the division of the stream of costs incurred between the present and the future in the process of measuring periodic income. The technical instruments used in reporting this division are the income statement and the balance sheet. . . . The income statement reports the assignment [of costs] to the current period; the balance sheet exhibits the costs incurred which are reasonably applicable to the years to come.[52]

The monograph described the periodic income determination process as the "matching of costs and revenues," giving it not only a catchy name but also strong intuitive appeal—a process of

---

[50] FASB Statement 12 was superseded by FASB Statement No. 115, *Accounting for Certain Investments in Debt and Equity Securities* (May 1993), which retained the provision requiring that unrealized holding gains and losses on certain securities be excluded from net income and directly added to or deducted from equity.

[51] W. A. Paton and A. C. Littleton, *An Introduction to Corporate Accounting Standards* (Ann Arbor, MI: American Accounting Association, 1940), p. 23.

[52] Paton and Littleton, *An Introduction to Corporate Accounting Standards*, p. 67.

relating the enterprise's efforts and accomplishments. The corollary was that most assets were "deferred charges to revenue," costs waiting to be "matched" against future revenues:

> The factors acquired for production which have not yet reached the point in the business process where they may be appropriately treated as "cost of sales" or "expense" are called "assets," and are presented as such in the balance sheet. It should not be overlooked, however, that these "assets" are in fact "revenue charges in suspense" awaiting some future matching with revenue as costs or expenses.
>
> The common tendency to draw a distinction between cost and expense is not a happy one, since expenses are also costs in a very important sense, just as assets are costs. "Costs" are the fundamental data of accounting. . . .
>
> The balance sheet thus serves as a means of carrying forward unamortized acquisition prices, the not-yet-deducted costs; it stands as a connecting link joining successive income statements into a composite picture of the income stream.[53]

Not surprisingly, those who had supported the accounting principles developed in the ARBs but were uncomfortable with those principles' apparent lack of theoretical support found highly attractive the theory that "matching costs and revenues" not only determined periodic net income but also justified the practice of accounting for most assets at their historical costs or an unamortized portion thereof.

However, just as the institutionalizing of a broad definition of accounting principles had caused problems for the Committee on Accounting Procedure itself and later for the APB, the institutionalizing of "matching costs with revenues," "costs are assets," and "avoiding distortion of periodic income" also caused problems for the FASB in developing a conceptual framework for financial accounting and reporting. The FASB found those expressions not only to be ingrained in accountants' vocabularies and widely used as reasons for or against particular accounting or reporting procedures but also to be generally vague, highly subjective, and emotion laden (pp. 2-32–2-45 of this chapter). They have proven to be of minimal help in actually resolving difficult accounting issues.

(iii) Failure to Reduce the Number of Alternative Accounting Methods.

The Institute's effort aimed at improving accounting by reducing the number of acceptable alternatives probably did improve accounting by culling out some "bad" practices.

> There are those who seem to believe that very little progress has been made towards the development of accounting principles and the narrowing of areas of differences in the principles followed in practice.
>
> It is difficult for me to see how anyone who has knowledge of accounting as it was practiced during the first quarter of this century and how it is practiced today can fail to recognize the tremendous advances that have taken place in the art.[54]

A number of the practices for whose acceptance Sanders, Hatfield, and Moore's *A Statement of Accounting Principles* had been lambasted[55] had disappeared by about 1950. It is uncertain, however, how much of that improvement was due to the ARBs and how much to other factors, such as the good professional judgment of corporate officials or auditors or the SEC's rejection of some egregious procedures.

Ironically, the end result was an overabundance of "good" practices that had survived the process. That plethora of sanctioned alternatives for accounting for similar transactions continued

---

[53] Paton and Littleton, *An Introduction to Corporate Accounting Standards*, pp. 25 and 67.

[54] Blough, "Development of Accounting Principles in the United States," p. 12.

[55] The report contained statements to the effect that (1) impairments of net worth in the form of catastrophic losses might be listed on the asset side, (2) deficits of new companies might be shown as assets, (3) capital losses might be carried as deferred charges if charging them against the income of a single period would distort profit, etc. (Storey, *The Search for Accounting Principles*, p. 30).

to thrive despite the committee's charge to reduce the number of alternative procedures because, just as Will Rogers never met a man he didn't like, the committee rarely met an accounting principle it didn't find acceptable.

> Two factors contributed to the increase in the number of accepted alternatives: (1) the committee on accounting procedure failed to make firm choices among alternative procedures, and (2) the committee was clearly reluctant to condemn widely used methods even though they were in conflict with its recommendations. For example, in its very first pronouncement on a specific problem—unamortized discount and redemption premium on refunded bonds [ARB 2]—the committee considered three possible procedures, of which it rejected one and accepted two.

> The committee had a clear preference—it praised the method of amortization of cost over the remaining life of the old bonds as consistent with good accounting thinking regarding the relative importance of the income statement and the balance sheet. It condemned immediate writeoff as a holdover of balance-sheet conservatism which was of "dubious value if attained at the expense of a lack of conservatism in the income account, which is far more significant" [ARB 2, page 13]. Nevertheless, the latter method had "too much support in accounting theory and practice and in the decisions of courts and commissions for the committee to recommend that it should be regarded as unacceptable or inferior" [ARB 2, page 20].

> ... The solution turned out to be a "live-and-let-live" policy. The major thing accomplished by the bulletin was the elimination of a method [amortization over the life of the new issue] which was not widely used anyway. And this type of solution was characteristic of the bulletins, rather than exceptional.

> The extreme to which this attitude was sometimes carried is exemplified in the Institute's inventory bulletin [ARB 29], a classic example of trying to please everyone. The committee accepted almost every conceivable inventory [pricing] procedure, except the discredited base-stock method. The committee therefore passed up the opportunity to narrow the range of acceptable alternative procedures in the area of inventory [pricing]. . . . Instead, the individual practitioner was left with the high-sounding but useless admonition that the method chosen should be the one which most clearly reflected periodic income.[56]

The proliferation of accepted alternative principles was probably inherent in an approach that championed disclosure and consistency in use of procedures over specific principles and consistency between principles.

Most of the controversial subjects covered by the ARB came back to haunt the Committee on Accounting Procedure's successor, the APB. The case-by-case, ad hoc, or piecemeal approach produced few lasting solutions to financial accounting and reporting problems.

(c) ACCOUNTING PRINCIPLES BOARD—1959–1973.   The American Institute of Accountants changed its name to the American Institute of Certified Public Accountants in June 1957, and in October of that year the new president of the AICPA, Alvin R. Jennings, proposed that the Institute reorganize its efforts in the area of accounting principles.[57] His recommendation came at a time when the Committee on Accounting Procedure was under fire for, among other things, failing to reduce the number of alternative accounting procedures. A growing number of Institute members sensed that the committee's firefighting approach to accounting principles had gone about as far as it could and expressed an urgent need for the committee to abandon that effort and to do what it had theretofore been reluctant to do—formulate or codify a comprehensive statement of accounting principles.

Jennings called for an increased research effort to reexamine the basic assumptions of accounting and to develop authoritative statements to guide accountants. He appointed a Special Committee

---

[56] Storey, *The Search for Accounting Principles*, pp. 49 and 50.

[57] Alvin R. Jennings, "Present-Day Challenges in Financial Reporting," *The Journal of Accountancy*, January 1958, pp. 28–34. [Reprinted in Stephen A. Zeff, *The Accounting Postulates and Principles Controversy of the 1960s* (New York and London: Garland Publishing, Inc., 1982).]

on Research Program, and its report, *Organization and Operations of the Accounting Research Program and Related Activities*, in December 1958, provided the basis for the organization of an APB and an Accounting Research Division. The committee set a lofty goal:

> The general purpose of the Institute in the field of financial accounting should be to advance the written expression of what constitutes generally accepted accounting principles, for the guidance of its members and others. This means something more than a survey of existing practice. It means continuing effort to determine appropriate practice and to narrow the areas of difference and inconsistency in practice. In accomplishing this, reliance should be placed on persuasion rather than on compulsion. The Institute, however, can, and it should, take definite steps to lead in the thinking on unsettled and controversial issues.[58]

The APB in September 1959 replaced the Committee on Accounting Procedure as the senior technical committee of the Institute with responsibility for accounting principles and authority to issue pronouncements on accounting principles without the need for approval of the Institute's membership or governing Council. The Board's 18 members were members of the Institute, and thus CPAs, who, like members of the Committee on Accounting Procedure, continued their affiliations with their firms, companies, and universities while serving without compensation on the Board.

The APB was originally envisioned as the instrument through which a definitive statement of accounting principles would finally be achieved—what the Wheat Report later would call a "'grand design' of accounting theory upon which all else would rest."[59] The report of the Special Committee on Research Program in 1958 outlined a hierarchy of postulates, principles, and rules to guide the APB's work:

> The broad problem of financial accounting should be visualized as requiring attention at four levels: first, postulates; second, principles; third, rules or other guides for the application of principles in specific situations; and fourth, research.
>
> Postulates are few in number and are the basic assumptions on which principles rest. They necessarily are derived from the economic and political environment and from the modes of thought and customs of all segments of the business community. The profession . . . should make clear its understanding and interpretation of what they are, to provide a meaningful foundation for the formulation of principles and the development of rules or other guides for the application of principles in specific situations. . . .
>
> A fairly broad set of co-ordinated accounting principles should be formulated on the basis of the postulates. The statement of this probably should be similar in scope to the statements on accounting and reporting standards issued by the American Accounting Association. The principles, together with the postulates, should serve as a framework of reference for the solution of detailed problems.
>
> Rules or other guides for the application of accounting principles in specific situations, then, should be developed in relation to the postulates and principles previously expressed. Statements of these probably should be comparable as to subject matter with the present accounting research bulletins. They should have reasonable flexibility.
>
> Adequate accounting research is necessary in all of the foregoing.[60]

---

[58] "Report to Council on the Special Committee on Research Program," *The Journal of Accountancy*, December 1958, pp. 62 and 63. [Reprinted in *Organization and Operations of the Accounting Research Program and Related Activities* (New York: American Institute of Certified Public Accountants, 1959); in Zeff, *Forging Accounting Principles in Five Countries*, pp. 248–265; and in Zeff, *The Accounting Postulates and Principles Controversy of the 1960s*.]

[59] *Establishing Financial Accounting Standards*, Report of the Study on Establishment of Accounting Principles (New York: American Institute of Certified Public Accountants, March 29, 1972), p. 15. [Often called the Wheat Report, after the group's chairman, Francis M. Wheat, a former SEC commissioner.]

[60] "Report to Council of the Special Committee on Research Program," p. 63.

The report of the Special Committee on Research Program contemplated that the APB would quickly concern itself with providing the conceptual context from which would flow the rules or procedures to be applied in specific situations. The APB would then use the postulates and principles in choosing between alternate rules and procedures to narrow the areas of difference and inconsistency in practice.

(i) Postulates and Principles.   Following that prescription, the new Accounting Research Division published Accounting Research Study No. 1, *The Basic Postulates of Accounting*, by Maurice Moonitz in 1961, and Accounting Research Study No. 3, *A Tentative Set of Broad Accounting Principles for Business Enterprises*, by Robert T. Sprouse and Maurice Moonitz in 1962. Accounting Research Studies (ARS) were not publications of the APB and thus did not constitute official Institute pronouncements on accounting principles. On the authority of the Director of Accounting Research, Maurice Moonitz, they were issued for wide exposure and comment.

In an article entitled "Why Do We Need 'Postulates' and 'Principles'?" Moonitz explained that postulates and principles were necessary to give accounting "the integrating structure it needs to give more than passing meaning to its specific procedures. It will provide 'experience' with the aid it needs from 'logic' to explain why it is that some procedures are appropriate and others are not."[61] An integrating structure would provide accounting with a mechanism by which to rid itself of procedures that clearly were not in harmony with the authoritatively stated principles.

Among the most significant contributions of those ARS was their development of the terms postulates and principles, especially postulates, which Moonitz explained in his article:

> "[P]ostulates" is used ... to denote those basic propositions of accounting which describe the accountant's understanding of the world in which he lives and acts. The propositions are therefore generalizations about the environment of accounting, generalizations based upon a more or less comprehensive view and understanding of that environment. The term "principles" is used to denote those basic propositions which stem from the postulates and refer expressly to accounting issues.[62]

To qualify as a postulate, a proposition had to meet two conditions: It must be "self-evident," an assertion about the environment in which accounting functions that is universally accepted as valid; and it must be "fruitful for accounting," that is, it must "relate to (be inferred from) a world that does exist and not to one that is a fiction." Moonitz also noted that self-evident is not, as some who commented on ARS 1 seemed to have believed, the same as trivial.[63] An example from ARS 1 to which he referred made his point: "Most of the goods and services that are produced are distributed through exchange, and are not directly consumed by the producers" (Postulate A-2.—Exchange). In that straightforward observation lie the reasons that accounting is concerned with production and distribution of goods and services and with exchange prices; if it is further observed that most exchanges are for cash, the reasons that accounting is concerned with cash prices and cash flows become apparent. As Moonitz observed, the "proposition is an extraordinarily fruitful one for accounting."[64]

Emphasis on a basis for accounting principles comprising self-evident propositions about the real-world environment in which accounting functions, and on which it reports, constituted a significant shift in thinking. Accountants' earlier emphasis, largely in a conceptual vacuum, had been

---

[61] Maurice Moonitz, "Why Do We Need 'Postulates' and 'Principles'?" *The Journal of Accountancy*, December 1963, p. 46. [Reprinted in Zeff, *The Accounting Postulates and Principles Controversy of the 1960s*.]

[62] Id., p. 43.

[63] Id., pp. 44 and 45.

[64] Maurice Moonitz, *The Basic Postulates of Accounting, Accounting Research Study No. 1* (New York: American Institute of Certified Public Accountants, 1961), p. 22. [Reprinted in Zeff, *The Accounting Postulates and Principles Controversy of the 1960s*.]

on the conventional nature of accounting and the resulting necessity for conventional procedures, allocations, opinion, and judgment to produce the numbers in income statements and balance sheets. That emphasis provided an unstable and uncertain basis for accounting principles.

> Accounting is often described as "conventional" in nature, and its principles as "conventions." The two terms, conventions and conventional, are ambiguous; the statement that accounting is conventional may be true or false depending on which meaning is intended. It is true if it refers to such things as the use of Arabic numerals, the use of the dollar sign, or the sequence in which assets, liabilities, revenues, and expenses are listed in financial statements because other symbols and forms could be used to convey precisely the same message. It is not true if the statement means that any proposition which accountants accept is a valid one. As a farfetched example, assume that all uninsured losses, without exception, were to be converted into "assets" by the expedient of calling them "deferred charges against future operations." This convention would not make assets out of losses; it would merely give the approval of accountants to a false assertion concerning the enterprise that suffered the losses, and would place accountants and accounting in an unfavorable light in the eyes of those who knew what had happened.
>
> Suppose, however, that the assertion about accounting principles as "conventions" is intended to convey the idea that they are generalizations, inferences drawn from a large body of data, and that they are not intended to be literal descriptions of reality. "Conventions" and "conventional" are clearly valid descriptions, then, but not because accounting is unique. Instead, accounting is like every other field of human endeavor in this one respect: Its basic propositions are generalizations or abstractions and not minute descriptions of every aspect of "reality."[65]

Postulates that were self-evident propositions about the real world and also fruitful for accounting were needed to provide a solid basis for accounting principles and rules—"a platform from which to start," "a place to stand"—and "a place to stand" was prerequisite to real improvement in accounting practice. "Failure by accountants to agree on a 'place to stand' will mean continued operation in mid-air, as unstable and uncertain in the future as in the past."[66]

In the more than 30 years since the two studies were published, their valuable contributions to accounting thought increasingly have been recognized. Some of the conclusions and recommendations of ARS 3, *A Tentative Set of Broad Accounting Principles for Business Enterprises*, such as use of replacement costs of inventories and plant and equipment and accounting for the effects of changes in the general price level, have remained controversial and still are largely unacceptable to many accountants. In contrast, most of the conclusions of ARS 1, *The Basic Postulates of Accounting*, long ago became commonplace in accounting literature. For example, the basic idea that the foundation for accounting principles lies in self-evident propositions about the environment in which accounting functions was incorporated into APB Statement No. 4, *Basic Concepts and Accounting Principles Underlying Financial Statements of Business Enterprises*, in 1970. By 1975 that basic idea had become an essential part of the FASB's conceptual framework.

When ARS 3 was published in April 1962, however, each copy contained a Statement of the Accounting Principles Board (later designated APB Statement 1) passing judgment on both studies: "The Board believes ... that while these studies are a valuable contribution to accounting thinking, they are too radically different from present generally accepted accounting principles for acceptance at this time."

It was not the APB's finest hour. Even though general dissatisfaction with the state of existing practice had been the reason for the APB's creation and the new emphasis on research, the Board and many others reacted as if they had been caught by surprise that the studies recommended some significant changes in existing practice. Moreover, instead of letting consideration of the studies follow the anticipated course of wide circulation and exposure and receipt of comments from interested readers before the Board considered the studies, the Board reacted first, spoiling

---

[65] Moonitz, "Why Do We Need 'Postulates' and 'Principles'?" pp. 45 and 46.
[66] Id., p. 45.

any opportunity of receiving unbiased comments on the studies. The experience seems to have adversely affected for years the Board's approach to postulates and principles.

The experience may have made the APB "disillusioned with, or at least skeptical toward, the potential that fundamental or 'theoretical' research might have for solving accounting problems. . . . [T]he Board seemed to abandon the hope of the Special Committee on Research Program that such research could serve as a foundation for pronouncements on accounting principles."[67] In any event, the Board did little or nothing more on accounting postulates and principles until 1965, except to authorize the project that in March 1965 became ARS No. 7, *Inventory of Generally Accepted Accounting Principles*, by Paul Grady, the second Director of Accounting Research. In 1965, the Board renewed efforts on fundamental matters—which it then called basic concepts and principles rather than postulates and principles—to comply with recommendations to the Institute's governing Council by the Special Committee on Opinions of the Accounting Principles Board (the Seidman Committee), but most Board members seemed to lack enthusiasm for the effort.

By the summer of 1962, when the Board hoped that it had put behind it the fuss over the postulates and principles studies, three years had passed since an Institute committee had issued a pronouncement on accounting principles. The Board turned its attention from postulates and principles and toward solving specific problems, just as had the Committee on Accounting Procedure.

(ii) The Accounting Principles Board, the Investment Credit, and the Seidman Committee. When the Board decided to tackle the thorny issue of accounting for the investment credit, which was enacted in federal income tax law for the first time in October 1962, it inadvertently created an ideal scenario for fueling doubts about its effectiveness and authority. The law provided that a company acquiring a depreciable asset other than a building could deduct up to 7 percent of the cost of the asset from its income tax otherwise payable in the year the asset was placed in service. Two accounting methods sprang up—the "flow-through" method, by which the entire reduction in tax was included in income of the year the asset was placed in service, and the "deferral" method, by which the tax reduction was included in net income over the productive life of the acquired property.

APB Opinion No. 2, *Accounting for the "Investment Credit,"* was issued in December 1962, setting forth the Board's choice of the deferral over the flow-through method. Some of the large accounting firms then popularly called the Big Eight almost immediately made it known that they would not expect their clients to abide by the Opinion. The SEC ruled that both methods had substantial authoritative support, making either acceptable and thereby effectively undercutting the Board's position. Fifteen months later, the Board issued APB Opinion No. 4 (Amending No. 2), *Accounting for the "Investment Credit,"* reaffirming its opinion that the investment credit should be accounted for by the deferral method. It recognized, however, the inevitable effect of the SEC's action on the authority of APB Opinion 2:

> [T]he authority of Opinions of this Board rests upon their general acceptability. The Board, in the light of events and developments occurring since the issuance of Opinion No. 2, has determined that its conclusions as there expressed have not attained the degree of acceptability which it believes is necessary to make the Opinion effective.
>
> In the circumstances the Board believes that . . . the alternative method of treating the credit as a reduction of Federal income taxes of the year in which the credit arises is also acceptable. [paragraphs 9 and 10]

The APB's authority had been severely undermined. Did APB Opinions still have to pass the test of general acceptance, as did the ARB before them, or did they constitute generally accepted accounting principles solely because the APB had issued them? The Board voted to bring the matter to the Executive Committee and the governing Council of the AICPA.

In May 1964, after an extended and heated debate, Council adopted a resolution "that it is the sense of this Council that [audit] reports of members should disclose material departures from

---

[67] Zeff, *Forging Accounting Principles in Five Countries*, pp. 177 and 178.

Opinions of the Accounting Principles Board.... " Pursuant to a directive in the resolution, the Institute formed a Special Committee on Opinions of the Accounting Principles Board to suggest ways of implementing the resolution and to review the entire matter of the status of APB Opinions and the development of accounting principles and practices for financial reporting.

The special committee reported to Council on its first charge in October 1964, and Council adopted a resolution and transmitted it to Institute members in a Special Bulletin, *Disclosure of Departures from Opinions of the Accounting Principles Board*. It declared that members of the Institute should see to it that a material departure from APB Opinions (or from ARBs still in effect)—even if the auditor concluded that the departure rested on substantial authoritative support—was disclosed in notes to the financial statements or in the auditor's report. Since Council adopted recommendations that "1. 'Generally accepted accounting principles' are those principles which have substantial authoritative support [and] 2. Opinions of the APB constitute 'substantial authoritative support,'" the authority of APB Opinions no longer depended on their passing a separate test of general acceptability.

The special committee, commonly referred to as the Seidman Committee after its second chairman, J. S. Seidman,[68] reported to Council on its second charge in May 1965, reiterating that an authoritative identification of generally accepted accounting principles was essential if an independent CPA was to fulfill his or her primary function of attesting to the conformity of financial statements with generally accepted accounting principles. Its Recommendation No. 1 was that:

At the earliest possible time, the [Accounting Principles] Board should:

a. Set forth its views as to the purposes and limitations of published financial statements....

b. Enumerate and describe the basic concepts to which accounting principles should be oriented.

c. State the accounting principles to which practices and procedures should conform.

d. Define such phrases in the auditor's report as "present fairly" and "generally accepted accounting principles." ...

e. Define the words of art employed by the profession, such as "substantial authoritative support," "concepts," "principles," "practices," "procedures," "assets," "liabilities," "income," and "materiality."[69]

The committee made that recommendation acknowledging that the Special Committee on Research Program had contemplated that the APB would have accomplished the task described by that time in its life, but it exculpated the Board: "This planned course ran into difficulty because current problems commanded attention and could not be neglected."[70]

However, the need for a solid conceptual foundation for accounting no longer could be neglected either:

[I]t remains true that until the basic concepts and principles are formulated and promulgated, there is no official bench mark for the premises on which the audit attestation stands. Nor is an enduring base provided by which to judge the reasonableness and consistency of treatment of a particular subject. Instead, footing is given to controversy and confusion.[71]

... Accounting, like other professions, makes use of words of art. Since accounting talks to the public, the profession's meaning, as distinguished from the literal dictionary meaning, must be explained to the public.

For example, ...

---

[68] The first chairman, William W. Werntz, died shortly after the special committee reported to Council on its first charge.

[69] *Report of Special Committee on Opinions of the Accounting Principles Board* (New York: American Institute of Certified Public Accountants, Spring 1965), p. 12.

[70] Id., p. 13.

[71] Id., p. 13.

What is meant by the expression "generally accepted accounting principles"? How is "generally" measured? What are "accounting principles"? Where are they inscribed, and by whom? ...

By "accepted," is the profession aiming at what is popular or what is right? There may be a difference. The ... Special Committee on Research Program said that "what constitutes generally accepted accounting principles ... means more than a survey of existing practice."

Then again, "accepted" by whom—the preparer of the financial statement, the profession, or the user?[72]

The profession has said that generally accepted accounting principles are those with "substantial authoritative support." What does that expression mean? What yardstick is to be applied to the words "substantial" and "authoritative"? What are the guidelines to prevent mere declaration, or use by someone, somewhere, from becoming the standard?

Many other expressions in accounting need explanation and clarification for the public. They include such words as "concepts," "principles," "practices," "procedures," "assets," "liabilities," "income," and "materiality."

Until the profession deals with all these matters satisfactorily, first for itself and then for understanding by the consumer of its product, there will continue to be an awkward failure of communication in a field where clear communication is vital.[73]

Accounting Principles Board Statement 4. Issued in October 1970, APB Statement No. 4, *Basic Concepts and Accounting Principles Underlying Financial Statements of Business Enterprises* was the Board's response to the Seidman Committee's recommendations. For those who had hoped for definitive answers to the Seidman Committee's questions or a statement of accounting's fundamental concepts and principles, APB Statement 4 was a disappointment. The Board gave every indication of having issued it primarily to comply, somewhat grudgingly, with the Seidman Committee's recommendations.

The definition of generally accepted accounting principles in APB Statement 4 and its description of their nature and how they become accepted, although couched in the careful language that characterized the Statement, merely reiterated what the Institute had been saying about them for over 30 years.

Generally accepted accounting principles incorporate the consensus[38] at a particular time as to ... [the items that should be recognized in financial statements, when they should be recognized, how they should be measured, how they should be displayed, and what financial statements should be provided].

... Generally accepted accounting principles encompass the conventions, rules, and procedures necessary to define accepted accounting practice at a particular time.... includ[ing] not only broad guidelines of general application, but also detailed practices and procedures.

Generally accepted accounting principles are conventional—that is, they become generally accepted by agreement (often tacit agreement) rather than by formal derivation from a set of

---

[38]Inasmuch as generally accepted accounting principles embody a consensus, they depend on notions such as *general acceptance* and *substantial authoritative support,* which are not precisely defined....

postulates or basic concepts. The principles have developed on the basis of experience, reason, custom, usage, and, to a significant extent, practical necessity.[74]

---

[72] Id., pp. 13 and 14.

[73] Id., p. 15.

[74] *Basic Concepts and Accounting Principles Underlying Financial Statements of Business Enterprises,* Statement of the Accounting Principles Board No. 4 (New York: American Institute of Certified Public Accountants, 1970), paragraphs 137–139.

Generally accepted accounting principles were a mixture of conventions, rules, procedures, and detailed practices that were distilled from experience and identified as principles primarily by observing existing accounting practice.

The basic concepts in Chapters 3–5 of APB Statement 4 were a mixed bag. On one hand, the definitions of assets, liabilities, and other "basic elements of financial accounting" were what George J. Staubus, who gave the Statement a generally positive review, called The Definitions Mess. All of the definitions were defective because the only essential distinguishing characteristic of assets (or liabilities) was that they were "recognized and measured as assets [or liabilities] in conformity with generally accepted accounting principles," and the other definitions depended on the definitions of assets and liabilities.[75]

On the other hand, the basic concepts also included new ideas (at least for Institute pronouncements) and normative propositions, and at least some of the concepts looked to what financial accounting ought to be in the future, not just to what it already was. These are examples:

- The basic purpose of financial accounting is to provide information that is useful to owners, creditors, and others in making economic decisions (paragraphs 40 and 73).

- Financial accounting is shaped to a significant extent by the nature of economic activity in individual business enterprises (paragraph 42).

- The transactions and other events that change an enterprise's resources, obligations, and residual interest include exchange transactions, nonreciprocal transfers, and other external events as well as production and other internal events (paragraph 62).

- Certain qualities or characteristics such as relevance, understandability, verifiability, neutrality, timeliness, comparability, and completeness make financial information useful (paragraphs 23 and 87–105).

- To make comparisons between enterprises as meaningful as possible, "differences between enterprises' financial statements should arise from basic differences in the enterprises themselves or from the nature of their transactions and not merely from differences in financial accounting practices and procedures" (paragraph 101).

Anyone familiar with the report of the Trueblood Study Group on objectives of financial statements and the FASB's conceptual framework will recognize that those and similar ideas later appeared in one or both of those sources.

Nevertheless, in describing itself, APB Statement 4 virtually ignored that it contained anything that was new, normative, or forward-looking, emphasizing instead that it looked only at the present and the past, even in describing its basic concepts. The Board was adamant that it had not passed judgment on the existing structure and apparently was almost equally reluctant to admit that it had broken new ground:

> The Statement is primarily descriptive, not prescriptive. It identifies and organizes ideas that for the most part are already accepted.... [T]he Statement contains two main sections that are essentially distinct—(a) Chapters 3–5 on the environment, objectives, and basic features of financial accounting and (b) Chapters 6–8 on present generally accepted accounting principles. The description of present generally accepted accounting principles is based primarily on observation of accounting practice. Present generally accepted accounting principles have not been formally derived from the environment, objectives, and basic features of financial accounting [that is, from the basic concepts.]*

> The aspects of the environment selected for discussion are those that appear to influence the financial accounting process directly. The objectives of financial accounting and financial statements discussed are goals toward which efforts *are presently directed*. [Emphasis added.] The accounting principles described are those that the Board believes are generally accepted *today*.

---

[75] George J. Staubus, "An Analysis of APB Statement No. 4," *The Journal of Accountancy*, February 1972, p. 39.

The Board has not evaluated or approved present generally accepted accounting principles except to the extent that principles have been adopted in Board Opinions. Publication of this Statement does not constitute approval by the Board of accounting principles that are not covered in its Opinions. [Emphasis in the original.] [paragraphs 3 and 4]

*[For some unexplained reason, the Statement does not use the term basic concepts after defining it in paragraph 1: "The term basic concepts is used to refer to the observations concerning the environment, the objectives of financial accounting and financial statements, and the basic features and basic elements of financial accounting discussed in Chapters 3–5 of the Statement" (paragraph 1, footnote 2). The rest of the Statement uses instead the full definition in footnote 2 or, as in this sentence, some shorter variation of it.]

The expected contribution of the basic concepts in the Statement was generally vague, and still in the future.

The Statement is a step toward development of a more consistent and comprehensive structure of financial accounting and of more useful financial information. It is intended to provide a framework within which the problems of financial accounting may be solved, although it does not propose solutions to those problems and does not attempt to indicate what generally accepted accounting principles should be. Evaluation of present accounting principles and determination of changes that may be desirable are left to future pronouncements of the Board. [paragraph 6]

Those paragraphs seemed to deflate unduly the most laudable parts of the Statement, almost as if the Board had gone out of its way to disparage the effort or otherwise to lower expectations about it. Instead of emphasizing that APB Statement 4 had begun to lay a basis for delineating what accounting ought to be and suggesting positive steps needed to build on it, the Board chose to characterize the Statement as primarily descriptive, thereby casting it into the category of uncritical description of what accounting already was. Once again, accounting principles had been defined as being essentially the product of experience.

However, there were by then too many people within and outside the profession who could no longer be satisfied with that view of accounting principles. Principles distilled from experience could lead only so far, and that point had long since been reached. For 15 to 20 years, principles distilled from experience had created more problems than they had solved, and a growing number of people interested in accounting principles had become convinced that principles had to be defined to mean a higher order of things than conventions or procedures. Dissatisfaction with the APB's performance in this area was mounting, and there was increasing pressure for the Board to state "the objectives of financial statements" as a basis for moving forward.

(iii) The End of the Accounting Principles Board.   At the same time, the APB was constantly under pressure from the SEC and others to confront current, specific problems encountered in practice and to issue Opinions on subjects seemingly far removed from the domain of principles, such as the presumed overstating of sales prices in some real estate sales with long-term financing, accounting for nonmonetary transactions, and reporting the effects of disposing of a segment of a business.

The SEC's urgency to deal with specific practice problems and widespread criticism of the use of the pooling of interests method influenced the APB and its staff to expend extra effort to produce an opinion on a highly controversial subject—accounting for business combinations—on which the Accounting Research Division had completed two related ARS: No. 5, *A Critical Study of Accounting for Business Combinations*, by Arthur R. Wyatt, and No. 10, *Accounting for Goodwill*, by George R. Catlett and Norman O. Olson.

Although the Board worked diligently and analyzed the problems about as well as could be expected in the absence of postulates and principles or other conceptual foundation, it became hopelessly deadlocked. It could find no solutions acceptable to a two-thirds majority to the problems of choosing between the purchase and pooling of interests methods for accounting for a business combination and of whether and how to capitalize goodwill and, if capitalized, whether to amortize it. Yet, it felt compelled to issue an Opinion because the SEC was almost certain to issue its own rule if the APB failed to do so.

The experience produced two Opinions in 1970, APB Opinion No. 16, *Business Combinations*, and No. 17, *Intangible Assets*, as well as more intense criticism of, and threats of legal action against, the Board. In a section entitled "Opinions 16 and 17—Vesuvius Erupts," Stephen A. Zeff reported that neither the Board's "hard-won compromise" nor the "'pressure-cooker' manner in which it was achieved" pleased anyone. "These two Opinions, perhaps more than any other factor, seem to have been responsible for a movement to undertake a comprehensive review of the procedure for establishing accounting principles."[76]

In January 1971, AICPA President Marshall S. Armstrong convened a conference to consider how the Institute might improve the process of establishing accounting principles, and two study groups were appointed to explore ways of improving financial reporting. The group chaired by Francis M. Wheat was formed to "examine the organization and operation of the APB and [to] determine what changes are necessary to attain better results faster."[77] The Wheat Group was primarily concerned with the processes and means by which accounting principles should be established. The Accounting Objectives Study Group, under the chairmanship of Robert M. Trueblood, was organized to review the objectives of financial statements and the technical problems in achieving those objectives.

The APB's days were numbered, although that was not yet clear, and perhaps not even suspected, in 1971, and the Board went on with its work. It issued almost half of its total of 31 Opinions after wheels were put in motion to develop an alternative structure that would eventually replace it.

Despite the criticisms the APB received for Opinions 16 and 17 and others and although some of its Opinions provided only partial solutions that would need to be revisited in the future, on balance its Opinions were successful. In several problem areas, the APB succeeded in remedying, sometimes almost completely and often to a significant degree, the greatest ill of the time by carrying out the charge it received at its creation: "to determine appropriate practice and to narrow the areas of difference and inconsistency in practice."[78] APB Opinions such as No. 9, *Reporting the Results of Operations*; No. 18, *The Equity Method of Accounting for Investments in Common Stock*; and No. 20, *Accounting Changes*, laid to rest long-standing controversies. APB Opinion No. 22, *Disclosure of Accounting Policies*, required implementation in 1972 of one of the key recommendations made in *Audits of Corporate Accounts* in 1932: Each company would disclose which methods it was using. Some of the most controversial APB Opinions—such as No. 5, *Reporting of Leases in Financial Statements of Lessee*; No. 8, *Accounting for the Cost of Pension Plans*; No. 11, *Accounting for Income Taxes*; No. 16, *Business Combinations*; No. 17, *Intangible Assets*; No. 21, *Interest on Receivables and Payables*; and No. 26, *Early Extinguishment of Debt*—caused some consternation and often fierce opposition, but both industry and public accountants learned to live with them, and later the FASB encountered opposition when it proposed changing some of them.

The report of the Wheat Group in March 1972, *Establishing Financial Accounting Standards*, concluded that many of the APB's problems were fatal flaws. The APB was weakened by nagging doubts about its independence, the inability of its part-time members to devote themselves entirely to the important problems confronting it, and the lack of coherence and logic of many of its pronouncements, which resulted from having to compromise too many opposing points of view. The group's solution was directed toward remedying those flaws, which, in its opinion, required a new arrangement.

The Wheat Report proposed establishment of a Financial Accounting Foundation, with trustees whose principal duties would be to appoint the members of a FASB and to raise funds for its operation. The Board would comprise seven members, all of whom would be salaried, full time, and unencumbered by other business affiliations during their tenure on the Board, and some of whom

---

[76] Zeff, *Forging Accounting Principles in Five Countries*, p. 216.
[77] Establishing Financial Accounting Standards, p. 87.
[78] "Report to Council of the Special Committee on Research Program," pp. 62 and 63.

would not have to be CPAs. The group recommended "Standards" Board rather than "Principles" Board because

> the APB (despite the prominence in its name of the term "principles") has deemed it necessary throughout its history to issue opinions on subjects which have almost nothing to do with "principles" in the usual sense [which "connotes things basic and fundamental, of a sort which can be expressed in few words, relatively timeless in nature, and in no way dependent upon changing fashions in business or the evolving needs of the investment community"].[79]

"Standard"—which connotes something established by authority or common consent as a pattern or model for guidance or a basis of comparison for judging quality, quantity, grade, level, and so on, and may need to be spelled out in some detail—was more descriptive than "principles" for most of what the APB did and what the FASB was expected to do.

The Wheat Group's diagnosis of the APB's terminal condition became the popular explanation, but it was not the only one. Oscar S. Gellein, a member of the APB during its final years and a member of the FASB during its early years, offered a perceptive analysis:

> The conditions most often identified with the problems of the APB were perceived conflicts of interests causing a waffling of positions and part-time effort where full-time effort was needed. In retrospect, those probably were not as significant as the absence of a structure of fundamental notions that would elevate the level at which debate begins and provide assurance of considerable consistency to the standards pronounced. The APB repetitively argued fundamentals. The same fundamentals were argued in taking up projects near the end of its tenure as were argued in connection with early projects. Even the most fundamental of fundamentals—assets, liabilities, revenue, expense—were never defined nor could the definitions be inferred from APB pronouncements.[80]

Thus, it may have been the Board's continual rejection of the ineluctable need to develop an underlying philosophy as a basis for accounting principles in favor of the Committee on Accounting Procedure's "brush fire" approach that most directly contributed to the way it was perceived and ultimately to its demise. The APB had never been able to achieve a consensus on the conceptual aspects of its work, which had effectively been pushed aside by the Board's efforts to narrow the areas of difference in accounting practice by a problem-by-problem treatment of pressing issues. Although the ARS on basic postulates and broad principles of accounting and APB Statement 4 had made conceptual contributions that would prove fruitful in the hands of the Study Group on the Objectives of Financial Statements and the FASB, the APB steadfastly refused to take credit for, or even acknowledge, those contributions. Thus, accounting was still without a statement of fundamental principles at the end of the APB's tenure, and its absence would continue to plague the profession until the FASB, mostly on its own initiative, did something about it.

(d) THE FINANCIAL ACCOUNTING STANDARDS BOARD FACES DEFINING ASSETS AND LIABILITIES. The FASB, which was not part of the AICPA, began operations in Stamford, Connecticut, on January 2, 1973, with Marshall S. Armstrong, the first chairman, and a small staff. The other six Board members and additional staff joined the group during the first half of the year, and the FASB was fully operational by the time it succeeded the APB at midyear.

Meanwhile, the Institute had approved a restated code of professional ethics that in a new Rule 203 covered for the first time infractions of the recommendations adopted by Council in 1964 regarding disclosure of departures from APB Opinions:

> A member shall not express an opinion that financial statements are presented in conformity with generally accepted accounting principles if such statements contain any departure from an

---

[79] Establishing Financial Accounting Standards, p. 13.

[80] Oscar S. Gellein, "Financial Reporting: The State of Standard Setting," *Advances in Accounting, Vol. 3*, Bill N. Schwartz, ed. (Greenwich, CT: JAI Press Inc., 1986), p. 13.

accounting principle promulgated by the body designated by Council to establish such principles. . . .

Council at its May 1973 meeting designated the FASB as the body to establish principles covered by Rule 203. The APB issued its final two Opinions—No. 30 and No. 31—and went out of business on June 30, 1973.

Later that year, the SEC's ASR No. 150, *Statement of Policy on Establishment and Improvement of Accounting Principles and Standards*, reaffirmed the policy set forth 35 years earlier in ASR 4 and declared that the Commission would recognize FASB Statements and Interpretations as having, and contrary statements as lacking, substantial authoritative support.

The FASB set its first technical agenda of seven projects in early April 1973, including a project called Broad Qualitative Standards for Financial Reporting. The Board undertook the project in expectation of receiving the report of the Trueblood Study Group, noting:

[A]s [the Board] develops specific standards, and others apply them, there will be a need in certain cases for guidelines in the selection of the most appropriate reporting. . . . [and] the report of the special AICPA committee on objectives of financial statements chaired by Robert Trueblood will be of substantial help in this project.[81]

The FASB received the report of the Trueblood Study Group, *Objectives of Financial Statements*, in October 1973.[82] The Study Group had concluded:

Accounting is not an end in itself. . . . [T]he justification for accounting can be found only in how well accounting information serves those who use it. Thus, the Study Group agrees with the conclusion drawn by many others that "The basic objective of financial statements is to provide information useful for making economic decisions." [page 61]

The report's other 11 objectives were more specific; for example, the next two identified the purposes of financial statements with meeting the information needs of those with "limited authority, ability, or resources to obtain information and who rely on financial statements as their principal source of information about an enterprise's economic activities" and with providing information useful to actual and potential owners and creditors in making decisions about placing resources available for investment or loan (page 62). The report also included a group of seven "qualitative characteristics of reporting" that information "should possess . . . to satisfy users' needs" (page 57).

Soon afterward, the FASB announced that the scope of "Broad Qualitative Standards for Financial Reporting" had been broadened because

[m]embers of the Standards Board believe that the . . . project should encompass the entire conceptual framework of financial accounting and reporting, including objectives, qualitative characteristics and the information needs of users of accounting information.[83]

The Board also for the first time used the title, "Conceptual Framework for Accounting and Reporting."

(i) Were They Assets? Liabilities? In the meantime, two other original projects confronted the new Board with the key questions of what constituted and what did not constitute an asset or a liability. The FASB's first technical agenda included some unfinished projects inherited from the APB. One was on accounting for research and development and similar costs, which eventually

---

[81] FASB, Status Report, June 18, 1973, pp. 1 and 4.

[82] *Objectives of Financial Statements*, Report of the Study Group on the Objectives of Financial Statements (New York: American Institute of Certified Public Accountants, October 1973). [Often called the Trueblood Report, after the group's chairman, Robert M. Trueblood.]

[83] FASB, News Release, December 20, 1973.

resulted in FASB Statement No. 2, *Accounting for Research and Development Costs* (October 1974), and FASB Statement No. 7, *Accounting and Reporting by Development* Stage Enterprises (June 1975); the other was on accruing for future losses, which eventually resulted in FASB Statement No. 5, *Accounting for Contingencies* (March 1975). Principal questions raised by those projects were: Do expenditures for research and development, start-up, relocation, and the like result in assets? Do "reserves for self-insurance," "provisions for expropriation of overseas operations," and the like constitute liabilities? decreases in assets?

The Board quite naturally turned to the definitions of assets and liabilities in APB Statement 4, which were the pertinent definitions in the authoritative accounting pronouncements. The definitions proved to be of no use to the FASB in deciding the major questions raised by the projects or to anyone else in trying to anticipate how the Board would decide the issues in the two projects.

The Board had to turn elsewhere for useful definitions of assets and liabilities to resolve the issues in those projects, and Board members learned that an early priority of the Board's conceptual framework project would have to be providing definitions of assets and liabilities and other elements of financial statements to fill a yawning gap in the authoritative pronouncements.

The reasons that the FASB found the definitions of assets and liabilities in APB Statement 4 to be useless underlay the Board's subsequent actions on the conceptual framework project. The related topics, the proliferation of questionable deferred charges and credits, the pervasive influence of the belief in "proper matching to avoid distorting periodic net income," and the common use of the expressions "assets are costs" and "costs are assets" help explain not only why Board members took the initiative in establishing a conceptual framework for financial accounting and reporting but also why the Board adopted the basic concepts that it did. Robert T. Sprouse used the term what-you-may-call-its to describe certain deferred charges and deferred credits routinely included in balance sheets as assets and liabilities without much consideration of whether they actually were assets or liabilities,[84] and the name has become widely used; expressions such as "proper matching," "nondistortion of periodic net income," and "assets are costs" originated in the 1930s and 1940s, as noted in describing the influence of the AAA on U.S. accounting practice, and became widely used in the 1950s, 1960s, and 1970s.

Assets, Liabilities, and What-You-May-Call-Its   The introduction to the definitions of assets and liabilities in APB Statement 4 said: "The basic elements of financial accounting—assets, liabilities . . . —are related to . . . economic resources, economic obligations . . ." (paragraph 130), suggesting that the Statement's discussion of economic resources and obligations provided a basis for the definitions of assets and liabilities. The Statement did define economic resources and economic obligations in a way that both accountants and nonaccountants would understand them to be, or to be synonymous with, what they also generally understood to be assets and liabilities:

> Economic resources are the scarce means (limited in supply relative to desired uses) available for carrying on economic activities. The economic resources of a business enterprise include: 1. *Productive resources* . . . the means used by the enterprise to produce its product . . . 2. *Products.* . . . 3. *Money* 4. *Claims to receive money* 5. *Ownership interests in other enterprises.*

> The economic obligations of an enterprise at any time are its present responsibilities to transfer economic resources or provide services to other entities in the future. . . . Economic obligations include: 1. *Obligations to pay money* 2. *Obligations to provide goods or services.* [paragraphs 57 and 58]

Moreover, the first sentence of the parallel definitions of assets and liabilities in paragraph 132 did identify assets with economic resources and liabilities with economic obligations:

$$\left\{ \begin{array}{l} \text{Assets} \\ \text{Liabilities} \end{array} \right\} \text{economic} \left\{ \begin{array}{l} \text{resources} \\ \text{obligations} \end{array} \right\} \text{of an enterprise that are recognized and measured}$$

in conformity with generally accepted accounting principles. . . .

---

[84] Robert T. Sprouse, "Accounting for What-You-May-Call-Its," *The Journal of Accountancy*, October 1966, pp. 45–53.

The second sentence of the definitions broke the relationships between assets and economic resources and between liabilities and economic obligations, however, by including what-you-may-call-its in both assets and liabilities:

$$\left\{ \begin{array}{l} \text{Assets} \\ \text{Liabilities} \end{array} \right\} \text{also include certain deferred} \left\{ \begin{array}{l} \text{charges} \\ \text{credits} \end{array} \right\} \text{that are not} \left\{ \begin{array}{l} \text{resources} \\ \text{obligations} \end{array} \right\}$$

but that are recognized and measured in conformity with generally accepted accounting principles.

The definitions actually defined nothing: Assets were whatever (economic resources and what-you-may-call-its) generally accepted accounting principles recognized and measured as assets, and liabilities were whatever (economic obligations and what-you-may-call-its) generally accepted accounting principles recognized and measured as liabilities. The definitions also were circular: Since the FASB was the body responsible for determining generally accepted accounting principles, research and development costs would be assets, and self-insurance reserves would be liabilities, if the Board said they were.

Nevertheless, APB Statement 4's definitions of assets and liabilities actually were descriptions of items recognized as assets and liabilities in practice. But why should balance sheets include as assets and liabilities items that lacked essential characteristics of what most people would understand to be assets and liabilities—items that involved no scarce means of carrying out economic activities, such as consumption, production, or saving, or items that involved no obligations to pay cash or provide goods or services to other entities?

Proper Matching to Avoid Distorting Periodic Net Income   The Board issued a Discussion Memorandum—a neutral document that describes issues and sets forth arguments for and against particular solutions or procedures but gives no Board conclusions—for each of the two projects and scheduled public hearings. At the hearings, respondents to the Discussion Memorandums were able to explain or clarify their analyses of the issues, and Board members could ask questions to pursue certain points made in comment letters and otherwise make sure they understood respondents' proposed solutions to the issues raised by the Discussion Memorandums and their underlying reasoning.

The Board discovered in the comment letters and the hearings that many respondents were less interested in what constituted assets and liabilities than in whether capitalizing and amortizing research and development costs and accruing self-insurance reserves "properly matched" costs with revenues and thus did not "distort periodic net income." Many of the respondents argued that "proper matching" required research and development and similar costs to be capitalized and amortized over their useful lives. Similarly, many argued that "proper matching" required self-insurance and similar costs to be accrued or otherwise "provided for" each period, whether or not the enterprise suffered damage from fire, earthquake, heavy wind, or other cause during the period. Unless the Board required proper matching of costs and revenues, many respondents counseled, periodic income of the affected enterprises would be distorted.

Board members were largely frustrated in their attempts to pin down what respondents meant by "proper matching" and "periodic income distortion," but the reasons for the proliferation of what-you-may-call-its emerged clearly. The following four snippets paraphrase what Board members heard at the hearings on research and development and similar costs and accounting for contingencies. Two of them are clear standing alone; two are understandable only if the questions being answered also are included.

    1. Q. In other words, you would focus on the measurement of income? You would not be concerned about the balance sheet?
    A. Yes. I think that is the major focus.

2. Much of the controversy over accrual of future loss has focused on whether a company had a liability for future losses or not. However, the impact on income should be overriding. The credit that arises from a provision for self-insurance is not a liability in the true sense, but that in and of itself should not keep it out of the balance sheet. APB Opinion 11 recognized deferred tax credits in balance sheets even though all agreed that the credit balances were not liabilities. Income statement considerations were considered paramount in that case, and similar thinking should prevail in accounting for self-insurance.

3. Defining assets does not really solve the problem of accounting for research and development expenditures and similar expenses. If some items that do not meet the definition of an asset are included in expenses of the current period, they may well distort the net income of that period because they do not relate to the revenues of that period. That accounting also may distort the net income of other periods in which the items more properly belong. The Board should focus on deferrability that gets away from the notion of whether or not those costs are assets and concentrates on the impact of deferral on the determination of net income.

4. **Q.** One of your criteria for capitalization is that net income not be materially distorted. Do you have any operational guidelines to suggest regarding material distortion?
   A. The profession has been trying to solve that one for a great many years and has been unsuccessful. I really do not have an answer.
   Q. Then, is material distortion a useful criterion that we can work with?
   A. Yes, I believe it is. Despite the difficulty, I think it is necessary to work with that criterion. It is a matter of applying professional judgment.[85]

Board members were not satisfied with the kinds of answers just illustrated.

Members of the FASB concluded early that references to vague notions such as "avoiding distortion" and "better matching" were neither an adequate basis for analyzing and resolving controversial financial accounting issues nor an effective way to communicate with one another and with the FASB's constituency.[86]

Many of the responses indeed were vague, and it soon became clear that proper matching and distortion of periodic net income were largely in the eye of the beholder. Respondents said essentially that although they had difficulty in describing proper matching and distorted income, they knew them when they saw them and could use professional judgment to assure themselves that periodic net income was determined without distortion in individual cases. The thinking and practice described in the comment letters and at the hearings seemed to make income measurement primarily a matter of individual judgment and provided no basis for comparability between financial statements. To Board members, the arguments for including in balance sheets items that could not possibly qualify as assets or liabilities—what-you-may-call-its—sounded a lot like excuses to justify smoothing reported income, thereby decreasing its volatility.

The experience generally strengthened Board members' commitment to a broad conceptual framework—one beginning with objectives of financial statements and qualitative characteristics (the Trueblood Report) and also defining the elements of financial statements and including concepts of recognition, measurement, and display—and affected the kind of concepts it would comprise.

(ii) Nondistortion, Matching, and What-You-May-Call-Its.   The proliferation of what-you-may-call-its and durability of apparently widely held and accepted notions of accounting such as

---

[85] Public Record—Financial Accounting Standards Board, 1974, Vol. 1, Discussion Memorandum on Accounting for Research and Development and Similar Costs Dated December 28, 1973 (1007), Part 2, pp. 171 and 172, 189 and 190; 1974, Vol. 3, Discussion Memorandum on Accounting for Future Losses Dated March 13, 1974 (1006), Part 2, pp. 18 and 19, 65.

[86] Robert T. Sprouse, "Commentary on Financial Reporting—Developing a Conceptual Framework for Financial Reporting," *Accounting Horizons*, December 1988, p. 127.

the overriding importance of "avoidance of distortion of periodic income" and "proper matching of costs with revenues" were the legacy of 40 years of accountants' emphasis on the accounting process and accounting procedures instead of on the economic things and events on which financial accounting is supposed to report. As a result, an accounting convention or procedure with narrow application but a catchy name was elevated to the focal point of accounting: Matching of costs and revenues to determine periodic net income for a period became the major function of financial accounting, and whatever was left over from the matching procedure (mostly "unexpired" costs and "unearned" receipts) was carried over to future periods as assets or liabilities, depending on whether the leftover items were debits or credits.

Although Paton and Littleton's AAA monograph, *An Introduction to Corporate Accounting Standards* (1940), popularized the term matching of costs and revenues and provided existing practice with what many saw as a theoretical basis that previously had been lacking, the roots of the emphasis on proper matching and nondistortion of periodic net income were older. For example, the basic rationale—that the single most important function of financial accounting was determination of periodic net income and that the function of a balance sheet was not to reflect the values of assets and liabilities but to carry forward to future periods the costs and credits already incurred and received but needed to determine net income of future periods—appeared in the report of the Institute's Special Committee on Cooperation with Stock Exchanges:

> It is probably fairly well recognized by intelligent investors today that the earning capacity is the fact of crucial importance in the valuation of an industrial enterprise, and that therefore the income account is usually far more important than the balance-sheet. In point of fact, the changes in the balance-sheets from year to year are usually more significant than the balance-sheets themselves.
>
> The development of accounting conventions has, consciously or unconsciously, been in the main based on an acceptance of this proposition. As a rule, the first objective has been to secure a proper charge or credit to the income account for the year, and in general the presumption has been that once this is achieved the residual amount of the expenditure or the receipt could properly find its place in the balance-sheet at the close of the period, the principal exception being the rule calling for reduction of inventories to market value if that is below cost.[87]

That thinking led in two related directions that came together only later as the argument that proper matching was needed to avoid distorting periodic net income, which was so popular in the comment letters and hearings on whether to defer research and development expenditures or accrue future losses. The nondistortion and matching arguments seem to have developed separately in the 1940s and 1950s and made common cause only later.

Nondistortion and the Balance Sheet as Footnote.   Since the purpose of income measurement was to indicate the earning power of an enterprise as well as to help appraise the performance of the enterprise and the effectiveness of management, periodic income was expected to be an indicator of the long-run or normal trend of income. The usefulness of the net income of a period as a long-run or normal measure was distorted therefore by including in it the effects of unusual or random events—gains or losses with no bearing on normal performance because they were extraordinary, caused by chance, or tended to average out over time—that could cause significant extraneous fluctuations in reported net income.

Emphasis on nondistortion of periodic net income surfaced in discussions of the effects of extraordinary and nonrecurring gains and losses in comparing the current operating performance and all-inclusive or clean-surplus theories of income, briefly described earlier, but also was later applied to accounting for recurring transactions and other events. The emphasis on stability and nondistortion of reported net income seems to have increased in the late 1940s and 1950s. Herman W. Bevis, who described the need to avoid distorting periodic net income in more detail and with more careful terminology than many accountants, set forth the underlying philosophy.

---

[87] *Audits of Corporate Accounts*, p. 10.

If the corporation watches the general economy, the latter also watches the corporation. For example, one of the important national economic indicators is the amount of corporate profits (and the dividends therefrom). Fluctuations in this particular index have important implications both for the private sector and with respect to the government's revenues from taxation; they also have a psychological effect on the economic mood of the nation. There is no doubt that, given a free choice between steadiness and fluctuation in the trend of aggregate corporate profits, the economic well-being of the nation would be better served by the former. Thus ... society will welcome any contribution that the accounting discipline can make to the avoidance of artificial fluctuations in reported yearly net incomes of corporations. Conversely, the creation by accounting of artificial fluctuations will be open to criticism.[88]

The primary accounting tool for avoiding artificial fluctuations was accrual accounting, which "reflects the fact that the corporation's activities progress much more evenly over the years than its cash outflow and inflow" and "attempts to transfer the income and expense effect of cash receipts and disbursements, other transactions, and other events from the year in which they arise to the year or years to which they more rationally relate."[89] However, accrual accounting was sometimes too general, and further guidance was needed. Bevis described four guidelines for repetitive transactions and events, which had been developed out of long experience, beginning with the transaction guideline and the matching guideline:

1. Record the effect on net income of transactions and events in the period in which they arise unless there is justification for recording them in some other period or periods.

2. Where a direct relationship between the two exists, match costs with revenues.[90]

To Bevis, in contrast to most accountants of the time, who tended to describe matching of costs and revenues very broadly, the matching guideline was of restricted application because "matching attempts to make a direct association of costs with *revenues*." Its application to a merchandising operation was obvious: "Carrying forward of the inventory of unsold merchandise so as to offset its cost against the revenue from its sale is clearly useful in determining the net income of each of the two years," although its use with some costing methods, such as LIFO, was at least questionable. Another clear application was to "the effecting of a sale [which] can be matched with a liability to pay a sales commission." Otherwise, however, "the ordinary business operation is so complex that revenues are the end product of a variety of corporate activities, often over long periods of time; objective evidence is lacking to connect the cost of most of the activities with any particular revenues." To emphasize that the matching guideline applied "to relatively few types of items," Bevis illustrated the kind of situations to which it clearly did not apply: "The matching guideline can become potentially dangerous when it attempts to match *today's real costs* with *hopes of tomorrow's revenues*, as in deferring research and development costs to be matched against hoped-for, but speculative, future revenues."[91]

In viewing matching narrowly, Bevis essentially agreed with George O. May, to whose memory the book was dedicated. May (in a report written with Oswald W. Knauth for the Study Group on Business Income) noted that it had become common, especially in academic circles, "to speak of income determination as being essentially a process of 'matching costs and revenues'" but warned: "Only in part are costs 'matched' against revenues, and 'matching' gives an inadequate indication of what is actually done.... [I]t would be more accurate to describe income determination as a process of (1) matching product costs against revenues, and (2) allocating other costs to periods."[92]

---

[88] Herman W. Bevis, *Corporate Financial Reporting in a Competitive Environment* (New York: The Macmillan Company, 1965), p. 30.

[89] Bevis, *Corporate Financial Reporting*, pp. 94 and 96.

[90] Id., pp. 97 and 100.

[91] Id., pp. 100 and 101.

[92] *Changing Concepts of Business Income*, Report of the Study Group on Business Income (New York: The Macmillan Company, 1952), pp. 28 and 29.

Bevis also noted that the matching guideline was "sometimes confused with the allocation of costs to periods. Taxes, insurance, or rent, for example, may be paid in advance and properly allocated to the years covered. However, this allocation is to a *period*, and one would be hard pressed to establish any direct connection between—i.e., to match—these costs and specific sales of the period to which they are allocated." Those kinds of allocations came not under the matching guideline but rather under the much broader systematic and rational guideline:

3. Where there is justification for allocating amounts affecting net income to two or more years, but there is no direct basis for measuring how much should be associated with each year, use an allocation method that is systematic and rational.[93]

An essential companion of the systematic and rational guideline was the nondistortion guideline:

4. From among systematic and rational methods, use that which tends to minimize distortions of periodic net income.[94]

Illustrations of "specific allocation practices that are designed to avoid or minimize distortions of net income among years" included self-insurance provisions, provisions for costs of dry-docking ships for major overhauls, and provisions for costs of relining of blast furnaces. For all of them, "a rational practice is to spread the costs over a reasonable period of time."

All three of the nondistortion practices described were potential what-you-may-call-its—deferred credits that did not qualify as liabilities. They were recognized not because they were liabilities incurred by the enterprise but because they would lessen the volatility of reported net income.

As already noted in describing the hearing on accruing future losses, not even those who advocated accruing self-insurance provisions and reserves argued that the reserves were liabilities. They argued for accruing the reserves to ensure proper matching and to avoid distorting periodic net income despite the fact that the resulting reserves were not liabilities. Similarly, the effect on net income, "to spread the costs over a reasonable period of time," was the principal consideration in accruing provisions for dry-docking ships and relining blast furnaces.

An enterprise does not incur a liability for costs that later will be expended in dry-docking a ship or relining a blast furnace by operating the ship or using the furnace. Rather, it begins to incur the pertinent liabilities only when it dry-docks the ship and begins to scrape off the barnacles or otherwise overhaul her or when it shuts down the furnace and starts the relining, but certainly not before making a contract with one or more other entities to do the work.

Costs of dry-docking a ship or relining a furnace might legitimately be recognized between dry-dockings or relinings by recognizing them as decreases in the carrying amount of the asset because accumulations of barnacles reduce the ship's efficiency or use of the furnace wears out the lining, but proponents of accruing costs to avoid distortion of periodic net income usually have not argued that way. Since their attention has focused almost entirely on the effect on reported net income, they have not been much concerned with "niceties" of whether periodically recognizing the cost increased liabilities or decreased assets. They have been likely to dismiss questions of that kind on the grounds that they are "merely geography" in the financial statements—an insignificant detail. Lack of concern about assets and liabilities was a distinguishing characteristic of true believers in the matching or nondistortion "gospel."

Bevis reflected that kind of focus on nondistortion of periodic net income and lack of concern about the resulting balance sheet:

[T]he amounts at which many assets and liabilities are stated in the balance sheet are a by-product of methods designed to produce a fair periodic net income figure. The objective is *not* to produce

---

[93] Bevis, *Corporate Financial Reporting*, p. 101.
[94] Id., p. 104.

a liquidating value or a current fair market value of assets. This approach is consistent with the primary interest of the stockholder in periodic income, as opposed to liquidating or "pounce" values in a not-to-be-liquidated enterprise.[95]

Indeed, he came up with the most imaginative—and pertinent—description in the entire nondistortion and proper-matching literature of the way proponents see a balance sheet—as a footnote to an income statement:

> [T]wo-thirds of the items on the asset side of the balance sheet [a "Composite Statement of Financial Position" of "100 Large Industrial Corporations" in the Appendix] ... are not assets in the sense of either being or expected to be directly converted to cash. They represent a huge amount of "deferred costs," mostly past cash expenditures, which are to be included as costs in future income statements.... Among all the footnotes explaining and elaborating on the income statement, this makes the balance sheet the biggest footnote of all.[96]

The same idea had been expressed less flatteringly by Professor William Baxter of the University of London (London School of Economics):

> [A group] of accountants bent on belittling the balance-sheet and elevating the revenue account. ...tend to dismiss the balance-sheet as a mere appendage of the revenue account—a mausoleum for the unwanted costs that the double-entry system throws up as regrettable by-products.[97]

Although Bevis defined matching narrowly and gave it only a limited place in periodic income determination, relying more on the rational and systematic guideline and the nondistortion guideline, his was probably a minority view. Most accountants who have emphasized the need for nondistorting income determination procedures have considered careful timing of recognition of revenues and expenses by proper matching to be critical in avoiding distortion of periodic income.

Proper Matching and "Assets Are Costs."   In contrast to Bevis's and May's narrow definitions of matching, most accountants have described matching of costs and revenues broadly, making matching either (1) one of two central functions of financial accounting or (2) *the* central function of financial accounting. Either way, matching encompasses allocations of costs using systematic and rational procedures, such as depreciation and amortization, which Bevis explicitly excluded from matching.

Accountants of the first group, whose use of matching has been the narrower of the two, have described periodic income determination as a two-step process: revenue recognition or "realization" and matching of costs with revenues (expense recognition). To them, matching not only recognized perceived direct relationships between costs and revenues, such as between cost of goods sold (product costs) and sales, but also recognized perceived indirect relationships between costs and revenues through mutual association with the same period. The latter would include relationships such as those between, on the one hand, costs recognized as expenses in the period incurred and depreciation and other costs allocated to the same period by a rational and systematic procedure and, on other hand, revenues allocated to the same period by "realization." That is, matching encompassed both matching product costs with specific revenues (Bevis's and May's definitions) and what usually has been called allocation—matching other costs with periods. For example, this definition clearly encompassed both kinds of matching:

---

[95] Bevis, *Corporate Financial Reporting*, p. 107.

[96] Id., p. 94.

[97] W. T. Baxter, ed., *Studies in Accounting* (London: Sweet & Maxwell Ltd., 1950), "Introduction." [Reprinted as "Introduction to the First Edition" in second and third editions: W. T. Baxter and Sidney Davidson, eds., *Studies in Accounting Theory* (London: Sweet & Maxwell Ltd., 1962) and Baxter and Davidson, eds., *Studies in Accounting* (London: The Institute of Chartered Accountants in England and Wales, 1977), p. x.]

Matching is one of the basic processes of income determination; essentially it is a process of determining relationships between costs . . . and (1) specific revenues or (2) specific accounting periods.[98]

Accountants of the second group have used matching of costs and revenues in the broadest possible sense—as a synonym for periodic income determination—making matching *the* central function of financial accounting. To them, matching encompassed both revenue recognition or "realization" and expense recognition. Matching dictated what has been included in income statements, as it did in both of these definitions:

> **matching** 1. The principle of identifying related revenues and expense with the same accounting period.[99]

> By means of accounting we seek to provide these test readings [of progress made] by a periodic matching of the costs and revenues that have flowed past "the meter" in an interval of time.[100]

The degree to which matching of costs and revenues had become the central function of financial accounting in the minds of many accountants by the time of the FASB's projects on research and development expenditures and similar costs and accruing future losses was indicated by Delmer Hylton's description in 1965, which was by no means an overstatement:

> Concurrent with the ascendency of the income statement in recent years, we have also witnessed increasing emphasis on the accounting convention known as "matching revenue with expense." In fact, it seems that most innovations in accounting in recent years have been justified essentially as better performing this matching process. In the minds of many accountants, this single convention outweighs all others; in other words, if a given procedure can be asserted to conform to the matching concept, nothing else need be said: the matter is settled and the procedure is justified.[101]

That is basically what Board members read and heard in the comment letters and public hearings on accounting for research and development expenditures and similar costs and accruing future losses. The need for proper matching of costs and revenues to avoid distorting periodic net income was the overriding consideration in many letters and in the prepared statements and answers of a significant number of those who appeared at the hearings and responded to Board members' questions. They showed little or no interest in whether research and development expenditures resulted in assets and whether reserves for self-insurance were liabilities.

Rather, those deferred charges and deferred credits belonged in the balance sheet because they were needed for proper matching to avoid distorting periodic net income. And what were most assets, anyway, except deferred or "unexpired" costs, as Paton and Littleton's monograph had said:

> [A]ssets are costs. "Costs" are the fundamental data of accounting, and. . . . it is possible to apply the term "cost" equally well to an asset acquired, a service received, and a liability incurred. Under this usage assets, or costs incurred, would clearly mean charges awaiting future revenue, whereas expenses, or costs applied, would mean charges against present revenue, . . .[102]

That usage followed from the monograph's view that periodic income measurement was not only a process of matching costs and revenues but also the focal point of accounting.

---

[98] APB Opinion No. 11, *Accounting for Income Taxes* (1967), paragraph 14(d).

[99] Eric L. Kohler, *A Dictionary for Accountants*, 5th edition (Englewood Cliffs, NJ: Prentice-Hall, Inc., 1975), p. 307.

[100] Paton and Littleton, *An Introduction to Corporate Accounting Standards* (1940), p. 15.

[101] Delmer Hylton, "On Matching Revenue with Expense," *The Accounting Review*, October 1965, p. 824.

[102] Paton and Littleton, *An Introduction to Corporate Accounting Standards*, pp. 25 and 26.

The factors acquired for production which have not yet reached the point in the business process where they may be appropriately treated as "cost of sales" or "expense" are called "assets," and are presented as such in the balance sheet.... [T]hese "assets" are in fact "revenue charges in suspense" awaiting some future matching with revenue as costs or expenses....

The fundamental problem of accounting ... is the division of the stream of costs incurred between the present and the future in the process of measuring periodic income.... The balance sheet ... serves as a means of carrying forward unamortized acquisition prices, the not-yet-deducted costs; it stands as a connecting link joining successive income statements into a composite picture of the income stream.[103]

Long before the time of the FASB projects on research and development costs and self-insurance reserves, however, Paton had recognized that matching had become an obsession of many accountants. It had been carried much too far and had been the cause of downgrading the meaning and significance of assets.

For a long time I've wished that the Paton and Littleton monograph had never been written, or had gone out of print twenty-five years or so ago. Listening to Bob Sprouse take issue with the "matching" gospel, which the P & L monograph helped to foster, confirmed my dissatisfaction with this publication.... The basic difficulty with the idea that cost dollars, as incurred, attach like barnacles to the physical flow of materials and stream of operating activity is that it is at odds with the actual process of valuation in a free competitive market. The customer does not buy a handful of classified and traced cost dollars; he buys a product, at prevailing market price. And the market price may be either above or below any calculated cost....

For a long time I've been touting the idea that the central element in business operation is the *resources* (in hand or in prospect) and that the main objective of operation is the efficient utilization of the available assets.[104]

His intermediate accounting textbook, published a mere dozen years after the monograph, was entitled *Asset Accounting*.[105]

(iii) An Overdose of Matching, Nondistortion, and What-You-May-Call-Its.   Board members had, as former chairman Donald J. Kirk once put it, cut their accounting teeth on matching, nondistortion, assets are costs, and similar notions. Some of them may have entertained some doubts about some of the ideas before serving on the Board, but it was the paramount importance that was attributed to those ideas in early comment letters and at the early hearings that made the Board increasingly uncomfortable with them. Those notions seemed to be open-ended; no one could explain the limits, if any, on matching or nondistortion procedures or how to verify that proper matching or nondistortion had been achieved. The experience made most, if not all, Board members highly skeptical about arguments that the need for proper matching to avoid distortion of periodic net income was the "be-all and end-all of financial accounting"[106] with little or no concern expressed about whether the residuals left over after matching actually were assets or liabilities.

Among other things, those early experiences had graphically demonstrated to Board members that once accountants had come to perceive assets primarily as costs, they often failed to distinguish assets in the real world from the entries in the accounts and financial statements. What-you-may-call-its were a consequence of the habit of using "costs" and "assets"

---

[103] Paton and Littleton, *An Introduction to Corporate Accounting Standards*, pp. 25 and 67.

[104] William A. Paton, "Introduction," in Williard E. Stone, ed., *Foundations of Accounting Theory: Papers Given at the Accounting Theory Symposium, University of Florida, March 1970* (Gainesville, FL: University of Florida Press, 1971), pp. x and xi.

[105] William A. Paton, with the assistance of William A. Paton, Jr., *Asset Accounting* (New York: The Macmillan Company, 1952).

[106] Sprouse, "Commentary on Financial Reporting—Developing a Conceptual Framework for Financial Reporting," p. 127.

interchangeably—"assets were costs; costs were assets"—without worrying about whether the costs actually represented anything in the real world.

The "Pygmalion Syndrome" (after the legendary sculptor who fell in love with his statue of a woman) was at work. That name was given by the noted physicist J. L. Synge to "the tendency of many people to confuse conceptual models of real-world things and events with the things and events themselves."[107] Perhaps the most common example has been the habit of lawyers, accountants, corporate directors and officers, stockholders, and others to describe a dividend as paid "out of surplus (retained earnings)." That habit led a prominent lawyer to chide:

> Distributions are never paid "out of surplus," they are paid out of assets; surplus cannot be distributed—assets are distributed. No one ever received a package of surplus for Christmas.[108]

The fact that the matching literature was so full of references to "unexpired" costs that "expired" when matched against revenues also caused a prominent professor of finance to admonish that accountants had confused matters by defining

> depreciation as "expired capital outlay"—in other words, as "expired cost"—thereby transferring the word from a value to a cost category. But this definition was a dodge rather than a solution, and the fact that it still enjoys some currency among accounting writers who must be aware of its spurious character illustrates the tenacity of convenient though specious phrases. For cost does not "expire." What may be said gradually to expire is the economic significance of the asset as it grows older, in short, its utility or its value. "Expired cost" is therefore mumbo jumbo, and a reversion to the old association of depreciation with loss in value would be a far more sensible alternative.[109]

As Board members began to look at problems likely to come onto the Board's agenda, they began to see more what-you-may-call-its in their future. In addition to self-insurance reserves and provisions for removing barnacles from ships or relining blast furnaces, which have already been described, a significant number of what-you-may-call-its were part of existing practice in the early 1970s, had been or were being proposed to become part of practice, or had recently been proscribed:

- Unamortized debt discount
- Deferred tax credits and deferred tax charges
- Deferred gains and losses on securities in pension funds
- Deferred gains on translating foreign exchange balances (The APB issued in late 1971 an exposure draft of a proposal to permit deferral of losses on foreign exchange balances but dropped the subject without issuing an Opinion.)
- Deferred gains or losses on sales of long-term investments
- Deferred gains or losses on sale-and-leaseback transactions
- Negative goodwill remaining after reducing to zero the noncurrent assets acquired in a business combination

Since several of those what-you-may-call-its were part of topics that might well come before the Board within a few years, Board members thought it essential to ensure that the Board would not have to face those kinds of matters without the necessary tools. They were not anxious to repeat

---

[107] Loyd C. Heath, "Accounting, Communication, and the Pygmalion Syndrome," *Accounting Horizons*, March 1987, p. 1.

[108] Bayless Manning, *A Concise Textbook on Legal Capital*, Second Edition (Mineola, NY: The Foundation Press, Inc., 1981), pp. 33 and 34.

[109] James C. Bonbright, *Principles of Public Utility Rates* (New York: Columbia University Press, 1961), pp. 195 and 196.

their experiences with research and development expenditures and similar costs and accruing future losses. They not only wanted to get in place a broad conceptual framework to provide a basis for sound financial accounting standards but also had some firm ideas of the kinds of concepts that were needed.

Kirk later described his own thinking at the time, and other Board members probably would concur with most of what he said:

> Among the projects on the Board's initial agenda were accounting for research and development costs and accounting for contingencies. The need for workable definitions of assets and liabilities became apparent in those projects and served as a catalyst for the part of the framework projects that became FASB Concepts Statement No. 3, *Elements of Financial Statements of Business Enterprises* (1980). . . .
>
> To me, the definitions were the missing boundaries that were needed to bring the accrual accounting system back under control. The definitions have, I hope, driven a stake part way through the "nondistortion" guideline. But I am realistic enough to know, having dealt with the subjects of foreign currency translation and pension cost measurement, that the aversion to volatility in earnings is so strong that the notion of "nondistortion" will not die easily.[110]

Kirk's reference to volatility of reported net income was not accidental—that has been and will continue to be a major bone of contention between the FASB and its constituents. Managements have been and continue to be concerned that volatility of periodic net income will affect adversely the market prices of their enterprises' securities and hence their cost of capital. The Board's general response to that concern has been that accounting must be neutral, and if financial statements are to represent faithfully an entity's net income, the presence of volatility must be reported to investors and creditors. For example, former Board member Robert T. Sprouse probably expressed the thinking of many Board members:

> I submit . . . that minimizing the volatile results of actual economic events should be primarily a matter for management policy and strategy, not a matter for accounting standards. To the extent volatile economic events actually occur, the results should be reflected in the financial statements. If it is true that volatility affects market prices of securities and the related costs of capital, it is especially important that, where it actually exists, volatility be revealed rather than concealed by accounting practices. Otherwise, financial statements do not faithfully represent the results of risks to which the enterprise is actually exposed.
>
> To me, the least effective argument one can make in opposing a proposed standard is that its implementation might cause managers or investors to make different decisions. . . . The very reason for the existence of reliable financial information for lenders and investors . . . is to help them in their comparisons of alternative investments. If stability or volatility of financial results is an important consideration to some lenders and investors, all the more reason that the degree of stability or volatility should be faithfully reflected in the financial statements.[111]

That kind of problem is nothing new. For example, almost 50 years earlier, Paton made essentially the same point as Sprouse in writing about the effects on income of the choice of inventory methods:

> [Sanders, Hatfield, and Moore] quote, with apparent approval, the following statement from Arthur Andersen: "The practice of equalizing earnings is directly contrary to recognized accounting principles." But . . . they go out of their way to support a European practice, the base-stock inventory method, which . . . has been vigorously revived and sponsored in recent years [in the United States] under the "last in, first out" label, which represents nothing more nor less than a major

---

[110] Donald J. Kirk, "Looking Back on Fourteen Years at the FASB: The Education of a Standard Setter," *Accounting Horizons*, March 1988, p. 15.

[111] Robert T. Sprouse, "Commentary on Financial Reporting—Economic Consequences: The Volatility Bugaboo," *Accounting Horizons*, March 1987, p. 88.

device for equalizing earnings, to avoid showing in the periodic reports the severe fluctuations which are inherent in certain business fields.... Actually, we do have good years and bad years in business, fat years and lean years. There is nothing imaginary about this condition—particularly in the extractive and converting fields, where this agitation centers.... It may be that in some situations the year is too short a period through which to attempt to determine net income (as surely the month and quarter often are), but if this is the case, the solution lies not in doctoring the annual report, but in lengthening the period. Certainly it is not good accounting to issue reports for a copper company, for example, which make it appear that the concern has the comparative stability of earning power of the American Telephone and Telegraph Co.[112]

The earlier description of the experiences of Board members that led them to support a broad conceptual framework project and to develop firm ideas about the kinds of concepts needed has focused on the projects on accounting for research and development expenditures and similar costs and accounting for contingencies, including accruing future losses. Those projects were highly significant experiences for Board members, as the preceding indicates, but later projects have provided additional or similar experiences. As the comments on volatility of income suggest, the education of Board members and members of the constituency is a continuing process in which the conceptual framework has been both a source of disagreement and controversy and a significant help in setting sound financial accounting standards.

(iv) Initiation of the Conceptual Framework.   Confronted with the fruits of decades of the profession's lethargy and inability to fashion a statement defining accounting's most basic concepts, the FASB, on its own initiative and motivated by the experiences of its members, decided to undertake the development of a statement of basic concepts that went beyond the objectives of financial statements to definition, recognition, measurement, and display of the elements of financial statements. In 1973 it initiated a conceptual framework project that was intended to be at once both the reasoning underlying procedures and a standard by which procedures would be judged.

A deliberative, authoritative body with responsibility for accounting standards finally had decided to do what the Committee on Accounting Procedure and the APB had been implored to do but had never felt strongly was a part of their mission. The FASB concluded that accounting did possess a core of fundamental concepts that were neither subject to nor dependent on the moment's particular, transitory consensus. Accounting had achieved the stage in its development that made it imperative and proper to place before its constituents a definitive statement of its fundamental principles.

2.3 THE FINANCIAL ACCOUNTING STANDARDS BOARD'S CONCEPTUAL FRAMEWORK

In an open letter to the business and financial community, which prefaced the booklet, *Scope and Implications of the Conceptual Framework Project* (December 2, 1976), Marshall S. Armstrong, the first chairman of the FASB, expressed some of the Board's aspirations for the conceptual framework project:

The conceptual framework project will lead to definitive pronouncements on which the Board intends to rely in establishing financial accounting and reporting standards. Though the framework cannot and should not be made so detailed as to provide automatically an accounting answer to a set of financial facts, it will determine bounds for judgment in preparing financial statements. The framework should lead to increased public confidence in financial statements and aid in preventing proliferation of accounting methods.

---

[112] William A. Paton, "Comments on 'A Statement of Accounting Principles,'" *The Journal of Accountancy*, March 1938, pp. 199 and 200.

The excerpt highlighted a significant characteristic of the conceptual framework project. Although Board members were aware of the widespread criticism directed at the Committee on Accounting Procedure and the Accounting Principles Board for their collective inability to provide the profession with an enduring framework for analyzing accounting issues, the FASB's stimulus was entirely different from that of its predecessors. It was not reacting to instructions or recommendations to establish basic concepts by groups such as the AICPA's Special Committees on Research Program or Opinions of the APB, the Wheat Group, or the SEC. Rather, the Board undertook the self-imposed task of providing accounting with an underlying philosophy because Board members had concluded that to discharge their standards-setting responsibilities properly, they needed a set of fundamental accounting concepts for their own guidance in resolving issues brought before the Board.

The idea that the conceptual framework was intended to benefit the FASB by guiding its ongoing work in establishing accounting standards was embodied in the Preface, entitled "Statements of Financial Accounting Concepts," to each Concepts Statement:

> The Board itself is likely to be the most direct beneficiary of the guidance provided by the Statements in this series. They will guide the Board in developing accounting and reporting standards by providing the Board with a common foundation and basic reasoning on which to consider merits of alternatives.

Armed with the conviction that a coordinated set of pervasive concepts was prerequisite to establishing sound and consistent accounting standards, the FASB in late 1973 formally expanded the scope of its original concepts project, "Broad Qualitative Standards for Financial Reporting," and changed its name. The new title—"Conceptual Framework for Accounting and Reporting: Objectives, Qualitative Characteristics and Information"—for the first time used the words "conceptual framework" by which the project would become identified.

The Board concluded at the outset that it was unrealistic to attempt to devise a complete conceptual framework and adopt it by a single Board action. It already had experienced an urgent need for a definitive statement about some of the most fundamental components of the envisioned conceptual framework—the objectives of financial reporting and definitions of the elements of financial statements. The absence of meaningful definitions of assets and liabilities in the accounting literature had already hindered the FASB's work on the other projects on its agenda.

The project was conceived as comprising six major parts, as illustrated by Exhibit 2.1. (A seventh part was added in 2000. See Section 2.3(b)(v).) The parts were expected to be undertaken in the order shown by moving down the pyramid and from left to right at each level.

The numbers in parentheses in Exhibit 2.1 reflect that although six Concepts Statements were issued, their numbers did not correspond to the order just described for the six boxes in the exhibit because (a) the Statement on qualities of useful information was finished before the Statement on elements of financial statements; (b) not-for-profit organizations were included within the scope of the framework, resulting in Concepts Statement 4, which pertained only to not-for-profit organizations, and in Concepts Statement 6, which amended Concepts Statement 2 and replaced Concepts Statement 3, making them applicable to not-for-profit organizations; and (c) little conceptual work was actually completed on the topics in the two lower levels of Exhibit 2.1, and what was done on all three topics was included in a single Concepts Statement, No. 5.

Exhibit 2.2 shows the six Concepts Statements by topic and date of issue and explains how they fit together in relation to Exhibit 2.1.

The conceptual framework constitutes the subject matter of the remainder of this chapter, which considers, among other things, the underlying philosophy of and emphasis in the framework, the effects on it of matters discussed earlier in the chapter, the ways that it has been and might be used by the FASB and others in improving financial accounting and reporting practice, and a more detailed look at some of the concepts. The discussion is divided into two sections: It looks at the conceptual framework first as a body of concepts that underlies financial accounting and reporting in the United States and then as five interrelated Concepts Statements, each focused on one of four parts of the framework: objectives of financial reporting, qualitative characteristics of accounting

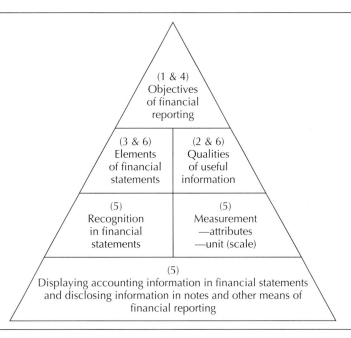

Exhibit 2.1   The FASB's Conceptual Framework for Financial Accounting and Reporting.

No. 1 "Objectives of Financial Reporting by Business Enterprises" (November 1978)

No. 2 "Qualitative Characteristics of Accounting Information" (May 1980)

No. 3 "Elements of Financial Statements of Business Enterprises" (December 1980)

No. 5 "Recognition and Measurement in Financial Statements of Business Enterprises" (December 1984)

No. 4 "Objectives of Financial Reporting by Nonbusiness Organizations" (December 1980)

[No. 2 amended by No. 6 to apply to not-for-profit organizations as well as to business enterprises]

No. 6 "Elements of Financial Statements" (December 1985)

[No. 3 superseded by No. 6, which applies to both business enterprises and not-for-profit organizations]

[No. 5 also briefly covers display in financial statements and disclosure in notes and other means of financial reporting]

Exhibit 2.2   The Six Concepts Statements.

information, elements of financial statements, and recognition and measurement and display in financial statements.

(a) THE FRAMEWORK AS A BODY OF CONCEPTS. The Concepts Statements as a group reflect a number of sources and other influences, most of which have already been introduced or otherwise noted, including:

- The Trueblood Study Group's report, *Objectives of Financial Statements* (October 1973), whose 12 objectives and seven "qualitative characteristics of reporting" and supporting discussion and analysis directly affected the two Concepts Statements on objectives and the one on qualitative characteristics and indirectly affected the others

- Board members' experiences in trying to set standards in the absence of an accepted conceptual basis, which was a significant factor both in the FASB's having a conceptual framework and in the kinds of concepts it comprises
- Conceptual work of the APB and Accounting Research Division, primarily ARS 1 and 3 on basic postulates and broad principles of accounting and the basic concepts part of APB Statement 4
- Conceptual work of others reported in the literature, including the work of individuals, the AAA's concepts and standards statements, and developments in Canada, the United Kingdom, Australia, New Zealand, and other countries
- Conceptual work of the FASB itself, including preparatory work on its original concepts project and development of Discussion Memorandums and Exposure Drafts that led to the Concepts Statements and related projects, such as that on materiality; and the fruits of "due process," such as some excellent comment letters and exchanges of views at a number of hearings

Some of the most fundamental concepts in the framework had their roots in those sources and influences. The three examples of fundamental concepts under the next three headings combine ideas from one or more Concepts Statements and illustrate those connections.

(i) Information Useful in Making Investment, Credit, and Similar Decisions.

Financial accounting and reporting is not an end in itself but is intended to provide information that is useful to present and potential investors, creditors, other resource providers, and other users outside an entity in making rational investment, credit, and similar decisions about it.

The FASB generally followed the report of the Trueblood Study Group on objectives of financial statements in focusing the objectives of financial reporting on information useful in investment, credit, and similar decisions, instead of on information about management's stewardship to owners or information based on the operating needs of managers. The description of Concepts Statement 1 later in this chapter shows the influence of the Trueblood Study Group's objectives on the FASB's objectives.

That focus on information for decision making represented a fundamental change in attitude toward the purposes of financial statements. Before the Trueblood Study Group's report, APB Statement 4 was the only AICPA pronouncement identifying financial reporting with the needs of investors and creditors for decision making rather than with the traditional accounting purpose of reporting on management's stewardship. A vocal minority, which still is heard from occasionally, has insisted that the primary function of accounting by an enterprise is to serve management's needs and that the objectives should reflect that purpose. It has never been obvious why proponents of that view think that a body such as the APB or FASB should be establishing objectives and setting standards for information that is primarily for internal and private use and that management can require in whatever form it finds most useful. The message intended apparently is that management, not the APB, FASB, or similar body, should decide what information financial statements are to provide to investors, creditors, and others.

The Study Group, which may have been influenced to some extent by APB Statement 4, emphasized the role of financial statements in investors' and creditors' decisions and identified the purposes of financial statements with the decisions of investors and creditors, existing or prospective, about placing resources available for investment or loan. The Study Group's recommendations became the starting point for the FASB to build a conceptual framework.

(ii) Representations of Things and Events in the Real-World Environment.

The items in financial statements represent things and events in the real world, placing a premium on representational faithfulness and verifiability of accounting information and neutrality of both standards setting and accounting information.

The FASB's decision to ground its concepts in the environment in which financial accounting takes place and the economic things, events, and activities that exist or happen there, instead of on accounting processes and procedures, was influenced significantly by Accounting Research Study 1 on basic postulates of accounting and the section of APB Statement 4 on basic concepts. The postulates in ARS 1 were, as already described, self-evident propositions about the environment in which accounting functions—a world that does exist and not one that is a fiction—that were fruitful for accounting.

For example, the observation that most of the goods and services produced in the United States are not directly consumed by their producers but are sold for cash or claims to cash suggests both why financial accounting is concerned with production and distribution of goods and services and with exchange prices and why investors, creditors, and other users of financial statements are concerned with cash prices and cash flows.

That focus of financial accounting on the environment and the things and events in it that are represented in financial statements constituted a fundamental change from the earlier emphasis on the conventional nature of accounting and the conventional procedures and allocations used to produce the numbers in financial statements. Thus, the Concepts Statements devote considerable space to describing activities such as producing, distributing, exchanging, saving, and investing in what they variously call the "real world," "economic, legal, social, political, and physical environment in the United States," or "U.S. economy," and what is involved in representing those economic things and events in financial statements. Concepts Statement 1 notes a significant consequence of that focus on things and events in the environment that is pertinent to the definitions of the elements of financial statements.

> The information provided by financial reporting pertains to individual business enterprises. . . . Since business enterprises are producers and distributors of scarce resources, financial reporting bears on the allocation of economic resources to producing and distributing activities and focuses on the creation of, use of, and rights to wealth and the sharing of risks associated with wealth. [paragraph 19]

Thus, the elements of financial statements are assets and liabilities and the effects of transactions and other events that change assets and liabilities—that change and transfer wealth.

(iii) Assets (and Liabilities)—The Fundamental Element(s) of Financial Statements.

The fundamental elements of financial statements are assets and liabilities because all other elements depend on them:

Equity is assets minus liabilities;

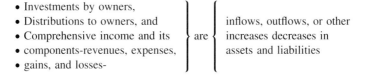

- Investments by owners,
- Distributions to owners, and
- Comprehensive income and its
- components-revenues, expenses,
- gains, and losses-

are

inflows, outflows, or other increases decreases in assets and liabilities

Because liabilities depend on assets—liabilities are obligations to pay or deliver assets—assets is the most fundamental element of financial statements.

Soon after its inception, the FASB needed definitions of assets and liabilities and found many examples of two types of definition in the accounting literature.

Definitions of one type identified assets with economic resources and wealth, emphasizing the service potential, or benefits, and economic values that an asset confers on the holding or owning entity. Similarly, they identified liabilities with amounts or duties owed to other entities, emphasizing the payment or expenditure of assets required of the debtor or owing entity to satisfy the claim. They were definitions that described things that most people could recognize as assets and liabilities because they had experience in their everyday lives as well as in their business activities with rights to use economic resources and with obligations to pay debts.

Three sets of definitions of assets and liabilities by the AAA, Robert K. Mautz, and Eric L. Kohler, respectively,[113] are examples of the numerous definitions the FASB considered that had those characteristics:

Assets are economic resources devoted to business purposes within a specific accounting entity; they are aggregates of service-potentials available for or beneficial to expected operations.	The interests or equities of creditors (liabilities) are claims against the entity arising from past activities or events which, in the usual case, require for their satisfaction the expenditure of corporate resources.
An asset may be defined as anything of use to future operations of the enterprise, the beneficial interest in which runs to the enterprise. Assets may be monetary or nonmonetary, tangible or intangible, owned or not owned.	Liabilities are claims against a company, payable in cash, in other assets, or in service, on a fixed or determinable future date.
asset Any owned physical object (tangible) or right (intangible) having economic value to its owner; an item or source of wealth ...	**liability** 1. An amount owing by one person (a debtor) to another (a creditor), payable in money, or in goods or services: the consequence of an asset or service received or a loss incurred or accrued ...

The FASB also found a second type of definition of assets and liabilities that included economic resources and obligations but also let in some ultimately undefinable what-you-may-call-its—such as deferred tax charges and credits, deferred losses and gains, and self-insurance reserves—items that are not economic resources or obligations of an entity but were included in its balance sheet as assets or liabilities "to achieve 'proper' matching of costs and revenues" or "to avoid distorting periodic net income" (pp. 2-33–2-47 of this chapter).

Prime examples of the second type of definition were those in APB Statement 4, paragraph 132, which explicitly included what-you-may-call-its in its definitions of assets and liabilities:

Assets—economic resources of an enterprise that are recognized and measured in conformity with generally accepted accounting principles. Assets also include certain deferred charges that are not resources but that are recognized and measured in conformity with generally accepted accounting principles.	*Liabilities*—economic obligations of an enterprise that are recognized and measured in conformity with generally accepted accounting principles. Liabilities also include certain deferred credits that are not obligations but that are recognized and measured in conformity with generally accepted accounting principles.

Those definitions were circular and open-ended, however, being both determinants of and determined by generally accepted accounting principles and saying in effect that assets and liabilities were whatever the Board said they were.

In trying to use the definitions in APB Statement 4 to set financial accounting standards for research and development expenditures and accruing future losses, Board members found that assets and liabilities defined as fallout from periodic recognition of revenues and expenses were too vague and subjective to be workable. That experience strongly reinforced the conceptual and practical superiority of definitions of assets and liabilities based on resources and obligations that exist in the real world rather than on deferred charges and credits that result only from bookkeeping entries.

---

[113] American Accounting Association, Committee on Concepts and Standards Underlying Corporate Financial Statements, *Accounting and Reporting Standards for Corporate Financial Statements and Preceding Statements and Supplements* (Iowa City, IA: American Accounting Association, 1957), pp. 3 and 7. Robert K. Mautz, "Basic Concepts of Accounting," *Handbook of Modern Accounting*, edited by Sidney Davidson (New York: McGraw-Hill Book Company, 1970), pp. 1–5 and 1–8 [chapter 1, pp. 5 and 8]. Kohler, *A Dictionary for Accountants*, pp. 39 and 291.

APB Statement 4's definitions proved to be of little help to the Board in deciding whether results of research and development expenditures qualified as assets or whether reserves for self-insurance qualified as liabilities because they permit almost any debit balance to be an asset and almost any credit balance to be a liability. They were hardly better than the definitions that they had replaced, which also included what-you-may-call-its and were circular and open-ended in the same ways:

> [T]he word "asset" is not synonymous with or limited to property but includes also that part of any cost or expense incurred which [according to generally accepted accounting principles] is properly carried forward upon a closing of books at a given date.

> ... Thus, plant, accounts receivable, inventory, and a deferred charge are all assets in a balance-sheet classification.

> The last named is not an asset in the popular sense, but if it may be carried forward as a proper charge against future income, then in an accounting sense, and particularly in a balance-sheet classification, it is an asset....

> ... Thus, the word ["liability"] is used broadly to comprise not only items which constitute liabilities in the popular sense of debts or obligations ... but also credit balances to be accounted for which do not involve the debtor and creditor relation. For example, capital stock, deferred credits to income, and surplus are balance-sheet liabilities in that they represent balances to be accounted for by the company; though these are not liabilities in the ordinary sense of debts owed to legal creditors.[114]

Definitions of that kind provide no effective limits or restraints on the matching of costs and revenues and the resulting reported net income. If balance sheets at the beginning and end of a period include debits and credits that are labeled assets and liabilities but that result from bookkeeping entries and are assets only "in an accounting sense" or "in a balance-sheet classification" or are only "balance-sheet liabilities," the income statement for the period will include components of income that are equally suspect—namely, debits and credits that are labeled revenues, expenses, gains, or losses but that result from the same bookkeeping entries as the what-you-may-call-its in the balance sheet. They have resulted not from transactions or other events that occurred during the period but from shifting revenues, expenses, gains, or losses from earlier or later periods to match costs and revenues properly or to avoid distorting reported periodic income.

Thus, when the Board defined the elements of financial statements in Concepts Statement 3 (and used the same definitions in Concepts Statement 6), it defined assets and liabilities in essentially the same way as the three sets of definitions by the AAA, Mautz, and Kohler, emphasizing the benefits that assets confer on their holders and the obligations to others that bind those with liabilities to pay or expend assets to settle them.

Assets are probable future economic benefits obtained or controlled by a particular entity as a result of past transactions or events. [Concepts Statement 6, paragraph 25]	Liabilities are probable future sacrifices of economic benefits arising from present obligations of a particular entity to transfer assets or provide services to other entities in the future as a result of past transactions or events. [Concepts Statement 6, paragraph 35]

---

[114] Accounting Research Bulletin No. 9 (Special), *Report of the Committee on Terminology* (May 1941), pp. 70 and 71. The definitions in ARB 9 were carried over to Accounting Terminology Bulletin No. 1, *Review and Résumé* (August 1953), paragraphs 26 and 27, but, for some unexplained reason, "deferred credits to income," the only part of the liability definition comparable to "deferred charges" in the asset definition, was deleted. Assets are probable future economic benefits obtained or controlled by a particular entity as a result of past transactions or events. [Concepts Statement 6, paragraph 25] Liabilities are probable future sacrifices of economic benefits arising from present obligations of a particular entity to transfer assets or provide services to other entities in the future as a result of past transactions or events. [Concepts Statement 6, paragraph 35]

The definitions that were adopted exclude all what-you-may-call-its. Deferred charges and credits that "need to be carried forward for matching in future periods" can no longer be included in assets and liabilities merely by meeting definitions no more restrictive than "assets are costs" and "liabilities are proceeds."

Although definitions identifying assets with economic resources and wealth and liabilities with amounts or duties owed to other entities had been common in the accounting literature from the turn of the century to the 1970s, the definitions in APB Statement 4 actually reflected accounting practice at the time the FASB was developing its definitions. Thus, its definitions represented a fundamental change from the emphasis on financial accounting as primarily a process of matching costs and revenues.

Misunderstanding and Controversy about the Financial Accounting Standards Board's Defining Assets and Liabilities as the Fundamental Elements.   Both of the other fundamental concepts described earlier—that the objective of financial reporting is to provide information useful in making investment, credit, and similar decisions and that items in financial statements represent things and events in the real-world environment—also constituted significant changes in perceptions of the purpose and nature of financial accounting and reporting. Both caused concern among many members of the FASB's constituency at the beginning and drew some criticism and opposition. With time, however, both concepts seem to have been understood reasonably well, their level of acceptance has increased, and active opposition has subsided.

In contrast, this third concept—that assets and liabilities are the fundamental elements of financial statements—still is undoubtedly the most controversial, and the most misunderstood and misrepresented, concept in the entire conceptual framework.

TWO VIEWS OF INCOME.   The FASB's emphasis on assets and liabilities in the definitions of the elements of financial statements became a focus of controversy in the development of the conceptual framework because it highlighted the tension in accounting thought and practice between two widely held and essentially incompatible views about income:

- Income is an enhancement of wealth or command over economic resources.
- Income is an indicator of performance of an enterprise and its management.

That difference of opinion about income usually has involved the question of whether certain items should be reported in the net income for a period or should be excluded from net income and reported directly in equity. It most often has been described as the issue of how to display the effects of unusual, extraordinary, or nonrecurring happenings and prior period adjustments, which underlay the disagreement between the SEC and the Institute's Committee on Accounting Procedure over the all-inclusive and current-operating-performance types of income statement, and has troubled accounting standards-setting bodies for more than half a century.

> Standard setters, including the Committee on Accounting Procedure, the Accounting Principles Board, and the Financial Accounting Standards Board, have issued more pronouncements dealing with display of the effects of unusual and nonrecurring events than any other subject.[115]

It also underlies differences between comprehensive income and earnings, recently manifesting itself most prominently in the issue of whether to extend the traditional display of unusual, nonrecurring, or extraordinary events—to exclude them from net income and report them directly in equity—to recurring but often volatile holding gains and losses that largely are beyond the control of an entity and its management.

Difference of opinion about whether income is wealth enhancement or performance indicator likewise underlay the controversy that followed issue of the FASB Discussion Memorandum on

---

[115] Oscar S. Gellein, "Periodic Earnings: Income? or Indicator?" *Accounting Horizons*, June 1987, p. 61. The pronouncements to which Gellein referred are:

definitions of elements of financial statements and their measurement (December 2, 1976), but the matter went deeper than financial statement display. In the FASB's conceptual framework, definitions of elements of financial statements are more fundamental than recognition, measurement, or display in financial statements (see Exhibit 2.1), and the Discussion Memorandum emphasized definition rather than display.

The Board referred to the two views of income or earnings as the *asset and liability view* and the *revenue and expense view* and described the difference between them for purposes of defining elements of financial statements as whether definitions of assets and liabilities should be the controlling definitions or should depend on definitions of revenues and expenses.

> The conceptual issue in choosing between the asset and liability view and the revenue and expense view concerns selecting the most fundamental elements whose precise definitions control the definitions of the other elements. [page 35]

Former Board member Oscar Gellein (writing in 1984) described the issue as one of identifying the elements that have what he called conceptual primacy and said that the question of which concepts had primacy was "[a] central issue [that] pervades the FASB's effort to construct a conceptual framework."[116] That question was the first issue in the Discussion Memorandum.

> Should the asset and liability view ... [or] the revenue and expense view ... be adopted as the basis underlying a conceptual framework for financial accounting and reporting?[117] [page 36]

According to the Discussion Memorandum, proponents of the asset and liability view hold that assets should be defined as the economic resources of an enterprise (its scarce means of carrying out economic activities such as exchange, production, saving, and investment), that liabilities should be defined as its obligations to transfer assets to other entities in the future, and that definitions of income and its components should depend on the definitions of assets and liabilities. Thus, no revenues or gains can occur unless an asset increases or a liability decreases, and no expenses or losses can occur unless an asset decreases or a liability increases. As a result, income reflects an increase in wealth of the enterprise, and a loss reflects a decrease in its wealth.

Proponents of the revenue and expense view, in contrast, hold that income is a measure of performance of an enterprise and its management, that income results from proper matching of costs and revenues, and that most nonmonetary assets and liabilities are by-products of the matching

---

Accounting Research Bulletins:

No. 8   *Combined Statement of Income and Earned Surplus* [Retained Earnings] (February 1941)

No. 32   *Income and Earned Surplus* (December 1947)

No. 35   *Presentation of Income and Earned Surplus* (October 1948)

No. 41   *Presentation of Income and Earned Surplus (Supplement to Bulletin No. 35)* (July 1951)

No. 43   *Restatement and Revision of Accounting Research Bulletins* (June 1953)

             Chapter 2(b), "Combined Statement of Income and Earned Surplus"

             Chapter 8, "Income and Earned Surplus"

APB Opinions:

No. 9   *Reporting the Results of Operations* [Income] (December 1966)

No. 20   *Accounting Changes* (July 1971)

No. 30   *Reporting the Results of Operations—Reporting the Effects of Disposal of a Segment of a Business, and Extraordinary, Unusual and Infrequently Occurring Events and Transactions* (June 1973)

FASB Statements:

No. 4   *Reporting Gains and Losses from Extinguishment of Debt* (an amendment of APB Opinion No. 30) (March 1975)

No. 16   *Prior Period Adjustments* (June 1977)

[116] Oscar S. Gellein, "Financial Reporting: The State of Standard Setting," *Advances in Accounting*, Vol. 3, edited by Bill N. Schwartz (Greenwich, CT: JAI Press, Inc., 1986), pp. 14 and 15.

[117] A third view described in the Discussion Memorandum, the nonarticulation view, is omitted.

process. Proper matching of costs and revenues involves timing their recognition to relate effort (expenses) and accomplishment (revenues) for a period. Thus, the effects of past expenditures or receipts that are deemed to be expenses or revenues of future periods are recognized as assets or liabilities (deferred charges or deferred credits) whether or not they relate to economic resources or obligations to transfer resources to other entities in the future.

ASSET AND LIABILITY VIEW AND CONCEPTUAL PRIMACY OF ASSETS AND LIABILITIES.   Although Concepts Statements 3 and 6 neither mentioned the asset and liability view and the revenue and expense view nor explained how or why the Board had settled on one of them, the definitions themselves left no doubt about which view the Board had endorsed. Following the steps it had set down in the Discussion Memorandum, it first identified assets and liabilities as "the most fundamental elements whose precise definitions control the definitions of the other elements" (page 35 of the Discussion Memorandum; quoted earlier on this page) and then used the most fundamental definitions—assets and liabilities—in defining all of the other elements. Equity is assets minus liabilities. Investments by and distributions to owners and comprehensive income and its components—revenues, expenses, gains, and losses—are inflows, outflows, or other increases and decreases in assets and liabilities. (Assets actually is the most fundamental element of financial statements because the definition of liabilities depends on the definition of assets—liabilities are obligations to pay or deliver assets.) The emphasis on assets and liabilities in the definitions of the elements of financial statements in Concepts Statement 3 showed that the Board had adopted the asset and liability view and rejected the revenue and expense view.

Assets and (to a lesser extent) liabilities have conceptual primacy, while income and its components—revenues, expenses, gains, and losses—do not.

> Every conceptual structure builds on a concept that has primacy. That is simply another way of saying some element must be given meaning before meaning can be attached to others. I contend that assets have that primacy. I have not been able to define income without using a term like asset, resources, source of benefits, and so on. In short, meaning can be given to assets without first defining income, but the reverse is not true. That is what I mean by conceptual primacy of assets. No one has ever been successful in giving meaning to income without first giving meaning to assets.[118]

The Board's early experiences had convinced it that definitions of assets and liabilities that depended on definitions of income and its components did not work. As already noted, those kinds of definitions proved to be of little help to the Board in deciding whether results of research and development expenditures qualified as assets or whether reserves for self-insurance qualified as liabilities because they permit almost any debit balance to be an asset and almost any credit balance to be a liability.

In addition, the Board had attempted to test whether revenues and expenses could be defined without first defining assets and liabilities. It asked respondents to the Discussion Memorandum to submit for its consideration precise definitions of revenues and expenses that were wholly or partially independent of economic resources and obligations (assets and liabilities) and capable of general application in a conceptual framework. That no one was able to do that without having to resort to subjective guides, such as proper matching and nondistortion of income, was a significant factor in the Board's ultimate rejection of the revenue and expense view.

> Attempts to identify a good match based on the primacy of revenue and expense have been unsuccessful so far. There is a serious question as to whether revenue and expense can be defined independent of assets and liabilities.[119]

---

[118] Oscar S. Gellein, "Primacy: Assets or Income?" *Research in Accounting Regulation*, Vol. 6, edited by Gary John Previts (Greenwich, CT: JAI Press, 1992), p. 198.

[119] Gellein, "Financial Reporting: The State of Standard Setting," p. 17.

Thus, revenues and expenses could not fulfill the function of concepts having primacy, which

are the concepts used to define other concepts. They prevent the systems from being open-ended and potentially circular. They are the concepts that are used to test for unity and maintenance of a consistent direction—they are the anchor.[120]

Instead, the Board found that definitions that made assets and liabilities essentially fallout of the process of matching revenues and expenses provided no anchor. They excluded almost nothing from income because they excluded almost nothing from assets and liabilities. The definitions were primarily conventional, not conceptual, and had made periodic income measurement largely a matter of individual judgment and personal opinion. The resulting accounting lacked the conceptual underpinning that provides, among other things, "the means for judging whether one solution is better than another.... [and] the restraints necessary to prevent proliferation of perceptions and resulting diversity of accounting methods for substantially similar circumstances."[121] That is, the Board found the revenue and expense view to be part of the problem rather than part of the solution.

In contrast, the Board's definitions of assets and liabilities limited what can be included in all of the other elements. The Board's choice of the asset and liability view limited the population of assets and liabilities to the underlying economic resources and obligations of an enterprise. The resulting definitions impose limits or restraints not only on what can be included in assets and liabilities but also on what can be included in income. The only items that can meet the definitions of income and its components—revenues, expenses, gains, and losses—are those that increase or decrease the wealth of an enterprise.

The Board based its definitions of elements of financial statements on the conceptual primacy of assets and liabilities for both conceptual and practical reasons. However, that decision was to put the Board at odds with many of its constituents because, among other reasons, "both [conceptual primacy], and the implications of the FASB position on it are still rather widely misunderstood."[122]

REVENUE AND EXPENSE VIEW AND ITS HOLD ON PRACTICE. The revenue and expense view had been the basis for accounting practice and for most authoritative accounting pronouncements for over 40 years when the Board looked closely at it in the 1970s. The FASB saw clear evidence of its pervasiveness in practice and in accountants' minds in its early projects on research and development expenditures and accruing future losses. An emphasis on the "proper matching of costs and revenues," a concern for avoiding "distortion of periodic net income," and a willingness to allow what-you-may-call-its to appear in balance sheets are all characteristics of the revenue and expense view of income, which has been described extensively earlier in this chapter without referring to it by that name.[123] When the Board issued the Discussion Memorandum, the revenue and expense view was the only view of accounting that most of its constituents knew.

Many of them apparently could not, or would not, believe that the Board's primary concern was the need for a set of definitions that worked. That reaction probably was to have been expected. Definitions of assets and liabilities have not been significant in the thinking underlying the revenue and expense view, which has focused on the need to measure performance by relating efforts expended with the resulting accomplishments and has emphasized proper matching and nondistortion of periodic net income as the means of achieving that association of effort and accomplishment.

---

[120] Gellein, "Financial Reporting: The State of Standard Setting," p. 15.

[121] Id., p. 13.

[122] Id., p. 14.

[123] Most accountants had never heard the terms "revenue and expense view" and "asset and liability view" until the FASB used them in its 1976 Discussion Memorandum on elements of financial statements.

Its proponents might find it difficult to believe that definitions of assets and liabilities could be considered to be fundamental concepts.

Unfortunately, the issue became highly emotional, and many of those who did not accept the Board's explanations looked for other explanations for its decision. Although the Board had defined assets and liabilities in a way that could accurately be described as venerable, many members of the Board's constituency found something unusual, perhaps even sinister, in the Board's definitions of elements of financial statements.

For example, a popular criticism of the asset and liability view charged the FASB with having the intent

- To downgrade the importance of net income and the income statement by making the balance sheet more important than the income statement
- To supplant accounting based on completed transactions and matching of costs and revenues with a "new" accounting based on the valuation of assets and liabilities at current values or costs

That many of the comment letters the Board received on the Discussion Memorandum echoed those charges mostly reflected the success of an illustrated-lecture tour by Robert K. Mautz, partner of Ernst & Ernst (now Ernst & Young LLP), in which he urged members of 65 to 70 chapters of the Financial Executives Institute to reject the asset and liability view.[124]

Board and staff members became concerned that discussion of the FASB's decision to base its definitions of elements of financial statements on the conceptual primacy of assets and liabilities had gone astray. The focus had been shifted from the definitions to some oversimplified and essentially irrelevant distinctions between the asset and liability and revenue and expense views concerning which financial statement is more useful and which measurement basis goes with which view.

> Conceptual primacy has nothing to do with the question of what information is most useful or of how it is measured. It refers only to the matter of definitional dependency.[125]

The Discussion Memorandum had tried to keep the emphasis on the definitions, explaining why the relative usefulness of income statements and balance sheets was never a real issue between the two views:

> [A]dvocates of the asset and liability view agree with advocates of the revenue and expense view that the information in a statement of earnings is likely to be more useful to investors and creditors than the information in a statement of financial position. That is, both groups agree that earnings measurement is the focus of financial accounting and financial statements. [paragraph 45]

Concepts Statement 1 was unequivocal in identifying information about income as most useful to investors, creditors, and other users:

> The primary focus of financial reporting is information about an enterprise's performance provided by measures of earnings and its components. Investors, creditors, and others who are concerned with assessing the prospects for enterprise net cash inflows are especially interested in that information. [paragraph 43][126]

---

[124] Pelham Gore, *The FASB Conceptual Framework Project, 1973–1985, An Analysis* (Manchester and New York: Manchester University Press, 1992), pp. 94 and 95.

[125] Gellein, "Financial Reporting: The State of Standard Setting," p. 15.

[126] That paragraph echoed paragraph 171 of *Tentative Conclusions on Objectives of Financial Statements of Business Enterprises*, which was issued in a package with the Discussion Memorandum: Earnings for an enterprise for a period measured by accrual accounting [is] generally considered to be the most relevant indicator of relative success or failure of the earning process of an enterprise in bringing in needed cash. Measures of periodic earnings are widely used by investors, creditors, security analysts, and others.

Thus, to say that the asset and liability view downgrades the significance of net income and the income statement by making the balance sheet more significant than the income statement at best reflects misunderstanding of the conceptual primacy of assets and liabilities and of the asset and liability view used by the Board. At worst, it misrepresents the Board's reasons for accepting the asset and liability view and rejecting the revenue and expense view of income.

The idea that the Board chose the asset and liability view to impose some kind of current value accounting on an unwilling world reflects the same misunderstanding and misrepresentation. None of the Concepts Statements except No. 5, *Recognition and Measurement in Financial Statements of Business Enterprises*, says anything about how assets or liabilities should be measured, and Concepts Statement 5 does not embrace a "new" accounting based on the valuation of assets and liabilities at current values or costs. If anything, it favors "historical-cost accounting" and erects barriers to current values or costs, for example, placing a higher hurdle for recognizing current values or costs than for recognizing historical costs: "Information based on current prices should be recognized if it is sufficiently relevant and reliable to justify the costs involved and more relevant than alternative information" (paragraph 90). Moreover, Concepts Statement 5 and numerous speeches made and articles written by Board members while the Concepts Statements were in progress furnish abundant evidence that Board members never were sufficiently of the same mind on the relative merits and weaknesses of current cost or value and so-called historical cost for measuring assets and liabilities for the Board accurately to be characterized as "having the intent" to adopt any particular measurement model for assets and liabilities.

Since Board members' continual public denials of that kind of intent and their explanations of what the Board actually was trying to accomplish were publicly brushed aside by many members of the Board's constituency, the unfortunate result was a generally unenlightening digression that served no purpose except to cast aspersions on Board members' veracity and integrity and to polarize opinion. It made little or no contribution to the conceptual framework, but it did reveal a deep-seated distrust of a conceptual framework, or perhaps of concepts generally, on the part of many accountants and a fear, easily triggered by, for example, labeling the asset and liability view a "valuation approach," that the FASB might be in the process of turning the world of accounting upside down.

The revenue and expense view is still deeply ingrained in many accountants' minds, and their first reaction to an accounting problem is to think about "proper matching of costs and revenues." Time will be needed for them to become accustomed to thinking first about effects of transactions or other events on assets and liabilities (or both) and then about how the effect on assets and liabilities has affected revenues, expenses, gains, or losses. Many will be able to make that adjustment only with difficulty, and a significant number simply will make no attempt to do so, clinging instead to the revenue and expense view. The FASB's experience suggests that a long tradition of ad hoc accounting principles has fostered a propensity to resist restraints on flexibility, especially those that limit an enterprise's ability to decide what can be included in income for a period.

Yet, the hold of the revenue and expense view on practice is destined to decline. Definitions reflecting the revenue and expense view have been weighed in the balance and found wanting, not only by the FASB but also by other standards-setting bodies.

> The conceptual frameworks of the standard-setting bodies [in Australia, Canada, the United Kingdom and the United States and the International Accounting Standards Committee] do rest on the bedrock of the balance sheet. This may be inevitable, given that advocates of a p[rofit] & l[oss] account-driven approach have so far failed to produce rigorous, coherent and consistent definitions of its elements that refer to underlying events rather than the recognition process itself.[127]

Countries besides the United States that have adopted or are in the process of adopting conceptual frameworks or statements also generally have developed definitions of elements of financial statements that reflect the conceptual primacy of assets and liabilities. Thus, standards setters in

---

[127] Brian Rutherford, "Accountancy Issues—They Manipulate, You Smooth. I Self-Hedge: Perhaps the World's Finest Know a Thing or Two After All," *Accountancy*, June 1995, p. 95.

Australia, Canada, and the United Kingdom, as well as the International Accounting Standards Committee, all have definitions that are generally similar to those of the FASB.

To those familiar with the FASB's experience with the Discussion Memorandum on elements of financial statements, the related Exposure Drafts, and Concepts Statement 3, what has happened recently in some of those countries is (in the words of Yogi Berra) *"déjà vu* all over again." At the annual Financial Times financial reporting conference in the United Kingdom in September 1993, for example,

> David Lindsell, senior technical partner at Ernst & Young, reiterated his firm's criticism of the A[ccounting] S[tandards] B[oard]'s conceptual approach (*Accountancy,* October 1993, page 11). Whereas the ASB's Statement of Principles makes the balance sheet the "focal point of the accounts" and "treats financial reporting primarily as a process of valuation," E&Y believes that the primary focus should be on "the measurement of earnings, and that the balance sheet should be seen as a residual statement, derived after measuring the company's profits and not the other way round."[128]

> Essentially E&Y accuses the ASB of focusing on the balance sheet at the expense of the p[rofit] & l[oss] account and argues for a return to pure historical cost accounting. . . . [S]ince E&Y went public with its criticism, it has heard from a lot of people, particularly finance directors, who have expressed sympathy with its arguments.[129]

International harmonization of accounting practice is likely to continue to be in the direction of phasing out the revenue and expense view.

However, change is likely to be rather deliberate, and at least in the United States, features of the revenue and expense view are likely to be part, though a shrinking part, of financial statements for some time to come. The Board has said that it "intends future change to occur in the gradual, evolutionary way that has characterized past change" (Concepts Statement 5, paragraph 2). And, although it precluded self-insurance reserves and similar what-you-may-call-its in balance sheets, the Board has permitted other what-you-may-call-its to avoid unduly disrupting practice. For example, it explicitly responded to concerns about volatility of reported net income expressed by respondents to the Exposure Draft that preceded FASB Statement No. 87, *Employers' Accounting for Pensions* (December 1985), concluding that to require accounting that was conceptually appropriate under the definitions in Concepts Statement 3 would be too great a change from past practice to be adopted in a single step. Thus, Statement 87 "retains three fundamental aspects of past pension accounting" despite their conflict with the Concepts Statements and accounting principles applied elsewhere (paragraph 84). One of the three—delaying recognition of actuarial gains and losses to spread over future periods the recognition of gains or losses that have already occurred to a liability for pensions or pension plan assets—requires recognizing in the accounts a number of what-you-may-call-its even though they do not qualify as assets or liabilities under the Board's definitions. The Board's perception of a need for expedients of that kind means that at least some "what-you-may-call-its" in balance sheets and the related arguments about "proper matching of costs and revenues" and "avoiding distortion of periodic net income" are likely to disappear only gradually.

(iv) Functions of the Conceptual Framework.   The Preface of each FASB Concepts Statement has carried the following, or a similar, description (this excerpt is from Concepts Statement 6):

> The conceptual framework is a coherent system of interrelated objectives and fundamentals that is expected to lead to consistent standards and that prescribes the nature, function, and limits of financial accounting and reporting. It is expected to serve the public interest by providing structure and direction to financial accounting and reporting to facilitate the provision of evenhanded

---

[128] "News—ASB under Fire," *Accountancy,* November 1993, p. 16.
[129] Brian Singleton-Green, "The ASB: Critics That Won't Be Pacified," *Accountancy,* November 1993, p. 26.

financial and related information that helps promote the efficient allocation of scarce resources in the economy and society, including assisting capital and other markets to function efficiently.

Establishment of objectives and identification of fundamental concepts will not directly solve financial accounting and reporting problems. Rather, objectives give direction, and concepts are tools for solving problems.

The FASB's conceptual framework is intended to be primarily a set of tools to help the Board in setting sound financial accounting standards and to help members of the Board's constituency not only understand and apply those standards but also contribute significantly to their development. It is not expected automatically to provide ready-made, unique, and obviously logical answers to complex financial accounting or reporting problems, but it should help to solve them by:

- Providing a set of common premises as a basis for discussion
- Providing precise terminology
- Helping to ask the right questions
- Limiting areas of judgment and discretion and excluding from consideration potential solutions that are in conflict with it
- Imposing intellectual discipline on what traditionally has been a subjective and ad hoc reasoning process

Those contributions of the conceptual framework have all been introduced at least indirectly earlier in this chapter, and the last two were cited as factors in the FASB's conclusions in the preceding discussion of assets as the fundamental element of financial statements. The following paragraphs add a few points on the first three.

A critical function of the conceptual framework is to provide a set of common premises from which to begin discussing specific accounting problems and developing solutions for them. The accounting profession's earlier efforts to establish accounting principles have shown that if experience is the frame of reference, no one can be sure of the starting point, if one exists at all, because everyone's experience is different. The FASB's predecessors tried to use experience as a common point of departure, but when confronted with the same problems, people with different experiences too often offered widely different solutions, and financial accounting was inundated with multiple solutions to the same problems. The problems of communication and understanding between those supporting the revenue and expense view and those supporting the asset and liability view offer a striking illustration.

A framework of coordinated concepts as the frame of reference, in contrast, can change that picture. The FASB and its constituency start from common ground, vastly increasing the likelihood that they can communicate with and understand each other on the complex and difficult problems that often arise in financial accounting and reporting. A set of common premises does not guarantee agreement, but it does avoid the problems and wasted time that result if those discussing a matter talk past each other because they actually are not talking about the same thing. It also promotes consensus once a problem is solved. For example, Donald J. Kirk, former chairman of the FASB, noted that the conceptual framework was undertaken "with the expectation that it would articulate definitions and concepts that would diminish the need for and details in standards; it was to be the 'relief' from the so-called 'firefighting' [approach] for which the FASB's predecessors had been criticized."[130]

A related purpose of the conceptual framework is to provide a precise terminology. Good terminology serves much the same function as a set of common premises: "Loose terminology encourages loose thinking. Precision in the use of words does not solve human controversies, but

---

[130] Donald J. Kirk, "Looking Back on Fourteen Years at the FASB: The Education of a Standard Setter," *Accounting Horizons*, March 1988, p. 11.

at least it paves the way for clear thinking."[131] The FASB's conceptual framework has contributed significantly to precise terminology through its careful definitions of the elements of financial statements in Concepts Statement 6 and the qualitative characteristics of accounting information in Concepts Statement 2.

The conceptual framework helps to ask the right questions. Indeed, the FASB has emphasized that contribution as much as any. For example, the definitions of elements of financial statements not only make clear which are the right questions but also the order in which to ask them:

What is the asset?

What is the liability?

Did an asset or liability or its value change?

Increase or decrease?

By how much?

Did the change result from:

An investment by owners?

A distribution to owners?

Comprehensive income?

Was the source of comprehensive income what we call:

Revenue?

Expense?

Gain?

Loss?

To start at the bottom and work up the list will not work. That is what ad hoc accounting has tried to do over many years, resulting in assets and liabilities in balance sheets that cannot meet the definitions.

The conceptual framework does not guarantee logical solutions to accounting problems. The results depend significantly on those who use the concepts to establish financial accounting standards. But it does provide valuable tools to standards setters.

> Standard setters' instincts alone are not adequate to maintain direction—to discriminate between a solution that better lends usefulness to a standard than another solution, and at the same time maintain consistency. Their instincts need conceptual guidance.
>
> ... The objectives build on the role of financial reporting and underlie the definitions of financial statement elements. Acceptance of the definitions provides the necessary discipline for order. Instead of arguing about the definitions, the FASB, as well as its constituents, now focuses attention on whether a matter in a given situation meets the conditions of a definition. That contributes to efficiency and furthers the chances of consistency.[132]

(b) THE FINANCIAL ACCOUNTING STANDARDS BOARD CONCEPTS STATEMENTS.   The Concepts Statements set forth the objectives and conceptual foundation of financial accounting that are the basis for the development of financial accounting and reporting standards. This section of the chapter discusses the individual Concepts Statements in a logical order according to their subject matter. The objectives of financial reporting constitute the subject matter of Concepts Statement No. 1, *Objectives of Financial Reporting by Business Enterprises*, and Concepts Statement No. 4, *Objectives of Financial Reporting by Nonbusiness Organizations*. The qualities that make accounting information useful for investment, credit, and other resource allocation decisions

---

[131] Austin Wakeman Scott, *Abridgement of the Law of Trusts* (Boston: Little, Brown and Company, 1960), p. 28.

[132] Gellein, "Financial Reporting: The State of Standard Setting," p. 13.

are described in Concepts Statement No. 2, *Qualitative Characteristics of Accounting Information*. Concepts Statements No. 3 and No. 6 define the *Elements of Financial Statements*. Finally, Concepts Statement No. 5, *Recognition and Measurement in Financial Statements of Business Enterprises*, describes a complete set of financial statements and what is meant by recognition and measurement.

(i) Objectives of Financial Reporting. After the FASB received the report of the Trueblood Study Group, *Objectives of Financial Statements*, in October 1973, it issued a Discussion Memorandum, *Conceptual Framework for Accounting and Reporting: Consideration of the Report of the Study Group on the Objectives of Financial Statements*, in June 1974. The Discussion Memorandum was based primarily on the Trueblood Report's 12 objectives of financial statements and seven qualitative characteristics of reporting. The Board held a public hearing in September and began to develop its own conclusions on the objectives.

Concepts Statement No. 1. In December 1976, the Board published for comment a draft entitled *Tentative Conclusions on Objectives of Financial Statements of Business Enterprises* and a Discussion Memorandum, *Conceptual Framework for Financial Accounting and Reporting: Elements of Financial Statements and Their Measurement*. Although the Trueblood Report included an objective of financial statements for governmental and not-for-profit organizations, the FASB had decided to concentrate its initial efforts on formulating objectives of financial statements of business enterprises. Following a public hearing on those publications the following August, the Board issued an Exposure Draft, *Objectives of Financial Reporting and Elements of Financial Statements of Business Enterprises*, in December 1977. Concepts Statement No. 1, *Objectives of Financial Reporting by Business Enterprises*, was issued in November 1978.

The change in title between the Tentative Conclusions and the Exposure Draft indicated a change in the Board's perspective from a focus on financial statements to financial reporting. To a significant extent, it reflected comments received on the Tentative Conclusions document. The change also emphasized that financial statements were the primary, but not the only, means of conveying financial information to users. During the Board's consideration of objectives, it had decided that for general purpose external financial reporting, the objectives of financial statements and the objectives of financial reporting are essentially the same, although, as the Statement said, some information is better provided by financial statements and other information is better provided by other means of financial reporting (paragraph 5).

That brief sketch of the background of the Statement has touched only certain points. Concepts Statement 1, like all of the Concepts Statements, contains an appendix on its background (paragraphs 57–63).

CONCEPTS STATEMENT NO. 1 AND THE TRUEBLOOD GROUP'S OBJECTIVES. The FASB accepted the starting point and basic objective in the report of the Trueblood Study Group and, although some differences in direction had begun to appear in the supporting discussion, accepted in a general way the group's second and third objectives. These excerpts are from the Study Group's report:

Accounting is not an end in itself. . . .

The basic objective of financial statements is to provide information useful for making economic decisions.

An objective of financial statements is to serve primarily those users who have limited authority, ability, or resources to obtain information and who rely on financial statements as their principal source of information about an enterprise's economic activities.

An objective of financial statements is to provide information useful to investors and creditors for predicting, comparing, and evaluating potential cash flows to them in terms of amount, timing, and related uncertainty. [pp. 61 and 62]

These excerpts are from Concepts Statement 1:

Financial reporting is not an end in itself but is intended to provide information that is useful in making business and economic decisions—for making reasoned choices among alternative uses of scarce resources in the conduct of business and economic activities. [paragraph 9]

The objectives in this Statement . . . stem primarily from the informational needs of external users who lack the authority to prescribe the financial information they want from an enterprise and therefore must use the information that management communicates to them. [paragraph 28]

Potential users of financial information most directly concerned with a particular business enterprise are generally interested in its ability to generate favorable cash flows because their decisions relate to amounts, timing, and uncertainties of expected cash flows. To investors, lenders, suppliers, and employees, a business enterprise is a source of cash in the form of dividends or interest and perhaps appreciated market prices, repayment of borrowing, payment for goods or services, or salaries or wages. They invest cash, goods, or services in an enterprise and expect to obtain sufficient cash in return to make the investment worthwhile. They are directly concerned with the ability of the enterprise to generate favorable cash flows and may also be concerned with how the market's perception of that ability affects the relative prices of its securities. [paragraph 25]

Financial reporting should provide information that is useful to present and potential investors and creditors and other users in making rational investment, credit, and similar decisions. [paragraph 34]

None of the other nine objectives of the Study Group was adopted in recognizable form in Concepts Statement 1. Many of them were about matters that the Board had decided to include in the recognition, measurement, and display parts of the conceptual framework.

Concepts Statement No. 4.   By 1977 the fiscal problems of a number of large cities, including New York and Cleveland, had prompted public officials and private citizens increasingly to question the relevance and reliability of financial reporting by governmental and not-for-profit organizations. That concern was reflected in many legislative initiatives and widely publicized allegations of serious deficiencies in the financial reporting of various kinds of not-for-profit organizations.

The Board began to consider concepts underlying general purpose external financial reporting by not-for-profit organizations by commissioning a research report to identify the objectives of financial reporting by organizations other than business enterprises. That report, *Financial Accounting in Nonbusiness Organizations*, by Robert N. Anthony, was published in May 1978. Rather than delay progress on the objectives of financial reporting by business enterprises by attempting to include not-for-profit organizations within its scope, the Board decided to proceed with two separate objectives projects. It issued a Discussion Memorandum based on the research report, followed by an Exposure Draft. Then, *Objectives of Financial Reporting by Nonbusiness Organizations* was issued as Concepts Statement 4 in December 1980. After Concepts Statement 4 was issued, the FASB changed the key term from nonbusiness to not-for-profit organizations.

Effects of Environment and Information Needs of Resource Providers.   Concepts Statement 1 and Concepts Statement 4 have the same structure. Both sets of objectives are based on the fundamental notion that financial reporting concepts and standards should be based on the information needs of users of financial statements who make decisions about committing resources to either business enterprises or not-for-profit organizations with the expectation of pecuniary reward or to not-for-profit organizations for reasons other than expectations of monetary return of or return on resources committed. From that broad focus, the Statements narrow the focus, on one hand, to the primary interest of investors, creditors, and other users in the prospects of receiving cash from their investments in or loans to business enterprises and the relationship of their prospects to those of the enterprise, and, on the other hand, to the needs of resource providers for information about a not-for-profit organization's services, its ability to continue to provide them, and the relationship of management's stewardship to the organization's performance. Finally, both Statements focus on the kinds of information that financial reporting can provide to meet the respective needs of both groups.

The objectives of financial reporting cannot be properly understood apart from the environmental context in which they have been developed—the real world in which financial accounting and reporting takes place. They are affected by the economic, legal, political, and social environment of the United States. The objectives "stem largely from the needs of those for whom the information is intended, which in turn depend significantly on the nature of the economic activities and decisions with which the users are involved" (Concepts Statement 1, paragraph 9). Thus, Concepts Statement 1 describes the highly developed exchange economy of the United States, in which:

- Most goods and services are exchanged for money or claims to money instead of being consumed by their producers.
- Most productive activity is carried on through investor-owned business enterprises whose operations are controlled by directors and professional managers acting in the interests of investor-owners.
- Well-developed securities markets tend to allocate scarce resources to enterprises that use them efficiently.
- Productive resources are generally privately rather than government owned, although government intervenes in the resource allocation process through taxation, borrowing and spending for government operations and programs, regulation, subsidies, or monetary and fiscal policy.

Cash is important in the economy "because of what it can buy. Members of the society carry out their consumption, saving, and investment decisions by allocating their present and expected cash resources" (Concepts Statement 1, paragraph 10). Entities' efficient allocation of cash and other economic resources is a means to the desired end of a well-functioning, healthy economy. The following excerpt from Concepts Statement 1 describes how financial reporting can contribute to achieving that social good. It refers to reporting about business enterprises, but its premise relates as well to the objectives of financial reporting of not-for-profit organizations.

> The effectiveness of individuals, enterprises, markets, and government in allocating scarce resources among competing uses is enhanced if those who make economic decisions have information that reflects the relative standing and performance of business enterprises to assist them in evaluating alternative courses of action and the expected returns, costs, and risks of each. The function of financial reporting is to provide information that is useful to those who make economic decisions about business enterprises and about investments in or loans to business enterprises. [paragraph 16]

Business enterprises and not-for-profit organizations have both similarities and differences in their operating environments that affect the information needs of those who make decisions about them and thus affect the objectives of financial reporting. Both kinds of entities have transactions with suppliers of goods and services who expect to be paid for what they provide, with employees who expect to be paid for their work, and with lenders who expect to be repaid with interest. Both entities may sell the goods or services they produce, although to survive, business enterprises charge prices sufficient to cover their costs, usually plus a profit, whereas not-for-profit organizations often may sell below cost or at nominal prices or may even give their outputs to beneficiaries without charge.

Not-for-profit organizations commonly need certain kinds of control arrangements more than do business enterprises. Although not-for-profit organizations must often compete not only with each other but also with business enterprises for goods and services, employees, and lendable funds, the operating performance of business enterprises generally is subject to the discipline of market controls to a greater extent than is the performance of not-for-profit organizations because business enterprises must compete in equity markets for funds to finance their operations while not-for-profit organizations do not. Spending mandates and budgets to control uses of resources are significant factors in obtaining and allocating resources for not-for-profit organizations to compensate for the lesser influence of direct market competition.

Business enterprises and not-for-profit organizations also differ in their relationships to some significant resource providers. Business enterprises have stockholders or other owners who invest with the expectation of receiving profits commensurate with the risks incurred. In contrast, not-for-profit organizations have no owners in the same sense as business enterprises and often receive significant amounts of resources by gift or donation from those who do not expect pecuniary returns. Those contributors are interested in the services the organizations provide and receive compensation for their contributions by nonfinancial means, such as by seeing the purposes and goals of the organizations advanced.

Objectives of Financial Reporting by Business Enterprises.   The objectives of financial reporting by business enterprises are derived from the information needs of investors, creditors, and others outside an enterprise who generally lack the authority to prescribe the information they want and thus must rely on information that management communicates to them. They are the primary users of the information provided by general purpose external financial reporting, whose primary objective is to

> provide information that is useful to present and potential investors and creditors and other users in making rational investment, credit, and similar decisions. [Concepts Statement 1, paragraph 34]

The objectives of general purpose external financial reporting are not derived from and do not comprehend satisfying the information needs of all potential users. Regulatory and taxing authorities, for example, have needs for special kinds of financial information that is not normally provided by financial reporting but also have the statutory authority to obtain the specific information they need. Thus they do not have to rely on information provided to other groups. Management is interested in the information provided by external financial reporting but also has ready access not only to that information but also to a great deal of internal information that is normally unavailable to those outside the enterprise. Management's primary role in external financial reporting is that of a provider or communicator of information for use by investors, creditors, and others outside the enterprise who must rely on management for information.

In emphasizing the information needs of investors, creditors, and similar users, the FASB recognized that external financial reporting cannot satisfy the particular and perhaps diverse needs of various individual users who look to the information provided by financial reporting for assistance in making resource allocation decisions. However, those who make investment, credit, and similar decisions do have common, overlapping interests in the ability of a business enterprise to generate favorable cash flows. It is the common interest in an enterprise's cash flow potential that the objectives of external financial reporting seek to satisfy.

The objectives in Concepts Statement 1 focus financial reporting on a particular kind of economic decision—the decision to commit or to continue to commit cash or other resources to a business enterprise with the expectation of payment or of future return of and return on the investment, usually in cash but sometimes in other goods and services. That kind of decision is made by investors, creditors, suppliers, employees, and other potential users of financial information, and they are interested in net cash inflows to the enterprise because their own prospects for receiving cash flows from investments in, loans to, or other participation in an enterprise depend significantly on its ability to generate favorable cash flows.

> Financial reporting should provide information to help present and potential investors and creditors and other users in assessing the amounts, timing, and uncertainty of prospective cash receipts from dividends or interest and the proceeds from the sale, redemption, or maturity of securities or loans. The prospects for those cash receipts are affected by an enterprise's ability to generate enough cash to meet its obligations when due and its other cash operating needs, to reinvest in operations, and to pay cash dividends and may also be affected by perceptions of investors and creditors generally about that ability, which affect market prices of the enterprise's securities. Thus, financial reporting should provide information to help investors, creditors, and others assess the amounts, timing, and uncertainty of prospective net cash inflows to the related enterprise. [Concepts Statement 1, paragraph 37]

Concepts Statement 1 explicitly recognizes that financial reporting does not and cannot provide all of the information needed by those who make economic decisions about business enterprises. It is but one source. Information provided by financial reporting needs to be combined with information about, among other things, the general economy, political climate, and prospects for an enterprise's particular industry or industries.

The objectives ultimately focus on the kind of information that fulfills the users' needs described and that the accounting system can provide better than other sources: information about assets, liabilities, and changes in them. Thus financial reporting should

> provide information about the economic resources of an enterprise, the claims to those resources (obligations of the enterprise to transfer resources to other entities and owners' equity), and the effects of transactions, events, and circumstances that change resources and claims to those resources. [Concepts Statement 1, paragraph 40]

That includes information about an enterprise's assets, liabilities, and owners' equity; information about enterprise performance provided by measures of comprehensive income (called earnings in Concepts Statement 1) and its components; information about liquidity, solvency, and funds flows; information about management stewardship and performance; and management's explanations and interpretations (paragraphs 41–54).

Objectives of Financial Reporting by Not-for-Profit Organizations.   The objectives of financial reporting by not-for-profit organizations are derived from the information needs of external resource providers who, like investors and creditors of business enterprises, generally cannot prescribe the information they want and thus must rely on information that management communicates to them. They are the primary users of the information provided by general purpose external financial reporting, whose primary objective is to

> provide information that is useful to present and potential resource providers and other users in making rational decisions about the allocation of resources to those organizations. [Concepts Statement 4, paragraph 35]

Resource providers encompass those who receive direct compensation for providing resources, including lenders, suppliers, and employees, as well as members, contributors, taxpayers, and others who are concerned with a not-for-profit organization's activities but who are not directly and proportionately compensated financially for their involvement.

The objectives flow from the common interests of those who provide resources to not-for-profit organizations in the services those organizations provide and in their continuing ability to provide services. Because the goals of not-for-profit organizations are to provide services rather than to generate profits,

> [f]inancial reporting should provide information to help present and potential resource providers and other users in assessing the services[17] that a [not-for-profit] organization provides and its ability to continue to provide those services. They are interested in that information because the services are the end for which the resources are provided. The relation of the services provided to the resources used to provide them helps resource providers and others assess the extent to which the organization is successful in carrying out its service objectives. [Concepts Statement 4, paragraph 38]

> [17]The term "services" in this context encompasses the goods as well as the services a [not-for-profit] organization may provide.

The kinds of controls imposed on the operations of not-for-profit organizations to compensate for the reduced influence of markets significantly affect the objectives of their financial reporting. Alternative controls, such as specific budgetary appropriations that may limit the amount an organization is allowed to spend for a particular program or donor-imposed restrictions on the use of resources, usually place a special stewardship responsibility on managers to ensure that resources are used for their intended purposes. Those kinds of spending mandates tend to have a pervasive effect on the conduct and control of the activities of not-for-profit organizations. Because of the nature of the resources entrusted to managers of not-for-profit organizations, Concepts Statement 4 identifies the evaluation of management stewardship and performance information as an objective of the financial reporting of not-for-profit organizations:

> Financial reporting should provide information that is useful to present and potential resource providers and other users in assessing how managers of a [not-for-profit] organization have discharged their stewardship responsibilities and about other aspects of their performance. [Concepts Statement 4, paragraph 40]

Management stewardship is of concern to investors and creditors of business enterprises and resource providers of not-for-profit organizations. Both kinds of resource providers hold management accountable not only for the custody and safekeeping of an organization's resources but also for their efficient and effective use. Concepts Statement 1 identifies comprehensive income as the common focus for assessing management's stewardship or accountability (paragraph 51). Since profit figures are not available for not-for-profit organizations, Concepts Statement 4 instead delineates information about an organization's performance as the focus for assessing management stewardship. It says that financial reporting can provide information about the extent to which managers have acted in accordance with provisions specifically designated by donors. Information about departures from budget mandates or donor-imposed stipulations that may adversely affect an organization's financial performance or its ability to provide a satisfactory level of services is important in assessing how well managers have discharged their stewardship responsibilities.

The objectives of not-for-profit organizations, like those of business enterprises, ultimately focus on the kind of information that the accounting system can provide better than other sources:

> Financial reporting should provide information about the economic resources, obligations, and net resources of an organization and the effects of transactions, events, and circumstances that change resources and interests in those resources. [Concepts Statement 4, paragraph 43]

Resources are the lifeblood of an organization in the sense that it must have resources to render services. Since resource providers tend to direct their interest to information about how an organization acquires and uses its resources, financial reporting should provide information about an organization's assets, liabilities, and net assets; information about its performance, such as about the nature of and relation between resource inflows and outflows and about service efforts and accomplishments; information about liquidity; and managers' explanations and interpretations (paragraphs 44–55).

Keeping the Objectives in Perspective.   Financial accounting information is not intended to measure directly the value of a business enterprise. Nor is it intended to determine or influence the decisions that are made with information it provides about business enterprises and not-for-profit organizations. Its function is to provide the neutral or unbiased information that investors, creditors, various resource providers, and others who are interested in the activities of business enterprises and not-for-profit organizations can use in making those decisions. If financial information were directed toward a particular goal, such as encouraging the reallocation of resources toward particular business enterprises or industries or in favor of certain programs or activities of not-for-profit organizations, it would not be serving its broader objective of providing information useful for resource allocation decisions.

Moreover, as Concepts Statement 1 says, financial reporting is not financial analysis:

> Investors, creditors, and others often use reported [income] and information about the components of [income] in various ways and for various purposes in assessing their prospects for cash flows from investments in or loans to an enterprise. For example, they may use [income] information to

help them (a) evaluate management's performance, (b) estimate "earning power" or other amounts they perceive as "representative" of long-term earning ability of an enterprise, (c) predict future [income], or (d) assess the risk of investing in or lending to an enterprise. They may use the information to confirm, reassure themselves about, or reject or change their own or others' earlier predictions or assessments. Measures of [income] and information about [income] disclosed by financial reporting should, to the extent possible, be useful for those and similar uses and purposes.

However, accrual accounting provides measures of [income] rather than evaluations of management's performance, estimates of "earning power," predictions of [income], assessments of risk, or confirmations or rejections of predictions or assessments. Investors, creditors, and other users of the information do their own evaluating, estimating, predicting, assessing, confirming, or rejecting. For example, procedures such as averaging or normalizing reported [income] for several periods and ignoring or averaging out the financial effects of "nonrepresentative" transactions and events are commonly used in estimating "earning power." However, both the concept of "earning power" and the techniques for estimating it are part of financial analysis and are beyond the scope of financial reporting. [paragraphs 47 and 48; *income* has been substituted for *earnings,* which the Board replaced with *comprehensive income* after Concepts Statement 1]

(ii) Qualitative Characteristics of Accounting Information. "The objectives of financial reporting underlie judgments about the qualities of financial information, for only when those objectives have been established can a start be made on defining the characteristics of the information needed to attain them" (Concepts Statement 2, paragraph 21). Having concluded in Concepts Statement 1 that to provide information useful for making investment, credit, and similar decisions is the primary objective of financial reporting, the FASB elaborated on the corollary to that objective in Concepts Statement 2: that the usefulness of financial information for decision making should be the primary quality to be sought in determining what to encompass in financial reporting. The qualities that make accounting information useful have been designated its "qualitative characteristics." The term was originally used by the Trueblood Study Group, but the idea of articulating the qualities of information that contribute to its usefulness in decision making has its genesis in the authoritative literature in APB Statement 4. That Statement described them as "qualitative objectives," which "aid in determining which resources and obligations and changes should be measured and reported and how they should be measured and reported to make the information most useful" (paragraph 84).

Both APB Statement 4 and the Trueblood Report are direct antecedents of the FASB Concepts Statements because emphasis on decision making by investors and creditors represented a departure from the AICPA's traditional view that financial statements primarily reported to present stockholders on management's stewardship of the corporation. Unless stewardship means mere custodianship, however, stockholders need essentially the same information for that purpose as they do for making investment decisions (Concepts Statement 1, paragraphs 50–53).

Concepts Statement No. 2. Concepts Statement No. 2, *Qualitative Characteristics of Accounting Information*, is described as a bridge between Concepts Statement 1 and the other Statements on elements of financial statements, recognition and measurement, and display. It connects the Statements on objectives, which concern the purposes of financial reporting, with the later Concepts Statements and Standards Statements, which deal with how to attain those purposes, by sharing "with its constituents [the Board's] thinking about the characteristics that the information called for in its standards should have. It is those characteristics that distinguish more useful accounting information from less useful information" (paragraph 1).

When Concepts Statement 2 was issued, the Board noted that its discussion of the qualitative characteristics referred primarily to business enterprises but that it had tentatively concluded that the qualities also applied to the financial reporting of not-for-profit organizations. In Concepts Statement 6, in 1985, the Board formally amended Concepts Statement 2 to apply to both business enterprises and not-for-profit organizations by giving it a new paragraph 4:

The qualities of information discussed in this Statement apply to financial information reported by business enterprises and by not-for-profit organizations. Although the discussion and the examples

in this Statement are expressed in terms commonly related to business enterprises, they generally apply to not-for-profit organizations as well. "Objectives of financial reporting by business
enterprises," "investors and creditors," "investment and credit decisions," and similar terms are
intended to encompass their counterparts for not-for-profit organizations, "objectives of financial
reporting by not-for-profit organizations," "resource providers," "resource allocation decisions,"
and similar terms.

Accountants are required to make a large number of choices—about the criteria by which assets
and liabilities and revenues and expenses are to be recognized and the attribute(s) of assets and
liabilities to be measured; about whether to allocate; about methods of allocation; about the level
of aggregation or disaggregation of the information to be disclosed in financial reports. Accounting
standards issued by the designated standards-setting body narrow the scope for individual choice,
but accounting choices will always have to be made, whether between choices for which no
standard has been promulgated or between alternative ways of implementing a standard.

> To maximize the usefulness of accounting information, subject to considerations of the cost of
> providing it, entails choices between alternative accounting methods. Those choices will be made
> more wisely if the ingredients that contribute to "usefulness" are better understood. [Concepts
> Statement 2, paragraph 5]

By defining the qualities that make accounting information useful, Concepts Statement 2 is
intended to enable the Board and its staff to provide direction for developing accounting standards
consistent with the objectives of financial reporting, which are oriented toward providing useful
information for making investment, credit, and similar decisions:

> The central role assigned here to decision making leads straight to the overriding criterion by which
> all accounting choices must be judged. The better choice is the one that, subject to considerations
> of cost, produces from among the available alternatives information that is most useful for decision
> making. [Concepts Statement 2, paragraph 30]

A Hierarchy of Accounting Qualities.   Concepts Statement 2 examines the characteristics that
make accounting information useful, and the FASB has gone to considerable effort to lay out
what usefulness means. Usefulness for making investment, credit, and similar decisions is the
most important quality in its "Hierarchy of Accounting Qualities": "The characteristics of information that make it a desirable commodity guide the selection of preferred accounting policies from
among available alternatives.... Without usefulness, there would be no benefits from information
to set against its costs. The hierarchy is represented in [Exhibit 2.3]" (Concepts Statement 2, paragraph 32).

Usefulness is a high-level abstraction. To serve as a meaningful criterion or standard against
which to judge the results of financial accounting, usefulness needs to be made more concrete
and specific by analyzing it into its components at lower levels of abstraction. The two primary
components of usefulness are relevance and reliability. While those concepts are more concrete
than usefulness, they are still quite abstract. That is why Concepts Statement 2 focuses at a
still more concrete level, where the concepts of predictive value and feedback value, timeliness,
representational faithfulness, verifiability, neutrality, and comparability together serve as criteria
for determining information's usefulness.

For accounting standards setting, usefulness cannot be interpreted to mean whatever a particular
individual interprets it to mean. A judgment that a piece of information is useful must be the result
of a careful analysis that confirms first that the information possesses the qualities at the most
concrete level of the hierarchy. Is it timely and does it have predictive or feedback value or both? Is
it representationally faithful, verifiable, and neutral? If it has those characteristics, it is relevant and
reliable. Only then, if information has survived that kind of examination, can it be deemed useful.

The exhibit also shows two constraints, primarily quantitative rather than qualitative in nature.
The pervasive constraint is that the benefits of information should exceed its cost. Information

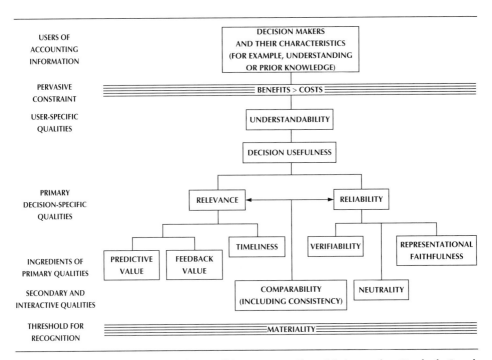

Exhibit 2.3   A hierarchy of accounting qualities. (*Source:* Financial Accounting Standards Board, *Statement of Financial Accounting Concepts No. 2*, par. 32.)

that would be useful for a decision may be just too expensive to justify providing it. The second constraint is a *materiality threshold*, meaning that "the requirement that information be reliable can still be met even though it may contain immaterial errors, for errors that are not material will not perceptibly diminish its usefulness" (paragraph 33).

The hierarchy distinguishes between user-specific and decision-specific qualities because whether a piece of information is useful to a particular decision by a particular decision maker depends in part on the decision maker. Usefulness depends on a decision maker's degree of prior knowledge of the information as well as on his or her ability to understand it.

> The better informed decision makers are, the less likely it is that any new information can add materially to what they already know. That may make the new information less useful, but it does not make it less relevant to the situation. If an item of information reaches a user and then, a little later, the user receives the same item from another source, it is not less relevant the second time, though it will have less value. For that reason, relevance has been defined in this Statement (paragraphs 46 and 47) in terms of the capacity of information to make a difference (to someone who does not already have it) rather than in terms of the difference it actually does make. The difference it actually does make may be more a function of how much is already known (a condition specific to a particular user) than of the content of the new messages themselves (decision-specific qualities of information). [Concepts Statement 2, paragraph 37]

Similarly, the ability to understand a pertinent piece of information relates more to the characteristics of users for whom the information is intended than to the information itself. Even though information may be relevant to a decision, it will not be useful to a person who cannot understand it.

In Concepts Statement 1, the Board said that information provided by financial reporting "should be comprehensible to those who have a reasonable understanding of business and economic activities and are willing to study the information with reasonable diligence" (paragraph 34). But information's relevance may transcend the ability of a user to recognize its import:

> Financial information is a tool and, like most tools, cannot be of much direct help to those who are unable or unwilling to use it or who misuse it. Its use can be learned, however, and financial reporting should provide information that can be used by all—nonprofessionals as well as professionals—who are willing to learn to use it properly. Efforts may be needed to increase the understandability of financial information. Cost-benefit considerations may indicate that information understood or used by only a few should not be provided. Conversely, financial reporting should not exclude relevant information merely because it is difficult for some to understand or because some investors or creditors choose not to use it. [Concepts Statement 1, paragraph 36]

> Understandability of information is governed by a combination of user characteristics and characteristics inherent in the information, which is why understandability and other user-specific characteristics occupy a position in the hierarchy of qualities as a link between the characteristics of users (decision makers) and decision-specific qualities of information. [Concepts Statement 2, paragraph 40]

The two primary decision-specific qualities that make accounting information useful for decision making are relevance and reliability. If either is missing completely from a piece of information, the information will not be useful. In choosing between accounting alternatives, one should strive to produce information that is both as relevant and as reliable as possible, but at times it may be necessary to sacrifice some degree of one quality for a gain in the other.

Relevance. "To be relevant to investors, creditors, and others for investment, credit, and similar decisions, accounting information must be capable of making a difference in a decision by helping users to form predictions about the outcomes of past, present, and future events or to confirm or correct expectations" (Concepts Statement 2, paragraph 47). That definition of relevance is more explicit than the dictionary meaning of relevance as bearing on or relating to the matter in hand. As alluded to earlier, prior knowledge of information may diminish its value but not its relevance and, hence, its usefulness, for it is information's ability to "make a difference" that makes it relevant to a decision.

Statements about relevance of financial statement information must answer the question "relevant to whom for what purpose?" For information to be judged relevant, an object to which it is relevant must always be understood.

PREDICTIVE VALUE AND FEEDBACK VALUE.   To be relevant, information must have predictive value or feedback value or both.

> Information can make a difference to decisions by improving decision makers' capacities to predict or by confirming or correcting their earlier expectations. Usually, information does both at once, because knowledge about the outcome of actions already taken will generally improve decision makers' abilities to predict the results of similar future actions. Without a knowledge of the past, the basis for a prediction will usually be lacking. Without an interest in the future, knowledge of the past is sterile. [Concepts Statement 2, paragraph 51]

David Solomons, consultant on and major contributor to Concepts Statement 2, said in his book, *Making Accounting Policy*, that "whereas predictive value is forward-looking and is derived directly from its power to guide decisions, feedback value is derived from what information tells about the past." He gives as an example of a balance sheet item with predictive value the allowance for uncollectible receivables, which is the amount of accounts receivable that is not expected to produce future cash flows. The most important figure in financial statements with feedback value is the earnings figure, which "conveys information about the success of the ventures that have been invested in and also about the performance of the managers who have been responsible for running the business."[133]

---

[133] David Solomons, *Making Accounting Policy: The Quest for Credibility in Financial Reporting* (New York: Oxford University Press, Inc., 1986), pages 89 and 90.

To say that accounting information has predictive value is not to say that in itself it constitutes a prediction (Concepts Statement 2, paragraph 53). Predictive value means value as an input into a predictive process, not value directly as a prediction. It is "the quality of information that helps users to increase the likelihood of correctly forecasting the outcome of past or present events" (Concepts Statement 2, glossary). Information about the present state of economic resources or obligations or about an enterprise's past performance is commonly a basis for expectations. Information is relevant if it can reduce the uncertainty surrounding a decision. It is relevant "if the degree of uncertainty about the result of a decision that has already been made is confirmed or altered by the new information; it need not alter the decision" (Concepts Statement 2, paragraph 49).

TIMELINESS.   To be relevant, information also must be timely. Timeliness means "[h]aving information available to a decision maker before it loses its capacity to influence decisions" (Concepts Statement 2, glossary). Information that is not available when it is needed or becomes available only long after it has value for future action is useless. "Timeliness alone cannot make information relevant, but a lack of timeliness can rob information of relevance it might otherwise have had" (Concepts Statement 2, paragraph 56).

Reliability.   Reliability is the quality of information that allows those who use it to depend on it with confidence. "The reliability of a measure rests on the faithfulness with which it represents what it purports to represent, coupled with an assurance for the user, which comes through verification, that it has that representational quality" (Concepts Statement 2, paragraph 59). The hierarchy of qualities decomposes reliability into two components, representational faithfulness and verifiability, with neutrality shown to interact with them.

REPRESENTATIONAL FAITHFULNESS.   Representational faithfulness is "correspondence or agreement between a measure or description and the phenomenon it purports to represent. In accounting, the phenomena to be represented are economic resources and obligations and the transactions and events that change those resources and obligations" (Concepts Statement 2, paragraph 63). The FASB's conceptual framework emphasizes that accounting is a representational discipline. It represents things in the financial statements that exist in the real world. Therefore, the correspondence between the accounting representation and the thing being represented is critical.

Concepts Statement 2 uses an analogy with mapmaking to illustrate what it means by representational faithfulness:

> A map represents the geographical features of the mapped area by using symbols bearing no resemblance to the actual countryside, yet they communicate a great deal of information about it. The captions and numbers in financial statements present a "picture" of a business enterprise and many of its external and internal relationships more rigorously—more informatively, in fact—than a simple description of it. [paragraph 24]

Just as the lines and shapes on a road map represent roads, rivers, and geographical boundaries, so also descriptions and amounts in financial statements represent cash, property, sales, and a host of things owned or owed by an entity as well as transactions and other events and circumstances that affect them or their values. The items in financial statements have a higher degree of reliability as quantitative representations of economic things and events in the real world—and therefore more usefulness to investors and other parties interested in an entity's activities—if they faithfully represent what they purport to represent. Since the benefit of the information is representational and not aesthetic, to take "artistic license" with the data decreases rather than increases its benefit. Just as a cartographer cannot add roads, bridges, and lakes where none exist, an accountant cannot add imaginary items to financial statements without spoiling the representational faithfulness, and ultimately the usefulness, of the information.

Striving for representational faithfulness does not comprehend creating an exact replica of the activities of an enterprise. Perfect information is as beyond the reach of accountants as it is of nonaccountants.

The financial statements of a business enterprise can be thought of as a representation of the resources and obligations of an enterprise and the financial flows into, out of, and within the enterprise—as a model of the enterprise. Like all models, it must abstract from much that goes on in a real enterprise. No model, however sophisticated, can be expected to reflect all the functions and relationships that are found within a complex organization. To do so, the model would have to be virtually a reproduction of the original. In real life, it is necessary to accept a much smaller degree of correspondence between the model and the original than that. One can be satisfied if none of the important functions and relationships are lost.... The mere fact that a model works—that when it receives inputs it produces outputs—gives no assurance that it faithfully represents the original. Just as a distorting mirror reflects a warped image of the person standing in front of it ..., so a bad model gives a distorted representation of the system that it models. The question that accountants must face continually is how much distortion is acceptable. [Concepts Statement 2, paragraph 76]

COMPLETENESS.   Completeness of information is an important aspect of representational faithfulness, and thus of reliability, because if financial statements are to faithfully represent an enterprise's financial position and changes in financial position, none of the significant financial functions of the enterprise or its relationships can be lost or distorted. Completeness is defined as "the inclusion in reported information of everything material that is necessary for faithful representation of the relevant phenomena" (Concepts Statement 2, glossary). Financial statements are incomplete, and therefore not representationally faithful, if, for example, an enterprise owns an office structure but reports no "building" or similar asset on its balance sheet.

Completeness also is necessary to relevance, the other primary quality that makes accounting information useful:

Relevance of information is adversely affected if a relevant piece of information is omitted, even if the omission does not falsify what is shown. For example, in a diversified enterprise a failure to disclose that one segment was consistently unprofitable would not, before the issuance of FASB Statement No. 14, *Accounting for Segments of a Business Enterprise,* have caused the financial reporting to be judged unreliable, but that financial reporting would have been (as it would now be) deficient in relevance. [Concepts Statement 2, paragraph 80]

Although completeness implies showing what is material and feasible, it must always be relative. Financial statements cannot show everything or they would be prohibitively expensive to provide.

VERIFIABILITY.   Verifiability is "the ability through consensus among measurers to ensure that information represents what it purports to represent or that the chosen method of measurement has been used without error or bias" (Concepts Statement 2, glossary). Verifiability is an essential component of reliability—to be reliable, accounting information must be both representationally faithful and verifiable: "The reliability of a measure rests on the faithfulness with which it represents what it purports to represent, coupled with an assurance for the user, which comes through verification, that it has that representational quality" (Concepts Statement 2, paragraph 59). Verifiability fulfills a significant but relatively narrow function.

In summary, verifiability means no more than that several measurers are likely to obtain the same measure. It is primarily a means of attempting to cope with measurement problems stemming from the uncertainty that surrounds accounting measures and is more successful in coping with some measurement problems than others.... [A] measure with a high degree of verifiability is not necessarily relevant to the decision for which it is intended to be useful. [Concepts Statement 2, paragraph 89]

Three ideas are the focus of the discussion in Concepts Statement 2 of verifiability and its relation to reliability:

1. Accounting information is verifiable if accounting measures obtained by one measurer can be confirmed or substantiated by having other measurers measure the same phenomenon with essentially the same results.

   > Verification implies consensus. Verifiability can be measured by looking at the dispersion of a number of independent measurements of some particular phenomenon. The more closely the measurements are likely to be clustered together, the greater the verifiability of the number used as a measure of the phenomenon.

   > Some accounting measurements are more easily verified than others. Alternative measures of cash will be closely clustered together, with a consequently high level of verifiability. There will be less unanimity about receivables (especially their net value), still less about inventories, and least about depreciable assets.... [Concepts Statement 2, paragraphs 84 and 85]

2. The purpose of verification is to confirm the representational faithfulness of accounting information—to provide a significant degree of assurance to a user that accounting measures essentially agree with or correspond to the economic things and events that they represent (Concepts Statement 2, paragraphs 59, 81, and 86). Accounting information may not be representationally faithful because measurer bias or measurement bias (or both) gives a measure the tendency to be consistently too high or too low instead of being equally likely to fall above and below what it represents. Measurer bias is introduced if a measurer, unintentionally through lack of skill or intentionally through lack of integrity, or both, wrongly applies the chosen measurement method. Measurement bias results from using a biased measurement method (Concepts Statement 2, paragraphs 77, 78, and 82). Representational faithfulness is adversely affected if information is intentionally biased to attain a predetermined result or induce a particular mode of behavior, a possibility that is discussed in the next section on neutrality.

3. The extent to which verifiability adds reliability to accounting information depends on whether

   > an accounting measure itself has been verified or only ... the procedures used to obtain the measure have been verified. For example, the price paid to acquire a block of marketable securities or a piece of land is normally directly verifiable, while the amount of depreciation for a period is normally only indirectly verifiable by verifying the depreciation method, calculations used, and consistency of application.... [Concepts Statement 2, paragraph 87]

   In present practice, for example, the result of measuring the quantity of an inventory is directly verifiable, while the result of measuring the carrying amount or book value of the inventory is only indirectly verifiable—the auditing process checks on the accuracy or verity of the inputs and recalculates the outputs but does not verify them.

   > For quantities there is a well-defined formal system (perpetual inventory system) which specifies the relevant empirical inputs (receipts and issues) and the output provides an expectation or prediction of the quantity on hand. The physical count is a separate [or direct] verification of that output.

   > For book values there is disagreement about the formal system (lifo or fifo) and disagreement about the relevant inputs (which costs are to be attached [to inventory] and which are to be expensed). The output [book value of the inventory on hand] ... is not separately verifiable.[134]

---

[134] Robert R. Sterling, "On Theory Construction and Verification," *The Accounting Review*, July 1970, p. 450, footnote 16.

Measures of the quantity of the inventory resulting from the perpetual inventory system and the physical count verify each other if they essentially agree. Independent measures of a phenomenon need not use the same measurement process. In the absence of a perpetual inventory system, however, verifying the quantity of the inventory requires at least two independent physical counts or a third way to measure the quantity of the inventory.

It makes a difference to the reliability of accounting information whether an accounting measure itself is verified or only the procedures used to obtain the measure are verified because even if disagreements about choice of method and relevant inputs are ignored or resolved, merely rechecking the mechanics does not verify the representational faithfulness of the measure, leaving its reliability in doubt.

Direct verification of accounting measures tends to minimize both personal bias introduced by a measurer (measurer bias) and bias inherent in measurement methods (measurement bias). Verification of only measurement methods tends to minimize measurer bias but usually preserves any bias there may be in the selection of measurement or allocation methods. [Concepts Statement 2, paragraph 87]

The elimination of measurer bias alone from information does not insure that the information will be reliable. Even though several independent measurers may agree on a single measurement method and apply it honestly and skillfully, the result will not be reliable if the method used is such that the measure does not represent what it purports to represent. [Concepts Statement 2, paragraph 86]

The distinguishing characteristic of accounting measures that normally are directly or separately verifiable as representing what they purport to represent is that they measure market prices in transactions between independent entities (Concepts Statement 2, paragraphs 65 and 67). Two or more independent measurers are likely to obtain essentially the same measures in each instance, and the separate measures will tend to cluster. Some will show more dispersion than others, and relatively few, if any, will be as tightly clustered as separate measures of cash, but whether or not they reasonably represent what they purport to represent is verifiable.

The distinguishing characteristic of accounting measures whose representational faithfulness normally cannot be verified because only the procedures used to obtain the measure are verifiable is that they result from allocations, which interpose between the resulting measures and the market prices on which they are based a calculation or other means of allotting the cost or other past price to time periods or individual assets. As a result, the inputs and procedures of the allocation process often are readily verifiable, but the outputs—the resulting measures—are not (Concepts Statement 2, paragraphs 65–67). Two or more independent measurers are unlikely to obtain essentially the same measures in each instance, and the separate measures will tend to be dispersed or scattered rather than clustered. The reliability of the accounting measures themselves cannot be verified because verifying only the procedures that produced them does not confirm or substantiate their representational faithfulness.

Since the point is likely to be misunderstood, it should explicitly be noted that the inability to verify the representational faithfulness of an accounting measure does not necessarily mean that the measure does not represent what it purports to represent. It generally means only that no one can know the extent to which the measure has or does not have that representational quality. Since the extent to which it represents faithfully the economic phenomenon it purports to represent is unknown, however, the measure cannot accurately be described as reliable.

Concepts Statement 2 also uses the difference between verifying a measure and verifying the method used to obtain it to show that reliability requires both representational faithfulness and verifiability. It illustrates how an accounting measure may be unreliable despite the verifiability of the allocation process that produced it using as an example the once-widespread practice, proscribed by FASB Statement No. 5, *Accounting for Contingencies*, for reasons described earlier in this chapter, of accruing "self-insurance reserves" by recognizing an annual expense or loss equal to a portion of expected future losses from fire, flood, or other casualties. Expectations of future losses could be actuarially computed for an enterprise with a large number of "self-insured" assets, and the methods of allocating expected losses to periods could be readily verified. Nevertheless, the representational faithfulness of the resulting measures would be extremely low, if not missing entirely. The "reserve for self insurance" in a balance sheet was a "what-you-may-call-it"—a deferred credit that did not qualify as a liability because the "self-insured" enterprise owed no one the amount of the reserve, or anything like it—and the allocated expense or loss in an income statement reported hypothetical effects of nonexistent transactions or events in years in which the enterprise suffered no casualties and, except by coincidence, grossly underreported losses incurred in years in which the enterprise's uninsured assets actually were damaged or destroyed by fire, flood, earthquake, hurricane, or the like.

Since the representational faithfulness of measures resulting from allocation procedures cannot be verified by rechecking the mechanics of how the measures were obtained, so-called historical cost accounting and other systems or models that depend heavily on allocations of prices in past transactions generally are considerably less reliable than is usually supposed. Concepts Statement 2 puts in perspective the oft-heard generalization that historical costs are "hard" information while current market prices are "soft" information—that historical cost information is reliable while current price information is not:

> More than one empirical investigation has concluded that accountants may agree more about estimates of the market values of certain depreciable assets than about their carrying values. Hence, to the extent that verification depends on consensus, it may not always be those measurement methods widely regarded as "objective" that are most verifiable. [paragraph 85]

Considerable confusion about reliability of accounting information results from the propensity of accountants and others to use reliable, objective, and verifiable interchangeably even though the three terms are not synonyms if used precisely. Reliable is a broader term than verifiable, comprising not only verifiability but also representational faithfulness. Objective is a narrower term than verifiable. It means being independent of the observer, implying that objective accounting information is free of measurer bias—not affected by the hopes, fears, and other thoughts and feelings of the measurer—but saying little or nothing about measurement bias. "Objectivity" and "objective" should assume the narrower meaning in accountants' vocabularies and be replaced by "verifiability" and "verifiable" to describe measures whose representational faithfulness can be confirmed through consensus of independent measurers and thus are reliable.

Neutrality.   Neutrality is concerned with bias and thus is a factor in reliability of accounting information. It is the "absence in reported information of bias intended to attain a predetermined result or to induce a particular mode of behavior" (Concepts Statement 2, glossary). Accounting information is neutral if it "report[s] economic activity as faithfully as possible, without coloring the image it communicates for the purpose of influencing behavior in *some particular direction*" (paragraph 100).

A common perception and misconception is that displaying neutrality means treating everyone alike in all respects. It would not necessarily show a lack of neutrality to require less disclosure of a small company than of a large one if it were shown that an equal disclosure requirement placed an undue economic burden on the small company. Solomons says that neutrality "does not imply that no one gets hurt." His response to the argument that accounting policy can never be neutral because in any policy choice someone gets his or her preference and someone else does not clarifies the meaning of neutrality:

> The same thing could be said of the draft, when draft numbers were drawn by lot. Some people were chosen to serve while others escaped. It was still, by and large, neutral in the sense that all males of draft age were equally likely to be selected. It is not a necessary property of neutrality that everyone likes the results; the absence of intentional bias is at the heart of the concept.[135]

---

[135] Solomons, *Making Accounting Policy*, p. 234.

Neutrality requires that information should be free from bias toward a predetermined result, but that is not to say that standards setters or those who provide information according to promulgated standards should not have a purpose in mind for financial reporting. Accounting should not be without influence on human behavior, but it should not slant information to influence behavior in a particular way to achieve a desired end.

> Neutrality in accounting is an important criterion by which to judge accounting policies, for information that is not neutral loses credibility. If information can be verified and can be relied on faithfully to represent what it purports to represent— *and if there is no bias in the selection of what is reported*—it cannot be slanted to favor one set of interests over another. [Concepts Statement 2, paragraph 107]

Former Board member Arthur R. Wyatt emphasized the crucial nature of the quality of neutrality in Concepts Statement 2 to the FASB's process and to the widespread acceptability of its resulting standards:

> Early on . . . the FASB undertook work to develop a conceptual framework, in part so that it could develop standards that had a logical cohesion, and in part so that the results of its deliberations could be evaluated to assess whether the resulting standards flowed from logical premises or may have been the result of lobbying activities or pressure politics.[136]

The Board unequivocally rejected the view that financial accounting standards should be slanted to foster a particular government policy or to favor one economic interest over another:

> The notion of neutrality within the Board's conceptual framework is that in resolving issues the Board will attempt to reach conclusions that result in reliable and relevant information and not conclusions that favor one segment of society to the detriment of one or more other segments. . . . [T]he notion of neutrality emphasizes that in developing the standard the Board . . . is not overtly striving to reallocate resources for the benefit of one group to the detriment of others.[137]

On several occasions, Donald J. Kirk, former Board chairman, also made the point that neutrality is essential to fulfilling the objective of providing relevant and reliable information to investors, creditors, and other users, and to prevent standards setting from becoming an exercise in directing resources to a preferred group. For example:

> [N]eutrality of information keeps financial reporting standards as a part of a measurement process, rather than a purposeful resource allocation process. . . . It is the emphasis on neutrality of information, as well as the independence of the standard setters from undue influence, that ensures the continued success of private sector standard setting.[138]

> To protect the public interest in useful accounting information, what is needed is *not* "good business sense," *nor* even "good public policy," but rather "neutrality" (i.e., "absence in reported information of bias intended to attain a predetermined result or to induce a particular mode of behavior"). The chairman of the SEC made the point about the importance of neutrality in his statement on oil and gas accounting:

> If it becomes accepted or expected that accounting principles are determined or modified in order to secure purposes other than economic measurement—even such virtuous purposes as energy production—we assume a grave risk that confidence in the credibility of our financial information system will be undermined.[139]

---

[136] Arthur R. Wyatt, "Accounting Standards and the Professional Auditor," *Accounting Horizons*, June 1989, p. 97.

[137] Id., p. 97.

[138] Kirk, "Looking Back on Fourteen Years at the FASB: The Education of a Standard Setter," p. 13.

[139] Donald J. Kirk, "Reflections on a 'Reconceptualization of Accounting': A Commentary on Parts I–IV of Homer Kripke's Paper, 'Reflections on the FASB's Conceptual Framework for Accounting and on

Neutrality in standards setting is so significant that it has been incorporated into the FASB's Mission Statement, and Concepts Statement 2 itself explains why neutrality is so critical to the Board and to the standards-setting process. The first and last words in the section entitled "Neutrality" are:

> Neutrality in accounting has a greater significance for those who set accounting standards than for those who have to apply those standards in preparing financial reports, but the concept has substantially the same meaning for the two groups, and both will maintain neutrality in the same way. Neutrality means that either in formulating or implementing standards, the primary concern should be the relevance and reliability of the information that results, not the effect that the new rule may have on a particular interest.
>
> The Board's responsibility is to the integrity of the financial reporting system, which it regards as its paramount concern. [Concepts Statement 2, paragraphs 98 and 110]

Comparability.   Comparing alternative investment or lending opportunities is an essential part of most, if not all, investment or lending decisions. Investors and creditors need financial reporting information that is comparable, both for single enterprises over time and between enterprises at the same time. Comparability is a quality of the relationship between two or more pieces of information—"the quality of information that enables users to identify similarities in and differences between two sets of economic phenomena" (Concepts Statement 2, glossary). Comparability is achieved if similar transactions and other events and circumstances are accounted for similarly and different transactions and other events and circumstances are accounted for differently.

Comparability has been the subject of much disagreement among accountants. Some have argued that enterprises and their circumstances are so different from one another that comparability between enterprises is an illusory goal, and to include it as an aim of financial reporting is to promise to investors and creditors something that ultimately cannot be delivered. In that view, the best that can be hoped for is that individual enterprises will use their chosen accounting procedures consistently over time to permit comparisons with other enterprises and that honorable auditors will be able to attest to the consistent application of "generally accepted accounting principles."

The problem with that view of comparability is that it allows an excessive degree of latitude in reporting practice. It was the dominant view during the 1930s and 1940s and did permit, or even encouraged, the proliferation of alternative accounting procedures that characterized the period, many in situations in which few significant differences in enterprises or circumstances were ever reasonably substantiated. The result was an intolerable lack of comparability, which was responsible for much of the criticism directed toward financial accounting and eventually led to the replacement of the Committee on Accounting Procedure by the APB.

Today, with the objectives of financial reporting focused on decision making, comparability is one of the most essential and desirable qualities of accounting information. Investors and creditors can no longer be expected to tolerate blanket claims of differences in circumstances to justify undue use of alternative accounting procedures. Only actual differences in transactions and other events and circumstances warrant different accounting.

Concepts Statement 2 notes that the need for comparable information is a fundamental rationale for standards setting:

> The difficulty in making financial comparisons among enterprises because of the use of different accounting methods has been accepted for many years as the principal reason for the development of accounting standards. [paragraph 112]

Some critics have focused on the standards setter's pursuit of comparability, calling it "uniformity," and mistakenly implying that standards are issued to require all enterprises to use the same

Auditing,'" *Journal of Accounting, Auditing & Finance*, Winter 1989, p. 95. The excerpt quoted is from Harold M. Williams, chairman, Securities and Exchange Commission, "Accounting Practices for Oil and Gas Producers" (Washington, D.C., 1978), p. 12.

accounting methods despite underlying differences. Comparability is, however, the antithesis of uniformity:

> Comparability should not be confused with identity, and sometimes more can be learned from differences than from similarities if the differences can be explained. The ability to explain phenomena often depends on the diagnosis of the underlying causes of differences or the discovery that apparent differences are without significance.... Greater comparability of accounting information, which most people agree is a worthwhile aim, is not to be attained by making unlike things look alike any more than by making like things look different. [Concepts Statement 2, paragraph 119]

In fact, uniformity of practice may be a greater threat to comparability than is too much flexibility in choice of accounting method. Investors and creditors can often discern and compensate for lack of comparability caused by alternative procedures, but they usually have no way of detecting a lack of comparability caused by forced uniformity of practice.

Consistency, meaning "conformity from period to period with unchanging policies and procedures" (Concepts Statement 2, glossary), has long been regarded as an important quality of information provided by financial statements. For example, it was an explicit part of the recommendation of the Special Committee on Cooperation with Stock Exchanges in 1932 (pp. 2-4 to 2-116 of this chapter). Auditors are required to point out changes in accounting principles or in the method of their application that have a material effect on the comparability of a client's financial statements.

Consistent use of accounting methods, whether from one period to another within a single firm or within a single period across firms, is a necessary but not a sufficient condition of comparability. Consistency in applying accounting methods over time contributes to comparability, provided that the methods consistently applied were reasonably comparable to begin with. Lack of comparability will never be transformed into comparability by consistent application. If what is measured and reported has representational faithfulness, an accurate analysis of similarities and differences will be possible, and comparability is enhanced. However, in the same way that lack of timeliness can deprive information of relevance it might otherwise have had, inconsistent use of comparable information can ruin whatever comparability the information might otherwise have had.

Concern for consistency does not mean that accountants should not be open to new and better methods and standards. A change need not inhibit comparability if its effects are properly disclosed.

Conservatism.   A word needs to be said about conservatism, an important doctrine in most accountant's minds, but not a separate qualitative characteristic in the FASB's hierarchy of qualities that make accounting information useful. The FASB has described conservatism as "a prudent reaction to uncertainty to try to ensure that uncertainties and risks inherent in business situations are adequately considered" (Concepts Statement 2, paragraph 95). That is quite different from the traditional meaning of conservatism in financial reporting, which usually connoted deliberate, consistent understatement of net assets and profits, summed up by the admonition to "anticipate no profits but anticipate all losses." That view developed during a time when balance sheets were considered the primary (and often only) financial statement, and bankers or other lenders were their principal external users. Since understating assets was thought to provide a greater margin of safety as security for loans and other debts, deliberate understatement was considered a virtue.

The traditional application of conservatism introduced into reporting a preference "that possible errors in measurement be in the direction of understatement rather than overstatement of net income and net assets" (APB Statement 4, paragraph 171). In practice that often meant depressing reported net income by excessive depreciation or undervaluation of inventory or deferring recognition of income until long after sufficient evidence of its existence became available.

That kind of conservatism has now become discredited because it conflicts with the information's comparability, with its representational faithfulness and neutrality, and thus with its reliability. Any kind of bias, whether overly conservative or overly optimistic, influences the timing of recognition of net income or losses and may mislead investors as they attempt to evaluate alternative investment opportunities. Information that adds to uncertainty is inimical to informed and rational decision making and betrays the fulfillment of the objectives of financial reporting.

> The appropriate way to treat uncertainty is to disclose its nature and extent honestly, so that those who receive the information may form their own opinions of the probable outcome of the events reported. That is the only kind of conservatism that can, in the long run, serve all of the divergent interests that are represented in a business enterprise. It is not the accountant's job to protect investors, creditors, and others from uncertainty, but only to inform them about it. Any attempt to understate earnings or financial position consistently is likely to engender skepticism about the reliability and the integrity of what is reported. Moreover, it will probably be ultimately self-defeating.[140]

Materiality.   The final item on the hierarchy, characterized as a constraint or *threshold for recognition*, is materiality, which is a *quantitative*, not a qualitative, characteristic of information. Materiality judgments pose the question: "Is this item large enough for users of the information to be influenced by it?" (Concepts Statement 2, paragraph 123). Materiality means:

> the magnitude of an omission or misstatement of accounting information that, in the light of surrounding circumstances, makes it probable that the judgment of a reasonable person relying on the information would have been changed or influenced by the omission or misstatement. [Concepts Statement 2, glossary]

Popular usage of "material" often makes it a synonym for "relevant," but the two are not synonymous in Concepts Statement 2. Information may be relevant in the sense that it is capable of making a difference and yet the amounts involved are immaterial—too small to matter in a decision. To illustrate the difference between materiality and relevance, Concepts Statement 2 (paragraph 126) provides an example of an applicant for employment who is negotiating with an employment agency. On one hand, information about the nature of the duties, salary, hours, and benefits is relevant, as well as material, to most prospective employees. On the other hand, whether the office floor is carpeted and whether the cafeteria food is of good quality are relevant, but probably not material, to a decision to accept the job. The values placed on them by the applicant are too small to influence the decision.

However, materiality judgments go beyond magnitude itself to the nature of the item and the circumstances in which the judgment has to be made. Items too small to be thought material if they result from routine transactions may be considered material if they arise in abnormal circumstances. Therefore, one must always think in terms of a threshold over which an item must pass, considering its nature and the attendant circumstances as well as its relative amount, that separates material from immaterial items.

Where the threshold for recognition occurs with regard to a materiality decision is a matter of judgment. Many accountants would like to have more quantitative guidelines or criteria for materiality laid down by the SEC, the FASB, or other regulatory agency. The FASB's view has been that materiality judgments can best be made by those who possess all the facts. In recognition of the fact that materiality guidance is sometimes needed, the appendices to Concepts Statement 2 include a list of quantitative guidelines that have been applied both in the law and in the practice of accounting. However, if and when those guidelines specify some minimum size stipulated for recognition of a material item, they do not preclude recognition of a smaller segment. There is still room for individual judgment in at least one direction.

Costs and Benefits.   Information is subject to the same pervasive cost-benefit constraint that affects the usefulness of other commodities: Unless the benefits to be derived from information equal or exceed the cost of acquiring it, it will not be pursued. Financial information is unlike other commodities, however, in being a partly private and partly public good since "the benefits of

---

[140] Solomons, *Making Accounting Policy*, p. 101.

information cannot always be confined to those who pay for it" (Concepts Statement 2, paragraph 135), and the balancing of costs and benefits cannot be left to the market.

Cost-benefit decisions about accounting standards generally have to be made by the standards-setting body—now the FASB. Both costs and benefits of accounting standards cut across the whole spectrum of the Board's constituency, with the benefits only partly accruing to those who bear the costs and the balance between costs and benefits reacting very imperfectly to supply and demand considerations. Moreover, individuals, be they providers, users, or auditors of accounting information, are not in a position to make cost-benefit assessments due to lack of sufficient information as well as probable biases on the matter.

Cost-benefit decisions are extremely difficult because both costs and benefits often are subjective and difficult or impossible to measure reliably. Cost-benefit analysis is at best a fallible tool. Although the Board is committed to doing the best it can in making cost-benefit assessments and Board members indeed have taken the matter seriously in facing the question in several standards in which it has arisen, cost-benefit measures and comparisons are too unreliable to be the deciding factor in crucial standards-setting decisions.

Impact of the Qualitative Characteristics.   In the 25 years since the Trueblood Study Group, and later the FASB, authoritatively clarified the objectives of financial reporting and the consequent primacy of usefulness of financial information for decision making, an evolution in accounting thought has slowly taken place:

> Once decision making is seen as the primary objective of financial reporting, it is inevitable that the usefulness of financial information for making decisions should be the primary quality to be sought in deciding what is to be reported and how that reporting is to be done. This is not quite the truism that it seems to be, for ... only a minority of the respondents to an FASB inquiry in 1974 favored the adoption of that objective. Since 1974 there has been a striking change in attitude among persons interested in financial reporting, and decision usefulness has become widely accepted as the most important quality that financial information should have.[141]

The qualitative characteristics have also had an impact on practice. Former FASB vice chairman Robert T. Sprouse, in an appearance at a Harvard Business School conference entitled "Conceptual Frameworks for Financial Accounting" in October 1982, described their contribution to accounting debate:

> I must confess that initially, although it was clear that certain identified qualitative characteristics of accounting information constituted an essential component of a conceptual framework for general purpose, external financial reporting, I was skeptical about their contribution to the standard setting process. It seemed to go without saying that accounting information should be relevant and reliable; I doubted that explicit acknowledgment of such qualities would be very useful to preparers, auditors, users, and standard setters in making decisions about financial reporting issues. I was wrong.
>
> The qualitative characteristics project has proven to be extremely valuable, particularly in improving communications among the many and varied organizations and individuals who are involved in resolving financial reporting issues. Statement No. 2 has established a language that has significantly enhanced the degree of precision and level of understanding in discussions of those matters. Increasingly, position papers and comment letters submitted to the FASB refer to specific qualitative characteristics to support positions that are advocated, recommendations that are proffered, and criticisms that are aimed at Board proposals. Similarly, in Board discussions and deliberations it is no longer sufficient to argue that something is relevant or irrelevant and reliable or unreliable. One must specify whether it is predictive value that is enhanced or lacking or whether representational faithfulness would be achieved or be absent, or whether it is some other

---

[141] Id., p. 86.

aspect of relevance or reliability that is affected. The result has been greater precision in thinking about issues and greater understanding in communicating about them.[142]

(iii) Elements of Financial Statements. Concepts Statement 1 said that "financial reporting should provide information about the economic resources of an enterprise, the claims to those resources (obligations of the enterprise to transfer resources to other entities and owners' equity), and the effects of transactions, events, and circumstances that change resources and claims to those resources" (paragraph 40). Concepts Statement 6 (and previously Concepts Statement 3) provides the means for carrying out that objective. It defines the elements of financial statements—the economic resources of an entity, the claims to those resources, and changes in them—about which information is relevant to investors, creditors, and other users of financial statements for investment, credit, and similar decisions.

> The elements defined in this Statement are a related group with a particular focus—on assets, liabilities, equity, and other elements directly related to measuring performance and status of an entity. Information about an entity's performance and status provided by accrual accounting is the primary focus of financial reporting.... [Concepts Statement 6, paragraph 3]

Concepts Statement No. 3. Concepts Statement No. 3, *Elements of Financial Statements of Business Enterprises*, issued in December 1980, defined 10 elements: assets, liabilities, equity, investments by owners, distributions to owners, and comprehensive income and its components: revenues, expenses, gains, and losses. The Statement introduced the term "comprehensive income," the name adopted by the Board for the concept that was called "earnings" in Concepts Statement 1 and the other conceptual framework documents previously issued, including the *Tentative Conclusions on Objectives of Financial Statements of Business Enterprises* (December 1976); the Discussion Memorandum, *Conceptual Framework for Financial Accounting and Reporting: Elements of Financial Statements and Their Measurement* (December 1976); and the Exposure Draft, *Objectives of Financial Reporting and Elements of Financial Statements of Business Enterprises* (December 1977). As its title shows, the first Exposure Draft in the conceptual framework project dealt with both objectives and elements.

During 1978, the Board divided the subject matter of the Exposure Draft. One part developed into Concepts Statement 1 on objectives, and another part became the basis for a revised Exposure Draft, *Elements of Financial Statements of Business Enterprises*, which was issued in December 1979. The substance of that Exposure Draft became Concepts Statement 3.

The Board's work on not-for-profit reporting was advancing concurrently, and Concepts Statement No. 4, *Objectives of Financial Reporting by Nonbusiness Organizations*, was issued with Concepts Statement 3 in December 1980. The four Concepts Statements constituted a single conceptual framework for financial accounting and reporting by all entities. The Board voiced its expectation in Concepts Statements 2 and 3 that the qualitative characteristics and definitions of elements of financial statements should apply to both business enterprises and not-for-profit organizations.

> Although the discussion of the qualities of information and the related examples in this Statement refer primarily to business enterprises, the Board has tentatively concluded that similar qualities also apply to financial information reported by nonbusiness organizations. [Concepts Statement 2, paragraph 4]

> Assets and liabilities are common to all organizations, and the Board sees no reason to define them differently for business and nonbusiness organizations. The Board also expects the definitions of

---

[142] *Conceptual Frameworks for Financial Accounting* [Proceedings of a conference at the Harvard Business School, October 1–2, 1982], H. David Sherman, ed. (Cambridge: President and Fellows of Harvard College, circa 1984), p. 33.

equity, revenues, expenses, gains, and losses to fit both business and nonbusiness organizations. [Concepts Statement 3, paragraph 2]

The Board saw no need for two separate statements on elements as it had for the objectives.

To solicit views on applying the qualitative characteristics and definitions of elements to both business enterprises and not-for-profit organizations, the Board issued an Exposure Draft, *Proposed Amendments to FASB Concepts Statements 2 and 3 to Apply Them to Nonbusiness Organizations*, in July 1983. The Board reaffirmed the conclusion that the qualitative characteristics applied to not-for-profit organizations and issued a revised Exposure Draft, *Elements of Financial Statements*, in September 1985. Concepts Statement No. 6, *Elements of Financial Statements*, was issued in December 1985, superseding Concepts Statement 3 and extending that Statement's definitions to not-for-profit organizations. Most of Concepts Statement 3 was carried over into the parts of Concepts Statement 6 concerned with business enterprises or with both kinds of entities. Paragraph numbers were changed, however, because Concepts Statement 6 has numerous paragraphs that relate only to not-for-profit organizations or that explain how the definitions in Concepts Statement 3 apply to not-for-profit organizations.

Concepts Statement No. 6.   Concepts Statement 6 defines the same 10 elements of financial statements that Concepts Statement 3 had defined: Seven are elements of the financial statements of both business enterprises and not-for-profit organizations—assets, liabilities, equity (business enterprises) or net assets (not-for-profit organizations), revenues, expenses, gains, and losses; and three are elements of financial statements of business enterprises only—investments by owners, distributions to owners, and comprehensive income. The Statement also defines three classes of net assets of not-for-profit organizations, characterized by the presence or absence of donor-imposed restrictions, and the changes in those classes during a period—changes in permanently restricted, temporarily restricted, and unrestricted net assets. For business enterprises, equity is defined only in total.

To try to avoid later confusion, Concepts Statement 6 is precise about what is an element and what is not. For example, cash, inventories, land, and buildings are items that fit the definition of assets, but they are not elements. Assets is the element:

> Elements of financial statements are the building blocks with which financial statements are constructed—the classes of items that financial statements comprise. *Elements* refers to broad classes, such as assets, liabilities, revenues, and expenses. Particular economic things and events, such as cash on hand or selling merchandise, that may meet the definitions of elements are not elements as the term is used in this Statement. Rather, they are called *items* or other descriptive names. This Statement focuses on the broad classes and their characteristics instead of defining particular assets, liabilities, or other items. [paragraph 5]

The Statement then emphasizes that the elements in financial statements stand for things and events in the real world:

> The items that are formally incorporated in financial statements are financial representations (depictions in words and numbers) of certain resources of an entity, claims to those resources, and the effects of transactions and other events and circumstances that result in changes in those resources and claims. That is, symbols (words and numbers) in financial statements stand for cash in a bank, buildings, wages due, sales, use of labor, earthquake damage to property, and a host of other economic things and events pertaining to an entity existing and operating in what is sometimes called the "real world." [paragraph 6]

The definitions are of the real-world things and events, not of what is recognized in financial statements. That is, the definition of assets, for example, refers to assets such as the inventory in the warehouse, not to the word "inventory" and the related amount in the balance sheet.

A thing or event and its representation in financial statements commonly are called by the same name. For example, both the amount deposited in a checking account and its representation in the balance sheet are called cash in bank.

Elements of financial statements are of two types: those that constitute financial position or status at a moment in time and those that are changes in financial position over a period of time. Assets, liabilities, and equity or net assets describe levels or amounts of resources or claims to or interests in resources at a moment in time. All other elements—revenues, expenses, gains, and losses (and for business enterprises, comprehensive income, and investments by and distributions to owners)—describe the effects of transactions and other events and circumstances that affect an entity over a period of time. The interrelation between the two types of elements is called articulation:

> The two types of elements are related in such a way that (a) assets, liabilities, and equity (net assets) are changed by elements of the other type and at any time are their cumulative result and (b) an increase (decrease) in an asset cannot occur without a corresponding decrease (increase) in another asset or a corresponding increase (decrease) in a liability or equity (net assets). Those relations are sometimes collectively referred to as *articulation*. They result in financial statements that are fundamentally interrelated so that statements that show elements of the second type depend on statements that show elements of the first type and vice versa. [Concepts Statement 6, paragraph 21]

The elements of financial statements are defined in relation to particular entities, which may be business enterprises, not-for-profit organizations, other economic units, or people. For example, items that qualify as assets under the definition are assets of particular entities.

Definition of Assets.   There is no more fundamental concept in accounting than assets. Assets, or economic resources, are the lifeblood of both business enterprises and not-for-profit organizations. Without assets—to exchange for, combine with, or transform into other assets—those entities would have no reason to exist.

> Economic resources or assets and changes in them are central to the existence and operations of an individual entity. Both business enterprises and not-for-profit organizations are in essence resource or asset processors, and a resource's capacity to be exchanged for cash or other resources or to be combined with other resources to produce needed or desired scarce goods or services gives it utility and value (future economic benefit) to an entity.

> Since resources or assets confer their benefits on an enterprise by being exchanged, used, or otherwise invested, changes in resources or assets are the purpose, the means, and the result of an enterprise's operations, and a business enterprise exists primarily to acquire, use, produce, and distribute resources. [Concepts Statement 6, paragraphs 11 and 15]

Because the concept of assets is so fundamental, one would think that the issue of what is or is not an asset would have been settled long ago. All accountants claim to know an asset when they see one, yet differences of opinion arise about whether some items called assets are assets at all and should be included in balance sheets. Those differences of opinion surfaced at the FASB's first hearings, as already described, and those experiences convinced early Board members that workable definitions of assets and liabilities were imperative.

The FASB decided on the conceptual primacy of assets and liabilities, meaning that the definitions of all the other elements of financial statements are derived from the definitions of assets and liabilities. Since the definition of assets is critical, Concepts Statement 6 provides a carefully worded definition with three essential facets, adds nine paragraphs explaining the characteristics of assets, and devotes a significant part of Appendix B to the Statement to elaborating the concept of assets. All of those sections are part of the definition of assets.

The definition of assets is in paragraph 25:

Assets are probable future economic benefits obtained or controlled by a particular entity as a result of past transactions or events.

Paragraph 26 then describes the trio of characteristics that qualify an item as an asset:

An asset has three essential characteristics: (a) it embodies a probable future benefit that involves a capacity, singly or in combination with other assets, to contribute directly or indirectly to future net cash inflows, (b) a particular entity can obtain the benefit and control others' access to it, and (c) the transaction or other event giving rise to the entity's right to or control of the benefit has already occurred.

The definition indicates the appropriate questions to ask in trying to decide whether or not a particular item is an asset: Is there a future economic benefit? If so, to which entity does it belong? What made it an asset of that entity?

FUTURE ECONOMIC BENEFITS.   Assets commonly are items that also can be characterized as economic resources—the scarce means through which people and other economic units carry out economic activities such as consumption, production, and exchange. All economic resources or assets have "service potential" or "future economic benefit," the scarce capacity to provide services or benefits to the people or other entities that use or hold them.

Future economic benefit is the essence of an asset (paragraphs 27–31). An asset has the capacity to serve the entity by being exchanged for something else of value to the entity, by being used to produce something of value to the entity, or by being used to settle its liabilities.

The most obvious evidence of future economic benefit is a market price. Anything that is commonly bought and sold has future economic benefit.... Similarly, anything that creditors or others commonly accept in settlement of liabilities has future economic benefit, and anything that is commonly used to produce goods or services, whether tangible or intangible and whether or not it has a market price or is otherwise exchangeable, also has future economic benefit. Incurrence of costs may be significant evidence of acquisition or enhancement of future economic benefits.... [Concepts Statement 6, paragraphs 172 and 173]

All value of economic (scarce) goods and services derives ultimately from the utility of consumers' goods and services, which are used primarily by individuals and families. Their capacity to satisfy human needs or wants creates demand not only for them but also for the producers' goods and services, used primarily by business enterprises and other producers, that provide economic benefit by being used, directly or indirectly, to produce consumers' goods and services or other producers' goods and services. Cash is the asset par excellence because of what it can buy. "It can be exchanged for virtually any good or service that is available or it can be saved and exchanged for them in the future" (Concepts Statement 3, paragraph 23) and is the medium for settling most liabilities.[143]

At least two questions need to be asked about the presence or absence of future economic benefit to determine whether or not an entity has an asset: Did the item obtained by an entity truly represent a future economic benefit in the first place, and does all or any of the future economic benefit to the entity remain at the time the issue of its being an asset is considered?

Concepts Statement 6 says that most assets presently included in financial statements qualify as assets under its definition because they have future economic benefits (paragraph 177). They include cash, accounts and notes receivable, interest and dividends receivable, and investments in

---

[143] L. Todd Johnson and Reed K. Storey, *Recognition in Financial Statements: Underlying Concepts and Practical Conventions*, FASB Research Report (Stamford, CT: Financial Accounting Standards Board, 1982), pp. 91–94.

the securities of other entities. Inventories of raw materials, work-in-process, and finished goods and productive resources such as property, plant, and equipment also qualify as assets, but some "assets" that have often been described in accounting literature as "deferred costs" or "deferred charges to revenues" either fail to qualify as assets or may perhaps represent assets but cannot reliably be recognized as assets.

Deferred costs that fail to qualify as assets are what-you-may-call-its—deferred costs that do not represent economic resources but are said to be assets "because they must be deferred and matched with future revenues to avoid distorting net income." For reasons described earlier, the Board firmly rejected the argument that "costs are assets," and Concepts Statement 6 is explicit:

> Although an entity normally incurs costs to acquire or use assets, costs incurred are not themselves assets. The essence of an asset is its future economic benefit rather than whether or not it was acquired at a cost....
>
> ... [I]ncurrence of a cost may be evidence that an entity has acquired one or more assets, but it is not conclusive evidence. Costs may be incurred without receiving services or enhanced future economic benefits. Or, entities may obtain assets without incurring costs—for example, from investment in kind by owners or contributions of securities or buildings by donors. The ultimate evidence of the existence of assets is the future economic benefit, not the costs incurred. [paragraphs 179 and 180]

Deferred costs that may or may not represent assets are victims of the pervasive uncertainty in business and economic affairs that often obscures whether or not some items have the capacity to provide future economic benefits to an entity and thus should be recognized as assets. A question arises whether an item received should be recognized as an asset or as an expense or loss if the value of future benefit obtained is uncertain or even doubtful or if the future benefit may be short-lived or of highly uncertain duration. Expenditures for research and development, advertising, training, development of new markets, relocation, and goodwill are examples of items for which management's intent clearly is to obtain or augment future economic benefits but for which there is uncertainty about the extent, if any, to which the expenditures succeeded in creating or increasing future economic benefits. That uncertainty led to FASB Statement No. 2, *Accounting for Research and Development Costs*, in which the Board for primarily practical reasons required entities to recognize the expenditures as expenses or losses rather than as assets. If research and development or advertising costs actually result in new or greater future economic benefit, that benefit qualifies as an asset. The practical problems are in determining whether future economic benefit is actually present and in quantifying it, especially if realization of benefits is far down the road, or perhaps never.[144]

Services provided by other entities can be assets of an entity only momentarily as they are received and used, and they commonly are recognized as expenses when received, but the right to receive services for specified or determinable future periods qualifies as an asset.

CONTROL BY A PARTICULAR ENTITY. The definition defines assets in relation to specific entities. An asset is an asset of some entity. No asset can simultaneously be an asset of more than one entity, although some physical assets may provide future economic benefits to two or more entities at the same time. That is, some assets comprise separable bundles of benefits that may be unbundled and held simultaneously by two or more entities so that each has an asset. For example, a building may provide future economic benefits to its owner, to an entity that leases space in it, and to an entity that holds a mortgage on it. Each has an interest in a different aspect of the same

---

[144] This paragraph paraphrases paragraphs 44, 45, and 173 of Concepts Statement 6 and briefly summarizes the conclusions of FASB Statement No. 2, *Accounting for Research and Development Costs*, whose development raised questions that helped Board members decide that a definition of assets was essential.

building, and each expects to receive cash flows from having one or more of the bundles of benefits.

An entity must control an item's future economic benefit to be able to consider the item as its asset. To enjoy an asset's benefits, an entity generally must be in a position to deny or regulate access to that benefit by others, for example, by permitting access only at a price.

> Thus, an asset of an entity is the future economic benefit that the entity can control and thus can, within limits set by the nature of the benefit or the entity's right to it, use as it pleases. The entity having an asset is the one that can exchange it, use it to produce goods or services, exact a price for others' use of it, use it to settle liabilities, hold it, or perhaps distribute it to owners. [Concepts Statement 6, paragraph 184]

An entity usually gains the ability to control an asset's future economic benefits through a legal right. However, an entity still may have an asset without having an enforceable legal right to it if it can obtain and control the benefit some other way, for example, by maintaining exclusive access to the asset's benefits by keeping secret a formula or process.

OCCURRENCE OF A PAST TRANSACTION OR EVENT.   Items become assets of an entity as the result of transactions or other events or circumstances that have already occurred. An entity has an asset only if it has the present ability to obtain that asset's future economic benefits. If an entity anticipates that it may in the future control an item's future economic benefits but as yet does not have that control, it cannot claim that item as its asset because the transaction, other event, or circumstance conferring that control has not yet occurred.

> Since the transaction or event giving rise to the entity's right to the future economic benefit must already have occurred, the definition excludes from assets items that may in the future become an entity's assets but have not yet become its assets. An entity has no asset for a particular future economic benefit if the transactions or events that give it access to and control of the benefit are yet in the future. [Concepts Statement 6, paragraph 191]

Similarly, once acquired, an asset continues as an asset of an entity as long as the transactions, other events, or circumstances that use up or destroy its future economic benefit or deprive the entity of its control are in the future.

Definition of Liabilities.   The definition of liabilities in paragraph 35 of Concepts Statement 6 has the same structure as the definition of assets in paragraph 25. The parallelism of the two definitions was deliberate.

> Liabilities are probable future sacrifices of economic benefits arising from present obligations of a particular entity to transfer assets or provide services to other entities in the future as a result of past transactions or events.

Paragraph 36 describes the three characteristics that an item must possess to be a liability:

> A liability has three essential characteristics: (a) it embodies a present duty or responsibility to one or more other entities that entails settlement by probable future transfer or use of assets at a specified or determinable date, on occurrence of a specified event, or on demand, (b) the duty or responsibility obligates a particular entity, leaving it little or no discretion to avoid the future sacrifice, and (c) the transaction or other event obligating the entity has already happened.

The definition prompts the following questions when trying to decide if a particular item constitutes a liability: Is there an obligation requiring a future sacrifice of assets? If so, which entity is obligated? What past transaction or event made it a liability of that entity?

REQUIRED FUTURE SACRIFICE OF ASSETS.   Liabilities commonly arise as the consequence of financial instruments, contracts, and laws invented to facilitate the functioning of a highly developed economy by permitting delays in payment and delivery in return for interest or other compensation as the price for enduring delay. Entities routinely incur liabilities to acquire the funds, goods, and services they need to operate and just as routinely settle the liabilities they incur, usually by paying cash. For example, borrowing cash results in an obligation to repay the amount borrowed, usually with interest; using employees' knowledge, skills, time, and effort results in an obligation to pay compensation for their use; or selling products with warranties results in an obligation to pay cash or to repair or replace the products that prove defective. Liabilities come in a vast array of forms, but they all entail a present obligation requiring a nondiscretionary future sacrifice of some economic benefit:

> The essence of a liability is a duty or requirement to sacrifice assets in the future. A liability requires an entity to transfer assets, provide services, or otherwise expend assets to satisfy a responsibility to one or more other entities that it has incurred or that has been imposed on it. [Concepts Statement 6, paragraph 193]

Although most liabilities arise from exchanges between entities, most of which are contractual in nature, some obligations are imposed by laws or governmental regulations that require sacrificing assets to comply.

Receipt of proceeds—cash, other assets, or services—without an accompanying cash payment is often evidence that a liability has been incurred, but it is not conclusive evidence. Other transactions and events generate proceeds—cash sales of goods or services or other sales of assets, cash from donors' contributions, or cash investments by owners—without incurring liabilities. Liabilities can be incurred without any accompanying receipt of proceeds, for example, by imposition of taxes. It is the obligation to sacrifice economic benefits in the future that signifies a liability, not whether proceeds were received by incurring it.

Most liabilities presently included in financial statements qualify as liabilities under the definition because they require a future sacrifice of assets. They include accounts and notes payable, wages and salaries payable, long-term debt, interest and dividends payable, and obligations to honor warranties and to pay pensions, deferred compensation, and taxes. Subscriptions or rents collected in advance or other "unearned revenues" from deposits and prepayments received for goods or services to be provided are also liabilities because they obligate an entity to provide goods or services to other entities in the future. Those kinds of items sometimes have been referred to as deferred credits or reserves in the accounting literature.

OBLIGATION OF A PARTICULAR ENTITY

> To have a liability, an entity must be obligated to sacrifice its assets in the future—that is, it must be bound by a legal, equitable, or constructive duty or responsibility to transfer assets or provide services to one or more other entities. [Concepts Statement 6, paragraph 200]

A liability entails an obligation—legal, moral, or ethical—to one or more other entities to convey assets to them or provide them with services in the future. Not all probable future sacrifices of assets are liabilities of an entity. An intent or expectation to enter into a contract or transaction to transfer assets does not constitute a liability until an obligation to another entity is taken on.

The obligation aspect of liabilities is not emphasized as strongly in the definition in the Concepts Statement as it perhaps might have been. The Board became enamored with making the one-sentence definitions of assets and liabilities parallel to accentuate the symmetry between future benefits of assets and future sacrifices of liabilities.

The definition of an asset emphasizes its "service potential" or "future economic benefit," "the scarce capacity to provide services or benefits to the entities that use them" (paragraph 28), the common characteristic possessed by all assets. The definition of a liability puts first "future sacrifices of assets" to make it parallel with the asset definition, but it would have been more precise to focus on an entity's *obligation* to another entity to transfer assets or to provide services to it in the future. Future sacrifices of assets, after all, are the consequence—not the cause—of an obligation to another entity. Liabilities are present obligations of a particular entity to transfer assets or provide services to other entities in the future requiring probable future sacrifices of economic benefits as a result of past transactions or events.

Some kinds of assets and liabilities are mirror images of one another. Receivables and payables are the most obvious example. Entity X has an asset (a receivable) because Entity Y has a liability (a payable) to transfer an asset (most commonly cash) to Entity X. Unless Entity Y has the liability, Entity X has no asset. Those relationships hold for rights to receive and obligations to pay or deliver cash, goods, or services. In fact, they hold for most contractual relationships involving a right to receive and an obligation to deliver. Receivables and payables cancel each other in national income accounting, for example, leaving land, buildings, equipment, and similar assets as the stock of productive resources of the economy.

Most kinds of assets are not receivables, and a host of assets have no liabilities as mirror images. For example, the benefit from owning a building does not stem from an obligation of another entity to provide the benefit. The building itself confers significant benefits on its owner. The owner may, of course, enhance the benefits from the building by obtaining the right to services provided by others, who incur corresponding obligations, but that is a separate contractual arrangement involving both rights and obligations for the contracting parties.

Consequently, the Board's concern with the symmetry between the future benefits of assets and the future sacrifices of liabilities tended to overshadow the obligation to another entity that is the principal distinguishing characteristic of a liability. The definition of liabilities in Concepts Statements 3 and 6 and the accompanying explanations might well have profited from a brief description such as that in FASB Statement No. 5, *Accounting for Contingencies*, paragraph 70.

> The economic obligations of an enterprise are defined in paragraph 58 of *APB Statement No. 4* as "its present responsibilities to transfer economic resources or provide services to other entities in the future." Two aspects of that definition are especially relevant to accounting for contingencies: first, that liabilities are *present* responsibilities and, second, that they are obligations to *other entities*. Those notions are supported by other definitions of liabilities in published accounting literature, for example:
>
> > Liabilities are claims of creditors against the enterprise, arising out of past activities, that are to be satisfied by the disbursement or utilization of corporate resources.[11]
> >
> > A liability is the result of a transaction of the past, not of the future.[12]

---

[11] American Accounting Association, *Accounting and Reporting Standards for Corporate Financial Statements and Preceding Statements and Supplements* (Sarasota, Fla: AAA, 1957), p. 16.
[12] Maurice Moonitz, "The Changing Concept of Liabilities," *The Journal of Accountancy*, May 1960, p. 44.

OCCURRENCE OF A PAST TRANSACTION OR EVENT.   Items become liabilities of an entity as the result of transactions or other events or circumstances that have already occurred. An entity has a liability only if it has a present obligation to transfer assets to another entity. Budgeting the payments required to enact a purchase results neither in acquiring an asset nor in incurring a liability because no transaction or event has yet occurred that gives the entity access to or control of future economic benefits or binds it to transfer assets.

Once incurred, a liability remains a liability of an entity until it is satisfied, usually by payment of cash, in another transaction or is otherwise discharged or nullified by another event or circumstance affecting the entity.

Nonessential Characteristics of Assets and Liabilities.   The word "probable" is included in the asset and liability definitions with its general, not accounting or technical, meaning and refers to that which can reasonably be expected or believed on the basis of available evidence or logic but is neither certain nor proved.[145] Its use was intended to indicate that something does not have to be certain or proved to qualify as an asset or liability. The first Exposure Draft did not contain the word "probable." It identified assets with "economic resources—cash and future economic benefits—" saying that a "resource other than cash ... must, singly or in combination with other resources, contribute directly or indirectly to future cash inflows ..." and identified liabilities with "obligations ... to other entities," saying that "the obligation must involve future sacrifice of resources ..."[146] The Board received many comment letters that said, in essence, "almost nothing can ever be an asset or liability because you have said that it has to be certain, and everything except cash is uncertain."

The Board thus inserted "probable" into the definition, but perhaps "expected" would have been a better word. As long as someone thinks that an item has value and is willing to pay for it, the item has value and meets the definition of assets, even if the expectation turns out to have been mistaken. It is easy to read more into the use of "probable" than was intended. "Probable" is not an essential part of the definitions; its function is to acknowledge the presence of uncertainty and to say that the future economic benefits or sacrifices do not have to be certain to qualify the items in question as assets and liabilities, not to specify a characteristic that must be present.

Although the application of the definitions of assets and liabilities commonly requires some assessment of probabilities, degrees of probability are not part of the definitions. The degree of probability of a future economic benefit (or of a future cash outlay or other sacrifice of future economic benefits) and the degree to which its amount can be estimated with reasonable reliability, both of which are required to recognize an item as an asset (or a liability), are recognition and measurement matters.

The asset and liability definitions screen out items that lack one or more of the three essential characteristics that assets and liabilities, respectively, must possess. Assets and liabilities have other features that help identify them. Assets may be acquired at a cost, tangible, exchangeable, or legally enforceable. Liabilities usually require the obligated entity to pay cash to one or more entities and are also legally enforceable. However, the difference between those features and the three characteristics identified by Concepts Statement 6 as essential to assets and liabilities is that the absence of a nonessential feature, by itself, is not sufficient to disqualify an item from being an asset or liability. For example, absence of a market price or exchangeability of an asset does not negate future economic benefit that can be obtained by use of the asset instead of by its exchange, although it may cause recognition and measurement problems. In contrast, absence of even one of the three essential characteristics does preclude an item from being an asset or liability:

> [A]n item does not qualify as an asset of an entity under the definition in paragraph 25 if (a) the item involves no future economic benefit, (b) the item involves future economic benefit, but the entity cannot obtain it, or (c) the item involves future economic benefit that the entity may in the future obtain, but the events or circumstances that give the entity access to and control of the benefit have not yet occurred (or the entity in the past had the ability to obtain or control the future benefit, but events or circumstances have occurred to remove that ability). Similarly, an item does not qualify as a liability of an entity under the definition in paragraph 35 if (a) the item entails no future sacrifice of assets, (b) the item entails future sacrifice of assets, but the entity is not obligated to make the sacrifice, or (c) the item involves a future sacrifice of assets that the entity will be obligated to make, but the events or circumstances that obligate the entity have not yet occurred (or the entity in the past was obligated to make the future sacrifice, but events or circumstances have occurred to remove that obligation). [Concepts Statement 6, paragraph 168]

---

[145] *Webster's New World Dictionary of the American Language*, Second College Edition (New York: Simon and Schuster, 1982), p. 1132.

[146] FASB Exposure Draft, *Objectives of Financial Reporting and Elements of Financial Statements of Business Enterprises* (December 29, 1977), paragraphs 47 and 49.

Equity or Net Assets.   Equity of business enterprises and net assets of not-for-profit organizations have the same definition.

> Equity or net assets is the residual interest in the assets of an entity that remains after deducting its liabilities.
>
> The equity or net assets of both a business enterprise and a not-for-profit organization is the difference between the entity's assets and its liabilities. [Concepts Statement 6, paragraphs 49 and 50]

Nevertheless, both terms should be used with care to assure that the referent is clear. Differences between business enterprises and not-for-profit organizations and the ways they carry out their respective missions, particularly the relative importance of transactions with owners to business enterprises and of gifts or donations to not-for-profit organizations, result in significant differences between the equity or net assets of the two kinds of entities.

> A major distinguishing characteristic of the equity of a business enterprise is that it may be increased through investments of assets by owners who also may, from time to time, receive distributions of assets from the entity. Owners invest in a business enterprise with the expectation of obtaining a return on their investment as a result of the enterprise's providing goods or services to customers at a profit. . . .
>
> In contrast, a not-for-profit organization has no ownership interest or profit purpose in the same sense as a business enterprise and thus receives no investments of assets by owners and distributes no assets to owners. Rather, its net assets often are increased by receipts of assets from resource providers (contributors, donors, grantors, and the like) who do not expect to receive either repayment or economic benefits proportionate to the assets provided but who are nonetheless interested in how the organization makes use of those assets and often impose temporary or permanent restrictions on their use. . . . [Concepts Statement 6, paragraphs 51 and 52]

Thus, whether a particular use of either equity or net assets refers to a business enterprise or a not-for-profit organization often is significant to investors, creditors, and other resource providers.

A footnote referenced to paragraph 50 notes that although the terms are interchangeable, "[t]his Statement generally applies the term *equity* to business enterprises, which is common usage, and the term *net assets* to not-for-profit organizations, for which the term *equity* is less commonly used." That terminology has the advantage of being both common and consistent, but what assures consistent clarity of meaning is Concepts Statement 6's careful use of the terms. It usually gives the complete names—equity of a business enterprise and net assets of a not-for-profit organization—using the shortcuts "equity" and "net assets" only if the referent is clear from the context. As a result, even if it interchanged the terms—net assets of a business enterprise or equity of a not-for-profit organization—the meaning would still be unmistakable.

EQUITY OR NET ASSETS AS A MEASURE OF WEALTH.   Although the term *wealth* is not part of most accountants' technical vocabularies, as explained earlier the definitions of the elements of financial statements in Concepts Statement 6 (carried over from Concepts Statement 3) make an enterprise's wealth and changes therein the major subject matter of financial accounting and reporting. The definitions of assets, liabilities, and equity in Concepts Statement 6 are all in terms of wealth. The Statement identifies assets with "economic resources. . . . the scarce means that are useful for carrying out economic activities, such as consumption, production, and exchange," whose "common characteristic . . . is 'service potential' or 'future economic benefit,' the scarce capacity to provide services or benefits to the entities that use them" (Concepts Statement 6, paragraphs 27 and 28). That is, the definition of assets refers to economic resources, rights to economic resources, and other things in the real-world environment in which financial accounting and reporting takes place that constitute wealth, and the definition of liabilities refers to obligations to transfer wealth to other entities. As a result, the definition of equity or net assets refers to net wealth of a business enterprise or a not-for-profit organization, and the remaining definitions refer to increases and decreases in wealth over time.

Equity of Business Enterprises.   Equity of business enterprises represents the ownership interests of those who invest funds in a business enterprise with the expectation of obtaining a return on their investment as a result of the enterprise's operating at a profit. Since equity ranks after liabilities as a claim to or interest in the assets of the enterprise, it is a *residual* interest. Changes in it result from profits and losses as well as from investments by and distributions to owners. Equity is often referred to as "risk capital," for in an uncertain world owners not only benefit if an enterprise is profitable but also are the first to bear the risk that an enterprise may be unprofitable.

> Equity in a business enterprise is the ownership interest, and its amount is the cumulative result of investments by owners, comprehensive income, and distributions to owners. That characteristic, coupled with the characteristic that liabilities have priority over ownership interest as claims against enterprise assets, makes equity not determinable independently of assets and liabilities. Although equity can be described in various ways, and different recognition criteria and measurement procedures can affect its amount, equity always equals net assets (assets minus liabilities). That is why it is a residual interest. [Concepts Statement 6, paragraph 213]

Liabilities and equity are mutually exclusive claims to or interests in an enterprise's assets by other entities, and liabilities take precedence over ownership interests. Although the line between equity and liabilities is clear in concept, it increasingly has been obscured in practice by introduction of financial instruments having characteristics of both liabilities and equity. Convertible debt instruments and redeemable preferred stock are common examples of securities with both debt and equity characteristics, which may cause problems in accounting for them.

Investments by and Distributions to Owners.   Equity of a business enterprise is increased and decreased by investments by owners and distributions to owners—unique transactions "between an enterprise and its owners *as owners* rather than as employees, suppliers, customers, lenders, or in some other nonowner role" (Concepts Statement 6, paragraphs 60 and 68).

> Investments by owners are increases in equity of a particular business enterprise resulting from transfers to it from other entities of something valuable to obtain or increase ownership interests (or equity) in it. Assets are most commonly received as investments by owners, but that which is received may also include services or satisfaction or conversion of liabilities of the enterprise.
>
> Distributions to owners are decreases in equity of a particular business enterprise resulting from transferring assets, rendering services, or incurring liabilities by the enterprise to owners. Distributions to owners decrease ownership interest (or equity) in an enterprise. [Concepts Statement 6, paragraphs 66 and 67; footnote reference omitted]

Not-for-profit organizations (pp. 2-96–2-97 of this chapter) have no comparable transactions.

A business enterprise may make discretionary distributions to owners, usually by the formal act of declaring a dividend, but it is not obligated to do so. Many enterprises have several classes of equity, each with different priority claims on enterprise assets in discretionary distributions or in the event of liquidation, depending on the degree to which they bear relatively more of the risk of unprofitability. All classes of equity depend to some extent on enterprise profitability for distributions of assets, and no class has an unconditional right or absolute claim to the assets of an enterprise except in the event of liquidation of the enterprise, and even then, owners must stand behind creditors, who have a priority right to enterprise assets (Concepts Statement 6, paragraph 62).

Comprehensive Income of Business Enterprises.   Investors, creditors, and others focus on comprehensive income to help them assess an enterprise's prospects for generating net cash inflows because, in the long run, it is through comprehensive income that they obtain a return on their investments, loans, or other association with an enterprise. Thus, the Concepts Statements recognize the significance of income and information about income of an enterprise to investors, creditors, and others.

> Equity is originally created by owners' investments in an enterprise and may from time to time be augmented by additional investments by owners. Equity is reduced by distributions by the enterprise to owners. However, the distinguishing characteristic of equity is that it inevitably is affected by the enterprise's operations and other events and circumstances affecting the enterprise (which together constitute comprehensive income . . .). [Concepts Statement 6, paragraph 63]

> The primary focus of financial reporting is information about an enterprise's performance provided by measures of [comprehensive income][147] and its components. [Concepts Statement 1, paragraph 43]

Concepts Statement 6 defines comprehensive income as

> the change in equity of a business enterprise during a period from transactions and other events and circumstances from nonowner sources. It includes all changes in equity during a period except those resulting from investments by owners and distributions to owners. [paragraph 70]

Comprehensive income and investments by and distributions to owners—class B in Exhibit 2.4—account for all changes in equity of a business enterprise during a period. The exhibit not only distinguishes the sources of changes in equity in class B from each other but also distinguishes them from other transactions and events affecting the enterprise during a period. Class A comprises exchange transactions that change assets or liabilities, or both, but do not change equity. They are common in most business enterprises. Events in class C are less familiar—changes within equity that do not affect assets or liabilities or change the amount of equity, such as stock dividends, conversions of preferred stock into common stock, and some stock recapitalizations.

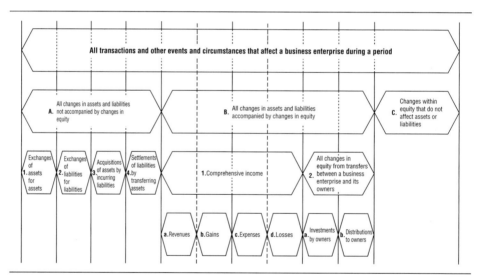

Exhibit 2.4   Transactions and other events that change assets, liabilities, and equity of business enterprises. (*Source:* Financial Accounting Standards Board, *Statement of Financial Accounting Concepts No. 6,* par. 64.)

---

[147] Concepts Statement 1 said *earnings*, but in Concepts Statement 3 (paragraph 1, footnote 1) the Board changed the name of the concept to *comprehensive income* and reserved the term *earnings* for possible use to designate a component part of comprehensive income. The Board used *earnings* in that way in Concepts Statement 5.

REVENUES, EXPENSES, GAINS, AND LOSSES.   Concepts Statements 3 and 6 define the components of comprehensive income—revenues, expenses, gains, and losses—as well as comprehensive income (paragraph references are from Concepts Statement 6):

> *Revenues* are inflows or other enhancements of assets of an entity or settlements of its liabilities (or a combination of both) from delivering or producing goods, rendering services, or other activities that constitute the entity's ongoing major or central operations. [paragraph 78]

> *Expenses* are outflows or other using up of assets or incurrences of liabilities (or a combination of both) from delivering or producing goods, rendering services, or carrying out other activities that constitute the entity's ongoing major or central operations. [paragraph 80]

> *Gains* are increases in equity (net assets) from peripheral or incidental transactions of an entity and from all other transactions and other events and circumstances affecting the entity except those that result from revenues or investments by owners. [paragraph 82]

> *Losses* are decreases in equity (net assets) from peripheral or incidental transactions of an entity and from all other transactions and other events and circumstances affecting the entity except those that result from expenses or distributions to owners. [paragraph 83]

Revenues and expenses represent actual or expected cash inflows and outflows usually associated with the ongoing major operations and earning and financing activities of an enterprise, leaving other more peripheral and incidental changes in equity to be described as various kinds of gains and losses.

Revenues and gains are similar, and expenses and losses are similar, but some differences are significant in conveying information about an enterprise's performance. Revenues and expenses result from an entity's ongoing major or central operations and activities—that is, from activities such as producing or delivering goods, rendering services, lending, insuring, investing, and financing. In contrast, gains and losses result from incidental or peripheral transactions of an enterprise with other entities and from other events and circumstances affecting it. Some gains and losses may be considered "operating" gains and losses and may be closely related to revenues and expenses. Revenues and expenses are commonly displayed as gross inflows or outflows of net assets, while gains and losses are usually displayed as net inflows or outflows.

... Distinctions between revenues and gains and between expenses and losses in a particular entity depend to a significant extent on the nature of the entity, its operations, and its other activities. Items that are revenues for one kind of entity may be gains for another, and items that are expenses for one kind of entity may be losses for another. For example, investments in securities that may be sources of revenues and expenses for insurance or investment companies may be sources of gains and losses in manufacturing or merchandising companies. Technological changes may be sources of gains or losses for most kinds of enterprises but may be characteristic of the operations of high-technology or research-oriented enterprises. ... [Concepts Statement 6, paragraphs 87 and 88]

The definitions of revenues, expenses, gains, and losses are less precise and serve a different purpose than the definitions of the six elements described in the preceding pages—assets, liabilities, equity, investments by owners, distributions to owners, and comprehensive income. Those six constitute the complete set of definitions of fundamental elements of financial statements of business enterprises. They are mutually exclusive and collectively are both necessary and sufficient to account for the wealth and net wealth of an enterprise at any time and for all changes in its net wealth during a period, including the changes comprising profit or loss (or income) for the period.[148]

---

[148] As noted earlier, the definitions in Concepts Statements 3 and 6 are of things and events in the real world and not of their representations in financial statements. Limitations on financial statements' reporting of an enterprise's wealth and changes in wealth stem from accounting's inability to recognize all wealth and changes in wealth in financial statements and accountants' historic reluctance to recognize even what can be recognized and measured with reasonable reliability.

In contrast, distinctions between revenues and gains and between expenses and losses are not needed to determine comprehensive income. Since comprehensive income is determined by changes in assets and liabilities, it can be derived without separating it into its various components.

Revenues, expenses, gains, and losses are useful not to define comprehensive income but to show how it is obtained.

> In the diagram [Exhibit 2.4], dashed lines rather than solid boundary lines separate revenues and gains and separate expenses and losses because of display considerations.... [T]his Statement ... do[es] not precisely distinguish between revenues and gains on the one hand or between expenses and losses on the other. Fine distinctions between revenues and gains and between expenses and losses, as well as other distinctions *within* comprehensive income, are more appropriately considered as part of display or reporting. [Concepts Statement 6, paragraph 64]

Definitions of the components of comprehensive income are significant because to satisfy the objectives of financial reporting, that is, to provide information intended to be useful to investors and creditors in assessing an enterprise's performance or profitability, requires more information about comprehensive income than just its amount. Investors and creditors want and need to know how and why equity has changed, not just the amount that it has changed. The sources of comprehensive income are significant to those attempting to use financial statements to help them with investment, credit, and similar decisions.

> Information about various components of comprehensive income is usually more useful than merely its aggregate amount to investors, creditors, managers, and others who are interested in knowing not only that an entity's net assets have increased (or decreased) but also *how* and *why*. The amount of comprehensive income for a period can, after all, be measured merely by comparing the ending and beginning equity and eliminating the effects of investments by owners and distributions to owners, but that procedure has never provided adequate information about an entity's performance. Investors, creditors, managers, and others need information about the causes of changes in assets and liabilities. [Concepts Statement 6, paragraph 219]

Comprehensive income is an all-inclusive income concept and results from many and varied sources. The primary source of comprehensive income is an enterprise's major or central operations, but income also can often be generated by peripheral or incidental activities in which an enterprise engages. Moreover, the economic, legal, social, political, and physical environment in which an enterprise operates creates events and circumstances—such as, price changes, interest rate changes, technological changes, impositions of taxes and regulations, discovery, growth or accretion, shrinkage, vandalism, thefts, expropriations, wars, fires, and natural disasters—that can affect comprehensive income but that may be partly or wholly beyond the control of individual enterprises and their managements (Concepts Statement 6, paragraphs 74 and 75; the examples are from paragraph 32).

Those many and varied transactions and other events that constitute sources of comprehensive income—central and peripheral, planned and unplanned, controllable and noncontrollable—result in receipts that may differ in stability, risk, and predictability. Thus the desire for information about the various sources of comprehensive income underlies the distinctions between revenues, expenses, gains, and losses.

Different components of income are useful to distinguish revenue generated from the production and sale of products from return on investments in marketable securities in an income statement. The primary purpose of separating comprehensive income into revenues and expenses and gains and losses is to make the display of information about an enterprise's sources of comprehensive income as useful as possible.

Net Assets of Not-for-Profit Organizations.   A not-for-profit organization has no ownership interests that can be sold or transferred or that convey entitlement to a share of a residual distribution of resources in the event of liquidation of the organization. It thus does not receive investments of assets by owners and is generally prohibited from distributing assets as dividends to its members or officers. Increases in its net assets result from receipt of assets from resource providers who expect to receive neither repayment nor return on the assets. However, some resource providers may impose permanent or temporary restrictions on the uses of the assets they contribute to be able to influence an organization's use of those assets. Thus, Concepts Statement 6 (paragraphs 92–94) divides net assets of not-for-profit organizations into three mutually exclusive classes—permanently restricted net assets, temporarily restricted net assets, and unrestricted net assets. Restrictions restrain the organization from using part of its resources for purposes other than those specified, for example, to settle liabilities or to provide services outside the purview of the restrictions.

Briefly, permanently restricted net assets is the part of net assets resulting from inflows of assets whose use by the organization is limited by donor-imposed stipulations that neither expire nor can be satisfied or otherwise removed by any action of the organization. Stipulations that require resources to be permanently maintained but that permit the organization to use the income derived from the donated assets are often called *endowments*.

Temporarily restricted net assets is the part of net assets governed by donor-imposed stipulations that can expire or be fulfilled or removed by actions of the organization in accordance with those stipulations. Once the stipulation is satisfied, the restriction is gone.

Unrestricted net assets is the part of net assets resulting from all revenues, expenses, gains, and losses that are not changes in permanently or temporarily restricted net assets. The only limits on unrestricted net assets are the broad limits encompassing the nature of the organization, which are specified in its articles of incorporation or bylaws, and perhaps limits resulting from contractual agreements (for example, loan covenants) entered into by the organization in the course of its operations.

Although a not-for-profit organization does not have ownership interests or comprehensive income in the same sense as a business enterprise, to be able to continue to achieve its service and operating objectives, it needs to maintain net assets such that resources made available to it at least equal the resources needed to provide services at levels satisfactory to resource providers and other constituents. To assess an organization's success at maintaining net assets, resource providers need information about the components of changes in net assets—revenues, expenses, gains, and losses. The definitions of revenues, expenses, gains, and losses of business enterprises also apply to not-for-profit organizations and

> include all transactions and other events and circumstances that change the amount of net assets of a not-for-profit organization. All resource inflows and other enhancements of assets of a not-for-profit organization or settlements of its liabilities that increase net assets are either revenues or gains and have characteristics similar to the revenues or gains of a business enterprise. Likewise, all resource outflows or other using up of assets or incurrences of liabilities that decrease net assets are either expenses or losses and have characteristics similar to expenses or losses of business enterprises. [Concepts Statement 6, paragraph 111]

A not-for-profit organization's central operations—its service-providing efforts, fund-raising activities, and most exchange transactions—by which it attempts to fulfill its service objectives are the sources of its revenues and expenses. Gains and losses result from activities that are peripheral or incidental to its central operations and from interactions with its environment, which give rise to price changes, casualties, and other effects that may be largely beyond the control of an individual organization and its management.

Accrual Accounting and Related Concepts. Concepts Statement 6 also defines several "terms of art" or significant financial accounting and reporting concepts that are used extensively in the conceptual framework.

TRANSACTIONS, EVENTS, AND CIRCUMSTANCES. *Transactions and other events and circumstances* affecting an entity is a phrase used throughout the conceptual framework to describe the sources or causes of changes in assets, liabilities, and equity. Real-world occurrences that are reflected in financial statements divide into two categories: events and circumstances. They can be further divided into this hierarchy:

Events
    Transactions
        Exchanges
        Nonreciprocal transfers
    Other external events
    Internal events
Circumstances

Events are by far the most important, encompassing external happenings, including transactions, and internal happenings. The breakdown of events into those various components highlights differences that are important to financial accounting.

> An event is a happening of consequence to an entity. It may be an internal event that occurs within an entity, such as using raw materials or equipment in production, or it may be an external event that involves interaction between an entity and its environment, such as a transaction with another entity, a change in price of a good or service that an entity buys or sells, a flood or earthquake, or an improvement in technology by a competitor. [paragraph 135]

Transactions are external events that include reciprocal transfers of assets and liabilities between an entity and other entities called *exchanges and nonreciprocal transfers* between an entity and its owners or between an entity and entities other that its owners in which one of the participants is often a passive beneficiary or victim of the other's actions:

> A transaction is a particular kind of external event, namely, an external event involving transfer of something of value (future economic benefit) between two (or more) entities. The transaction may be an exchange in which each participant both receives and sacrifices value, such as purchases or sales of goods or services; or the transaction may be a nonreciprocal transfer in which an entity incurs a liability or transfers an asset to another entity (or receives an asset or cancellation of a liability) without directly receiving (or giving) value in exchange. Nonreciprocal transfers contrast with exchanges (which are reciprocal transfers) and include, for example, investments by owners, distributions to owners, impositions of taxes, gifts, charitable or educational contributions given or received, and thefts. [paragraph 137]

Investments by and distributions to owners are nonreciprocal transfers because they are events in which an enterprise receives assets from owners and acknowledges an increased ownership interest or disperses assets to owners whose interests decrease. They are not exchanges from the point of view of the enterprise because it neither incurs any obligations nor sacrifices any of its assets in exchange for owners' investments, and it receives nothing of value to itself in exchange for the assets it distributes with the payment of a dividend.

Circumstances, in contrast, are not events but the results of events. They provide evidence of often imperceptible events that may already have happened but that are discernible only in retrospect by the resulting state of affairs. They are important in financial reporting because they often have accounting consequences.

> Circumstances are a condition or set of conditions that develop from an event or a series of events, which may occur almost imperceptibly and may converge in random or unexpected ways to create situations that might otherwise not have occurred and might not have been anticipated. To see the circumstance may be fairly easy, but to discern specifically when the event or events that caused it occurred may be difficult or impossible. For example, a debtor's going bankrupt or a thief's stealing gasoline may be an event, but a creditor's facing the situation that its debtor is bankrupt or a warehouse's facing the fact that its tank is empty may be a circumstance. [paragraph 136]

ACCRUAL ACCOUNTING. The objectives of financial reporting are served by accrual accounting, which generally provides a better indication of an entity's assets, liabilities, and performance than does information about cash receipts and payments. Accrual accounting is defined in paragraph 139 of Concepts Statement 6:

> Accrual accounting attempts to record the financial effects on an entity of transactions and other events and circumstances that have cash consequences for the entity in the periods in which those transactions, events, and circumstances occur rather than only in the periods in which cash is received or paid by the entity. Accrual accounting is concerned with an entity's acquiring of goods and services and using them to produce and distribute other goods or services. It is concerned with the process by which cash expended on resources and activities is returned as more (or perhaps less) cash to the entity, not just with the beginning and end of that process. It recognizes that the buying, producing, selling, distributing, and other operations of an entity during a period, as well as other events that affect entity performance, often do not coincide with the cash receipts and payments of the period.

Accrual accounting is based not only on cash transactions but also on all the transactions, events, and circumstances that have cash consequences for an entity but involve no concurrent cash movement. By accounting for noncash assets, liabilities, and comprehensive income, accrual accounting links an entity's operations and other transactions, events, and circumstances that affect it with its cash receipts and outlays, thereby providing information about its assets, liabilities, and changes in them that cannot be obtained by accounting only for its cash transactions.

Concepts Statement 6 also provides technical definitions of the following procedures used to apply accrual accounting [emphasis added]:

> *Accrual* is concerned with expected future cash receipts and payments: It is the accounting process of recognizing assets or liabilities and the related liabilities, assets, revenues, expenses, gains, or losses for amounts expected to be received or paid, usually in cash, in the future. *Deferral* is concerned with past cash receipts and payments—with prepayments received (often described as collected in advance) or paid: It is the accounting process of recognizing a liability resulting from a current cash receipt (or the equivalent) or an asset resulting from a current cash payment (or the equivalent) with deferred recognition of revenues, expenses, gains, or losses. Their recognition is deferred until the obligation underlying the liability is partly or wholly satisfied or until the future economic benefit underlying the asset is partly or wholly used or lost. [paragraph 141]

> *Allocation* is the accounting process of assigning or distributing an amount according to a plan or a formula. It is broader than and includes *amortization,* which is the accounting process of reducing an amount by periodic payments or write-downs. Specifically, amortization is the process of reducing a liability recorded as a result of a cash receipt by recognizing revenues or reducing an asset recorded as a result of a cash payment by recognizing expenses or costs of production. [paragraph 142]

> *Realization* in the most precise sense means the process of converting noncash resources and rights into money and is most precisely used in accounting and financial reporting to refer to sales of assets for cash or claims to cash.... *Recognition* is the process of formally recording or incorporating an item in the financial statements of an entity. [paragraph 143]

> *Matching* of costs and revenues is simultaneous or combined recognition of the revenues and expenses that result directly and jointly from the same transactions or other events. In most entities, some transactions or events result simultaneously in both a revenue and one or more expenses. The revenue and expense(s) are directly related to each other and require recognition at the same time. In present practice, for example, a sale of product or merchandise involves both revenue (sales revenue) for receipt of cash or a receivable and expense (cost of goods sold) for sacrifice of the product or merchandise sold to customers.... [paragraph 146]

That is a narrow definition of matching, similar to the definitions of Herman W. Bevis and George O. May (pp. 2-37 to 38 of this chapter). The definition excludes from matching the systematic and rational allocation of revenues or costs to periods by a formula and makes matching a single process in measuring comprehensive income, not a synonym for the entire periodic income determination process, as it commonly has been.

Concepts Statement 6 also includes an example on debt discount, premium, and issue cost (paragraphs 235–239) to illustrate precise technical differences between some of those terms.

(iv) Recognition and Measurement.   Recognition and measurement originally had been viewed as separate components of the conceptual framework. Two research studies on recognition matters were commissioned by the FASB: *Recognition of Contractual Rights and Obligations: An Exploratory Study of Conceptual Issues* (1980), by Yuji Ijiri, and *Survey of Present Practices in Recognizing Revenues, Expenses, Gains, and Losses* (1981), by Henry R. Jaenicke. Those studies focused, respectively, on the timing of the initial recognition of assets and liabilities and on the related subsequent timing of recognition of revenues and expenses. A third study, *Recognition in Financial Statements: Underlying Concepts and Practical Conventions*, by L. Todd Johnson and Reed K. Storey, was published in 1982.

Meanwhile, a project on financial reporting and changing prices was to consider measurement. The direction of the original measurement project was changed, however, because of the urgency caused by the increasing prices of the late 1960s and 1970s and the SEC's issuance of ASR No. 190, *Notice of Adoption of Amendments to Regulation S-X Requiring Disclosure of Certain Replacement Cost Data*, which required certain publicly held companies to disclose replacement cost information about inventories, cost of sales, productive capacity, and depreciation. Instead of remaining part of the conceptual framework, the measurement project resulted in FASB Statement No. 33, *Financial Reporting and Changing Prices* (1979).

Concepts Statement No. 5.   Recognition decisions often cannot be separated from measurement decisions, particularly if the decision relates to when to recognize changes in assets and liabilities. Recognition and measurement were eventually combined in the conceptual framework because most Board members became convinced that certain recognition questions, which were among the most important to be dealt with, were so closely related to measurement issues that it was unproductive to try to handle them separately. The product of that union was Concepts Statement No. 5, *Recognition and Measurement in Financial Statements of Business Enterprises*, issued in December 1984.

Financial Statements.   Concepts Statement 5 includes concepts that relate recognition and measurement to the earlier Concepts Statements. For example, it is the part of the conceptual framework in which the FASB describes the financial statements that should be provided and how those financial statements contribute to the objectives of financial reporting.

> Financial statements are a central feature of financial reporting—a principal means of communicating financial information to those outside an entity. In external general purpose financial reporting, a financial statement is a formal tabulation of names and amounts of money derived from accounting records that displays either financial position of an entity at a moment in time or one or more kinds of changes in financial position of the entity during a period of time. Items that are recognized in financial statements are financial representations of certain resources (assets) of an entity, claims to those resources (liabilities and owners' equity), and the effects of transactions and other events and circumstances that result in changes in those resources and claims. The financial statements of an entity are a fundamentally related set that articulate with each other and derive from the same underlying data. [paragraph 5]

To satisfy the objectives of financial reporting—to provide information that is useful to investors and creditors and other users in making rational investment, credit, and similar decisions; to provide information to help them assess the amounts, timing, and uncertainty of prospective net cash inflows to an enterprise; and to provide information about the economic resources, claims to those resources (obligations to transfer resources to other entities and owners' equity), and changes in and claims

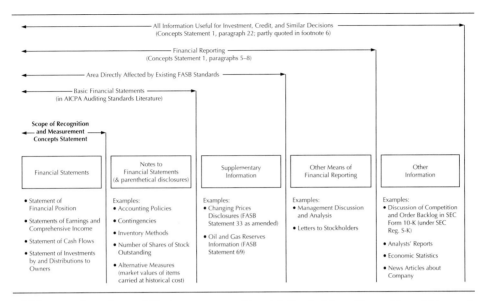

Exhibit 2.5   Information useful for investment, credit, and similar decisions. (*Source:* Financial Accounting Standards Board, Statement of Financial Accounting Concepts No. 5, par. 5.)

to those resources—requires a full set of articulated financial statements that report:

Financial position at the end of the period

Earnings (net income) for the period

Comprehensive income (total nonowner changes in equity) for the period

Cash flows during the period

Investments by and distributions to owners during the period. [Concepts Statement 5, paragraph 13]

A full set of financial statements provides information about an entity's financial position and changes in its financial position. Financial position, as depicted in a balance sheet, is determined by the relationship between an entity's economic resources (assets) and obligations (liabilities), leaving a residual (net assets or owners' equity). In addition, information about earnings, comprehensive income, cash flows, and transactions with owners are different kinds of information about the effects of transactions and other events and circumstances that change assets and liabilities during a period—that is, they are information about different kinds of changes in financial position.

Not all information useful for investment, credit, and similar decisions that financial accounting is able to provide can be reported in financial statements. Concepts Statement 5 includes a diagram (Exhibit 2.5) illustrating the many kinds of information that investors and creditors may contemplate consulting when deciding whether to invest in or loan funds to an enterprise. Financial statements provide only part of the information useful for investment, credit, and similar decisions. Financial reporting also encompasses notes to financial statements and parenthetical disclosures, which provide information about accounting policies or explain information recognized in the financial statements. Supplementary information about the effects of changing prices or management discussion and analysis provides information that may also be relevant for making decisions but is deemed not to meet the criteria necessary for recognition in financial statements. Financial statements are unique because the information they provide is distinguished by its capacity and need to withstand the scrutiny of accounting recognition.

Concepts Statement 5, expanding the one-sentence definition in Concepts Statement 3, defines *recognition* as

> the process of formally recording or incorporating an item into the financial statements of an entity as an asset, liability, revenue, expense, or the like. Recognition includes depiction of an item in both words and numbers, with the amount included in the totals of the financial statements. For an asset or liability, recognition involves recording not only acquisition or incurrence of the item but also later changes in it, including changes that result in removal from the financial statements. [paragraph 6]

A slight shift in emphasis discloses another characteristic of recognition: "Recognition attempts to represent or depict in financial statements the effects on an entity of real-world economic things and events.[149] That description is congruent with the idea expressed throughout the conceptual framework that financial reporting is concerned with providing information about things and events that occur in the real world in which accounting takes place.

Concepts Statement 5 affirms the value of information disclosed in notes or other supplementary information as essential to understanding the information recognized in financial statements, but it also makes it clear that

> disclosure by other means is *not* recognition. Disclosure of information about the items in financial statements and their measures that may be provided by notes or parenthetically on the face of financial statements, by supplementary information, or by other means of financial reporting is not a substitute for recognition in financial statements for items that meet recognition criteria. Generally, the most useful information about assets, liabilities, revenues, expenses, and other items of financial statements and their measures (that with the best combination of relevance and reliability) should be recognized in the financial statements. [paragraph 9]

Although information provided by notes to financial statements or by other means is valuable and ought to be made available to investors, creditors, and other users, it is not a substitute for recognition in the body of financial statements with the amounts included in the financial statement totals.

COMPREHENSIVE INCOME AND EARNINGS.   Concepts Statement 5 says that a full set of financial statements should report both comprehensive income and earnings. Since the distinction between comprehensive income and earnings in the Statement is another manifestation of the difference of opinion about whether income is an enhancement of wealth (command over economic resources) or an indicator of performance of an enterprise and its management, the Statement implies that financial statements should report both kinds of information. Present practice reports neither earnings nor comprehensive income, although a statement of net income based on present generally accepted accounting principles may report either or both if there are no changes in accounting principles or no holding gains or losses reported as direct increases or decreases in equity instead of in net income.

Comprehensive income was defined in Concepts Statement 3 as an all-inclusive income concept:

> Comprehensive income is the change in equity (net assets) of an entity during a period from transactions and other events and circumstances from nonowner sources. It includes all changes in equity during a period except those resulting from investments by owners and distributions to owners. [paragraph 56]

The same definition was carried over into Concepts Statement 6, paragraph 70.

---

[149] Johnson and Storey, *Recognition in Financial Statements*, p. 2.

Comprehensive income is the only concept of income defined in the FASB's conceptual framework.[150] Although Concepts Statement 5 referred a half dozen times to "the concept of earnings" and gave earnings much more attention than comprehensive income, neither Concepts Statement 5 nor any other Concepts Statement defined earnings or its close relative net income. Instead, Concepts Statement 3, paragraph 1, footnote 1 [carried over into Concepts Statement 6], explained that the Board had changed to *comprehensive income* the name of the concept that was called *earnings* in Concepts Statement 1 and other conceptual framework documents previously issued and had reserved the term earnings for possible use to designate a component part of comprehensive income.

Later, Concepts Statement 5 did use the term earnings to describe a component part of comprehensive income that corresponds to net income in current practice, except that it excludes the so-called catch-up adjustment required by paragraph 19(b) of APB Opinion No. 20, *Accounting Changes*, to be included in net income.[151]

Earnings and comprehensive income have the same broad components—revenues, expenses, gains, and losses—but are not the same because certain classes of gains and losses are included in comprehensive income but are excluded from earnings. [paragraph 42]

The Statement described a two-step relationship between earnings and comprehensive income:

Revenues − expenses + most gains − most losses = Earnings

   ± Cumulative effect on prior years of a change in accounting principle = Net income

   ± Gains and losses included in comprehensive income but excluded from net income[152]

   − Comprehensive income.

The Concepts Statements describe but do not define earnings and net income because they cannot be defined. Both result from applying generally accepted accounting principles and are determined by what is done in practice at a particular time—the meaning of each changes with

---

[150] Comprehensive income is one of six mutually exclusive elements of financial statements of business enterprises whose definitions are necessary and sufficient to form a complete or closed set. The other five are assets, liabilities, equity, investments by owners, and distributions to owners (p. 2-95 of this chapter).

[151] Both earnings and net income as Concepts Statement 5 uses the terms are what Concepts Statements 3 and 6 described as intermediate components of comprehensive income: "Comprehensive income consists of not only its basic components—revenues, expenses, gains, and losses—but also various intermediate components or measures that result from combining the basic components .... in various ways to obtain several measures of enterprise performance with varying degrees of inclusiveness ... Those intermediate" components or measures are, in effect, subtotals of comprehensive income and often of one another ... (Concepts Statement 3, paragraph 62; Concepts Statement 6, paragraph 77 is almost the same.) Each Statement explains that: "Although cash resulting from various sources of comprehensive income is the same, receipts from various sources may vary in stability, risk, and predictability ... indicating a need for information about various components of comprehensive income" (paragraphs 61 and 76, respectively).

[152] This term, which is more descriptive and accurate than Concept Statement 5's *other nonowner changes in equity*, was used in FASB Statement No. 109, *Accounting for Income Taxes* (February 1992), and implied in a number of other FASB Statements. This entry is from Statement 109's glossary:

Gains and losses included in comprehensive income but excluded from net income

Under present practice, gains and losses included in comprehensive income but excluded from net income include certain changes in market values of investments in marketable equity securities classified as noncurrent assets, certain changes in market values of investments in industries having specialized accounting practices for marketable securities, adjustments from recognizing certain additional pension liabilities, and foreign currency translation adjustments. Future changes to generally accepted accounting principles may change what is included in this category. [paragraph 289]

changes in generally accepted accounting principles. Thus, paragraph 35 of Concepts Statement 5 says:

> The Board expects the concept of earnings to be subject to the process of gradual change or evolution that has characterized the development of net income. Present practice has developed over a long time, and that evolution has resulted in significant changes in what net income reflects, such as a shift toward what is commonly called an *all-inclusive income statement*. Those changes have resulted primarily from standard-setting bodies' responses to several factors, such as changes in the business and economic environment and perceptions about the nature and limitations of financial statements, about the needs of users of financial statements, and about the need to prevent or cure perceived abuse(s) in financial reporting. Those factors sometimes may conflict or appear to conflict. For example, an all-inclusive income statement is intended, among other things, to avoid discretionary omissions of losses (or gains) from an income statement, thereby avoiding presentation of a more (or less) favorable report of performance or stewardship than is justified. However, because income statements also are used as a basis for estimating future performance and assessing future cash flow prospects, arguments have been advanced urging exclusion of unusual or nonrecurring gains and losses that might reduce the usefulness of an income statement for any one year for predictive purposes.

Those kinds of arguments also have been advanced urging exclusion of recurring gains and losses that increase the volatility of reported net income, and the FASB has to some extent responded. For example, FASB Statement No. 12, *Accounting for Certain Marketable Securities* (1975), and FASB Statement No. 52, *Foreign Currency Translation* (1981), excluded from net income certain holding gains and losses (gains and losses from holding assets or owing liabilities while their prices change). Briefly, Statement 12 required the carrying amount of a marketable equity securities portfolio to be the lower of its aggregate cost and market value but required that changes in the carrying amount of a noncurrent marketable equity securities portfolio "be included in the equity section of the balance sheet [that is, not included in net income] and shown separately" (paragraph 11). Similarly, Statement 52 provided that "translation adjustments [as defined in the Statement] shall not be included in determining net income but shall be reported separately and accumulated in a separate component of equity" (paragraph 13). The Board had taken a step away from the APB's decision to make reported net income all-inclusive—"net income should reflect all items of profit and loss recognized during the period with the sole exception of the prior period adjustments" (APB Opinion No. 9, *Reporting the Results of Operations* [December 1966], paragraph 17)—and had set the stage for the distinction between earnings and comprehensive income that it made in Concepts Statement 5.

As might have been expected, comprehensive income generally has been criticized for being too inclusive, among other things including volatile holding gains and losses that are excluded from net income or earnings. For example, John W. March's dissent to Concepts Statement 5 reflected the common view that periodic income determination should focus on performance rather than report gains and losses from all sources that increase or decrease wealth. These are the first and penultimate paragraphs of his dissent:

> Mr. March dissents from this Statement because (a) it does not adopt measurement concepts oriented toward what he believes is the most useful single attribute for recognition purposes, the cash equivalent of recognized transactions reduced by subsequent impairments or loss of service value—instead it suggests selecting from several different attributes without providing sufficient guidance for the selection process; (b) it identifies all nonowner changes in assets and liabilities

---

Concepts Statement 5, FASB Statement 109, and other FASB Statements refer only to *gains and losses* that are included in comprehensive income but excluded from earnings. In some kinds of enterprises, however, increases and decreases in equity from holding assets or owing liabilities while their prices change involve activities that constitute ongoing major or central operations and thus qualify as revenues and expenses instead of gains and losses.

as comprehensive income and return on equity, thereby including in income, incorrectly in his view, capital inputs from nonowners, unrealized gains from price changes, amounts that should be deducted to maintain capital in real terms, and foreign currency translation adjustments; (c) it uses a concept of income that is fundamentally based on measurements of assets, liabilities, and changes in them, rather than adopting the Statement's concept of earnings as the definition of income; and (d) it fails to provide sufficient guidance for initial recognition and derecognition of assets and liabilities.

The description of earnings (paragraphs 33–38) and the guidance for applying recognition criteria to components of earnings (paragraphs 78–87) is consistent with Mr. March's view that income should measure performance and that performance flows primarily from an entity's fulfillment of the terms of its transactions with outside entities that result in revenues, other proceeds on resource dispositions (gains), costs (expenses) associated with those revenues and proceeds, and losses sustained. However, Mr. March believes that those concepts are fundamental and should be embodied in definitions of the elements of financial statements and in basic income recognition criteria rather than basing income on measurements of assets, liabilities, and changes in them.[153]

As March suggested, Concepts Statement 5 contains good, brief descriptions of the goal of periodic income determination in the minds of those who think it should focus on performance.

> ... Earnings is a measure of performance for a period and to the extent feasible excludes items that are extraneous to that period—items that belong primarily to other periods.... [paragraph 34]

> Earnings focuses on what the entity has received or reasonably expects to receive for its output (revenues) and what it sacrifices to produce and distribute that output (expenses). Earnings also includes results of the entity's incidental or peripheral transactions and some effects of other events and circumstances stemming from the environment (gains and losses). [paragraph 38]

Concepts Statement 5, as noted earlier, devoted much more attention to earnings than to comprehensive income, and for more than 10 years the Board did nothing more about its conclusion that a full set of financial statements reports comprehensive income (paragraph 13). Most people had, to their knowledge, never seen a statement that reports comprehensive income and may have had difficulty picturing it and its relation to an income statement in present practice.

As a result of Statements 12 and 52 and other FASB Statements of which they were forerunners, net income is less all-inclusive than it was, say, after issuance of APB Opinion No. 30, *Reporting the Results of Operations—Reporting the Effects of Disposal of a Segment of a Business, and Extraordinary, Unusual and Infrequently Occurring Events and Transactions* (June 1973). Since the FASB has not required a statement of comprehensive income, pronouncements such as Statements 12 and 52 that exclude volatile holding gains and losses from net income and bury them directly in equity have made it possible for many U.S. enterprises to report periodic income that reflects their domestic and foreign operations as less risky than they actually are.

That may be about to change. The Board recently has been talking about how to report both earnings, or its close relative net income, and comprehensive income and has issued an Exposure Draft, *Reporting Comprehensive Income* (June 20, 1996).[154] The Board's effort seems to have been encouraged by *Financial Reporting in the 1990s and Beyond* (1993), a report by the Financial Accounting Policy Committee of the Association for Investment Management and Research (AIMR) intended to express the views of AIMR members on financial reporting.

> Throughout the report, there are repeated recommendations that the FASB needs to develop its concept of "comprehensive income." [page 5]

---

[153] March's dissent to Concepts Statement 5 constituted a retroactive dissent to Concepts Statement 3, to which he had assented. The dissent explicitly repudiated Concepts Statement 3's definition of comprehensive income and would replace it in the definitions of the elements of financial statements with Concepts Statement 5's "concept of earnings."

[154] Author's note: FASB Statement No. 130, *Reporting Comprehensive Income*, was issued in June 1997.

We refer to comprehensive income several times above and have urged the FASB to construct the bridge from concept to standard. It is needed for better and more useful financial reporting in several areas.

... The F[inancial] A[ccounting] P[olicy] C[ommittee] has consistently supported the all-inclusive income statement format.... We consider income to include all of an enterprise's wealth changes except those engendered from transactions with its owners. We have profound misgivings about the increasing number of wealth changes that elude disclosure on the income statement. Yet individual items may be interpreted differently. That calls for a display of comprehensive income that allows components of different character to be seen and evaluated separately. [page 63]

Capital Maintenance.   Maintenance of capital is a financial concept or abstraction needed to measure comprehensive income. Since comprehensive income is a residual concept, not all revenues of a business enterprise for a period are comprehensive income because the sacrifices necessary to produce the revenues must be considered. Capital used up during the period must be recovered from revenues or other increases in net assets before any of the return may be considered comprehensive income. A concept of capital maintenance is critical for distinguishing an enterprise's return *on* investment from return *of* investment because an enterprise receives a profit or income—a return on investment—only after its capital has been maintained or recovered.

Two major concepts of capital maintenance exist, the financial capital concept and the physical capital concept (which is often described as maintaining operating capability, that is, maintaining the capacity of an enterprise to provide a constant supply of goods or services).

In Concepts Statement 5, the Board decided that the concept of financial capital maintenance is the basis for a full set of articulated financial statements.

A return on financial capital results only if the financial (money) amount of an enterprise's net assets at the end of a period exceeds the financial amount of net assets at the beginning of the period after excluding the effects of transactions with owners. The financial capital concept is the traditional view and is the capital maintenance concept in present financial statements. [paragraph 47]

Financial capital maintenance can be measured either in units of money (for example, nominal dollars) or in units of constant purchasing power (e.g., 1982–1984 dollars or 2007 dollars).

The Board rejected the physical capital concept, which holds that

a return on physical capital results only if the physical productive capacity of the enterprise at the end of the period (or the resources needed to achieve that capacity) exceeds the physical productive capacity at the beginning of the period, also after excluding the effects of transactions with owners. [paragraph 47]

The general procedure for maintaining physical capital is to value assets, such as inventories, property, plant, and equipment at their current replacement costs and to deduct expenses, such as cost of goods sold and depreciation, at replacement costs from revenues to measure periodic return on capital. The increases and decreases in replacement costs of those assets while they are held by the enterprise are included in owners' equity as a "capital maintenance adjustment" rather than in return on capital as "holding gains and losses." The idea underlying the measurement of return on capital in the physical capital concept is that increases in wealth that are merely increases in prices of things that an enterprise must continue to hold to engage in operations do not constitute return on capital but part of the capital to be maintained.

The principal difference between the two concepts is in the treatment of holding gains and losses resulting from the effects of price changes during a period on assets while held and on liabilities while owed.

Under the financial capital concept, if the effects of those price changes are recognized, they are conceptually holding gains and losses ... and are included in the return on capital. Under the physical capital concept, those changes would be recognized but conceptually would be capital maintenance adjustments that would be included directly in equity and not included in return on capital. Both earnings and comprehensive income as set forth in this Statement, like present net income, include holding gains and losses that would be excluded from income under a physical capital maintenance concept. [paragraph 48]

Measurement and Attributes.   By definition, recognition includes the depiction of an item in both words and numbers. The need to quantify the information about an item to be recognized introduces the issue of its *measurement*.

> Measurement involves choice of an attribute by which to quantify a recognized item and choice of a scale of measurement (often called "unit of measure"). [Concepts Statement 5, paragraph 3]

Attribute is defined and explained in footnote 2 to paragraph 2 of Concepts Statement 1:

> "Attributes to be measured" refers to the traits or aspects of an element to be quantified or measured, such as historical cost/historical proceeds, current cost/current proceeds, etc. Attribute is a narrower concept than measurement, which includes not only identifying the attribute to be measured but also selecting a scale of measurement (for example, units of money or units of constant purchasing power). "Property" is commonly used in the sciences to describe the trait or aspect of an object being measured, such as the length of a table or the weight of a stone. But "property" may be confused with land and buildings in financial reporting contexts, and "attribute" has become common in accounting literature and is used in this Statement.

Since recognition often involves recording changes in assets and liabilities, it often raises the question of whether the amount of an attribute should be changed or whether a different attribute should be used in its place. In any event, since the changes in an asset or liability and in the attribute occur at the same time, it is often difficult to separate recognition from measurement problems.

Five different attributes of assets and liabilities are used in present accounting practice. The following is based on paragraph 67 of Concepts Statement 5, which describes the attributes and gives examples of the kinds of assets for which each attribute is commonly reported:

1. *Historical cost.* The amount of cash or its equivalent paid to acquire an asset, usually adjusted after acquisition for amortization or other allocations (for example, property, plant, equipment, and most inventories).
2. *Current cost.* The amount that would have to be paid if the same or an equivalent asset were acquired currently (for example, some inventories).
3. *Current market value.* The amount that could be obtained by selling an asset in orderly liquidation (for example, marketable securities).
4. *Net realizable value.* The nondiscounted amount into which an asset is expected to be converted in due course of business less direct costs necessary to make that conversion (for example, short-term receivables).
5. *Present (or discounted) value of future cash flows.* The present value of future cash inflows into which an asset is expected to be converted in due course of business less present values of cash outflows necessary to obtain those inflows (for example, long-term receivables).

Recognition and Measurement—Description Rather Than Concepts.   The preceding pages have described several areas in which Concepts Statement 5 has furthered the conceptual framework, at least to some extent—in identifying what a full set of financial statements comprises, in expanding and clarifying what constitutes recognition, in explaining the relationship between comprehensive income and its component part, earnings, and in endorsing financial capital maintenance.

Although the Statement's name implies that it gives conceptual guidance on recognition and measurement, its conceptual contributions to financial reporting are not really in those two areas.

As a result of compromises necessary to issue it, much of Concepts Statement 5 merely describes present practice and some of the reasons that have been used to support or explain it but provides little or no conceptual basis for analyzing and attempting to resolve the controversial issues of recognition and measurement about which accountants have disagreed for years.

The FASB knew all along that recognition and measurement concepts would be controversial. Each component of the conceptual framework—the objectives, the qualitative characteristics, the elements of financial statements, recognition and measurement—is successively less abstract and more concrete than the one before. Recognition and measurement are the most concrete and least abstract of the components because they are necessarily at the point at which concepts and practice converge. They are the components in which practicing accountants have been most interested because they determine what actually gets into the numbers and totals in the financial statements. While few practitioners may be interested in what they may see as abstractions—such as objectives, qualitative characteristics, and definitions—most are interested in a change in revenue recognition or the measured attribute of an asset, or perhaps in reporting the effects of inflation, and they usually feel that they have a vested interest in the Board's decisions regarding recognition and measurement and in resisting changes that may adversely affect their future reporting.

Accountants have strongly held, and ultimately polarizing, views about which is the most relevant and reliable attribute to be measured and about the circumstances needed for recognizing changes in attributes and changes in the amounts of an attribute. Proponents of the present model—which often is mislabeled historical cost accounting because it is actually a mixture of historical costs, current costs, current exit values, net realizable values, and present values—fiercely defend it and broach no discussion of alternatives for fear that any change would portend its abandonment in favor of current value accounting, a term that is used generically to refer to the continuous use of any attribute other than historical cost. Similarly, proponents of various current cost or current value models are equally unyielding, often almost as critical of other current value or current cost models that compete with their own favorite model as they are of the historical-cost model for its failure to recognize the realities of changing values and changing prices.

The Board was as badly split on recognition and measurement as the constituency. Although most Board members could see the deficiencies in the current model, a majority of the Board could not accept a current value or current cost measurement system, even at a conceptual level. Therefore, instead of indicating a preferred accounting model or otherwise offering conceptual guidance about measurement, Concepts Statement 5 merely acknowledged that present practice consists of a mix of five attributes for measuring items in financial statements and said that the Board "expects the use of different attributes to continue" (paragraph 66). Beyond that, it said that "information based on current prices should be recognized if it is sufficiently relevant and reliable to justify the costs involved and more relevant than alternative information" (paragraph 90), which was extremely weak guidance. Whereas a neutral exposition of alternatives was appropriate for a Discussion Memorandum, a litany of present measurement practices with neither conceptual analysis or evaluation nor guidance for making choices was not proper for a Concepts Statement.

In merely describing current practice, Concepts Statement 5 is a throwback to statements of accounting principles produced by the "distillation of experience" school of thought—an essentially practical, not a conceptual, effort. Its prescriptions for improving practice are reminiscent of those of the Committee on Accounting Procedure or the APB: Measurement problems will be resolved on a case-by-case basis. Unfortunately, that approach worked only marginally well for those now-defunct bodies.

Oscar Gellein called the discussion of recognition in the Exposure Draft that ultimately became part of Concepts Statement 5 "a helpful distillation of current recognition practices." However, he also saw that the Statement would not advance financial reporting in the area of recognition and measurement:

> The umbrella is broad enough to cover virtually all current practices, but not conceptually directed toward either narrowing those practices or preventing their proliferation. . . . Recognition is the

watershed issue in the conceptual framework in the sense that hierarchically it is the ultimate stage of conceptual concreteness. Without that kind of conceptual guidance, there is the risk of reversion to ad hoc rules in determining accounting methods.[155]

David Solomons criticized Concepts Statement 5 for distorting the process of formulating future accounting standards.[156] He noted that in several places it asserts that concepts are to be developed as the standards-setting process evolves, citing these examples:

> The Board expects the concept of earnings to be subject to the process of gradual change or evolution that has characterized the development of net income. [paragraph 35]

> Future standards may change what is recognized as components of earnings. . . . Moreover, because of the differences between earnings and comprehensive income, future standards also may recognize certain changes in net assets as components of comprehensive income but not as components of earnings. [paragraph 51]

> The Board believes that further development of recognition, measurement, and display matters will occur as the concepts are applied at the standards level. [paragraph 108]

Solomons was not at all persuaded by the Board's apparent argument, represented by those excerpts, that concepts could be a by-product of the standards-setting process:

> These appeals to evolution should be seen as what they are—a cop-out. If all that is needed to improve our accounting model is reliance on evolution and the natural selection that results from the development of standards, why was an expensive and protracted conceptual framework project necessary in the first place? It goes without saying that concepts and practices should evolve as conditions change. But if the conceptual framework can do no more than point that out, who needs it? And, for that matter, if progress is simply a matter of waiting for evolution, who needs the FASB?[157]

Concepts Statement 5 almost seems to have anticipated the challenges to its legitimacy as a Statement of recognition and measurement concepts and capitulated in its second and third paragraphs, which could serve as its epitaph:

> The recognition criteria and guidance in this Statement are generally consistent with current practice and do not imply radical change. Nor do they foreclose the possibility of future changes in practice. The Board intends future change to occur in the gradual, evolutionary way that has characterized past change.

> This Statement also . . . notes that . . . the Board expects the use of different attributes. . . . [and] nominal units of money (that is, unadjusted for changes in purchasing power over time) . . . to continue.

Concepts Statement 5 does make some noteworthy conceptual contributions—they are just not on recognition and measurement.

(v) Using Cash Flow Information and Present Value in Accounting Determinations. Cash flow information and present value are used in some accounting determinations now, but their application is not consistent. Further, those devices are not used in other accounting determinations in which they might be used. The reason for both of those conditions has been the lack of an authoritative framework within which to consider the issues involved.

---

[155] Gellein, "Financial Reporting: The State of Standard Setting," p. 14.

[156] David Solomons, "The FASB's Conceptual Framework: An Evaluation," *The Journal of Accountancy*, June 1986, p. 122.

[157] Id., p. 122.

To rectify that lack, the FASB initiated a project in October 1988 that culminated in publication of its Concepts Statement No. 7, *Using Cash Flow Information and Present Value in Accounting Measurements*, in February 2000. The Statement considers issues in determining amounts but not issues in recognition. It is confined to determinations at initial recognition, fresh-start determinations, and amortization based on future cash flows, in situations other than those in which transactions involving cash or other assets paid or received are involved or in which observations of fair values in the marketplace are available.

The Board defines *fair value* of an asset (or liability) in its Concepts Statement No. 7 much the same as it always has:

> The amount at which an asset (or liability) could be bought (or incurred) or sold (or settled) in a current transaction between willing parties, that is, other than in a forced or liquidation sale.

That definition is ambiguous. It does not say who the "willing parties" are. One of the willing parties must be the owner of the asset. If the owner is not willing to sell, there would be no "current transaction." The other must be a prospective buyer who is willing to pay at least as much as the minimum amount for which the owner is willing to sell. For many if not most assets, no such buyer exists.

The FASB avoids the ambiguity in its definition of *fair value* in its Preliminary Views, *Reporting Financial Instruments and Certain Related Assets and Liabilities at Fair Value*, issued on December 14, 1999:

> Fair value is an estimate of the price an entity would have realized if it had sold an asset or paid if it had been relieved of a liability on the reporting date in an arm's-length exchange motivated by normal business considerations. That is, it is an estimate of an exit price determined by market interactions. [par. 47]

Why the FASB issued two different definitions of *fair value* at about the same time is not clear. Subsequently in this supplement, the assumption is made that *fair value* refers to the maximum amount any buyer is willing to pay for the asset, that is, the asset's current selling price, which generally agrees with the definition in the Preliminary Views.

Cash flow information and present value are linked. Present value is considered for use only in connection with the use of future cash flow information in accounting determinations. The Statement provides a framework for using future cash flows at the basis for accounting determinations. The framework describes the objective of using present value in such determinations and provides general principles for its use, especially when the amount of future cash flows, their timing, or both are uncertain.

Fundamental Questions Relevant to Determinations that Use Present Value Techniques.   The Statement addresses the following fundamental questions relevant to determinations that use future cash flows and present value techniques:

- What is the objective, or objectives, of present value when it is used in determinations at initial recognition of assets or liabilities?
- Does the objective differ in subsequent fresh-start determinations of assets and liabilities?
- Do determinations of liabilities require objectives, or present problems, different from those of determinations of assets?
- How should estimates of cash flows and interest rates be developed?
- What is the objective, or objectives, of present value when it is used in the amortization of existing assets and liabilities?
- If present value is used in the amortization of assets and liabilities, how should the technique be applied when estimates of cash flows change?

The Time Value of Money.   Present value techniques (discounting using the compound interest formula) are used for the purpose of incorporating in accounting determinations the time value of money. The time value of money refers to the fact that the earlier money is to be obtained, the more valuable the prospective receipt is; and the later money needs to be paid, the less burdensome the obligation to pay it is. Those facts are reflected in accounting determinations involving future cash receipts or future cash payments that incorporate present value techniques. The Board justifies its consideration of present value techniques based on the facts that present value is one of the foundations of economics and corporate finance, that the computation of present value is part of most modern asset-pricing models, and that the present value of future cash flows is implicit in all market prices.

The Board does not say what the implicit relationship is. It is the following: (1) The seller believes that the present value of the future cash receipts the seller could obtain in the future from using the object being sold is *less than* the amount of money represented by the price involved in the sale or *less than* the present value the seller could receive from an alternative investment the seller could make with the proceeds of sale—that is why the seller is willing to sell at the price of the sale—and (2) the buyer believes that the present value of the future cash receipts the buyer will receive in the future from using the object being sold is *more than* the amount of money represented by the price involved in the sale—that is why the buyer is willing to buy at the price of the sale. Thus, the price of the sale does not equal the present value as seen by either the buyer or the seller.

The Statement illustrates the time value of money with (1) an asset with a contractual cash receipt of $10,000 due in one day, certain of receipt (though nothing about the future is certain); (2) an asset with a contractual cash receipt of $10,000 due in 10 years, certain of receipt; (3) an asset with a contractual cash receipt of $10,000 dues in one day, with the receipt to be equal to or less than $10,000; (4) an asset with a contractual cash receipt of $10,000 due in 10 years, with the receipt to be equal to or less than $10,000; and (5) an asset with an expected cash receipt of $10,000 due in 10 years, with the receipt to be at least $8,000 but not more than $12,000. By reporting the assets all at the amounts contracted or expected to be received, they would all be reported at the gross amounts of $10,000. That would be misleading, because they are not economically the same—they differ on timing and certainty of receipt—and a buyer who wants to maximize his or her resources would not agree to pay the same amount for all of the assets.

Elements of Present Value Determinations.   Discounting the gross amounts $10,000 using present value techniques and discount rates and periods that reflect the diverse timing and diverse certainty of receipt of the assets would reflect the time value of money and work to counteract the misleading effect. The following are the elements of such a present value calculation:

- An estimate of the amounts and timing of anticipated future cash receipts and payments related to the asset
- Anticipated possible variations in those amounts or timing
- The interest rate that would reflect the pure time value of money (i.e., not involving uncertainty), which is the risk-free interest rate (U.S. government securities or U.S. government–backed securities are considered to be risk free. But are they? Confederate debt and the bonds of Tsar Nicholas II, for example, were not.)
- The interest-rate premium for bearing the uncertainty
- Other, sometimes unidentifiable, factors, such as illiquidity and market imperfections

Using Present Value to Approximate Fair Value at Initial Recognition and for Fresh-Start Determinations.   Fair value incorporates all of those elements. When used in accounting determinations at initial recognition and fresh-start determinations, present values are used only to approximate fair values that cannot be determined directly from the market.

The Board states that the fair value, if determinable, would encompass the consensus view of those interested in buying the asset, of the asset's utility, future cash flow, uncertainties surrounding the cash flows, and discount in the price demanded for the uncertainties. (There is, however, no such consensus view. There is only one view for each prospective buyer, which differs among prospective buyers. The term *consensus* implies that the prospective buyers agree. The fair value is the maximum price any prospective buyer would be willing to pay for the asset, not a consensus price.)

The usual determination of the amount of an asset at initial recognition is its cash price in the exchange in which it is acquired if it is acquired in an exchange in which there is a cash price (the Board notes an exception related to unstated rights or privileges described in APB Opinion No. 21).

If an asset is acquired other than in such an exchange, the Board states that its amount should be determined when acquired at fair value. If the asset is acquired in a nonmonetary exchange, its amount should be determined to be the fair value of the asset surrendered to obtain it, in conformity with APB Opinion No. 29.

Fair value can be determined most satisfactorily by reference to the price in a recent exchange for cash involving an asset similar to the asset whose amount is being determined. If there is no such exchange, the Board contends that amounts may have to be determined by estimating the future cash flows involved with the asset and applying present value techniques. The objective in determining the discount rate in the present value calculation is that contained in APB Opinion No. 21:

> The objective is to approximate the rate which would have resulted if an independent borrower and an independent lender had negotiated a similar transaction under comparable terms and conditions with the option to pay the cash price upon purchase or to give a note for the amount of the purchase which bears the prevailing rate of interest to maturity.

The principles that apply to determinations at initial recognition apply equally for fresh-start determinations. Because an asset subject to a fresh-start determination is not then acquired in an exchange involving a cash price, its amount cannot be determined directly at such a price. Determining its amount is necessarily confined to concepts involving fair value, as discussed above for assets acquired other than in exchanges involving a cash price.

The Board lists the following existing accounting conventions alternative to fair value that incorporate the elements of a present value calculation listed above to diverse extents: value-in-use (entity-specific determinations), effective-settlement determinations for liabilities, and cost-accumulation or cost-accrual determinations. Each of those conventions contains factors that are specific to the reporting entity: It adds factors not contemplated in the price of an exchange involving the kind of asset involved and assumptions of the entity's management not made by buyers and sellers in the market, or it excludes factors contemplated by buyers and sellers in the market, or both. The alternative conventions are related to the fact that the best estimate by the entity's management of the present value of uncertain future cash flows may differ from the fair value of those cash flows. The reasons the management's expectations might differ from those expected by buyers and sellers in the market include:

- The management might intend to use the asset or settle the liability in a manner different from that contemplated by the buyers and sellers.
- The management might prefer to retain the risk involved in a liability rather than transfer the risk to another party.
- The entity might benefit, for example, from tax or zoning variances, private information, trade secrets, or processes not otherwise available.
- The entity might be able to take advantage of internal resources not available at the entity's cost to realize or pay amounts involved in the asset or liability.

Those items represent contemplated future comparative advantages enjoyed by the reporting entity relative to the asset or liability over those enjoyed by other buyers or sellers in the market.

If the amount of an asset or liability is determined at initial recognition or at a fresh start using one of those alternative conventions and the offset to the amount is to revenue or expense, the contemplated future comparative advantage is reported in income at initial recognition or fresh-start determination. If the amount of an asset or liability is determined at those times using fair value, the contemplated future comparative advantage is reported in the periods in which it realizes assets or settles liabilities at amounts that differ from fair value.

Some suggest that the amounts of assets and liabilities be determined at initial recognition or at a fresh start at amounts that incorporate the contemplated future comparative advantages, because they contend that that would better help users of financial statements assess the amounts and timing of prospective cash receipts to them. The FASB points out, however, that such reporting ignores the uncertainties involved in the prospective cash flows. It further points out that though knowledge of management's expectations is often useful and informative, the market is the final arbiter of asset and liability values, and that fair value, which incorporates those values, results in neutral, complete, and representational faithful determinations of the economic characteristics of the asset or liability. Further, the alternative conventions imply various discount rates, such as an asset-earning rate, an incremental-borrowing rate, or an embedded interest rate, with no conceptual basis for choosing among them. For all of those reasons, the FASB has decided that, as stated above, the amount of an asset or liability should be determined at initial recognition or at a fresh start at fair value. It points out, however, that a lack of other data might sometimes require incorporating the expectations of the reporting entity's management in implementing the fair value principle.

Implementing the Determination of Fair Value Using Present Value Techniques.   To implement the determination of fair value using present value techniques, the risk-free interest rate must be determined, future cash flows must be estimated, the uncertainty involved in those cash flows must be estimated, and other factors affecting the estimated cash flow, such as possible variations in their amounts or timing, illiquidity, or market imperfections, must be considered. There are two ways to incorporate those factors in the calculation. First, the uncertainty and the other factors may be used to determine risk-adjusted estimates of the future cash flows and the pure risk-free interest rate applied to them. Second, the risk-free interest rate may be adjusted for the uncertainty and the other factors to determine a risk-adjusted interest rate and applied to the unadjusted estimated future cash flows.

Before getting into the details of determining the factors required for the calculation of present value, the Board lists general principles to follow to avoid biasing the calculation:

- To the extent possible, estimated cash flows and interest rates should reflect assumptions that would be considered in contemplating an arm's-length transaction for cash.
- Interest rates used should reflect assumptions consistent with those inherent in the estimated cash flows. For example, an interest rate of 12 percent should be applied to contractual cash flows of a loan with characteristics that reflect that rate.
- Estimated cash flows and interest rates should not be deliberately overstated or understated to obtain a desired reporting result.
- The estimated cash flows and interest rates should reflect the range of possible outcomes.

If the asset or liability consists of contractual cash flows (a promised series of future cash receipts or payments), they should be used as the future cash flows in the calculation. A single interest rate, often described as "the rate commensurate with the risk," is consistent for assets and liabilities with contractual cash flows with the manner in which marketplace participants describe assets and liabilities, such as a "12 percent bond." Such an approach is useful for determinations in which comparable assets and liabilities can be observed in the marketplace.

However, that approach is unsuited for complex problems of amount determination, including determination of the amounts of nonfinancial assets and liabilities for which there is no market for the asset or liability or for a comparable asset or liability. If no contractual cash flows are involved, the cash flows must be estimated. To determine the present value of such an asset or liability, the observable rate of interest of a comparable asset or liability must be used. The comparable asset or liability must have cash flows whose characteristics are similar to those of the asset or liability whose amount is being determined. The following must be done to do so:

- Identify the set of cash flows that will be discounted.
- Identify another asset or liability in the marketplace that appears to have similar cash flow characteristics.
- Compare the cash flow sets from the two items to make sure that they are similar (e.g., are both sets contractual cash flows, or is one contractual and the other an estimated cash flow?).
- Evaluate whether there is an element in one item that is not present in the other (e.g., is one less liquid than the other?).
- Evaluate whether both sets of cash flows are likely to behave (vary) in a similar fashion under changing economic conditions (FASB Concepts Statement No. 7, par. 44).

In complex situations, the future cash flows should be determined by the expected cash flow approach. That approach uses the sum of probability-weighted amounts in a range of possible estimated amounts. The Board illustrates that as follows for uncertain amounts. The probabilities of cash flows are $100 with a probability of 10 percent, $200 with a probability of 60 percent, and $300 with a probability of 30 percent. The expected cash flow is ($100 × 10%) + ($200 × 60%) + ($300 × 30%) = $220. It illustrates that for uncertain timing of receipts or payments as follows. An estimated cash flow of $1,000 may be received or paid in one year with a probability of 10 percent, in two years with a probability of 60 percent, or in three years with a probability of 30 percent. The comparable interest rates are 5 percent for one year, 5.25 percent for two years, and 5.5 percent for three years. The expected present value is ([$1,000 discounted at 5% for one year = $952.38[158]] × 10%) + ([$1,000 discounted at 5.25% for two years = $902.73[159]] × 60%) + ([$1,000 discounted at 5.5% for three years = $851.61[160]] × 30%) = $95.24 + $541.64 + $255.48 = $892.36.

Those illustrations go beyond the use of present value techniques for "contractual rights to receive money or contractual obligations to pay money on fixed or determinable dates" (APB Opinion No. 21, par. 2). Such techniques cannot reflect uncertainties in timing. Calculations such as those illustrated are not routinely used by accountants. They are required, however, in determinations of pensions, other postretirement benefits, and some insurance liabilities. They are allowed for determination of impairment of long-lived assets and estimating the fair value of financial instruments. The Board answers those who may object to applying probabilities to highly subjective estimates of future cash flows by stating that the approach without applying probabilities uses the same subjective estimates without the "computational transparency" of the illustrated approach.

The Board discusses these situations as examples in which the information needed to implement the calculations is limited:

- The estimated amount is between $50 and $250, with no amount more likely than another. The estimated expected cash flow is ($50 + $250) ÷ 2 = $150.
- The estimated amount is between $50 and $250, and $100 is most likely. The probabilities are not known. The estimated expected cash flow is ($50 + $100 + $250) ÷ 3 = $133.33.
- It is estimated that there is a 10 percent probability that the amount will be $50, a 30 percent probability that the amount will be $250, and a 60 percent probability that the amount will be $100. The estimated expected cash flow is ($50 × 10%) + ($250 × 30%) + ($100 × 60%) = $140.

---

[158] $952.38 × 1.05 = $1,000.
[159] $902.73 × 1.0525 × 1.0525 = $1,000.
[160] $851.61 × 1.055 × 1.055 × 1.055 = $1,000.

Obtaining the data to make such complex calculations can be expensive. The Board states that, as usual, the cost of implementing this technique should be commensurate with the benefits to be obtained from it by the users of financial statements.

The Board notes objections to the expected cash flow technique in selected circumstances. For example, an asset or liability has an expected cash flow of $10 with a 90 percent probability and an expected cash flow of $1,000 with a 10 percent probability. The technique arrives at a fair value of ($10 × .9) + ($1,000 × .1) = $109. They say that represents neither the $10 nor the $1,000. The Board says the $109 represents the fair value, which neither the $10 nor the $1,000 represents.

Relationship to Accounting for Contingencies.   Statement of Concepts No. 7 focuses on determination of amounts, not on recognition. In contrast, FASB Statement of Standards No. 5 and FASB Interpretation No. 14 focus on recognition of loss "contingencies." (That is a misnomer. Statement No. 5 calls for recognition of a loss if it is probable that an asset *has been* impaired or a liability or an increase in a liability *has been* incurred and that future events will confirm the loss. There is nothing contingent about such events.) Nevertheless, the Statements interact.

For example, determining the fair value of a loan involves expectations about potential default, but recognizing a loss under Statement No. 5 requires that it be probable that a loss has been incurred. The Board presents an illustration that it states raises issues that are "intractable" and beyond the scope of Statement No. 7. If the preceding illustration is changed to make the 90 percent probability a cash flow of $0, the expected cash flow is $100 but Statement No. 5 would seem to call for recognition of the liability at $0. Or, if a reporting entity had 10 potential liabilities with the characteristics of this illustration with the outcomes of the 10 independent of one another, some would conclude that a probable loss is $1,000, because one in 10 will probably materialize. Statement No. 5 would on that basis report a loss of $1,000, but Statement No. 7 would report no loss.

Some losses are reported by adjustment to the existing amortization or reporting convention not involving a current interest rate, not through a fresh-start determination. Such adjustments are beyond the scope of Statement No. 7. A fresh-start determination such as required by FASB Statement of Standards No. 121 is consistent with Statement No. 7.

FASB Interpretation No. 14 prescribes a determination of an amount equal to the minimum value in the range involved. That is inconsistent with Statement No. 7.

Risk and Uncertainty.   The fair value estimate should include the amount sellers are able to receive for bearing the risk inherent in the cash flows from the asset, if it is identifiable, determinable, and significant. Including an arbitrary adjustment for risk or arbitrarily excluding an adjustment for risk in unacceptable. Matrix pricing, option-adjusted spread models, and fundamental analysis are ways to estimate the risk adjustment. However, if no reliable estimate of the risk premium can be obtained or if it is small compared with the potential error in estimating the future cash flows, the risk-free interest rate may be preferable to use.

The uncertainty involved in the risk of owning the asset should be described clearly. For example, a lender on 1,000 loans may set the interest rate based on the view that some loans will default, whereas another lender on 1,000 loans may set the interest rate based on the view that 150 loans will default. Determination of the present value in those situations should make the distinction.

A purchaser of an asset with a given certain expected future cash flow would pay more for the asset than for an asset with the same expected future cash flow but that involves uncertainty. That is because people prefer to avoid uncertainty (are "risk-averse"). For that reason, the Board concludes that uncertainty should be factored into determination of present value to approximate fair value. The risk premium, the premium for uncertainty, is often difficult to determine. The Statement describes approaches to the problem, including portfolio theory, behavioral finance theory, and the Capital Asset Pricing Model, including problems with and disputes over each.

Relevance and Reliability.   Calculations to determine fair values in the absence of readily observable market values, whether to determine future cash flows or present values, use estimates and therefore are inherently imprecise. Nevertheless, though different conclusions may be reached about the amount and timing of future cash flows and adjustments for uncertainty and risk, the use of expected future cash flows and simplifying assumptions permits the determination of present values that are sufficiently reliable and much more relevant than undiscounted amounts.

Present Value in the Determination of Liability Amounts.   The Statement discusses techniques to estimate the fair value of a liability at initial recognition or at a fresh start. The objective is to estimate the value of the assets to either settle the liability with the holder or transfer the liability to an entity of comparable credit standing. One way is to estimate the price at which the liability can be sold as an asset to another entity. The other way is to estimate the price the reporting entity would have to pay another entity to assume the liability. Both of those involve the credit standing of the reporting entity. The price at which the liability can be sold or that the reporting entity would have to pay another entity to assume the liability is affected by the perceived risk of holding the liability as an asset. The greater the perceived risk, the less another entity would agree to pay to obtain the liability as an asset (the greater the required effective interest rate), and vice versa.

In complex liabilities, such as a liability with a range of possible outflows, the effect of risk may be more effectively included by computing expected cash flows.

Including the reporting entity's credit standing in the determination of the amount at which to report a liability at initial recognition and at a fresh start has been controversial, with some contending that such reporting involves a paradox—income is reported when the reporting entity's credit standing declines. The FASB is adamant, however: "... there is no rationale for why, in initial or fresh-start measurement, the recorded amount of a liability should reflect something other than the price that would exist in the marketplace."[161] In fact, Lorensen has presented such a rationale, an argument in favor of reporting a liability at its risk-free funding rate.[162]

The FASB goes on to disagree that there is a paradox:

> A change in credit standing represents a change in the relative positions of the two classes of claimants (shareholders and creditors) to an entity's assets. If the credit standing diminishes, the fair value of creditors' claims diminishes. The amount of shareholders' residual claim to the entity's assets may appear to increase, but that increase probably is offset by losses that may have occasioned the decline in credit standing. Because shareholders usually cannot be called on to pay a corporation's liabilities, the amount of their residual claims approaches, and is limited by, zero. Thus, a change in the position of borrowers necessarily alters the position of shareholders, and vice versa.

> The failure to include changes in credit standing in the measurement of a liability ignores economic differences between liabilities. Consider the case of an entity that has two classes of borrowing. Class One was transacted when the entity had a strong credit standing and a correspondingly low interest rate. Class Two is new and was transacted under the entity's current lower credit standing. Both classes trade in the marketplace based on the entity's current credit standing. If the two liabilities are subject to fresh-start measurement, failing to include changes in the entity's credit standing makes the classes of borrowings seem different—even though the marketplace evaluates the quality of their respective cash flows as similar to one another. (Statement of Concepts No. 7, par. 86–88)

The main objection to the FASB's defense is that it relies on the effects on parties separate from the reporting entity: the creditors and the shareholders. The financial report on a reporting entity should be solely about effects of events on the reporting entity, not on any other entity. Regardless of changes in the values of claims to the creditors or rights of shareholders, the reporting entity has the same obligation to make the same payments, unchanged by changes affecting the creditors or shareholders.

---

[161] Statement of Concepts No. 7, par. 85.

[162] Leonard Lorensen, "Accounting Research Monograph No. 4," *Accounting for Liabilities* (New York: AICPA, 1992).

The FASB states that the reporting entity's reported shareholders' equity "may appear" to increase using the kind of reporting it prefers in the face of a decline in the credit standing of the reporting entity. In fact, it does increase. The FASB says that the increase probably is offset by losses that may have occasioned the decline in credit standing. The message is that it is correct to, in effect, reverse reporting such losses. No justification for such a reversal is offered or apparent.

Though, as the FASB states, the marketplace evaluates the quality of the respective cash flows of the Class One and Class Two liabilities it illustrates as similar to one another, their promised cash flows are different, because their interest payments are different, reflecting the difference in the credit standing between the times they were incurred. Under the reporting recommended by Lorensen, they would appear different. Were their required cash flows the same, they would appear the same under the reporting recommended by Lorensen.

Interest Methods of Allocation. All methods of so-called systematic and rational allocation use formulas selected at the beginning of the periods of allocation. They are said to report changes in value, utility, or substance of assets and liabilities over time, though the FASB states that "they are not measurements." Interest methods of allocation use the compound interest formula, for example, for amortization of discount or premium as prescribed by APB Opinion No. 21. They are considered most relevant to circumstances in which a borrowing and a lending is involved, similar assets or liabilities are allocated using the interest method, a set of estimated future cash flows is closely associated, and the calculation at initial recognition was based on present value.

Applying an interest method of allocation requires description of the kind of cash flow (promised, expected, etc.), the kind of interest rate to be used (effective or other), application of the rate (constant effective or a series of annual), and how to report changes in the amount or timing of the estimated cash flows. Changes in market interest rates are ignored. Changes in estimates of cash flows are included in a fresh-start calculation or affect the interest amortization plan. The plan may be affected by a prospective approach, computing a new effective interest rate, a catch-up approach, adjusting the carrying amount of the asset or liability to the amount it would have been had the new estimate been made originally, or a retrospective approach based on actual cash flows to date and newly estimated remaining cash flows. The FASB expresses a preference for the catch-up approach. Though some consider the retrospective approach best, the cost of applying it may be prohibitive.

2.4 INVITATION TO LEARN MORE

This chapter is more of a generous introduction to the FASB's conceptual framework than a comprehensive description or analysis of it. About half of the chapter is concerned with the antecedents of the conceptual framework, why the FASB undertook it, and why it contains the particular set of concepts that it does. The framework cannot really be understood without that background. The descriptions of the various Concepts Statements emphasized their major conclusions and some of the explanation they provide but did not go into them deeply enough to provide a substitute for reading them. Readers are urged to read the Concepts Statements themselves.

The FASB has used the completed parts of the framework with considerable success. The Board's constituents also have learned to use the framework, partly at least because they have discovered that they are more likely to influence the Board if they do. Both the Board and the constituents have also found that at times the concepts appear to work better than at other times, and undoubtedly they sometimes could have been more soundly applied. As much of the chapter suggests, some parts of the conceptual framework are still controversial, partly at least because long-held views die hard. The framework remains unfinished, although the Board gives no sign of completing it in the near future.

Despite the fact that the Board has left it incomplete, the FASB's conceptual framework

- Is the first reasonably successful effort by a standards-setting body to formulate and use an integrated set of financial accounting concepts

- Has fundamentally changed the way financial accounting standards are set in the United States
- Has provided a model for the International Accounting Standards Committee and several national standards-setting bodies in other English-speaking countries, which not only have set out their own concepts but also clearly have been influenced by the FASB's Concepts Statements, sometimes to the point of adopting the same or virtually the same set of concepts

The Concepts Statements can continue to contribute significantly to better financial accounting and reporting standards. However, the conceptual framework is primarily a set of tools in the hands of standards setters. To live up to their promise, sound concepts require "the right blend of characteristics in standard setters—independence of mind, intellectual integrity, judicial temperament, and a generous portion of wisdom."[163]

Looking forward, challenges will be presented by the current business environment—where joint ventures, licensing arrangements and multiple subsidiaries blur the lines of the traditional entity, and perhaps challenge the concepts of financial reporting and accounting.[164]

2.5 SOURCES AND SUGGESTED REFERENCES

Accounting Research Bulletin No. 43, *Restatement and Revision of Accounting Research Bulletins.* New York: American Institute of Accountants, 1953.

American Accounting Association, Committee on Concepts and Standards Underlying Corporate Financial Statements. *Accounting and Reporting Standards for Corporate Financial Statements and Preceding Statements and Supplements.* Iowa City, Iowa: American Accounting Association, 1957.

American Accounting Association, Executive Committee. "A Tentative Statement of Accounting Principles Underlying Corporate Financial Statements." *The Accounting Review,* June 19, 1936, pp. 187–191. [Reprinted in *Accounting and Reporting Standards for Corporate Financial Statements and Preceding Statements and Supplements*, pp. 60–64.]

Anton, Hector R. "Objectives of Financial Accounting: Review and Analysis." *The Journal of Accountancy,* January 1976, pp. 40–51.

APB Statement No. 4, *Basic Concepts and Accounting Principles Underlying Financial Statements of Business Enterprises.* New York: American Institute of Certified Public Accountants, 1970.

Audits of Corporate Accounts: Correspondence between the Special Committee on Cooperation with Stock Exchanges of the American Institute of Accountants and the Committee on Stock List of the New York Stock Exchange, 1932–1934. New York: American Institute of Accountants, 1934. [Reprinted, New York: American Institute of Certified Public Accountants, 1963; and in Zeff, *Forging Accounting Principles in Five Countries* (full reference below), pp. 237–247.]

Baxter, W. T., ed. Introduction. *Studies in Accounting.* London: The Macmillan Company, 1950. [Reprinted as "Introduction to the First Edition" in second and third editions: Baxter, W. T. and Sidney Davidson, eds. *Studies in Accounting Theory.* London: Sweet & Maxwell Ltd., 1962; and Baxter and Davidson, eds. *Studies in Accounting.* London: The Institute of Chartered Accountants in England and Wales, 1977.]

Berle, A. A., Jr. "Accounting and the Law." *The Accounting Review,* March 1938, pp. 9–15. [Reprinted in *The Journal of Accountancy*, May 1938, pp. 368–378.]

Bevis, Herman W. *Corporate Financial Reporting in a Competitive Environment.* New York: The Macmillan Company, 1965.

---

[163] Kirk, "Looking Back on Fourteen Years at the FASB: The Education of a Standard Setter," p. 17.

[164] Steven H. Wallman, "The Future of Accounting and Disclosure in an Evolving World: The Need for Dramatic Change." *Accounting Horizons.* September, 1995. For a further discussion of issues facing contemporary and future financial reporting see also: *Financial Reporting in the 1990s and Beyond*, a report of the Association for Investment Management and Research (AIMR), Peter H. Knutson, principal author, Charlottesville, VA, AIMR, 1993 and *A Comprehensive Business Reporting Model: Financial Reporting for Investors.* Charlottesville VA: CFA Institute, 2005.

Blough, Carman G. "Development of Accounting Principles in the United States." *Berkeley Symposium on the Foundations of Financial Accounting*. Berkeley: Schools of Business Administration, University of California, 1967, pp. 1–14; discussions by Carl Devine, pp. 15–19, and Stephen A. Zeff, pp. 20–25.

Bonbright, James C. *Principles of Public Utility Rates*. New York: Columbia University Press, 1961.

Byrne, Gilbert R. "To What Extent Can the Practice of Accounting Be Reduced to Rules and Standards?" *The Journal of Accountancy*, November 1937, pp. 364–379. [Reprinted in Moonitz, Maurice, and A. C. Littleton, eds. *Significant Accounting Essays*. Englewood Cliffs, New Jersey: Prentice-Hall, Inc., 1965, pp. 103–115.]

Carey, John L. *The Rise of the Accounting Profession to Responsibility and Authority, 1937–1969*. New York: American Institute of Certified Public Accountants, 1970.

CFA Institute. *A Comprehensive Business Reporting Model: Financial Reporting for Investors*. Charlottesville VA: CFA Institute, 2005. 62 pages.

Chambers, R. J. "Why Bother with Postulates?" *Journal of Accounting Research*, Spring 1963, pp. 3–15. [Reprinted in Zeff, *The Accounting Postulates and Principles Controversy of the 1960s* (full reference below).]

Changing Concepts of Business Income. Report of the Study Group on Business Income. New York: The Macmillan Company, 1952.

Chatfield, Michael. Postulates and Principles. Chapter 20 in *A History of Accounting Thought*, revised ed. Huntington, New York: Robert E. Krieger Publishing Company, 1977.

"Comments on 'Accounting for Income Taxes.'" A Statement by the Committee on Accounting Principles and Practice of the New Jersey Society of Certified Public Accountants. *The Journal of Accountancy*, March 1945, pp. 235–240.

Conceptual Framework for Financial Accounting and Reporting: Elements of Financial Statements and Their Measurement. FASB Discussion Memorandum. Stamford, Connecticut: Financial Accounting Standards Board, December 2, 1976.

Conceptual Frameworks for Financial Accounting (Proceedings of a conference at the Harvard Business School, October 1–2, 1982), edited by H. David Sherman. Cambridge: President and Fellows of Harvard College, circa 1984.

Disclosure of Departures from Opinions of the Accounting Principles Board. Special Bulletin. New York: American Institute of Certified Public Accountants, 1964. [Reprinted in Zeff, *Forging Accounting Principles in Five Countries* (full reference below), pp. 266–268.]

Establishing Financial Accounting Standards. Report of the Study on Establishment of Accounting Principles. New York: American Institute of Certified Public Accountants, March 29, 1972. (Often called the Wheat Report, after the chairman, Francis M. Wheat, a former SEC commissioner.)

Financial Reporting in the 1990s and Beyond. A position paper prepared by Peter H. Knutson. Charlottesville, Virginia: The Association for Investment Management and Research, 1993.

Gellein, Oscar S. "Financial Reporting: The State of Standard Setting." In *Advances in Accounting*, Vol. 3, edited by Bill N. Schwartz. Greenwich, Connecticut: JAI Press Inc., 1986, pp. 3–23.

———, "Periodic Earnings: Income? or Indicator?" *Accounting Horizons*, June 1987, pp. 59–64.

———, "Primacy: Assets or Income?" In *Research in Accounting Regulation*, Vol. 6, edited by Gary John Previts. Greenwich, Connecticut: JAI Press, Inc., 1992, pp. 198–199.

Gilman, Stephen. *Accounting Concepts of Profit*. New York: The Ronald Press Company, 1939, pp. 167–257.

Gore, Pelham. *The FASB Conceptual Framework Project, 1973–1985, An Analysis*. Manchester and New York: Manchester University Press, 1992.

Grady, Paul, ed. *Memoirs and Accounting Thought of George O. May*. New York: The Ronald Press Company, 1962.

Greer, Howard C. "What Are Accepted Principles of Accounting?" *The Accounting Review*, March 1938, pp. 25–30.

Heath, Loyd C. "Accounting, Communication, and the Pygmalion Syndrome." *Accounting Horizons*, March 1987, pp. 1–8.

Hylton, Delmer. "On Matching Revenue with Expense." *The Accounting Review*, October 1965, pp. 824–828.

Jennings, Alvin R. "Present-Day Challenges in Financial Reporting." *The Journal of Accountancy*, January 1958, pp. 28–34. [Reprinted in Zeff, *The Accounting Postulates and Principles Controversy of the 1960s* (full reference below).]

Johnson, L. Todd, and Reed K. Storey. *Recognition in Financial Statements: Underlying Concepts and Practical Conventions.* FASB Research Report. Stamford, Connecticut: Financial Accounting Standards Board, 1982.

Kirk, Donald J. "Commentary on the Limitations of Accounting—A Response [to Eugene H. Flegm]." *Accounting Horizons,* September 1989, pp. 98–104.

————, "Looking Back on Fourteen Years at the FASB: The Education of a Standard Setter." *Accounting Horizons,* March 1988, pp. 8–17.

————, "Reflections on a 'Reconceptualization of Accounting': A Commentary on Parts I–IV of Homer Kripke's Paper, 'Reflections on the FASB's Conceptual Framework for Accounting and on Auditing.'" *Journal of Accounting, Auditing & Finance,* Winter 1989, pp. 83–105.

Knutson, Peter H. A report of the AIMR Financial Accounting Policy Committee, *Financial Reporting in the 1990s and Beyond.* Charlottesville, VA: AIMR, 1993. 98 pages. The AIMR is now known as the CFA Institute.

Kohler, Eric L. *A Dictionary for Accountants,* fifth ed. Englewood Cliffs, NJ: Prentice-Hall, Inc., 1975.

Lawler, John. "A Talk with George O. May." *The Journal of Accountancy,* June 1955, pp. 40–45.

Littleton, A. C. "Tests for Principles." *The Accounting Review,* March 1938, pp. 16–24.

Luper, Oral L., and Paul Rosenfield. "The APB Statement on Basic Concepts and Principles." *The Journal of Accountancy,* January 1971, pp. 46–51.

Manning, Bayless. *A Concise Textbook on Legal Capital,* 2d ed. Mineola, New York: The Foundation Press, Inc., 1981.

Mautz, Robert K. Basic Concepts of Accounting. In *Handbook of Modern Accounting,* edited by Sidney Davidson. New York: McGraw-Hill, 1970, pp. 1-1–1-15.

May, George O. "The Influence of Accounting on the Development of an Economy." *The Journal of Accountancy,* January 1936, pp. 11–22.

————, "Improvement in Financial Accounts." *The Journal of Accountancy,* May 1937, pp. 333–369.

————, "Principles of Accounting." *The Journal of Accountancy,* December 1937, pp. 423–425.

————, "Terminology of the Balance Sheet." *The Journal of Accountancy,* January 1942, pp. 35–36.

————, *Financial Accounting: A Distillation of Experience.* New York: The Macmillan Company, 1943.

————, "The Nature of the Financial Accounting Process." *The Accounting Review,* July 1943, pp. 189–193.

————, "Should the LIFO Principle Be Considered in Depreciation Accounting When Prices Vary Widely?" *The Journal of Accountancy,* December 1947, pp. 453–456.

————, "Business Combinations: An Alternative View." *The Journal of Accountancy,* April 1957, pp. 33–36.

————, "Income Accounting and Social Revolution." *The Journal of Accountancy,* June 1957, pp. 36–41.

————, "Generally Accepted Principles of Accounting." *The Journal of Accountancy,* January 1958, pp. 23–27.

Moonitz, Maurice. *The Basic Postulates of Accounting.* Accounting Research Study No. 1. New York: American Institute of Certified Public Accountants, 1961. [Reprinted in Zeff, *The Accounting Postulates and Principles Controversy of the 1960s* (full reference below).]

————, "The Changing Concept of Liabilities." *The Journal of Accountancy,* May 1960, pp. 41–46.

————, "Why Do We Need 'Postulates' and 'Principles'?" *The Journal of Accountancy,* December 1963, pp. 42–46. [Reprinted in Zeff, *The Accounting Postulates and Principles Controversy of the 1960s* (full reference below).]

————, *Obtaining Agreement on Standards in the Accounting Profession.* Studies in Accounting Research No. 8. Sarasota, Florida: American Accounting Association, 1974.

"News—ASB under Fire." *Accountancy,* November 1993, p. 16.

Objectives of Financial Statements. Report of the Study Group on the Objectives of Financial Statements. New York: American Institute of Certified Public Accountants, October 1973. (Often called the Trueblood Report, after the chairman, Robert M. Trueblood.)

Paton, William A., with the assistance of William A. Paton, Jr. *Asset Accounting.* New York: The Macmillan Company, 1952.

Paton, William A. "Comments on 'A Statement of Accounting Principles.'" *The Journal of Accountancy,* March 1938, pp. 196–207.

_____, Introduction. In *Foundations of Accounting Theory: Papers Given at the Accounting Theory Symposium, University of Florida, March 1970*, edited by Williard E. Stone. Gainesville, Florida: University of Florida Press, 1971.

Paton, William A., and A. C. Littleton. *An Introduction to Corporate Accounting Standards.* Ann Arbor, Michigan: American Accounting Association, 1940.

Report of Special Committee on Opinions of the Accounting Principles Board. New York: American Institute of Certified Public Accountants, Spring 1965. (Often called the Seidman Report, after the chairman, J. S. Seidman.)

"Report to Council of the Special Committee on Research Program." *The Journal of Accountancy,* December 1958, pp. 62–68. [Reprinted in Zeff, *Forging Accounting Principles in Five Countries* (full reference below), pp. 248–265; and in Zeff, *The Accounting Postulates and Principles Controversy of the 1960s* (full reference below).]

Rutherford, Brian. "Accountancy Issues—They Manipulate. You Smooth. I Self-hedge: Perhaps the World's Finest Know a Thing or Two After All." *Accountancy,* June 1995, p. 95.

Sanders, Thomas Henry; Henry Rand Hatfield; and Underhill Moore. *A Statement of Accounting Principles.* New York: American Institute of Accountants, 1938. [Reprinted, Columbus, Ohio: American Accounting Association, 1959.]

Shattke, R. W. "An Analysis of Accounting Principles Board Statement No. 4." *The Accounting Review,* April 1972, pp. 233–244.

Scott, Austin Wakeman. *Abridgement of the Law of Trusts.* Boston: Little, Brown and Company, 1960.

Scope and Implications of the Conceptual Framework Project. Stamford, Connecticut: Financial Accounting Standards Board, December 2, 1976.

Singleton-Green, Brian. "The ASB: Critics That Won't Be Pacified." *Accountancy,* November 1993, p. 26.

Solomons, David. "The FASB's Conceptual Framework: An Evaluation." *The Journal of Accountancy,* June 1986, pp. 114–124.

_____, *Making Accounting Policy: The Quest for Credibility in Financial Reporting.* New York: Oxford University Press, Inc., 1986.

Sprouse, Robert T. "Accounting for What-You-May-Call-Its." *The Journal of Accountancy,* October 1966, pp. 45–53.

_____, "Commentary on Financial Reporting—Developing a Conceptual Framework for Financial Reporting." *Accounting Horizons,* December 1988, pp. 121–127.

_____, "Commentary on Financial Reporting—Economic Consequences: The Volatility Bugaboo." *Accounting Horizons,* March 1987, p. 88.

Sprouse, Robert T., and Maurice Moonitz, *A Tentative Set of Broad Accounting Principles for Business Enterprises.* Accounting Research Study No. 3. New York: American Institute of Certified Public Accountants, 1962.

Staubus, George J. "An Analysis of APB Statement No. 4." *The Journal of Accountancy,* February 1972, pp. 36–43.

Sterling, Robert R. "On Theory Construction and Verification." *The Accounting Review,* July 1970, pp. 444–457.

Storey, Reed K. "Conditions Necessary for Developing a Conceptual Framework." FASB *Viewpoints*, March 3, 1981. [Excerpted in *The Journal of Accountancy*, June 1981, pp. 84–96, and (with unauthorized revisions by the editor, some of which changed the meaning) in *Financial Analysts Journal*, May-June 1981, pp. 51–58.]

_____, *The Search for Accounting Principles.* New York: American Institute of Certified Public Accountants, 1964. [Reprinted, Houston, Texas: Scholars Book Company, 1977.]

Storey, Reed K. and Sylvia Story, "The Framework of Financial Accounting and Concepts." Special Report. Norwalk, Connecticut: FASB, 1998.

Trouant, D. L. *Financial Audits.* New York: American Institute Publishing Co., Inc., 1937.

Walker, R. G. "The SEC's Ban on Upward Asset Revaluations and the Disclosure of Current Values." *Abacus,* March 1992, pp. 3–35.

Wallman, Steven H. "The Future of Accounting and Disclosure in an Evolving World: The Need for Dramatic Change" *Accounting Horizons.* September, 1995. Wyatt, Arthur R. "Accounting Standards and the Professional Auditor." *Accounting Horizons,* June 1989, pp. 96–102.

Wyatt, Arthur R. "Commentary on Interface Between Teaching/Research and Teaching/Practice." *Accounting Horizons,* March 1989, pp. 125–128.

Zeff, Stephen A. *The Accounting Postulates and Principles Controversy of the 1960s.* New York and London: Garland Publishing, Inc., 1982.

————, *Forging Accounting Principles in Five Countries: A History and An Analysis of Trends.* Champaign, Illinois: Stipes Publishing Company, 1972.

CHAPTER 3

SECURITIES AND EXCHANGE COMMISSION REPORTING REQUIREMENTS

Debra J. MacLaughlin, CPA
BDO Seidman LLP
Wendy Hambleton, CPA
BDO Seidman LLP

3.1 THE SECURITIES AND EXCHANGE COMMISSION

(a) CREATION OF THE SECURITIES AND EXCHANGE COMMISSION.   Congress created the Securities and Exchange Commission (the SEC, or the Commission) through the Securities Exchange Act of 1934 (the 1934 Act). The Securities Act of 1933 (the 1933 Act) was administered by the Federal Trade Commission before the SEC was established.

The 1933 Act and 1934 Act (the Securities Acts) are the main securities statutes of importance to accountants. The Commission also administers the Public Utility Holding Company Act of 1935, the Trust Indenture Act of 1939, the Investment Company Act of 1940, and the Investment Advisers Act of 1940. In addition, the Commission administers the Securities Investor Act of 1970 and also serves as adviser to the U.S. District Court in connection with Federal Bankruptcy Act reorganization proceedings involving registrants. The SEC's Web site is *www.sec.gov*.

(b) ORGANIZATION OF THE SECURITIES AND EXCHANGE COMMISSION.   The Commission is an independent agency of five commissioners. No more than three may be of the same political party. They are appointed by the President (with advice and consent of the Senate) to five-year terms, one term expiring each year.

One commissioner is designated by the President to act as chairman. The Commission has a professional staff, consisting of lawyers, accountants, engineers, financial analysts, economists, and administrative and clerical employees, which is organized into 11 divisions and offices (other than administrative offices). The following are the divisions and offices and their responsibilities:

1. *Office of International Affairs*. Created in 1989, this office is primarily responsible for negotiating understandings between the SEC and foreign securities regulators and for coordinating enforcement programs pursuant to those agreements. It also consults with other divisions and offices concerning the effect of the internationalization of the securities markets on their responsibilities and programs.

2. *Division of Market Regulation*. Regulates securities exchanges, national securities associations, and brokers-dealers, and administers the statistical functions.

3. *Division of Enforcement*. Supervises enforcement activities under the statutes administered by the Commission. Institutes civil, administrative, and injunctive actions. Refers criminal prosecution to the Justice Department in collaboration with the General Counsel.

4. *Division of Investment Management*. Administers the Investment Company Act of 1940, the Investment Advisors Act of 1940, and the Public Utility Holding Company Act of 1935. Investigates and inspects broker-dealers and deals with problems of the distribution methods, services, and reporting standards of investment firms.

5. *Division of Corporation Finance*. Accountants will deal primarily with this division on SEC matters. This division is described in greater detail in Subsection 3.1(c).

6. *Office of Administrative Law Judges*. Rules on admissibility of evidence and makes decisions at hearings held on the various statutes administered by the Commission. The decisions, when appealed, are reviewed by the Commission.

7. *Office of the General Counsel*. The General Counsel is the chief law officer of the Commission. Coordinates the SEC's involvement in judicial proceedings and provides legal advice and assistance.

8. *Office of the Chief Accountant*. The Chief Accountant, currently Robert Herdman, is the Commission's principal adviser on accounting and auditing matters. The Office of the Chief Accountant:

    a. Develops policy with respect to accounting and auditing matters and financial statement requirements

    b. Supervises implementation of policies on accounting and auditing matters

    c. Reviews complex, new, or controversial accounting and auditing problems of registrants

    d. Considers registrants' appeals of decisions by the Division of Corporation Finance on accounting matters

    e. Serves as liaison with professional societies [Financial Accounting Standards Board (FASB), American Institute of Certified Public Accountants (AICPAs), Cost Accounting Standards Board (CASB), Government Accounting Standards Board (GASB), and Financial Executives Institute (FEI)] and federal and state agencies

    f. Considers accountants' independence

    g. Prepares Financial Reporting Releases (FRRs) and (in conjunction with the Division of Corporation Finance), Staff Accounting Bulletins (SABs)/Staff Legal Bulletins (SLBs)

    h. Assists counsel in administrative proceedings relating to accounting and auditing matters

  9. *Office of Economic Analysis.* Assists the Commission in formulating regulatory policy and prepares statistical information relating to the capital markets. Uses an economic monitoring system to provide timely and useful economic information about the effects of certain SEC regulations on issuers, investors, broker-dealers, and other participants in the capital markets.

  10. *Office of Municipal Securities.* Serves as a clearinghouse and point of coordination of the Commission's municipal securities activities. The office provides expertise to the Commission and staff members, assists in municipal securities initiatives throughout the Commission, and works toward assuring a full understanding of Commission policy decisions relating to municipal securities. In addition, it provides technical assistance in legislative matters and in the development and implementation of major Commission initiatives in the municipal securities area.

  11. *Office of Investor Education and Assistance.* Created by the SEC specifically to serve individual investors. The Office makes sure the concerns and problems encountered by individual investors are known throughout the SEC and considered when the agency takes action. Investor assistance specialists are available to answer questions and analyze complaints. They may also refer complaints to the appropriate SEC Division or Office. In certain situations, a copy of the complaint is sent to the brokerage firm or company involved, requesting a written response. This sometimes helps in the resolution process.

The main offices of the Commission are located at 450 5th Street NW, Washington, DC 20549. There are also five regional and six district offices.

- The regional offices are the field representatives of the Commission. It is their responsibility to provide enforcement and inspection capabilities throughout the country.
- The district offices are generally under the supervision of the regional office within its zone. Their primary function is to assist the Commission in its regulatory investigative activities.

(c) DIVISION OF CORPORATION FINANCE.   Because accountants generally deal more with the Division of Corporation Finance than with the other SEC divisions, its duties and operations are considered here in greater detail.

(i) Responsibilities.   The Division's principal responsibility is to ensure that financial information included in SEC filings is in compliance with the rules and regulations of the SEC. Its duties include these six:

  1. Setting standards for information to be included in filed documents

  2. Reviewing and processing filings under the applicable securities acts

  3. Reviewing and processing proxy statements

  4. Reviewing reports of insider trading in equity securities of registrants

5. Determining compliance with the applicable statutes and rules

6. Preparing SABs and SLBs in conjunction with the Office of the Chief Accountant

The SEC does not pass on the merits of any proposed security issue. Although the SEC sets accounting and disclosure requirements that, in some cases, may be over and above those required by generally accepted accounting principles (GAAP), it does not generally prescribe the use of specific auditing procedures other than those related to certain regulated industries. It is the responsibility of the independent public accountant to determine whether the financial statements included in the filing have been audited in accordance with generally accepted auditing standards.

(ii) Organization.   The Division is supervised by a director who is aided by a deputy director, 7 associate directors, and 11 assistant directors.

The Division also has a chief counsel who interprets the securities laws and a chief accountant who supervises compliance in accounting and auditing matters. The chief accountant does not set policy; in novel or complex accounting situations, he may confer with the Commission's Chief Accountant.

Each Assistant Director office is staffed by attorneys, accountants, and examiners. Each office is responsible for certain specific industries, so that each reviewer will be familiar with a registrant's type of business and will treat accounting and reporting matters consistently. A registrant is assigned to an industry group and then to a particular office based on the company's primary Standard Industrial Classification (SIC) Code.

Once a company's initial filing is assigned to an Assistant Director office for review, all subsequent matters relating to that company are generally handled by that office. To determine the name of the appropriate Assistant Director, go to the Division of Corporation Finance's home page on the SEC's Web site. A company's assignment can be determined from the section "CF Company Assignment Listings."

The Assistant Director offices have access to the Office of Engineering for assistance in technical areas such as mining and valuation.

If a company is a new small business issuer (SBI), it will generally be assigned to the Office of Small Business regardless of its industry.

(iii) Review Procedures.   Filings with the Division are customarily reviewed by an accountant and an attorney or financial analyst. The accountant's review will be directed toward determining adequate disclosure and compliance with GAAP and the applicable rules of the SEC. This review will also determine the appropriateness of the accounting and disclosures based on information in the textual section of the filing.

Comments from the review may result in issuing the registrant a "deficiency letter" or "letter of comments." The Assistant Director approves comments made by the attorney or financial analyst, and an assistant chief accountant clears comments made by the accountant. If there are troublesome accounting problems, the Division's Chief Accountant may confer with the Office of the Chief Accountant. In unusual situations, the Office of the Chief Accountant may bring the matter to the Commission's attention.

To minimize SEC comments regarding potential problem areas in the filing, the registrant may request a prefiling conference with the Commission's staff. Such conferences may also be held after the filing to resolve matters in the letter of comment. The SEC has developed protocol for contacting the Office of the Chief Accountant or the Division of Corporation Finance for accounting issues. This protocol can also be found on the SEC's Web site in the section "Information for Accountants." After a registrant has provided the written information, it can also request a fact to face meeting to resolve the issue if necessary.

The registrant also may refer matters to the Office of the Chief Accountant and, in rare instances, to the Commission. This can occur either before filing or after receipt of the letter of comments.

Because of the significant volume of filings it receives on an annual basis, the Division has adopted a selective review program. Registration and proxy statements are given priority over the

1934 Act reports because of the tight time schedules associated with such filings. The selective review criteria are directed at reviewing all key filings, and registrants should expect all registration statements for initial public offerings to be thoroughly reviewed. If a registration or proxy statement is selected for review, the registrant will be notified.

Normally the Division attempts to review a registration statement and provide initial comments within 30 days after the filing date. Comments are generally provided in writing, and upon request will be sent via fax. However, when timing is critical a reviewer may agree to read them over the phone and confirm them in writing.

Periodic reports under the 1934 Act may be reviewed on a selective basis after the filing date. Depending on the number and severity of the deficiencies, the staff will either require the registrant to amend the periodic report or may only require that the changes be implemented in future filings.

The 1934 Act permits the SEC to suspend trading in any security "for a period not exceeding 10 days" if it is in the public interest and is necessary to protect investors. Based on a Supreme Court decision, the SEC does not have the authority to issue suspensions beyond the initial 10 days.

(iv) EDGAR—Electronic Data Gathering Analysis and Retrieval System.   In its efforts to improve its review process, provide greater dissemination of information, and make the filing process more efficient for filers, the Commission developed its Electronic Data Gathering, Analysis, and Retrieval (EDGAR) system. With a few exceptions, most forms filed with the SEC are required to be filed electronically. Other information, such as responses to comment letters, may also be required to be filed electronically. Responses to comment letters and other correspondence do not become publicly available. Anyone with access to the Internet can review public filings made via EDGAR. The SEC's Web site contains a section related to EDGAR and how to use the system.

(v) Extension of Time to File.   If a filing is not expected to be made on a timely basis, the SEC rules require that companies submit a notification on Form 12b-25 indicating the reason for extension, no later than one business day after the due date of the report. In addition, the rules provide relief where reports are not timely filed if a timely filing would involve unreasonable effort or expense. Under this provision, a report will be considered to be filed on a timely basis if the following three provisions are met:

1. The required notification on Form 12b-25 (a) discloses that the reasons causing the inability to file on time could not be eliminated without unreasonable effort or expense, and (b) undertakes that the document will be filed no later than the 15th day following the due date (by the fifth day with respect to Form 10-Q).

2. There is a statement, attached as an exhibit to Form 12b-25, from any person other than the registrant (e.g., the independent accountant) whose inability to furnish a required opinion, report, or certification was the reason the report could not be timely filed without unreasonable effort or expense.

3. The report is filed within the represented time period.

This procedure does not require a response by the SEC.

Periodic reports that are filed late with the SEC may (1) prevent the registrant from using short-form registration statements on Forms S-2 and S-3, (2) cause injunctive action to compel filing, (3) make Rule 144 unavailable for the sale of shares by company officers, directors, or insiders (thus requiring registration of those shares before they can be sold), or (4) result in suspension of trading in the registrant's securities. The exchange may often act quickly to suspend trading of a security if the company has not filed information on a timely basis.

(d) RELATIONSHIP BETWEEN THE ACCOUNTING PROFESSION AND THE SECURITIES AND EXCHANGE COMMISSION.   The SEC and the accounting profession have cooperated with each other in developing GAAP. Through its FRRs, SABs, and SLBs, the SEC has informed the accounting profession of its opinions on accounting and reporting. In addition, the Chief Accountant and certain members of his staff attend meetings of the FASB [including the Emerging Issues Task Force (EITF)] and technical committees of the AICPA.

In turn, as stated in FRR No. 1 (Section 101):

> . . . the Commission intends to continue its policy of looking to the private sector for leadership in establishing and improving accounting principles and standards through the FASB with the expectation that the body's conclusions will promote the interests of investors. For the purpose of this policy, principles, standards, and practices promulgated by the FASB in its Statements and Interpretations will be considered by the Commission as having substantial authoritative support, and those contrary to such FASB promulgations will be considered to have no such support.

Although there has been an attempt to eliminate the differences between GAAP requirements and SEC accounting and reporting requirements, there are still certain key differences. The following lists some of the additional requirements for SEC registrants:

- Assets subject to lien (S-X Rule 4-08(b))—requires the disclosure of the nature and approximate amount of assets mortgaged, pledged, or subject to liens.
- Financial information of unconsolidated subsidiaries and 50 percent or less owned equity method investees (S-X Rule 4-08(g) and 3-09)—depending on the significance of the investment, the SEC may require separate audited financial statements of the investee.
- Income tax expense (S-X Rule 4-08(h))—additional disclosure regarding the components of income tax expense (domestic foreign, other, etc.) and a numerical reconciliation between the reported income tax expense and the pretax income multiplied by the statutory rate.
- Related party transactions (S-X Rule 4-08(k))—disclose related party balances on the face of the financial statements.
- Disclosure of the composition of "other" current assets, current liabilities, assets, and liabilities if the total exceeds certain thresholds (S-X Rule 5-02.8, 5-02.17, 5-02.20, 5-20.24).
- Guarantor financial statements (S-X Rule 3-10)—depending on the significance and other criteria regarding the guarantors, the SEC may require separate financial information regarding guarantor and nonguarantor entities included in the consolidated financial statements.

For more detailed information related to these and other differences, see Section 3.4.

(e) SARBANES-OXLEY ACT OF 2002.   In response to several significant restatements by public companies in late 2001 and early 2002, both the House of Representatives and the U.S. Senate proposed bills that could affect almost everyone associated with public companies. The two bills were quickly reconciled into the Sarbanes-Oxley Bill, which the President signed in late July 2002 and thus became the Sarbanes-Oxley Act (the Act).

The Act is very broad in scope and, while it appears to be quite specific, numerous questions of interpretation have arisen and will continue to arise. Future clarification and, possibly, expansion, whether through decisions of the yet-to-be-established Public Company Accounting Oversight Board (Board) and the SEC or through additional legislation, will be forthcoming.

The following is a broad overview of certain provisions of the Act.

(i) Implications for Public Company Officers and Directors.

Certifications.   Chief Executive Officer (CEO) and chief financial officer (CFO) certifications regarding annual and quarterly reports will now be required in accordance with two separate provisions of the Act. In certifications provided in response to Section 302 of the Act, the officers must each state:

- They have reviewed the report.

- Based on their knowledge:
  - The report contains no untrue material fact and does not omit a material fact that would make the statements misleading, and
  - The financial statements and other financial information in the report present fairly, in all material respects, the operations and financial condition of the company.
- They are responsible for establishing and maintaining internal controls.
- They have designed internal controls to ensure that material information relating to the issuer and its consolidated subsidiaries is made known to such officers by others within the company and its consolidated subsidiaries during the period in which the periodic reports are being prepared.
- They have evaluated the effectiveness of internal controls within 90 days prior to the report and have presented their conclusions about such effectiveness based on their evaluation.
- They have disclosed to the issuer's auditors and the audit committee all significant deficiencies and/or material weaknesses in the controls and any fraud involving management or other employees who have a significant role in the issuer's internal controls.
- They have indicated in the report whether there were any significant changes in internal controls or other factors that might significantly affect internal controls subsequent to the date of their evaluation, including any corrective actions taken in response to deficiencies and/or material weaknesses.

(Rules regarding this section were issued by the SEC in August 2002. See Section 3.1(f) below on recent SEC proposed rules and other guidance.)

Pursuant to Section 906 of the Act, such officers must also provide a certification for each periodic report containing financial statements filed with the SEC that:

- The periodic report complies fully with the requirements of Section 19(a) or 15(d) of the Securities Exchange Act of 1934.
- The information provided presents fairly, in all material respects, the financial condition and results of operations of the company.

(The provision for certification under Section 906 was effective upon signing of the Act.)

Maximum penalties for knowing violations of this section of the Act are fines of up to $1 million and/or imprisonment for up to 10 years, willful violations carry fines of up to $5 million and/or imprisonment of up to 20 years.

Internal Control Reports.   Companies must also file a report on internal control with their annual reports. This report must acknowledge management's responsibility for establishing and maintaining an adequate internal control structure and procedures for financial reporting and include an assessment as to the effectiveness of such structure as of its fiscal year-end. The internal controls discussed here may go well beyond the internal controls covering the preparation of financial statements; this report also appears to cover the internal controls related to the procedures for financial reporting including disclosures in Management Discussion and Analysis (MDA) and elsewhere in its public filings.

(This provision is effective upon issuance of rules by the SEC.)

Loans to Officers and Directors.   The Act, subject to certain limited exceptions, makes it unlawful for a company to extend credit to its directors and executive officers. However, existing loans are grandfathered, provided they are not materially modified or renewed.

(This provision was effective upon signing the Act.)

Penalties for Violations of Securities Laws.   Under the Act, corporate officers are subject to new penalties. If a company restates its financial statements due to material noncompliance with financial reporting requirements, as a result of misconduct, any bonuses and other incentive-based or equity-based compensation received by the CEO and CFO during the 12 months following the filing of the noncompliant document, as well as any profits realized from the sale of securities during that period, must be returned to the company.

(This provision is effective upon signing of the Act.)

There are other provisions in the Act addressing corporate code of ethics, insider trading, and other issues.

(ii) Implications for Audit Committees.

General Audit Committee Requirement and Responsibilities.   All public companies must have an audit committee. If one is not appointed, the entire board will be deemed to be functioning as the audit committee. The committee will be responsible for the following:

- Appointment, compensation, and oversight of auditors, including resolution of any disagreements between management and the auditors
- Establishing procedures for receiving and addressing complaints, including anonymous submissions, concerning accounting, internal control, or auditing matters
- Engaging independent counsel or other advisers, as necessary, with funding to be provided by the company

Each audit committee member must be independent. Under the independence definition in the Act, the member may not receive fees from the company for any consulting, advisory, or other services (other than for services on the board) and may not be affiliated with either the company or its subsidiaries in any capacity other than as a director. The SEC is to issue rules requiring the national securities exchanges to prohibit from listing any security from any issuer that does not meet the above requirements for its audit committee.

(SEC to issue rules by April 2003.)

Financial Expertise Requirement and Disclosure.   Companies must disclose whether or not at least one member of the audit committee qualifies as a "financial expert." When making such a determination, a company should consider an individual's:

- Educational and professional background
- Knowledge of GAAP and financial statements
- Experience in preparing or auditing financial statements for comparable companies
- Experience with internal accounting controls
- Understanding of audit committee functions

(SEC to issue rules by January 2003.)

(iii) Implications for Independent Auditors.

Public Company Accounting Oversight Board.   The Act requires the creation of the Public Company Accounting Oversight Board. The Board will have five financially literate members (two current or former certified public accountants [CPAs] and three non-CPAs). Members, appointed by the SEC after consultation with the Chairman of the Federal Reserve Board and the Secretary of the Treasury, may not be connected with any public accounting firm other than as retired members receiving fixed continuing payments, and in general may not be employed or engaged in any other professional or business activity. The Board, as well as an accounting standards board (expected to continue to be the FASB), will be funded through fees collected from public companies, which will be assessed based on a percentage of each company's market capitalization to total market capitalization for all public companies.

The Board's duties will be to establish or adopt standards (e.g., auditing, quality control, ethics, independence) related to the preparation of audit reports, conduct inspections of registered accounting firms, and conduct investigations and disciplinary proceedings, as necessary. When conducting investigations, the Board will be able to request and compel testimony, through subpoena requests, of public accounting firms and issuers. The Board will have the authority, subject to SEC review, to impose sanctions on accounting firms that are not in compliance with the Act. The Board's activities will replace the current firm on firm peer review and the AICPA's current role of determining appropriate actions in cases of violation of rules by accountants.

Public Accounting Firms.   All accounting firms that audit public companies will be required to register with the Board. This requirement also extends to foreign accounting firms that audit a public company (a foreign private issuer as well as a U.S. company). Registered firms serving more than 100 public companies will be subject to annual quality reviews conducted by the Board. All other firms will be reviewed, at a minimum, on a triennial basis.

(Firms to be registered by 180 days after the SEC determines the Board is suitably organized.)

Auditor Independence Standards.   The Act imposes new restrictions on the types of services a public accounting firm can perform for a public company when it is serving as that company's auditor. Prohibited services include:

- Bookkeeping services
- Financial information systems design and implementation
- Appraisal or valuation services, fairness opinions, or contribution-in-kind reports
- Actuarial services
- Internal audit outsourcing services
- Management functions or human resources
- Broker or dealer, investment adviser, or investment banking services
- Legal services and expert services unrelated to the audit

(Effective upon registration of accounting firms.)

Other nonaudit services, including tax services, may be provided but only if approved in advance by the company's audit committee. Approval of all nonaudit services must be disclosed in periodic reports.

(Effective upon registration of accounting firms.)

A registered accounting firm may not audit a public company if the engagement and/or concurring partner has performed audit services for that company for the past five years. At a minimum, this would dictate mandatory rotation every five years. Accounting firms are also prohibited from auditing a public company if the CEO, CFO, controller, or chief accounting officer was employed by the firm and participated in the company's audit during the one year preceding the initiation of the audit.

(Effective upon registration of accounting firms.)

A company's public accounting firm must attest to and report on management's assessment of its internal controls (discussed above) as part of the audit engagement. This report must describe the scope of the testing of the internal control structure, present findings, evaluate controls, and describe material weaknesses and noncompliance noted.

(Effective upon registration of accounting firms.)

Financial Disclosures.   The SEC must require disclosure in quarterly and annual reports of material off-balance sheet transactions, arrangements, obligations, and other relationships with related parties that may have a material current or future effect on financial condition and results of operations.

Additionally, pro forma financial information included in any periodic report, annual report, or press release:

- May not contain any untrue statement of a material fact or omit a material fact necessary to ensure the information is not misleading
- Must be reconciled to financial condition and results of operations prepared in accordance with GAAP

Most likely these rules will be based on the disclosures previously suggested by the SEC in FRR No. 61, *Commission Statement about Management's Discussion and Analysis of Financial Condition and Results of Operations*, and FRR No. 59, *Cautionary Advice Regarding the Use of "Pro Forma" Financial Information in Earnings Releases*.

(Rules to be issued by the SEC by January 26, 2003.)

(f) SEC PROPOSED RULE MAKING AND OTHER GUIDANCE. In addition to the Act that was proposed by Congress, the SEC had proposed certain rule making and provided certain cautionary advice and other forms of guidance during late 2001 and 2002, as well. Some of the rules the SEC had proposed are basically covered by requirements in the Act; however, some are not specifically addressed. The SEC issued the following:

- FRR No. 59, *Cautionary Advice Regarding the Use of Pro Forma Financial Information in Earnings Releases*, in December 2001. The release, available on the SEC Web site under "Regulatory Actions: Other Commission Orders and Notices," highlights that:
  ○ The antifraud provisions of the federal securities laws apply to a company issuing pro forma financial information (even though quarterly press releases are not required to be filed with the SEC).
  ○ Departures from GAAP raise particular concerns if the basis of presentation is not clearly disclosed. For example, if a company announces "earnings before unusual or nonrecurring transactions," it should describe the particular transactions that are omitted and apply the same methodology to all comparable periods.
  ○ Statements about a company's results, although literally true, may be misleading if they omit *material* information. For example, investors are likely to be deceived if a company uses pro forma to recast a GAAP loss as if it were a profit.
  ○ Companies are encouraged to follow the earnings press release guidelines jointly developed by the Financial Executives International (FEI) and the National Investors Relations Institute, which advocate clear disclosure as to how the announced results deviate from GAAP, as well as the amounts of those deviations. This guidance is available on the FEI Web site, *www.fei.org*, under "News & Info—Pro Forma Guidelines."
- FRR No. 60, *Cautionary Advice Regarding Disclosure about Critical Accounting Policies*, in December 2001. The basic thrust of the release is that reported financial position and operating results often imply a degree of precision, continuity, and certainty that is unfounded. Consequently, even a technically accurate application of GAAP may not provide a clear understanding of the company's financial well-being and the possibility, likelihood, and implication of changes in its financial and operating status. In the release, the staff encourages companies to adopt a disclosure regimen that stresses:
  ○ A management focus on and evaluation of the critical accounting policies used in the financial statements
  ○ MD&A disclosures that are balanced and fully responsive, and include explanations and effects of critical accounting policies, the judgments made in their application, and the likelihood of materially different reported results under different conditions or assumptions

○ An audit committee review of the selection, application, and disclosure of critical accounting policies (i.e., evaluation of the criteria used by management in selection of accounting principles and methods)

○ Consultation with the SEC staff regarding critical accounting policies if management, the audit committee, or the auditors are uncertain about the application of specific GAAP

- FRR No. 61, *Commission Statement about Management's Discussion and Analysis of Financial Condition and Results of Operations*, in January 2002. This release provides additional guidance on MD&A and encourages registrants to include specific discussions in their MD&As on:

○ Liquidity and financing, especially any off-balance sheet items

○ Certain trading activity of nonexchange-traded contracts accounted for at fair value

○ Related-party transactions, highlighting the business purpose of the transaction and any ongoing contractual commitments as a result of the transaction

This release also suggests that registrants include a table summarizing all contractual obligations and commercial commitments in a single location in the MD&A. The release reminds registrants that the information in their MD&A should be the most relevant to investors and should be in a format that is easily understandable.

The above three releases were not formal rule making, but presented the SEC's thoughts on certain issues. The SEC followed up with additional formal rule making later in 2002. The following rules were proposed by the SEC:

(i) Acceleration of Periodic Report Filing Dates and Disclosure Concerning Web Site Access to Reports.   On April 11, 2002, the SEC proposed to shorten the time frame that certain companies would have to file their annual Form 10-K and quarterly Form 10-Q reports. Annual reports would be due 60 (rather than 90) days after year-end and quarterly reports would be due 30 (rather than 45) days after quarter end.

The accelerated due dates would be required by "accelerated filers," defined by the Release as a company that has:

- A public float of $75 million or more
- Been subject to the Exchange Act reporting requirements for at least 12 calendar months
- Filed at least one annual report

The proposal would require companies to remain as "accelerated filers" until they meet the requirement of a small business filer (less than $25 million in public float and less than $25 million in revenues for two consecutive years).

SBIs that file on Forms 10-KSB and 10-QSB and foreign private issuers would not be affected by these proposed changes. These proposed changes would be effective for fiscal years ending after October 31, 2002, and would affect the due date for December 31, 2002, annual reports.

(ii) Form 8-K Disclosure of Certain Management Transactions (Release No. 33-8090).   On April 12, 2002, the SEC released a proposed amendment to Form 8-K that would require certain public companies to file current reports under a new item 10 to report information about:

- Director and executive officer transactions in company equity securities (including derivative securities transactions and transactions with the company)
- Director and executive officer arrangements for the purchase or sale of company equity securities
- Cash loans to directors and executive officers made or guaranteed by the company or an affiliate of the company

The due dates for the Form 8-K would vary based on the monetary volume of the transactions. Reports of transactions and loans with an aggregate value of $100,000 or more would be due within two business days after the reportable event. Reports for transactions greater than $10,000 but less than $100,000 and grants and awards under employee benefit plans would be due by the close of business on the second business day of the following week. Reports of transactions and loans with an aggregate value less than $10,000 would be deferrable until the aggregate cumulative value of those unreported events for the same director or executive officer exceeds $10,000.

The date of a reportable event would be the date on which the parties enter into an agreement. In the case of an open market securities transaction, the date would be the trade date, not the settlement date.

The amendments would be effective for directors and executive officers of companies with a class of equity securities registered under Exchange Act Section 12. Executive officers, as defined by Exchange Act Rule 3b-7, would include a company's president; any vice president in charge of a principal business unit, division or function; and any other officer or person who performs a policy-making function for the company, including officers of subsidiaries. The proposed amendments are intended to provide investors with disclosure of potentially useful information as to management's views of the performance or prospects of the company, or financial arrangements that may represent additional compensation. The SEC believes that such disclosure should enable them to make better-informed and more timely investment and voting decisions.

(iii) Disclosure in Management's Discussion and Analysis about the Application of Critical Accounting Policies (Release No. 33-8098).

On May 10, 2002, the SEC released a proposed rule to require a separately captioned section in MD&A regarding the critical accounting estimates made by companies in applying accounting policies and initial adoption of certain accounting policies. The proposal builds on the disclosures the SEC encouraged registrants to make in FRR No. 60, *Cautionary Advice Regarding Disclosure about Critical Accounting Policies*, issued in December 2001. According to the SEC staff, most companies fell short of the type of thoughtful discussions contemplated by the SEC.

(iv) Critical Accounting Estimates.

According to the proposal, an accounting estimate is considered critical if:

- It requires the company to make assumptions about matters that are highly uncertain at the time it is made; and
- Different estimates that the company reasonably could have used in the current period, or changes in the accounting estimate that are reasonably likely to occur from period to period, would materially affect on the company's reported financial condition, changes in financial condition, or results of operations.

The following disclosures about critical accounting estimates would be required:

- A discussion that identifies and describes the estimate, the methodology used, certain assumptions, and reasonably likely changes
- An explanation of the significance of the estimate to the company's financial condition, changes in financial condition and results of operations, and, where material, an identification of the line items in the company's financial statements affected by the estimate
- A quantitative discussion of changes in the overall financial performance and, to the extent material, line items in the financial statements if the company were to assume that the estimate was changed, either by using reasonably possible near-term changes in certain assumptions or the reasonably possible range of the estimate
- A quantitative and qualitative discussion of any material changes made to the estimate in the past three years, the reasons for the changes, and the effect on line items in the financial statements and overall financial performance

- A statement of whether the company's senior management has discussed the development and selection of the estimate, and the MD&A disclosure regarding it, with the company's audit committee

- If the company operates in more than one segment, an identification of the segments of the company's business affected by the estimates

- A discussion of the estimate on a segment basis, mirroring the one required on a company-wide basis, to the extent that a failure to present that information would result in an omission that renders the disclosure materially misleading

(v) Initial Adoption of Accounting Policies.   The proposal would require disclosure if an accounting policy was adopted (other than one resulting from the mandated adoption of new accounting literature) and it materially affected the company's reported financial condition, changes in financial condition, or results of operations. A company would be required to disclose:

- The events or transactions that gave rise to the initial adoption

- The accounting principle adopted and the method of applying that principle

- The effects on the company's reported financial condition, changes in financial condition, and results of operations (discussed on a qualitative basis)

- If applicable, that the company was permitted a choice among acceptable accounting principles, what the alternatives were, and why the company made the choice it did (including, where material, qualitative disclosure of the effects on the company's reported financial presentation that the alternatives would have had)

- If no accounting literature exists addressing the events or transactions giving rise to the initial adoption, an explanation of the company's decision as to which accounting principle to use

These disclosures would cover the financial statements for the most recent fiscal year and any subsequent interim period presented. They would be required in all annual reports, registration statements, and proxy and information statements. The proposal would also require quarterly updates to report material changes.

These disclosures would be required for all public companies, including foreign private issuers, with one exception. SBIs that have not had revenues from operations during the last two fiscal years (or last fiscal year and subsequent interim period presented) would be exempt.

The rest of this chapter discusses rules that are in place prior to the adoption of the Sarbanes-Oxley Act and prior to the adoption of any of the above-listed proposed rules by the SEC.

(g) QUALIFICATIONS AND INDEPENDENCE OF PUBLIC ACCOUNTANTS PRACTICING BEFORE THE SEC.   To qualify for practice before the SEC, the public accountant auditing the financial statements must be independent, in good standing in the profession, and entitled to practice under the laws of his place of residence or principal office (Rule 2-01 of Regulation S-X).

In November 2000, the SEC issued amendments to modernize its rules for determining whether an auditor is independent and to expand proxy disclosure requirements for nonaudit services. The new rules, which take a more moderate approach than those originally proposed by the SEC, were adopted unanimously after extensive negotiations with the AICPA and other representatives of the accounting profession. The new independence rules apply to all auditors (including non-U.S. auditors) that submit audit reports in SEC filings. The amendments generally took effect on February 5, 2001, although certain restrictions have become effective over an 18-month transition period. The rule changes are based on the assumption that investor confidence in auditor independence depends on whether the auditor is in fact independent and whether a reasonable investor would conclude, in light of all relevant facts and circumstances, that the auditor is capable of exercising objective and impartial judgment.

In summary, the rules:

- Significantly reduce the number of audit firm employees and their family members whose investments in, or employment with, audit clients impair an auditor's independence
- Identify certain nonaudit services that would impair an auditor's independence
- Require certain disclosures in annual proxy statements regarding nonaudit services provided by the auditor during the last fiscal year

The SEC and others have expressed concern that the performance of nonaudit services for audit clients might impair the fact or appearance of independence. Rather than prohibit auditors from providing any nonaudit services to audit clients, the SEC adopted a two-pronged approach. First, the rule specifies nine nonaudit services that, if provided by auditors to an audit client, may be deemed inconsistent with an auditor's independence. Second, the new rule requires the following disclosures in annual proxy statements filed after February 5, 2001:

- Fees billed or expected to be billed for the audit of the annual financial statements in Form 10-K or 10-KSB and the reviews of the financial statements included in Forms 10-Q or 10-QSB for that year
- Fees billed for information technology services
- Total fees for other services provided (e.g., tax services unrelated to the income tax accrual, work on registration statements, M&A work, or other consulting)
- Whether the board of directors or the audit committee has considered whether the nonaudit services are compatible with maintaining the auditor's independence

The required disclosures need only be made in the proxy statement relating to an annual meeting of shareholders at which directors are to be elected. Companies reporting solely under Section 15(d) of the Exchange Act and foreign private issuers need not make the disclosures since they are not subject to the proxy rules.

(h) SEC'S FOCUS ON ACCOUNTING FRAUD.   SEC officials have expressed concern over the increase in two types of accounting fraud—"cooked books" and "cute accounting." "Cooking" the books involves falsifying books and records either by creating or accelerating revenues or by deferring or concealing expenses. "Cute" accounting involves misapplying or stretching accounting principles and interpretations to obtain the desired, albeit distorted, financial picture. Both the accounting profession and corporate officials have been reminded by the SEC of their responsibilities to the public investor. More specifically:

- The SEC will carefully review Form 8-K reports to monitor changes in accountants. CPA firms should use caution when taking on new clients. A firm should review the work of the predecessor accountants to determine whether the change in accountants was the result of a company's refusing to comply with GAAP or violating federal securities laws. The SEC will take action against companies that "shop" for the most favorable accounting interpretations. The enforcement division will pursue not only these companies but also accounting firms that attempt to gain clients by disregarding GAAP.
- Accountants should treat with healthy skepticism any changes in accounting policies or individual transactions that increase revenues or reduce expenses.
- Accountants should avoid the tendency to rationalize otherwise questionable accounting positions. Firms should not take the view that "if it is not proscribed, it's permitted," but instead should use accounting procedures that follow both the letter and the spirit of SEC and FASB pronouncements.

- Companies have a duty to disclose adverse nonpublic information (e.g., loss of a major customer) in the management's discussion and analysis section of Form 10-K. Furthermore, independent accountants are obligated not to sign off on filings if significant information is missing.

The SEC is concerned with "opinion shopping" and requires companies and their former auditors to make certain disclosures upon a change in outside auditor. FRR No. 31 provides additional guidance as to these disclosures.

FRR 31 explains that "the term *disagreements* should be interpreted broadly, to include any difference of opinion on any matter of accounting principles or practices, financial statement disclosure, or auditing scope or procedures, which if not resolved to the former accountant's satisfaction would have caused it to refer to the subject matter of the disagreement in connection with its report." It further explains that preliminary differences of opinion that are "based on incomplete facts" are not disagreements if the differences are resolved by obtaining more complete factual information.

When an independent accountant who was the principal accountant for the company or who audited a significant subsidiary and was expressly relied on by the principal accountant resigns, declines to stand for reelection, or is dismissed, the registrant must also disclose:

- Whether the former accountant resigned, declined to stand for reelection, or was dismissed, and the date of this action
- Whether there was an adverse opinion, disclaimer of opinion, or qualification or modification of opinion as to uncertainty, audit scope, or accounting principles issued by such accountant for either of the two most recent years, including a description of the nature of the opinion
- Whether the decision to change accountants was recommended by or approved by the audit committee or a similar committee, or by the board of directors in the absence of such special committee

Finally, the rules also require disclosure of certain "reportable events" during the two most recent fiscal years or any subsequent interim period preceding the resignation or dismissal of the accountant. "Reportable events" include:

- The auditors having advised the registrant that the internal controls necessary to develop reliable financial statements do not exist
- The auditors having advised the registrant that information has come to the auditor's attention that led him or her to no longer be able to rely on management's representations, or that has made him or her unwilling to be associated with the financial statements
- The auditors having advised the registrant of his or her need to significantly expand the audit scope or information having come to the auditor's attention during the last two fiscal years and any subsequent interim period that, if further investigated, may (a) materially impact the fairness or reliability of either a previously issued audit report or the underlying financial statements or the financial statements issued or to be issued for a subsequent period or (b) cause him or her to be unwilling to rely on management's representations or to be associated with the financial statements and because of the change in auditors, the auditor did not expand his or her scope or conduct a further investigation
- The auditors having advised the registrant that information has come to the auditor's attention that what he or she has concluded materially impacts the fairness or reliability of either (a) a previously issued audit report or the underlying financial statements or (b) the financial statements relating to a subsequent period, and unless the matters are resolved to the auditor's satisfaction, the auditor would be prevented from rendering an unqualified report and, because of the change in auditors, the matter has not been resolved

Disagreements and reportable events are intended to include both oral and written communications to the registrant. Because these communications deal with sensitive areas that may impugn the integrity of management, they will have to be handled with extreme care on the part of all involved.

The time frame for reporting these changes is as follows:

- The Form 8-K reporting the change should be filed by the end of the fifth business day following the day the former auditor is dismissed or notifies its client of its resignation or decision not to stand for reelection.

- The letter from the former auditor should be filed by the registrant by the end of the tenth business day following the filing of the initial Form 8-K. Further, the letter must be filed within two business days after it is received by the registrant.

- The registrant should request the former auditor to furnish its letter "as promptly as possible." To facilitate prompt responses, the new rule requires the registrant to provide the former auditor with a copy of its report no later than the day the initial Form 8-K is filed with the SEC.

- The auditor who is aware that a required filing related to a change of accountants has not been made by the registrant should consider advising the registrant in writing of that reporting responsibility with a copy to the Commission.

The SEC has recently proposed changing the time frame from five business days for the initial reporting of the change to two business days.

In addition, the SEC Practice Section of the AICPA has a rule requiring auditors to communicate auditor changes directly to the SEC. Under that rule, when a firm has resigned, declined to stand for reelection, or has been dismissed, it should notify the former client within five business days that the auditor-client relationship has ceased and should simultaneously send a copy to the SEC (generally by fax with a follow-up hard copy).

(i) FOREIGN CORRUPT PRACTICES ACT.   The Foreign Corrupt Practices Act of 1977 (FCPA) deals with (1) payments to foreign officials and (2) internal accounting control.

(i) Payments to Foreign Officials.   The Act makes it illegal to offer anything of value to any foreign official, foreign political party, and so on (other than employees of foreign governments, and so on, whose duties are ministerial or clerical), for the purpose of exerting influence in obtaining or retaining business. The prohibition against payments to foreign officials, as stated in this law, applies to all U.S. domestic concerns regardless of whether they are publicly or privately held. The Act may also apply to foreign subsidiaries of U.S. companies.

(ii) Internal Accounting Control.   The FCPA makes it illegal for companies subject to SEC jurisdiction to fail to:

- Keep books and records, in reasonable detail, that accurately and fairly reflect the transactions and disposition of the company's assets
- Devise and maintain a system of internal accounting controls that will provide reasonable assurance that:

    Transactions are properly recorded in accordance with management's authorization

    Financial statements are prepared in conformity with GAAP and accountability for assets is maintained

    Access to company assets is permitted only with management's authorization

    The recorded assets are checked and differences reconciled at reasonable intervals

Shortly after the Act became effective, the SEC issued Accounting Series Releases (ASRs) No. 242, which states: "It is important that issuers subject to the new requirements review their accounting procedures, systems of internal accounting controls and business practices in order that they may take any actions necessary to comply with requirements contained in the Act." To aid management in evaluating internal accounting control (which could be beneficial in judging whether a company complies with the accounting requirements of the FCPA), the AICPA formed a Special Advisory Committee on Internal Accounting Control. This committee issued a report that defines internal accounting control, develops related objectives (categorized by the committee as authorization, accounting, and asset safeguarding), and discusses what management should be doing with respect to an evaluation of these controls.

According to the committee's report, the internal accounting control environment should be a significant factor in management's assessment of the company's system. Along those lines, the report of the Special Advisory Committee on Internal Control (1979) states: "It is unlikely that management can have reasonable assurance that the broad objectives of internal accounting control are being met unless the company has an environment that establishes an appropriate level of control consciousness."

The role of top management and the board of directors in establishing an appropriate internal accounting control environment is significant. The report considers the factors that shape such an environment to include "creating an appropriate organizational structure, using sound management practices, establishing accountability for performance, and requiring adherence to appropriate standards for ethical behavior, including compliance with applicable laws and regulations."

A strong control environment may include, for example, clearly defined accounting policies and procedures, clearly established levels of responsibility and authority, periodic evaluations of employees to determine that their performance is consistent with their responsibilities, budgetary controls, and an effective internal audit function. A strong control environment will provide more assurance that the company's internal accounting control procedures are followed. On the other hand, a poor internal accounting control environment could negate the effect of specific controls (e.g., employees may hesitate to challenge management override of control procedures).

After assessing the control environment, management should evaluate the internal accounting control system. There are several approaches to such an evaluation, depending, for example, on the organizational structure of the company and its type of business. The report uses a "cycle" approach in illustrating an evaluation of internal accounting control, although other approaches may be acceptable (e.g., by function or operating unit). Under the cycle approach, transactions are grouped into convenient cycles (e.g., revenues, expenditures, production or conversion, financing, and external financial reporting) and appropriate internal accounting control criteria are identified for each cycle. In addition, the existing control procedures and techniques used by the company to meet the related criteria should be evaluated.

Meeting internal accounting control criteria generally reduces the risk of material undetected errors and irregularities. Of course, there are inherent limitations to any system of internal accounting control. Even though internal accounting control procedures are performed and the related criteria are met, collusion or override can circumvent existing procedures. Even a strong system of internal accounting control can provide only reasonable assurance for the timely detection of errors or irregularities. However, nonachievement of criteria increases the likelihood that (1) transactions not authorized by management will occur, (2) transactions will not be properly recorded, and (3) assets will be subject to unauthorized access.

The FCPA's legislative history recognizes that the aggregate cost of specific internal controls should not exceed the expected benefits to be derived. Therefore, the report concludes that if it is determined that an internal accounting control criterion is not met, management should evaluate the "cost/benefit" considerations of modifying existing procedures or adding new ones. In determining the aggregate cost, consideration should be given to the direct and indirect dollar cost (e.g., additional personnel, new forms), and whether the new or modified procedure slows the decision-making process or has other deleterious effects on the company. To measure the expected benefit, management should evaluate the likelihood that an error or irregularity could result in a loss to the company or in a misstatement in its financial statements, and evaluate the extent of such loss or misstatement.

Because the system of internal accounting control depends on employees' performing their assigned duties, the report indicates that management should establish a program to obtain reasonable assurance that the controls continue to function properly. The nature of the monitoring program will vary from company to company and will depend on the company's size and organizational structure, the degree of managerial involvement in its day-to-day operations, and the complexity of its accounting system. Ordinarily, monitoring occurs through supervision, representations, audits, or other compliance tests, and so on.

(j) AUDIT COMMITTEES. Companies whose securities are traded on the New York Stock Exchange are required by the exchange to have audit committees comprising independent members of the board of directors. This requirement is a condition for original and continued listing. Directors who are members of present management or who serve the company in an advisory capacity, such as consultants or legal counsel, and relatives of executives are not considered independent directors. Former company executives who serve as directors can serve on the audit committee if, in the opinion of the board, that person will exercise independent judgment and will materially aid and assist the function of the committee.

The American Stock Exchange, NASDAQ, National Market System, and NASDAQ Small Cap Market require that listed companies have an audit committee with majority membership held by independent directors (and have at least two independent members on their board of directors).

As previously mentioned, the *Report of the National Commission on Fraudulent Financial Reporting* (1987) recommends that audit committees comprising only independent directors be required for all public companies.

(k) CONTACT WITH SEC STAFF. Contact with the staff of the SEC can be both formal and informal and can occur in three situations:

1. *Investigation*. The SEC staff can make an informal investigation when they believe the securities laws have been violated. Such investigations may be prompted by market activity in a stock that is not justified by publicly available information, or by news accounts of possible wrongdoing, complaints from the investing public, references from stock exchanges and the National Association of Securities Dealers, or references from other law enforcement agencies. Persons do not have to assist the staff in their investigation and instead can force the staff to proceed immediately to a formal investigation, authorized by the Commission when justified. The formal order of investigation will name the SEC staff members who are authorized to issue subpoenas for the production of witnesses and documents.

2. *Registration*. The SEC review of 1933 Act registration statements is described later. The company issuing the securities and its lawyers, underwriters, and accountants work closely with SEC staff to produce a document that the SEC will not contend lacks full disclosure.

3. *Interpretation*. As a general rule, the U.S. legal system does not allow persons to obtain interpretations of the law before an act is committed. Only through litigation can a person know whether a violation has occurred. However, administrative agencies often provide some exceptions to the rule.

A formal interpretation from the SEC is obtained by receiving a no-action letter. This communication is a staff promise not to recommend to the Commission that it take action if the facts submitted by the applicant and described in the letter are found to be accurate. The Commission has always honored its staff's no-action letters. Typical no-action letters involve exemption from 1933 Act registration and refusals by corporations to include a stockholder proposal in the company's proxy material.

The SEC will respond to informal questions related to interpretations of rules and the like. In certain circumstances the staff will respond to questions without requiring disclosures of the name of the registrant. Generally, these "no-name" inquiries are on more general questions. In fact-specific questions, the staff will often request a written submission regarding the facts and circumstances and will request that the name of the registrant be disclosed in the submission.

(l) CURRENT REFERENCE SOURCES.   To keep abreast of SEC developments, accountants and others mainly consult the following publications:

- The *SEC Docket* is a weekly compilation of the full text of all SEC releases, including ASRs, and the *SEC News Digest* is a daily summary of important SEC developments. Both can be ordered from the Superintendent of Documents, Government Printing Office, Washington, DC 20402.
- *The Federal Securities Law Reporter*, published by Commerce Clearing House (New York), is a loose-leaf service containing all federal securities laws, SEC rules, forms, interpretations and decisions, and court decisions on securities matters.
- *The Securities Regulation and Law Reports*, published by the Bureau of National Affairs, Inc. (Washington, DC), presents weekly summaries of most of the information of the kind contained in Commerce Clearing House publications with the full text of some releases and court decisions.
- The SEC's Web site, *www.sec.gov*, provides the full extent of all SEC releases and of speeches made by members of the Commission and its staff.

3.2 THE SECURITIES ACT OF 1933

(a) TRANSACTIONS COVERED.   The preamble to the 1933 Act states that the Act is intended "to provide full and fair disclosure of the character of securities sold in interstate and foreign commerce and through the mails, and to prevent frauds in the sale thereof, and for other purposes."

This statement is misleadingly broad. The 1933 Act does not cover the most common sale of securities: sales of issued and outstanding securities. Those transactions, on a stock exchange, in the over-the-counter (OTC) market or otherwise, are regulated by the 1934 Act. The 1933 Act covers only the original sale of the security by the issuer, along with sales by persons in control of an issuer.

There are two primary aspects to the 1933 Act regulation of securities offerings:

1. The sale must be registered with the SEC, and purchasers must be furnished with much of the information contained in the registration statement in the form of a prospectus (1933 Act, Sections 5, 6).
2. Purchasers of the securities who suffer losses within a specified time period may recover their losses if the registration statement contained a materially misleading statement (1933 Act, Section 11). Recovery can be obtained from the issuer. However, the proceeds from the sale may have been squandered; therefore, recovery is permitted from directors, underwriters, and any expert, such as an accountant, if the material misrepresentation was in the audited financial statements. All defendants, other than the issuer, may avoid liability by proving their due diligence in reviewing the registration statement.

(b) AUDITORS' RESPONSIBILITIES.   As to the audited financial statements, auditors must prove that they had, "after reasonable investigation, reasonable ground to believe, and did believe, at the time . . . the registration statement became effective, that the statements [in the audited financial statements] were true and that there was no omission to state a material fact required to be stated therein or necessary to make the statements therein not misleading . . ." [1933 Act, § 11(b)(3)]. The Act states: "The standard of reasonableness shall be that required of a prudent man in the management of his own property" [1933 Act, Section 11(c)].

The *BarChris* case (*Escott v. BarChris Construction Corp.*, 283 F. Supp. 643, U.S. District Court, Southern District of New York, 1968) was the first, and remains the most important, case regarding liability for a misleading 1933 Act registration statement. A major accounting firm was among the defendants found not to have fulfilled due diligence requirements. The court stated: "Accountants should not be held to a standard higher than that recognized in their profession." However, the court relied heavily on the failure of the firm to follow its own guidelines for reviewing events since the date of the statements for the purpose of ascertaining whether the audited financial statements were misleading at the time the registration statement became effective. The complete text of the *BarChris* case appears in *Regulating Transactions in Securities*.[1]

(c) MATERIALITY.   When the securities acts require plaintiffs to prove that information was false, untrue, or misleading, they must also show that the information was material to investors. In general, neither the statutes nor the SEC's rules and regulations offer quantitative tests or useful verbal descriptions of the meaning of "materiality." For example, as to the information required to be filed in a 1933 Act registration statement, information is material if "an average prudent investor ought reasonably to be informed [of it]" (1933 Act, Rule 405).

Many cases involve attempts to further define materiality. In the *BarChris* case, the judge used the test of "a fact which if it had been correctly stated or disclosed would have deterred or tended to deter the average prudent investor from purchasing the securities in question." Starting in the mid-1970s, some courts admitted that they would have to apply materiality standards in a flexible manner, reflecting the context in which the misleading statement was made (e.g., a 1933 Act registration statement, a 1934 Act registration statement or periodic report, a proxy statement, a case involving insider trading or tipping, etc.).

In SAB No. 99, *Materiality*, August 12, 1999, the SEC staff states that accountants and independent auditors should not rely exclusively on quantitative benchmarks to determine materiality in preparing or auditing financial statements. Misstatements are not immaterial simply because they fall beneath a numerical threshold. This subject is one the SEC is considering in connection with its campaign to counter earnings management (see Section 3A.1).

(i) Assessing Materiality.   A company or its independent auditor becomes aware that combined misstatements or omissions overstate net income four percent and earnings per share $0.02 (four percent). No item in the consolidated financial statements is misstated by more than five percent, nor are there any particularly egregious circumstances, such as self-dealing or misappropriation. Management and the independent auditor conclude that the accounting is permissible.

The staff concludes that the materiality of items may not be determined based simply on whether they fall beneath any percentage threshold set by management or the independent auditor. The staff does not object to the use of a percentage threshold as an initial step in determining materiality. But that is only the beginning. A full analysis of relevant conditions is required. Materiality concerns the significance of an item to users of financial statements. A matter is material if it is substantially likely that a reasonable person would consider it important. The context of the surrounding circumstances or the total mix of information requires assessment. Both quantitative and qualitative factors are involved. The FASB, the AICPA auditing literature, and the U.S. Supreme Court have emphasized these matters concerning materiality.

The staff thus believes that there are numerous circumstances in which misstatements below five percent could be material, that qualitative factors could cause quantitatively small misstatements to be material. Following are examples of such factors:

- Whether the misstatement is based on a precise measurement or on an estimate and the degree of imprecision inherent in the estimate. A misstatement of a given amount in the former case is more likely to be material than in the latter case.
- Whether the misstatement masks a change in earnings trends or other trends.

---

[1] J.L. Wiesen, *Regulating Transactions in Securities*. West Publishing Co.: St. Paul, MN: 1975.

- Whether the misstatement hides a failure to meet analysts' consensus expectations for the company.
- Whether the misstatement changes a loss into income or vice versa.
- Whether the misstatement affects the company's compliance with regulatory requirements.
- Whether the misstatement affects the company's compliance with contractual requirements.
- Whether the misstatement increases management's compensation, for example, by satisfying requirements for the award of incentive compensation.

The potential market reaction to a misstatement is too blunt an instrument to be used by itself in determining its materiality. However, the demonstrated volatility of the price of a company's securities in response to certain kinds of disclosures may provide guidance as to whether investors consider quantitatively small misstatements material. Expectations based, for example, on a past pattern of market performance that a known misstatement may cause a significant positive or negative market reaction should be considered in determining the materiality of the item.

The intent of management may provide significant evidence of materiality, particularly if management has intentionally misstated items to manage reported earnings (see Chapter 4), presumably believing that the amounts and trends that result would be significant to users of the financial statements. The staff believes that investors generally would consider significant a management practice to overstate or understate earnings just short of a percentage threshold to manage earnings and an accounting practice that, in essence, made all earnings amounts subject to a management-directed margin of misstatement.

The location of an item may affect its materiality. For example, a misstatement of the revenue and operating profit of a relatively small segment represented by management to be important to future profitability is more likely to be material to investors than a misstatement of the same percentage of a routine segment.

(ii) Aggregating and Netting Misstatements.   In determining the effects on the financial statements taken as a whole, each misstatement should be considered separately, and the aggregate effect should also be considered. The effects on individual line item amounts, subtotals, and totals should be considered. Misstatements of material amounts, such as of revenue, are not cured by misstatements of other amounts, such as of expenses. In considering the effect of misstatements on subtotals or totals, care should be taken in offsetting a misstatement of an amount based on an estimate and an amount capable of precise measurement.

Immaterial misstatements of prior reporting periods may aggregate and together with the current period's immaterial misstatement be material in the current period.

(iii) Intentional Immaterial Misstatements.   Management has managed earnings by intentionally adjusting various financial statement items in a manner not in conformity with GAAP. The adjustments are not material separately or in the aggregate.

The staff concludes that in certain circumstances, intentional immaterial misstatements are unlawful. The staff believes that the FASB's statement in each of its Statements of Standards that it need not be applied to immaterial items does not cover intentional misstatements. Sections 13(b)(2)–(7) of the Exchange Act require registrants to make and keep books, records, and accounts, which, in reasonable detail, accurately and fairly reflect the transactions and dispositions of the assets of the registrant and must maintain internal accounting controls sufficient to provide reasonable assurances that, among other things, transactions are recorded as necessary to permit the preparation of financial statements in conformity with GAAP. In this context, "reasonable assurance" and "reasonable detail" are not based on materiality but on the level of detail and degree of assurance that would satisfy prudent officials in the conduct of their own affairs. Reasonableness in this context is not solely based on the significance of the item to investors. It reflects instead a judgment as to whether an issuer's failure to correct a known misstatement implicates the purposes underlying the accounting provisions of Sections 13(b)(2)–(7) of the Exchange Act. Statements on

Auditing Standards No. 82 also clearly implies that immaterial misstatements may be fraudulent financial reporting.

Also, U.S.C. Sections 78 m(4) and (5) provides that criminal liability may be imposed if a person knowingly fails to implement a system of internal accounting controls or knowingly falsifies books, records, or accounts. These factors should be considered in assessing whether a misstatement results in a violation of a registrant's duty to keep books and records that are accurate in reasonable detail:

- It is reasonable to treat misstatements that are clearly inconsequential differently from more significant ones.
- It is likely never reasonable to record or not to correct known misstatements in an ongoing senior management effort to manage earnings.
- Small misstatements need not be corrected if it would involve major expenditures. But not correcting any misstatement at little cost is not reasonable.
- Not correcting an item that agrees with one of two or more reasonable interpretations of authoritative accounting guidance may be reasonable. However, if there is little ground for reasonable disagreement, the case for not correcting a misstatement is correspondingly weaker.

An independent auditor who discovers an illegal act as defined by Section 10A(b) of the Exchange Act, regardless of whether it is perceived to materially affect the financial statements being audited irrespective of netting, must, unless it is clearly inconsequential, among other things, inform the appropriate level of management and be sure that the audit committee is adequately informed. The independent auditor may also have to reevaluate the degree of audit risk in the engagement, determine whether to revise the nature, timing, and extent of audit procedures, and consider whether to resign. The intentional misstatement may also suggest to the independent auditor the existence of reportable conditions or material weaknesses in internal accounting control designed to detect and deter improper financial reporting or a lax tone set by top management. The independent auditor must report such conditions to the audit committee.

Authoritative literature takes precedence over industry practice that is contrary to GAAP.

The staff encourages registrants and their independent auditors to discuss beforehand proposed accounting treatments for or disclosures of transactions or events not specifically covered by existing accounting literature.

(iv) Implementation Questions.   The SEC staff issued an undated document, SAB No. 99, *Materiality, Implementation Questions and Answers on Assessing Materiality*, that provides personal views of SEC officials and other nonauthoritative information:

- A long-applied quantitative rule of thumb, in the absence of qualitative factors, is that a misstatement over 10 percent is presumed to be material, one between 5 percent and 10 percent may be material, and one under 5 percent is usually not material. Misstatement over five percent may be immaterial but the higher the percentage gets, the more likely it is material.
- Income from continuing operations is generally the most appropriate benchmark for quantitative evaluation of the materiality of income statement misstatements. That may not be so for a company that operates at or near breakeven or if results of operations vary between income and losses from period to period. An appropriate substitute benchmark could be measures discussed in management's discussion and analysis (MD&A) or on which industry or analysts' reports focus. Normalized income from continuing operations may be used for companies whose income is volatile. Revenues, total equity, or total assets may be a useful benchmark for companies operating at or near breakeven.
- Analysts' consensus expectations, stock price volatility, and potential market reaction to misstatement should be considered together. The independent auditor should consider whether

management may be under pressure to adjust earnings up or down to meet analysts' expectations or reduce stock price volatility. If so, that might mean that quantitatively immaterial misstatements are material. The independent auditor should discuss the matter with management and the audit committee. Nevertheless, neither management, the audit committee, nor the independent auditor should be expected to be able to accurately anticipate specific market reactions. But if, for example, in the last six quarters, a penny change one way or another in earnings per share leads to a 20 percent change in stock market price, that may make something currently material. However, in about 45 percent of earnings surprises studied, the associated stock movements and the earnings surprises were in opposite directions.

- The relative significance of the consequences that could significantly affect the company, such as a debt default, determines whether the violation of a specified contractual requirement, the existence or concealment of a possible unlawful transaction, or noncompliance with regulatory requirements affects materiality beyond quantitative factors.

(d) SMALL BUSINESS INTEGRATED DISCLOSURE SYSTEM.   In 1992, the SEC adopted new rules to allow small businesses to raise capital in the public markets at a lower cost and with fewer impediments. The new rules also reduce reporting requirements for small businesses. The principal aspects of the new rules are:

- Creation of Regulation S-B and Forms SB-2, 10-KSB, 10-QSB, and 10-SB, representing a separate integrated disclosure system for filings by SBIs under the 1933 Act and reporting under the 1934 Act. In general, SBIs are companies that have annual revenues and a public float of less than $25 million each.
- Regulation S-B is designed to be more "user friendly" than Regulations S-X and S-K.
- Changes to Regulation A under the 1933 Act, which exempts certain public offerings from registration, to increase the dollar limitation and allow issuers to obtain indications of potential investor interest (or "test the water") before taking on the cost of preparing the offering circular [see Subsection 3.2(e)(ii)].
- Changes to Regulation D under the 1933 Act (exempt private offerings) to allow general solicitation in certain offerings [see Subsection 3.2(e)(i)].

For SBIs, Regulation S-B now replaces Regulation S-X and S-K as the central repository of both financial statements and nonfinancial disclosure requirements. An SBI is defined as a company having the following:

- Revenues of less than $25 million
- Market value of securities held by nonaffiliates (i.e., "public float") of less than $25 million

For a company filing an Initial Public Offering (IPO) or an initial registration statement, the revenue test is applied to the latest completed fiscal year to be included in the filing. The public float for an initial registration statement is a date within 60 days of the filing. For a company making an IPO, the public float is determined on the date of filing based on the number of shares held by nonaffiliates before the offering and the estimated IPO price. Reporting companies apply the revenues test to the latest completed fiscal year and the public float test as of a date within 60 days prior to year-end.

However, to relieve companies of having to switch back and forth between disclosure systems, an SBI will only lose that status if it fails the same test (revenue or public float) for two consecutive years. Also, a reporting company that is not an SBI may become one by meeting both tests for two consecutive years.

Accompanying the creation of Regulation S-B was the adoption of:

- Form SB-2, for offerings of securities for cash by small issuers
- Form 10-KSB, for annual reports of small issuers

- Form 10-QSB, for quarterly reports by small issuers
- Form 10-SB, for initial 1934 Act registration by small issuers

Form SB-2 has no dollar limit on the size of the offering, and may be used for any cash offering, not just initial offerings.

Forms 10-KSB, 10-QSB, and 10-SB are patterned after their "big brothers" with the disclosure to be governed by Regulation S-B. SBIs will continue to use Form 8-K and Form S-4, but referring to Regulation S-B instead of S-X or S-K. Finally, small issuers that are eligible to use short form registration statements S-2 or S-3 can continue to do so, again using Regulation S-B requirements. The principal financial statement concessions in Regulation S-B are:

- Presenting financial information for one less year than in a "normal" filing; only two years of income and cash flow statements, and one balance sheet; and
- Eliminating the requirements currently contained in Regulation S-X for certain disclosures that exceed those called for by GAAP.

Exhibit 3.1 presents a comparison of the key differences between the requirements of Regulation S-X to those under Regulation S-B. Exhibit 3.2 illustrates principal differences between Regulation S-K and Regulation S-B. The main distinctions are the elimination of the requirement for five years of selected financial data, market risk disclosures, certain executive compensation disclosures, and the approach to MD&A. Except for those differences noted in Exhibit 3.2, Regulation S-B contains a simplified version of each of the requirements of Regulation S-K. The SEC hopes that the simplified language of the rules will reduce the cost of preparing filings.

In April 1993, the SEC adopted additional revisions to its rules and forms used by SBIs. The following is a summary of those revisions:

- Created a subset of SBIs (called *transitional small business issuers*), for which 1933 Act and 1934 Act reporting is further eased by allowing the use of Regulation A level disclosures together with audited financial statements. Transitional SBIs are generally companies that have not registered more than $10 million of securities in any 12-month period (other than securities registered on Forms S-8) and have not made a filing using a nontransitional format.
- Adopted a new registration statement Form SB-1, which permits transitional SBIs to register up to $10 million of securities under the 1933 Act using the Regulation A level disclosure with two years of audited financial statements.
- Amended Form 10-SB to allow SBIs to file their initial 1934 Act registration using Regulation A disclosure with audited financial statements.

Topic	Difference
Annual periods to be presented	Reg. S-B only requires two years of operations and cash flows and only the most recent year-end balance sheet.
Financial statements of acquired businesses	Under Reg. S-B, no more than two years of operating and cash flow statements are required.
Financial statement disclosures	Most of the disclosures required by Reg. S-X that exceed the requirements of GAAP are not required under Reg. S-B.
Separate financial statement of significant equity investees	Not required under Reg. S-B.
Financial statements schedules	Not required under Reg. S-B.
Interim financial statements	Reg. S-B provides different thresholds for combining captions in condensed financial statements.

Exhibit 3.1   Differences between Regulation S-X and Regulation S-B.

Topic	Difference
Description of business	Registration statements need to discuss the business historical development for only three years, under Reg. S-B, instead of five. Segment information and disclosures about foreign operations are not called for by Reg. S-B; however, they are still required in the financial statements by GAAP.
Selected financial data	Not required under Reg. S-B.
Selected quarterly financial information	Not required under Reg. S-B.
Management's discussion and analysis of financial condition and results of operations	Required under Reg. S-B only if the company has had revenues from operations in each of the last two years or the latest year and any current year interim period being reported. Other companies must present a plan of operations for the next 12 months, including a discussion of how cash needs will be met.
Market risk disclosures	Not required under Reg. S-B. SBIs that file using large issuer forms are also not required to provide this information.
Executive compensation	Disclosures (i) about benefits paid or accrued under pension or retirement plans, (ii) about the potential value of option/SAR grants, (iii) of a stock performance graph, (iv) of a compensation committee report, (v) of a 10-year option repricing history, and (vi) interlocking directorships are generally not required under Reg. S-B.

Exhibit 3.2   Principal differences between Regulation S-K and Regulation S-B.

- The SEC amended the year-end updating requirements of Regulation S-B. Previously all 1933 Act filings for initial public offerings had to be updated to include year-end financial statements if they became effective after 45 days after year-end. The amendment was to defer the updating requirements until 90 days after year-end if certain tests relating to profitability over the prior three years are met.
- Provided automatic waiver for SBIs as to the filing of some or all of the financial statements of significant acquired businesses where such financial statements are not readily available and the acquisition does not exceed certain materiality levels.
- Amended Rule 502 of Regulation D to permit eligible nonreporting issuers to provide same kind of information as required in Part II of Form 1-A.
- Revised Rule 254 to provide that a written "test the waters" solicitation document complying with Regulation A will not constitute a prospectus.
- Allowed a transitional SBI to satisfy the proxy rules requirement for the delivery of an annual report by providing only the financial statements included in its Form 10-KSB.
- Allows transitional SBIs to use new optional disclosures formats in Schedule 14A.

(e) EXEMPTIONS FROM REGISTRATION.   The following is a discussion of the exemptions from the registration process and the simplified filings available to a company contemplating an offering under the 1933 Act.

The 1933 Act gives to the SEC the authority to establish rules for exempting securities from registration, if offered in small issues or if offered to a limited number of investors. Rules 501 through 509 of the 1933 Act, referred to as *Regulation D*, cover limited offerings and sales of securities, whereas Rules 251 through 263, called *Regulation A*, cover the small offering exemptions.

(i) Regulation D.   Regulation D was adopted in 1982 to allow small businesses to raise capital without the burdens imposed by the registration process.

The regulation comprises Rules 501–508. Rules 501–503 contain definitions, terms, and conditions that generally apply throughout the regulation. Rules 504–506 provide the three exemptions from registration under Regulation D as follows:

- Rule 504 relates to offerings where the aggregate sales price does not exceed $1 million in a 12-month period. This exemption is not available to companies subject to the 1934 Act reporting requirements or to an investment company registered under the Investment Company Act of 1940 or certain development stage companies.

  Rule 504 under Regulation D allows a company that does not report under the 1934 Act to issue in any 12-month period up to $1 million of its securities without delivering any specified disclosure or offering document. Previously, offerings under Rule 504 could use general solicitation (cold calling, the use of advertisements, or general invitation to seminars or presentations) only if the offering had been registered under the securities or "blue sky" law of at least one state that requires registration and prospectus delivery. Additionally, unless the offer had been "blue-skied" in this manner, the securities issued were "restricted" securities under the 1933 Act. The resale of restricted securities is more difficult and, accordingly, investors generally pay less for these securities to compensate for the limited liquidity.

  To increase the use of Rule 504, the SEC eliminated the blue sky registration prerequisite to the use of general solicitation or the issuance of unrestricted securities. Thus, if the offering is limited to states that have no registration or prospectus requirement for such sales, a company that is not subject to 1934 Act reporting can publicly offer up to $1 million of unrestricted securities annually without preparing any specified form of disclosure document.

- Rule 505 relates to offerings up to $5 million in a 12-month period to an unlimited number of "accredited" investors (defined below) and to a limit of 35 other purchasers not meeting the accredited investor definition. This exemption is unavailable to registered investment companies.

- Rule 506 permits offerings, without regard to the dollar amount, to no more than 35 purchasers meeting certain sophistication standards, and an unlimited number of accredited investors. This exemption requires, among other things, that the issuer reasonably believe that the nonaccredited purchaser, or representative, has adequate knowledge and experience in finance and business to evaluate the merits and risks of the securities offered. This rule has no qualifications as to the issuer.

- Rule 507 addresses the disqualifying provision relating to exceptions under Rules 504, 505, and 506.

- Rule 508 relates to the insignificant deviations from a term, condition, or requirement of Regulation D.

Accredited Investor.   An accredited investor includes institutions or individuals who come within, or whom the issuer reasonably believes come within, any of the following nine categories:

1. An institutional investor, such as a bank, insurance company, or an investment company registered under the Investment Company Act of 1940
2. A private business development company, as defined in the Investment Advisers Act of 1940
3. An employee benefit plan qualifying under the Employee Retirement Income Security Act (ERISA) with total assets over $5 million, if the plan's investment decisions are made by a bank, insurance company, or registered investment adviser
4. A tax-exempt organization under the Internal Revenue Code with total assets in excess of $5 million
5. Any director, executive officer, or general partner of the issuer
6. Any trust, with total assets in excess of $5 million, not formed for the specific purpose of acquiring the securities offered whose purchase is directed by a sophisticated person

7. A person whose individual net worth or joint net worth with spouse at the time of the purchase exceeds $1 million

8. A person whose individual income for each of the two most recent years is in excess of $200,000 and reasonably expects income in excess of $200,000 in the current year

9. Any entity in which all the equity owners are accredited investors

Disclosure Requirements.   The disclosure requirements of Regulation D depend on the nature of the issuer and the size of the offering depending on these three items:

1. An issuer offering securities under Rule 504 and 504a or to only accredited investors is not required to furnish disclosures.

2. Companies not subject to the 1934 Act reporting requirement must furnish:
   ○ For offerings up to $2 million, the same kind of information as would be required in Part II of Form 1-A, except that the issuer's balance sheet, which shall be dated within 120 days of the start of the offering, must be audited.
   ○ For offerings up to $7.5 million, the same information required by Part I of Form SB-2 (see below) or other registration statement, if the issuer is not qualified to use Form SB-2. Generally, financial statements for the two latest years are required, with only the most recent year audited.
   ○ For offerings over $7.5 million, the same information specified in Part I of Form SB-2, Form S-1, or other registration statement that would be required in a full registration.

   Certain reduced disclosures may be permitted by the SEC if obtaining an audit would result in "unreasonable effort and expense" to the company.

   Limited partnerships may furnish income tax basis financial statements if their preparation in conformity with GAAP would be unduly burdensome or costly.

3. Companies subject to the 1934 Act reporting requirements are required to furnish:
   ○ Either: The latest annual stockholders' report, related proxy statement and, if requested, Form 10-K,

   Or: The information (but not the Form itself) contained in the most recent Form 10-K or registration statement on Form S-1 or Form 10.
   ○ Most recent interim filings.

If the securities are offered to even one nonaccredited investor, the issuer is liable to provide the information required in item 2 or item 3 above to all potential purchasers.

Conditions to Be Met.   In addition to the qualifications to be met by issuers under Rules 504 and 505, Regulation D includes the following limitations and conditions:

- Except as provided in Rule 504, no form of general solicitation or general advertising can be used by the issuer or any person acting on its behalf to offer the securities. The issuer or the person acting on its behalf (e.g., an underwriter) must have a preexisting relationship with the offeree.
- Except as provided in Rule 504, securities sold under Regulation D will be "restricted" securities with limited transferability. Each stock certificate issued should include a legend stating the security is restricted as to transferability.

(ii) Regulation A.   Regulation A allows a company to publicly offer its securities without registration under the 1933 Act. Instead, an offering statement (Form 1-A) is filed and qualified with the SEC. Two principal attractions of Regulation A are that only two years of financial statements are necessary, and the financial statements may be unaudited if audited information is not already available. Further, the completion of a Regulation An offering does not automatically subject the issuer to 1934 Act reporting. However, Regulation A's relatively low dollar limit of $1.5 million of offerings in any 12-month period, and its strict prohibition against any communications designed to gauge investor interest before the offering statement is filed, caused a decline in the exemption's use over the years.

To revitalize Regulation A, the SEC raised the limit to $5 million in any 12-month period (of which $1.5 million can be sales by selling security holders) and will now allow issuers to "test the waters" before filing the offering statement with the SEC. Also, Form 1-A has been revised to allow the optional use of a "user-friendly" question and answer form (the SCOR form) used by several states for the registration of Regulation D offerings. Under the revised rules for prefiling communications, issuers can solicit indications of interest through the distribution or publication of preliminary materials. In general, the contents of these materials is unregulated, except that it is limited to factual information. However, the preliminary materials must include a brief general description of the company's business and products, the business experience of the chief executive officer, and a statement that no money is being solicited or accepted until the qualification and delivery of the offering circular. Any solicitation of interest material must be filed with the SEC on the date it is first used, and oral communications to gauge investor interest are permitted once the solicitation of interest document is filed. However, the rules also require that the use of the solicitation statement must be discontinued once the preliminary offering statement has been filed, and they call for a 20-day lapse between the last use of the solicitation statement and the first sale of any securities.

Regulation A has also been changed to: (1) conform the process of filing, amending, and qualifying the offering statement to the registration process under the 1933 Act; (2) provide guidance on what offerings within any 12-month period must be counted toward the $5 million limit ("integrations"); and (3) eliminate the availability of Regulation A to companies that report under the 1934 Act, companies not incorporated in the United States or Canada, so-called blank-check companies (i.e., those with no specific business except to find and acquire a presently unidentified business), and offerings of undivided interests in oil, gas, or other mineral rights.

(iii) Other Exemptions.   Other exemptions from the registration requirement are:

- Offerings restricted to residents of the state in which the issuer is organized and does business, provided the issuer has at least 80 percent of its revenue and assets within the state and at least 80 percent of the net proceeds of the offering are used within the state (Rule 147)
- Securities of some governmental agencies
- Offerings of small business investment companies (Regulation E)

(f) OTHER INITIATIVES.   The SEC made several amendments to Form S-3 in October 1992 to make it available to more issuers. The changes include:

- The time period for which an issuer must previously have been a reporting company was reduced from 36 months to 12 months;
- The requirement that the market value of an issuer's voting and nonvoting common stock held by nonaffiliates must be $150 million or more has been reduced to $75 million; and
- The requirement for an annual trading volume of 3 million shares was eliminated.

(g) "GOING PRIVATE" TRANSACTIONS.   Companies repurchase their shares from the public and, in turn, become privately held. "Going private" transactions include leveraged buyouts, in which a group of investors (normally including company officers) borrows money to purchase company stock, using the assets of the acquired company as collateral for the loan.

In response to numerous complaints from shareholders about going private transactions, the SEC adopted Rule 13e-3, which prohibits going private transactions that are fraudulent, deceptive, or manipulative. Under the rule, companies are required to state whether the transaction is fair to stockholders unaffiliated with management and to provide a detailed discussion of the material factors on which that belief is based. Among the factors that should be addressed are (1) whether the transaction is structured so that approval of at least a majority of unaffiliated stockholders is required and (2) whether the consideration offered to unaffiliated stockholders constitutes fair value in relation to current and historical market prices, net book value, going concern value, liquidation value, purchase price in previous purchases, and any report, opinion, or appraisal obtained on the fairness of the consideration.

Rule 13e-4, relating to an issuer's tender offer for its own securities, also imposes stringent disclosure requirements and other responsibilities on registrants. The rule requires that (1) an issuer's tender offer remain open for at least 20 business days, (2) a shareholder tendering his stock have the right to withdraw within the first 15 business days or after 40 business days following the announcement if the company has not acted on its offer, (3) officers, directors, and major shareholders disclose all their stock transactions during the 40 business days preceding the purchase offer, and (4) an issuer accept tendered securities on a pro rata basis if a greater number of securities is tendered than the issuer is obliged to accept within 20 days of an offer.

(h) INITIAL FILINGS.   The information requirements for initial and annual filings have tended to merge in recent years. The rules applicable to Form 10-K now require much of the same financial statement information required in a registration statement. As a result, the Form 10-K has been referred to as a *mini S-1*. However, there are some unique aspects of initial filings.

The following are the most commonly used forms for registration under the 1933 Act:

S-1	General form to be used when no other form is specifically prescribed. Disclosures are similar to those required for Form 10-K.
S-2	For companies that have been reporting to the SEC for 36 or more months but do not meet a "float" test ($75 million or more of voting and nonvoting stock by nonaffiliates). Certain Form S-2 disclosure obligations can be satisfied by delivering the annual report to stockholders along with the prospectus. The more complete information in Form 10-K is incorporated by reference into the prospectus.
S-3	For companies that have been reporting to the SEC for 12 or more months and meet the above float test. Form S-3 allows maximum incorporation by reference and requires the least disclosure in the prospectus [see Subsection 3.2(f)].
S-4	For securities to be issued in certain business combinations and that are to be redistributed to the public.
S-6	For unit investment trusts registered under the Investment Company Act of 1940 on Form N-8B-2.
S-8	For securities to be offered to employees under certain stock option, stock purchase, or similar plans.
S-11	For registration of securities issued by certain real estate investment trusts and by companies whose primary business is acquiring and holding real estate.
S-14	For registration of securities issued in connection with the formation of a bank holding company.
F-1, F-2, F-3, and F-4	Registration of the securities of certain foreign private issuers.
F-7, F-8, F-9, F-10,	For registration of offerings by certain Canadian issuers that and F-80 are entitled to sell securities in the United States on the basis of the prospectus prepared under Canadian requirements.

Effective October 1, 1998, the SEC adopted a rule that requires issuers to write the cover page, summary, and risk factors section of prospectuses in plain English. The SEC also gave guidance to issuers of prospectuses on how to make the entire prospectus clear, concise, and understandable. Further, it issued *A Plain English Handbook: How to Create Clear SEC Disclosure Documents*, which provides techniques and tips on how to create plain English disclosure documents.

The rule was adopted because prospectuses issued before adoption of the rule often used complex, legalistic language not understandable by any except financial or legal experts. The SEC determined that that was unacceptable because prospectuses are intended to provide full and fair disclosure to investors, not all of whom are such experts. The proliferation of complex transactions and securities combined with the complex, legalistic language to magnify the problem. The goal is to result in prospectuses that are simpler, clearer, more useful, and, therefore, more widely read.

The organization, language, and design of the covered sections of the prospectus should conform to plain English principles and be easy to read. Qualities of writing involved in plain English include short sentences; definite, concrete, everyday language; the active voice; tabular presentation or bullet lists for complex information whenever possible; no legal jargon or highly technical business terms; and no multiple negatives. The sections should be designed to make them inviting to the readers. The text should be formatted and the document designed to highlight information important to investors.

The SEC requires registrants to use the following techniques in writing prospectuses:

- Sections, paragraphs, and sentences must be clear and concise.
- Short explanatory sentences and bullet lists should be used whenever possible.
- Terms used should ordinarily be made understandable in context. Terms should be defined in glossaries only if they cannot be made understandable in context and if defining the terms that way facilitates understanding of the disclosure.
- Avoid legal and highly technical business terminology.
  The SEC requires registrants to avoid the following conventions:
  ○ Legalistic or overly complex presentations that cloud the substance of the disclosure.
  ○ Vague boilerplate explanations readily subject to differing interpretations.
  ○ Complex information taken from legal documents without clear and concise explanation.
  ○ Repetition that adds to the length of the prospectus without adding to the quality of the information.

The goal of the guidance on how to make the entire prospectus clear, concise, and understandable is to rid the entire prospectus of legalese and repetition so that information important to investors is not blurred.

The SEC staff assists registrants in complying with the rule.

3.3 THE SECURITIES EXCHANGE ACT OF 1934

(a) SCOPE OF THE ACT.   The 1934 Act has six principal parts:

1. Creation and operation of the SEC
2. Regulation of stock exchanges and the OTC market
3. Regulation of brokers and dealers
4. Corporate disclosure requirements
5. Regulation of corporate managers, large stockholders, and preparers of filed statements
6. Prohibition against fraud in securities transactions

(b) CORPORATE DISCLOSURE REQUIREMENTS.

(i) Registration of Securities.   Unlike the registration of securities transactions under the 1933 Act, registration under the 1934 Act is a one-time registration for an issue of securities.

Issuers of securities registered on a national securities exchange (listed securities), and companies that have assets exceeding $1 million and 500 or more shareholders of record, must register by filing Form 10. This form requires the following 15 items of information:

1. Business
2. Financial information
3. Properties
4. Security ownership of certain beneficial owners and management
5. Directors and executive officers
6. Executive compensation
7. Certain relationships and related transactions
8. Legal proceedings
9. Market price of and dividends on the registrants' common equity and related stockholder matters
10. Recent sales of unregistered securities
11. Description of registrants' securities to be registered
12. Indemnification of directors and officers
13. Financial statements and supplementary data
14. Changes in and disagreements with accountants on accounting and financial disclosure
15. Financial statements and exhibits

(ii) Periodic Reports.   Registrants under the 1934 Act (as defined earlier), or any issuer that ever sold securities pursuant to an effective 1933 Act registration statement and has 300 or more shareholders of record, must file periodic reports with the Commission. Principally, these reports are Form 10-K (an annual report), Form 10-Q (a quarterly report), and Form 8-K (a special events report).

These reporting requirements may be eliminated for companies with equity securities registered under Section 12(b) or 12(g) of the 1934 Act if:

- The number of holders of record of a class of security decreases at any time to less than 300 (and the company has filed at least one Form 10-K)
- The company certifies that it had fewer than 500 holders of record *and* on the last day of each of the last three fiscal years the total assets have not exceeded $10 million (and the company has filed at least three Form 10-Ks since its most recent registered securities offering)

For companies with a class of security registered under the 1933 Act [i.e., not Section 12(b) or 12(g) companies], these reporting requirements, as required solely by Section 15(d) of the 1934 Act, may be suspended if:

- Ownership falls below 300 persons at the *beginning* of a fiscal year, and a 1933 Act filing does not become effective during that year (a company whose securities were registered with the SEC on or before August 20, 1964, may discontinue filing if the value of the outstanding securities of the registered class falls below $1 million, even though there are at least 300 holders of record); or

- The company certifies that it had fewer than 500 holders of record and, on the last day of each of its last three fiscal years, its total assets have not exceeded $10 million *and* a 1933 Act filing does not become effective during that year.

A company that desires an exemption from periodic reporting should file Form 15 with the SEC.

There are two changes in Exchange Act Rule 12b-15, which covers the procedures for amending previous Exchange Act filings:

1. The cover page procedure was changed by rescinding Form 8. In its place, registrants are now required to make amendments under cover of the form being amended. The fact that the filing is an amendment will be designated by adding the letter "A" after the form title (e.g., Form 10-K/A).

2. Amendments are now required to set forth the complete text of each item amended, rather than only revised words or lines as previously permitted.

3.4 FORM 10-K AND REGULATIONS S-X AND S-K

Form 10-K is the annual report required to be filed by companies whose securities are registered with the SEC. The due date of the filing is 90 days after the end of the registrant's fiscal year.

The filings are reviewed by the Division of Corporation Finance. As indicated in Subsection 3.1(c)(iii), the staff may review Form 10-K on a selective basis after the filing date. However, the filings that are reviewed are subjected to close scrutiny.

The SEC issues a set of instructions concerning the preparation of Form 10-K. Form 10-K is prepared using Regulation S-X, which prescribes requirements for the form, content, and periods of financial statements and for the accountant's reports, and Regulation S-K, which prescribes the other disclosure requirements.

The Form 10-K text (as distinguished from financial statements and related notes) generally is prepared by the company's attorneys, or by the company with assistance, if necessary, from the attorneys.

The accountant should read the entire Form 10-K text for the omission of pertinent information in the financial statements and to avoid inconsistencies between the financial statements and the text. Also, he may become aware of information in the text that he believes to be misleading (see SAS No. 8).

Form 10-K and related documents must be submitted electronically (unless the registrant has requested and received a hardship exemption) in accordance with Regulation S-T.

(a) REGULATION S-X.   The form and content of and requirements for financial statements included in filings with the SEC are set forth in Regulation S-X. Regulation S-X rules, in general, are consistent with GAAP but contain certain additional disclosure items not provided for by GAAP, as discussed later.

Regulation S-X is organized into 13 articles as follows:

- *Article 1—Application of Regulation S-X*. Contains certain definitions that are used throughout Regulation S-X.
- *Article 2—Qualifications and Accountants' Reports*. Contains the SEC rules on the qualification and independence of accountants and the requirements for accountants' reports.
- *Article 3—General Instructions as to Financial Statements*. Contains the instructions as to the various types of financial statements (e.g., registrant, businesses acquired or to be acquired, significant unconsolidated subsidiaries) required to be filed, and the periods to be covered.
- *Article 3A—Consolidated and Combined Financial Statements*. Governs the preparation of consolidated or combined financial statements by a registrant.

- *Article 4—Rules of General Application*. Contains certain disclosure requirements not provided for by GAAP and also contains accounting rules for registrants engaged in oil- and gas-producing activities.
- *Article 5—Commercial and Industrial Companies*. Contains the instructions as to the contents of and disclosures for the balance sheet and income statement line items for commercial and industrial companies as well as the requirements for financial statement schedules.
- *Articles 6– to 9*. Contains financial statement and schedule instructions, in a manner similar to Article 5, for certain special types of entities as follows:

Article 6	Registered Investment Companies
Article 6A	Employee Stock Purchase, Savings, and Similar Plans
Article 7	Insurance Companies
Article 9	Bank Holding Companies

Note that Article 8 on Committees issuing certificates of deposit was removed in 1985.

- *Article 10—Interim Financial Statements*. Contains instructions as to the form and content of the interim financial statements required by Article 3 and by the quarterly report on Form 10-Q.
- *Article 11—Pro Forma Financial Information*. Contains presentation and preparation requirements for pro forma financial statements and a financial forecast filed in lieu of a pro forma statement of income.
- *Article 12—Form and Content of Schedules*. Sets out the detailed requirements for the various financial statement schedules required by Articles 5, 6, 6A, 7, and 9.

(b) ACCOUNTANTS' REPORTS.   The form and content of accountants' reports are prescribed by Rule 2-02 of Regulation S-X.

In those situations where other independent accountants have audited the financial statements of any branch or consolidated subsidiary of the registrant, Rule 2-05 of Regulation S-X sets forth the reporting requirements. Section 543 of the AICPA's Codification of Statement on Auditing Standards requires disclosure in accountants' reports that exceeds the requirements of Rule 2-05. Therefore, that Statement should govern the form of accountants' reports when another auditor performs part of the audit.

Where part of an audit is made by an independent accountant other than the principal accountant and his report is referred to by the principal accountant, or when the prior period's financial statements are audited by a predecessor accountant, the separate report of the other accountant must be included in the filing. However, such separate reports are not required to be included in annual reports to stockholders.

The SEC generally will not accept opinions that are qualified for scope or fairness of presentation. The SEC will reject opinions that contain an explanatory paragraph that addresses the uncertainty of the registrant's ability to recover its investment in specific assets, for example, a significant receivable, an investment, or certain deferred costs. Since GAAP require such assets to be stated not in excess of their net recoverable amount, the SEC staff views such modifications as indicative of a scope of limitation (i.e., the auditor was unable to determine that the asset was stated at or below net recoverable value).

However, the SEC will accept an audit report that contains a "going concern" paragraph if prepared in conformity with SAS No. 59 and if the filing contains full and fair disclosure as to the registrant's financial difficulties and the plans to overcome them. Also, an audit report with a fourth explanatory paragraph describing an accounting change is acceptable.

Any filings made via EDGAR include a typed signature of the accountant. The registrant is required to keep a manually signed copy of the accountant's report in its files for five years after the filing of the related document.

(c) GENERAL FINANCIAL STATEMENT REQUIREMENTS.   Article 3 of Regulation S-X establishes uniform instructions governing the periods to be covered for financial statements included in most registration statements and reporting forms filed with the SEC. These are:

- Audited balance sheets as of the end of the last two fiscal years.
- Audited statements of income, stockholders' equity, and cash flows for each of the last three fiscal years. The same financial statements are required in annual reports to stockholders furnished pursuant to Section 14a-3 of the proxy rules (Regulation 14A).

Additionally, for 1933 Act filings, Article 3, in general, requires in specified circumstances unaudited interim financial statements for a current period along with financial statements for the comparable period of the prior year. It also allows audited statements of income, stockholders' equity, and cash flows for a nine-month period to substitute for one of the required fiscal year periods in certain specified circumstances or when permitted by the staff.

Article 3 codifies the staff position that 1933 Act filings by companies that have not yet completed their first fiscal year must include audited financial statements as of a date within 135 days of the date of the filing.

(d) CONSOLIDATED FINANCIAL STATEMENTS.   Rule 3A-02 requires a registrant to file consolidated financial statements that clearly exhibit the financial position and results of operations of the registrant and its subsidiaries. A brief description of the principles followed in consolidating the financial statements and in determining the entities included in consolidation is required to be disclosed in the notes to the financial statements. If there has been a change in the entities included in the consolidation or in their fiscal year-ends, such changes should also be disclosed.

The latest year of consolidated subsidiaries must be within 93 days of the registrant's fiscal year-end. For such differences in year-end the registrant must disclose the closing date of the subsidiary and the effect of intervening events that materially affect the financial position or results of operation. Where fiscal years differ by more than 13 days, statements of the subsidiary should be adjusted to a period that more nearly corresponds with the fiscal period of the parent.

(e) REGULATION S-X MATERIALITY TESTS.   The following summarizes some of the additional disclosures required by Rules 5-02 and 5-03 of Regulation S-X, based on stated levels of materiality. These disclosures may be made either on the face of the financial statements or in a note.

- *Notes receivable*. Show separately if amount represents more than 10 percent of aggregate receivables.
- *Other current assets and other assets*. State separately any amount in excess of five percent of total current assets and total assets, respectively.
- *Other current liabilities and other liabilities*. State separately any amount in excess of five percent of total current liabilities and total liabilities, respectively.
- *Net sales and gross revenues*. State separately each component representing 10 percent of total sales and revenues.

(f) CHRONOLOGICAL ORDER AND FOOTNOTE REFERENCING.   The SEC has no preference as to the chronological order (i.e., left to right or right to left) used in presenting the financial statements. However, the same order must be used consistently throughout the filing, including numerical data in narrative sections.

The financial statements are not required to be referenced to applicable notes unless it is appropriate for an effective presentation.

(g) ADDITIONAL DISCLOSURES REQUIRED BY REGULATION S-X.   Regulation S-X requires certain significant disclosures to the financial statements not required by GAAP. The following is a summary of the nine most common additional requirements (exclusive of those relating to specialized industries). However, if amounts involved are immaterial, disclosures may be omitted.

1. *Assets Subject to Lien [Rule 4-08(b)]*. The nature and approximate amount of assets mortgaged, pledged, or subject to liens and an identification of the related obligation.

2. *Restrictions on the Payment of Dividends [Rule 4-08(e)]*. A description of the most restrictive limit on the payment of dividends by the registrant and the amount of retained earnings or net income restricted or free of restrictions. Additionally, the amount of consolidated retained earnings representing the undistributed earnings of 50 percent-or-less-owned equity method investees must be disclosed.

   As discussed in more detail later in this section, disclosure may also be required of restrictions on the ability of subsidiaries to transfer funds to the parent, and in some cases separate parent-company-only financial information may be required. The disclosure requirements are based on specified materiality tests.

3. *Financial Information of Unconsolidated Subsidiaries and 50 percent%-or-Less-Owned Equity Method Investees [Rules 3-09 and 4-08(g)]*. This requirement is discussed in detail later in this section.

4. *Related Party Transactions [Rules 1-02(t) and 4-08(k)]*. Regulation S-X requires disclosure of material-related party balances on the face of the balance sheet, income statements, and statement of cash flows (in addition to the footnote disclosures required by SFAS No. 57).

5. *Income Taxes [Rule 4-08(h)]*. The additional SEC disclosures relating to income taxes are discussed in Subsections 3.1(d) and 3.4(g).

6. *Redeemable Preferred Stock [Rule 5-02(28)]*. The presentation and disclosure requirements for preferred stocks or other equity securities having certain mandatory redemption features are discussed in Subsection 3.4(m).

7. *Defaults [Rule 4-08(c)]*. Disclose the facts and amounts concerning any default in principal, interest, sinking fund, or redemption requirement, or any breach of a covenant that has not been cured. If a waiver has been obtained, the registrant must state the amount involved and the period of the waiver.

8. *Warrants or rights outstanding [Rule 4-08(i)]*. Disclose the title and aggregate amount of securities underlying warrants or rights outstanding; and the date and price at which the warrants or rights are exercisable.

9. *Accounting policies for certain derivative instruments [Rule 4-08(n)] (effective for all filings made after June 15, 1997)*. Disclose the accounting policies used for derivative financial instruments and derivative commodity instruments and the methods of applying these policies that materially affect the determination of financial position, cash flows, or results of operations. The disclosure should include: (1) a discussion of the methods used to account for derivatives, (2) the types of derivatives accounted for under each method, (3) the criteria required to be met for use of each accounting method, (4) the accounting method used if the specific criteria are not met, (5) the accounting for the termination of derivatives designed as hedges, (6) the accounting for derivatives if the designated item matures or is otherwise terminated, and (7) where and when derivatives and their related gains and losses are reported in the financial statements.

(h) OTHER SOURCES OF DISCLOSURE REQUIREMENTS.   The SEC publishes the opinions of the Commission on major accounting questions and on the form and content of financial statements and financial disclosures in FRRs. These opinions [originally called *Accounting Series Releases*], which supplement Regulations S-X and S-K, have been codified by the SEC to present their contents in an organized manner. The SEC's "Codification of Financial Reporting Policies" contains all current releases relating to financial statement information.

SABs are interpretations and practices followed by the Division of Corporation Finance and the Office of the Chief Accountant. SABs are not SEC rules; instead, they are a means of documenting the SEC staff's views on matters relating to accounting and disclosure practices. An SAB usually deals with a specific question posed to the SEC relating to a specific situation. However, the staff has indicated that the guidance included in the SABs should be applied in similar cases. Although the SABs are not formal rules of the SEC, they do reflect the staff's current thinking and represent the position that will be taken on various accounting and disclosures matters. As a result, SABs, should be followed when preparing information to be included in a filing with the SEC.

The new SLBs, issued for the first time in 1997, reflect the views of the SEC staff, but are not rules or regulations (similar to SABs).

(i) RESTRICTIONS ON TRANSFER BY SUBSIDIARIES AND PARENT-COMPANY-ONLY FINANCIAL INFORMATION.   Regulation S-X emphasizes the disclosure of restrictions on subsidiaries' ability to transfer funds to the parent by requiring the following disclosures in certain instances:

- Footnote disclosure describing and quantifying the restrictions on the subsidiaries [Rule 4-08(e)].
- Condensed parent-company-only financial information as a financial statement schedule [Rules 5-04 and 12-04].

The following footnote disclosures are required when the sum of (1) the proportionate share of subsidiaries' consolidated and unconsolidated net assets (after intercompany eliminations) that are restricted from being loaned or advanced, or paid as a dividend to the parent without third party consent *and* (2) the parent's equity in undistributed earnings of 50 percent-or-less-owned equity method investees exceed 25 percent of consolidated net assets as of the latest fiscal year-end:

- Any restrictions on all subsidiaries' ability to transfer funds to the parent in the form of cash dividends, loans, or advances
- The separate total amounts of consolidated and unconsolidated subsidiaries' restricted net assets at the end of the latest year

In addition, the rules require presentation of condensed parent company financial position, results of operations, and cash flows in a financial statement schedule (Schedule I) when the restricted net assets of consolidated subsidiaries exceed 25 percent of consolidated net assets at the end of the latest year (Rules 5-04 and 12-04). The condensed data may be in Form 10-Q format and should disclose, at a minimum, material contingencies, the registrant's long-term obligations and guarantees, cash dividends paid to the parent by its subsidiaries and investees during each of the last three years, and a five-year schedule of maturities of the parent's debt.

In determining the amount of restricted net assets, where the limitations on funds that may be loaned or advanced differ from any dividend restriction, the least restrictive amount should be used in the computation. For example, if a subsidiary is prohibited from paying dividends, but can loan funds to the parent without limitation, the subsidiary's net assets will be considered unrestricted. Illustrations of situations involving restrictions may include loan agreements that require a subsidiary to maintain certain working capital or net assets levels. The amount of the subsidiary's restricted net assets should not exceed the amount of its net assets included in consolidated net assets (acquisition of a subsidiary in a "purchase" transaction can result in a significant difference in this regard). Furthermore, consolidation adjustments should be "pushed down" to the subsidiary for the purpose of this test.

In computing net assets, redeemable preferred stock and minority interests should be excluded from equity.

(j) FINANCIAL INFORMATION REGARDING UNCONSOLIDATED SUBSIDIARIES AND 50-PERCENT-OR-LESS-OWNED EQUITY METHOD INVESTEES.   Depending on their significance, Regulation S-X can require the presentation of:

- Footnote disclosure of summarized financial statement information for unconsolidated subsidiaries and 50 percent-or-less-owned equity method investees
- In addition to the footnote disclosure, the presentation of separate financial statements for one or more unconsolidated subsidiaries or 50 percent-or-less-owned equity method investees

It should be noted that SFAS No. 94, *Consolidation of All Majority-Owned Subsidiaries*, has reduced the number of unconsolidated subsidiaries to a relatively narrow group of subsidiaries for which control is temporary or ineffectual.

Summarized financial statement footnote information as to assets, liabilities, and results of operations of unconsolidated subsidiaries and 50 percent-or-less-owned equity method investees is required when any one of the following tests [significant subsidiary tests of Rule 1-02(w)] are met on an individual or aggregate basis [Rule 4-08(g)].

- *Investment test*. The amount of the registrant's and its other subsidiaries' investments in and advances to of such subsidiaries and other companies exceeds 10 percent of the total assets of the parent and its consolidated subsidiaries as shown in the most recent consolidated balance sheet. For a proposed business combination to be accounted for as a pooling of interests, this condition is also met when the number of common shares exchanged or to be exchanged exceeds 10 percent of the registrant's total common shares outstanding at the date the combination is initiated.
- *Asset test*. The amount of the registrant's and its other subsidiaries' proportionate share of the total assets (after intercompany eliminations) of such subsidiaries and other companies exceeds 10 percent of the total assets of the parent and its consolidated subsidiaries as shown in the most recent consolidated balance sheet.
- *Income test*. The registrant's and its other subsidiaries' equity in the income from continuing operations before income taxes and extraordinary items and cumulative effect of an accounting change of such subsidiaries or other companies exceeds 10 percent of the income of the registrant and its consolidated subsidiaries for the most recent fiscal year. However, if such consolidated income is at least 10 percent lower than the average of such income for the last 5 fiscal years, then the average income may be substituted in the determination. Any loss year should be excluded when computing average income. Additionally, when preparing the income statement test on an aggregate basis, unconsolidated subsidiaries, and 50 percent-or-less-owned equity method investees that report losses should not be aggregated with those reporting income.

The summarized information should include (Rule 1-02(bb)):

- *For financial position*. Current and noncurrent assets and liabilities, redeemable preferred stock, and minority interests. In the case of specialized industries where classified balance sheets ordinarily are not presented, the major components of assets and liabilities should be shown.
- *For results of operations*. Gross revenues or net sales, gross profit, income (loss) from continuing operations before extraordinary items and cumulative effect of accounting changes, and net income (loss).

The summarized data is required for the same periods as the audited consolidated financial statements (insofar as it is practicable). In presenting the data, unconsolidated subsidiaries should not be combined with 50 percent-or-less-owned investees. Furthermore, if the significant subsidiary test is met, the summarized information should be provided for *all* such companies; requests to omit some entities on the basis of immateriality (i.e., less than 10 percent) will not be routinely granted by the Commission.

In addition to the requirement for footnote disclosure of summarized financial information, separate financial statements are required for any unconsolidated subsidiary or 50 percent-or-less-owned equity method investee that individually meets the Rule 1-02(w) test using 20 percent instead of 10 percent. These separate statements should cover, insofar as is practicable, the same periods as the audited consolidated financial statements and should be audited for those periods in which the 20 percent test is met.

The SEC has eliminated the asset test when determining whether separate audited financial statements of all (both domestic and foreign) equity investees must be provided under Reg. S-X rule 3-09. However, it should be noted that the SEC did not change the Reg. S-X Rule 4-08(g) requirement to provide summary financial information in the notes to the financial statements if equity investees are significant based on any of the three (i.e., assets, investment, and income) significance tests.

Combined or unconsolidated financial statements may be presented when two or more unconsolidated subsidiaries, or two or more 50 percent-or-less-owned investees, meet the 20 percent test.

The inclusion of those separate financial statements required by Rule 3-09 does not eliminate the need to present summarized footnote information pursuant to Rule 4-08(g), and the existence of one 20 percent entity will also automatically trigger the footnote disclosure of summarized information for all entities on an aggregate basis.

The following represent two informal interpretations by the SEC staff of the significant subsidiary test under Rule 1-02(w)(2):

1. Rule 1-02(w)(2) of Regulation S-X states that a subsidiary is significant if the parent's (registrant's) and its other subsidiaries' proportionate share of the total assets (after intercompany eliminations) of the subsidiary exceeds 10 percent of consolidated assets.

   The following interpretations are directed to the phrase "after intercompany eliminations."

   The term *tested subsidiary* (used below) refers to the subsidiary being tested to determine whether it is a significant subsidiary. Receivables of the tested subsidiary from members of the consolidated group should be eliminated before determining the consolidated group's proportionate share of total assets of the tested subsidiary. Receivables from unconsolidated subsidiaries and 50 percent-or-less-owned persons of the tested subsidiary should not be eliminated before determining the consolidated group's proportionate share of total assets of the tested subsidiary.

   No adjustments would be made to consolidated assets included in the denominator of the fraction, because all appropriate intercompany eliminations are already made in consolidation. Although the phrase "after intercompany eliminations" is not used in Rule 1-02(w)(3), adjustments to income from continuing operations before income taxes for intercompany profits should be made to the entity being tested similar to those made in recording earnings of the entity in consolidation.

2. Rule 1-02(w)(3) states that a subsidiary is significant if the parent's and its other subsidiaries' equity in the income from continuing operations before income taxes, extraordinary items, and cumulative effect of an accounting change of the subsidiary exceeds 10 percent of such income of the parent and its consolidated subsidiaries, provided that if such income of the parent and its consolidated subsidiaries is at least 10 percent lower than the average of such income for the last five fiscal years such average may be substituted in the determination.

   The alternative five-year average income substitution is only applicable to the parent and its consolidated subsidiaries, and is not applicable to the subsidiary being tested. In computing the five-year average income, loss years should be assigned a zero, and the denominator should be five. This rule may not be used if the registrant reported a loss, rather than income, in its latest fiscal year.

In situations where there is a loss figure for one but not both sides of the equation in the computation of the income test, the income test should be made by determining the percentage effect of the parent's and its other subsidiaries' equity in the income or loss from continuing operations before income taxes, extraordinary items, and the cumulative effect of an accounting change of the tested subsidiary on the income or loss of the parent and its subsidiaries, excluding the income or loss of the tested subsidiary.

(k) DISCLOSURE OF INCOME TAX EXPENSE.   Rule 4-08(h) of Regulation S-X requires detailed disclosures relating to income tax expense. These rules related originally to companies that were using APB No. 11 (but have been updated for SFAS No. 96 and SFAS No. 109). Companies generally only have to make the disclosures required by SFAS No. 109, except that all companies should disclose foreign versus pretax income and the five percent materiality thresholds must be applied as discussed next [see Subsection 3.1(d)]. The primary purposes of the rule are to enable readers of financial statements to:

- Evaluate current and potential cash drains that may result from the payment of income taxes
- Distinguish between one-time and continuing tax advantages enjoyed by the company

The rule originally stated that the income statement or related footnotes must disclose domestic and foreign pretax income (if five percent or more of pretax income) and the components of income tax expense including:

- Taxes currently payable.
- The net tax effect of timing differences (i.e., depreciation, warranty costs). The reasons for timing differences should be included in a separate schedule. If no individual difference is five percent or more of the tax computed at the statutory rate, this separate schedule may be omitted.

Those portions of the preceding components that represent U.S. federal, foreign, and other income taxes should be shown separately. Amounts applicable to foreign or other income taxes need not be separately disclosed if each is less than five percent of the total of the related component.

With the adoption of SFAS No. 96 and 109, the SEC eliminated the requirement to disclose the net tax effect of timing differences. In practice, the components of deferred tax assets and liabilities are displayed in accordance with SFAS No. 109 (based on a five percent threshold).

In some cases, income tax expense will be included in more than one caption in the income statement. For example, income taxes may be allocated to continuing operations, discontinued operations, extraordinary items, and cumulative effect of an accounting change. In that event, it is not necessary to disclose the components of income tax expense (e.g., currently payable, deferred, foreign) included in each caption. Instead, there may be an overall summary of such components, together with a listing of the total amount of income taxes included in each income statement caption. (The totals of the "overall summary" and the "listing" should be in agreement.) An example of footnote disclosure in this situation is contained in SAB Topic 6-1.

The rule requires the registrant to provide a reconciliation (in percentages or dollars) between the reported income tax expense (benefit) and the amount computed by multiplying pretax income (loss) by the statutory federal income tax rate. If none of the individual reconciling items exceeds five percent of such amount, and the total difference to be reconciled is less than five percent of such amount, the reconciliation may be omitted. Even if the five percent test is not met, the reconciliation still should be submitted to the extent that it is considered significant in evaluating the trend of earnings, or if similar information is presented in the reconciliation for another period. When an item is reported on a net of tax basis (e.g., extraordinary item), the taxes attributable to that item should also be reconciled with the statutory federal income tax rate.

In those cases where the registrant is a foreign entity, the statutory rate prevailing in the foreign country should be used in making the computations outlined above.

(l) DISCLOSURE OF COMPENSATING BALANCES AND SHORT-TERM BORROWING ARRANGEMENTS.   Regulation S-X calls for disclosure of compensating balances [Rule 5-02(1)] and short-term borrowing arrangements [Rule 5-02(19)]. The purpose of the rules is to provide information on liquidity of the registrant (i.e., short-term borrowings and maintenance of compensating balances) and cost of short-term borrowing.

(i) Disclosure Requirements for Compensating Balances.   A compensating balance is that portion of any demand deposit (i.e., certificate of deposit, checking account balance) maintained by a company as support for existing or future borrowing arrangements.

Compensating balances that are legally restricted under an agreement should be segregated on the balance sheet. An example is a situation where a certificate of deposit must be held for the duration of a loan. If the compensating balance is maintained against a short-term borrowing arrangement, it should be included as a current asset; if held against a long-term borrowing arrangement, it should be treated as a noncurrent asset.

The existence of a compensating balance arrangement, regardless of whether the balance is legally restricted and even if the arrangement is not reduced to writing, requires the following six disclosures in the notes to financial statements for the latest fiscal year:

1. A description of the arrangement.
2. The amount of the compensating balance, if determinable (e.g., a percentage of short-term borrowings, a percentage of unused lines of credit, an agreed-upon average balance).
3. The required balance, under certain arrangements, may be expressed as an average over a period of time. The average required amount may differ materially from that held at year-end.
4. Material changes in amounts of compensating balance arrangements during the year.
5. Noncompliance with a compensating balance requirement, and possible bank sanctions whenever such sanctions may be immediate and material.
6. Compensating balances maintained for the benefit of affiliates, officers, directors, principal stockholders, or similar parties.

There is a materiality guideline for determining whether disclosure or segregation is required. Usually, compensating balances that exceed 15 percent of liquid assets (current cash balances and marketable securities) are considered material.

Some considerations in computing compensating balances include the following:

- A compensating balance may include funds that would be held in any case as a minimum operating balance. Such operating balances should not be subtracted from the compensating balance. It may be desirable, however, to disclose the dual purpose of such amounts in the footnotes.
- Amounts disclosed or segregated in the financial statements should be on the same basis as the cash amounts shown in those statements. However, the book amounts and bank amounts for cash may differ because of outstanding checks, deposits in transit, and funds subject to collection. To reconcile the book and bank accounts, the compensating balance amount agreed to by the bank should be adjusted by the estimated "float" (i.e., outstanding checks less deposits in transit).

(ii) Disclosure Requirements for Short-Term Borrowings.   The notes to financial statements should disclose the weighted average interest rate on short-term borrowings outstanding as of the date of each balance sheet presented; and the amount and terms of unused lines of credit [Rule 5-02(19)]. There must be separate disclosure for lines that support a commercial paper borrowing or similar arrangement. If a line of credit may be withdrawn under certain circumstances, this situation also must be disclosed.

A company may maintain lines of credit with a number of banks. If the aggregate amount of credit lines exceeds the debt limit under any one agreement, only the usable credit should be disclosed.

(m) REDEEMABLE PREFERRED STOCK.   Rules 5-02(28), (29), and (30) require that amounts relating to equity securities should be separately classified as (1) preferred stock with mandatory redemption requirements, (2) preferred stock without mandatory redemption requirements, and (3) common stock. Redeemable preferred stock, or another type of stock with the same characteristics, may not be concluded under the general heading of "stockholders' equity" or combined with other stockholders' equity captions, such as additional paid-in capital and retained earnings.

The rule defines redeemable preferred stock as any class of stock (not just preferred) that (1) the issuer undertakes to redeem at a fixed or determinable price on a fixed or determinable date or dates, (2) is redeemable at the option of the holder, or (3) has conditions for redemption that are not solely within the control of the issuer, such as provisions for redemption out of future earnings.

The rule also requires registrants to provide a general description of each issue of redeemable preferred stock, including its redemption terms, the combined aggregate amounts of expected redemption requirements each year for the next five years, and other significant features similar to those for long-term debt.

The rules do not require any change in the calculation of debt/equity ratios for the purpose of making materiality computations to determine if an item requires disclosure or for determining compliance with existing loan agreements. However, where ratios or other data involving amounts attributable to stockholders' equity are presented, such ratios or other data should be accompanied by an explanation of the calculation. If the amounts of redeemable preferred stock are material and the ratios presented are calculated treating the redeemable preferred stock as equity, the ratios should also be presented as if the redeemable preferred stock were classified as debt.

According to SAB, Topic 3-C, when preferred stock is issued for less than its mandatory redemption value, the stated value should be increased periodically by accreting the difference, using the interest method, between stated value and the redemption value. The periodic accretions should be included with cash dividend requirements of preferred stock in computing income applicable to common stock unless the preferred stock is a common stock equivalent.

Although Rules 5-02(28), (29), (30) and the related FRR Section 211 speak to preferred stocks that require redemption, the SEC staff applies those provisions to any equity security that has conditions requiring redemption that are outside the control of the issuer. Several EITF consensus positions have applied FRR Section 211, by analogy, to stock purchase warrants and stock issued under certain employee stock plans.

With the general decline in interest rates, it is not uncommon for companies to find that the dividend rates on their outstanding preferred stocks exceed what they believe to be a current rate. The response of many companies in this position has been to either (1) redeem these preferred stocks (typically at a premium to their carrying values), or (2) induce their conversion. As long as redemption of the preferred stock is not outside the control of the issuer (i.e., the security is not a "mandatorily redeemable" preferred stock), accounting practice for such transactions has been to record the excess of (1) the fair value of the consideration transferred to the preferred stockholders over (2) the carrying amount of the preferred stock as a charge to additional paid-in capital and to give no recognition to these amounts in computing net income or earnings per share. However, the SEC staff has stated that it believes that such amounts should be treated as reductions of income applicable to common shareholders (in a manner similar to the treatment of dividends on preferred stock) for earnings per share calculation purposes.

(n) REGULATION S-X SCHEDULES.   The schedules required by Regulation S-X support information presented in the financial statements and can be filed 120 days after the balance sheet date as an amendment on Form 10-K/A. Each schedule has detailed instructions as to what information is required. It is essential to understand these instructions and tie the schedules in to the related items in the financial statements. The information required by any schedule may be included in the financial statements and related notes, in which case the schedule may be omitted.

The schedules are required to be audited if the related financial statements are audited.

Schedule No.	Description
I	Condensed financial information of registrant
II	Valuation and qualifying accounts
III	Real estate and accumulated depreciation
IV	Mortgage loans on real estate
V	Supplemental information concerning property-casualty insurance operations

The S-X schedules are required in Forms 10-K, S-1, S-4, and S-11, but are not required in Forms S-2, S-3, 10-KSB, SB-1, and SB-2.

(o) REGULATION S-K. Regulation S-K contains the disclosure requirements for the "textual" (nonfinancial statement) information in filings with the SEC. Regulation S-K is divided into the following 10 major classifications:

1. *General*. Including the Commission's policy on projections.
2. *Business*. Including a description of property and legal proceedings (Items 101, 102, and 103).
3. *Securities of the Registrant*. Including market price and dividends (Items 201 and 202).
4. *Financial Information*. Including selected financial data, supplementary financial information, management's discussion and analysis of financial condition and results of operations (MD&A), and disagreements with accountants and market risk disclosures (Items 301–305).
5. *Management and Certain Security Holders*. Including directors, executive officers, promoters, and control persons; executive compensation; security ownership of certain beneficial owners and management; and certain relationships and related transactions (Items 401–405).
6. *Registration Statement and Prospectus Provisions* (Items 501–512).
7. *Exhibits* (Item 601).
8. *Miscellaneous* (Items 701 and 702).
9. *List of Industry Guides* (Items 801 and 802).
10. *Roll-Up Transactions* (Items 901–915).

(p) STRUCTURE OF FORM 10-K. Form 10-K comprises four parts that are structured to facilitate incorporation by reference from the annual stockholders' report and the proxy statement for the election of directors. This format reflects the SEC's ongoing program of promoting the integration of reporting requirements under the 1933 and 1934 Acts.

Part I
Item 1   Business
Item 2   Properties
Item 3   Legal Proceedings
Item 4   Submission of Matters to a Vote of Security Holders

Part II
Item 5   Market for Registrant's Common Equity and Related Stockholder Matters
Item 6   Selected Financial Data
Item 7   Management's Discussion and Analysis of Financial Condition and Results of Operations
Item 7A   Quantitative and Qualitative Disclosures about Market Risk
Item 8   Financial Statements and Supplementary Data
Item 9   Changes in and Disagreements with Accountants on Accounting and Financial Disclosures

Part III
Item 10   Directors and Executive Officers of the Registrant
Item 11   Executive Compensation
Item 12   Security Ownership of Certain Beneficial Owners and Management
Item 13   Certain Relationships and Related Transactions
Part IV
Item 14   Exhibits, Financial Statement Schedules, and Reports on Form 8-K

(i) Part I of Form 10-K.   The information called for by Parts I and II *may* be incorporated by reference from the annual stockholders' report if that report contains the required disclosures. Where information is incorporated by reference, Form 10-K should include a cross-reference schedule indicating the item numbers incorporated and the related pages in the referenced material. The cross-referencing would be included on the cover page and in Item 14 of Form 10-K.

Item 1—Business (Item 101 of Regulation S-K).   This caption requires the disclosures specified by Regulation S-K relating to the description of business, which are segregated into the following major categories:

- General development of the business during the latest fiscal year. The registrant should discuss the year organized and its form of organization, any bankruptcy proceedings, business combinations, acquisitions or dispositions of material assets not in the ordinary course of business, or any changes in the method of conducting its business.
- Financial information about industry segments for the last three fiscal years (or for each year the registrant has been engaged in business, whichever period is shorter). If significant trends relating to segments are identified in the five-year Selected Financial Data required under Item 6, it may be advisable to include the segment data for the additional years in Item 1.
- Narrative description of business. This caption requires a description of the registrant's current and planned business for each reportable segment and should include information on principal products and services, markets, distribution methods, new products, sources and availability of raw materials, patents, seasonality of business, practices relating to working capital items, dependence on major customers, backlog, government contracts, and competition. In addition, research and development activities, number of employees, and compliance with environment-related laws (including disclosure of material estimated capital expenditures for environmental control facilities for the succeeding fiscal year) should be discussed. The number of employees disclosed should be as of the latest practicable data.
- Financial information about foreign operations and export sales as specified in SFAS No. 14 for the last three fiscal years (or shorter period, if applicable). Export sales should be disclosed in the aggregate or by appropriate geographic area to which the sales are made.

Item 2—Properties (Item 102 of Regulation S-K).   A description of the principal properties owned or leased should be identified. The registrant should briefly discuss the location and general character of the property and indicate any outstanding encumbrances. The industry segments in which the properties are used should be included.

The suitability, adequacy, capacity, and utilization of the facilities should be considered. The SEC has indicated this item will be read in conjunction with the staff's review of the discussion of "capital resources" in the MD&A (Item 7 of Form 10-K).

Additional information is required for registrants engaged in oil- and gas-producing activities.

Item 3—Legal Proceedings (Item 103 of Regulation S-K).   This caption primarily requires disclosure of legal proceedings that are pending or that were terminated during the registrant's fourth quarter, and involve claims for damages in excess of 10 percent of consolidated current assets. Such disclosure generally includes the name of the court or agency, the date instituted, the principal parties, a description of the factual basis alleged to underlie the proceeding, and the relief sought (if pending). For terminated proceedings, disclosure would include termination date and description of disposition. Disclosure is not required for litigation that is ordinary, routine, and incidental to the company's business.

Environmental actions brought by a governmental authority are required to be disclosed unless the registrant believes that any monetary sanctions will be less than $100,000. Any material bankruptcy, receivership, or similar proceeding of the registrant should also be described.

In determining whether disclosure under Item 3 is required, FRR No. 36 indicates that amounts a company may be required to pay toward remedial costs do not represent sanctions under Items 103.

Any legal proceedings to which a director, officer, affiliate, or owner of record (actually or beneficially) of more than five percent of the voting stock is a party adverse to the registrant should also be disclosed.

Item 4—Submission of Matters to a Vote of Security Holders.   Matters submitted during the fourth quarter to security holders' vote, through the solicitation of proxies or otherwise, must be reported under this caption. The date of the meeting held, names of officers elected, description of other matters voted on, and the voting results, where applicable, would be included.

(ii) Part II of Form 10-K.

Item 5—Market for Registrant's Common Equity and Related Stockholder Matters (Item 201 and 701 of Regulation S-K).   The following information is required under this caption:

- The registrant should provide information relating to principal trading markets and common stock prices for the last two years. If the principal market is an exchange (i.e., New York, American, or other stock exchange), the quarterly high and low sales prices should be disclosed. Where there is no established public trading market, a statement should be furnished to that effect. If the principal market is not an exchange (i.e., the securities are traded on the NASDAQ, or in the OTC market), the high and low bid information should be disclosed.

- The approximate number of shareholders for each class of common stock as of the latest practicable date is required to be disclosed.

- The frequency and amount of any cash dividends declared on common stock during the past two years and any restrictions on the registrant's present ability to pay dividends are required. If no dividends have been paid, the registrant should so state. When dividends have not been paid in the past although earnings indicated an ability to do so, and the registrant does not intend to pay dividends in the foreseeable future, a statement to that effect should be included under this item. Registrants with a dividend-paying history are encouraged, but not required, to indicate whether dividends will continue in the future. Such forward-looking information is covered by the SEC's safe-harbor rules on projections.

  When there are restrictions (including restrictions on the ability of subsidiaries to transfer funds to the registrant) that materially limit the registrant's dividend-paying ability, a discussion of these matters should be included in this caption or should be cross-referenced to the applicable portion of MD&A or to the required disclosures in the notes to the financial statements.

- For any sales of unregistered securities sold by the registrant: (1) the securities sold including the title, amount, and date; (2) the name of persons or class of persons to whom the securities were sold; (3) the consideration received; (4) the exemption from registration claimed; and (5) the terms of conversion if applicable.

- For first registration statements filed under the Securities Act, the issuer must report on the use of proceeds in the first periodic report filed after the registration statement's effective date and in each subsequent periodic report (i.e., Form 10-K and 10-Q) until the offering is terminated or all proceeds applied, whichever is later. The reports must quantify use of proceeds to date (i.e., to invest in property and plant, to acquire businesses, or to repay debt) and identify any direct or indirect payments to directors, officers, or 10 percent or more stockholders.

Item 6—Selected Financial Data (Item 301 of Regulation S-K).   This item is intended to highlight significant trends in the registrant's financial condition, as well as its results of operations. The following summary should be provided, in columnar form, for the last five fiscal years (or shorter period, if applicable) and any additional years necessary to keep the information from being misleading:

- Net sales (or operating revenues)
- Income (loss) from continuing operations and related earnings per common share data
- Total assets
- Long-term obligations (including long-term debt, capital leases, and preferred stock subject to mandatory redemption features)
- Cash dividends declared per common share (if a dividend was not declared, the registrant should state so)

A registrant may provide additional information to enhance the understanding of, or highlight trends in, its financial position or results of operations.

Item 7—Management's Discussion and Analysis of Financial Condition and Results of Operations (MD&A) (Item 303 of Regulation S-K).   The SEC expects each registrant to tailor the MD&A to its own specific circumstances. As a result there are no prescribed methods of disclosing the required information. The primary focus is centered on the company's earnings, liquidity, and capital resources for the three-year period covered by the financial statements. MD&A may also include other relevant information that promotes an understanding of a registrant's financial condition, changes in financial condition, or results of operations.

The use of boilerplate analysis is discouraged. MD&A should not merely repeat numerical data, such as dollar or percentage changes, contained in or easily derived from the financial statements. Instead, the registrant should provide meaningful commentary as to *why* changes in liquidity, capital resources, and operations have occurred. The reasons an expected change did not occur should also be included. The emphasis should be on trends, regardless of whether they are favorable or not.

The discussion on each topic should not be solely from a historical perspective. A registrant must also discuss any known trends, demands, commitments, events, or uncertainties that are reasonably likely to have a material effect on future financial condition, liquidity, or results of operations (such as unusually large promotional expenses, large price increases, and strikes).

The SEC's continuing focus on the importance of MD&A attained a new level in 1992 with the first-ever enforcement action taken solely due to the inadequacy of MD&A disclosures. While the SEC has tacked on MD&A allegations in previous cases of improper financial reporting, *In the Matter of Caterpillar, Inc.* (Accounting and Auditing Enforcement Release No. 363), there was no financial reporting question.

Seriously deficient MD&As may result in an enforcement action, even if the financial statements and other narrative disclosures are in compliance. Companies would be wise to review their procedures for complying with the MD&A requirements. Particular issues that should be evaluated include:

- The adequacy of "systems" in place to gather the information necessary to prepare MD&A (this would include both information about past results and information about known trends, demands, commitments, events, or uncertainties)
- The extent to which matters that are significant enough to require discussion at the board of directors level are considered for disclosure in MD&A

- The extent to which the company's MD&A does more than update boilerplate and provides the investor with an opportunity to see the company "through the eyes of management"

In 1989, the SEC completed an MD&A project that was intended to study MD&As in actual filings to determine what could be done to improve the information therein. An interpretive release (FRR No. 36) providing guidance for the improvement of MD&A was issued on May 18, 1989. FRR No. 36 and ASR No. 299 contain examples illustrating particular points that the staff believes require emphasis. The following discussion of the financial areas that are to be addressed in MD&A incorporates this guidance.

- *Liquidity and Capital Resources*
  Liquidity and capital resources may be discussed together because of their interrelationship. Disclosure is required of internal and external sources of liquidity.
    In this context, liquidity relates to a company's ability to generate sufficient cash flow on both a long-term and short-term basis. The liquidity discussion should go beyond a review of working capital at specific dates. It should cover sources of liquidity, trends, or unusual demands indicating material changes in liquidity, and remedial action required to meet any projected deficiencies. The discussion of liquidity should not be limited to cash flow. The registrant should consider changes in other working capital items and future sources of liquidity, such as financing capabilities and securities transactions.
    Any expected substantial excess of cash outlay for income taxes over income tax expense for any of the next three years should also be discussed in the liquidity section. In order to determine this information, the registrant must estimate future temporary differences, as well as reversals of prior years' temporary differences.
    For entities with going concern opinions, the registrant should disclose its financial difficulties and plans to overcome the difficulties, and provide a detailed discussion of its ability or inability to generate sufficient cash to support its operations during the 12-month period following the date of the financial statements.
    Indicators of liquidity should be disclosed in the context of the registrant's particular business. For example, working capital may be an appropriate measure of liquidity for a manufacturing company, but might not be so for a bank. Even if working capital is considered to be a measure of a company's liquidity, indicators ordinarily should go beyond working capital. Depending on the nature of the company, liquidity indicators may also include unused credit lines, debt-equity ratios, bond ratings, and debt covenant restrictions.
    If the financial statements, as required by Regulation S-X, disclose restrictions on the ability of subsidiaries to transfer funds to the parent, the liquidity discussion should indicate the impact of these restrictions on the parent.
    Capital resources are not specifically defined by the Commission but equity, debt, and off-balance sheet financing arrangements are used as examples. MD&A should describe any material commitments for capital expenditures, their purpose, and the planned source of funds to pay for those capital items. Trends in capital resources, including anticipated changes between the mix of equity, debt, and any off-balance sheet financing arrangements, should be discussed.
    Forward-looking information, such as the total anticipated cost of a new plant or the company's overall capital budget, is encouraged by the SEC but not required. Although this information would be useful and is expressly covered by the SEC's safe harbor rule for projections, the advisability of including such information ordinarily should be reviewed with legal counsel. Known data that will have an impact on future operations (e.g., known increases in labor or material costs, commitments for capital expenditures) is not considered forward-looking data and is required to be disclosed.

- *Results of Operations*
  A description is required of any unusual or infrequent events or transactions and any trends or uncertainties that are expected to affect future sales or earnings. The extent to which

sales changes are attributable to volume and prices also should be described. In addition, events that management expects to cause a material change in the relationship between costs and revenues should be discussed, along with the expected change. Furthermore, for the latest three years, the effect of inflation and price changes should be discussed (because SFAS No. 33 has been eliminated by the FASB, Item 303's reference to the requirements of that statement is no longer relevant, unless the registrant elects to continue to disclose such information).

For accounting standards (i.e., FASB, SOPs) that have been issued but not yet adopted, a brief description of the standard and its anticipated adoption date, the method of adoption, and impact on the financial statements to the extent reasonably estimable is required. Also for net deferred tax assets, if material, the registrant should discuss uncertainties surrounding realization of the assets and management assumptions.

The SEC believes that, in some cases, a discussion of interrelationships may be the most helpful way of describing the reasons for changes in several individual items. For example, certain costs may be directly related to sales so that a discussion of the reasons for a change in sales may also serve to explain the changes in a related item. A repetition of the same explanation is neither required nor useful.

The SEC has been very focused on disclosures related to segments. They believe that MD&A should adequately explain variances on a segment-by-segment basis. MD&A should also highlight any instances where a segment contributes a disproportionate amount of income or loss as compared to its revenue levels.

The Commission has stated that its focus on MD&A disclosures will continue, and principal targets of enforcement will include the failure of companies to address continued operating trends and financial institutions not candidly addressing loan loss problems. The SEC has also warned that the antifraud provisions applicable to filings under the securities acts also apply to all public statements made by persons speaking on behalf of the registrant. Therefore, company spokespersons should exercise care when making statements that can reasonably be expected to be made known to the financial community and ultimately relied upon by the public investor.

Item 7A—Quantitative and Qualitative Disclosures About Market Risk (Item 305 of Regulation S-K).   The disclosures are not required for SBIs.

The disclosures must be made in all filings containing annual financial statements. Summarized quantitative disclosures must also be provided for the preceding fiscal year, although comparative information is not required for the first fiscal year in which the information is presented.

The quantitative and qualitative disclosures are intended to help investors better understand specific market risk exposures of registrants, thereby allowing them to better manage market risks in their investment portfolios.

Item 305 requires separate disclosures for instruments entered into for:

- Trading purposes
- Purposes other than trading

In addition, within each of these portfolios, market risk must be described separately for each category of risk (e.g., interest rate risk, foreign currency exchange rate risk, and commodity price risk). Materiality is to be evaluated based on both:

- The materiality of the fair values of the market risk-sensitive instruments outstanding at the end of the latest fiscal year
- The materiality of potential near-term (generally up to one year) losses in future earnings, fair values, and cash flows from reasonably possible near-term changes in market rates or prices

If market risk is determined to be material under *either* definition (present or future), market risk disclosures are required.

Based on this definition of materiality, entities with no derivatives (e.g., banks with significant fixed rate loans outstanding, entities with material amounts of marketable securities, or entities with receivables or payables denominated in foreign currencies) will be required to make Item 305 disclosures.

- *Quantitative Disclosures*

  The quantitative information requirements are very detailed and specific. In summary, the information can be disclosed in three different ways. The alternatives are:

  1. A tabular presentation that shows fair values, contract terms, and expected future cash flow amounts for market risk-sensitive instruments

  2. A sensitivity analysis showing the potential loss in future earnings, fair values, or cash flows of market risk-sensitive instruments resulting from one or more selected hypothetical changes in interest rates, foreign currency exchange rates, commodity prices or other relevant market rate or price changes over a selected period of time

  3. Value at risk disclosures that express the potential loss in earnings, fair values, or cash flows of market risk-sensitive instruments over a selected period of time, with a selected likelihood of occurrence, from changes in interest rates, foreign currency exchange rates, commodity prices, or other relevant market rates or prices

  The rules provide great flexibility in selecting the method to be used for each portfolio (trading and nontrading) and category of risk. Furthermore, the methods, once selected, can be changed if the registrant discloses the reason for the change and provides comparable disclosures for the current and previous years. Additionally, registrants who believe providing quantitative year-end information may hurt their competitive position may provide the sensitivity analysis or value-at-risk disclosures for the average, high, and low amounts for the fiscal year.

  In addition, disclosures regarding the methods and assumptions used are required. Registrants must also discuss (after the initial year) the reasons for material quantitative changes in market risk exposures as compared to the preceding fiscal year.

  Registrants are also encouraged, but not required, to provide market risk disclosures regarding market risk-sensitive instruments and transactions other than those specifically required by Item 305 (e.g., commodity positions, anticipated transactions), and disclosures for these items may be combined with the disclosures for the required instruments. Disclosure for these items was not required because their cash flows may be difficult to estimate. For example, a U.S. company that imports a significant portion of the products it sells from Japan may find it difficult to estimate the impact on anticipated transactions of changes in the yen/dollar exchange rate.

  Registrants are therefore also required to discuss limitations that cause the quantitative information to not fully reflect the market risk exposures of the entity. Such limitations include (1) failing to provide the voluntary disclosures discussed in the preceding paragraph and (2) the fact that market risks related to leverage, options, or prepayment features may not be fully communicated through the required disclosures.

  The SEC believes that much of the information to prepare the tabular presentation is currently available and that the additional recordkeeping costs to implement this approach should not be significant, particularly since (1) financial institutions already disclose a significant amount of the information required in a tabular presentation pursuant to Industry Guide 3 and (2) the tabular presentation alternative is similar to the gap analysis commonly provided by financial institutions. On the other hand, the SEC believes that the sensitivity analysis or value at risk disclosure alternatives may require significant additional costs if a registrant does not already use one of these methodologies to manage market risk.

- *Qualitative Disclosures*

  The qualitative disclosures are intended to make the quantitative information more meaningful by placing it in the context of the registrant's business. Registrants are required to describe (1) the primary market risk exposures at the end of the latest fiscal year, (2) how those exposures are managed (i.e., description of objectives, strategies, and instruments, if any, used), and (3) known or expected changes in exposures or risk management practices as compared to those in effect during the most recently completed fiscal year.

The Private Securities Litigation Reform Act of 1995 established a safe harbor from liability in private lawsuits for certain forward-looking statements. This safe harbor was extended to the Item 305 disclosures. The safe harbor does not apply to financial statements, so the Item 305 disclosures must be made outside the financial statements.

Item 8—Financial Statements and Supplementary Data.

- *Financial Statements*

    Article 3 of Regulation S-X contains uniform instructions governing the periods to be covered by financial statements included in annual stockholders' reports and in most 1933 Act and 1934 Act filings. The basic financial statement requirements for Form 10-K are:

    Audited balance sheets as of the end of the most recent two fiscal years

    Audited statements of income, changes in stockholders' equity, and cash flows for the most recent three fiscal years

    These financial statements may be incorporated into the 10-K by reference from the annual stockholders' report.

    The financial statement schedules required by Regulation S-X, as well as any separate financial statement required by Rule 3-09, are not included in Item 8 but instead are presented in Item 14.

- *Supplementary Financial Information* (Item 302 of Regulation S-K)

    Selected Quarterly Financial Data

    All domestic companies that do not qualify as a SBI are required to disclose certain quarterly financial data in SEC filings containing financial statements. The SEC urges public companies that are exempt from the amendments to comply on a voluntary basis. This information should also be included in annual reports sent to stockholders.

    The following data is required to be disclosed for each full quarter within the latest two fiscal years and any subsequent interim periods for which income statements are presented:

    Net sales, gross profit, income (loss) before extraordinary items and cumulative effect of a change in accounting, per share data based upon such income (loss) (basic and diluted) and net income (loss). The registrant may also be required to disclose per share data for discontinued operations, extraordinary items, and net income (losses) (in accordance with SFAS 128). SAB Topic 6-G-1 states that companies in specialized industries should, in lieu of "gross profit," present quarterly data in the manner most meaningful to their industry.

    A description of the effect of any disposals of segments of a business and extraordinary, unusual, or infrequently occurring items.

    The aggregate effect and nature of year-end or other adjustments that are material to the results of the quarter.

    An explanation, in the form of a reconciliation, of differences between amounts presented in this item and data previously reported on Form 10-Q filed for any quarter (e.g., where a pooling of interests occurs or where an error is corrected).

The interim data disclosures are not required for parent-company-only financial statements that are presented in a schedule in Item 14 of Form 10-K. The data also need not be included for supplemental financial statements for unconsolidated subsidiaries or 50 percent-or-less-owned companies accounted for by the equity method unless the subsidiary or affiliate is a registrant that does not meet the conditions for exemption from the disclosure rule. Statement on Auditing Standards No. 71 requires auditors to perform certain review procedures with respect to the quarterly data. It also provides guidance for an auditor's reporting responsibilities regarding the review of quarterly financial data. Specifically, the auditor's report should be expanded if the selected quarterly financial data is omitted or has not been reviewed.

Although the rules do not require auditors' involvement with quarterly reports on Form 10-Q prior to their filing, many registrants may request their auditors to review the interim data on a prefiling basis in order to permit early consideration of significant accounting matters and early modification of accounting procedures that might be improved and to minimize the necessity of revising the quarterly data when year-end financial statements are prepared.

Information about Oil- and Gas-Producing Activities

Information specified in paragraphs 9–34 of SFAS No. 69 is required to be provided for significant oil- and gas-producing activities [as defined in Rule 4-10(a) of Regulation S-X].

Item 9—Changes in and Disagreements with Accountants on Accounting and Financial Disclosures (Item 304 of Regulation S-K).   The SEC has long been concerned about the relationships between the registrant and its independent accountants. During the 1980s, the growing number of allegations about "opinion shopping" encouraged the SEC to adopt new disclosure requirements to provide increased public disclosure of possible opinion-shopping situations. In FRR No. 31, dated April 7, 1988, the Commission stated:

> The auditor must, at all times, maintain a "healthy skepticism" to ensure that a review of a client's accounting treatment is fair and impartial. The willingness of an auditor to support a proposed accounting treatment that is intended to accomplish the registrant's reporting objectives, even though that treatment might frustrate reliable reporting, indicates that there may be a lack of such skepticism and independence on the part of the auditor. The search for such an auditor by management may indicate an effort by management to avoid the requirements for an independent examination of the registrant's financial statements. Engaging an accountant under such circumstances is generally referred to as "opinion shopping." Should this practice result in false or misleading financial disclosure, the registrant and the accountant would be subject to enforcement and/or disciplinary action by the Commission.

In 1986 and 1988, the SEC made significant amendments to Item 304 to require additional disclosures about changes in and disagreements with accountants. Disagreements and "other reportable events" are required to be disclosed in Form 8-K and in proxy statements sent to shareholders. The same disclosures are generally required in Form 10-K. However, if a Form 8-K has been filed reporting a change in accountants and there were no reported disagreements or reportable events, the Form 10-K does not require a repetition of the disclosures.

(iii) Part III of Form 10-K.   The information required in this part may be incorporated by reference from the proxy statement relating to election of directors if such statement is to be filed within 120 days after year-end. If the information is omitted from the Form 10-K and the proxy statement ultimately is not filed within the 120-day period, it will be necessary to amend the Form 10-K by filing a Form 10-K/A to include the omitted information. The reportable information and captions are described in the following subsections.

Item 10—Directors and Executive Officers of the Registrant (Items 401 and 405 of Regulation S-K).   The information reportable under this caption includes a listing of directors and executive officers, and information about each individual. Directors would include all persons nominated or chosen to become directors.

The SEC defines executive officers as the president, secretary, treasurer, vice-president in charge of a principal function or business, or any person with policy-making functions affecting the entire entity even if he has no title.

Disclosure of family relationships among directors and executive officers and a brief account of their previous business experience for the past five years is also required. Any involvement in certain legal or bankruptcy proceedings during the past five years should be disclosed.

Registrants that were organized within the last five years or that have recently become subject to the reporting requirements of the Exchange Act are also required to disclose certain legal and bankruptcy proceedings that have occurred during the past five years and involve a promoter or control person.

Also, pursuant to Item 405 of Regulation S-K, the registrant must disclose certain information on the identity of officers, directors, or owners of more than 10 percent of any class of stock who during the latest year were late in the filing of any of the "insider trades" reports (Forms 3, 4, and 5) required under Section 16 of the 1934 Act.

Item 11—Executive Compensation (Item 402 of Regulation S-K).   In October 1992 and subsequently, the SEC adopted new rules regarding executive compensation disclosures. The new rules focus on the disclosure of compensation information of the chief executive officer and the four most highly compensated executive officers other than the CEO whose salary and bonus exceed $100,000 in the most recent fiscal year. Information must also be disclosed for (1) any person who served as CEO during the past fiscal year and (2) up to two additional executives whose compensation would have been required to be disclosed if that person had not left the company. This determination is based on, and the amounts to be disclosed are, the actual amounts paid during the period of employment. The amounts are not to be annualized. Briefly, the principal new disclosure requirements include the following:

- Summary compensation table provides a three-year summary of compensation paid. It includes annual compensation (salary, bonuses, etc.), earned long-term compensation [including restricted stock awards, the number of options and stock appreciation rights (SARs) granted, long-term incentive plan payouts, and restricted stock holdings], and all other compensation. By requiring information covering three years, this table is designed to provide investors with information to evaluate trends in executive compensation.

- Option/SAR grants table summarizes the number and terms of options/SARs granted during the last fiscal year. It also requires information about the potential value of the grants. The potential value may be measured by one of the following two methods: (1) using an option pricing model (such as the Black-Scholes model) or (2) using assumed annual appreciation rates of 5 percent and 10 percent over the term of the grant. Companies using an option pricing model are required to describe the assumptions and adjustments underlying the calculation.

- Option/SAR value table summarizes options/SARs exercised during the last fiscal year and the aggregate value received. It also summarizes, as of the end of the fiscal year, the number of unexercised options/SARs held and their "in-the-money" value.

- Long-term incentive awards table summarizes rights awarded under long-term incentive plans during the last fiscal year, the periods until payout, and, for payouts that are not based on stock price, information about the range of potential payouts.

- Stock performance graph shows the cumulative total return to shareholders (stock price appreciation plus dividends) over the previous five years in comparison to returns on a broad market index (such as the S&P 500) and a peer group index.

- Compensation committee report is prepared by the compensation committee of the board of directors (or, in the absence of such a committee, the full board). It must discuss the compensation policies for executive officers and, for the last fiscal year, the specific relationship of corporate performance to executive compensation. It also must discuss the bases for CEO's compensation for the most recent fiscal year, including the factors and criteria on which the CEO's compensation was based.

The new rules also require disclosure of information about benefits under defined benefit pension plans, compensation of directors, employment contracts and termination agreements, repricing of options/SARs, and interlocking director relationships.

The new disclosures must be provided in new registration statement, periodic reports, and proxy and information statements filed after January 1, 1993. The SBIs are not required to provide all of the new disclosures. The SBIs may phase in the summary compensation table information over three years. In addition, SBIs are not required to provide:

- Information about the potential value of grants in the option/SAR grants table
- A stock performance graph
- A compensation committee report
- Defined benefit pension plan information
- A portion of the information required (the 10-year repricing history) when options/SARs are repriced
- Information about interlocking director relationships

Equity Compensation Plans. Over the past 10 years, the use of equity compensation has increased dramatically. There has been a similar increase in investors' concerns about the potential dilutive effect of a registrant's equity compensation plans, the absence of full disclosure to shareholders about these plans, and the adoption of many plans without shareholder approval. In December 2001, in response to these concerns, the SEC adopted rules on "Disclosure of Equity Compensation Plan Information."

The following disclosures are required for all equity compensation plans (including individual compensation arrangements) in effect as of the end of the most recent fiscal year:

- The number of securities to be issued upon exercise of outstanding options, warrants, and rights
- The weighted average exercise price of outstanding options, warrants, and rights
- The number of securities remaining available for future issuance under equity compensation plans

The information should be provided on an aggregate basis and categorized between those plans that were approved by shareholders and those that were not. For each plan that has not been approved by shareholders, the registrant should include a brief description of the material features of the plan. Copies of such plans should also be filed as exhibits unless they are immaterial in amount or significance.

These disclosures are required in annual reports on Forms 10-K and 10-KSB for fiscal years ending on or after March 15, 2002. They are also required in proxy statements for meetings of shareholders occurring on or after June 15, 2002, where the registrant is submitting a compensation plan for shareholder approval.

Item 12—Security Ownership of Certain Beneficial Owners and Management (Item 403 of Regulation S-K). The information reportable under this caption is required for owners of more than five percent of any class of voting securities and for all officers and directors. The name and address of the owner, the amount and nature of beneficial ownership, and the class and percentage ownership of stock should be presented in the prescribed tabular form.

Item 13—Certain Relationships and Related Transactions (Item 404 of Regulation S-K). Certain transactions in excess of $60,000 must be disclosed that have taken place during the last fiscal year or are proposed to take place, directly or indirectly, between the registrant and any of its directors (including nominees), executive officers, more-than-five percent stockholders, or any member of their immediate family. In addition, special rules apply to disclosure of payments between the registrant and entities in which directors have an interest (including significant customers, creditors, and suppliers, and law firms or investment banking firms where fees exceeded five percent of the firm's gross revenues).

If the registrant is indebted, directly or indirectly, to any individual mentioned above, and such indebtedness has exceeded $60,000 at any time during the last fiscal year, Item 13 requires that the individual, nature of the liability, the transaction in which the liability was incurred, the outstanding balance at the latest practicable date, and other pertinent information be disclosed.

(iv) Part IV of Form 10-K.

Item 14—Exhibits, Financial Statement Schedules, and Reports on Form 8-K.   This item relates to Regulation S-X schedules, the financial statements required in Form 10-K but not in the annual stockholders' report (i.e., financial statements of unconsolidated subsidiaries or 50 percent-or-less-owned equity method investees, or financial statements of affiliates whose securities are pledged as collateral), and exhibits required by Item 601 of Regulation S-K (including a list of the registrant's significant subsidiaries) and, for electronic filers only, a financial data schedule.

All financial statements, schedules, and exhibits filed should be listed under this item. Where any financial statement, financial statement schedule, or exhibit is incorporated by reference, the incorporation by reference should be set forth in a schedule included in this item.

The financial statement schedules at Item 14 must be covered by an accountant's report. If the financial statements in Item 8 have been incorporated by reference from the annual stockholders' report, Item 14 should include a separate accountant's report covering the schedules. Such a report usually makes reference to the report incorporated by reference in Item 8, indicates that the audit referred to in that report also included the financial statement schedules, and expresses an opinion on whether the schedules present fairly the information required to be presented therein. When the financial statements are *not* incorporated by reference from the annual report, the 10-K must include an opinion on both the financial statements required by Item 8 and the financial statement schedules required by Item 14. This is accomplished by either of two methods:

1. The report appearing in Item 8 may cover only the financial statements with a separate report included in Item 14 on the financial statement schedules.
2. The report appearing in Item 8 may cover both the financial statements and financial statement schedules by including the schedules in the scope paragraph and by adding a third paragraph that contains an opinion on the schedules.

In addition, the registrant should state whether any reports on Form 8-K have been filed during the last quarter, listing the items reported, any financial statements filed, and the dates of the reports.

(v) Signatures.

The required signatories include the principal executive officer, principal financial officer, controller or principal accounting officer, and at least a majority of the board of directors. The name of each person who signs the report must be typed or printed beneath his signature. Signatures for any electronic submission are in typed form rather than manual format. However, manually signed pages (or other documents acknowledging the typed signature) must be obtained *prior* to the electronic filing. The registrant must retain the original signed version of the document for a period of five years after the filing and provide it to the SEC or the staff upon request.

(vi) Relief for Certain Wholly Owned Subsidiaries.

When a registrant has certain wholly owned subsidiaries, themselves registrants, such subsidiaries are permitted to omit certain data from their own Form 10-K filings (Items 4, 6, 7, 10, 11, 12, and 13) provided they disclose, among other things, an MD&A (similar to the type of MD&A required for Form 10-Q) [see Subsection 3.5(a)].

(vii) Variations in the Presentation of Financial Statements in Form 10-K.

Form 10-K may be presented in various ways, including the following:

- The annual stockholders' report is incorporated by reference in Form 10-K. This approach is encouraged by the SEC.

- The entire Form 10-K (text and financial information) is included in the annual stockholders' report.
- Copies of the financial statements and schedules are attached to the text.

(q) ANNUAL REPORT TO STOCKHOLDERS.   In recent years, the information included in annual reports to stockholders has moved toward compliance with the reporting requirements of Form 10-K.

Rules 14a-3 and 14c-3 of the 1934 Act give the SEC the right to regulate the financial statements included in the stockholders' annual report. Although an annual stockholders' report must be sent to the SEC, technically it is not a "filed" document. Therefore, the annual stockholders' report is not subject to the civil liability provisions of Section 18 of the 1934 Act unless it is an integral part of a required filing, such as when incorporated by reference in Form 10-K. Yet, an annual stockholders' report is subject to the antifraud provisions set forth in Section 10b and Rule 10b-5 of the 1934 Act. The trend toward conforming the annual stockholders' report with Form 10-K is part of the Commission's integrated disclosure system, which requires annual stockholders' reports to contain, in addition to the financial statements, the following:

- Selected quarterly financial data for certain registrants and information regarding changes in and disagreements with accountants (Items 302 and 304 of Regulation S-K)
- Selected five-year financial data (Item 301 of Regulation S-K)
- Management's discussion and analysis of the company's financial condition and operating results (Item 303 of Regulation S-K)
- Information called for by Item 201 of Regulation S-K regarding dividend policy and market prices
- Quantitative and qualitative disclosures about market risk (Item 305 of Regulation S-K)
- A brief description of the business during the most recent year
- Information relating to segments, classes of similar products or services, foreign and domestic operations, and export sales (Item 101 of Regulation S-K)
- Employment information for each director and executive officer

The similar disclosure requirements allow registrants to use extensive incorporation by reference to the annual stockholders' report in SEC filings. As such, the annual stockholders' report is often expanded to meet the disclosure requirements of Items 1 through 4 of Form 10-K to allow incorporation by reference. In some cases, the Form 10-K and the annual report are even combined into one document.

The annual stockholders' report also must contain a statement, in boldface, that the company will provide the annual report on Form 10-K, without charge, in response to written requests and must indicate the name and address of the person to whom such a written request is to be directed. The statement may alternatively be included in the proxy statement.

(i) Financial Statements Included in Annual Report to Stockholders.   Audited balance sheets for the latest two years and statements of income and cash flows for the latest three years are required.

The financial statements are required to be in accordance with Regulation S-X except that Articles 3, 11 and 12, other than Rules 3-03(e), 3-04, and 3-20 do not have to be followed. (Article 3 sets forth the financial statements to be included in SEC filings. Article 11 deals with pro forma information. Article 12 deals with financial statements schedules. Rule 3-03(e) requires the business segment disclosure of SFAS No. 14, Rule 3-04 covers changes in other stockholders' equity, and Rule 3-20 addresses the currency for financial statements of foreign private issuers.) The financial statements must be as large and legible as 8-point modern type and the notes must be at least 10-point modern type.

Financial statement schedules and exhibits, which may otherwise be required in Form 10-K, may be omitted.

If the financial statements for a prior period have been audited by a predecessor accountant, the separate report of the predecessor may be omitted in the annual report to stockholders if it is referred to in the successor accountant's report. The separate report of the predecessor accountant would, however, be required in the Form 10-K, in Part II, or in Part IV as a financial statement schedule.

(ii) Content of Annual Report to Stockholders.   The SEC has long recognized that the annual stockholders' report is the most effective method of communicating financial information to stockholders. It believes these reports should be readable and informative and prefers that they be written without boilerplate. The SEC allows registrants to use their discretion in determining the format of the annual stockholders' report, as long as the information required is included and can easily be located. To improve the presentation of data, the SEC encourages the use of charts and other graphic illustrations, as long as they are consistent with the information in the financial statements.

Under APB Opinion No. 28, publicly traded companies that neither separately report fourth-quarter results to stockholders nor disclose the results for that quarter in the annual report are required to disclose the following information in a note to the financial statements: (1) disposals of segments of a business and extraordinary, unusual, or infrequently occurring items recognized in the fourth quarter, and (2) the aggregate effect of year-end adjustments that are material to the results of that quarter.

(iii) Reporting on Management and Audit Committee Responsibilities in the Annual Report to Stockholders.   The National Commission on Fraudulent Financial Reporting (1987) has recommended the following:

- All public companies should be required by the SEC to include in an annual stockholders' report, a report signed by top management, acknowledging management's responsibilities for the financial statements and internal controls and providing management's assessment of the effectiveness of the internal controls.
- All public companies should be required by the SEC to include in an annual stockholders' report, a letter from the chairman of the audit committee describing its activities.

Similar recommendations have been made by both the AICPA and the FEI in the past. Many companies already include "management reports" containing information similar to that suggested by the National Commission.

(iv) Summary Annual Reports.   The concept of "summary annual reports" has been discussed by the Financial Executives International for several years. The basic argument is that the annual report contains much information that is not relevant or meaningful to the average investor; therefore, an alternative reporting vehicle should be permitted by the SEC. For various reasons, the Commission rejected such proposals until January 20, 1987, when it issued a no-action letter in response to a proposal by General Motors (GM). In that letter, the SEC staff did not object to the GM proposal to provide a "glossy report" to its shareholders separate from its SEC filings and to include the required annual report as a part of the proxy material and Form 10-K. The glossy report would include summary financial data similar to, though more extensive than, that contained in a quarterly report. It would also include a discussion of significant accounting events in a financial narrative section and an opinion of the public accountants covering the summary financial information. The proxy material and the Form 10-K would then become "stand alone" documents with no incorporation by reference from the glossy report. In its explanation, the SEC staff focused on the following five factors in GM's proposal, which is likely to set a precedent for other registrants attempting to prepare such summary annual reports:

1. The release of the full audited financial statements with the earnings press release, and the extensive circulation of the release to the market
2. The filing of Form 10-K with the Commission at or prior to the release of the glossy report
3. The proposed auditors' report on the financial information to be included with the summary financial data in the glossy report
4. Inclusion of the annual report to shareholders, as required by Rule 14a-3(b) in both the Form 10-K and an appendix to the annual election of directors proxy statement
5. Inclusion of a statement in the glossy report, as well as the proxy statement, to provide the Form 10-K upon request

However, GM did not implement its new glossy report for its 1986 year-end. Since January 1987 a number of companies have prepared and issued summary annual reports.

3.5 FORM 10-Q

In addition to the comprehensive annual report on Form 10-K, the Commission requires a registrant to file a Form 10-Q for each of the first three quarters of its fiscal year. Form 10-Q is due 45 days after the end of the quarter; one is not required for the fourth quarter. If the registrant is a listed company, it also must file Form 10-Q with the appropriate stock exchange. The following are the basic requirements of Form 10-Q:

- The form is required to be filed by any company (1) whose securities are registered with the SEC, and (2) which is required to file annual reports on Form 10-K.
- Information must be submitted on a consolidated basis.
- Financial statements must be reviewed by an independent auditor in accordance with Statement on Auditing Standards No. 71 (including any amendments to SAS No. 71).

A uniform set of instructions for interim financial statements is included in Article 10 of Regulation S-X, as an extension of the SEC's integrated disclosure program. In addition, certain requirements for the current Form 10-Q are contained in FRR Sections 301, 303, 304, and 305. Interpretations of the rules are provided in SAB Topic 6-G.

A registrant may elect to incorporate by reference all of the information required by Part I to a quarterly stockholder report or other published document containing the information. Other information also may be incorporated by reference in answer or partial answer to an item in Part II, provided the incorporation by reference is clearly identified. The SEC permits a combined quarterly stockholder report and Form 10-Q *if* the report contains all information required by Part I and all other information (cover page, signature, Part II) is in the combined report or included on Form 10-Q with appropriate cross-referencing.

(a) STRUCTURE OF FORM 10-Q.   Form 10-Q consists of two parts. Part I contains financial information, and Part II contains other information such as legal proceedings and changes in securities.

(i) Part I—Financial Information.

Item 1—Financial Statements.   The financial statements should be prepared in accordance with Rule 10-01 of Regulation S-X, APB Opinion No. 28, and SFAS No. 3. An understanding of these requirements is essential in preparing Form 10-Q.

The financial statements may be condensed and should include a condensed balance sheet, income statement, and statement of cash flows for the required periods. The statements are not required to be audited or reviewed by independent accountants.

Balance sheets as of the end of the latest quarter and the end of the preceding fiscal year are required. A comparative balance sheet as of the end of the previous year's corresponding interim date need only be included when, in the registrant's opinion, it is necessary for an understanding of seasonal fluctuations.

Only the major captions set forth in Article 5 of Regulation S-X are required to be disclosed, except that the components of inventory (raw materials, work-in-process, finished goods) shall also be presented on the balance sheet or in the notes. Thus, even if a company uses the gross profit method or similar method to determine cost of sales for interim periods, management will have to estimate the inventory components.

There is also a materiality rule for disclosure of major balance sheet captions. Those that are less than 10 percent of total assets *and* that have not changed by more than 25 percent from the preceding fiscal year's balance sheet may be combined with other captions.

Income statements for the latest quarter and the year to date and for the corresponding periods of the prior year are to be provided. Statements may also be presented for the 12-month period ending with the latest quarter and the corresponding period of the preceding year.

For example, if a company reports on a November 30, 1990, fiscal year-end, its Form 10-Q for the quarter ended August 31, 1990, would include comparative income statements for the nine months ended August 31, 1990 and 1989, and for the three months ended August 31, 1990 and 1989.

Only major captions set forth in Article 5 of Regulation S-X are required to be disclosed. However, a major caption may be combined with others if it is less than 15 percent of average net income for the latest three fiscal years *and* has not changed by more than 20 percent as compared to the related caption in the income statement for the corresponding interim period of the preceding year (except that bank holding companies must present securities gains or losses as a separate item, regardless of the amount or percentage change). In computing average net income, only the amount classified as "net income" should be used. Loss years should be excluded unless losses were incurred in all three years, in which case the average loss should be used. As with the balance sheet, retroactive reclassification of the prior year is required to conform with the current year's classification in the income statement.

Statements of cash flows for the year to date and for the corresponding period of the prior year are to be presented. In addition, the statement may be presented for the 12-month periods ending with the latest quarter and the corresponding period of the prior year. The statement of cash flows may be condensed, starting with a single amount for net cash flows from operating activities. Additionally, individual items of financing and investing cash flows, and disclosures about noncash investing or financing transactions, need only be presented if they exceed 10 percent of the average net cash flows from operating activities for the last three years. In computing the average, any years that reflect a net cash outflow from operations should be excluded, unless all three years reflect a net cash outflow, in which case the average outflow should be used for the test.

Seven other important provisions of the rules relating to financial information are as follows:

1. Detailed footnote disclosures and Regulation S-X schedules are not required. However, disclosures must be adequate so as not to make the presented information misleading. It would appear that the two preceding sentences are contradictory. There is, however, a presumption that financial statement users have read or have access to the audited financial statements containing detailed disclosures for the latest fiscal year, in which case most continuing footnote disclosures could be omitted.

    Regulation S-X specifically requires disclosure of events occurring since the end of the latest fiscal year having a material impact on the financial statements, such as changes in:

    a. Accounting principles and practices.

    b. Estimates used in the statements.

    c. Status of long-term contracts.

    d. Capitalization, including significant new borrowings, or modification of existing financing arrangements.

e. If material contingencies exist, disclosure is required even if significant changes have not occurred since year-end.

f. In addition, based on existing pronouncements and informal statements by the SEC, the following matters, if applicable, should be considered for disclosure:

    i. Significant events during the period (i.e., unusual or infrequently occurring items, such as material write-downs of inventory or goodwill)

    ii. Significant changes in the nature of transactions with related parties

    iii. The basis for allocating amounts of significant costs and expenses to interim periods if different from those used for the annual statements

    iv. The nature, amount, and tax effects of extraordinary items

    v. Significant variations in the customary relationship between income tax expense and income before taxes

    vi. The amount of any last-in, first-out (LIFO) liquidation expected to be replaced by year-end or the effect of a material liquidation during the quarter

    vii. Significant new commitments or changes in the status of those previously disclosed

Although it is not mentioned in the rules, registrants may consider it desirable to indicate with a legend on Form 10-Q that the financial statements are condensed and do not contain all GAAP-required disclosures that are included in a full set of financial statements.

2. The interim financial statements should contain a statement representing that they reflect all normally recurring adjustments that are, in management's opinion, necessary for a fair presentation in conformity with GAAP. Such adjustments would include estimated provisions for bonuses and for profit-sharing contributions normally determined at year-end.

3. The registrant may furnish additional information of significance to investors, such as seasonality of business, major uncertainties, significant proposed accounting changes, and backlog. In that connection, it would ordinarily be appropriate to include a statement that the interim results are not necessarily indicative of results to be obtained for the full year.

4. For disposals of a significant portion of the business or for combinations accounted for as purchases, the effect on revenues and net income (including earnings per share) must be disclosed. In addition, in the case of purchases, pro forma disclosures in accordance with SFAS No. 141 are required.

5. If the prior period information has been retroactively restated after the initial reporting of that period, disclosure is required of the effect of the change.

6. Disclosure is required of earnings and dividends per share of common stock, the basis of the computation, and the number of shares used in the computation for all periods presented. The registrant must file an exhibit, showing in reasonable detail the computation of earnings per share in complex situations. However, the SEC staff has informally indicated that such exhibits may no longer be needed in light of SFAS No. 128 and its required disclosures.

7. If an accounting change was made, the date of the change and the reasons for making it must be disclosed. In addition, in the first Form 10-Q filed after the date of an accounting change, a letter from the accountants (referred to as a *preferability letter*) must be filed as an exhibit in Part II, indicating whether they believe the change to be a preferable alternative accounting principle under the circumstances. If the change was made in response to an FASB requirement, no such letter need be filed.

The SEC staff acknowledges that where objective criteria for determining preferability have not been established by authoritative bodies, the determination of the preferable accounting treatment should be based on the registrant's business judgment and business planning (e.g., expectations regarding the impact of inflation, consumer demand for the company's products, or a change in marketing methods). The staff believes that the registrant's judgment and business planning, unless they appear to be unreasonable, may be accepted and relied on by the accountant as the basis of the preferability letter.

If circumstances used to justify a change in accounting method become different in subsequent years, the registrant may not change back to the principle originally used without again justifying that the original principle is preferable under current conditions.

Item 2—Management's Discussion and Analysis of Financial Condition and Results of Operations [Item 303(b) of Regulation S-K].   The MD&A must be provided pursuant to Item 303(b) of Regulation S-K and should discuss substantially the same issues covered in the MD&A for the latest Form 10-K, specifically focusing on:

- Material changes in financial condition for the period from the latest fiscal year-end to the date of the most recent interim balance sheet and, if applicable, the corresponding interim period of the preceding fiscal year
- Material changes in results of operations for the most recent year-to-date period, the current quarter, and the corresponding periods of the preceding fiscal year

In preparing the discussion, companies may presume that users of the interim financial information have access to the MD&A covering the most recent fiscal year. The MD&A should address any seasonal aspects of its business affecting its financial condition or results of operations and identify any significant elements of income from continuing operations that are not representative of the ongoing business. The impact of inflation does not have to be discussed.

The MD&A should be as informative as possible. As discussed, the registrant should avoid the use of boilerplate analysis and not merely repeat numerical data easily derived from the financial statements.

Item 3—Quantitative and Qualitative Disclosures about Market Risk (Item 305 of Regulation S-K).   Market risk information is required to be presented if there have been material changes in the market risks faced by a registrant or in how those risks are managed since the end of the most recent fiscal year. Interim information is not required until after the first fiscal year-end in which the disclosures are made.

(ii) Part II—Other Information.   The registrant should provide the following information in Part II under the applicable captions. Any item that is not applicable may be omitted *without* disclosing that fact.

Item 1—Legal Proceedings (Item 103 of Regulation S-K).   A legal proceeding has to be reported in the quarter in which it first becomes a reportable event or in subsequent quarters in which there are material developments. For terminated proceedings, information as to the date of termination and a description of the disposition should be provided in the Form 10-Q covering that quarter.

Item 2—Changes in Securities and Use of Proceeds (Item 701 of Regulation S-K).   Any changes to any class of registered securities and the effect that the changes have on the shareholder rights should be disclosed. Changes in working capital restrictions and limitations on dividend payments would constitute a "change."

Any sales of equity securities not registered under the Securities Act, not previously reported, including a description of the securities sold, the purchasers, the consideration received, the exemption from registration claimed, and the terms of conversions (if any), should be disclosed.

For first registration statements filed under the Securities Act, the issuer must report on the use of proceeds in the first periodic report filed after the registration statement's effective date, and in each subsequent periodic report (i.e., Form 10-K or 10-Q) until the offering is terminated or all proceeds applied, whichever is later. The registrant must quantify the use of proceeds to date (i.e., to invest in property and plant, to acquire businesses, to repay debt), and identify any direct or indirect payments to directors, officers, or 10 percent or more stockholders.

Item 3—Defaults on Senior Securities.   Disclosure is required of a default (with respect to principal or interest) not cured within 30 days of the due date, including any grace period, if the related indebtedness exceeds five percent of consolidated assets. A default relating to dividend arrearages on preferred stock should also be disclosed.

Item 4—Submission of Matters to a Vote of Security Holders.   Matters submitted to security holders' vote, through the solicitation of proxies or otherwise, must be reported under this caption.

Item 5—Other Information.   Events not previously reported on Form 8-K may be reported under this caption. Such information would not be required to be repeated in a report on Form 8-K.

Item 6—Exhibits and Reports on Form 8-K.   This caption should include a listing of exhibits filed with Form 10-Q (Item 601 of Regulation S-K) and a listing of Form 8-K reports filed during the quarter, showing the dates of any such reports, items reported, and financial statements filed.

Inapplicable exhibits may be omitted without referring to them in the index. Where exhibits are incorporated by reference, that fact should be noted.

(iii) Omission of Information by Certain Wholly Owned Subsidiaries.   Certain wholly owned subsidiaries are permitted to omit Items 2, 3, and 4 of Part II provided certain conditions are met and to streamline the disclosures required in Item 2 of Part I.

(iv) Signatures.   The form must be signed by the principal financial officer or chief accounting officer of the registrant, as well as another duly authorized officer. If the principal financial officer or chief accounting officer is also a duly authorized signatory, one signature is sufficient provided the officer's dual responsibility is indicated.

Signatures for any electronic submission are in typed form rather than manual format. However, manually signed pages (or other documents acknowledging the typed signatures) must be obtained *prior* to the electronic filing. The registrant must retain the original signed document for a period of five years after the filing of the related document and provide it to the SEC or the staff upon request.

3.6 FORM 8-K

(a) OVERVIEW OF FORM 8-K REQUIREMENTS.   A company that is required to file annual reports on Form 10-K is required to file current reports on Form 8-K if any of specified reportable events take place. If the registrant is a listed company, it must also file the Form 8-K with the appropriate stock exchange.

Form 8-K is required to report the occurrence of the events specified in Items 1–3, 8, and 9 below, and it must be filed with the SEC within 15 days after the occurrence of the earliest event reported. A report covering an Item 4 or 6 must be filed within five days after the occurrence of the event. A report covering an event in Item 5 is to be filed "promptly" (because the filing of Form 8-K for events includable in Item 5 is optional, there is no mandatory filing deadline). FRR No. 18 has amended the filing requirements of Form 8-K by providing an extension of up to 60 days to file financial statements of acquired businesses as an amendment to Form 8-K that are reportable in Item 2.

If substantially the same information required for Form 8-K has been previously reported by the registrant in a filing with the SEC (such as in Part II of Form 10-Q), there is no need to include it on a Form 8-K.

If a registrant issues a press release or other document within the specified period above, which includes the information meeting some or all of the requirements of Form 8-K, the information may be incorporated by reference to the document. The document incorporated by reference should be included as an exhibit to Form 8-K.

See Section 3.1(f), SEC Proposed Rule Making and Other Guidance, discussed previously.

(b) EVENTS TO BE REPORTED.

(i) Item 1—Changes in Control of Registrant.   Detailed information is required as to a change in control of the registrant, including the identity of acquiring or selling parties, source and amount of consideration, date and description of transaction, percentage of ownership of acquiring party, terms of loans and pledges, and any arrangements or understanding among the parties [see Item 403(c) of Regulation S-K].

(ii) Item 2—Acquisition or Disposition of Assets.   Disclosure is required of any acquisitions or dispositions of a significant amount of assets, other than in the ordinary course of business. Disclosures would include the transaction date, description of the assets, the purchase or sales price, the parties involved and any relationships between them, sources of funds used, and the use of assets acquired.

An acquisition or disposition is "significant" if:

- The net book value of the assets or the purchase price or sales price exceeds 10 percent of the registrant's consolidated assets before the transaction, *or*
- The business (100 percent interest) bought or sold meets the test of a significant subsidiary, *or*
- The purchase or sale involves an interest (less than 100 percent) in a business that meets the test of a significant subsidiary, substituting 20 percent for 10 percent, and is required to be accounted for by the equity method.

Financial statements may be required to be filed for the acquired business, depending on its relative significance. The determination of significance is made by applying the significant subsidiary tests in comparing the latest annual financial statements of the acquired business to the registrant's latest annual consolidated financial statements filed at or before the acquisition (Rule 3-05 of Regulation S-X). For pooling of interests transactions, the significant subsidiary tests include a comparison of the number of common shares exchanged with the registrant's common shares outstanding at the date the transaction is initiated. The income and asset test should be as of the latest fiscal year; *provided, however*, that if the registrant has, since the end of the most recent fiscal year, consummated an acquisition for which historical and pro forma financial information has been filed on Form 8-K, then the pro forma amount in that Form 8-K for the latest fiscal year may be used. (*Note:* Registrants who believe their specific circumstances warrant the use of later financial information in other situations should consult with the Division of Corporation Finance, which will evaluate such requests on a case-by-case basis.)

- If, based on such tests, none of the conditions exceeds 20 percent, financial statements are not required.
- If any condition exceeds 20 percent, but none exceeds 40 percent, financial statements are required for the latest year prior to acquisition (audited) and for any interim periods required by Rules 3-01 and 3-02 of Regulation S-X (unaudited).
- If any condition exceeds 40 percent, but does not exceed 50 percent, financial statements are required for the two most recent years (audited), and for any interim periods (unaudited).
- If any condition exceeds 50 percent, financial statements are required for the three latest years (audited), as required in Form 10-K, and for any interim periods (unaudited). However, only two years of financial statements are required if the acquired business revenues, in its most recent year, are less than $25 million.

If the acquired business or equity investee is a foreign entity, the entity's financial statements previously could be either (1) presented in U.S. GAAP or (2) presented in local GAAP if a reconciliation from local GAAP to U.S. GAAP was provided.

These reconciliation requirements have been changed in the following ways:

- Reconciliations of local GAAP financial statements to U.S. GAAP are now required only if the significance level of the acquired business or equity investee exceeds 30 percent. [However, it should be noted that (1) the requirements to provide local GAAP financial statements remain and (2) as discussed further below, reconciliation work will still be required.]
- The reconciliations to U.S. GAAP may now be made in accordance with Item 17 of Form 20-F. (Item 17 is a simplified reconciliation requirement that does not require all of the disclosures required by U.S. GAAP and Reg. S-X.)

Even if the reconciliation of U.S. GAAP does not need to be presented, reconciliation work will still be required with respect to the financial statements of foreign equity investees. This is because (1) the local GAAP financial statements of the foreign equity investees must still be converted to U.S. GAAP in order to properly apply the equity method of accounting and (2) the SEC did not change the Reg. S-X Rule 4-08(g) requirement to provide summary financial information regarding equity investees in accordance with U.S. GAAP in the notes to the primary financial statements.

The requirement as to the age of financial statements has also been changed. Domestic issuers may now update the financial statements of acquired foreign businesses or foreign equity investees included in their filings on the same time schedule as foreign issuers. Audited financial statements for the most recently completed fiscal year are now not required until six months after the year-end, and unaudited interim financial statements are now required only to the extent necessary to make the most recent financial statements included in the filing more than 10 months old.

Regulation S-X governs the form and content of these financial statements. S-X schedules are not required.

If a portion of a business is being acquired, such as a division or a single product line, the registrant should provide audited financial statements only on the portion of the business acquired. Therefore, the registrant may, depending on the circumstances and with the permission of the SEC, present a "statement of assets acquired and liabilities assumed" (excluding amounts not included in the acquisition, such as intercompany advances) instead of a balance sheet and a "statement of revenues and direct expenses" for the business acquired instead of an income statement. A registrant, when acquiring a division or product line whose operations are included in the consolidated financial statements of a larger entity, should determine as soon as possible if the accountant reporting on the consolidated financial statements of the seller is able to report on the portion being acquired.

A significant acquisition or disposition under Item 2 will also require presentation of pro forma financial information, giving effect to the event. The purpose of pro forma data is to provide investors with information about the continuing impact of a transaction and assist them in analyzing future prospects of the registrant. The main provisions of the rule (Regulation S-X, Article 11) are as follows:

- The pro forma financial statements should consist of a condensed balance sheet as of the end of the most recent period and condensed income statements for the latest fiscal year and the interim period from the latest fiscal year-end to the date of the pro forma balance sheet (interim data for the corresponding period of the prior year is optional).
- Only the major captions of Article 5 of Regulation S-X need be presented. For the balance sheet, captions that amount to less than 10 percent of total assets may be combined; income statement captions less than 15 percent of average net income for the latest three years may likewise be combined.
- The pro forma statements should be preceded by an introductory paragraph describing the transaction and should be accompanied by explanatory notes.

- Ordinarily, the statements should be in columnar form, presenting historical statements, pro forma adjustments, and the pro forma totals. Care should be taken in combining pro forma adjustments to the same line item. Sufficient detail must be provided to allow for a clear understanding of amount and nature of required adjustments. For a purchase business combination, the footnotes should tabularly indicate the components and allocation of the purchase price.
- If the acquired business's fiscal year differs from that of the registrant by more than 93 days, the income statement of the acquired business for the latest year should be updated, if practicable. This could be done by adding and deducting comparable interim periods. In that case, there should be disclosure of the periods combined and the revenues and income for periods excluded or for periods included more than once (e.g., an interim period included both as part of the fiscal year and subsequent interim period).
- The pro forma income statement should end with income (loss) from continuing operations before nonrecurring charges or credits directly related to the transaction (e.g., severance pay, gain or loss on the transaction, professional and printing costs). Material nonrecurring items and related tax effects that will affect net income within the next 12 months should be disclosed separately. Nonrecurring items included in the historical financial statements that are not directly attributable to the transaction should *not* be excluded from the pro forma financial statements.

    If the assets acquired include assets relating to operations that the acquirer intends to dispose of, the staff will not object to the presentation of those assets as a single line item in the pro forma balance sheet, provided the operations are not expected to be continued for more than a short period (i.e., 12 months) prior to disposal.
- Adjustments to the pro forma income statement should assume the transaction was consummated at the beginning of the earliest fiscal year and should include factually supportable adjustments that are directly attributable to the transaction and expected to have a continuing effect. Adjustments to the balance sheet should assume the transaction had occurred at the balance sheet date, and should include factually supportable adjustments that are directly attributable to the transaction (regardless of whether they have a continuing impact or are nonrecurring).

    If an acquired entity was previously part of another entity, adjustments might be necessary when corporate overhead, interest, or income taxes had not been allocated by management on a reasonable basis. Similarly, if the acquired business was an S corporation or a partnership, adjustments should be made to reflect estimated officer salaries and income taxes. For dispositions, the adjustments should include deletion of the divested business and adjustments of expenses incurred on behalf of that business (e.g., advertising costs). For transactions accounted for as a purchase, the adjustments should reflect goodwill amortization, depreciation, other effects of APB Opinion No. 16, and interest on debt incurred to make the acquisition.
- Tax effects of pro forma adjustments should be shown separately and ordinarily should be calculated at the statutory rate in effect during the periods presented.
- In certain unusual instances, there may only be a limited number of clearly understandable adjustments, in which case a narrative description of the transaction may be substituted for the pro forma statements.
- Historical and pro forma per share data, including the number of shares used in the computation, should be disclosed on the face of the pro forma income statement. If common shares are to be issued in the transaction, the per share data should be adjusted to reflect assumed issuance at the beginning of the period presented.
- A financial forecast may be presented in lieu of the pro forma income statement. The forecast should be in the same detail as the pro forma income statements and should cover at least 12 months from the date of the most recent balance sheet included in the filing

or the estimated consummation date of the transaction, whichever is later. Historical information for a recent 12-month period should be presented in a parallel column. The forecast should be presented in accordance with AICPA guidelines, with clear disclosure of underlying assumptions.

The determination of what constitutes a "business" for the purpose of determining whether financial statements are required to be included in the filing is a "facts and circumstances" test. This would require an evaluation of whether there is sufficient continuity of the acquired entity's operations before and after the transaction so that presentation of prior financial data is meaningful for an understanding of future operations. There is a presumption that a subsidiary or division is a business, although a smaller component or an entity also could qualify. Among the matters to be considered are:

- Whether the type of revenue-producing activity will remain generally the same
- Whether physical facilities, employee base, marketing system, sales force, customer base, operating rights, production methods, or trade names will remain

If it is impractical to file the required historical or pro forma financial statements for an acquired business within the 15-day filing period, Form 8-K provides for an extension of up to 60 days to file the information. The extension is available when (1) providing the information within 15 days is impractical, (2) the registrant states so in Form 8-K, (3) the registrant states the date the financial statements are expected to be filed, and (4) the registrant provides the financial information as soon as practical within the 60-day period.

In stating that an extension of time is required, the registrant would provide all available information required under Items 2 and 7 for the business acquisition. The registrant may, at its option, include unaudited financial statements in the initial report on Form 8-K. No further extensions beyond the 60 days will be considered. The SEC has emphasized that the availability of the extension should not be an invitation for nontimely filing of the required information.

Generally the SEC staff will not issue a blanket waiver of the requirement for the financial statements of an acquired operation. However, where it can be shown that obtaining the required audited financial statements involves undue cost or difficulty, the SEC staff will generally issue a "no-action" letter. Such a letter would indicate that the SEC staff will not recommend an enforcement action against the registrant that is based solely on the failure to file the required audited financial statements and pro forma financial information as part of the report on Form 8-K. However, this does not constitute a waiver, and until the required audited financial statements are filed or the registrant's consolidated financial statements include the acquired operations for an equivalent period, the registrant will be unable to file registration statements under the 1933 Act, except as discussed below, and exempt offerings pursuant to Rules 505 and 506 of Regulation D may not be made to purchasers who are not accredited investors. The foregoing restriction does not apply to the following types of offerings:

- Offerings or sales of securities upon the conversion of outstanding convertible securities or upon the exercise of outstanding warrants or rights
- Dividend or interest reinvestment plans
- Employee benefit plans
- Transactions involving secondary offerings
- Sales of securities pursuant to Rule 144

(iii) Item 3—Bankruptcy or Receivership.   If a receiver or similar agent has been appointed for the registrant in a bankruptcy proceeding, disclosure is required concerning the proceeding, the receiver, the court involved, and certain other matters.

(iv) Item 4—Changes in Registrant's Independent Accountants.   Certain disclosures are required in Form 8-K as a result of the resignation by (or declination to stand for reelection after completion of the current audit) or dismissal of a registrant's independent accountant, or the engagement of a new accountant. Such changes in the accountant for a significant subsidiary on whom the principal accountant expressed reliance in his report would also be reportable events.

The Commission has become increasingly concerned about changes in accountants and the potential for opinion shopping. The 8-K disclosure requirements about changes in accountants were significantly changed in 1988 by FRR No. 31. Then the timing requirements for 8-K filings involving Item 4 were changed in 1989 by FRR No. 34.

When an independent accountant who was the principal accountant for the company or who audited a significant subsidiary and was expressly relied on by the principal accountant resigns (or declines to stand for reelection) or is dismissed, the registrant must make the following four disclosures:

1. Whether the former accountant resigned, declined to stand for reelection, or was dismissed, including the date thereof and whether:

    a. there was an adverse opinion, disclaimer of opinion, or qualification or modification of opinion as to uncertainty, audit scope, or accounting principles issued by such accountant for either of the two most recent years, including a description of the nature of the opinion.

    b. the decision to change accountants was recommended by or approved by the audit committee or a similar committee or by the board of directors in the absence of such special committee.

2. Whether during the two most recent fiscal years and any subsequent interim period preceding the resignation, declination, or dismissal there were any disagreements with the former accountant on any matter of accounting principles or practices, financial statement disclosure, or auditing scope or procedure, which disagreement(s), if not resolved to the satisfaction of the former accountant, would have caused the accountant to make reference to the subject matter of the disagreement(s) in connection with his or her report. If such disagreement occurred, the registrant must disclose:

    a. The nature of the disagreement

    b. Whether any audit committees (or similar body) or board of directors discussed the subject matter of the disagreement with the former accountant

    c. Whether the registrant has authorized the former accountant to respond fully to the successor accountant concerning the matter

    The term *disagreements* should be interpreted broadly but should not include preliminary differences of opinion that are "based on incomplete facts" if the differences are resolved by obtaining more complete factual information.

3. Whether there were any "reportable events" during the two most recent fiscal years or any subsequent interim period preceding the resignation, declination, or dismissal, including:

    a. The auditor having advised the registrant that the internal controls necessary to develop reliable financial statements do not exist.

    b. The auditor having advised the registrant that information has come to the auditor's attention that led him or her to no longer be able to rely on management's representations or that has made him or her unwilling to be associated with the financial statements.

    c. The auditor having advised the registrant that there is a need to significantly expand the audit scope or that information has come to the auditor's attention during the last two fiscal years and any subsequent interim period that, if further investigated, may (1) materially impact the fairness or reliability of either a previously issued audit report or the underlying financial statements or the financial statements issued or to be issued for a subsequent period or (2) cause the auditor to be unwilling to rely on management's representations or to be associated with the financial statements and due to the change in auditors, the auditor did not expand his scope or conduct a further investigation.

d. The auditor having advised the registrant that information has come to the auditor's attention that he or she has concluded materially impacts the fairness or reliability of either (1) a previously issued audit report or the underlying financial statements or (2) the financial statements relating to a subsequent period and, unless the matter is resolved to the auditor's satisfaction, the auditor would be prevented from rendering an unqualified report and, due to the change in auditors, the matter has not been resolved.

4. When a new independent accountant has been engaged, the registrant must identify the newly engaged accountant and the date of the engagement. In addition, if, during the two most recent fiscal years or subsequent interim period, the registrant or someone on its behalf consulted the newly engaged accountant regarding the application of accounting principles as to any specific transaction, either completed or proposed, the type of audit opinion that would be rendered on the registrant's financial statements, or any matter of disagreement or a reportable event with the former accountant. If such a consultation took place, the Form 8-K must:

a. Describe the accounting issue and the newly engaged accountant's view. Any written opinion issued by the new accountant must be filed as an exhibit, and the new accountant must be provided the opportunity to review the disclosure and furnish a letter to the SEC that clarifies or expresses disagreement with the registrant's disclosure of its views.

b. State whether the former accountant was consulted regarding such issues and, if so, describe the former accountant's views.

Disagreements and reportable events are intended to be communicated to the registrant orally and in writing. Because these are sensitive areas that may impugn the integrity of management, communication will have to be handled with extreme care on the part of all involved.

In early 1989, the Commission finalized its "early warning release," which significantly reduced the time period permitted in filing a Form 8-K relating to a change in accountants. FRR No. 34 reduced the time period for filing the Item 4 disclosure from 15 calendar days to five business days. It also provided (1) that the letter from the registrant's former independent accountant must be filed within 10 business days after the filing that disclosed the change, (2) that the registrant must file such letter within two business days of receipt, and (3) that the former accountant may provide an interim letter to the registrant, which also must be filed within two business days of receipt. In late 1989, the AICPA's SEC Practice Section adopted a rule requiring member CPA firms to notify the SEC within five business days of terminating a relationship with a registrant-client. A notification letter is sent simultaneously to the registrant-client and the Chief Accountant of the SEC.

Additionally, Item 304 of Regulation S-K requires the registrant to disclose similar information about auditor changes during the two years preceding the filing of registration statements for initial public offerings.

(v) Item 5—Other Events. The registrant may, at its option, report any information that it believes to be important to the stockholders but that is not specifically required to be reported on Form 8-K. Examples would be the commencement of material litigation, plant closings due to fire or strike, the discovery of mineral resources, and any important new products or product lines. The year 2000 issue may also warrant disclosure.

(vi) Item 6—Resignation of Registrant's Directors. A Form 8-K should be filed if a director has resigned or declines to stand for reelection because of a disagreement with management related to the company's operations and has furnished the company with a letter describing the disagreement and requesting the event be disclosed.

The registrant should summarize the disagreement and may include a statement presenting its views if it considers the director's description incorrect or incomplete. The director's letter should be filed as an exhibit with Form 8-K.

(vii) Item 7—Financial Statements, Pro Forma Financial Information, and Exhibits.   Financial statements of acquired businesses, if applicable, and all required pro forma information should be included, as discussed earlier. The exhibits outlined in Item 601 of Regulation S-K should also be furnished.

(viii) Item 8—Change in Fiscal Year.   A Form 8-K reporting a change in a registrant's fiscal year must disclose the date the change was decided on, the date of the new fiscal year, and whether the report on the transition (i.e., "short") period will be filed on Form 10-Q or Form 10-K. Exchange Act Rules 15 d-10 and 13a-10 provide, in general, that reports for transition periods of less than six months may be filed on Form 10-Q, while those for periods of six months or more must be filed on Form 10-K. If the transition period is one month or less, and certain requirements are met, separate transition reports do not have to be filed.

(ix) Item 9—Regulation FD Disclosures.   Regulation FD requires material information that is made known to certain individuals to be made available to all investors. One method of disseminating this information is by filing a Form 8-K. The due dates for Item 9 disclosures are based on the FD rules and vary based on the facts and circumstances.

(x) Signatures.   The Form 8-K requires the signature of one duly authorized officer of the registrant. The same procedures described for Forms 10-K and 10-Q apply.

3.7 PROXY STATEMENTS

(a) OVERVIEW.   Because of the geographic dispersion of the owners of a public company, it is unlikely that a quorum could be obtained at any meeting that required a vote of the shareholders. As a result, the use of proxies and proxy statements developed to facilitate such votes. A proxy is broadly defined as any authorization given to someone by security holders to act on their behalf at a stockholders' meeting. The term "proxy" also refers to the document used to evidence such authorization. Persons soliciting proxies must comply with Regulation 14A and the 1934 Act, which prescribes the content of documents to be distributed to stockholders before, or at the same time, such solicitation occurs.

The informational content of the proxy statement provided to the stockholders depends on the action to be taken by the stockholders. Schedule 14A prescribes the informational content required based on the specific circumstances.

When the vote is solicited for (1) an exchange of one security for another, (2) mergers or consolidations, or (3) transfers of assets, the transaction constitutes an "offer to sell securities." As such, a registration statement is required under the 1933 Act and can be filed on Form S-4 (Form F-4 for foreign private issuers in similar transactions).

(b) REGULATION 14A.   The SEC derives its authority to regulate the solicitation of proxies from the Exchange Act and from the Investment Company Act of 1940. Section 14(a) of the Exchange Act states:

It shall be unlawful for any person, by the use of the mails or by any means or instrumentality of interstate commerce or of any facility of a national securities exchange or otherwise, in contravention of such rules and regulations as the Commission may prescribe as necessary or appropriate in the public interest or for the protection of investors, to solicit or to permit the use of his name to solicit any proxy or consent or authorization in respect of any security (other than an exempted security) registered pursuant to Section 12 of this title.

Based on this statutory authority, the SEC established Regulation 14A to regulate proxy solicitations. Regulation 14A comprises the following Rules:

Because of the complexity of these rules, most are not discussed in detail here. However, it is important to remember that proxies and proxy statements are different from other SEC filings because they are required to be sent directly to the security holders. Registration statements are filed directly with the SEC. Annual reports on Form 10-K are filed with the SEC and are furnished to the shareholder only on request. Typically, the proxy materials must be given to the shareholders at least 20 days prior to the meeting date. Companies listed on the New York Stock Exchange provide shareholders 30 days to review the materials.

The proxy rules require companies to provide shareholders with proxy cards to give them more opportunity to participate in corporate elections. Shareholder proxy cards must (1) indicate whether the proxy is solicited on behalf of the board of directors, (2) enable shareholders to abstain from voting on directors and other proxy matters as well as to approve or disapprove each matter, and (3) allow shareholders to vote for or withhold authority to vote for each nominee for the board of directors.

(c) SEC REVIEW REQUIREMENTS. Except as noted below, Rule 14a-6 requires that preliminary copies of the proxy statements and related materials be filed with the SEC at least 10 calendar days prior to the date definitive copies of such material are first sent or given to security holders. Such materials should be appropriately marked as "Preliminary Copies" and the date definitive materials are to be mailed to the shareholders must be stated in the filing. Earlier submission (usually more than 20 days) is advisable to allow time for any changes that may be required as a result of the SEC's selective review process.

In 1988, the SEC provided some relief in the area of proxy material review. Preliminary proxy materials need not be filed with the Commission if the solicitation relates to any meeting of security holders at which the only matters to be acted on include these six:

1. The election of directors.
2. The election, approval, or ratification of accountant(s).
3. A security holder proposal included pursuant to Rule 14a-8.
4. With respect to a registered investment company or business development company, a proposal to continue, without change, any advisory or other contract or agreement that has been the subject of a proxy solicitation for which proxy material has previously been filed.
5. With respect to an open-end registered investment company, a proposal to increase the number of shares authorized to be issued.
6. The approval or ratification of certain compensation plans (i.e., restricted stock, SARs, or stock options) or amendments to such plans. This exemption does not, however, extend to the approval of awards made pursuant to such plans.

Information in preliminary proxy material will be made available to persons requesting it after the definitive proxy is filed, unless an application for confidential treatment for such information is made at the time of filing the preliminary proxy material and approved by the SEC. Such preliminary material will also be made available to persons requesting it if no definitive filing is anticipated.

Before the registrant files the preliminary material, the accountant should read the entire text and compare it with the financial statements. This procedure is intended to avoid inconsistencies and misleading comments of which the accountant may have knowledge and to ascertain that the financial statements include disclosures mentioned in the text that are appropriate for a fair presentation of the financial statements in conformity with GAAP.

As previously discussed, effective January 1, 1998, the SEC no longer accepts paper filings that are required to be submitted electronically. Signatures for any electronic submission are in typed form rather than manual format. However, manually signed pages must be obtained prior to the electronic filing and retained for five years.

If the audit has not been completed, the SEC requires that a letter from the independent accountant accompany the preliminary material. The letter should state that the accountant has considered the preliminary material and will allow the use of his or her report on the financial statements. This letter is addressed to the registrant, who, in turn, submits it to the SEC. When preparing the letter, the accountant should avoid using general terms such as "considered" or "reviewed" in describing the work and should avoid expressing approval, either directly or indirectly, of the sufficiency of disclosures in the text. The accountant should state that he or she has read the preliminary proxy statements and will upon completion of the audit allow use of the report on the financial statements. The financial statements covered by the report, and the date of the report, should be specified in the letter. When a proxy statement is prepared for a proposed merger, the letter should relate only to the company with which the accountant is familiar.

Copies of the definitive material that are mailed to stockholders should be filed with the SEC no later than the date such material is mailed to the stockholders.

If changed circumstances or new events arising between the time the proxy solicitation is mailed and the stockholders' meeting date cause the proxy material to be materially false and misleading, the corrected material should be disseminated promptly to the stockholders and to the SEC (with markings clearly indicating the changes).

3.8 SOURCES AND SUGGESTED REFERENCES

BDO Seidman, *MD&A Checklist*. New York: BDO Seidman, 2002.

Securities Regulation and Law Report. Bureau of National Affairs, Washington, DC, weekly reporting service.

CHAPTER 4

INTRODUCTION TO INTERNAL CONTROL ASSESSMENT AND REPORTING

Michael J. Ramos

4.1 INTRODUCTION

The Sarbanes-Oxley Act of 2002 made significant changes to many aspects of the financial reporting process. One of those changes is a requirement that management evaluate the effectiveness of its internal control over financial reporting and provide a report on this evaluation. Additionally, the company's independent auditors are required to audit this internal control report in conjunction with their traditional audit of the company's financial statements.

This chapter summarizes management's evaluation and reporting requirements and provides a structured, comprehensive approach for compliance. The material in this chapter has been excerpted from *How to Comply with Sarbanes-Oxley Section 404: Assessing the Effectiveness of Internal Control*, by Michael Ramos, published by John Wiley & Sons.

4.2 DEFINITION OF INTERNAL CONTROL

For the purposes of complying with the internal control reporting requirements of the Sarbanes-Oxley Act, the SEC rules provide the working definition of the term *internal control over financial reporting*. Rule 13a-15(f) defines internal control over financial reporting as follows:

> The term internal control over financial reporting is defined as a process designed by, or under the supervision of, the issuer's principal executive and principal financial officers, or persons performing similar functions, and effected by the issuer's board of directors, management and other personnel, to provide reasonable assurance regarding the reliability of financial reporting and the preparation of financial statements for external purposes in accordance with generally accepted accounting principles and includes those policies and procedures that:
>
> **1.** Pertain to the maintenance of records that in reasonable detail accurately and fairly reflect the transactions and dispositions of the assets of the issuer;
> **2.** Provide reasonable assurance that transactions are recorded as necessary to permit preparation of financial statements in accordance with generally accepted accounting principles, and that receipts and expenditures of the issuer are being made only in accordance with authorizations of management and directors of the issuer; and
> **3.** Provide reasonable assurance regarding prevention or timely detection of unauthorized acquisition, use or disposition of the issuer's assets that could have a material effect on the financial statements.

When considering the SEC's definition, you should note the following:

- The term *internal control* is a broad concept that extends to all areas of the management of an enterprise. The SEC definition narrows the scope of an entity's consideration of internal control to the preparation of the financial statements—hence the use of the term *internal control over financial reporting*.
- The SEC intends its definition to be consistent with the definition of internal controls that pertain to financial reporting objectives that was provided in the Committee of Sponsoring Organizations (COSO) of the Treadway Commission COSO Report.
- The rule makes explicit reference to the use or disposition of the entity's assets—that is, the safeguarding of assets.

4.3 MANAGEMENT'S REQUIRED REPORTS ON INTERNAL CONTROL

(a) ANNUAL REPORTING REQUIREMENTS.   Section 404 of the Sarbanes-Oxley Act requires chief executive officers (CEOs) and chief financial officers (CFOs) to evaluate and report on the effectiveness of the entity's internal control over financial reporting. This report is contained in the company's Form 10K, which is filed annually with the SEC. The SEC has adopted rules for its registrants that effectively implement the requirements of the Sarbanes-Oxley Act, Section 404.

Under the SEC rules, the company's 10K must include:[1]

A. *Management's Annual Report on Internal Control Over Financial Reporting.* Provide a report on the company's internal control over financial reporting that contains:

  1. A statement of management's responsibilities for establishing and maintaining adequate internal control over financial reporting.

  2. A statement identifying the framework used by management to evaluate the effectiveness of the company's internal control over financial reporting.

  3. Management's assessment of the effectiveness of the company's internal control over financial reporting as of the end of the most recent fiscal year, including a statement as to whether or not internal control over financial reporting is effective. This discussion must include disclosure of any material weakness in the company's internal control over financial reporting identified by management. Management is not permitted to conclude that the registrant's internal control over financial reporting is effective if there are one or more material weaknesses in the company's internal control over financial reporting.

  4. A statement that the registered public accounting firm that audited the financial statements included in the annual report has issued an attestation report on management's assessment of the registrant's internal control over financial reporting.

B. *Attestation Report of the Registered Public Accounting Firm.* Provide the registered public accounting firm's attestation report on management's assessment of the company's internal control over financial reporting.

C. *Changes in Internal Control Over Financial Reporting.* Disclose any change in the company's internal control over financial reporting that has materially affected, or is reasonably likely to materially affect, the company's internal control over financial reporting.

The company's annual report filed with the SEC also should include management's fourth-quarter report on the effectiveness of the entity's disclosure controls and procedures, as described in the next section.

(i) Effective Dates.   The requirement to disclose material changes in the entity's internal control (item (c) above) became effective on August 14, 2003. The effective date for the other provisions of the rules described above—that is, management's report on the effectiveness of internal control and the related auditor attestation—become effective at different times, depending on the filing status of the company.

- *Accelerated filer.* A company that is an accelerated filer as of the end of its first fiscal year ending on or after November 15, 2004, must begin to comply with the internal control reporting and attestation requirements in its annual report for that fiscal year.[2]
- *Nonaccelerated filer.* Smaller companies are required to comply with the full requirements of the new rules for their first fiscal year ending on or after July 15, 2007.
- *Foreign private issuers.* The effective data for foreign private issuers depends on whether the issuer is an accelerated or non-accelerated filer. Accelerated filers are required to comply for their first fiscal year ending on or after July 15, 2006. Non-accelerated foreign private issuers have until July 15, 2007.

---

[1] See Regulation S-K, Item 308 (17 CFR §229.308).
[2] "Accelerated filer" is defined in Exchange Act Rule 12b-2. Generally, companies with a market capitalization of $75 million or more are considered accelerated filers.

(b) QUARTERLY REPORTING REQUIREMENTS.   Section 302 of the Sarbanes-Oxley Act requires quarterly reporting on the effectiveness of an entity's "disclosure controls and procedures." Item 307 of SEC Regulation S-K implements this requirement for the company's quarterly Form 10-Q filings by requiring management to:

> Disclose the conclusions of the company's principal executive and principal financial officers, or persons performing similar functions, regarding the effectiveness of the company's disclosure controls and procedures as of the end of the period covered by the report, based on the evaluation of these controls and procedures.

In addition to reporting on disclosure controls, the company's quarterly reports also must disclose material changes in the entity's internal control over financial reporting.

Note that for these quarterly filings:

- Management is *not* required to evaluate or report on internal control over financial reporting. That evaluation is required on an *annual basis only*.
- The company's independent auditors are *not* required to attest to management's evaluation of disclosure controls.

(i) Disclosure Controls and Procedures.   With these rules, the SEC introduces a new term, *disclosure controls and procedures*, which is different from *internal controls over financial reporting* defined earlier. SEC Rule 13a-15(e) defines disclosure controls and procedures as those that are:

Designed to ensure that information required to be disclosed by the issuer in the reports that it files or submits under the Act is

- recorded,
- processed,
- summarized, and
- reported

within the time periods specified in the Commission's rules and forms. Disclosure controls and procedures include, without limitation, controls and procedures designed to ensure that information required to be disclosed by an issuer in the reports that it files or submits under the Act is accumulated and communicated to the issuer's management, including its principal executive and principal financial officers, or persons performing similar functions, as appropriate to allow timely decisions regarding required disclosure [emphasis added].

Thus, "disclosure controls and procedures" would encompass the controls over all material financial and nonfinancial information in Exchange Act reports. Information that would fall under this definition that would not be part of an entity's internal control over financial reporting might include the signing of a significant contract, changes in a strategic relationship, management compensation, or legal proceedings.

(ii) The Disclosure Committee.   In relation to its rule requiring an assessment of disclosure controls and procedures, the SEC also advised all public companies to create a disclosure committee to oversee the process by which disclosures are created and reviewed, including the:

- Review of 10-Q, 10K, and other SEC filings; earnings releases; and other public information for the appropriateness of disclosure
- Determination of what constitutes a significant transaction or event that requires disclosure
- Determination and identification of significant deficiencies and material weaknesses in the design or operating effectiveness of disclosure controls and procedures

- Assessment of CEO and CFO awareness of material information that could affect disclosure

The existence and effective operation of an entity's disclosure committee can have a significant effect on the nature and scope of management's work to evaluate the effectiveness of the entity's internal control. For example:

- The effective functioning of a disclosure committee may be viewed as an element that strengthens the entity's control environment.
- The work of the disclosure committee may create documentation that engagement teams can use to reduce the scope of their work.

4.4 MANAGEMENT CERTIFICATIONS

In addition to providing a report on the effectiveness of its disclosure controls and internal control over financial reporting, the company's principal executive officer and principal financial officer are required to sign two certifications, which are included as exhibits to the entity's 10-Q and 10K. These two certifications are required by the following sections of the Sarbanes-Oxley Act:

1. Section 302, which requires a certification to accompany each quarterly and annual report filed with the SEC
2. Section 906, which added a new Section 1350 to Title 18 of the U.S. Code, and which contains a certification requirement subject to specific federal criminal provisions. This certification is separate and distinct from the Section 302 certification requirement.

Exhibit 4.1 provides the text of the Section 302 certification. This text is provided in SEC Rule 13a-14(a) and should be used exactly as set forth in the rule.

Exhibit 4.2 provides an example of the Section 906 certification. Note that some certifying officers may choose to include a "knowledge qualification," as indicated by the optional language within the parentheses. Officers who choose to include this language should do so only after consulting with their SEC counsel. Unlike the Section 302 certification, which requires a separate certification for both the CEO and CFO, the company can provide only one 906 certification, which is then signed by both individuals.

(a) SUBCERTIFICATION.   A great deal of the information included in financial statements and other reports filed with the SEC originates in areas of the company that are outside the direct control of the CEO and CFO. Because of the significance of information prepared by others, it is becoming common for the CEO and CFO to request those individuals who are directly responsible for this information to certify it. This process is known as *subcertification*, and it usually requires the individuals to provide a written affidavit to the CEO and CFO that will allow them to sign their certifications in good faith.

Items that may be the subject of subcertification affidavits include:

- Adequacy of specific disclosures in the financial statements or other reports filed with the SEC, such as *Management's Disclosure and Analysis* included in the entity's 10Q or 10K.
- Accuracy of specific account balances.
- Compliance with company policies and procedures, including the company's code of conduct.
- Adequacy of the design and/or operating effectiveness of departmental internal controls and disclosure controls.
- Accuracy of reported financial results of the department, subsidiary, or business segment.

I, [identify the certifying individual], certify that:

1. I have reviewed this [specify report] of [identify registrant];

2. Based on my knowledge, this report does not contain any untrue statement of a material fact or omit to state a material fact necessary to make the statements made, in light of the circumstances under which such statements were made, not misleading with respect to the period covered by this report;

3. Based on my knowledge, the financial statements, and other financial information included in this report, fairly present in all material respects the financial condition, results of operations and cash flows of the registrant as of, and for, the periods presented in this report;

4. The registrant's other certifying officer(s) and I are responsible for establishing and maintaining disclosure controls and procedures (as defined in Exchange Act Rules 13a-15(e) and 15 d-15(e)) and internal control over financial reporting (as defined in Exchange Act Rules 13a-15(f) and 15 d-15(f)) for the registrant and have:

    a. Designed such disclosure controls and procedures, or caused such disclosure controls and procedures to be designed under our supervision, to ensure that material information relating to the registrant, including its consolidated subsidiaries, is made known to us by others within those entities, particularly during the period in which this report is being prepared;

    b. Designed such internal control over financial reporting, or caused such internal control over financial reporting to be designed under our supervision, to provide reasonable assurance regarding the reliability of financial reporting and the preparation of financial statements for external purposes in accordance with generally accepted accounting principles;

    c. Evaluated the effectiveness of the registrant's disclosure controls and procedures and presented in this report our conclusions about the effectiveness of the disclosure controls and procedures, as of the end of the period covered by this report based on such evaluation; and

    d. Disclosed in this report any change in the registrant's internal control over financial reporting that occurred during the registrant's most recent fiscal quarter (the registrant's fourth fiscal quarter in the case of an annual report) that has materially affected, or is reasonably likely to materially affect, the registrant's internal control over financial reporting; and

5. The registrant's other certifying officer(s) and I have disclosed, based on our most recent evaluation of internal control over financial reporting, to the registrant's auditors and the audit committee of the registrant's board of directors (or persons performing the equivalent functions):

    a. All significant deficiencies and material weaknesses in the design or operation of internal control over financial reporting which are reasonably likely to adversely affect the registrant's ability to record, process, summarize, and report financial information; and

    b. Any fraud, whether or not material, that involves management or other employees who have a significant role in the registrant's internal control over financial reporting.

Exhibit 4.1   Section 302 Certification SEC Rule 13a-14(a)/15 d-14(a).

In connection with the [annual/quarterly] report of [name of registrant] (the "Company") on Form (10-K/10-Q) for the period ended (the "Report"), the undersigned in the capacities listed below, hereby certify, pursuant to 18 U.S.C. ss. 1350, as adopted pursuant to Section 906 of the Sarbanes-Oxley Act of 2002, that

    i. The Report fully complies with the requirements of Section 12(a) or 15(d) of the Securities Exchange Act of 1934; and

    ii. The information contained in the Report fairly presents, in all material respects, the financial condition and results of operations of the company.

Exhibit 4.2   Section 906 Certification 18 U.S.C. Section 1350.

4.5 THE INDEPENDENT AUDITOR'S RESPONSIBILITIES

Exhibit 4.3 describes the relationship between the various rule-making bodies, companies, and their auditors regarding the reporting on internal control. As described previously, management of public companies is required to report on the effectiveness of the entity's internal control on an annual basis and the company's independent auditors are required to audit this report. The SEC is responsible for setting rules to implement the Sarbanes-Oxley Act requirements. Those rules include guidance for reporting by the CEO and CFO on the entity's internal control over financial reporting and disclosure controls, but they do not provide any guidance or set standards for the independent auditors. The Public Company Accounting Oversight Board (PCAOB) sets the auditing standards, which have a direct effect on auditors and how they plan and perform their engagements.

In addition, the auditing standards will have an *indirect effect* on the company as it prepares for the audit of the internal control report. Just as in a financial statement audit, the company should be able to support its conclusions about internal control and provide documentation that is sufficient for the auditor to perform an audit. Thus, in preparing for the audit of its internal control report, it is vital for management, and those who assist them, to have a good understanding of what the independent auditors will require. In practice, the auditing standards, and related interpretative guidance, have become the de facto definitive guidance for both management and auditors on the assessment of internal control effectiveness.

4.6 THE AUDIT STANDARDS

In June 2004, the SEC approved PCAOB Auditing Standard No. 2, *An Audit of Internal Control Over Financial Reporting Performed in Conjunction With an Audit of Financial Statements*. This standard requires auditors for the first time to conduct two audits of their publicly traded clients: the traditional audit of financial statements and a new audit of internal control. The standard provides definitive guidance for independent auditors on the performance of their audit of internal control.

The Auditing Standard has a significant effect on the way in which company management conducts its own required assessment in internal control effectiveness. For example, the standard:

- Requires auditors to assess the quality of the company's self-assessment of internal control. In providing this guidance, the standard describes certain required elements of management's process that must be present for the auditor to conclude that the process was adequate.

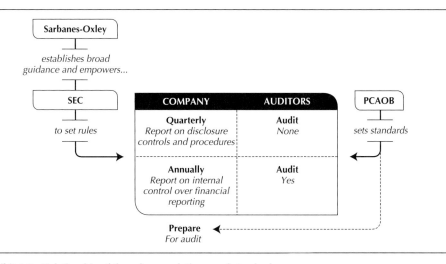

Exhibit 4.3   Relationship of the rules, regulations, and standards.

- Requires auditors to assess the adequacy of the company's documentation of internal control. The standard goes on to provide definitive guidance on what management's documentation should contain for the auditor to conclude that it is adequate. Lack of adequate documentation is considered a control deficiency that may preclude an unqualified opinion on internal control or may result in a scope limitation on the auditor's engagement.

- Allows the auditor to rely on the work performed by the company in its self-assessment process to support his or her conclusion on internal control effectiveness. However, to rely on this work to the maximum extent, certain conditions regarding the nature of the work and the people who performed it must be met.

- Establishes the definition of a *material weakness* in internal control. To conclude that internal control is effective, management should have reasonable assurance that there were no material weaknesses in internal control as of the reporting date.

Subsequent to the approval of the Auditing Standard, both the PCAOB and the SEC have released periodically documents of answers to frequently asked questions. These documents set forth the PCAOB and SEC staff's opinions and views on certain matters. Although both the PCAOB and the SEC both point out that these opinions and views do not represent official "rules," you should be prepared to justify any departure from the answers to questions discussed in these documents. An important step in planning a SOX 404 compliance engagement is to make sure you have read the most current staff positions issued by the PCAOB and the SEC

(a) OVERALL OBJECTIVE OF THE AUDITORS' ENGAGEMENT. The auditor's objective in an audit of internal control is to express an opinion about management's assessment of the effectiveness of the company's internal control over financial reporting. This objective implies a two-step process.

1. First, management must perform its own assessment and conclude on the effectiveness of the entity's internal controls.

2. Next, the auditors will perform their own assessment and form an independent opinion as to whether management's assessment of the effectiveness of internal control is fairly stated.

Thus, internal control is assessed twice, first by management and then by the independent auditors. That the auditors will be auditing internal control—and in some cases, reperforming some of the tests performed by the entity—does not relieve management of its obligation to document, test, and report on internal control.

To form his or her opinion, the auditor will:

- Evaluate the reliability of the process used by management to assess the entity's internal control

- Review and rely on the results of *some* of the tests performed by management, internal auditors, and others during their assessment process

- Perform his or her own tests

(b) EVALUATION OF MANAGEMENT'S ASSESSMENT PROCESS. The SEC rules relating to the scope of managements assessment of internal control effectiveness are rather general. In practice, companies frequently encounter situations for which the SEC has not provided guidance. In those situations, companies will commonly look to the Auditing Standard to help determine which business units or controls should be included in their assessment.

AS No. 2 provides extensive guidance on the required scope of management's self-assessment of the company's internal control. This guidance is in the context of the external auditor's evaluation of the quality of the company's assessment process, stating that the external auditor should determine whether management's evaluation includes certain elements.

If the company's self-assessment process does *not* include all the elements listed in the standard, the external auditor will conclude that the process was inadequate, in which case he or she will be forced to determine that a scope limitation had been placed on the engagement and modify the "clean opinion" on internal control. As a practical matter, most companies take steps to ensure that their assessment process includes all the required elements listed in the auditing standard.

The auditing standard provides detailed guidance on what is required of management's process, stating that management should address the following elements.

- Determining which controls should be tested, including controls over all relevant assertions related to all significant accounts and disclosures in the financial statements. Generally, such controls include:
  - Controls over initiating, authorizing, recording, processing, and reporting significant accounts and disclosures and related assertions embodied in the financial statements.
  - Controls over the selection and application of accounting policies that are in conformity with generally accepted accounting principles.
  - Antifraud programs and controls.
  - Controls, including information technology general controls, or which other controls are dependent.
  - Controls over significant nonroutine and nonsystematic transactions, such as accounts involving judgments and estimates.
  - Company level controls (as described in paragraph 53), including:
    - The control environment, and
    - Controls over the period-end financial reporting process, including controls over procedures used to enter transaction totals into the general later, to initiate, authorize, record, and process journal entries in the general ledger; and to record recurring and nonrecurring adjustments to the financial statements (e.g., consolidating adjustments, report combinations, and reclassifications).
- Evaluating the likelihood that failure of the control could result in a misstatement, the magnitude of such a misstatement, and the degree to which other controls, if effective, achieve the same control objectives.
- Determining the locations or business units to include in the evaluation for a company with multiple locations or business units (See paragraphs B1 through B17).
- Evaluating the design effectiveness of controls.
- Evaluating the operating effectiveness of controls based on procedures sufficient to assess their operating effectiveness. Examples of such procedures include testing of the controls by internal audit, testing of controls by others under the direction of management, using a service organization's reports (see paragraphs B18 through B29), inspection of evidence of the application of controls, or testing by means of a self-assessment process, some of which might occur as part of management's ongoing monitoring activities. Inquiry alone is not adequate to complete this evaluation. To evaluate the effectiveness of the company's internal control over financial reporting, management must have evaluated controls over all relevant assertions related to all significant accounts and disclosures.
- Determining the deficiencies in internal control over financial reporting that are of such a magnitude and likelihood of occurrence that they constitute significant deficiencies or material weaknesses.
- Communicating findings to the external auditor and to others, if applicable.
- Evaluating whether findings the reasonable and support management's assessment.

How to Comply with Sarbanes-Oxley Section 404: Assessing the Effectiveness of Internal Control provides detailed guidance to help you comply with each of these required elements of management's assessment process. The *Sarbanes-Oxley 404 Implementation Toolkit* provides an integrated set of forms, checklists, example questions, and other practice aids to help you perform an assessment of internal control.

(c) DOCUMENTATION.   The external auditors are required to evaluate the adequacy of management's documentation of internal control. Again, the consequences of not complying with the requirements of the Auditing Standard are severe.

Paragraph 42 of the standard provides the requirements for the documentation of internal control. That paragraph requires management's documentation to include the following.

- The design of controls over all relevant assertions related to all significant accounts and disclosures in the financial statements. The documentation should include the five components of internal control over financial reporting as discussed in paragraph 49, including the control environment and company-level controls as described in paragraph 53;
- Information about how significant transactions are initiated, authorized, recorded, processed, and reported;
- Sufficient information about the flow of transactions to identify the points at which material misstatements due to error or fraud could occur;
- Controls designed to prevent or detect fraud, including who performs the controls and the related segregation of duties;
- Controls over the period-end financial reporting process;
- Controls over safeguarding of assets (See paragraphs C1 through C6); and
- The results of management's testing and evaluation.

(d) SCOPE OF TEST WORK.   The auditing standard also provides guidance on the nature, timing, and extent of the auditor's procedures for a number of situations, including:

- Extent of testing of multiple locations, business segments, or subsidiaries
- Required tests when the entity uses a service organization to process transactions
- Updated test work required when the original testing was performed at an interim date in advance of the reporting date

Interpretive guidance issued by the staffs of the SEC and PCAOB provide information on how to address additional situations that may raise questions about the scope of the work.

(e) USE OF WORK OF INTERNAL AUDITORS AND OTHERS.   Both Sarbanes-Oxley and the PCAOB Auditing Standard describe a two-pronged approach for providing financial statement users with useful information about the reliability of a company's internal control:

- First, management assesses and reports on the effectiveness of the entity's internal control.
- Second, the company's external auditors audit management's report and issue a separate, independent opinion on the effectiveness of the company's internal control.

In this scheme, it is vital that the two participants perform their duties independently of each other.

By the same token, the practical aspects of implementing the requirements of Sarbanes-Oxley Section 404 suggest that external auditors should be able to use, to some degree, the work performed by management in its self-assessment of internal control in their audit. To do otherwise, to completely prohibit external auditors form using some of management's work, would make the cost of compliance quite steep.

Thus, the Auditing Standard balances two competing goals: objectivity and independence of the parties involved versus the use of management's work by the external auditor as a means of limiting the overall cost of compliance.

Note: The company is *prohibited* in its self-assessment of internal control from relying on the work performed by the external auditors in their audit.

Keep in mind that the company is required to perform a thorough, detailed assessment of the company's internal control. As much as possible, management will want to provide the results of its work to the external auditors, so the auditors will not have to duplicate the company's efforts.

(i) The External Auditor's Use of the Company's Internal Control Work.   Paragraphs 108 through 126 of the Auditing Standard provide extensive guidance on the degree to which the company's work on internal control can be used by the external auditors. The relevant section is titled "Using the Work of Others" The standard indicates that the work of "others" includes the relevant work performed by:

- Internal auditors.
- Other company personnel.
- Third parties working under the direction of management or the audit committee.

The external auditor's ability to rely on the work of others has its limits. Paragraph 108 of the standard describes the fundamental principle in the external auditor's using the work of others. The external auditor must "perform enough of the testing himself or herself so that the external auditor's own work provides the principal evidence for the external auditor's opinion." The standard goes on to describe a framework for ensuring that the external auditors comply with this principle. Essentially:

- The external auditor is prohibited from using the company's work in certain areas of the audit.
- For all other areas, the external auditor may use the company's work, if certain conditions are met.

(ii) Work That Must Be Performed by the External Auditors.   There are two areas where the external auditors are prohibited from using the company's work in their audit.

- *Control environment*. The external auditors are prohibited from using the work of company management and others to reduce the amount of work they perform on controls in the control environment. This does not mean that they can *ignore* your work in this area. To the contrary, paragraph 113 of the standard requires the external auditor to "consider the results of worked performed in this area by others because it might indicate the need for the external auditor to increase his or her own work."
- *Walkthroughs*. External auditors are required to perform at least one walkthrough for each major class of transactions. A walkthrough involves tracing a transaction from origination through the company's information systems until it is reflected in the company's financial reports. Chapter 3 of this Practice Aid discusses the requirements for walkthroughs in more detail.

Note that paragraph 115 of the standard states that "controls specifically established to prevent and detect fraud" are part of the control environment. Thus, the external auditors will be testing antifraud programs and controls themselves.

(iii) Using the Work of Others.   For all areas other than the control environment and the walkthroughs, the external auditors may use the company's tests on internal control during their audit. Paragraph 109 of the standard summarizes the steps that the external auditor's must follow to use the work of others to support his or her conclusions reached in the audit of internal control. To determine the extent to which the external auditor may use of company's work, the external auditor is required to:

a. Evaluate the nature of the controls subjected to the work of others. In general, auditors will probably want to perform their own tests on the controls related to accounts that have a high risk of material misstatement. For the controls for less risky accounts they will be more inclined to rely on the work of the company.

b. Evaluate the competence and objectivity of the individuals who performed the work. The more competent and objective the company's project team, the more likely the external auditors will be to rely on their work.

c. Test some of the work performed by others to evaluate the quality and effectiveness of their work.

To allow the company's external auditors to make as much use as possible of the company's own assessment of internal control, company management should have a clear understanding of the conditions that must be met for the external auditor's to use the work. To help the external auditors determine that those criteria have been met, you may wish to *document your compliance with the key requirements* of the auditing standard and make this documentation available to the external auditors early on in their audit planning process. For example, you should consider:

- Obtaining the bios or resumes of project team members showing their education level, experience, professional certification, and continuing education.
- Documenting the company's policies regarding the assignments of individuals to work areas.
- Documenting the "organizational status" of the project team and how they have been provided access to the board of directors and audit committee.
- Determining that the internal auditors follow the relevant internal auditing standards.
- Establishing policies that ensure that the *documentation* of the work performed includes:
  - A description of the scope of the work
  - Work programs
  - Evidence of supervision and review
  - Conclusions about the work performed

(f) DETERMINATION OF MATERIAL WEAKNESS. The SEC reporting rules require entity management to disclose material weaknesses in internal control. Engagements to assess the effectiveness of internal controls should be planned and performed in a way that will detect material misstatements. Thus, it is critical that you have a working definition of the term. The auditing standard provides the following definitions.

- A control deficiency exists when the design or operation of a control does not allow management or employees, in the normal course of performing their assigned functions, to prevent or detect misstatements on a timely basis.
- A significant deficiency is a control deficiency, or combination of control deficiencies, that adversely affects the company's ability to initiate, authorize, record, process, or report external financial data reliably in accordance with generally accepted accounting principles such that there is more than a remote likelihood that a misstatement of the company's annual or interim financial statements that is more than inconsequential will not be prevented or detected. *Note:* A misstatement is inconsequential if a reasonable person would conclude, after considering the possibility of further undetected misstatements, that the misstatement, either individually or when aggregated with other misstatements, would clearly be immaterial to the financial statements. If a reasonable person could not reach such a conclusion regarding a particular misstatement, that misstatement is more than inconsequential.

- A material weakness is a significant deficiency, or combination of significant deficiencies, that results in more than a remote likelihood that a material misstatement of the annual or interim financial statements will not be prevented or detected.

(g) WORKING WITH THE INDEPENDENT AUDITORS. To render an opinion on either the financial statements or the effectiveness of internal control, the company's independent auditors are required to maintain their independence, in accordance with applicable SEC rules. These rules are guided by certain underlying principles, which include:

- The audit firm must not be in a position where it audits its own work.
- The auditor must not act as management or as an employee of the client.

The PCAOB Auditing Standard incorporates the SEC's principles in its auditing standard and then expands on these principles in important ways. Although maintaining independence is primarily the responsibility of the auditors several of the independence requirements of AS No. 2 impose certain responsibilities on management and the audit committee. These requirements include:

- *Preapproval by the audit committee.* Each internal control-related service to be provided by the auditor must be preapproved by the audit committee. In its introduction to the standard, the PCAOB clarifies that "the audit committee cannot pre-approve internal control-related services as a category, but must approve each service."

  For proxy or other disclosure purposes, the company may designate some auditor services as "audit" or "nonaudit" services. The requirement to preapprove internal control services applies to *any* internal control-related services, regardless of how they might be designated.
- *Active involvement of management.* Management must be "actively involved" in a "substantive and extensive" way in all internal control services the auditor provides. Management can not delegate these responsibilities, nor can it satisfy the requirement to be actively involved by merely accepting responsibility for documentation and testing performed by the auditors.
- *Independence in fact and appearance.* The company's audit committee and external auditors must be diligent to ensure that independence both in fact and appearance is maintained.

No matter how detailed the independence rules may become, they can not possibly address every possible interaction between the company and its auditors. During the initial implementation of SOX 404 many situations arose that called into question whether the auditor could interact with the company in a particular way and still maintain its independence.

For example, if the company was unsure whether it's documentation of internal control would be acceptable, could it approach its auditors for advice? If the auditors made recommendations on how to improve the documentation and the company then incorporated those recommendations, wouldn't that put the audit firm in the position of auditing its own work when it reviewed that documentation? The form and content of the company's documentation of its internal control is the responsibility of management. If the auditor becomes significantly involved in that decision, doesn't that imply that they are acting in the capacity of management?

In the initial implementation of SOX 404, it became common for auditors provide as little advice as possible to their clients on internal control matters. Concerned about possibly violating the independence rules they chose to largely remove themselves from their client's efforts.

As a practical matter, both the SEC and the PCAOB understood that the public interest is not well-served if the independent auditors are completely uninvolved from the company's efforts to understand and assess its internal control. There must be some sharing of information between the company and its auditors, and the auditors must be able to provide help and advice on some matters.

In June of 2004 the SEC and PCAOB issued some guidance in this area. Essentially that guidance allows the auditor to provide "limited assistance to management in documenting internal controls and making recommendations for changes to internal controls. However, management has the ultimate responsibility for the assessment, documentation and testing of the company's internal control."

The PCAOB provided more extensive guidance on how company management may solicit advice from and share advice with their auditors on internal control matters. The guidance from the staff was in answer to a question directed specifically to an auditor's review of the company's draft financial statements or their providing advice on the adoption of a new accounting principle or emerging issue—services that historically have been considered a routine part of a high quality audit.

The PCAOB staff stated that, "some type of information-sharing on a timely basis between management and the auditor is necessary." However, when management seeks the assistance of the company's auditors to help with its internal control assessment, it should make it clear that management retains the ultimate responsibility for internal control. The PCAOB places the burden on management to clearly communicate with the auditors the nature of the advice they are seeking and the purpose for which the auditor is being involved.

4.7 A TOP-DOWN, RISK-BASED APPROACH FOR EVALUATING INTERNAL CONTROL

As indicated previously, both the SEC and PCAOB periodically issue staff position papers to clarify how AS 2 applies in specific circumstances. On May 16, 2005, in response information that was gathered about the first year of implementation, both the SEC and PCAOB issued guidance that addressed the most significant problems encountered with the implementation of AS 2. Of the five main areas addressed in the guidance, the following are the most relevant to company management.

- Use a risk-based, top-down approach. The PCAOB emphasized that auditors should use a top-downapproach, and company management would be wise to use this same approach. In a top-down approach, you begin with an evaluation of entity-level controls and from there move to the testing of detailed activity-level controls.

    One of the key principles of the top-down approach is that the decision of which controls to document and test is based an assessment of risk. Controls that mitigate significant risks should be documented and assessed. Those that mitigate less significant risks would be subject to considerably less, if any testing and evaluation.

    The risk-based, top-down approach is described in more detail in the next section of this chapter.

- Auditors and company management should engage in direct and timely communication with each other. As described in the previous section of this chapter, during the first year of compliance, there was often a lack of communication between the two. With its May 16 guidance, the PCAOB makes it clear that auditor should be responsive to client requests for advice, provided that company management take final responsibility for internal control.

- Auditors should make as much use as possible of the work on internal control performed by the company. This guidance should help companies keep down the cost of compliance, but it also means that companies have to perform their assessment with qualified individuals in a way that is consistent with the requirements of AS 2.

(a) PRINCIPLES OF A RISK-BASED, TOP-DOWN APPROACH.   Controls operate at two levels within any organization. Entity-level controls are pervasive and can affect many different financial statement accounts. For example, a company's hiring and training policies will affect the way in which individual control procedures are performed. Companies that hire qualified people and train them properly will have much greater success when it comes times for those people to perform their jobs. The converse also is true. In that sense, hiring and training policies can have an effect on many different financial statement accounts.

Activity-level controls, on the other hand, are restricted to one transaction type. For controls over case disbursements will affect cash disbursements only and will have no impact on other accounts, such as the recording of goodwill or the depreciation of fixed assets.

In the year of implementation, many companies and their auditors adopted a bottom-up approach in which they started by identifying all of the companies activity-level controls and then documenting and testing each of these to determine whether internal control as a whole was effective. As you can imagine, this approach was extremely time-consuming and costly. Moreover, not only is it not required, it is not even contemplated by AS 2.

The method described by the auditing standard is the exact opposite of this approach. In a top-down approach you begin at the top, at the entity-level. You then identify the most significant accounts and transaction types at the organization and the control objectives for those accounts and transactions. Once you determine the control objectives, you identify those controls that are in place to meet those objectives. Those controls, and only those controls, are then tested and evaluated.

By using a top-down approach the company:

- Tests only those controls related to significant accounts and transactions, which eliminates the need to understand the process and assess controls in those areas that do not affect the likelihood that the company's financial statements could be materially misstated.
- Tests the minimum number of controls necessary to meet the control objective. Redundant controls (and there are many of these) are not tested.

Implementing a top-down approach requires company management to exercise its judgment. How do you decide which accounts and transactions are "significant" and which are insignificant? If you are not going to test all the control activities for significant accounts and transactions, how do you determine which ones to test?

To make these and other decisions you should consider the related risk of material misstatement of the financial statements. As described in more detail in Chapter 2 of this book, control activities are designed to meet identified risks of misstatement. For example, one of the risks of misstatement is that the company may fail to record all of its accounts payable as of year-end. To mitigate this risk, management will design and implement procedures at the company to make sure that that all payables get recorded.

Do these controls need to be documented and tested? It depends on the relative significance of the risk of failing to record all accounts payable. What is the likelihood that the failure to record all accounts payable would result in a material misstatement of the company's financial statements? The answer to this question will help you determine whether to document and test the controls over accounts payable.

Performing an assessment of internal control is not a "paint-by-numbers" exercise. It is a process that requires a great deal of judgment. The primary benchmark for making these judgments risk, that is the risk that the financial statements would be materially misstated if the identified control was ineffective.

4.8 COORDINATING WITH THE INDEPENDENT AUDITORS

It is vital that you coordinate your project with the entity's independent auditors. This coordination process begins at the planning phase of the project and continues at each subsequent phase. Proper coordination between your team and the independent auditors will facilitate an effective and efficient audit. A lack of coordination with the auditors could result in a variety of negative, unforeseen consequences, including:

- Duplication of effort
- Reperformance of certain tests

- Performance of additional tests or expansion of the scope of the engagement
- Misunderstandings relating to the definition or reporting of material weaknesses

You should reach a consensus with the entity's independent auditors on key planning decisions, including:

- The overall engagement process and approach
- The scope of your project, including locations or business units to be included
- Preliminary identification of significant controls
- The nature of any internal control deficiencies noted by the auditors during their most recent audit of the entity's financial statements
- Tentative conclusions about what will constitute a significant deficiency or material weakness
- The nature and extent of the documentation of controls
- The nature and extent of the documentation of tests of controls
- The degree to which the auditors will rely on the results of your test work to reach their conclusion

During the early phases of the project, it may not be possible to obtain a definitive understanding with the auditors on all significant planning matters. In those situations, you should still work with the auditors to reach a consensus regarding:

- A clear understanding of the issue(s) that need resolution
- The additional information required to reach a resolution
- The process to be followed to resolve the matter
- An estimated time frame for the process to be completed and the issue(s) to be resolved

4.9 A NEW ERA

The passage of the Sarbanes-Oxley Act signaled the start of a new era in financial reporting, on par with the requirement of 70 years ago that the company's financial statements be audited by an independent CPA. Then, the capital markets looked to the CPA profession for help in implementing this new requirement. Now members of the profession—whether in public practice or employed in industry—seem equally well positioned to make a significant contribution as our country's financial reporting process embarks on another new direction.

CHAPTER 5

PUBLIC COMPANY ACCOUNTING OVERSIGHT BOARD

Don Pallais, CPA

5.1 BACKGROUND

Congress created the Public Company Accounting Oversight board (PCAOB) as a response to the Enron, WorldCom, and other accounting-related scandals. The Sarbanes-Oxley Act of 2002 created new requirements for publicly held companies and others (Chapter 4 discusses that Act in more detail) and revamped the regulatory system for auditors of public companies. The authority for standard-setting for audits of financial statements of publicly held companies and for quality control for firms that perform those audits was taken from the American Institute of Certified Public Accountants (AICPA), where it had been since the 1930s, and bestowed on the PCAOB.

The PCAOB opened its doors in January 2003 and held its first meeting that month. The Securities and Exchange Commission (SEC) reported, on April 25, 2003, that the PCAOB was organized and had the capacity to carry out its legislated duties, the final critical step in its establishment.

5.2 PUBLIC COMPANY ACCOUNTING OVERSIGHT BOARD AUTHORITY

Sarbanes-Oxley defines the PCAOB's authority and revises the Securities Act of 1934 to recognize it. PCAOB was established to:

oversee the audit of public companies that are subject to the securities laws, and related matters, in order to protect the interests of investors and further the public interest in the preparation of informative, accurate, and independent audit reports for companies the securities of which are sold to, and held by and for, public investors [sec. 101(a)].

The PCAOB's authority is subordinate to that of the SEC. Sarbanes-Oxley did not affect the SEC's authority to enforce the nation's securities laws, including regulating auditors, taking action against them, or setting accounting, auditing, or independence standards. The SEC maintains budgetary authority over the PCAOB and must approve proposed substantive rules before they take effect.

The PCAOB regulates auditors of issuers, which are described under Sarbanes-Oxley as follows:

The term "issuer" means an issuer (as defined in section 3 of the Securities Exchange Act of 1934 (15 USC 78c)), the securities of which are registered under section 12 of that Act (15 USC 78 l), or that is required to file reports under section 15(d) (15 USC 78o(d)), or that files or has filed a registration statement that has not yet become effective under the Securities Act of 1933 (15 USC 77a et seq.), and that it has not withdrawn [sec. 2(a)(7)].

It has authority over both domestic and foreign auditing firms that prepare or issue audit reports on U.S. public companies, or that play a substantial role in the preparation or issuance of such reports.

The PCAOB's primary public-interest functions include:

- Registering accounting firms that audit public companies.
- Establishing and maintaining standards for auditing, quality control, ethics, and independence related to the preparation of audit reports for public companies.
- Conducting inspections of registered firms.
- Conducting investigations and disciplinary proceedings against registered firms and associated individuals, including imposing sanctions when justified.

The PCAOB is not charged with standard-setting or regulatory authority over audits on nonpublic companies. Those audits are regulated at the state level and the state boards of accountancy (or similar bodies) continue to recognize the AICPA as the standard-setter for those audits. Although state boards of accountancy can choose to adopt PCAOB standards instead of those of the AICPA, Sarbanes-Oxley §209 explicitly notes that "the standards approved by the [PCAOB] should not be presumed to be applicable ... for small and medium sized nonregistered public accounting firms."

5.3 STRUCTURE

Although overseen by the SEC, the PCAOB is not an agency of the U.S. government and its staff members are not government employees. It is a nonprofit corporation that can be dissolved only by an act of Congress.

The PCAOB's Washington office is home to the board, the executive staff, and the standards-setting function. It is located at 1666 K Street, NW, Washington, DC 20006-2803. The phone number is (202) 207-9100 and its Web site is *www.pcaobus.org*. It has several satellite offices around the country, primarily involved with inspections.

(a) BOARD MEMBERS.   There are five members of the board. The board members serve full-time and cannot engage in any other professional or business activity. They are appointed by the SEC, in consultation with the Chairman of the Federal Reserve and the Secretary of the Treasury. Two, and only two, of the members are to be current or former CPAs; however, a CPA cannot be appointed chairperson if he or she practiced as a CPA within five years of appointment to the board.

Board members serve five-year terms, except for the initial members who were appointed to staggered terms. No member can serve more than two terms.

(b) STAFF. The board is supported by a staff of several hundred accountants, attorneys, and others. Many of the accountants were partners in auditing firms before joining the PCAOB staff.

The board has established organizational functions as follows:

- Division of Registration and Inspections, which creates the registry of accounting firms and performs inspections of the firms.
- Office of the Chief Auditor and Professional Standards, which advises the board on standards-setting.
- Division of Enforcement and Investigations, which performs investigations of possible violations of law or professional standards and recommends disciplinary actions to the board.
- Office of General Counsel, which provides legal advice and assists the board's rulemaking functions.
- Office of Operations, which is responsible for information technology, human resources, and finance.
- Office of Research and Analysis, which provides the board with assessment of risk and related insights.
- Offices of public affairs and government relations, which assist the board in communications with the public, Congress, and the news media.
- International affairs staff, which advises the board on international issues.

(c) ADVISORY GROUPS. The board has the authority to create advisory groups to make recommendations regarding standards. It has officially convened a Standing Advisory Group to assist the board in reviewing existing standards, in formulating new ones, and in evaluating proposed standards projects. Periodically, the board convenes ad hoc groups to advise the staff on specific practice issues.

5.4 FUNDING

The PCAOB is not a government agency and is not funded by the government, although its budget is subject to SEC approval. The bulk of the funding comes from an allocation of accounting support fees assessed on public companies. The PCAOB also receives registration and annual fees from auditing firms.

The PCAOB has the authority to assess monetary penalties against auditors, but the amounts so collected do not fund PCAOB activities. Under Sarbanes-Oxley, the penalties are donated to a merit scholarship program for undergraduate and graduate students in accredited accounting degree programs.

5.5 REGISTRATION

Under Sarbanes-Oxley, only firms registered with PCAOB may "prepare or issue, or . . . participate in the preparation or issuance of, any audit report with respect to any issuer" [sec. 102(a)]. Thus, any firm—domestic or foreign—that plays a substantial role in an audit of a public company must be registered. However, a firm can voluntarily register with the board even if it does no audits of public clients.

It is illegal for a nonregistered firm to audit or participate in the audit of a public company. Accordingly, a firm must maintain its registration and needs to consider whether other firms that it relies on for the audits of subsidiaries or other elements of the company are registered.

Registered firms must follow the PCAOB standards in auditing, quality control, and independence; pay the required registration fees; undergo periodic inspections; and cooperate with PCAOB-initiated investigations.

The application form for registration, called *Form 1*, asks for a substantial amount of information, including:

- The names of all public companies audited during the preceding calendar year, and those that the firm expects to audit during the current calendar year.
- The annual fees the firm received from each public company for audit services, other accounting services, and nonaudit services.
- A statement of the firm's quality control policies for accounting and auditing services.
- A list of all accountants associated with the firm who participate in or otherwise contribute to audits.
- Information relating to relevant criminal, civil, or administrative actions or disciplinary proceedings pending against the firm or any associated person of the firm.

The application form is completed and submitted electronically. Sarbanes-Oxley calls for some of this information to be publicly available, which the PCAOB expects to provide via the Internet. Firms can request that certain proprietary or confidential information be protected from public disclosure.

The board has 45 days to review a firm's application. The board can either: approve it; request more information from the firm, triggering another 45-day review period; or call for a hearing to determine whether the application should be approved. In the latter case, the acceptance decision is made by a hearing officer, although at the request of either party, it is reviewable by the board. Alternatively, the firm may elect to treat the call for a hearing as a written notice of disapproval that can be appealed directly to the SEC.

There is a registration fee and an annual fee, which are assessed based on the number of public clients the firm audits.

A firm may withdraw from PCAOB registration, but the board may delay the withdrawal for up to 18 months while it carries out inspection, investigation, or disciplinary proceedings.

5.6 STANDARDS

Sarbanes-Oxley gave the PCAOB the authority to approve or establish standards for auditing, quality control, and independence. The board determined that, rather than adopt the standards of others (except for the transitional interim standards), it will establish its own standards. Thus, standards applicable to audits of public companies are established by PCAOB; standards for audits of nonpublic companies—known as *generally accepted auditing standards*—continue to be established by the AICPA. The PCAOB standards are not characterized as generally accepted because their authority does not derive from general acceptance, but rather from regulatory authority.

(a) AUDITORS SUBJECT TO THE STANDARDS.   The PCAOB's practice standards apply to all auditors, including staff and independent contractors (called *associated persons*), who participate in an audit of a public company. Registered firms also must comply with the board's quality control standards.

Auditors of nonpublic companies may choose to apply PCAOB standards either voluntarily or to meet the needs of clients or financial statement users. If an auditor of a nonpublic company complies with the PCAOB auditing standards and the audit report specifically refers to compliance with the PCAOB's auditing standards, the auditor need not comply with the board's independence standards, nor does the reference imply that the auditor is subject to the securities laws or PCAOB regulatory requirements such as inspections.

The AICPA has issued an auditing interpretation (AU 9508.89) explaining that if an auditor applies PCAOB standards in the audit of a nonpublic company, the auditor must also comply with generally accepted auditing standards and the audit report should refer to both sets of standards.

(b) INTERIM STANDARDS.   Although the PCAOB had immediate authority over standards, it chose to adopt as interim standards the professional standards that existed on April 16, 2003. The standards adopted were the following as they existed on that date:

- Generally accepted auditing standards as established by the AICPA.
- Statements on Standards for Attestation Engagements, and related interpretations.
- Statements on Quality Control Standards and certain AICPA SEC Practice Section Requirements of Membership.
- Rule 102 of the AICPA Code of Professional Conduct and related interpretations and rulings.
- Rule 101 of the AICPA Code of Professional Conduct and related interpretations and rulings and Independence Standards Board Standards Nos. 1, 2, and 3 and interpretations 99-1, 00-1, and 00-2. The board recognizes, though, that to the extent an SEC independence rule differs from the AICPA or ISB rules, the SEC rule takes precedence.

The PCAOB's intention in adopting the interim standards were to methodically review them and revise, replace, or supplement them as necessary.

(c) SARBANES-OXLEY MANDATED STANDARDS.   Although the board will issue new standards and amend or replace the interim standards, Sarbanes-Oxley explicitly calls for the PCAOB to require:

- Audit firms to prepare work papers and other information related to the audit report, in sufficient detail to support the auditor's conclusions, and to maintain them for at least seven years.
- A concurring or second-partner review and approval of audit reports.
- An audit report that includes a description of tests and findings related to the entity's internal control, including an evaluation of the effectiveness of internal control, an evaluation of the assessment of internal control made by management, and a description of material weaknesses in control or material noncompliance with controls the auditor discovered.
- Quality control standards that deal with:
  - Monitoring of professional ethics and independence
  - Consultation on accounting and auditing questions
  - Supervision of audit work
  - Hiring, professional development, and advancement of personnel
  - Acceptance and continuation of engagements
  - Internal inspection

Sarbanes-Oxley requires auditors to report directly to the audit committee or, when there is none, the board of directors. It also requires the auditor to report on a timely basis to the audit committee all critical accounting policies and procedures used; alternative accounting treatments discussed with management, along with their ramifications and the treatment the auditor preferred; and other written communications between the firm and management, such as management letters or schedules of unadjusted differences.

The auditor of a public company, under the law, may also provide to that company nonaudit services, such as tax services, only with the advance approval of the company's audit committee. However, the law specifically prohibits auditors of public companies from also providing the following services to those companies:

- Bookkeeping or other accounting services.
- Financial information systems design and implementation.
- Appraisal or valuation services, fairness opinions, or contribution-in-kind reports.

- Actuarial services.
- Internal audit outsourcing services.
- Management or human resource functions.
- Broker or dealer, investment advisor, or investment banking services.
- Legal services and expert services unrelated to the audit.

Sarbanes-Oxley requires that partners on an audit rotate off after performing audit services for that company for five consecutive years. It also prohibits auditors from taking certain senior financial positions with the companies they audit if they worked on the audit less than a year before the initiation of the current audit.

(d) STANDARD-SETTING.   Standards are approved on a majority vote of the board members. The members are assisted by the chief auditor's staff and, as necessary, ad hoc participation from outsiders.

The board is assisted by its Standing Advisory Group (SAG). Chaired by the chief auditor, the SAG reviews existing standards, evaluates proposals to amend standards, and recommends new standards to the board. Its contribution is advisory only, but it provides the views of a diverse spectrum of backgrounds and viewpoints.

The board's standard-setting process involves the following steps:

1. The proposed standard is discussed by the board at an open meeting. The briefing papers that provide background and recommendations are available on the PCAOB Web site and the board's meetings are Webcast and archived on the Web site.

2. The proposed standard is issued for comment. An exposure draft is made available on the PCAOB Web site for at least 21 days. Hard copies of the exposure draft are generally not produced or mailed out for comment.

3. The draft, revised as appropriate following exposure, is discussed and approved for issuance by the board at a public meeting. The approved rule is made available on the PCAOB Web site.

4. The final rule is filed with the SEC for its review. The SEC has the final approval power over PCAOB rules.

5. The SEC publishes a notice of filing for the PCAOB's rule in the *Federal Register* and comments are received for at least 35 days.

6. The SEC decides whether to approve the PCAOB standard. The SEC can only accept or reject the rule; it cannot make revisions. If the rule is approved, it is printed in the *Federal Register* and becomes a PCAOB standard.

(e) FORM OF GUIDANCE.   PCAOB standards contain three parts: a release, the standard, and the background and basis for conclusions. The PCAOB staff has indicated that all three sections, having been approved by the board, are authoritative and auditors are required to follow the guidance in all three.

The PCAOB staff also issues interpretive guidance in the form of Staff Questions and Answers. Although this guidance does not constitute rules of the board and is not approved by the board, the staff considers it in interpreting the rules when questions arise in inspections or investigations.

5.7 INSPECTIONS

The PCAOB is charged by Congress with conducting:

a continuing program of inspections to assess the degree of compliance of each registered public accounting firm and associated persons of that firm with [Sarbanes-Oxley], the rules of the

[PCAOB], the rules of the [SEC], or professional standards, in connection with its performance of audits, issuance of audit reports, and related matters involving issuers [Sarbanes-Oxley § 104(a)].

The Division of Registration and Inspection is responsible for the inspection program.

(a) REQUIRED INSPECTIONS. All firms that audit public companies are required to undergo PCAOB inspection. A registered firm with no public clients is not subject to inspection.

Foreign registered firms may request that the board rely on a non-U.S. inspection. In that case, the board will determine the degree, if any, to which it will rely on the non-U.S. inspection. The board considers the level of the non-U.S. inspection program's independence, rigor, and inspection work program.

Sarbanes-Oxley calls for annual inspections of firms with more than 100 public clients and inspections at least every three years for firms with 100 or fewer public clients, although it allows the PCAOB to adjust this schedule. In addition, the PCAOB may also conduct special inspections at its own discretion or SEC request.

(b) INSPECTION SCOPE. The PCAOB inspection is similar in concept to the peer reviews of public-company auditors that had been administered by the AICPA, but there are some significant differences. The inspection is not done by another public accounting firm, but by the PCAOB staff. Whereas peer reviews were intended primarily as a way to improve the firm's practice, inspections can be more punitive: negative results may be communicated to the SEC or state boards of accountancy and disclosed to the public. In addition, an identified deficiency might lead to a PCAOB investigation.

Before arriving at the firm to be inspected, the PCAOB requests a substantial amount of information from the firm to help determine the inspection scope. The information requested includes the firm's financial statements, business model, internal policies and procedures, client lists, proposals, withdrawals, and latest internal inspection or peer review results.

Inspections focus on two general aspects of a firm's practice: practice management and individual audits. The focus for smaller firms is different than for larger ones, taking into account the structural differences resulting from smaller size.

In assessing the firm's practice management, the inspectors review policies and procedures and interview personnel. They focus on seven significant areas:

1. The tone at the top; that is, management's commitment to quality auditing practices, and whether the expectation for quality practices is communicated unambiguously to the partners and staff.

2. Whether compensation and promotion within the firm are driven by technical proficiency, not just the ability to generate new business.

3. How the firm monitors compliance with applicable independence rules, including those related to nonaudit services both for the firm and those in its alliances and joint ventures.

4. What factors the firm considers in client acceptance and continuance, including whether the engagements accepted are within the firm's competence and how the audit work addresses identified risks.

5. The effectiveness of the firm's internal inspection process, including consideration of actions the firm takes to address identified problems.

6. The effectiveness of the firm's audit policies and procedures, including how policies are identified, developed, and communicated.

7. How the firm coordinates the use of foreign affiliates for audits of foreign subsidiaries of U.S. clients, including how the firm satisfies itself about the foreign affiliates' knowledge of U.S. technical requirements.

Individual engagements are selected for review based on factors such as the office or partner involved significant client or industry risks, or other information suggesting that the engagement might be of particular interest. The focus of the engagement review is to assess the quality of the audit work and related documentation, evaluate the knowledge and ability of the engagement team, determine whether the work was performed or reviewed timely, and identify the need for improvements or new standards.

The inspection involves detailed review of the work papers and interviews with those who did the work, including staff at all levels and nonaudit personnel, such as tax or information technology specialists. The PCAOB inspectors may also interview members of the engagement clients' audit committees to gain their perspectives on the audit and auditor communications.

(c) INSPECTION RESULTS.   At the conclusion of the inspection, the PCAOB prepares a draft report, which is made available to the firm. A firm that disagrees with the findings can file a response within 30 days. The board then reviews the draft report and the firm's response, if any, and after due consideration, issues a final report. A firm that continues to disagree with the findings can appeal to the SEC to review the PCAOB report.

The final inspection report is sent to the SEC. The report is made available to the public except that criticisms or defects identified in the firm's quality control system are not made public unless they are not corrected to the board's satisfaction within a year of the inspection report. The public disclosure excludes certain confidential or proprietary information and information privileged under the rules of evidence.

The board may refer information emanating from the review, along with the firm's response to the report, to relevant state licensing authorities.

5.8 INVESTIGATIONS

The PCAOB's Office of Investigations and Enforcement can investigate possible violations by registered firms of Sarbanes-Oxley, PCAOB rules, securities laws applicable to auditors, or professional standards. Allegations of potential violations might come from PCAOB inspections, information forwarded to the PCAOB (its Web site has a facility for such reporting), or public information that comes to the PCAOB's attention.

Informal inquiries and formal investigations, along with related documents provided to PCAOB, are confidential until presented in connection with a public proceeding. Thus, until made public, they are protected from discovery by plaintiffs' counsel. The PCAOB may, however, make such documents available to the SEC, U.S. or state attorneys general, or other applicable federal or state regulatory authorities.

In conducting an investigation, the board can call for testimony, audit work papers, or other documents from a firm or other person involved in the audit. Registered firms are required to cooperate with the investigation; failure to do so can be the basis for disciplinary action.

The board may also request testimony or documents from others, such as the public company whose audit is under investigation. The PCAOB may request the SEC to issue a subpoena to compel cooperation of these individuals or organizations.

If the board chooses, it can hold formal proceedings to determine whether an individual or firm should be disciplined. These proceedings are not public, unless agreed to by the relevant parties. However, they are on the record, before a trier of fact, and involve testimony under oath and the offering of evidence. Firms or individuals subject to the hearing may be accompanied by counsel.

The board has the authority to sanction any registered firm or associated individual who it determines violated Sarbanes-Oxley, PCAOB rules, securities laws relating to the preparation and issuance of audit reports, or professional standards. Sanctions may include:

- Suspension or revocation of registration.
- Temporary or permanent suspension or bar of a person from further association with any registered public accounting firm.

- Temporary or permanent limitation on the activities, functions, or operations of the firm or person (e.g., prohibiting a firm from accepting new audit clients for a period of time, requiring a firm to assign a reviewer or supervisor to an associated person, requiring a firm to terminate one or more audit engagements, and requiring a firm to make functional changes in the firm or the engagement team).
- A civil money penalty for each such violation to a maximum of $100,000 for an individual and $2 million for a firm or, if the violation is intentional, reckless, or knowing or involves repeated instances of negligence, $750,000 for an individual and $15 million for a firm.
- Censure.
- Additional professional education or training.
- Requiring the firm to engage an independent monitor, subject to the approval of the board, to observe and report on the firm's future compliance with relevant laws or standards.
- Requiring the firm to engage counsel or another consultant to design policies to comply with relevant laws or standards.
- Requiring the firm or associated person to adopt or implement policies, or to undertake other actions, to improve audit quality or to comply with relevant laws or standards.
- Requiring a firm to obtain an independent review and report on one or more engagements.

Any sanctions imposed can be appealed to the SEC.

For investigations of foreign firms, the board may rely on the investigation or sanction of the firm by a non-U.S. authority.

The PCAOB reports the name of the individual or firm sanctioned, a description of the sanction and the basis for its imposition, and other information the board deems appropriate to the SEC, the appropriate state or foreign licensing authority, and the public.

CHAPTER 6

EARNINGS MANAGEMENT

Paul Rosenfield, CPA

6.1 EARNINGS MANAGEMENT BY DISTORTING THE APPLICATION OF GENERALLY ACCEPTED ACCOUNTING PRINCIPLES

On September 28, 1998, Chairman Arthur Levitt of the Securities and Exchange Commission (SEC) referred to a "widespread, but too little-challenged custom: earnings management." He referred to the practice as *a game of nods and winks*, *accounting being perverted*, *cutting corners*, and *wishful thinking . . . winning the day over faithful representation*. He stated his fear that "we are witnessing an erosion in the quality of earnings, and therefore the quality of financial reporting. Managing may be giving way to manipulation; integrity may be losing out to illusion. . . . in the gray area between legitimacy and outright fraud"[1]

The SEC defines "earnings management" as "distorting the application of generally accepted accounting principles."[2] Levitt said that "Flexibility in accounting allows it to keep pace with business innovations. Abuses such as earnings management occur when people exploit this pliancy." He said that the practice "reflect[s] the desires of management rather than the underlying financial performance of the company." He said earnings may be managed by "gimmicks."[3] Those gimmicks distort the application of generally accepted accounting principles (GAAP) to serve the desires of management, for example, by (1) reporting higher overall earnings than the underlying financial performance of the reporting entity justifies, (2) reporting earnings in periods other than when they occur to obtain a desired result, and (3) stabilizing reported earnings. (Levitt said, "Trickery is employed to obscure actual financial volatility.")[4]

---

[1] Speech at New York Center for Law and Business, September 28, 1998.
[2] Securities and Exchange Commission, "Fact Sheet," p. 2.
[3] Speech at New York Center for Law and Business, September 28, 1998.
[4] Id.

One force driving this phenomenon is the feeling among managers that they have to make their estimates, that reported quarterly or annual earnings that are less than the reporting entity or analysts had predicted spells doom. Levitt stated: "I recently read of one major U.S. Company that failed to meet its so-called numbers by one penny, and lost more than six percent of its stock value in one day.... [And] [A]uditors, who want to retain their clients, are under pressure not to stand in the way."[5]

Levitt listed these ways to distort the application of GAAP to manage earnings:

- "Big bath" restructuring charges (see item 2 below).
- Creative acquisition accounting, in which an ever-growing portion of the acquisition price is classified as in-process research and development, which can be written off in a one-time charge rather than included in goodwill to be charged ratably against income. The SEC sent a letter on September 9, 1999, to the American Institute of Certified Public Accountants (AICPA), which it publicized on its Web site, *www.sec.gov*, asking the AICPA to describe best practice in the area and giving some guidance. The AICPA is now working on the project; meanwhile, the SEC's letter apparently has had the effect of reducing the practice.
- "Cookie jar reserves," in which unrealistic assumptions are used to estimate liabilities for items such as sales returns, loan losses, or warranty costs. Companies reach into the cookie jars and report income when needed in bad times. The SEC issued proposed rule S7-03-00 dealing with this matter on January 27, 2000.
- "Immaterial" misapplications of accounting principles (see item 1 below).
- Premature reporting of revenue (see item 3 below).

The SEC has dealt with those techniques by enforcement actions. In addition, it has issued the following Staff Accounting Bulletins on three of them:

1. In Staff Accounting Bulletin No. 99, issued on August 12, 1999, the SEC staff stated its view that no misstatement is immaterial if its purpose is to manage earnings (see Section 3.2(c)).
2. In Staff Accounting Bulletin No. 100, issued on November 24, 1999, the SEC staff stated its views on reporting on charges that typically result from consolidation or relocation of operations or the disposition or abandonment of operations or productive assets (see Section 9.4(b)).
3. In Staff Accounting Bulletin No. 101, issued on December 3, 1999, the SEC staff stated its views on issues in reporting of revenue, in part because of revenue reporting issues encountered by registrants that came to the Commission's attention, including issues related to earnings management (see Section 17.3(h)).

Chapter 5 discusses recent egregious examples of earnings management (and of hiding debt, etc.) by distorting the application of GAAP, by Enron, WorldCom, and a number of other reporting entities.

6.2 EARNINGS MANAGEMENT BY THE FAULTY DESIGN OF GENERALLY ACCEPTED ACCOUNTING PRINCIPLES[6]

As discussed in Section 6.1, the SEC (and most others) has assumed that GAAP itself acts as a bar to earnings management, defining it in terms of the *application* of GAAP. Schipper likewise contends that "... GAAP, auditors, audit committees, and legal rules—constrain reporting. In

---

[5] Id.

[6] This section is taken from Paul Rosenfield, "What Drives Earnings Management? It Is GAAP Itself," *Journal of Accountancy*, October 2000.

addition, economic conditions influence accruals. Some components of earnings are therefore not susceptible to management. . . ."[7] Healy and Wahlen state that "Earnings management occurs when managers use judgment in financial reporting and in structuring transactions to alter financial reports to either mislead some stakeholders about the underlying economic performance of the company or to influence contractual outcomes that depend on reported accounting numbers."[8]

However, the SEC has been considering the view that distorting the application of GAAP is the smaller of the two causes of earnings management, and that the larger cause is the faulty design of GAAP itself.

The faulty design of GAAP may permit earnings to be managed, for example, by permitting reporting entities to report income that they have not earned. For example, consider this statement by Johnson and Petrone, two Financial Accounting Standards Board (FASB) staff members, about a formerly acceptable method of accounting for business combinations: "[The pooling-of-interests method of reporting after a business combination] essentially is a means . . . to report higher earnings without having to earn them. . . ."[9] However, the desire to report income as high as possible, as real and as well known as it is, is tempered by fears of attracting increased demands from suppliers of inputs, such as stockholders and employees, and from the government. In contrast, the issuers of financial reports have no such reservations about another way to manage earnings that is facilitated by the faulty design of GAAP, to avoid significant fluctuations from period to period in reported income. Their desire for stability of income reporting exceeds their desire for higher reported income. Their acceptance of income tax allocation, for example, demonstrates that. Stability of income reporting is the fundamental goal of traditional financial reporting. Heath reported that "One former FASB member told me recently that 95 percent of the comments the Board receives from financial statement preparers fall into one of three categories: Don't make any changes, don't move so fast, and don't make income volatile—don't let it fluctuate."[10] Wyatt, a former member of the FASB, states that ". . . the artificial smoothing of real world volatility [is] a common feature of FASB standards. . . ."[11]

A view of Chief Accountant Turner of the SEC, that "No accounting system [other than ours] provides comparable transparency to a reporting entity's underlying economic events and transactions,"[12] is a commendable objective. It conforms with this observation by the FASB: "An analogy with cartography [map making] has been used to convey some of the characteristics of financial reporting. . . ."[13] However, our GAAP as currently designed fails for two reasons to provide such transparency. Because the reasons are pervasive, the failure is systemic. First, application of current GAAP results in failure to report on a major portion of the underlying economic events that meet the FASB's qualitative criteria for reporting on events in its Concepts Statement No. 2. Second, application of current GAAP introduces noise into the system that hopelessly clouds the portrayal of the effects of the events it does permit reporting entities to report on and thereby prevents achievement of transparency in reporting on them. It does all that for the single purpose of managing earnings.

Because of the realization convention, the events current GAAP permits reporting entities to report on are mainly confined to changes in quantities of assets and liabilities. Those are underlying events that affect reporting entities, of course. But they are not the only underlying events that affect reporting entities. As the FASB states, ". . . all entities are [also] affected by price changes, interest

---

[7] Katherine Schipper, "Commentary on Earnings Management," *Accounting Horizons*, December 1989, p. 98.

[8] Paul M. Healy and James M. Wahlen, "A Review of the Earnings Management Literature and Its Implications for Standard Setting," *Accounting Horizons*, December 1999, p. 368.

[9] L. Todd Johnson and Kimberley R. Petrone, "Why Not Eliminate Goodwill?" *FASB Status Report*, November 17, 1999, p. 12.

[10] Loyd C. Heath, "How About Some Constructive Input to the FASB?" *Financial Executive*, September/October 1990, p. 57.

[11] Arthur R. Wyatt, "Professionalism in Standard-Setting," *The CPA Journal*, July 1988, p. 25.

[12] Lynn Turner, Letter to P. Rosenfield, October 27, 1999.

[13] FASB, Statement of Concepts No. 2, "*Qualitative Characteristics of Accounting Information*," par. 24.

rate changes, technological changes . . . and similar events. . . ."[14] The FASB goes on to state that "To compare . . . performance by comparing only realized gains [gains reported when quantities change] implies a definition of performance that many people would regard as incomplete and, therefore, as an unreliable representation."[15] Consider the exchange by a reporting entity of 10 shares of a widely traded stock worth $150 a share for $1,500. That does not affect the reporting entity much if at all. But a prior change in its price from $100 to $150 a share while held did affect the reporting entity, as anyone who holds such stock can testify (are investors indifferent about increases in the current selling prices of their stocks?). The FASB concludes that "Information based on current prices should be recognized if it is sufficiently relevant and reliable to justify the costs involved and more relevant than alternative information."[16]

The FASB does not, however, conform with those praiseworthy observations it makes. In 1978, the FASB stated in the foreword to its "Objectives" that it ". . . recognizes that in certain respects current generally accepted accounting principles may be inconsistent with those that may derive from the objectives and concepts set forth in [its Concepts] Statement[s] . . . In due course, the Board expects to reexamine its pronouncements, pronouncements of predecessor standard-setting bodies, and existing financial reporting practice in the light of newly enunciated objectives and concepts." But in the ensuing 25 years to this writing, it has not evaluated the current broad principles by applying the objectives and concepts, and there is no sign that it will do so in the foreseeable future. (In fact, in its Concepts Statement No. 7, paragraph 16, issued in 2000, the Board stated that it ". . . does not intend to revisit existing accounting standards and practice solely as result of issuing this Statement.") Kripke noted ". . .the [FASB]'s failure to attempt to make progress. . .by applying its own qualitative characteristics. . . ."[17] The American Accounting Association characterizes the result: "The most general criticism to be leveled at financial statements in their present form is that they are seriously *incomplete*. . . . One respect in which financial statements are now incomplete is that, because they are substantially transaction-based, they fail to recognize some value changes occurring during a period that aren't associated with a transaction."[18]

Systematic and rational allocation causes the noise current GAAP introduces. The adoption in the 1930s of the *definition* of accounting as a process of allocation[19] and the retention of that definition to this day demonstrates that allocation is endemic to financial reporting. Allocation infects most of financial reporting, including, for example, depreciation, and reporting on inventories, investments, income taxes, pensions, goodwill and other intangibles, and liabilities. Allocation seems necessary because of the events whose effects are not reported on, because, in the absence of allocation, not reporting on those effects would result in reporting all assets and liabilities while they are held or owed at their original amounts, an obviously unsatisfactory result.

Allocation uses smooth ("systematic") formulas, such as the straight-line and double-declining-balance formulas for depreciation and the compound interest formula for reporting on liabilities, each selected at the beginning of the period of allocation, supposedly to represent the effects of underlying economic events that are expected to occur in the future. We financial reporters cannot be that prescient about events that may occur in the future, after we select the formulas. And events do not occur as regularly as the formulas imply.

Moreover, allocation does not even represent the effects of underlying economic events. It merely takes amounts from the financial reporting territory, such as costs, enters them in the financial reporting map, and massages them there. As Hendriksen and van Breda state: ". . . annual

---

[14] FASB, Statement of Concepts No. 6, "*Elements of Financial Statements*," par. 218.

[15] Statement of Concepts No. 2, par. 118.

[16] FASB, Statement of Concepts No. 5, "*Recognition and Measurement in Financial Statements of Business Enterprises*."

[17] Homer Kripke, "Reflections on the FASB's Conceptual Framework for Accounting and on Auditing," *Journal of Accounting, Auditing & Finance*, Winter 1989, p. 25.

[18] American Accounting Association, "Report of the American Accounting Association Committee on Accounting and Auditing Measurement, 1989–90," *Accounting Horizons*, September 1991, p. 83.

[19] American Accounting Association, "A Tentative Statement of Accounting Principles Affecting Corporate Reports," *The Accounting Review*, June 1936.

[depreciation] is simply a fraction of the total ... cost.... [and] has no necessary relation to ... occurrences within the year.... [it] has no real world connotations."[20] The AICPA said the same: "Definitions are unacceptable which imply that *depreciation for the year* is a measurement ... of anything that actually occurs within the year."[21] (Also see Thomas[22] and Section 19.8.)

If financial reporting reported on the effects of the economic events it fails to report on, allocation would be unnecessary. But reporting on those effects would result in reported income being less stable than it is under current GAAP. The issuers want more stable income reporting, so they prevent GAAP from resulting in reporting on those effects. As Zeff states: "... [there is] intense political lobbying against proposals that special interests find to be obnoxious even though the proposed reforms are seen as serving the interests of financial statement users."[23] The issuers usually disguise their desire and power to prevent introduction of more volatility in income reporting. Ihlanfeldt, an issuer, provides an undisguised example in the following narrow area: "... field-testing...sponsored by the Financial Executives Research Foundation...confirmed that application of the FASB's tentative conclusions would have introduced a high degree of volatility into companies' annual pension expense.... This resulted in the Board making changes in the final standard that helped to reduce volatility.... they did listen—but it was not without considerable prodding."[24]

We defend allocation mainly on the basis of realization and objectivity. Both are smoke screens to cover up the real goal of those who support it, to stabilize reported income. The smooth formulas allocation uses have that result. Hatfield, a leader of the profession in the early twentieth century, stated that "... depreciation is only part of a broader scheme whose purpose is to equalize charges between different years."[25] Sterling said that "The very purpose of measurement is to discover variations in empirical phenomena. By contrast, it seems that the purpose of allocation is to make the empirical phenomena appear to be smooth regardless of the actual variations."[26] Lee said that "... allocations [are] designed to produce smoothed income flows."[27] And Devine said that "... depreciation is clearly a device for smoothing irregular capital budgeting outlays."[28] We use allocation for managing earnings, as former Chief Accountant Schuetze of the SEC, said, for "... smoothing the hills and valleys of change."[29]

The power of realization and allocation to stabilize income reporting, embodied in the current design of GAAP, dwarfs the power individual issuers have to stabilize income reporting by distorting the application of GAAP. Those concepts are the main engines of earnings management today, and they should therefore be eliminated.

6.3 SOURCES AND SUGGESTED REFERENCES

FASB, Statement of Concepts No. 1, "*Objectives of Financial Reporting by Business Enterprises*".

Arthur, Levitt, Speech at New York Center for Law and Business, September 28, 1998.

Securities and Exchange Commission, "Fact Sheet", p. 2.

---

[20] Eldon S. Hendriksen and Michael F. van Breda, *Accounting Theory*, Fifth Edition (Boston: Richard D. Irwin, Inc., 1992), pp. 527, 528.

[21] American Institute of Certified Public Accountants (American Institute of Accountants until 1957), "Review and Résumé," *Accounting Terminology Bulletin No. 1*, p. 24.

[22] Arthur L. Thomas, "The FASB and the Allocation Fallacy," *Journal of Accountancy*, November 1975.

[23] Stephen Addam Zeff, "A Perspective on the U.S. Public/Private-Sector Approach to Standard Setting and Financial Reporting," Inaugural Lecture, State University of Limburg, June 3, 1994, p. 26.

[24] William J. Ihlanfeldt, "The Rule-Making Process: A Time for Change," in Previts, *Standard Setting*, p. 28.

[25] Henry Rand Hatfield, *Modern Accounting* (New York: D. Appleton and Company, 1916), p. 134.

[26] Robert R. Sterling, *Toward a Science of Accounting* (Houston: Scholars Book Co., 1979), p. 226.

[27] T. A. Lee, "The Simplicity and Complexity of Accounting," in Sterling, *Simplified*, p. 45.

[28] Carl Thomas Devine, *Essays in Accounting Theory*, Volume II (American Accounting Association, 1985), p. 79n.

[29] Walter Schuetze, "Keep It Simple," *Accounting Horizons*, June 1991, p. 113.

CHAPTER 7

FORGETTING OUR DUTIES TO THE USERS OF FINANCIAL REPORTS: THE LESSON OF ENRON

Paul Rosenfield, CPA

7.1 NEGLECT OF OUR DUTIES

Financial reports are consumer products. The American Institute of Certified Public Accountants (AICPAs) Special Committee on Financial Reporting knew that. It called its report *Improving Business Reporting—A Customer Focus*. Its members knew the users of the reports are the parties whom the whole endeavor of financial reporting should benefit. But the rest of us have forgotten that, if we ever realized it—so much so that Walter Schuetze, a former Chief Accountant of the Securities and Exchange Commission (SEC), felt he had to remind us of it, forcefully, recently:

> We accountants are doing accounting for accountants' sake, not for use by investors, creditors, underwriters, analysts, boards of directors, and regulators who are the people that we accountants should aim to please.... Accounting should not be done for the benefit of accountants.[1]

The 2001 Enron collapse, the largest bankruptcy in U.S. history, accompanied by the worst financial reporting breakdown in decades—if not the worst ever—and by the destruction of Arthur Andersen & Co., one of the five largest international Certified Public Accountant (CPA) firms, dramatized the neglect of our duties to our basic clients, our customers, the users of financial reports. Melissa Klein quoted Goldwasser as saying that "Andersen ... lost sight of their duties to the public."[2] The Enron financial reporting breakdown was accompanied by other reported large-scale breakdowns, for example, at WorldCom—whose reported breakdown was called

---

[1] Walter Schuetze, "What Are Assets and Liabilities? Where Is True North? Accounting that My Sister Would Understand," *Abacus*, February 2001, pp. 4 and 16.
[2] Melissa Klein, "Guilty Verdict Draws Mixed Reactions," *Accounting Today*, July 8–21, 2002, p. 38.

"... the most sweeping bookkeeping deception in history...,"[3] Cedant Corporation, Global Cross-ing, Qwest Communications, Rite Aid, Waste Management, The Baptist Foundation, Vivendi Universal (a French company), and Xerox.

Arthur Levitt, a former SEC chairman, testified before Congress that "What has failed is nothing less than the system for overseeing our capital markets."[4] C. William Thomas said in the *Journal of Accountancy* that "... the Enron implosion has wreaked more havoc on the accounting profession than any other case in U.S. history."[5] Anna Quindlen wrote in *Newsweek* that "In a post-Enron economy... [t]he American people are afraid... that huge corporate entities that once promised secure employment and investments are hollow at the core."[6] And Daniel Kadlec said that "... a fat slice of corporate America ... has been ethically bankrupt for years. We're only now getting a look at the red ink on the moral balance sheets ..."[7]

If the issuers of Enron's financial reports had had the welfare of the users of its financial reports as their primary goal in its financial reporting, Enron might have survived its hard times and pros-pered. The reports might have told the users all they needed to know. The reports and the actions of Enron they facilitated might not have brought down Enron, its officers, its employees, its investors, and its independent auditors. The affair might not had sullied the very reputation of our profession.

7.2 OURSELVES TO BLAME

We have only ourselves to blame. The central place of the users of financial reports had been formally explored in the official financial reporting literature, starting in the late 1960s, by the American Accounting Association in *A Statement of Basic Accounting Theory*:

> Accounting information must be useful to people ... reports [should] be prepared with the intended user's needs in mind.

And by the AICPA, in APB Statement No. 4, *Basic Concepts and Accounting Principles Underlying Financial Statements of Business Enterprises*:

> The basic purpose of financial accounting and financial statements is to provide quantitative financial information about a business enterprise that is useful to statement users, particularly owners and creditors, in making economic decisions.

In 1978 and 1980, the Financial Accounting Standards Board (FASB), added its voice:

> Financial reporting is ... intended to provide information that is useful in making business and economic decisions ... [Its] objectives ... stem largely from the needs of those for whom the information is intended ...[8]

But we have forgotten our duties to the users, or, more likely, have never really thought about them. The average CPA feels he is too busy trying to apply the rules to think about whether the reports he produces or audits are most informative to the users. CPAs believe they have fulfilled their responsibilities as long as they have obeyed the letter of the rules. As Schuetze suggests, we have done financial reporting for our benefit, not for the benefit of the users.

---

[3] Daniel Kadlec, "WorldCon," *Time*, July 8, 2002, p. 21.

[4] Jonathan Alter, "Which Boot Will Drop Next?" *Newsweek*, February 4, 2002, p. 25.

[5] C. William Thomas, "The Rise and Fall of Enron," *Journal of Accountancy*, April 2002, p. 44.

[6] Anna Quindlen, "The Axis of Re-Election," *Newsweek*, March 4, 2002, p. 65.

[7] Daniel Kadlec, "WorldCon," *Time*, July 8, 2002, p. 21.

[8] FASB, Statement of Concepts No. 1, "*Objectives of Financial Reporting by Business Enterprises*," par. 9.

The FASB has rarely referred to the users since 1980. In 1994, the FASB staff asked the Financial Accounting Standards Advisory Council the following in a questionnaire it sent to the Council: "What interim steps can the Board take to incorporate the user focus...into current projects and forthcoming standards?" in effect confessing that the Board had forgotten to focus on the users. And the Council's responses to the FASB's annual agenda questionnaire of 1994 included a statement by the Chairman of the Special Committee on Financial Reporting, who was a member of the Council and later the Chairman of the FASB, that "The focus on users' needs ... [by the Special Committee] was unprecedented and should require the Board to give prompt attention to the [Special Committee's] report and recommendations." The focus on users' needs wasn't unprecedented, only forgotten.

The subject of this Handbook has been thought of as *financial accounting* (thus the name *Financial Accounting Standards Board*), simply preparing documents seemingly with the only purpose to recite history: George J. Staubus pointed out that "... nearly all of our current generally accepted accounting principles (GAAP) were solidified before the profession became interested in objectives."[9] Even the names of the processes involved given by the FASB perpetuate that misconception. The FASB calls the two main processes *measurement* and *recognition*. Assets, liabilities, revenues, expenses, and the like are "measured" (often simply calculated) and then "recognized" in, incorporated "into," financial statements: "Recognition is the process of formally recording or incorporating an item into the financial statements of an entity as an asset, liability, revenue, expense, or the like." Issuance by the issuers and use by the users is not suggested. Such a process may involve only one party, the issuers in their role as preparers, who look inward.

On the contrary, we are not simply in the business of *accounting*—of measuring and recognizing— which requires only one party; we are essentially in the business of *reporting*, which requires two parties, the issuers and the users. Heath commented to that effect:

> If the [FASB] were to be renamed today, it might well be called the ... Financial Reporting Policy Board ... The word "reporting" rather than "accounting" better conveys the breadth of [the] subject.[10]

7.3 THE CENTRAL FAILURE

Lots of things went wrong to cause the financial reporting breakdown that accompanied the Enron collapse:

> In many ways, Enron and its dealings with Arthur Andersen are an anomaly, a perfect storm where greed, lax oversight, and outright fraud combined to unravel two of the nation's largest companies. But a certain moral laxity has come to pervade even the bluest of the blue chips.[11]

> Shareholder deception, supine boards, and Special Purpose Entities seem to have rendered the U.S. corporate governance model a Swiss cheese of loopholes.[12]

They are all symptomatic of a central failure in the system. Carmichael and Gerboth identified that failure:

Carmichael:

> FASB has bogged down in the specifics.... The predictable result has been that creative Big Five accountants and chief financial officers have simply structured ever more ingenious ways

---

[9] George J. Staubus, *Making Accounting Decisions*, (Houston: Scholars Book Company, 1977), p. 16.

[10] Loyd C. Heath, "Commentary on Accounting Literature," *Accounting Horizons*, March 1988, p. 110.

[11] John A. Byrne et. al., "How to Fix Corporate Governance," *BusinessWeek*, May 6, 2002, p. 70.

[12] John Rossant et. al., "The Corporate Cleanup Goes Global," *BusinessWeek*, May 6, 2002, p. 80.

around them. "FASB has had all along an unwillingness to specify the objectives of their pronouncements."[13]

Gerboth:

Every new rule breeds a profusion of finagles, and time is on the side of the finagler.... The mark of a profession is a commitment to excellence ... that commitment ... will not long survive ... the notion that the job of the professional is to search out and exploit the loopholes in his own standards.[14]

The lesson of Enron is that we have forgotten our duties to the users of financial reports. We financial reporters have been trying to do the minimum, to conform with merely the letter but not the spirit of generally accepted accounting principles: "... almost all managers stop when they reach [the] minimums [defined by GAAP]."[15] Perhaps that has been abetted by the failure Carmichael identified, the FASB's failure to specify the objectives of their pronouncements, its failure to impart the spirit of the principles.

7.4 A GOOD START

A good start would be for us financial reporters, with or without prodding by the FASB, to begin conforming with the following principle:

A financial report should provide and explain clearly all the information the users of the report need for their decisions that the report can provide, within reasonable cost constraints.

To remind us of that responsibility, the following could be inserted in the independent auditor's standard report:

Further, in our opinion, the financial report provides and explains clearly all the information the users of the report need for their decisions that the report can provide, within reasonable cost constraints.

---

[13] Quoted in Steve Liesman, Jonathan Weil, and Scot Paltrow, "When Rules Keep Debt Off the Books," *Wall Street Journal*, January 18, 2002.
[14] Dale Gerboth, "Commentary on the Accounting Game," *Accounting Horizons*, December 1987, pp. 98 and 99; "Commentary: The Limits of Technique," *Accounting Horizons*, March 1988, p. 107.
[15] Paul B. W. Miller and Paul R. Bahnson, "The Book Is Out on Quality Financial Reporting," *Accounting Today*, July 22–August 4, 2002, p. 15.

CHAPTER 8

MANAGEMENT DISCUSSION AND ANALYSIS*

Sydney Garmong, CPA

Crowe Chizek and Company LLC

Small business registrants should refer to Regulation S-B for both nonfinancial and financial disclosure requirements.

8.1 OVERVIEW

(a) INTRODUCTION. Management must include, as part of Form 10-K filings, a section entitled "Management Discussion and Analysis of Financial Condition and the Results of Operations" (commonly referred to as *Management Discussion & Analysis* [MD & A]). The governing regulation is Section 229.303 of Regulation S-K and is referred to as *Item 303*. As stated in Item 303, the objective of the MD&A is "to provide to investors and other users information relevant to an assessment of the financial condition and results of operations of the registrant as determined by evaluating the amounts and certainty of cash flows from operations and from outside sources." The

---

*Sydney Garmong, CPA is an executive in the Financial Institution Group at Crowe Chizek and Company LLC in Washington DC. The information contained in this chapter is the view of the author and does not necessarily represent the views of Crowe Chizek and Company LLC.

MD&A should permit shareholders and users to see and understand the specific decisions made through the eyes of management. The Securities and Exchange Commission (SEC) has stated:

> The Commission has long recognized the need for a narrative explanation of the financial statements, because a numerical presentation and brief accompanying footnotes alone may be insufficient for an investor to judge the quality of earnings and the likelihood that past performance is indicative of future performance. MD&A is intended to give the investor an opportunity to look at the company through the eyes of management by providing both a short- and long-term analysis of the business of the company. The Item asks management to discuss the dynamics of the business and to analyze the financials. [Securities Act Release No. 6711, April 24, 1987, 52 FR 13715]

The SEC has especially emphasized the need for prospective disclosures:

> The MD&A requirements are intended to provide, in one section of a filing, material historical and prospective textual disclosure enabling investors and other users to assess the financial condition and results of operations of the registrant, with particular emphasis on the registrant's prospects for the future. [1989]

This is notably similar to the statement given by the Financial Accounting Standards Board (FASB) on the purpose of financial reporting in general:

> Financial reporting should include explanations and interpretations to help users understand financial information provided. For example, the usefulness of financial information as an aid to investors, creditors, and others in forming expectations about a business enterprise may be enhanced by management's explanations of the information. Management knows more about the enterprise and its affairs than investors, creditors, or other "outsiders" and can often increase the usefulness of financial information by identifying certain transactions, other events, and circumstances that affect the enterprise and explaining their financial impact on it. [par. 54 of FASB Concepts Statement, "Objectives of Financial Reporting by Business Enterprises"]

Additionally, the Financial Analysts Federation has endorsed the MD&A:

> We have supported the efforts of the SEC to make these disclosures meaningful. The MD&A, when properly prepared, can be extremely valuable in helping users understand the results of operations and, by extension, the factors which will affect future operating results. (Letter, dated September 30, 1986, from Anthony Cope, Chairman, SEC Liaison Committee of the Financial Analysts Federation to Jonathan Katz, Secretary, SEC)

In sum, both the SEC and the investment community strongly support the MD&A requirement. Furthermore, in light of SEC enforcement actions, particular care should be exercised in drafting the MD&A. Toward this end, the auditing profession has undertaken steps to provide examination and review services with respect to the MD&A, as discussed in detail in section 8.4.

(b) A BRIEF HISTORY.   The requirement for a management discussion section originated in 1968 when the SEC adopted the *"Guides for Preparation and Filing of Registration Statements"* (Securities Act Release No. 33-4936). These guides required a Summary of Earnings, which was to address unusual conditions affecting net income. In 1974, this Summary was mandated for filings under the Securities Exchange Act and was broadened to include a discussion of underlying trends in profitability. Although specific topics to be discussed were not specified, recommendations were made. The SEC wanted to keep the requirements flexible, allowing management to discuss those items peculiar to its business, in order to prevent a "boilerplate" presentation. However, corporations generally fulfilled the requirement by providing percentage changes of financial statement line items (which investors could calculate themselves) without providing substantive reasons for the changes.

In 1977, the SEC's Advisory Committee on Corporate Disclosure reiterated that corporate management, in fact, be given broad latitude in their discussions, but that better direction be provided. To elicit more meaningful prospective analyses, the SEC granted protection under safe harbor rules in 1979.[1] Then in 1980, the MD&A requirement was substantially expanded and rewritten. Although "soft" information was to be provided, the overriding belief was that the potential relevance surpassed problems of verifiability. The 1980 requirements changed the MD&A from a summary of earnings only to an analysis of liquidity, capital resources, as well as results of operations.

Subsequent to the issuance of the above regulation in 1980, the auditing profession initiated proposals to change the MD&A requirement. In 1986, Coopers & Lybrand proposed increased discussion of business risk and that the MD&A be subject to auditor review procedures. The remaining (then) "Big Eight" firms jointly issued *The Future Relevance, Reliability, and Credibility of Financial Information; Recommendations to the American Institute of Certified Public Accountants (AICPA) Board of Directors*, which also called for increased risk disclosure, but recommended that it be removed from the MD&A and that it be audited. In 1987, the AICPA issued an Exposure Draft of a proposed *Statement on Standards for Attestation Engagements, Examination of Management's Discussion and Analysis* (1987). The AICPA ultimately issued a final attestation standard as discussed in Section 8.4[2].

All of this activity generated a response from the SEC. In 1987, the SEC issued its *Concept Release*, which reaffirmed the purpose of the MD&A and requested public comment. The SEC received 196 responses, almost all of which opposed changes to the 1980 regulation. Some respondents did, however, suggest additional guidance through an interpretive release and stricter enforcement. Therefore, the SEC, in 1988, began a special review to assess the adequacy of disclosure and to identify common deficiencies. The first phase of the review covered 218 companies in 12 industries. The SEC found deficiencies in 206 filings (95 percent). A second phase of the review covered 141 companies in another 12 industries. Of these, 139 (99 percent) received comment letters; 53 of these were required to file amendments, and six were referred to the SEC's Division of Enforcement.

Nonetheless, the SEC concurred with the prevailing view that no changes to existing MD&A requirements were necessary. In May 1989, the SEC did issue, an Interpretive Release, "Management's Discussion and Analysis of Financial Condition and Results of Operations; Certain Investment Company Disclosures", which provided guidance, particularly on prospective or "forward-looking" disclosures.[3] This is significant in that the examples included in the Release can serve as standards against which the SEC can measure the adequacy of registrant disclosures. The entire 1989 Release is known as *FR-36*. (See *www.sec.gov/rules/interp/33-8350.htm*.

With respect to currently known trends, the 1989 Release points out that management must assess whether the trend, demand, commitment, event, or uncertainty is likely to happen. If a matter is not likely, no disclosure is required. However, management must be able to make a determination that a matter is not likely. If management cannot make such a determination, it must evaluate the consequences based on the assumption that the event will happen, and then disclose the effects if the consequences are material. The Release distinguishes currently known trends from anticipated trends.

---

[1] The safe harbor rule protects issuers from liability for forward-looking information, if such information has a reasonable basis and is disclosed in good faith. Otherwise, fraud actions under Rule 10b-5 may be brought against the firm.

[2] In 1975, Statement on Auditing Standards No. 8 (AU Section 550) was issued. The statement addressed the auditor's responsibility with respect to "Other Information in Documents Containing Audited Financial Statements" and stated that while the auditor is not obligated to perform any procedures to corroborate information outside of the financial statements (such as the MD&A), such information should be read to determine whether it is consistent with the financial statements.

[3] Although the 1989 Release emphasizes prospective analysis, the historical analysis of the 1980 Release is also required. The 1989 Release interprets, but does not supersede, the 1980 release. Therefore, by continuing to require a discussion of historical changes, as well as prospective events, the SEC underscores its belief that a better understanding of the causes of past performance is necessary for investors to assess the likelihood that the past is indicative of the future.

Examples of known trends affecting future operations include reductions in the registrant's product prices, erosion in market share, changes in insurance coverage, likely nonrenewal of a material contract, discontinuation of a growth trend, and implementation of recently enacted legislation. With respect to future liquidity, the release indicates that the SEC expects registrants to discuss both short- and long-term liquidity, and to use the framework of the statement of cash flows as a basis of discussion (i.e., future operating, investing, and financing cash flows).[4,5]

To underscore the SEC's insistence on enhanced prospective disclosures, the SEC issued the following warning:

> Where a material change in a registrant's financial condition (such as a material increase or decrease in cash flows) or results of operations appears in a reporting period and the likelihood of such change was not discussed in prior reports, the Commission staff as part of its review of the current filing will inquire as to the circumstances existing at the time of the earlier filings to determine whether the registrant failed to discuss a known trend, demand, commitment, event or uncertainty as required by Item 303. [1989]

Exhibit 8.1 provides the full text of the Section 229.303 (Item 303), "Management's Discussion and Analysis of Financial Condition and Results of Operations", of Regulation S-K. Exhibit 8.2 lists, in chronological order, the major SEC releases related to the MD&A.

(c) RECENT DEVELOPMENTS.

(i) Non-GAAP Measures.   On December 4, 2001, the SEC issued a release entitled *Cautionary Advice Regarding the Use of "Pro Forma" Financial Information in Earnings Releases*, which is also referred to as *FR-59*. The SEC issued this release to registrants that present their earnings and results of operations on the basis of methodologies other than generally accepted accounting principles (GAAP). These often referred to as *pro forma* financial information. The SEC states that pro forma financial information can serve useful purposes for public companies who wish to focus investors' attention on critical components of financial results to provide a meaningful comparison to results for the same period of prior years or to emphasize the results of core operations. However, the SEC observed that to a large extent, this has been the intended function of disclosures in a company's MD&A section of its reports.

In response to Section 401(b) of the Sarbanes-Oxley Act of 2002 and to codify guidance in FR-59, the SEC amended Regulation S-K. The SEC subsequently adopted new rules and amendments to address public companies' disclosure or release of certain financial information that is calculated and presented on the basis of methodologies other than in accordance with GAAP. The final rule, "Conditions for Use of Non-GAAP Financial Measures", was issued on January 22, 2003. The disclosure regulation, Regulation G, which requires public companies that disclose or release such non-GAAP financial measures to include, in that disclosure or release, a presentation of the most directly comparable GAAP financial measure and a reconciliation of the disclosed non-GAAP financial measure to the most directly comparable GAAP financial measure. The final rule also adopted amendments to provide additional guidance to those registrants that include non-GAAP financial measures in SEC filings.

---

[4] As a matter of interest, the 1989 Release mentions one known, future, material event that need not be disclosed. Merger negotiations do not have to be discussed in the MD&A unless the registrant has otherwise disclosed them. The SEC acknowledges that the risk of disclosure may jeopardize the transaction.

[5] There are other disclosure items, which are required under different SEC releases and which may be disclosed in the MD&A. For instance, the SEC's Financial Reporting Release No. 6 (1982) mentions the MD&A as an appropriate place to discuss the degree of exposure to exchange rate risks, the functional currencies used to measure significant foreign operations, and the nature of the translation component of equity. Also, in its Staff Accounting Bulletin (SAB) No. 74 (1987), the SEC states that the MD&A may be used to discuss the impact (if known or reasonably estimable) of a future adoption of a recently issued accounting standard.

TITLE 17—COMMODITY AND SECURITIES EXCHANGES
CHAPTER II—SECURITIES AND EXCHANGE COMMISSION
PART 229_STANDARD INSTRUCTIONS FOR FILING FORMS UNDER SECURITIES ACT
Subpart 229.300_Financial Information
Section 229.303 (Item 303) Management's discussion and analysis of financial condition and results of operations.

a. *Full fiscal years.* Discuss registrant's financial condition, changes in financial condition and results of operations. The discussion shall provide information as specified in paragraphs (a)(1) through (5) of this Item and also shall provide such other information that the registrant believes to be necessary to an understanding of its financial condition, changes in financial condition, and results of operations. Discussions of liquidity and capital resources may be combined whenever the two topics are interrelated. Where in the registrant's judgment a discussion of segment information or of other subdivisions of the registrant's business would be appropriate to an understanding of such business, the discussion shall focus on each relevant, reportable segment or other subdivision of the business, and on the registrant as a whole.

1. *Liquidity.* Identify any known trends or any known demands, commitments, events, or uncertainties that will result in or that are reasonably likely to result in the registrant's liquidity increasing or decreasing in any material way. If a material deficiency is identified, indicate the course of action that the registrant has taken or proposes to take to remedy the deficiency. Also identify and separately describe internal and external sources of liquidity, and briefly discuss any material unused sources of liquid assets.

2. *Capital resources.*

   i. Describe the registrant's material commitments for capital expenditures as of the end of the latest fiscal period, and indicate the general purpose of such commitments and the anticipated source of funds needed to fulfill such commitments.

   ii. Describe any known material trends, favorable or unfavorable, in the registrant's capital resources. Indicate any expected material changes in the mix and relative cost of such resources. The discussion shall consider changes between equity, debt, and any off-balance-sheet financing arrangements.

3. *Results of operations.*

   i. Describe any unusual or infrequent events or transactions or any significant economic changes that materially affected the amount of reported income from continuing operations and, in each case, indicate the extent to which income was so affected. In addition, describe any other significant components of revenues or expenses that, in the registrant's judgment, should be described in order to understand the registrant's results of operations.

   ii. Describe any known trends or uncertainties that have had or that the registrant reasonably expects will have a material favorable or unfavorable impact on net sales or revenues or income from continuing operations. If the registrant knows of events that will cause a material change in the relationship between costs and revenues (such as known future increases in costs of labor or materials or price increases or inventory adjustments), the change in the relationship shall be disclosed.

   iii. To the extent that the financial statements disclose material increases in net sales or revenues, provide a narrative discussion of the extent to which such increases are attributable to increases in prices or to increases in the volume or amount of goods or services being sold or to the introduction of new products or services.

   iv. For the three most recent fiscal years of the registrant, or for those fiscal years in which the registrant has been engaged in business, whichever period is shortest, discuss the impact of inflation and changing prices on the registrant's net sales and revenues and on income from continuing operations.

Continues

Exhibit 8.1   Item 303 of Regulation S-K.

---

4. *Off-balance-sheet arrangements.*

   i. In a separately-captioned section, discuss the registrant's off-balance-sheet arrangements that have or are reasonably likely to have a current or future effect on the registrant's financial condition, changes in financial condition, revenues or expenses, results of operations, liquidity, capital expenditures, or capital resources that are material to investors. The disclosure shall include the items specified in paragraphs (a)(4)(i)(A), (B), (C), and (D) of this Item to the extent necessary to an understanding of such arrangements and effect and shall also include such other information that the registrant believes is necessary for such an understanding.

      A. The nature and business purpose to the registrant of such off-balance-sheet arrangements;

      B. The importance to the registrant of such off-balance-sheet arrangements in respect of its liquidity, capital resources, market risk support, credit risk support, or other benefits;

      C. The amounts of revenues, expenses, and cash flows of the registrant arising from such arrangements; the nature and amounts of any interests retained, securities issued, and other indebtedness incurred by the registrant in connection with such arrangements; and the nature and amounts of any other obligations or liabilities (including contingent obligations or liabilities) of the registrant arising from such arrangements that are or are reasonably likely to become material and the triggering events or circumstances that could cause them to arise; and

      D. Any known event, demand, commitment, trend, or uncertainty that will result in or is reasonably likely to result in the termination, or material reduction in availability to the registrant, of its off-balance-sheet arrangements that provide material benefits to it, and the course of action that the registrant has taken or proposes to take in response to any such circumstances.

   ii. As used in this paragraph (a)(4), the term *off-balance-sheet arrangement* means any transaction, agreement, or other contractual arrangement to which an entity unconsolidated with the registrant is a party, under which the registrant has:

      A. Any obligation under a guarantee contract that has any of the characteristics identified in paragraph 3 of FASB Interpretation No. 45, *Guarantor's Accounting and Disclosure Requirements for Guarantees, Including Indirect Guarantees of Indebtedness of Others* (November 2002) ("FIN 45"), as may be modified or supplemented, and that is not excluded from the initial recognition and measurement provisions of FIN 45 pursuant to paragraphs 6 or 7 of that Interpretation;

      B. A retained or contingent interest in assets transferred to an unconsolidated entity or similar arrangement that serves as credit, liquidity, or market risk support to such entity for such assets;

      C. Any obligation, including a contingent obligation, under a contract that would be accounted for as a derivative instrument, except that it is both indexed to the registrant's own stock and classified in stockholders' equity in the registrant's statement of financial position, and therefore excluded from the scope of FASB Statement of Financial Accounting Standards (SFAS) No. 133, *Accounting for Derivative Instruments and Hedging Activities* (June 1998), pursuant to paragraph 11(a) of that Statement, as may be modified or supplemented; or

      D. Any obligation, including a contingent obligation, arising out of a variable interest (as referenced in FASB Interpretation No. 46, *Consolidation of Variable Interest Entities* [January 2003], as may be modified or supplemented) in an unconsolidated entity that is held by, and material to, the registrant, where such entity provides financing, liquidity, market risk, or credit risk support to, or engages in leasing, hedging, or research and development services with, the registrant.

Exhibit 8.1   *Continued.*

5. Tabular disclosure of contractual obligations.

   i. In a tabular format, provide the information specified in this paragraph (a)(5) as of the latest fiscal year end balance sheet date with respect to the registrant's known contractual obligations specified in the table that follows this paragraph (a)(5)(i). The registrant shall provide amounts, aggregated by type of contractual obligation. The registrant may disaggregate the specified categories of contractual obligations using other categories suitable to its business, but the presentation must include all of the obligations of the registrant that fall within the specified categories. A presentation covering at least the periods specified shall be included. The tabular presentation may be accompanied by footnotes to describe provisions that create, increase, or accelerate obligations, or other pertinent data to the extent necessary for an understanding of the timing and amount of the registrant's specified contractual obligations.

Contractual obligations		Payments due by period			
	Total	Less than 1 year	1–3 years	3–5 years	More than 5 years
[Long-Term Debt Obligations]					
[Capital Lease Obligations]					
[Operating Lease Obligations]					
[Purchase Obligations]					
[Other Long-Term Liabilities Reflected on the Registrant's Balance Sheet under GAAP]					
Total					

   ii. *Definitions:* The following definitions apply to this paragraph (a)(5):

     A. *Long-Term Debt Obligation* means a payment obligation under long-term borrowings referenced in FASB SFAS No. 47 *Disclosure of Long-Term Obligations* (March 1981), as may be modified or supplemented.

     B. *Capital Lease Obligation* means a payment obligation under a lease classified as a capital lease pursuant to FASB SFAS No. 13 *Accounting for Leases* (November 1976), as may be modified or supplemented.

     C. *Operating Lease Obligation* means a payment obligation under a lease classified as an operating lease and disclosed pursuant to FASB SFAS No. 13 *Accounting for Leases* (November 1976), as may be modified or supplemented.

     D. *Purchase Obligation* means an agreement to purchase goods or services that is enforceable and legally binding on the registrant that specifies all significant terms, including: fixed or minimum quantities to be purchased; fixed, minimum, or variable price provisions; and the approximate timing of the transaction.

Instructions to Paragraph 303(a):

1. The registrant's discussion and analysis shall be of the financial statements and of other statistical data that the registrant believes will enhance a reader's understanding of its financial condition, changes in financial condition and results of operations. Generally, the discussion shall cover the three year period covered by the financial statements and shall use year-to-year comparisons or any other formats that in the registrant's judgment enhance a reader's understanding. However, where trend information is relevant, reference to the five year selected financial data appearing pursuant to Item 301 of Regulation S-K may be necessary.

Continues

Exhibit 8.1   *Continued.*

2. The purpose of the discussion and analysis shall be to provide to investors and other users information relevant to an assessment of the financial condition and results of operations of the registrant as determined by evaluating the amounts and certainty of cash flows from operations and from outside sources.

3. The discussion and analysis shall focus specifically on material events and uncertainties known to management that would cause reported financial information not to be necessarily indicative of future operating results or of future financial condition. This would include descriptions and amounts of (A) matters that would have an impact on future operations and have not had an impact in the past, and (B) matters that have had an impact on reported operations and are not expected to have an impact upon future operations.

4. Where the consolidated financial statements reveal material changes from year to year in one or more line items, the causes for the changes shall be described to the extent necessary to an understanding of the registrant's businesses as a whole; *Provided, however,* That if the causes for a change in one line item also relate to other line items, no repetition is required and a line-by-line analysis of the financial statements as a whole is not required or generally appropriate. Registrants need not recite the amounts of changes from year to year which are readily computable from the financial statements. The discussion shall not merely repeat numerical data contained in the consolidated financial statements.

5. The term *liquidity* as used in this Item refers to the ability of an enterprise to generate adequate amounts of cash to meet the enterprise's needs for cash. Except where it is otherwise clear from the discussion, the registrant shall indicate those balance sheet conditions or income or cash flow items which the registrant believes may be indicators of its liquidity condition. Liquidity generally shall be discussed on both a long-term and short-term basis. The issue of liquidity shall be discussed in the context of the registrant's own business or businesses. For example a discussion of working capital may be appropriate for certain manufacturing, industrial, or related operations but might be inappropriate for a bank or public utility.

6. Where financial statements presented or incorporated by reference in the registration statement are required by Rule 4-08(e)(3) of Regulation S-X to include disclosure of restrictions on the ability of both consolidated and unconsolidated subsidiaries to transfer funds to the registrant in the form of cash dividends, loans, or advances, the discussion of liquidity shall include a discussion of the nature and extent of such restrictions and the impact such restrictions have had and are expected to have on the ability of the parent company to meet its cash obligations.

7. Any forward-looking information supplied is expressly covered by the safe harbor rule for projections. See Rule 175 under the Securities Act, Rule 3b-6 under the Exchange Act and Securities Act Release No. 6084 (June 25, 1979).

8. Registrants are only required to discuss the effects of inflation and other changes in prices when considered material. This discussion may be made in whatever manner appears appropriate under the circumstances. All that is required is a brief textual presentation of management's views. No specific numerical financial data need be presented except as Rule 3-20(c) of Regulation S-X otherwise requires. However, registrants may elect to voluntarily disclose supplemental information on the effects of changing prices as provided for in SFAS No. 89, "Financial Reporting and Changing Prices" or through other supplemental disclosures. The Commission encourages experimentation with these disclosures in order to provide the most meaningful presentation of the impact of price changes on the registrant's financial statements.

9. Registrants that elect to disclose supplementary information on the effects of changing prices as specified by SFAS No. 89, "Financial Reporting and Changing Prices," may combine such explanations with the discussion and analysis required pursuant to this Item or may supply such information separately with appropriate cross reference.

10. All references to the registrant in the discussion and in this Item shall mean the registrant and its subsidiaries consolidated.

Exhibit 8.1   *Continued.*

11. Foreign private registrants also shall discuss briefly any pertinent governmental economic, fiscal, monetary, or political policies or factors that have materially affected or could materially affect, directly or indirectly, their operations or investments by U.S. nationals.

12. If the registrant is a foreign private issuer, the discussion shall focus on the primary financial statements presented in the registration statement or report. There shall be a reference to the reconciliation to United States generally accepted accounting principles, and a discussion of any aspects of the difference between foreign and United States generally accepted accounting principles, not discussed in the reconciliation, that the registrant believes is necessary for an understanding of the financial statements as a whole.

Instructions to Paragraph 303(a)(4):

1. No obligation to make disclosure under paragraph (a)(4) of this Item shall arise in respect of an off-balance-sheet arrangement until a definitive agreement that is unconditionally binding or subject only to customary closing conditions exists or, if there is no such agreement, when settlement of the transaction occurs.

2. Registrants should aggregate off-balance-sheet arrangements in groups or categories that provide material information in an efficient and understandable manner and should avoid repetition and disclosure of immaterial information. Effects that are common or similar with respect to a number of off-balance-sheet arrangements must be analyzed in the aggregate to the extent the aggregation increases understanding. Distinctions in arrangements and their effects must be discussed to the extent the information is material, but the discussion should avoid repetition and disclosure of immaterial information.

3. For purposes of paragraph (a)(4) of this Item only, contingent liabilities arising out of litigation, arbitration, or regulatory actions are not considered to be off-balance-sheet arrangements.

4. Generally, the disclosure required by paragraph (a)(4) shall cover the most recent fiscal year. However, the discussion should address changes from the previous year where such discussion is necessary to an understanding of the disclosure.

5. In satisfying the requirements of paragraph (a)(4) of this Item, the discussion of off-balance-sheet arrangements need not repeat information provided in the footnotes to the financial statements, provided that such discussion clearly cross-references to specific information in the relevant footnotes and integrates the substance of the footnotes into such discussion in a manner designed to inform readers of the significance of the information that is not included within the body of such discussion.

b. *Interim periods.* If interim period financial statements are included or are required to be included by Article 3 of Regulation S-X, a management's discussion and analysis of the financial condition and results of operations shall be provided so as to enable the reader to assess material changes in financial condition and results of operations between the periods specified in paragraphs (b) (1) and (2) of this Item. The discussion and analysis shall include a discussion of material changes in those items specifically listed in paragraph (a) of this Item, except that the impact of inflation and changing prices on operations for interim periods need not be addressed.

1. *Material changes in financial condition.* Discuss any material changes in financial condition from the end of the preceding fiscal year to the date of the most recent interim balance sheet provided. If the interim financial statements include an interim balance sheet as of the corresponding interim date of the preceding fiscal year, any material changes in financial condition from that date to the date of the most recent interim balance sheet provided also shall be discussed. If discussions of changes from both the end and the corresponding interim date of the preceding fiscal year are required, the discussions may be combined at the discretion of the registrant.

2. *Material changes in results of operations.* Discuss any material changes in the registrant's results of operations with respect to the most recent fiscal year-to-date period for which an income statement is provided and the corresponding year-to-date period of the preceding fiscal year. If the registrant is required to or has elected to provide an income statement for the most recent

Continues

Exhibit 8.1 *Continued.*

fiscal quarter, such discussion also shall cover material changes with respect to that fiscal quarter and the corresponding fiscal quarter in the preceding fiscal year. In addition, if the registrant has elected to provide an income statement for the twelve-month period ended as of the date of the most recent interim balance sheet provided, the discussion also shall cover material changes with respect to that twelve-month period and the twelve-month period ended as of the corresponding interim balance sheet date of the preceding fiscal year. Notwithstanding the above, if for purposes of a registration statement a registrant subject to paragraph (b) of Rule 3-03 of Regulation S-X provides a statement of income for the twelve-month period ended as of the date of the most recent interim balance sheet provided in lieu of the interim income statements otherwise required, the discussion of material changes in that twelve-month period will be in respect to the preceding fiscal year rather than the corresponding preceding period.

Instructions to Paragraph (b) of Item 303

1. If interim financial statements are presented together with financial statements for full fiscal years, the discussion of the interim financial information shall be prepared pursuant to this paragraph (b) and the discussion of the full fiscal year's information shall be prepared pursuant to paragraph (a) of this Item. Such discussions may be combined.

2. In preparing the discussion and analysis required by this paragraph (b), the registrant may presume that users of the interim financial information have read or have access to the discussion and analysis required by paragraph (a) for the preceding fiscal year.

3. The discussion and analysis required by this paragraph (b) is required to focus only on material changes. Where the interim financial statements reveal material changes from period to period in one or more significant line items, the causes for the changes shall be described if they have not already been disclosed: *Provided, however,* That if the causes for a change in one line item also relate to other line items, no repetition is required. Registrants need not recite the amounts of changes from period to period which are readily computable from the financial statements. The discussion shall not merely repeat numerical data contained in the financial statements. The information provided shall include that which is available to the registrant without undue effort or expense and which does not clearly appear in the registrant's condensed interim financial statements.

4. The registrant's discussion of material changes in results of operations shall identify any significant elements of the registrant's income or loss from continuing operations which do not arise from or are not necessarily representative of the registrant's ongoing business.

5. The registrant shall discuss any seasonal aspects of its business which have had a material effect upon its financial condition or results of operation.

6. Any forward-looking information supplied is expressly covered by the safe harbor rule for projections. See Rule 175 under the Securities Act, Rule 3b-6 under the Exchange Act and Securities Act Release No. 6084 (June 25, 1979).

7. The registrant is not required to include the table required by paragraph (a)(5) of this Item for interim periods. Instead, the registrant should disclose material changes outside the ordinary course of the registrant's business in the specified contractual obligations during the interim period.

c. *Safe harbor.*

1. The safe harbor provided in section 27A of the Securities Act of 1933 and section 21E of the Securities Exchange Act of 1934 ("statutory safe harbors") shall apply to forward-looking information provided pursuant to paragraphs (a)(4) and (5) of this Item, provided that the disclosure is made by: an issuer; a person acting on behalf of the issuer; an outside reviewer retained by the issuer making a statement on behalf of the issuer; or an underwriter, with respect to information provided by the issuer or information derived from information provided by the issuer.

Exhibit 8.1   *Continued.*

2. For purposes of paragraph (c) of this Item only:

 i. All information required by paragraphs (a)(4) and (5) of this Item is deemed to be a *forward looking statement* as that term is defined in the statutory safe harbors, except for historical facts.

 ii. With respect to paragraph (a)(4) of this Item, the meaningful cautionary statements element of the statutory safe harbors will be satisfied if a registrant satisfies all requirements of that same paragraph (a)(4) of this Item.

47 FR 11401, Mar. 16, 1982, as amended at 47 FR 29839, July 9, 1982; 47 FR 54768, Dec. 6, 1982; 52 FR 30919, Aug. 18, 1987; 68 FR 5982, 5999, Feb. 5, 2003.

Exhibit 8.1   *Continued.*

(ii) Critical Accounting Estimates. On December 12, 2001, the SEC issued a release entitled *Cautionary Advice Regarding Disclosure About Critical Accounting Policies*, which is also referred to as *FR-60*. While the SEC's rules governing MD&A have long required disclosure about trends, events, or uncertainties known to management that would materially affect reported financial information, the SEC observed that disclosure responsive to these requirements could be enhanced. For example, environmental and operational trends, events, and uncertainties typically are identified in MD&A, but the implications of those uncertainties for the methods, assumptions, and estimates used for recurring and pervasive accounting measurements are not always addressed. Communication between investors and public companies could be improved if management explained in MD&A the interplay of specific uncertainties with accounting measurements in the financial statements.

The SEC encourages public companies to include in their MD&A full explanations, in plain English, of their critical accounting policies, the judgments and uncertainties affecting the application of those policies, and the likelihood that materially different amounts would be reported under different conditions or using different assumptions. The objective of this disclosure is consistent with the objective of MD&A.

The SEC pointed out that investors may lose confidence in a company's management and financial statements if sudden changes in its financial condition and results occur but were not preceded by disclosures about the susceptibility of reported amounts to change, including rapid change. In FR-60, the SEC alerted public companies to the importance of employing a disclosure regimen as follows:

1. Each company's management and auditor should bring particular focus to the evaluation of the critical accounting policies used in the financial statements. As part of the normal audit process, auditors must obtain an understanding of management's judgments in selecting and applying accounting principles and methods. Special attention to the most critical accounting policies will enhance the effectiveness of this process. Management should be able to defend the quality and reasonableness of the most critical policies, and auditors should satisfy themselves thoroughly regarding their selection, application, and disclosure.

2. Management should ensure that disclosure in MD&A is balanced and fully responsive. To enhance investor understanding of the financial statements, companies are encouraged to explain in MD&A the effects of the critical accounting policies applied, the judgments made in their application, and the likelihood of materially different reported results if different assumptions or conditions were to prevail.

3. Prior to finalizing and filing annual reports, audit committees should review the selection, application, and disclosure of critical accounting policies. Consistent with auditing standards, audit committees should be apprised of the evaluative criteria used by management in their selection of the accounting principles and methods. Proactive discussions between the audit committee and the company's senior management and auditor about critical accounting policies are appropriate.

The following are SEC releases pertinent to the MD&A regulation in chronological order.

- Securities Act Release No. 4936 (Dec. 9, 1968) (33 FR 18617), *Guides for preparation and filing of registration statements under the Securities Act of 1933.* This was the first requirement for a narrative discussion of the results of operations, which was incorporated in registration statements.

- Securities Act Release No. 5520 (Sept., 3, 1974) (39 FR 31894), *Commission's guidelines for registration and reporting.* This required a narrative discussion about the results of operations to accompany all periodic financial statements.

- Securities Act Release No. 5992 (November 7, 1978) (43 FR 53251), *Guide for reports or memoranda concerning registrants.* This release set forth a "safe harbor" for forward-looking information. As a result, the government or private plaintiffs are prevented from alleging fraud in suits where forward-looking projections fail to materialize, as long as they have a reasonable basis and are disclosed in good faith.

- Securities Act Release No. 6231 (September 2, 1980) (45 FR 63630), *Amendments to annual report form, related forms, rules, regulations, and guides; integration of Securities' Acts Disclosure System.* This release expanded the required discussion to include liquidity, capital resources, as well as the results of operations. It also required discussion of certain prospective information. It remains in force.

- Securities Act Release No. 6349 (September 28, 1981) 23 SEC Docket 962 [not published in the Federal Register]. This release reported deficiencies in complying with the 1980 requirement and gave examples of disclosures to assist companies in drafting the MD&A.

- Securities Act Release No. 6711 (April 24, 1987) (52 FR 13715) This release was referred to as the Concept Release. Its main purpose was to seek comment from various parties to proposed changes in the MD&A requirements made by the accounting profession.

- Securities Act Release No. 6835 (May 18, 1989) (54 FR 22427), *Management's Discussion and Analysis of Financial Condition and Results of Operations; Certain Investment Company Disclosures.* This release gave more examples of MD&A disclosures, particularly those pertaining to prospective information. See *www.sec.gov/rules/interp/33-6835.htm.*

- Securities Act Release Nos. 33-8039, 34-45124, FR-59 (December 4, 2001) (Federal Register: December 10, 2001, Volume 66, Number 237), *Cautionary Advice Regarding the Use of "'Pro Forma'" Financial Information in Earnings Releases.* This release provides cautionary advice regarding the use of "pro forma" financial information in earnings releases.

- Securities Act Releases Nos. 33-8040; 34-45149; FR-60 (December 12, 2001) (Federal Register: December 17, 2001, Volume 66, Number 242), *Cautionary Advice Regarding Disclosure About Critical Accounting Policies.* This release provides cautionary advice regarding disclosure about critical accounting policies.

- Securities Act Release Nos. 33-8056; 34-45321; FR-61 (January 22, 2002) (Federal Register: January 25, 2002, Volume 67, Number 17), *Commission Statement about Management's Discussion and Analysis of Financial Condition and Results of Operations.* This release sets forth certain views of the SEC regarding disclosure in Management's Discussion and Analysis concerning liquidity and capital resources including off-balance-sheet arrangements; certain trading activities that include non-exchange-traded contracts accounted for at fair value; and effects of transactions with related and certain other parties.

- Securities Act Release Nos. 33-8098; 34-45907 (Federal Register: May 20, 2002 (Volume 67, Number 97). Proposed rule, *Disclosure in Management's Discussion and Analysis About the Application of Critical Accounting Policies.* The SEC proposed disclosure requirements that would enhance investors' understanding of the application of companies' critical accounting policies. The proposals would encompass disclosure in two areas: accounting estimates a company makes in applying its accounting policies and the initial adoption by a company of an accounting policy that has a material impact on its financial presentation. This proposal remains outstanding at date of this publication.

- Securities Act Release Nos. 33-8182; 34-47264; FR-67 (Federal Register: February 5, 2003, Volume 68, Number 24), *Disclosure in Management's Discussion and Analysis about Off-Balance-Sheet Arrangements and Aggregate Contractual Obligations.* This final rule requires a registrant to provide an explanation of its off-balance-sheet arrangements in a separately captioned subsection of the Management's Discussion and Analysis section of a registrant's disclosure documents. The amendments also require registrants (other than small business issuers) to provide an overview of certain known contractual obligations in a tabular format.

- Securities Act Release Nos. 33-8350; 34-48960; FR-72, (Federal Register: December 29, 2003 (Volume 68, Number 248) *Commission Guidance Regarding Management's Discussion and Analysis of Financial Condition and Results of Operations.* This interpretation is intended to elicit more meaningful disclosure in MD&A in a number of areas, including the overall presentation and focus of MD&A, with general emphasis on the discussion and analysis of known trends, demands, commitments, events, and uncertainties, and specific guidance on disclosures about liquidity, capital resources, and critical accounting estimates.

Exhibit 8.2   MD & A Related SEC Releases.

4. If companies, management, audit committees, or auditors are uncertain about the application of specific GAAP principles, they should consult with our accounting staff. We encourage all those whose responsibility it is to report fairly and accurately on a company's financial condition and results to seek out our staff's assistance. We are committed to providing that assistance in a timely fashion; our goal is to address problems before they happen.

On May 10, 2002, the SEC proposed a rule entitled *Disclosure in Management's Discussion and Analysis about the Application of Critical Accounting Policies*. The proposal encompassed disclosure in two areas as follows:

- Accounting estimates a company makes in applying its accounting policies. Under the first part of the proposals, a company would have to identify the accounting estimates reflected in its financial statements that required it to make assumptions about matters that were highly uncertain at the time of estimation. Disclosure about those estimates would then be required if different estimates that the company reasonably could have used in the current period, or changes in the accounting estimate that are reasonably likely to occur from period to period, would have a material impact on the presentation of the company's financial condition, changes in financial condition or results of operations. A company's disclosure about these critical accounting estimates would include a discussion of: the methodology and assumptions underlying them; the effect the accounting estimates have on the company's financial presentation; and the effect of changes in the estimates.
- The initial adoption by a company of an accounting policy that has a material impact on its financial presentation. Under the second part of the proposals, a company that has initially adopted an accounting policy with a material impact would have to disclose information that includes: What gave rise to the initial adoption; the impact of the adoption; the accounting principle adopted and method of applying it; and the choices it had among accounting principles. Companies would place all of the new disclosure in the MD&A section of their annual reports, registration statements and proxy and information statements. In addition, in the MD&A section of their quarterly reports, U.S. companies would have to update the information regarding their critical accounting estimates to disclose material changes.

This proposal remains outstanding.

(iii) Off-Balance-Sheet Arrangements and Contractual Obligations.   On January 22, 2002, the SEC issued a statement entitled, *Commission Statement about Management's Discussion and Analysis of Financial Condition and Results of Operations*, which is also referred to as FR-61. The release addressed disclosures matters including liquidity and capital resources, including off-balance-sheet arrangements; certain trading activities that include non-exchange traded contracts accounted for at fair value; and the effects of transactions with related and certain other parties. On January 28, 2003, the SEC issued a final rule entitled, *Disclosure in Management's Discussion and Analysis about Off-Balance-Sheet Arrangements and Aggregate Contractual Obligations*, to formally amend Regulation S-K. The final rule was issued in response to Section 401 of the Sarbanes-Oxley Act of 2002 and to codify guidance FR-61.

MD&A must include a separately-captioned section for the disclosure about off-balance-sheet arrangements. The final rule requires an explanation to investors why a registrant engages in off-balance-sheet arrangements and an understanding of the business activities advanced through off-balance-sheet arrangements. To the extent necessary, the following items should be disclosed:

- The nature and business purpose of the off-balance-sheet arrangements,
- The importance of the off-balance-sheet arrangements for liquidity, capital resources, market risk, or credit risk support,
- The financial impact of the arrangements (e.g., revenues, expenses, cash flows, or securities issued) and the exposure to risk (e.g., retained interests or contingent liabilities) and

- Known events, demands, commitments, trends, or uncertainties.

GAAP requires disclosure of obligations and commitments to make future payments under contracts, such as debt and lease agreements. However, the SEC believes the aggregated information about contractual obligations in a single location provides useful context for investors to assess liquidity and capital resource needs and demands. The contractual obligations example table in the final rule is almost identical to the table in FR-61. The rules specify that the following categories of contractual obligations must be included within the table in substantially the same form as displayed in Exhibit 8.1. The rules do allow a registrant to cross-reference to information in the footnotes to the financial statements.

(iv) General Guidance on MD&A. On December 19, 2003, the SEC issued interpretative guidance entitled, *Commission Guidance Regarding Management's Discussion and Analysis of Financial Condition and Results of Operations* which is also referred to as FR-72. This guidance is intended to elicit more meaningful disclosure in MD&A in a number of areas, including the overall presentation and focus of MD&A, with general emphasis on the discussion and analysis of known trends, demands, commitments, events and uncertainties, and specific guidance on disclosures about liquidity, capital resources, and critical accounting estimates. It provides guidance to assist companies in preparing MD&A disclosure that is easier to follow and understand; and in providing information that more completely satisfies the SEC's previously enunciated principal objectives of MD&A. The release captures the objective of the MD&A as follows:

> The purpose of MD&A is not complicated. It is to provide readers information necessary to an understanding of [a company's] financial condition, changes in financial condition and results of operations. The MD&A requirements are intended to satisfy three principal objectives:
>
> - To provide a narrative explanation of a company's financial statements that enables investors to see the company through the eyes of management;
> - To enhance the overall financial disclosure and provide the context within which financial information should be analyzed; and
> - To provide information about the quality of, and potential variability of, a company's earnings and cash flow, so that investors can ascertain the likelihood that past performance is indicative of future performance

MD&A should be a discussion and analysis of a company's business as seen through the eyes of those who manage that business. Management has a unique perspective on its business that only it can present. As such, MD&A should not be a recitation of financial statements in narrative form or an otherwise uninformative series of technical responses to MD&A requirements, neither of which provides this important management perspective. Through this release we encourage each company and its management to take a fresh look at MD&A with a view to enhancing its quality. We also encourage early top-level involvement by a company's management in identifying the key disclosure themes and items that should be included in a company's MD&A.

Based on our experience with many companies' current disclosures in MD&A, we believe there are a number of general ways for companies to enhance their MD&A consistent with its purpose. The recent review experiences of the staff of the Division of Corporation Finance, including its Fortune 500 review, have led us to conclude that additional guidance would be especially useful in the following areas:

- The overall presentation of MD&A;
- The focus and content of MD&A (including materiality, analysis, key performance measures and known material trends and uncertainties);
- Disclosure regarding liquidity and capital resources; and
- Disclosure regarding critical accounting estimates.

Therefore, in this release, we emphasize the following points regarding overall presentation:

- Within the universe of material information, companies should present their disclosure so that the most important information is most prominent;
- Companies should avoid unnecessary duplicative disclosure that can tend to overwhelm readers and act as an obstacle to identifying and understanding material matters; and
- Many companies would benefit from starting their MD&A with a section that provides an executive-level overview that provides context for the remainder of the discussion.

We also emphasize the following points regarding focus and content:

- In deciding on the content of MD&A, companies should focus on material information and eliminate immaterial information that does not promote understanding of companies' financial condition, liquidity and capital resources, changes in financial condition, and results of operations (both in the context of profit and loss and cash flows);
- Companies should identify and discuss key performance indicators, including non-financial performance indicators, that their management uses to manage the business and that would be material to investors;
- Companies must identify and disclose known trends, events, demands, commitments, and uncertainties that are reasonably likely to have a material effect on financial condition or operating performance; and
- Companies should provide not only disclosure of information responsive to MD&A's requirements, but also an analysis that is responsive to those requirements that explains management's view of the implications and significance of that information and that satisfies the objectives of MD&A.

8.2 CURRENT REQUIREMENTS

(a) OVERALL PRESENTATION. As discussed in FR-72, *Commission Guidance Regarding Management's Discussion and Analysis of Financial Condition and Results of Operations*, SEC provides the several recommendations to assist registrants in improving their MD&A disclosures. The SEC believes that the presentation of the MD&A of too many companies may have become unnecessarily lengthy, difficult to understand and confusing.

In order to engender better understanding, companies should prepare MD&A with a strong focus on the most important information, provided in a manner intended to address the objectives of MD&A. The SEC recommends, in FR-72, consideration of the following:

- Companies should consider whether a tabular presentation of relevant financial or other information may help a reader's understanding of MD&A.
- Companies should consider whether the headings they use assist readers in following the flow of, or otherwise assist in understanding, MD&A, and whether additional headings would be helpful in this regard.
- Many companies' MD&A could benefit from adding an introductory section or overview that would facilitate a reader's understanding.
- While all required information must of course be disclosed, companies should consider using a "layered" approach. Such an approach would present information in a manner that emphasizes, within the universe of material information that is disclosed, the information and analysis that is most important.

(b) CONTENT AND FOCUS. As discussed in FR-72, SEC asserts that many companies can improve their MD&A by focusing on the most important information disclosed in MD&A. Disclosure should emphasize material information that is required or promotes understanding and de-emphasize immaterial information that is not required and does not promote understanding. The MD&A requirements call for companies to provide investors and other users with material information that is necessary to an understanding of the company's financial condition and operating performance, as well as its prospects for the future. While the desired focus of MD&A for a particular company will depend on the facts and circumstances of the company, some guidance about the content and focus of MD&A is generally applicable. The SEC offers the following advice as follows:

1. Focus on Key Indicators of Financial Condition and Operating Performance
2. Focus on Materiality
3. Focus on Material Trends and Uncertainties
4. Focus on Analysis

For the full text of FR-72, see *www.sec.gov/rules/interp/33-8350.htm*.

(c) GENERAL REQUIREMENTS.   The MD&A is required to cover the three most recent fiscal years and the two inter-year comparisons. Registrants need not discuss the earliest year in comparison to the preceding year unless the discussion is necessary for an understanding of a trend of the registrant's financial position or results of operations. The general requirements, as summarized from Item 303, include:

- Discuss registrant's financial condition, changes in financial condition and results of operations.
- With respect to all of the above categories, registrants are required to identify any currently known trends, demands, commitments, events, or uncertainties that are reasonably expected to have material affects on the registrant's liquidity, capital resources, and results of operations, or that would cause reported financial information not to be necessarily indicative of future operating results or financial condition.
- Provide such other information that the registrant believes to be necessary to an understanding of its financial condition, changes in financial condition and results of operations.
- The above must also be discussed by business segments to the extent necessary, in the registrant's judgment, for an understanding of the business as a whole.
- Both positive and negative aspects of a company's financial condition and results of operations should be addressed.
- Where the consolidated financial statements reveal material changes from year to year in one or more line items, the causes for the changes shall be described to the extent necessary to an understanding of the registrant's businesses as a whole.

The required disclosures are ultimately conditional upon passing both a "materiality" and a "cost" threshold. Immaterial effects or events need not be (but may be) disclosed.[6] As stated

---

[6] The SEC discussed materiality in SAB No. 99, *Materiality*, August 12, 1999. See § 3.2(c). Further, the SEC relies on the decisions rendered by the Supreme Court in two separate cases. In TSC Industries Inc. v. Northway (1980), the Court stated that "an omitted fact is material if there is a substantial likelihood that reasonable shareholders would consider it important." The court further explained, "To fulfill the materiality requirement, there must be a substantial likelihood that the disclosure of the omitted fact would have been viewed by the reasonable investor as having significantly altered the 'total mix' of information made available." In Basic, Inc. v. Levinson (1988), the Court addressed materiality as it relates to possible future events: "Materiality will depend at any given time upon a balancing of both the indicated probability that the event will occur and the anticipated magnitude of the event in light of the totality of the company activity." Finally, and most important, for both past events and possible future events, the Court states, "Materiality depends on the facts and is to be determined on a case by case basis." Therefore, materiality is a relative concept.

in Item 303: "The information provided pursuant to this Item need only include that which is available to the registrant without undue effort or expense and which does not clearly appear in the registrant's financial statements."

The full requirements are contained in Exhibit 8.1. Regulation S-K requires disclosure in the following areas:

a. Liquidity

b. Capital Resources

c. Results of Operations

d. Off-balance-sheet arrangements

e. Tabular disclosure of contractual obligations

(d) CRITICAL ACCOUNTING ESTIMATES. Many estimates and assumptions involved in the application of GAAP have a material impact on reported financial condition and operating performance and on the comparability of such reported information over different reporting periods. As previously discussed, the SEC's December 2001 Release, FR-60, reminded companies that, under the existing MD&A disclosure requirements, a company should address material implications of uncertainties associated with the methods, assumptions, and estimates underlying the company's critical accounting measurements. In its follow up statement, FR-72, the SEC states that:

> When preparing disclosure under the current requirements, companies should consider whether they have made accounting estimates or assumptions where:
>
> • The nature of the estimates or assumptions is material due to the levels of subjectivity and judgment necessary to account for highly uncertain matters or the susceptibility of such matters to change; and
>
> • The impact of the estimates and assumptions on financial condition or operating performance is material.
>
> If so, companies should provide disclosure about those critical accounting estimates or assumptions in their MD&A.

(e) EFFECT OF NEWLY ISSUED BUT NOT YET EFFECTIVE ACCOUNTING STANDARDS. Public companies must discuss the effect of newly issued, but not yet effective, accounting standards. SEC SAB (SAB.T.11 M), *Disclosure of the Impact That Recently Issued Accounting Standards Will Have on the Financial Statements of the Registrant When Adopted in a Future Period* (SAB No. 74), requires disclosure of the expected impacts on financial information to be reported in the future, and is required in the financial statements if the change to the new accounting standard will be accounted for in future periods by restatement of the current financials. Additionally, disclosure in the financials is to be considered when the change will be accounted for prospectively or as a change in accounting principle.

8.3 RELATED ACCOUNTING LITERATURE

STATEMENT OF POSITION (SOP) 94-6

The financial statements disclosures under GAAP have similar objectives as the MD&A disclosures. In 1994, the AICPA's Accounting Standards Executive Committee (AcSEC) issued SOP 94-6, *Disclosure of Certain Significant Risks and Uncertainties*. The SOP 94-6 requires an entity to disclose, in the notes to the financial statements, forward-looking information about certain significant estimates and concentrations. This is a GAAP requirement, rather than a MD&A requirement, and is applicable to both public and private entities. As discussed in par. 2 in the introduction to the statement:

> The disclosures focus primarily on risks and uncertainties that could significantly affect the amounts reported in the financial statements in the near term or the near-term functioning of the

reporting entity. The risks and uncertainties this SOP deals with can stem from the nature of the entity's operations, from the necessary use of estimates in the preparation of the entity's financial statements, and from significant concentrations in certain aspects of the entity's operations.

Namely, an entity must disclose:

a. Nature of operations
b. Use of estimates in the preparation of financial statements
c. Certain significant estimates
d. Current vulnerability due to certain concentrations

The first two disclosures are always required. Disclosures about risks (related to concentrations) and uncertainties (concerning estimates) are required if specified criteria are met. The Statement became effective for fiscal years ending after December 15, 1995. The following is a discussion of the required disclosures as summarized from SOP 94-6. For a complete understanding, readers should refer to the full text of the statement.

(a) NATURE OF OPERATIONS.   Financial statements should include a description of the major products or services the reporting entity sells or provides and its principal markets, including the locations of those markets. If the entity operates in more than one business, the disclosure should also indicate the relative importance of its operations in each business and the basis for the determination — for example, assets, revenues, or earnings.

(b) USE OF ESTIMATES IN THE PREPARATION OF FINANCIAL STATEMENTS.   Financial statements should include an explanation that the preparation of financial statements in conformity with GAAP requires the use of management's estimates.

(c) CERTAIN SIGNIFICANT ESTIMATES.   Uncertainties concerning estimates that affect financial statement amounts (such as a valuation allowance for deferred tax assets or the carrying amount of inventory or a long-term contract) if it is at least reasonably possible the estimates will change within a year and the effect of the change could be material to the financial statements. The Statement requires disclosures regarding significant estimates used to determine the carrying amounts of assets or liabilities and the disclosures of gain or loss contingencies if the estimates meet the following specified criteria:

• The information must be known before issuance of financial statements.
• It is at least reasonably possible that the estimate of the effect of the situation known at the financial statement date may change in the near term.
• The effect of the change would be material.

(d) CURRENT VULNERABILITY DUE TO CERTAIN CONCENTRATIONS.   Risks related to concentrations in volume of business, sources of supply, revenue, or market or geographic area if it is at least reasonably possible that the concentrations could have a severe impact on operations within a year. The Statement requires disclosures regarding vulnerability to risk of loss resulting from specified concentrations, as described below, if the following criteria are met:

• The concentration exists at balance sheet date.
• The concentration makes the entity vulnerable to risk of near-term severe impact (a severe impact is a significant, financially disruptive effect on operations), and
• It is at least reasonably possible that events that could cause the severe impact will occur in the near term.

The concentration is in one of the following areas:

- Volume of business with a particular customer, supplier, lender, grantor, or contributor
- Revenue from particular products, services, or fund-raising events
- Source of supply of materials, labor, services, or licenses or other rights
- Market or geographic area in which operations are conducted

8.4 EXTERNAL AUDITOR INVOLVEMENT

The external auditor is required follow Statement of Auditing Standards (SAS) No. 8, *Other Information in Documents Containing Audited Financial Statements*, when other information, such as the MD&A, is presented with the audited financial statements and the independent auditor's report. SAS 8 was issued by the AICPA in December 1975 and in the codification, the reference is AU Section 550, *Other Information in Documents Containing Audited Financial Statements*. As excerpted from par. 4 of SAS 8, the auditor has the responsibility to read the other information, such as the MD&A:

> .04 Other information in a document may be relevant to an audit performed by an independent auditor or to the continuing propriety of his report. The auditor's responsibility with respect to information in a document does not extend beyond the financial information identified in his report, and the auditor has no obligation to perform any procedures to corroborate other information contained in a document. However, he should read the other information and consider whether such information, or the manner of its presentation, is materially inconsistent with information, or the manner of its presentation, appearing in the financial statements.

For a complete understanding, readers should refer to the full text of the standard.

Management may wish to engage the external auditor to perform additional procedures related to the MD&A. To accommodate such an engagement, the AICPA issued, in 2001, Statement on Standards for Attestation Engagements (SSAE) 10, *Attestation Standards: Revision and Recodification*, which is relevant to the external auditor's association with MD&A. In the codification, the reference is AT Section 701: *Management's Discussion and Analysis*. This statement provides performance and reporting guidance and applies to engagements where management has opted to engage the external auditor to examine and to review the MD&A included in audited financial statements or in other documents. The full text of AT Section 701 can be accessed at the AICPA's website *www.aicpa.org/download/numbers/div.auditstd/AT-00701.pdf*. On April 16, 2003, the PCAOB adopted certain pre-existing AICPA standards as its interim standards to be used by external auditors on an initial, transitional basis. PCAOB Rules 3200 T, 3300 T, 3400 T, 3500 T, and 3600 T describe the standards that the PCAOB adopted and require registered public accounting firms and their associated persons to comply with these interim standards to the extent not superseded or amended by the PCAOB, excerpted as follows:

> Rule 3200 T. Interim Auditing Standards. In connection with the preparation or issuance of any audit report, a registered public accounting firm, and its associated persons, shall comply with generally accepted auditing standards, as described in the AICPA Auditing Standards Board's SAS No. 95, as in existence on April 16, 2003 (Codification of Statements on Auditing Standards, AU § 150 (AICPA 2002)), to the extent not superseded or amended by the Board.

> Rule 3300 T. Interim Attestation Standards. In connection with an engagement (i) described in the AICPA's Auditing Standards Board's SSAE No. 10 (Codification of Statements on Auditing Standards, AT § 101.01 (AICPA 2002)) and (ii) related to the preparation or issuance of audit reports for issuers, a registered public accounting firm, and its associated persons, shall comply with the AICPA Auditing Standards Board's Statements on Standards for Attestation Engagements, and related interpretations and Statements of Position, as in existence on April 16, 2003, to the extent not superseded or amended by the Board.

CHAPTER 9

GLOBAL ACCOUNTING AND AUDITING

Richard C. Jones, PhD, CPA
Hofstra University

9.1 INTRODUCTION

This chapter summarizes the key organizations and factors involved in the process of developing a global accounting and auditing structure. The discussion begins with an overview of the environment and goals of developing a global framework followed by a discussion of the key organizations involved in this difficult and challenging process.

(a) MOVEMENT TOWARD A GLOBAL SET OF STANDARDS.   Since the 1970s, the global financial environment has changed dramatically. Such changes are in part attributable to changes in the business and political climate in which companies operate. The key factors influencing the global business and political climate include increasing competition among companies operating in different countries, the emergence of additional market-based economies, and rapid improvements in information technology. At the same time, with the improvements in telecommunications and other technological innovations, the world's financial centers are increasingly interconnected, allowing corporations and borrowers to look beyond their home country's borders for capital. An increasing number of foreign companies routinely raise or borrow capital in U.S. financial markets,[1] and U.S. investors have shown great interest in investing in foreign enterprises. This globalization of the securities markets has challenged securities regulators around the world to adapt to meet the needs of market participants while maintaining the desired levels of investor protection and market integrity.

Currently issuers wishing to access capital markets in different national jurisdictions must comply with the national jurisdiction's securities filing regulations and financial reporting requirements, which often contain special reporting requirements for cross-border registrants. Such filing and reporting requirements also differ significantly among the various national jurisdictions. Thus, companies attempting to access capital in several different national securities markets must adapt their reporting to meet the requirements of the diverse cross-border filing regulations. Such differences in financial exchange listing and reporting requirements can increase the company's costs of accessing capital markets and might create inefficiencies in cross-border capital flows.

In response to the flow of financial capital across national borders, national and international regulatory authorities, and standard-setting organizations have been working to establish a process for developing high quality International Accounting Standards (IASs) that can be applied in a consistent and comparable manner worldwide. Consistent with the goal of establishing high quality global accounting standards, national and international regulatory organizations have been working closely with national auditing standard-setting organizations to develop a structure for ensuring that audit firms adhere to the highest quality auditing practices.

With respect to developing a global set of high quality accounting standards, representatives of the Securities and Exchange Commission (SEC) have indicated that the following criteria will be considered when assessing the acceptability of proposed IASs:[2]

- The standards must constitute a comprehensive, generally accepted basis of accounting.
- The standards must be of high quality, resulting in comparability, transparency, and full disclosure.
- The standards must be rigorously interpreted and applied.

Further, with the increasing flow of capital across national borders and the movement toward a global set of accounting standards, capital market regulatory authorities and market participants are also calling for the development of a global set of standards governing the audit profession. For example, in its May 2000 concepts statement on international accounting and auditing,[3] the SEC of the United States called for a global financial reporting and independent audit infrastructure that ensures that accounting standards are rigorously interpreted and applied, and that ensures that instances of inappropriate application of financial accounting and reporting standards and

---

[1] As noted in the Panel on Audit Effectiveness Report and Recommendations (August 31, 2000), in 1999 more than 1,200 foreign companies representing 57 countries were registered to issue securities in the United States.

[2] Taken from a December 2000 speech by John M. Morrissey, former Deputy Chief Accountant, U.S. Securities and Exchange Commission.

[3] SEC Concepts Release, *International Accounting Standards*, Exchange Act Release Nos. 33-7801, 34-42430; International Series No. 1215 (February 2000).

problematic practices are identified and resolved in a timely fashion. Elements of this global financial reporting and independent audit infrastructure include:

- Effective, independent, and high-quality accounting and auditing standard setters
- High-quality auditing standards
- Audit firms with effective quality controls worldwide
- Profession-wide quality assurance
- Active regulatory oversight

(b) ACHIEVING CONVERGENCE OF ACCOUNTING AND AUDITING STANDARDS. A common concern of those involved in developing and regulating global accounting and auditing standards is insuring transparency in the standard-setting process and convergence between global standards and the associated national standard-setting bodies.

Convergence refers to establishing a single set of high-quality global standards, either accounting or audit, applicable to all users of those standards. Such standards should reduce alternatives and eliminate differences among comparable national standards and international standards and should be applied by users in a consistent and comparable manner worldwide. Achieving convergence requires the close participation and coordination of standard setting among national and international standard-setting organizations. In response to that challenge, the International Accounting Standards Board (IASB, formerly the International Accounting Standards Committee [IASC]) and the International Auditing and Assurance Standards Board (IAASB, formerly the International Audit Practices Committee [IAPC]) have modified their approach to setting standards to promote a close working relationship among national and international standard setters. In addition, as will be discussed in this chapter, the IASB and the IAASB have been working closely with the International Organization of Securities Commissions (IOSCO) and other international regulators to achieve global endorsement. Further, during 2001, the IASB achieved a key step in that goal when IOSCO recommended the use of a core set of IASB accounting standards for use in all cross-border filings.

In June 2001, the seven largest accounting firms released a report comparing the national accounting standards of 62 countries with the associated international standards. The report, *Generally Accepted Accounting Principles (GAAP) 2001*, also includes an analysis of each country's progress made toward convergence with IASs since the GAAP 2000 report was issued. Some of the major findings of the GAAP 2001 report are:

- Almost one third of the countries responding to the GAAP 2001 survey are actively pursuing a standard-setting agenda that promotes convergence of national standards with the international standards.
- About one half of the countries included in the study retain national accounting standards with major differences from the international standards. These countries provided no indication that they intend to revise their standards to converge with the international standards.
- The areas that contain the most significant differences between national and IASs include certain financial reporting recognition and measurement issues and certain financial statement disclosure requirements. The recognition and measurement issues for which the GAAP 2001 report identified major differences include: (1) financial instruments, (2) impairment losses, (3) provisions and reserves for losses and contingent liabilities, (4) employee benefit liabilities, (5) income taxes, and (6) accounting for business combinations. Additionally, the report noted that disclosures regarding related party transactions and disclosure of segment information continue to differ significantly among the examined reporting countries.
- A major challenge in the process of increasing convergence among national and IAS setters is the current IASB effort to eliminate the accounting alternatives contained in IASs.

The GAAP 2001 report calls on national standard setters, government and stock market regulators, financial statement preparers, users of financial reporting, and other concerned parties to work together to promote convergence with international standards.

9.2 INTERNATIONAL STANDARD-SETTING ORGANIZATIONS

The increasingly global economic landscape demands a similarly global professional accounting framework that supports the development of standards for accounting and reporting and standards for the conduct and performance of the audit. Recently, that framework has emerged around several international organizations that retain a global focus. Those organizations include:

- IASB
- International Federation of Accountants (IFAC)
- European Union (EU)

The IASB and IFAC are private organizations whose membership is composed of professional accounting organizations from developed and lesser developed countries. In 2001, the IASB replaced the IASC, which was perceived to have certain structural limitations that restricted its ability to gain widespread endorsement. Similarly, through its IAASB, IFAC takes the lead in developing global auditing standards.

The EU represents the governments of its 25 member states and is composed of governmental ministers. Although ceding much of the responsibility for issuing international and national standards to the IASB and IFAC, the EU has occasionally issued Directives on the audit and accounting policies and procedures of its member states. The goal of the Directives is to promote convergence of audit and accounting approaches within the EU.

(a) INTERNATIONAL ACCOUNTING STANDARDS BOARD.   The IASB began in 1966 with the formation of the Accountants' International Study Group (AISG). The members of the AISG were representatives of the accounting profession from Canada, the United Kingdom, and the United States. The AISG was formed to perform comparative studies of the major accounting issues among the three originating countries.

In 1973, the AISG formed a committee consisting of representatives from professional accounting organizations from Australia, Canada, France, Germany, Japan, Mexico, the Netherlands, the United Kingdom and Ireland, and the United States. In June 1973, those nine professional organizations founded the IASC. The founding countries constituted the initial board of the IASC.

In 1977, with the formation of the IFAC, the international professional activities of the IASC were organized under IFAC, which later agreed that the IASC would have complete autonomy in setting IASs and in the issuance of discussion documents on international accounting issues.

The business of the IASC was conducted by a board comprised of representatives from national accounting standard-setting bodies from 13 countries and representatives of the International Coordinating Committee of the Financial Analysts' Associations, the Federation of Swiss Holding Companies, and the International Association of Financial Executives Institutes. Additionally, the Indian and South African delegations included representatives from Sri Lanka and Zimbabwe, respectively. Regular observers of IASC meeting included representatives of the European Commission and the Financial Accounting Standards Board (FASB) of the Unites States, among others.

The work of the IASC was developed and published by its board after a due process involving consultation on a worldwide basis. The due process procedures, which involved the issuance of exposure drafts of proposed standards, provided financial information users, preparers, and auditors with the opportunity to express their views on the proposed standard. In setting its technical agenda and in developing IASs, the IASC board consulted with various advisory bodies including an International Consultative Group, member bodies, and other standard-setting organizations.

Once an agenda topic was chosen, a steering committee was established to conduct the appropriate research and to move the project through its various due process documents leading up to the issuance of an IAS. An IASC board member chaired the steering committee, and the committee included representatives from accountancy bodies from at least three other national standard-setting bodies. Over its life, the IASC issued 39 IASs addressing a broad range of accounting issues including the preparation of cash flow statements, accounting for leases, business combinations, and earnings per share.

In 1997, the IASC board formed the Strategy Working Party (SWP) to consider the structure of the IASC after it completes a "Core Standards" development process.[4] SWP issued its discussion paper *Shaping IASC for the Future*, setting the working party's recommendations on the necessary structural changes to the IASC in meeting its long-term objectives. The SWP's recommendations, though extensive, retained many elements of the existing IASC structure. Those recommendations included:

- Formation of a 12-member board of trustees with the authority to appoint IASC board members, including the chair and vice chair of both the Strategic Development Committee and the Standing Interpretations Committee.
- Increasing the size and representation on the IASC board. The board would consist of 20 country seats, an increase from the existing 13 seats, and five seats for other interested parties, an increase from the existing four seats. The board would retain final approval on all International Standards on Auditing (ISAs) and exposure drafts of proposed IASs.
- Replacing the existing steering committees, which had the responsibility of preparing the draft IASs and exposure drafts of proposed ISAs, with the Standards Development Committee (SDC), which would take on some of the responsibilities of the IASC board, including approving the final interpretations of the International Financial Reporting Interpretations Committee (IFRIC). In addition, the SDC rather than the IASC board would represent the organizational link with the national standard-setting organizations and any consultative advisory groups.
- A technical director and technical staff would support the work efforts of the SDC and IFRIC.

The IASC received 84 written comments on the SWP's recommendations. In general, commentators argued that the recommendations did not go far enough in ensuring an independent international standard-setting organization that considered the concerns of its broad range of constituents. In its final report, the SWP noted:[5]

> The comment letters and consultations with interested parties also reflected various views on the attributes that are considered desirable to establish the legitimacy of a standard setting organization. The primary attributes identified were the representativeness of the decision making body, the independence of its members, and technical expertise. As applied to the IASC structure, the legitimacy of IASC's Standards is considered by some to be established through direct participation of key constituents in the decision making process. The other view is that legitimacy is established if the development of Standards is undertaken by an autonomous body of relatively few, full-time and highly skilled experts who are independent of perceived economic incentives which might interfere with their role on the decision making body.

Based on the SWP's final recommendations, the IASC was renamed the IASB and restructured around the basic objectives of the development of a high-quality set of global accounting standards, formation of an independent standard-setting board, and broad geographic representation among its members.

---

[4] In 1995, the IASC board entered into an agreement with IOSCO to complete a core set of international accounting standards by 1999. Upon successful completion of the agreed-upon core set of standards, IOSCO agreed to review the standards and consider endorsement of IASs for cross-border securities offerings among its member countries. In 1998, the IASC completed 39 core standards. IOSCO reviewed such standards and, in 2000, IOSCO recommended 30 of those standards for cross border offerings and listings.

[5] "Recommendations on Shaping the IASC for the Future: A Report of the International Accounting Standards Committee," prepared by the Strategic Working Party of the International Accounting Standards Committee. International Accounting Standards Committee, London, 1999, p. 6.

(i) The Structure of the International Accounting Standards Board.[6]   The IASB is the standard-setting body of the larger IASC Foundation (the Foundation). The Foundation's objectives are to:

- Develop a single set of high quality, understandable, and enforceable global accounting standards that require high quality, transparent, and comparable information in financial statements and other financial reporting to users make economic decisions;
- Promote the use and rigorous application of those standards; and
- Consider the special needs of small and medium-sized entities and emerging economies; and
- Bring about convergence of national and IASs to high quality solutions.

The operating structure of the Foundation consists of the Trustees, the IASB (also called the *Board*), the Standards Advisory Council (SAC), and the IFRIC.

(ii) The International Accounting Standards Board Trustees.   The trustees are appointed for a three-year, renewable term. The trustees consist of 22 individuals originally selected by the subsequent trustees.

Further, to ensure broad global representation, the convened group must consist of (1) six representatives appointed from North America, (2) six representatives appointed from Europe, and (3) six representatives appointed from the Asia/Pacific region. The remaining four representatives can be from any region, so long as overall geographic balance is maintained.

The composition of the trustees should provide a balance of professional backgrounds, including auditors, preparers, users, academics, and other officials serving the public interest. Two trustees will normally be senior partners of prominent international accounting firms.

Trustees must meet at least twice each year. They have the following responsibilities:

- Handle fund-raising activities for the IASB
- Appoint the members of the IASB, including those with liaison responsibilities with national standard-setting organizations, monitor its effectiveness, and annually review the IASB's strategy
- Appoint the members of the SAC and the IFRIC
- Approve the annual budget
- Promote the IASB and the objective of rigorous application of its standards
- Establish and amend the operating procedures for the IASB, the Standard Interpretations Committee, and the Standards Advisory Committee

(iii) The International Accounting Standards Board.   Whereas the Trustees group has broad geographic representation, representation on the IASB is based on the individual's technical accounting proficiency and practical experience.

- Demonstrated technical competency and knowledge of financial accounting and reporting
- The ability to analyze accounting issues and to consider the implications of the analysis for the decision process
- Effective oral and written communication skills
- Capability to consider varied viewpoints and impartial and well-reasoned decision making
- Understanding of the global financial, business, and economic environment in which the IASB operates
- Ability to work in a collegial environment

---

[6] Details on the structure of the IASC Foundation are available on its web site (*www.iasb.org*).

- Integrity, objectivity, and discipline
- Commitment to the Foundation's mission and to serving the public interest

IASB board members are appointed by the Trustees and consists of 14 members, 12 are full time and two are part time.

The IASB has full responsibility for all technical accounting matters including the preparation and issuance of the International Accounting Standards (renamed "International Financial Reporting Standards [IFRSs]") and the associated exposure drafts of financial reporting standards. Other IASB responsibilities include:

- Publish exposure drafts on all projects and regularly publish a draft statement of principles or other discussion document for public comment on major projects
- Retain full discretion over the technical agenda of the IASB and over the assignment of technical projects, in organizing the conduct of the technical work, including the outsourcing of technical accounting research or other work to national standard setters or other organizations
- Establish procedures for reviewing comments received from the IASB constituency on documents issued for public comment
- Form steering committees or other types of specialist advisory groups to provide advice on major projects
- Consult the SAC on major projects, agenda decisions, and work priorities

Each IASB member has one vote on any issue presented for vote by the Board. Nine members of the 14 members must approve a financial reporting standard, exposure draft, final standard, or IFRIC interpretation for publication and issuance. Other IASB decisions, including publication of a discussion paper, require a simple majority of the IASB members present at a meeting attended by at least 60 percent of the Board.

Except for certain administrative matters, the IASB opens its meeting to the public. When deemed necessary, the IASB may use a public hearing meeting format to discuss specified agenda topics or approve the use of field tests to ensure that proposed accounting approaches are practical and workable.

Except in limited circumstances, IASB exposure drafts of proposed financial reporting standards, discussion documents, and other similar public documents receive a comment period of 90 days. Under exceptional circumstances, the IASB may issue an exposure draft for 60 days.

(iv) The Standards Advisory Council.   The SAC, which consists of at least 30 members with diverse geographic and professional backgrounds, provides a forum for organizations and individuals with an interest in international financial reporting to participate in the standard-setting process. Members of the SAC are appointed for renewable three-year terms.

As constituted, the SAC's objectives are:

- Advising the IASB on agenda decisions and Board priorities
- Informing the IASB of the diverse views of representative organizations and individuals on major standard-setting projects
- Providing advice to the IASB and the Trustees on other issues, as requested

In addition, the IASB must consult the SAC in advance of any proposed changes to the IASB Constitution.

The SAC meets with the IASB at least three times each year. Meetings between the SAC and the IASB are open to the public.

(v) The International Financial Reporting Interpretations Committee.   The IFRIC consists of 12 members appointed by the trustees. The Director of Technical Activities, a staff position, or other senior member of the IASB staff is the chair of the IFRIC and a nonvoting member. In addition, the trustees may appoint representatives of regulatory organizations to observe the meetings of the IFRIC. Although not granted voting status, the regulatory observers are permitted to speak at the meetings. Currently, representatives from the International Organizations of Securities Commissions and the European Commission are observers of IFRIC meetings.

Members of the IFRIC include accountants in public practice and industry and financial statement users.

In the absence of specific authoritative guidance, the IFRIC reviews emerging accounting issues that might be subject to divergent or unacceptable accounting treatment, with the goal of reaching consensus on the appropriate accounting approach. The framework of the IASB and existing IFRSs guide IFRIC interpretations. As constituted, the IFRIC's responsibilities include:

- Interpreting the application of IFRSs and providing timely guidance on financial reporting issues not specifically addressed in existing international accounting guidance
- Working with national standard-setting organizations to bring about convergence of national accounting standards and IFRSs to high quality solutions
- Publishing draft interpretations for public comment and, when developing a final Interpretation, considering comments received and issuing a final Interpretation within a reasonable time period

Before issuance, IFRIC's drafts and final Interpretations must be approved by the IASB.

The IFRIC meets as often as necessary, currently about every two months. Each IFRIC member has one vote and is expected to represent their own independent views rather than the views of any firm, organization, or other constituency with which they may be associated. Although an IFRIC member may send an alternate, as approved by the IFRIC Chair, such alternates may speak at meetings but are not granted voting privileges.

Except for meetings during which certain administrative matters are discussed, the IFRIC's meetings are open to the public.

(vi) International Financial Reporting Standards.   IFRSs are authoritative guidance on how particular economic events and transactions should be reported in a company's financial statements and reports.

IFRSs are established within the context of a conceptual accounting framework that was approved in 1989. The framework assists the IASB in the development of future standards; in its periodic review of existing standards; and in promoting the convergence of regulations, accounting standards, and procedures relating to the presentation of financial statements. However, the framework is not an authoritative IAS and does not define standards for any particular measurement or disclosure issue. The framework addresses general-purpose financial statements that a company prepares and presents to meet the common information needs of a wide range of financial information users. It covers the following topics:

- Defines the objectives of financial statements and underlying assumptions
- Identifies the qualitative characteristics of financial statements
- Defines the basic elements of financial statements and the concepts for recognition and measurement of the financial statement elements
- Defines the concepts of capital and capital maintenance

At present, the IASB has no authority to require compliance with IFRSs. However, for cross-border securities issuances, many countries allow foreign companies to apply IFRSs when those companies prepare financial reports for issuance to the public. Such countries may require certain reconciliations or additional footnote explanations of differences between reported information and local accounting and financial reporting standards. Among the countries that permit application of IFRSs are Australia, Canada, Germany, Hong Kong, Japan, the United Kingdom, and the United States. In addition, IOSCO reviewed 30 international standards for consideration for cross-border reporting by its member countries. Based on that review and subject to the appropriate reconciliation, disclosures, and interpretations, in May 2000, the President's Committee of IOSCO recommended that IOSCO members permit multinational issuers to use the 30 approved standards to prepare their financial reporting information for cross-border offerings and listings. Further, as of January 1, 2005, the EU requires all publicly listed companies to prepare their financial statements in conformity with IFRSs. As of January 2005, Australia adopted IFRSs as its national accounting standards. Starting in 2007, New Zealand will require IFRSs.

Procedures for the Development of International Financial Reporting Standards. Potential IASB financial accounting and reporting topics may be suggested to the IASB by its Board members, members of the SAC, national accounting standard-setting organizations, regulatory organizations, the IASB staff, and other interested individuals and IASB constituents. Once an item is added to its technical agenda, the IASB is given responsibility for determining the scope of that project. Development of an IFRS may involve the following steps:

- Establishment of an Advisory Committee to consult with the IASB on issues involved in the project
- Preparation and issuance of a discussion document to obtain comments on the topic and proposed guidance from interested parties
- Preparation and issuance of an Exposure Draft for public comment, after deliberation and consideration of the public comments received
- Issuance of a final IFRS, after deliberation and consideration of public comments received on the Exposure Draft

International Financial Reporting Standards Issued. At present, the IASB has 34 outstanding standards. Of those, IOSCO recommended 30 of the IFRS for use by its member countries for cross-border securities filings. Since receiving IOSCO's recommendation, the IASB issued IAS 40, "Investment Property," and IAS 41, "Agriculture." The outstanding IFRS are listed in Exhibit 9.1.

(b) INTERNATIONAL FEDERATION OF ACCOUNTANTS.[7] IFAC is a nongovernmental global professional organization of national accounting groups that represent accountants employed in public practice, business and industry, the public sector, and education that interact regularly with the accounting profession. IFAC was established in 1977 as a result of the growth in international trade and multinational business enterprises coupled with a significant increase in investors' attraction to investments outside of their national borders and the associated increase in cross-border capital flows.

IFAC's stated mission is "to strengthen the worldwide accountancy profession and [to] contribute to the development of strong international economies by establishing and promoting adherence to high-quality professional standards, furthering the international convergence of such standards and speaking out on public interest issues," where applicable. IFAC accomplishes its mission through its communications with national professional accounting organizations that are its official members and through its interactions with the many other professional organizations that rely on or have an interest in the activities of the international accounting profession.

In 2001, IFAC issued a paper, *Enhancing Financial Reporting and Auditing* (the Paper), containing initiatives proposed to strengthen IFAC and improve the global professional accounting

---

[7] Information on IFAC and its structure is available at the organization's web site (*www.ifac.org*).

Accounting Standards Issued		Publication Date
IFRS 1	First-Time Adoption of International Financial Reporting Standards	June 2003
IFRS 2	Share-Based Payment	February 2004
IFRS 3	Business Combinations	March 2004
IFRS 4	Insurance Contracts	March 2004
IFRS 5	Non-Current Assets Held for Sale and Discontinued Operations	March 2004
IAS 1	Presentation of Financial Statements	December 2003
IAS 2	Inventories	December 2003
IAS 7	Cash Flow Statements	December 1992
IAS 8	Accounting Policies, Changes in Accounting Estimates and Errors	December 2003
IAS 10	Events After the Balance Sheet Date	December 2003
IAS 11	Construction Contracts	December 1993
IAS 12	Income Taxes	October 1996
IAS 14	Segment Reporting	August 1997
IAS 16	Property, Plant, and Equipment	December 2003
IAS 17	Leases	December 2003
IAS 18	Revenue	December 1993
IAS 19	Employee Benefits	December 1993
IAS 20	Accounting for Government Grants and Disclosure of Government Assistance	January 1983
IAS 21	The Effects of Changes in Foreign Exchange Rates	December 2003
IAS 23	Borrowing Costs	December 1993
IAS 24	Related Party Disclosures	December 2003
IAS 26	Accounting and Reporting by Retirement Benefit Plans	January 1987*
IAS 27	Consolidated and Separate Financial Statements	December 2003
IAS 28	Investments in Associates	December 2003
IAS 29	Financial Reporting in Hyperinflationary Economies	July 1989*
IAS 30	Disclosures in the Financial Statements of Banks and Similar Financial Institutions	August 1990*
IAS 31	Interests in Joint Ventures	December 1990*
IAS 32	Financial Instruments: Disclosure and Presentation	December 2003
IAS 33	Earnings Per Share	December 2003
IAS 34	Interim Financial Reporting	June 1998
IAS 36	Impairment of Assets	June 1998
IAS 37	Provisions, Contingent Liabilities, and Contingent Assets	September 1998
IAS 38	Intangible Assets	September 1998
IAS 39	Financial Instruments: Recognition and Measurement	December 2003
IAS 40	Investment Property	December 2003
IAS 41	Agriculture	December 2001

*Statements were later reformatted.

Exhibit 9.1   International Financial Reporting Standards.

self-regulatory structure. The main elements of the initiatives include:

- Strengthening the processes and broadening the membership of the IAASB (formerly the International Auditing Practices Committee)
- Establishing a self-regulatory regime for firms performing transnational audits, comprising the Forum of Firms and its executive arm, the Transnational Audit Committee (an IFAC standing committee)
- Establishing a global Public Oversight Board

- Introducing a program for monitoring the compliance by IFAC member bodies with IFAC standards and other pronouncements

IFAC's current structure reflect implementation of many of the recommendations proposed in the Paper.

(i) Membership. Membership in IFAC is open to accountancy organizations recognized by law or general consensus within their countries as substantial national organizations of good standing within the accounting profession. At present, IFAC has 163 member organizations in 119 countries representing more than 2 million accountants.

Members of IFAC are expected to:

- Effort to fulfill IFAC's mission and objectives;
- Provide financial support of IFAC;
- Demonstrate compliance with the obligations set out in the Statements of Membership Obligations (SMOs), which are issued or revised periodically. SMOs are issued by the IFAC Board and provide clear benchmarks to current member organizations to assist them in meeting their membership requirements.

(ii) Governance of the International Federation of Accountants. IFAC is governed by an organization consisting of IFAC Council, the Board, and seven standing technical committees: Transnational Auditors Committee (TAC), Compliance Committee, International Assurance and Auditing Standards Board, Ethics Committee, Public Sector Committee, Education Committee, and Financial and Management Accounting Committee (FMAC).

Council. The Council consists of one representative from each member body of IFAC. The Council meets one time each year and is responsible for deciding constitutional questions and electing the IFAC board. Council members retain one vote on any issue addressed to the Council during its meeting. Other responsibilities include:

- Appointing a nominating committee
- Electing board members, based on the recommendations of the nominating committee
- Electing from its members, based on the recommendations of the nominating committee, the deputy president, who replaces the president for a term of two years
- Monitoring the progress and achievement of IFAC
- Admitting and expelling members, as appropriate
- Determining the basis for financial contributions from members
- Determining IFAC's strategic initiatives, budgetary priorities, and other major policy matters

The International Federation of Accountants Board. The Council, based on the recommendations of the nominating committee elects the board. The board consists of the president, the deputy president, and 20 individuals from 19 countries. The board has broad regional representation as no more than two members may be from any single country.[8] The board is elected for up to three-year terms and meets three times each year.

The responsibilities of the Board include:

- Appointing and replacing members to IFAC Committees
- Implementation of the IFAC self-regulatory structure
- Overseeing the relationship between IFAC and its member organizations

---

[8] Except that the country of the president may have an additional representative on the board. See Part 5 of the IFAC Constitution dated November 2004.

- Determining the timing, frequency, and location of the periodic World Congress of Accountants
- Setting policy and overseeing IFAC operations and implementation of its work program
- Recommending to the Council the basis for assessment of the financial contributions to be paid to IFAC by its members
- Distributing a report, including audited financial statements, on IFAC activities to its members on an annual basis
- Approving changes to the constitution of the Forum of Firms

The Standing Committees.   The standing committees work toward achieving the broad objectives of IFAC by issuing guidance that member organizations are committed to implement in their own countries. The standing committees include:

- *Transnational Auditors Committee (TAC).* TAC is the executive committee of the Forum of Firms. Membership in the Forum of Firms is open to all accounting firms that perform or wish to perform audits of transnational audits. Member firms will be expected to conform to certain quality control standards and will be subject to an evolving global peer review process to assess the firm's compliance with the quality control standards. TAC is responsible for coordinating the global peer review process and supervising the development of additional guidance regarding transnational audit work.
- *Compliance Advisory Panel.* The Compliance Advisory Panel (the CAP) oversees the implementation and operation of the IFAC compliance program. The CAP also makes recommendations to the IFAC Board about the membership application process including recommending new applicants for membership.
- *IAASB International Auditing and Assurance Standards Board.* The IAASB works to improve the uniformity of auditing practices and related services by issuing pronouncements on a variety of audit and assurance functions and by promoting global acceptance of their standards. Below is a discussion of IAASB and a listing of its standards.
- *Ethics Committee.* The Ethics Committee consults and advises the board on all aspects of ethical issues, develops appropriate guidance on these issues for the board's ultimate approval, and promotes an understanding of ethical issues among its member bodies. In addition, the Ethics Committee continually monitors and stimulates debate on a wide range of ethical issues to ensure that its guidance is responsive to the expectations of its constituency.
- *International Public Sector Accounting Standards Board.* The International Public Sector Accounting Standards Board issues accounting and auditing pronouncements and conducts educational and research programs aimed at improving the financial management and accountability of national governments, regional and local governments, related governmental agencies, and the constituencies they serve.
- *Education Committee.* The Education Committee develops standards and guidelines, conducts research, and facilitates the exchange of information to ensure that accountants are adequately trained. An important Education Committee focus is assisting developing nations in the advancement of accounting education.
- *Professional Accountants in Business Committee (PAIB).* PAIB publishes guidance, sponsors research programs, and facilitates the international exchange of ideas to develop and support financial and management accounting professionals. FMAC also works to increase public awareness, understanding, and demand for the services of these professionals worldwide.
- *Nominating Committee.* The Nominating Committee makes recommendations regarding the composition of IFAC boards, committees, and task forces.

Occasionally, IFAC's Council appoints small working groups, ad hoc committees, or special task forces to address significant issues that warrant focused attention. Currently, there are two task forces:

1. Small and Medium Practices Task Force
2. Anti-Money Laundering Task Force
3. Task Force on Rebuilding Public Confidence in Financial Reporting

(iii) International Standards on Auditing.   The IAASB issues ISAs and guidance on the application of the ISAs. The IAASB consists of 18 members appointed by the IFAC Board. The chairman is a full time position and the remaining seventeen members are volunteer, part-time positions. Members are appointed by the IFAC Board based on recommendations from the IFAC Nominating Committee. Each member may bring one technical adviser to meetings. The technical advisers are nonvoting representatives but are granted privilege of the floor. The IAASB has broad geographical representation. Current members include representatives from Australia, Brazil, France, Germany, Italy, Japan, Lebanon, Malaysia, Serbia and Montenegro, the United Kingdom, and the United States.

The IAASB meets about four times each year. Meetings, which are open to the public, are held in New York and several locations around the world. In 2006, the scheduled meeting locations are Hong Kong, New York, Brussels, and London. Information about meeting locations, the agenda, and minutes are available on the IFAC Website (*www.ifac.org*).

In developing its auditing and assurance guidance, the IAASB establishes subcommittees to prepare and present draft auditing standards and statements. Subcommittees are composed of IAASB committee members, technical auditors from member organizations, and IFAC staff. The IAASB deliberates on draft standards and statements at its regular meetings. After extensive discussion and debate, the subcommittee prepares an exposure draft of a statement or standard for public issuance. Comments received on the exposure draft are summarized and discussed at subsequent subcommittee meetings, and a revised document is prepared for discussion at an IAASB meeting. The IAASB deliberates on the revised draft and associated public comments and makes recommendations to the subcommittee, which are used to prepare a final document.

Each IAASB member has one vote on any document received. A final standard (ISAs) requires approval of at least 75 percent of attending members.

The IAASB issues three types of formal guidance:

1. *ISAs*, which are applied in the audit of financial statements and adapted to the audit of other information and related services.
2. *International Standards on Assurance Engagements (ISAEs)*, which are applied to high-level assurance engagements performed by professional accountants in public practice when such engagements are not covered by an ISA or an International Auditing Practices Statement (IAPS). At present, the IAASB has issued one standard on assurance engagements, ISA 100.
3. *International Auditing Practices Statements (IAPSs)*, which provide practical assistance to auditors in implementing ISAs and promoting good practice. IAPSs do not have the authority of ISAs.

Neither ISAs nor ISAEs override local or national auditing or assurance services regulations, respectively.

The IAASB also issues various discussion papers with the intention of promoting discussion or debate on auditing and assurance issues affecting the accounting profession, presenting findings, or describing situations of interest relating to auditing and assurance issues. A discussion paper does not carry the authority of either an ISA or an IAPS.

In July 1994, the then IAPC issued a codified set of ISAs. The codification consists of a preface, framework, glossary, and numbered sections on the associated auditing and assurance guidance. Rather than issuing individual standards and revising sections of the codification, IAASB guidance revises the subject matter section of the codification. For example, the IAASB might issue a revision of Section 100 on Assurance Engagements. Thus, individual ISAs are not numbered.

The codification's format follows the conduct of an audit, from planning through fieldwork and on to a conclusion and reporting; it also unites the all-important risk assessment standards in their proper place in the audit process (see Exhibit 9.2).

Prior to the issuance of the codification, IOSCO endorsed the ISAs. At that time, IOSCO stated that the ISAs represent a comprehensive set of auditing standards and, for multinational reporting purposes, securities regulatory authorities could rely upon that audits conducted in accordance with the ISAs. However, to date, IOSCO has not endorsed the codification. The IAASB and IOSCO are actively working together in order to obtain such endorsement. Along with other preparers, regulators, and users of financial information, IOSCO is a representative to the IAASB Consultative Advisory Group, which contributes their views to the IAASB during the development of auditing and assurance guidance.

In its "facts sheet," the IAASB notes that its ISAs are used as the basis for national auditing standards in more than 70 countries.

(c) EUROPEAN UNION.   In 1957, the Treaty of Rome created the EU. A decade later, in 1967, three existing communities—the European Economic Community, the European Coal and Steel Community, and the European Atomic Energy Community—were merged. In 1993, the European Community became the EU. Currently, a single Commission, a Council of Ministers (the Council), and a European Parliament exercise the powers and responsibilities incorporated in the separate treaties comprising the EU.

The Council represents the governments of its member states. The Council is the EU's decision-making body. It deliberates proposals developed by the representatives in the Commission. A qualified majority vote by Council is generally required for approval of all proposals. Council votes are weighted based on the population of the individual member countries.

(i) Council Directives.   EU Directives are one approach used to harmonize company law throughout its member states. Directives are developed through a complex and lengthy process including ratification by its member states. Once ratified, each member state adopts and implements the Directive, although national authorities are given some latitude on matters of implementation.

Directives address all aspects of company law including accounting and auditing. Of the 13 relevant company Directives that have been issued, two have significantly influenced European efforts to converge accounting and financial reporting—the Fourth and Seventh Directives. These are discussed below. In addition, the Eighth Directive addresses the qualification of accounting professionals authorized to conduct statutory audits.

The Fourth Directive was issued in 1978. It is applicable to public and private companies with the exception of banks and insurance companies. The Fourth Directive indicates that, in preparing financial reports, companies must provide a "true and fair" view of a their assets, liabilities, financial position, and results of operations. The guidance of the Fourth Directive includes:

- The format for a company's balance sheet and profit and loss statement
- The minimum footnote disclosure requirements and the contents of the annual report
- A section addressing the valuation rules and concepts considered in preparing financial statements and reported information

The Seventh Directive was issued in 1983. It applies to groups of companies that include at least one public or private limited liability company. The Seventh Directive requires member states to mandate, under certain specified criteria, consolidation accounting between parent companies and their controlled subsidiaries. A parent company is deemed to have control if it has: (1) a majority of voting rights, (2) the ability to appoint a majority of the subsidiary's board of directors, (3) right to exercise dominant influence over a limited liability company pursuant to a control contract, or a majority of voting rights, or (4) control of a majority of voting rights pursuant to agreements with

Subject Matter Number	Document Title
	Glossary of Terms
	Preface to ISAs
100–199	*Introductory Matters*
200–299	*General Principles and Responsibilities*
200	Objective and General Principles Governing an Audit of Financial Statements
210	Terms of Audit Engagements
220	Quality Control for Audit Work
220 R	Quality Control for Audits of Historical Financial Information
230	Documentation
240	The Auditor's Responsibility to Consider Fraud in an Audit of Financial Statements
250	Consideration of Laws and Regulations in an Audit of Financial Statements
260	Communications of Audit Matters with Those Charged with Governance
300–499	*Risk Assessment and Response to Assessed Risks*
300	Planning an Audit of Financial Statements
315	Understanding the Entity and Its Environment and Assessing the Risks of Material Misstatement
320	Audit Materiality
330	The Auditor's Procedures in Response to Assessed Risks
402	Audit Considerations Relating to Entities Using Service Organizations
500–599	*Audit Evidence*
500	Audit Evidence
501	Audit Evidence—Additional Considerations for Specific Items
505	External Confirmations
510	Initial Engagements—Opening Balances
520	Analytical Procedures
530	Audit Sampling and Other Selective Testing Procedures
540	Audit of Accounting Estimates
545	Auditing Fair Value Measurements and Disclosures
550	Related Parties
560	Subsequent Events
570	Going Concerns
580	Management Representations
600–699	*Using Work of Others*
600	Using the Work of Another Auditor
610	Considering the Work of Internal Auditing
620	Using the Work of an Expert
700–799	*Audit Conclusions and Reporting*
700	The Auditor's Report on Financial Statements
700 R	The Independent Auditor's Report on a Complete Set of General-Purpose Financial Statements
701	Modification to the Independent Auditor's Report
710	Comparatives
720	Other Information in Documents Containing Audited Financial Statements
800–899	*Specialized Areas*
800	The Auditor's Report of Special Purpose Audit Engagements
1000–1100	*International Auditing Practices Statements*
1000	Inter-Bank Confirmation Procedures
1004	The Relationship Between Banking Supervisors and Banks' External Auditors
1005	The Special Consideration in the Audit of Small Entities
1006	Audits of the Financial Statements of Banks
1010	The Consideration of Environmental Matters in the Audit of Financial Statements
1012	Auditing Derivative Financial Instruments
1013	Electronic Commerce: Effect on the Audit of Financial Statements
1014	Reporting by Auditors on Compliance with International Financial Reporting Standards

Exhibit 9.2   Codification of International Auditing Standards and International Auditing Practices Statements.

other shareholders.[9] The Directive also includes guidance on the techniques of consolidation and associated footnote disclosures.

(ii) EU Procedures.   The EU legislative process operates on three main levels, with different procedures applying at each of them. For instruments of general validity (Regulations and Directives), there is the proposal procedure, the cooperation procedure introduced by the Single European Act, and the co-decision procedure introduced by the Treaty on EU. The three procedures are mutually exclusive.

The proposal procedure is, as it always was, the basis for the adoption of all general EU instruments; it is applicable where neither the cooperation procedure nor the co-decision procedure is stated to apply. It rests on a division of labor between the Council and the Commission. Put very briefly, the Commission proposes and the Council disposes. But before the Council actually reaches a decision, there are various stages to be completed in which, depending on the subject of the measure, it may also come before the European Parliament and the Economic and Social Committee. The procedures followed by the EU in developing Directives under the proposal procedure are:

- The Commission consults with officials for the member states and their specialists on specific suggestions for harmonizing company law or accountings.
- The staff of the Commission prepares a working paper for purposes of discussion by the Commission and national experts.
- A formal draft Directive is prepared and approved by the Commission, submitted to the Council, and published.
- The Council submits the formal draft Directive to the Economic and Social Committee and to the European Parliament for comments.
- After receipt of comments, the proposal is deliberated by the Council and negotiated with delegates of the member states, as needed.
- The Directive is approved by Council and issued to the member states.
- The member states are then required to bring into their respective national law, within specified time periods, the regulations and administrative provisions needed to comply with the Directive.
- The effective time period for compliance has varied from six months to as much as five years for certain provisions.

(iii) EU—Recent Developments.   In recent years, the EU has stressed its goal in support of convergence of accounting and financial reporting standards around those issued by the IASC (now IASB). For example:

- In 1999, the EC issued its action plan to improve the Single Market for Financial Services over a five-year period. In that action plan, the Commission noted that the standards of the IASC represent the benchmark for companies that intend to participate in cross-border securities transactions.
- In 2000, the EC issued a report, *EU Financial Reporting Strategy: The Way Forward*, which contains its recommendations on an approach to European convergence. In that report, the EC recommends making it mandatory for all EU-listed companies to prepare consolidated financial statements in accordance with IASs. Further, the report proposed amending existing Directives and developing an IAS endorsement mechanism with the goal of achieving European application of IASs by January 1, 2005. In June 2002, the EC adopted a regulation requiring listed companies to prepare consolidated financial reports in accordance with IAS (now IFRSs).

---

[9] Adapted from Frederick D. S. Choi, Carol Ann Frost, and Gary K. Meek, *International Accounting*, Third Edition Prentice-Hall, Upper Saddle River, NJ, 1999, p. 270.

- The EU, through its various committees on accounting issues, has been a vocal supported and critic of IASB proposals. For example, in 2004, the EU objected to certain provisions of the revised IAS on accounting and reporting for derivative transactions. Rather than reject the revised standard in total, the EU accepted a modified version of the final standard, IAS No. 39, and requested that the IASB reconsider certain provisions. In response, the IASB reconsidered those provisions and issued amendments. In 2005, the EU accepted the amended standard for use by listed companies in EU member states. It's clear that the EU intends to continue to be an active participant in IASB activities.

- In 2005, the EU approved amendments to the Eighth Directive. Consistent with some of the provisions of the Sarbanes-Oxley Act of 2002 in the U.S., the amendments will establish public oversight of the auditing profession and increase audit committee oversight over the acceptance and conduct of the corporate audit. In addition, similar to the acceptance of IFRSs issued by the IASB, the amendment will make the application of IAASB auditing standards mandatory for all statutory audits. The amendments are expected to take effect for audits beginning in 2007.

The EU's recent activities make it clear that, subject to its review and evaluation of IFRSs, its objective is promote convergence of accounting standards with the guidance of the IASB.

(d) OTHER MAJOR GLOBAL STANDARD-SETTING ORGANIZATIONS.   In the last five years, the IASB and IFAC have taken the lead in developing and promoting IFRSs and international auditing and assurance standards, respectively. However, other organizations remain very influential in the global standard-setting arena. Following is a brief discussion of those organizations.

(i) International Organization of Securities Commissions.   IOSCO was created in 1983. Its members represent national securities regulators and representatives from national securities exchanges that have responsibility for securities regulation and the administration of securities laws. IOSCO's objectives are to:

- Promote high-quality standards for regulating securities markets around the world and to maintain just, efficient, and sound markets

- Exchange information on regulatory processes and procedures to promote the development of domestic securities markets

- Establish standards and effective security procedures to ensure the efficient and effective flow of securities transactions

- Provide mutual assistance to promote the integrity of securities markets by a rigorous application of established standards and by effective enforcement actions against market offenders

IOSCO has more than 170 members across its three membership categories—ordinary, associate, and affiliate members. Its activities to promote convergence began in 1989 when IOSCO released a report stating that cross-border offerings would be facilitated by the development of a global set of accounting standards. At that time, IOSCO decided to focus its activities on the efforts of the IASC (now the IASB). Since 1989, IOSCO has:

- Identified the necessary components of a core set of accounting standards that the IASC would have to develop in order to create an acceptable body of standards for companies involved in cross-border securities filings (1993)

- Reviewed the available set of IASB accounting standards and identified the issues that would have to be addressed before IOSCO would consider recommending those standards to its members (1994)

- Agreed with the IASB on a work plan for development of a core set of accounting standards, which, if successfully completed, would result in IOSCO considering those standards for endorsement (1995)

- Upon the IASB completing the "core standards work program," began its review of the IASB standards and interpretations completed under the agreed to work program (1999)
- Recommended that, for future cross-border securities filings, its members permit those filings to be prepared using an approved set of 30 IASB standards, supplemented where necessary to address issues of national or regional concern (2000)

In its report on the IASB core standards, IOSCO discusses the supplemental treatments that IOSCO members may want to consider when deciding on the implementation. IOSCO is also working with the IAASB to develop a similar work plan to consider recommending IAS to its members for cross-border auditing and assurance engagements.

(ii) International Forum on Accountancy Development.   Following the late 1990s East Asian economic crises, representatives from large international accounting firms, governments, regulators, multinational lending organizations, investor groups, and others created the International Forum on Accountancy Development (IFAD). Initially, IFAD was formed to address the accounting framework and structure in developing and emerging nations. IFAD members and observers include representatives from 29 member organizations including IFAC, IASB, the International Monetary Fund, the World Bank and regional development banks, the Organization for Economic Development and Cooperation, the Basel Committee on Banking Supervision, and large international accounting firms.

After its initial meeting, IFAD issued a report, *Raising Reporting and Auditing Practices Worldwide—The Vision* (the Vision). Though revised and significantly expanded, IFAD's goals and initiatives are based on the recommendations contained in the Vision document. IFAD's objectives are to:[10]

- Promote understanding by national governments of the value of transparent financial reporting, in accordance with sound corporate governance
- Assist in defining expectations as to how the accounting profession should carry out its responsibilities to support the public interest
- Encourage governments to focus more directly on the needs of developing countries and economies in transition
- Help harness funds and expertise to build accounting and auditing capacity in developing countries
- Contribute to a common strategy and framework of reference for accountancy development
- Promote cooperation between governments, the accounting and other professions, international financial institutions, regulators, standard-setting organizations, and issuers and providers of financial capital
- Develop guidelines to identify the characteristics of a strong financial architecture and the roles of the accounting profession within that architecture

In order to implement its objectives, IFAD formed the International Steering Committee (ISC). ISC members consist of representatives from banking regulators, international financial institutions, international accounting firms, and financial statement users and preparers.

The ISC retained day-to-day responsibility for monitoring the progress toward the implementation of IFAD's objectives at a country level primarily by:

- Working in partnership as an international community
- Developing an approach and criteria to be taken by country project teams

---

[10] Taken from IFAD's web site.

- Providing a forum for coordination and communication between the public- and private-sector organizations on matters related to improving global financial reporting practices
- Establishing benchmarks for measuring success toward achieving IFAD's objectives
- Reviewing progress at the country level
- Giving both general and specific directions and facilitating solutions where the country teams are having difficulties

In its short tenure, IFAD has completed several major projects including:

1. GAAP 2001, which updates and expands a report issued by large accounting firms, *GAAP 2000: A Survey of National Accounting Rules in 53 Countries*. GAAP 2001 compares the financial reporting and disclosures rules in 60 countries with those of the IASB and highlights instances of inconsistency.
2. International Financial Framework project, which examines global and national capital formation environment and identifies the role of the accounting profession in that overall financial framework.

With completion of the 2002 GAAP convergence publication, IFAD completed its work program.

(iii) The Intergovernmental Working Group of Experts on International Standards of Accounting and Reporting.   Established in 1982, by a resolution of the Economic and Social Council of the United Nations, the Intergovernmental Working Group of Experts on International Standards of Accounting and Reporting's (ISAR's) original mandate was to promote the international harmonization of corporate accounting and reporting practices. However, with the shift of focus of accounting and financial reporting convergence efforts to the activities of the IASB, ISAR's work activities has shifted somewhat. Using an integrated program of research, intergovernmental dialogue, consensus building, and technical cooperation, the ISAR's objectives are to:[11]

- Make a positive contribution to national and regional accounting and auditing standard setting
- Take actions to ensure comparability of disclosure by transnational corporations
- Serve as an international body for considering accounting and auditing issues to improve the availability and comparability of information disclosed by transnational corporations
- Review international accounting and reporting developments
- Establish working priorities taking into account the needs of home and host countries, particularly those of developing countries
- Consult appropriate international bodies on matters pertaining to the development of international accounting and reporting standards and elicit views of interested parties
- Report to the Commission on Investment, Technology, and Related Financial Issues (formerly the Commission on Transnational Corporations) on steps to be taken in pursuit of the long-term objective of international harmonization of accounting and reporting standards

In recent years, the ISAR's has issued reports on a variety of topics including: *Accounting and Reporting by Small and Medium-Sized Enterprises* (dated July 16, 2001) and *Global Curriculum for the Professional Education of Professional Accountants* (dated December 28, 1998). In addition, the organization has addressed issues such as environmental accounting and reporting and review of existing corporate governance policies and procedures. In addition, the ISAR retains continuous liaison activities with the IASB, IFAC, and IFAD.

---

[11] Adapted from the ISAR's web site (*www.unctad.org/isar/*).

9.3 SOURCES AND SUGGESTED REFERENCES

Arthur Andersen & Co., BDO Seidman, Deloitte Touche Tohmatsu, Ernst & Young, Grant Thornton, KPMG Peat Marwick, and PricewaterhouseCoopers, *GAAP 2001: A Survey of National Accounting Rules Benchmarked Against International Accounting Standards*. Available on IFAD's web site (*www.ifad.net*), June 2001.

Blanchet, Jeannot, "Global Standards Offer Opportunity," *Financial Executive*, March/April 2002, pp. 2–3.

Casabona, Patrick, and Shoaf, Victoria, "International Financial Reporting Standards: Significance, Acceptance, and New Developments", *Review of Business*, Winter 2002, pp. 16–20.

Choi, Frederick S., Frost, Carol Ann, and Meek, Gary K., *International Accounting*, Third Edition. Prentice-Hall, Upper Saddle River, NJ, 1999.

Dalessio, A. N., Seiler, M. E., and Jones, R. C., International Accounting and Standards, included in the *Accountants' Handbook*, Ninth Edition, edited by D. R. Carmichael, Steven B. Lilien, and Martin Mellman. John Wiley and Sons, Inc., New York. 1999.

Craig, James L., Carmichael, Douglas R., and Guy, Dan M., "Are International Auditing Standards Ready to Replace U.S. GAAS," *The CPA Journal*, June 2000, pp. 20–24.

FEE, the European Federation of Accountants, "The Role of Accounting and Auditing in Europe." Available on the FEE web site (*www.fee.be*), May 2002.

Guy, Dan M., and Carmichael, D. R., *International Standards on Auditing & Related Services, 2002*. Practitioners Publishing Company, Texas, 2001.

IFAC and Staff, *2004 IFAC Handbook of Auditing and Ethics Pronouncements*. International Federation of Accountants, New York, 2004.

Oliverio, Mary Ellen, "The New Structure for International Accounting Standards," *The CPA Journal*, May 2000, pp. 20–26.

Plaistowe, Ian, "Our Global Goal," *Accountancy*, May 2001, p. 1.

Public Oversight Board and Staff, *The Panel on Audit Effectiveness Report and Recommendations,* Stamford, CT, 2000.

Ravlic, Tom, "The IOSCO Role: Making International Rules," *Australian CPA*, August 1999, pp. 54–56.

Securities Exchange Commission and Staff, *SEC Concepts Release: International Accounting Standards (File No. S7-04-00)*. Available on the U.S. SEC web site (*www.sec.gov*), February 2000.

Strategy Working Party of the International Accounting Standards Committee, *Recommendations on Shaping the IASC for the Future: A Report of the International Accounting Standards Committee*. International Accounting Standards Committee, London, 1999.

Taylor, Michael, "The IOSCO Objectives and Principles of Securities Regulation," *Financial Regulation Report*, June 1998, pp. 3–6.

Technical Committee of IOSCO, *IASC Standards: Report of the Technical Committee of IOSCO*. Available on the IOSCO web site (*www.iosco.org*), May 2000.

Tidrick, Donald E., "A Conversation with James J. Leisenring, IASB Member," *The CPA Journal*, March 2002, pp. 48–51.

Tie, Robert, "IFAC, Firms to Apply International Standards Consistently," *Journal of Accountancy*, April 2000, p. 20.

VALUABLE WEB SITE SOURCES

IASB, International Accounting Standards Board (*www.iasc.org.uk*)

Deloitte's IAS Plus, a comprehensive source on international financial reporting (*www.iasplus.com*)

IFAC, International Federation of Accountants (*www.ifac.org*)

IOSCO, International Organization of Securities Commissions (*www.iosco.org*)

EU, European Union (*europa.eu.int/comm/internal_market/en/company/*)

CHAPTER 10

FINANCIAL STATEMENTS: FORM AND CONTENT

Jan R. Williams, PhD, CPA

College of Business Administration University of Tennessee

10.1 INTRODUCTION

Financial statements are one of management's primary means of communicating with external parties about the financial activities of the enterprise. Through financial statements, interested parties outside a company are able to learn a great deal about the financial effects of business transactions and the accumulated resources and obligations of the reporting enterprise.

This chapter presents an overview of the form and content of financial statements as a means of introducing these important communication tools. The purpose is to introduce financial statements, to illustrate how they interrelate or articulate with each other, and to suggest the types of information that can be gleaned from them. Later chapters develop in more depth the specific content and underlying accounting principles of specific financial statements.

The following sections review the objectives of financial reporting, including financial statements, and identify the principles supporting the preparation of financial statements. Next there are individual reviews and illustrations of the primary financial statements—the balance sheet, the income statement, the statement of stockholders' equity, and the statement of cash flows. Articulation of financial statements is then covered, followed by a discussion of the role of supplemental and note disclosure. The chapter ends with a discussion of some of the limitations of financial statements as communication tools.

10.2 PRINCIPLES UNDERLYING FINANCIAL STATEMENTS

(a) OBJECTIVES OF FINANCIAL REPORTING. The Financial Accounting Standards Board (FASB) is the authoritative body responsible for establishing financial reporting standards in the United States. The FASB has established several objectives of financial reporting. *Financial reporting* is a broad term used to identify all means by which investors, creditors, and other interested parties learn about the financial activities of an enterprise. One of the most important parts of the financial reporting environment is the preparation and distribution of financial statements, particularly statements that are audited by an independent Certified Public Accountant (CPA).

Three primary objectives of financial reporting, which are carried out in part through the preparation of financial statements, are as follows:

1. To provide information that is useful to present and potential investors and creditors and other users in making rational investment, credit, and similar decisions (Statement of Financial Accounting Concepts (SFAC) No. 1, par. 34)

2. To provide information to help current and potential investors and creditors and other users assess the amounts, timing, and uncertainty of prospective cash receipts from dividends and interest and the proceeds from the sale, redemption, or maturity of securities or loans (SFAC No. 1, par. 37)

3. To provide information about the economic resources of the enterprise, claims to those resources and the effects of transactions, events, and circumstances that change resources and claims to resources (SFAC No. 1, par. 40)

In explaining these objectives, the FASB points out that information provided should be comprehensible to those who have a reasonable understanding of business and economic activities and are willing to study the information with reasonable diligence. Thus, the orientation of financial statements is toward the reasonably informed user of financial information—neither the extreme highest in terms of knowledge (e.g., professional financial analysts) nor the extreme lowest (e.g., the naive investor with little knowledge of business activities).

(b) SELECTED UNDERLYING PRINCIPLES.   Many broad principles underlie the preparation of financial statements. The following paragraphs briefly set forth several principles that are important for an introductory understanding of the financial statements.

(i) Multiple Sources of Information.   Financial statements are only one of many sources of financial information about a reporting enterprise. Management may communicate financial and other information to interested parties in a variety of ways, some of which are through governmental organizations such as the Securities and Exchange Commission (SEC). News releases and direct contact with owners and others are other means of communication within the financial reporting framework. Many times these communications include financial statements or refer to information taken from financial statements.

(ii) Approximate Measures.   The content of financial statements results, in part, from approximate rather than exact measures of business activities. Many estimates and assumptions are required to partition ongoing business activities into relatively short periods of time, such as one year. Although the financial statements have an appearance of precision because items are measured in terms of a monetary unit, determining many of the amounts requires judgments that impose uncertainty and imprecision into the resulting financial statement items.

(iii) Historical Orientation.   The orientation of financial statements is primarily historical inasmuch as they report activities and events that have already occurred. Reporting on historical events, however, sometimes requires estimates of the future.

(iv) General Purpose Financial Statements.   The primary financial statements are general purpose in nature in that they are designed to meet the information needs of a wide variety of financial statement users and are not specifically tailored to the unique needs of any particular user group. These general purpose statements are intended primarily for external users who lack the authority to dictate the specific information they receive. Users who do have the authority to dictate the nature of such information are not the primary audience of general purpose financial statements.

(v) Accrual Accounting.   Financial statements are based on accrual accounting principles. Accrual accounting attempts to measure the financial impact of events and transactions when they occur and not simply when the cash consequences of those events and transactions take place. The cash effects of certain transactions may occur earlier or later than the transaction itself, and accountants attempt to report at the time of the substantive financial effects rather than only the cash effects.

(vi) Explanatory Notes and Disclosures.   The usefulness of financial statements is believed to be enhanced by explanations and details outside the body of the statements themselves. For this reason, financial statements are frequently accompanied by notes and other supplemental disclosures providing a variety of information that would otherwise not be available. A discussion of supplemental and note disclosure is presented later in this chapter.

A complete set of financial statements generally includes a balance sheet, an income statement, a statement of stockholders' equity, and a statement of cash flows. In the following sections, each of these statements is illustrated and described. Because of the overview nature of this chapter, all of the disclosures that would normally accompany the statements are not presented. Rather, the focus is on the basic structure of each statement, the definitions of the primary elements of the statements, and the interrelationship of the statements.

10.3 BALANCE SHEET

A balance sheet, also called a *statement of financial position*, is a listing of the quantifiable resources that an enterprise has to operate with as well as a listing of claims against those resources represented by both creditors and owners. In the report form of the statement, the quantifiable resources, called *assets*, are first listed, followed by the claims of creditors and owners. In the account form of the statement, the assets are typically presented on the left and the claims to the assets on the right side of the statement. An important relationship in the balance sheet is that the claims to the assets equal or "balance" exactly the amount of the assets presented.

Another way to view the balance sheet is that it represents the quantifiable resources of the enterprise and a description of the three primary sources from which those resources have been garnered. The first source is creditors—those who have loaned or otherwise provided resources to the company for its use, expecting a return on those loaned amounts as well as eventual repayment of them. The second source is the owners, called *stockholders* in a corporation, who have committed resources to the company, expecting some combination of return and enhanced value of the investment through the effective employment of resources by the enterprise. The third source also is considered an owner source but results from the assets earned by the enterprise having been retained for its future use rather than having been distributed back to the owners on a periodic basis.

Exhibit 10.1 illustrates a balance sheet for the hypothetical Morristown Products, Inc. It is prepared in the report form, first listing assets, followed by liabilities and stockholders' equity. This is a *classified balance sheet*, with the various major categories further categorized as described next.

(a) ASSETS.   Assets are defined as probable future economic benefits obtained or controlled by the enterprise as a result of past transactions or events (SFAC No. 6, par. 25). Assets have three essential characteristics: (1) They embody a probable future economic benefit in the form of a direct or indirect future net cash inflow; (2) a particular enterprise (e.g., the owner) can obtain the benefit and control others' access to it; and (3) the transaction or other event giving rise to the enterprise's right to control the benefit has already occurred (SFAC No. 6, par. 26). Assets are typically presented in the balance sheet in terms of current and noncurrent classifications.

(i) Current Assets.   Current assets are assets that are expected to become cash, sold, or consumed in the near future (Accounting Research Bulletin (ARB) No. 43, Ch. 3, par. 4). These assets are considered "liquid" in that they represent cash or near-cash resources from which the company can satisfy obligations as they become due. The primary purpose of listing current assets is to communicate information about the various stages of a company's short-term cash-to-cash cycle, including the amount invested in each stage of that cycle. Exhibit 10.2 depicts a typical short-term cash cycle for a company that invests cash in merchandise inventory. That inventory is held until sold to customers on credit, thus creating accounts receivable that are subsequently converted into cash. Assuming the purchase of inventory takes place at a dollar amount below the price of the sale of that same inventory, the eventual addition to cash when the receivable is collected is greater than the original reduction in cash when the item was purchased. This short-term or operating cycle is intended to be a primary source of increased cash, which is then available for future use in continued operations.

Current assets are typically listed in their order of liquidity in the balance sheet, beginning with cash itself. Some companies hold certain highly liquid investments as cash equivalents and combine them with cash as a current asset in the balance sheet. In Exhibit 10.1 cash is followed by

MORRISTOWN PRODUCTS, INC.
Balance Sheet
December 31, 2000, 2001, and 2002
(In thousands of dollars)

	2002	2001	2000
Assets			
Current assets			
Cash	$ 8	$ 13	$ 10
Marketable securities	6	5	5
Accounts receivable	50	40	45
Merchandise inventory	100	90	75
Prepaid expenses	7	4	5
	$171	$152	$140
Property, plant, and equipment			
Equipment	$100	$100	$100
Building	250	200	200
Land	60	60	50
	$410	$360	$350
Less: accumulated depreciation	(105)	(90)	(75)
	305	270	275
Investments	67	67	50
Total assets	$543	$489	$465
Liabilities			
Current liabilities			
Accounts payable	$ 52	$ 45	$ 40
Accrued expenses	40	32	35
	$ 92	$ 77	$ 75
Noncurrent liabilities			
Bonds payable	200	200	200
Total liabilities	$292	$277	$275
Stockholders' equity			
Preferred stock	$ 20	$ 20	$ 20
(500 shares @ $40 par value)			
Common stock	110	110	100
(10,000 shares @ $10 par value in 2000;			
11,000 shares @ $10 par value in			
2001 and 2002)			
Additional paid-in capital	35	35	30
Retained earnings	86	47	40
Total stockholders ' equity	$251	$212	$190
Total liabilities and stockholders' equity	$543	$489	$465

Exhibit 10.1   Sample balance sheet.

marketable securities, accounts receivable, merchandise inventory, and prepaid expenses, in that order. Marketable securities are considered current assets if management invests in them when excess cash is available and disinvests when that cash is again needed for operating purposes. If the intent of management is to retain the investment for a longer period of time, the securities would not be classified as current. Marketable securities presented in the current asset section of a balance sheet may be thought of as secondary sources of cash that are readily available to the company when needed. Accounts receivable represent the result of credit sales transactions that

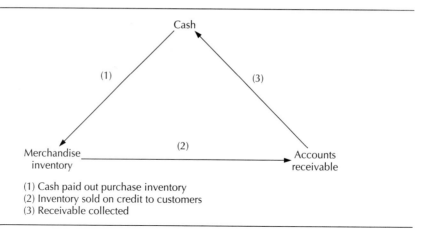

(1) Cash paid out purchase inventory
(2) Inventory sold on credit to customers
(3) Receivable collected

Exhibit 10.2   Short-term operating cycle.

have not yet been collected in cash. Merchandise inventory represents the company's investment in assets held for resale and expected to be sold in the near future. Prepaid expenses represent advance payments of items that will be used by the company in the coming accounting period. Prepaid expenses are different from other current assets in that they will not become cash in the near future, but they conserve the use of cash in the near future.

The time period for distinguishing current assets from other assets is usually one year. Some companies, however, have a short-term cash-to-cash cycle, or operating cycle, of more than one year. For example, if inventory is required to be held through an aging process, the time between the initial investment of cash in inventory and the eventual return of that cash through the sale of the inventory may be quite long. If a company's operating cycle is longer than one year, the longer period of the cycle is used to identify current assets. If the company has several cycles within a year, a year is used.

(ii) Noncurrent Assets.   Noncurrent assets are assets that do not meet the definition of current assets. These may represent a variety of resources available to the enterprise and may vary considerably among enterprises, depending on the nature of the business activity in which the enterprise is involved. Many companies require property, plant, and equipment, sometimes referred to as *fixed* or *plant assets*, in order to operate. In Exhibit 10.1, Morristown Products, Inc., presents equipment, buildings, and land under a property, plant, and equipment caption. The amounts so presented generally represent the cost of those assets to the enterprise. Over time that cost is recognized as an expense in the income statement of the enterprise, a subject covered in Subsection 10.4(b) of this chapter. The accumulation of those expense amounts is identified in the balance sheet as "accumulated depreciation" and is subtracted from the cost of the assets. Over time, the accumulated depreciation would ordinarily increase in amount as illustrated in Exhibit 10.1.

A variety of other noncurrent assets may be held by a company at any particular point in time. The balance sheet of Morristown Products, Inc., illustrates one such asset, investments. These are most likely securities of other enterprises that the company is holding with the intent of not converting to cash in the near future. Thus, they are properly identified as other than current assets.

(b) LIABILITIES.   Liabilities are probable future sacrifices of economic benefits arising from present obligations of the reporting enterprise to transfer assets or provide services to other entities in the future as a result of past transactions or events (SFAC No. 6, par. 35). Liabilities have three essential characteristics: (1) They embody a present duty or responsibility that is expected to be settled by probable future transfer of assets; (2) the duty or responsibility obligates a particular enterprise; and (3) the transaction or event obligating the enterprise has already occurred (SFAC

No. 6, par. 36). Liabilities are typically presented in the balance sheet in terms of current and noncurrent classifications.

(i) Current Liabilities.   Current liabilities are liabilities that are expected to be satisfied with the use of current assets (ARB No. 43, Ch. 3, par. 7). Ordinarily, current liabilities are those that will be due within one year or operating cycle, if longer. There are instances where such short-term obligations are not presented as current liabilities, however, because they are not expected to be satisfied using current assets. For example, if a company has a long-term debt obligation outstanding and throughout the period of the debt provides for repayment by investing in a fund to be used only for that purpose, the debt obligation is not a current liability in its last year, because the asset source used for repayment is not a current asset.

In Exhibit 10.1, two examples of current liabilities are illustrated—accounts payable and accrued expenses. The former most likely results from the purchase of merchandise inventory from suppliers and represents debts that will be paid within a very short time. Accrued expenses may arise from a variety of sources related to the application of accrual accounting procedures and may represent the enterprise's obligation to pay wages to employees, interest to creditors, taxes to government, and other similar items.

(ii) Noncurrent Liabilities.   Noncurrent liabilities are liabilities that do not meet the definition of current liabilities. They are part of the long-term financing of the enterprise and are expected to be repaid at some distant date. Bonds payable is used as an example of such an arrangement in Exhibit 10.1.

(iii) Working Capital and the Current Ratio.   Current assets and current liabilities are listed and their totals reported in the balance sheet as previously explained. The excess of total current assets over total current liabilities is referred to as *working capital*. The total of current assets compared to the total of current liabilities is commonly referred to as the *current ratio*. Working capital and the current ratio are thought to be helpful in evaluating the entity's ability to meet its obligations as they come due (i.e., the entity's liquidity).

(c) STOCKHOLDERS' EQUITY.   Equity is the residual interest in the enterprise after deducting liabilities from assets (SFAC No. 6, par. 49). A corporate organization titles that equity as "stockholders' equity." Other forms of business organization, such as sole proprietorships and partnerships, commonly refer to it simply as *owner's equity* or *owners' equity*.

(i) Contributed Equity.   Corporations sell stock as evidence of ownership in the company. This stock may be labeled preferred or common stock. Although a detailed discussion of these types of stock is beyond the scope of this chapter, preferred stock will receive distributions of assets to owners, called *dividends*, before common stock. Also, should the company liquidate, preferred stockholders have a preference in receiving assets over common stockholders. The stocks typically have an identified par or stated value at which they are carried in the corporate balance sheet, as illustrated in Exhibit 10.1 ($40 par for preferred and $10 par for common).

Because preferred and common stock will not necessarily sell to stockholders at precisely their par values, additional accounts may be found in the stockholders' equity section of the balance sheet representing additional sources of assets. In Exhibit 10.1, the account "additional paid-in capital" is an example of such an account. The preferred stock, common stock, and additional paid-in capital accounts combined represent the contributed or paid-in equity of the enterprise—those amounts that have been committed to the enterprise by owners for the enterprise's use.

(ii) Retained Earnings.   The final element of stockholders' equity is retained earnings. This amount represents a source of enterprise assets from profitable past operations beyond the amount of such assets that have been distributed to owners in the form of dividends. Typically companies do not distribute assets to stockholders that are equal to the amount of their earnings. Rather, they withhold a portion of earned assets for future operations, including expansion of business activities and other uses.

The balancing feature can be seen in Exhibit 10.1 inasmuch as the assets equal the total of the liabilities and stockholders' equity (e.g., $543,000 in 2002). The balance sheet is based on this primary underlying principle, and it represents a basic tenet of financial reporting. The balance sheet has been described as a still photograph of a business at a point in time, in terms of its assets, liabilities, and owners' equity—a simple but appropriate analogy that identifies what this important financial statement attempts to communicate.

(iii) Subclassifying Stockholders' Equity.   In explaining the term *equity*, the FASB has observed that distinctions within equity, such as those between common and preferred stock, between contributed and earned capital, and between stated or legal capital and other equity, are primarily matters of presentation, implying that this information may be of limited value to financial statement users (SFAC No. 6, footnote 29).

10.4 INCOME STATEMENT

Continuing the analogy of the balance sheet as a still photograph of an enterprise at a point in time, the income statement can then be described as a motion picture that identifies certain dimensions of the enterprise over a period of time. Exhibit 10.3 shows the relationship of the balance sheet and the other financial statements, including the income statement, in terms of time. Exhibit 10.4 provides an income statement for Morristown Products, Inc., for the years 2001 and 2002. This income statement relates to, or articulates with, the balance sheet presented earlier in Exhibit 10.1. It describes the profit-directed activities of the company in terms of its revenues and expenses, leading to a final figure of net income or net loss.

(a) REVENUES.   Revenues are inflows or other enhancements of assets of an enterprise or settlement of its liabilities from delivering or producing goods, rendering services, or carrying out other activities that constitute the entity's ongoing major or central operations (SFAC No. 6, par. 78). The nature of an enterprise's revenues depends on the type of business activity. For a manufacturing enterprise, revenues consist of sales of its manufactured product to retailers or other enterprises that will sell to the ultimate consumer. For a service enterprise, revenues represent the value of the services provided to its customers or clients for a period of time. Revenues are typically the first items listed in an income statement, as is the case in Exhibit 10.4 with the "sales" figure for Morristown Products, Inc.

(b) EXPENSES.   Expenses are outflows or other using up of assets or incurrences of liabilities from delivering or producing goods, rendering services, or carrying out other activities that constitute the entity's ongoing major or central operations (SFAC No. 6, par. 80). Sacrifices of resources are necessary in order for an enterprise to create revenues. These sacrifices are in the form of asset outflows or creation of liabilities that, in turn, will result in asset outflows when those liabilities are eventually paid. Expenses attempt to measure these asset outflows or reductions. Many expense

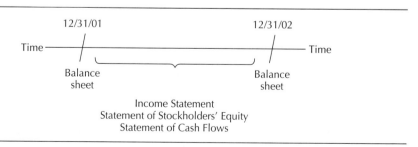

Exhibit 10.3   Relationship of financial statements.

MORRISTOWN PRODUCTS, INC.
Income Statement
For years ended December 31, 2001 and 2002
(In thousands of dollars)

	2002	2001
Sales	$ 500	$ 400
Cost of sales	240	180
Gross margin	$ 260	$ 220
Expenses:		
Selling and administrative	$ 135	$ 155
Depreciation	15	15
	150	170
Income from operations	$ 110	$ 50
Interest expense	20	20
Income before income taxes	$ 90	$ 30
Provision for income taxes	27	9
Net income	$ 63	$ 21
Earnings per share	$5.60	$1.87

Exhibit 10.4   Sample income statement.

categories are presented in the typical income statement of a business enterprise, as is the case in Exhibit 10.4—cost of sales, selling and administrative, depreciation, interest, provision for income taxes. All of these represent various types of expenses that are required to create the asset enhancements or revenues related to these expenses.

The income statement is based on an accounting principle called *matching*. Revenues ordinarily can be readily associated with specific business activity that relates to specific periods of time. Once the revenues for a period of time have been identified, the accountant then attempts to associate with those revenues all expenses that relate to (1) that same period of time and/or (2) the generation of those specific revenues. These amounts are then "matched," meaning that the expenses are subtracted from the revenues, to determine the results of operations for the period. The result is called *net income* if revenues exceed expenses; it is called *net loss* if expenses exceed revenues.

(c) PRESENTATION ISSUES.   In a multiple-step income statement, illustrated in Exhibit 10.4, several subtotals appear within the statement. Examples are "gross margin," "income from opera-tions," and "income before income tax." These descriptions are intended to help the reader of the statement understand the important relationships that underlie the statement. Gross margin mea-sures the difference between sales and cost of sales. Cost of sales is the direct cost of acquiring (or manufacturing) the items sold. Gross margin is a broad concept of profit in that it deducts from sales only the direct cost of those items sold and does not include other costs of business oper-ations that are necessary, but less direct. Income from operations attempts to measure the excess of sales over those expenses that are most closely tied to ongoing business operations. In the case of Morristown Products, Inc., in Exhibit 10.4, interest payments on borrowings and income taxes have been omitted from the determination of income from operations on the basis that they are less closely related to ongoing business activities than are the other expenses identified earlier in the statement—cost of sales, selling and administrative, and depreciation. Income before income taxes indicates the profitability of the company after recognizing all related expenses except income tax. Net income is the final indication of profitability for the period of time covered. The subtotals preceding net income in Exhibit 10.4 are not found in all income statements but are placed there at the discretion of the preparer for the convenience and understanding of the financial statement reader. An income statement that omits these subtotals is called a *single-step income statement*.

Earnings per share (EPS) is an indication of the net income recalculated on a per-share-of-common-stock basis. Referring again to Exhibit 10.4, in 2001 net income per share of common stock was $1.87, and for 2002 the amount was $5.60. This figure is calculated by taking the amount of net income, reducing it by any dividend requirements for preferred stock, and dividing the result by the weighted average number of shares of common stock outstanding for the year.

Income statements may include gains and losses other than those illustrated in Exhibit 10.4. Gains and losses may result from a variety of peripheral business activities: that is, they do not relate to the primary, ongoing central activities of the enterprise. These types of gains and losses occur less frequently than revenues and expenses that are defined as the enterprise's primary revenue-producing activities.

10.5 STATEMENT OF STOCKHOLDERS' EQUITY

A required disclosure in a complete set of financial statements of a corporation is an identification of the changes in stockholders' equity in terms of dollars by major category and numbers of shares of stock (Accounting Principles Board (APB) Opinion No. 12, par. 10). This disclosure can be made in several different forms, such as a note or supplemental schedule to the other financial statements, or a separate financial statement. Because many companies today make this presentation in the form of a separate financial statement, Exhibit 10.5 takes that approach in Morristown Products, Inc.'s statement of stockholders' equity.

Like the income statement, the statement of stockholders' equity covers a period of time rather than a specific point in time. The columns represent the major categories of stockholders' equity: contributed equity—preferred stock, common stock, and additional paid-in capital—and retained earnings. The statement begins with the balance at the end of the period prior to that covered in the statement. In Exhibit 10.5, the statement covers 2001 and 2002, so the statement begins with the balances in the stockholders' equity accounts at the end of 2000.

The rows in the statement indicate activities that resulted in changes in the major categories of stockholders' equity—sale of common stock, net income, and dividends. Notice that the sale of common stock in 2001 affects only the contributed equity accounts inasmuch as they are intended to include those amounts contributed to the enterprise by stockholders. In this case, common stock increased by the par value of the shares sold, $10,000, and additional paid-in capital increased by $5,000. This means that the stock sold for 1.5 times its par value, or $15 per share. The increase in the number of shares is disclosed in the caption to the left describing the sale of common stock.

MORRISTOWN PRODUCTS, INC.
Statement of Stockholders' Equity
For years ended December 31, 2001 and 2002
(In thousands of dollars)

| | Contributed Equity | | | |
	Preferred Stock	Common Stock	Additional Paid-in Capital	Retained Earnings
Dec. 31, 2000	$20	$100	$30	$40
Sale of 1000 shares of common stock		10	5	
Net income				21
Dividends				(14)
Dec. 31, 2001	$20	$110	$35	$47
Net income				63
Dividends				(24)
Dec. 31, 2002	$20	$110	$35	$86

Exhibit 10.5   Sample statement of stockholders' equity.

Net income and dividends affect only retained earnings, as illustrated in Exhibit 10.5. Net income increases the retained earnings balance, and dividends decrease that balance.

Exhibit 10.5 shows the relationship of the financial statements covered earlier to the statement of stockholders' equity. For example, the net income amount included in the retained earnings column of Exhibit 10.5 is taken directly from the income statement for each year as indicated in Exhibit 10.4. Also, the various stockholders' equity accounts at December 31 of each year correspond to the amounts presented in the company's balance sheet at the end of each year in Exhibit 10.1. For example, the December 31, 2002, balances of preferred stock ($20,000), common stock ($110,000), additional paid-in capital ($35,000), and retained earnings ($86,000) in the balance sheet correspond to the amounts in the final row of the statement of stockholders' equity in Exhibit 10.5.

10.6 STATEMENT OF CASH FLOWS

One of the central objectives of financial reporting is to provide information that is useful to external parties in assessing the amount, timing, and uncertainty of prospective cash flows to them. One factor of particular importance in this assessment is the cash position of the enterprise itself. As a result, the fourth financial statement is the statement of cash flows.

The statement of cash flows presents information about an enterprise's cash receipts and payments during a period of time (SFAS No. 95, par. 4). This statement is similar in concept to the income statement and statement of stockholders' equity in that it covers a period of time rather than a point in time, as does the balance sheet. In its simplest form, the statement of cash flows simply indicates the enterprise's primary sources of cash and the primary ways the enterprise used that cash. These changes are presented in a manner that reconciles the change in cash from the beginning to the end of the accounting period.

The statement of cash flows for Morristown Products, Inc., is included in Exhibit 10.6. This statement is presented in three categories—cash flows from operating activities, cash flows from investing activities, and cash flows from financing activities. At the bottom of the statement, the net change in cash is presented as a reconciling figure to show how the cash balance either increased or decreased between the beginning and ending of the accounting period covered by the statement.

(a) OPERATING ACTIVITIES.   Cash flows from operating activities generally describe the cash-flow effects of those transactions presented in the enterprise's income statement. Because the income statement is prepared on an accrual basis, revenues and expenses reported in that statement may not represent the cash effects of those transactions during the same accounting period. For example, revenues are generally recognized at the point of sale, but cash may not be received from the sale until the company collects the related receivable at a later date. Expenses, on the other hand, may have been paid before or after the period in which the expense is recognized in the income statement. Depreciation, for example, represents an expense that attempts to measure the cost of services rendered during a period of time by the enterprise's plant assets. The cash to purchase those assets may have been paid in an earlier accounting period.

The following three types of cash inflows from operating activities are presented in the statement of cash flows, as appropriate (SFAS No. 95, par. 22):

1. Cash receipts from sales of goods or services
2. Cash receipts from returns on loans to and investments in other enterprises
3. Other cash receipts that do not stem from transactions classified as investing and financing activities

Cash outflows from operating activities typically presented in the statement of cash flows are (SFAS No. 95, par. 23):

1. Cash payments to acquire goods for manufacture or sale
2. Cash payments to suppliers and employers for goods or services

MORRISTOWN PRODUCTS, INC.
Statement of Cash Flows
For the years ended December 31, 2001 and 2002
(In thousands of dollars)

	2002	2001
Cash Flows from Operating Activities		
Cash received from customers	$ 490	$ 405
Cash paid to suppliers	(243)	(190)
Cash paid for selling and administrative expenses	(130)	(157)
Cash paid for interest	(20)	(20)
Cash paid for income taxes	(27)	(9)
Net cash provided by operating activities	$ 70	$ 29
Cash Flows from Investing Activities		
Payment to purchase land		$ (10)
Payment to purchase investments		(17)
Payment to purchase marketable securities	$ (1)	
Payment to purchase building	(50)	
Net cash used in investing activities	(51)	(27)
Cash Flows from Financing Activities		
Sale of common stock		$ 15
Payment of dividends	(24)	(14)
Net cash provided by (used in) financing activities	(24)	1
Net increase (decrease) in cash	$ (5)	$ 3
Cash at beginning of year	13	10
Cash at end of year	$ 8	$ 13

Reconciliation of Net Income to Net Cash Provided by Operating Activities

Net income	$ 63	$ 21
Adjustments to reconcile net income to net cash provided by operating activities:		
Depreciation	$ 15	$ 15
Change in current assets and liabilities:		
Accounts receivable	(10)	5
Inventory	(10)	(15)
Prepaid expenses	(3)	1
Accounts payable	7	5
Accrued expenses	8	(3)
	7	8
Net cash provided by operating activities	$ 70	$ 29

Exhibit 10.6   Sample statement of cash flows.

3. Cash payments to governments for taxes, duties, fines, and other fees or penalties

4. Cash payments to lenders and other creditors for interest

5. Other cash payments that are not classified as investing and financing cash outflows

The types of cash flows from operating activities of a particular enterprise depend on the nature of that enterprise's activities. Exhibit 10.6 presents the cash flows from operating activities first in the statement of cash flows in five categories that are deemed appropriate for this enterprise's particular business activities. The result is a figure of net cash flows from operating activities (e.g., $70,000 for 2002), implying a netting of positive and negative cash flows within that category.

The relationship of net cash flows from operating activities to the company's net income is shown in a disclosure presented as part of the statement of cash flows. In that disclosure, net income is adjusted for noncash items to show the reader of the statement why net income and net cash flows from operating activities are different amounts. For example, for 2002 net income was $63,000 and net cash flows from operating activities was $70,000. The difference is due to several noncash items that affected net income but did not provide or use cash during the year. (This disclosure is found at the bottom of the statement of cash flows in Exhibit 10.6.)

(b) INVESTING ACTIVITIES.   Cash flows from investing activities present the enterprise's cash-flow activities in terms of investments in assets. Specifically, cash inflows are ordinarily presented in one of the following three categories (SFAS No. 95, par. 16):

1. Receipts from collections or sales of loans made by the enterprise to other enterprises
2. Receipts from sales of equity instruments of other enterprises
3. Receipts from the sales of property, plant and equipment, and other productive assets

Cash outflows from investing activities are typically presented in one of the following three categories (SFAS No. 95, par. 17):

1. Payments for loans made to other enterprises and investments in other enterprise's debt instruments
2. Payments to acquire equity instruments of other enterprises
3. Payments to purchase property, plant and equipment, and other productive assets

In Exhibit 10.6, the cash flow from investing activities is presented for Morristown Products, Inc., resulting in negative cash flow of $51,000 for 2002. During the year the company had only two types of transactions in investing category—purchase of marketable securities and purchase of building—both of which represent negative cash flows.

(c) FINANCING ACTIVITIES.   Financing activities represent positive and negative cash flows of the enterprise from debt and equity financing transactions. Typical cash inflows from financing activities are (SFAS No. 95, par. 19):

- Proceeds from selling stock
- Proceeds from issuing bonds, mortgages, notes, and other debt instruments

Negative cash flows from financing activities are (SFAS No. 95, par. 20):

- Payments of dividends or other distributions to owners
- Repayments of amounts borrowed

Referring again to Exhibit 10.6, the third major section of the statement of cash flows of Morristown Products, Inc., is the cash flows from financing activities. For 2002 the net amount is a reduction of $24,000, resulting from a single transaction—payment of dividends. For 2001, on the other hand, the net amount from financing activities is a positive $1,000 amount when the amount received from the sale of common stock ($15,000) is offset by the amount of dividends paid ($14,000).

10.7 ARTICULATION OF FINANCIAL STATEMENTS

Reference has been made several times to the relationship of the four financial statements in the above presentation. Selected specific examples have shown where the items in one of the statements relate directly to the items in another financial statement.

The four financial statements are derived from the same underlying transactions and the same financial measurements of those transactions. The statements present different types of information about the enterprise's activities during a period of time and thus are not alternatives to each other. All are necessary for the reader to get as complete an understanding as is possible through the medium of financial statements.

Attempting to demonstrate the articulation of financial statements in a single illustration is an impossible undertaking. Exhibit 10.7 attempts to illustrate several of the most important relationships that underlie the four financial statements presented earlier—the balance sheet, the income statement, the statement of stockholders' equity, and the statement of cash flows. These eight relationships identified by numbers in parentheses in Exhibit 10.7 are summarized in the following list:

1. Revenues and expenses, presented in the income statement, result in changes in assets and liabilities in the balance sheet.

2. Net income flows into the statement of stockholders' equity and is an important determinant of the end-of-period balance in retained earnings.

3. The ending balances of contributed equity accounts in the statement of stockholders' equity correspond to the same amounts in the stockholders' equity section of the balance sheet.

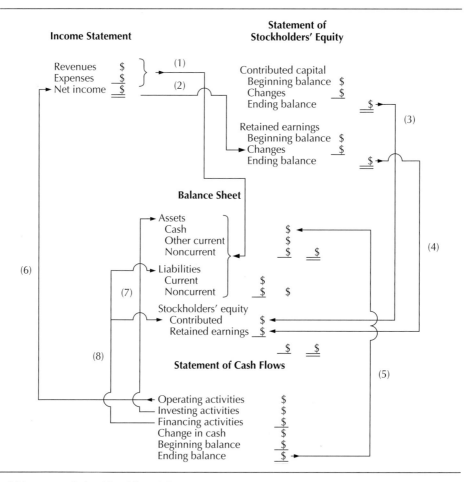

Exhibit 10.7   Relationship of financial statements.

4. The ending balance of retained earnings in the statement of stockholders' equity corresponds to the balance in retained earnings in the stockholders' equity section of the balance sheet.

5. The ending cash balance in the statement of cash flows corresponds to the amount of cash presented on the balance sheet.

6. Cash flows from operating activities in the statement of cash flows reflects the cash effects of those transactions included in the determination of net income. A reconciliation of net income and net cash flows from operating activities is presented as part of the statement of cash flows.

7. Investing activities in the statement of cash flows reflect positive and negative cash flows from changes in assets whose ending balances are included in the balance sheet.

8. Financing activities in the statement of cash flows reflect positive and negative cash flows from debt and equity financing transactions. The end-of-period balances in debt and equity are presented in the balance sheet.

10.8 FINANCIAL STATEMENT DISCLOSURE

One of the underlying principles of financial statement preparation is adequate or fair disclosure. This means that financial statements and the notes and other supplemental information accompanying them must include all available relevant information to keep them from being misleading. In determining whether a specific item of information should be disclosed, the accountant must judge whether that information would make a difference in the decision of a reasonably prudent reader of the financial statements. If the information would be important to such a person, it should be disclosed.

Many disclosure requirements are specified in the authoritative accounting literature, such as the Statements of Financial Accounting Standards of the FASB. Because of the extensive nature of these requirements, accountants frequently use checklists to ensure that they have not overlooked important information. An example excerpt from such a checklist is presented in Exhibit 10.8 for the balance sheet categories of "Inventories" and "Related-Party Transactions and Economic Dependency." The parenthetical references within the checklist refer to the authoritative literature from which the disclosure requirement is derived. The three columns to the right indicate the alternative responses for the financial statement preparer: "Yes" (disclosure has been made), "No" (disclosure has not been made, but is required), and "N/A" (disclosure is not applicable in this case).

Disclosure takes several forms. The strongest form of disclosure is to include the information in the body of the financial statements. In fact, the statements themselves are a form of disclosure. Including certain words, phrases, and dollar amounts in the statement is one means of disclosing the information. Classification within the financial statements is also an important form of disclosure.

A great deal of information is presented in conjunction with financial statements but outside the body of the statements. This information is typically labeled as notes to the financial statements. These notes include both text and numerical information that intend to further inform the reader of the financial statements about matters that have been included in summary fashion in the statements or have been excluded entirely from the financial statements. Notes to the financial statements should not be interpreted by the reader as secondary or unimportant. In fact, notes often occupy more page space than the statements themselves and include very important information that would not be available if the reader were limited to the information that can be contained in the financial statements themselves.

(a) BROAD DISCLOSURE REQUIREMENTS.   The following paragraphs discuss several areas of broad disclosure requirements that do not relate to any one financial statement element. Rather, they are more pervasive in nature and apply to the financial statements as a whole.

(i) Accounting Policies.   The basic elements of the financial statements are identified and measured by applying accounting policies, many of which have been established by the FASB and

	Yes	No	N/A

E. Inventories

1. Are the major classes of inventory disclosed (e.g., finished goods, work in process, raw materials)?
[Generally Accepted]

2. Is the method of determining inventory cost (e.g., LIFO, FIFO) disclosed?
[ARB 43, Ch. 3A, par. 9 (AC I78.120)]

3. Is the basis for stating inventory disclosed (e.g., lower of cost or market)?
[ARB 43, Ch. 4, par. 14 (AC I78.120); APB 22, par. 13 (AC A10.106)]

4. Are valuation allowances for inventory losses shown as a deduction from the related inventory?
[APB 12, par. 3 (AC V18.102)]

5. Are the net losses on firm purchase commitments for goods for inventory disclosed in the income statement?
[APB 43, Ch. 4, par. 17 (AC VI78.121 and .122)]

T. Related Party Transactions and Economic Dependency

1. For related party transactions, do disclosures include:
   a. The nature of the relationships involved?
   b. For each period for which an income statement is presented:
      1. A description of the transaction, including transactions to which no amounts or nominal amounts were ascribed?
      2. Other information deemed necessary to an understanding of the effects of the transaction on the financial statements?
      3. The dollar amount of transactions?
      4. The effect of any changes in the method of establishing the terms from that used in the preceding period?
   c. Amounts due from or to related parties as of the date of each balance sheet presented and, if not otherwise apparent, the terms and manner of settlement?
   [SFAS 57, pars. 2–4 (AC R36.102–.104)]

2. If representations about transactions with related parties are made, do they avoid the implication that the related party transactions were consummated at arm's length, or if such implications are made, can they be substantiated?
[SFAS 57, par. 3 (AC R36.103)]

3. If (a) the reporting entity and one or more other enterprises are under common ownership or management control and (b) the existence of the control could result in operating results or financial position of the reporting entity being significantly different from that if the enterprise were autonomous, is the nature of the controlled relationships disclosed (even if there are no transactions between the enterprises)?
[SFAS 57, pars. 2 and 4 (AC R36.102 and .104)]

4. Are the nature and extent of leasing transactions with related parties appropriately disclosed?
[SFAS 13, par. 29 (AC L10.125)]

5. Are combined financial statements considered for entities under common control?
[ARB 51, pars. 22 and 23 (AC C51.121 and .122)]

Exhibit 10.8   Sample financial statement disclosure checklist. (*Source:* American Institute of Certified Public Accountants, *Checklists and Illustrative Financial Statements for Corporations,* 2001.)

other policy-setting bodies within the accounting profession. In some areas, alternative policies are available, and companies are required to disclose to readers of financial statements those policies that have been adopted in the preparation of the financial statements (APB Opinion No. 22, par. 8).

The inventory accounting policy statement is particularly important because of the disclosure about the accounting method used in determining the amount of inventories. Companies may account for inventories by a variety of techniques, such as first in, first out (FIFO), last in, first out (LIFO), and several averaging methods. The method used in determining the amount of inventory may have an important impact on the amounts in the income statement, balance sheet, and other financial statements and is considered important information in interpreting financial statements.

(ii) Related Party Transactions.   Related parties are individuals or companies with the ability to influence the financial transactions of each other. Disclosure of related party transactions may be important for a complete understanding of the financial statements of companies engaged in such transactions.

Notes to financial statements should include a description of transactions between related parties, such as transactions between a principal stockholder and the company, between a corporate officer and the company, and between a subsidiary company and its parent company (SFAS No. 57, par. 2).

(iii) Subsequent Events.   Financial statements cover a specific time period or point in time. These statements are not immediately available at the end of the accounting period but are usually published several weeks later. The period of time between the end of the accounting period and the issuance of the financial statements is called the *subsequent period*.

During the subsequent period, events may occur or information may become available that should be communicated in the financial statements. If the information reflects conditions that existed at the end of the previous accounting period, the items and amounts in the financial statements may require adjustment in order to appropriately reflect the company's financial position and results of operations for the previous period Statements on Auditing Standards ((SAS) No. 12, par. 3). If the information reflects conditions that arose after the end of the previous accounting period, it may be necessary to disclose that information in the form of notes to the statements so that they reflect all relevant information (SAS No. 12, pars. 5–6).

(iv) Doubt Concerning Continued Existence.   Financial statements are typically prepared on the assumption that the enterprise is a going concern. This means that, in the absence of information to the contrary, it is reasonable to expect the company to continue in existence for the foreseeable future.

Should accountants preparing the financial statements determine that this assumption is not reasonable and that a significant question about continued existence exists, that information must be disclosed in notes to the financial statements (SAS No. 59, par. 10)?

(v) Contingent Liabilities.   Contingent liabilities are liabilities that involve a great deal of uncertainty as to their existence and amount. They frequently exist as a result of lawsuits against an enterprise or other situations that may, in the future, require the enterprise to transfer assets in settlement of a claim.

If certain conditions are met, contingent liabilities should be formally entered into the accounting records and become a part of the financial statements. Many contingent liabilities, however, are less certain and are typically disclosed in notes to the financial statements. This is frequently the case with pending lawsuits where the certainty of loss, including the amount of loss, is unknown when the financial statements are issued. Disclosure in this manner puts the reader on notice as to the possible negative consequences of events that have already taken place but do not meet the objectivity standards necessary for inclusion in the body of the financial statements (SFAS No. 5, par. 10).

(vi) Significant Risks and Uncertainties.   The volatility of the business and economic environment dictates a need for disclosure about significant risks and uncertainties that confront business enterprises. Following are four areas for which information is required in conjunction with financial statements:

1. Nature of operations (i.e., description of major products or services and principal markets)
2. Use of estimates in the preparation of financial statements (i.e., explanation that the preparation of financial statements in conformity with generally accepted accounting principles (GAAP) requires the use of management's estimates)
3. Certain significant estimates (i.e., disclosure of specific estimates that have material impact on the financial statements)
4. Current vulnerability due to certain concentrations (i.e., disclosure of (a) concentrations in the volume of business with a particular customer, supplier, lender, grantor, or contributor; (b) concentrations in revenue from particular products, services, or fund-raising events; (c) concentrations in the available sources of materials, labor, or services; and (d) concentrations in the market or geographic area in which an entity conducts its operations (American Institute of Certified Public Accountant (AICPA) Statement of Position No. 94-6, par. 10–22))

(vii) Disclosure Recommendations of the AICPA Special Committee on Financial Reporting. A special committee of the AICPA, charged with making broad recommendations to improve financial reporting through improved disclosure, has recommended enhanced supplementary disclosures that are intended to help users of financial statements evaluate the reporting entity's prospects. Included among the recommendations of this group are:

- Standard setters should develop a comprehensive model of business reporting, indicating the types and timing of information that users need to value and assess the risk of their investments.
- Improve understanding of costs and benefits of business reporting, recognizing that definitive quantification of costs and benefits is not possible.
- Improve financial statement disclosures in the following areas:
  ○ Business segment information
  ○ Innovative financial instruments
  ○ Identity, opportunities, and risks of off-balance sheet financing arrangements
  ○ Effects of core and noncore activities and events and measure at fair value noncore assets and liabilities
  ○ Uncertainty of measurements of certain assets and liabilities
  ○ Reporting on fourth quarter separately and including business segment information in interim reports

In addition to the above specific recommendations, the Special Committee made general recommendations that standard setters search for and eliminate less relevant disclosures, improve the display in financial statements, expand interim reporting requirements, improve comparability and consistencies of information, and provide key statistics and ratios to assist users of financial statements (AICPA, *Improving Business Reporting—A Customer Focus*, pp. 123–125).

(b) DISCLOSURES RELATED TO SPECIFIC FINANCIAL STATEMENT ELEMENTS.   Whereas the examples of disclosure discussed above are broad in nature and do not relate to specific financial statement elements, other disclosures focus attention on individual items in the balance sheet, income statement, or other financial statements. Examples of several of these disclosures are briefly identified and discussed in the following subsections.

(i) Debt and Equity Investments.   Companies may have invested cash in debt and equity instruments of other companies and, as a result, may have investments among the assets in their balance sheets. Accepted accounting procedures call for separating these investments into three portfolios—trading, available-for-sale, and held-to-maturity—based primarily on the intent of management for holding the investment. Trading securities may include both debt and equity investments and are presented as current assets in the balance sheet. Available-for-sale securities include both debt and equity investments for which the enterprise has no immediate plans to sell, but does not plan to hold indefinitely (equity securities) or until maturity (debt securities). Held-to-maturity investments include only those debt investments for which the intent is to hold until maturity. Available-for-sale and held-to-maturity investments are usually presented as noncurrent assets.

Information disclosed in notes to the balance sheet about these investments includes their fair value, gross unrealized holding gains and losses, and amortized cost by category, as well as information about realized gains and losses included in the income statements (SFAS No. 115, par. 19, 21).

(ii) Inventories. In addition to disclosing information about the accounting policy employed in accounting for inventories, detailed information about the dollar amounts of inventories must be disclosed. For example, a manufacturing company may have several types of inventories—raw materials, work-in-process, and finished goods. The financial statements or related notes should include an indication of the dollar amounts of each of these types of inventories (ARB No. 43, Ch. 4, par. 3).

(iii) Plant Assets and Depreciation. Plant assets include land, buildings, equipment, furniture, fixtures, and other long-lived assets that are required to accomplish the business purposes of an enterprise. Plant assets are subject to depreciation whereby a portion of the cost of the asset is written off as an expense during those years in which the asset is used. The remaining unamortized cost is presented in the balance sheet as an asset.

Information about the amount of plant assets in individual categories, such as equipment and fixtures, is believed to be important to readers of financial statements. In addition, information about the cost of those assets and the portion of the cost that has been written off as depreciation to date is also important. This information may be presented in the body of the financial statements but is often found among notes to the financial statements (APB Opinion No. 12, par. 5).

(iv) Long-Term Debt. The amount of long-term debt is presented in the enterprise's balance sheet. That amount may be made up of many different debt issues, having different interest rates, maturity dates, and other characteristics. Information about the details of individual debt issues that make up the total of long-term debt is frequently found among the notes to financial statements in order to avoid unnecessary details in the statements themselves.

(v) Capital Structure. A corporation may have one or more types of preferred and common stock in its capital structure. Information about the characteristics of individual issues of capital stock, such as the number of shares the corporation is authorized to issue, the par or stated value, and the dividend rate, is disclosed in the financial statement or related notes. If an entity has issued redeemable stock (i.e., stock that must be repurchased by the issuing company at a future date), the amount of the redemption requirement must be disclosed for each of the next five years, usually in notes to the financial statements. Also, the preference of preferred stock in liquidation must be presented in the aggregate on the face of the balance sheet (SFAS No. 129, par. 4–8).

The above are a few examples of the types of information that are usually disclosed in conjunction with financial statements. Disclosures in a variety of other areas, such as leases, pensions, and income taxes, can be quite long and complex. They include a great deal of information that would otherwise be unknown to the user of the financial statements.

(c) SPECIAL DISCLOSURES OF PUBLICLY HELD COMPANIES. Publicly held companies must adhere to a higher disclosure standard in certain areas than companies that are not publicly held. Due to the unique reporting responsibilities of publicly held companies, the FASB has limited certain disclosure requirements to publicly held companies. Several of these are briefly discussed in the following paragraphs.

(i) Segment Disclosures. Publicly held companies are required to report detailed information about their reportable operating segments. This information is generally reported as supplemental to the financial statements and is prepared on the same basis as is used internally for evaluating segment performance. Operating segments are components of an enterprise about which separate financial information is available that is evaluated regularly by the chief operating decision maker in deciding how resources should be allocated within the enterprise (SFAS No. 131, par. 10). Segment reporting requirements also include information about operations in different geographic areas and reliance on major customers (SFAS No. 131, par. 38–39).

(ii) Earnings per Share. The EPS figures are required only in the income statements of publicly held companies. These are presented as part of the income statement and indicate the amount of net income attributable to each share of outstanding common stock, after providing for dividends that would be required on preferred stock. Nonpublic companies are not required to make these disclosures in their income statements (SFAS No. 21, par. 12). Public companies whose capital structure includes financial instruments and other contractual arrangements that would reduce EPS (called *potential common stock*) are required to make a dual presentation of EPS—basic EPS and diluted EPS. Basic EPS reflects the historical amount of EPS of common stock, and diluted EPS is a pro forma amount that anticipates the dilutive effect of potential common stock (SFAS No. 128, par. 8, 11).

(iii) Interim Reporting. Companies may provide information to their stockholders and others on a more frequent basis than annually. Many companies provide information regularly on a quarterly basis.

Publicly held companies that report regularly on an interim basis must meet certain specific disclosure standards. These standards specify the information that must be presented, as a minimum, in these reports (APB Opinion No. 28, par. 30).

(d) DISCLOSURE OVERLOAD. The accounting profession as well as the investing community have expressed concern that too much disclosure may be required by the authoritative accounting literature, causing users to get lost in the details and miss the primary message being communicated. Standards overload, if in fact such exists, is believed by many to be caused by the fact that reporting needs of users of the financial statements of large, public companies drive the establishment of standards, most of which are then applicable to all companies, including smaller, private companies. The AICPA special committee referred to earlier recently searched, without much success, for current disclosure requirements that could be eliminated. While it was unable to find current requirements that do not provide useful information for the complex business environment and types of transactions companies engage in, it did recommend that standard setters and regulators continue the search in hopes of simplifying financial statement disclosures.

10.9 LIMITATIONS OF FINANCIAL STATEMENTS

Financial statements are important means of communications between management and external parties, primarily investors and creditors. These statements are subject to certain limitations, several of which are introduced in this final section.

(a) STABLE MONETARY UNIT ASSUMPTION. Financial statements are prepared with an underlying assumption of a stable monetary unit. Accountants recognize that the monetary unit does, in fact, change in value over time. In the United States, the monetary unit is the dollar, and in recent years the changes in value have been declines as the general level of prices has risen consistently. Experiments have been undertaken to measure the impact of changing prices on the financial statements. To date, however, no single approach has been accepted, nor is any adjustment for changing prices required in financial statements prepared in accordance with accepted accounting principles.

Perhaps the best way to describe the underlying assumption is not as a stable monetary unit but rather as a monetary unit with changes in value from period to period that are not large enough to have a material impact on the financial statements. Astute readers of financial statements should be generally aware that some distortion may exist because of the impact of changing prices and that the failure to adjust for such changes represents a limitation of financial statements.

(b) HISTORICAL ORIENTATION.   Financial statements are essentially historical representations of business activity. They are frequently used to anticipate the future and their historical orientation imposes a limitation on their value in this regard. Despite the historical orientation of the statements, accountants must consider the future to make many of the judgments that are required in reporting about past activities. For example, in determining an appropriate amount of depreciation on a plant asset for an accounting period, the accountant must make an assumption concerning how long the reporting entity will use that asset.

(c) JUDGMENT AND ESTIMATION.   While financial statements have an appearance of great precision, they are tentative in nature and require judgment and estimation. Any attempt to partition ongoing business activity into relatively short periods of time, such as a year or quarter, requires judgment and estimation about future events and about the outcome of incomplete past events. Although accountants attempt to apply an objectivity standard to the extent possible, in many instances they must resort to judgment and estimation to determine important amounts that affect the elements of the financial statements.

(d) MANAGEMENT ABILITY TO INFLUENCE CONTENT.   Within limits, management has the ability to influence the content of financial statements. Certain end-of-period activities can have an important effect on the relationships that investors and creditors consider particularly important in assessing the financial activities of the enterprise.

(e) UNRECORDED ITEMS.   The accounting system does not attempt to capture all aspects of business activity that may be important factors in the success of the enterprise. One example of an item that may be very important to the future well-being of the enterprise is its human resources. For many companies, its management personnel and labor force may be its most valuable "asset," but nowhere in the balance sheet does this item appear.

Financial statements are limited to those elements that can be measured with reasonable objectivity and that are required by GAAP. They should be viewed as only partial representations, rather than complete representations, of the business enterprise.

(f) FLEXIBILITY VERSUS UNIFORMITY.   An ongoing debate in the accounting profession is flexibility versus uniformity. This controversy asks the question: Should enterprises have latitude in the manner in which they identify and measure the elements of the financial statements (i.e., flexibility), or should all enterprises follow precisely the same rules and procedures in preparing statements (i.e., uniformity)?

At present, elements of both flexibility and uniformity exist in GAAP. In some areas, enterprises have great latitude in accounting for and presenting certain items in their financial statements. In other areas, enterprises are essentially limited to a single process or procedure. The FASB seeks to identify areas of financial reporting where unjustified differences exist in practice. One objective of the FASB is to narrow these areas of difference in practice so that all enterprises account for similar transactions in essentially the same manner. This is a long process, however, and undoubtedly both flexibility and uniformity in different areas of accounting can be expected to exist for years to come.

10.10 SOURCES AND SUGGESTED REFERENCES

Accounting Principles Board, "Omnibus Opinion—1967," APB Opinion No. 12. AICPA, New York, 1967.

———, "Disclosure of Accounting Policies," APB Opinion No. 22. AICPA, New York, 1972.

———, "Interim Financial Reporting," APB Opinion No. 28. AICPA, New York, 1973.

American Institute of Certified Public Accountants, Accounting Research Bulletin No. 43, Ch. 3, "Working Capital." AICPA, New York, 1953.

———, Accounting Research Bulletin No. 43, Ch. 4, "Inventory Pricing." AICPA, New York, 1953.

———, "Checklists and Illustrative Financial Statements for Corporations." AICPA, New York, 2001.

———, "Improving Business Reporting—A Customer Focus, Comprehensive Report of the Special Committee on Financial Reporting," 1994.

———, Statement of Position 94-6, "Disclosure of Certain Significant Risks and Uncertainties." AICPA, New York, 1994.

———, "Subsequent Events," Statement on Auditing Standards No. 12. AICPA, New York, 1972.

———, "The Auditor's Consideration of an Entity's Ability to Continue as a Going Concern," Statement on Auditing Standards No. 59. AICPA, New York, 1988.

Financial Accounting Standards Board, "Objectives of Financial Reporting by Business Enterprises," Statement of Financial Accounting Concepts No. 1. FASB, Stamford, CT, 1978.

———, "Accounting for Contingencies," Statement of Financial Accounting Standards No. 5. FASB, Stamford, CT, 1975.

———, "Elements of Financial Statements," Statement of Financial Accounting Concepts No. 6. FASB, Stamford, CT, 1985.

———, "Accounting for Certain Investments in Debt and Equity Securities," Statement of Financial Accounting Standards No. 115. FASB, Norwalk, CT, 1993.

———, "Disclosures about Segments of an Enterprise and Related Information," Statement of Financial Accounting Standards No. 131. FASB, Stamford, CT, 1997.

———, "Disclosure of Information about Capital Structure," Statement of Financial Accounting Standards No. 129. FASB, Stamford, CT, 1997.

———, "Earnings Per Share," Statement of Financial Accounting Standards No. 128. FASB, Stamford, CT, 1997.

———, "Related Party Disclosures," Statement of Financial Accounting Standards No. 57. FASB, Stamford, CT, 1982.

———, "Statement of Cash Flows," Statement of Financial Accounting Standards No. 95. FASB, Stamford, CT, 1987.

———, "Suspension of the Reporting of Earnings Per Share and Segment Information by Nonpublic Enterprises," Statement of Financial Accounting Standards No. 21. FASB, Stamford, CT, 1978.

CHAPTER 11

INCOME STATEMENT PRESENTATION AND EARNINGS PER SHARE

Juan Aguerrebere, Jr., CPA
Perez Abreu, Aguerrebere, Sueiro LLC

11.1 OFFICIAL PRONOUNCEMENTS ON INCOME STATEMENT PRESENTATION

An enterprise reports its results of operations in a set of financial statements that includes an income statement. The format of the income statement and its components of income have been the subject of controversy, and as a result numerous pronouncements of professional accounting bodies have addressed related issues. For the most part the central issues discussed in these pronouncements involve the distinction between normal recurring items of profit and loss and other items that affect the determination of income.

One such pronouncement, Accounting Principles Board (APB) Opinion No. 9, "Reporting the Results of Operations," states that net income reported on an income statement should reflect all items of profit and loss recognized during the period with the exception of prior period adjustments. The APB also refined the appropriate reporting format in APB Opinion No. 30, "Reporting the Results of Operations—Reporting the Effects of Disposal of a Segment of a Business, and Extraordinary, Unusual and Infrequently Occurring Events and Transactions." Both of these Opinions required that extraordinary items, as defined in Section 6.3, be segregated from the results of continuing and ordinary operations of the entity. Opinion No. 30 expanded the categories to be segregated from continuing and ordinary operations by specifying the treatment of discontinued operations and unusual or infrequently occurring items.

11.2 DISCONTINUED OPERATIONS

In general, the term *discontinued operations* refers to the operations of a "segment of a business" which has been or is planned to be abandoned or otherwise disposed of. The term *segment of a business* is defined as a component of an entity whose operations encompass a separate major line of business or class of customer. A component can be a subsidiary, division, joint venture, or unconsolidated investee. This definition of segment of a business should not be confused with the use of the term *segment* in Statement of Financial Accounting Standards (SFAS) No. 14, "Financial Reporting for Segments of a Business Enterprise."

(a) MEASUREMENT DATE.   The component should be reported as discontinued during the first reporting period in which management having the requisite authority commits itself to a formal plan of disposal. This is referred to as the *measurement date*. Once the decision to dispose of the component has been made, the component's operating results prior to the measurement date should be presented on the income statement as a separate category before extraordinary items. Any financial statements for a prior period, presented for comparative purposes, should be restated to conform to this presentation.

The formal plan of disposal should include (1) an identification of the major assets to be disposed, (2) the expected method of disposal, (3) the expected period required to complete the disposal, which should generally be within 12 months of the plan's adoption, (4) an estimate of the results of operations from the measurement date to the disposal date (phase-out period), and (5) the estimated proceeds to be realized by disposal.

(b) DISPOSAL DATE.   The *disposal date* is the closing date if a sale is contemplated. Any gain or loss on the actual disposal of the segment, combined with the operating results of the discontinued operations, should be disclosed separately on the face of the income statement or in a note. Income taxes applicable to both items should also be disclosed on the face of the income statement or in a note to the financial statements.

(c) EXAMPLES OF DISCONTINUED OPERATIONS.   APB Opinion No. 30 states that the discontinuance of a part of a segment of a business, that is the phasing out of a product line or class of service, or a shift in production or marketing emphasis or location is incidental to the evolution of an entity and, accordingly, does not qualify for treatment as a discontinued operation. Although in theory the criteria may seem straightforward, accountants have had difficulty interpreting these broad criteria in practice. Recognizing this difficulty, the American Institute of Certified Public Accountants (AICPA) issued "Accounting Interpretation of APB Opinion No. 30" in November 1973 to provide guidance on the classifications found in Opinion No. 30. The interpretations provide the following examples as situations that qualify as discontinued operations:

1. The sale of a major division that represents an entity's only activity in a specific industry; the assets and results of operations of the division are clearly separable.
2. The sale by a meat-packing company of a 25 percent interest in a professional ball club that they had accounted for under the equity method.
3. The sale by a communications company of all its radio stations (constituting 30 percent of total consolidated revenues). The remaining activities are television stations and a publishing company. The assets and results of operations of the radio station are clearly separable both physically and operationally.
4. The disposal by a food distributor of one of its two food divisions, which use significantly different channels of distribution. One division sells food wholesale primarily to supermarket chains, and the other division sells food through its chain of fast food restaurants, some of which are franchised and some of which are company-owned. Although both divisions are in the business of distribution of food, the sale of food through fast food outlets is vastly different in nature from wholesaling food to supermarket chains. Thus, by having two major classes of customers, the company has two segments of business.

(d) RECORDING DISCONTINUED OPERATIONS.   The method of recording the discontinuation or disposition of a business segment is determined by whether there is a gain or a loss. A gain should be recognized when it is realized, usually at the disposal date. Losses, on the other hand, should be anticipated and recorded at the measurement date. The gain or loss on disposal is calculated at the measurement date, using estimates of the results of operations during the phaseout period. The APB was concerned that the gain or loss on disposal could conceal normal write-downs on a going-concern basis, for example, inventory or receivable adjustments. Thus it stated that such write-downs should be included in results of operations prior to the measurement date unless clearly and directly associated with the disposal decision. The Emerging Issues Task Force (EITF) in Issue No. 85-36, "Discontinued Operations with Expected Gain and Interim Operating Losses," considered the need for clarification of APB Opinion No. 30 and the related interpretations thereof in accounting for any expected losses from the measurement date to the disposal date when a gain on disposal was expected. The Task Force consensus stated that estimated losses from operations should only be deferred until the disposal date if there is reasonable assurance that a net gain will be realized. The Task Force also reached consensus on two underlying issues. The first consensus applied the previous consensus to sales that do not meet the criteria of a segment. Second, it stated that all multiple disposals of segments under the same formal plan should be reported as a combined amount. However, if the criteria for discontinued segments are not met, these disposals, such as a portion of a line of business, should not be combined.

(e) ACCOUNTING FOR DISCONTINUED OPERATIONS SUBSEQUENTLY RETAINED.

The EITF, "Accounting for Discontinued Operations Subsequently Retained" in Issue 90-16, considered a situation in which a company decides to dispose of a segment of its business in accordance with APB No. 30. In accruing the loss on disposition of the segment, the company wrote down assets to net realizable value. The assets would not have been treated as impaired and no loss would have been accrued if the company had not decided to discontinue the operations of that segment. In the next period, management decided to retain the segment. The following accounting issues are present:

- Issue 1—Should any of the accrued losses on writing down the segment to net realizable value be reversed now that the segment is no longer being discontinued?
- Issue 2—Should the financial statements of the prior period be restated or reclassified as a result of the subsequent decision to retain the business segment?

The EITF reached a consensus that the remaining estimated accrued loss should be reversed in the period the company decides to retain the business segment. The portion of the prior period loss related to actual operations of the business in the prior period should not be reversed. There is to be continual evaluation of the business segment following impairment guidelines as practiced by the company, and any individual asset impairments are to be classified as continuing operations.

The EITF concluded that the reversal is not an error and the prior periods should not be restated. However, the business segment's results of operations reported in prior periods should be reclassified from discontinued to continuing operations. The remaining estimated accrued loss should continue to be reported as discontinued segments in the prior period financial statement. In the current reporting period, continuing operations should include current period operating results of the segment. The remaining unaccrued loss should be reversed as part of discontinued operations.

For those filing with the Securities and Exchange Commission, the observer called for the following six additional disclosures:

1. Reason for reversal of decision
2. Total segment assets, liabilities, revenues, and operating results of the segment previously reported as discontinued
3. Amount of loss recognized when the segment was recorded at net realizable value and basis for calculation
4. Disclosure of impairment losses recorded by business segment (Losses due to asset impairment must be classified before income from continuing operations.)

5. Disclosure of amount and components of amounts of accrued losses subsequently reversed

6. Management discussion and analysis (MD&A)

(f) ALLOCATION OF COSTS AND EXPENSES. The EITF also considered the questions of whether interest or general corporate overhead could be allocated to a discontinued operation. The Task Force reached a consensus that general corporate overhead may not be allocated. Interest may be allocated, although it is not required to be allocated. If interest is allocated, the calculation of the method to be used is described in EITF Issue No. 87-24, "Allocation of Interest to Discontinued Operations." The SEC observer indicated that public companies must clearly disclose the accounting policy to allocate interest, the method used to determine the amount of interest allocated and the amount allocated to premeasurement date, and estimated predisposal date periods.

(g) DISCLOSURE OF DISCONTINUED OPERATIONS. Certain disclosures are required for the periods from the measurement date to the disposal date:

- Identification of the discontinued segment
- Expected disposal date and manner of disposal (sale or abandonment)
- Remaining assets and liabilities of segment at the balance sheet date
- Results of operations and any proceeds from disposal of the segment during the period from the measurement date to the balance sheet date (and a comparison with any prior estimates)

Disclosure of per share data, although not separately required for discontinued operations, is commonly given on the face of the income statement or in the notes.

In the Staff Accounting Bulletin (SAB) 93, "Accounting and Disclosure Regarding Discontinued Operations," the SEC considered seven clarification issues with respect to discontinued operations: (1) the method of disposal is not determined, (2) the disposal plan requires more than one year to complete, (3) accounting for the abandonment of a business segment, (4) disposal of an operation with significant interest retained, (5) classification and disclosure of contingencies relating to discontinued operations, (6) accounting for subsidiaries that management intends to sell, and (7) accounting for the spin-off of a subsidiary.

(i) Method of Disposal Not Determined. The SEC considered the circumstances where an entity adopts and announces a plan to discontinue a segment but has not determined the manner by which certain material operations will be discontinued (sale, spin-off, or liquidation). The SAB indicates that in such circumstances paragraph 14 of APB 30 has not been complied with since the "expected method of disposal . . . and the expected proceeds or salvage to be realized by disposal" are not known.

(ii) Plan of Disposal Requiring More than One Year. Where there are multiple sales of assets or divisions contemplated under a plan of disposal, all such sales should occur within one year. The SEC believes that to qualify under paragraphs 15–17 of APB 30 for classification outside of continuing operations, the plan of disposal must contemplate the consummation of the disposal of all portions of the business segment within 12 months of the plan's adoption. The staff of the SEC believes that the accounting estimates needed under accounting for a discontinued operation cannot be developed with sufficient reliability if projections beyond 12 months from the plan's adoption are required.

(iii) Accounting for Abandonment of a Business Segment. If a company adopts a plan of discontinuance but is required by contract or regulation to continue to provide services for periods remaining under existing contracts which may exceed one year, discontinued operation accounting may be appropriate. The staff will not object if discontinued accounting is used when the company will not accept new business (other than it is required to do under existing contracts or regulations) within 12 months of a plan's adoption. The operating results of the segment through final termination must be estimable with reasonably accuracy.

(iv) Disposal of Operation with Significant Interest Retained.   When a company sells a majority interest in a segment but retains an interest sufficient to require equity accounting under APB 18, discontinued accounting is not appropriate. The staff believes that the transaction should be accounted for as a disposal of a portion of a line of business.

(v) Classification and Disclosure of Contingencies Relating to Discontinued Operations.
If a company had appropriately accounted for the disposal of a segment in a previous year, but had continuing obligations under the contract so that estimates were required, revisions of those estimates are to be classified as discontinued operations as indicated in paragraph 25 of APB 30. However, the staff believes that any changes in the carrying value of assets received in the exchange as consideration should be classified within continuing operations.

(vi) Accounting for Subsidiaries That Management Intends to Sell.   When a company plans to sell a segment but discontinued accounting is not yet appropriate, the company cannot deconsolidate the segment under the view that control is temporary under SFAS 94. The staff believes that the concept of control as indicated in SFAS 94 does not encompass planned sales. The concept of temporary control is intended to encompass events that are outside the control of the entity.

(vii) Accounting for the Spin-Off of a Subsidiary.   If a company spins off a subsidiary, it should not ordinarily account for the transaction by restating previous financial statements as a change in entity under paragraph 30 of APB 20, as if the company never had an investment in the subsidiary. In limited circumstances involving an initial public offering (IPO), the staff has not objected to such accounting if the spin-off was completed prior to the effectiveness of the offering and certain conditions are met.

11.3 EXTRAORDINARY ITEMS

An extraordinary item is an event or transaction that meets two criteria: It must be both unusual in nature and infrequent in occurrence. Otherwise, an event or transaction is generally presumed to be either an ordinary or a usual activity of the entity. Being either unusual in nature or infrequent in occurrence does not qualify it as an extraordinary item [see Subsection 11.3(e)].

(a) UNUSUAL NATURE.   As mentioned above, the first criteria an item must meet to be considered extraordinary is to be unusual. The underlying event or transaction should be clearly unrelated to the ordinary and typical activities of the entity. This definition encompasses the specific characteristics of the entity, including, for example, the industry in which it operates, the geographical location of its operations, and the extent of government regulation. Thus an event or transaction may be unusual for one industry but normal for another.

(b) INFREQUENTLY OCCURRING.   The second criterion for an extraordinary item to meet is that the event or transaction is not reasonably expected to recur in the foreseeable future and is not considered to be frequently occurring. This definition considers the same features as items of unusual nature, such as industry, geographical location, and government regulation. Thus this criterion may be met by one company whereas the same underlying event would not be infrequent to another company. Past history of the company provides evidence to assess the probability of recurrence of an event.

(c) APPLICATION OF CRITERIA.   Certain gains and losses are, by definition (APB Opinion No. 30, par. 23), considered not extraordinary items, such as:

- Write-down of receivables, inventories, equipment leased to others, or intangible assets
- Gains or losses from foreign exchange transactions or translations (including major devaluations and revaluations)

- Gains or losses on the disposal of a segment of a business (discontinued operations)
- Gains or losses from the sale or abandonment of property, plant, or equipment used in a business
- Effects of a strike (including an indirect effect such as a strike against a major supplier)
- Adjustment of accruals on long-term contracts

Only in rare instances may an event or transaction included in first and fourth bullets above clearly meet the criteria and be included in extraordinary items. Such instances would occur if the gain or loss on such an event or transaction is the direct result of a major casualty, an expropriation, or a prohibition under a newly enacted law.

(d) EXCEPTIONS TO CRITERIA.   Some items that apparently would not meet the criteria of an extraordinary item must be classified as such under existing authoritative literature. Two such items that fit this description are gains and losses on extinguishment of debt as cited in SFAS No. 4, "Reporting Gains and Losses from Extinguishment of Debt," and gain on the restructuring of debt in a troubled situation as discussed in SFAS No. 15, "Accounting by Debtors and Creditors for Troubled Debt Restructurings." The accounting and reporting for extinguishments and troubled debt restructurings are discussed in Chapter 20.

(e) REPORTING AN EXTRAORDINARY ITEM.   The effect of an extraordinary item should be segregated if its effect is material to income before extraordinary items, to the trend in earnings before extraordinary items, or to other appropriate criteria. The materiality of individual events or transactions is considered separately and not aggregated unless the effects result from a single identifiable transaction or event that meets the criteria of an extraordinary item. The preference expressed in APB Opinion No. 30 is for individual descriptive captions and amounts for each extraordinary event or transaction on the face of the income statement. However, disclosure in the notes to financial statements describing the nature of the event or transaction comprising the extraordinary item and the principal items entering the calculation of the gain or loss is acceptable. The extraordinary item should be shown net of applicable income taxes.

Per share amounts for income before extraordinary items and net income should be given on the face of the income statement. There is no requirement to give the per share amount of the extraordinary items, but such disclosure is common.

11.4 MATERIAL GAINS AND LOSSES—UNUSUAL OR INFREQUENTLY OCCURRING, NOT EXTRAORDINARY

A material event or transaction that is either unusual or infrequently occurring, but not both, is by definition not an extraordinary item. Material gains or losses of this nature should be shown separately on the face of the income statement as a component of income from continuing operations. These items are not shown net of tax, nor is per share disclosure permitted on the face of the income statement. However, note disclosure may be given that presents the item net of tax and discloses the per share effects. The discussion that follows covers four special items and their reporting: disposal of part of a segment, restructuring charges, takeover defense, and sale of stock by a subsidiary.

(a) DISPOSAL OF PART OF A SEGMENT OF A BUSINESS.   The gain or loss on the disposal of part of a segment of a business is not an extraordinary item or a discontinued operation. Thus it may be reported as a separate component of continuing operations. The measurement principles used to calculate gain or loss on disposal are described in paragraph 15 of SFAS No. 121, "Accounting for the Impairment of Long-Lived Assets and for Long-Lived Assets to Be Disposed Of." Unlike the disposal of a segment, a company is not permitted to accrue expected operating losses when a commitment date is reached to dispose of part of a segment. The results of operations prior to the measurement date should not, however, be shown separately on the income statement. This information may be disclosed in the notes to financial statements along with per share data.

Some examples of situations not qualifying as discontinued operations that were also given in the interpretations of APB Opinion No. 30 are:

- Sale of a major subsidiary in one country by an entity that has other activities in the same industry in other countries
- Sale of an interest in an equity investee in the same line of business as the investor
- Sale of assets related to the manufacture of wool suits when the entity manufactures suits from synthetic products elsewhere (considered only product line disposal)

(b) RESTRUCTURING CHARGES.   During the middle to late 1980s, enterprises began to restructure their operations. These corporate restructurings involved sales of equipment or facilities, severance of employees, and relocation of operations. The EITF considered the income statement presentation (ordinary or extraordinary) of such restructurings but was unable to reach a consensus in EITF Issue No. 86-22, "Display of Business Restructuring Provisions in the Income Statement." It only stated that entities should use their own judgment. The SEC subsequently addressed this issue in SAB No. 67, "Income Statement Presentation of Restructuring Charges," issued in December 1986. The SEC position stated that restructuring charges should be shown as a component of continuing operations and separately disclosed if material. Since Staff Accounting Bulletins (SABs) do not apply to nonpublic companies, the EITF considered in Issue No. 87-4, "Restructuring of Operations: Implications of SEC Staff Accounting Bulletin No. 67," whether the SEC position was GAAP for nonpublic companies. The Task Force indicated that following the SAB provisions is not required for nonpublic enterprises to be in accordance with GAAP. The Task Force agreed that consistent with its views expressed in Issue No. 86-22, nonpublic companies should exercise judgment in selecting the most meaningful income statement presentation.

The SEC observer later provided clarification of the extent of SAB No. 67, such as:

- SAB No. 67 was not intended to address the presentation of a simple sale of assets or a portion of a line of business.
- The SAB restates the position of the SEC observer that showing "earnings from operations before provisions for restructuring of operations," which is acceptable under EITF Issue No. 86-22, is not acceptable for SEC registrants.

In the early 1990s, companies were reporting restructuring charges on an increasing basis. Restructuring charges as reported comprised various broad types of expenses. Restructuring charges included costs of severance and termination, costs to eliminate or consolidate product lines, costs to close or relocate operations or plants, costs to restrain employees to use newly developed systems, and losses on impairment or disposal of assets. In EITF Issue 94-3, "Liability Recognition for Certain Employee Termination Benefits and Other Costs to Exit an Activity Including Certain Costs Incurred in a Restructuring," the Task Force reached the following tentative conclusions.

a. *A liability for employee termination benefits* should be recognized when management approves the plan if all the following conditions exist:

  1. Prior to the date of the financial statements, management with the appropriate authority to involuntarily terminate employees approves and commits the company to the plan (termination plan) that establishes the benefits to be received upon termination.

  2. Prior to the date of the financial statements, the plan and benefit arrangements are communicated to employees in sufficient detail to enable affected employees to calculate their benefits.

  3. The plan specifies the number of employees, job classification, or function and their location.

4. The period of time to complete the plan of termination indicates that significant changes are not likely. The foregoing provisions do not apply to termination benefits paid as part of the disposal of a segment, pursuant to an ongoing benefit plan, or under the terms of a defined compensation contract.

b. Costs that have no future economic benefit should be accrued on the commitment date. The commitment date is the date when all the following conditions are met.

1. Management with the appropriate authority commits the company to the exit plan.

2. The plan identifies all actions to be taken (i.e., activities to be continued or closed/sold, including method of disposition and expected date of plan completion).

3. Actions required to implement the plan begin as soon as possible after the commitment date, and the period of time to complete the plan indicates that changes to the plan are not likely.

The costs to be recognized under the exit plan can have no future benefit to continued operations. Costs meeting this requirement should be recognized at the commitment date if they are not associated with or are not incurred to generate revenues after the commitment date of the exit plan and meet either criterion (1) or (2) below.

1. The cost is incremental to other costs incurred prior to the commitment date and is incurred as a direct result of the exit plan.

2. The costs will be incurred under a contractual commitment existing prior to the commitment date and will not economically benefit the company.

Costs should be recorded when they are reasonably estimable. Any unrecognized costs should be recorded when they can be reasonably estimated.

Results of operations after the commitment date are not exit costs. Costs to sell assets under the exit plan are also not exit costs. Costs not qualifying as exit costs should not be recognized at the commitment date but when an obligation is actually incurred.

The EITF Issue 94-3 has significant disclosure requirements and also provides many examples to illustrate applications of its provisions.

(c) TAKEOVER DEFENSE. A question created by the takeover surge is the appropriate presentation of takeover defense expenses on the income statement. The FASB issued Financial Technical Bulletin (FTB) No. 85-6, which makes the following two statements:

1. A company should not classify the cost to defend itself from a takeover or the costs attributable to a "standstill" agreement as an extraordinary item.

2. If a company repurchases shares for a price significantly in excess of current market from an unwanted suitor, it must include stated or unstated rights. Accordingly, only the amount representing fair value should be accounted for as the cost of Treasury shares, any excess should be accounted for according to its substance, presumably charged to expense. The SEC has stated that in applying FTB No. 85-6 quoted market represents fair value; use of appraised values that differ from public market values is not acceptable.

(d) SALES OF STOCK BY A SUBSIDIARY. Prior to the issuance in 1983 of SAB No. 51, "Accounting for Sales of Stock by a Subsidiary," most parent companies had accounted for the effects on its equity in the subsidiary of a sale of additional stock by a subsidiary as a capital transaction. In SAB No. 51, the SEC indicated that it had reconsidered this position where the sale of such shares by the subsidiary is not part of a broader corporate reorganization. The SEC, in its reconsideration, stated that it accepts the advisory conclusions of the AICPA issues paper "Accounting in Consolidation for Issuances of a Subsidiary's Stock," which indicates that profit or loss should be recognized in these situations. The SEC concluded that if gains (losses) are recognized from issuances of a subsidiary's stock as income statement items, they should be shown as a separate line item (without regard for materiality) and clearly designated as nonoperating. Subsequently SAB No. 81, "Gain Recognition on the Sale of a Business or Operating Assets to a Highly Leveraged Entity," was issued in 1989, indicating that gain recognition may not be appropriate where a subsidiary is sold to a highly leveraged entity. Further, SAB No. 84, "Accounting for Sales of Stock by a Subsidiary," which was also issued in 1989, gives additional guidance on recognizing a sale of stock by a subsidiary as a gain.

The income statement treatment in consolidation of gains or losses for the sale of stock by a subsidiary represents a choice among acceptable accounting methods and, once chosen, should be applied consistently to all stock transactions for any subsidiary that meet the conditions for income statement treatment. In SAB 84, the staff also deals with other interpretation matters, such as what constitutes a broader corporate reorganization.

The Financial Accounting Standards Board has exposure drafts under consideration that will affect accounting for guarantees and consolidation of special purpose entities. On final approval, the proposed exposure drafts will affect the accounting and income statement presentation for these areas.

11.5 ACCOUNTING CHANGES

The FASB stated in SFAS No. 154 "Accounting Changes and Error Corrections," that:

> A presumption exists that an accounting principle once adopted shall not be changed in accounting for events and transactions of a similar type. Consistent use of the same accounting principle from one accounting period to another enhances the utility of financial statements for users by facilitating analysis and understanding of comparative accounting data.

FASB No. 154 defines the term *accounting change* to mean "a change in (1) an accounting principle, (2) an accounting estimate, or (3) the reporting entity. The correction of an error in previously issued financial statements is not an accounting change."

(a) GENERAL CHANGES IN ACCOUNTING PRINCIPLE.   A change in accounting principle involves the adoption of a generally accepted accounting principle different from the one previously used for reporting purposes. Thus a change in accounting principle involves a choice among two or more generally accepted accounting principles and the method of applying the chosen principle. It does not include (1) initial adoption of an accounting principle to report first-time or previously immaterial events or transactions, or (2) adoption or modification of an accounting principle because of events or transactions that are clearly different in substance from previously occurring events or transactions.

SFAS No. 154 provides that an entity should change an accounting principle only if the change is required by a newly issued accounting pronouncement or the entity can justify its use based on the basis that it is preferable.

(b) ACCOUNTING FOR CHANGES IN ACCOUNTING PRINCIPLE.   An accounting change should be reported through retrospective application of the new principle to all prior periods, unless it is unpractical to do so. Retrospective application involves the following:

a. The cumulative effect of the change on periods prior to those presented shall be presented as adjustments to carrying values of the assets and liabilities as of the beginning of the first period presented.

b. An offsetting adjustment, if any, to the opening balance of retained earnings.

c. Financial statements for each individual prior period presented shall be adjusted to reflect the effects of applying the new principle.

Sometimes it is not practical to determine the cumulative effect of applying a change in accounting principle to all prior periods presented. In such cases, the new accounting principle should be applied to the carrying amounts of the assets and liabilities as of the beginning of the earliest period to which the new principle can practically be applied. Finally, if it is impractical to determine the cumulative effect on any prior period, the new accounting principle shall be applied prospectively to the current and future periods.

(i) Impracticability of Determining Effects.   SFAS No. 154 indicates that it should be consider impractical to apply the effects of a change in accounting principle retrospectively only if one of the following conditions exist:

    a. After making every reasonable effort to do so, you are unable to apply the requirement.

    b. Retrospective application requires assumptions about management's intent in a prior period that cannot be independently substantiated.

    c. Retrospective application requires significant estimates of amounts, and it is impossible to distinguish objectively information about those estimates that (1) provides evidence about circumstances that existed on the date(s) at which those amounts would arise under retrospective application, and (2) would have been available when the financial statements for that prior period were issued.

(ii) Direct and Indirect Effects.   SFAS 154 requires that the entity include in the restated periods only the direct effects of a change in accounting principle, including any related income tax effects. Indirect effects, such as changes profit sharing or royalty payments, should not be recognized in restated periods. Instead, such amounts should be recognized in the period the change is made.

(c) CHANGES IN ACCOUNTING ESTIMATE.   Changes in accounting estimates are a normal part of the operations of an entity, and the estimation of the effects of future events is an inherent part of preparing financial statements. Accounting estimates involve the judgments that management of the entity must make concerning incomplete transactions or events on the basis of the information presently available. Obviously these estimates change as new or better information becomes available or new events occur. Examples of items that require estimates are (1) uncollectible receivables, (2) inventory obsolescence, (3) service lives and salvage value of depreciable assets, (4) warranty costs, (5) amortization period of deferred charges, and (6) recoverable mineral reserves.

Changes in estimates are sometimes difficult for the accountant to distinguish from an accounting principle change as they cannot clearly be classified as either one or the other. For example, a change from deferral and amortization of an expense item to expensing as incurred, when the future benefits of the deferred item are doubtful, may have been made in partial or complete recognition of a change in estimated future benefits. Such changes in principle that are inseparable from changes in estimate are treated as changes in estimate.

The effects, if material, of a change in estimate on income from continuing operations and net income (including per share amounts) for the current year and for future years, if applicable, should be disclosed in a note describing the change. A change in estimate should not be accounted for retroactively or by reporting pro forma amounts. Disclosure of changes in estimates made in the ordinary course of business (e.g., uncollectible receivables, percentage complete on long-term contracts, or inventory obsolescence) is not required; however, it is recommended if the effect of a change in estimate is material.

(d) CHANGES IN REPORTING ENTITY.   A change in reporting entity is a change in accounting principle. This type of change results in financial statements of a different reporting entity and usually is limited mainly to (1) presenting consolidated or combined financial statements in place of financial statements of individual reporting entities, (2) changing specific subsidiaries or companies included in the financial statements of the consolidated or combined group of companies, and (3) changing among cost, equity, and consolidation methods of accounting for subsidiaries or other investments in common stock. The financial statements for the period of a change in reporting entity should disclose the nature and reason for the change and the effect on income before extraordinary items and net income (including per share amounts). A change in reporting entity due to a pooling of interests should be reported as provided in APB Opinion No. 16, "Business Combinations." In June 2001, the FASB issued SFAS No. 141, "Business Combinations." SFAS No. 141 requires that all business combinations be accounted for by using the purchase method of accounting. The provisions of SFAS No. 141 apply to all business combinations initiated after June 30, 2001. SFAS No. 141 also applies to all business combinations accounted for using the purchase method for which the date of acquisition is July 1, 2001, or later.

(e) CORRECTION OF AN ERROR.   Although not an accounting change, the correction of an error in previously issued financial statements involves factors similar to those encountered in reporting a change in accounting principle. Errors arise from (1) mathematical mistakes, (2) oversight or misuse of facts existing at the time when financial statements are prepared, and (3) mistakes in the application of accounting principles, including a change from an unacceptable accounting principle to a generally accepted accounting principle.

Corrections of errors should be reported as prior period adjustments (see Section 11.6). The nature of the error and the effect on income before extraordinary items and net income (including per share amounts) should be disclosed in the period when the error was discovered and corrected.

(f) MATERIALITY.   Materiality, applicable to accounting changes and corrections of errors, is considered in relation to both the effects of individual changes and the aggregate effect of all changes. A change or correction may be material to (1) income before extraordinary items or net income of the current year, or (2) the trend in earnings. In both cases the disclosures referred to above should be made. If the change or correction is not material according to these criteria but is reasonably certain to have a material effect in later periods, disclosure of the change or correction should be made whenever the period of change is presented. SAB No. 40 stated that, if prior periods' income statements are not restated because the amounts are immaterial, the cumulative effect of the change should be included in the determination of income for the period in which the change was made. However, if the cumulative effect is material to the current period's income, or to the trend in earnings, prior period income statements would have to be adjusted.

(g) DISCLOSURES REQUIRED FOR ACCOUNTING CHANGES.   The following disclosures are required when an entity effects a change in accounting principle:

1. The nature and reason for the change, including an explanation of why the new principle is preferable
2. The effect of the change on income from continuing operations, net income, any other affected financial statement line item, and any affected per-share amounts for the current period and any prior periods retrospectively adjusted
3. The cumulative effect of the change on retained earnings or other components of equity or net assets as of the beginning of the earliest period presented
4. If retrospective application to all periods is impracticable, disclosure of the reasons therefore, and a description of the method used for the change
5. If indirect effects of a change are recognized, the financial statements should disclose (1) a description of the indirect effects including the amounts that have been recognized in the current period, and (2) if practicable, the amount of the total recognized indirect effects of the accounting change that are attributable to each prior period presented

(h) PREFERABILITY LETTER. The first Form 10-Q, quarterly financial statements, filed with the SEC subsequent to an accounting change, must include a preferability letter prepared by the company's accountants. A preferability letter for a change made in the fourth quarter of the fiscal year may be submitted in the company's annual report on Form 10-K. If this is not done, the preferability letter must be submitted when filing the next Form 10-Q.

Disclosure of a change in accounting principle should include an explanation of why the new accounting principle is preferable. Auditing standards require that the accountant assess the reasonableness of management's justification for the change in accounting principle before concurring. In FRR No. 1 (ASR No. 177), the SEC issued requirements beyond those specified in professional standards. By amending Form 10-Q, FRR No. 1 (ASR No. 177) requires the accountant to issue a letter indicating whether the newly adopted accounting principle is preferable under the circumstances. A letter need not be issued, however, if the change in accounting principle was mandated by the FASB or another authoritative standards setter such as AcSEC or EITF.

11.6 PRIOR PERIOD ADJUSTMENTS

Corrections of errors should be reported as prior period adjustments, as specified in paragraph 10 of SFAS No. 16, "Prior Period Adjustments," as amended by SFAS No. 109. The disclosure of their effects, both gross and net of taxes, on net income of prior periods is required in the financial statements for the year of the adjustment. Disclosure of the effects on each prior period presented and on per share earnings are also required.

In the deliberations leading to the issuance in 1977 of SFAS No. 16, questions arose as to the statement's applicability to interim as well as annual financial statements. The FASB concluded that certain practices regarding interim information and prior period adjustments should be continued and others should be discontinued. A section entitled "Adjustments Related to Prior Interim Periods of the Current Fiscal Year" was included in SFAS No. 16. Interim reporting is covered in Chapter 13.

11.7 REPORTING OF UNUSUAL EVENTS AND TRANSACTIONS

The following listings should provide guidance to accountants in the reporting of events and transactions as extraordinary, or material gains and losses not considered extraordinary, and accounting changes. The reporting of these items requires considerable judgment.

A listing for discontinued operations is not presented because the reporting of this type of event does not vary in practice. Furthermore, the issuance of SFAS No. 16 has restricted the type of items to be reported as prior period adjustments to the extent that such a listing is not necessary.

The primary source used to obtain this listing is: *Accounting Trends and Techniques* (AICPA, 1994).

Extraordinary Items

Adjustment of prior period extraordinary item	Expropriation
Debt extinguishments	Major casualties (fire)

Material Gains and Losses Not Considered Extraordinary

Diminished value of assets	Partial closing of operation facility
Discontinuance of part of a business	Plant relocation expenses
Environmental claims	Restructuring charges
Excess insurance proceeds	Retirement plans expense
Gain/loss from sale of assets	Settlement of claims
Gain on sale of equity interest	Strike expense
Litigation settlement	Takeover defense

Accounting Changes	
Change in depreciation method	Computational error
Change in method of determining inventory costs	Subsequent discovery of facts existing at date of accountants' report
Change from the full-cost method to successful efforts method of oil and gas properties	*Change in Reporting Entity*
Change from LIFO method to FIFO method of inventory valuation	*Effects impractical to determine*
Change to conform to FASB statements that require or permit retroactive restatement	Change from FIFO cost to LIFO method inventory valuation
	Change in depreciation method for new assets only
Correction of an Error	
Change from unacceptable principle to GAAP	*Change in Estimate*
	Of allowance for doubtful accounts
	Of depreciable lives
	Of income taxes
	Of restructuring costs

11.8 SEC INCOME STATEMENT PRESENTATION REQUIREMENTS FOR SPECIFIC INDUSTRIES

(a) RETAIL COMPANIES.   The SEC expressed its views in SAB No. 1 (codified in 1981 in SAB No. 40) on including leased or licensed departments' revenues in the caption "Total revenues," as is common in the financial statements of department stores. The SEC stated that this practice is acceptable but the amounts should be disclosed separately in the income statement or notes thereto. Further, the service fee income from finance subsidiaries of retail companies should be separately disclosed in the income statement or a note.

(b) UTILITIES.   SFAS No. 90 "*Regulated Enterprises—Accounting for Abandonments and Disallowances of Plant Costs*," issued in 1986, implies that a utility must charge a portion of the cost of an abandoned power plant to expense. In addition, any costs of a completed plant expected to be disallowed should also be charged to expense. The SEC was asked if these charges could be shown as extraordinary. The SEC responded in SAB No. 72, "*Classification of Charges for Abandonments and Disallowances*," issued in 1987, that these costs do not meet the criteria of APB Opinion No. 30 for unusual and infrequently occurring and should be shown as part of continuing operations.

(c) CASINO-HOTELS.   In 1987, the SEC stated in SAB No. 69, "*Income Statement Presentation*," that registrants having casino and hotel operations should show the income from these operations separately. Thus, casino, hotel, and restaurant operations are commonly disclosed separately. In June 1997, the FASB issued SFAS No. 131, "*Disclosures about Segments of an Enterprise and Related Information.*" SFAS No. 131 requires public enterprises to report certain information about operating segments in complete sets of financial statements of public enterprises and in condensed financial statements of their interim reporting periods. It also requires public enterprises to report certain information about their products and services, the geographic areas in which they operate, and their major customers. SFAS No. 131 requires general-purpose financial statements to include selected information reported based on a single segment. SFAS No. 131 requires that an enterprise report a measure of segment profit or loss and certain items included in determining segment profit or loss, segment assets, and certain related items. The reported information should correspond with the periods presented in the income statement of the public enterprise.

11.9 REPORTING COMPREHENSIVE INCOME

The FASB (the Board) was urged to address concerns of various users of financial statements regarding the practice of reporting some comprehensive income items directly within a balance sheet equity component. To promote harmonization of international standards, the FASB also discussed the concept of comprehensive income with various international accounting standards setting organizations. After exposing the FASB's tentative conclusions in this area, the Board issued FASB No. 130, "Reporting Comprehensive Income," in June 1997. This standard supplements and adds to but does not modify the previous discussion on income statement presentation.

(a) DEFINITION AND SCOPE. The Statement establishes standards for reporting and display of comprehensive income and its components. The scope of this standard covers all enterprises that provide a full set of financial statements (financial position, results of operations, and cash flows). The provisions of the statement need not be followed by enterprises that do not have any elements of comprehensive income in any period presented nor by not-for-profit entities reporting under statement No. 117, "Financial Statements of Not-For Profit Organizations." Publicly held enterprises are required to apply this statement in externally reported summarized data or financial statements.

Thus, U.S. generally accepted accounting principles generally follow the all-inclusive concept of reporting (i.e., all items of income and expense flow through the income statement). In prior standards, certain specific exceptions to the all-inclusive income concept were made. Certain items that reflect changes in assets or liabilities were not reported in the income statement but were shown as a separate component of equity (i.e., items of foreign currency translation). The statement adopts the definition of comprehensive income used in concepts statement 6: "the change in equity [net assets] of a business enterprise during a period from transactions and other events and circumstances from nonowner sources. It includes all changes in equity during a period except those resulting from investments by owners and distributions to owners."

"Comprehensive income" is used to describe all components of comprehensive income including the results of operations. "Other comprehensive income" refers to those items that under GAAP are included in comprehensive income but not results of operations.

(b) PURPOSE. This standard was issued to better assist users of financial statements in gaining an understanding of and assessing an enterprise's activities and the timing and magnitude of cash flows. The FASB also believes that information on the separate components of comprehensive income needs to be disclosed to gain a more complete understanding of the enterprise's activities; accordingly, such disclosure of the components of comprehensive income is required.

(c) DISPLAY AND CLASSIFICATION. All components of comprehensive income are to be reported in the periods when recognized. The Board believes that information about the components of comprehensive income may be more important than the total amount of comprehensive income. Therefore, the statement divides comprehensive income into two broad captions, net income and other comprehensive income.

(i) Net Income. Previous standards that require reporting of income from continuing operations, discontinued operations, extraordinary items, and cumulative effects of changes in accounting principles are unchanged by this standard.

(ii) Other Comprehensive Income. Existing standards require separate classification of foreign currency items, minimum pension liability adjustments, and unrealized gains and losses on certain investments securities, are unchanged by this standard. The Board believes that leaving this requirement intact provides a familiar format for users of financial statements.

(iii) Reclassification Adjustments. Reclassification adjustments that arise because of the double counting of certain items as part of net income for a period that were previously displayed as part of other comprehensive income need to be separately shown. For example, securities gains realized in the current period could have previously been included as unrealized gains in a previous comprehensive income statement. Accordingly, these must be offset in the period in which they are shown in net income to avoid including them twice in comprehensive income. The presentation of reclassification adjustments may be disclosed gross on the face of financial statements or net on the financial statements with appropriate disclosure in the notes to financial statements. The Board decided that it was not practicable to calculate the adjustment for minimum pension liability; therefore, a net display should be used for this item.

(d) ALTERNATIVE FORMATS.   The Statement does not mandate a specific format for reporting comprehensive income. However, it does require that net income be separately displayed as a component of comprehensive income. Therefore, a one-statement approach or a two-statement approach may be used. These approaches are similar to current practice for displaying a statement of retained earnings. In addition, tax effects of the items displayed as elements of other comprehensive income may be shown either gross on the face of the statement or in notes to the financial statements. This treatment is similar to reclassification adjustments.

(e) OTHER ISSUES.   As a consequence of this change in display of other comprehensive income, the Board needed to consider its effects on other financial reporting criteria. Items such as reporting of prior period adjustments, statement of cash flows, other items reported in equity, and the reporting of equity investees needed to be considered.

(i) Prior Period Adjustments.   The Board concluded that the reporting and display of any prior period adjustments would not conflict with current reporting of comprehensive income because of the retroactive restatement provisions of prior period adjustments.

(ii) Statement of Cash Flows.   It is possible that use of either the indirect method or the direct method reconciliation of the operating section of the statement of cash flows would be affected if elements of comprehensive income were noncash items. The Board concluded that the cash flow statement should not be amended for the impact of any of these items since it would not substantively add informational content.

(iii) Other Items Reported in Equity.   The display of certain other items reported in equity were considered. The Board considered whether the display of deferred compensation expense arising from the issuance of shares before services are rendered (APB Opinion No. 25) or SFAS No. 123 or employee stock ownership plans (SOP 76-3) should be addressed in this statement. The Board concluded that these items have elements of both equity and expense characteristics, accordingly it was beyond the scope of the consideration of comprehensive income at this time and these items should be considered equity transactions. Similarly, taxes not payable due to reorganization accounting (SOP 90-7) gains and losses resulting from indexed contracts in company shares (EITF No. 94-7) should be considered as equity transactions.

(iv) Equity Investees.   If an equity investee displays items of other comprehensive income, the investor is permitted to combine its proportionate share of such amounts with its own comprehensive income items and display the aggregate amount regardless of which format is used.

11.10 EARNINGS PER SHARE

In 1993, the FASB decided to amend the existing accounting literature on computing "earnings per share (EPS)" as detailed in APB Opinion No. 15, as amended. Users of financial statements believed that Opinion No. 15 was complex and had arbitrary provisions. Further, most of the rest of the world followed the methodology issued by the International Accounting Standards Committee (IASC). Accordingly, to simplify the computation of EPS and to harmonize U.S. standards with international standards, FAS No. 128, "EPS" was issued, and concurrently the IASC issued IAS 33, "EPS," which was substantially the same provision as FAS No. 128.

(a) TERMS RELATED TO EARNINGS PER SHARE.   The terms "basic EPS" and "diluted EPS" are used to identify required per share data.

(i) Basic EPS. The amount of earnings for the period available to each share of common stock presumed to be outstanding during the reporting period.

(ii) Diluted EPS. The amount of earnings for the period available to each share of common stock outstanding during the reporting period and to each share that would have been outstanding assuming all dilutive potential common shares were outstanding during the reporting period.

(iii) Contingently Issuable Shares. Shares issuable for little or no cash consideration upon satisfaction of certain conditions pursuant to a contingent stock agreement. These shares include (a) shares issuable in future upon satisfaction of specified conditions, (b) shares that have been issued but are returnable if specified conditions are not met, and (c) shares that are held in escrow which are returnable.

(iv) Antidilution. An increase in EPS or a decrease in loss per share amounts.

(v) Weighted Average Shares. The mean average of outstanding shares and those presumed to be outstanding during the period. Shares are presumed to be outstanding when there is no circumstance under which the shares would not be issued. These would include shares issued in poolings of interests and contingently issuable shares where the contingent conditions have been met.

Most other definitions or terms used in FAS No. 128 are similar to those terms used in APB No. 15 and in current practice.

(b) BASIC EARNINGS PER SHARE. Basic EPS is considered to be a measure of financial performance over the reporting period. It is required to be presented on the face of the income statement. Basic per share amounts are at a minimum required to be shown for income from continuing operations and net income. The calculation of basic EPS is computed by dividing the appropriate income statement amount (i.e., income available to common shareholders) by the weighted average number of outstanding common shares during the period.

(c) DILUTED EARNINGS PER SHARE. Diluted EPS is intended to measure performance after giving effect to the maximum potentially dilutive common shares outstanding during the period. Diluted EPS is calculated as follows: Numerator same as basic EPS, then amended for effect of dilutive shares; denominator is basic EPS plus number of additional common shares that would have been outstanding if the potentially dilutive shares have been issued. These dilutive shares could arise from options, warrants, convertible securities, or shares issuable under acquisition or compensation agreements.

The numerator is adjusted to reflect the (1) add back to any convertible preferred dividends, or (2) after-tax effected interest on convertible debt associated with the respective dilutive securities and any nondiscretionary effects of the add backs, if any, such as pension or compensation expense. Also net of tax conversion is assumed to be at the most advantageous price to the security holder. Changes subsequent to the reporting period (i.e., active conversions or market price changes if applicable) are not adjusted retroactively.

(i) Antidilution. As with Opinion No. 15, only the potential shares that are dilutive are used. If the potential conversion, exercise, and so forth are antidilutive, it is not assumed for the computation. This situation can arise if there is a loss from continuing operations for the period or the options or warrants are out of the money. Antidilution is measured against income from continuing operations after preferred dividends if there are multiple income captions required to be shown.

(ii) Options, Warrants, and Their Equivalents. The treasury stock method should be used to reflect the dilutive effect of call options, warrants, and their equivalents (stock purchase contracts, partially paid subscriptions, and nonvested stock granted to employees). Under this method, exercise is assumed only when the average market price during the reporting period exceeds the exercise price. If options are exercised or expired, the period of time during the reporting period prior to such exercise or expiration must be added to the denominator. The treasury stock method assumes that:

- For unexercised securities (options, warrants, etc.) that were outstanding at the beginning of the period, common shares are assumed issued.
- The proceeds from any assumed exercise are used to purchase shares at an average market price during the period regardless if that is not the intent. Unlike APB Opinion No. 15, the modified treasury stock method (20 percent limitations) is not used.
- The resulting incremental shares are included in the denominator.

(iii) Convertible Securities.   Convertible securities are those that could result in the issuance of common shares for convertible debt or preferred stock. The impact of the potential issuance of the common shares on diluted EPS is determined using the if-converted method. The if-converted method is calculated as follows:

- When dealing with convertible preferred, the applicable dividends are added to the numerator. The amount of such dividends to add back is the amount deducted from income from continuing operations. Remember, only convertible preferred dividends are added back for diluted EPS. Nonconvertible preferred dividends always reduced income available to common shareholders for both basic and diluted EPS.
- If the convertible security is debt, then (a) applicable interest expense is added to the numerator, (b) the numerator is adjusted for other nondiscretionary income adjustments assuming a recalculation for the add back of interest in (A) above are made, and (B) the income tax effects of items (a) and (b), if any, are also added or subtracted from the numerator.
- The denominator should be increased for the common shares issuable upon the assumed conversion of the preferred stock or debt at the beginning of the period. As with all diluted EPS calculations, if the effect of conversion upon income from continuing operations is antidilutive, conversion should not be assumed. If actual conversion occurs or the conversion period lapses, then conversion for diluted EPS is assumed for the period of time prior to conversion, redemption, or lapse. This results in any issued common shares being considered outstanding for diluted EPS calculations for the full period. After actual conversion, these shares are included as outstanding in the weighted average calculation for both basic and diluted EPS and are assumed converted for the period of time prior to conversion for diluted EPS calculations.

(iv) Contingently Issuable Shares.   Under FAS No. 128, contingently issuable shares are included in basic EPS only when all necessary conditions prior to exercise have been satisfied, but the shares were not issued. However, for diluted EPS such shares are included in the denominator as of the beginning of the interim period in which the conditions were satisfied.

The calculation of diluted EPS prior to the end of the contingency period (period before all necessary conditions have been satisfied) assumes that the end of the reporting period is the end of the contingency period. Accordingly, the denominator would be increased for the number of shares that would be issuable based upon the conditions as they exist at the end of the reporting period if, and only if, the effect is dilutive.

(v) Calculation Sequence.   It is possible that the sequence of assumed conversions could affect the amount of dilution. Thus a convertible security may be dilutive by itself but antidilutive when combined with other potential issuances of common stock. To reflect maximum dilution, each security or issue of security is stratified from the most dilutive to the least dilutive. If the effect of including the next issue of security in the calculation of dilutive EPS results in higher EPS, then such securities are antidilutive to the diluted EPS calculation as a whole and should not be included. Therefore, the resultant dilutive EPS will reflect the lowest earnings per common share. Options and warrants will usually not be impacted by this rule since the use of the treasury stock method does not increase the numerator.

(vi) Interim Calculations. Each reporting period is treated as a discrete period for both basic and diluted EPS. Quarterly diluted EPS calculations under the treasury stock method should use the average market price for the period. For annual calculations, the sum of the shares used in each quarter divided by 4 should be used only if all quarters were profitable. If a loss was experienced, the effect on the quarters would be antidilutive. For annual calculations, when a loss was experienced during at least one quarter, the average market price for the period should be used for the treasury stock method. Thus, it is still possible that diluted EPS for the year or year-to-date amounts may not equal the sum of the respective quarters.

It is also possible that contingently issuable shares under performance preferred would also be considered outstanding for one quarter and not another. Year-to-date calculations, if all quarters are profitable, are the same as above. If a quarter is a loss, the inclusion of all contingently issuable shares would be antidilutive to the quarter and therefore excluded. However, as with the treasury stock method, these contingently issuable shares would be included in year-to-date calculations if they are dilutive.

Interim period EPS are not restated because of the resolution of the contingent issuance criteria.

11.11 PRESENTATION

The presentation under FAS No. 128 is similar to that of APB Opinion No. 15. Enterprises that have a simple capital structure need report on the face of the income statement only basic EPS. Basic EPS should be shown for at least income from continuing operations and net income. Enterprises with more complex capital structures (i.e., those with potential common shares) should show both basic and diluted EPS for these captions.

If the enterprise has another required reporting caption on the income statement (i.e., extraordinary items, cumulative effect of accounting change), it can present the EPS information (basic and dilutive) on the face of the income statement or in the notes to the financial statements.

The EPS data should be presented for all periods for which an income statement or summary of earnings is presented. If diluted EPS is shown for any period, it should be shown for all periods. In a situation in which basic and diluted EPS are the same for all periods shown, they may be shown as one line item. Unlike APB Opinion No. 15, there is no materiality exception for presenting diluted EPS. Thus, if diluted EPS is different from basic EPS for any period, it must be shown regardless of the size of the difference. Although the terms "basic EPS" and "diluted EPS" are used in FAS No. 128, there is no requirement to use that specific terminology. Traditional language such as "earnings per common share" and "earnings per common share—after dilution" are also appropriate.

11.12 DISCLOSURE

The FAS No. 128 requires the following three items for each period an income statement is presented:

1. A reconciliation of the numerators and denominators used in the calculation of basic and diluted EPS for income from continuing operations. This requirement pertains to the net effect of each class of potential dilution. Accordingly, supporting calculations or methodology (i.e., weighted average shares or treasury stock calculations) need not be shown.

2. The effect of preferred dividends on basic EPS in arriving at income from continuing operations available to common shareholders must be given. Theoretically, this could be met by including the preferred dividend requirement as a reconciling item of the numerator above. It should be noted that the SEC requires disclosure of income available to common shareholders on the face of the income statement when the difference between this calculation and net income is material.

3. Disclosure must be made of any securities that were omitted from the diluted EPS calculation because their effect was antidilutive but could be dilutive in the future.

If any transactions occur after the end of the period but before the financial statements are issued that would have changed the number of shares or potential shares materially, these must be disclosed. This disclosure requirement is similar to supplementary EPS under APB Opinion No. 15, although no calculation needs to be given.

- *Stock dividends and splits.* If a stock dividend, split, or reverse split occurs, all per share calculations should be retroactively restated. This should be done even if the dividend or split occurs after the period but before the issuance of the financial statements. A stock right issued whose terms have an exercise price at issuance, less than the stock's face value, should be treated the same as a stock dividend.

- *Prior period adjustments.* Certain accounting standards require retroactive restatement of financial statements for changes in accounting or error correction. The affected EPS data should be restated. When restating such data, all calculations are made as if new. Accordingly, items that either were or were not included in the original calculation could change. Potential shares that were dilutive could become antidilutive and vice versa. The effect of any restatement should be disclosed and expressed in per share terms.

- *Effective date.* FAS No. 128 is effective for both interim and annual statements for periods ending after December 15, 1997. Earlier application is not permitted. Subsequent to this date, all EPS data (both interim and annual) need to be restated to conform to FAS No. 128. This requirement includes summaries presented outside the financial statements.

11.13 EFFECT ON EXISTING LITERATURE

Exhibit 11.1 summarizes the effect of FAS No. 128 on pronouncements that were not specifically amended by FAS No. 128.

11.14 COMPUTATIONAL GUIDANCE

(a) WEIGHTED AVERAGE.   Basically, EPS is earnings available for common shareholders divided by the number of shares outstanding. More precisely, it is:

$$\frac{\text{Net income after deducting dividends on preferred stock and other claims of senior securities}}{\text{Weighted average number of common shares outstanding during the period after appropriate adjustments}}$$

Adjustments are required for stock dividends or splits (including those affected after the balance sheet date but prior to issuance of the financial statements) and after adjustments to reflect the number of shares issued in poolings of interest retroactively to the beginning of year.

The following example illustrates the computation of the weighted average number of shares outstanding. Assume that the changes in a company's outstanding common shares during a year are as follows:

Date	Change in Common Shares	Number of Shares
January 1	Outstanding at start of year	900
January 16	Issued on exercise of options	100
April 1	Issued as 10% stock dividend	100
August 11	Issued in pooling of interests	500
September 2	Repurchase of treasury shares	(200)
October 19	Issued for cash	400
December 31	Outstanding at end of year	1,800

Computation of the weighted average number of shares on a "days outstanding" basis would be as follows:

Date	Increase (Decrease)	Cumulative Total		Days Outstanding		Shares Days
January 1		900				
Plus adjustments for:						
10% stock dividend	+90					
Shares issued in pooling	+500					
January 1 adjusted		1,490	×	15	=	22,350
January 16 issuance of options	100					
Plus adjustments for:						
10% stock dividend	+10	1,600	×	229	=	366,400
September 2 Treasury repurchase	−200	1,400	×	47	=	65,800
October 19 cash issuance	+400	1,800	×	74	=	133,200
				365		587,750

The weighted average number of shares outstanding for the year would be

$$\frac{587,750}{365} = 1,610 \text{ shares}$$

In computing the weighted average number of outstanding shares, 90 of the 100 shares issued on April 1 as a 10 percent stock dividend are treated as outstanding retroactively to January 1, and 10 of the 100 stock dividend shares are treated as outstanding retroactively to January 16 (the date on which the options to which those shares related were exercised), for the following reason. When a stock dividend occurs, ownership in the company has been divided into a greater number of shares, each of which represents a proportionately smaller piece of the company. Retroactive recognition of the stock dividend for EPS computation purposes simply equates the prestock dividend shares with the poststock dividend shares. A stock split would be handled similarly. Prior years' EPS would also be restated for stock dividends and splits.

The 500 shares issued on August 11 in a business combination accounted for as pooling of interests are treated as outstanding retroactively to January 1 (with recomputation of prior years' EPS) because the earnings of the combining companies are pooled retroactively.

11.15 SPECIAL EARNINGS PER SHARE REPORTING REQUIREMENT FOR COMPANIES REGISTERED WITH THE SECURITIES AND EXCHANGE COMMISSION

Item 601 of Regulation S-K requires an exhibit to the principal filing forms (Forms S-1, S-2, S-4, S-11, 10, 10-Q, and 10-K) as follows: A statement setting forth in reasonable detail the computation of per share earnings, unless the computation can be clearly determined from the material in the registration statement or report. Since FAS No. 128 expressly requires disclosure of the number of shares used in computing EPS and the computation itself, many SEC registrants that filed the computational exhibit will no longer need to file them. In addition, SAB No. 40 requires explanatory disclosure of material changes in EPS amounts that are due principally to changes in the number of shares outstanding rather than to changes in net income. For example, disclosure is required if EPS increases materially as a result of the purchase of treasury shares by the issuer, even though aggregate earnings may remain relatively unchanged. Such disclosure would be made in "Management's Discussion and Analysis of the Summary of Earnings," which SEC registrants are required to present.

Where an IPO is occurring and stock, options, warrants, and other potentially dilutive securities have been granted or issued during the one year prior to the IPO and the exercise or issuance price is less than the public offering price, the SEC, in SAB No. 64, "Applicability of Guidance in Staff Accounting Bulletins; Reporting Income or Loss Applicable to Common Stock; Accounting for Redeemable Preferred Stock; Issuances of Shares Prior to an Initial Public Offering," issued in 1986, stated that all EPS calculations should be made assuming use of the treasury stock method as if these securities had been outstanding for all periods. The SEC, in SAB No. 83, "Earnings per Share Computations in an Initial Public Offering," added that the inclusion of potentially dilutive securities in an IPO (as required by SAB No. 64) does not change the registrant's responsibility under GAAP to determine if compensation expense should be recorded.

11.16 SOURCES AND SUGGESTED REFERENCES

Accounting Principles Board, "Reporting the Results of Operations," APB Opinion No. 9. AICPA, New York, 1966.

———, "Omnibus Opinion," APB Opinion No. 12. AICPA, New York, 1967.

———, "Business Combinations," APB Opinion No. 16. AICPA, New York, 1970.

———, "Accounting Changes," APB Opinion No. 20. AICPA, New York, 1971.

———, "Reporting the Results of Operations—Reporting the Effects of Disposal of a Segment of a Business, and Extraordinary, Unusual and Infrequently Occurring Events and Transactions," APB Opinion No. 30. AICPA, New York, 1973. American Institute of Certified Public Accountants, "Statement of Position 93-6, "Employers' Accounting for Employee Stock Ownership Plans." AICPA, New York, 1993.

———, "Accounting Trends and Techniques." AICPA. New York, 1994.

———, Financial Accounting Standards Board, "Discontinued Operations with Expected Gain and Interim Operating Loss, EITF Issue No. 85-36. FASB, Stamford, CT, 1985.

———, "Display of Business Restructuring Provisions in the Income Statement, EITF Issue No. 86-22. FASB, Stamford, CT, 1986.

———, "Restructuring of Operations: Implications of SEC Staff Accounting Bulletin No. 67," EITF Issue No. 87-4. FASB, Stamford, CT, 1987.

———, "Accounting for Discontinued Operations Subsequently Retained," EITF No. 90-16. FASB, Norwalk, CT, March 19, 1991.

———, "Convertible Bonds with Issuer Option to Settle for Cash upon Conversion," EITF Issue No. 90-19, FASB, Norwalk, CT, July 11, 1991.

———, "Liability Recognition for Certain Employee Termination Benefits and Other Costs to Exit an Activity Including Certain Costs Incurred in a Restructuring," EITF Issue No. 94-3. FASB, Norwalk, CT, September 22, 1994.

_____, "Allocation of Interest to Discontinued Operations," EITF Issue No. 87-24. FASB Stamford, CT, 1987.

_____, "Reporting Gains and Losses from Extinguishment of Debt," Statement of Financial Accounting Standards No. 4. FASB, Stamford, CT, 1975.

_____, "Financial Reporting for Segments of a Business Enterprise," Statement of Financial Accounting Standards No. 14. FASB, Stamford, CT, 1976.

_____, "Accounting by Debtors and Creditors for Troubled Debt Restructuring," Statement of Financial Accounting Standards No. 15. FASB, Stamford, CT, 1977.

_____, "Prior Period Adjustments," Statement of Financial Accounting Standards No. 16. FASB, Stamford, CT, 1977.

_____, "Regulated Enterprises—Accounting for Abandonments and Disallowances of Plant Costs," Statement of Financial Accounting Standards No. 90. FASB, Stamford, CT, 1986.

_____, "Consolidation of All Majority-Owned Subsidiaries," Statement of Financial Accounting Standards No. 94. FASB, Stamford, CT, 1987.

_____, "Accounting for the Impairment of Long-Lived Assets and for Long-Lived Assets to be Disposed of," Statement of Financial Accounting Standards No. 121. FASB, Norwalk, CT, 1995.

_____, "Earnings per Share," Statement of Financial Accounting Standards No. 128. FASB, Norwalk, CT, 1997.

_____, "Disclosures about Segments of an Enterprise and Related Information," Statement of Financial Accounting Standards No. 131. FASB, Norwalk, CT, 1997.

_____, "Business Combinations," Statement of Financial Accounting Standards No. 141. FASB, Norwalk, CT, 2001.

_____, "Accounting for a Purchase of Treasury Shares at a Price Significantly in Excess of the Current Market Price of Shares and the Income Statement Classification of Costs Incurred in Defending against a Takeover Attempt," FASB Technical Bulletin No. 85-6. FASB, Stamford, CT, 1985.   Securities and Exchange Commission, "Codification of SAB Nos, 1–38," Staff Accounting Bulletin No. 40. SEC, Washington, DC, 1981.

_____, "Accounting for Sales of Stock by a Subsidiary," Staff Accounting Bulletin No. 51. Washington, DC, 1983.

_____, "Income Statement Presentation of Restructuring Charges," Staff Accounting Bulletin No. 67. SEC, Washington, DC, 1986.

_____, "Income Statement Presentation," Staff Accounting Bulletin No. 69. SEC, Washington, DC, 1987.

_____, "Classification of Charges for Abandonments and Disallowances," Staff Accounting Bulletin No. 72. SEC, Washington, DC, 1987.

_____, "Gain Recognition on the Sale of a Business or Operating Assets to a Highly Leveraged Entity," Staff Accounting Bulletin No. 81. SEC, Washington, DC, 1989.

_____, "Accounting for Sales of Stock by a Subsidiary," Staff Accounting Bulletin No. 84. SEC, Washington, DC, 1989.

_____, "Accounting and Disclosure Regarding Discontinued Operations," Staff Accounting Bulletin No. 93. SEC, Washington, DC, 1993.

_____, "Codification of Financial Reporting Polices," Financial Reporting Release No. 1, ASR No. 177. SEC, Washington, DC, 1982.

CHAPTER 12

ACCOUNTING FOR BUSINESS COMBINATIONS

Paul Pacter, PhD, CPA

Director IAS Global Office Deloitte Touche Tohmatsu

12.1 BACKGROUND

For the 30 years prior to June 30, 2001, accounting for business combinations in the United States was governed by Accounting Principles Board (APB) Opinion No. 16, "Business Combinations," APB Opinion No. 17, "Intangible Assets," and their various amendments and interpretations. Those standards provided for two methods of accounting for business combinations—the pooling of interests method and the purchase method—and for amortization of goodwill and other intangible assets recognized under the purchase method over a period not longer than 40 years.

Effective July 1, 2001, those pronouncements were replaced by Statement of Financial Accounting Standards (SFAS) No. 141, "Business Combinations," and SFAS No. 142, "Goodwill and Other Intangible Assets." The new standards fundamentally change the method of accounting for business combinations and goodwill and other intangible assets. SFAS No. 141 requires that all business combinations be accounted for by a single method—the purchase method. And whereas Opinion No. 17 had presumed that goodwill and all other intangible assets were wasting assets (i.e., finite lived) that should be amortized in determining net income, SFAS No. 142 makes no such presumption. Instead, under SFAS No. 142, goodwill and intangible assets that have indefinite useful lives are not amortized but rather are tested at least annually for impairment. Any intangible assets that have finite useful lives continue to be amortized over their useful lives, but without the constraint of an arbitrary 40-year ceiling.

SFAS No. 141 does not change many of the provisions of Opinion No. 16 related to the application of the purchase method. For example, it does not significantly change the guidance for determining the cost of an acquired entity and allocating that cost to the assets acquired and liabilities assumed, the accounting for contingent consideration, and the accounting for preacquisition contingencies.

12.2 SCOPE

For purposes of applying Statement No. 141, a *business combination* occurs when an entity acquires all or a portion of the net assets that constitute a business or equity interest of one or more entities and obtains control over the entity or entities. (For purposes of that Statement, *entity* refers to the participants in a business combination; the term can refer to any of the various forms in which the participants may exist.) Control is generally indicated by "ownership by one company" (ARB No. 1, *Consolidated Financial Statements*, paragraph 2, as amended by SFAS No. 94, "Consolidation of All Majority-Owned Subsidiaries").

The Statement applies to combinations involving either incorporated or unincorporated entities. The provisions of the statement apply equally to a business combination in which (a) one or more entities are merged or become subsidiaries, (b) one entity transfers its net assets or equity interests to another (including all or a portion of the net assets that constitutes a business or equity interests of the entity), or (c) each entity transfers its net assets or equity interests to a newly formed entity. Each represents a business combination regardless of whether the form of consideration given is cash, other assets, a business or a subsidiary of the entity, debt, common or preferred stock, or a combination of those forms. An exchange of a business for a business also constitute a business combination.

The acquisition of some or all of the equity interests held by minority stockholders of a subsidiary is not a business combination. However, the acquisition of some or all of the stock held by minority stockholders of a subsidiary—regardless of whether acquired by the parent, the subsidiary itself, or another affiliate—is accounted for by the purchase method under SFAS No. 141. The term *business combination* as used in the Statement also excludes both (a) transfers by an entity of some or all of its net assets to a newly formed substitute entity chartered by the transferor entity and (b) transfers of net assets or exchanges of shares between entities under common control, such as between a parent corporation and its subsidiary or between two subsidiary corporations of the same parent. The assets and liabilities transferred in such transactions are recorded in the accounts of the entity that received the net assets or shares at the amounts recorded in the accounts of the entity that made the transfer as the date of the transfer or exchange.

12.3 THE PURCHASE METHOD OF ACCOUNTING

Application of the purchase method of accounting involves:

- Identifying the acquiring company
- Determining the date used to record the acquisition
- Determining the cost of the acquired entity. This includes:
  - Valuing the consideration paid or, in some cases, the net assets acquired
  - Accounting for the direct costs of the business combination
  - Accounting for contingent consideration
- Identifying the assets acquired and liabilities assumed
- Allocating the purchase price—that is, allocating the cost of the acquired entity to the assets acquired and the liabilities assumed
- Accounting subsequent to the business combination

(a) IDENTIFYING THE ACQUIRING COMPANY.   The acquiring entity is the entity that obtains control over the other entity or entities involved in the business combination. An entity that distributes cash or other assets or incurs liabilities to acquire the assets or equity interests of another entity and obtain control over the other entity is generally the acquiring entity. The identities of the acquiring entity and the acquired entity are usually evident in a business combination effected by the issuance of stock. The acquiring entity normally issues the stock and commonly is the larger entity. However, the facts and circumstances surrounding a business combination sometimes indicate that a smaller entity acquires a larger one. Also, in some business combinations, the combined entity assumes the name of the acquired entity or it is the acquired entity that issues the stock, which is commonly referred to as a *reverse acquisition*.

In identifying which entity is the acquiring entity in a business combination involving two or more entities, all pertinent facts are considered, particularly the relative voting rights in the combined entity after the combination and the composition of the board of directors and the senior management of the combined entity. In identifying which of the shareholder groups retained or received the larger portion of the voting rights in the combined entity, the existence of any major voting block, unusual or special voting arrangements, and options, warrants, or convertible securities is considered.

If a new entity is formed to issue stock to effect a business combination, one of the existing combining entities is considered the acquiring entity on the basis of the evidence available. The guidance in the two preceding paragraphs applies to that determination.

The Securities and Exchange Commission (SEC) Staff Accounting Bulletin (SAB) No. 40, Topic 2, Item A.2, provides additional guidance in identifying the acquiring company and indicates that other factors must also be considered in identifying which company is the acquiror. These considerations include:

- Restrictions on the ability of the former officers or directors of one of the companies to solicit proxies or to participate in voting matters of the combined company
- Predominant control by the management and board of directors of one of the combining companies of management and the board of directors of the combined company
- The extent to which the assets, revenues, net earnings, and current market value of one of the combining companies significantly exceed those of the other combining companies
- The market value of the securities to be received or retained by the former common stockholders of the companies involved in the combination
- The nature of the combined company's business operations compared with operations of the separate entities

The application of the guidance in paragraphs 15–19 of SFAS No. 141 and SAB No. 40, Topic 2, may result in treating the legal acquiror as the acquiree for purchase accounting purposes. Such is the case in a reverse acquisition as described below.

(i) Reverse Acquisitions.   The term *reverse acquisition* refers to a business combination accounted for by the purchase method in which the company that issues its shares or gives other consideration to effect a business combination is determined to be the acquiree. This is typically based on the fact that the shareholders of the issuer will have less than a majority of voting control of the combined entity. Reverse acquisitions often involve a shell company or a blind pool created for the purpose of raising capital and using such assets to acquire an interest in an operating company by issuing its shares to acquire all of the stock of an operating company. A reverse acquisition is frequently characterized by the continued operations of the operating company under its precombination management, with little or no management involvement by officers and directors of the shell or blind pool.

In a reverse acquisition, the legal acquiror continues in existence as the legal entity whose shares represent the outstanding common stock of the combined company. In some instances, the legal acquiror is a public company whose shares are listed on an exchange. By effecting a reverse acquisition, the accounting acquiror can thereby gain access to the public market without going through an initial public offering.

(ii) Applying Purchase Accounting to a Reverse Acquisition.   In applying purchase accounting to a reverse acquisition, the assets of the legal acquiror must be revalued and the purchase price allocated to those assets acquired and liabilities assumed. The equity section of the combined company's balance sheet should reflect the legal acquiror's equity securities outstanding. The retained earnings or accumulated deficit of the accounting acquiror should carry over to the combined company, and the difference resulting from purchase price adjustments and adjustments to the legal acquiror's common stock and other equity securities is charged or credited to paid-in capital.

For example, a blind investment pool, P, acquired all of a company's (A's) outstanding common stock in exchange for 48 newly issued shares of P's common stock. As a result of the combination, A's former shareholders hold approximately 70% of the outstanding shares of the combined company. In addition, the operations of A continue to be the principal operations of the combined company, and the management and the board of directors of A continue as the predominant management and the board of directors of the combined company. (Assume the disposition of shares by an affiliate of A violates the use of pooling of interests accounting.) The separate balance sheets and consolidated statements of P and A would be as follows:

	Company P		Company A	
	Historical Cost	Fair Value	Historical Cost	Fair Value
Assets				
Cash	$ 95	$ 95	$ 20	$ 20
Receivables			40	40
Inventory			30	40
Fixed assets—net			75	85
Other assets	5		15	15
Total assets	$ 100	$ 95	$ 180	$ 200
Liabilities and Equity				
Payables	$ 10	$ 10	$ 25	$ 25
Accrued liabilities			15	15
Debt	50	50	70	65
Common stock	20	20	25	25
Paid-in capital	30	30	25	25
Retained earnings	(10)	(15)	20	45
Total liabilities and equity	$ 100	$ 95	$ 180	$ 200

Consolidating Balance Sheet

Assets				
Cash	$ 95	$ 20		$ 115
Receivables		40		40
Inventory		30		30
Fixed assets—net		75		75
Other assets	5	15	$ (5)[a,d]	15
Total assets	$ 100	$ 180	$ (5)	$ 275
Liabilities and Equity				
Payables	$ 10	$ 25		$ 35
Accrued liabilities		15		15
Debt	50	70		120

(Continues)

	Company P		Company A	
	Historical Cost	Fair Value	Historical Cost	Fair Value
Common stock	20	25	$ 23[b]	68
Paid-in capital	30	25	(38)[a,b,c]	17
Retained earnings	(10)	20	10[c]	20
Total liabilities and equity	$ 100	$ 180	$ (5)	$ 275

[a]To reflect reduction in fair value of P's other assets.
[b]To reflect issuance of 48 shares of P common stock to A's shareholders for A's common stock.

P shareholders	20 shares (30% of outstanding common stock)
A shareholders	48 shares (70% of outstanding common stock)
	68 shares

[c]To reflect elimination of beginning accumulated deficit of P.
[d]For simplicity, the deferred tax consequence attributable to the reduction in the carrying amount of P's other assets, which ordinarily results in a temporary difference under SFAS No. 109, is ignored.

(b) DETERMINING THE COST OF THE ACQUIRED EQUITY. Accounting for a business combination by the purchase method follows principles normally applicable under historical-cost accounting to recording acquisitions of assets and issuances of stock and to accounting for assets and liabilities after acquisition. The cost of an acquired company is required to be measured by the fair value of the consideration given or the fair value of the acquired company, whichever is the more clearly evident. The fair value of the consideration given will generally be more clearly evident because of the difficulties associated with measuring the fair value of the acquired company. Although the fair value of the individual assets acquired and liabilities assumed must be determined in connection with the accounting for a business combination by the purchase method, it is often difficult to value goodwill or other intangible assets separately or to determine the existence of negative goodwill.

If the quoted market price is not the fair value of stock, either preferred or common, the consideration received is estimated even though measuring directly the fair values of assets received is difficult. Both the consideration received, including goodwill, and the extent of the adjustment of the quoted market price of the stock issued is weighed to determine the amount to be recorded. All aspects of the acquisition, including the negotiations, are studied, and independent appraisals may be used as an aid in determining the fair value of securities issued. Consideration other than stock distributed to effect an acquisition may provide evidence of the total fair value received.

The cost of an acquired entity and the values assigned to assets acquired and liabilities assumed are determined as of the date of acquisition (Section 12.3(l)). The statement of income of an acquiring entity for the period in which a business combination occurs includes income of the acquired entity after the date of acquisition by including the revenue and expenses of the acquired operations based on the cost to the acquiring entity.

(i) Fair Value of Consideration Given. Many business combinations are effected through the issuance of cash or other assets or securities, the incurrence or assumption of liabilities, or a combination thereof. Frequently, information required to measure the value of the consideration given is readily available. Cash is measured at its face amount, and assets, such as marketable securities, at fair value. Paragraph 22 of SFAS No. 141 requires that consideration also be given to the market price of securities for a reasonable period before and after the date the terms of the combination are agreed to and announced. Liabilities are measured at the present value of future cash payments.

Situations frequently encountered where valuation issues arise are those where the consideration given includes securities that are closely held, restricted or thinly traded, preferred stock, debentures, or treasury stock. The valuation of securities that are not readily traded is typically performed by someone with an appropriate level of expertise to make such judgments, such as a reputable investment banker. The following three paragraphs discuss various considerations in these situations.

Preferred stock issued to effect a business combination may have characteristics of debt securities or equity securities, or it may have significant characteristics of both types of securities. Consideration should be given to the fair value of the acquiree and the debt versus equity characteristics of the preferred stock, including:

- The stated dividend rate of the preferred stock compared with market rates for similar securities
- The tax implications to the holders of the securities and the effect of such implications on the value of similar securities
- Redemption, liquidation, or conversion rights that will affect the valuation of the stock
- Any other factors that may have a unique bearing on the fair value of such securities

Debentures or other debt instruments issued to effect an acquisition should be recorded at their fair value (i.e., present value based on market rates of interest determined in accordance with APB Opinion No. 21) and a premium or discount recorded if the stated interest rate differs materially from the current yield for a comparable security.

When the consideration given in a business combination includes treasury stock, the principles of fair value still apply. That is, the purchase price is measured by the fair value of the securities given as consideration following the requirements of paragraph 22 of SFAS No. 141 as previously discussed. In all likelihood, this fair value will differ from the carrying value or cost of the treasury shares. Thus, a charge or credit to additional paid-in capital will be necessary for the difference between the value and the recorded cost of the treasury shares.

The cost of a purchase business combination is generally determined at the initiation date of the combination with recognition that security prices may need a short period of time to reflect market valuations associated with the proposed combination.

(ii) Options of the Acquiree. The acquiree in a business combination may have options outstanding at the initiation date. In such instances, the acquiror may assume the obligation of the acquiree to issue shares upon exercise of the options, it may require the acquiree to redeem all of the outstanding options, or it may permit the options to remain outstanding without change. If the options are permitted to remain outstanding without change, their existence ordinarily has no impact on the purchase price because it is assumed that the purchase price reflects any dilution expected to result from their exercise. The exercise of the options will result in creation of, or addition to, minority interest in the acquired company. Accordingly, consideration would need to be given to the outstanding options in the allocation of the purchase price. If the acquiror assumes the acquiree's obligation to issue shares upon exercise of the options, an adjustment of the purchase price is required.

If the options are assumed by the acquiror, an amount equal to the difference between the exercise price and the fair value of the securities at the acquisition date, issuable by the acquiree upon exercise, should be recorded as a part of the purchase price. However, the exercise of such options should not be assumed in recording the shares issuable in connection with the business combination. Such shares may be common stock equivalents or other potentially dilutive securities, and consideration should be given to them in the computation of earnings per share of the combined company in accordance with SFAS No. 128. However, only the difference between the exercise price and the fair value of the securities issuable should be recorded on the acquisition date. For example, if the fair value of the acquiror's stock is determined to be $100 per share and the exercise price of outstanding options is $45 per share, the difference, $55 per share, should be included in the computation of the purchase price with a corresponding credit to additional paid-in capital. The $45 option exercise price should not be recorded until the option is exercised.

The Emerging Issues Task Force (EITF) discussed Issue No. 85-45, "*Business Combinations: Settlement of Stock Options and Awards*," at its February 1986 meeting and reached the following consensus:

> ... APB Opinion No. 25, "*Accounting for Stock Compensation Plans*" requires that, if the target company settles stock options voluntarily, at the direction of the acquiring company, or as part of the plan of acquisition, the settlement should be accounted for as compensation expense in the separate financial statements of the target company.

Accordingly, if the acquiror settles outstanding options for cash or stock, or by assuming the obligation for these options, the consideration given results in an adjustment to the purchase price of the acquisition. If, on the other hand, the acquiree settles the options for cash or other consideration before, after, or as part of the acquisition, compensation expense would be recorded by the acquiree.

(iii) Fair Value of the Acquired Company.   As noted earlier, there may be instances where the fair value of the company acquired is more clearly evident than the fair value of the consideration given. For example, this might be the case where the acquiree is a shell company or a blind pool where assets are essentially monetary assets subject to reasonable independent valuations. In other situations where the purchase price must be determined based on the value of the assets acquired, reference should be made to industry price/earnings ratios, opinions of investment bankers, independent appraisals of the acquiree's net assets (including intangibles and goodwill), the value indicated by the negotiations, recent security transactions for both companies to the combination, and any other indicators of value that are available.

(iv) When to Value Shares Issued in a Business Combination.   Shares issued in a business combination should be valued at the acquisition date, which is the date that the acquirer takes possession and control of the acquired entity's assets and liabilities and the seller receives its payment. SFAS No. 141 allows the parties, for convenience, to make a written designation that the effective date is the end of an accounting period between the dates the business combination is initiated and consummated. If such date is designated and used for accounting purposes, the cost of the acquisition and the income recognized by the acquirer must be reduced by interest imputed at an appropriate current rate, to compensate for recognizing income before the consideration is transferred. As a result, both income and goodwill are reduced. See additional discussion in Section 12.3(1) of this chapter.

(c) DIRECT COSTS OF THE BUSINESS COMBINATION.   SFAS No. 141 states in paragraph 24:

> The cost of an entity acquired in a business combination includes the direct costs of the business combination. Costs of registering and issuing equity securities shall be recognized a reduction of the otherwise determinable fair value of the securities. However, indirect and general expenses related business combinations shall be expensed as incurred.

Direct costs of acquisitions have typically been held to mean those costs that would not have been incurred if the acquisition had not been initiated.

Interpretation No. 33 indicates that only "out-of-pocket" or incremental costs (costs of services provided from sources outside the company) should be included in the purchase price because internal costs ordinarily involve an allocation of costs that would have been incurred whether or not the acquisition had taken place.

If a business combination is effected through the issuance of equity securities, the cost of the acquired company should be measured by the fair value of those equity securities. The resulting credit to shareholders' equity should be reduced by the cost of registration and issuance of those securities.

Interpretation No. 35 requires that, if registration costs will not be incurred or paid until after the acquisition date, such costs should be accrued as a liability with a corresponding reduction in the amount credited to additional paid-in capital. The result of this adjustment will generally be recognized as a charge to goodwill.

Typical direct costs of acquisition include the following:

- Debt placement and other bank-related fees in connection with debt incurred to finance the acquisition
- Refinancing fees associated with the acquiree's debt that require refinancing upon a change in ownership
- Prepayment penalties associated with the acquiree's debt that is prepaid in order to restructure the financing of the combined company and provide the acquisition lender with the first mortgage on all assets of the combined company
- Fees paid to investment bankers (see also discussion of SAB No. 77 below)
- Fees paid for outside accounting, legal, engineering, or appraisal services

In March 1988, the SEC issued SAB No. 77, which addresses the treatment of certain debt issue costs incurred in connection with financing used in a business combination accounted for by the purchase method. The SAB uses the example of a company that retained an investment banker to provide the following services:

- Advisory services in structuring the acquisition
- Arrangement of "bridge financing" on an interim basis
- Structuring of "permanent financing" at a subsequent date

The SAB requires that the investment banker's fees (whether separately billed or not) be allocated to the services provided and that the fees for the bridge financing and permanent financing be accounted for as debt issue costs rather than direct costs of the acquisition.

(i) Acquisition Costs Incurred by the Acquiree.   An acquiree may incur accounting, legal, engineering, and other consulting fees in connection with a business combination. These costs would normally be expensed by the acquiree unless it can be demonstrated that the costs are nonduplicative direct costs of the acquisition and are clearly incurred by the acquiree for the benefit of the acquiror. Nonduplicative acquisition costs are those that are more clearly associated with the distinct activities of the acquiror rather than with the costs that benefit the combined companies or the acquiree's stockholders; such costs would normally have been incurred by the acquiror absent an arrangement between the parties for the acquiree to pay such costs.

In the absence of a reimbursement arrangement between the acquiror and the acquiree, costs incurred by the acquiree incidental to the acquisition should be expensed. These acquisition costs must be evaluated based on the facts and circumstances of the specific acquisition.

(ii) Plant Closing Costs and Employee Severance Costs.   Subparagraph 37k of SFAS No. 141 indicates that, in allocating the purchase price to the assets acquired and liabilities assumed, a liability should be recorded for plant closing expenses incidental to the acquisition. The Financial Technical Bulletin (FTB) No. 85-5 addresses the costs of closing duplicate facilities resulting from an acquisition. It distinguishes between costs of closing plants owned by the acquiree and costs of closing the acquiror's plants. It indicates that only the direct costs of an acquisition should be included in the cost of the acquired company. It does not permit the cost of closing the acquiror's facilities, which become duplicative as a result of the acquisition, to be considered part of the cost of acquisition. Such plant closing costs would include employee severance costs, relocation costs, and other costs incidental to the closing of duplicate facilities. The Technical Bulletin also indicates that plant closing expenses, in general, are not part of the direct costs of the acquisition which are added to the value of securities or assets given to effect the acquisition in arriving at the total purchase price. Rather, a plant closing liability is one factor to be considered in allocating the cost of the acquired company to the individual assets acquired and liabilities assumed. It is ordinarily assumed that the costs of plant closing, employee relocation, and severance plans were comprehended in the negotiations and are an integral part of the bargained purchase price in a business combination. The costs of such plant closing, employee relocation, and severance plans should, therefore, be an allocation of the purchase price and not an additional cost of the acquisition.

(iii) Payments to Employees: Acquisition Cost versus Employee Compensation Arrangements.
An acquisition agreement may include provisions for consideration to be paid to employees of the acquiree. The intent of such arrangements may be to compensate employees of the acquiree for past services, to act as a "golden handcuff" in retaining key executives of the acquiree during a specified period subsequent to the acquisition, or to serve as additional consideration in the purchase acquisition.

Payments made, or to be made, to employees of an acquiree should be evaluated carefully to determine if the substance of the transaction is compensation for services performed subsequent to the acquisition or a cost of the acquisition. Many of the considerations discussed earlier in this chapter with regard to employee/shareholder arrangements in a pooling should be considered in determining the purchase price in a business combination accounted for by the purchase method.

A provision that requires employees to remain in the service of the combined company for a specified extended period of time before payments are received, or where such payments seem to approximate normal compensation levels for the employees, generally indicates that the substance of such payments is compensation for services to be rendered in the period subsequent to the acquisition rather than additional cost of the acquisition.

Conversely, if only a short service period is required for the employees to vest, it could indicate that little or no benefit will be received in a period subsequent to the acquisition. Payments significantly in excess of employees' normal compensation may also indicate that the substance of the payments may represent compensation for services rendered prior to the acquisition or an additional cost of acquiring the target company.

Employee payments determined to be part of the acquisition cost represent a liability assumed in the acquisition rather than a direct cost of the acquisition that increases the total purchase price.

(iv) Discretionary Costs in Purchase Business Combinations.
In many purchase business combinations, the management of the acquiring company expects to incur certain costs shortly after the merger to integrate the operations of the two companies or to exit certain activities or terminate or relocate certain employees of either the acquired or acquiring company. In May 1995, the EITF addressed those matters and reached a consensus in Issue No. 95-3, "Recognition of Liabilities in Connection with a Purchase Business Combination."

To the extent that an expected future cost is accrued as a liability at the time of a business combination, the cost of the acquisition increases. Since the identifiable assets are not affected, the amount of the accrued liability normally results in an increase to goodwill.

Issue No. 95-3 addresses three broad groups of costs expected to be incurred as a result of a purchase business combination:

1. Costs to exit an activity or to involuntarily terminate or relocate employees of the *acquired* company
2. Costs to exit an activity or to involuntarily terminate or relocate employees of the *acquiring* company
3. Costs to integrate the activities of the acquired company with those of the acquiring company

Examples would include salaries of management personnel during the integration phase and costs of training acquired personnel, upgrading the acquired company's physical facilities or computer systems, relocating acquired equipment, and consolidating or restructuring certain functions.

In resolving Issue No. 95-3, the EITF concluded that only the first group of costs (costs to exit an activity or to involuntarily terminate or relocate employees of the *acquired* company) are potentially recognizable as liabilities at the time of a purchase business combination, and then only under the conditions described below. The second group of costs (costs related to activities or employees of the *acquiring* company) may not be accrued as liabilities and, thereby, added to the purchase cost, because the cost of a purchase acquisition is never allocated to the assets of the acquiring company (see Financial Accounting Standards Board Technical Bulletin No. 85-5). The third group of costs—expenditures to integrate the activities of the acquired company with those of the acquiring company and any other exit, termination, or relocation costs relating to the acquired company that do not qualify for liability accrual—should be either expensed or capitalized when incurred based on the nature of the expenditure and the capitalization policy of the combined company.

Expected costs to exit an activity of the acquired company should be recognized as a liability as of the date of a purchase business combination if:

- The cost was incurred pursuant to a formal plan (Issue No. 95-3 identifies criteria for such a plan including requirements that the plan be based on conditions existing as of the date of the merger and that it be finalized not longer than one year after the merger).
- Action to implement the plan begins as soon as the plan is finalized.
- The cost is not incurred to generate revenues of the combined entity after the merger.
- The cost has no future economic benefit to the combined company.
- Either (a) the cost is incremental to other costs incurred by either the acquired or the acquiring company prior to the merger and will be incurred as a direct consequence of the plan to exit an activity of the acquired company or (b) the cost is the result of a premerger contractual obligation of the acquired company.

Expected costs to involuntarily terminate or relocate employees of the acquired company should be recognized as a liability as of the date of the purchase business combination if:

- The cost was incurred pursuant to a formal plan that clearly identifies the number of employees to be terminated or relocated, their job classifications or functions, and their locations.
- The details of the termination or relocation plan and related benefits are finalized and communicated to employees not longer than one year after the merger date.
- Action to implement the plan begins as soon as the plan is finalized.

If an estimated liability is accrued at the time of the combination and the actual amount ultimately turns out to be less, the excess should reduce the cost of the acquired company, that is, reduce goodwill. If the cost ultimately turns out to be more than the original accrual, the portion of that excess arising in the first year after the combination is added to the cost of the acquired company; any excess cost incurred beyond a year after the merger is charged to expense when incurred.

Issue No. 95-3 specifies certain disclosures that must be made in the notes to the financial statements of the combined company both in the period in which the merger occurs and thereafter until the plan to exit activities or terminate or relocate employees is completed.

(d) CONTINGENT CONSIDERATION. A purchase or merger agreement may include provisions for additional consideration, such as cash payments or the issuance of additional stock, in the event that one or more future events occur. In such situations, the ultimate purchase price may vary depending on the outcome of these contingencies. This presents an accounting problem in initially recording the acquisition.

SFAS No. 141 requires that "cash and other assets distributed, securities issued unconditionally, and amounts of contingent consideration that are determinable at the date of acquisition shall be included in determining the cost of an acquired entity and recorded at that date." Other consideration that is issuable upon resolution of a contingency should be disclosed but not recorded as a liability unless the outcome of the contingency is "determinable beyond a reasonable doubt."

To the extent a contingent consideration liability is recognized, it should be recorded at its present value. The discount should be accreted over the remaining terms of the contingency period in accordance with the provisions of APB Opinion No. 21.

(i) Contingencies Based on Earnings.   SFAS No. 141 requires that additional consideration that is contingent upon maintaining or achieving specified levels of earnings be recorded when resolved. These types of contingencies result in an adjustment to the purchase price of the acquiree based on the fair value of the consideration issued or issuable, with the fair value measured as of the date the contingency is resolved. The fair value of the consideration issued should be allocated to the assets acquired, generally as an adjustment to goodwill or negative goodwill.

As with all aspects of a business combination, evaluation should be made of the substance of contingency arrangements as well as their form.

The EITF addressed the question of whether contingent consideration that is embedded in a financial instrument or that is itself a separate financial instrument should be recorded by the issuer at fair value at acquisition date or recognized only when the contingency is resolved. In Issue No. 97-8, EITF concluded that the contingent consideration should be recorded at fair value at acquisition date.

Some agreements provide that a portion of the consideration be placed in escrow to be distributed or to be returned to the transferor when specified events occur. Either debt or equity securities may be placed in escrow, and amounts equal to interest or dividends on the securities during the contingency period may be paid to the escrow agent or to the potential security holder. Such amounts are accounted for according to the accounting for the securities. That is, until the disposition of the securities in escrow is resolved, payments to the escrow agent are not recorded as interest expense or dividend distributions. An amount equal to interest and dividends later distributed by the escrow agent to the former stockholders is added to the cost of the acquired assets at the date distributed and amortized over the remaining life of the assets.

Contingent consideration is usually recorded when the contingency is resolved and consideration is issued or becomes issuable. In general, the issuance of additional securities or distribution of other consideration at resolution of contingencies based on earnings results in an additional element of cost of an acquired entity. In contrast, the issuance of additional securities or distribution of other consideration at resolution of contingencies based on security prices does not change the recorded cost of an acquired entity.

(ii) Contingencies Based on Security Prices.   Another type of contingency arrangement addressed by SFAS No. 141 is one in which the acquiror guarantees attainment of a specified price for its stock or maintenance of a specified security price during the contingency period. If the contingency price is not met, additional consideration in the form of cash, equity, or debt securities is given upon resolution of the contingency to make the current value of the total consideration equal the specified amount. The Statement's use of the term *specified amount* refers to the total guaranteed value of the acquisition, including the value of the contingency. For example, if Company A proposes to acquire Company B for stock value at $10 million and cash of $50 million, but guarantees that the stock will have a value of $15 million after three years or Company A will pay cash or issue additional shares of stock sufficient to meet the $15 million guaranteed value, then the purchase price of Company B would be $65 million, represented by the $50 million cash exchanged, plus the $15 million of guaranteed stock value.

The authoritative literature does not provide guidance on discounting the guaranteed portion to be paid at the end of the contingency period. In practice, discounting has been used in some situations and not used in others. The SEC has taken the position in certain cases, primarily where the guarantee is issuable in stock rather than cash or other consideration, that acquisition cost associated with a guaranteed price contingency for stock should be determined without regard to discounting.

The issuance of additional securities or distribution of other consideration does not affect the cost of the acquired entity, regardless of whether the amount specified is a security price to be maintained or a higher security price to be achieved. On a later date when the contingency is resolved and additional consideration is distributable, the acquiring entity records the current fair value of the additional consideration issued or issuable. However, the amount previously recorded for securities issued at the date of acquisition is simultaneously reduced to the lower current value of the securities. Reducing the value of debt securities previously issued to their later fair value results in recording a discount on debt securities. The discount is amortized from the date the additional securities are issued.

A tax reduction resulting from imputed interest on contingently issuable stock reduces the fair value recorded for contingent consideration based on earnings and increases additional capital recorded for contingent consideration based on security prices.

The substance of some agreements for contingent consideration is to provide compensation for services or use of property or profit sharing, and the additional consideration given is accounted for as expenses of the appropriate periods.

Accounting for contingent consideration based on conditions other than those described are inferred from the procedures discussed. For example, if the consideration contingently issuable depends on both future earnings and future security prices, additional cost of the acquired entity is recorded for the additional consideration contingent on earnings, and previously recorded consideration is reduced to the current value of the consideration contingent on security prices. Similarly, if the consideration contingently issuable depends on later settlement of a contingency, an increase in the cost of acquired assets, if any, is amortized over the remaining life of the assets.

(iii) Earnings per Share Consequences of Contingent Share Arrangements.   Paragraphs 30 through 35 of SFAS No. 128 provide guidance on the appropriate accounting for earnings per share under contingent share arrangements. In general terms, that Statement requires that both primary and diluted earnings per share be adjusted to reflect contingently issuable shares when the conditions that give rise to the issuance of such contingent shares are currently being met. Additionally, if the conditions are not currently being met or must be met over a period of years, the number of contingently issuable shares included in diluted earnings per share is based on the number of shares, if any, that would be issuable if the end of the current reporting period were the end of the contingency period. Previously reported earnings per share data should not be restated to give retroactive effect to shares subsequently issued as a result of attainment of a specified increased earning level.

Paragraph 32 of SFAS No. 141, which provides guidance on accounting for shares contingently issuable based on market price of the stock at a future date, states:

> The number of shares contingently issuable may depend on the market price of the stock at a future date. In that case, computations of diluted EPS shall reflect the number of shares that would be issued based on the current market price at the end of the period being reported on if the effect is dilutive.

(iv) Adjustment of Acquisition Cost or Compensation Expense?   SFAS No. 141 does not provide clear guidance as to when contingent consideration is an adjustment of the original acquisition cost and when it is compensation expense. An adjustment of the acquisition cost normally increases goodwill and is amortized over the remaining amortization period of the goodwill previously recognized in the acquisition. Recognizing contingent consideration as compensation expense is a current charge against earnings. Paragraph 27 of SFAS No. 141 states that, "in general, the issuance of additional securities or distribution of other consideration at resolution of contingencies based on earnings shall result in an additional element of cost of an acquired entity." On the other hand, paragraph 34 says that "if the substance of the agreement for contingent consideration is to provide compensation for services or use of property or profit sharing, the additional consideration given shall be accounted for as an expense of the appropriate periods." While paragraph 34 does not identify the kinds of contingencies that *may* make the additional consideration compensation expense, in practice they tend to be contingencies based on maintaining or achieving a level of earnings. In several recent cases, the SEC staff has taken the position that if the contingent consideration is based on earnings or other measure of financial performance and is paid to "key employees" (individuals who are in a position to directly affect financial performance, such as directors, officers, or senior managers), the contingent consideration is compensation expense.

The EITF addressed the matter in EITF Issue No. 95-8, "Accounting for Contingent Consideration Paid to the Shareholders of an Acquired Enterprise in a Purchase Business Combination." The EITF reached a consensus that judgment is required to determine whether the consideration transferred to settle an earnings- or performance-based contingency is compensation or is an additional purchase price for the acquired company. The published consensus identifies a number of factors and circumstances to consider in exercising that judgment. Examples that indicate compensation rather than additional purchase price include a requirement of continued employment for payment of the contingent amount, extra payments to those selling shareholders who remain as key employees of the combined company, and contingent payments structured on terms similar to those of former profit-sharing arrangements of the acquired company.

(e) ACQUISITION OF MINORITY INTERESTS.   The discussion to this point has been concerned with various types of business combinations. An acquisition of stock held by minority stockholders of a subsidiary is not a business combination; paragraph 14 of SFAS No. 141, however, requires such acquisitions to be accounted for by the purchase method. Use of the purchase method of accounting is required whether the stock is acquired by the parent, the subsidiary itself, or other subsidiaries of the same parent. Additionally, the purchase method should be used if the effect of a transaction, irrespective of its form, is to reduce or eliminate the minority interest in a subsidiary. The adjustments necessary to give effect to the application of the purchase method are not ordinarily recognized in the separate financial statements of the subsidiary, and, accordingly, shares purchased directly by the subsidiary, or by the parent or other companies controlled by the parent and contributed to the subsidiary, should be accounted for as a capital transaction by the subsidiary. A more comprehensive discussion of the effects of purchase accounting on the separate financial statements of an acquired company (pushdown accounting) is included in Subsection 12.3(i).

The purchase of fractional shares or shares held by dissenting stockholders as part of a plan of combination is not an acquisition of minority interest. In this circumstance, the general provisions of the Statement would apply.

Interpretation No. 26 provides additional guidance on the acquisition of minority interest and indicates that purchase accounting is applicable when:

- A parent exchanges its common stock, assets, or debt for common stock held by minority shareholders of its subsidiary
- The subsidiary buys as treasury stock the common stock held by minority shareholders
- Another subsidiary of the parent exchanges its common stock or assets or debt for common stock held by the minority shareholders of an affiliated subsidiary

The above examples of acquisitions of minority interests raise questions regarding the appropriate accounting in certain circumstances when considered in relation to Interpretation No. 39, which discusses combinations and exchanges between entities under common control. FTB No. 85-5 addresses the issues of downstream mergers and stock transactions between companies under common control. FTB No. 85-5 emphasizes the point made in Interpretation No. 26 that acquisition of minority interest through a downstream merger should be accounted for by the purchase method, even though some would argue that such transactions may represent a combination of entities under common control.

FTB No. 85-5 also discusses in detail the accounting for stock transactions between companies under common control in relation to the acquisition of the minority interest of one subsidiary by issuing stock of another subsidiary. The accounting for such transactions between subsidiaries under common control depends on whether the minority shareholders are party to the exchange of shares. Paragraph 6 of the Technical Bulletin indicates that, if shares owned by minority shareholders are exchanged by the minority shareholders for shares of ownership in another subsidiary of the parent, the transaction is recognized by the parent company as the acquisition of a minority interest and should be accounted for by the purchase method. If, however, minority shareholders are not party to an exchange of shares between the two subsidiaries (assuming one partially owned subsidiary issues its shares in exchange for the parent's shares of another subsidiary), the minority interest in the issuing subsidiary remains outstanding. This transaction should be accounted for in a manner similar to that for a pooling of interests under the guidance of Interpretation No. 39, because the substance of the transaction is simply a rearrangement of the parent's investment in its subsidiaries without change in the composition of any of the existing minority interests.

As can be seen from the above example, although the minority stockholders' interest in net assets of the subsidiaries has changed in each case, the accounting will depend on whether the minority shareholders participated in the transaction or if the exchange of shares occurred only between the parent and/or its subsidiaries.

(i) Exchange of Ownership Interests Between Entities under Common Control.   The EITF Issue No. 90-5 deals with two situations that may arise when a parent company transfers its ownership in one subsidiary Sub A to another subsidiary Sub B in exchange for additional shares of Sub B. The parent's investment in Sub A differs from the value of the net assets in Sub A's financial statements because pushdown accounting appropriately was not applied.

The Task Force concluded that the consolidated financials of Sub B should reflect the assets and liabilities of Sub A at the historical cost in the consolidated financials of Sub B's parent and not at the historical cost in Sub A's financials. The parent's carrying amount is historical cost under Interpretation No. 39. The Task Force also noted that Sub B must be a substantive operating company.

The Task Force stated further that the acquisition be treated as a purchase acquisition in the consolidated statements of Sub B, conforming to the guidance contained in Technical Bulletin 85-5, regardless of whether cash or stock is used to effect the transaction. However, if the exchange lacks substance, it should be accounted for based on carrying amounts. If stock is used, there must be an objective and reliable basis for measuring the value of the stock issued in order to record the transaction at fair value.

(ii) Accounting for Simultaneous Common Control Mergers.   A recent set of issues that came before the Task Force (EITF Issue No. 90-13) involved transactions in which a parent company (Parent) obtains control of another company (Target) and almost simultaneously, as part of the planned transaction, Target issues additional shares to Parent in exchange for Parent's interest in a subsidiary (Subsidiary).

The Task Force concluded that the two-step transaction cannot be separated, but should be viewed as one transaction. Interpretation No. 39 does not apply, and Parent should account for the transfer of Subsidiary to Target as a purchase of Target under the Opinion. Furthermore, Parent should account for the transaction as a partial sale of Subsidiary to Target's minority shareholders and as a partial acquisition of Target. Gain or loss would be recognized by Parent on the portion of Subsidiary sold.

In preparing Parent's consolidated statements, Parent should step up Target's assets and liabilities to the extent acquired by Parent and step up Subsidiary's assets and liabilities to the extent Subsidiary was sold.

In the separate financial statements of Target, the transaction should be accounted for as a reverse acquisition of Target by Subsidiary. In Target's separate financials, its assets and liabilities would be reflected at fair value to the extent acquired. Subsidiary's assets and liabilities should not be revalued. The Task Force noted that this treatment is consistent with reverse acquisition accounting (Subsidiary has acquired an interest in Target) and gain or loss is not recognized at the Target-Subsidiary level.

Subsidiary:	
70% of the $100 historical cost	$ 70
30% of the $250 fair value	75
Target:	
70% of the $500 fair value	350
30% of the $200 historical cost	60
Basis of combined entity	$ 555
Parent's basis in Target	$ 420
Minority interest	135
	$ 555

Target's and Subsidiary's assets and liabilities would be valued in Target's separate financial statements at amounts totaling $510, based on the following calculation:

Subsidiary historical cost	$ 100
Target:	
70% of the $500 fair value	350
30% of the $200 historical cost	60
Basis of combined entity	$ 510

Exhibit 12.1   Example of the application of the EITF consensus on Issue No. 90-13, "Accounting for Simultaneous Common Control Mergers," Exhibit 90-13A.

The illustration in Exhibit 12.1 is reproduced from EITF Issue No. 90-13, with permission.

(f) IDENTIFYING ASSETS ACQUIRED AND LIABILITIES ASSUMED.   Before doing the allocation procedures described in Sections 12.3(f) and (g), the acquiring entity does the following:

- Review the purchase consideration if other than cash to make sure that it has been valued in conformity with the guidance in Section 12.3(b)
- Identify all of the assets acquired and liabilities assumed, including intangible assets

SFAS No. 141 recommends use of the following illustrative lists as a reference tool in identifying intangible assets acquired in a business combination.

- *Customer-based or market-based assets* — intangible assets that relate to customer structure or market factors of the business:
    1. Lists (advertising, customer, dealer, mailing, subscription, etc.)
    2. Customer base
    3. Financial institution depositor or borrower relationships
    4. Customer routes
    5. Delivery system, distribution channels
    6. Customer service capability, product or service support
    7. Effective advertising programs
    8. Trademarked brand names
    9. Newspaper mastheads
    10. Presence in geographic locations or markets
    11. Value of insurance-in-force, insurance expirations
    12. Production backlog
    13. Concession stands
    14. Airport gates and slots

15. Retail shelf space

16. Files and records (credit, medical)

- *Contract-based assets*—intangible assets that have a fixed or definite term:

  1. Agreements (consulting, income, licensing, manufacturing, royalty, standstill)

  2. Contracts (advertising, construction, consulting, customer, employment, insurance, maintenance, management, marketing, mortgage, presold, purchase, service, supply)

  3. Covenants not to compete

  4. Easements

  5. Leases (valuable or favorable terms)

  6. Permits (construction)

  7. Rights (broadcasting, development, gas allocation, landing, lease, mineral, mortgage servicing, reacquired franchise, servicing, timber cutting, use, water)

- *Technology-based assets*—intangible assets that relate to innovations or technological advances within the business:

  1. Computer software and license, computer programs, information systems, program formats, Internet domain names and portals

  2. Secret formulas and processes, recipes

  3. Technical drawings, technical and procedural manuals, blueprints

  4. Databases, title plants

  5. Manufacturing processes, procedures, production line

  6. Research and development

  7. Technological know-how

- *Statutory-based assets*—intangible assets with statutorily established useful lives:

  1. Patents

  2. Copyrights (manuscripts, literary works, musical compositions)

  3. Franchises (cable, radio, television)

  4. Trademarks, trade names

- *Workforce-based assets*—intangible assets that relate to the value of the established employees or workforce of a company:

  1. Assembled workforce, trained staff

  2. Nonunion status, strong labor relations, favorable wage rates

  3. Superior management or other key employees

  4. Technical expertise

  5. Ongoing training programs, recruiting programs

- *Corporate organizational and financial assets*—intangible assets relating to the organizational structure of an entity:

  1. Savings value of escrow fund

  2. Favorable financial arrangements, outstanding credit rating

  3. Fundraising capabilities, access to capital markets

  4. Favorable government relations

All identifiable assets acquired and liabilities assumed in a business combination, regardless of whether recorded separately in the financial statements of the acquired entity, are assigned a portion of the total cost of the acquired entity based on their fair values at the date of acquisition. Among other sources of relevant information, independent appraisals and actuarial or other valuations may be used as an aid in determining the fair values. The tax basis of an asset or liability is not a factor in determining its fair value.

(g) ALLOCATION OF PURCHASE PRICE.   The bookkeeping mechanics of allocating the purchase price may be accomplished in several ways depending in part on the structure of the transaction (i.e., purchase of stock or assets) and of the continuing organization (i.e., parent/subsidiary or parent only) and future reporting requirements.

In the case of an asset purchase, the assets and liabilities acquired are recorded on the acquiror's books. In the case of a stock purchase to be operated as a wholly owned subsidiary, the parent company could record the purchase as an investment and apply the equity method to account for future activities of the subsidiary. The purchase price allocation in this case would be accomplished off the books and only recorded with consolidating entries as part of the consolidation process. Alternatively, the purchase price allocation could be pushed down to the subsidiary's books. Under pushdown accounting, all subsidiary assets (tangible and intangible) and liabilities are adjusted to fair market value at the time of the acquisition with an offsetting adjustment to the subsidiary's equity accounts resulting in agreement between the total of these equity accounts and the parent's investment account. The applicability of pushdown accounting is further discussed in Subsection 12.3(i).

Paragraph 35 of SFAS No. 141 provides general guidance on the allocation of the purchase price to the assets acquired and liabilities assumed of an acquired company. It requires that all of the identifiable assets acquired, including intangible assets, be allocated a portion of the cost of the acquired company, normally equal to the asset's fair value at the date of acquisition. The Statement requires that the excess of cost of the acquired company over the sum of the amounts assigned to tangible and identifiable intangible assets acquired, less values assigned to liabilities assumed, be recorded as goodwill. Acquired identifiable intangible assets that cannot be reliably measured are included in the amount recorded as goodwill. Reliability embodies the characteristics of representational faithfulness and verifiability, as discussed in FASB Concepts Statement No. 2, "Qualitative Characteristics of Accounting Information," and does not mean that intangible assets must be precisely measurable. Paragraph 37 of the Statement provides specific guidance on the assignment of fair values to individual assets acquired and liabilities assumed in the acquisition.

An acquiring entity should record periodically as a part of income the accrual of interest on assets and liabilities recorded at the acquisition date at the discounted values of amounts to be received or paid. An acquiring entity does not record as a separate asset the goodwill previously recorded by an acquired entity and does not record deferred income taxes recorded by an acquired entity before its acquisition.

(i) Excess of the Fair Value of Acquired Net Assets over Cost.   In some cases, the sum of the fair values of identifiable assets acquired less liabilities assumed may exceed the cost of the acquired entity (excess). In those cases, the amounts that otherwise would be assigned to acquired intangible assets that are of a type that do not have an observable market are limited to the amount that would not create or increase an excess. If the excess is less than the fair values of those acquired intangible assets, it is allocated as a pro rata reduction of the fair values that otherwise would be assigned. If the excess is greater than the fair values of those intangible assets, the remaining excess is then allocated as a pro rata reduction of the fair values that otherwise would be assigned to all of the acquired depreciable nonfinancial assets and all of the acquired intangible assets that are of a type that have an observable market.

If any excess remains after those assets are reduced to zero, that excess is recognized as an extraordinary gain, as described in paragraph 11 of APB Opinion No. 30, "Reporting the Results of Operations—Reporting the Effects of Disposal of a Segment of a Business, and Extraordinary, Unusual and Infrequently Occurring Events and Transactions." The extraordinary gain is recognized in the period in which the business combination is completed unless the combination involves contingent consideration that, if paid or issued, would be recognized as an additional element of cost of the acquired entity. If an extraordinary gain is recognized before the end of the allocation period, any subsequent adjustments to that extraordinary gain that result from changes to the purchase price allocation are recognized as an extraordinary item.

For contingent consideration based on earnings, an amount equal to the lesser of the maximum amount of the contingent consideration or excess is recognized as if it were a liability. When the contingency is resolved, the contingent consideration issued or issuable over the amount that was recognized as if it were a liability is recognized as an additional cost of the acquired entity. If the amount initially recognized as if it were a liability exceeds the fair value of the consideration issued or issuable, that excess is allocated as a pro rata reduction of the amount assigned to assets acquired. Any amount that remains after reducing those assets to zero is recognized as an extraordinary gain.

(ii) Purchase Price Allocated to Inventories. The objective of allocating the purchase price to the various components of inventories is to assure that the acquiror recognizes only profits associated with value added to the acquired inventory subsequent to the acquisition date and does not recognize profit associated with purchased value of the inventories. Accordingly, in assigning the purchase price to finished goods and work-in-process inventories, SFAS No. 141 requires that the valuation be based on selling price less the sum of (1) costs to complete, if applicable; (2) costs of disposal; and (3) a reasonable profit margin for the completion and selling effort and the postacquisition completion effort. It is generally not appropriate to assign the acquiree's carrying value to the cost of acquired inventories, because the acquiree's cost does not reflect the manufacturing profit that is recognized by the acquiree through the normal selling process. This manufacturing profit should be considered as part of the fair value assigned to the inventory.

Raw materials should be valued at replacement cost on the date of the acquisition, because no value has been added to the raw materials through manufacturing or holding. Replacement cost of raw materials inventories should be determined as of the business combination acquisition date because significant changes in replacement cost could have occurred subsequent to the original purchase of the raw materials by the acquiree.

Care should be taken in evaluating the various types of inventory to assure that inventories are valued according to their appropriate classification: raw materials, work-in-process, or finished goods. For example, Company A acquired the olive distribution operations of Company B. The acquisition date was in February. Spot market prices for raw olives as of February were used to value the raw olive inventories of the olive-processing operation. Traditionally, the olive company purchased its olive inventories in September and October when the olive harvests occurred and distilled them for a period of approximately six months prior to sale to distributors. Because the valuation of the olive inventories occurred in February during a period when raw olives were at a premium because of low supply, the value assigned to the olives was significantly higher than the company's normal cost of olives and the subsequent selling price of the distilled olives. As a result, sales in the subsequent year resulted in substantial losses to the company. In this case, the nature of the olive market is so seasonal that the February spot price was an inappropriate valuation for the olive inventories. In addition, the olives should have been valued as work-in-process inventories, since the distillation process was under way. A valuation based on estimated selling price during the following selling season, discounted for cost of completing the distillation process and selling the olives through the company's distribution network, was the appropriate method of valuing the olive inventories.

(iii) Last-In First-Out Inventories. Inventories accounted for under the last-in first-out (LIFO) method by the acquired company should be valued at fair value in accordance with the provisions of SFAS No. 141 at the acquisition date. This fair value of the acquired inventories thereby becomes the LIFO base layer valuation for postacquisition purposes. Carryover of the acquiree's LIFO basis inventories for book purposes is not appropriate because that is not fair value at acquisition date. The effect of differences between book and tax bases arising from the allocation of purchase price is discussed in Section 12.3(g)(iii) of this chapter.

(iv) Determining Costs to Complete, Selling Costs, and Normal Profit Margin. The valuation of finished goods and work-in-process inventories requires consideration of costs to complete, selling costs, and normal profit margin for the completion and selling effort. The calculation of a normal profit margin should be based on an allocation of a normal gross profit among the preacquisition and postacquisition activities associated with the inventories. One guideline for determining the reasonable profit allowance (spoken of in SFAS No. 141, paragraph 37c) is to identify a reasonable dollar value profit margin for the particular item of inventory for the industry. This amount should then be reduced by the estimated selling costs associated with the product. The resulting amount should then be allocated between the preacquisition and postacquisition activities based on the ratio of selling expenses and completion costs to total manufacturing costs plus selling expenses.

(v) Allocation to Noncurrent Tangible and Intangible Assets. The appraised value of non-current tangible and identifiable intangible assets is generally the best measure of fair value for allocating the purchase price of the acquisition. SFAS No. 141, consistent with SFAS No. 144, "Accounting for the Impairment or Disposal of Long-Lived Assets," specifically suggests the following two methods for allocating purchase price to plant and equipment, depending on the type of expected future use for those assets:

1. If the equipment is to be used for an extended period, the valuation should be based on current replacement costs for similar capacity, unless the expected future use of the assets indicates a lower value to the acquiror. The use of appraisal information or relevant published indices would be appropriate to establish replacement cost.
2. Equipment to be sold or held for later sale rather than used in postacquisition operations should be valued at current net realizable value.

SFAS No. 141 requires that intangible assets that can be identified and named should be valued separately from goodwill and other identifiable assets acquired in the acquisition. Intangible assets typically found in an acquisition include those listed in Section 12.3(e) of this chapter (see also paragraph A14 of SFAS No. 141). The critical factor in assessing whether a particular intangible asset should be valued separately in an acquisition is whether the intangible asset arises from contractual or legal rights or is capable of being separated from the entity and sold.

Identifiable intangible assets with fair values that are reliably measurable should not be included in goodwill. An intangible asset is recognized as an asset apart from goodwill if it arises from contractual or other legal rights (regardless of whether those rights are transferable or separable from the acquired entity or from other rights and obligations). If an intangible asset does not arise from contractual or other legal rights, it is recognized as an asset apart from goodwill only if it is separable, that is, it is capable of being separated or divided from the acquired entity and sold, transferred, licensed, rented, or exchanged (regardless of whether there is an intent to do so). However, for purposes of Statement No. 141, an intangible asset that cannot be sold, transferred, licensed, rented, or exchanged individually is considered separable if it can be sold, transferred, licensed, rented, or exchanged in combination with a related contract, asset, or liability. For purposes of Statement No. 141, an assembled workforce is not recognized as an intangible asset apart from goodwill.

(vi) Assignment of Purchase Price to Leases. FASB Interpretation No. 21, "Accounting for Leases in a Business Combination," provides guidance on valuing capital leases acquired. The Interpretation indicates that the acquiror shall retain the previous classification of leases acquired in a business combination unless the provisions of the leases are modified as indicated in paragraph 9 of SFAS No. 13, "Accounting for Leases." The amounts assigned to the asset and liability as a capital lease in a purchase combination should be determined independently of each other. The liability should be equal to the present value of the remaining lease payments, discounted at an appropriate current interest rate as of the acquisition date. The capital lease asset should be valued based on the underlying value of the asset itself. One method of estimating such a value in a situation in which the remaining useful life of the asset exceeds the lease terms would be to calculate the present value of the current fair rental value for similar used equipment using an appropriate current interest rate as of the acquisition date. The Interpretation also indicates that subsequent to the initial recording, the leases should be accounted for in accordance with SFAS No. 13.

(vii) Research and Development Acquired. FIN No. 4 indicates that identifiable assets resulting from research and development (R&D) activities of an acquired company should be recorded in the business combination and that the purchase price should be allocated to the research and development asset. Some research and development assets acquired might include patents received or applied for, blueprints, formulas and specifications, designs for new products or processes, materials and supplies, equipment and facilities, and projects in process.

After allocation of the purchase price, an evaluation should be made to determine whether the identifiable R&D assets are to be used in the general research and development activities of the combined enterprise or will be used in a particular research and development project and have no alternative future use. Paragraph 12 of SFAS No. 2 indicates that costs of research and development activities should be expensed unless the asset has alternative future use.

The EITF addressed Issue No. 86-14, "Purchased Research and Development Projects in a Business Combination," at its July 1986 and May 1987 meetings. The Task Force agreed that FIN No. 4 required a portion of the purchase price to be allocated to the R&D projects in process that have value and that the amount allocated to the R&D project would be charged to expense as a research and development cost if the project does not have an alternative future use. Some Task Force members questioned whether the rationale for such allocation of purchase price and subsequent write-off should be reconsidered by the FASB. At the May 1987 meeting, the FASB staff indicated that the Board does not favor reconsidering the guidance in FIN No. 4 or SFAS No. 2. Accordingly, FIN No. 4 continues to require an allocation of purchase price to identifiable results of research and development.

(viii) Allocation of Purchase Price to Assets to Be Sold. EITF Issue No. 87-11, "Allocation of Purchase Price to Assets to Be Sold," addresses several questions regarding the allocation of purchase price to a subsidiary of an acquiree when the acquiror plans to sell the subsidiary within one year of the acquisition date and use the proceeds from the sale to reduce the acquisition debt. At its November 1987 meeting, the EITF reached a consensus that the allocation of purchase price should reflect the acquiror's intent to sell the subsidiary and that this action, if taken within one year of the acquisition, should not result in any impact on the acquiror's consolidated statement of operations as a result of the cash flows from (1) the subsidiary's postacquisition operations, (2) interest on the portion of the acquisition debt used to acquire the subsidiary, or (3) proceeds of the sale. This consensus applies solely to net assets that are expected to be sold within one year of the date of acquisition.

Prior to this consensus, the SEC had required that the acquiror have a firm contract to sell the assets at the acquisition date before it would permit discounting of the net realizable value. The SEC staff accepted the EITF consensus and will require the accounting described above for those instances where the operations to be sold were identified as of the purchase date and, as of that date, there was a reasonable expectation that the operations would be sold within one year. At the December 1987 EITF meeting, the SEC representative indicated that the SEC staff would also require the following disclosures in the financial statements and pro forma information that cover the reporting periods in which the consensus is applied:

- A description of the operations held for sale, a description of the method used to assign amounts to those assets, the expected disposal date, and the method used to account for those assets.
- Disclosures of the operation's profit or loss during the period that has been excluded from the consolidated income statement, together with a schedule reconciling that amount to the earnings received or losses funded by the parent that have been accounted for as an adjustment to the carrying amount of the assets. Allocated interest cost should be separately identified.

- Disclosure of any gain or loss on the ultimate disposition that has been treated as an adjustment of the original purchase price allocation.

In addition, the SEC expects registrants to review differences between actual and estimated cash flow and the estimated sales proceeds in order to determine if a loss should be reported for events that occur during the holding period.

In EITF Issue No. 90-6, the Task Force considered two events not addressed in Issue No. 87-11: (1) The acquiring company does not complete the sale of an operating unit (a line of business or a portion of a line of business) of an acquired company within one year of the purchase date, but the acquiring company still intends to sell the operating unit; and (2) the acquiring company decides not to sell the operating unit.

The Task Force concluded that Issue No. 87-11 be applied only to identified net assets held for sale that constitute a segment or a portion of a segment of a business. As to the "holding period," a company may continue to apply the accounting of Issue No. 87-11 for up to one year from the purchase date if it is actively attempting to find a buyer and remains committed to a formal plan of sale. In addition, Issue No. 87-11 accounting may be continued for a short period beyond one year only in the event a firm contract exists for a sale to be completed soon after the end of the one-year period. At the end of the holding period, the acquiring company should discontinue accounting for the operating unit to be sold in accordance with Issue No. 87-11. Thereafter, the results of operations and incremental interest expense incurred in financing the purchase of the operating unit should be reported in the consolidated operations of the acquiring company generally as a single line item. The amounts pertaining to the operating unit (operating results, gain or loss on disposal, and interest expense) should be reported as part of income or loss from continuing operations, unless the operating unit qualifies as a segment of a business, in which case Opinion No. 30 applies.

Task Force members also considered other matters, such as the need to allocate the carrying value of the acquired unit at the end of the holding period, at least on a memo basis, to determine the operating results of the operations of the unit. Because the unit is still held for sale, no cumulative adjustment is made to reflect a reallocation of the unit's purchase price or reversal of the effects of applying Issue No. 87-11 accounting. There is also a need to continually re-evaluate the net realizable value of the unit. A decrease in net realizable value should be reflected as losses to the acquiring company if attributable to specific identifiable economic events occurring subsequent to the purchase date. Other changes in net realizable value identified within the (Opinion No. 30) allocation period not so attributable should be accounted for as an adjustment to the allocation of the purchase price.

If a decision is made not to sell the operating unit of the acquired company within the holding period, the Task Force concluded that the purchase price of the acquired company should be reallocated. This reallocation should be based on amounts as of the purchase date as though the operating unit had never been held for sale, including reversal of the effects of having applied Issue No. 87-11 accounting to the transaction.

When a decision not to sell is reached after the end of the holding period, the purchase price of Company B should not be reallocated based on amounts as of the purchase date. Rather, the carrying amount of Subsidiary S as of the date the decision is made to keep Subsidiary S should be allocated to the current fair values of its identifiable assets and liabilities on that date and the remainder, if any, to goodwill. The current carrying amount of Subsidiary S at that date should be net of any impairment in the value of Subsidiary S since the date of purchase. Any such impairment is recognized as a current loss from operations. Any change in goodwill resulting from the allocation is amortized over its remaining life in accordance with Opinion No. 17.

The SEC observer indicated that it is expected that the registrant be able to demonstrate that the operation to be sold had been identified at the purchase date and there was at least a reasonable expectation of sale within one year. A mere intent to sell is insufficient. Moreover, the consensus for Issue Nos. 87-11 and 90-6 require, rather than merely permit, that kind of accounting in those circumstances.

The SEC staff would expect the financial statements and pro forma information covering all reporting periods to include:

- A description of the operations held for sale, the method used to assign amounts to those assets, the method used to account for those assets, and the expected disposal date.
- Disclosure of the operation's profit or loss that has been excluded from the consolidated income statement during the period together with a schedule reconciling that amount to the earnings received or losses funded by the parent that have been accounted for as an adjustment to the carrying amount of the assets. The amount of allocated interest cost should be separately identified.
- Disclosure of any gain or loss on the ultimate disposition that has been treated as an adjustment of the original purchase price allocation.
- Discussion in Management's Discussion and Analysis of Financial Condition and Results of Operations (MD&A) of any material effect on results of operations, liquidity, capital resources and known trends, commitments, or contingencies.

A decision not to sell after the holding period should be disclosed, including the reasons and an explanation of the adjustments including (1) the carrying amount of the subsidiary that will be allocated to the current fair values of its identifiable assets and liabilities (including the amount of operating profit or losses and interest capitalized pursuant to the consensus for Issue No. 87-11), and (2) the effect on comparability of the reporting periods.

The need to continually monitor cash flows, actual versus estimated, is required to determine whether an impairment loss should be reported in the income statement for events that have occurred subsequent to the purchase date.

(ix) Allocation of Purchase Price to Pensions. SFAS No. 87 requires that business combinations accounted for by the purchase method include recognition of a liability to the extent the projected benefit obligation exceeds plan assets or, alternatively, recognition of an asset to the extent the plan assets exceed the projected benefit obligation. In applying the guidance of SFAS No. 87, any previously existing unrecognized net gain or loss, unrecognized prior-service cost, and unrecognized net obligation or net asset existing at the date of initial application of SFAS No. 87 are eliminated. Postacquisition pension expense for the acquired plan is based only on service cost, interest cost, and the actual return on assets until such time as unrecognized gains or losses and unrecognized prior service costs arise through the postacquisition operations of the plan. The liability or asset recorded for acquired pension costs is amortized or accreted based on the difference between pension funding and pension expense. If it is anticipated that the plan will be terminated or curtailed, the effects of such actions should be taken into consideration in measuring the projected benefit obligation used to determine the appropriate amount of the asset or liability to be recorded.

The SFAS No. 87 approach to allocation of purchase price to a pension liability or asset may result in a significantly larger liability or asset than would have been recognized under the Opinion, because it takes into consideration the total projected benefit obligation, which includes the effect of future salary increases and comprehends both vested and nonvested benefits.

The effect of this increased allocation to the pension liability will usually result in the recognition of a greater amount of goodwill in most business combinations. This will result in additional charges to income subsequent to the acquisition.

The pension assets and liabilities to be recorded in the acquisition of a company with both overfunded and underfunded plans should not be offset in allocating the purchase price.

(x) Postretirement Benefits of the Acquiree. Paragraphs 86 through 88 of FASB Statement No. 106, *Employers' Accounting for Postretirement Benefits Other than Pensions* (SFAS No. 106), provide guidance on accounting for postretirement plans acquired in a business combination that is accounted for by the purchase method. That guidance indicates that when an employer is acquired in a business combination that is accounted for by the purchase method under the Opinion and that employer sponsors a single-employer defined benefit postretirement plan, the allocation of the purchase price to individual assets acquired and liabilities assumed shall include a liability for the accumulated postretirement benefit obligation (APBO) in excess of the fair value of the plan assets or an asset for the fair value of the plan assets in excess of the APBO. The APBO assumed shall be measured based on the benefits attributed by the acquired entity to employee service prior to the date the business combination is consummated, adjusted to reflect (a) any changes in assumptions based on the purchaser's assessment of relevant future events and (b) the terms of the substantive plan to be provided by the purchaser to the extent they differ from the terms of the acquired entity's substantive plan.

Further, if the postretirement benefit plan of the acquired entity is amended as a condition of the business combination (e.g., if the change is required by the seller as part of the consummation of the acquisition), the effects of any improvements attributed to services rendered by the participants of the acquired entity's plan prior to the date of the business combination shall be accounted for as part of the APBO of the acquired entity. Otherwise, if improvements to the postretirement benefit plan of the acquired entity are not a condition of the business combination, credit granted for prior service shall be recognized as a plan amendment. If it is expected that the plan will be terminated or curtailed, SFAS No. 106 requires that the effects of those actions shall be considered in measuring the APBO. Otherwise, no future changes to the plan should be anticipated.

In addition, any previously existing unrecognized net gain or loss, unrecognized prior service cost, or unrecognized transition obligation or transition asset is eliminated for the acquired employer's plan. Subsequently, to the extent that the net obligation assumed or net assets acquired are considered in determining the amounts of contributions to the plan, differences between the purchaser's net periodic postretirement benefit cost and amounts it contributes will reduce the liability or asset recognized at the date of the combination.

(xi) Postemployment Benefits of the Acquiree.   The FASB Statement No. 112, *Employers' Accounting for Postemployment Benefits*, sets standards of accounting for an employer's cost of providing benefits to former or inactive employees after employment but before retirement. Examples of such benefits would be salary continuation, severance pay, and disability, medical, and life insurance coverage. In a sense, SFAS No. 112 is a companion to SFAS No. 106, which covers the costs of providing benefits to former employees after retirement date. SFAS No. 112 is less detailed than SFAS No. 106. For instance, it does not contain guidance on how to account for postemployment benefits acquired in a purchase business combination that would parallel the guidance in paragraphs 86-88 of SFAS No. 106. In the absence of explicit guidance in SFAS No. 112, the guidance in SFAS No. 106 should, logically, be analogized to postemployment benefit obligations of the acquired company that are assumed by the acquiring company (see Subsection 12.3(g)(x)).

(xii) Assignment of Purchase Price to Liabilities Existing at the Acquisition Date.   SFAS No. 141 requires that liabilities assumed in the acquisition be recorded at their fair value. Such liabilities include warranty accruals, vacation pay, deferred compensation, unfavorable leases, contracts, and commitments, as well as accounts and notes payable and other forms of long-term debt. Liabilities should be recorded at the present value of amounts to be paid and discounted at current interest rates. The objective of allocating fair value to liabilities assumed in the acquisition is to arrive at amounts assigned as though the acquiror had incurred the liabilities as of the acquisition date.

Certain components of equity should also be evaluated to determine if the substance of the security is more closely related to debt than to equity. For example, mandatory redeemable preferred stock, which is typically classified outside of the equity section due to the redemption characteristics, should generally be recorded at fair value at the date of acquisition. The amount of cash the preferred shareholders will receive is fixed, as in a debt arrangement, and generally the other redemption and dividend terms are fixed as well. There is little difference in substance between assuming long-term debt of a target company and assuming mandatorily redeemable preferred stock. Both types of securities represent potential claims against the company for cash.

The EITF discussed Issue No. 84-35a, "Liabilities Accrued in a Purchase Business Combination," at its February 1985 meeting. Several types of liabilities were discussed, and no consensus was reached as to individual types of liabilities that should be accrued. However, the FASB staff expressed its belief that the literature is clear: Liabilities that exist at the acquisition date should be accrued at their fair values.

(xiii) Income Tax Effects on the Purchase Price Allocation.   The following discussion of accounting for income taxes in connection with business combinations accounted for by the purchase method is based on the guidance provided in SFAS No. 109, "Accounting for Income Taxes."

The SFAS No. 109 requires recognition of a deferred tax liability or asset at the acquisition date for the income tax consequences of differences between the assigned values and the tax bases of the assets acquired and the liabilities assumed (except the portion of goodwill for which amortization is not deductible for tax purposes, unallocated "negative goodwill," leveraged leases, and acquired APB Opinion No. 23 differences). This change may seem to imply little more than a requirement to "gross up" the tax effects that would have been previously recognized on a "net-of-tax" basis under the Opinion and APB Opinion No. 11. However, the change is much more significant:

- A net deferred tax asset is recognized in a purchase transaction if realization of the tax benefits for deductible temporary differences and carryforwards is more likely than not.
- If separate tax returns are expected to be filed in future years, only the available evidence of the acquired entity should be considered in determining if realization of acquired tax benefits is more likely than not.
- Tax benefits for temporary differences and carryforwards of the acquirer that were not recognized prior to the business combination may be recognized in the purchase price allocation by reducing the valuation allowance if realization is more likely than not.
- Discounting of the income tax consequences of temporary differences and carryforward benefits to their present values is prohibited.

Consistent with prior practice, no deferred income taxes are recorded for the amount assigned to goodwill that is not deductible for tax purposes. Also, deferred income taxes are not recorded for the difference between the financial reporting amount assigned to a leveraged lease acquired in a purchase business combination and the tax basis of that lease. EITF Issue No. 96-7 concludes that deferred taxes are not provided on the difference between book and tax bases of in-process research and development costs at acquisition date, and therefore in-process R&D is written off on a gross basis.

This accounting applies to both taxable and nontaxable purchase business combinations. A taxable business combination is distinguished from a nontaxable one in that, in a taxable transaction, the purchase price is assigned to the assets acquired and liabilities assumed both for income tax and financial reporting purposes, whereas in a nontaxable business combination, the predecessor's tax bases are carried forward. In both taxable and nontaxable business combinations, the amounts assigned to the individual assets acquired and liabilities assumed for financial statement purposes are often different from the amounts assigned or carried forward for tax purposes. A deferred tax liability or asset is recognized for each of these differences using the recognition and measurement criteria of SFAS No. 109.

The following example from paragraph 260 of SFAS No. 109 illustrates the recognition and measurement of a deferred tax liability and asset in a nontaxable business combination. The assumptions are as follows:

- The enacted tax rate is 40 percent for all future years, and amortization of goodwill is not deductible for tax purposes.
- An enterprise is acquired for $20,000, and the enterprise has no leveraged leases.

- The tax basis of the net assets acquired is $5,000, and the assigned value (other than goodwill) is $12,000. Future recovery of the assets and settlement of the liabilities at their assigned values will result in $20,000 of taxable amounts and $13,000 of deductible amounts that can be offset against each other. Therefore, no valuation allowance is necessary.

The amounts recorded to account for the purchase transaction are as follows:

Assigned value of the net assets (other than goodwill) acquired	$12,000
Deferred tax liability for $20,000 of taxable temporary differences	(8,000)
Deferred tax asset for $13,000 of deductible temporary differences	5,200
Goodwill—nondeductible	10,800
Purchase price of the acquired enterprise	$20,000

If a valuation allowance is recognized for the deferred tax asset for an acquired entity's deductible temporary differences or operating loss or tax credit carryforwards at the acquisition date, SFAS No. 109 indicates that the tax benefits for those items that are first recognized (i.e., by elimination of that valuation allowance) in financial statements after the acquisition date shall be applied (a) first to reduce to zero any goodwill related to the acquisition, (b) second to reduce to zero other noncurrent intangible assets related to the acquisition, and (c) third to reduce income tax expense.

(xiv) Deferred Taxes Associated with Acquired Identifiable Intangible Assets with No Tax Basis.
Differences in the tax and book bases of purchased intangible assets result in temporary differences under SFAS No. 109 even if the asset has no tax basis or if the amortization of the asset is not currently deductible for tax purposes. This is often the case in a nontaxable business combination where, for accounting purposes, a significant portion of the purchase price is allocated to identifiable intangible assets such as franchise rights, patents, mortgage servicing rights, or other intangible assets with no tax basis.

The FASB staff concluded in Question 16 of their special report, *A Guide to Implementation of Statement 109 on Accounting for Income Taxes* (the Special Report), that these intangible assets should not be treated in a manner similar to goodwill. Question 16 states, in part:

> A deferred tax liability or asset should be recognized for temporary differences related to intangible assets other than goodwill in accordance with the recognition and measurement requirements of Statement 109. Goodwill recognized in a business combination accounted for as a purchase is a residual—it is the excess of purchase price over the assigned values of the identifiable net assets acquired. Other intangible assets such as customer lists and trademarks are not residuals and are not included among the exceptions (which include goodwill) to comprehensive recognition of deferred taxes identified in paragraph 9 [of the Statement].

SFAS No. 109 indicates that "unallocated negative goodwill" does not represent a temporary difference. However, negative goodwill that is allocated to (as a reduction of) the fair value of noncurrent assets will affect the deferred tax liability associated with the difference between book and tax bases for those assets. Accordingly, in determining the deferred tax liability for a business combination in which negative goodwill is allocated to noncurrent assets, the negative goodwill must be computed simultaneously with the deferred tax liability.

(xv) Tax Deductibility of Goodwill Amortization.
The Omnibus Budget Reconciliation Act of 1993 was enacted on August 10, 1993, and provides that the tax basis of goodwill can be amortized over 15 years. For business combinations consummated after the enactment date, the guidance contained in paragraph 262 and 263 of SFAS No. 109 should be followed. Thus, if the combination results in goodwill for financial reporting purposes that exceeds goodwill for tax purposes, the excess will not result in a reported tax benefit. If, however, tax goodwill exceeds

goodwill for financial reporting purposes, a tax benefit will be reported when those tax benefits are realized in tax returns in future years.

(xvi) Allocation of Purchase Price When Less than 100 Percent Acquired.   Paragraph 35 of SFAS No. 141 states that, in a purchase business combination, the acquiring company should record at fair value the assets acquired and liabilities assumed. However, if the acquiring company in a purchase business combination acquires less than 100 percent of the outstanding common shares of the acquired company, the Statement does not specify whether the identifiable assets and liabilities of the acquired company should be recorded at (a) 100 percent of their fair value on the date of the acquisition or (b) the acquiring company's proportionate share of their value on the date of the acquisition plus the minority interest's proportion of the preacquisition carrying amounts. In the first case, minority interest is recorded at minority's share of the fair value of the identifiable assets and liabilities. In the second case, minority interest is recorded at minority's share of the subsidiary's carrying amount. While the differences could be substantial, they do not affect the measurement of consolidated net income or earnings per share. They do affect the balance sheet and various amortizations and the amount of minority interest in consolidated income reported in the income statement.

Both approaches are followed in practice today, though the second approach (measure minority's share based on the acquired company's carrying amount) is far more common. The FASB is addressing this issue in a project on Business Combinations—Purchase Method Procedures currently on its agenda.

(xvii) Concerns of Securities and Exchange Commission Staff.   In the past several years, the SEC staff has required a number of registrants to restate their financial statements by reallocating portions of the cost of purchase business combination out of goodwill and into specifically identifiable assets—assets whose amortization periods are likely to be shorter than that for goodwill. Under SFAS No. 141, the acquisition cost must be allocated first to all identifiable assets acquired and liabilities assumed "regardless of whether they had been recorded in the financial statements of the acquired entity" (paragraph 35). Paragraph 37 contains some general guides for assigning amounts to individual assets acquired and liabilities assumed other than goodwill. These days, with an increasing number of acquisitions of service and technology companies, significant portions of the acquisition cost may be attributable to other kinds of self-created identifiable intangible assets that were not recorded on the acquiree's books but that must be recognized under SFAS No. 141. The SEC staff has also taken the position that a portion of the acquisition cost that is assigned to purchased research and development should be capitalized and amortized as an intangible asset, and not written off in its entirety immediately after the acquisition, if it meets the "alternative future use" test in paragraph 11c, "Intangibles purchased from others," of SFAS No. 2, "Accounting for Research and Development Costs." Normally, R&D would have an alternative future use if technological feasibility or marketability can be established.

(h) PREACQUISITION CONTINGENCIES.   SFAS No. 141 provides guidance on the accounting for preacquisition contingencies in purchase business combinations. The Statement defines a preacquisition contingency as "a contingency of an entity that is acquired in a business combination that is in existence before the consummation of the combination."

The guidance of SFAS No. 5, "Accounting for Contingencies," should be used in determining whether a condition, situation, or set of circumstances constitutes a contingency of the acquiree at the date of acquisition. Contingencies arising from the acquisition itself are not preacquisition contingencies (e.g., litigation over the acquisition or the tax effects of the acquisition). These contingencies are the acquiring company's contingencies rather than preacquisition contingencies.

In the allocation of the purchase price, preacquisition contingencies should be assigned a value based on their fair value if that can be determined during the allocation period or based on a reasonable estimate. After the one-year allocation period suggested by SFAS No. 141, the resolution of a preacquisition contingency should be recorded as an adjustment to income in the period of resolution. In measuring the fair value of a preacquisition contingency, the use of present value techniques is not prohibited if sufficient information is available to justify their use.

The passage of time, in and of itself, does not change the resolution of a preacquisition contingency from an adjustment of purchase price to an income statement adjustment. For example, assume Company A purchased Company B in June 1986. In the purchase allocation, a liability of $10 million was recorded as "a provision for possible IRS adjustments and other contingencies." As of December 1986, it was determined that the most probable amount due the IRS was $2 million, based on the status of "in-process" IRS examinations. In July 1987, all of the preacquisition contingencies were settled and the total amount to be paid was approximately $2 million. In this case, the allocation period would basically end in December 1986, because the company is no longer waiting for information in order to make the allocation of purchase price required by paragraph 5 of SFAS No. 38 (now replaced by SFAS No. 141). On the basis of the information available in December 1986, Company A could allocate the purchase price using a reasonable estimate of the fair value of the preacquisition contingency. Accordingly, income statement recognition in July 1987 for resolution of the liability would be inappropriate, and the final adjustment should be reflected as an adjustment to the purchase price.

EITF Issue No. 93-7, "Uncertainties Related to Income Taxes in a Purchase Business Combination," discusses a number of uncertainties related to income taxes that may exist at the time of or arise in connection with a purchase business combination. Examples include uncertainties about the allocation of the purchase price to individual assets and liabilities for income tax purposes in a taxable business combination, uncertainties about the carryover bases of assets, liabilities, and carryforwards at the date of acquisition in a nontaxable combination, or uncertainties about tax returns of the acquired company for periods prior to the acquisition date. The issues are whether SFAS No. 141 is applicable to any income tax uncertainties and, if not, how income tax uncertainties should be accounted for under SFAS No. 109.

The EITF concluded that all income tax uncertainties that exist at the time of or arise in connection with a purchase business combination should be accounted for pursuant to SFAS No. 109. Further, the Task Force reached a consensus that the guidance contained in Question 17 of the Special Report on SFAS No. 109 should be applied to changes in estimates and final settlements of all income tax uncertainties that predate or result from a purchase business combination with the exception of uncertainties related to the valuation allowance of a deferred tax asset. The consensus does not, however, apply to changes in judgment about the realization of deferred tax assets because SFAS No. 109 provides guidance for changes in a valuation allowance related to an acquired deductible difference or carryforward. Further, the Task Force noted that the requirement for reduction of a valuation allowance established at the acquisition date applies only to initial recognition of an acquired benefit; all other changes in the valuation allowance due to a change in judgment about the realizability of the deferred tax asset should be included in income from continuing operations.

As indicated in Question 17 of the Special Report, deferred tax assets and liabilities at the date of a purchase business combination should be based on management's best estimate of the ultimate tax basis that will be accepted by the tax authority, and liabilities for prior tax returns of the acquired entity should be based on management's best estimate of the ultimate settlement. At the date of a change in management's best estimate of the ultimate tax basis of acquired assets, liabilities, and carryforwards, and at the date that the tax basis is settled with the tax authority, deferred tax assets and liabilities should be adjusted to reflect the revised tax basis and the amount of any settlement with the tax authority for prior-year income taxes. Similarly, at the date of a change in management's best estimate of items relating to the acquired entity's prior tax returns, and at the date that the items are settled with the tax authority, any liability previously recognized should be adjusted. The effect of those adjustments should be applied to increase or decrease the remaining balance of goodwill attributable to that acquisition. If goodwill is reduced to zero, the remaining amount of those adjustments should be applied initially to reduce to zero other noncurrent intangible assets related to that acquisition, and any remaining amount should be recognized in income.

The Task Force observed that interest on the final settlement with the tax authority that accrues subsequent to the acquisition date should not be included in the goodwill adjustment.

The Task Force also reached a consensus that the guidance in Question 17 of the Special Report is applicable to all purchase business combinations, regardless of whether the combination occurred prior to the adoption of SFAS No. 109 and regardless of the transition method used to adopt SFAS No. 109. SFAS No. 141 applies to all other preacquisition contingencies, and the application of the EITF consensus should be limited solely to income tax uncertainties relating to purchase business combinations.

(i) PUSHDOWN ACCOUNTING. In October 1979, the American Institute of Certified Public Accountants (AICPA) Accounting Standards Executive Committee (AcSEC) prepared an Issues Paper entitled "Pushdown Accounting." The Issues Paper's advisory committee dealt with determining the percentage change in ownership that would justify a new basis of accounting.

Members of AcSEC supported 90 percent as a minimum change of ownership that would justify pushdown accounting. At the time AcSEC decided to support pushdown accounting, it was not supported by practice or by other authoritative accounting or regulatory bodies. In January 1983, the Federal Home Loan Bank Board issued guidance in R-Memorandum No. 55 (which was superseded by R-55a in 1986) consistent with the Issues Paper, which permits but does not require pushdown accounting. The SEC also agreed in SAB No. 54 that "the Staff believes that purchase transactions that result in an entity becoming substantially wholly-owned (as defined in Rule 1-02(z) of Regulation S-X) establish a new basis of accounting for the purchased assets and liabilities."

When initially applied in practice, a new basis of accounting in the separate financial statements of an acquired entity was generally applied when the change in ownership was at least 90 percent. However, since the AICPA Issues Paper was published in 1979, practice has developed to permit pushdown accounting when the change in ownership is 80 percent or greater. In the case of a step acquisition, pushdown accounting may be applied when an individual, company, or control group obtains 80 percent ownership or more of the acquired entity.

As noted above, the SEC's position on pushdown accounting has been based on an entity becoming "substantially wholly-owned" rather than the "substantial change in ownership" concept discussed in the 1979 AcSEC Issues Paper. The SEC staff has indicated that SAB No. 54 was intended to require pushdown accounting when an entity became "substantially wholly-owned" even if accomplished through a step acquisition that takes a number of years to complete. In addition, the SEC will address each situation on an individual "facts and circumstances" basis.

In June 1985, the EITF discussed Issue No. 85-21, "Changes of Ownership Resulting in a New Basis of Accounting." Several accounting issues regarding the application of pushdown accounting were discussed. No consensus views were reached by the EITF, and the EITF chairman indicated that pushdown issues would be dealt with in the standards phase of the FASB's consolidations project to the extent that it was addressed in the AcSEC Issues Paper on pushdown accounting.

As with all aspects of business combinations, an evaluation should be made of the change in ownership that results in the application of pushdown accounting to assure that the substance of the acquisition and the change in ownership, not just the legal form, determine the appropriate accounting. For example, 80 percent of a company (X) is owned by the public (Group A) and 20 percent is owned by two individuals, the president and a board member (Group B). Two unrelated individuals propose to form a holding company (HC) and capitalize it with $1 million. Then through a series of transactions with Group A and Group B shareholders, HC will acquire 90 percent of X's stock. HC will be 78 percent owned by the two unrelated individuals which formed HC and 22 percent by Group B. Even though X is 90 percent owned by HC, the application of pushdown accounting would be questionable. In evaluating the acquisition, one should look at the total change in ownership of X held by the two unrelated individuals after the transaction. After the acquisition, the unrelated individuals that formed HC own 78 percent of HC's 90 percent ownership interest in X, or approximately 70 percent. Between the Group A shareholders and Group B shareholders, there is a continuing ownership interest in X of 30 percent. It is unlikely that one could argue that a 70 percent change in ownership justifies the use of pushdown accounting.

(i) Pushdown of Parent Company Debt.   In applying the concepts of pushdown accounting, questions often arise regarding the pushdown of the acquiror's debt to its subsidiary. For example, a company (A) forms a subsidiary to acquire the net assets of another company. A has borrowed 100 percent of the purchase price, which exceeds the recorded basis of the net assets acquired. A intends to service this debt from the earnings of the subsidiary, whose cash flows are expected to be sufficient to cover the debt service on the loan. Should A's debt be pushed down to the subsidiary?

The subject of pushdown of parent company debt to a subsidiary was discussed by the EITF without reaching a consensus. In December 1987, the SEC released SAB No. 73, "Pushdown Basis of Accounting for Parent Company Debt Related to Subsidiary Acquisition." The SAB requires that debt incurred or mandatory redeemable preferred stock issued by a parent to acquire substantially all of the common stock of a subsidiary should be pushed down along with the related purchase price adjustment if:

- The subsidiary is to assume the debt of the parent in a current or planned transaction
- The proceeds of a debt or equity offering of the subsidiary will be used to retire all or part of the parent company's debt
- The subsidiary pledges its assets as collateral or otherwise guarantees the parent company's debt

(ii) Exceptions to Pushdown of Parent Company Debt.   SAB No. 73 does not require debt to be pushed down to the subsidiary if only the subsidiary's stock is pledged as collateral for the debt since, in the case of default, such a pledge would not give the parent's debtholders priority over the subsidiary's debtholders but rather would simply transfer the parent's common stock investment to the parent's debtholders. In addition, the SAB provides guidance on the required disclosures in the notes to financial statements and the registrant's "Management's Discussion and Analysis of Financial Condition and Results of Operations."

The SEC has also indicated, in regard to the pushdown of parent-company debt to the separate financial statements of a subsidiary when pushdown accounting itself is not required because of the specific exclusions outlined in SAB No. 54, that pushdown of parent-company debt generally becomes an issue only when pushdown accounting is applied. However, the SEC may require pushdown accounting (and pushdown of the related parent-company debt) in situations where there is public debt, preferred stock, or significant minority interest, depending on the individual facts and circumstances.

(j) ALLOCATION PERIOD.   SFAS No. 141 does not specifically address the period of time subsequent to the acquisition date over which the research and fact gathering must be accomplished and the purchase price allocated. The reasonableness of the allocation period should be determined through an analysis of the specific facts and circumstances surrounding the business combination, including:

- The size and complexity of the entity acquired
- Information available to the acquiror prior to the consummation date
- The acquiror's management's knowledge of and expertise in the acquiree's business
- Demonstration by management of its ongoing efforts to avail itself of relevant information

In connection with the accounting for preacquisition contingencies (discussed in Subsection 12.3(h) of this chapter), Appendix F of SFAS No. 141 defines the "allocation period" for preacquisition contingencies as follows:

The period required to identify and measure the fair value of the assets acquired and the liabilities assumed in a business combination. The allocation period ends when the acquiring entity is no longer waiting for information that it has arranged to obtain and that is known to be available or obtainable. Thus, the existence of a preacquisition contingency for which an asset, a liability, or an impairment of an asset cannot be estimated does not, of itself, extend the allocation period. Although the required period will vary with circumstances, the allocation period should usually not exceed one year from the consummation of a business combination.

It is not unusual for a company to acquire another company in a business combination to be accounted for by the purchase method at or near the end of a reporting period or its fiscal year. The allocation of the purchase price may not be completed by the date the acquiror's financial statements are issued. In such cases, a preliminary allocation should be made and disclosure should be made in the financial statements that further adjustments may arise as a result of finalization of the ongoing study. Changes subsequent to the issuance of financial statements in the allocation of purchase price should then be evaluated by determining (1) if the original allocation, as reported, was the result of preliminary evaluation of an ongoing data-gathering and evaluation process, which in management's opinion was not expected to differ significantly upon finalizing the study; and (2) whether the study was finalized in a reasonable period of time subsequent to the acquisition. Adjustments to preliminary amounts generally result in corresponding adjustments to goodwill.

The nature of an asset and not the manner of its acquisition determines an acquirer's subsequent accounting for the cost of that asset. The basis for measuring the cost of an asset—regardless of whether it is the amount of cash paid, the fair value of an asset received or given up, the amount of a liability incurred, or the fair value of stock issued—has no effect on the subsequent accounting for the cost, which is retained as the carrying amount of the asset, depreciated, amortized, or otherwise matched with revenue.

After initial recognition, goodwill and other intangible assets acquired in a business combination are accounted for in accordance with the provisions of SFAS No. 142, "Goodwill and Other Intangible Assets."

(k) SAB STAFF ACCOUNTING BULLETIN NO. 61. In May 1986, the SEC issued SAB No. 61, "Adjustments to Allowances for Business Combination Loan Losses-Purchase Method Accounting." The SAB indicates that, with rare exceptions, the SEC does not believe changes in allowances for loan losses are necessary as part of the allocation process in applying purchase accounting adjustments. The SEC believes that, assuming the appropriate methodology is followed by each party to the business combination, each company's estimate of the uncollectible portion of a loan portfolio would fall within a range of acceptability.

However, the SEC concedes that a purchase accounting adjustment may be required to reflect a difference in valuation of a portfolio of loans or receivables if the acquiror's intent with regard to ultimate recovery of the loans or receivables is demonstrably different from the plans or assumptions used by the acquiree in estimating its loan loss reserve. For example, the acquiree may have intended to hold the loans to maturity or to assist a troubled borrower through a long-term workout on the loan, whereas the acquiror plans to sell such loans or foreclose on the underlying collateral. The net carrying value of the loans recorded in purchase allocation should therefore be based on the acquiror's plan of recovery.

Loan losses and allowances for uncollectible accounts and similar reserves are typically not considered preacquisition contingencies. Reasonable methods of estimating such losses or allowances should be used by the acquiree and evaluated by the acquiror at the date of acquisition. Subsequent adjustments to the allowances to reflect the ultimate outcome or resolution of the receivables is presumed to be based on changes in the economic factors surrounding the particular receivable, the nature of the receivable, and the evaluation of the collectibility of the receivables in light of events occurring subsequent to the business combination. Accordingly, such changes in the related valuation accounts should not be accounted for as adjustments to the cost of the business combination.

The provisions and guidance of SAB No. 61 have also been applied to other assets acquired in a purchase business combination. The SEC staff has indicated the guidance should be interpreted broadly with its provisions applied to items such as warranty reserves, inventory obsolescence reserves, and bad debt reserves of nonfinancial institutions, among others.

(l) DATE USED TO RECORD THE ACQUISITION.   Paragraph 48 of SFAS No. 141 indicates that the date of the acquisition is ordinarily the date of consummation of the acquisition (i.e., the date assets are received and other assets are given or securities are issued). Accordingly, such date is normally used for purposes of recording the business combination. SFAS No. 141 also provides for the use of a convenience date, whereby the parties to the combination may designate as the effective date the end of an accounting period that falls between the initiation date and the consummation date. One condition for using a convenience date is that the written agreement for the acquisition provides that effective control of the acquired company is transferred to the acquiror by the effective date without restriction, except for those restrictions required to protect the stockholders of the acquiree. The restrictions permitted are those that prohibit significant changes in operations or disposal of assets, require normal payment of dividends, and the like.

In the event a convenience date is used, SFAS No. 141 requires that adjustments be made to the cost of the acquired company and net income for imputed interest at an appropriate current rate on the assets given, liabilities incurred, or stock issued as of the transfer date to acquire the company.

Factors that should be evaluated in determining if control has passed to the acquiror include the following:

- The combination has been approved by both companies' boards of directors.
- The acquiree does not do anything between the effective date and consummation date outside the ordinary course of business.
- Management of the combined entity takes over the day-to-day operations of the acquiree.
- Only one set of postacquisition accounting records is maintained from the effective date forward.
- Combined operational meetings involving employees of both companies are held.

Use of a convenience date subsequent to the consummation date is not permitted by SFAS No. 141.

(m) DISCLOSURE IN FINANCIAL STATEMENTS.   The notes to the financial statements of a combined entity disclose the following information in the period in which a material business combination is completed:

   a. The name and a brief description of the acquired entity and the percentage of voting equity interests acquired
   b. The primary reasons for the acquisition, including a description of the factors that contributed to a purchase price that results in recognition of goodwill
   c. The period for which the results of operations of the acquired entity are included in the income statement of the acquiring entity
   d. The cost of the acquired entity and, if applicable, the number of shares of equity interests (such as common shares, preferred shares, or partnership interests) issued or issuable, the value assigned to those interests, and the basis for determining that value
   e. A condensed balance sheet disclosing the amount assigned to each major asset and liability caption of the acquired entity at the acquisition date
   f. Contingent payments, options, or commitments specified in the acquisition agreement and the accounting treatment that will be followed should any such contingency occur
   g. The amount of purchased research and development assets acquired and written off in the period and the line item in the income statement in which the amounts written off are aggregated
   h. For any purchase price allocation that has not been finalized, that fact and the reasons for it; in subsequent periods, the nature and amount of any material adjustments made to the initial allocation of the purchase price

i. The following information if the amount assigned to goodwill or to other intangible assets acquired is significant in relation to the total cost of the acquired entity:

  1. For intangible assets subject to amortization:

   a. The total amount assigned and the amount assigned to any major intangible asset class

   b. The amount of any significant residual value, in total and by major intangible asset class

   c. The weighted-average amortization period, in total and by major intangible asset class

   d. The weighted-average amortization period

   e. Any residual value assumed in determining the amount to be amortized (if significant in relation to the carrying amount of the intangible asset class)

  2. For intangible assets not subject to amortization, the total amount assigned and the amount assigned to any major intangible asset class

  3. For goodwill:

   a. The total amount of goodwill and the amount that is expected to be deductible for tax purposes

   b. The amount of goodwill by reportable segment (if the combined entity is required to disclose segment information in conformity with SFAS No. 131, "Disclosures about Segments of an Enterprise and Related Information") unless not practicable

The notes to the financial statements of an acquiring entity disclose the following information in the period in which individually immaterial business combinations have been completed if those combinations are material in the aggregate:

a. The number of entities acquired and a brief description of those entities

b. The aggregate cost of the acquired entities, the number of shares of stock issued or issuable, and the value assigned to those shares

c. The aggregate amount of any contingent payments, options, or commitments and the accounting treatment that will be followed should any such contingency occur (if potentially significant in relation to the aggregate cost of the acquired entities)

d. The information described in item i above if the aggregate amount assigned to goodwill or to other intangible assets acquired is significant in relation to the aggregate cost of the acquired entities

In the period in which an extraordinary gain is recognized related to a business combination, the notes to the financial statements disclose the information required by paragraph 11 of APB Opinion No. 30. The notes to the financial statements also disclose, for any material business combination completed after the balance sheet date but before the financial statements are issued, the information required in items a to i above (unless not practicable).

(i) Pro Forma Disclosures.   Paragraph 54 of SFAS No. 141 requires that pro forma results of operations be presented as supplemental information for the period in which the companies are combined and for the immediately preceding period.

(ii) Classification of Acquired Securities.   The FASB Statement No. 115, "Accounting for Certain Investments in Debt and Equity Securities," requires an investor to classify its investments in debt and equity securities into three categories (held-to-maturity securities, trading securities, and available-for-sale securities) and prescribes different accounting for each. When such securities are obtained in a business combination accounted for by the purchase method, they should be classified based on the intent and ability of the acquiring company. This may mean reclassification from how those securities were classified in the financial statements of the acquired company. It may also mean a different classification in the separate statements of the acquired subsidiary versus consolidation.

(iii) Disclosures in Interim Financial Information.   The summarized interim financial information of a public business entity discloses the following information if a material business combination is completed during the current year up to the date of the most recent interim statement of financial position presented:

    a. The information described in items a to h above.

    b. Supplemental pro forma information that discloses the results of operations for the current interim period and the current year up to the date of the most recent interim statement of financial position presented and for the corresponding periods in the preceding year as though the business combination had been completed as of the beginning of the period being reported on. That pro forma information displays, at a minimum, revenue, income before extraordinary items and the cumulative effect of accounting changes (including those on an interim basis), net income, and earnings per share.

    c. The nature and amount of any material, nonrecurring items included in the reported pro forma results of operations.

(n) DISCLOSURES IN SECURITIES AND EXCHANGE COMMISSION FILINGS.   In Financial Reporting Release No. 47, the SEC revised its rules with respect to disclosures relating to significant business acquisitions in filings under the 1933 and 1934 Securities Acts. These amendments reduce the number of years for which the acquired company's financial statements must be provided and, in some cases, eliminate the requirement to provide those financial statements in registration statements altogether.

(o) ILLUSTRATION OF THE PURCHASE METHOD OF ACCOUNTING.   A case is presented in Exhibit 12.2 to illustrate the purchase method of accounting for a business combination.

EXAMPLE—THE PURCHASE METHOD OF ACCOUNTING FOR A BUSINESS COMBINATION
Consolidated Balance Sheet
Date of Combination ($ in thousands)

Assume two companies decide to combine. In the merger negotiations, the companies agree to exchange common stock for common stock. The larger of the two companies (Issuing Co.) agrees to exchange one of its shares for 5.333 shares of the smaller company (Combining Co.). Combining Co. has been fair-valued at $15,000,000 by a reputable investment banker. Issuing Co. will pay $15/share in cash for fractional shares. The transaction is accounted for by the purchase method.

	Historical		Adjustments	
	Acquiror	**Acquiree**	**Dr. (Cr.)**	**Consolidated**
Assets				
Current Assets:				
Cash and cash equivalents	$ 3,746	$ 2,469	$ (717)[a]	$ 5,498
Accounts receivable	7,511	4,728		12,239
Inventories	4,293	2,253	467[c]	7,013
Total current assets	15,550	9,450	(250)	24,750
Property, plant, and equipment:				
Land	2,704	402	1,148[c]	4,254
Buildings and improvements	9,688	2,796	54[c]	
Machinery and equipment	10,068	8,965	35[c]	19,068
	22,460	12,163	1,237	35,860
Less accumulated depreciation	7,210	2,663	2,663[c]	7,210
Property, plant, and equipment—net	15,250	9,500	3,900	28,650
				(Continues)

Exhibit 12.2   The purchase method of accounting.

	Historical		Adjustments	
	Acquiror	Acquiree	Dr. (Cr.)	Consolidated
Notes receivable	2,591	1,116	34[c]	3,741
Cost in excess of net assets acquired	2,368	474	(474)[c]	2,368
Other assets	1,741	960	(250)*	2,419
Total assets	$37,500	$21,500	$ 2,928	$61,928
Liabilities and Shareholders' Equity				
Current Liabilities:				
Accounts payable	$ 2,884	$ 1,469		$ 4,353
Accrued liabilities	3,150	2,772		5,922
Current portion of long-term debt	1,673	603		2,276
Current taxes payable	1,043	1,381		2,424
Total current liabilities	8,750	6,225		14,975
Long-term debt	9,500	2,970	$ (450)[c]	12,920
Deferred income taxes	3,650	1,005	505**	4,150
Shareholders' Equity:				
Common stock	500	1,000	643***	857
Paid-in capital	2,275	4,375	(9,551)****	16,201
Retained earnings	12,825	5,925	5,925[c]	12,825
Total shareholders' equity	15,600	11,300	(2,983)	29,883
Total liabilities and shareholders' equity	$37,500	$21,500	$ (2,928)	$61,928

[a]Acquisition of 47,800 shares of Acquiree, $1 par value, common stock not tendered by dissenting or fractional shareholders for cash totaling $717.

[b]To reflect the issuance of 178,538 shares of Acquiror $2 par value common stock to effect the combination with Acquiree. Such stock has been independently valued at $14,283.

[c]To reflect the fair value of assets and liabilities of Acquiree obtained in exchange for stock and cash:

	Fair Value
Cash and cash equivalents	$ 2,469
Accounts receivable	4,728
Inventories	2,720
Land	1,550
Buildings and improvements	2,850
Machinery and equipment	9,000
Accumulated depreciation	0
Notes receivable	1,150
Cost in excess of net assets acquired	0
Other assets	178
Accounts payable	(1,469)
Accrued liabilities	(2,772)
Current portion of long-term debt	(603)
Current taxes payable	(1,381)
Long-term debt	(3,420)
Deferred Income taxes	0
	15,000
Less: Cash paid[a]	(717)
Fair value of stock exchanged[b]	(14,283)
	$ 0

[d]Adjustment to reflect the impact of the readjustment of tax basis of assets of Acquiree and tax differences of Acquiree utilized by the combination entity.

		*** 48[a]	**** 669[a]
(782)[c]	** 1,005[c]	(357)[b]	(13,926)[b]
500[d]	(500)[d]	952[c]	3,706[c]
(282)	505	643	(9,551)

Exhibit 12.2   Continued.

(p) EFFECTIVE DATA AND TRANSMISSION.   Except for combinations between two or more mutual enterprises, SFAS No. 141 is effective as follows:

  a. The provisions of the Statement apply to all business combinations initiated after June 30, 2001. The pooling-of-interests method may not be used for those business combinations. The following definition of "initiated" applies here:

> A plan of combination is initiated on the earlier of (1) the date that the major terms of a plan, including the ratio of exchange of stock, is announced publicly or otherwise formally made known to the stockholders of any one of the combining companies or (2) the date that stockholders of a combining company are notified in writing of an exchange offer. Therefore, a plan of combination is often initiated even though consummation is subject to the approval of stockholders and others.

  b. The provisions of the Statement also apply to all business combinations accounted for by the purchase method for which the acquisition date is July 1, 2001, or later.

The Statement is not effective for combinations between two or more mutual enterprises until interpretive guidance is issued related to the application of the purchase method to such transactions. The FASB stated that it intends to consider issues related to such application of the purchase method.

The following transition provisions apply to business combinations for which the acquisition date was before July 1, 2001, that were accounted for using the purchase method:

  a. The carrying amount of acquired intangible assets that do not meet the criteria for recognition apart from goodwill (and any related deferred tax liabilities if the intangible asset amortization is not deductible for tax purposes) is reclassified as goodwill as of the date SFAS No. 142 is initially applied in its entirety. (See Chapter 17.)
  b. The carrying amount of (1) any recognized intangible assets that meet those recognition criteria or (2) any unidentifiable intangible assets recognized in conformity with paragraph 5 of SFAS No. 72, "Accounting for Certain Acquisitions of Banking or Thrift Institutions," that have been included in the amount reported as goodwill (or goodwill and intangible assets) are reclassified and accounted for as an asset apart from goodwill as of the date Statement 142 is initially applied in its entirety.
  c. Other than as set forth in **a.** and **b.**, an entity does not change the amount of the purchase price assigned to the assets acquired and liabilities assumed in a business combination for which the acquisition date was before July 1, 2001.

As of the earlier of the first day of the fiscal year beginning after December 15, 2001, for the date Statement 142 is initially applied in its entirety, the amount of any unamortized deferred credit related to an excess over cost arising from (a) a business combination for which the acquisition date was before July 1, 2001, or (b) an investment accounted for by the equity method acquired before July 1, 2001, is written off and recognized as the effect of a change in accounting principle. The effect of the accounting change and related income tax effects are presented in the income statement between the captions *extraordinary items* and *net income*. The per share information presented in the income statement includes the per share effect of the accounting change.

12.4 LEVERAGED BUYOUT

(a) DEFINITION.   Authoritative accounting literature does not provide a definition of a leveraged buyout (LBO) transaction. However, an LBO can best be described as a financing technique for acquiring a company wherein a large portion of the purchase price is derived from borrowings, often some or all of which are secured by the underlying assets of the entity being acquired. In most LBO transactions, management of an existing company (OLDCO) and one or more new investors form a HC (NEWCO) to acquire all of OLDCO's outstanding common stock.

(b) STRUCTURE.   There is no predetermined manner in which to structure an LBO; a structure is designed to meet the requirements of each transaction, giving appropriate consideration to existing and forecasted cash flows, capital expenditure and working capital needs, income tax considerations, potential dispositions, and lender requirements. There are, however, common elements in the structure of each LBO transaction.

(i) Legal Form.   NEWCO's are generally formed to acquire OLDCO. Typically, there is no real economic incentive or disincentive to form NEWCO, although for practical purposes many companies acquired in an LBO transaction are publicly owned and are acquired through a tender offer and a NEWCO is generally formed to hold the tendered OLDCO shares prior to the closing of the tender offer. NEWCO may also be used to effect a squeeze-out merger, which is a mechanism used to acquire untendered shares. Depending on OLDCO's state of incorporation, a squeeze-out can generally be accomplished after two-thirds of OLDCO's stockholders have tendered their OLDCO stock to NEWCO. At that point, NEWCO may have the legal right to effect a merging of NEWCO into OLDCO, without shareholder approval, and force an exchange of cash or NEWCO securities for the untendered OLDCO stock.

Nonpublic companies acquired in an LBO generally have a limited number of stockholders; therefore, establishing NEWCO simply to acquire shares may be regarded as an unnecessary expense. However, for accounting purposes, the need to form NEWCO to acquire OLDCO is very important. That is, without forming NEWCO, the transaction can only be accounted for as a restructuring/recapitalization for which no change in accounting basis is appropriate.

(ii) Management Participation.   In most if not all LBOs, management has the critical role of managing OLDCO's assets to assure repayment of borrowings and maximize value to NEWCO's stockholders. Accordingly, management's involvement in structuring the LBO transaction and, more importantly, their continued involvement in managing OLDCO after the acquisition is often crucial to the success of the LBO transaction. Accordingly, key members of OLDCO management are generally given a substantive incentive to assure the continued successful operation of OLDCO. This is typically accomplished through management's investment in NEWCO.

Management may be granted options to acquire additional NEWCO stock, generally at a price based on the fair market value of the stock at the date of the LBO transaction. A vesting period of several years is often required before management is entitled to receive unrestricted ownership of the stock. The options and warrants provide the stockholders of NEWCO with a mechanism by which to assure continued employment of key management. The granting of options and warrants also provides management the ability to acquire NEWCO equity at bargain rates (assuming that the fair market value of the stock rises) at a future date, thus obviating the need for them to make up-front cash investments.

(iii) Financing Arrangements.   The borrowing required to fund an LBO may come from a variety of sources: commercial banks, insurance companies, other financial institutions, public investment, and so on. As mentioned above, financing arrangements are dependent upon cash flow needs for operations, debt service, and dividend distributions. Frequently, however, the financing consists of bank and institutional term loans, private investor debt and equity investments placed by investment bankers, and a bridge loan. The bridge loan is made available by the lenders until less expensive permanent financing is obtained.

Another factor that may affect the legal form of the transaction is the nature of the security required by lenders. That is, NEWCO as the acquiror generally incurs the indebtedness to acquire OLDCO. One or more lending institutions, however, may desire more security on their loans than a pledge of OLDCO stock owned by NEWCO. More specifically, some lending institutions require their loans to be placed in the legal entity that contains the operating assets, that is, OLDCO.

A number of LBO transactions have also included financing through the issuance of debt and/or equity securities to the former owners of OLDCO. Certain securities in an LBO may take the form of what is known as *paid-in-kind* (PIK) securities. These securities, for a specified period of years, pay interest or dividends by issuing additional securities. Such securities provide NEWCO relief from its cash flow needs in the early years following the LBO.

Numerous LBOs have also issued NEWCO common stock to OLDCO shareholders. This provides such shareholders with the potential for large profits frequently generated from postacquisition sales of assets, or public offerings of NEWCO stock at prices in excess of the LBO acquisition price.

(iv) Tax Considerations.   A multitude of factors affect the taxability of the transaction to OLDCO and its stockholders. There are, however, some common strategies to minimize income taxes to both parties. For example, OLDCO's management may wish to exchange part or all of its equity interest in OLDCO for an equity interest in NEWCO without paying tax on the appreciation in the OLDCO stock. This can be accomplished through the use of an acquisition HC to which management transfers its OLDCO stock in exchange for NEWCO stock.

As another example, if a corporate seller of OLDCO has been filing a consolidated return, the buyer and seller may jointly make a §338(h)(10) election, the effect of which is to treat a stock acquisition as an asset purchase for tax purposes. This will allow higher depreciation deductions to offset postacquisition taxable income. The election may be beneficial to both the seller and the buyer for nontax reasons since the transaction is actually a stock rather than an asset transfer.

Other tax strategies will depend on the specific facts and circumstances of the entities and individuals involved in the transaction.

(c) HISTORICAL PERSPECTIVE.   The determination of whether an LBO transaction was a purchase business combination, a step-acquisition, or a treasury stock transaction was a difficult accounting problem that accountants had to solve as the pace of LBO transactions increased. In an LBO transaction in which OLDCO shareholders become NEWCO shareholders, the price paid by NEWCO to acquire their OLDCO stock could be considered as purchase price, a capital transaction, or a mixture of both.

Because generally accepted accounting principles (GAAP) was not clear regarding the accounting for LBO transactions, accountants were required to make some difficult decisions regarding the proper manner in which to account for the transactions. Not surprisingly, the decisions produced a variety of accounting results that often meant the difference between the write-up of assets to fair value or a reduction of equity. In many cases, a reduction of equity resulted in NEWCO reporting a negative net worth. Although the underlying economics of LBO transactions are not changed based on whether the accounting results produce a write-up of assets or a reduction of equity, it is almost undeniable that a company attempting to raise capital will have an easier time doing so if it has positive, rather than negative, equity.

The Securities and Exchange Commission staff, along with the accounting profession, naturally became concerned regarding the diversity in accounting results and in the proper accounting for LBO transactions. Therefore, while the SEC staff internally adopted guidelines for determining the circumstances in which an LBO transaction should be accounted for as a purchase business combination, they raised the issue of accounting for LBO transactions at the EITF's May 1986 meeting so that the accounting profession would be more directly involved in establishing accounting guidance. The SEC staff and the profession were especially interested in resolving this issue because of its significance to investors, particularly when OLDCO shareholders become NEWCO shareholders.

The EITF reached a consensus on Issue No. 86-16, "Carryover of Predecessor Cost in Leveraged Buyout Transactions," in July 1987. This consensus, however, did not address the accounting for transactions in which an OLDCO shareholder decreased his ownership interest in NEWCO relative to what he owned in OLDCO (these situations are sometimes referred to as *leveraged sell-offs*). At about the same time, the SEC staff communicated to the EITF that LBO transactions seemed to be evolving and that they may not resemble the LBO transaction described in Issue No. 86-16.

In June 1988, the FASB staff raised Issue No. 88-16, "Basis in Leveraged Buyout Transactions When the Previous Owner's Interest Declines." In dealing with Issue No. 88-16, the EITF formed a working group to formulate a proposal to deal with the varied matters covered by this issue. In the course of the various EITF and working group meetings, it was decided that one comprehensive consensus should be prepared that would encompass the matters addressed in Issue Nos. 86-16 and 88-16. In doing so, the EITF's conclusions were largely influenced by a desire on the part of the SEC staff to limit diversity in practice, prevent potential accounting abuses, and limit the number of circumstances requiring consultation with the SEC staff. The result of the EITF's efforts, reached by consensus at its May 1989 meeting, is predominantly an objective set of rules that define the accounting for all LBO transactions.

(d) ACCOUNTING FOR THE LEVERAGED BUYOUT TRANSACTION. EITF Issue No. 88-16 indicates that the substance of the LBO transaction must be evaluated to determine whether it constitutes:

- A financial restructuring/recapitalization for which no change in accounting basis would be appropriate
- A step acquisition for which a partial change in accounting basis would be appropriate
- A purchase by new controlling investors for which a partial or complete change in basis, based on the fair value of the transaction, would be appropriate

The EITF's consensus guidance consists of an elaborate set of criteria that define when a new accounting basis is appropriate (situations in second and third bulleted items above), and how to determine that new accounting basis.

In the context of basis adjustments to assets and liabilities acquired, LBOs are considered to be analogous to purchase business combinations discussed previously in this chapter.

The EITF consensus is divided into three sections. The first section addresses the circumstances in which a change in control has occurred, the second section addresses the calculation of NEWCO's recorded investment in OLDCO, and the third section addresses limitations on recording the basis otherwise calculated in the second section.

(e) CHANGE IN CONTROL. The EITF consensus specifies this general provision:

A partial or complete change in accounting basis is appropriate only when there has been a change in control of voting interest; that is, a new controlling shareholder or group of shareholders must be established.

This provision stems from the underlying assumption that the establishment of a new controlling shareholder or control group results in a transaction similar to a purchase business combination, as opposed to a recapitalization-restructuring for which a change in basis is not appropriate.

The consensus guidance establishes specific objective and subjective criteria to be evaluated in determining whether a new controlling shareholder or control group (defined below) has been established. Included in this determination is a definition of which shareholders are part of the control group. The consensus guidance also describes the accounting result if a change in control has not occurred.

(i) Objective Criteria. Except for the most straightforward circumstance under which a change in control has occurred, that is, a single new shareholder gains the ability to unilaterally exercise control over NEWCO, the guidance in this section is based on two underlying assumptions:

1. New shareholders that meet the definition for inclusion in the NEWCO control group will act in concert to exercise control over NEWCO. This assumption concludes that by virtue of (a) the significance of the shareholders' economic interests in NEWCO, and (b) the contemporaneous acquisition of NEWCO interests, such shareholders have similar goals and will consistently act together to control NEWCO.

2. Members of management have a commonality of interest among themselves that distinguishes them from being "typical" shareholders. This commonality of interest is derived from management's shared responsibility to achieve the objectives of the enterprise, and their authority to establish policies and make decisions by which those objectives will be pursued.

The foregoing assumptions address circumstances wherein there has been a step acquisition by one or more parties. However, the EITF also recognized that there were some circumstances in which certain shareholders in the NEWCO control group had a step acquisition while other shareholders in the NEWCO control group decreased their ownership interest in NEWCO in relation to their percentage ownership interest in OLDCO. In this latter situation, it was not always clear whether there had been a change in control. Accordingly, the EITF provided explicit guidance to address this issue. This particular portion of the EITF consensus guidance was heavily debated because, in some circumstances, following the guidance could produce a potentially contentious result. For example, as Exhibit 12.3 demonstrates, Investor 2 has been excluded from the NEWCO3 control group for the reason indicated, yet Investors 1 and 2 clearly have a majority ownership in OLDCO and in NEWCO. The question follows then: If Investors 1 and 2 could have controlled OLDCO *and* NEWCO, has there actually been a change in control?

In applying the objective tests for determining whether there has been a change in control, the NEWCO shareholders were divided into three groups—management, shareholders with a greater percentage of residual interest in NEWCO than they held in OLDCO, and shareholders with the same or lower percentage of residual interest in NEWCO than they held in OLDCO. Each group of shareholders was believed to have characteristics distinct from the other groups.

Management shareholders are presumed to be part of the control group because they are presumed to have the ability to significantly influence the terms of the LBO transaction and the operations of OLDCO after the LBO transaction. Further, their participation in the LBO transaction indicates a commonality of interest between them and other members of the control group.

The following examples illustrate the change in control criterion as described in Section 1(a) of the consensus (all ownership interests are fully diluted).

	OLDCO	NEWCO1	NEWCO2	NEWCO3	NEWCO4
Management	20%	60%	30%	0	40%
Investor 1	40	40	10	45%	20
Investor 2	40	0	0	15	0
Investor 3	0	0	30	20	20
Investor 4	0	0	30	20	20
Total	100%	100%	100%	100%	100%

NEWCO1 would qualify as a change in control under the criterion in Section 1(a)(i) of the consensus guidance (management obtains unilateral control of NEWCO1).

NEWCO2 would qualify as a change in control under the criterion in Section 1(a)(ii) of the consensus guidance because Investors 3 and 4, who are members of the NEWCO2 control group, obtain unilateral control of NEWCO2.

Assuming Investor 2 is not a member of the NEWCO3 control group, for example, because Investor 2 has no capital at risk in NEWCO other than a common stock interest, NEWCO3 would qualify as a change in control under the criterion in Section 1(a)(iii) of the consensus guidance.

NEWCO4 would not qualify as a change in control because management and Investor 1 are in NEWCO4's control group. A subset of the NEWCO4 control group (management and Investor 1) owned a majority voting interest in OLDCO. See Section 1(c) of the consensus guidance for the criteria for inclusion in the control group.

Exhibit 12.3   Examples of the change in control criterion used in the EITF consensus on Issue No. 88-16. (Reprinted from Exhibit 88-16B of the EITF consensus.)

However, in some instances, management has clearly not participated with the other members of the control group in promoting the LBO transaction, such as when management has pursued its own bid to acquire OLDCO and loses its quest to a rival bidder.

Therefore, in those unusual circumstances, the EITF believed that the commonality of interest linking management with the other members of the control group was absent, and management should not be presumed part of the NEWCO control group.

When the presumption that management is part of the NEWCO control group has been overcome, management is nevertheless considered a single shareholder in applying other tests required by the EITF consensus because management is still considered to have a commonality of interest among themselves. This logic would seem to be borne out in situations such as the competing management bid described above.

When management is included in the NEWCO control group, it is included without regard to management's ownership interest in NEWCO. That is, there is no de minimis exception provided because of the significant influence that management is deemed to have in controlling NEWCO.

The NEWCO shareholders that have increased their ownership interest in relation to the percentage ownership interest that they had in OLDCO are divided into two groups based on their percentage ownership in NEWCO. This division was made so that shareholders representing the passive investing public could be excluded from the control group.

The NEWCO shareholders that have *decreased* their relative ownership interest were generally perceived as trying to pass control of OLDCO on to new shareholders. For example, the president of OLDCO owns 100 percent of OLDCO's outstanding stock and desires to retire, but either has an interest in retaining an "equity kicker" or the new owners are unable to borrow sufficient funds to buy out all of the president's equity in OLDCO. However, there were other examples in which it appeared that control was not being passed on to new owners. Accordingly, the EITF devised two tests designed to determine whether a shareholder was aligned with other members of the control group and, therefore, should be included in or excluded from the control group.

The first test, a voting-interest test, is applied to each individual shareholder. It determines whether a shareholder is aligned with other control group members based on the significance of that shareholder's voting ownership interest in NEWCO. This test employs a complicated set of criteria for determining what constitutes a voting interest.

For the individual shareholder being tested, all dilutive securities owned by that shareholder must be considered exercised when calculating the percentage voting interest. This fully diluted amount represents the maximum ownership interest that can be obtained by the shareholder. Dilutive securities held by other shareholders are treated as having been exercised when their terms are no less favorable than the terms of the dilutive securities held by the shareholder being tested. However, the effect of dilution cannot reduce the continuing shareholder's voting interest percentage below that which he can currently exercise.

Rights held by a continuing shareholder to purchase NEWCO stock at fair value at the time of exercise need not be considered in the voting-interest test if such rights are not exercisable for a substantive period of time (currently at least one year).

The second test, a capital-at-risk test, is also applied to individual shareholders. It determines whether a shareholder is aligned with other control group members based on the significance of the shareholder's economic interest in NEWCO. Although authoritative accounting literature defines control and significant influence based on the percentage of voting interest, many believe that a person holding a significant economic interest does have significant influence or may effectively control an entity.

(ii) Subjective Criteria. A basic tenet of accounting theory is that the substance of the transaction, rather than merely its legal form, should prevail in recording the event. For example, the EITF believed it would be inappropriate for a new shareholder to form NEWCO, have NEWCO acquire 100 percent of the outstanding common stock of OLDCO, sell 100 percent of NEWCO's common stock back to the original OLDCO stockholders, and conclude that a change in control had occurred. Accordingly, the EITF identified a number of factors that should be considered in assessing whether the change in control, determined as a result of applying the objective guidance, is truly a substantive change in control.

(iii) No Change in Control.   The consensus guidance states the following when a change in control has not occurred:

> If a change in control is deemed not to have occurred as a result of applying the above guidance, the transaction should be considered a recapitalization–restructuring for which a change in accounting basis is not appropriate.

In other words, the transaction is accounted for as what is alternatively referred to as a *redemption*, *distribution*, or *effective dividend*.

(f) DETERMINING THE CARRYING AMOUNT OF NEWCO'S INVESTMENT IN OLDCO. The EITF consensus sets forth this general provision:

> The form of a transaction by which the investor obtains its interest in NEWCO does not change the accounting to be applied. In general, if an investor in NEWCO owned a residual interest in OLDCO, then the lesser of that investor's residual interest in OLDCO or NEWCO is carried over at the investor's predecessor basis.

Again, although the acquisition of OLDCO by NEWCO could take many different forms as a result of legal, tax, or other implications, the EITF concluded that the substance of the transaction should provide the basis for recording the transaction.

The following paragraphs describe the calculation of the carrying amount of NEWCO's investment in OLDCO. They address OLDCO interests acquired from all continuing shareholders (i.e., those OLDCO shareholders who have acquired a NEWCO interest), differentiating between those who are and those who are not part of the NEWCO control group.

Continuing shareholders who are part of the NEWCO control group are viewed as having acquired OLDCO in step fashion. Accordingly, the historical cost accounting principles applicable to a step acquisition are applied. To the extent that a shareholder owns the same percentage of residual interest in NEWCO as in OLDCO, no recordable event has occurred with respect to that residual interest; that is, no exchange has taken place, and the historical cost basis in the OLDCO investment should not be changed. If there is a net increase in ownership, then the carrying amount of NEWCO's investment in OLDCO is generally determined in a manner that is similar to a step acquisition, and the increase in ownership is recorded at fair value.

Some continuing shareholders who are members of the NEWCO control group, however, actually decrease their relative ownership interests. These continuing shareholders are viewed as having retained a portion of their original interest in OLDCO. The portion of the OLDCO investment that has not been disposed of is one in which no exchange has taken place. Accordingly, the proportional historical cost basis for that portion of the investment that is retained is not changed.

Continuing shareholders who are not part of the NEWCO control group are further subdivided between those who own less than five percent of NEWCO and those who own five percent or more of NEWCO, but who own no more of NEWCO (as a percentage) than they held in OLDCO. (This latter group of shareholders was previously excluded from the control group because they had less than a 20 percent voting interest or less than 20 percent of the cumulative capital-at-risk in NEWCO.)

The first group, the passive investing public, is not considered parties to the step acquisition of OLDCO. Therefore, their OLDCO interests acquired by NEWCO may be valued at fair value. The latter group of shareholders cannot, by prior definition, be considered the passive investing public since they own five percent or more of NEWCO. Although these individuals were excluded from the NEWCO control group under the "Change in Control" section discussed above, they, if viewed as a group, could have significant influence as NEWCO investors. Accordingly, their OLDCO interests will be valued by NEWCO at their predecessor basis if they collectively have significant influence (i.e., they own 20 percent or more) of NEWCO. If they do not collectively have significant influence over NEWCO, then their OLDCO interests may be valued at fair value.

The OLDCO interests acquired by NEWCO from noncontinuing shareholders may be valued at fair value as an exchange has clearly taken place.

In EITF Issue No. 90-12, the Task Force reached a consensus on the question of how NEWCO's investment in OLDCO should be allocated to individual assets and liabilities of OLDCO in an LBO within the scope of Issue 88-16, in which a portion of NEWCO's investment in OLDCO is valued at predecessor basis. The Task Force concluded that the allocation should be similar to a step acquisition (partial purchase method). The consensus does not require or change the practice in Issue No. 88-16 applications, retained earnings, and accumulated depreciation are reduced to zero after the allocation.

The SEC observer noted that a partial purchase application would split a Net Operating LessNOL carryforward, whereas in this case the entire NOL carryforward must be viewed as an acquired carryforward.

(g) LIMITATION OF THE CARRYING AMOUNT OF NEWCO'S INVESTMENT IN OLDCO. The following paragraphs address the valuation of OLDCO based on the ability to validate the value of NEWCO securities issued to acquire OLDCO. Notwithstanding any conclusion reached under the previous section, this section may limit NEWCO's ability to record all or a portion of its investment in OLDCO at fair value. The EITF's general provision is stated as follows:

> The fair value of any securities issued by NEWCO to acquire OLDCO should be objectively determinable. Fair value should not be used, whether or not the NEWCO securities are publicly traded, unless at least 80% of the fair value of consideration paid to acquire OLDCO equity interests comprises monetary consideration (the monetary test).

The EITF consensus defines the element of the numerator and denominator in determining what percentage of the consideration paid by NEWCO constitutes monetary consideration.

If less than 80 percent of the total consideration paid by NEWCO to acquire OLDCO constitutes monetary consideration, then the OLDCO value as reported by NEWCO is limited to the percentage of monetary consideration paid. Accordingly, NEWCO may be required to record a larger portion of its investment in OLDCO at predecessor basis (i.e., larger than that which otherwise results from the application of step-acquisition accounting principles) as a result of an inability to objectively and reliably measure the value of the transaction.

The EITF consensus also addresses circumstances in which NEWCO equity interests have been acquired from OLDCO assets and, therefore, cannot result in NEWCO equity. For example, the controlling NEWCO shareholder may obtain his NEWCO equity interest from OLDCO assets by way of a loan or unusual bonus or other payment. In these circumstances, the cash paid results in a debit to NEWCO equity and a credit to the value of the OLDCO investment.

(h) LEVERAGED BUYOUT ACCOUNTING ILLUSTRATED.   Exhibit 12.4 illustrates the application of the EITF consensus guidance. This example is reprinted from Example 5 of Exhibit 88-16F of the EITF consensus. The consensus contains several additional examples of accounting for LBOs.

(i) INTERNATIONAL ACCOUNTING STANDARDS BOARD INTERNATIONAL FINANCIAL REPORTING STANDARD NO. 3 "BUSINESS COMBINATIONS."

(i) IFRS 3   International Financial Reporting Standards (IFRS) 3, "Business Combinations" was issued in March of 2004, and superseded IAS 22. IFRS 3 defines a business combination as the bringing together of separate entities or business into one reporting entity. To be accounted for as a combination under IFRS 3, the entity being acquired generally must meet the following definition of a business:

> an integrated set of activities and assets conducted and managed for the purpose of providing:

	OLDCO			NEWCO	
	Shares	Book Value	Fair Value	Shares	Fair Value
Management	24	$ 2,400	$ 2,880	60	$ 2,880
Public	76	7,600	9,120	40	1,920
Total	100	$10,000	$12,000	100	$ 4,800

Method of Acquisition of OLDCO Interest
Source of cash:
  Debt $ 7,200
Cash paid to public $ 7,200
NEWCO common stock issued to public in
  exchange for OLDCO common stock
  (40 shares × $48)   1,920
NEWCO common stock issued to
  management in exchange for OLDCO
  common stock (60 shares × $48)   2,880
  OLDCO fair value $12,000

Application of the 80% Monetary Test
Monetary consideration $ 7,200
Total consideration $12,000
Portion monetary   60%

Accounting

The transaction meets the criteria of Section 1(a) of the consensus (management obtains unilateral control); therefore, a change in basis is appropriate.

Management's 24% interest should be recorded at predecessor basis in accordance with Section 2 of the consensus. The monetary test in Section 3 of the consensus is not met; therefore, only 60% of the OLDCO interests acquired should be recorded at fair value. The remaining interest acquired from OLDCO public shareholders should be recorded based on OLDCO's book value as a surrogate for public's predecessor basis.

	Percent	Amount
Summary of Accounting		
Valuation:		
Predecessor basis (24 shares × $110)	24	$ 2,640
OLDCO book value [(76% − 60%) × $10,000]	16	1,600
Fair value (60% ×$12,000)	60	7,200
Total investment in OLDCO		11,440
Less NEWCO debt		(7,200)
NEWCO equity		$ 4,240
Analysis of NEWCO Equity Account		
Stock issued to management valued at predecessor basis		$ 2,640
Stock issued to public valued at OLDCO book value		1,600
NEWCO equity		$ 4,240

Exhibit 12.4   Example of the application of the EITF consensus on Issue No. 88-16. (Reprinted from Exhibit 88-16F of the EITF consensus.)

   a. a return to investors, or

   b. lower costs or other economic benefits directly and proportionately to policyholders or participants.

However, certain acquisitions of assets are treated as a combination even if they do not meet the above definition. If an entity acquires a group of assets that do not meet the definition of a business, it should allocate the cost of the group of assets among the individual assets based on their relative fair values. If goodwill arises from the transaction, the transaction is accounted for as a business combination.

The following types of transactions generally meet IFRS 3's definition of a business combination:

- The purchase of all assets, liabilities and rights to the activities of an entity
- The purchase of some of the assets, liabilities and rights to activities of an entity that together meet the definition of a business
- The establishment of a new legal entity in which the assets, liabilities and activities of combined businesses will be held

Like SFAS No. 141, IFAS 3 requires the acquisition (purchase) method to be used for all business combinations.

Some differences exist in the requirements of IFRS 3 as compared to SFAS Nos. 141:

- The definition of a business under IFRS differs from that contained in SFAS No. 141
- The date of measurement of the cost of a business combination under IFAS 3 is as the date of acquisition, whereas the date of measurement under SFAS 141 is the date of announcement
- Under IFRS 3 in-process research and development acquired is recognized as an asset on the books of the combined entity and amortized over its useful life. SFAS 141 requires the immediate write-off of acquired in-process research and development
- Under SFAS 141, the entity fair values only the proportion of the assets attributable to the acquirer. Therefore, minority interest is not valued at the fair value of its share of the assets. Under IFRS 3, the entity must recognize the fair value of 100 percent of the assets, with a corresponding increase to minority interest
- Under SFAS 141, negative goodwill is accounted for by first reducing the carrying amounts of certain non-monetary assets and liabilities with any excess taken to net income. In contrast, IFRS 3 requires all negative goodwill (after a reassessment of asset values) to be taken to net income

The FASB and the International Accounting Standards Board (IASB) have on their agendas a joint project to amend both IFAS 3 and SFAS 141 to further harmonize the two standards.

12.5 SOURCES AND SUGGESTED REFERENCES

Accounting Principles Board, "Earnings per Share," APB Opinion No. 15. AICPA, New York, 1969.

_____, "Business Combinations," APB Opinion No. 16. AICPA, New York, 1970.

_____, "Intangible Assets," APB Opinion No. 17. AICPA, New York, 1970.

_____, "Interest on Receivables and Payables," APB Opinion No. 21. AICPA, New York, 1971.

_____, "Accounting for Stock Issued to Employees," APB Opinion No. 25. AICPA, New York, 1972.

_____, "Business Combinations: Accounting Interpretations of APB Opinion No. 16," Interpretations Nos. 1–39. AICPA, New York, 1970–1973.

American Institute of Certified Public Accountants, "Pushdown Accounting," Issues Paper. AICPA, New York, 1979.

Federal Home Loan Bank Board, "Pushdown Accounting," R-Memorandum No. 55. FHLBB, Washington, DC, 1983.

Financial Accounting Standards Board, "Business Combinations: Sale of Duplicate Facilities and Accrual," EITF Issue No. 84-35. FASB, Stamford, CT, 1984.

_____, "Liabilities Accrued in a Purchase Business Combination," EITF Issue No. 84-35a. FASB, Stamford, CT, 1984.

_____, "Securities That Can Be Acquired for Cash in a Pooling of Interests," EITF Issue No. 85-14. FASB, Stamford, CT, 1985.

_____, "Changes of Ownership Resulting in a New Basis of Accounting," EITF Issue No. 85-21. FASB, Stamford, CT, 1985.

_____, "Business Combinations: Settlement of Stock Options and Awards," EITF Issue No. 85-45. FASB, Stamford, CT, 1986.

_____, "Pooling with 10 Percent Cash Payout Determined by Lottery," EITF Issue No. 86-10. FASB Stamford, CT, 1986.

_____, "Purchased Research and Development Projects in a Business Combination," EITF Issue No. 86-14. FASB, Stamford, CT, 1986.

_____, "Carryover of Predecessor Cost in Leveraged Buyout Transactions," EITF Issue No. 86-16. FASB, Stamford, CT, 1986.

_____, "Allocation of Purchase Price to Assets to Be Sold," EITF Issue No. 87-11. FASB, Stamford, CT, 1987.

_____, "Effect of a Standstill Agreement on Pooling of Interests Accounting," EITF Issue No. 87-15. FASB, Stamford, CT, 1987.

_____, "Whether the 90 Percent Test for a Pooling of Interests Is Applied Separately to Each Company or on a Combined Basis," EITF Issue No. 87-16. FASB, Stamford, CT, 1987.

_____, "Poolings of Companies That Do Not Have a Controlling Class of Common Stock," EITF Issue No. 87-27. FASB, Stamford, CT, 1987.

_____, "Basis in Leveraged Buyout Transactions When the Previous Owner's Interest Declines," EITF Issue No. 88-16. FASB, Norwalk, CT, 1988.

_____, "Exchange of Ownership Interests Between Entities under Common Control," EITF Issue No. 90-5. FASB, Norwalk, CT, April 19, 1990.

_____, "Accounting for Certain Events Not Addressed in Issue No. 87-11, Relating to an Acquired Operating Unit to Be Sold," EITF Issue No. 90-6. FASB, Norwalk, CT, September 7, 1990.

_____, "Accounting for a Business Combination Involving a Majority-Owned Investee of a Venture Capital Company," EITF Issue No. 90-10. FASB, Norwalk, CT, May 9, 1991.

_____, "Allocating Basis to Individual Assets and Liabilities for Transactions Within the Scope of Issue No. 88-16," EITF Issue No. 90-12. FASB, Norwalk, CT, July 12, 1990.

_____, "Accounting for Simultaneous Common Control Mergers," EITF Issue No. 90-13. FASB, Norwalk, CT, September 7, 1990.

_____, "Effect of Acquisition of Employer Shares for/by an Employee Benefit Trust on Accounting for Business Combinations," EITF Issue No. 93-2. FASB, Norwalk, CT, 1993.

_____, "Uncertainties Related to Income Taxes in a Purchase Business Combination," EITF Issue No. 93-7. FASB, Norwalk, CT, May 1993.

_____, "Recognition of Liabilities in Connection with a Purchase Business Combination," EITF Issue No. 95-3. FASB, Norwalk, CT, 1995.

_____, "Accounting for Contingent Consideration Paid to the Shareholders of an Acquired Enterprise in a Purchase Business Combination," EITF Issue No. 95-8. FASB, Norwalk, CT, 1995.

_____, "Recognition of Liabilities in Anticipation of a Business Combination," EITF Issue No. 95-14. FASB, Norwalk, CT, 1995.

_____, "Accounting for Deferred Taxes on In-Process Research and Development Activities Acquired in a Purchase Business Combination," EITF Issue No. 96-7. FASB, Norwalk, CT, May 23, 1996.

_____, "Accounting for a Business Combination When the Issuing Company Has Targeted Stock," EITF Issue No. 96-8. FASB, Norwalk, CT, May 23, 1996.

_____, "Accounting for Contingent Consideration Issued in a Purchase Business Combination," EITF Issue No. 97-8. FASB, Norwalk, CT, July 23–24, 1997.

_____, "Effect on Pooling-of-Interests Accounting of Certain Contingently Issuance Exercisable Options or Other Equity Instruments," EITF Issue No. 97-9. FASB, Norwalk, CT, July 23–24 and September 18, 1997.

_____, "Determination of the Useful Life of Renewable Intangible Assets under FASB Statement No. 142, *Goodwill and other Intangible Assets*," EITF Issue 03-9. FASB, Norwalk, CT, July 31, 2003.

_____, "FASB Special Report—A Guide to Implementation of Statement 109 on Accounting for Income Taxes—Questions and Answers." FASB, Norwalk, CT, March 1992.

_____, "Applicability of FASB Statement No. 2 to Business Combinations Accounted for by the Purchase Method," FASB Interpretation No. 4. FASB, Stamford CT, 1975.

_____, "Applying APB Opinions No. 16 and 17 When a Savings and Loan Association or a Similar Institution Is Acquired in a Business Combination Accounted for by the Purchase Method," FASB Interpretation No. 9. FASB, Stamford, CT, 1976.

_____, "Accounting for Leases," Statement of Financial Accounting Standard No. 13. FASB, Stamford, CT, 1976.

_____, "Accounting for Leases in a Business Combination," FASB Interpretation No. 21. FASB, Stamford, CT, 1978.

_____, "Accounting for Research and Development Costs," Statement of Financial Accounting Standards No. 2. FASB, Stamford, CT, 1974.

_____, "Accounting for Contingencies," Statement of Financial Accounting Standards No. 5. FASB, Stamford, CT, 1975.

_____, "Accounting for Preacquisition Contingencies of Purchased Enterprises," Statement of Financial Accounting Standards No. 38. FASB, Stamford, CT, 1980.

_____, "Disclosure of Postretirement Health Care and Life Insurance Benefits," Statement of Financial Accounting Standards No. 81. FASB, Stamford, CT, 1984.

_____, "Employers' Accounting for Pensions," Statement of Financial Accounting Standards No. 87. FASB, Stamford, CT, 1985.

_____, "Accounting for Income Taxes," Statement of Financial Accounting Standards No. 109. FASB, Stamford, CT, 1992.

_____, "Employers' Accounting for Postemployment Benefits," Statement of Financial Accounting Standards No. 112. FASB, Norwalk, CT, 1992.

_____, "Accounting for Certain Investments in Debt and Equity Securities," Statement of Financial Accounting Standards No. 115. FASB, Norwalk, CT, 1993.

_____, "Accounting for the Impairment of Long-Lived Assets and for Long-Lived Assets to Be Disposed Of," Statement of Financial Accounting Standards No. 121. FASB, Norwalk, CT, 1995.

_____, "Business Combinations," Statement of Financial Accounting Standards No. 141. FASB, Norwalk, CT, 2001.

_____, "Goodwill and Other Intangible Assets," Statement of Financial Accounting Standards No. 142. FASB, Norwalk, CT, 2001.

_____, "Accounting for the Impairment or Disposal of Long-Lived Assets," Statement of Financial Accounting Standards No. 144. FASB, Norwalk, CT, 2001.

_____, "Issues Relating to Accounting for Business Combinations," FASB Technical Bulletin No. 85-5. FASB, Stamford, CT, 1985.

International Financial Reporting Standard No. 3, "Business Combinations," IASB, London, 2004.

Securities and Exchange Commission, "Determination of the Acquiring Corporation," Staff Accounting Bulletins Topic 2, Item A-2 (SAB No. 40). SEC, Washington, DC, 1981.

_____, "Application of Pushdown Basis of Accounting in Financial Statements of Subsidiaries Acquired by Purchase," Staff Accounting Bulletin No. 54. SEC, Washington, DC, 1983.

_____, "Adjustment of Allowances for Business Combination Loan Losses—Purchase Method Accounting," Staff Accounting Bulletin No. 61. SEC, Washington, DC, 1986.

_____, "Views on ASR Nos. 130 and 135 Regarding Risk Sharing in Business Combinations Accounted for as a Pooling-of-Interests," Staff Accounting Bulletin No. 65. SEC, Washington, DC, 1986.

_____, "Pushdown Basis of Accounting for Parent Company Debt Related to Subsidiary Acquisition," Staff Accounting Bulletin No. 73. SEC, Washington, DC, 1987.

_____, "Effect of Certain De Minimis Sales by Affiliates in Compliance with the Requirements of ASR Nos. 130 and 135," Staff Accounting Bulletin No. 76. SEC, Washington, DC, 1988.

_____, "Views Regarding Allocation of Debt Issue Costs in a Business Combination Accounted for as a Purchase," Staff Accounting Bulletin No. 77. SEC, Washington, DC, 1988.

_____, "Business Combinations," Staff Accounting Bulletin No. 96. SEC, Washington, DC, 1996.

————, "Pooling of Interests Accounting," Accounting Series Release No. 130. SEC, Washington, DC, 1972.

————, "Revised Guidelines for the Application of Accounting Series Release No. 130," Accounting Series Release No. 135. SEC, Washington, DC, 1973.

————, "Effect of Treasury Stock Transactions on Accounting for Business Combinations," Accounting Series Release No. 146. SEC, Washington, DC, 1973.

————, "Statement of Policy and Interpretations in Regard to Accounting Series Release No. 146," Accounting Series Release No. 146-A. SEC, Washington, DC, 1974.

————, "Streamlining Disclosure Requirements Relating to Significant Business Acquisitions," Financial Reporting Release No. 47. SEC, Washington, DC, 1996.

CHAPTER 13

CONSOLIDATION, TRANSLATION, AND THE EQUITY METHOD

Steven Rubin, CPA

Deloitte & Touche LLP

This Chapter was reviewed and updated for this Eleventh Edition by Francis E. Scheuerell Jr., CPA, CMA and the Editors. Mr. Scheuerell is a partner, Financial Reporting Services of Callaway Partners, LLC in Atlanta, Georgia.

13.1 OVERVIEW

Consolidation, translation, and the equity method are related sets of accounting practices used mainly in the preparation of consolidated financial statements.

(a) CONSOLIDATION.   Consolidated financial statements present the financial position, results of operations, and cash flows of a consolidated group of companies essentially as if the group were a single enterprise with one or more branches or divisions. With limited exceptions, a consolidated group of companies includes a parent company and all subsidiaries in which the parent company has a direct or indirect controlling financial interest. Because the reporting entity for consolidated financial statements transcends the legal boundaries of single companies, consolidated financial statements have special features, which require consideration in preparing and interpreting them.

(i) Control.   Consolidation is required when one company, the parent, owns—directly or indirectly—more than 50 percent of the outstanding voting shares of another company, unless control is likely to be temporary or does not rest with the parent. For instance, a majority-owned subsidiary is not consolidated if it (1) is in legal reorganization or bankruptcy or (2) operates under foreign exchange restrictions, controls, or other governmentally imposed uncertainties so severe that they cast doubt on the parent's ability to control the subsidiary. Majority-owned subsidiaries excluded from consolidation because control is likely to be temporary or does not rest with the parent are called *unconsolidated subsidiaries*.

Investments in unconsolidated subsidiaries, like other investments that give an investor the ability to exercise significant influence over the investee's operating and financial activities, are accounted for by the equity method, which is discussed below.

(ii) Irrelevant Factors.   The fact that a particular subsidiary is located in a foreign country, has a large minority interest, or engages in principal activities substantially different from those of its parent is irrelevant to the consolidation requirement. That was not always the case, however. Until 1988, those factors were quite relevant and, indeed, were considered to be legitimate reasons for excluding a particular subsidiary from consolidation. The rules were changed by the issuance of Statements of Financial Accounting (SFAS) No. 94, "Consolidation of All Majority-Owned Subsidiaries," and that no longer is the case. The SFAS No. 94 requires consolidation of all majority-owned subsidiaries unless control is temporary or does not rest with the majority owners.

A difference in fiscal periods of a parent and a majority-owned subsidiary does not in itself justify the subsidiary's exclusion from consolidation. In that case, the subsidiary has to prepare, for consolidation purposes, financial statements for a period that corresponds with or closely approaches the parent's fiscal period.

If, however, the difference between the parent's and the subsidiary's fiscal periods does not exceed about three months, the subsidiary's financial statements may be consolidated with those of the parent even though they cover different periods. In that case, recognition has to be given in the consolidated financial statements by disclosure or otherwise of this fact and the effect of any intervening events that materially affect consolidated financial position or results of operations.

(iii) Intercompany Amounts.   Only legal entities can own assets, owe liabilities, issue capital stock, earn revenues, enjoy gains, and incur expenses and losses. A group of companies as such cannot do those things. So the elements of consolidated financial statements are the elements of the financial statements of the members of the consolidated group of companies—the parent company and its consolidated subsidiaries. They are the assets owned by the member companies, the liabilities owed by the member companies, the equity of the member companies, and the revenues, expenses, gains, and losses of the member companies.

Some elements of the financial statements of member companies are not elements of the consolidated financial statements, however. The elements of the financial statements of a reporting entity are relationships and changes in relationships between the reporting entity and outside entities. But some elements of the financial statements of members of a consolidated group are relationships and changes in relationships between member companies, called *intercompany amounts*. (They would more accurately be described as intragroup amounts.) Intercompany amounts are excluded from consolidated financial statements.

It is convenient to prepare consolidated financial statements by starting with the financial statements of the member companies, which include intercompany amounts. The intercompany amounts are removed by adjustments and eliminations in consolidation. The items are:

- *Intercompany stockholdings*. Ownership by the parent company of capital stock of the subsidiaries and ownership, if any, by subsidiaries of capital stock of other subsidiaries or of the parent company.
- *Intercompany receivables and payables*. Debts of member companies to other member companies.
- *Intercompany sales, purchases, fees, rents, interest, and the like*. Sales of goods or provision of services from member companies to other member companies.
- *Intercompany profits*. Profits recorded by member companies in transactions with other member companies reflected in recorded amounts of assets of member companies at the reporting date.
- *Intercompany dividends*. Dividends from members of the consolidated group to other members of the consolidated group.

After the intercompany amounts are eliminated, the consolidated financial statements present solely relationships and changes in relationships with entities outside the consolidated reporting entity. They present:

- Amounts receivable from and amounts payable to outside entities
- Investments in outside entities
- Other assets helpful in carrying out activities with outside entities
- Consolidated equity equal to the excess of those assets over those liabilities
- Changes in those assets, liabilities, and equity, including profits realized or losses incurred by dealings with outside entities

Consolidated financial statements present the financial affairs of a consolidated group of companies united for economic activity by common control.

(iv) Variable Interest Entities.   In 2003, the Financial Accounting Standards Board (FASB) issued FASB Interpretation (FIN) No. 46 (Revised December 2003), "Consolidation of Variable Interest Entities (VIEs)—An Interpretation of Accounting Research Bulletin (ARB) No. 51", to clarify the circumstances where and how VIEs should be consolidated. As defined in paragraph 2c of FIN 46 R, interests in a VIE are contractual, ownership, or other interests in an entity that change with changes in the fair value of the entity's net assets, thus the term *variable interest entity*. VIEs are often are created for a specific purpose (e.g., to facilitate the securitization of receivables). In FIN No. 46 R, VIEs are defined by the nature and amount of their equity investment and the rights and obligations of their equity investors

FIN 46 defines a VIE as a legal entity whose equity, by design, has any of the following characteristics:

- The equity investors do not have an obligation to absorb the expected losses of the entity,
- The equity investors do not have the right to receive the expected returns,
- The total equity at risk is not sufficient to finance the entity's activities without additional financial support,
- The equity investors do not have the ability to make decisions through voting rights, or,
- The voting rights of equity investors are not proportional to their expected share of losses or residual returns and substantially all of the entity's activities are on behalf of an entity with few voting rights.

In general, VIEs should be consolidated by their primary beneficiaries (e.g., the party that will absorb the majority of the losses or receive the majority of the benefits), even when the primary beneficiary is not the majority owner.

The issue of accounting for such entities received considerable public attention and accounting focus after revelations about the role of certain unconsolidated entities in possibly obscuring the underlying economic effect of certain transactions relating to Enron's financial statements. FIN 46 will make it harder to exclude debt from the balance sheet via specialized finance affiliates, and likely will require more entities to be consolidated.

Entities holding a majority of voting stock will still follow the ownership-based guidelines for consolidation in ARB No. 51, *Consolidated Financial Statements*.

Variable interests may include:

- Investments in common or preferred stock
- Loans or notes
- Guarantees
- Certain insurance contracts and derivative contracts
- Leases, and service or management contracts.

Not all entities that qualify as VIEs are consolidated. For example, when a VIE has sufficient equity at risk such that the VIE can operate on a stand-alone basis, there may be no need for another entity to consolidate the VIE.

This topic continues to be a complex area of practice. Familiarity with the Interpretation's concepts and requirements is evolving, but FIN 46 provides much needed guidance to shore up perceived weaknesses in the consolidation requirements when VIEs exist.

FIN 46 also identifies certain required disclosures for primary beneficiaries as well as for unconsolidated VIEs.

(v) Disclosures.   Consolidation policy, that is, the composition of the consolidated group, needs to be disclosed in the notes to the consolidated financial statements. Also, a member of a consolidated group that files a consolidated tax return discloses the following information related to income taxes in its own separately issued financial statements:

- The amount of current and deferred tax expense for each statement of earnings presented and any tax-related balances due to or from other group members as of each balance sheet date
- The principal provisions of the method by which the consolidated amount of current and deferred tax expense is allocated to members of the consolidated group and the nature and effect of any changes in that method

(b) BUSINESS COMBINATIONS.   A company can start a subsidiary by having it incorporated and investing resources in it. Including such a subsidiary in consolidated financial statements presents no special problem. The amount of the investment recorded by the parent company equals the initial equity of the subsidiary, each of which is eliminated in consolidation. Business combinations are the subject of Chapter 12 in this Handbook.

(c) TRANSLATION.   Financial statements of a parent company are stated in the domestic unit of currency, such as the U.S. dollar for U.S. parent companies. Financial statements of a foreign subsidiary are stated in a foreign unit of currency, a unit of currency other than the domestic unit of currency, such as the U.K. pound for U.K. subsidiaries. Such foreign currency financial statements cannot be consolidated with domestic currency financial statements; the result would be a set of financial statements stated in more than one unit of currency, which would make them unintelligible.

Before the financial statements of a foreign subsidiary can be consolidated with the financial statements of its parent company, therefore, the amounts in its foreign currency financial statements are changed to amounts stated in the domestic unit of currency. Changing the amounts from those stated in the foreign unit of currency to those stated in the domestic unit of currency is called *translation*, analogous to translation from one language to another. Translation is discussed and illustrated in Section 13.2.

Translation uses foreign exchange rates. Such rates are ratios of exchange, prices of units of one kind of currency in terms of units of another kind of currency, such as $(U.S.) 1.50 for £(U.K.) 1. Foreign exchange rates change, as all other prices do. That causes two problems in translation: (1) how to select the foreign exchange rates to use for translation; and (2) how to treat translation differences, items unique to translated financial statements caused by translating amounts in a single set of financial statements at two or more foreign exchange rates.

(d) EQUITY METHOD.   The equity method is used to account for investments that give an investor the ability to exercise significant influence over the investee's operating and financial activities, including investments in majority-owned subsidiaries that do not qualify for consolidation. The investee may be a corporation, a partnership, or a joint venture. An investment accounted for by the equity method is initially recorded at cost. After that, the investment's carrying amount is increased or decreased for the investor's share of changes in the underlying net assets of the investee and for certain other transactions and other events. Principles relating to the equity method are discussed in Section 13.3.

(e) COMBINED FINANCIAL STATEMENTS.   Circumstances exist in which combined financial statements of commonly controlled corporations are likely to be more meaningful than their separate financial statements. Such circumstances include, for example, ownership by one person of a controlling interest in several corporations related in their operations.

If combined financial statements are prepared, they present only relationships and changes in relationships with entities outside the combined group. That means that intercompany sales and purchases, profit, and receivables and payables are eliminated. Intercompany stockholdings, if any, are eliminated.

The separate components of equity of each corporation are aggregated with the corresponding separate components of the other corporations. Presentation of a table showing each corporation's portion of each component of combined equity in either the balance sheet or the notes, though not required by the authoritative accounting literature, would likely enhance the usefulness of the combined statements.

(f) CONSOLIDATING STATEMENTS.   If all else fails to present information on a group of related companies in a helpful way, consolidating statements are often used as an effective means of presenting the pertinent information. Such statements are essentially presentations as in worksheets used to derive consolidated financial statements together with notes and other kinds of necessary disclosures.

(g) SECURITIES AND EXCHANGE COMMISSION RULES AND REGULATIONS ON CONSOLIDATED FINANCIAL STATEMENTS.   Beyond the concepts and procedures involving all consolidated financial statements, the Security and Exchange Commission (SEC), in its Regulation S-X, has published regulations for registrants that file their consolidated financial statements with the commission.

(i) Selection of Reporting Entity.   The rules require that the application of principles for inclusion of subsidiaries in consolidated financial statements "clearly exhibit the financial position and results of operations of the registrant and its subsidiaries." A company not majority owned may not be consolidated. A subsidiary whose financial statements are as of a date or for periods different from those of the registrant may not be consolidated unless all the following conditions apply:

- The difference is not more than 93 days.
- The closing date of the subsidiary's financial information is expressly indicated.
- The necessity for using different closing dates is briefly explained.

Due consideration must be given to consolidating foreign subsidiaries operating under political, economic, or currency restrictions. If such foreign subsidiaries are consolidated, the effects, if determinable, of foreign exchange restrictions on the consolidated financial position and results of operations must be disclosed.

(ii) Intercompany Items and Transactions.   Intercompany items and transactions between members of a consolidated group generally are eliminated in consolidated financial statements, and unrealized intercompany profits and losses on transactions with investees accounted for by the equity method are also eliminated. If such items are not eliminated, the registrant is required to state its reason for not doing so.

(iii) Other Disclosures.   The SEC rules require brief descriptions in the notes to consolidated financial statements of the principles of consolidation followed and any changes in principles or in the composition of the companies constituting the consolidated group since the last set of consolidated financial statements was filed with the commission.
The rules require that consolidated financial statements also present:

- An explanation and reconciliation of differences between (1) the amount at which investments in consolidated subsidiaries are carried on the registrant's books and (2) the equity of the registrant in the assets and liabilities of the subsidiaries
- An explanation and reconciliation between (1) dividends received from unconsolidated subsidiaries and (2) earnings of unconsolidated subsidiaries
- An analysis of minority interest in capital stock, in retained earnings, and in net income of consolidated subsidiaries

13.2 FOREIGN CURRENCY TRANSLATION

A subsidiary or another unit within a consolidated group of companies (or within a company or an affiliated group of companies), such as a joint venture, a division, or a branch, may be a foreign operation, an operating unit that prepares foreign currency financial statements. Before such statements can be included in domestic currency consolidated financial statements, they ordinarily have to be translated into the domestic currency used in the consolidated financial statements, the currency of the parent company's country. The SFAS No. 52, "Foreign Currency Translation," sets forth current generally accepted accounting procedures (GAAP) for translation.

(a) OBJECTIVES OF TRANSLATION.   The SFAS No. 52 states objectives to be achieved in translation in the face of changes in foreign exchange rates, ratios of exchange between two currencies. The principles in SFAS No. 52 were adopted with the intention of achieving those objectives. The basic objective is:

- *Compatibility with expected effects.* Information concerning foreign operations should be generally compatible with the expected effects of changes in foreign exchange rates on the parent company's cash flows and equity. If a change in an exchange rate is expected to have an overall beneficial effect, translation should reflect that. If a change is expected to have an overall adverse effect, translation should likewise reflect that. The expected effects of a change in a foreign exchange rate on the carrying amounts of all assets and liabilities of a foreign operation should therefore be recognized currently.

Other major objectives are:

- *Conformity with GAAP.* Translation should produce amounts that conform with GAAP. For example, inventories and land, buildings, and equipment should be stated at acquisition cost after translation.
- *Retaining results and relationships.* The financial results and relationships in the foreign currency financial statements of a foreign operation should be retained in its statements after translation. Profits should translate into profits and losses should translate into losses. Relationships before translation, such as a current ratio of two to one or a ratio of gross profit to sales of 35 percent, should be the same after translation.

In SFAS No. 52, the FASB also considered whether to adopt another objective:

To use a "single unit of measure" for financial statements that include translated foreign amounts. (par. 70)

It did not adopt that objective (par. 75). It forces accountants to put into financial statements the equivalent of the four that results from adding one yard and three feet, thus making them meaningless and worthless. The FASB not only acknowledged that the principles in SFAS No. 52 require accountants to violate the single-unit-of-measure rule of arithmetic, but it defended it strenuously:

[The FASB] believes that, for an enterprise operating in multiple currency environments, a true "single unit of measure" does not, as a factual matter, exist. . . . The Board concluded that for many foreign entities, adhering to a "single unit of measure" was artificial and illusory. (pars. 85, 88)

But no unit of measure exists until it is defined for the purpose at hand. Moreover, if no single unit of measure could be soundly defined for multiple currency environments, sound consolidation, or combination involving foreign operations would be impossible.

The single unit of measure should be the unit used in the parent company's financial statements.

(b) ASSUMPTIONS CONCERNING TRANSLATION.   SFAS No. 52 states these assumptions concerning translation on which the principles in the statement are based:

- *Two types of foreign operations.* Foreign operations are of two types, which differ from each other so much that translation procedures for the two types have to differ. The two types are (1) self-contained and integrated foreign operations and (2) components or extensions of the parent company's domestic operations.

- *Self-contained and integrated foreign operations.* A foreign operation may be relatively self-contained and integrated in a foreign country. Such an operation should be treated in consolidated financial statements as a net investment of the parent company. The entire net investment, not merely certain assets and liabilities of the foreign operation, is exposed to the risk of changes in the exchange rate between the currency of the foreign country and the domestic currency. Though such changes affect the parent company's net investment, they do not affect its cash flows. The effects of such changes on a foreign operation should therefore be excluded from reported consolidated net income unless the parent company sells part or all of its investment in the foreign operation or completely or substantially liquidates its investment in the foreign operation.

- *Components or extensions of parent company domestic operations.* A foreign operation may be a direct and integral component or an extension of the parent company's domestic operations, such as an import or export business. It should be treated as an integral part of the parent company's operations. Changes in the exchange rate between the currency of the country in which the foreign operation is conducted and the domestic currency directly affect certain individual assets and liabilities of the foreign operation, for example, its foreign currency receivables and payables, and thereby affect the parent company's cash flows. The effects should be recognized currently in reported consolidated net income.

- *Functional currencies.* The most meaningful measuring unit for the assets, liabilities, and operations of a foreign operation is the currency of the primary economic environment in which the operation is conducted, its functional currency. Consolidated financial statements should therefore use one measuring unit for each functional currency of the operating units in the consolidated group of companies, including the domestic currency, which is the functional currency of the parent company. If only one measuring unit were used, the resulting information generally would be incompatible with the expected effects of changes in foreign exchange rates on the parent company's cash flows and equity. It would therefore be contrary to the basic objective of translation.

- *Highly inflationary economies.* Currencies of countries with highly inflationary economies are unsatisfactory as measuring units for financial reporting. A highly inflationary economy is one that has cumulative inflation of approximately 100 percent or more over three years. An operation in the environment of such a currency should be treated as if the domestic currency were its functional currency.

- *Effective hedges.* Some contracts, transactions, and balances are, in effect, hedges of foreign exchange risks. They should be treated that way regardless of their form.

(c) TASKS REQUIRED FOR TRANSLATION.   SFAS No. 52 (par. 69) states that to achieve the objectives of translation and to conform with its assumptions, these four major tasks are required for each foreign operation:

1. Identifying the functional currency of the [operation's] economic environment
2. Measuring all elements of the financial statements in the functional currency
3. Using the current exchange rate for translating from the functional currency to the reporting currency, if they are different
4. Distinguishing the economic impact of changes in exchange rates on a net investment from the impact of such changes on individual assets and liabilities that are receivable or payable in currencies other than the functional currency

(i) Identifying the Functional Currency. SFAS No. 52 indicates that identifying the functional currency of a foreign operation by determining the primary economic environment in which the operation is conducted is essentially a matter of management judgment. Management assesses the economic facts and circumstances pertaining to the foreign operation in relation to the objectives of translation, discussed above. Economic factors are considered both individually and collectively to determine the functional currency, so that the financial results and relationships are measured with the greatest degree of relevance and reliability.

Exercise of management's judgment is simplified if a foreign operation is either clearly self-contained and integrated in a particular foreign country, so that the currency of that country obviously is its functional currency, or clearly a direct and integral component or extension of the parent company's operations, so that the domestic currency obviously is its functional currency.

The functional currency of a foreign operation normally is the currency of the environment in which it primarily generates and expends cash. But sometimes observable facts are ambiguous in pointing to the functional currency. For example, if a foreign operation conducts significant amounts of business in two or more currencies, its functional currency might not be easily identifiable. For those operations, individual economic facts and circumstances need to be assessed.

Appendix A of SFAS No. 52 provides guidance for making those assessments in particular circumstances. The guidance is grouped in sets of indicators: cash flow indicators, sales price indicators, sales market indicators, expense indicators, financing indicators, and intercompany transactions and arrangements indicators.

(ii) Measuring in the Functional Currency. Most foreign operations prepare their financial statements in their functional currencies. Some, however, prepare their financial statements in other foreign currencies. Before the financial statements of a foreign operation are translated from its functional currency to the domestic currency, its foreign currency financial statements obviously have to be stated in its functional currency. If its financial statements are stated in another currency because its records are maintained in the other currency, they have to be remeasured into the functional currency before translation.

SFAS No. 52 (par. 10) distinguishes between remeasurement and translation. It states the goal of remeasurement to be "to produce the same results as if the . . . books of record had been maintained in the functional currency."

Remeasurement requires, as does translation, use of foreign exchange rates. For remeasurement, they are the rates between the foreign currency in which the financial statements of a foreign operation are stated and its foreign functional currency. Unlike translation, however, remeasurement requires the use of historical foreign exchange rates in addition to the current foreign exchange rate. Historical rates are rates at dates before the reporting date as of which certain financial statement items are recorded, such as items recorded at acquisition cost.

Remeasurement takes three steps. First, amounts to be remeasured at historical rates are distinguished from amounts to be remeasured at current rates. Second, the amounts are remeasured using the historical and current rates, as appropriate. Third, all exchange gains and losses identified by remeasurement are recognized currently in income. Such gains and losses are identified by remeasuring amounts at rates current at the reporting date, mainly monetary assets and liabilities not denominated in the functional currency, that differ from rates current at the preceding reporting date or an intervening date at which they were acquired.

Amounts remeasured at historical rates generally are amounts stated in historical terms, such as acquisition cost, and related revenue and expenses, such as depreciation.

SFAS No. 52 specifies that amounts resulting from interperiod income tax allocation and amounts related to unamortized policy acquisition costs of stock life insurance companies are to be remeasured using the current rate.

To remeasure an amount recorded in a currency other than the functional currency at the lower of cost and market, its cost in the foreign currency is first remeasured using the historical exchange rate. That amount is compared with market in the functional currency, and the remeasured amount is written down if market is lower than remeasured cost. If the item had been written down in the records because market was less than cost in the currency in which it was recorded, the write-down is reversed if market in the functional currency is more than remeasured cost.

If an item is written down to market in the functional currency, the resulting amount is treated as cost in subsequent periods in which it is held in applying the lower of cost and market rule.

The financial statements of a foreign operation in a highly inflationary economy are remeasured to the domestic currency the way they would be remeasured were the domestic currency its functional currency.

(iii) Translation Using the Current Rate.   Amounts remeasured into the domestic currency need not be translated, because the domestic currency is used as the reporting currency in the consolidated financial statements. Amounts measured in a foreign currency or remeasured into a foreign currency are all translated using the current foreign exchange rate between the foreign currency and the domestic currency.

For assets and liabilities, that is the rate at the reporting date. For income statement items, that is the rates as of the dates during the reporting period at which the items are recorded. An appropriately weighted average rate may be used to translate such items if they are numerous.

(iv) Translation Adjustments.   Translation adjustments result from translating all amounts in foreign currency financial statements at rates current at the reporting date or during the reporting period different from rates current at the previous reporting date or during the previous reporting period. Remeasurement of a foreign operation's foreign currency financial statements involves recognition in current income of exchange gains and losses. In contrast, translation adjustments are not recognized in current income but are accumulated in a separate component of equity.

The translation adjustments pertaining to a foreign operation are transferred from equity to gain or loss on disposition of the foreign operation when it is partly or completely sold or completely or substantially liquidated.

(d) TREATMENT OF FOREIGN COMPONENTS OR EXTENSIONS OF PARENT COMPANY OPERATIONS.   The functional currency of a foreign operation that is a component or extension of the parent company's operations is the domestic currency. If it prepares its financial statements in a foreign currency, those financial statements are remeasured into the domestic currency by procedures discussed above. No translation is required for such a foreign operation.

(e) TREATMENT OF FOREIGN CURRENCY TRANSACTIONS.   Some transactions of a unit in a consolidated group of companies may take place in a currency other than the functional currency of the unit. For example, a unit whose functional currency is the Mexican peso may buy a machine on credit for U.K. pounds or may sell securities on credit for French francs. Except in a forward exchange contract (discussed below), the amounts in such a foreign currency transaction are measured at the transaction date at the foreign exchange rate at that date—in the example, between the peso and the pound or between the peso and the franc.

At the next reporting date or at an intervening date at which the receivable or payable is settled, the receivable or payable is remeasured at the rate current at that date. Changes in its amount as measured in the functional currency since the previous reporting date or an intervening date at which it was acquired are transaction gains or losses, to be included in current reported consolidated net income, except as discussed later.

To illustrate: Corporation P, whose functional currency is U.S. dollars, borrowed £(U.K.)1,000,000 on January 1, 20X1, and agreed to repay £100,000 on December 31, 20X1, and £1,100,000 on December 31, 20X2. Exchange rates were $1.60/£1 at January 1, 20X1, and $1.50/£1 at December 31, 20X1.

The payment of £100,000 on December 31, 20X1, is remeasured as interest expense of $150,000. The liability in dollars at December 31, 20X1, is remeasured for the change in exchange rate and

		U.S. Dollars
Liability		
January 1, 20 × 1	£1,000,000 × $1.60/£1 =	$1,600,000
December 31, 20 × 1	£1,000,000 × $1.50/£1 =	1,500,000
Transaction gain		$ 100,000

Exhibit 13.1   Corporation P, transaction gain on forward exchange contracts for the year 20×1.

a transaction gain of $100,000 is determined, for presentation in P's income statement for the year 20X1, as shown in Exhibit 13.1.

(f) FORWARD EXCHANGE CONTRACTS. Forward exchange contracts are contracts that require currencies of two countries to be traded in specified amounts at specified future dates and specified rates, called *forward rates*. Such contracts are foreign currency transactions that require special treatment.

(i) Discounts or Premiums on Forward Exchange Contracts. A forward exchange contract may involve a discount or premium, a difference between the foreign exchange rate specified in the contract and the rate at the date the contract is entered into, multiplied by the amount of foreign currency specified in the contract. Ordinarily, a discount or premium is allocated to income over the duration of the forward exchange contract. However, a discount or premium may be treated differently in these circumstances:

If the contract is designated as and is effective as a hedge of a net investment in a foreign operation (discussed further on). If so, the discount or premium may be included with translation adjustments and thus not be reported in income.

If the contract meets the tests of a hedge of an identifiable foreign currency commitment (also discussed farther on). If so, the discount or premium may be included in the amount at which the foreign currency transaction related to the commitment is stated.

(ii) Gains or Losses on Forward Exchange Contracts. A gain or loss on a forward exchange contract to be reported in the current reporting period is computed by multiplying the amount of the foreign currency to be exchanged by the difference between (1) the foreign exchange rate at the reporting date and (2) the rate (a) on the date on which the contract was made or (b) the previous reporting date, whichever is later. A gain or loss on a forward exchange contract is recognized in income as a transaction gain or loss in the period of the gain or loss, unless it is in one of the categories of transaction gains and losses excluded from net income, discussed later.

To illustrate a forward exchange contract: On January 1, 20X1, P and Q enter into a contract in which Q agrees to buy £(U.K.)1,000,000 from P for $(U.S.)1,550,000, incorporating a forward rate of $1.55/£1, on December 31, 20X2. The exchange rate at January 1, 20X1, is $1.60/£1. The contract therefore involves a premium to P and a discount to Q of £1,000,000 × ($1.60/£1 − $1.55/£1) = $50,000.

Q makes this entry:

Foreign currency receivable	$1,600,000	
Payable to P		$1,550,000
Discount on foreign exchange contract		50,000

P makes this entry:

Receivable from Q	$1,550,000	
Premium on foreign exchange contract	50,000	
Foreign currency payable		$1,600,000

P and Q allocate the $50,000 to forward exchange gain or loss over the years 20X1 and 20X2. P makes this entry in each of the two years:

Amortization of premium on forward exchange contract	$ 25,000	
Premium on forward exchange contract		$ 25,000

Q makes this opposite entry in each of the two years:

Discount on forward exchange contract	$ 25,000	
Amortization of discount on forward exchange contract		$ 25,000

The exchange rate changes to $1.50/£1 at December 31, 20X1, and $1.45/£1 at December 31, 20X2. P records these entries based on the changes in the exchange rate:

December 31, 20X1

Foreign currency payable	$ 100,000	
Forward exchange gain		$ 100,000

£1,000,000 × ($1.60/£1 − $1.50/£1) = $100,000

December 31, 20X2

Foreign currency payable	$ 50,000	
Forward exchange gain		$ 50,000

£1,000,000 × ($1.50/£1 − $1.45/£1) = $50,000

Q records these opposite entries based on the changes in the exchange rate:

December 31, 20X1

Foreign exchange loss	$ 100,000	
Forward currency receivable		$ 100,000

December 31, 20X2

Forward exchange loss	$ 50,000	
Foreign currency receivable		$ 50,000

On settlement of the contract on December 31, 20X2, P makes this entry:

Foreign currency payable	$1,450,000	
Cash	$ 100,000	
Receivable from Q		1,550,000

To record payment of $1,450,000 to buy £1,000,000 to give to Q, receipt of $1,550,000 from Q, and cancellation of the forward exchange receivable from Q.

Q makes this opposite entry:

Payable to P	$1,550,000	
Foreign currency receivable		$1,450,000
Cash		100,000

To record receipt of $1,450,000 on sale of £1,000,000 received from P, payment of $1,550,000 to P, and cancellation of the forward exchange payable to P

The contract may be summarized as shown in Exhibit 13.2.

The net gain of P and loss of Q of $100,000 equal the difference between the forward rate and the rate on the settlement date times the amount of currency transferred:

$$($1.55/£1 − $1.45/£1) × £1,000,000 = $100,000$$

	Gain by P, Loss by Q, U.S. Dollars
Foreign exchange gain or loss on contract:	
The year 20 × 1—£1,000,000 × ($1.60/£1 − $1.50/£1) =	$100,000
The year 20 × 2—£1,000,000 × ($1.50/£1 − $1.45/£1) =	$ 50,000
	150,000
Premium or discount on contract	(50,000)
Net gain or loss over the life of the contract	$100,000

Exhibit 13.2   -Corporation P or Corporation Q, gain or loss on forward exchange contracts beginning in the year 20×1

(g) EXCLUSION OF TRANSACTION GAINS AND LOSSES FROM INCOME. Gains and losses on some foreign currency transactions are not recognized in income when they occur.

(i) Treatment as Translation Adjustments. SFAS No. 52 (par. 20) requires amounts that otherwise fit the definition of gains and losses on foreign currency transactions to be treated as translation adjustments if

a. [They] are designated as, and are effective as, economic hedges of a net investment in a foreign entity, commencing as of the designation date [or]

b. [They are] intercompany foreign currency transactions that are of a long-term investment nature (that is, settlement is not planned or anticipated in the foreseeable future), when the [units that are parties] to the transaction[s] are consolidated, combined, or accounted for by the equity method in the reporting [entity's] financial statements.

(ii) Deferral of Transaction Gains and Losses. Recognition of transaction gains and losses in consolidated income is deferred for such gains and losses resulting from transactions intended to hedge identifiable foreign currency commitments; they are included in accounting for the transaction resulting from the commitment. However, recognition of losses is not deferred if deferral would lead to recognition of losses in subsequent periods.

SFAS No. 52 (par. 21) states two conditions that have to be met for a foreign currency transaction to be considered a hedge of an identifiable foreign currency commitment:

1. The foreign currency transaction is designated as, and is effective as, a hedge of a foreign currency commitment.

2. The foreign currency commitment is firm.

(h) OTHER TOPICS IN FOREIGN CURRENCY TRANSLATION. Other topics concerning translation by the current rate method include income tax considerations, intercompany profit eliminations, selection of exchange rates, approximations, and required disclosures.

(i) Income Tax Considerations. Treatment of foreign operations involves these special income tax accounting treatments:

- *Unremitted earnings*. Deferred taxes are not recognized on translation adjustments that meet the tests in APB Opinion No. 23, "Accounting for Income Taxes—Special Areas," concerning unremitted earnings.

- *Intraperiod allocation*. Income taxes related to transaction gains and losses or translation adjustments reported in separate components of the income statement or the statement of changes in equity are allocated to the separate components.

(ii) Intercompany Profit Eliminations. An exception in the current rate method to the use of the current exchange rate for translation is the method to eliminate intercompany profits on transactions between combined or consolidated companies or between affiliates accounted for by the equity method. They are eliminated at the rates at the dates of the transactions, because those are the rates at which the profits are embedded in the recorded amounts. Such eliminations precede applying the current exchange rates to the foreign currency amounts.

To illustrate: Corporation P, a domestic parent company, sold a parcel of land last year to Corporation S, its foreign subsidiary, at a profit of $24,000, when the exchange rate was $1/Z8 (Polish zlotys). S recorded the land in zlotys. The current exchange rate is Z6 = $1. The profit is eliminated at Z8/$1. The remaining amount at which S has the land recorded is translated at Z6/$1. However, exchange restrictions between dollars and zlotys may be severe enough to call into question the soundness of including S in the consolidated reporting entity.

(iii) Selection of Exchange Rates. The current foreign exchange rate is used for most translation required by SFAS No. 52. Circumstances in which the rates at the dates of transactions are used instead are discussed above. These are other special considerations in selecting exchange rates:

> If the two currencies involved could not be exchanged on the date of the transaction or the reporting date, the rate at which they could be exchanged at the first succeeding date is used.

> If the inability to exchange the two currencies is not merely temporary, including the foreign operation in a consolidated group or accounting for it by the equity method is questioned.

> Foreign currency transactions are translated at the rates at which they could have been settled at the dates of the transactions. Resulting receivables and payables are translated subsequently at the rates at which they could be settled at the reporting dates.

> If there is more than one rate at a particular date, the rate at which foreign currency could be exchanged for domestic currency to remit dividends is used.

> If the reporting date of the foreign currency financial statements being translated differs from the reporting date of the reporting entity in which the foreign operation is included, the current rate is the rate in effect on the reporting date of the foreign currency financial statements.

(iv) Approximations. Approximations of the results of applying the required translation principles are acceptable if the cost of applying them to every detail exceeds the benefits of such precision and the results do not materially differ from what they would be by applying them to every detail. Judgment is required to determine whether to use approximation, because determining the extent of the differences precisely would require the very calculations to be avoided by approximations.

(i) DISCLOSURES CONCERNING FOREIGN OPERATIONS. These disclosures are required concerning foreign operations:

- The total transaction gains or losses, including, for this purpose, gains and losses on forward contracts other than those excluded from income
- An analysis of the changes in the separate component of equity for translation adjustments, including at least:
  > The beginning and ending accumulated balances

  > The net change from translation adjustments and gains and losses from hedges and intercompany balances treated the way translation adjustments are treated

  > Income taxes allocated to translation adjustments

  > Transfers from the equity component into income because of the partial or complete sale of an investment in a foreign operation or the complete or substantial liquidation of a foreign operation

13.3 THE EQUITY METHOD

The equity method, which is the focus of APB Opinion No. 18, is used to account for investments in unconsolidated subsidiaries, corporate joint ventures, and common stock that provide the investor with the ability to exercise significant influence over the operating and financial policies of the investee.

Under the equity method, an investor initially records an investment at cost. It adjusts the carrying amount of the investment at the end of the period in which it is acquired and in succeeding periods by the investor's proportionate share of changes in the investee's assets and liabilities and for the effects of intercompany profits. The principles for determining the cost of an investment accounted for by the equity method are essentially the same as those for determining the cost of an investment leading to a business combination accounted for by the purchase method, discussed in Chapter 12.

(a) DIFFERENCES BETWEEN CONSOLIDATION AND THE EQUITY METHOD. An investor's net income for a period and its equity at a point in time with its investment accounted for by the equity method are generally the same as they are with the investee consolidated. Application of SFAS No. 34, "Capitalization of Interest Cost," and SFAS No. 58, "Capitalization of Interest Cost in Financial Statements That Include Investments Accounted for by the Equity Method" cause differences, however.

Under SFAS No. 34, the total amount of interest cost capitalized in a set of consolidated financial statements cannot exceed the total amount of interest cost incurred by all the members of the consolidated group after intercompany amounts are eliminated. Under SFAS No. 58, however, for investments accounted for by the equity method, the total amount of interest cost capitalized in the investor's financial statements cannot exceed the total amount of interest cost incurred solely by the investor. That is, interest costs incurred by an investee accounted for by the equity method are excluded in accounting for amounts in the investor's financial statements on which interest is capitalized. Interest cost incurred by the investee can be capitalized only on amounts in the investee's financial statements.

(b) USING THE EQUITY METHOD. An investor generally uses the equity method to account for each of the following types of investments.

(i) Unconsolidated Subsidiaries. If a subsidiary does not qualify for consolidation, its financial statement elements are not combined with corresponding elements of the parent company line by line, but are instead reported in the parent company's balance sheet and income statement on one line on each statement, the one called *investment in unconsolidated subsidiary* or the like and the other called *investment revenue* or the like.

(ii) Joint Ventures. An enterprise may be formed and operated by a number of other enterprises as a joint venture—a separate business or means to carry out a specific project for the benefit of its investors, also called *venturers*. The venturers pool their resources, knowledge, and talents and share risks for the purpose of ultimately sharing rewards. In many joint ventures, each venturer has more than just a passive interest or investment; each participates—either directly or indirectly—in managing the venture. Investments in joint ventures are generally accounted for by the equity method.

(iii) Investments in Common Stock Involving Significant Influence. In the absence of evidence to the contrary, an investor with an investment of from 20 percent to 50 percent of the voting common stock of an investee is presumed to have the ability to exercise significant influence over the financial and operating policies of the investee and, because of that, uses the equity method to account for such an investment. Conversely, in the absence of evidence to the contrary, an investor with an investment of less than 20 percent of the common stock of an investee is presumed not to have the ability to exercise significant influence over the financial and operating policies of the investee and, therefore, does not use the equity method to account for such an investment but uses the method discussed in Subsection 13.4(a).

The ability to exercise significant influence may be inferred from, for example:

- Representation on the investee's board of directors
- Participation in policy-making processes
- Material intercompany transactions
- Interchange of managerial personnel
- Technological dependency

The inability to exercise significant influence may be inferred from, for example:

- Opposition by the investee that challenges the investor's ability to exercise significant influence, such as litigation or complaints to government authorities
- An agreement by the investor surrendering significant rights as a stockholder
- Concentration of the majority ownership of the investee among a few stockholders, who operate the investee without regard to the views of the investor
- Inability of the investor to obtain representation on the investee's board of directors after attempting to do so
- Inability of the investor to obtain financial information necessary to apply the equity method after attempting to do so

No one item in either of those lists is the sole determining factor as to whether an investor has the ability to exercise significant influence over the investee. Instead, all items are considered collectively.

If an investor owns two investments of, say, 20 percent each in unrelated corporations, one investment might qualify for the equity method and the other not, because their circumstances differ. Judgment is always necessary in determining whether an investment gives an investor the ability to exercise significant influence over the investee.

(c) APPLYING THE EQUITY METHOD.   Application of the equity method is discussed and illustrated below.

Under the equity method, the investor's initial investment, in essence, comprises three bundles:

Bundle A. A proportionate share of the book values of the investee's assets and liabilities on the date of the purchase.
plus
Bundle B. A proportionate share of the differences between the book values and the fair values of the investee's assets and liabilities on the date of the initial investment (commonly referred to as *net unrealized appreciation* or *unrealized depreciation*). The principles for determining the fair values of the investee's assets and liabilities parallel the principles in applying the purchase method of accounting for business combinations, discussed in Chapter 12.
plus
Bundle C. Goodwill, which is the excess at the date of purchase of (1) the cost of the investment over (2) the investor's proportionate share of the fair values of the investee's assets and liabilities (the sum of $A + B$) at the date of the purchase. If (2) exceeds (1), this bundle is negative goodwill. The principles of accounting for goodwill and negative goodwill under the equity method parallel the principles to account for them in consolidation.

The investor adjusts the carrying amount of the investment in succeeding periods by its proportionate share of changes in each bundle and for the effects of intercompany profits.

(i) Bundle A. Changes in the investee's equity are caused by earnings or losses from operations, extraordinary items, prior period adjustments, the payment of cash or property dividends, and other transactions by the investor or the investee in stock of the investee.

The investor charges the investment account for its proportionate share of the investee's earnings from operations and credits investment revenue. If the investee reports a loss, the investor credits the investment account for its proportionate share of the investee's loss from operations and charges investment revenue. A negative balance in the investment revenue account for a reporting period is disclosed as a loss from investment. The investor adjusts its investment account for its proportionate share of the investee's prior period adjustments and extraordinary items and correspondingly charges or credits prior period adjustments and extraordinary items in its own financial statements.

An investor recognizes receipt of a cash dividend by crediting its investment account.

(ii) Bundle B. The portion of the investment that represents the investor's proportionate share of the differences between the fair values and the book values of each of the investee's assets and liabilities at the date of the investment (unrealized appreciation or depreciation) is amortized to investment revenue over the remaining estimated useful lives of the underlying assets and liabilities.

(iii) Bundle C. The portion of the difference between the cost of an investment and the amount of underlying equity in assets and liabilities of an investee accounted for by the equity method that represents goodwill, known as *equity method goodwill*, is not amortized. Equity method goodwill is not tested for impairment in conformity with FASB Statement No. 142. Equity method investments continue to be tested for impairment in conformity with paragraph 19(h) of APB Opinion No. 18, "The Equity Method of Accounting for Investments in Common Stock."

(iv) Intercompany Profit or Loss. Intercompany profit or loss on assets bought from or sold to an investee is eliminated in the period of sale by adjusting the investment and the investment revenue accounts. That entry is reversed in the period in which the asset is sold to unrelated parties. The amount of unrealized profit or loss to be eliminated depends on whether the underlying transactions are considered to be at arm's length. If the transactions are not considered to be at arm's length, all the intercompany profit or loss is eliminated. If, however, the underlying transactions are considered to be at arm's length, only the investor's proportional share of the unrealized profit or loss is eliminated.

(v) Special Considerations. Applying the equity method sometimes involves the following special considerations.

Preferred Dividends. An investor computes its proportionate share of the investee's net income or loss after deducting cumulative preferred dividends, regardless of whether they are declared.

Investee's Capital Transactions. An investor accounts for transactions between the investee and its stockholders (e.g., issuances and reacquisitions of its stock) that directly affect the investor's proportionate share of the investee's equity in the same way that such transactions of a consolidated subsidiary are accounted for.

Time Lag. An investor's reporting period may differ from that of the investee or the financial statements of the investee may not be available in time for an investor to record in its financial statements the information necessary to apply the equity method currently. In either case, the investor applies the equity method using the investee's most recent available financial statements. The same lag in reporting is used each period for consistency.

Permanent Decline in Value.   The recorded amount of an investment accounted for by the equity method is normally not reduced for declines in market value. But if the decline brings that market value below the carrying amount of the investment and is judged to be permanent, the investment is written down to its recoverable amount, usually market value, and a loss is charged to current income. The distinction between a decline that is permanent and one that is not is often not clear. However, evidence of a permanent decline might be demonstrated by, for example, the investor's inability to recover the carrying amount of the investment, the investee's inability to sustain an earnings capacity that would justify the carrying amount of the investment, or a history of losses or market values substantially below cost.

To illustrate: On January 1, 20X4, Corporation P accounts for its investment in Corporation S by the equity method. The carrying amount is $24,000 and the market value of the investment is $13,000. If the decline is judged to be permanent, P discontinues applying the equity method and records this entry to reduce the investment to its recoverable amount, in this case market value:

Investment loss	$11,000	
Investment in Corporation S		$11,000

If the market subsequently recovers, $13,000, not $24,000, is the basis at which to resume applying the equity method.

Excessive Losses.   A company that accounts for an investment by the equity method ordinarily discontinues applying that method when the carrying amount of the investment in and net advances to the investee is reduced to zero, unless the investor has guaranteed obligations or is otherwise committed to providing further financial support for the investee. An investor resumes applying the equity method after the investee returns to profitable operations and the investor's proportionate share of the investee's subsequent net income equals the proportionate share of net losses the investor did not recognize during the period that application of the equity method was suspended.

Changed Conditions.   If an investment no longer qualifies for the equity method because the investor no longer has the ability to exercise significant influence over the investee, the investor stops applying the equity method and starts applying the cost method from that point on. The investor does not retroactively adjust the carrying amount of the investment to reflect what the carrying amount of the investment would have been had that method been applied since the investment was acquired.

To illustrate: On January 1, 20X4, Corporation P's investment in Corporation S ceases to give P the ability to exercise significant influence over S. On that date the investment in Corporation S is reported in P's financial statements at $28,000. That becomes the investment's cost for purposes of applying the cost method from that point on.

If an investment accounted for by the cost method subsequently qualifies for the equity method because the investor subsequently gains the ability to exercise significant influence over the investee, the investor stops applying the method and starts applying the equity method from that point on. In that case, in contrast, the investor does retroactively adjust the carrying amount of the investment to what it would have been had it been accounted for by the equity method starting with its first acquisition by the investor, in a manner consistent with the accounting for a step-by-step acquisition of a subsidiary.

To illustrate: P acquired stock of S on January 1, 20X3, for $24,000. The investment did not give P the ability to exercise significant influence over S. The investment is reported in P's balance sheet on December 31, 20X3, at $24,000, in accordance with the cost method. Had the investment previously qualified for the equity method, the investment in S would have been reported in P's balance sheet at $32,000.

On January 1, 20X4, P gains the ability to exercise significant influence over S without a change in its holding of S's stock. P therefore increases its investment account to $32,000, as follows:

Investment in Corporation S	$8,000	
Retained earnings		$8,000

It applies the equity method from then on the way it would have been applied had P first obtained the ability to exercise significant influence when it first acquired the investment.

(d) DISCLOSURES CONCERNING THE EQUITY METHOD. The following information about investments accounted for by the equity method, as applicable, is disclosed on the face of the financial statements, in the notes to the financial statements, or in supporting schedules or statements:

- The names of the investees and the percentages of ownership.
- Reasons investments of 20 percent or more of the voting stock of an investee are not accounted for by the equity method.
- Reasons investments of less than 20 percent of the voting stock of an investee are accounted for by the equity method.
- The amounts of net unrealized appreciation or depreciation and how the amounts are amortized.
- The amounts of goodwill and how they are amortized.
- The quoted market prices of the investments, if available.
- Summarized information about the assets, liabilities, and results of operations of investments in unconsolidated subsidiaries or in corporate joint ventures, if they are material individually or collectively in relation to the financial position or results of operations of the investor. The information can be either about each investment accounted for by the equity method or combined information of all investments accounted for by the equity method.
- Descriptions of possible conversions, exercises of warrants or options, or other contingent issuances of stock of investees that may significantly affect the investor's shares of reported earnings.

13.4 SUMMARY OF MAJOR PRONOUNCEMENTS

The following sections summarize some of the major pronouncements that deal with the topics covered in this chapter.

(a) CONSOLIDATION.

- ARB No. 43, Chapter 12, "Foreign Operations and Foreign Exchange," provides criteria for the treatment of foreign subsidiaries in consolidated financial statements.
- ARB No. 51, *Consolidated Financial Statements,* describes the purpose of consolidated financial statements and selection of a consolidation policy, and it discusses concepts underlying consolidation and procedures to prepare consolidated financial statements.
- SFAS No. 94, *Consolidation of All Majority-Owned Subsidiaries,* amends ARB No. 51 to require consolidation of all majority-owned subsidiaries unless control is temporary or does not rest with the majority owners.
- FIN No. 46(R). "Consolidation of Variable Interest Entities—An Interpretation of ARB No. 51." Revised, December 2003.
- EITF Issue No. 87-15, "Effect of a Standstill Agreement on Pooling-of-Interests Accounting," holds that the existence of a standstill agreement does not by itself preclude an otherwise qualifying business combination from being accounted for by the pooling-of-interests method. A standstill agreement is an agreement that prohibits a more than 10 percent shareholder from acquiring additional shares of the enterprise or its successors for a specified period.

- In EITF Issue No. 87-27, "Poolings of Companies That Do Not Have a Controlling Class of Common Stock," concludes that a business combination may still qualify for the pooling-of-interests method even if the issuing company has to convert voting preferred stock into voting common stock so as to create a controlling class of common stock.

- In EITF Issue No. 88-27, "Effect of Unallocated Shares in an ESOP on Accounting for Business Combinations," specifies the circumstances in which unallocated shares held by an employee stock option plan should and should not be considered "tainted" for purposes of determining whether a business combination should be accounted for by the pooling of interests method.

- FTB No. 85-5, "Issues Relating to Accounting for Business Combinations, Including Costs of Closing Duplicate Facilities of an Acquirer; Stock Transactions between Companies under Company Control; Downstream Mergers; Identical Common Shares for a Pooling of Interests; Pooling of Interests by Mutual and Cooperative Enterprises," clarifies the following matters:

  That costs incurred to close duplicate facilities as a result of a business combination should not be considered part of the cost of the business combination

  How a parent company should account for minority interest in an exchange of stock between two of its subsidiaries

  That an exchange by a partially owned subsidiary of its common stock for the outstanding common stock of its parent should be accounted for under the purchase method

  That the pooling-of-interests method may not be used to account for a business combination in which one company issues common stock identical to other outstanding common shares except that the issuer retains a right of first refusal to reacquire the shares issued in certain specified circumstances

  That the conversion of a mutual or cooperative enterprise to a stock company within two years of a business combination does not by itself bar the combination from being accounted for by the pooling-of-interests method

- EITF Issue No. 94-2, "Treatment of Minority Interests in Certain Real Estate Investment Trusts," and the related EITF Issue 95-7, "Implementation Issues Related to the Treatment of Minority Interests in Certain Real Estate Investment Trusts," specify how, and at what amount, the sponsor's interest and partnership income or loss should be reported in the financial statements of a real estate investment trust (REIT).

- EITF Issue No. 96-16, "Investor's Accounting for an Investee When the Investor Has a Majority of the Voting Interest but the Minority Shareholder or Shareholders Have Certain Approval or Veto Rights," describes circumstances in which certain rights held by the minority interest may preclude consolidation by the controlling shareholder.

- EITF Issue No. 97-2, "Application of FASB Statement No. 94 and APB Opinion No. 16 to Physician Practice Management Entities," discusses circumstances in which interests in practice management entities should and should not lead to the consolidation of the entity's financial statements.

- EITF Issue No. 97-6, "Application of Issue No. 96-20 to Qualifying Special-Purpose Entities Receiving Transferred Financial Assets Prior to the Effective Date of FASB Statement No. 125," reached a consensus that was nullified by the issuance of FASB Statement No. 140.

- EITF Issue No. 99-16, "Accounting for Transactions with Elements of Research and Development Arrangements," discusses reporting by an enterprise that is a party to a research and development arrangement through which it obtains the results of research and development funded partially or entirely by others.

- EITF Issue No. 00-4, "Majority Owner's Accounting for a Transaction in the Shares of a Consolidated Subsidiary and a Derivative Indexed to the Majority Interest in That Subsidiary," discusses reporting by a parent company that owns a majority of a subsidiary's outstanding common stock and consolidates the subsidiary at the inception of a derivative contract of a type described in the Issue.

- EITF Issue No. 02-5, "Definition of 'Common Control,'" in relation to FASB Statement No. 141, "Business Combinations," discusses how to determine whether separate entities are under common control, in the context of Statement No. 141, when common majority ownership exists by an individual, a family, or a group affiliated in some other manner.

(b) FOREIGN CURRENCY TRANSLATION.

- ARB No. 43, Chapter 12, "Foreign Operations and Foreign Exchange," provides criteria for the treatment of foreign subsidiaries in consolidated financial statements.
- SFAS No. 52, "Foreign Currency Translation," specifies the accounting for foreign operations reported in the financial statements of a domestic company. It supersedes SFAS No. 8, "Accounting for the Translation of Foreign Currency Transactions and Foreign Currency Financial Statements."
- FIN No. 37, "Accounting for Translation Adjustments upon Sale of Part of an Investment in a Foreign Entity," prescribes that the accounting in SFAS No. 52 that applies to a sale or complete or substantially complete liquidation of an investment in a foreign entity also applies to a partial disposal by an enterprise of its ownership interest.
- EITF Issue No. 90-17, "Hedging Foreign Currency Risks with Purchased Options," provides guidance on the accounting for purchased foreign currency options that are not specifically addressed in SFAS No. 52.
- EITF Issue No. 91-1, "Hedging Intercompany Foreign Risks," concludes that (a) transactions between members of a consolidated group with different functional currencies can result in foreign currency risk that may be hedged for accounting purposes and (b) the appropriate accounting for the risk depends on the type of hedging instrument used.
- EITF Issue No. 91-4, "Hedging Foreign Currency Risks with Complex Options and Similar Transactions," led to (a) a consensus on the type of information that should be disclosed by an entity that hedges foreign currency risks with complex or similar transactions and (b) an SEC staff position regarding the deferral of gains or losses on complex options and similar transactions.
- EITF Issue No. 92-4, "Accounting for a Change in Functional Currency When an Economy Ceases to Be Considered Highly Inflationary," states that an entity with a foreign subsidiary operating in an economy that ceases to be considered highly inflationary should restate the functional currency accounting bases of nonmonetary assets and liabilities as of the date of cessation.
- EITF Issue No. 92-8, "Accounting for the Income Tax Effects under FASB Statement No. 109 of a Change in Functional Currency When an Economy Ceases to Be Considered Highly Inflationary," states that deferred income taxes associated with temporary differences arising from a change in functional currency when an economy ceases to be considered highly inflationary should be reflected as an adjustment to the cumulative translation adjustment component of stockholders' equity.
- EITF Issue 93-10, "Accounting for Dual Currency Bonds," discusses whether the effect of foreign currency exchange rates on dual currency bonds (bonds whose principal is repayable in U.S. dollars, but whose periodic interest is payable in a foreign currency) should be recognized (a) as an adjustment of future interest expense or (b) currently as an adjustment of the liability's carrying amount.

- EITF Issue No. 97-7, "Accounting for Hedges of the Foreign Currency Risk Inherent in an Available-for-Sale Marketable Equity Security," concludes that foreign currency transaction gains or losses on a foreign currency forward exchange contract or foreign-currency-denominated liability should be reported in the Statement 115 separate component of stockholders' equity.

- EITF Issue No. 01-5, "Application of FASB Statement No. 52 to an Investment Being Evaluated for Impairment That Will Be Disposed Of," discusses whether a reporting enterprise should include the accumulated foreign currency translation adjustment in the carrying amount of the investment in assessing impairment of an investment in a foreign entity that is held for disposal if the planned disposal will cause some or all of the accumulated foreign currency translation adjustments to be reclassified to net income.

(c) EQUITY METHOD.

- APB Opinion No. 18, "The Equity Method of Accounting for Investments in Common Stock," specifies the circumstances in which an investment in common stock should be accounted for by the equity method of accounting and the principles that apply to the method.

- SFAS No. 58, "Capitalization of Interest Cost in Financial Statements That Include Investments Accounted for by the Equity Method," specifies the circumstances in which investments accounted for by the equity method should be considered qualifying assets for purposes of interest capitalization.

- FIN No. 35, "Criteria for Applying the Equity Method of Accounting for Investments in Common Stock," clarifies that the presumptions concerning the applicability of the equity method may be overcome by predominant evidence to the contrary, based on an evaluation of all facts and circumstances relating to the investment.

- FTB No. 79-19, "Investor's Accounting for Unrealized Losses on Marketable Securities Owned by an Equity Method Investee," emphasizes that an investor should not combine the portfolios of its marketable securities with the portfolios of the marketable securities of its investees that are accounted for by the equity method, for purposes of determining the investor's unrealized losses on marketable securities.

- FASB Statement No. 142, "Goodwill and Other Intangible Assets," indicates the treatment of equity method goodwill after it is first recognized.

- EITF Issue No. 98-13, "Accounting by an Equity Method Investor for Investee Losses When the Investor Has Loans to and Investments in Other Securities of the Investee," provides guidance on how the equity method loss pickup from the application of APB Opinion No. 18, when the carrying amount of the common stock has been reduced to zero, interact with the applicable literature relating to investments in the other securities of the investee, FASB Statement No. 114, or FASB Statement No. 115.

- EITF Issue No. 00-1, "Investor Balance Sheet and Income Statement Display under the Equity Method for Investments in Certain Partnerships and Other Ventures," discusses whether there are circumstances in which proportionate gross presentation is appropriate under the equity method of accounting for an investment in a legal entity.

- EITF Issue No. 00-8, "Accounting by a Grantee for an Equity Instrument to Be Received in Conjunction with Providing Goods or Services," discusses issues involved contemporaneous exchange of equity instruments for goods or services with contingent conditions.

- EITF Issue No. 00-12, "Accounting by an Investor for Stock-Based Compensation Granted to Employees of an Equity Method Investee," discusses accounting for stock-based compensation based on the investor's stock granted to employees of an investee accounted for under the equity method when no proportionate funding by the other investors occurs and the investor does not receive any increase in the investor's relative ownership percentage of the investee.

- EITF Issue No. 01-2, "Interpretations of APB Opinion No. 29," discusses how to account for the exchange of an equity method investment for a similar equity method investment.

13.5 SOURCES AND SUGGESTED REFERENCES

Rosenfield, Paul, "Accounting for Foreign Operations," *Journal of Accountancy*, August 1987.

CHAPTER 14

STATEMENT OF CASH FLOWS

Judith Weiss, CPA

14.1 NATURE AND BACKGROUND OF THE STATEMENT OF CASH FLOWS

(a) PRONOUNCEMENTS ON THE STATEMENT OF CASH FLOWS.   Statement of Financial Accounting (SFAS) No. 95, "Statement of Cash Flows," issued in December 1987, establishes standards for providing a statement of cash flows in general purpose financial statements. The SFAS No. 95 superseded Accounting Principles Board (APB) Opinion No. 19, "Reporting Changes in Financial Position," issued in 1971, which first elevated the funds statement to the status of a basic financial statement. The SFAS No. 95 changes the focus of the funds statement from one based on various definitions of funds, principally working capital or cash, to a focus on changes in cash. Under APB Opinion No. 19, funds were defined variously as cash, cash and short-term investments, quick assets, or working capital. The current uniform focus on cash should result in greater financial statement comparability. The cash focus also conforms more closely to the underlying concepts of SFAC No. 5, "Recognition and Measurement in Financial Statements of Business Enterprises," issued in 1984. The SFAC No. 5 (par. 13) states that a full set of financial statements for a period should show, among other things, cash flows during the period. Paragraph 52 points out:

> A statement of cash flows directly or indirectly reflects an entity's cash receipts classified by major sources and its cash payments classified by major uses during a period. It provides useful information about an entity's activities in generating cash through operations to repay debt, distribute dividends; or reinvest to maintain or expand operating capacity; about its financing activities, both debt and equity; and about its investing or spending of cash. Important uses of information about an entity's current cash receipts and payments include helping to assess factors such as the entity's liquidity, financial flexibility, profitability, and risk.

The change in emphasis of the funds statement from working capital to cash actually predates SFAS No. 95. In 1981, the Financial Executive Institute (FEI) encouraged its members to change the focus of the funds statement to cash and cash equivalents. By 1987, "Accounting Trends and Techniques" (AICPA, 1987), which surveys the financial accounting and reporting practices of 600 corporations, observed that in 1980 approximately 90 percent of the funds statements used a working capital concept of funds. By 1986, only 34 percent followed that approach, whereas 66 percent had adopted a form of cash approach.

Since its issuance in 1987, SFAS No. 95 has been amended by the following pronouncements:

- SFAS No. 102, "Statement of Cash Flows—Exemption of Certain Enterprises and Classification of Cash Flows from Certain Securities Acquired for Resale"
- SFAS No. 104, "Statement of Cash Flows—Net Reporting of Certain Cash Receipts and Cash Payments and Classification of Cash Flows from Hedging Transactions"
- SFAS No. 115, "Accounting for Certain Investments in Debt and Equity Securities"
- SFAS No. 117, "Financial Statements for Not-for-Profit Organizations"
- SFAS No. 133, "Accounting for Derivative Instruments and Hedging Activities"

(b) BACKGROUND.   Historically, the funds statement was often prepared by accountants to explain the discrepancy between an enterprise's reported net income and the funds available for dividends, debt repayment, and capital expenditure. However, the funds statement was not recognized by managers and financial analysts to be a significant analytic tool until after World War II. During the 20 years that followed, it began to appear in a growing number of annual reports, but great diversity remained in terminology, content, and form. In 1963, APB Opinion No. 3, "The Statement of Source and Application of Funds," provided some guidelines for preparation and presentation of the funds statement; this Opinion, however, only recommended presenting the statement of changes in financial position as supplementary information. The growing number of companies presenting a funds statement in their annual reports and the requirement by several regulatory agencies that a funds statement be included in reports filed with them finally prompted the APB to issue Opinion No. 19. Opinion No. 19, however, permitted but did not require enterprises to report cash flow information in the statement of changes in financial position. Since that Opinion was issued, the significance of information about an enterprise's cash flows has increasingly been recognized. Nevertheless, certain problems continued to limit the utility of the statement:

- Ambiguity of terms such as funds
- Lack of comparability arising from diversity in focus
- Differences in definition of funds flow from operations (cash or working capital)
- Differences in the format of the statement (sources and uses format or activity format)

The diversity in the form and content of the statement has been attributed to the lack of clear objectives for the statement.

The Financial Accounting Standards Board (FASB)'s initial involvement in cash flow reporting started in December 1980, with the publication of a Discussion Memorandum, "Reporting Funds Flows, Liquidity, and Financial Flexibility," which discussed funds flow reporting issues. This was followed in November 1981 by an Exposure Draft of a Proposed Concepts Statement, "Reporting Income, Cash Flows, and Financial Position of Business Enterprises," which discussed the role of a funds statement and guides for reporting components of funds flows, and concluded that the focus should be cash rather than working capital. However, a Statement was not issued. Further work led to the issuance of SFAC No. 5, followed by an Exposure Draft, "Statement of Cash Flows," in July 1986, and the issuance in 1987 of SFAS No. 95.

(c) OBJECTIVES OF THE STATEMENT OF CASH FLOWS.   The SFAS No. 95 (par. 4) sets forth the primary purpose of a statement of cash flows—"to provide relevant information about the cash receipts and cash payments of an enterprise during a period." The statement of cash flows should help investors, creditors, and others to:

- Assess the enterprise's ability to generate positive future net cash flows
- Assess the enterprise's ability to meet its obligations, its ability to pay dividends, and its needs for external financing
- Assess the reasons for differences between net income and associated cash receipts and payments
- Assess the effects on an enterprise's financial position of both its cash and noncash investing and financing transactions during the period

According to the FASB, these objectives would be achieved by a statement of cash flows that reports the cash effects during a period of a company's operations and its investing and financing transactions, supplemented by a reconciliation of net income and operating cash flows. Additionally, noncash financing and investing activities should be reported because they may result in future cash flows.

There are limits to the extent to which a statement of cash flows can be used to assess future cash flows. A cash flows statement shows the details of an enterprise's current cash receipts and cash payments. However, a cash flows statement, according to SFAC No. 5 (par. 24),

> ... provides an incomplete basis for assessing prospects for future cash flows because it cannot show interperiod relationships. Many current cash receipts, especially from operations, stem from activities of earlier periods, and many current cash payments are intended or expected to result in future, not current, cash receipts. Statements of earnings and comprehensive income, especially if used in conjunction with statements of financial position, usually provide a better basis for assessing future cash flow prospects of an entity than do cash flow statements alone.

However, the reconciliation of net income to net cash flows from operations called for by SFAS No. 95 may further the utility of the statement as a vehicle for assessing future cash flows from operations. The prescribed reconciliation reveals the nature and amounts of differences between net income and net operating cash flows. A time series analysis of such differences studied in conjunction with changes in net income and changes in cash flows from operations may provide a useful tool for assessing future cash flows from operations.

(d) SCOPE OF STATEMENT OF FINANCIAL ACCOUNTING NO. 95.   The SFAS No. 95 (par. 3) requires that a business enterprise providing a set of financial statements that reports both financial position and results of operations should provide a statement of cash flows for each period that presents results of operations. This requirement applies to all business enterprises including financial institutions, investment companies, and small businesses.

(i) Financial Institutions.   Financial institutions, especially banks, contended that a cash flows statement would not be meaningful for them because cash is the "product" of their earning activities and is therefore the equivalent of inventory. The Board took the view that "to survive, a bank, like a manufacturer, must generate positive (or at least neutral) cash flows from its operating, investing, and financing activities over the long run" (SFAS No. 95, par. 59). Banks obtain cash from deposits, money market operations and other purchases of funds, issuing long-term debt and equity securities, loan repayments by borrowers, investment sales and maturities, and net interest and fees earned. Banks' cash outflows cover deposit withdrawals, liability maturities, loan commitments, expenditures for investment and other purposes, and operating costs. The Board's view is that those activities are integral to a bank's operating, investing, and financing activities and should be disclosed in its financial statements.

(ii) Not-for-Profit Organizations.   The SFAS No. 95 does not include not-for-profit organizations within its scope. However, SFAS No. 117 amends SFAS No. 95 to require that all not-for-profit organizations provide a statement of cash flows that focuses on the organization as a whole and conforms to SFAS No. 95.

(iii) Exemption of Defined Benefit Plans from SFAS No. 95 Requirements.   SFAS No. 102 exempts from the requirements of SFAS No. 95 defined benefit pension plans that present financial statements in accordance with SFAS No. 35, "Accounting and Reporting by Defined Benefit Pension Plans." The Board concluded that SFAS No. 35 presents a comprehensive list of basic financial statements that defined benefit pension plans are required to provide; SFAS No. 95 was not intended to modify SFAS No. 35. Additionally, other employee benefit plans that are not covered by SFAS No. 35, such as health and welfare plans, that present financial information similar to the information required by SFAS No. 35 (including the presentation of assets at fair value) are likewise not required to provide a statement of cash flows. The Board noted, however, that a statement of cash flows would provide relevant information if the plan invests in assets that are not highly liquid (real estate) or obtains financing for its investments.

(iv) Exemption of Investment Companies.   In SFAS No. 95, the Board concluded that information about cash flows is relevant for investment companies and that such companies should not be exempted from a requirement to provide a statement of cash flows. After further study, the Board reconsidered its earlier conclusion and in SFAS No. 102 decided that a highly liquid investment company that provides a statement of change in net assets would be providing much of the same information contained in a statement of cash flows. Therefore, requiring such companies to provide additionally a statement of cash flows would not be cost-effective. SFAS No. 102 (par. 6) states that a statement of cash flows is not required to be provided by:

    a. an investment company that is subject to the registration and regulatory requirements of the Investment Company Act of 1940 (1940 Act),

b. an investment enterprise that has essentially the same characteristics as those subject to the 1940 Act, or

c. a common trust fund, variable annuity account, or similar fund maintained by a bank, insurance company, or other enterprise in its capacity as a trustee, administrator, or guardian for the collective investment and reinvestment of moneys.

To be exempt, an enterprise must meet all of the following conditions in SFAS No. 102 (par. 7):

a. During the period, substantially all of the enterprise's investments were highly liquid (e.g., marketable securities and other assets for which a market is readily available).

b. Substantially all of the enterprise's investments are carried at market value.

c. The enterprise had little or no debt, based on average debt outstanding during the period, in relation to average total assets.

d. The enterprise provides a statement of change in net assets.

(e) FOCUS ON CASH AND CASH EQUIVALENTS.   The decision of the Board to focus the statement of cash flows on flows of cash rather than on flows of working capital was based on the belief that the cash approach is more consistent with the objectives of the statement and is reinforced by the actual trend in accounting practice toward a cash approach and away from a working capital approach.

Cases have demonstrated that a positive working capital does not necessarily indicate liquidity. Furthermore, decisions of investors, creditors, and others focus on assessments of future cash flows. In focusing on cash, the Board decided to include cash equivalents, that is, short-term, highly liquid investments in which companies frequently invest cash in excess of immediate needs.

(i) Cash.   Cash includes currency on hand, demand deposits with banks and other financial institutions, and other accounts that have the general characteristics of demand deposits, which allow deposits and withdrawals at any time and without prior notice or penalty.

(ii) Cash Equivalents.   To ensure a measure of uniformity in the focus on flows of cash, the Board provided guidance on the short-term, highly liquid investments that would qualify as cash equivalents. SFAS No. 95 (par. 8) states that cash equivalents are short-term, highly liquid investments that are both:

a. Readily convertible to known amounts of cash

b. So near their maturity that they present insignificant risk of changes in value because of changes in interest rates.

Paragraph 8 states further, "Generally only investments with original maturities of three months or less qualify under that definition." Original maturity is further defined as maturity to the entity holding the investment. The Statement clarifies that the maturity date must be three months from the date of its acquisition by the entity. Thus, a Treasury note purchased three years ago and held does not become a cash equivalent when its remaining maturity is three months.

Cash equivalents include Treasury bills, commercial paper, money market funds, and federal funds sold (for an enterprise with banking operations). The purchase and the sale of those investments are viewed as part of an entity's cash management activities and not as cash flow activities, that is, operating, investing, or financing activities. Thus, the details of such transactions need not be reported in the statement of cash flows.

Although the Board provided guidance on what may be included in cash equivalents, SFAS No. 95 does not require *all* cash equivalents to be classified as "cash and cash equivalents." For example, an enterprise could decide to include cash equivalents as investments, especially where its operation consists of investing in short-term, highly liquid investments. The Board decided that items meeting the definition of cash equivalents that are part of a larger pool of investments properly considered investing activities need not be segregated and treated as cash equivalents. Banks and other financial institutions carry Treasury bills and so on in their trading and investment accounts. For these reasons the Board requires an enterprise to disclose its policy for determining which items are treated as cash equivalents. A change in policy of classifying cash equivalents is considered a change in accounting principle to be effected by restating financial statements for earlier years presented for comparative purposes.

(iii) Correspondence to Balance Sheet Cash Amount.   The total amount of cash and cash equivalents at the beginning and end of the period in the statement of cash flows must be the same amounts as similarly titled line items or subtotals in the statement of financial position as of those dates.

(iv) Restricted Cash.   Cash or cash equivalents may be restricted by management for some noncurrent purpose. Under these circumstances, the cash or cash equivalents should be classified as noncurrent based on management's intent. The amount would be reported as a use of cash and classified as operating, investing, or financing depending on the intended application.

(f) GROSS AND NET CASH FLOWS.   In SFAS No. 95, the Board adopted the position that reporting gross cash flows is more informative and relevant than reporting net cash flows. Thus, the repayment of a loan and the borrowing on a new loan should be reported separately as a cash outflow and a cash inflow, rather than being offset and reported on a net cash flow basis. However, exceptions to this principle appear in paragraph 13, which states:

> Items that qualify for net reporting because their turnover is quick, their amounts are large, and their maturities are short are cash receipts and payments pertaining to (a) investments (other than cash equivalents), (b) loans receivable, and (c) debt providing that the original maturity of the asset or liability is three months or less.

That exclusion includes short-term debt such as revolving credit arrangements and commercial paper obligations. For certain other items, such as demand deposits of a bank and customer accounts payable of a broker-dealer, the enterprise is essentially holding or disbursing cash for its customers. Knowledge of gross changes of such items is not necessary to an understanding of an entity's cash flows. The Board also decided that cash flows from credit card receivables may be reported net.

In addition, SFAS No. 104 amends paragraph 13 by exempting banks, savings institutions, and credit unions from gross reporting of cash receipts and cash payments for (1) deposits made at other financial institutions and withdrawals from those deposits, (2) time deposits accepted and repayments of those deposits, and (3) loans to customers and collections of the principal on those loans. If information about such enterprises is included in consolidated financial statements, the net amounts of cash receipts and cash payments related to the subsidiary's deposits or lending activities should be reported separately from the consolidated entity's gross amounts of cash receipts and cash payments for other investing and financing activities, including subsidiaries of the financial institutions described above that are not themselves financial enterprises.

Presenting cash flows from operating activities by the indirect method, which is permitted by SFAS No. 95, results in net reporting of operating cash receipts and cash payments.

(g) CLASSIFICATION OF CASH RECEIPTS AND CASH PAYMENTS.   Also, SFAS No. 95 requires that cash receipts and cash payments be classified into investing, financing, or operating activities. The Board decided that grouping cash flows in this manner enables evaluation of relationships within and among the three kinds of activities. The Statement provides guidelines to ensure comparability across enterprises, and it defines investing and financing activities. Operating activities include all transactions and other events that are not defined as investing or financing activities.

(i) Investing Activities.   Investing activities include the following cash outflows and cash inflows: Cash outflows for:

- Acquisition of property, plant, and equipment or other productive assets
- Purchase of debt instruments not designated as cash equivalents or entity instruments
- Investments in another company
- Loans made to another entity

Cash inflows from:

- Proceeds from the disposal of property, plant, and equipment, as well as other productive assets
- Proceeds from the sale or collection of loans and debt (not cash equivalents)
- Sale or return of investments on equity instruments
- Collections on loans

The SFAS No. 115 amends SFAS No. 102 to require that cash flows from purchases, sales, and maturities of *available-for-sale* securities be classified as cash flows from investing activities and reported gross in the statement of cash flows. That classification also applies to *held-to-maturity* securities. Cash flows from purchases, sales, and maturities of securities that are carried at market value and classified as trading securities continue to be classified as cash flows from operating activities. Mark-to-market changes, that is, write-ups and write-downs to market value, are eliminated or reversed because they do not reflect changes in cash flows.

Exhibit 14.1 provides a survey abstracted from 1988 annual reports of transactions related to investing activities, including disposition of segments, discontinued operations, investments in related parties, life insurance proceeds received from officers, and other related-party additions to other accounts receivable.

(ii) Financing Activities.   Financing activities include the following cash inflows and cash outflows: Cash inflows from:

- Proceeds from the sale or issuance of equity securities
- Proceeds from the issuance of bonds, mortgages, notes, and other short- or long-term debt instruments

Cash outflows for:

- Payment of dividends to shareholders
- Other distributions to owners
- Outlays for repurchase of equity securities
- Repayment of short- or long-term borrowings

SFAS No. 117, which provides accounting guidance for not-for-profit organizations and amends SFAS No. 95 to extend its provisions to those enterprises, amends SFAS No. 95 to require that the following items be classified as financing activities in the cash flow statements of not-for-profit organizations:

- Receipts of restricted resources that in accordance with the donors' stipulations must be used for long-term purposes

Acquisition of franchises

Additions to equipment and leasehold improvements

Additions to long-term notes receivable (Super Valu Stores)

Additions to other accounts receivable

Additions to preopening costs

Additions to software products

Capital contributions to unconsolidated subsidiaries

Capital expenditures

Cash proceeds from divestiture and restructuring

Cash proceeds from sale of investments*

Change in other assets

Collections of notes receivable

Contributions to 50%-or-less owned affiliates

Disposals of leased assets

Disposition of assets related to discontinued developmental activities

Dissolution of investment in affiliate

Distributions to minority interests (McFaddin Ventures)

Dividends received (First Cities Industries, Inc.)

Equity investments*

Expenditures on suspended construction project

Expenses and income taxes related to sale of segment (Quantum Chemical Corporation)

(Increases) decreases in marketable securities*

Increase in deferred acquisition cost

Increase in deferred turnarounds and charges and other assets

Investments in joint venture

Investments in life insurance policies*

Investments in preferred stock

Investments in related parties

Investments in unconsolidated subsidiaries

Net change in cattle breeding herd

Notes receivable advances to ESOP (Frozen Food Express Industries)

Nuclear fuel expenditures

Nuclear fuel sales to lessors

Payments on long-term notes receivable (Super Valu Stores)

Payments received from officers and other related parties

Proceeds from collection of notes receivable

Proceeds from disposition of carried interest

Proceeds from dispositions of unconsolidated subsidiaries

Proceeds from insurance claims related to investments

Proceeds from sale of insurance subsidiary

Proceeds from sale of property, plant, and equipment

Proceeds from sale of property

Proceeds from sale of segment

Proceeds from sale of technology, net of expenses

Purchase of another company

Purchase of patents and other assets

Purchase of tax benefits

Reduction of investments in related companies

Reduction of restricted investment in marketable securities

Short-term investments

(Restriction) release of short-term investments

*See Subsection 14.1(g)(i) for a discussion of the effects of SFAS No. 115 on the treatment of investments in securities and related cash flows.

Exhibit 14.1   Types of investing transactions appearing in corporate annual reports.

- Receipts from contributions and investment income that in accordance with the donors' stipulations are restricted for the purposes of acquiring, constructing, or improving property, plant, and equipment or other long-lived assets or establishing or increasing a permanent endowment or term endowment

In Emerging Issues Task Force (EITF) Issue 95-13, "Classification of Debt Issue Costs in the Statement of Cash Flows," the Task Force reached a consensus that a borrower should classify cash payments for debt issue costs as a financing activity in the statement of cash flows.

Exhibit 14.2 provides a survey abstracted from 1988 annual reports of transactions related to financing activities, including proceeds from warrants, principal payments on loans payable to shareholders, payments received from Employee Stock Ownership Plan (ESOP), and proceeds from sale and leaseback under operating leases.

(iii) Operating Activities.   Operating activities comprise all transactions and other events that are not investing and financing activities, including the following cash inflows and outflows:

Cash transactions costs of exchange	Payments received from ESOP
Cost of issuing debentures	Payments of short-term debt assumed in acquisitions
Cost of refinancing debt	Principal payments on capital lease obligations
Decrease in convertible subordinated debenture as result of extinguishment	Principal payments on loans payable shareholders
Dividends to minority shareholders	Principal payments on notes payable and installment contracts
Dividends paid	Proceeds from exercise of stock options
Exercise of stock options, including income tax benefit	Proceeds from issuance of long-term debt
Exercise of warrants	Proceeds from issuance of pollution control bonds
Issuance of preferred stock	Proceeds from revolving bank loans
Loan to ESOP	Proceeds from sale and leaseback under operating lease, less deferred gains
Net borrowings under working capital facilities	Purchases of treasury stock
Net increase in privately placed paper	Redemption of common stock
Net payments under line of credit	Redemption of common stock warrants
Net proceeds from public offerings	Redemption of preferred stock
Payments to acquire treasury stock	Redemption of revolving bank loan
Payments of long-term debts, including current maturities	Retirement of common stock, purchase of treasury stock, and other equity transactions
	Stock option plan

Exhibit 14.2   Types of financing transactions appearing in corporate annual reports.

Cash inflows from:

- Receipts from the sale of goods or services, or the collection or sale of receivables arising from those sales
- Interest on investment in debt securities and loans
- Dividends on investments in equity securities
- Receipts on other transactions not defined as investing or financing

Cash outflows for operating activities include:

- Payments for the acquisition of inventory
- Payments to employees for services
- Payments for taxes
- Interest payments, reduced by amounts capitalized; capitalized interest is an investing cash flow
- Payments to suppliers for other expenses
- Payments on other transactions not defined as investing or financing

(iv) Components of Cash Flows from Operating Activities. Cash flows from operating activities are the cash effects of transactions and other events affecting income determination. Interest received on loans and dividends received on equity securities are included in cash flows from operating activities, although they are investment related. SFAS No. 117, however, amends SFAS No. 95 to state that not-for-profit organizations should *not* classify interest and dividends as operating cash receipts if those receipts are restricted by their donors for long-term purposes. Interest paid on loans is included as a cash flow from an operating activity, although the expenditure itself is finance related. Capitalized interest, however, is part of the cost of the nonmonetary asset and is treated as investment related.

All income taxes paid are treated as operating cash flows. Allocation of income taxes among activities is considered to be arbitrary and, therefore, is not required.

SFAS No. 102 requires that cash flows resulting from the acquisition of securities and other assets that are carried at market value in a trading account be classified as operating cash flows. This position is reaffirmed in SFAS No. 115, which states that cash flows relating to securities classified as trading securities are operating cash flows. Cash flows relating to loans acquired specifically for resale and carried at market value or the lower of cost or market value should also be classified as operating cash flows.

In EITF Issue No. 00-15, "Classification in the Statement of Cash Flows of the Income Tax Benefit Received by a Company upon Exercise of a Nonqualified Employee Stock Option," the Task Force discussed how an enterprise that accounts for employee stock options under APB Opinion No. 25, "Accounting for Stock Issued to Employees," should classify in its cash flow statement presented under the indirect method an income tax benefit that reduces the enterprise's tax liability when an employee exercises fixed stock options. Because under the provisions of APB No. 25 an employer recognizes no compensation expense, an income tax benefit is credited to equity rather than to an expense. The Task Force reached a consensus that under those circumstances, a reduction in an enterprise's income tax liability should be classified as an operating activity. The EITF also reached a consensus that a disclosure in the notes to the financial statements is required if a material income tax benefit is not presented as a separate line item in the statement of cash flows or in the statement of stockholders' equity.

During its discussion of EITF Issue 02-6, "Classification in the Statement of Cash Flows of Payments Made to Settle an Asset Retirement Obligation within the Scope of FASB Statement No. 143, 'Accounting for Asset Retirement Obligations,'" the EITF reached a consensus that an enterprise should classify a cash payment to settle an asset retirement obligation as an operating activity in its statement of cash flows.

(v) Additional Classification Guidance. If a cash inflow or outflow relates to more than one activity category, its classification should be determined according to the item's predominant source of cash flow. For instance, the acquisition, production, and sale of equipment used or rented by a firm is generally investment related. This presumption is overcome, however, if such equipment is used or rented for a short period and then sold. Under those circumstances, the acquisition or production of that asset as well as the subsequent sale is classified as part of operating activities.

All cash payments from customers or payments made to suppliers, including cash from installment sales, are classified as operating cash flows.

Each cash flow is classified according to its nature, even if it is intended as a hedge. For example, the purchase or sale of a futures contract is an investing activity, regardless of whether that contract is intended to hedge a firm commitment or purchase inventory.

SFAS No. 104, as amended by SFAS No. 133, amends SFAS No. 95 to permit cash flows resulting from derivative instruments that are accounted for as fair value or cash flow hedges in accordance with SFAS No. 133 to be classified in the same category as the cash flows from the items being hedged provided there is disclosure of accounting policy. However, cash flows from an instrument that is no longer accounted for as a hedge of an identifiable transaction or event should be classified based on the nature of the instrument.

Gains and losses resulting from the redemption of a firm's own debt are financing related and are categorized as cash flows related to the retirement of outstanding debt.

Gains and losses resulting from asset disposals are investment related. Receipts from the disposal of property, plant, or equipment include the proceeds of an insurance settlement.

Advance payments on the purchase of productive assets are considered to be investing cash flows. Any debt to the seller of the productive asset is a financing transaction.

All principal payments on mortgages, including seller-financed mortgages or debt on productive assets, are classified as financing cash flows.

Cash proceeds from business interruption insurance should be classified as an operating activity, whereas insurance proceeds to recover damages to plant and equipment are classified as an investing activity.

Ordinary dividends received are classified as an operating activity. On the other hand, liquidating dividends received would be classified as an investing activity. When a note is repaid, the difference between the amount paid and the carrying value should be reported as interest.

Insurance paid should be classified as an operating activity even if required to obtain a loan.

Accounts payable transactions that are financing activities, for example, accounts payable for factory equipment purchased, should be classified as financing activities. Factory equipment purchased would be classified as an investing cash outflow net of financing costs.

14.2 GUIDANCE ON STATEMENT PRESENTATION

The statement of cash flows for a period reports separately the net cash provided for or used by operating, investing, and financing activities. The cash flows reconcile beginning and ending amounts of cash and cash equivalents. Separate disclosure of cash flows pertaining to extraordinary or discontinued items is no longer required. The factory equipment would be classified as an investing cash outflow, net of the financing.

The new Statement permits the use of either the direct or indirect method of presenting cash flows from operating activities. However, companies are encouraged to present cash flows from operating activities using the direct method.

Supporters of the direct approach point out that the presentation is consistent with that of investing and financing cash flows (i.e., gross operating cash receipts and cash payments are presented). Moreover, information about operating cash receipts and payments is useful when making credit decisions and assessing a company's ability to service existing debt.

The indirect approach (which reconciles net income with net operating cash flows) is favored by some because

- It provides a useful link between the statement of cash flows and the income statement and balance sheet.
- Financial statement users are more familiar with it.
- It is generally less expensive.
- The direct approach, which presents income statement on a cash rather than an accrual basis, may erroneously suggest that net cash flow from operating activities is as good as, or better than, net income as a measure of performance.[1]

(a) DIRECT METHOD. This method involves showing the major classes of operating cash receipts (cash collected from customers or earned on investments) and cash payments (cash paid to suppliers or to creditors for interest). The net cash flow from operating activities is the difference between cash received from operations and cash payments for operations.

Companies reporting under the direct method are required to report separately the following classes of operating cash receipts and payments:

- Cash collected from customers, including lessees and licensees
- Interest and dividends received
- Other operating cash receipts, if any
- Cash paid to employees and other supplies of goods and services
- Interest paid
- Income taxes paid
- Other operating payments

---

[1] J. J. Mahoney, M. V. Sever, and J. A. Theis, "Cash Flow: FASB Opens the Floodgates," *Journal of Accountancy*, May 1988, pp. 25–38.

Companies are also encouraged to provide additional breakdowns beyond the minimum items required under the direct method. For instance, a manufacturer can separate purchases of inventory from selling, general, and administrative expenditures.

Exhibit 14.3 illustrates the direct approach used in the 1993 annual report of United States Surgical Corporation.

(b) INDIRECT METHOD.   Companies choosing not to use the direct method must calculate net cash from operating activities indirectly by adjusting from net income for the effects of these major classes of reconciling items:

- Deferrals of past cash receipts and cash payments (inventory, deferred income, prepaid expenses, and deferred expenses)
- Accruals of expected future cash receipts and payments (accounts receivable and notes receivable from sales transactions; interest receivable; accounts payable and notes payable from transactions with suppliers; interest payable; taxes payable; excess of income under the equity method over dividends; and other accruals)
- Investing or financing-related items and noncash expenses (depreciation; amortization; provision for bad debts; goodwill; gains and losses on the extinguishment of debt; gains and losses on the disposal of property, plant, and equipment, and gains and losses on the disposal of discontinued operations)

This technique is referred to as the *indirect or reconciliation method*.

The 1994 edition of *Accounting Trends and Techniques*, published by the American Institute of Certified Public Accountants (AICPA), indicates that of the 600 annual reports examined, 585 applied the indirect method to report operating cash flow.

(c) RECONCILIATION OF NET CASH FLOWS FROM OPERATING ACTIVITIES TO NET INCOME.   A reconciliation of net cash flows from operating activities to net income must be provided only if the direct method is used. The reconciliation separately reports major classes of reconciling items. At a minimum, changes in inventory, payables, and receivables that are related to operating items are separately reported; however, enterprises are encouraged to provide further breakdowns of reconciling items. For instance, changes in receivables from the sale of goods might be reported separately from other receivables.

If the direct method is used, the reconciliation should be provided in a separate schedule. If the indirect method is used, the reconciliation may be included in a separate schedule or within the statement of cash flows. Additionally, under the indirect method, both income taxes paid and interest paid (exclusive of capitalized amounts) must be separately disclosed. In determining net cash from operating activities, all adjustments to net income should be clearly identified as reconciling items.

Exhibit 14.4 illustrates the indirect approach using the presentation contained in the 2001 annual report of EMC Corporation.

(d) SURVEY OF ADJUSTMENTS USING THE INDIRECT METHOD.   Exhibit 14.5 provides a survey abstracted from annual reports of reconciling items in converting net income to net cash flow from operations under the indirect method. Under the indirect method shown in the exhibit, there are a number of gain and loss adjustments, including gain on sale of investments, gain on debt extinguishments, and gain on sale of hedges. Other adjustments typically are extraordinary items, cumulative effect of accounting changes, and discontinued operations.

(e) NONCASH TRANSACTIONS.   Noncash transactions—for example, nonmonetary exchanges, the conversion of debt to equity, the acquisition of a machine by incurring a liability—should be reported in related disclosures. Those disclosures may be either narrative or

UNITED STATES SURGICAL CORPORATION

Consolidated Statements of Cash Flows

	Year Ended December 31,		
	1993	1992	1991
	(In thousands)		
Cash flows from operating activities:			
Cash received from customers	$1,103,300	$1,087,700	$773,700
Cash paid to vendors, suppliers, and employees	(941,200)	(905,900)	(710,600)
Interest paid	(18,300)	(15,600)	(11,400)
Income tax paid	(12,800)	(18,400)	(22,800)
Net cash provided by operating activities	131,000	147,800	28,900
Cash flows from investing activities:			
Additions to property, plant, and equipment	(216,400)	(270,700)	(146,900)
Other assets	(31,100)	(31,100)	(15,100)
Net cash used in investing activities	(247,500)	(301,800)	(162,000)
Cash flows from financing activities:			
Long-term debt borrowings under credit agreements	2,614,400	1,840,800	725,600
Long-term debt repayments under credit agreements	(2,495,900)	(1,696,000)	(605,000)
Common stock issued from stock plans	12,100	48,000	41,800
Dividends paid	(13,700)	(16,400)	(14,700)
Acquisition of common stock for treasury		(16,100)	(12,500)
Net cash provided by financing activities	116,900	160,300	135,200
Effect of exchange rate changes	(2,000)	(6,400)	(2,500)
Net decrease in cash	(1,600)	(100)	(400)
Cash, beginning of year	2,500	2,600	3,000
Cash, end of year	$ 900	$ 2,500	$ 2,600
Reconciliation of net income (loss) to net cash provided by operating activities:			
Net income (loss)	$ (138,700)	$ (138,900)	$ 91,200
Adjustments to reconcile net income (loss) to net cash provided by operating activities:			
Depreciation and amortization	83,200	59,400	40,300
Amortization of deferred compensation	—	4,200	4,100
Asset writedowns—restructuring	73,800	—	—
Adjustment of property, plant, and equipment valuation allowances	17,400	3,900	7,500
Receivables—decrease (increase)	67,800	(108,200)	(68,900)
Inventories—(increase)	(48,400)	(75,800)	(110,500)
Adjustment of inventory reserves	44,200	29,900	24,200
Other current assets—(increase) decrease	(23,900)	9,900	(13,600)
Accounts payable and accrued expenses—increase	34,300	51,400	38,500
Income taxes payable and deferred—decrease increase	(24,300)	(14,100)	15,700
Income tax benefit from stock options exercised	14,400	50,000	—
Other Assets—decrease	28,100	—	—
Other adjustments—net	3,100	(1,700)	400
Total adjustments	269,700	8,900	(62,300)
Net cash provided by operating activities	$ 131,000	$ 147,800	$ 28,900

Exhibit 14.3   Illustration of annual report using the direct method.

EMC CORPORATION
Consolidated Statements of Cash Flows
For the Years Ended December 31,

	2001	2000	1999
	(in thousands)		
Cash Flows from Operating Activities:			
Net income (loss)	$ (507,712)	$1,782,075	$1,010,570
Adjustment to reconcile net income (loss) to net cash provided by operating activities:			
Depreciation and amortization	654,698	516,798	424,803
Non-cash restructuring, inventory, and other special charges	449,364	21,000	59,526
Other than temporary declines in equity investments	106,560	—	—
Amortization of deferred compensation	19,514	27,027	22,311
Provision for doubtful accounts	32,711	27,537	25,817
Deferred income taxes	(227,429)	35,349	(122,973)
Net loss on disposal of property, plant, and equipment	2,282	18,523	9,896
Tax benefit from stock options exercised	137,901	207,694	58,033
Minority interest	29	2,235	135
Changes in assets and liabilities, net of acquired assets and liabilities:			
Accounts and notes receivable	806,022	(647,577)	(409,364)
Inventories	127,581	(406,985)	2,417
Other assets	(19,303)	(155,306)	(73,319)
Accounts payable	(78,429)	147,675	70,798
Accrued expenses	201,301	200,033	158,191
Income taxes payable	(157,007)	228,089	88,442
Deferred revenue	69,637	109,594	67,116
Other liabilities	13,558	(5,105)	(2,834)
Net cash provided by operating activities	1,631,258	2,108,656	1,389,565
Cash Flows from Investing Activities:			
Additions to property, plant, and equipment	(889,309)	(858,423)	(542,209)
Proceeds from sales of property, plant, and equipment	17,310	200	1
Capitalized software development costs	(120,724)	(102,772)	(88,201)
Purchases of short- and long-term available-for-sale securities	(4,981,376)	(2,644,077)	(2,752,925)
Sales of short- and long-term available-for-sale securities	4,445,271	1,961,208	1,445,237
Maturity of short- and long-term available-for-sale securities	126,683	35,000	—
Purchases of short- and long-term held-to-maturity securities	—	—	(191,254)
Maturity of short- and long-term held-to-maturity securities	—	—	940,483
Business acquisitions, net of cash acquired	(111,455)	(233,554)	—
Net cash used by investing activities	(1,513,600)	(1,842,418)	(1,188,868)

Exhibit 14.4   Illustration of annual report using the indirect method.

EMC CORPORATION
Consolidated Statements of Cash Flows
For the Years Ended December 31,

	2001	2000	1999
	(in thousands)		
Cash Flows from Financing Activities:			
Issuance of common stock	170,284	234,057	101,424
Issuance of subsidiary stock	—	376,607	—
Purchase of treasury stock	(18,258)	—	—
Cash portion of McData Corporation spin-off dividend	(141,981)	—	—
Redemption of 6% convertible subordinated notes due 2004	—	(155)	—
Payment of long-term and short-term obligations	(16,859)	(10,244)	(30,435)
Issuance of long-term and short-term obligations	40,206	11,392	2,256
Net cash provided by financing activities	33,392	611,657	73,245
Effect of Exchange Rate Changes on Cash	(5,252)	(4,083)	1
Net Increase in Cash and Cash Equivalents	151,050	877,895	273,942
Cash and Cash Equivalents at Beginning of Period	1,983,221	1,109,409	835,466
Cash and Cash Equivalents at End of Period	$2,129,019	$1,983,221	$1,109,409
Noncash Activity:			
—Conversion of convertible subordinated notes, net of debt issuance costs	$ —	$ 665,397	$ 57,101
—Capital lease obligations	24,490	—	—
—Options associated with business acquisitions	1,050	11,372	—
—Distribution of net assets in McData Corporation dividend	234,152	—	—

Exhibit 14.4   *Continued.*

summarized within a schedule. The objective of those disclosures is to clearly relate cash and noncash aspects of transactions involving similar items. If a transaction is part cash and part noncash, only the cash portion is reported in the statement of cash flows.

Exhibit 14.6 provides an example of a narrative presentation of noncash activities used by Allied Signal, Inc.

(i) Survey of Noncash Items in Cash Flow Disclosures.   Exhibit 14.7 provides a survey abstracted from annual reports of common types of noncash items appearing in corporate annual reports. Among the types of noncash items are fair value of treasury stock issued for businesses acquired, surrender of leases and release from debt and other obligations on discontinuing development activities, bank borrowings and subsequent loan proceeds to ESOPs, transfer of property including debt to a real estate trust in exchange for trust shares, abandonment of a plant, bank foreclosures on real estate, dividends declared but unpaid, exchange of nonmonetary assets, and acquisition of subsidiaries or nonmonetary assets by issuing equity securities.

Accounts payable

Accretion of note discount

Accrued compensation and employee benefits

Accrued income taxes

Accrued interest payable

Accrued liabilities

Accrued retirement benefits

Advanced revenue

Allowance for funds used during construction

Amortization of deferred gains

Amortization of goodwill

Amortization of restricted award shares

Amortization of software products

Amount due from affiliate

Assets held for resale

Changes in certain noncash, assets and
liabilities, net of effects of businesses acquired,
and noncash transactions

Common shares awarded under restricted stock
plan

Common stock portion of class action settlement

Cumulative effect of change in method of
accounting for income taxes

Customer advances

Decrease in refundable federal and local taxes

Deferred compensation

Deferred contract research and development
revenue from related parties

Deferred income taxes

Deferred investment credit, net

Deferred revenue

Depletion

Depreciation

Employee stock award program

Equity in unremitted earnings of unconsolidated
affiliates in excess of dividends received from
unconsolidated affiliates

Extraordinary credit resulting from use of net
operating loss carryforwards

Extraordinary item, net of deferred income taxes

Gain on discontinued development activities

Gain on discontinued operations

Gain on extinguishment of debt

Gain on foreign currency hedge

Gain on partial sale of subsidiary

Gain on sale of investments

Impairments

Income tax benefit from stock option plans

Increase in cash surrender value of life insurance

Increase in deferred items

Increase in escrow bonding arrangement

Inventories

Issuance of common stock in settlement of
litigation

Issuance of debt in payment of interest on debt

Loss from discontinued operations

Loss on disposal property and equipment

Loss on equity investments

Manufacturing consolidation accrual

Minority interest in subsidiaries' earnings

Net earnings from discontinued operations

Pension settlement gain

Prepaid expenses and other current assets

Prepaid income taxes

Provision for losses on accounts receivable

Provision for losses on direct financing leases

Provision for losses on short-term investments

Provision for possible losses on disposition of
restaurant

Provision for self-insurance reserve

Rate deferrals

Receivables

Restructuring charge

Restructuring costs

Share of related-party losses

Sublease revenues and other credits

Tax benefits related to employee stock options

Writedown of assets and related termination
costs

Exhibit 14.5   Types of adjustments used under the indirect method in arriving at net cash provided by operating activities appearing in annual reports.

(ii) Noncash Items Not Disclosed.   Not all noncash items are required to be disclosed. For example, if operating activities are presented under the direct method, then the following noncash items are not disclosed in the statement, although they will appear in the reconciliation of net income to net operating cash flow under the indirect method:

- Depreciation of plant and equipment
- Amortization of intangibles
- Amortization of bond discount and premium
- Increase in investments carried at equity

**GENERAL ELECTRIC COMPANY
AND CONSOLIDATED AFFILIATES
2001 ANNUAL REPORT**

26 Supplemental Cash Flows Information

Changes in operating assets and liabilities are net of acquisitions and dispositions of principal businesses.

"Payments for principal businesses purchased" in the Statement of Cash Flows is net of cash acquired and includes debt assumed and immediately repaid in acquisitions.

"All other operating activities" in the Statement of Cash Flows consists primarily of adjustments to current and noncurrent accruals and deferrals of costs and expenses, increases and decreases in progress collections, adjustments for gains and losses on assets, increases and decreases in assets held for sale, and adjustments to assets.

Noncash transactions include the following: in 2001, the acquisition of Imatron Inc. for GE common stock valued at $205 million; in 2000, the acquisition of Harmon Industries for shares of GE common stock valued at $346 million; and in 1999, GE's contribution of certain media properties in exchange for a noncontrolling interest in NBCi, a former publicly traded company (described in note 2).

Certain supplemental information related to GE and GECS cash flows is shown below.

For the years ended December 31 (in millions)	2001	2000	1999
GE			
Purchases and sales of GE shares for treasury			
Open market purchases under share repurchase program	$ **(3,137)**	$ (2,226)	$ (1,866)
Other purchases	**(1,571)**	(3,116)	(5,622)
Dispositions (mainly to employee and dividend reinvestment plans)	**2,273**	5,811	6,486
	$ **(2,435)**	$ 469	$ (1,002)
GECS			
Financing receivables			
Increase in loans to customers	$**(140,758)**	$(100,938)	$(95,201)
Principal collections from customers—loans	**121,004**	87,432	86,379
Investment in equipment for financing leases	**(20,315)**	(15,454)	(18,173)
(Principal collections from customers—financing leases	**11,641**	7,873	13,634
Net change in credit card receivables	**(14,815)**	(9,394)	(10,740)
Sales of financing receivables	**29,291**	14,405	11,473
	$ **(13,952)**	$ (16,076)	$(12,628)
All other investing activities			
Purchases of securities by insurance and annuity businesses	$ **(53,452)**	$ (35,911)	$(26,271)
Dispositions and maturities of securities by insurance and annuity businesses	**45,403**	25,960	23,979
Proceeds from principal business dispositions	**2,572**	(605)	279
Other	**(2,080)**	(1,617)	(6,270)
	$ **(7,557)**	$ (12,173)	$ (8,283)
			(*Continues*)

Exhibit 14.6   Illustration of narrative presentation and schedule of noncash activities.

For the years ended December 31 (in millions)	2001	2000	1999
Newly issued debt having maturities longer than 90 days			
Short-term (91 to 365 days)	$ **12,622**	$ 12,782	$ 15,799
Long-term (longer than one year)	**16,118**	32,297	30,082
Proceeds—nonrecourse, leveraged lease debt	**2,012**	1,808	1,724
	$ **30,752**	$ 46,887	$ 47,605
Repayments and other reductions of debt having maturities longer than 90 days			
Short-term (91 to 365 days)	$ **(29,195)**	$ (27,777)	$(21,211)
Long-term (longer than one year)	**(6,582)**	(3,953)	(5,447)
Principal payments—nonrecourse, leveraged lease debt	**(274)**	(177)	(266)
	$ **(36,051)**	$ (31,907)	$(26,924)
All other financing activities			
Proceeds from sales of investment contracts	$ **9,080**	$ 8,826	$ 7,236
Redemption of investment contracts	**(7,033)**	(9,061)	(7,127)
Preferred stock issued by GECS affiliates	—	—	513
Capital contributions from GE	**3,043**	—	—
Cash received upon assumption of Toho Mutual Life Insurance Company insurance liabilities	—	13,177	—
	$ **5,090**	$ 12,942	$ 622

Exhibit 14.6 *Continued.*

Acquisition of company by contributing property, investments, and working capital	Note received on sale of business
Acquisition of equity interests of minority shareholders in subsidiaries	Preferred stock converted into common stock
Acquisition of limited partner interests in exchange for common shares	Purchase of property, plant, and equipment for notes
Borrowing from a bank and subsequently loaning proceeds to ESOP	Reclassification of current marketable securities to noncurrent stock issued to employees
Capital lease obligations entered into for new lease	Reclassification of short-term borrowings of commercial paper and bank loans
Common stock dividends paid on convertible stock	Sale of property, plant, and equipment for notes
Common stock exchanged for treasury stock	Sale of secured assets held for sale for assumption of debt
Conversion of convertible subordinated debenture	Surrender of leases and release from debt and other obligations on discontinuing development activities
Deferred compensation from awarding restricted stock awards	Transfer of real property, including debt assumed to a real estate trust in exchange for trust shares
Fair value of treasury stock issued for businesses acquired	Treasury stock issued for compensation plans
Issuance of common shares on conversion of director's note payable	Treasury stock issued on conversion of debentures
Issuance of common stock in payment of floating rate subordinated notes	
Liabilities assumed in business acquisition	

Exhibit 14.7   Types of noncash transactions disclosed in corporate annual reports.

Some noncash transactions may affect only operating items and may not be disclosed at all, such as exchange of inventory for services.

Other transactions not disclosed are stock dividends and stock splits.

(f) CASH FLOWS FROM DISCONTINUED OPERATIONS.   Separate disclosure of cash flows from discontinued operations is not required. However, a company may segregate, within the operating section of the statement of cash flows, its cash flows from discontinued operations from cash flows related to continuing operations. If so, this form of presentation should be made for each comparative period included within the statement of cash flows. Income taxes paid need not be allocated between continuing and discontinued operations.

On discontinuing an operation, certain losses and expenses related to disposal are typically identified. They might include anticipated losses on disposal including pension and other postemployment-related events such as termination and severance-related costs. To the extent those anticipated losses and expenses have no immediate cash effect or are investment related, those items will be included in the reconciliation of net income to net cash flows from operations under the indirect method.

Cash received on the disposal of discontinued operations is an investment activity, and related disposal gains and losses are reconciling items in deriving net cash from operating activities. Separating of operating cash paid or generated by a discontinued component of an entity both before and after the measurement date from net cash provided or used in the disposal of that component is clearly difficult and somewhat arbitrary. As part of a disposal of a component of an entity, cash flows attributable to transactions such as cash reversions accompanying pension plan terminations and settlements and payments of termination benefits on severance are all operating activities. All income taxes paid regardless of whether related to continuing or discontinued operations are classified as operating.

Operating cash flow from discontinued operations according to some should be reported as an operating activity even though income or loss between the measurement date and disposal date is included in the gain or loss on disposal. However, cash flows from discontinued operations may be shown separately from cash flow from continuing operations on a pretax basis, followed by a single amount for income taxes paid. This step avoids allocating the tax paid between the two groups.

Kmart Corporation, in its 1988 annual report, separates continuing and discontinued operations in its statement of cash flows from operations (Exhibit 14.8). Kmart includes cash provided or used by discontinued operations as an operating cash flow and, in addition, shows reconciling adjustments to income to derive cash flows from discontinued operations.

(g) EXTRAORDINARY ITEMS.   Cash provided from or used by extraordinary items need not be separately disclosed.

A company can choose to show separately the cash flows from extraordinary items within operating activities, using a treatment similar to that for discontinued operations.

A cash settlement of litigation that qualifies as an extraordinary item would be classified as an operating activity and could be shown separately in the statement of cash flow as an extraordinary operating activity.

Extraordinary items are classified according to the underlying nature of the transaction. Accordingly, a gain or loss on the extinguishment of debt is a reconciling adjustment to net income and is related to financing activities. Extraordinary gains without a cash effect on operations or those that are investment or financing related are presented as reconciling adjustments to net income in deriving net cash from operating activities.

(h) ACCOUNTING CHANGES AND PRIOR PERIOD ADJUSTMENTS.   The cumulative effect of accounting changes not involving cash is reconciling adjustments to net income in arriving at net cash from operating activities.

KMART CORPORATION
Reconciliation of Net Income to
Net Cash Flow from Operating Activities

(Millions)	1988	1987	1986
Operations			
Income from continuing retail operations	$692	$570	$ 472
Noncash charges (credits) to earnings:			
Depreciation and amortization	401	377	344
Deferred income taxes	12	58	90
Undistributed equity income	(36)	(23)	(23)
Increase in other long-term liabilities	67	52	44
Other—net	56	13	20
Cash provided by (used for) current assets and current liabilities:			
(Increase) decrease in inventories	(418)	(677)	387
Increase (decrease) in accounts payable	102	312	(65)
Other—net	90	(59)	129
Total provided by continuing retail operations	966	623	1,398
Discontinued operations			
Gain (loss) from discontinued operations	—	28	(251)
Items not affecting cash—net	—	(95)	249
Cash provided by (used for) discontinued operations	(58)	214	—
Total provided by (used for) discontinued operations	(58)	147	(2)
Net cash provided by operations	$908	$770	$1,396

Exhibit 14.8   Illustration of annual report showing separate disclosure of cash flows from discontinued operations.

Taxes incurred in connection with an accounting change or prior period adjustment are an operating item. If there is a cash effect of an accounting error, it may be desirable to report it separately in the cash flow statement.

(i) Business Combinations.   In reporting business combinations, the statement of cash flows should reflect a single item under investing activities, for example, "Cash paid to purchase a company (net of cash acquired)." If a business is sold, then the line item would indicate "Cash received from sale of business (net of cash sold)."

Other companies show the cash paid in the purchase acquisition net of cash received.

14.3 WORKSHEET TECHNIQUE

The format of the statement of cash flows differs based on the approach used to present cash flows from operations—the direct method or the indirect method. If the direct method of presentation is adopted (as recommended in SFAS No. 95), the worksheet technique requires the use of a preclosing trial balance for the current period. On the other hand, a postclosing trial balance for the current period is more suitable for the indirect method. It is essential to understand both techniques because SFAS No. 95 requires a reconciliation of net income to net cash flow from operations as supplementary disclosure when the direct method is used in the statement of cash flows. However, Exhibit 14.11, later in this chapter, illustrates a shortcut technique for converting cash flow from operations prepared under the indirect method to the direct method. Preparation of the statement of cash flows requires an analysis of the annual changes in balance sheet accounts and the increases in income and expenses of the period in order to identify all cash flows from operating, investing, and financing activities. Revenue and expense accounts must be adjusted from the accrual basis to a cash basis. Cost of goods sold should also be analyzed for inventory adjustments, and so on. The adjustment for depreciation should be for the total amount incurred, and the change in inventories should be inclusive of the amount of depreciation capitalized in inventory. These amounts reconcile with balance sheet changes, although not with APB Opinion No. 12, requiring disclosure of depreciation expense. Gains and losses must be adjusted to reflect the underlying nature and amount of cash effects, that is, investing, financing, or operating. Noncash transactions are either eliminated (depreciation) or are disclosed separately (acquisition of long-lived assets for debt or stock) as noncash activities.

(a) DIRECT METHOD. Exhibit 14.9 illustrates the application of the worksheet technique using the direct method. In Column 1, the 12/31/X0 balances of Baruch Corporation reflect postclosing figures. The balances as of 12/31/X1, shown in Column 4, are those of the preclosing trial balance. Columns 2 and 3 reflect those entries needed to determine cash flows from operating, financing, and investing activities and to reconcile the changes in account balances from 12/31/X0 to 12/31/X1 (letters in parentheses refer to list on pages 14–24 and 14–25).

An analysis of the accounts for 20X1 revealed the following:

INCOME ACCOUNTS

Depreciation expense	
Selling expense	$ 1,500
G & A expenses	2,000
Patent amortization in G & A expenses	500
Amortization of bond discount in interest expense	250
Loss on sale of plant assets in selling expense	2,000

OTHER TRANSACTIONS

Purchases of equipment	$15,000
Equipment sold for $8,000, cost $12,500, accumulated depreciation—$2,500	
loss of $2,000 included in selling expense	
Gain on bond retirement	
Bonds retired	
Face value	$12,000
Book value	11,000
Cash paid	9,100
(Tax on gain included in income tax expense—$600)	
Bonds converted to common stock	
Face value	$19,000
Book value	18,000
Converted into $1,650 shares of $10 par value capital stock	
Paid in 20X1	
Dividend payable 12/31/X1	$ 6,000
Notes payable 12/31/X1	23,000
Accounts receivable are all from merchandise customers	
Accounts payable are all from inventory suppliers	

Based on the foregoing analysis of changes in the accounts, the following worksheet entries are needed to determine cash flows from the three activities for 20X1 (letters correspond to relevant entries in Exhibits 14.9 and 14.10).

BARUCH CORPORATION
Worksheet for Statement of Cash Flows—Direct Method
12/31/X1

	Balances 12/31/X0	Changes		Balances 12/31/X1
	DR(CR)	DR	CR	DR(CR)
Accounts				
Cash	$ 25,000	$ 18,750 (Q)		$ 43,750
Accounts receivable, net	22,500		$9,750 (A)	12,750
Inventory	67,500	5,000 (B)		72,500
Property, plant, and equipment	100,000	15,000 (G)	12,500 (F)	102,500
Accumulated depreciation	(19,000)	2,500 (F)	3,500 (C)	(20,000)
Patents, net	4,000		500 (D)	3,500
Unamortized bond discount	3,000		250 (E)	750
			1,000 (H)	
			1,000 (I)	
	$203,000			$215,750
Accounts payable	$ (14,000)	750 (B)		$ (13,250)
Accrued G & A expenses payable	(1,000)	1,000 (M)		0
Dividends payable	(6,000)	6,000 (J)	5,000 (K)	(5,000)
Income taxes payable	(18,000)		7,500 (P)	(25,500)
Notes payable	(23,000)	23,000 (L)		0
Convertible bonds payable	(47,000)	12,000 (H)		(16,000)
		$019,000 (I)		
Deferred income taxes	(7,500)	1,000 (P)		(6,500)
Capital stock	(56,000)		16,500 (I)	(72,500)
Additional contributed capital	(12,500)		1,500 (I)	(14,000)
Retained earnings	(18,000)			(18,000)
Dividends		5,000 (K)		5,000
	$203,000			$165,750
Sales			440,000 (A)	$(440,000)
Cost of goods sold		220,000 (B)		220,000
Selling expenses		1,500 (C)		91,000
		2,000 (F)		
		87,500 (N)		
G & A expenses		2,000 (C)	1,000 (M)	42,500
		500 (D)		
		41,000 (O)		
Interest expense		17,500 (E)		17,500
Income tax expense		20,900 (P)		20,900
Extraordinary gain on debt extinguishment (before tax)			1,900 (H)	(1,900)
				50,000
				$215,750
Operating Activities				
Cash collected from customers		449,750 (A)		
Cash paid to suppliers			225,750 (B)	
Cash paid for selling expenses			87,500 (N)	
Cash paid for G & A expenses			41,000 (O)	
Cash paid for interest expense			17,250 (E)	
Cash paid for income taxes			14,400 (P)	
		$449,750	$385,900	

Exhibit 14.9   Illustrative worksheet showing direct method.

	Balances 12/31/X0	Changes		Balances 12/31/X1
	DR(CR)	DR	CR	DR(CR)
Investing Activities				
Sale of equipment		$ 8,000 (F)		
Purchase of equipment			$ 15,000 (G)	
		8,000	15,000	
Financing Activities				
Dividends paid			6,000 (J)	
Cash paid to retire convertible bonds		————	9,100 (H)	
Payment of notes payable			23,000 (L)	
			38,100	
Net change in cash			18,750 (Q)	
		$959,650	$959,650	
Noncash disclosures—items (I) and (K)				

Exhibit 14.9   Continued.

BARUCH CORPORATION
Worksheet for Statement of Cash Flows—Indirect Method
12/31/X1

	Balances 12/31/X0	Changes		Balances 12/31/X1
	DR(CR)	DR	CR	DR(CR)
Accounts				
Cash	$ 25,000	$ 18,750 (Q)		$ 43,750
Accounts receivable, net	22,500		$ 9,750 (A)	12,750
Inventory	67,500	5,000 (B)		72,500
Property, plant, and equipment	100,000	15,000 (G)	12,500 (F)	102,500
Accumulated depreciation	(19,000)	2,500 (F)	3,500 (C)	(20,000)
Patents, net	4,000		500 (D)	3,500
Unamortized bond discount	3,000		250 (E)	750
			1,000 (H)	
			1,000 (I)	
	$203,500			$215,750
Accounts payable		750 (B)		$ (13,250)
Accrued expenses payable	1,000	1,000 (M)		0
Dividends payable	6,000	6,000 (J)	5,000 (K)	(5,000)
Income taxes payable	18,000		7,500 (P)	(25,500)
Notes payable	23,000	23,000 (L)		0
Convertible bonds payable	47,000	12,000 (H)		(16,000)
		19,000 (I)		
Deferred income taxes	7,500	1,000 (P)		(6,500)
Capital stock	56,000		16,500 (I)	(72,500)
Additional contributed capital	12,500		1,500 (I)	(14,000)
Retained earnings	18,000	5,000 (K)	50,000 (X)	(63,000)
	$203,500			$215,750
				(Continues)

Exhibit 14.10   Illustrative worksheet for statement of cash flows showing indirect method.

	Balances 12/31/X0	Changes		Balances 12/31/X1
	DR(CR)	DR	CR	DR(CR)
Operating Activities				
Net income		50,000 (X)		
Depreciation		3,500 (C)		
Patent amortization		500 (D)		
Amortization of bond discount		250 (E)		
Gain on retirement of convertible bonds			1,900 (H)	
Loss on sale of equipment		2,000 (F)		
Decrease in accounts receivable		9,750 (A)		
Increase in inventory			5,000 (B)	
Decrease in accrued expense payable			1,000 (M)	
Decrease in accounts payable			750 (B)	
Decrease in deferred income taxes			1,000 (P)	
Increase in income taxes payable		7,500 (P)		
		73,500	9,650	
Investing Activities				
Sale of equipment		$ 8,000 (F)		
Purchase of equipment			$ 15,000 (G)	
Net cash outflow from investing activities				
Financing Activities				
Dividends paid			6,000 (J)	
Cash paid to retire convertible bonds			9,100 (H)	
Payment of notes payable			23,000 (L)	
			38,100	
Net change in cash			18,750 (Q)	
		$190,500	$190,500	
Noncash disclosures—items (I) and (K)				

Exhibit 14.10   *Continued.*

X. Net income $50,000.

A. To record operating activity—cash inflow from customers, $449,750. Includes sales, $440,000, plus decrease in accounts receivable, $9,750. (The provision for bad debts would also need to be analyzed but is not included in this illustration.)

B. To record operating activity—cash paid to suppliers. Includes cost of goods sold, $220,000, plus increase in inventory, $5,000, and decrease in accounts payable, $750.

C. To eliminate the noncash depreciation charge of $3,500 from selling expense, $1,500, and administrative expense, $2,000.

D. To eliminate the noncash charge for patent amortization of $500 from administrative expense.

E. To record operating activity—cash paid for interest expense, $17,500, less $250 amortization of discount.

F. To record investing activity—proceeds on sale of equipment, $8,000; to eliminate loss of $2,000 from selling expense; and to reconcile cost of equipment, $12,500, and accumulated depreciation, $2,500, with changes in those accounts.

G. To record investing activity—cash purchase of equipment, $15,000.

H. To record financing activity—cash paid to retire bonds, $9,100; to reflect change in bonds payable, $12,000, and reduction of unamortized bond discount, $1,000; and to eliminate extraordinary gain of $1,900.

I. To eliminate the effects of a noncash transaction—conversion of bonds payable to common stock, which will be reported separately among the noncash changes. Bonds payable reduced by $19,000, unamortized bond discount reduced by $1,000, and capital stock and additional contributed capital increased by $16,500 and $1,500, respectively.

J. To record financing activity—payment of dividends of $6,000.

K. To eliminate the effects of a noncash transaction—declaration of dividends of $5,000, to be reported separately.

L. To record financing activity—the repayment of notes payable, $23,000.

M. To increase G & A expenses to reflect the payment of accrued G & A expenses payable.

N. To record operating activity—payment of selling expenses.

O. To record operating activity—payment of G & A expenses.

P. To record operating activity—payment of income taxes determined as follows:

12/31/X1 Balance—Income tax payable		$18,000
Add: Income tax expense	$20,900	
Decrease in deferred income tax	1,000	21,900
		39,900
Income tax paid		14,400
12/31/X2 Balance—Income tax payable		$25,500

Q. To reflect the increase in cash of $18,750 as a balancing amount.

(b) INDIRECT METHOD.   Although SFAS No. 95 recommends using the direct method, it permits using the indirect method. Furthermore, if the direct method is used, SFAS No. 95 requires a reconciliation of net income to net cash flow in a separate schedule.

The worksheet for the indirect method starts with postclosing trial balances for both the prior period and the current period. Net income is then adjusted to net cash flow from operations by removing the effects of accruals and deferrals, and adjusting for the effects of all items whose cash effects are either investing or financing cash flows or are noncash transactions.

The major classes of accounts to portray operating cash flows under the indirect method are the following:

- Net change in receivables, payables, and inventory
- Net change in interest and dividends earned but not received
- Net change in interest accrued but not paid
- Depreciation and amortization
- Net change in deferred taxes
- Net gain or loss on sale of property

The worksheet is illustrated in Exhibit 14.10 using the same data as in Exhibit 14.9. After an initial adjustment (keyed (X)) to remove net income from the change in retained earnings, which sets up the amount as a starting point for cash flow from operations, the remaining adjustments and eliminations track those of the direct method except that the adjustments for operating items are to net income rather than revenues and expenses (letters refer to list on pages 14–24 and 14–25). After the initial adjustment, entries are keyed in the same manner as explanations to adjustments that appear on Exhibit 14.9.

(c) CONVERSION OF INDIRECT TO DIRECT METHOD OF OPERATING CASH FLOW.
Exhibit 14.11 illustrates a shortcut technique for converting operating cash flows from one method
to the other. Thus, there is no need to prepare two separate worksheets. Once an initial worksheet is
completed, under the indirect method, showing cash flows from operating, investing, and financing
activities, then the operating cash flow data and the relevant adjustments on that worksheet can be
used to prepare operating cash flow under the direct method in Exhibit 14.11.

14.4 FOREIGN CURRENCY CASH FLOWS

(a) CONSOLIDATING FOREIGN OPERATIONS.   SFAS No. 95 requires companies with foreign operations or foreign currency (FC) transactions to include in the consolidated statement of
cash flows the reporting currency equivalent of FC cash flows using exchange rates in effect at
the time of the cash flows. Weighted average exchange rates may be used if the results are not
materially different from those rates at the cash flow dates.

The procedure would require companies with foreign operations to prepare a separate statement
of cash flows in the FC for each foreign operation or by groups of companies using the same FC,
translate them into the reporting currency, and then consolidate those statements with the statement
of cash flows for domestic operations.

The procedures to prepare the statement of cash flows apply irrespective of whether the functional currency is the local FC or the reporting currency (U.S. dollars).

**(b) PRESENTATION OF THE EFFECTS OF EXCHANGE RATE CHANGES ON CASH
BALANCE.**   The effect of exchange rate changes on cash balances held in FCs are not cash
flows, but they must be included in the statement of cash flows because they affect the consolidated balance sheet change in cash and cash equivalents. To facilitate the reconciliation of the
change in cash and cash equivalents, SFAS No. 95 requires that the effect of exchange rate changes
on cash balances held in FCs be reported as a separate item in the statement of cash flows. The
item does not represent an operating, financing, or investing activity. Therefore, in the statement
the item should follow those activities and precede the net change in cash and cash equivalents.
EMC Corporation in its 2001 annual report (see Exhibit 14.4) shows the effects of exchange rate
changes on cash to arrive at the net increase in cash for the year.

(c) EXCHANGE RATE GAINS OR LOSSES.   Exchange rate gains or losses recognized in the
income statement and not relating to cash flows are presented as a reconciling item in the reconciliation of net income and net cash flow from operating activities, similar to the presentation of
other noncash gains or losses.

**(d) DETERMINING EXCHANGE GAIN OR LOSS MODIFIED BY STATEMENT OF
FINANCIAL ACCOUNTING NO. 95.**   The following simplified example illustrates the method
required by SFAS No. 95 for determining exchange rate gain or loss.

Assume that:

Inactive Overseas Company, a foreign subsidiary whose functional currency is the FC, had
little activity in 20X1. In fact, the only event occurring was the sale of land on June 30,
20X1, for (FC) 20, which was at the book value.

Other Information:

Cash January 1, 20X1:   (FC) 100
Cash December 31, 20X1:   (FC) 120

Exchange rates from FC to U.S. dollars were .12 at January 1, 20X1, .13 at June 30, 20X1,
and .15 at December 31, 20X1.

When preparing the statement of cash flows, the dollar amount used in reporting sale of land
and exchange rate gain or loss as follows:

BARUCH CORPORATION
Worksheet to Convert Cash Flow from Operations from Indirect to Direct Method

Income Statement (DR) CR

	Net Income	Sales	Cost of Goods Sold	Selling and G&A Expenses	Interest Expense	Income Taxes	Gain on Debt Retirement
Net income	$50,000	$440,000	$(220,000)	$(133,500)	$(17,500)	$(20,900)	$1,900
Depreciation	3,500			3,500			
Patent amortization	500			500			
Amortization of bond discount	250				250		
Decrease in deferred income taxes	(1,000)					(1,000)	
Gain on retirement of convertible bonds	(1,900)						(1,900)
Loss on sale of equipment	2,000			2,000			
Decrease in accounts receivable	9,750	9,750					
Increase in inventory	(5,000)		(5,000)				
Decrease in accrued expense payable	(1,000)			(1,000)			
Decrease in accounts payable	(750)		(750)				
Increase in income taxes payable	7,500					7,500	
Net cash inflow from operations	$63,850	$449,750 Cash Received from Customers	$(225,750) Cash Paid to Suppliers	$(128,500) Cash Paid for Selling and G&A Expenses	$(17,250) Cash Paid for Interest	$(14,400) Cash Paid for Taxes	$ 0

Exhibit 14.11 Illustrative worksheet converting operating cash flows from indirect to direct method.

OVERSEAS COMPANY
Balance Sheets

To illustrate how to prepare a local currency statement of cash flows and translate it to the reporting currency equivalent of the local currency cash flows, assume the following financial information for Overseas Company, a wholly owned West German subsidiary of a U.S. company with cash flows in Deutsche marks (DM).

| | December 31 | | Increase/ |
	19X7	19X6	(Decrease)
Assets			
Current Assets			
Cash and equivalents	752,222 DM	535,784 DM	216,438 DM
Accounts receivable	1,400,000	1,685,000	(285,000)
Inventories	1,500,000	1,600,000	(100,000)
Prepaid expenses	75,000		75,000
	3,727,222	3,820,784	(93,562)
Property and Equipment	2,400,000	2,250,000	150,000
Accumulated depreciation	(410,000)	(260,000)	(150,000)
	1,990,000	1,990,000	
	5,717,222 DM	5,810,784 DM	(93,562) DM
Liabilities and Shareholder's Equity			
Current Liabilities			
Accounts payable and accrued expenses	2,036,281 DM	1,740,429 DM	295,852 DM
Due to parent	867,052	946,372	(79,320)
	2,903,333	2,686,801	216,532
Long-Term Debt	1,600,000	2,000,000	(400,000)
Deferred Income Taxes	60,000	45,000	15,000
Shareholder's Equity			
Capital stock	600,000	600,000	200,000
Retained earnings	353,889	278,983	74,906
	1,153,889	1,078,983	74,906
	5,717,222 DM	5,810,784 DM	(93,562) DM

Exhibit 14.12   Foreign currency cash flows: Preparing and translating a foreign currency statement of cash flows (Part A).

Source: (Ernst & Young, "Statement of Cash Flows—Understanding and Implementing FASB Statement No. 95," 1988. Used by permission.)

DOLLAR AMOUNT FOR REPORTING SALE OF LAND

	Foreign Currency	Exchange Rate	Translated Amount (Amount Reported)
Investing activities:			
Cash from sale of land	20FC	.13	$2.60
Exchange gain			3.40

OVERSEAS COMPANY
Statements of Income and Retained Earnings
Year Ended December 31, 19X7

Sales	7,800,000 DM
Other income	31,211
	7,831,211
Costs and expenses	
Cost of goods sold	6,410,000
General and administrative	650,000
Depreciation	150,000
Interest	220,000
	7,430,000
	401,211
Foreign currency transaction gain	79,320
Income before income taxes	480,531
Income taxes	
Current	290,625
Deferred	15,000
	305,625
Net income	174,906
Retained earnings at beginning of year	278,983
	453,889
Less dividends paid	100,000
Retained earnings at end of year	353,889 DM

Assume the following additional information:

The exchange rate of DM to U.S. dollars was .317 at 12/31/X6, .406 at 12/31/X7, and the weighted average rate for 19X7 was .346.

The only change in property and equipment was a purchase at the beginning of the year; the increase in the amount due to parent was because of changes in exchange rates for U.S. dollar denominated intercompany debt; the decrease in long-term debt was because of repayments during the year; and the dividends of DM 100,000 were paid at year end. Changes in all other balances occurred ratably during the year.

Exhibit 14.12   Foreign currency cash flows: Preparing and translating a foreign currency statement of cash flows (Part B).

SFAS No. 95 translates cash inflows and outflows using the exchange rate at the date of the transaction: 20FC (.13). Accordingly, the exchange gain is calculated as the sum of the exchange gain from holding 100FC for the year and 20FC for half a year: 100FC (.15 − .12) + 20FC (.15 − .13) = $340. The exchange gain must be identified separately in the statement of cash flows.

(e) FOREIGN CURRENCY TRANSACTIONS.   FC transactions are transactions denominated in a currency other than the local currency of the entity engaging in the transaction. The reporting currency equivalent of FC cash flows should be classified in the statement of cash flows according to the nature of the transaction. Companies will have to analyze the FC transaction gains and losses to determine whether they should be presented as reconciling items in arriving at cash flow from operations.

For example, in a repayment of FC denominated debt, a realized exchange gain or loss would be a reconciling item in operating cash flow, whereas the repayment would be classified as a financing activity.

OVERSEAS COMPANY
Statement of Cash Flows
Year Ended December 31, 19X7

Foreign Currency as Functional Currency

Assuming the functional currency is the Deutsche mark, the statement of cash flows using the indirect approach would appear as follows in DM and U.S. dollars:

	Local Currency	Exchange Rate	Reporting Currency
Operating Activities			
Net income	174,906 DM	.346[1]	$60,517
Adjustments to reconcile net income to net cash provided by operating activities:			
Depreciation	150,000	.346[1]	51,900
Deferred taxes	(015,000)	.346[1]	5,190
Decrease in accounts receivable	285,000	.346[1]	98,610
Decrease in inventories and prepaid expenses	25,000	.346[1]	8,650
Increase in accounts payable and accrued expenses	295,852	.346[1]	102,365
Foreign currency transaction gain	(79,320)	.346[1]	(27,445)
NET CASH PROVIDED BY OPERATING ACTIVITIES	866,438		299,787
Investing Activities			
Purchases of property and equipment	(150,000)	.317[2]	(47,550)
NET CASH USED BY INVESTING ACTIVITIES	(150,000)		(47,550)
Financing Activities			
Repayment of long-term debt	(400,000)	.346[1]	(138,400)
Cash dividends to parent	(100,000)	.406[2]	(40,600)
NET CASH USED BY FINANCING ACTIVITIES	(500,000)		(179,000)
Effect of exchange rate changes on cash	N/A		62,321
Increase in Cash and Equivalents	(216,438)		135,558
Cash and cash equivalents at beginning of year	535,784	.317[3]	169,844
CASH AND CASH EQUIVALENTS AT END OF YEAR	752,222 DM	.406[3]	$305,402

[1] Weighted average rate.

[2] Rate at time of transaction. Note: This example assumes all purchases of property and equipment were made at the beginning of the year to demonstrate the statement of cash flow implications. More commonly companies will purchase property and equipment throughout the year and will translate these purchases using a weighted average rate.

[3] Rate at respective period end.

Exhibit 14.12   Foreign currency cash flows: Preparing and translating a foreign currency statement of cash flows (Part C).

(f) TRANSLATION OF FOREIGN OPERATIONS—A CASE.   Exhibit 14.12 (Parts A–D), which illustrates translation of foreign operations, is reproduced with permission from Ernst & Young's 1988 booklet, "Statement of Cash Flows—Understanding and Implementing FASB Statement No. 95."

14.5 DISCLOSURE

(a) SUMMARY OF REQUIRED DISCLOSURES.   SFAS No. 95 requires the following disclosures supplementary to the statement of cash flows:

The amount reported as the effect of exchange rate changes on cash and cash equivalents can be viewed as a "plug" figure in the statement, but it can be proved this way:

Effect on beginning cash balance			
Beginning cash balance in local currency	535,784 DM		
Net change in exchange rate during year	.089		$ 47,684
(.406–.317)			
Effect from operating activities			
Cash provided in local currency	866,438		
Year-end exchange rate	.406		351,774
Less: U.S. dollar operating cash flows reported			299,787
			51,987
Effect from investing activities			
Cash used in local currency	(150,000)		
Year-end exchange rate	.406		(60,900)
Less: U.S. dollar investing cash flows reported			(47,550)
			(13,350)
Effect from financing activities			
Cash used in local currency	(500,000) DM		
Year-end exchange rate	.406		(203,000)
Less: U.S. dollar financing cash flows reported			(179,000)
			(24,000)
Effect of exchange rate changes on cash			$ 62,321
Cash provided by operating activities using the direct method would be presented this way:			
Cash received from customers	8,085,000 DM[1]	.346[2]	$2,797,410
Other cash received	31,211	.346[2]	10,799
Cash paid to suppliers and employees	(6,744,773)[1]	.346[2]	(2,333,692)
Interest paid	(230,000)[3]	.346[2]	(79,580)
Income taxes paid	(275,000)[3]	.346[2]	(95,150)
	866,438 DM		$ 299,787

[1] This amount could be derived using the same methodology illustrated in Section 4.
[2] Weighted average exchange rate during the year.
[3] Difference between these amounts and corresponding amounts reported as expenses in the statement of income are due to changes in beginning and end- of-year interest and income tax accruals included in accounts payable and accrued expenses.

Exhibit 14.12   Foreign currency cash flows: Preparing and translating a foreign currency statement of cash flows (Part D).

- A statement of company policy in classifying cash equivalents
- Details of noncash investing and financing transactions
- A reconciliation of net income and net cash flow from operating activities if the direct method is used to present operating cash flows, or net cash flow from operations is presented as a single amount in the statement
- Disclosure of interest paid (net of interest capitalized) and income taxes paid if the indirect method is used to present cash flow from operations

(b) CASH FLOWS PER SHARE.   SFAS No. 95 specifies that cash flow per share is not to be reported. The FASB concluded that the reporting of cash flow per share information "would falsely imply that cash flow, or some component of it, is a possible alternative to earnings per share as a measure of performance." This conclusion is consistent with an earlier Securities and Exchange

---

FINANCIAL INSTITUTION, INC.
Statement of Cash Flows
Year Ended December 31, 20X1

The statement of cash flows and the reconciliation of net income to net cash provided by operating activities for Financial Institution, Inc., provided in paragraph 147 of SFAS No. 95 are superseded by the following:

Increase (Decrease) in Cash and Cash Equivalents

Cash flows from operating activities:		
Interest received	$ 5,350	
Fees and commissions received	1,320	
Proceeds from sales of trading securities	20,550	
Purchase of trading securities	(21,075)	
Financing revenue received under leases	60	
Interest paid	(3,925)	
Cash paid to suppliers and employees	(795)	
Income taxes paid	(471)	
Net cash provided by operating activities		$ 1,014
Cash flows from investing activities:		
Proceeds from sales of investment securities	2,225	
Purchase of investment securities	(4,000)	
Net increase in credit card receivables	(1,300)	
Net decrease in customer loans with maturities of 3 months or less	2,250	
Principal collected on longer term loans	26,550	
Longer term loans made to customers	(36,300)	
Purchase of assets to be leased	(1,500)	
Principal payments received under leases	107	
Capital expenditures	(450)	
Proceeds from sale of property, plant, and equipment	260	
Net cash used in investing activities		(12,158)
Cash flows from financing activities:		
Net increase in demand deposits, NOW accounts, and savings accounts	3,000	
Proceeds from sales of certificates of deposit	63,000	
Payments for maturing certificates of deposit	(61,000)	
Net increase in federal funds purchased	4,500	
Net increase in 90-day borrowings	50	
Proceeds from issuance of nonrecourse debt	600	
Principal payment on nonrecourse debt	(20)	
Proceeds from issuance of 6-month note	100	
Proceeds from issuance of long-term debt	1,000	
Repayment of long-term debt	(200)	
Proceeds from issuance of common stock	350	
Payments to acquire treasury stock	(175)	
Dividends paid	(240)	
Net cash provided by financing activities		10,965
Net decrease in cash and cash equivalents		(179)
Cash and cash equivalents at beginning of year		6,700
Cash and cash equivalents at end of year		$ 6,521
		(Continues)

Exhibit 14.13   Illustration of statement of cash flow for a financial institution.

Reconciliation of Net Income to Net Cash Provided by Operating Activities:

Net income		$ 1,056
Adjustments to reconcile net income to net cash provided by operating activities:		
Depreciation	$ 100	
Provision for probable credit losses	300	
Provision for deferred taxes	58	
Loss on sales of investment securities	75	
Gain on sale of equipment	(50)	
Increase in trading securities (including unrealized appreciation of $25)	(700)	
Increase in taxes payable	175	
Increase in interest receivable	(150)	
Increase in interest payable	75	
Decrease in fees and commissions receivable	20	
Increase in accrued expenses	55	
Total adjustments		(42)
Net cash provided by operating activities		$ 1,014

Exhibit 14.13   *Continued.*

Commission (SEC) prohibition against reporting cash flow per share in filings with the Commission. In Financial Reporting Release (FRR) Section 202.04 (ASR No. 142), the Commission expressed the view that cash flow per share could be misleading, especially since at that time there were no standards for computing that amount.

14.6 APPLICATION OF STATEMENT OF CASH FLOWS TO SPECIAL INDUSTRIES

The principles of SFAS No. 95 apply to enterprises other than commercial entities, including financial institutions, insurance companies, health care entities, and investment companies. Not-for-profit organizations were not included in the scope of SFAS No. 95 because the Board had not decided whether not-for-profit organizations should be required to provide a statement of cash flows. SFAS No. 117 requires all not-for-profit organizations to provide a statement of cash flows that focuses on the organization as a whole and that conforms with the provisions of SFAS No. 95. SFAS No. 95 does not apply to governmental entities. However, because certain funds, such as proprietary and similar trust funds, follow the financial reporting practices of similar private-sector enterprises, most implementation issues faced by these governmental entities are not unique. Thus, such funds may present a statement of cash flows. The Government Accounting Standards Board (GASB) statement No. 9 establishes standards of cash flow reporting for governmental entities.

SFAS No. 102, Appendix B, which is partially reproduced here in Exhibit 14.13, presents a statement of cash flows and the reconciliation of net income to net cash flows provided by operating activities for a financial institution. Note that the gross concept of cash flows is applicable to financial institutions, which is a change from past practice of certain institutions of showing the net change in investments, loans, and deposit accounts in the statement of change in financial position. Also, Exhibit 14.13 offers additional guidance on the requirements of SFAS No. 95 for financial institutions in presenting cash flow data. SFAS No. 104 amends SFAS No. 95 to permit banks, savings institutions, and credit unions to report in a statement of cash flows certain net cash receipts and cash payments for (1) deposits placed with other financial institutions and withdrawals of those deposits, (2) time deposits accepted and repayments of those deposits, and (3) loans made to customers and principal collections of those loans.

14.7 SOURCES AND SUGGESTED REFERENCES

Accounting Principles Board, "The Statement of Sources and Application of Funds," APB Opinion No. 3. AICPA, New York, 1963.

———, "Omnibus Opinion," APB Opinion No. 12. AICPA, New York, 1967.

———, "Reporting Changes in Financial Position," APB Opinion No. 19. AICPA, New York, 1971.

American Institute of Certified Public Accountants, "Accounting Trends and Techniques." AICPA, New York, 1987.

Clark, H. G., and Lorensen, L., *Illustrations of Cash-Flow Financial Statements*. AICPA, New York, 1989.

Ernst & Young, "Statement of Cash Flows—Understanding and Implementing FASB Statement No. 95." Ernst & Young, Cleveland, OH, January 1988.

Financial Accounting Standards Board, "Reporting Funds Flows Liquidity, and Financial Flexibility," Discussion Memorandum. FASB, Stamford, CT, 1981.

———, "Reporting Income, Cash Flows, and Financial Position of Business Enterprises," Exposure Draft of Proposed Concepts Statement. FASB, Stamford, CT, 1981.

———, "Recognition and Measurement in Financial Statements of Business Enterprises," Statement of Financial Accounting Concepts No. 5. FASB, Stamford, CT, 1984.

———, "Accounting and Reporting by Defined Benefit Pension Plans," Statement of Financial Accounting Standards No. 35. FASB, Stamford, CT, 1980.

———, "Foreign Currency Translation," Statement of Financial Accounting Standards No. 52. FASB, Stamford, CT, 1981.

———, "Statement of Cash Flows," Statement of Financial Accounting Standards No. 95. FASB, Stamford, CT, 1987.

———, "Statement of Cash Flows—Exemption of Certain Enterprises and Classification of Cash Flows from Certain Securities Acquired for Resale," Statement of Financial Accounting Standards No. 102. FASB, Stamford, CT, 1989.

———, "Statement of Cash Flows—Not Reporting of Certain Cash Receipts and Cash Payments and Classification of Cash Flows from Hedging Transactions," Statement of Financial Accounting Standards No. 104. FASB, Norwalk, CT, 1989.

———, "Accounting for Certain Investments in Debt and Equity Securities," Statement of Financial Accounting Standards No. 115. FASB, Norwalk, CT, 1993.

———, "Financial Statements. Not-for-Profit Organizations," Statement of Financial Accounting Standards No. 117. FASB, Norwalk, CT, 1993.

———, "Accounting for Derivative Instruments and Hedging Activities," Statement of Financial Accounting Standards No. 133. FASB, Norwalk, CT, 1998.

———, EITF Issue No. 95-13, "Classification of Debt Issue Costs in the Statement of Cash Flows," EITF ABSTRACTS, FASB, Norwalk, 2001.

———, EITF Issue No. 00-15, "Classification in the Statement of Cash Flows of the Income Tax Benefit Received by a Company upon Exercise of a Nonqualified Employee Stock Option," EITF ABSTRACTS, FASB, Norwalk, 2001.

Mahoney, J. J., Sever, M. V., and Theis, J. A., "Cash Flow: FASB Opens the Floodgates," *Journal of Accountancy*, May 1988, pp. 25–38.

Securities and Exchange Commission. "Reporting Cash Flow, per Share Information," Accounting Series Release No. 142, §202.04, SEC, Washington, DC, 1982.

CHAPTER 15

INTERIM FINANCIAL STATEMENTS

Anthony J. Mottola, CPA

Mottola & Associates, Inc.

15.1 IMPORTANCE OF INTERIM FINANCIAL INFORMATION: TIMELY DISCLOSURE

As the age of information gathers greater momentum in a new millennium, so the appetite for financial information has increased, as have the sensitivity and reaction of the securities markets for that information. In this climate, interim financial information plays an increasingly important role. Financial statements continue to evolve from a historical archive, through being a basis for making decisions about the future, to confirming the results of previously announced expectations.

Recent Securities and Exchange Commission (SEC) proposals would have the chief executive officer (CEO) and chief financial officer (CFO) sign the interim disclosures of public companies to stress their involvement in the process and the accuracy of the data communicated to the public, as well as shorten the time frames for filing the disclosures. And in the post-Enron/post-Andersen environment, the involvement of the independent auditor is likely to increase. Today's markets respond with almost equal vigor to the press release of quarterly earnings, followed by the issuance of related interim financial statements as they do to year-end audited financial information.

Publication of financial information at interim dates enables users to assess an enterprise's current performance, compare and contrast that performance with previous expectations announced by management or predicted by analysts, and revise or confirm expectations of future performance.

The great preponderance of effort in the development of generally accepted accounting principles (GAAP) has been devoted to resolving issues associated with annual financial reporting. Increasingly, estimates of future cash flows find their way into the valuations that affect the amounts reported in annual financial statements. With the continuing integration of "current value" measurements into the "historical cost" financial reporting model, a growing number of substantive issues affects the preparation and presentation of interim financial information. That, coupled with the marketplace's reactions to restatements of reported results, increases the significance of the task of preparing interim financial statements.

15.2 APPLICATION OF GENERALLY ACCEPTED ACCOUNTING PRINCIPLES TO INTERIM FINANCIAL STATEMENTS

(a) **ALTERNATIVE VIEWS.**   The fundamental issue is whether interim financial statements are to be viewed as a presentation of an autonomous period or as an integral part of the annual reporting period. If interim statements are considered to be an autonomous presentation of financial data—the discrete view—deferrals and accruals should be determined following the same accounting principles and practices that apply to annual periods. If, however, such statements are deemed to be an integral part of the annual period—the integral view—reporting at the end of each interim period is affected by judgments made at that date as to results of operations for the balance of the year.

(i) **The Discrete View.**   The premise that expenses should be matched with revenue creates allocation problems in applying the discrete view. Some enterprises, such as outdoor construction contractors, sports arenas, and resorts, have highly seasonal revenue yet incur fixed costs throughout the year. Sophisticated cost allocation techniques have to be developed to enable management to reasonably estimate total costs and profit margins so that each interim period reflects expenses in direct proportion to the revenue generated.

In some industries, significant expenditures normally associated with an annual period, such as the costs of major repairs or advertising campaigns, may benefit more than one interim period. However, under the discrete view such expenditures affect interim earnings when incurred. Furthermore, some business costs, such as volume discounts to customers or an employer's share of social security taxes, may be incurred in one interim period but relate to activities of all interim periods.

(ii) **The Integral View.**   The integral view minimizes short-term fluctuations in reported interim earnings that reverse or are offset in later interim periods. However, the integral view introduces another source of volatility: the limitations of the estimation process.

The prediction and estimation required of management in preparing interim statements following the integral view may result in errors that distort operating results in later interim periods. For example, revenue from an advertising campaign conducted during a prior interim period may be substantially below the original estimate, and the deferral of advertising costs to the current interim period may further depress current reported earnings. Conversely, if accruals made in early interim periods for costs that are not incurred, such as major repairs that are postponed, are reversed in a later interim period, higher reported earnings will be reflected.

(b) CONCERNS COMMON TO BOTH VIEWS.   Few companies have developed and refined procedures to accumulate information to prepare interim financial statements. Many companies have no formal closing procedures. Thus accounting estimates, such as allowances for doubtful receivables and losses from commitments and contingencies, are not based on detailed information. Physical inventories are generally not taken because such procedures cannot be cost justified. Management must balance its needs for additional evidence against the desirability of releasing interim results on a timely basis. Also, the potential for imprecision in interim financial statements is greater since estimates are subject to the same range of error as those in annual statements, but the numbers associated with the shorter period are smaller.

(c) CURRENT VIEW OF APPLICATION OF GENERALLY ACCEPTED ACCOUNTING PRIN-CIPLES TO INTERIM REPORTING.   Present practice is still largely governed by the conclusions set forth in paragraphs 9 and 10 of Accounting Principles Board (APB) Opinion No. 28, "Interim Financial Reporting," wherein the Board essentially adopted the integral view:

The usefulness of [interim] information rests on the relationship that is has to the annual results of operations. Accordingly, the Board has concluded that each interim period should be viewed primarily as an integral part of an annual period.

The results for interim reporting generally should follow the accounting principles and practices used to prepare the most recent annual financial statements, unless a change in accounting is being adopted as of the current interim period.

However, the Board has concluded that certain accounting principles and practices followed for annual reporting purposes may require modification at interim reporting dates so that the reported results for the interim period may better relate to the results of operations for the annual period.

In many of its pronouncements, the Financial Accounting Standards Board (FASB) prescribes how to apply its provisions to interim financial statements. Some, such as accounting for marketable equity securities, use the values in effect at the date of the preparation of the financial statements. Others, such as certain accounting for income taxes, require estimates of the results of the full year's operations as a basis for making estimates of interim results.

15.3 MEASUREMENT PRINCIPLES FOR INTERIM REPORTING

(a) REVENUE.   As stated in paragraph 11 of APB Opinion No. 28, "revenue from products sold or services rendered should be recognized as earned during an interim period on the same basis as followed for the full year." Revenue is recognized when realized, that is, when the earnings process is complete or virtually complete and when an exchange has taken place. In some situations, this approach may distort interim results. For example, major plant repairs or the need to retool equipment, a strike, or a serious material shortage may cause distortion. These situations require disclosure in interim financial statements so that the statements will not be misleading; however, they do not constitute a justification for departing from the basic principle of revenue recognition.

(b) COSTS AND EXPENSES.   Since revenue recognition practices are the same for annual and interim reporting, differences in earnings measurements hinge on how the remaining components of the operating statement are recognized and displayed in interim financial statements. In SFAC No. 5, "Recognition and Measurement in Financial Statements of Business Enterprises" (pars. 85–87), the Board provides further recognition guidance by stating:

expenses and losses are generally recognized when an entity's economic benefits are used up in delivering or producing goods, rendering services, or other activities that constitute its ongoing major or central operations or when previously recognized assets are expected to provide reduced or no further benefits.

The Board also set forth two principles that specify the basis for recognizing the expenses and losses that are deducted from revenue to determine income or loss. They are "consumption of benefits" and "loss or lack of future benefit."

Under the consumption of benefits principle, the relationship between expenses and revenue is presumed to be either direct or related to revenue recognized during the period. For example, expenses such as cost of goods sold are matched with revenue. Similarly, expenses such as selling and administrative salaries are recognized during the period in which cash is spent or liabilities are incurred for goods and services that are used up either immediately or soon thereafter. Determining the cost of products sold involves several assumptions regarding the flow of costs [last-in, first-out (LIFO), first-in, first-out (FIFO), etc.] and the interrelationship between inventory and costs of goods sold.

Costs that do not have a direct cause-and-effect relationship with revenue, but that clearly provide benefits to more than one accounting period, should be allocated as expenses in a systematic and rational manner to the periods during which the related assets are expected to provide benefits. Examples of such costs include depreciation of fixed assets, amortization of intangible assets, and allocation of rent and prepaid insurance. These types of expenses involve assumptions about the pattern of benefits and the relationship between expenses and benefits. The period(s) over which such expenses are allocated and the allocation method should appear reasonable to an unbiased observer and should be consistent from period to period.

Under the loss or lack of future benefit principle, "An expense or loss is recognized if it becomes evident that previously recognized future economic benefits of an asset have been reduced or eliminated, or that a liability has been incurred or increased without associated economic benefits."

Therefore, costs recognized immediately as expenses are: (1) costs incurred currently that provide no discernible future benefits; (2) costs incurred previously and deferred that no longer provide discernible benefits; and (3) other costs for which allocation among several periods would serve no useful purpose. Examples include officers' salaries and amounts paid to settle lawsuits.

(c) COSTS ASSOCIATED WITH REVENUE.   Paragraph 13 of APB Opinion No. 28 is consistent with the pervasive principles cited above. It states: "Those costs and expenses that are associated directly with or allocated to the products sold or to the services rendered for annual reporting purposes (including, for example, material costs, wages and salaries and related fringe benefits, manufacturing overhead, and warranties) should be similarly treated for interim reporting purposes." However, Opinion No. 28 also recognizes the propriety of certain departures from annual inventory pricing practices, as described below.

(i) Gross Profit Estimation.   For many companies that do not maintain perpetual inventory records, a physical inventory at the end of each reporting period would be cost prohibitive. Also, the time required to take and price the inventory and to summarize the results might cause unacceptable delays in the release of interim financial information. Thus management determines the cost of goods sold (and inventory) at interim dates by applying estimated gross profit rates to revenue recognized during the interim period. This technique is based on an assumption that the percentage of gross profit (or a composite rate for the different classes of products sold) will be the same in successive accounting periods. Estimated gross profit rates should be reasonably determined from results of prior periods and current budgets. Although use of gross profit rates or other estimation techniques different from those used for the annual determination of inventory and cost of goods sold may be justified, users of interim financial data should be advised that a different method involving a greater degree of judgment was employed. Thus Opinion No. 28 requires that companies disclose the method used at interim dates and any significant adjustments resulting from reconciliations with the annual physical inventory.

(ii) LIFO.   As discussed in Chapter 18, the LIFO method associates the most recent inventory quisitions with the most recent sales for purposes of determining the cost of goods sold. If ntory quantities remain stable from year to year, the value of inventory will also remain stable "current" year's costs will be associated with the "current" year's revenue.

American Institute of Certified Public Accountants (AICPA) addressed the problems of IFO for interim reporting in an issues paper entitled "LIFO and Interim Financial

Reporting." In particular, the issues paper presents the problems and different approaches involved in estimating the interim effect of LIFO and determining the appropriate balance sheet presentation of the provision to offset the effect of an interim, temporary LIFO inventory liquidation. The paper points out the difficulty of implementing LIFO for interim reporting because LIFO is, by tax law definition, an annual calculation.

Since an estimate for the interim cost of sales must be computed, several approaches for making this estimate are used:

- *Approach A.* Specify quarterly calculation of the LIFO effect based on year-to-date amounts.
- *Approach B.* Project the expected annual LIFO cost and allocate that projection to the quarters equally or in relation to certain operating criteria.
- *Approach C.* Make a complete quarterly LIFO determination; that is, determining an appropriate LIFO index at the end of each quarter, applying that price change to specifically determined inventories at the end of each quarter, and using that information to make discrete quarterly computations, including determination of quarterly increments and decrements (few, if any, companies are believed to use this approach due to cost, effort, and time involved).

The AICPA Task Force concluded, "Only the first two approaches are acceptable as long as the application results in reasonable matching of most recently incurred costs with revenues, considering such things as the effects of significant changes in prices, operating levels, and mix."

The APB Opinion No. 28 (par. 14) requires that interim earnings not reflect a LIFO inventory liquidation if management expects to replenish that inventory by year end. According to the LIFO issues paper, the authoritative literature does not state how the adjustment should be treated in the balance sheet. Possible accounting treatments of the adjustment for interim balance sheet purposes include:

- *Treatment X.* Record the pretax income effect of the LIFO inventory liquidation as a deferred credit in the balance sheet's current liabilities section, with inventory reflecting the liquidation.
- *Treatment Y.* Record as a liability (perhaps included in accounts payable) an amount sufficient to reinstate the inventory balance to the amount before liquidation plus the amount necessary to offset the income statement liquidation effect.
- *Treatment Z.* Record as a credit to inventory (in rare circumstances the credit could be greater than the inventory balance), the effect of which in some cases is to do nothing.

The Task Force believes for practical considerations that either Treatment X or Z is reasonable. Regarding the issue of increments expected to be liquidated by year end, the Task Force believes companies using specific goods LIFO should adjust interim costs if temporary interim inventory increments occur, to produce a reasonable matching of most recently incurred costs with current revenues.

Finally, in the case where a LIFO liquidation is not expected to be reinstated by year end, the interim statements can reflect the effect of the liquidation. The Task Force believes that "to the extent it can be reasonably determined considering the cost-benefit factors involved, a company should recognize the effect of an interim LIFO inventory liquidation not expected to be reinstated by year-end in the period in which it occurs." However, the Task Force also believes a company using a dollar-value LIFO and Approach B may spread the expected effect of the liquidation using an approach similar to the one it uses for allocating the LIFO adjustment (normally a charge).

(iii) Illustrations of LIFO Liquidation. Exhibit 15.1 illustrates the accounting for a LIFO liquidation as of March 31, 20X2. Management does not expect to replenish a LIFO liquidated layer. A sample footnote is provided. Additionally, the case reviews the year-end reporting under the assumption management was incorrect and inventory is replenished.

ZZ COMPANY
Condensed Consolidated Balance Sheets
(Interim)

	March 31, 20X2	March 31, 20X1	December 31, 20X1
Assets:			
Cash	$ 30,000	$ 15,000	$ 19,000
Receivables	100,000	150,000	125,000
Inventories	80,000*	80,000	90,000
Total Assets	$210,000	$245,000	$234,000
Liabilities:			
Accounts Payable	65,000	40,000	50,000
Deferred Credit	15,000*	0	0
Accrued Expenses	5,000	15,000	28,000
	85,000	55,000	68,000
Stockholders' Equity	125,000	190,000	166,000
Total Liabilities and Stockholders' Equity	$210,000	$245,000	$234,000

ZZ COMPANY
Condensed Consolidated Balance Sheets
(Annual)

	December 31, 20X2	December 31, 20X1
Assets:		
Cash	$ 35,000	$ 19,000
Receivables	140,000	125,000
Inventories	65,000**	90,000
Total Assets	$240,000	$234,000
Liabilities:		
Accounts Payable	50,000	50,000
Accrued Expenses	10,000	18,000
	60,000	68,000
Stockholders' Equity	180,000	166,000
Total Liabilities and Stockholders' Equity	$240,000	$234,000

*LIFO liquidation occurs at interim, but management expects to reinstate that inventory at year end. During the first three months of 20X2, a liquidation of LIFO inventory occurred, but it is expected that the reduction will reverse at year end. Therefore, a deferred credit of $15,000 is established, which is the difference between the cost to replace this temporary inventory reduction and the LIFO cost assigned to the quantities.

**At year end, management is incorrect, and inventory is not reinstated. During 20X2, a reduction of inventory quantities resulted in a liquidation of LIFO inventory layers carried at costs prevailing in prior years, which are lower than current costs. Had these inventory layers been replaced, the higher cost of replacement would have been charged to cost of sales, thereby decreasing net income by $15,000.

Exhibit 15.1   Accounting for a LIFO liquidation where management does not expect to replenish the LIFO layer.

(iv) Market below Cost.   Normally, inventory is presented in annual financial statements at cost or market value, whichever is lower. A write-down to market value establishes a new "cost basis" that is not adjusted for subsequent recoveries. For the purposes of interim reporting, this general practice is modified to conform to the integral view of interim statements. If the market value of inventory declines below cost at an interim date, but the loss can reasonably be expected to be recovered either before the inventory is sold or, in the case of LIFO inventory, inventory amounts will be restored by year end, the loss need not be recognized in interim results of operations since no loss is expected to be incurred in the annual period. So-called temporary market declines not requiring immediate recognition tend to result from unusual circumstances, such as a temporary oversupply in the market, or relate to a product with an established pattern of seasonal price fluctuations. On the other hand, if management is unable to conclude that it is reasonable to expect a market recovery before either the inventory is sold or, in the case of LIFO inventory, before year end, the inventory loss should be recognized in the current interim period. Any recovery of such losses in subsequent interim periods of the same annual period should be reported as a gain.

Exhibit 15.2 illustrates the accounting for a LIFO liquidation whereas of March 31, 20X2, management expects to replenish the LIFO layer. At year end, management proves incorrect and inventory has been liquidated.

(v) Standard Cost.   Companies that use standard cost accounting systems for determining product costs generally should defer at interim reporting dates purchase price and capacity variances that are expected to be absorbed by the end of the annual period. Unanticipated variances should be reported at the end of an interim period in a manner consistent with practices used at year end.

All these modifications of annual practices involve a high degree of judgment on the part of management, and methods should be established by management to obtain the data necessary to make informed decisions.

(d) OTHER COSTS AND EXPENSES.   Costs other than product costs are recognized as expenses in annual periods based on expenditures made in the period, accruals for expenditures to be incurred in subsequent periods, or amortization of expenditures made previously that benefit more than one period. In paragraph 15 of APB Opinion No. 28, the Board concluded that the following three standards should apply to such costs in interim periods:

1. Costs and expenses should be charged to income in interim periods as incurred or be allocated among interim periods based on an estimate of time expired, benefit received, or activity associated with the periods. Procedures adopted for assigning specific cost and expense items to an interim period should be consistent with those followed in reporting annual results of operations. However, when a specific item charged to expense for annual reporting purposes benefits more than one interim period, it may be allocated among the interim periods in question.

2. Costs and expenses incurred in an interim period that cannot be readily identified with the activities or benefits of other interim periods should be charged to the interim period in which they are incurred. The nature and amount of such costs should be disclosed, unless items of a comparable nature are included in both the current interim period and the corresponding interim period of the preceding year.

3. Such costs and expenses should not be arbitrarily assigned to an interim period.

4. Gains and losses arising in an interim period that would not be deferred at year end should not be deferred to later interim periods.

As the foregoing indicates, there is sufficient latitude in the standards for interim reporting to allow for different treatment of similar items among companies. However, it would be inappropriate to believe that standard setters intended to permit an entity to treat a particular type of cost, in the same circumstances, one way in one interim report and another way in a subsequent interim report. Rather, the need for alternative methods can be attributed to differences in the circumstances of business enterprises, including the ability to gather information necessary to determine whether costs should be accrued or deferred.

XYZ COMPANY
Condensed Consolidated Balance Sheets
(Interim)

	March 31, 20X2	March 31, 20X1	December 31, 20X1
Assets:			
Cash	$ 30,000	$ 15,000	$ 19,000
Receivables	100,000	150,000	125,000
Inventories	65,000*	80,000	90,000
Total Assets	$195,000	$245,000	$234,000
Liabilities:			
Accounts Payable	50,000	40,000	50,000
Accrued Expenses	5,000	15,000	18,000
	55,000	55,000	68,000
Stockholders' Equity	140,000	190,000	166,000
Total Liabilities and Stockholders' Equity	$195,000	$245,000	$234,000

XYZ COMPANY
Condensed Consolidated Balance Sheets
(Annual)

	December 31, 20X2	December 31, 20X1
Assets:		
Cash	$ 30,000	$ 19,000
Receivables	140,000	125,000
Inventories	80,000**	90,000
Total Assets	$250,000	$234,000
Liabilities:		
Accounts Payable	30,000	50,000
Accrued Expenses	25,000	18,000
	55,000	68,000
Stockholders' Equity	195,000	166,000
Total Liabilities and Stockholders' Equity	$250,000	$234,000

LIFO liquidation occurred at interim, but management expects that inventory will not be reinstated. During the first three months of 20X2, a reduction of inventory quantities resulted in a liquidation of LIFO inventory layers carried at costs prevailing in prior years, which are lower than current costs. Had these inventory layers been replaced, the higher cost of replacement would have been charged to cost of sales, thereby decreasing net income by $15,000.
**At year end, management is incorrect and inventory is reinstated.* No footnote disclosure is required.

Exhibit 15.2   Accounting for a LIFO liquidation where management expects to replenish the LIFO layer.

If allocation is appropriate, it should be based on a "systematic and rational" method consistently applied. Acceptable allocation methods are (1) ratably over time, (2) proportionately as benefits are received, and (3) in relation to the activity associated with the interim period, perhaps in light of anticipated activity for the annual period. For example, insurance expense should be allocated ratably over the life of the policy; advertising expense should be allocated to the periods when benefits are received; and royalty expense should be allocated on the basis of activity during the interim period. In the last example, if royalty rates vary based on aggregate volume for the annual period, amounts accrued at interim dates will be based on anticipated annual volume.

Although Opinion No. 28 illustrates the application of the standards outlined above, the number of examples given is limited. The following six illustrations provide further clarification:

1. Expenses for which a liability is accrued should be allocated based on time expired. Examples are interest, rent, property taxes, franchise taxes not based on income, vested vacation pay, and pension expense.

2. Nondiscretionary expenditures incurred randomly that benefit the whole year should be allocated to all interim periods, usually on a time basis. Examples are normal recurring repairs, cost of printed annual reports, and normal recurring professional fees (audit, legal, etc.).

3. Expenditures for which a liability is incurred late in the year but that relate to activity during the year should be estimated and accrued, usually on a revenue basis. Examples are quantity sales discounts based on annual sales volume and incentive compensation and bonus plans.

4. Expenses resulting from accounting judgments that are susceptible to interim approximations should be estimated and accrued, on either a time or revenue basis. Examples are provisions for bad debts, change in useful lives or fixed assets, provisions for product warranty, and provisions for obsolete inventory.

5. Expenses resulting from amortization of balance sheet amounts should usually be allocated on a time basis. Examples are fixed asset depreciation and amortization of deferred charges.

6. Expenses connected with random, unexpected losses should be expensed as incurred. Examples are losses on contracts and casualty losses.

(e) INCOME TAX PROVISIONS. The supplanting of Statement of Financial Accounting Standards (SFAS) No. 96 by SFAS No. 109 changed the accounting for income taxes from the deferred method prescribed by APB No. 11 to the asset/liability method. SFAS No. 109 is consistent with the FASB's conceptual framework, which has at its core the balance sheet and the concomitant definitions of asset and liability. APB No. 11 (deferred method) emphasized the matching of revenues with expenses whereas SFAS No. 109 approaches the accounting for income taxes through the valuation of current and deferred tax assets and liabilities. The income tax expense for a given period is the sum of current income taxes payable or refundable and the valuation of the deferred tax assets and liabilities, if any. Determining an appropriate provision for income taxes in interim periods is complex.

An enterprise should develop its best estimate of the effective tax rate for the full year and use that rate in providing for taxes in interim statements. The income tax expense (benefit) should be allocated among continuing operations, discontinued operations, extraordinary items, and shareholders' equity. Amounts included in continuing operations include changes in tax laws or tax rates, changes in tax status, and changes in estimates relating to the realization of deferred tax assets. Shareholders' equity should be charged or credited with the tax effects of such matters as the following: (a) adjustments of retained earnings for certain changes in accounting principles or corrections of errors, (b) changes in contributed capital, (c) changes in the tax basis of assets acquired in a business combination accounted for as a pooling of interests for which a tax benefit was previously recognized, and (d) differences in recognition of expenses applicable to employee stock options for accounting and tax purposes. See Chapter 22 for a more complete discussion of tax allocation between reporting periods.

As is true of other aspects of interim financial reporting, the selection of an effective tax rate should be neither arbitrary nor static. It should reflect the company's tax posture, budgets, and intentions regarding operations during the annual period, and should be reevaluated and modified at each interim reporting date in the light of current information.

The annual effective tax rate established and used should take into consideration such factors as capital gain rates, available tax planning alternatives employed in computing ordinary income or loss, and foreign tax credits. It should also be recognized that the effects of new tax legislation cannot be taken into account prior to the enactment of such legislation. Tax benefits for the amount of taxes paid in prior years that are refundable by carryback of a loss of the current year can be recognized. Under FASB No. 109, an enterprise may recognize as an asset the benefits of a loss carryforward at the end of a fiscal year or arising in an interim period provided the probability that the enterprise will generate profits in future periods is judged to be "more likely than not."

The tax expense for an interim period is the product of the estimated annual effective tax rate and the year-to-date ordinary income or loss less the tax expense for the previous interim period calculated in a comparable manner.

Exhibit 15.3 illustrates the calculation of income tax expense assuming a tax rate change occurring in the second quarter. A suggested footnote is also included with the example.

(f) DISPOSAL OF A SEGMENT OF A BUSINESS AND EXTRAORDINARY ITEMS. APB Opinion No. 30, "Reporting the Results of Operations," requires that extraordinary items and the effects of disposing of a segment of a business be reported separately from the results of operations and net of their tax effect. Events of an abnormal nature that do not meet the criteria for an extraordinary item should also be reported separately from income from continuing operations. This facilitates the comparison of reported earnings with those of prior periods.

These matters are accorded substantially the same treatment in interim statements, although the measurement of materiality is somewhat more complex. In paragraph 21 of Opinion No. 28, the APB specified that the measurement of materiality with respect to extraordinary items should relate to estimated income for the full year. It seems reasonable and consistent with the integral view

---

CALCULATION OF INCOME TAX EXPENSE

Assume:
The effective tax rate is 40% in the first quarter and 30% in the second quarter

First Quarter:

	3 Months Ended
Income before income taxes	$500 (Assumed)
Provision for income taxes (40%)	200
Net Income	$300

Second Quarter:

	6 Months Ended
Income before income taxes	$800
Provision for income taxes (30%)	240
Net Income	$560
Interim F/S would appear as follows:	

	6 Months Ended June 30, 20X2	Second Quarter	First Quarter (As Previously Reported)
Income before income tax	$800	$300	$500
Provision for income tax	240	40	200
Net Income	$560	$260	$300

The difference in effective tax rates is reported in the second quarter under SFAS No. 96. The footnote disclosure might be as follows:

The provision for income taxes and the related liability have been reduced to give effect to the decline in federal income tax rates from 40% to 30% from January 1, 20X2, the effective date of the rate change. (If applicable, a similar adjustment would be made to any deferred tax balances.)

Exhibit 15.3   Calculation of income tax expense with a tax rate change in the second quarter from 40% to 30%.

to apply the same measurement criteria to the disposal of a segment of a business. Consequently, if disposals of business segments and extraordinary items are not material to estimated income for the annual period, they should not be reported separately, on a net-of-tax basis, in interim statements. However, if those items are material to the results of operations for the interim period or to the trend in interim earnings, they should be separately identified in the income statement and explained in a note.

Contingencies such as pending or threatened litigation and other major uncertainties should be reconsidered for each interim report. The accounting and disclosure requirements relating to contingencies are the same for interim as for annual reporting when a complete set of interim financial statements is presented.

(g) ACCOUNTING CHANGES.   Any change in accounting principle made in an interim period should be reported by retrospective application to prior periods. However, if it is impractical to apply the principle to prior interim periods of the fiscal year of the change, the change must be postponed until the beginning of the next fiscal year. See Chapter 9 for a complete discussion of accounting changes.

15.4 DISCLOSURE OF INTERIM FINANCIAL INFORMATION

(a) VARIATIONS IN DISCLOSURE.   The nature and extent of disclosures of financial information by business enterprises continues to evolve. Factors influencing disclosure include nature of shareholders (i.e., a public versus private enterprise); centralized management location versus widely decentralized management and widely diverse operations; and the increasing desire to present information in addition or supplemental to financial information in accordance with GAAP, to focus users on additional, sometimes alternative, measurements.

Owner-managers of closely held businesses may conclude that they obtain sufficient information from their day-to-day involvement in company affairs. However, even they might need to prepare and make available a complete set of financial statements each quarter to comply with provisions of credit agreements. Within and among the breadth of American business, there are a variety of possible scenarios. Even without specific requirements for external reporting at interim dates, private enterprises should be mindful of the potential need to prepare interim data on a comparative basis should they ever seek a wider distribution of their securities.

With increasing frequency, measurements of periodic results of operations other than net income in compliance with GAAP are being reported by business enterprises and the news media and discussed by public company management with analysts and investors. Descriptions such as "recurring earnings," "core earnings," or "operating income excluding special charges" and others have found their way into press releases, interim and annual reports, and other financial communications. These measures typically exclude a range of expenses that do not meet the criteria for being reported as extraordinary items. Whatever the alternative yardstick used, preparers would be well advised to make sure such alternative is clearly defined and presented together with reconciliation with income pursuant to GAAP.

(b) MINIMUM DISCLOSURE FOR PUBLIC COMPANIES.   There is a need to balance the desire for completeness of presentation with the desire for timeliness of dissemination of interim information. To that end, standard setters have established a minimum of nine disclosure requirements (APB No. 28, unless otherwise indicated) to be made by public companies to their security holders:

1. Sales or gross revenue, provision for income taxes, extraordinary items (including related income tax effects), cumulative effect of a change in accounting principles or practices, net income, and comprehensive income.
2. Information about reportable operating segments including:
   a. Revenue from external customers.

  b. Intersegment revenue (i.e., components of the enterprise for which there is available separate financial information that is evaluated regularly by the chief decision maker for assessments of performance and allocations of resources).

  c. A measure of segment profit or loss (not necessarily the same as GAAP, particularly with respect to joint costs, transfer pricing, etc.).

  d. Total assets for which there have been a material change from the amount disclosed in the latest annual report (e.g., a major increase in productive capacity or the disposal of a portion of a segment).

  e. A description of differences from the last annual report in the basis of segmentation or in the basis of measurement of segment profit or loss.

  f. A reconciliation of the sum of segment profit or loss reported in item c above with the enterprise's consolidated income net income. However, if extraordinary items, taxes, and the cumulative effect of changes in accounting principles are not allocated to segments, the disclosure and reconciliation can be made to consolidated income before those items. Each reconciling item must be separately identified and described.

3. Basic and diluted earnings per share (FASB No. 128). Applicable to annual periods beginning after December 15, 1997. Financial statements for prior periods presumably disclosed primary and fully diluted earnings per share pursuant to APB No. 15. Those financial statement amounts will be restated when presented after the adoption of FASB No. 128.

4. Seasonal revenue, costs, or expenses.

5. Significant changes in estimates or provisions for income taxes.

6. Disposal of a segment of a business and extraordinary, unusual, or infrequently occurring items (with explanations).

7. Contingent items, including significant changes in the risk associated with derivative securities and other off-balance sheet financing techniques.

8. Changes in accounting principles or estimates (e.g., the impairment of long-lived assets or intangibles per FASB No. 121) with appropriate explanations.

9. Any significant changes in financial position (i.e., liquid assets, net working capital, long-term liabilities, or stockholders' equity).

The foregoing data should be presented for the current quarter and current year to date or last 12 months to date, together with comparable data for the preceding year.

To avoid inappropriate inferences by users about fourth-quarter earnings when separate reports for this quarter are not issued, the APB requires that the annual financial statements include a note containing either the data specified above or, at a minimum, (1) disposals of segments of a business; (2) extraordinary, unusual, or infrequently occurring items; and (3) the aggregate effect of year-end adjustments that are material to the results of the quarter. The latter item identifies the cumulative impact of the results of the estimation process during the year.

The APB based these minimum requirements on the presumption that users of summarized interim financial data will have read the latest published annual report, including the annual financial statements, and that interim disclosures will be viewed in that context. This presumption carries the integral view into the reporting process.

(c) DISCLOSURE REQUIREMENTS OF STOCK EXCHANGES. The interim information required to be disclosed by companies whose securities trade in the major domestic securities markets is generally less extensive than the minimum set forth in APB Opinion No. 28. Thus the minimum disclosures of Opinion No. 28 apply.

The New York Stock Exchange (NYSE) and the American Stock Exchange (AMEX) require listed companies to release interim financial information on a quarterly basis. Exceptions to quarterly filings are granted in unusual cases where quarterly filings would be impracticable or misleading. Fourth quarter reports are not required since that period is covered by the annual financial statements.

From: John Doe   James Smith
    ABC Company   XYZ Public Relations Co.
    1 Main Street   2 Main Street
    Anytown, U.S.A.   Anytown, U.S.A.

                           FOR IMMEDIATE RELEASE

ABC COMPANY REPORTS HIGHER FIRST QUARTER EARNINGS
REVENUES INCREASE 10%; EARNINGS PER SHARE UP 15%

Anytown, U.S.A., (Date) ABC Company reported higher revenues, net earnings, and earnings per share for the first three months of the year. In making the announcement John Doe, CFO, reported that first-quarter revenues rose to $11,000,000, an increase of 10% over the $10,000,000 in the same period last year. Net earnings rose 15% to $1,500,000 versus $1,304,348 for the first three months of last year. Similarly, earnings per share for the quarter were $1.50, a 15% increase from the $1.30 reported last year.

Unit sales of widgets were up, reflecting the Company's increasing share of the market. Mr. Doe noted that the Company had opened an additional manufacturing facility which increased the Company's productive capacity by 10%.

	For the Quarters Ended June 30		
	20X2	**20X1**	**% Increase**
Operating revenues	$11,000,000	$10,000,000	10
Earnings before income taxes	3,000,000	2,608,696	15
Federal and other income taxes	1,500,000	1,304,348	15
Net earnings	1,500,000	1,304,348	15
Earnings per share of common stock (based on the weighted average number of shares outstanding)	$1.50	$1.30	15

Exhibit 15.4   Example of a press release of quarterly results.

The quarterly information must be released to the exchanges on a timely basis. The NYSE assumes that a listed company will provide the information "as soon as it is available and following a pattern of major companies in its industry." The AMEX requires the information be submitted within 45 days. The interim data must also be distributed as a press release to major newspapers of general circulation (at least in New York), to national newswire services, and to Dow Jones & Company, Inc. Distribution to security holders is encouraged but not mandatory. Copies of all releases should also be filed with the appropriate exchange. See Exhibit 15.4 for an example of a press release.

The National Association of Securities Dealers (NASD), the self-regulatory organization for the over-the-counter (OTC) market, requires companies whose securities are publicly traded to file with it a copy of the quarterly report mandated by the SEC no later than two weeks after its SEC filing date.

It is fast becoming common practice for business enterprises to publish such data, together with other management commentary, on the business's Web site. Care should be taken to make sure any additional information does not conflict with the basic disclosures.

(d) SECURITIES AND EXCHANGE COMMISSION REQUIREMENTS FOR INTERIM REPORTING.   The SEC promulgates financial accounting and disclosure requirements that it deems to be in the public interest or necessary for the protection of investors. In addressing the need for disclosure between annual periods, the Commission has accepted the concept that interim results should be viewed as an integral part of the annual period. Thus, for example, Financial

Reporting Release (FRR) No. 1 [Accounting Series Release (ASR) No. 177], "Notice of Adoption of Amendments to Form 10-Q and Regulation S-X Regarding Interim Financial Reporting," states, "The Commission ... believes that detailed footnote disclosures required annually need not be updated quarterly in the absence of highly unusual circumstances." However, Rule 10-01(a)(5) or Article 10 of Reg. S-X requires that when material contingencies exist, they should be disclosed even though no significant changes have occurred since year end.

The SEC requires public companies to file with it quarterly information on Form 10-Q. In addition, unusual or significant events occurring within a quarter, for example, changes in control of the company, a major acquisition or disposal of assets, a change in independent accountants, and other events deemed to be materially important to security holders, are to be reported monthly on Form 8-K. In the case of a material acquisition or disposition of assets, audited interim financial statements are required. When a company changes its independent accountant, any disagreement between the company and the former accountant that would have resulted in a modified audit report if not satisfactorily resolved must also be reported to the SEC on Form 8-K. Additionally, the independent accountant must provide a letter to the company, within 10 business days of the date the accountant receives the company's disclosure, expressing his views regarding the company's disclosure to the SEC. The accountant's letter should ordinarily not exceed 200 words.

The information to be filed quarterly with the SEC for the current and immediately preceding periods includes:

- A condensed balance sheet at the end of the quarter
- Condensed statements of income, retained earnings, and cash flows for the quarter and the year to date
- An exhibit setting forth the earnings per share computation in reasonable detail
- Notes describing in detail any material events (e.g., lawsuit settlements, etc.) or other changes deemed to be materially important to shareholders

Exhibit 15.5 illustrates some of these requirements. Management must also discuss the reasons for material changes in the amounts of revenue and expense in (1) the current quarter, compared to both the preceding quarter and the corresponding quarter of the prior year, and (2) the current year to date compared to the corresponding period of the prior year.

Regulation S-X, Article 10, Rule 10-01 outlines the Commission's requirements for interim financial statements. Essentially, interim financial statements follow the general form and content of the presentation prescribed for annual reporting. The exceptions, however, include:

- Interim financial statements may be unaudited.
- Interim balance sheets and statements of income shall only include major captions.
- The statement of changes in financial position may be abbreviated.
- Disclosures shall be included to make the information presented not misleading.
- If the registrant entered into a business combination, treated for accounting purposes as a pooling of interests, the interim financial statements shall reflect the combined results of the pooled businesses.
- Where a material business combination is accounted for as a purchase occurs during the current fiscal year, pro forma disclosure shall be made of the results of operations for the current year up to the date of the most recent interim balance sheet provided as though the companies had combined at the beginning of the period being reported on.
- The registrant must state the date of any material accounting change and the reasons for making it.

The SEC requires companies seeking to register securities for sale to the public to file registration statements including financial statements. Under Regulation S-X, the SEC does not require interim financial data more current than the most recent quarterly reporting date. Additionally, the

ABC COMPANY
Condensed Statement of Financial Condition

	June 30	
	20X2	**20X1**
Assets:		
Cash	$ 2,000	$ 2,500
Receivables	5,000	3,500
Inventory	5,000	4,500
Other Current Assets	3,000	2,500
Property, Plant & Equipment, Net	6,000	5,500
Other Assets	2,000	2,500
Total Assets	$23,000	$21,000
Liabilities:		
Accounts Payable	1,000	1,500
Notes Payable	3,000	2,500
Accrued Expenses and Other Liabilities	2,000	2,500
Bonds Payable	8,000	6,500
Total Liabilities	$14,000	$13,000
Stockholders' Equity:		
Common Stock	2,000	2,000
Paid-in Capital	3,000	3,000
Retained Earnings	4,000	3,000
Total Stockholders' Equity	9,000	8,000
Total Liabilities and Stockholders' Equity	$23,000	$21,000

ABC COMPANY
Condensed Statements of Income and Retained Earnings
For the Three Months and Six Months Ended June 30, 20X2

	3 Months Ended June 30, 20X2	6 Months Ended June 30, 20X2
Sales	$10,000	$20,000
Cost of goods sold	8,550	17,150
Gross profit	1,450	2,850
Selling and administrative expenses	150	250
Income before taxes	1,300	2,600
Provision for income taxes	300	600
Net income	1,000	2,000
Retained earnings beginning of period	3,500	3,000
Dividends	500	1,000
Retained Earnings June 30, 20X2	$ 4,000	$ 4,000
Earnings per share (assume 2,000 shares)	$ .50	$ 1.00
Cash provided by operations	$ 1,000	$ 2,000
Cash flows from investing:		
Capital expenditures	$ (1,500)	$ (3,500)
Cash used in investing	(1,500)	(3,500)
Cash flows from financing:		
Proceeds from issuance of long-term debt	$ 500	1,500
Dividends	(500)	(1,000)
Cash from financing	0	500
Increase (decrease) in cash	(500)	(1,000)
Cash, beginning of period	2,500	3,000
Cash, end of period	$ 2,000	$ 2,000
Interest paid in period	$ 250	$ 450
Income taxes paid in period	$ 300	$ 600

Exhibit 15.5   Examples of SEC requirements for interim reporting.

Commission allows data to be presented in condensed financial statements in the same degree of detail as in Form 10-Q.

In the interim period in which the enterprise adopts and applies a new accounting standard for the first time, all of the disclosures prescribed by the standard for annual financial statements should be included with the interim financial statements. However, such disclosures need not be updated for subsequent interim periods of the same year. Also, in general, the fair value of financial instruments needs to be disclosed and addressed in the Management Discussion and Analysis only if there has been a significant change in value or market conditions, highlighting those instruments that are particularly susceptible to slight movements in market conditions.

15.5 ROLE OF THE INDEPENDENT AUDITOR

(a) ROLE OF THE INDEPENDENT AUDITOR. Consistency in the application of accounting principles facilitates meaningful comparisons of a company's performance over time. Although new circumstances affecting a company or general business conditions may make modifications in accounting principles desirable, changes cannot be made arbitrarily. In FRR No. 1 (ASR No. 177), the SEC stated,

> Since a substantial burden of proof falls upon management to justify a change, the Commission believes that the burden has not been met unless the justification is sufficiently persuasive to convince an independent accounting expert that in his judgment the new method represents an improved method of measuring business operations in the particular circumstances involved.

Thus, the independent auditor must provide the company with a letter, to be filed as an exhibit to the first Form 10-Q filed after adoption of an accounting change, indicating whether the change is to an alternative principle that, in his judgment, is preferable in the circumstances. See Exhibit 15.6 for a sample letter from an accountant. The subject of preferability letters is discussed further in Chapter 7.

The SEC requires public companies to have their interim financial statements reviewed in accordance with standards established or adopted by the Public Company Accounting Oversight Board (PCAOB). The registered accountant performing the service may or may not issue a report on the review.

(b) THE OBJECTIVES AND PROCEDURES FOR A REVIEW OF INTERIM FINANCIAL INFORMATION. Statement on Auditing Standards (SAS) No. 100 (as adopted by the PCAOB) differentiates between the objectives of a review of interim financial information and the objectives of an audit of financial statements in accordance with generally accepted auditing standards (GAAS). The objective of a "review" is to provide the accountant, based on applying his knowledge of financial reporting through inquiries and analytical procedures, with a basis for reporting whether material modifications should be made for such information to conform with GAAP. The objective of an audit of financial statements in conformity with GAAS is to provide a reasonable basis for the auditor to express an opinion on the financial statements taken as a whole. A review is not an audit, because the review does not include (a) tests of accounting records, (b) obtaining corroborating evidential matter in response to inquiries, or (c) the application of certain other procedures ordinarily performed during an audit. A review does not ensure that an accountant will become aware of all significant matters that would be disclosed in an audit.

The process of reviewing interim financial information primarily involves inquiry and analysis. The SAS No. 100 provides guidance on the conduct of a limited review. Among other things, it:

- Requires that the accountant establish an understanding with the client.
- Clarifies the knowledge of the entity's internal control structure that the accountant needs to obtain when the accountant is engaged to review interim financial information but has not audited the most recent annual financial statements.

mm/dd/yy

Basic Corporation
6 Main Street
Anytown, U.S.A.

Gentlemen:

We are providing this letter to you for inclusion as an exhibit to your Form 10-Q filing pursuant to Item 601(b)(18) of Regulation S-K.

We have read management's justification for the change in accounting for inventories from the first-in first-out method to the last-in first-out method contained in the Company's Form 10-Q for the quarter ended March 31, 20X2. Based on our reading of the data and discussions with Company officials of the business judgment and business planning factors relating to the change, we believe management's justification to be reasonable. Accordingly, in reliance on management's determination as regards elements of business judgment and business planning, we concur that the newly adopted accounting principle described above is preferable in the Company's circumstances to the method previously applied.

We have not examined any fiscal statements of Basic Corporation as of any date or for any period subsequent to December 31, 20X1, nor have we audited the application of the change in accounting principle disclosed in Form 10-Q of Basic Corporation for the quarter ended March 31, 20X2; accordingly, our comments are subject to revision on completion of an audit of the financial statements that include the accounting change.

Very truly yours,

Adam, Bailey & Clarke

Exhibit 15.6   Illustrative letter from independent accountant concurring with accounting change adopted by management.

- Incorporates additional guidance on accounting estimates and performing analytical procedures in connection with a review of interim financial information.
- Requires the accountant, in performing a review of interim financial information, to obtain assurance that the audit committee, or those with equivalent authority and responsibility, is adequately informed of:

    —Any irregularities or illegal acts of which the accountant becomes aware during the review, unless those irregularities or illegal acts are clearly inconsequential.

    —Significant deficiencies in internal control of which the accountant becomes aware during the review.

    —Matters identified in SAS Nos. 61 and 100 that have an effect on interim financial information and should be the subject of communications with audit committees.

    —Notes that an entity may publish various documents that contain information in addition to interim financial information and the independent accountant's review report on that information. In those circumstances, the accountant may wish to refer to the guidance in SAS No. 8, "Other Information in Documents Containing Audited Statements" (AICPA, Professional Standards, Vol. 1, AU sec. 550).

15.6 SOURCES AND SUGGESTED REFERENCES

Accounting Principles Board, "Earnings per Share," APB Opinion No. 15. AICPA, New York, 1969.

———, "Accounting Changes," APB Opinion No. 20. AICPA, New York, 1971.

———, "Interim Financial Reporting," APB Opinion No. 28. AICPA, New York, 1973.

———, "LIFO and Interim Financial Reporting," Identification and Discussion of Certain Financial Accounting and Reporting Issues Concerning LIFO Inventories, AICPA Issues Paper. AICPA, New York, November 30, 1984.

———, "Reporting the Results of Operations," APB Opinion No. 30. AICPA, New York, 1973.

———, "Basic Concepts and Accounting Principles Underlying Financial Statements of Business Enterprises," APB Statement No. 4. AICPA, New York, 1970.

———, AICPA Auditing Standards Board, Statement on Auditing Standards No. 100, AICPA, New York, 2002.

———, "Communication of Matters About Interim Financial Information Filed or to Be Filed with Specified Regulatory Agencies—An Amendment to SAS No. 36, Review of Interim Financial Information," Statement on Auditing Standards No. 66. AICPA, New York, July 1981.

Bows, Albert J., and Wyatt, Arthur R., "Improving Interim Financial Reporting," *Journal of Accountancy*, Vol. 136, 1973.

Carlson, T. E., "Needed: A New Interpretation for Interim Reports," *Management Accounting*, Vol. 59, 1978.

Financial Accounting Standards Board, "Recognition of Inventory Market Declines at Interim Reporting Dates," EITF Abstracts Issue No. 86-13. FASB, Stamford, CT, May 1, 1986.

———, "Objectives of Financial Reporting by Business Enterprises," Statement of Financial Accounting Concepts No. 1. FASB, Stamford, CT, 1978.

———, "Recognition and Measurement in Financial Statements of Business Enterprises," Statement of Financial Accounting Concepts No. 5. FASB, Stamford, CT, December 1984.

———, "Elements of Financial Statements (a replacement of FASB Concepts Statement No. 3—incorporating an amendment of FASB Concepts Statement No. 2)," Statement of Financial Accounting Concepts No. 6. FASB, Stamford, CT, December 1985.

———, "Interim Financial Accounting and Reporting," Discussion Memorandum. FASB, Stamford, CT, 1978.

———, "Accounting for Income Taxes in Interim Periods: An Interpretation of APB Opinion No. 28," FASB Interpretation No. 18. FASB, Stamford, CT, 1977.

———, "Reporting Accounting Changes in Interim Financial Statements: An Amendment of APB Opinion No. 28," Statement of Financial Accounting Standards No. 3. FASB, Stamford, CT, 1974.

———, "Financial Reporting for Segments of a Business Enterprise—Interim Financial Statements: An Amendment of FASB Statement No. 14," Statement of Financial Accounting Standards No. 18. FASB, Stamford, CT, 1977.

——— "Accounting for Income Taxes," Statement of Financial Accounting Standards No. 96. FASB, Stamford, CT, December 1, 1987.

——— "Accounting for Income Taxes," Statement of Financial Accounting Standards No. 109. FASB, Stamford, CT, February 1992.

Rappaport, Louis H., *SEC Accounting Practice and Procedure*. John Wiley & Sons, New York, 1972.

Schiff, Michael, *Accounting Reporting Problems*. Financial Executives Institute, New York, 1978.

Securities and Exchange Commission, "Notice of Adoption of Amendments to Form 10-Q and Regulation S-X Regarding Interim Financial Reporting," Accounting Series Release No. 177. SEC, Washington, DC, 1975.

——— "Codification of Financial Reporting Policies," Financial Reporting Release No. 1. SEC, Washington, DC, April 1982.

——— "Interim Financial Statements," Rule 10-01, Article 10, Regulation S-X, Bowne. New York, June 1987.

——— "Interpretation of Accounting Series Release No. 177," Staff Accounting Bulletin No. 6, SEC, Washington, DC, 1976.

"SEC Seeking Views on Whether to Propose Timely Review of Interim Financial Data," *Securities Regulation & Law Report*. BNA Publishing, Washington, DC, June 23, 1989.

Securities Exchange Act of 1934, Regulation 14A: Solicitation of Proxies. SEC, Washington, DC, 1978.

——— "Accounting for Income Taxes—Deferral of the Effective Date of FASB Statement No. 96," Statement of Financial Accounting Standards No. 103. FASB, Norwalk, CT, December 1989.

——— "Accounting for Income Taxes—Deferral of the Effective Date of FASB Statement No. 96," Statement of Financial Accounting Standards No. 108. FASB, Norwalk, CT, December, 1991.

_____ "Reporting Comprehensive Income," Statement of Financial Accounting Standards No. 130. FASB, Norwalk, CT, 1997.

_____ "Disclosures about Segments of an Enterprise and Related Information," Statement of Financial Accounting Standards No. 131. FASB, Norwalk, CT, 1997.

_____ "Rescission of FASB Statement No. 75 and Technical Corrections," Statement of Financial Accounting Standards No. 135. FASB, Norwalk, CT, 1999.

_____ "Accounting for Certain Derivative Instruments and Certain Hedging Activities (an amendment of FASB Statement No. 133)," Statement of Financial Accounting Standards No. 138. FASB, Norwalk, CT, 2000.

CHAPTER 16

ANALYZING FINANCIAL STATEMENTS

Gerald I. White, CFA
Grace & White, Inc.

Ashwinpaul C. Sondhi, PhD
A. C. Sondhi and Associates, LLC

16.1 SCOPE OF FINANCIAL STATEMENT ANALYSIS

(a) EXTERNAL USERS OF PUBLISHED FINANCIAL STATEMENTS.   This section is concerned with the techniques of financial analysis employed by users of financial statements who are external to the company. As such, the techniques described are generally limited to analysis of published financial statements or similar statements privately circulated. Principal emphasis is on the financial statements of companies whose shares are publicly traded. Chapter 44 of this *Handbook* is concerned with the valuation of companies whose shares are not publicly traded.

Management has available far more extensive internal financial data for control of the business and deployment of resources. In many respects it may employ the same analytical approaches as the external user, but in greater detail.

The common characteristic of external users is their general lack of authority to prescribe the information they want from an enterprise. They depend on general-purpose external financial reports provided by management. The objectives of these external users are aptly described by the Financial Accounting Standards Board (FASB) in SFAC No. 1, "Objectives of Financial Reporting by Business Enterprises" (par. 34):

INFORMATION USEFUL IN INVESTMENT AND CREDIT DECISIONS

Financial reporting should provide information that is useful to present and potential investors and creditors and other users in making rational investment, credit, and similar decisions. The information should be comprehensible to those who have a reasonable understanding of business and economic activities and are willing to study the information with reasonable diligence.

(b) USER GROUPS AND THEIR ANALYTICAL OBJECTIVES.   External users of financial information encompass a wide range of interests but can be classified in three general groups: (1) investors—both creditors and equity investors; (2) government—regulatory bodies, tax authorities, the executive and legislative branches; and (3) the general public and special interest groups—labor unions, consumer groups, and so on. Each group has a particular objective in financial statement analysis but, as the FASB stated, the primary users are equity investors and creditors. The information supplied to investors and creditors, however, is likely to be generally useful to other user groups as well. Hence financial accounting standards are geared to the purposes and perceptions of investors. That is the group for whom the analytical techniques in this chapter are geared.

The underlying objective of financial analysis is the comparative measurement of risk and return in order to make investment or credit decisions. These decisions are based on some estimates of the future, be it a month, a year, or a decade. General-purpose financial statements, which describe the past, provide one basis for projecting future cash flows. Many of the techniques used in this analytical process are broadly applicable to all types of decisions, but there are also specialized techniques concerned with specific investment interests or, put another way, specific risks and returns.

(i) Equity Investors.   The equity investor is primarily interested in the long-term earning power of the company and its ability to pay dividends. Since the equity investor bears the residual risk in an enterprise, his analysis is the most comprehensive of any user and encompasses techniques employed by all other external users. Because the residual risk is the greatest and most volatile, the equity investor has focused increasing attention on measuring comparative risks and diversifying these risks in investment portfolios.

(ii) Creditors.   This subgroup of investors emphasizes several specialized analytical approaches. Short-term creditors, such as banks and trade creditors, place more emphasis on the immediate *liquidity* of the business because they seek an early payback of their investment. Long-term investors in bonds, such as insurance companies and pension funds, are primarily concerned with the long-term asset position and earning power of the company. They seek assurance of the payment of interest and the capability of retiring or refunding the obligation at maturity. Creditor risks are usually less than equity risks and are more easily quantifiable.

(c) SOURCES OF FINANCIAL INFORMATION.   The term *financial statements* normally encompasses four statements: the income statement, the balance sheet, the statement of changes in stockholders' equity (or changes in retained earnings), and the statement of cash flows. The notes to the financial statements are an integral part of the entire set and provide substantial amounts of supplementary information, such as the operations of major segments of the business, the financial position of pension plans, and off-balance sheet (OBS) obligations.

These statements are presented in both the annual and the quarterly reports to shareholders and in filings with the Securities and Exchange Commission (SEC). The SEC filings (registration statements for new security offerings, the 10-K annual report, 10-Q quarterly report, and 10-K report) often contain additional valuable information not presented in reports to shareholders. Shareholder reports, on the other hand, often contain useful supplementary financial and statistical data and a narrative report by management. Therefore, any comprehensive analysis of a company should review both of these basic sources.

Industry data and other information about a company also may be obtained from sources outside the company. This discussion is confined to company-originated financial data.

(d) FRAMEWORK FOR ANALYSIS.   Investment analysis should begin with an evaluation of macroeconomic conditions including trends in the gross national product (GNP), personal consumption, and capital expenditures along with other relevant macrovariables. This analysis should be developed on a domestic and international level for insights into the relative investment potential across countries and industrial sectors. The competitive, economic, and technological factors affecting selected industries should be analyzed next; finally, there should be a comprehensive analysis of various firms in these industries. The analysis framework to achieve forecasts of earning power and market value can be outlined as follows:

1. Economywide factors
      GNP
      Personal consumption expenditures
      Capital expenditures
      Interest rates

          Currency rates

          Other relevant macrovariables

2. Industrywide factors

          Product life cycle—sales and earnings

          Unit cost and unit sales price

              Trends over time

              Relative to other firms

          Economic and technological forces affecting industry competition

              Threat of new entrants

              Bargaining power of buyers

              Rivalry among existing competitors

              Threat of substitute products

              Bargaining power of suppliers

3. Firm-specific analyses

          Firm strategies in given economic and industrywide environment

          Earning power

          Leverage analysis

16.2 INCOME STATEMENT ANALYSIS

This section discusses the evaluation of earning power and risk through analyses of the revenue and expense components of the income statements. Various analytical techniques used to study trends and variability in revenues and the impact of costs incurred on risk are described.

(a) THE CONCEPTS OF EARNING POWER AND RISK.   In the long run, earning power is the basis for credit and the source of cash return (interest or dividends) to the investor. The analyst seeks to project earning power over some future period associated with the length of the risk period. Therefore, it is the focus of income statement analysis.

    Earning power is an analytical concept and cannot be separately identified in the income statement. It is defined as the ability of a company to generate continuing earnings from the operating assets of the business over a period of years. Its characteristics include normality, stability (or variability), and growth. Normality is the normal level of earnings, absent strikes, floods, and other unusual nonrecurring events. It excludes extraordinary items such as accounting adjustments and nonrecurring capital gains or charges. Stability is the absence of variation around a trend line. Growth is the rate of change in the trend line of earnings over a defined period. Generally, earning power is better represented by operating earnings than by total net income, which often includes unusual or random elements. The analyst normalizes and averages operating earnings data to determine earning power, which he then projects and capitalizes.

    The risk element in earning power is the variability between actual and expected earnings, or the predictability of earnings. The earnings of some companies may fluctuate with some regularity in a cyclical pattern, whereas for others the fluctuations are irregular and unpredictable. Fluctuation is tantamount to uncertainty, which increases as fluctuations become increasingly irregular and unpredictable. Thus, stocks of copper companies are considered more risky than, say, those of household product companies, because their earnings are much less predictable.

(b) SALES AND REVENUE ANALYSIS.   Sales and other operating revenues are the lifeblood of a business. The analyst compares the company's revenue factors with the industry and with competing companies and seeks to associate economic changes with internal company trends. He makes comparisons by analysis of trend and variability and attempts to ascertain the relative importance of price and volume.

Year	Company A Steady Growth		Company B Cyclical Pattern		Company C Unusual Development	
	Amount	% Change	Amount	% Change	Amount	% Change
1	$ 21.5		$ 8.1	20.5		
2	23.0	7.0	23.6	30.4	$ 21.5	4.9
3	24.0	4.3	28.1	19.1	23.0	7.0
4	25.7	7.1	35.7	17.0	24.5	6.5
5	28.1	9.3	29.0	(18.8)	26.0	6.1
6	29.6	5.3	27.5	(5.2)	26.5	1.9
7	31.3	5.7	26.0	(5.4)	28.0	5.7
8	34.5	10.2	29.0	11.5	29.0	3.6
9	35.0	1.4	32.0	10.3	40.0	10.3
10	36.3	3.7	40.0	25.0	50.0	25.0
10-year Total	$289.0		$289.0		$289.0	
% Change years 1–10		68.8		121.0		143.9
Compound growth rate years 1–10 (%)		6.0		9.2		10.4
Least squares growth rate (%)		6.0		4.8		9.1
Standard deviation		5.3		6.1		9.2

Exhibit 16.1   Measures of sales trends.

(i) Trend Analysis. The most appropriate measure of a trend is determined by the revenue pattern. A stable trend is easily measured by a compound annual growth rate calculated on the end point values, but a highly variable pattern is better measured by a least squares calculation. Three patterns of sales trends are illustrated in Exhibit 16.1.

Company A shows fairly steady growth, and a compound growth rate calculated between years 1 and 10 is a reasonable measure of trend. It can be presumed to have some predictive power, subject to an analysis of all factors affecting sales.

Company B shows a cyclical pattern with a compound growth rate calculated from year 1 to year 10 of 9.2 percent, although total sales for 10 years are the same as Company A. Obviously, a growth rate calculated from the bottom of one cycle to the peak of another one does not provide a sound basis for prediction. Two better methods can be used. One is to measure from one peak to the next peak (or from trough to trough). Thus year 1 (trough) to year 7 (trough) shows a compound growth rate of 6.0 percent; or year 4 (peak) to year 10 (peak), a rate of 1.9 percent. A second method is to fit a least squares trend line to the data. The slope of this line shows a growth rate of 4.8 percent, which is probably a more realistic long-term measure for this company.

Company C experiences an explosive sales growth at the end of the decade, enabling it to attain the same 10-year total as Companies A and B. The compound growth rate over the whole period is 10.4 percent, and the least squares growth rate is 9.1 percent. When it is realized that the growth rate in the first 8 years is only 5.1 percent compared with 31.3 percent in the last 2, the 10-year compound growth fails to describe the sales trend. In fact, there is no satisfactory measure to project the sales trends of Company C in comparison with the other companies. The company's recent sales experience must be analyzed before any projection can be made.

(ii) Variability. These three companies illustrate widely differing sales patterns, leading to different levels of confidence in their persistence in future years. One indication of variability is the simple year-to-year percentage change in sales. Company A's year-to-year increases are close to the 10-year compound growth rate, whereas Company B swings widely above and below its 10-year trend line growth of 4.8 percent annually. The standard deviation is the statistical tool that measures the variation from the trend line. For Company A it can be expected that about two-thirds of the expected values will fall within ±5.3, or 18 percent of the mean, whereas for Company C the range is ±9.2, or 32 percent of the mean. A's variability is less, and the certainty of its sales trend is greater, although not absolute.

(iii) Components of Sales Trends.   A sales trend can be understood better if the components of price and volume can be separated. Not many companies provide such information, but it often can be derived indirectly. If Company A sells a single product, the price of which is known, volume can be easily computed. For Company A, for example, the price rose at a 4.0 percent annual rate during the 10-year period.

Volume growth can be calculated as follows:

$$\text{Volume growth over 10 years} = \frac{\text{Sales (year 10)}}{\text{Price (year 10)}} - \frac{\text{Sales (year 1)}}{\text{Price (year 1)}}$$

By dividing year 10 sales by year 10 price we obtain a volume figure for that year. A similar exercise for the base year (year 1) provides a comparable figure. Conversely, volume may be known (e.g., steel production), so price can be derived from this equation, substituting volume for price.

Occasionally the components of sales change are presented in a variance analysis in an annual report. This is illustrated as follows:

Total sales increase in year 2	$150,000
Increase due to price ((Price 2 − Price 1) × Volume 1)	86,000
Increase due to volume ((Volume 2 − Volume 1) × Price 2)	64,000

In large diversified companies, gross sales are an aggregate of many diverse activities, and many other components of sales should be analyzed. In recent years companies have been required to report sales (and earnings and other data) of the principal segments and geographic sources of the business.

Within a single product line or segment there are also differences in the characteristics of sales components. One example is sales versus service revenues, or sales versus leasing. Most companies provide this breakdown where it is important. Sales of an expensive machine (e.g., a computer) may be expected to fluctuate from year to year, but service revenues will tend to build up steadily as the number of installed machines increases. Alternatively, buyers may shift between buying and leasing, although product shipments remain unchanged. The volatility and the current profitability of these revenue streams are quite different, and both must be analyzed to fully understand the sales trend.

When examining sales trends, the analyst must be wary of the effects of acquisitions and divestitures as well as the effects of changes in exchange rates. These issues are discussed in Subsections 16.3(h) and 16.3(j).

(iv) Comparative Trend Analysis.   A company cannot be analyzed in a vacuum. The outside forces affecting it and its responses are an important aspect of financial analysis. Sales can be tested against competition in the company's markets and general economic trends. There are a number of ways to do this, none very difficult. Exhibit 16.2 is illustrative. Company D is gaining a share of the market. Company E had an earlier cyclical recovery but merely maintained its position relative to the economy over the full business cycle. Its greater cyclical variability is an important aspect of the appraisal of the company. Company F's slow revenue growth is due to lagging volume compared to its industry.

Although the comparison of similar companies is a necessary part of analysis, it is fraught with peril. No two companies are identical. Differences in sales trends may result from any of the following:

- End markets may have different growth or cyclical characteristics.
- Major customers may differ; differences in customer sales trends will be reflected in new orders.

Year	Company D Sales % Industry	Company E Sales % GNP	Company F Volume Index[a]	
			Company	Industry
1	23.5	.00065	100	100
2	27.4	.00072	105	105
3	28.1	.00075	112	117
4	29.3	.00070	113	120
5	30.2	.00068	115	123
5-year average	27.7	.00070	109	113

[a]Year 1 = 100.

Exhibit 16.2   Comparative sales trend analysis.

- Companies that are considered secondary suppliers will show greater variability than "primary" suppliers.
- Some companies have greater vertical integration than others in the same industry.
- In industries with high transportation costs, regional conditions may vary greatly (e.g., cement).

(c) COST AND EXPENSE ANALYSIS.   Many of the same analytical techniques applied to revenue analysis can also be utilized in expense analysis, but the predominant technique is profit margin analysis. The great diversity of business operations precludes any general standard for such ratios; they are best used in internal trend analysis and company comparisons.

(i) Classification of Costs.   In a typical industrial company the principal expense categories are cost-of-goods-sold and selling, general, and administrative expenses. Sometimes these categories are subdivided. Sometimes depreciation is shown separately rather than included in other categories. Because of these and other classification problems, these categories are rarely comparable from company to company.

For purposes of analysis, one should focus on gross profit (sales less cost of goods sold) or on operating income (before other income and expense, interest income and expense, and income taxes). Using income before interest charges facilitates the comparison of companies with different financial structures.

(ii) Margin Analysis.   A company's ability to control costs in relation to revenues is an important factor in earning power. Five ratios or margins are generally used to measure cost control in industrial companies, as follows:

1. $\text{Gross margin} = 1 - \dfrac{\text{Cost of good sold}}{\text{Sales}}$

2. $\text{Expense ratio} = \dfrac{\text{Selling, general and administrative expenses}}{\text{Sales}}$

3. $\text{Operating margin} = \dfrac{\text{Operating income}}{\text{Sales}}$

4. $\text{Pretax margin} = \dfrac{(\text{Operating income} + \text{other income} - \text{interest})}{\text{Sales}}$

5. $\text{Profit margin} = \dfrac{\text{Net income before extraordinary items}}{\text{Sales}}$

These ratios must be interpreted in relation to other companies in the same industry and over time within the company. Any given ratio has little meaning out of context. Margins must also be related to other facets of the business, such as the capital required and the turnover ratio, as will be explained in a later part of this section.

For example, a retail food chain typically will show a low operating margin because it rapidly passes through a high volume of products at a very low unit cost. Although a low operating margin would normally suggest considerable uncertainty about the continuity of operating income, the rapid turnover provides more opportunity to keep selling prices in line with costs.

In contrast, a capital intensive industrial company may have a much wider operating margin, but typically it will have a higher proportion of fixed costs and more volatile sales. An electric utility company will show both a wide operating margin and steady sales, but its capital costs (e.g., interest) are also large.

Some lines of business have a very low gross margin, that is, the cost of the product is a high percentage of sales, meaning that value added by the company is modest. In such cases, the dynamics of expenses can be related better to the gross margin than to sales. Today, commercial banks offset interest costs, which are far larger than any other expense, against interest income to derive a net interest margin. In effect, this spread is the real measure of a bank's revenue from its lending and investing activities. Other expenses are measured against the total of net interest income and other revenues, such as trust fees.

(iii) Analytical Adjustments.   When possible, nonrecurring items should be removed from earnings prior to analysis. These items include the following:

- Gains or losses from refinancing
- Capital gains or losses on asset sales
- Write-offs, especially "restructurings provisions" [see Subsection 16.3(f)]
- Transitional impacts of new accounting standards
- Results of discontinued operations
- Foreign currency translation gain or loss
- Settlement in a major lawsuit

These items may or may not have great significance for cash flow, but usually they are nonrecurring or infrequent, and therefore cannot be projected in an assessment of future earning power. A loss on a facility closedown is largely an accounting adjustment that in effect recognizes a prior loss of earning power. It will not affect future years except perhaps indirectly in sales and costs. Foreign currency translation gains and losses are accounting adjustments arising from fluctuations in foreign exchange, and their economic significance to the business is often hard to judge. A gain from debt retirement is really a capital transaction unrelated to the operations of the business.

(iv) Operating Leverage.   The analyst should attempt to separate variable, semivariable, and fixed costs. This will permit better analysis of cost control in a fluctuating business environment. Companies usually do not reveal this information, but an analysis of cost and expense movement over a business cycle may give a general indication. All costs are variable in the long run but over a business cycle, high fixed costs have a leverage effect on operating income.

In Exhibit 16.3, Company X's variable costs are a steady 50 percent of sales, whereas its fixed costs average only 20 percent of sales. Company Y has only 20 percent in variable costs but 40 percent in fixed costs and 30 percent in semivariable costs. In year 1, sales and profit margins are the same. With 10 percent increase in sales in year 2, Company Y shows a 65 percent gain in operating income compared with 45 percent for X. In the third year sales drop 18 percent, and Y suffers a 76 percent drop in operating income compared with 62 percent for X. Company Y has a more highly leveraged operating structure, making its income more sensitive to a change in sales.

	Company X			Company Y		
	Year 1	Year 2	Year 3	Year 1	Year 2	Year 3
Sales Expense	$1,000	$1,100	$900	$1,000	$1,100	$900
Variable[a]	$ 500	$ 550	$450	$ 200	$ 220	$180
% of sales	50.0	50.0	50.0	20.0	20.0	20.0
Semivariable[b]	200	205	195	300	315	280
% of sales	20.0	18.6	21.7	30.0	28.6	31.1
Fixed[c]	200	200	200	400	400	400
% of sales	20.0	18.2	22.2	40.0	36.4	44.4
Total expense	900	955	845	900	935	860
% of sales	90.0	86.8	93.9	90.0	85.0	95.5
Operating income	$ 100	$ 145	$ 55	$ 100	$ 165	$ 40
% of sales	10.0	13.2	6.1	10.0	15.0	4.5

[a]Variable costs: direct labor, materials, and supplies.
[b]Semivariable costs: administrative expense, fuel, maintenance.
[c]Fixed costs: depreciation, rents, and interest.

Exhibit 16.3   Operating leverage.

(v) **Fixed Charges.**   Fixed charges consist of interest and related expense and an interest factor on capitalized leases, both of which are contractual commitments and are deductible for income taxes. Preferred stock dividends are a fixed charge ahead of the common stock, but they lack the firm contractual commitment of debt and they are not deductible for income taxes.

The key measure of the burden of fixed charges is the interest coverage ratio. This is calculated as follows:

$$\text{Interest coverage ratio} = \frac{\text{Income before interest and taxes}}{\text{Fixed charges}}$$

This is expressed as "times fixed charges covered," for example, 2.75 × (times).

If there are senior and subordinated classes of debt, the coverage ratio for the senior debt is calculated separately by using only the interest cost of the senior debt as the divisor. Coverage for the subordinated debt is calculated on an overall basis, as above.

Interest on borrowed funds used for large construction and development projects is now required to be capitalized under Statement of Financial Accounting Standards (SFAS) No. 34, "Capitalization of Interest Cost." However, such capitalized interest should be added to interest expense in computing coverage ratios. Nor should interest earned be deducted from interest payable, although it can be included with other income. The bondholder is interested in earnings protection for all interest, regardless of accounting reductions.

The quality perception of fixed income securities is heavily influenced by the coverage ratio. But here again the ratio must be related to the type of business. A ratio of 2.50 times for an electric utility is satisfactory because earnings are stable and it is a regulated monopoly providing a basic service. For an industrial company, a ratio of 5.00 × or 6.00 × would be more appropriate for a highly rated issue because of more variable earnings in competitive markets.

The margin of safety is another ratio used to measure the adequacy of protection for fixed charges.

$$\text{Margin of safety} = \frac{\text{Income after fixed charges before income taxes}}{\text{Sales}}$$

It is simply the percentage of revenues remaining after fixed charges or, in other words, the pretax margin. In terms of a bond, it shows the percentage by which revenue can decline without endangering full coverage of interest expense. It is useful in conjunction with the coverage ratio. For example, a company may have a small debt and a correspondingly high interest coverage ratio, but a low margin of safety. This could indicate that any adversity could quickly wipe out interest coverage despite the low debt.

(vi) Preferred Dividend Coverage.   The coverage of preferred dividends should be calculated on a comprehensive basis, using the following formula:

$$\text{Preferred dividend coverage} = \frac{\text{Income before interest and taxes}}{\text{Fixed charges} + \text{Pretax preferred dividends}}$$

Because preferred dividends are paid out of income after income taxes, they must be "grossed up" before being inserted in the formula. Preferred dividends must be divided by (1 minus the marginal income tax rate) to compute the pretax earnings needed to pay the preferred dividend.

The prior deductions method, which simply divides net income by preferred dividends, is not a permissible method unless there is no interest expense. Otherwise this method gives a misleading indication of coverage (see Exhibit 16.4 for fixed charge coverage ratios).

(d) INCOME TAX ANALYSIS.   In 1993, SFAS 109 (1992) replaced prior standards. The accounting methods themselves are described in Chapter 24 of this *Handbook*. The purpose of this section is to discuss the information available from footnote disclosures required by SFAS 109 and the inferences than can be drawn from such data.

Pervasive differences in the objectives and methods of financial reporting and accounting for income taxes generate temporary differences in periodic tax liability and tax expense. (Note: Some differences are permanent in that revenues and expenses in the financial statements are never recognized on the tax return and vice versa. These differences are not discussed here since they do not generate deferred taxes and their cash consequences are unambiguous.) These differences are reported as deferred tax liabilities or deferred tax assets but their cash consequences are not always obvious. In the United States, these differences are usually significant because tax-book conformity is required only in the case of last-in, first-out inventory valuation.

The SFAS 109 uses a modified liability method; the balance sheet accrual is intended to represent the future cash flow consequences of past events. Thus, a change in tax rates results in the balance sheet asset or liability being "marked to market" to reflect that change.

Debt

$50, senior: Annual interest charges @ 10% = $5
$25, junior (subordinated): Annual interest charges @ 12% = $3
1 million shares of preferred stock: Annual dividend @ $1/share = $1

Partial Income Statement

Income before interest and taxes	$16
Interest: Senior debt	(5)
Junior debt	(3)
Pretax income	$ 8
Taxes @ 37.5%	3
Net income	5
Preferred dividend	(1)
Net income available for common stock	$ 4

Coverage Ratios

Senior debt: $16 \div 5 = 3.2x$
Total debt: $16 \div 8 = 2.0x$ (Not $11 \div 3 = 3.67$)
Preferred: $16 \div (5 + 3 + (1 \div .625)) = 16 \div 9.6 = 1.67x$ (Not $5 \div 1 = 5.0$)

Exhibit 16.4   Fixed charge coverage ratios for Company P ($ in millions).

Deferred tax assets are fully recorded under the new standard. However, it requires firms to record a valuation allowance when an evaluation of future taxable income suggests that it is more likely than not that some or all of the deferred tax assets may not be realized. As changes in the valuation allowance are included in periodic income tax expense, such changes affect reporting earnings and can be used to manage earnings. In addition, changes in the valuation allowance complicate the assessment of effective tax rates.

Statement No. 109 also changed some of the "indefinite reversal" provisions of Accounting Principles Board (APB) Opinion Nos. 23 and 24. In particular, companies are required to provide deferred taxes on the reinvested earnings (subsequent to December 15, 1992) of domestic affiliates accounted for under the equity method. However, the provision of deferred taxes on the undistributed earnings of foreign affiliates remains discretionary.

The major issue of deferred tax accounting remains largely unsolved. What the financial analyst would like to know is what income tax payments (or refunds) can be expected in future years. Unfortunately, no mechanical accounting method answers that question satisfactorily.

Fortunately, the disclosure requirements of SFAS No. 109, which expanded those of prior standards, provide useful raw material for analysis of the impact of income taxes on the firm. A brief discussion of the usefulness of these disclosures follows.

1. Disclosure of all deferred tax assets and liabilities (prior to SFAS No. 109, some were buried in other accounts). The required disclosure of all components of tax expense is also helpful. With these disclosures it should be possible to reconcile income tax expense with income taxes paid (often impossible given past disclosures).

2. Reconciliation of effective tax rate with statutory rate: This permits the analyst to understand the permanent differences between taxable and reported income as well as sources of income with tax rates that differ significantly from the statutory rate. This information facilitates forecasts of future net income under varying assumptions regarding the sources of pretax income.

3. Sources of deferred tax assets and liabilities for the current year and on a cumulative basis: This permits the analyst to evaluate the financial reporting methods of the firm. Significant sources may include depreciation, impairment, and other "restructuring" charges, revenue and expense recognition methods, and postretirement benefits.

4. The amount of any valuation allowance and the change for the year. As the valuation allowance is highly judgmental, this disclosure makes the decision transparent so that the analyst can evaluate both the decision (which may signal operating expectations) and its impact on reported income and equity.

5. Unrecognized tax loss carryforwards, which may be available, in some circumstances, to shelter future income.

6. Unrecognized deferred tax liabilities related to the reinvested earnings of foreign affiliates and (pre-1992) domestic affiliates. This disclosure facilitates the comparison of firms making different choices in this area. In addition, the income tax effects of possible intercompany dividends and dispositions can be evaluated.

Ultimately, therefore, as in most areas of financial reporting, disclosure requirements are the most valuable provisions of the new accounting standard. While companies must report a precise number for income tax expense, disclosures permit analysts to better understand the range of possible outcomes.

(e) EARNING POWER ANALYSIS.   Having analyzed reported net income, the analyst can proceed to the comparison of one company with another and to the projection of future earnings. The types of ratio and trend analysis already discussed are applicable here:

- Net income margin on sales

- Trend over last 5 and 10 years, measured by compound growth rate, least squares trend, or averages for periods
- Variability over the same period as measured by the standard deviation from trend, or between cyclical peaks and troughs

These measures can be used to compare the company with others in the same industry and with companies in other industries. These comparisons will usually reveal which companies have the most favorable trends in earning power.

16.3 ACCOUNTING AND REPORTING ISSUES

The impacts of various accounting and reporting issues on reported earnings, analyses of risk, and earning power are discussed below.

(a) THE QUALITY OF EARNINGS.   Financial statements prepared in accordance with generally accepted accounting principles (GAAP) may fall short of meeting the needs of investment analysts for various reasons. GAAP-based financial reporting provides a record of significant accounting events but does not report all relevant economic events. The selection and quantification of economic events qualifying for accounting recognition is highly variable across firms. Within GAAP, managements have considerable latitude in their choice of methods (last-in, first-out [LIFO] versus first-in, first-out, [FIFO]; accelerated versus straight-line depreciation) and estimates (service lives; residual values) resulting in inconsistencies and measurement biases across firms and over time. Thus, an evaluation of the "Quality of Earnings" is an essential component of a comprehensive analysis of financial statements.

Bernstein and Siegel define quality of earnings as a measure (qualitative) of the comparative integrity, reliability, and predictive ability of reported earnings.[1] Thus, the quality of earnings is determined by the degree to which selected accounting policies reflect economic reality and represent future earning power. This determination must be made across firms and over time for the firm, allowing an assessment of comparability (similarity of accounting policies between companies) and consistency (continuity over time). Various accounting issues requiring particular attention are discussed in the following sections.

(b) INVENTORY.   The principal methods of valuing inventories are LIFO, FIFO, and average cost, which are explained in Chapter 16. LIFO accounting results in lower reported income, lower current taxes, and better forecasts of future earnings when price levels are increasing and inventory quantities are constant or increasing. Despite tax benefits, many major industrial companies have not adopted LIFO. Earnings comparisons across firms can be misleading if no adjustment is made for differences in inventory accounting. Average cost earnings will fall between those computed using LIFO or FIFO. The LIFO earnings of a FIFO firm may be approximated by computing the LIFO effect as follows:

$$\text{LIFO effect} = \text{FIFO beginning inventory} \times \text{percent change in}$$

$$\text{specific price level (for major segment(s) of the firm)}$$

The LIFO effect is the difference in cost of goods sold between the LIFO and FIFO methods. Given the effective tax rate for the firm, the impact on income taxes and reported income can be determined. It is easier to determine the FIFO earnings of a LIFO firm since it will disclose the LIFO reserve or the difference between LIFO and FIFO ending inventories. The difference between

---

[1] L. A. Bernstein and J. G. Siegel, "The Concept of Earnings Quality," *Financial Analysts Journal*, Vol. 35, No. 4, July–August 1979, pp. 72–75.

two consecutive LIFO reserves is the LIFO effect for that time period. The LIFO reserve should be added to the LIFO ending inventory balance to approximate the current cost of inventories on hand. Earnings reported using LIFO will generally not reflect the same trend/growth rate represented by the same earnings stream under FIFO. A liquidation of LIFO layers will increase reported income and current taxes. This impact on net income is generally disclosed in the footnotes. However, liquidations may signal changes in future earnings and/or investment in the affected segment. The analyst should not confuse liquidations with declines in the LIFO reserve that are a result of decreases in inventory prices.

LIFO inventory accounting comes in different forms. A firm may use a single LIFO "pool" or many pools; that choice has an impact on LIFO liquidations. Pools generally contain products that are substantially identical. A second variant is pricing, as firms can construct internal price indices rather than using government produced indices. Users should watch for "changes in accounting estimates" in these areas. Note that the LIFO variant used for financial reporting purposes may differ from that used for tax reporting, despite the conformity requirement.

(c) DEPRECIATION. Periodic depreciation expense allocates the cost of long-lived assets to operating periods during which the assets are used in production. The expense is a function of the chosen depreciation method, asset lives, and residual values. Although a substantial number of companies use accelerated depreciation methods for income tax reporting, few do so for financial reporting. Those that do so will report lower and more conservative net income. The cash impact of depreciation is due to the tax savings generated by the depreciation method used for income tax reporting. The use of different depreciation methods in tax and financial reporting results in a difference between the tax liability and reported tax expense—that is, a deferred tax expense, which is disclosed in the footnotes. This deferred tax amount divided by the federal statutory tax rate gives an approximation of the difference in depreciation expense and can be used to adjust reported net income. Since depreciation expense is based on historical cost, it tends to overstate income when price levels are increasing. Thus, accelerated depreciation methods may provide a reasonable approximation of replacement or current cost depreciation.

Asset lives also affect reported depreciation expense. Management has some latitude in the determination of asset lives since judgment and experience are used in this choice. Footnote disclosure of depreciation policies can be used to compare asset lives of similar companies in the same industry. A comparison of the ratio of depreciation expense to gross fixed assets will frequently eliminate the effects of different depreciation curves and different useful lives.

The average age of fixed assets used in operations may be computed by dividing the accumulated depreciation by depreciation expense. The ratio of gross property, plant, and equipment to depreciation expense reflects the average life assumption used in reporting. Increasing investment due to expansion or declining investment due to deteriorating business conditions will distort these ratios, suggesting the need for caution in interpreting trends in these ratios over time and across firms.

The third component of the depreciation calculation is residual value. Changes in estimates of residual value reduce the depreciable base and, therefore, depreciation expense.

The depreciation policy adopted for idled/underutilized facilities should be analyzed for inferences regarding the quantification and timing of unamortized costs expected to be recovered through future operations. Changes in depreciation policy may mask a deteriorating financial condition or pervasive asset impairment.

(d) EXPENSE DEFERRALS. Discretionary costs are subject to management control and earnings can be managed when expenses (such as marketing or research) are accelerated or deferred. The decision whether to capitalize or expense can also significantly affect reported income. The capitalization decision also increases reported cash flow from operations as expenditures are included in cash flow for investment. For example, some firms capitalize software development costs while others do not. While SFAS No. 34 requires the capitalization of interest, not all firms do so.

Particular areas of concern are:

- Deferral of marketing expenditures and sales commissions
- Accrual or deferral of major maintenance expenditures
- Credit loss accruals
- Warranty accruals

(e) REVENUE RECOGNITION.   Revenue is generally recognized when goods are sold or as services are rendered. Since the activities of one period may generate cash flows in subsequent periods, both the quantification and timing of revenue recognition present problems. The timing of sales and services, uncertainties regarding the collection of expected inflows, and expected future costs of providing services should be evaluated in the context of the firm's operations and compared to prevailing industry practices. Various specialized industries including franchising, real estate, motion pictures, and television require particular attention. The increasing emphasis on fee-based services in the financial sector of the economy and the growth of leasing also present challenging revenue recognition problems.

Revenue recognition has been a particular problem in recent years. Particular areas of concern include:

- Sales incentives such as discounts, undocumented right of return, and the granting of stock options
- Barter arrangements that create difficult measurement issues
- Recording revenue when an agreement is signed rather than over the agreement's term
- Recognizing revenues for which the firm is merely an agent
- Reporting shipping and handling costs as revenues
- Premature recognition of revenues although the earnings process is not yet complete

(f) DISCONTINUED OPERATIONS, EXTRAORDINARY GAINS (LOSSES), AND UNUSUAL ITEMS.   The assessment of future earning power is a function of the predictability of income statistics. Thus, analysts are concerned with revenues and expenses directly related to the normal and recurring operations since they reflect future earning power. The inclusion of unusual or nonrecurring events would distort the predictability of reported income. Inconsistently applied definitions or interpretations of recurring versus nonrecurring events would reduce comparability across firms and may provide a basis for manipulation or smoothing of income. However, unusual and extraordinary data may be relevant to the evaluation of managerial efficiency.

Existing reporting standards require separate reporting of material, unusual, *and* infrequent events in the income statement. These events are evaluated with reference to the specific and similar firms in the same industry in light of the firm's environment. Qualifying extraordinary items are reported separately, net of tax effects, after operating income. The related earnings-per-share amounts also are disclosed separately. Examples include expropriation of assets by foreign governments and gains or losses due to debt extinguishment.

Events that are either unusual or infrequent but not both may be reported on a separate line in the income statement but cannot be reported net of taxes. Additional footnote disclosure often accompanies these events, and it may provide insights into their effect on future earning power and cash flows.

SFAS No. 121 requires the recognition of impairments when one or more impairment indicators are present and the expected gross cash flows from the assets are less than their carrying amount. The loss is measured as the difference between the fair value of the asset(s) or the present value of the cash flows and the carrying value of the asset(s). This two-step approach to recognition and measurement will leave the timing of recognition and amount of the impairment loss substantially at the discretion of management.

Impairments of long-lived assets, write-downs or write-offs (henceforth inclusively referred to as *impairments*), and restructurings are generally reported on a separate line in the income statement. Impairments and write-downs are due to substantial changes in technological or market conditions and eliminate past cash flows related to assets the firm may idle or continue to operate at reduced levels. Their contribution to future earnings and cash flows is uncertain as to timing and amount.

Restructuring provisions often include impairments and may reflect significant reorganizations of business. The nonimpairment related components of restructuring include termination or severance costs in addition to various other current and future cash outflows.

The operating results of and the gain (loss) due to disposal of qualifying discontinued segments also must be reported separately, net of taxes, after income from continuing operations. The related earnings-per-share effects also are presented separately. Discontinued segments are reported separately if their assets, results of operations, and other activities can be clearly segregated from the assets, results of operations, and other activities of the firm. This segregation must be accomplished physically, operationally, and for financial reporting purposes.

(g) CHANGING PRICES. As financial statements are largely based on historical costs, price changes tend to reduce the usefulness of such statements. Whereas periods of high inflation have ushered in attempts to provide inflation-adjusted data, most recently with SFAS No. 33, most financial statements provide little assistance to the user in gauging the effects of changing prices on the enterprise.

SFAS No. 33 employed two complementary approaches: Common dollar reporting, which uses a unit of general purchasing power as the unit of measure and has the advantages of ease of preparation and ease of audit, and current cost reporting, which uses so-called current buying prices as the measurement attribute. Chapter 15 discusses those approaches, the reasons SFAS No. 33 failed, and why that was a mixed blessing.

In the case of monetary assets, adjustment is generally not required because price changes have little direct impact on the fair value of such assets. The areas of interest are generally "physical assets," especially inventories, fixed assets, and investments.

When the LIFO method of inventory valuation is used, the analyst can use required disclosures to make the necessary adjustments. Adding back the LIFO reserve (which must be disclosed) provides a reasonable estimate of the current value of inventories. When FIFO or average cost is used, inventories are already stated at close to current value.

The current cost of fixed assets is more difficult to estimate. Although both Accounting Series Release (ASR) No. 190 and SFAS No. 33 required estimates of such current cost from companies subject to their requirements, there was considerable leeway in application. Going back to such data (SFAS No. 33 data was last required in 1985) may provide a starting point, but great care must be taken. Some data were arrived at by simply indexing original cost using general construction cost indicators. Such approximations will fail to capture the true value of real estate holdings.

For public companies, the 10-K annual report filed with the SEC may contain a considerable amount of information about the location and extent of real estate holdings. For some categories (shopping centers, hotels, etc.) industry rules of thumb may enable one to translate physical data (e.g., square footage) into market value data.

Clues may be available in the financial statements. Real estate taxes paid may indicate assessed values. When borrowings are secured by specific holdings, some inference about value can be made. The income (or cash flow) generated by real estate investments may be an indication of value. Assets acquired via a purchase method acquisition can be assumed to have been written up at that time; if goodwill was created, one can assume that the write-up was the maximum possible.

When natural resources are included in fixed assets, additional information may be provided. Companies with reserves of oil and natural gas are required (SFAS No. 69) to provide information about the physical quantities and their discounted present value based on current costs and prices. Although such data are based on estimates and preparers strongly discourage their use, these data are widely used in the financial community to value such reserves. For other natural resource holdings (coal, precious metals, etc.), only physical data must be disclosed. The analyst must make assumptions in order to value these holdings, but the result is usually closer to fair value than the historical cost of such holdings.

Investments may also require adjustment. If investee financial statements are available, they can be used to value the holding, perhaps by comparison with public companies in the same industry. In making such comparisons, the user should take care to adjust for differences in accounting methods and financial leverage. When investments include holdings of public companies, current market value can be used in place of cost.

The discussion thus far has focused on balance sheet valuation. However, the income statement should also be adjusted for changing prices. To the extent that income includes "holding gains" resulting from price increases, whether realized or unrealized, the financial markets may discount reported earnings.

In the area of inventories, the use of LIFO removes the effect of rising prices from reported earnings. For non-LIFO inventories an approximation must be made. If the company is in one line of business, a government or private price index may be employed to estimate the inflation component. The percentage price change should be multiplied by the starting inventory, and the result (after tax) should be subtracted from operating net income. For multiple lines of business, this should be done on a segmented basis when possible.

Current cost depreciation may be difficult to estimate because of the required assumptions. If the amount of capital spending that does not create higher capacity can be estimated, it may be the best answer. This is because economic depreciation can be defined as the expenditures necessary to leave end-of-year capacity equal to that at the beginning of the period.

(h) FOREIGN OPERATIONS.   Financial statements of companies with operations outside of the United States are made more complex by the effects of changing currency rates. Despite some opinion to the contrary, SFAS No. 52 *did not* result in the removal of all such impacts from financial statements.

The functional currencies chosen by a company for its foreign operations have an important effect on how currency changes affect reported earnings. Assets and liabilities of foreign subsidiaries are remeasured from local currencies into functional currencies using the principles of SFAS No. 8. Thus, all translation gains and losses resulting from the remeasurement process are included in earnings immediately. In some cases, where the U.S. dollar has been chosen as the functional currency for all foreign operations, there is considerable potential earnings volatility.

Under SFAS No. 52, the translation of functional currency balance sheets into the reporting currency (U.S. dollar for U.S. companies) generates gains or losses that are deferred to a separate component of stockholders equity. Such gains or losses accumulate indefinitely unless a foreign subsidiary is sold or impairment is recognized.

The U.S. dollar must be used as the functional currency in a hyperinflationary economy (defined as three-year cumulative inflation exceeding 100 percent). As a result translation gains and losses are included in earnings.

The difference between remeasurement (SFAS No. 8) and translation (SFAS No. 52) is not simply that of recognition of gains and losses. The balance sheet exposure is defined differently as well. Remeasurement uses the temporal method. For most companies, this means that inventories and fixed assets are translated using historical rates; almost all other assets and liabilities are translated at current exchange rates. The exposure to currency fluctuation under SFAS No. 8 is, in practice, the net monetary asset position. Under SFAS No. 52, in contrast, the exposure is the net investment, regardless of the composition of assets and liabilities. It is, therefore, quite possible for a currency rate change to result in gains under remeasurement (SFAS No. 8) but losses under translation (SFAS No. 52).

Unfortunately, the disclosure requirements of SFAS No. 52 are minimal. Unless the financial statement preparer is willing to provide additional information about functional currencies, the analyst must resort to guessing.

Even when the translation effects of foreign currency changes are excluded from the income statement, reported sales and earnings may be materially affected by such changes. Revenues and costs incurred in foreign currencies are translated into the reporting currency using average exchange rates for the period. When the reporting currency rises, for example, foreign currency earnings and sales will appear to be smaller. Given the large fluctuations of the dollar against other major currencies in recent years, these impacts have had a significant impact on the apparent sales and earnings trends of companies with large foreign operations.

Prior to the effective date of SFAS No. 95, cash flow statements were often distorted by currency rate changes. Real changes and translation effects were mixed together, reducing the usefulness of cash flow data. SFAS No. 95, however, requires that reporting currency cash flow statements be translated directly from functional currency statements. As a result, translation impacts are excluded. Use of average exchange rates still has an impact on the trend of cash flow data, however.

The analysis of foreign operations cannot be confined to looking at the accounting consequences of exchange rate changes. Such changes may have real economic consequences that are quite different from the accounting impacts.

For foreign operations that are completely isolated from external influences, it may be possible to ignore the economic consequences of currency rate changes. In such cases, changes in the U.S. dollar equivalent of the subsidiary net worth may be a fair indicator of changes in economic net worth.

For most foreign operations, however, changing exchange rates do have an impact on local operations. To the extent that local operations compete with imports from or exports to other countries, currency rate changes will affect real profitability. Regardless of whether operations are accounted for using SFAS No. 8 or SFAS No. 52, it is unlikely that the accounting impacts will mirror the economic changes. In some cases (e.g., import competitive), the two may diverge; a rising local currency will increase the translated net worth while decreasing the real profitability (and hence real net worth) of the foreign subsidiary.

Analysis of a company with foreign operations, therefore, requires two types of analysis. First, the user must understand how the reported results of foreign operations have been affected by the rate changes. Second, he must examine the underlying economic relationships in order to understand the trend of real profitability of such operations.

(i) POSTEMPLOYMENT BENEFITS.   Companies with defined benefit pension plans must account for such plans in accordance with SFAS No. 87 issued in 1985. Because current accounting standards permit considerable latitude in making actuarial assumptions and provide for deferred recognition of differences between assumptions and realized results, both income statement and balance sheet may contain considerable "noise."

The balance sheet generally includes only the cumulative differences between accrued pension cost and contributions actually made. The best measure of pension fund status is normally the difference between the fair value of fund assets and the projected benefit obligation. The gap between the amounts reflected on the balance sheet and the funded status results from deferred recognition of actuarial gains and losses, plan amendments, and the initial impact of SFAS No. 87.

Replacing the amounts actually recognized with the funded status will reflect the actual plan status, as if the plan had been consolidated with the corporate parent. In some cases, when plan termination can be assumed, the accumulated benefit obligation may be a better measure of the liability. Note that both liability measures are highly sensitive to the choice of discount rate. That rate can vary from company to company and, for the same company, from year to year.

Pension cost and operation expense consists of four components: (1) service cost; (2) interest on the projected benefit obligation; and (3) assumed return on assets (ROA) may be considered the "normal" portion of pension cost; while (4) amortization components vary from year to year. Note that even the "normal" costs are sensitive to the choice of discount rate and assumed rate of ROA. Comparability and consistency cannot be assumed.

Issued in December 1990, SFAS No. 106 established new accounting standards for employers providing postemployment benefits other than pensions Other Post Employment Benefits(OPEB). The accounting for such benefits is discussed in Chapter 38.

From the analysis point of view, the new standard was an enormous improvement. As in the case of pensions (SFAS No. 87), disclosures permit analysts to see behind the accounting conventions to the economics of the plans.

In contrast to SFAS No. 87, SFAS No. 106 permitted two methods of adoption. Employers could either recognize the transition liability (plan assets less the accumulated postretirement benefit obligation) immediately or amortize that liability over the remaining service life of active plan participants (or, if greater, over 20 years). Because these plans were largely unfunded, the transition liability for many firms was very large.

Almost all firms chose to recognize the transition liability when adopting the standard, resulting in large reductions to earnings and equity in some cases. An extreme example was General Motors, which recognized an after-tax charge of $20.8 billion, reducing book value per share to $1.98 at December 31, 1992. Relatively few companies chose to amortize the transition liability; many that did so were regulated utilities.

There were several advantages of immediate recognition. First, future earnings were enhanced relative to amortization, due to the absence of amortization expense. Second, higher earnings and reduced equity sharply increased reported return on equity (ROE). Third, plan amendments that reduce benefits create positive amortization that increases future reported income.

The disclosure requirements of SFAS Nos. 87 and 106 were amended by SFAS No. 132 (1998). The major effect of the new standard is explicit disclosure of the effects of acquisitions, divestitures, plan amendments, and foreign currency changes on plan assets and liabilities. Prior to that standard, such events often precluded the analysis of economic changes (as opposed to changes recognized in the financial statements) in benefit plans during the period. SFAS No. 132 also requires explicit disclosure of such key amounts as employer contributions and benefit payments.

(i) Analysis of SFAS No. 106 Disclosures.   Because of the importance of transition method, determination of management choice in the area is the first priority. For firms that chose immediate recognition, plan status should be examined, in the same way as the status of pension plans is reviewed. For firms that chose amortization of the transition liability, the (after-tax) unrecognized liability should be deducted from net worth. Amortizing firms will also report reduced future income relative to firms choosing immediate recognition; such amortization should be added back to reported income for comparability.

The second area of focus should be plan amendments. Because of the sharply rising cost of health care (the major component of the OPEB liability), many firms have introduced cost-sharing, caps, and other provisions intended to limit the employer obligation. Such plan amendments, in many cases, reduce the SFAS No. 106 liability. Such experience gains ultimately reduce plan expense and increase reported income.

(ii) Impact of Actuarial Assumptions.   Companies that have adopted SFAS No. 106 will have made a number of assumptions required to estimate both the benefit obligation and the postretirement benefit cost. Some of these assumptions, which must be disclosed, are the same assumptions required by SFAS No. 87:

- Discount rate
- Expected long-term rate of return on plan assets
- Rate of compensation growth

In the case of postretirement benefits, the last two of these items are rarely significant. Because plan assets are minimal, the return assumption has little impact on benefit cost. The rate of compensation growth is also unimportant for most nonpension benefit plans. The discount rate, however, remains highly significant.

Because the discount rate is used to compute the present value of the benefit obligation, the latter is highly sensitive to the choice of rate. If experience with pensions is a guide, there will be considerable variation among companies, and the chosen rate will vary over time. A higher discount rate will reduce the benefit obligation (and therefore the transition liability) and the service cost (present value of benefits earned in current year) component of benefit cost.

For postretirement health care benefits, which are the most important nonpension benefits in most cases, the benefit obligation is also extremely sensitive to assumptions regarding the future cost of medical care. The most important of these assumptions is the health care cost trend rate. SFAS No. 106 requires disclosure of:

- The trend rate used for the next year
- The pattern of rates used thereafter

For example, Westvaco discloses in its 1999 annual report that:

> The annual rate of increase in health care costs was assumed at six percent for 1998, five percent for 1999, and remaining at that level thereafter.

Such disclosures should be compared with those of other companies as lower trend rates result in reduced measures of both the liability and expense of postretirement health care plans.

These disclosures are intended to improve the comparability of the benefit obligations and costs of different employers when they are based on different assumptions. They also reveal the sensitivity of the benefit obligation to the trend rate assumption.

Du Pont, for example, disclosed (1994) that a one-percentage-point increase in trend rates for each future year would increase the Accumulated Pension Benefit Obligation APBO by approximately $251 million (4.6 percent) and the combined service and interest cost by approximately $44 million (16.5 percent). General Electric (GE), however, stated that a one percent increase in trend rates would not have had a material effect on the December 31, 1995, APBO or the annual cost of retiree health plans.

The different degree of sensitivity to changes in the trend rate is dramatic. The very low sensitivity of GE suggests that it has substantial cost-sharing provisions in its plan that limit the impact of unexpected inflation in health care costs. These provisions may include employee contributions and plan limits (caps). Du Pont appears to be much more at risk should health care costs exceed those assumed.

Westvaco, for example, discloses that a one-percentage-point increase (decrease) would increase (decrease) the APBO by $288,000 or 1.4 percent ($252,000 or 1.3 percent) and the combined service and interest cost would increase (decrease) by $70,000 or 2.9 percent ($63 or 2.6 percent). The low sensitivity of the Westvaco plans reflects lifetime benefit caps that limit the effect of unexpected inflation in health care costs.

In contrast, Ohio Casualty reports in its 2000 annual report that a 1 percent increase (decrease) in the assumed health care cost trend rate would increase (decrease) the APBO by 12 percent (10 percent) and benefit cost by 16 percent (13 percent). Companies like Ohio Casualty with higher sensitivity are much more at risk should health care costs exceed those assumed.

This two-sided disclosure shows the effect on the firm of both higher and lower health care inflation. Because cost sharing provisions in plans differ, these effects are neither uniform nor symmetrical.

(iii) Impact of Mergers and Acquisitions.   As in the case of pensions, postretirement benefits must be explicitly recognized when an acquisition is accounted for using the purchase method of accounting. The transition liability is therefore shown on the acquirer's balance sheet following the effective date of the acquisitions. Such recognition means that no adjustment to net worth is required for purposes of analysis except for gains and losses deferred subsequent to the date of the acquisition.

(j) MERGERS AND ACQUISITIONS.   Companies that make significant acquisitions transform their financial statements. Analysis of such companies must attempt to understand the effects of these transactions.

The adoption of SFAS No. 141 (2001) by the FASB eliminated use of the pooling method in the United States (but that method is still permitted by International Accounting Standards Board (IASB) standards and those of many other countries). Under the purchase method, the assets and liabilities of the acquired company are revalued to current market; any excess of the purchase price over the fair value of nets assets acquired become goodwill. SFAS No. 142 (2001) replaced goodwill amortization with the requirement of periodic assessment of goodwill for impairment.

Under the purchase method, the acquired firm is included in financial statements effective with the acquisition date. This creates an illusion of growth, especially when many small acquisitions make it impossible to track the contribution of each acquisition to operating results. Some firms become dependent on frequent acquisitions. If their stock price declines or access to credit is restricted, the growth trend may disappear.

The inclusion of the assets and liabilities of the acquired firm creates a discontinuity, instantly changing the financial ratios of the enterprise. The mix of historical cost (the assets and liabilities of the acquirer are not restated) and fair values (acquired firm) also hampers analysis. When the acquired firm was public and/or the acquisition is significant, there may be adequate disclosure to permit analysis of the effect of the acquisition on ratios and other performance indicators. When the acquired firm is reported as a segment, segment data may permit the analyst to track the effect of the acquisition on future operating results.

(k) PUSH DOWN ACCOUNTING. When an entity that has been acquired in an acquisition accounted for by the purchase method issues its own financial statements, those statements may reflect that transaction. In most cases the purchase method adjustments will be "pushed down" into the financial statements of the acquiree.

This is often seen when an acquired company has publicly held debt or preferred stock and, therefore, continues to publish separate financial statements. Such statements may also be presented to bank lenders, creditors, and customers.

The footnotes of these financial statements will normally show the effect of the purchase method adjustments. Users of such statements should bear in mind that the purchase method adjustments will distort ratios derived from both balance sheet and income statement data.

When companies that have been taken private through leveraged buyouts are taken public again, their statements will usually reflect "push down" accounting. Comparisons of such entities with others that have not gone through the revaluation process must take into account the effects of "push down" on the balance sheet and income statement.

(l) ANALYSIS OF SEGMENT DATA. SFAS No. 131 (1997) requires firms to provide data on each reportable segment of their business, both annually and for interim periods. The standard uses the management approach under which segment disclosures depend on the firm's internal organization. These data, augmented by the management discussion and analysis, are generally helpful in assessing the firm's operating results. However, the following four problems limit the usefulness of these data:

1. Reported segment data depend on the data reported to top management. Thus, firms that have skimpy internal information systems may report less data.
2. Segment data may be based on a different accounting system than the U.S. GAAP used for consolidated reporting. For example, data for regulated subsidiaries can be reported using regulatory GAAP if such data are used for internal reporting purposes. Similarly, foreign subsidiaries may report using local GAAP if such data are reported to top management.
3. Reported segment data depend on internal allocation policies. Thus comparisons of firms with different policies will be difficult. The main use of segment data will remain the analysis of trends within each company.
4. Geographic segment data reporting requirements are reduced from those of SFAS No. 14. Companies with large foreign operations, therefore, may provide less data about such segments, whose results may fluctuate due to economic and foreign currency volatility.

(m) ANALYSIS OF INTERIM RESULTS. When analyzing a company's financial statements, the latest annual data are normally supplemented by subsequent interim reports. Although use of interim data is essential because of its timeliness, some caution must be exercised.

For public companies, the user should always obtain the 10-Q quarterly reports filed with the SEC. Shareholder reports are often highly abbreviated. The 10-Q will contain financial statements that may be the equivalent of those found in the annual report except for footnotes.

The lack of footnotes sometimes limits the usefulness of interim reports. Whereas major accounting changes should be disclosed in the 10-Q, changes in estimates may not be. Some of the financial data may be condensed as well.

However, the major reason for caution in the use of interim data is the possibility of drawing misleading conclusions. Companies with a high degree of seasonality will produce interim results that are not an indicator of annual performance. Retailers, for example, produce a disproportionate part of earnings in the quarter that includes the Christmas selling period. A secondary peak around Easter is also normal. Interim results of seasonal companies should, therefore, be compared with the interim results of the corresponding period for prior years.

Accounting for income taxes may create some difficulty in interpreting interim results. As income tax expense is determined on an annual basis, interim tax expense must be estimated based on assumptions about the full year. Income tax expense for the first quarter, for example, must be determined by using the estimated tax rate for the full year. This rate must be reestimated each quarter. Changes in the estimated tax rate may distort quarterly results.

The LIFO inventory accounting is also determined on an annual basis and depends on prices and physical inventory levels at the end of the year. Here again, quarterly results depend on estimates of the year-end position, and a new estimate must be made each quarter.

More generally, there is more scope for companies to "manage" earnings on a quarterly basis. Expenses can be deferred (or accrued) in ways that would not be permitted at a fiscal year-end. In addition, transactions may be accounted for differently once the auditors have had their say.

Now, SFAS No. 131 (1997) requires abbreviated segment reporting on an interim basis, effective in 1999. Such data should facilitate the analysis of interim data and the use of such data to forecast future operating results.

(n) INTERNATIONAL REPORTING DIFFERENCES. The continued growth of international capital markets and trade has resulted in increasingly multinational enterprises with complex financial statements consolidating operations in various countries and prepared using their different reporting standards. However, the absence of globally accepted accounting standards makes it difficult to analyze and compare investments across countries. A brief discussion of various efforts to harmonize standards and achieve comparability follows.

(i) International Accounting Standards Board (IASB). Reorganized in 2001, the IASB has established standards that provide a credible alternative to U.S. GAAP. Its multinational members have produced 41 standards as of June 30, 2002, a Framework for the Preparation and Presentation of Financial Statements (similar to the FASB's conceptual framework), and a Standing Interpretations Committee (similar to the FASB's Emerging Issues Task Force [EITF]).

A number of non-U.S. companies have adopted International Accounting StandardsIAS standards, and they are expected to largely replace non-U.S. standards by 2005 for companies seeking access to capital markets. Full acceptance, however, depends on acceptance by the SEC for filings in the United States.

(ii) Reporting by Foreign Issuers in the United States. Foreign firms may directly sell securities in the United States or their securities may be traded as depositary shares American Depository Receipts(ADRs). These companies may follow the registration and reporting requirements applicable to domestic companies or elect to report as foreign registrants on Forms 20-F and 6-K, which are comparatively less comprehensive. Foreign firms filing Form 20-F must reconcile reported income and equity to U.S. GAAP. The reconciliations contain information useful in understanding accounting differences and comparing alternative investments.

(o) ANALYSIS OF INVESTMENTS.   The recognition of market values in historical cost financial statements has been one of the major accounting controversies of recent years. Strong support for "mark to market" accounting from the SEC has resulted in actions by the FASB that increase both disclosures of market values and their use in financial statements.

There are two basic issues. One is whether market value should supplant historic cost for investments. The argument for market value is greater relevance; the argument for historic cost is based on reliability. This issue, in practice, comes down to where to draw the line. There is little argument against carrying marketable equity securities, for example, at market value but enormous opposition to "marking to market" bank loans and fixed income investments expected to be held to maturity. A related issue concerns the advisability of marking to market only the asset side of the balance sheet while leaving liabilities at historic cost.

The second issue is the disposition of unrealized gains and losses. The choice is between immediate recognition in reported income and deferral via stockholders' equity.

SFAS No. 115 (1993) requires firms to categorize investments in debt and equity securities[2] as follows:

- *Debt securities classified as held to maturity*. Such investments are measured at amortized cost. Any realized gains or losses are included in reported income. This classification requires that the firm have both the intent and the ability to hold the securities until maturity.

- *Trading securities (debt and equity)*. These investments are measured at fair (market) value as current assets. Unrealized (as well as realized) gains and losses are included in reported income.

- *Securities available for sale (debt and equity)*. These securities, carried either as current or noncurrent assets, are also measured at fair value. However, unrealized gains and losses are reported as a separate component of stockholders' equity and excluded from reported earnings until sold.

SFAS No. 107 (1992) requires supplemental disclosure of market values for certain financial instruments, mainly investments. While exception is made when it is "impractical" to provide such disclosure, the result of the standard was a sharp increase in information available regarding the market value of long-term investments.

From the analysis point of view, there are three objectives when a firm has investments:

1. All investment income should be removed from operating income; market value changes in particular (whether realized or unrealized) obscure the reported results of operations.

2. The total return (including market value changes) should be compared with benchmark return data in order to evaluate the investment performance of the investments.

3. When analyzing the balance sheet, all portfolios should be marked to market, given the greater relevance of market values. For unrealized gains and losses, deferred taxes should be provided when sale would generate tax payments or refunds.

Based solely on management intent, SFAS No. 115 made no real difference as it simply replaced one arbitrary set of classifications with another. Investment returns will still have to be disentangled from operating results and investments carried at cost have to be marked to market for analysis.

The SFAS No. 107 disclosures, however limited, should be valuable in providing estimates of market value for asset classes other than highly marketable equity and debt (for which market

---

[2] The new standard maintained the prior practice of considering preferred shares with fixed redemption provisions (or which are redeemable at the option of the investor) as debt securities while nonredeemable preferreds are considered equity.

values are already disclosed). These disclosed values should be used, for analytic purposes, in place of historic cost in order to "mark to market" investment portfolios.

For financial institutions, however, the analyst must recognize that the assets are only half the story. To the extent that such institutions "match" the characteristics (such as duration) of asset and liability portfolios, market value changes for assets should be accompanied by approximately equal market value changes for liabilities. While, under SFAS No. 107, financial firms are not prohibited from disclosing market values for liabilities, few do so given difficult measurement problems. Thus, while the analyst may be able to evaluate the investment performance of the asset portfolios, an evaluation of the effect of market value changes on real (economic) net worth of financial institutions may be elusive.

(p) STOCK COMPENSATION PLANS.   SFAS No. 123 (1995) requires disclosure of extensive data regarding stock options and similar compensation plans. Firms are required to disclose the pro forma effect on net income and earnings per share (EPS) of recording the cost of such plans as an expense.

As the FASB made income statement recognition of stock compensation expense voluntary, virtually no firm included these costs in net income. However, a few firms (e.g., Coca-Cola and GE) have now decided to report these costs in net income. For analysis and valuation, when only pro forma data are available, they should be used instead of reported net income and EPS. As stock compensation plans often represent a significant element of compensation, omitting their cost overstates income relative to firms that use other forms of compensation that must be expensed.

(q) EARNINGS PER SHARE.   The SFAS No. 128 (1997) revised the reporting requirements; firms must now report basic EPS and diluted EPS.

Basic EPS excludes the effect of all dilutive securities; diluted EPS is very similar to the fully diluted EPS required by APB 15. For valuation, only diluted EPS should be used. For trend analysis, however, especially over short time periods, basic EPS may be more useful as it ignores the effect on EPS of stock prices.

16.4 BALANCE SHEET ANALYSIS

(a) ELEMENTS OF THE BALANCE SHEET.   The balance sheet reports the status of the company's financial position at a point in time, in contrast to the income statement, which reflects the flow of operating and earning activities during a period. Because earnings are essential for an enterprise's financial health, primary analytical emphasis has focused on earning power, but balance sheet analysis is equally important for a comprehensive understanding of a company's financial position and progress.

The main components of the balance sheet are the enterprise's assets or financial resources and the equities or claims against those resources. Assets represent probable future economic benefits obtained or controlled by the enterprise as a result of past transactions or events. Assets may be physical or tangible, for example, inventories, plant and equipment, and natural resources. Some assets are intangible in that they represent legal claims or rights to economic resources, for instance, patents and copyrights.

Equities are either external claims against the enterprise's resources (i.e., liabilities), or they represent the "residual" interests of the firm's owners, called *stockholders'* or *owners' equity*. Liabilities are probable future sacrifices of economic resources because of the enterprise's present obligations to transfer resources or provide services to external claimants in the future as a result of past transactions or events. Examples are accounts payable, taxes, and bonds payable.

Owners' equity is the residual interest of the owners of the enterprise and represents the excess of the assets over liabilities. It includes preferred and common stock, additional paid-in capital, and the earnings retained in the enterprise. Owners' equity represents the capital invested in the firm by its owners.

SFAS No. 130 (1997) reorganizes the stockholders' equity section by introducing the concept of comprehensive income, defined as:

> the change in equity of a business enterprise during a period from transactions and other events and circumstances from nonowner sources. It includes all changes in equity during a period except those resulting from investments by owners and distributions to owners (SFAC 6 (1985), paragraph 70, emphasis added).

Thus, comprehensive income includes both net income and direct-to-equity adjustments (other comprehensive income) such as:

- Cumulative translation adjustments under SFAS No. 52
- Minimum pension liability under SFAS No. 87
- Unrealized gains and losses on available-for-sale securities under SFAS No. 115
- Deferred gains and losses on cash flow hedges under SFAS No. 133

While SFAS No. 130 does not change financial statement measurements, it does organize the elements of other comprehensive income to facilitate their analysis. These elements represent economic changes that have not yet been recognized in net income, but often have implications for securities valuation; they can be ignored only at the analyst's peril.

Assets and liabilities are defined as economic resources and claims against these resources. However, the financial reporting system emphasizes the recording of accounting events, rather than economic events. Many relevant economic events receive no recognition in financial statements; for example, the impact of price-level changes on reported quantifications of assets and liabilities is virtually ignored since financial statements are based on historical costs.

The selection of economic events that receive accounting recognition is discretionary and highly variable across firms. Leases, which in substance may be installment purchases of assets, may not receive accounting recognition if the lease contract is structured to avoid capitalization criteria in accounting standards. Managements may also select from different methods and use different estimates in quantifying selected accounting events, for example, inventory valuation, depreciation methods, service lives, and pension costs. These factors lead to significant inconsistencies and measurement biases in the financial statements of different firms and of the same firm over time.

The explosive growth in OBS financing transactions such as sales or securitization of receivables, take-or-pay contracts, and leases has increased the divergence between reported accounting and economic assets and liabilities. These transactions are generally structured as executory contracts, thereby avoiding accounting recognition [see Subsection 16.4(c)(vii)].

Balance sheet classification of reported assets and liabilities is based on their respective time cycles for realization. Current assets and liabilities are expected to be realized or paid within a 12-month period or within the normal operating cycle of the firm, whichever is longer. Long-term assets are intended for use in the business, such as plant and equipment, or are not intended for sale, such as investments in affiliates. Long-term liabilities such as bonds payable are due after one year. Owners' equity represents the residual interest and as such is the permanent capital invested in the firm. Balance sheet analysis revolves around the interrelationships among its various components.

(b) LIQUIDITY ANALYSIS.   Short-term lenders, suppliers, and creditors focus on the liquidity of the firm in their assessment of its risk level. The evaluation concerns the firm's ability to meet its maturing obligations at a given point in time; equally important are changes in that ability over time. Cash or cash equivalents become available through liquidation of short-term debt and equity instruments, collection of receivables, and conversion of inventories into receivables through sales, thence into cash. In ongoing businesses, continuing operations require new investments in inventories and receivables to replace those converted to cash. Thus, receivables and inventories are to a considerable extent "permanent capital," not liquid assets, except for seasonal businesses that experience troughs and peaks. However, as financial markets evolve, securitization of receivables and more effective inventory financing and management techniques may erode the "permanence" of capital invested in these liquid assets.

(i) Analytical Ratios. Two ratios are traditionally used in the assessment of short-term liquidity and financial flexibility: the current ratio and the quick ratio. They apply primarily to industrial, merchandising, and service companies rather than to utilities or financial services companies. These two ratios are defined as follows:

1. Current ratio $= \dfrac{\text{Current assets (cash and equivalents, receivables and inventories)}}{\text{Current liabilities (payables, accruals, taxes and debt due in 1 year)}}$

2. Quick ratio $= \dfrac{\text{Cash and equivalents plus receivables}}{\text{Current liabilities}}$

The application of these ratios is illustrated in Exhibit 16.5.

Company N begins the year (column A) with a current ratio of 2.0, which reflects an ample margin of current assets over current liabilities; the quick ratio of 1.2 indicates that liquid assets alone exceed all current liabilities. The quick ratio is a more conservative measure of relative liquidity in that it assumes liquidity is provided only by cash, cash equivalents, and receivables that normally can be realized in the short run without loss. Inventories usually are further removed from realization and may be subject to loss. Inventories of actively traded commodities, for example, wheat, can be very liquid and should be included among liquid assets in the quick ratio for relevant industries.

Using the Ratios.   The measures of liquidity provide an indication of the firm's short-run ability to meet its obligations, but they are superficial standing alone, are limited in that they provide a picture at a specific point in time, and may be distorted at year end.

The year-to-year trends and business characteristics also must be analyzed along with continued evaluation of the trend of earnings. A good liquidity position and financial flexibility can erode rapidly with losses and vice versa. If Company N's liquidity position changes in one year from column A to column B, an obvious deterioration has occurred. All liquidity ratios are lower, and receivables and inventory are higher, increasing the current assets. Current liabilities have increased since short-term bank debt has been used to finance the increase in current assets.

The analyst and short-term creditor should review the trends in and impact on operating cash flow and earnings through an analysis of trends in sales (by segments, where possible), the collectibility of receivables, and the salability of inventories to evaluate sources of increase in risk

	A	B	C
Cash	$10,000	$ 10,000	$25,000
Receivables	20,000	35,000	20,000
Inventory	20,000	55,000	20,000
Current assets	$50,000	$100,000	$65,000
Bank loan	—	35,000	—
Payables	5,000	15,000	5,000
Accruals	10,000	15,000	10,000
Taxes	10,000	10,000	15,000
Current liabilities	25,000	75,000	30,000
Net working capital	$25,000	$ 25,000	$35,000
Ratios			
1. Current ratio	2.00	1.33	2.17
2. Quick ratio	1.20	0.60	1.50

Exhibit 16.5   Liquidity ratios for Company N.

and decrease in financial flexibility. The ratio of operating cash flow to average current liabilities may provide insights into causes of changes in the current ratio:

$$\text{Operating cash flow to current liabilities} = \frac{\text{Cash provided by operations}}{\text{Average current liabilities}}$$

Empirical research by Casey and Bartczak suggests that healthy firms exhibit ratios of 40 percent or better.[3]

However, the changes in and trends of liquidity ratios should be interpreted with caution. When the current ratio exceeds 1.00, equal increases (decreases) in current assets and current liabilities will decrease (improve) the current ratio but need not reflect a decline (improvement) in financial flexibility. Temporary plant shutdowns or recessions may reduce current liabilities or allow the firm to use up inventories with a resulting improvement in current ratios. In contrast, the firm may build up inventories, financing the increase with short-term debt in anticipation of increased sales. These actions may be appropriate but would depress current ratios.

The firm's liquidity position is also susceptible to manipulation. At year end, purchases may be delayed or receivables sold and proceeds used to retire short-term debt. The use of averages in the ratios and a comparison of ratios over time will mitigate this problem to some extent. Acquisitions and divestitures also significantly distort current ratios. However, some disclosures required by SFAS No. 95, "Statement of Cash Flows," will allow analysts to adjust for these effects.

Lenders providing short-term bank debt and publicly traded long-term debt generally control the liquidity risk by imposing requirements for maintenance of minimum current ratios or working capital. These indenture restrictions or debt covenants are disclosed in footnotes to financial statements and often are included in filings with the SEC 10-K reports. The analyst should monitor the firm's maintenance of liquidity ratios specified in debt covenants and evaluate accounting changes, for example, switching to FIFO inventory valuation from LIFO, which may mask deteriorating financial conditions.

The analyst should use footnote disclosures of significant accounting policies to adjust published figures to a more realistic basis. If the LIFO method is used for inventory accounting, the reported book value of inventories may well be far below current value. Footnote disclosures of LIFO reserves should be used to gross up LIFO inventories to equivalent FIFO amounts, improving the current ratio and augmenting comparability with FIFO companies. The marketable securities also should be adjusted from book to market values, allowing for tax effects. These adjustments would make the current assets more representative of the firm's liquidity position.

Seasonal and Cyclical Factors.   Most seasonal businesses have fiscal years ending at the conclusion of the sales cycle when the financial position is most liquid. At interim periods the current ratios may change considerably from the previous year end without any change in net working capital and financial flexibility.

Assume that Company N in Exhibit 16.5 is in the Christmas trade and columns A and C represent its financial position at successive January 31 fiscal year ends, whereas column B reflects its position on October 31. To build inventories for the seasonal peak, the company borrows from its bank and finances receivables by allowing payables and accruals to build up in the normal course of business. At year end, inventories are liquidated, receivables collected, bank loans repaid, and net profit of $10,000 is added to the net working capital or liquidity position. During the year, Company N also increases long-term debt to expand the plant.

Although the ratios in column B are the same as in the trend analysis in the first case, the circumstances are different. The lower liquidity ratios reflect a temporary condition just before the inventories begin to move into sales. At the end of the season (column C), the liquidity position has returned to "normal" with some improvement due to profitable operations. The analyst

---

[3] C. J. Casey and N. J. Bartczak, "Using Operating Cash Flow Data to Predict Financial Distress: Some Extension," *Journal of Accounting Research*, Spring, 1985, pp. 384–401.

should evaluate firm performance relative to the normal pattern of the Christmas trade and industry performance. If the merchandise does not move at Christmas, the year-end position will be column B, rather than column C.

Highly cyclical industries or building contractors may display this same pattern of change over a longer period as volume increases and then subsides.

A Fast Turnover Business. A retail grocery chain, for example, is mostly a cash business and usually has few or no receivables. It can operate adequately on a current ratio of less than 2.0. Cash is being received as quickly as sales are made, and payables and accruals accumulate and turn over at longer intervals. High daily cash receipts and quick inventory turnover allow such firms to raise cash for unanticipated needs very quickly.

A Slow Turnover Business. A steel company, on the other hand, will have very large inventories and receivables and typically will have a current ratio of 3.0, 4.0, or higher. However, the receivables and inventory are necessary for operations and may not be immediately available to meet current obligations. Hence, a steel company may be no more liquid than the retail grocery chain despite its nominally higher current ratio.

Companies with diverse businesses may include fast and slow turnover segments, manufacturing, retail, and financial operations and divisions with different or conflicting restrictions on current ratios. To the extent possible, the analyst should adjust for these differences using information in footnotes and segment reports.

(ii) Activity Ratios. Liquidity analysis can be augmented by an assessment of how effectively the firm uses its liquid assets. Various activity ratios are used to analyze the operating cycle, that is, the flow of materials into finished merchandise into receivables into cash.

The inventory turnover ratio provides an indicator of the efficiency of the firm's operations. It is calculated as follows:

$$\frac{\text{Cost of goods sold}}{\text{Average inventory}}$$

The number of days that inventory is on hand can be calculated as:

$$\frac{365}{\text{Inventory turnover}}$$

The turnover ratio and the number of days that inventory is on hand should be analyzed for trends over time and compared to similar firms in the industry. The latter comparison requires an adjustment for any differences in inventory methods. Ideally, for industries experiencing rising prices, the cost of goods sold should be stated in LIFO terms and the inventory balances should reflect current costs (FIFO). Thus both numerator and denominator would reflect current costs. Use of LIFO inventory cost to compute turnover will inflate that ratio, especially if the LIFO reserve is high relative to LIFO cost.

The receivables turnover and the average number of days that receivables are outstanding indicate the effectiveness of the firm's credit policies and the length of time it takes to convert the receivables to cash:

$$\text{Receivables turnover} = \frac{\text{Net credit sales}}{\text{Average receivables}}$$

$$\text{Number of days receivables are outstanding} = \frac{365}{\text{Receivables turnover}}$$

This ratio is only meaningful when compared to credit terms used by the firm and, if possible, similar firms in the industry. If the credit terms are net 30 days but receivables are outstanding for

50 days on average, the collections are slow. When receivables have been sold, the analyst should use footnote data to adjust turnover calculations [see Subsection 16.4(c)(vii)].

The total number of days that inventories are on hand and the number of days that receivables are outstanding indicate the length of the operating cycle of the firm—the amount of time it takes the firm to convert materials into cash. A review of these ratios over time and with similar companies would allow a cash flow forecast and indicate whether short-term obligations can be met with cash flows from operations. Thus, activity ratios are particularly relevant to short-term creditors such as banks. Creditors should also monitor the earnings power, which is essential to maintain solvency and meet maturing obligations. Without adequate margins, the operating cycle will not produce the cash required to repay debts.

(c) ANALYSIS OF LONG-TERM ASSETS AND LIABILITIES.   Generally, noncurrent assets are stated at their historical cost book values adjusted for depreciation and as such rarely reflect their economic worth. However, noncurrent assets represent the firm's investments in manufacturing technologies and are relevant to an analysis of its growth prospects.

Investments in nonaffiliated companies are reported at acquisition costs and may well be marketable securities, in which case their current market value can be added to liquid assets that are a part of current assets. Investments in affiliated enterprises and joint ventures are reported at cost plus the proportionate interest in the investee's undistributed earnings. They may represent investments in emerging technologies or acquisitions of operating capacity in partnership with other firms. These investments usually are not available for sale, but they should be analyzed for elements of value different from carrying value. Footnotes often provide separate financial data for such investees. Direct borrowing may support these investments, or the firm may provide indirect guarantees of underlying debt. Since the investor reports its proportionate interest in the net assets of these investees, the debt component of these investments requires analysis. (See discussion on OBS financing techniques.)

Property, plant, and equipment normally represent permanent investment, and their value to the firm is best measured by their contribution to income. The net carrying value is based on historical cost, which provides some idea of relative magnitude but usually is not indicative of current value. Supplementary disclosures under SFAS No. 33 provide some measure of current value. However, these disclosures are no longer mandatory, making analysis difficult if not impossible.

Some types of property have a degree of liquidity, and secondary markets may provide current market values. Substituting these values for net book values may provide insights into a company's economic worth. Reserves of natural resources and commercial real estate are examples.

Oil and gas companies disclose the present values of their reserves of oil and gas; the analyst can use these data to derive an indication of market value. The adjusted valuations have a more practical analytical use than historical book values. Coal reserves and the timber content of forest properties are other examples of natural resource properties to which a similar analysis can be applied. Real estate investment trusts and hotel companies sometimes report the market value of their commercial properties and the change in those values as a measure of income, supplementing their standard historical cost accounts.

Deferred charges are accounting numbers that do not represent assets but are incurred expenditures not yet reflected in income. Normally these have minor significance, but they should be examined carefully when they are large or increasing. Reported income may be overstated in such instances.

(i) Fixed Asset Turnover Ratio.   A measure of the efficiency of capital investment can be derived as follows:

$$\frac{\text{Net sales}}{\text{Average fixed assets}}$$

This ratio reflects the sales generated by investments in productive capacity. Some caveats should be noted. Growing companies would report increasing investments in fixed assets resulting in a relatively low turnover. Significant acquisitions accounted for under the purchase method may also lower the turnover. In contrast, cutbacks in investments, discontinued operations, and write-offs will improve the ratio but with possibly negative implications for earning power. Finally, increased reliance on leasing accounted for as operating leases would have a favorable but comparatively misleading impact on this turnover ratio.

(ii) Capitalization Analysis. The analysis of a company's capital structure—the amount of debt relative to equity—is essential for an evaluation of its use of financial leverage and the measurement of its ability to meet its long-term obligations. The use of debt in the capital structure adds fixed costs through contractual interest payments, exerting a leverage effect on the residual return to stockholders. The higher the rate of ROA relative to the fixed after-tax cost of debt capital, the higher the residual return accruing to stockholders. However, the fixed nature of interest payments has an adverse effect on this return during recessions or declines in demand as the rate of ROA falls. Given the priority of debt claims relative to equity, a highly leveraged capital structure will have a negative impact on equity holders when adversity strikes. Conservative debt ratios enhance access to capital markets and improve the investment quality of the common stock.

The firm's ability to meet fixed interest and principal repayment obligations is a function of its earnings and cash-generating ability. The proportion of debt to equity capital and the stability of earnings and operating cash flows determine the riskiness of the firm's capital structure.

Long-term creditors use bond covenants to limit debt levels. Covenants that restrict dividend payments based on measures of cumulative profitability or net worth serve to restrict the firm's ability to strengthen stockholders' position relative to that of bondholders. The analyst should monitor the firm's maintenance of various ratios and relationships specified by bond covenants. The recent wave of highly leveraged mergers and recapitalizations and their impact on bondholders emphasizes the importance of a detailed analysis of the protection implied by debt covenants.

(iii) Capitalization Table. The capital structure of a company is usually presented in a capitalization table derived from the balance sheet. It shows the position and proportion of capital issues in relation to each other and the total capital of the company. Exhibit 16.6 illustrates such a table.

(iv) Debt Ratios. Three ratios (defined below) are used to evaluate the relationship between debt and equity. A comprehensive definition of debt includes current debt, long-term debt, capitalized lease obligations, and contractual obligations not afforded accounting treatment as liabilities, for example, take-or-pay payments and certain operating leases. Subsections 16.4(c)(vi) and (vii) discuss the analysis of these OBS financing transactions. Preferred stock may have some characteristics of debt and should be evaluated for the most appropriate classification. A detailed discussion of preferred stock follows this section. All subsidiary debt should be included in total capitalization to determine the total debt supported by the company's capital.

Debt ratios that are based on the balance sheet may be calculated as:

$$\text{Debt to total capital ratio} = \frac{\text{Total current and long-term debt} + \text{capitalized leases}}{\text{Total capital (total debt} + \text{leases} + \text{stockholder's equity)}}$$

This figure expresses debt as a percentage of total capital. Exhibit 16.6 shows that this ratio is 77.1 percent (73.3 percent in 2000) for Lyondell Chemical Company.

The debt-to-equity ratio is defined as:

$$\frac{\text{Total current and long-term debt} + \text{capitalized leases}}{\text{Total stockholders' equity}}$$

This ratio is often used interchangeably with the debt-to-capital ratio, which is preferred. In 2001, this ratio was 336.2 percent (274.7 percent in 2000) for Lyondell Chemical Company.

LYONDELL CHEMICAL COMPANY
Capitalization Table
(in US$ millions)

	12/31/2000		12/31/2001	
	Amount	% of Total Capital (BV)	Amount	% of Total Capital (BV)
Short-term debt	10	0.19	7	0.14
Long-term debt	3,844	73.12	3,846	76.94
Total Debt (Book Value)	**3,854**	**73.31**	**3,853**	**77.08**
Common stockholders' equity				
(Book Value)[1]	$1,403	26.69	$1,146	22.92
Total capital (Book Value)	**$5,257**	**100.00**	**$4,999**	**100.00**
Common stockholders' equity				
(Market Value)[2]	$1,800		$1,685	
Total capital (Market Value)	**$5,654**		**$5,538**	
Debt		%		%
to equity (BV)		274.7		336.2
to capital (BV)		73.3		77.1
Debt		%		%
to equity (MV)		214.09		228.71
to capital (MV)		68.16		69.58

Notes (2001 Calculations):
[1] From Balance Sheet, includes common stock, paid-in-capital, and retained earnings less treasury stock.
[2] From supplementary information in the Balance Sheet, based on number of shares outstanding and the closing market price on 12/31/2001 (117.56 × $14.33).

Exhibit 16.6 Sample capitalization table.

Total debt at book value should also be compared to the market value of total capital instead of book value:

$$\frac{\text{Total debt at book value}}{\text{Total debt and preferred stock} + \text{common stock at market}}$$

(70.96 percent (70.03 in 2000) for Lyondell Chemical Company on 12/31/2001).

When the market value of total capital is well above book value, the debt ratio will be lower than the book value-based ratio; it will be presumed that the company's earning power and/or market conditions are favorable for issuance of debt to raise needed capital or refund existing debt. However, a continued trend of market value of equity at less than book value may signal deteriorating credit and restricted financial flexibility. Although this ratio will vary because of market fluctuations, it is a useful analytical tool.

These derivations can be altered to focus on senior debt, for example, mortgage bonds and bank debt, when the capital structure includes junior debt, for example, debentures or subordinated debt. The junior debt is subtracted from the numerator and added to the denominator, thereby becoming a part of the capital base that supports the senior debt. The debt ratio for senior debt alone is thus more favorable than for the entire debt.

The debt ratios must be viewed in context. The type of business, the variability and trend of earnings and other relevant factors must be evaluated. For example, a finance company, which has liquid financial assets, and an electric utility, which may be a regulated monopoly providing a basic service, will normally carry higher debt ratios than a cyclical manufacturing company.

(v) Preferred Stock Ratios.   Preferred stock also has a claim on assets prior to the common stock, and its position and leverage effect are easily shown in the capitalization table. The preferred stock ratio can be classified by seniority, that is, senior preferred stock and junior preference stock.

Adjustments may be necessary for the correct balance sheet presentation of preferred stocks. For purposes of analysis, preferred stock should be shown at liquidating value rather than at stated value because this is the true measure of its claim on assets. Any excess of liquidating value over stated value should be charged against retained earnings in the common equity.

A second issue is the classification of preferred stock subject to mandatory redemption. The SEC now requires that such stock be shown apart from stockholders' equity. This is based on the notion that mandatory redemption through a sinking or purchase fund makes the preferred stock a "temporary" form of capital analogous to debt. Stockholders' equity is considered "permanent" capital.

Preferred stock may be considered permanent capital (i.e., stockholders' equity) on legal grounds because failure to make dividend or sinking fund payments will normally not cause default or bankruptcy, as with a bond. The principal effect of such failure probably would be to block dividends on the common stock. This common equity nature is stronger in the case of convertible preferred, especially when conversion can be forced by calling the preferred.

However, nonconvertible, mandatorily redeemable preferred has the economic characteristics of debt. Thus, it should be treated as subordinated debt for purposes of analysis.

(vi) Off-Balance-Sheet (OBS) Obligations.   Balance sheet based analyses of capital structure and leverage may understate firm risk because OBS activities and executory contracts do not receive accounting recognition. The OBS transactions are designed to transfer or share the risk of the firm's operations, and they have real current or future cash flow consequences. For example, long-term lease contracts may be, in substance, installment purchases of long-term assets, but they have been structured to avoid capitalization requirements of accounting standards, thereby eliminating balance sheet recognition of the asset and the related liability. Nonrecognition in the financial statements limits the usefulness of capital structure and risk indicators unless proper adjustments are made.

Executory contracts involve commitments to purchase or pay for a commodity or service over a period of time. No liability is recognized since no accounting obligation arises until an exchange transaction is completed. This legalistic definition of liabilities has contributed to their nonrecognition in financial statements.

Firms may engage in these transactions to avoid reporting adverse debt-to-equity ratios and to reduce the probability of technical default under restrictive covenants in debt indentures. Historical cost basis financial statements, which suppress the current value of assets, increase the incentive to engage in OBS transactions to keep liabilities off the books. A detailed review of footnote disclosures of OBS transactions and executory contracts is essential for a comprehensive analysis of capital structure.

(vii) Examples of Off-Balance-Sheet Financing Techniques.   The most common examples of the use of OBS financing techniques follow. When analyzing a company, the analyst must watch for such transactions and make the appropriate adjustments when computing financial ratios.

Accounts Receivable.   Legally separate, wholly owned finance subsidiaries are often created to purchase receivables from the parent, which uses the proceeds to retire debt. When such subsidiaries are unconsolidated, the parent firms report significantly lower debt–equity ratios. Parent companies in the past used the "equity" method to account for their finance subsidiaries, that is, the consolidated balance sheet reported the parent's net investment in these units, suppressing the debt used to finance receivables. The FASB eliminated this nonconsolidation option (SFAS No. 94), and all post-1987 financial statements must consolidate the assets and liabilities of controlled finance subsidiaries (after relevant intercompany eliminations). The analyst should compute consolidated debt–equity ratios because the parent generally supports finance subsidiary borrowings through extensive income-maintenance agreements and direct or indirect guarantees of its debt.

Receivables also may be financed by sale (or securitization) to unrelated parties with proceeds used to reduce debt. These transactions are effectively collateralized borrowing when receivables are transferred with recourse to the "seller." Footnote disclosures should be analyzed to determine whether the risks and rewards of controlling these receivables have been transferred to the "buyer." Where the "seller" retains these risks and rewards, the analyst should reinstate the receivables and treat the proceeds as debt in computing the debt–equity ratio as well as the current ratio, receivables turnover, and the return on average total capital.

Inventories.   Firms may finance inventory and raw material purchases through take-or-pay commitments whereby they contract to purchase or pay for minimum quantities over a specified time period. The present value of these future obligations should be included in computing debt ratios. Companies typically use take-or-pay contracts to ensure supplies of raw materials or availability of manufacturing capacity. Natural resource companies may use through-put contracts to guarantee distribution needs by contracting with pipelines to purchase or transport minimum quantities. Firms organize joint ventures with related companies or third parties where the take-or-pay commitments effectively guarantee the joint venture's long-term debt service requirements. In some cases, direct guarantees of joint venture or related companies debt are disclosed in footnotes. The obligations under take-or-pay and through-put arrangements and the direct guarantees should be included in the computation of debt–equity ratios.

Natural resource firms may finance inventories through commodity-indexed debt where interest and/or principal repayments are a function of the price of underlying commodities. Changing commodity prices should be monitored to determine their impact on these liabilities and the debt–equity ratios.

Fixed Assets.   Firms acquire rights to fixed assets through lease contracts structured to avoid capitalization criteria in accounting standards. Footnote disclosure of these operating leases details minimum payments for each of the next five years and the total payments thereafter. Where this payment schedule depicts relatively stable and long-term payments over a period roughly equivalent to the average economic/useful life of similarly owned long-term assets or those under capitalized leases, the analyst should capitalize these operating leases to adjust reported debt levels. The reported fixed assets, depreciation expense, and interest expense also should be adjusted in order to correctly calculate various affected ratios.

Joint Ventures.   Firms acquire, control, or obtain access to distribution and manufacturing capacity through joint ventures and/or investments in affiliated and nonaffiliated companies. In some cases the joint venture offers economies of scale and needed capacity or provides for a negotiated sharing of technologies, raw materials, or financial risk. The owners of these ventures enter into take-or-pay or through-put arrangements where the minimum, guaranteed payments are designed to cover required debt service obligations. These agreements constitute the collateral for the venture's borrowings in the absence of substantial equity investments by various parties to the joint venture. Direct or indirect guarantees of venture's debt may also be present.

Generally, the firms account for their investment in the joint ventures using the equity method, since no single firm holds a controlling interest. Thus, the balance sheet reports only the nominal net investment in the venture. Footnotes may disclose the assets, liabilities, and results of operations of the venture in a summarized format. These disclosures should be used for proportionate consolidation of the joint venture with the firm. Any direct or indirect guarantees of venture debt should be evaluated for adjustment to reported debt levels.

Investments.   Some firms have issued long-term debt convertible into the common stock of related firms, held as investments. Potential motives for these transactions include lower interest costs on debt, benefits of tax deductibility of interest payments, the 80 percent exclusion from taxable income of dividends received from eligible investments, and control of the amount and timing of capital gains on conversion.

Currency and Interest-rate Exposure.   Long-term debt in foreign currency denominations may increase the firm's exchange-risk exposure. The mix of fixed and variable rate debt exposes the firm to interest-rate risk.

Some firms also engage in interest rate and/or currency swaps related to outstanding debt. For example, a bond may be issued payable in fixed-rate Australian dollars and the proceeds swapped for variable-rate Swiss francs. The foreign currency-denominated debt may also be convertible into commodities or natural resources. Footnote disclosures vary widely, ranging from an acknowledgment of swap transactions to detailed analyses of the effect of swaps on currency- and interest-rate exposure. The analyst should monitor these disclosures to evaluate risk exposure.

Exhibit 16.7 ties together this discussion of OBS techniques, using Lyondell Chemical Company as an example. Lyondell makes extensive use of joint ventures, operating leases, and other OBS techniques. Adjustments for these obligations increase debt from $3,853 to $5,291 ($3,854 to $5,207 in 2000), or 37 percent (35 percent in 2000). Even after adjustment of stated equity to significantly higher market value, the debt-to-capital ratio rises from 77.1 percent (as computed in Exhibit 16.6) to 97.5 percent (from 73.3 percent to 95.4 percent in 2000). However, this exhibit is incomplete; a comprehensive adjustment requires additional analysis of the operations and financial structure of Lyondell's affiliates and other guarantees it provides to those affiliates and its partners in various joint ventures. The analyst should also recognize Lyondell's proportionate share of the present value of operating leases and noncancelable purchase obligations of its affiliates.

(viii) Property Analysis.   The long-term capital of the company is often compared with its permanent investment in property and equipment. This is analogous to the ratio of mortgage loan to value in the financing of residential and commercial buildings. Since plant and equipment are carried at historical cost and normally are not available for sale, this ratio has limited practical significance. A better measure is the ratio of debt to total net tangible assets including net current assets.

A debt-to-property analysis may be more useful in the case of natural resource companies or companies with large real estate holdings. Frequently, the market value of natural resources holdings exceeds historical cost book values. Theoretically this market value is an indicator of funds available to support debt in an emergency. For some companies these excess market values can be significant, and may augment the potential value of the entire company in an acquisition.

16.5 CASH FLOW ANALYSIS

Effective in 1987, SFAS No. 95 replaced the "funds statement" with a statement of cash flows. From an analytic viewpoint, the change is most beneficial. The funds statement generally added little information to that available from the balance sheet and income statement.

In contrast, the statement of cash flows provides significant additional data for analysis. This improvement is mainly due to the provisions of SFAS No. 95 requiring that:

1. The effect of acquisitions be removed from the balance sheet changes used to compute cash flows
2. The effects of changes in exchange rates be removed from balance sheet changes used to compute cash flows
3. Cash flows be separated into operating, investing, and financing activities

The first two requirements result in cash flow data that are unclouded by the effects of acquisitions and exchange rate factors. The third requirement means that such accounts as accounts receivable, accounts payable, accrued liabilities, long-term liabilities, and accounts labeled "other" or "miscellaneous" must be segregated into operating, investing, and financing functions by the financial statement preparer. As a result of these requirements, the statement of cash flows is far more accurate than the "do it yourself" estimates that were formerly necessary.[4]

---

[4] A. C. Sondhi, G. H. Sorter, and G. I. White, "Cash Flow Redefined: FAS 95 and Security Analysis," *Financial Analysts Journal*, November–December 1988, pp. 19–20.

LYONDELL CHEMICAL COMPANY
Capitalization Table
(in US$ millions)

	12/31/2000		12/31/2001	
	Amount	% of Adjusted Total Capital (BV)	Amount	% of Adjusted Total Capital (BV)
Total Debt (Book Value)[1]	$3,854	70.61	$3,853	71.03
Adjustments:				
41% of Equistar's long-term liabilities[2]	922	16.89	958	17.66
58.75% of Lyondell-CITGO's long-term liabilities[2]	276	5.06	294	5.42
Fair value of long-term debt[3]	(77)	−1.41	—	—
Guarantees and contingent liabilities[4]	—	—	—	—
Capitalization of Lyondell's operating leases[5]	232	4.25	223	4.12
Adjusted Total Debt	$5,207	95.40	$5,291	97.55
Common stockholders' equity (BV)	$1,403	25.71	$1,146	21.13
Adjustments:				
Goodwill[6]	−$1,152	−21.11	−$1,102	−20.32
LIFO reserves[6]	—		—	
Fair value of investments and long-term receivables[6]	—		$ 89	1.64
Excess (shortfall) of present value of DCF over capitalized costs over capitalized costs of oil & gas reserves[6]	—		—	
Adjusted Common Stockholders Equity (BV)	$ 251	4.60	$ 133	2.45
Total capital (BV)	$5,257		$ 4999	
Total capital (BV)	$5,458	100.00	$5,424	100.00
Common stockholders' equity (Market Value)[7]	$1,650		$1,577	
Total capital (MV)	$5,504		$5,430	
Adjusted total capital (MV)	$6,857		$6,868	
Adjusted Debt		%		%
to adjusted equity (BV)		2,074.4		3,978.4
to adjusted capital (BV)		95.4		97.5
Adjusted Debt		%		%
to equity (MV)		315.56		335.53
to adjusted capital (MV)		94.60		97.44

Notes (2001 Calculations):
[1] From Exhibit 16.6.
[2] From supplementary information in the Annual Report.
[3] From Note 14, difference between fair value and carrying amount of debt, interest rate swaps, and other derivatives.
[4] Guarantees of the debt of affiliated companies, subsidiaries, and other relevant contingent liabilities should be included in adjustments to total debt. See discussion in the text and Lyondell's footnotes detailing its relationship and obligations to affiliates.
[5] From Note 15, present value of future rental payments under operating leases (see text for an explanation of the discount rate used).
[6] From Balance Sheet and footnotes.
[7] From Exhibit 16.6.

Exhibit 16.7   Sample adjusted capitalization table

(a) **DIRECT VERSUS INDIRECT METHODS.**   SFAS No. 95 permits the statement of cash flows to be prepared using either the direct or indirect methods. Although the indirect method is used by virtually all preparers, the direct method is more suitable for analysis. In most cases, therefore, direct method statements must be prepared by the analyst. This can be done by rearranging the data given in the indirect method format. For example, combining sales with the change in operating accounts receivable produces cash receipts.[5]

As there is some evidence that the components of cash flow from operating activities are better indicators than the total, the analyst should use whatever detail is available. The ratio of each component to cash receipts, for example, should be looked at over time.

Cash flow used for investments should be compared with cash flow from operations. The difference is often called *free cash flow*, and may be a useful indicator of the cash-generating ability of the enterprise. However, the analyst must compare the results of this exercise with the a priori expectations based on the type of business. For example, a company experiencing rapid growth may have little or no operating cash flow and free cash flow may be negative. In this case the analyst would be primarily concerned with how this cash deficit was being financed. A proper balance between debt and equity should be struck.

However, a *cash cow* should generate cash flow from operations well in excess of capital needed for investment purposes. In this case the analyst would be concerned with the use of the excess cash flow. If the free cash flow generated did not conform to the prior expectation, this would also be a cause for concern.

(b) **COMPARING CASH FLOWS.**   Cash flow analysis is best done using data for a number of years. Cash flow for one period may be distorted by random events (strikes, abnormal volume due to price changes, etc.). Also keep in mind that, for cyclical companies, the business cycle will affect cash flows. Cyclical expansions generally require additional working capital; contractions generate cash as working capital is reduced.

For periods of less than one year, additional caution is required because of seasonality. The statement of cash flows for less than one year should be compared only with the statement for the corresponding period of prior years when the business is at all seasonal. Otherwise, normal seasonal working capital variations will dominate any real trends.

When comparing different companies, allowance must be made for differences in financial structure. Under the provisions of SFAS No. 95, cash flow from operating activities includes income from investments and interest expense (but not dividends paid). In order to facilitate intercompany comparisons, interest expense (after-tax) should be removed from operating cash flow and included in financing cash flow. When income from investments is significant, it should be removed (after-tax) from operating cash flow and included in investing cash flow. With these adjustments, cash flow from operations can be evaluated, and companies can be compared with the effects of financing decisions removed.

16.6 INTEGRATED ANALYSIS OF FINANCIAL STATEMENTS

A company's ROA provides a comprehensive measure of its profitability during a given period of time and is calculated as follows:

$$\text{Return on assets} = \frac{\text{Net income}}{\text{Average total assets}}$$

The trends in this ratio allow an evaluation of the company's performance over time. It also should be compared with the ratio for similar firms over time and with an industry average. This

---

[5] J. Livnat and A. C. Sondhi, "Debt Capacity and Financial Contracting: Finance Subsidiaries," *Journal of Accounting, Auditing and Finance*, Spring 1989, pp. 237–265.

return measure is affected by accounting and tax policy choices and the degree of leverage used by a firm over time and across firms. A measure using earnings before interest and income taxes (EBIT) overcomes these limitations and provides a measure of operating profitability unaffected by differences in leverage and tax effects. It is calculated as:

$$\frac{\text{Earnings before interest and taxes}}{\text{Average total assets}}$$

Further insights into operating performance over time may be obtained by evaluating the components of these return measures. One component is the net income (or EBIT) margin, which is a measure of the profitability in relation to sales. The second component, the asset turnover ratio, evaluates the effectiveness of the firm's use of assets in generating sales. Each component can be analyzed in greater detail to determine the underlying relationships affecting current return and their potential impact on returns over time. The net income (or EBIT) margin can be decomposed further to evaluate changes in different sources of revenues and proportions of various expense categories over time. Inventory, receivables, and fixed asset turnover ratios can be analyzed to evaluate trends in the fixed asset turnover:

Net income margin or EBIT margin	×	Asset turnover	=	Return on assets
$\dfrac{\text{Net income}}{\text{Net sales}}$				$\dfrac{\text{Net income}}{\text{Average total assets}}$
or	×	$\dfrac{\text{Net income}}{\text{Average total assets}}$	=	or
$\dfrac{\text{EBIT}}{\text{Net sales}}$				$\dfrac{\text{EBIT}}{\text{Average total assets}}$
↓		↓		
Analysis of relevant revenue and expense breakdowns		Analysis of inventory, receivables, and fixed asset turnover		

Exhibit 16.8 shows that Ashland's ROA has improved from 3.75 percent in 1997 to 5.80 percent in 2001. In 1998, Ashland reported a decline in ROA due to a significant drop in asset turnover (beginning in 1998, previously consolidated units were reported on the equity method, significantly reducing reported sales) despite an increase in the profit margin. In 2000, a decline in the profit margin was not overcome by an improvement in asset turnover. However, the decline in the net income reflected a loss on discontinued operations. Excluding this loss, the profit margin (based on continuing operations) would have been 6.41 percent and the ROA 7.56 percent. In 2001, asset turnover declined but was more than offset by a significant improvement in reported profit margin. When we compute profit margins using income from continuing operations, 2001 reflects a decline in performance as compared to 2000. EBIT return rose nearly 190 percent to 11.05 percent in 2001 from 3.82 percent in 1997. However, 1997 and 1998 are not comparable to the other years because of the change to the equity method in 1998. From 1999 to 2001, EBIT margins have improved by approximately 21 percent.

Investors should also calculate the firm's ROE as:

$$\frac{\text{Net income}}{\text{Average common equity}}$$

ASHLAND, INC. AND CONSOLIDATED SUBSIDIARIES

Year	Profit Margin[1] Net Income / Sales	×	Asset Turnover[2] Sales / Avg. Total Assets	=	Return on Assets[3] Net Income / Avg. Total Assets	×	Leverage[4] Avg. Total Assets / Avg. common equity	=	Return on Equity[5] Net Income / Avg. common
	(%)				(%)				(%)
1997	2.11	×	1.78	=	3.75	×	3.72	=	13.96
1998	3.11	×	0.94	=	2.93	×	3.13	=	9.17
1999	4.26	×	1.09	=	4.63	×	2.88	=	13.36
2000	0.88	×	1.18	=	1.04	×	3.25	=	3.36
2001	5.40	×	1.07	=	5.80	×	3.43	=	19.89

Net Income – Growth Rates (1997–2001)

	%
% Change	18.46
Compound Growth rate	9.89

Notes (2001 Calculations)
[1] Profit margin (%) = (Net Income/Sales) × 100 = (417/7719) × 100 = 5.4%
[2] Asset Turnover = Sales/Average total assets (7719/((7284+7092)/2)) = 1.07
[3] ROA = Profit Margin × Asset Turnover = 5.4 × 1.07 = 5.80%
[4] Leverage = Average Total Assets × Average Common Equity = (((7284+7092)/2)/((2266+1965)/2))) = 3.43
[5] ROE = ROA × Leverage = 5.80 × 3.43 = 19.89

Some numbers in this table do not multiply out precisely because of rounding; the ratios in this table were derived from Ashland Inc.'s Annual Reports.

Continues

Exhibit 16.8   Analysis of return on equity.

ASHLAND, INC. AND CONSOLIDATED SUBSIDIARIES

Year	Preinterest & Tax Margin[1] EBIT Sales		Asset Turnover[2] Sales Avg. Total Assets		Preinterest Return on Assets[3] EBIT Avg. Total Assets		Interest on Assets[4] Interest Expense Avg. Total Assets		Postinterest Return on Assets[5] EBT Avg. Total Assets		Leverage[6] Avg. Total Assets Avg. Common Equity		Pretax Return on Equity[7] EBT Avg. Common Equity
	(%)				(%)		(%)		(%)				(%)
1997	3.82	×	1.78	=	6.79	−	2.29	=	4.50	×	3.72	=	16.75
1998	6.84	×	0.94	=	6.45	−	1.88	=	4.57	×	3.13	=	14.28
1999	9.15	×	1.09	=	9.95	−	2.24	=	7.71	×	2.88	=	22.24
2000	8.55	×	1.18	=	10.07	−	2.93	=	7.14	×	3.25	=	23.18
2001	11.05	×	1.07	=	11.87	−	2.39	=	9.48	×	3.43	=	32.51

EBIT—Growth Rates (1997–2001)

	%
% Change	68.91
Compound Growth rate	13.78

Notes (2001 Calculations)

[1] Pre-interest and tax margin (%) = (EBIT/Sales) × 100 = (853/7719) × 100 = 11.05%

[2] Asset Turnover = Sales/Average Total Assets (7719/((7284 + 7092)/2)) = 1.07

[3] Preinterest ROA = Preinterest and tax margin × Asset Turnover = 11.05 × 1.07 = 11.87

[4] Interest on Assets = (Interest expense × Average Total Assets) × 100 = (172/((7719 + 7092)/2)) × 100 = 2.39

[5] Postinterest ROA = Preinterest ROA − Interest on Assets = 11.87 − 2.39 = 9.48

[6] Leverage = Average Total Assets × Average Common Equity = (((7284 + 7092)/2)/((2266 + 1965)/2)) = 3.43

[7] Pretax ROE = Postinterest ROA × Leverage = 9.48 × 3.43 = 32.51

Exhibit 16.8 *Continued.*

The ROE should be analyzed over time and across firms, and it should be compared to the average ROE for the industry in which the firm operates. Ashland's ROE was 13.96 percent in 1997; it fell to 9.17 percent in 1998 and to 3.36 percent in 2000. As noted previously, the ROE reported in 2000 is affected by loss from discontinued operations. ROE from continuing operations would have been 24.5 percent, which is significantly higher than the 19.89 percent reported for 2001.

The trends in ROE can be further analyzed in terms of its components:

$$ROE = \frac{\text{Net income}}{\text{Average total assets}} \times \frac{\text{Average total assets}}{\text{Average common equity}}$$

$$\text{or}$$

$$= \text{Profit margin} \times \text{Asset turnover} \times \text{Leverage ratio}$$

$$= \frac{\text{Net income}}{\text{Net sales}} \times \frac{\text{Net sales}}{\text{Average total assets}} \times \frac{\text{Average total assets}}{\text{Average common equity}}$$

An analysis of these components shows that the decline (from 1997 to 2000) in ROE stemmed from the year 2000 fall in profit margins, lower asset turnover in 1998–2000 relative to 1997, and a resulting lower ROA. Significantly higher profit margins in 2001 generated the highest reported ROE. Note that asset turnover (1.07x) remains lower than that reported in 1997 (1.78x) and the improvement is all due to the higher profit margin. However, an ROE measure based on income from continuing operations shows a lower ROE in 2001 compared to 2000.

The third component, assets/equity, is a leverage measure: The higher the ratio, the lower the proportion of assets financed by common equity. This ratio has increased steadily from 2.26 in 1990 to 3.30 in 1993 and declined slightly to 3.07 in 1994. The firm has decreased debt in 1993 and 1994 (it reported decreasing interest expense as a percentage of average total assets) while improving operating performance and generating higher cash flows.

16.7 FIXED INCOME ANALYSIS

Investors in fixed income securities are concerned with the safety of the expected interest payments and redemption of debt at maturity. The safety of interest payments is a function of the margin of earnings in excess of interest so that an unexpected decline in earnings will not jeopardize payment. Redemption at maturity depends on internal cash flows, the relationship of debt to equity, and other industry- and economy-wide factors. Thus, fixed-income investors need a comprehensive analysis of all financial statements to develop insights into the investment risk relative to expected return.

(a) EARNINGS PROTECTION. The key ratios are fixed charge coverage and the margin of safety, which are discussed in Subsection 16.2(c)(v). The adequacy of the coverage ratio depends on the volatility of earnings. The greater the volatility, the higher the ratio necessary to assure protection under adverse circumstances. A low ratio, say 2.5 times, is adequate for a finance company, whose earnings are stable. In fact, captive finance subsidiaries (i.e., those conducting at least 70 percent of their operations with the parent) have income-maintenance agreements with the parent whereby it guarantees coverage ratios from 1.05 to 1.50 times fixed charges. A much higher ratio, five to six times, is desirable for an industrial company whose earnings fluctuate because of the business cycle.

Another test of earnings adequacy is earning power—the return before interest expense on the total invested capital. This is given by the following equation:

$$\text{Return on invested capital} = \frac{\text{Earnings before interest and taxes}}{\text{Average invested capital}}$$

This is a useful long-term measure of strength. The margin of safety provided by the return on investment depends on the cost of debt. A return of 14 percent on invested capital is adequate when rates are 5–7 percent, but not at substantially higher rates. The current trend toward recapitalization using high-yield debt significantly increases vulnerability and reduces the protection available to the creditors if it is not accompanied by a sustained increase in return on total invested capital.

Redemption at maturity should be evaluated by the analysis of cash flows and the balance sheet in conjunction with the income statement to determine the assurance of payment at maturity. First, the maturity schedule of the outstanding debt, as given in footnotes to the financial statements, must be reviewed. The company may have a continuing run of maturing obligations, including sinking funds, or it may have a few widely spaced larger maturities. The analyst then should evaluate the firm's ability to meet the specified repayment schedule and amounts through internally generated funds that is, operating cash flows. The measure is as follows:

$$\text{Years to pay} = \frac{\text{Total fixed obligations}}{\text{Operating cash flows}}$$

This ratio states the number of years required to pay off all debt by application of all internally generated cash flows. The logic is that debt maturities will have the first priority on all available funds. Normally this ratio ought to be in a range of three to five years. At 8 to 10 years, the repayment burden could be onerous. The recent trend toward increased use of debt has increased the ratio relative to past experience. High levels of internally generated cash flows will signify low years-to-pay and high credit standing.

In summary, whereas actual appropriation of all internal cash flow to debt reduction for several years would hamper the future growth of the business and be tantamount to liquidation, a high ratio of cash flow to debt gives a company considerable flexibility in financing its business internally and/or externally and therefore is a good indicator of credit quality. A useful adjustment to this ratio would require a deduction from operating cash flows of capital expenditures required to maintain productive capacity, a crude measure of which may be provided by the current cost equivalent of depreciation. The resulting ratio is more conservative but would facilitate a more comprehensive analysis. The analyst should also compute this ratio after adjusting for all OBS obligations. These adjustments would enable the analyst to compare different reported and OBS-inclusive capital structures.

The company's overall credit standing should be reviewed on the expectation that a new issue can be sold to refund a large maturing issue or recapitalize the firm. Here again, the investor should evaluate long-term earning power, interest coverage, the ratio of debt to total capital, OBS financing activities, and bond covenants to determine whether a refunding issue or recapitalization would be accepted in the marketplace. Many industrial bonds have sinking funds that retire most of the issue by maturity, but that is not the case for most utilities. Utilities must maintain a balanced capital structure and adequate coverage in order to maintain continued access to the bond market.

Exhibit 16.9 details bond protection ratios for Ashland over the 1997–2001 period. Generally, all the measures of protection and safety for creditors have improved over the 1997–2001 period.

16.8 FINANCE COMPANY DEBT ANALYSIS

Finance companies have a large body of outstanding debt, and its quality is measured by slightly different criteria adapted to the special circumstances of this business, which involves the financing of sales and receivables of their parents and that of other, unaffiliated companies. Finance company assets are composed largely of financial obligations of third parties that are self-liquidating through relatively frequent payments of both principal and interest, allowing significantly greater leverage than that observed for industrial companies. Earnings depend on the loss experience on loans, the interest rate spread between loans and borrowings, and expense control. Finance subsidiaries and their industrial parents also have extensive operating agreements that call for income maintenance and direct or indirect parent guarantees of subsidiary debt, augmented by extensive debt covenants.

ASHLAND, INC. AND CONSOLIDATED SUBSIDIARIES

	1997	1998	1999	2000	2001
Pretax Interest Coverage (x)[1]	2.97	3.44	4.44	3.44	4.96
Pretax Fixed Charge Coverage (x)[2]	2.07	2.27	2.98	2.54	3.34
EBITDA Coverage (%)[3]	6.34	4.83	6.07	4.64	6.41
Free Cash Flow/Total Debt (%)[4]	(3.29)%	130.15%	(10.78)%	(23.91)%	(4.26)%
Margin of Safety (%)[5]	2.54%	4.85%	7.09%	6.07%	8.82%
Pretax Return on Permanent Capital (%)[6]	10.35%	10.20%	15.24%	14.72%	17.01%
Operating Income/Net Sales (%)[7]	2.81%	0.73%	2.53%	2.46%	0.30%
Long-Term Debt/Capitalization (%)[8]	45.55%	42.05%	42.23%	46.78%	44.56%
Total Debt/Capitalization (%)[9]	47.90%	45.20%	47.36%	54.14%	46.50%
Current Assets/Total Debt[10]	1.58	1.02	1.02	0.09	1.08
Net Tangible Assets/Total Debt[11]	2.53	3.27	3.07	2.73	3.31

Notes (2001 Calculations)

[1] EBIT/(Interest expense + Capitalized interest) = 853/172 = 4.96

[2] ((EBIT + Gross rents)/(Interest expense + Capitalized interest + Gross rents)) = (853 + 119)/(172 + 119) = 3.34

[3] EBITDA/(Interest expense + Capitalized interest) = 1103/172 = 6.41

[4] Free operating cash flow/Total debt = (−87/2044) × 100 = −4.26%

[5] EBT/Net sales = (681/7719) = 8.82%

[6] [EBIT/(Average (Total debt + Deferred taxes + Minority interest + Equity)] × 100 = 17.01%

[7] Operating income/Net sales = (23/7719) × 100 = 0.30%

[8] Long-term debt/(Debt + Equity) = (1959/4396) × 100 = 44.56%

[9] Total debt/(Debt + Equity) = (2044/4396) × 100 = 46.50%

[10] Current assets/Total debt = 2213/2044 = 1.08

[11] Total assets − Intangibles/Total debt = (7284 − 528)/2044 = 3.31

Exhibit 16.9   Bond protection ratios for an industrial company.

The ratios used to measure these factors are fundamentally the same as for other businesses, but they are usually expressed in a different form, and the standards are different. The analyst should also evaluate the operating agreement and bond covenants to evaluate finance company debt risk.[6]

SFAS No. 94 requires the consolidation of leasing and finance subsidiaries that were previously reported under the equity method because of their nonhomogeneous operations. The standard requires continued disclosure of disaggregated information on finance subsidiaries. To the extent possible, the analyst should evaluate separate finance company data to evaluate the riskiness of finance company debt. An analysis of the parent–subsidiary contractual relationship is necessary for an evaluation of recourse to the parent. Lenders to the parent are concerned with both the risk in parent debt and the degree of support the parent is contractually obligated to provide to its subsidiaries. The effect of consolidation on traditional ratios will not always be in the expected direction and of anticipated magnitude because of differences between parent and subsidiary size, profitability, and growth rates over time and across firms. Disaggregated disclosures are necessary for a separate evaluation of finance company and parent debt. To the extent that continued availability of disaggregated disclosure is affected by FASB actions with respect to consolidated financial reporting, analysts will need to monitor these developments.

(a) THE OPERATING AGREEMENT.   Operating agreements govern the transactions between the parent and its financing subsidiary. An income maintenance agreement is used to provide a parent guarantee that the subsidiary's net income will be a prespecified multiple of its fixed charges; direct payments to the subsidiary are required when this multiple is not reached, thereby protecting investments in subsidiary debt. Operating agreements require that receivables be sold to subsidiaries at discounts competitive with those prevailing in the financial markets. Uncollectibles are charged to the parent, and the subsidiary often has the right to withhold a predetermined portion of the purchase price (a holdback reserve), which is refunded when receivables have been collected. Some agreements contain provisions for repossession and payments in the event of default.

In summary, the operating agreement serves to reduce the volatility and risk in subsidiary earnings and cash flows, thereby enhancing the protection available to the finance company's debt holders.

(b) ASSET PROTECTION RATIOS.   Since receivables are the principal assets of finance companies, asset protection for the debt is measured by the proportion of receivables to debt, as follows:

$$\frac{\text{Gross receivables} - \text{unearned finance charges}}{\text{Total debt}}$$

This ratio should range from 110 percent to 120 percent, and it indicates the margin of liquid or financial assets over total debt. A similar ratio should also be calculated on senior debt. Refunding and call provisions in debt covenants provide additional protection. Generally, significant declines in receivables trigger a requirement to redeem outstanding debt at specified premiums. This covenant also limits investment in nonfinancial assets, which may be constrained by other, direct covenants.

(c) RESERVE AND LOSS RATIOS.   The quality of financial assets is critical to the earning power and credit quality of a finance company. This quality is measured by the rate of losses on collection of receivables and the adequacy of balance sheet reserves to absorb losses. The level of holdback reserves also indicates the continued parent equity in the subsidiary. Loss as a percentage of average receivables is defined as:

$$\frac{\text{Net losses on charge} - \text{offs for the year}}{\text{Average receivables (gross receivables} - \text{unearned finance charges)}}$$

---

[6] J. Ronen and A. C. Sondhi, "Debt Capacity and Financial Contracting: Finance Subsidiaries," *Journal of Accounting, Auditing and Finance*, Spring 1989, pp. 237–265.

This ratio will vary depending on the type of business (retail versus wholesale; mix of products financed). A rising trend is an important signal. Losses can also be measured against net interest income on a trend basis.

Reserves as a percentage of receivables is defined as:

$$\frac{\text{Reserve for losses}}{\text{Gross receivables} - \text{unearned finance charges}}$$

The reserve is used to absorb losses and is replenished by charges to operations. To provide a proper cushion, the reserve should be 1.25–2 times annual losses.

(d) LOAN SPREADS. Earnings in the finance (and banking) industry are developed by lending funds at a higher rate than that paid on borrowed funds (i.e., the net interest earned). This spread should be evaluated against the net investment in receivables to derive a rate of return:

$$\frac{\text{Net interest earned (interest revenues} - \text{interest expense)}}{\text{Average receivables (gross receivables} - \text{unearned charges)}}$$

(e) LIQUIDITY. Finance companies are constantly in the market, rolling over short-term paper, refunding longer issues, and selling new debt. Liquidity therefore becomes a function of an adequate balance of debt between all sectors of the money market without an undue concentration of maturities, coupled with adequate bank lines of credit. To maintain the confidence of the market to accept paper under various economic conditions, consistent earnings trends, controlled operations, and debt levels are designed to accomplish these objectives, and the analyst should monitor these ratios and covenants over time to manage risk and return tradeoffs.

(f) CAPITALIZATION. Subordinated debt is usually a significant segment of the finance company's capital structure and must be evaluated separately from senior debt. Subordinated debt and equity together represent the capital base supporting the high levels of debt observed in finance companies. Senior debt is normally restricted to a multiple of the capital base, the aggregate of total debt, the liquid net worth, or a multiple of net worth. Covenants also contain similar restrictions on allowed subordinated debt. The ratio of senior debt to the capital base is frequently 2.5:1–3.5:1 for independent finance companies. Captives may use higher ratios because of access to parent company capital and some guarantees of minimum earnings. Bank credit departments use a similar ratio—"borrowing ratio"—which eliminates nonliquid assets from the capital base. The ratio of senior debt to capital is:

$$\frac{\text{Total senior debt}}{\text{Subordinated debt} + \text{net worth}}$$

Thus, the allowed debt (senior and subordinated) is restricted to some multiple of equity or, in the case of subsidiaries, to the parent's equity investment, and may incorporate subordinated debt owed to parent in the capital base. Along with requirements to maintain receivables levels, these covenants preserve collateral available in the finance company. The ratios described above and the covenants should be monitored by the analyst to evaluate finance company debt.

16.9 GLOSSARY

Liquidity Analysis

1. Current ratio $= \dfrac{\text{Current assets (cash and equivalents, receivables and inventories)}}{\text{Current liabilities (payables, accruals, taxes, and debt due in 1 year)}}$

2. Quick ratio $= \dfrac{\text{Cash and equivalents plus receivables}}{\text{Current liabilities}}$

3. Operating cash flow to current liabilities $= \dfrac{\text{Cash provided by operations}}{\text{Average current liabilities}}$

Activity Ratios

4. Inventory turnover $= \dfrac{\text{Cost of goods sold}}{\text{Average inventory}}$

The number of days inventory is on hand can be calculated as:

$$\frac{365}{\text{Inventory turnover}}$$

5. Receivables turnover $= \dfrac{\text{Net credit sales}}{\text{Average receivables}}$

6. Number of days receivables are outstanding $= \dfrac{365}{\text{Receivables turnover}}$

7. Fixed asset turnover ratio $= \dfrac{\text{Net sales}}{\text{Average fixed assets}}$

Margin Analysis

8. Gross margin $= 1 - \dfrac{\text{Cost of goods sold}}{\text{Sales}}$

9. Expense ratio $= \dfrac{\text{Selling, general, and administrative expenses}}{\text{Sales}}$

10. Operating margin $= \dfrac{\text{Operating income}}{\text{Sales}}$

11. Pretax margin $= \dfrac{\substack{\text{Income before income tax} \\ \text{(Operating income + other income – interest)}}}{\text{Sales}}$

12. Profit margin $= \dfrac{\text{Net income before extraordinary items}}{\text{Sales}}$

Debt Ratios

13. Interest coverage ratio $= \dfrac{\text{Income before interest and taxes}}{\text{Fixed charges}}$

14. Margin of safety $= \dfrac{\text{Income after fixed charges before income taxes}}{\text{Sales}}$

15. Preferred dividend coverage $= \dfrac{\text{Income before interest and taxes}}{\text{Fixed charges + pretax preferred dividends}}$

16. Debt to total capital ratio $= \dfrac{\text{Total current and long-term debt + capitalized leases}}{\text{Total capital(total debt + leases + stockholders' equity)}}$

17. Debt-to-equity ratio $= \dfrac{\text{Total current and long-term debt + capitalized leases}}{\text{Total stockholders' equity}}$

or

$$\frac{\text{Total debt at book value}}{\text{Total debt and preferred stock + common stock at market}}$$

Integrated Analysis of Financial Statements

18. Return on assets $= \dfrac{\text{Net income}}{\text{Average total assets}}$

or

19. $\dfrac{\text{Earnings before interest and taxes}}{\text{Average total assets}}$

Decomposition of Margin and Return Ratios

20. Net income margin
or
EBIT margin

$\times$ Asset turnover = Return on assets

$$\frac{\text{Net income}}{\text{Net sales}}$$

or

$$\frac{\text{EBIT}}{\text{Net sales}}$$

$$\times \frac{\text{Net sales}}{\text{Average total assets}} =$$

$$\frac{\text{Net income}}{\text{Average total assets}}$$

or

$$\frac{\text{EBIT}}{\text{Average total assets}}$$

$\downarrow$

Analysis of relevant
revenue and expense
breakdowns

$\downarrow$

Analysis of inventory,
receivables, and fixed
asset turnover

21. $\text{ROE} = \dfrac{\text{Net income}}{\text{Average common equity}}$

Decomposition of Return on Equity

22. $\text{ROE} = \dfrac{\text{Net income}}{\text{Average total assets}} \times \dfrac{\text{Average total assets}}{\text{Average common equity}}$

or

$= \text{Profit margin} \times \text{Asset turnover} \times \text{Leverage ratio}$

$= \dfrac{\text{Net income}}{\text{Net sales}} \times \dfrac{\text{Net sales}}{\text{Average total assets}} \times \dfrac{\text{Average total assets}}{\text{Average common equity}}$

Other Earnings and Asset Protection Ratios

23. $\text{Return on invested capital} = \dfrac{\text{Earnings before interest and taxes}}{\text{Average invested capital}}$

24. Number of years to pay off debt by application of internally generated cash flows =

$$\frac{\text{Total fixed obligations}}{\text{Operating cash flows}}$$

25. $\text{Asset protection ratio} = \dfrac{\text{Gross receivables} \ - \ \text{unearned finance charges}}{\text{Total debt}}$

26. Reserve and loss ratio =

$$\frac{\text{Net losses on charge} - \text{offs for the year}}{\text{Average receivables(gross receivables} - \text{unearned finance charges)}}$$

27. Reserves as a percentage of receivables =

$$\frac{\text{Reserve for losses}}{\text{Gross receivables} - \text{unearned finance charges}}$$

28. $\text{Loan spreads} = \dfrac{\text{Net interest earned (interest revenues} \ - \ \text{interest expense)}}{\text{Average receivables (gross receivables} \ - \ \text{unearned charges)}}$

29. $\text{Ratio of senior debt to capital} = \dfrac{\text{Total senior debt}}{\text{Subordinated debt} \ + \ \text{net worth}}$

16.10 SOURCES AND SUGGESTED REFERENCES

Bernstein, L. A., and Siegel, J. G., "The Concept of Earnings Quality," *Financial Analysts Journal*, Vol. 35, No. 4, July–August 1979, pp. 72–75.

Casey, C. J., and Bartczak, N. J., "Using Operating Cash Flow Data to Predict Financial Distress: Some Extensions," *Journal of Accounting Research*, Spring 1985, pp. 384–401.

————, "Financial Reporting and Changing Prices," Statement of Financial Accounting Standards No. 33. FASB, Stamford, CT, 1979.

————, "Capitalization of Interest Cost," Statement of Financial Accounting Standards No. 34. FASB, Stamford, CT, 1979.

————, "Foreign Currency Translation," Statement of Financial Accounting Standards No. 52. FASB, Stamford, CT, 1981.

————, "Disclosures about Oil and Gas Producing Activities," Statement of Financial Accounting Standards No. 6. FASB, Stamford, CT, 1982.

————, "Employers' Accounting for Pensions," Statement of Financial Accounting Standards No. 87. FASB, Stamford, CT, 1985.

————, "Consolidation of All Majority-Owned Subsidiaries," Statement of Financial Accounting Standards No. 94. FASB, Stamford, CT, 1987.

————, "Statement of Cash Flows," Statement of Financial Accounting Standards No. 95. FASB, Stamford, CT, 1987.

————, "Disclosure about Fair Values of Financial Instruments," Statement of Financial Accounting Standards No. 107. FASB, Norwalk, CT, 1991.

————, "Accounting for Income Taxes," Statement of Financial Accounting Standards No. 109. FASB, Norwalk, CT, 1991.

————, "Accounting for Certain Investments in Debt and Equity, Securities, Exposure Draft." FASB, Norwalk, CT, 1990.

————, "Employers' Disclosures about Pensions and Other Postretirement Benefits," Statement of Financial Accounting Standards No. 132. FASB, Norwalk, CT, 1998.

————, "Accounting for Derivative Instruments and Hedging Activities," Statement of Financial Accounting Standards No. 133. FASB, Norwalk, CT, 1998.

————, "Business Combinations," Statement of Financial Accounting Standards No. 141. FASB, Norwalk, CT, 2001.

————, "Goodwill and Other Intangible Assets," Statement of Financial Accounting Standards No. 142. FASB, Norwalk, CT, 2001.

Livnat, J., and Sondhi, A. C., "Estimating the Components of Operating Cash Flows." Working Paper, New York University, December 1989.

Ronen, J., and Sondhi, A. C., "Debt Capacity and Financial Contracting: Finance Subsidiaries," *Journal of Accounting, Auditing and Finance*, Spring 1989, pp. 237–265.

Securities and Exchange Commission, "Notice of Adoption of Amendments to Regulation S-X Requiring Disclosure of Certain Replacement Cost Data," Accounting Series Release No. 190. SEC, Washington, DC, 1976.

Sondhi, A. C., Sorter, G. H., and White, G. I., "Cash Flow Redefined: FAS 95 and Security Analysis," *Financial Analysts Journal*, November–December 1988, pp. 19–20.

White, G. I., Sondhi, A. C., and Fried, D., *The Analysis and Use of Financial Statements* (Third Edition.). John Wiley & Sons, Inc., New York, 2003.

CHAPTER 17

PRICE-CHANGE REPORTING

Paul Rosenfield, CPA

17.1 FINANCIAL ACCOUNTING STANDARDS BOARD STATEMENT NO. 33

The Financial Accounting Standards Board (FASB) conducted an experiment in its Statement No. 33, "Financial Reporting and Changing Prices," issued in 1979, in which certain companies were required to present one set of supplementary information stated in a unit of measure defined in terms of the general purchasing power of the dollar reflecting changes in the general level of prices—inflation reporting—and one set adjusted to current buying prices—current cost reporting. (Other bases reflecting price changes that have been advocated for financial reporting, such as current selling prices and the discounted amount of future cash receipts and payments, were not part of FASB Statement No. 33 and are not considered in detail in this chapter.)

This chapter was updated for the Eleventh Edition by the editors.

(a) INFLATION REPORTING. The unit of measure in a set of financial statements is defined in terms of the unit of the money of a country (or of much of a continent, in the case of Euros). Money has three kinds of powers in terms of which the unit of measure for financial statements can be defined. The first is its debt-paying power, which U.S. paper money implies is its primary or only power: "This note is legal tender for all debts, public, and private." U.S. dollars have only one kind of power to discharge debts denominated in U.S. dollars, which never changes. Tendering one U.S. dollar always discharges one U.S. dollar of debt.

The second kind of power of money of interest in financial reporting is its specific purchasing power. Money can be used to buy specific things: Most things for sale in a country are exchangeable for the money or promises of the money of the country. A specific purchasing power of a given quantity of money is its power to buy a single specific kind of good or service. That power depends on the price of that good or service. There is one kind of specific purchasing power for each kind of good or service money can buy. Prices, ratios of exchange, are stated in numbers of units of money. The prices of specific kinds of goods and services can change, so the specific purchasing powers of the quantity of money can change.

The third kind of power of money of interest in financial reporting is its general purchasing power. A general purchasing power of a given quantity of money is its power to buy a specified group of diverse kinds of goods and services, often called a basket of goods and services. A quantity of money at a point in time has one kind of general purchasing power for each kind of basket that can be specified. Skinner observed that "Some people argue that an index of prices in general has no meaning,"[1] but specifying a basket specifies a general purchasing power; it exists because it is a power that exists to buy a selection of things that exist. The prices of the goods and services in the basket can change, so each kind of general purchasing power of the quantity of money can change.

Nevertheless, "... most accountants and users of financial statements have been inculcated with a model of financial reporting that assumes stability of the [general purchasing power of the] monetary unit...."[2] We financial reporters should not act as though something important to financial reporting is the opposite of what it is.

A specified quantity of money, such as that specified in a price, thus involves debt-paying power, specific purchasing power, and general purchasing power. When money is spent (sacrificed), the holder of the money gives up powers (incurs costs) of those kinds. When money is received, the recipient receives powers of those kinds.

Current generally accepted accounting principles (GAAP) in the United States use a unit of measure defined in terms of the debt-paying power of the unit of money. One of the sets of financial statements mandated by FASB Statement No. 33 incorporated a definition of the unit of measure in terms of the general purchasing power of the unit of money.

(b) CURRENT COST REPORTING. "Current buying prices" is a shorthand expression. There are three ways to express current buying prices longhand, stated below. Not considering those longhand expressions has misled proponents of replacing acquisition costs with current buying prices (current costs) as the general basis for financial statements. All such longhand expressions make it clear that current buying prices do not belong in statements of financial position or income statements. (Some have suggested that current buying prices may be helpful as surrogates for or predictors of supposed future events or as surrogates for other attributes.)

The overriding reason they do not belong in financial statements is that once a reporting entity buys an asset, it is finished with the buying market for the asset. It cannot buy an asset it owns while it owns it (obviously); as Sterling states, there are "... entry values of unowned assets...."[3]

---

[1] Ross M. Skinner, *Accounting Standards in Evolution* (Holt, Rinehart, and Winston of Canada, Limited, 1987), p. 554.
[2] FASB, Statement of Standards No. 89, "Financial Reporting and Changing Prices," Lauver dissent.
[3] Robert R. Sterling, *Toward a Science of Accounting* (Houston: Scholars Book Co., 1979), p. 101, emphasis added.

(*Entry values* and *exit values* are common, even more abbreviated expressions for current buying and selling prices.) Nevertheless, Sterling stated that "I mean by 'entry values' the process of valuing assets at their current purchase price. . . . [but] the relevance of entry values of owned assets escapes me."[4] But it is impossible to "valu[e] assets at their current purchase price," and there is no issue of whether current buying prices of owned assets are or are not relevant. *Such prices don't exist*. This exemplifies the trap of referring to "entry price" or "entry value" rather than using the following longhand expression: "the price at which the reporting entity can currently buy an asset it owns," which can be seen as obvious nonsense. (In contrast, current selling prices exist. A reporting entity can sell assets it holds, though it cannot buy assets it holds.) Others fell into the same trap:

> A given asset [owned by a firm] may have several different market prices [including] what it would cost [the firm] to purchase [it] now. . . . (Thomas, Main, p. 36)

> A current . . . price for an asset [owned by a firm] can be obtained from . . . markets . . . in which the firm could buy the asset. . . . (Edwards and Bell, Income, p. 75)

> Current costs represent the exchange price that would be required today [for an entity] to obtain the same asset or its equivalent. (Hendriksen and van Breda, Theory, p. 495)

Edwards and Bell even state that a reporting entity can buy an asset it owns from a competitor! "If the asset being valued is a good in process or a finished good . . . the cost to purchase it from a competitive firm would. . . ."[5]

Like time and cause and effect, assets go in only one direction; for assets, that direction is from purchase to use, if any, and to sale. After an asset is bought by a reporting entity, the entity can only either use it or send it to its selling markets for the asset or its products (if a reporting entity has to dump an asset it holds, it may sell it in the same place it bought it, but that is still a selling market for the reporting entity, and it sells it for its selling price in that market). But we financial reporters spin theories to avoid that conclusion, though current buying prices are even worse than acquisition costs, because acquisition costs at least are attributes of the assets. Current buying prices violate the number one qualitative criterion for financial statements, representativeness,[6] because they purport to represent nothing about the assets held by the reporting entity.

Note that this does not refer to the price at which the reporting entity can currently buy an asset *similar* to an asset it owns, which is another kind of current buying price and a second longhand expression for current buying prices. Systems using these kinds of current buying prices have also been advocated for replacement of acquisition cost as the general basis for financial statements. The fatal defect of this proposal is that such prices are not attributes of the assets held by the reporting entity. They are attributes of assets not held by the reporting entity—assets it does not hold but can buy. Though theories are spun attempting to justify the proposal, such prices should not be used because they are not part of the history of the reporting entity (except for the history of its buying opportunities, which should not be presented in financial statements), and financial statements are supposed to be confined to reporting financial aspects of its history.

A third longhand expression for current buying prices is the amount of money it would cost to recoup the value lost when a reporting entity is deprived of an asset—its so-called deprival value. The fatal defect of proposals to use this idea of current buying prices as the basis for the amounts at which to measure assets in financial statements is that it involves a factor that is contrary to fact—fiction. If an asset held is to be measured at deprival value, the underlying assumption is that the reporting entity has been deprived of it. However, the reporting entity cannot both hold it and have been deprived of it. A report of history should not involve fiction.

---

[4] Id., p. 124.

[5] Edgar O. Edwards and Philip W. Bell, *The Theory and Measurement of Business Income* (Berkeley: University of California Press, 1961), p. 91.

[6] This is the first part of the FASB's criterion of representational faithfulness (the second part is faithfulness). FASB Statement of Concepts No. 2, "Qualitative Characteristics of Accounting Information."

The use of current buying prices follows the law of the hammer, which states that if you give a four-year-old a hammer, he will discover that everything needs hammering. If you give a financial reporting theorist current buying prices, he will discover that financial statements cannot do without them. That is the opposite of how advances in technology should proceed. A technical problem should first be identified and analyzed and a mechanism then sought to solve it, rather than vice versa.

One of the sets of financial statements mandated by FASB Statement No. 33 incorporated current buying prices as the attribute to emphasize in financial statements.

17.2 THE RELATIONSHIP BETWEEN INFLATION REPORTING AND CURRENT COST REPORTING

Inflation reporting involves the definition of the unit of measure. In contrast, current cost reporting, one of the varieties of current value reporting, involves selection of attributes to measure. Exhibit 17.1 illustrates the relationship.

They are separate responses to separate problems: "...the question of current cost is one of 'value,' and the question of general price level adjustments is one of 'scale.' These are two separate issues."[7] However, the separation is often disregarded, for example: "... general price level accounting and current-value accounting are competing alternative measures for dealing with problems created by inflation."[8]

The effect on income statements in general of changing the attribute that's measured is merely to change the periods in which income is reported: "...[the] choice of attributes to be measured ... do[es] not affect the amounts of comprehensive income ... over the life of an enterprise but do[es] affect the time and way parts of the total are identified with the periods that constitute the entire life."[9] Changing the unit of measure, in contrast, changes the amount of overall reported income.

17.3 THE FAILURE OF FINANCIAL ACCOUNTING STANDARDS BOARD STATEMENT NO. 33

The FASB in effect rescinded its Statement No. 33 by issuing its Statement No. 89, in 1986. Flegm celebrated Statement No. 33's failure: "One of the challenges that academics should address ...

	Historical Cost	Current Value
Units of money	1	2
Units of general purchasing power (general price-level restatement)	3	4

Exhibit 17.1   Relationship between General Price-Level Restatement and Current Value Accounting (*Source*: Paul Rosenfield, "The Confusion between General Price-Level Restatement and Current Value Accounting," *Journal of Accountancy*, October 1972.)

[7] Vernon Kam, *Accounting Theory*, 2nd ed. (New York: John Wiley & Sons, 1990), p. 449.
[8] Ahmed Riahi Belkaoui, *Accounting Theory*, 3rd ed. (New York: The Dryden Press, 1993), p. 305.
[9] FASB, Statement of Concepts No. 6, "Elements of Financial Statements," par. 73.

is why Statement No. 33 was such a dismal failure...."[10] This chapter takes up that challenge.

(a) THE BACKGROUND OF FINANCIAL ACCOUTING STANDARDS BOARD STATEMENT NO. 33.

Before the stock market crash of 1929, many companies increased the amounts at which they reported their assets, mainly their land, buildings, and machinery, to make them more current, based on the belief that investors were influenced by reported asset amounts more than by reported income amounts, in contrast with the opposite belief today. After the crash, the write-ups were reversed and many companies even wrote their assets down below acquisition cost.

Many people said those increased asset amounts contributed to the increase in prices of common stocks leading up to the crash; for example, Brown referred to "The speculative orgy of the prede-pression days based on frequent and optimistic revaluations of assets, dividend distributions based on inflated values, and heavy reliance on book values of stock...."[11] Investors who had lost money rightly or wrongly placed part of the blame on us financial reporters who had made or permitted the write-ups. Thus burned, we financial reporters changed rules, instituted new rules—"... in the United States...upward revaluation was virtually outlawed in the 'thirties...."[12]—and vowed we would never again permit assets to be reported at amounts greater than their acquisition costs: Littleton, an influential professor at the time, said that "...few people wish to see enterprises and accounting tangle again with the revaluation approach often used in the 1920s and 1930s."[13]

It was said that the financial reporters of that day would all have to die before reporting of assets at greater than acquisition cost would again be permitted; as the economist Paul Samuelson said, "knowledge advances 'funeral by funeral.' "[14] The historian Jacques Barzun agrees: "...old resisters could be gradually argued into their graves."[15] Even today, issuers of financial reports feel much the same. For example, Flegm recently said that "It was common practice in the 1920s to 'create' values through such questionable practices as writing up one's assets, but the 1929 stock market crash and the subsequent congressional hearings which resulted in the establishment of the Securities and Exchange Commission (SEC) ended such 'voodoo accounting.' "[16]

After more than a generation, double-digit inflation plus a nudge from the chief accountant of the SEC caused us financial reporters to reconsider. First, the SEC in 1976[17] and then the FASB in 1979 in FASB Statement No. 33 temporarily required large companies to present supplementary information reflecting current prices of assets held—often higher than their acquisition costs—and reflecting the financial effects of inflation. For the moment, though, the primary financial statements reflect the Depression mentality of acquisition cost now and evermore. The American Institute of Certified Public Accountants (AICPA) Special Committee on Financial Reporting reflected that mentality in 1994: "Despite the periodic call to do so, [standard setters] should not pursue a value-based accounting model."[18]

(b) THE DEFECTS OF FINANCIAL ACCOUTING STANDARDS BOARD STATEMENT NO. 33.

FASB Statement No. 33 had two major defects: (1) its use of supplementary statements and (2) its use of current buying prices.

---

[10] Eugene H. Flegm, "The Limitations of Accounting," *Accounting Horizons*, September 1989, p. 95.

[11] Clifford D. Brown, "The Emergency of Income Reporting," in Coffman et al., *Perspectives*, p. 69.

[12] R. J. Chambers, "Second Thoughts on Continuously Contemporary Accounting," *Abacus*, September 1970, p. 40.

[13] A. C. Littleton, *Structure of Accounting Theory* (New York: American Accounting Association, 1953), p. 213.

[14] Nicholas Wade, "From Ants to Ethics: A Biologist Dreams of Unity of Knowledge," *New York Times*, May 12, 1998, p. F6.

[15] Jacques Barzun, *From Dawn to Decadence* (New York: HarperCollins Publishers, Inc., 2000), p. 38.

[16] Eugene H. Flegm, Letter to the Editor of *Barron*'s, January 13, 1986, p. 48.

[17] Accounting Series Release 190.

[18] AICPA, Special Committee on Financial Reporting, *Comprehensive Report of the Special Committee on Financial Reporting*, "Improving Business Reporting—A Customer Focus," 1994, p. 95.

(i) The Use of Supplementary Statements. The FASB thought that "Supplementary financial statements, complete or partial, may be useful, especially to introduce and to gain experience with new kinds of information."[19] Solomons said as much: "The easiest way for the board to innovate is through requirements to provide supplementary information. That way, change—even radical change—can be introduced for a trial period without disrupting GAAP."[20] But people said they did not know what to do with the information, and that is why the experiment failed. The FASB terminated the experiment.

The reason people did not know what to do with the supplementary information was that it competed with the usual financial statement information stated in a unit of measure defined in terms of the debt-paying power of the dollar, which pertained to the same things as the supplementary information but gave different amounts. The debt-paying power information was familiar; the supplementary information was unfamiliar: "... the presentation of financial statements on the traditional basis supplemented by statements on any contemporary basis will only increase, not diminish, confusion. ...; ... where the supplementary information is contradictory of the principal information ... recipients know not what to do with it."[21] The competition was too much for the supplementary information. That was the best way to condemn inflation reporting.

Inflation reporting should not be toyed with. One set of financial statements should be presented. The unit of measure in the financial statements should be defined in terms of the consumer general purchasing power of the unit of money. (Mexico, Chile, and Venezuela, e.g., did that.) People would know what to do with such financial statements—the same things they do with current-style financial statements, only better.

(ii) The Use of Current Buying Prices. As discussed above, current buying prices should not be used in financial statements. Two other possible replacements for acquisition costs should be considered—current selling prices and discounted future cash receipts and payments.

(c) A MIXED BLESSING. The failure of FASB Statement No. 33 was a mixed blessing. It was defectively designed: It involved supplementary statements, which denigrated the experimental information, and it used a factor that it called an attribute of assets that is not an attribute of assets. It is fortunate that it failed. An unfortunate effect of its failure, however, is that interest in reflecting changing prices in financial statements in the periods in which they change has at least temporarily diminished since then. Thus, earnings management by the faulty design of GAAP, which is discussed in Chapter 6, continues to be facilitated.

(d) A NOBLE FAILURE. Though a failure, FASB Statement No. 33 was a noble failure, not, as Flegm called it, a dismal failure, because it marked a significant departure from the kind of financial reporting practiced throughout most of the twentieth century, going back at least to the stock market crash. For a shining moment, the profession abandoned its terror of reflecting changes in the prices of assets while they are held, at least in supplementary statements.

17.4 SOURCES AND SUGGESTED REFERENCES

AICPA, Special Committee on Financial Reporting, *Comprehensive Report of the Special Committee on Financial Reporting*, "Improving Business Reporting—A Customer Focus," 1994.

---

[19] FASB, Statement of Concepts No. 5, "Recognition and Measurement in Financial Statements of Business Enterprises."

[20] Policy, p. 196. I once said much the same: "One thing I know is that we cannot get the general price-level statements to be the only statements now. That would be absolutely impossible, considering the educational job that would be required for both accountants and users, to cite just one problem." (Rosenfield, "Critique," p. 162.) Experience with FASB Statement No. 33, as discussed in the text, has caused me to repent of that sentiment.

[21] R. J. Chambers, "Accounting Education for the Twenty-first Century," *Abacus*, Vol. 23, No. 2, 1987, p. 195; and *Accounting, Finance, and Management* (Chicago: Arthur Andersen & Co., 1969), p. 440.

Barzun, Jacques, *From Dawn to Decadence* (New York: HarperCollins Publishers, Inc., 2000).

Belkaoui, Ahmed Riahi, *Accounting Theory,* 3rd ed. (New York: The Dryden Press, 1993).

Brown, Clifford D., The Emergence of Income Reporting, in Coffman et al., *Perspectives.*

Chambers, R. J., *Accounting, Finance, and Management* (Chicago: Arthur Andersen & Co., 1969).

———, "Second Thoughts on Continuously Contemporary Accounting," *Abacus,* September 1970.

———, "Accounting Education for the Twenty-first Century," *Abacus,* Vol. 23, No. 2, 1987.

Coffman, Edward N., Tondkar, Rasoul H., and Previts, Gary John, *Historical Perspectives of Selected Financial Accounting Topics* (Homewood, IL: Irwin, 1993).

Edwards, Edgar O., and Bell, Philip W., *The Theory and Measurement of Business Income* (Berkeley: University of California Press, 1961).

Financial Accounting Standards Board, Statement of Concepts No. 2, "Qualitative Characteristics of Accounting Information."

———, Statement of Concepts No. 5, "Recognition and Measurement in Financial Statements of Business Enterprises."

———, Statement of Concepts No. 6, "Elements of Financial Statements."

———, Statement of Standards No. 89, "Financial Reporting and Changing Prices."

Flegm, Eugene H., Letter to the Editor of *Barron's*, January 13, 1986.

———, "The Limitations of Accounting," *Accounting Horizons,* September 1989.

Hendriksen, Eldon S., and van Breda, Michael F., *Accounting Theory,* 5th ed. (Boston: Richard D. Irwin, Inc., 1992).

Kam, Vernon, *Accounting Theory,* Second edition. (New York: John Wiley & Sons, 1990).

Littleton, A. C., *Structure of Accounting Theory* (New York: American Accounting Association, 1953).

Rosenfield, Paul, Critique: Inflation and the Lag in Accounting Practice, in Sterling and Bentz, *Perspective.*

———, "The Confusion Between General Price-Level Restatement and Current Value Accounting," *Journal of Accountancy,* October 1972.

Skinner, Ross M., *Accounting Standards in Evolution* (Canada: Holt, Rinehart and Winston of Canada, Limited, 1987).

Solomons, *Making Accounting Policy* (New York: Oxford University Press, 1986).

Sterling, Robert R., *Toward a Science of Accounting* (Houston: Scholars Book Co., 1979).

Sterling, Robert R., and Bentz, William F., *Accounting in Perspective* (Dallas: South-Western Publishing Co., 1971).

Thomas, Arthur L., *Financial Accounting: The Main Ideas,* Second edition. (Belmont, CA: Wadsworth Publishing Company, Inc., 1975).

Wade, Nicholas, "From Ants to Ethics: A Biologist Dreams of Unity of Knowledge," *New York Times,* May 12, 1998.

CHAPTER 18

CASH, TRANSFERS OF FINANCIAL ASSETS, LOANS, AND INVESTMENTS

Luis E. Cabrera, CPA

American Institute of Certified Public Accountants

This chapter was updated from the Tenth Edition for recent changes in professional literature by Sydney Garmong, CPA, Crowe Chizek and Company LLC. The information contained in this chapter does not necessarily represent the views of Crowe Chizek and Company LLC.

18.1 INTRODUCTION TO CASH

(a) NATURE AND IMPORTANCE OF CASH.   Cash is both the beginning and the end of the operating cycle (cash–inventory–sales–receivables–cash) in the typical business enterprise, and almost all transactions affect cash either directly or indirectly. Cash transactions are probably the most frequently recurring type entered into by a business because (except for barter transactions) every sale leads to a cash receipt and every expense to a cash disbursement. It is recognized as the most liquid of the assets, and thus has prominence for users who are focusing on issues of liquidity.

Cash derives its primary importance from its dual role as a medium of exchange and a unit of measure. As a medium of exchange, it has a part in the majority of transactions entered into by an enterprise. Assets are acquired and realized, and liabilities are incurred and liquidated, in terms of cash. Thus, cash is generally the most active asset possessed by a company. As a unit of measure, it sets the terms on which all properties and claims against the enterprise are stated in its financial statements. Price-change reporting, which addresses disclosures for fluctuations in value as general and specific price levels rise and fall, is discussed in Chapter 17.

(b) CASH ACCOUNTING AND CONTROL.   The major challenge in accounting for cash is maintaining adequate control over the great variety and quantity of cash transactions. Cash receipts may come from such diverse sources as cash sales, cash on delivery (C.O.D.) transactions, collections on accounts and notes receivable, loans, security issues, income from investments, and sales of such properties as retired assets, scrap, and investments. Disbursements may be made for a variety of expense items, for cash purchases and in payment of various liabilities, for dividends and for taxes. Thus, the variety of cash transactions in itself presents inherent problems.

The quantity of cash transactions constitutes another source of difficulty. To handle expeditiously the volume of cash transactions calls for appropriate equipment, careful organization and segregation of duties, planning of procedures, and design of appropriate forms. Information as to available cash balances is of daily interest to the management of every business, and this information must be accurate and prompt if it is to be useful.

(c) MISREPRESENTED CASH BALANCES.   Companies sometimes misrepresent their cash balance to improve the appearance of their financial liquidity. This practice is sometimes called *window dressing*. Smith and Skousen describe this practice as follows:

> Certain practices designed to present a more favorable financial condition than is actually the case may be encountered. For example, cash records may be held open for a few days after the close of a fiscal period and cash received from customers during this period reported as receipts of the preceding period. An improved cash position is thus reported. If this balance is then used as a basis for drawing predated checks in payment of accounts payable, the ratio of current assets to current liabilities is improved. The current ratio may also be improved by writing checks in payment of obligations and entering these on the books even though checks are not to be mailed until the following period.[1]

---

[1] Jay M. Smith, Jr. and K. Fred Skonsen, *Intermediate Accounting*, Tenth Edition. (South-Western Publishing Co., Cincinnati, Ohio, 1990).

18.2 ACCOUNTING FOR AND REPORTING CASH

(a) CLASSIFICATION AND PRESENTATION.   The presentation of cash in the balance sheet is largely an issue of appropriate classification and description. Because of its importance in evaluating an entity's financial condition, cash must be stated as accurately as possible. This calls for careful analysis of each component of cash so that no items will improperly be included in, or excluded from, current assets. In this connection, ARB No. 43, "Restatement and Revision of Accounting Research Bulletins" (Ch. 3, pars. 4–6), states, in part:

> For accounting purposes, the term current assets is used to designate cash and other assets or resources commonly identified as those which are reasonably expected to be realized in cash or sold or consumed during the normal operating cycle of the business. Thus the term comprehends in general such resources as (a) cash available for current operations and items which are the equivalent of cash. . . .

> This concept of the nature of current assets contemplates the exclusion from that classification of such resources as: (a) cash and claims to cash which are restricted as to withdrawal or use for other than current operations, are designated for expenditure in the acquisition or construction of noncurrent assets, or are segregated for the liquidation of long-term debts. . . .

As the one asset that is liquid, that is, expendable with no intermediary transactions or conversions, cash assumes the position of prime importance in the balance sheet and is generally presented as the first item among the assets of the enterprise. Four examples of presentation are:

1. Cash and cash equivalents
2. Cash
3. Cash and equivalents
4. Cash includes certificates of deposit or time deposits

Generally, the form shown in example 1 above is widely used, but the important point is that cash subject to withdrawal restrictions should not be combined with cash of immediate availability. In this regard, O'Reilly, et al state in Montgomery's Auditing: "The cash caption on the balance sheet should include cash on hand and balances with financial institutions that are immediately available for any purpose and cash equivalents."

Statement of Financial Accounting Standards (SFAS) No. 95, "Statement of Cash Flows" (par. 8), states that cash equivalents are short-term highly liquid investments that are both:

- Readily convertible to known amounts of cash
- So near their maturity that they present insignificant risk of changes in value because of changes in interest rates

Paragraph 8 also states that "generally only investments with original maturities of three months or less qualify under that definition." Original maturity is further defined as maturity to the entity holding the investment. The Statement clarifies that the maturity date must be three months from the date of its acquisition by the entity. Thus, a Treasury note purchased three years ago and held does not become a cash equivalent when its remaining maturity is three months. Cash equivalents include Treasury bills, commercial paper, and money market funds.

(b) DEFINITION OF CASH.   Cash exists both in physical and book entry forms: physical in the form of coin and paper currency as well as other negotiable instruments of various kinds, and book entry in various forms such as commercial bank deposits and savings deposits. In addition to coin and paper currency, other kinds of physical cash instruments that are commonly reported as cash for financial accounting purposes include certificates of deposit, bank checks, demand bills of exchange (in some cases), travelers' checks, post office or other money orders, bank drafts, cashiers' checks, and letters of credit.

All these forms of cash involve credit and depend for their ready acceptance on the integrity and liquidity of some person or institution other than those offering or accepting them as cash. This is true even for coin and paper currency which is, ultimately, dependent on the credit of the government issuing it. Given this integrity and liquidity, the book entry forms and other physical instruments are properly viewed as cash because of their immediate convertibility into cash in its currency form at the will of the holder. Convertibility in the case of savings accounts, certificates of deposit, and other time deposits may be something less than immediate depending on stipulated conditions imposed by the depository, but the assurance of such convertibility makes these items a generally accepted form of cash. However, only investments with original maturities of three months or less qualify for presentation as cash equivalents, as described above.

(c) RESTRICTED CASH.   Cash restricted as to use by agreement, such as amounts deposited in escrow or for a specified purpose subject to release only at the order of a person other than the depositor, should not be classified in the balance sheet as cash and, unless deposited to meet an existing current liability, should presumably be excluded from current assets. Cash is sometimes received from customers in advance payment for work being performed under contract or under similar circumstances. Such cash is properly designated as cash in the balance sheet, but may be properly classified as a current asset only if the resulting customer's deposit is classified as a current liability. Cash restricted as to withdrawal because of inability of the depository to meet demands for withdrawal (such as deposits in banks in receivership) is not a current asset and should not be designated in the balance sheet as cash without an appropriate qualifying caption.

In regard to cash awaiting use for construction or other capital purposes or held for the payment of long-term debt, O'Reilly, et al. state:

> Cash sometimes includes balances with trustees, such as sinking funds or other amounts not immediately available, for example, those restricted to uses other than current operations, designated for acquisition or construction of noncurrent assets, or segregated for the liquidation of long-term debt. Restrictions are considered effective if the company clearly intends to observe them, even though the funds are not actually set aside in special bank accounts. The facts pertaining to those balances should be adequately disclosed, and the amounts should be properly classified as current or noncurrent.[2]

(d) BANK OVERDRAFTS.   Overdrafts may be of two kinds: (1) an actual bank overdraft, resulting from payment by the bank of checks in an amount exceeding the balance available to cover such checks; (2) a book overdraft, arising from issuance of checks in an amount in excess of the balance in the account on which drawn, although such checks have not cleared through the bank in an amount sufficient to exhaust the account.

Actual bank overdrafts represent the total of checks honored by the bank without sufficient funds in the account to cover them; such an overdraft is the bank's way of temporarily loaning funds to its customer. Accordingly, bank overdrafts (other than those that arise in connection with a "zero-balance" or similar arrangement with a bank) represent short-term loans and should be classified as liabilities if the right of offset does not exist.

Book overdrafts representing outstanding checks in excess of funds on deposit should generally be classified as liabilities and cash reinstated at the balance sheet date. Such credit book balances should not be viewed as offsets to other cash accounts except where the legal right of setoff exists within the same bank due to the existence of other positive balances in that bank.

FASB Interpretation (FIN) No. 39, "Offsetting of Amounts Related to Certain Contracts," provides guidance on whether the right of offset has been met. Where right of setoff does not exist,

---

[2] Vincent M. O'Reilly et al, *Montgomery's Auditing*, Twelfth Edition. (John Wiley & Sons, New York, 1998) Section 17.17.

the credit balance can be viewed as a reinstatement of the liabilities that were cleared in the bookkeeping process. When outstanding checks in excess of funds on deposit are reclassified, it is preferable that they be separately classified; if they are included in accounts payable, the amounts so included should be disclosed, if material. Reclassifying as a liability *all* outstanding checks (including those covered by funds on deposit in the bank account concerned) is generally not considered acceptable.

(e) FOREIGN BALANCES.   Cash in foreign countries may properly be included in the balance sheet as cash if stated at its equivalent in U.S. currency at the prevailing rate of exchange and if no exchange restrictions exist to prevent the transfer of such monies to the domicile of the owner. Depending on circumstances and the extent to which such cash balances may be subject to exchange control or other restrictions, the amount of cash so included should be considered for disclosure, either by being stated separately, parenthetically, or otherwise. The question of exchange restrictions (or economic conditions) preventing transfer of cash across national boundaries is of prime importance, and cash in foreign countries should be classified as a current asset only if appropriate review establishes that no significant restrictions or conditions exist with respect to the amounts involved. If restrictions exist but ultimate transfer seems probable, the cash may be included in the balance sheet in a noncurrent classification.

Difficulty in stating foreign cash balances at their equivalent in U.S. currency occurs when more than one rate of exchange exists. In this situation, the use of an exchange rate related to earnings received from the foreign subsidiary for the purpose of translating foreign currency accounts is recommended. SFAS No. 52, "Foreign Currency Translation," (pars. 26–28) provides guidance on the selection of exchange rates.

(f) COMPENSATING CASH BALANCES.   It is not uncommon for banks to require that a current or prospective borrower maintain a compensating balance on deposit with the bank. Frequently, the required compensating balance is based on the average outstanding loan balance. A compensating deposit balance may also be required to assure future credit availability (including maintenance of an unused line of credit). The compensating balance requirement may be (1) written into a loan or line of credit agreement, (2) the subject of a supplementary written agreement, or (3) based on an oral understanding. In some instances, a fee is paid on an unused line of credit (or commitment) to ensure credit availability.

The Securities and Exchange Commission (SEC) originally defined compensating balances in ASR No. 148 as follows:

> A compensating balance is defined as that portion of any demand deposit (or any time deposit or certificate of deposit) maintained by a corporation (or by any other person on behalf of the corporation) which constitutes support for existing borrowing arrangements of the corporation (or any other person) with a lending institution. Such arrangements would include both outstanding borrowings and the assurance of future credit availability.

For SEC registrants, requirements for the disclosure of restrictions on the withdrawal or use of cash and cash items, such as compensating balance arrangements, are set forth in Rule 5-02.1 of Regulation S-X as follows:

CASH AND CASH ITEMS.

Separate disclosure shall be made of the cash and cash items which are restricted as to withdrawal or usage. The provisions of any restrictions shall be described in a note to the financial statements. Restrictions may include legally restricted deposits held as compensating balances against short-term borrowing arrangements, contracts entered into with others, or company statements of intention with regard to particular deposits; however, time deposits and short-term certificates of deposit are not generally included in legally restricted deposits. In cases where compensating balance arrangements exist but are not agreements which legally restrict the use of cash amounts shown on the balance sheet, describe in the notes to the financial statements these arrangements and the amount involved, if determinable, for the most recent audited balance sheet required and for any subsequent unaudited balance sheet required in the notes to the financial statements. Compensating balances that are maintained under an agreement to assure future credit availability shall be disclosed in the notes to the financial statements along with the amount and terms of such agreement.

Guidelines and interpretations for disclosure are in FRR No. 203 and Staff Accounting Bulletin (SAB) Topic 6H. These provide useful information in evaluating the need for segregation and disclosure of compensating balance arrangements, including determination of the amount to be disclosed. Cash float and other factors should be considered.

Although no other authoritative literature requires compensating balance disclosures in the financial statements of non-SEC registrants, disclosure of material compensating balances will usually be necessary for fair presentation of the financial statements in accordance with generally accepted accounting principles (GAAP). Consequently, the disclosure of material compensating balance arrangements in financial statements of non-SEC reporting companies, whether maintained under a written agreement or under an informal agreement confirmed by the bank, is usually considered necessary as an "informative disclosure" under the third standard of reporting. It should be noted that compensating balances may also relate to an agreement or an understanding relative to future credit availability (including unused lines of credit). Compensating balances related to future credit availability should be disclosed as well as those related to outstanding borrowings.

(i) Disclosure.   In circumstances where compensating balances relative to outstanding loans and future credit availability are not legally restricted as to withdrawal, note disclosure is appropriate.

(ii) Segregation in the Balance Sheet.   Cash that is not subject to withdrawal should be classified as a noncurrent asset to the extent such cash relates to the noncurrent portion of the debt that causes its restriction. To the extent legally restricted cash relates to short-term borrowings, it may be included with unrestricted amounts on one line in financial statements of non-SEC reporting companies provided the caption is appropriate and there is disclosure of the restricted amounts in the notes, for example, "Cash and restricted cash (Note 3)." Rule 5-02.1 of Regulation S-X requires SEC-reporting companies to disclose separately funds legally restricted as to withdrawal, but FRR No. 203.02.b is more specific in its requirement to segregate all legally restricted cash in the balance sheet.

No single example is appropriate for the disclosure of all compensating balance arrangements and future credit availability (including unused lines of credit) because the terms of loan agreements vary greatly. However, the following hypothetical examples illustrate methods of disclosing the details of compensating balance agreements and future credit availability.

The following is an example of disclosure where withdrawal of the compensating balance was legally restricted at the date of the balance sheet.

CASH ITEMS DISCLOSED ON BALANCE SHEET

SEC-Reporting Companies

Current assets

Cash	$3,500,000
Restricted cash compensating balances (Note X)	6,000,000

Non-SEC Reporting Companies

Current assets

Cash and restricted cash (Note X)	$9,500,000

Note X. Compensating Balances

A maximum of $100,000,000 is available to the company under a revolving credit agreement. Under the terms of the agreement, the company is required to maintain on deposit with the bank a compensating balance, restricted as to use, of 10 percent of the outstanding loan balance. At December 31, 20XX, $6,000,000 of the cash balance shown in the balance sheet was so restricted after adjusting for differences of "float" between the balance shown by the books of the company and the records of the bank.

For SEC-reporting companies, the following disclosure should be added to the above note:

This "float" amount consisted of $3,000,000 of unpresented checks less $500,000 of deposits of delayed availability at the agreed-upon schedule of 1.5 days' deposits.

The following is an example of disclosure for both SEC and non-SEC reporting companies where withdrawal of the compensating balance was not legally restricted at the date of the balance sheet.

Current assets

Cash (Note X)	$10,000,000

Note X. Compensating Balances

Under an informal agreement with a lending bank, the company maintains on deposit with the bank a compensating balance of 5 percent of an unused line of credit and 10 percent of the outstanding loan balance. At December 31, 20XX approximately $5,800,000 of the cash balance shown in the balance sheet represented a compensating balance.

(g) UNUSED LINES OF CREDIT.   Rules 5-02.19 and 22 of Regulation S-X require that the amount and terms (including commitment fees and the conditions under which commitments may be withdrawn) of unused lines of credit or unused commitments for financing arrangements be disclosed. The term *unused lines of credit* is used for short-term financing arrangements; the term *unused commitments* refers to long-term financing arrangements. The requirements of Regulation S-X are as follows:

5.02.19 ACCOUNTS AND NOTES PAYABLE. (b) The amount and terms (including commitment fees and the conditions under which lines may be withdrawn) of unused lines of credit for short-term financing shall be disclosed, if significant, in the notes to the financial statements. The weighted average interest rate on short term borrowings outstanding as of the date of each balance sheet presented shall be furnished in a note. The amount of these lines of credit which support a commercial paper borrowing arrangement or similar arrangements shall be separately identified.

5.02. 22. BONDS, MORTGAGES, AND OTHER LONG TERM DEBT, INCLUDING CAPI-TALIZED LEASES. (b) The amount and terms (including commitment fees and the conditions under which commitments may be withdrawn) of unused commitments for long-term financing arrangements that would be disclosed under this rule if used shall be disclosed in the notes to the financial statements if significant.

Many future credit arrangements are informal. Even formal arrangements may be withdrawn by lending institutions on very short notice, usually resulting from an adverse change in the financial position of a company. Therefore, limitations relating to the subsequent use of such lines of credit make it particularly difficult to provide informative and adequate disclosure so that the reader does not get a more favorable picture than is warranted. Because of the uncertainty of the duration of some lines of credit, disclosure of these types of lines of credit in financial statements requires the exercise of individual judgment based on the facts of the particular situation, and disclosures should include the limitations and conditions of subsequent use. Unused lines of credit or commitments that may be withdrawn at the mere option of the lender need not be disclosed but, if disclosed, the nature of the arrangement should be disclosed as well.

Disclosure of lines of credit and other borrowing arrangements is generally not considered to be essential information in financial statements of non-SEC reporting companies. In certain cases, however, such as when unused lines of credit support outstanding commercial paper, this type of information may be significant in evaluating financial position. Where this is so, disclosure of future credit availability under written or informal agreements would be necessary for a *fair presentation*, provided the unused credit may not be withdrawn solely at the option of the would-be lender. A fee paid on an unused line of credit or commitment would provide evidence of a binding agreement, as would maintenance of a compensating balance for this purpose.

(i) Fee Paid for Future Credit Availability.   A commitment fee has an effect on the cost of borrowing that is similar to that of a compensating balance. If a fee is paid to a lending bank for an unused line of credit or commitment, such fee should be disclosed if significant (Rule 502.19b of Regulation S-X).

(ii) Disclosure.   The following is an example of disclosure of binding bank credit arrangements. Information of this nature may be combined with note disclosure of indebtedness.

Note X. Unused Lines of Credit

Bank lines of credit under which notes payable of $105,000,000 were outstanding at December 31, 20XX, aggregated $152,500,000. The use of these lines generally is restricted to the extent that the Company is required periodically to liquidate its indebtedness to individual banks for 30 to 60 days each year. Borrowings under such agreements are at interest rates ranging from 1/4 -to 1/2 of 1% above the prime rate, plus a commitment fee of 1/4 to 1/2 of 1% on the unused available credit. Commitments by the banks generally expire one year from the date of the agreement and are generally renewed.

For SEC-reporting companies the following disclosure should be added to the above note:

Total commitment fees paid on the unused lines of credit amounted to $175,000 for 20XX, $195,000 for 20XX, and $180,000 for 20XX.

(h) CONCENTRATION OF CREDIT RISK.   Disclosures related to cash balances should include the existence of uninsured cash balances that represent a significant concentration of credit risk. American Institute of Certified Public Accountants (AICPA) Technical Practice Aid No. 2110.06, "Disclosure of Cash Balances in Excess of Federally Insured Amounts," provides the following guidance:

Inquiry. Should the existence of cash on deposit with banks in excess of Federal Deposit Insurance Corporation (FDIC)-insured limits be disclosed in the financial statements? Reply. The existence of uninsured cash balances should be disclosed if the uninsured balances represent a significant concentration of credit risk. Credit risk is defined in FASB Statement No. 105, "Disclosure of Information about Financial Instruments with Off-Balance-Sheet Risk and Financial Instruments with Concentrations of Credit Risk," Paragraph 7 (AC F25.107), as "the possibility that a loss may occur from the failure of another party to perform according to the terms of the contract." As a result, bank statement balances in excess of FDIC-insured amounts represent credit risk.

An example of disclosure for this circumstance might be:

The Company maintains its cash in bank deposit accounts which, at times, may exceed federally insured limits. The Company has not experienced any losses in such account. The Company believes it is not exposed to any significant credit risk on cash and cash equivalents.

(i) FAIR VALUE DISCLOSURES.   SFAS No. 107, "Disclosure about Fair Value of Financial Instruments," requires disclosure of fair values of all financial instruments. The disclosure should include the method and significant assumptions used to estimate fair value. Due to the short-term maturity of cash and cash equivalents, this requirement is often met by the following sample disclosure:

Cash and Cash Equivalents. The carrying amount approximates fair value because of the short-term maturity of those instruments.

18.3 TRANSFERS OF FINANCIAL ASSETS

(a) **INTRODUCTION.** With some transfers of financial assets, the transferor has some continuing involvement with the transferred assets or with the transferee. Over the past few decades, these arrangements have grown in volume, variety, and complexity. Those transfers raise the issues of whether transferred financial assets should be considered to be sold and a related gain or loss recorded or whether the assets should be considered to be collateral for borrowings and the transfer not recognized. An entity may sell financial assets and receive in exchange cash or other assets that are unrelated to the assets sold so that the transferor has no continuing involvement with the assets sold. Alternatively, an entity may borrow money and pledge financial assets as collateral, or engage in any of a variety of transactions that transfer financial assets to another entity with the transferor having some continuing involvement with the assets transferred. Examples of continuing involvement include recourse or guarantee obligations, servicing, agreements to repurchase or redeem, and put or call options on the assets transferred. Many transactions disaggregate financial assets into separate components by creating undivided interests in pools of financial assets that frequently reflect multiple participations (often referred to as *tranches*) in a single pool. The components created may later be recombined to restore the original assets or may be combined with other financial assets to create still different assets. An entity also may enter into transactions that change the characteristics of an asset that the entity continues to hold. An entity may sell part of an asset, or an undivided interest in the asset, and retain part of the asset. In some cases, it has not been clear what the accounting should be. An entity may settle a liability by transferring assets to a creditor and obtaining an unconditional release from the obligation. Alternatively, an entity may arrange for others to settle or set aside assets to settle a liability later. To address these issues, the Financial Accounting Standards Board (FASB) issued guidance as described below.

The FASB issued its SFAS No. 140, "Accounting for Transfers and Servicing of Financial Assets and Extinguishments of Liabilities," in September 2000 to replace its Statement No. 125, "Accounting for Transfers and Servicing of Financial Assets and Extinguishment of Liabilities."[3] Though it replaces Statement No. 125 in its entirety, Statement No. 140 carries forward most of the provisions of Statement No. 125. Like Statement No. 125, the Statement No. 140 employs a "financial-components approach" that focuses on control and recognizes that financial assets and liabilities can be divided into several components. Under that approach, after a transfer of financial assets, an entity recognizes the financial and servicing assets it controls and the liabilities it has incurred, derecognizes financial assets when control has been surrendered, and derecognizes liabilities when extinguished.

Statement No. 140 distinguishes transfers of financial assets that are sales from transfers that are secured borrowings, and addresses servicing assets and liabilities, financial assets subject to prepayment and secured borrowing and collateral, and extinguishments of liabilities. It also provides implementation guidance for assessing isolation of transferred assets, conditions that constrain a transferee, conditions for an entity to be a qualifying special purpose entity (SPE), accounting for transfers of partial interests, measurement of retained interests, servicing of financial assets, securitizations, transfers of sales-type and direct financing lease receivables, securities lending transactions, repurchase agreements including "dollar rolls," "wash sales," loan syndications and

---

[3] On August 11, 2005, the FASB issued three exposure drafts to amend Statement 140: (1) "Accounting for Transfers of Financial Assets", (2) "Accounting for Servicing of Financial Assets" and (3) "Accounting for Certain Hybrid Financial Instruments". In February 2006, the FASB issued Statement No. 155, "Accounting for Certain Hybrid Financial Instruments", to resolves issues addressed in Statement 133 Implementation Issue No. D1, "Application of Statement 133 to Beneficial Interests in Securitized Financial Assets." The FASB expects to issue a final standard for servicing assets in the first quarter of 2006 and for transfers of financial assets in the second quarter of 2006. Readers should be alert to final issuances.

participations, risk participations in banker's acceptances, factoring arrangements, transfers of receivables with recourse, and extinguishments of liabilities. Statement 140 also provides guidance about whether a transferor has retained effective control over assets transferred to qualifying SPE through removal-of-accounts provisions, liquidation provisions, or other arrangements.

Statement No. 125 was effective for transfers and servicing of financial assets and extinguishments of liabilities occurring after December 31, 1996, and on or before March 31, 2001, except for certain provisions. Statement 127 deferred until December 31, 1997, the effective date (a) of paragraph 15 of Statement 125 and (b) for repurchase agreement, dollar-roll, securities lending, and similar transactions, of paragraphs 9–12 and 237(b) of Statement 125. Statement No. 140 is effective for transfers and servicing of financial assets and extinguishments of liabilities occurring after March 31, 2001 and is effective for recognition and reclassification of collateral and for disclosures relating to securitization transactions and collateral for fiscal years ending after December 15, 2000. Disclosures about securitization and collateral accepted need not be reported for periods ending on or before December 15, 2000, for which financial statements are presented for comparative purposes. Statement No. 140 is to be applied prospectively with certain exceptions. Other than those exceptions, earlier or retroactive application of its accounting provisions is not permitted.

The following is a brief overview about securitizations. Securitizations are also discussed in Chapter 31. As discussed in paragraph 73–76 of Statement No. 140:

> financial assets such as mortgage loans, automobile loans, trade receivables, credit card receivables, and other revolving charge accounts are commonly transferred in securitizations. Securitizations of mortgage loans may include pools of single-family residential mortgages or other types of real estate mortgage loans, for example, multifamily residential mortgages and commercial property mortgages. Securitizations of loans secured by chattel mortgages on automotive vehicles as well as other equipment (including direct financing or sales-types leases) are also common. Both financial and nonfinancial assets can be securitized; life insurance policy loans, patent and copyright royalties, and even taxi medallions have also been securitized. But securitizations of nonfinancial assets are outside the scope of Statement No. 140.

> An originator of a typical securitization (the transferor) transfers a portfolio of financial assets to an SPE, commonly a trust. In "pass-through" and "pay-through" securitizations, receivables are transferred to the SPE at the inception of the securitization, and no further transfers are made; all cash collections are paid to the holders of beneficial interests in the SPE. In "revolving-period" securitizations, receivables are transferred at the inception and also periodically (daily or monthly) thereafter for a defined period (commonly three to eight years), referred to as the *revolving period*. During the revolving period, the SPE uses most of the cash collections to buy additional receivables from the transferor on prearranged terms.

> Beneficial interests in the SPE are sold to investors, and the proceeds are used to pay the transferor for the assets transferred. The beneficial interests may comprise either a single class having equity characteristics or multiple classes of interests, some having debt characteristics and others having equity characteristics. The cash collected from the portfolio is distributed to the investors and others as specified by the legal documents that established the SPE.

> Pass-through, pay-through, and revolving-period securitizations that meet the criteria in paragraph 9 of Statement No. 140 for transfers in which the transferor surrenders control over the financial assets and thus qualify for sale accounting. All financial assets obtained or retained and liabilities incurred by the originator of a securitization that qualifies as a sale are recognized and measured as provided in Section 18.4(c)(ii); that includes the implicit forward contract to sell new receivables during a revolving period, which may become valuable or onerous to the transferor as interest rates or other market conditions change.

Revolving-period securitizations and isolation of transferred assets in securitizations are discussed in paragraphs 77–84 of the statement.

A qualifying SPE, also referred to as a *QSPE*, is not consolidated in the financial statements of a transferor or its affiliates. A qualifying SPE is a trust or other legal vehicle that meets all the conditions described in paragraph 35 of Statement No. 140.

(b) GENERAL PROVISIONS. Transfers of all or a portion of a financial asset, for example, a loan, are accounted for as either sales or secured borrowings with a pledge of collateral, depending on the circumstances. Transfers of financial assets should be accounted for as a sale if the transferor surrenders control over those financial assets. Control is considered to have been surrendered if and only if all the following three conditions are met. Paragraph 9 of Statement 140 states that:

a. "The transferred assets have been isolated from the transferor—put presumptively beyond the reach of the transferor and its creditors, even in bankruptcy or other receivership." Paragraphs 27–28 provide implementing guidance. The nature and extent of evidence required to support an assertion that has been accomplished depend on the facts and circumstances. All available evidence that supports or questions the assertion is considered. Judgment is required as to:

  ○ Whether the contract or circumstances permit the transferor to revoke the transfer
  ○ The kind of bankruptcy or other receivership into which the transferor or SPE might be placed
  ○ Whether a transfer of financial assets would likely be deemed a true sale at law
  ○ Whether the transferor is affiliated with the transferee
  ○ Other factors under pertinent law

  Derecognition requires evidence providing reasonable assurance that the transferred assets would be beyond the reach of the powers of a bankruptcy trustee or other receiver for the transferor or any consolidated affiliate of the transferor that is not a special-purpose corporation or other entity designed to make remote the possibility that it would enter bankruptcy or other receivership.

b. "Each transferee (or, if the transferee is a qualifying SPE, each holder of its beneficial interests) has the right to pledge or exchange the assets (or beneficial interests) it received, and no condition both constrains the transferee (or holder) from taking advantage of its right to pledge or exchange and provides more than a trivial benefit to the transferor." Paragraphs 29–35 provide implementing guidance.

c. "The transferor does not maintain effective control over the transferred assets through either (1) an agreement that both entitles and obligates the transferor to repurchase or redeem them before their maturity or (2) the ability to unilaterally cause the holder to return specific assets, other than through a cleanup call." (As discussed in the Glossary, a cleanup call is "an option held by the servicer or its affiliate, which may be the transferor, to buy the remaining transferred financial assets or the remaining beneficial interests not held by the transferor, its affiliates, or its agents in a qualifying SPE—or in a series of beneficial interests in transferred assets within a qualifying SPE, if the amount of outstanding assets or beneficial interests falls to a level at which the cost of servicing the assets or beneficial interests becomes burdensome in relation to the benefits of servicing.") Paragraphs 47–54 provide implementing guidance.

As stated in paragraph 10 of Statement No. 140, on completion of any transfer of financial assets, the transferor should:

a. "Continue to carry in its statement of financial position any retained interest in the transferred assets, including, if applicable, servicing assets,, beneficial interests in assets transferred to a qualifying SPE in a securitization and retained undivided interests." Paragraph 58–59, 61–67, and 73–84 of Statement No. 140 provides implementing guidance.

b. "Allocate the previous carrying amount between the assets sold, if any, and the retained interests, if any, based on their relative fair values at the date of transfer."

(c) TRANSFERS ACCOUNTED FOR AS A SALE. Once a transfer of financial assets that meets the aforementioned conditions is completed, the transfer is accounted for as a sale only to the extent that consideration other than beneficial interests (i.e., rights to receive all or a portion of specified cash flows) in the transferred assets is received in exchange. As stated in paragraphs 11 and 12, the transferor shall:

  a. "Derecognize all assets sold.

  b. Recognize all assets obtained and liabilities incurred in consideration as proceeds of the sale, including cash; put or call options held or written, such as guarantee or recourse obligations; forward commitments, such as commitments to deliver additional receivables during the revolving periods of some securitizations; swaps, such as provisions that convert interest rates from fixed to variable; and servicing liabilities, if applicable." Paragraph 56, 57, and 61–67 of Statement No. 140 provides implementing guidance.

  c. "Initially measure at fair value assets obtained and liabilities incurred in a sale or, if it is not practicable to estimate the fair value of an asset or a liability, apply alternative measures." Paragraph 71–72 of Statement No. 140 provides implementing guidance.

  d. "Recognize in earnings any gain or loss on the sale."

The transferee shall recognize all assets obtained and any liabilities incurred and initially measures them at fair value (in aggregate, presumptively the price paid). If a transfer of financial assets in exchange for cash or other considerations (other than beneficial interests in the transferred assets) does not meet the criteria for a sale, the transferor and the transferee account for the transfer as a secured borrowing with pledge of collateral," as discussed below.

(d) SECURED BORROWINGS AND COLLATERAL.   As discussed in paragraph 15 of Statement 140, "a debtor may grant a security interest in certain assets to a lender (the secured party) to serve as collateral for its obligation under a borrowing, with or without recourse to other assets of the debtor. An obligor under other kinds of current or potential obligations, for example, interest rate swaps, also may grant a security interest in certain assets to a secured party. If collateral is transferred to the secured party, the custodial arrangement is commonly called a *pledge*. Secured parties sometimes are permitted to sell or repledge (or otherwise transfer) collateral held under a pledge. The same relationships occur, under different names, in transfers documented as sales that are accounted for as secured borrowings. The accounting for noncash collateral by the debtor (or obligor) and the secured party depends on whether the secured party has the right to sell or repledge the collateral and on whether the debtor has defaulted.

  a. If the secured party (transferee) has the right by contract or custom to sell or repledge the collateral, the debtor (transferor) reclassifies the asset and reports it in its statement of financial position separately (e.g., as security pledged to creditors) from other assets not so encumbered.

  b. If the secured party sells collateral pledged to it, it recognizes the proceeds from the sale and its obligation to return the collateral. The sale of collateral is a transfer subject to the provisions of this Statement.

  c. If the debtor defaults under the terms of secured contract and is no longer entitled to redeem the pledged asset, it derecognizes the pledged asset, and the secured party recognizes the collateral as its asset initially measured at fair value or, if it has already sold the collateral, derecognizes its obligation to return the collateral.

  d. Except as provided in item c above, the debtor continues to carry the collateral as its asset, and the secured party does not recognize the pledged asset."

(e) FINANCIAL ASSETS SUBJECT TO PREPAYMENT.   As discussed in paragraph 14: "Interest-only strips, retained interests in securitizations, loans, other receivables, or other financial assets that can contractually be prepaid or otherwise settled in such a way that the holder would not recover substantially all of its recorded investment, except for instruments that are within the scope of

Statement 133, shall be subsequently measured like investments in debt securities classified as available-for-sale or trading under Statement 115, as amended."

(f) SERVICING ASSETS AND LIABILITIES.   Paragraph 13 of Statement 140 discusses servicing assets and liabilities as follows:

> Each time an entity undertakes an obligation to service financial assets it recognizes either a servicing asset or a servicing liability for the servicing contract, unless it transfers the assets to a qualifying SPE in a guaranteed mortgage securitization, retains all of the resulting securities, and classifies them as debt securities held to maturity in conformity with FASB Statement No. 115. If the servicing asset or liability was purchased or assumed rather than undertaken in a sale or securitization of the financial assets being serviced, it shall measured initially at its fair value, presumptively the price paid. A servicing asset or liability shall be amortized in proportion to and over the period of estimated net servicing income (if servicing revenues exceed servicing costs) or net servicing loss (if servicing costs exceed servicing revenues). A servicing asset or liability shall be assessed for impairment or increased obligation based on its fair value. Paragraph 61–64 of Statement No. 140 provides implementing guidance.

Servicing of mortgage loans, credit card receivables, or other financial assets commonly includes collecting principal, interest, and escrow payments from borrowers; paying taxes and insurance from escrowed funds; monitoring delinquencies; executing foreclosure if necessary; temporarily investing funds pending distribution; remitting fees to guarantors, trustees, and others providing services; and accounting for and remitting principal and interest payments to the holders of the interests in the financial assets. While servicing is inherent in all financial assets, it becomes a distinct asset or liability only when contractually separated from the underlying assets by sale or securitization of the assets with servicing retained or separate purchase or assumption of the servicing. Servicing is most common in the financial institution and mortgage banking industries. Accordingly, this topic is also addressed in Chapter 31.

(g) REPURCHASE AGREEMENTS AND "WASH SALES."   As discussed in paragraphs 96–100 of Statement 140:

> Government securities dealers, banks, other financial institutions, and corporate investors commonly use repurchase agreements to obtain or use short-term funds. Under those agreements, the transferor ("repo-party") transfers a security to a transferee ("repo-counterparty" or "reverse party") in exchange for cash and concurrently agrees to reacquire the security at a future date for an amount equal to the cash exchanged plus a stipulated "interest" factor.

Other securities or letters of credit sometimes are exchanged. Those transactions are accounted for in the same manner as securities lending transactions.

> Repurchase agreements can be put into effect in a variety of ways. Some are similar to securities lending transactions in that the transferee has the right to sell or repledge the securities to a third party during the term of the agreement. In others, the transferee does not have the right to sell or repledge the securities during the term of the agreement. For example, in a tri-party repurchase agreement, the transferor transfers securities to an independent third-party custodian that holds them during the term of the agreement. Also, many repurchase agreements are for short terms, often overnight, or have indefinite terms that allow either party to terminate the arrangement on short notice. However, other repurchase agreements are for longer terms, sometimes until the maturity of the transferred asset. Some repurchase agreements call for repurchase of securities that need not be identical to the securities transferred.

> If the criteria in paragraph 9 are met, the transferor accounts for a repurchase agreement as a sale of financial assets and a forward repurchase commitment, and the transferee accounts for the agreement as a purchase of financial assets and a forward resale commitment. Other transfers accompanied by an agreement to repurchase the transferred assets that are accounted for as sales include transfers with agreements to repurchase at maturity and transfers with repurchase

agreements in which the transferee has not obtained collateral sufficient to fund substantially all the cost of buying replacement assets.

Furthermore, "wash sales" previously not recognized if the same financial asset was bought soon before or after the sale are accounted for as sales. Unless there is a concurrent contract to repurchase or redeem the transferred financial assets from the transferee, the transferor does not maintain effective control over the transferred assets.

As with securities lending transactions, under many agreements to repurchase transferred assets before their maturity the transferor maintains effective control over the assets. Repurchase agreements that do not meet all the criteria in paragraph 9 are treated as secured borrowings. Fixed-coupon and dollar-roll repurchase agreements, and other contracts under which the securities to be repurchased need not be the same as the securities sold, qualify as borrowings if the return of substantially the same securities as those concurrently transferred is assured. Therefore, those transactions are accounted for as secured borrowings by both parties to the transfer.

If a transferor has transferred securities to an independent third-party custodian, or to a transferee, under conditions that preclude the transferee from selling or repledging the assets during the term of the repurchase agreement (as in most tri-party repurchase agreements), the transferor has not surrendered control over those assets.

Loan syndications, loan participations, and banker's acceptances are most common in the financial institution industry and are also addressed in Chapter 31.

(h) LOAN SYNDICATIONS.   As discussed in paragraphs 102–103 of Statement 140:

Borrowers often borrow amounts greater than any one lender is willing to lend. Therefore, groups of lenders commonly jointly fund the loans. That may be accomplished by a syndication under which several lenders share in lending to a single borrower, but each lender loans a specific amount to the borrower and has the right to repayment from the borrower.

A loan syndication is not a transfer of financial assets. Each lender in the syndication accounts for the amounts it is owed by the borrower. Repayments by the borrower may be made to a lead lender that then distributes the collections to the lenders of the syndicate. In those circumstances, the lead lender is simply functioning as a servicer and, therefore, does not recognize the aggregate loan as an asset.

(i) LOAN PARTICIPATIONS.   As discussed in paragraphs 104–106 of Statement 140:

Groups of banks or other entities also may jointly fund large borrowings through loan participations in which a single lender makes a large loan to a borrower and subsequently transfers undivided interests in the loan to other entities.

Transfers by the originating lender may take the legal form of either assignments or participations. The transfers are usually nonrecourse, and the transferor ("originating lender") continues to service the loan. The transferee ("participating entity") may or may not have the right to sell or transfer its participation during the term of the loan, depending on the terms of the participation agreement.

If the loan participation agreement gives the transferee the right to pledge or exchange those participations and the other criteria in paragraph 9 are met, the transfers to the transferee are accounted for by the transferor as sales of financial assets. A transferor's right of first refusal on a bona fide offer from a third party, a requirement to obtain the transferor's permission that shall not be unreasonably withheld, or a prohibition on sale to the transferor's competitor if other potential willing buyers exist is a limitation on the transferee's rights but presumptively does not constrain a transferee from exercising its right to pledge or exchange. However, if the loan participation agreement constrains the transferees from pledging or exchanging their participations, the transferor presumptively receives a more than trivial benefit, has not relinquished control over the loan, and accounts for the transfers as secured borrowings.

(j) BANKERS' ACCEPTANCES AND RISK PARTICIPATIONS IN THEM. As discussed in paragraphs 107–110 of Statement 140:

Banker's acceptances provide a way for a bank to finance a customer's purchase of goods from a vendor for periods usually not exceeding six months. Under an agreement among the bank, the customer, and the vendor, the bank agrees to pay the customer's liability to the vendor on presentation of specified documents that provide evidence of delivery and acceptance of the purchased goods. The principal document is a draft or bill of exchange drawn by the customer that the bank stamps to signify its "acceptance" of the liability to make payment on the draft on its due date.

Once the bank accepts a draft, the customer is liable to repay the bank at the time the draft matures. The bank recognizes a receivable from the customer and a liability for the acceptance it has issued to the vendor. The accepted draft becomes a negotiable financial instrument. The vendor typically sells the accepted draft at a discount either to the accepting bank or in the marketplace.

A risk participation is a contract between the accepting bank and a participating bank in which the participating bank agrees, in exchange for a fee, to reimburse the accepting bank in the event that the accepting bank's customer fails to honor its liability to the accepting bank in connection with the banker's acceptance. The participating bank becomes a guarantor of the credit of the accepting bank's customer.

An accepting bank that obtains a risk participation does not derecognize the liability for the banker's acceptance, because the accepting bank is still primarily liable to the holder of the banker's acceptance even though it benefits from a guarantee of reimbursement by a participating bank. The accepting bank does not derecognize the receivable from the customer because it has not transferred the receivable: It controls the benefits inherent in the receivable, and it is still entitled to receive payment from the customer. However, the accepting bank records the guarantee purchased, and the participating bank records a liability for the guarantee issued.

(k) FACTORING ARRANGEMENTS. As discussed in paragraph 112 of Statement 140: "Factoring arrangements are a means of discounting accounts receivable on a nonrecourse, notification basis. Accounts receivable are sold outright, usually to a transferee (the factor) that assumes the full risk of collection, without recourse to the transferor in the event of a loss. Debtors are directed to send payments to the transferee. Factoring arrangements that meet the criteria in paragraph 9 of SFAS 140 are accounted for as sales of financial assets because the transferor surrenders control over the receivables to the factor."

(l) TRANSFERS OF RECEIVABLES WITH RECOURSE. As discussed in paragraphs 113 of Statement 140:

In a transfer of receivables with recourse, the transferor provides the transferee with full or limited recourse. The transferor is obligated under the recourse provision to make payments to the transferee or to repurchase receivables sold under certain circumstances, typically for defaults up to a specified percentage. The effect of a recourse provision on the application of the criteria in paragraph 9 may vary by jurisdiction. In some jurisdictions, transfers with full recourse may not place transferred assets beyond the reach of the transferor and its creditors, but transfers with limited recourse may. A transfer of receivables with recourse is accounted for as a sale, with the proceeds of the sale reduced by the fair value of the recourse obligation, if the criteria in paragraph 9 are met. Otherwise, a transfer of receivables with recourse is accounted for as a secured borrowing.

(m) EXTINGUISHMENTS OF LIABILITIES. As discussed in paragraphs 114 of Statement 140:

If a creditor releases a debtor from primary obligation on the condition that a third party assumes the obligation and that the original debtor becomes secondarily liable, the release extinguishes the original debtor's liability. However, in those circumstances, regardless of whether explicit consideration was paid for the guarantee, the original debtor becomes a guarantor. As such, it recognizes a guarantee obligation in the same manner as would a guarantor that had never been primarily liable to the creditor, with due regard for the likelihood that the third party will carry out its obligations. The guarantee obligation is initially measured at fair value, and that amount reduces or increases the loss recognized on extinguishment.

(n) DISCLOSURES.   FASB Statement No. 140 (par. 17) requires a reporting entity to disclose certain matters relating to collateral, certain debt extinguishments, assets designated for satisfying scheduled payments, description on assets and liabilities for which it not practicable to estimate fair values, servicing assets and liabilities, securitized assets and retained interests. Additional issues and disclosure requirements that are more prevalent for financial institutions—for example, servicing assets and liabilities—are discussed in Chapter 31. Issues and disclosure requirements related to extinguishments of liabilities are discussed in Chapter 25.

18.4 LOANS

(a) INTRODUCTION.   Although not the primary focus of their business, manufacturers, whole-salers, retailers, and service companies may nevertheless originate loans in connection with their revenue-generating activities. FASB Statement 114, "Accounting by Creditors for Impairment of a Loan," which applies to all creditors and defines a loan, in paragraph 4, as:

> a contractual right to receive money on demand or on fixed or determinable dates that is recognized as an asset in the creditor's statement of financial position. Examples include but are not limited to accounts receivable (with terms exceeding one year) and notes receivable.

However, there are certain requirements, as discussed below, for any type of credit arrangement, including trade receivables. In contrast, one of the most significant activities for financial institutions is the origination and acquisition of loans in order to generate interest revenue. Chapter 31 discusses matters of interest to financial institutions and entities involved in lending and deposit taking activities.

(b) INITIAL RECOGNITION AND MEASUREMENT.   Upon origination or acquisition, loans are generally recorded at their present value. Par. 8a of Statement of Position(SOP) 01-6, "Account-ing by Certain Entities (Including Entities with Trade Receivables) That Lend to or Finance the Activities of Others," states that:

> Loans and trade receivables that management has the intent and ability to hold for the foreseeable future or until maturity or payoff should be reported in the balance sheet at outstanding principal adjusted for any chargeoffs, the allowance for loan losses (or the allowance for doubtful accounts), any deferred fees or costs on originated loans, and any unamortized premiums or discounts on purchased loans.

Generally, interest income on loans is accrued at the contractual rate, and premiums and discounts are amortized using the interest method in accordance with FASB Statement 91, "Accounting for Nonrefundable Fees and Costs Associated with Originating or Acquiring Loans and Initial Direct Costs of Leases." In addition, loans are generally presented in the statement of financial position at amortized cost. Accounting Principles Board (APB) Opinion No. 21, "Interest on Receivables and Payables" discusses the appropriate accounting when the face amount of a note does not reasonably represent the present value1 of the consideration given or received in the exchange. APB 21 (par. 3) excludes from its scope "receivables and payables arising from transactions with customers or suppliers in the normal course of business which are due in customary trade terms not exceeding approximately one year" and "transactions between parent and subsidiary companies and between subsidiaries of a common parent."

Noninterest bearing loans, loans with unrealistic interest rates, and loans obtained in exchange for property, goods, or services with fair values materially different from the principal amount of the loan lead to the recognition of premiums and discounts. APB Opinion No. 21 (par. 16) requires discounts and premiums to be reported "as a direct deduction from or addition to the face amount of the [loan]." Appendix A of APB Opinion No. 21 provides illustrations of the appropriate balance sheet presentation.

Nonrefundable fees and costs associated with an entity's lending activities are discussed in FASB Statement No. 91, Such considerations are most prevalent for financial institutions and the accounting for these fees and costs is discussed in Chapter 31.

Some acquired loans may have experienced a decline in credit quality. SOP 03-3, "Accounting for Certain Loans or Debt Securities Acquired in a Transfer" addresses the accounting and reporting for those loans. Loans that have been acquired should be evaluated to determine whether the provisions of SOP 03-3 should be applied.

(c) LOAN IMPAIRMENT AND INCOME RECOGNITION. Statement of Financial Accounting Concepts No. 6, "Elements of Financial Statements," defines assets as "probable future economic benefits obtained or controlled by a particular entity as a result of past transactions or events" (par. 25). FASB Statement No. 5, "Accounting for Contingencies" and FASB Statement No. 114 address the accounting by creditors for impairment of certain loans. The Statements indicate that a loan is impaired when, based on current information and events, it is probable that a creditor will be unable to collect all amounts due according to the contractual terms of the loan agreement." It applies to all creditors. While both statements address loan impairment, Statement No. 5 generally addresses smaller balance homogenous loans while Statement No. 114 addresses all loans except those specifically excluded (par. 6):

- "Large groups of smaller-balance homogeneous loans that are collectively evaluated for impairment...."
- Loans that are measured at fair value or at the lower of cost or fair value, for example, in accordance with [SFAS] No. 65, "Accounting for Certain Mortgage Banking Activities," or other specialized industry practice.
- Leases as defined in [SFAS] No. 13, "Accounting for Leases."
- Debt Securities as defined in [SFAS] No. 115, "Accounting for Certain Investments in Debt and Equity Securities."

SFAS No. 114 does not specify how a creditor should identify loans that are to be evaluated for impairment. However, in practice, a number of different mechanisms are employed to identify loans for impairment evaluation. These mechanisms include but are not limited to past due reports, reports from regulatory examiners, reviews of incomplete loan files of financial institutions, identification of those borrowers facing financial difficulties or operating in industries facing such difficulties, and loss statistics pertaining to certain categories of loans.

(i) Impairment Measurement Guidelines. The measurement of impairment should take into account both contractual interest payments and contractual principal payments consistent with the original payment terms of the loan agreement. For loans within the scope of Statement No. 114, the creditor should measure impairment based on the present value of expected future cash flows discounted at the loan's effective interest rate. A loan's effective interest rate is defined as "the rate of return implicit in the loan (i.e., the contractual interest rate adjusted for any net deferred loan fees or costs, premium, or discount existing at the origination or acquisition of the loan)" (par. 14).

The Statement provides that as a practical expedient, creditors may alternatively measure impairment based on a loan's observable market price or the fair value of the collateral if the loan is collateral dependent. If the latter approach is used, the measurement of impairment should take into account estimated costs to sell the collateral, on a discounted basis. Furthermore, when a creditor determines that foreclosure is probable, impairment must be measured based on the fair value of the collateral.

In any event, a valuation allowance should be established if the recorded investment in the loan (including accrued interest, net deferred loan fees or costs, and unamortized discount or premium) exceeds the impaired measure. The recognition of such an allowance is accompanied by a corresponding charge to bad debt expense.

(ii) Income Recognition.   Once a loan has been impaired, some entities, particularly financial institutions, suspend the accrual of interest because such accruals do not in those circumstances reflect economic reality.

The recognition of interest income on impaired loans was initially addressed by SFAS No. 114 (pars. 17–19). Subsequent to its issuance, however, a number of commentators requested an extension of the effective date of the Statement due to the difficulty of applying the new guidelines. As a result, the FASB issued SFAS No. 118 to "allow a creditor to use existing methods for recognizing interest income on impaired loans" (par. 3). Statement 118 eliminated the original income recognition provisions of paragraphs 17–19 of SFAS No. 114. However, SFAS No. 114 (par. 17), as amended, recognizes that accounting methods for the recognition of interest income include using "a cost-recovery method, a cash-basis method, or some combination of those methods."

(d) TROUBLED DEBT RESTRUCTURINGS.   Occasionally, a loan may be restructured to meet a borrower's changing circumstances and a new loan is recognized. However, if "the creditor for economic or legal reasons related to the debtor's financial difficulties grants a concession to the debtor that it would not otherwise consider" (par. 2), the transaction should be accounted for in accordance with SFAS No. 15, "Accounting by Debtors and Creditors for Troubled Debt Restructurings." The following types of restructuring arrangements are discussed in SFAS No. 15:

- Transfers of assets of the debtor or an equity interest in the debtor to fully or partially satisfy the debt
- Modification of debt terms, including reduction of one or more of the following: (1) interest rates with or without extension of maturity date(s), (2) face or maturity amounts, and (3) accrued interest

Creditors that receive assets or an equity interest in the debtor in full satisfaction of the loan should account for the restructuring at the fair value of the assets or equity interest received or the fair value of the loan, whichever is more clearly determinable. In the case of a partial satisfaction of the loan, the fair value of the loan may not be used (par. 28, fn. 16).

SFAS No. 114 amended SFAS No. 15 to require that a creditor account for a troubled debt restructuring involving a modification of terms in accordance with SFAS No. 114. However, the effective interest rate to be used in these situations is the original contractual rate and not the rate specified in the restructuring agreement. Furthermore, creditors must disclose "the amount of commitments, if any, to lend additional funds to debtors owing receivables whose terms have been modified in troubled debt restructurings" (SFAS No. 15, par. 40b).

Loans restructured through a modification of terms before the effective date of SFAS No. 114 may continue to be accounted for and disclosed in accordance with SFAS No. 15 as long as the loan, as restructured, is not impaired. Any subsequent impairment will require the application of SFAS No. 114.

(e) NOTES RECEIVED FOR CAPITAL STOCK.   An entity may sometimes receive a note from the sale of capital stock or as a contribution to paid-in capital. The Emerging Issues Task Force (EITF), in EITF 85-1, "Classifying Notes Received for Capital Stock," addressed the issue of whether an entity should report the note receivable as a reduction of shareholders' equity or as an asset. The EITF "reached a consensus that reporting the note as an asset is generally not appropriate, except in very limited circumstances when there is substantial evidence of ability and intent to pay within a reasonably short period of time." One situation where such a note receivable may be reported as an asset is the payment of the note prior to issuance of the financial statements.

(f) DISCLOSURES.   There are a number of standards which require disclosures related to loans as follows:

- APB Opinion 22, Disclosure of Accounting Policies, paragraphs 8 and 12
- SOP 01-6, Accounting by Certain Entities (Including Entities With Trade Receivables) That Lend to or Finance the Activities of Others, paragraph 13–17
- APB Opinion No. 12, Omnibus Opinion—1967, paragraphs 2 and 3
- FASB Statement No. 5, Accounting for Contingencies, paragraphs 9–11
- SOP 94-6, Disclosure of Certain Significant Risks and Uncertainties, paragraphs 13 and 14
- FSP-SOP 94-6-1, Terms of Loan Products That May Give Rise to a Concentration of Credit Risk
- FASB Statement No. 114, Accounting by Creditors for Impairment of a Loan, as amended by FASB Statement No. 118, Accounting by Creditors for Impairment of a Loan—Income Recognition and Disclosures, paragraph 20A
- SOP 03-3, Accounting for Certain Loans or Debt Securities Acquired in a Transfer, paragraph 14–16
- FASB Statement No. 107, Disclosures about the Fair Value of Financial Instruments

18.5 DEBT SECURITIES

(a) INTRODUCTION.   An entity may invest in debt securities (e.g., bonds) to generate interest revenue and/or to realize gains from their sale at increased market prices. SFAS No. 115 is the primary standard applicable to investments in debt securities. The FASB has also issued a special report entitled, "A Guide to Implementation of Statement 115 on Accounting for Certain Investments in Debt and Equity Securities," which contains a series of questions and answers (herein referred to by question number as *FASB Q&A*) useful in understanding and implementing the Statement. Paragraph 137 of SFAS No. 115 defines, in part, debt securities as those securities that represent "a creditor relationship with an enterprise." These securities include:

- "U.S. Treasury securities, U.S. government agency securities, municipal securities, corporate bonds, convertible debt, commercial paper, all securitized debt instruments, such as collateralized mortgage obligations (CMOs) and real estate mortgage investment conduits (REMICs), and interest-only and principal-only strips.
- A CMO (or other instrument) that is issued in equity form but is required to be accounted for as a nonequity instrument regardless of how that instrument is classified (i.e., whether equity or debt) in the issuer's statement of financial position.
- Preferred stock that by its terms either must be redeemed by the issuing enterprise or is redeemable at the option of the investor.
- Structured notes that are in the form of debt securities."

Except as mentioned below, SFAS No. 115 "applies to all debt securities, including securities that have been grouped with loans in the statement of financial position" (EITF Topic No. D-39, "Questions Related to the Implementation of FASB Statement No. 115"). These include (1) a bank's originated and securitized mortgage loans that continue to be reported as loans in the Call Report, (2) bank investments in unrated industrial development bonds classified as loans in the Call Report, and (3) "Brady Bonds." In addition, FASB Technical Bulletin No. 94-1, "Application of Statement 115 to Debt Securities Restructured in a Troubled Debt Restructuring," indicates that "Statement 115 applies to all loans that meet the definition of a *security* in that Statement. Thus, any loan that was restructured in a troubled debt restructuring involving a modification of terms, including those restructured before the effective date of Statement 114, would be subject to the provisions of Statement 115 if the debt instrument meets the definition of a security" (par. 3).

Excluded from the definition of debt securities are unsecuritized loans, options on debt securities, accounts receivable, option contracts, financial futures contracts, forward contracts, and lease contracts. In addition, since SFAS No. 115 generally requires that investments in debt securities be presented at fair value, enterprises that already use similar measurement guidelines in accounting for these investments—for example, brokers and dealers in securities, defined benefit pension plans, and investment companies—need not apply the requirements of the Statement. In this regard, SFAS No. 115 (par. 4) states, the "Statement does not apply to enterprises whose specialized accounting practices include accounting for substantially all investments in debt and equity securities at market value or fair value, with changes in value recognized in earnings (income) or in the change in net assets."

Not-for-profit organizations are also excluded from the Statement's provisions. However, the Statement applies "to cooperatives and mutual enterprises, including credit unions and mutual insurance companies" (par. 4).

As previously discussed in Section 18.3(e), certain financial assets subject to prepayment are measured like investment in debt securities. Those assets include interest-only strips, retained interests in securitizations, loans, other receivables, or other financial assets that can contractually be prepaid or otherwise settled in such a way that the holder would not recover substantially all of its recorded investment, except for instruments that are within the scope of Statement 133.

EITF 99-20, "Recognition of Interest Income and Impairment on Purchased and Retained Beneficial Interests in Securitized Financial Assets," provides interest income recognition and measurement guidance for interests retained in a securitization transaction accounted for as a sale. The scope of EITF 99-20 includes retained beneficial interests in securitization transactions that are accounted for as sales under Statement 140 and certain purchased beneficial interests in securitized financial assets. The scope includes beneficial interests that (par. 5):

a. Are either debt securities under Statement 115 or required to be accounted for like debt securities under Statement 115 pursuant to paragraph 14 of Statement 140.

b. Involve securitized financial assets that have contractual cash flows (for example, loans, receivables, debt securities, and guaranteed lease residuals, among other items). Thus, the consensus in this Issue does not apply to securitized financial assets that do not involve contractual cash flows (e.g., common stock equity securities, among other items). The Task Force observed that the guidance in Issue No. 96-12, "Recognition of Interest Income and Balance Sheet Classification of Structured Notes," may be applied to those beneficial interests involving securitized financial assets that do not involve contractual cash flows.

c. Do not result in consolidation of the entity issuing the beneficial interest by the holder of the beneficial interests.

(b) INITIAL RECOGNITION AND MEASUREMENT. Upon acquisition, debt securities are classified into one of three categories: (1) held-to-maturity, (2) available-for-sale, or (3) trading. Generally, these securities are initially recorded at cost with appropriate identification of premium or discounts. EITF Issue No. 94-8, "Accounting for Conversion of a Loan into a Debt Security in a Debt Restructuring," states that "the initial cost basis of a debt security of the original debtor received as part of a debt restructuring should be the security's fair value at the date of the restructuring."

(i) Held-to-Maturity. An entity that has the positive intent and ability to hold a debt security to maturity should classify such security as a held-to-maturity security. Otherwise, the security should be classified as trading or available-for-sale. A positive intent and ability to hold a security to maturity does not exist if management's intent to hold the security to maturity is uncertain, if the intent is "to hold the security for only an indefinite period" (par. 9), or if there is a "mere absence of an intent to sell" (par. 59). FASB Q&A No. 18 states that "given the unique opportunities for profit embedded in a convertible security, it generally would be contradictory to assert the positive intent and ability to hold a convertible debt security to maturity and forego the opportunity to exercise the conversion feature." In determining positive intent and ability, the following additional guidance is available:

- SFAS No. 115 (par. 9) states that "a debt security should not, for example, be classified as held-to-maturity if the enterprise anticipates that the security would be available to be sold in response to ... needs for liquidity (e.g., due to the withdrawal of deposits, increased demands for loans, surrender of insurance policies, or payment of insurance claims)," or changes in (1) "market interest rates and related changes in the security's prepayment risk," (2) "the availability of and the yield on alternative investments," (3) "funding sources and terms," or (4) "foreign currency risk."

- SFAS No. 115 (par. 7), as amended, provides that "a security may not be classified as held-to-maturity if that security can contractually be prepaid or otherwise settled in such a way that the holder of the security would not recover substantially all of its recorded investment." SFAS No. 140 (par. 14) also requires that "interest-only strips, loans, other receivables, or retained interests in securitizations that can contractually be prepaid or otherwise settled in such a way that the holder would not recover substantially all of its recorded investment shall be subsequently measured like investments in debt securities classified as available-for-sale or trading under Statement 115."

(ii) Trading. Debt securities classified as trading securities are those that are "bought and held principally for the purpose of selling them in the near term (thus held for only a short period of time)" (par. 12a). These include mortgage-backed securities held for sale in conjunction with mortgage banking activities.

(iii) Available-for-Sale. Debt securities that are not classified as held-to-maturity or trading securities are classified as available-for-sale securities.

(c) ACCOUNTING AFTER ACQUISITION. Gains and losses realized upon the sale of debt securities are included in earnings. As previously discussed in Section 18.3, sale accounting is only appropriate for transfers of financial assets in which the transferor surrenders control over those financial assets pursuant to the provisions of SFAS No. 140, paragraph 9. Otherwise, the transferor should account for the transfer as a secured borrowing with pledge of collateral pursuant to SFAS No. 140, paragraph 15.

Generally, interest income is recognized at the contractual rate and premiums and discounts are amortized using the interest method. As discussed above, certain beneficial interests should follow the guidance in EITF 99-20. In addition, the retrospective interest method should be used for recognizing income on structured note securities that are classified as available-for-sale or held-to-maturity and that meet one or more of the conditions set forth in EITF Issue No. 96-12, "Recognition of Interest Income and Balance Sheet Classification of Structured Notes." Structured notes are debt instruments whose cash flows are linked to the movement in one or more indexes, interest rates, foreign exchange rates, commodities prices, prepayment rates, or other market variables.

The amount at which a debt security is presented in the statement of financial position depends on its classification as discussed below. This will require a determination of fair value—"the amount at which a financial instrument could be exchanged in a current transaction between willing parties, other than in a forced or liquidation sale. If a quoted market price is available for an instrument, the fair value to be used in applying [the] Statement is the product of the number of trading units of the instrument times its market price" (par. 137). If a quoted market price is not available for a debt security, pricing techniques such as "discounted cash flow analysis, matrix pricing, option-adjusted spread models, and fundamental analysis" (par. 111) can be used to obtain an estimate of fair value.

The appropriateness of a security's classification must be reassessed at each reporting date. In making this assessment, prior sales and transfers should be considered. Transfers to another category are discussed below.

(i) Held-to-Maturity. Debt securities classified as held-to-maturity are carried at amortized cost. Like loans, premiums and discounts pertaining to these securities are generally amortized using the interest method in accordance with FASB Statement 91.

In assessing the appropriateness of the held-to-maturity designation at each reporting date, SFAS No. 115 (par. 8) provides that transfers or sales due to the following changes in circumstances do not refute the held-to-maturity classification of other debt securities:

- Evidence of a significant deterioration in the issuer's creditworthiness.
- A change in tax law that eliminates or reduces the tax-exempt status of interest on the debt security (but not a change in tax law that revises the marginal tax rates applicable to interest income).
- A major business combination or major disposition (such as sale of a segment) that necessitates the sale or transfer of held-to-maturity securities to maintain the enterprise's existing interest rate risk position or credit risk policy.
- A change in statutory or regulatory requirements significantly modifying either what constitutes a permissible investment or the maximum level of investments in certain kinds of securities, thereby causing an enterprise to dispose of a held-to-maturity security.
- A significant increase by the regulator in the industry's capital requirements that causes the enterprise to downsize by selling held-to-maturity securities.
- A significant increase in the risk weights of debt securities used for regulatory risk-based capital purposes.

It is not appropriate to apply these exceptions to situations that are similar, but not the same as, those listed above. However, the Statement indicates that "in addition to the foregoing changes in circumstances, other events that are isolated, nonrecurring, and unusual for the reporting enterprise that could not have been reasonably anticipated may cause the enterprise to sell or transfer a held-to-maturity security without necessarily calling into question its intent to hold other debt securities to maturity" (par. 8).

The FASB Q&A No. 29 indicates that "the sale of a held-to-maturity security in response to a tender offer will call into question an investor's intent to hold other debt securities to maturity in the future." In addition, FASB Q&A No. 24 notes that "sales of held-to-maturity securities to fund an acquisition (or a disposition, for example, if deposit liabilities are being assumed by the other party) are inconsistent with [SFAS No. 115] paragraph 8."

(ii) Trading. Debt securities classified as trading securities are carried at fair value. The resulting unrealized gain or loss is reflected in earnings.

(iii) Available-for-Sale. Debt securities classified as available-for-sale are, like debt securities classified as trading, carried at fair value. The resulting unrealized gain or loss is reflected as a separate component of equity, net of related deferred income taxes (or in other comprehensive income). These unrealized gains and losses should include the entire change in the fair value of foreign currency-denominated available-for-sale debt securities, and not just the portion attributable to changes in exchange rates.

The FASB staff has announced that "when an entity has decided to sell an available-for-sale security whose fair value is less than its cost and the entity does not expect the fair value of the security to recover prior to the expected time of sale, a write-down for other-than-temporary impairment should be recognized in earnings in the period in which the decision to sell is made" (EITF Topic No. D-44, which was superseded with the issuance of FSP FAS 115-1, "The Meaning of Other-Than-Temporary Impairment and Its Application to Certain Investments").

(iv) Transfers between Categories. Changes in the classification of investments in debt securities are accounted for at fair value. The following table summarizes the proper accounting for transfers:

Transfer From	Transfer To	Accounting Principles
Trading	Available-for-Sale	Previously recognized unrealized gains and losses are not reversed.
	Held-to-Maturity	Previously recognized unrealized gains and losses are not reversed.
Available-for-Sale	Trading	Unrealized gains and losses, including those already reflected in equity (or accumulated other Comprehensive income; see Section 18.5(c)), are recognized in earnings.
	Held-to-Maturity	Unrealized gains and losses at the date of transfer remain in equity (or accumulated other Comprehensive income; see Section 18.5(c)) but are amortized over the remaining life of the security Using the interest method. Premiums and discounts created by the transfer at fair value are also amortized using the interest method.
Held-to-Maturity	Trading	Unrealized gains and losses are recognized in earnings.
	Available-for-Sale	Unrealized gains and losses are reflected in equity, net of related deferred income taxes

(d) IMPAIRMENT. Temporary declines in the fair value of securities below amortized cost are not recognized since it is generally held that such declines will ultimately reverse. However, the evaluation of whether or not an impairment is considered other-than-temporary has been a long standing practice issue. In order to provide some guidance on evaluating other than temporary impairment, the FASB issued FSP FAS 115-1, "The Meaning of Other-Than-Temporary Impairment and Its Application to Certain Investments," in November 2005. While the FSP clarifies the accounting in a few areas, it largely refers to existing accounting literature and incorporates the existing guidance from the SEC. The FSP refers to a basic three-step model:

- Step 1: Determine whether an investment is impaired (i.e., fair value is less than cost). Generally, cost equals amortized cost less any previous write-downs.
- Step 2: Determine whether the impairment is other-than-temporary. Other-than-temporary does not necessarily mean permanent and an investment does not have to be deemed permanently impaired in order to require a write-down.
- Step 3: If the impairment is deemed to be other-than-temporary, recognize an impairment loss equal to the difference between the carrying amount and its fair value, measured as of the balance sheet date. Further, the fair value becomes the new cost basis of the investment and should not be adjusted for subsequent recoveries in fair value.

FSP FAS-115-1 refers to Paragraph 16 of Statement 115 for determining whether an impairment is other than temporary:

For individual securities classified as either available-for-sale or held-to-maturity, an enterprise shall determine whether a decline in fair value below the amortized cost basis is other than temporary. (If a security has been the hedged item in a fair value hedge, the security's "amortized cost basis" shall reflect the effect of the adjustments of its carrying amount made pursuant to paragraph 22(b) of Statement 133.) For example, if it is probable that the investor will be unable to collect all amounts due according to the contractual terms of a debt security not impaired at acquisition, an other-than-temporary impairment shall be considered to have occurred. [Footnote 4] If the decline in fair value is judged to be other than temporary, the cost basis of the individual security shall be written down to fair value as a new cost basis and the amount of the write-down shall be included in earnings (that is, accounted for as a realized loss). The new cost basis shall not be changed for subsequent recoveries in fair value. Subsequent increases in the fair value of available-for-sale securities shall be included in other comprehensive income pursuant to paragraph 13; subsequent decreases in fair value, if not an other-than-temporary impairment, also shall be included in other comprehensive income.

Footnote 4: A decline in the value of a security that is other than temporary is also discussed in FSP FAS 115-1 and FAS 124-1, "The Meaning of Other-Than-Temporary Impairment and Its Application to Certain Investments," AICPA Statement on Auditing Standards No. 92, "Auditing Derivative Instruments, Hedging Activities, and Investments in Securities," and in SEC Staff Accounting Bulletin No. 59, "Accounting for Noncurrent Marketable Equity Securities."

As referenced in Statement 115, AICPA Statement on Auditing Standards No. 92, "Auditing Derivative Instruments, Hedging Activities, and Investments in Securities," paragraph 47, provides the following guidance:

Impairment Losses. Regardless of the valuation method used, generally accepted accounting principles might require recognizing in earnings an impairment loss for a decline in fair value that is other than temporary. Determinations of whether losses are other than temporary often involve estimating the outcome of future events. Accordingly, judgment is required in determining whether factors exist that indicate that an impairment loss has been incurred at the end of the reporting period. These judgments are based on subjective as well as objective factors, including knowledge and experience about past and current events and assumptions about future events. The following are examples of such factors.

Fair value is significantly below cost and —

— The decline is attributable to adverse conditions specifically related to the security or to specific conditions in an industry or in a geographic area.

— The decline has existed for an extended period of time.

— Management does not possess both the intent and the ability to hold the security for a period of time sufficient to allow for any anticipated recovery in fair value.

The security has been downgraded by a rating agency.

The financial condition of the issuer has deteriorated.

Dividends have been reduced or eliminated, or scheduled interest payments have not been made.

The entity recorded losses from the security subsequent to the end of the reporting period.

As referenced in Statement 115, SEC SAB 59 (as amended by SAB 103, "Update of Codification of Staff Accounting Bulletins") provides the following guidance as Topic 5: "Miscellaneous Accounting, Other Than Temporary Impairment of Certain Investments in Debt and Equity Securities":

M. Other Than Temporary Impairment of Certain Investments in Debt and Equity Securities (SAB NO. 59)

Facts: Paragraph 16 of Statement 115 specifies that "[f]or individual securities classified as either available-for-sale or held-to-maturity, an enterprise shall determine whether a decline in fair value below the amortized cost basis is other than temporary... If the decline in fair value is judged to be other than temporary, the cost basis of the individual security shall be written down to fair value as a new cost basis and the amount of the write-down shall be included in earnings (that is, accounted for as a realized loss)."

Statement 115 does not define the phrase "other than temporary." In applying this guidance to its own situation, Company A has interpreted "other than temporary" to mean permanent impairment. Therefore, because Company A's management has not been able to determine that its investment in Company B is permanently impaired, no realized loss has been recognized even though the market price of B's shares is currently less than one-third of A's average acquisition price.

Question: Does the staff believe that the phrase "other than temporary" should be interpreted to mean "permanent"?

Interpretive Response: No. The staff believes that the FASB consciously chose the phrase "other than temporary" because it did not intend that the test be "permanent impairment," as has been used elsewhere in accounting practice. [Footnote 12]

Footnote 12: Footnote 4 to Statement 115 refers to this SAB for a discussion of considerations applicable to a determination as to whether a decline in market value below cost, at a particular point in time, is other than temporary. FASB's implementation guide "A Guide to Implementation of Statement 115 on Accounting for Certain Investments in Debt and Equity Securities," SAS 92, "Auditing Derivative Instruments, Hedging Activities, and Investments in Securities," AICPA Audit Guide, "Auditing Derivative Instruments, Hedging Activities, and Investments in Securities," and EITF Topic D-44 also address issues related to the determination of whether a decline in fair value of a investment security is other than temporary.

The value of investments in marketable securities classified as either available-for-sale or held-to-maturity may decline for various reasons. The market price may be affected by general market conditions which reflect prospects for the economy as a whole or by specific information pertaining to an industry or an individual company. Such declines require further investigation by management. Acting upon the premise that a write-down may be required, management should consider all available evidence to evaluate the realizable value of its investment.

There are numerous factors to be considered in such an evaluation and their relative significance will vary from case to case. The staff believes that the following are only a few examples of the factors which, individually or in combination, indicate that a decline is other than temporary and that a write-down of the carrying value is required:

a. The length of the time and the extent to which the market value has been less than cost;

b. The financial condition and near-term prospects of the issuer, including any specific events which may influence the operations of the issuer such as changes in technology that may impair the earnings potential of the investment or the discontinuance of a segment of the business that may affect the future earnings potential; or

c. The intent and ability of the holder to retain its investment in the issuer for a period of time sufficient to allow for any anticipated recovery in market value.

Unless evidence exists to support a realizable value equal to or greater than the carrying value of the investment, a write-down to fair value accounted for as a realized loss should be recorded. In accordance with the guidance of paragraph 16 of Statement 115, such loss should be recognized in the determination of net income of the period in which it occurs and the written down value of the investment in the company becomes the new cost basis of the investment."

In addition to retaining the disclosure requirements of the superseded EITF 03-1, The Meaning of Other-Than-Temporary Impairment and Its Application to Certain Investments, and referring to existing GAAP and SEC guidance, the FSP also clarifies the following:

- If the impairment is considered other-than-temporary, then the impairment should be measured as the difference between fair value and cost basis at the balance sheet date. (paragraph 15 of the FSP)

- For post-impairment income recognition, income must be recognized on expected, not contractual, cash flows. (paragraph 16 of the FSP)

- If the decision is made to sell an investment in a loss position, the loss should be recorded in the period the decision is made rather than when the actual sale occurs, incorporating existing guidance in EITF Topic D-44, "Recognition of Other-Than-Temporary Impairment upon the Planned Sale of a Security Whose Cost Exceeds Fair Value." (paragraph 14 of the FSP)

The guidance in the final FSP is effective for reporting periods beginning after December 15, 2005. Earlier application is permitted. However, the existing disclosures, previously required under EITF 03-1, remain in place for December 31, 2005 year-ends.

(e) REPORTING COMPREHENSIVE INCOME.   In June 1997, the FASB issued SFAS No. 130, "Reporting Comprehensive Income." The transition section of the Statement provides, among other things, that the Statement is effective for fiscal years beginning after December 15, 1997. Earlier application is permitted and reclassification of financial statements for earlier periods provided for comparative purposes is required. The previous discussion on available-for-sale debt securities parenthetically refers to other comprehensive income to facilitate the transition to the new requirements. Readers should be alert to the following major changes resulting from the adoption of Statement No. 130.

Subsequent to the adoption of SFAS No. 130, unrealized gains and losses previously reported net of applicable deferred income taxes in a separate component of shareholders' equity under SFAS No. 115 will have to be reported in other comprehensive income. In addition, the unrealized gain or loss at the date of transfer into the available-for-sale category from the held-to-maturity category will also have to be reported in other comprehensive income.

The new requirements will require reclassification adjustments "to avoid double counting in comprehensive income items that are displayed as part of net income for a period that also had been displayed as part of other comprehensive income in that period or earlier periods" (par. 18). SFAS No. 130 (Appendix C) provides illustrations of the calculation of reclassification adjustments for Statement 115 available-for-sale securities. The reporting and display of comprehensive income and its components in a full set of general-purpose financial statements is discussed further in Chapter 10.

(f) DISCLOSURES.   The references applicable to disclosure requirements are:

- FASB No. 105, paragraph. 20.
- FASB Statement 115, paragraph 19–22
- SOP 03-3, paragraphs 14–16
- FAS 115-1 and FAS 124-1: "The Meaning of Other-Than-Temporary Impairment and Its Application to Certain Investments," paragraph 17

18.6 EQUITY SECURITIES

(a) INTRODUCTION.   Equity securities are often purchased to generate dividend income, to realize gains from their sale to other parties, and/or to achieve control over another enterprise. Except as discussed below, SFAS No. 115, as amended, is the primary standard applicable to investments in equity securities that have readily determinable fair values. As mentioned earlier, the FASB has also issued a special report entitled, "A Guide to Implementation of Statement 115 on Accounting for Certain Investments in Debt and Equity Securities," which contains a series of questions and answers useful in understanding and implementing the Statement.

SFAS No. 115 (par. 137) defines an equity security as "any security representing an ownership interest in an enterprise (e.g., common, preferred, or other capital stock) or the right to acquire (e.g., warrants, rights, and call options) or dispose of (e.g., put options) an ownership interest in an enterprise at fixed or determinable prices." This definition excludes "convertible debt or preferred stock that by its terms either must be redeemed by the issuing enterprise or is redeemable at the option of the investor." FASB Q&A No. 3 indicates that this "definition does not include written equity options because they represent *obligations* of the writer, not investments. Is also does not include cash-settled options on equity securities or options on equity-based indexes, because those instruments do not represent ownership interests in an enterprise. Options on debt securities are not within the scope of the Statement." In addition, the Statement does not apply to:

- "Enterprises whose specialized accounting practices include accounting for substantially all investments in debt and equity securities at market value or fair value, with changes in value recognized in earnings (income) or in the change in net assets" (par. 4).
- Not-for-profit organizations. However, the Statement applies "to cooperatives and mutual enterprises, including credit unions and mutual insurance companies" (par. 4).
- "Investments in equity securities accounted for under the equity method nor to investments in consolidated subsidiaries" (par. 4). Consolidation and the equity method of accounting are discussed in Chapter 11 of this *Handbook*.
- Equity securities that do not have readily determinable fair values (e.g., restricted stock).

FASB Q&A No. 4 notes that "APB Opinion No. 18, "The Equity Method of Accounting for Investments in Common Stock," describes the cost method and the equity method of accounting for investments in common stock and specifies the criteria for determining when to use the equity method. Equity securities that do not have readily determinable fair values that are not required to be accounted for by the equity method are typically carried at cost, as described in paragraph 6 of Opinion 18, adjusted for other-than-temporary impairment."

(b) INITIAL RECOGNITION AND MEASUREMENT.   Upon acquisition, equity securities are generally recorded at cost, presumably fair value at acquisition, and classified into one of two categories: (1) available-for-sale or (2) trading. The FASB Q&A No. 38 provides that the initial basis under Statement 115 of a marketable equity security that should no longer be accounted for under the equity method would be the previous carrying amount of the investment. The Q&A notes that "paragraph 19(1) of APB Opinion No. 18, "The Equity Method of Accounting for Investments in Common Stock," states that the earnings or losses that relate to the stock retained should remain as a part of the carrying amount of the investment and that the investment account should not be adjusted retroactively."

(c) ACCOUNTING AFTER ACQUISITION.   Gains and losses realized on the sale of equity securities are included in earnings and dividend income is recognized upon declaration. As previously discussed in the section , sale accounting is only appropriate for transfers of financial assets in which the transferor surrenders control over those financial assets pursuant to the provisions of SFAS No. 140, paragraph 9. Otherwise, the transferor should account for the transfer as a secured borrowing with pledge of collateral pursuant to SFAS No. 140, paragraph 15.

Equity securities are carried at fair value. As with debt securities, the accounting for the resulting unrealized gain or loss depends on the equity security's classification. Changes in the fair value of equity securities classified as trading are reflected in earnings while changes in the fair value of equity securities classified as available-for-sale are reflected in a separate component of shareholder's equity (or other comprehensive income), net of the related deferred income tax effects.

(d) IMPAIRMENT.   Declines in fair value that are deemed to be "other-than-temporary" should be accounted for as realized losses, resulting in a new cost basis for the security. Impairment is discussed above in Section 18.5(d). For equity securities with readily determinable market values, the impairment guidance in paragraph 16 of Statement 115 (see above) should be followed. For investments in equity securities that carried on the cost method, FSP-FAS 115-1 refers to Paragraph 6 of APB 18 for determining whether an impairment is other than temporary:

a. THE COST METHOD. An investor records an investment in the stock of an investee at cost, and recognizes as income dividends received that are distributed from net accumulated earnings of the investee since the date of acquisition by the investor. The net accumulated earnings of an investee subsequent to the date of investment are recognized by the investor only to the extent distributed by the investee as dividends. Dividends received in excess of earnings subsequent to the date of investment are considered a return of investment and are recorded as reductions of cost of the investment. A series of operating losses of an investee or other factors may indicate that a decrease in value of the investment has occurred which is other than temporary and should accordingly be recognized. [Footnote 3a]

Footnote 3a: FSP FAS 115-1 and FAS 124-1, "The Meaning of Other-Than-Temporary Impairment and Its Application to Certain Investments," discusses the methodology for determining impairment and evaluating whether the impairment is other than temporary.

Paragraph 10 of FSP FAS-115-1 discusses the impairment considerations for cost-method investments for which the fair value is not readily determinable.

(e) TRANSFERS BETWEEN CATEGORIES.   The transfer of equity securities between categories is accounted for in the same manner as the transfer of debt securities discussed above. Of course, transfers to or from the held-to-maturity category do not apply.

(f) REPORTING COMPREHENSIVE INCOME.   As discussed in Section 18.5(c), in June 1997, the FASB issued SFAS No. 130, "Reporting Comprehensive Income." The transition section of the Statement provides, among other things, that the Statement is effective for fiscal years beginning after December 15, 1997. Earlier application is permitted and reclassification of financial statements for earlier periods provided for comparative purposes is required. The previous discussion on available-for-sale equity securities parenthetically refers to other comprehensive income to facilitate the transition to the new requirements. Readers should be alert to the major changes resulting from the adoption of Statement 130. The reporting and display of comprehensive income and its components in a full set of general-purpose financial statements is discussed further in Chapter 10.

(g) DISCLOSURES.   The references applicable to disclosure requirements are:

- FASB Statement 105, paragraph. 20.
- FASB Statement 115, paragraph 19, 21–22
- FAS 115-1 and FAS 124-1: "The Meaning of Other-Than-Temporary Impairment and Its Application to Certain Investments," paragraph 18.

18.7 SOURCES AND SUGGESTED REFERENCES

American Institute of CPAs. "Accounting by Certain Entities (Including Entities with Trade Receivables) That Lend to or Finance the Activities of Others" Statement of Position 01-6, AICPA, New York.

_____ "Accounting for Certain Purchased Loans and Debt Securities Acquired in a Transfer" Statement of Position 03-3, AICPA, New York.

_____ "Disclosure of Certain Significant Risks and Uncertainties" Statement of Position 94-6 AICPA.

Bort, Richard, *Corporate Cash Management Handbook*. Warren, Gorham & Lamont, Boston, 1989

Committee on Accounting Procedure, "Restatement and Revision of Accounting Research Bulletins," *Accounting Research Bulletin No. 43*. AICPA, New York, 1953.

Financial Accounting Standards Board. "A Guide to Implementation of Statement 115 on Accounting for Certain Investments in Debt and Equity Securities." Special Report FASB, Norwalk, CT, 1995.

_____ "Accounting for Changes That Result in a Transferor Regaining Control of Financial Assets Sold" EITF Issue No. 02-9. FASB, Norwalk, CT,

_____ "Accounting for Contingencies" Statement of Financial Accounting Standards No. 5. FASB, Stamford, CT, 1975.

_____ "Accounting for Conversion of a Loan into a Debt Security in a Debt Restructuring," EITF Issue No. 94-8. FASB, Norwalk, CT, 1997

_____ "Accounting for Nonrefundable Fees and Costs Associated with Originating or Acquiring Loans and Initial Direct Costs of Leases," Statement of Financial Accounting Standards No. 91, FASB, Norwalk, CT.

———— "Accounting for Transfers and Servicing of Financial Assets and Extinguishments of Liabilities," Statement of Financial Accounting Standards No. 140, FASB, Norwalk, CT, 2000.

———— "Accounting by Debtors and Creditors for Troubled Debt Restructurings," Statement of Financial Accounting Standards No. 15. FASB, Stamford, CT, 1977.

———— "Accounting by Creditors for Impairment of a Loan," Statement of Financial Accounting Standards No. 114. FASB, Norwalk, CT, 1993.

———— "Accounting by Creditors for Impairment of a Loan—Income Recognition and Disclosures," Statement of Financial Accounting Standards No. 118. FASB, Norwalk, CT, 1994.

———— "Accounting for Certain Investment in Debt and Equity Securities," *Statement of Financial Accounting Standards* No. 115. FASB, Norwalk, CT, 1993.

———— "Accounting for Transfers and Servicing of Financial Assets and Extinguishment of Liabilities," *Statement of Financial Accounting Standards* No. 140. FASB, Norwalk, CT, 2001.

———— "Balance Sheet Treatment of a Sale of Mortgage Servicing Rights with a Subservicing Agreement." EITF Issue 90-21 FASB, Norwalk, CT.

———— "Classifying Notes Receivable for Capital Stock," EITF Issue 85-1, FASB, Norwalk, CT.

———— "Consolidation of All Majority-Owned Subsidiaries," Statement of Financial Accounting Standards No. 94. FASB, Stamford, CT, 1987.

———— "Determination of What Risks and Rewards, If Any, Can Be Retained and Whether Any Unresolved Contingencies May Exist in a Sale of Mortgage Loan Servicing Rights" EITF Issue 95-5, FASB, Norwalk, CT.

———— "Financial Reporting and Changing Prices," Statement of Financial Accounting Standards No. 89. FASB, Stamford, CT, 1986.

———— "Foreign Currency Translation," Statement of Financial Accounting Standards No. 52. FASB, Stamford, CT, 1981.

————. "Questions and Answers Related to Servicing Activities in a qualifying Special-Purpose Entity under FASB Statement No. 140." Topic D-99. FASB, Norwalk, CT.

———— "Questions Related to the Implementation of FASB Statement No. 115," EITF Topic No. D-39. FASB, Norwalk, CT.

———— "Recognition of Interest Income and Impairment on Purchased and Retained Beneficial Interests in Securitized Financial Assets," EITF Issue No. 99-20, FASB, Norwalk, CT.

———— "Reporting Comprehensive Income," Statement of Financial Accounting Standards No. 130. FASB, Norwalk, CT, 1997.

———— "Terms of Loan Products That May Give Rise to a Concentration of Credit Risk" FASB Staff Position-SOP 94-6-1.

———— "The Applicability of FASB Statement No. 115 to Desecuritizations of Financial Assets," EITF Topic No. D-51. FASB, Norwalk, CT.

———— "The Meaning of Other-Than-Temporary Impairment and Its Application to Certain Investments" EITF Issue 03-1. FASB, Norwalk, CT.

Keiso, Donald E., Weygandt, Jerry D., and Warfield, Terry D. *Intermediate Accounting,* Twelfth Edition., John Wiley & Sons, New York, 2006.

Meigs, Walter B., Larsen, E. John, and Meigs, Robert F., *Principles of Auditing,* Ninth Edition. Irwin, Homewood, IL, 1988.

O'Reilly, Vincent M., Mc Donnell, Patrick J., Winograd, Barry N., Gerson, James, S. and Jaenicke, Henry R., *Montgomery's Auditing,* Twelfth Edition. John Wiley & Sons, New York, 1998.

Securities and Exchange Commission, "Notice of Adoption of Amendments to Regulation S-X and Related Interpretations and Guidelines Regarding Disclosure of Compensating Balances and Short-Term Borrowing Arrangements," Accounting Series Release No. 148. SEC, Washington, DC, November 1973.

Smith, Jay M., Jr., and Skousen, K. Fred, *Intermediate Accounting,* Tenth Edition., South-Western Publishing Co., Cincinnati, OH, 1990.

CHAPTER 19

REVENUES AND RECEIVABLES

Alan S. Glazer, PhD, CPA
Franklin & Marshall College

Henry R. Jaenicke, PhD, CPA
Drexel University

19.1 NATURE AND MEASUREMENT OF REVENUE

(a) DEFINITION AND COMPONENTS OF REVENUE.   Statement of Financial Accounting Concepts (SFAC) No. 6, "Elements of Financial Statements" (pars. 78, 79, and 82), issued in December 1985, defines revenues and gains as follows:

Revenues are inflows or other enhancements of assets of an entity or settlements of its liabilities (or a combination of both) from delivering or producing goods, rendering services, or other activities that constitute the entity's ongoing major or central operations.

Revenues represent actual or expected cash inflows (or the equivalent) that have occurred or will eventuate as a result of the entity's ongoing major or central operations. The assets increased by revenues may be of various kinds—for example, cash, claims against customers or clients, other goods or services received, or increased value of a product resulting from production. Similarly, the transactions and events from which revenues arise and the revenues themselves are in many forms and are called by various names—for example, output, deliveries, sales, fees, interest, dividends, royalties, and rent—depending on the kinds of operations involved and the way revenues are recognized.

Gains are increases in equity (net assets) from peripheral or incidental transactions of an entity and from all other transactions and other events and circumstances affecting the entity except those that result from revenues or investments by owners.

SFAC No. 6 (pars. 87–89) distinguishes revenues from gains (and expenses from losses) as follows:

Revenues and gains are similar, and expenses and losses are similar, but some differences are significant in conveying information about an enterprise's performance. Revenues and expenses result from an entity's ongoing major or central operations and activities—that is, from activities such as producing or delivering goods, rendering services, lending, insuring, investing, and financing. In contrast, gains and losses result from incidental or peripheral transactions of an enterprise with other entities and from other events and circumstances affecting it. Some gains and losses may be considered "operating" gains and losses and may be closely related to revenues and expenses. Revenues and expenses are commonly displayed as gross inflows or outflows of net assets, while gains and losses are usually displayed as net inflows or outflows.

The definitions and discussion of revenues, expenses, gains, and losses in this Statement give broad guidance but do not distinguish precisely between revenues and gains or between expenses and losses. Distinctions between revenues and gains and between expenses and losses in a particular entity depend to a significant extent on the nature of the entity, its operations, and its other activities. Items that are revenues for one kind of entity may be gains for another, and items that are expenses for one kind of entity may be losses for another. For example, investments in securities that may be sources of revenues and expenses for insurance or investment companies may be sources of gains and losses in manufacturing or merchandising companies. Technological changes may be sources of gains or losses for most kinds of enterprises but may be characteristic of the operations of high-technology or research-oriented enterprises. Events such as commodity price changes and foreign exchange rate changes that occur while assets are being used or produced or liabilities are owed may directly or indirectly affect the amounts of revenues or expenses for most enterprises, but they are sources of revenues or expenses only for enterprises for which trading in foreign exchange or commodities is a major or central activity.

Since a primary purpose of distinguishing gains and losses from revenues and expenses is to make displays of information about an enterprise's sources of comprehensive income as useful as possible, fine distinctions between revenues and gains and between expenses and losses are principally matters of display or reporting (paragraphs 64, 219–220, and 228).

The Financial Accounting Standards Board (FASB) currently is reconsidering the definition of revenue it provided in SFAC No. 6 in order to clarify whether transactions give rise to revenues or gains (see Section 19.4(d)). This chapter does not distinguish between gains and revenues because the distinction is not important in resolving the major issues of revenue recognition and measurement. The distinction is significant, however, in considering income statement presentation of earnings, particularly whether asset inflows and outflows should be shown gross or net and where gains and losses should be reported.

(b) CLASSIFICATION OF REVENUE.   O'Reilly, Hirsch, Defliese, and Jaenicke note that:

Most companies have one or more major sources of revenues and several less significant types of miscellaneous revenues, commonly referred to as other income. The term used for a given type of revenue usually depends on whether it is derived from one of the enterprise's principal business activities. For example, sales of transformers by an electrical supply company would be "sales," while such transactions would be "other income" to an electric utility. Conversely, interest and dividends from investments would be "other income" to almost all enterprises except investment companies, for which interest and dividends are a primary source of revenues.[1]

(c) MEASUREMENT, EARNING, REALIZATION, AND RECOGNITION OF REVENUE.

There is general agreement on the meaning of the terms "measurement" and "earning" as they apply to revenue. However, there has been disagreement regarding usage of two other terms—realization and recognition—that are significant in establishing the accounting period in which revenue should be reported.

(i) Measurement of Revenue.   SFAC No. 5, "Recognition and Measurement in Financial Statements," states that revenues "are generally measured by the exchange values of the assets (goods or services) or liabilities involved ..." (par. 83). That measurement criterion, coupled with the FASB definition of revenues, thus excludes from revenues those items commonly referred to as *revenue adjustments*, such as bad debts, discounts, returns, and allowances. (See the discussion below under "Revenue Adjustments and Aftercosts.") In certain circumstances, the time value of money should be acknowledged, and interest implicit in a revenue transaction should be classified separately.

Revenue can be measured by the prices (i.e., "gross" amounts) of goods or services sold to customers or the differences (i.e., "net" amounts) between those prices and the amounts due to third parties that supply the goods or services. Staff Accounting Bulletin (SAB) No. 101 (Topic 13-A.5, Question 10), "Revenue Recognition," discusses two major questions to be answered when deciding whether to record revenue at gross or net amounts:

1. Does the entity act as a principal (where its compensation, in substance, is gross profit from the transaction) or as an agent or broker (where its compensation, in substance, is a commission or fee)?

2. Does the entity take title to the goods sold or otherwise bear the risks and rewards of ownership (such as the risk of loss for collection, delivery, or returns)?

The Standards Executive Committee (SEC) staff concluded that if the entity functions as a principal and bears the risks and rewards of ownership, revenue should be reported at gross amounts, with separate reporting of cost of sales. If, instead, the entity functions as an agent and does not bear those risks and rewards—for example, Internet companies, travel agents, and retailers that stock little or no inventory, do not take title to goods sold to customers, and use third-party service providers to fill orders and ship products to customers—revenue should be reported at net amounts.

Additional factors to consider are provided in Emerging Issues Task Force (EITF) Issue No. 99-19, "Reporting Revenue as a Principal versus Net as an Agent." Although its consensus acknowledges that the decisions often involve judgment, the Task Force provides a list of indicators supporting revenue measurement at gross amounts:

- The entity, rather than the supplier, is primarily responsible for meeting customers' needs and ensuring customer satisfaction (i.e., entity is the "primary obligor").
- The entity has the risk of loss before a customer order is placed or after a customer return (i.e., entity bears "general inventory risk").
- The entity has the risk of loss after a customer order is placed or during shipping (i.e., entity bears "physical loss in inventory risk").
- The entity has latitude in setting the selling price.
- The entity adds value, such as by physically changing the product or performing part of the service.

---

[1] V. M. O'Reilly, M. B. Hirsch, P. L. Defliese, and H. R. Jaenicke, *Montgomery's Auditing*, Eleventh Edition (John Wiley & Sons, New York, 1990), p. 371.

- The entity has discretion in choosing from among the different suppliers for the product or service.
- The entity is involved in determining and communicating product or service specifications to the supplier.
- The entity is responsible for collecting the sales price from the customer and paying the supplier, regardless of whether the customer pays the total price (i.e., entity bears "credit risk").

Three indicators also are provided that support recognizing revenue at net amounts:

1. The supplier, rather than the entity, is primarily responsible for meeting the customer's needs and ensuring customer satisfaction (i.e., supplier is the "primary obligor").

2. The entity earns a fixed amount, expressed either in terms of dollars or a percentage of the gross amount billed to the customer.

3. The entity has little or no credit risk.

No single indicator determines which method should be used. For example, although an entity's not taking title to products sold to customers generally indicates a lack of "general inventory risk" and, therefore, net revenue reporting, an entity's taking title to products is not sufficient, by itself, to justify gross reporting.

The EITF's consensus on Issue No. 99-19 also discusses disclosures that may be appropriate for entities reporting revenues at net amounts. The EITF notes that SEC rules require separate presentation of revenues from the sales of products and revenues from the sales of services, and the latter category would normally include commissions and fees recognized from activities reported at net amounts. In addition, the consensus permits disclosure of gross transaction volume for those revenues reported at net amounts. Gross amounts can be reported either parenthetically on the face of the income statement or in the related notes, but they may not be labeled "revenues" or be included in a column that reports net income or loss.

Depending on when revenue is recognized (see Section 19.5(d), the measurement process requires varying degrees of estimation. The later revenue is recognized in the earning process, the less need there is to use estimates in measuring it.

(ii) Earning of Revenue. Agreement also exists on the question of what "earning" revenue means. According to paragraph 83b of SFAC No. 5, revenues are not recognized until earned. An entity's revenue-earning activities involve delivering or producing goods, rendering services, or other activities that constitute its ongoing major or central operations. Revenues are considered to have been earned when the entity has substantially accomplished what it must do to be entitled to the benefits represented by the revenues. Understanding when revenue should be recognized thus may require a knowledge of the nature of the specific earning process in certain industries.

(iii) Revenue Realization and Recognition. To "recognize" revenue means to report it in the entity's financial statements or to record it in the entity's accounts by crediting a revenue account and simultaneously debiting an asset or a liability. At the time revenue is recognized, closely related expenses (such as cost of goods sold) also are recognized, although the particular accounting system (e.g., a periodic inventory system) may cause the actual bookkeeping entry to be made later in the accounting period. At the point of revenue recognition, the accounting for related assets switches from recording entry values, that is, amounts based on purchase prices (such as the historical cost of an asset), to recording exit values, that is, amounts based on selling prices (such as the selling price of an asset sold in the ordinary course of business). "In traditional accounting terminology, the accountant is said to 'recognize revenue' when he switches from one measurement approach to the other."[2]

---

[2] G. J. Staubas, *Making Accounting Decisions* (Scholars Book Co., Houston, 1977), p. 172.

The *realization principle* has been used in relation to the recognition of revenue. Unfortunately, use of the term *realization* has not been uniform, and for that reason some authors prefer to avoid it. The term is so deeply embedded in accounting terminology, however, that it cannot be ignored.

Some authors have used realization in a very broad sense to mean that the necessary conditions for recognizing revenue have been met. The 1957 revision of the American Accounting Association (AAA) *Accounting and Reporting Standards for Corporate Financial Statements*, for example, states: "The essential meaning of realization is that a change in an asset or liability has become sufficiently definite and objective to warrant recognition in the accounts."[3] Under this broad view, the point of realization (recognition) is movable, and specific rules must be provided to define when it occurs in different types of revenue transactions and earning processes.

A widely held view, however, has been that realization takes place at a single specific point in time, such as the sale date, and recognition of revenue at all other points in time is a departure from or an exception to the realization principle. Some departures or exceptions are considered acceptable in specific circumstances, based on the presence of certain characteristics. Accounting Principles Board (APB) Statement No. 4, "Basic Concepts and Accounting Principles Underlying Financial Statements of Business Enterprises" (pars. 150–152), illustrates this view of the realization principle:

> Revenue is conventionally recognized at a specific point in the earning process of a business enterprise, usually when assets are sold or services are rendered. This conventional recognition is the basis of the pervasive measurement principle known as realization.
>
> **P-2 Realization.** Revenue is generally recognized when both of the following conditions are met: (1) the earning process is complete or virtually complete, and (2) an exchange has taken place.
>
> The exchange required by the realization principle determines both the time at which to recognize revenue and the amount at which to record it. Revenue from sales of products is recognized under this principle at the date of sale, usually interpreted to mean the date of delivery to customers. Revenue from services rendered is recognized under this principle when services have been performed and are billable. Revenue from permitting others to use enterprise resources, such as interest, rent, and royalties is also governed by the realization principle. Revenue of this type is recognized as time passes or as the resources are used.
>
> Revenue from sales of assets other than products is recognized at the date of sale. Revenue recognized under the realization principle is recorded at the amount received or expected to be received.
>
> Revenue is sometimes recognized on bases other than the realization rule. For example, on long-term construction contracts revenue may be recognized as construction progresses. This exception to the realization principle is based on the availability of evidence of the ultimate proceeds and the consensus that a better measure of periodic income results. Sometimes revenue is recognized at the completion of production and before a sale is made. Examples include certain precious metals and farm products with assured sales prices. The assured price, the difficulty in some situations of determining costs of products on hand, and the characteristic of unit interchangeability are reasons given to support this exception.

A third meaning of realization restricts the term to its dictionary meaning of "conversion into actual money" or, in slightly modified form, "conversion of nonmonetary assets into monetary assets." This meaning of the term is divorced completely from any notion of revenue recognition, although revenues may, coincidentally, be recognized when cash ("actual money") or other monetary assets are received. The FASB uses the term essentially in this third sense in SFAC No. 6 (par. 143):

> Realization in the most precise sense means the process of converting noncash resources and rights into money and is most precisely used in accounting and financial reporting to refer to sales of

---

[3] American Accounting Association (AAA), Committee on Accounting Concepts and Standards, *Accounting and Reporting Standards for Corporate Financial Statements*, 1957 Revision (AAA, Sarasota, FL, 1957), p. 3.

assets for cash or claims to cash. The related terms realized and unrealized therefore identify revenues or gains or losses on assets sold and unsold, respectively. Those are the meanings of realization and related terms in the Board's conceptual framework.

Recognition is the process of formally recording or incorporating an item in the financial statements of an entity...

(d) REVENUE RECOGNITION ALTERNATIVES. Revenue can be recognized at various points in the earning process, depending on the circumstances.

Paragraph 84 of SFAC No. 5 notes that revenue is commonly recognized "at time of sale," although six other points are described:

1. After production and delivery—if a sale, cash receipt, or both occur before production and delivery of goods or services.

2. During production—if a contract exists for which reliable estimates of revenue, total costs, and progress can be made.

3. As time passes—if reliable, contractually based measures established in advance are available for services rendered or rights to use assets are provided continuously over a period of time.

4. At completion of production—if a product or service can be sold at a price that can be reliably determined with little effort before delivery.

5. At the time of exchange for nonmonetary assets—if the fair value of goods or services sold or of nonmonetary assets received can be reliably measured.

6. As cash is collected—if collectibility of assets received from the sale of goods or services is doubtful.

The use of each alternative (or basis) in different circumstances is discussed below. The general criteria for recognizing revenue and specific factors to be considered in applying those criteria are considered later in this chapter (see Section 19.3).

(i) Delivery. Recognizing revenue when a product is delivered or service rendered, often referred to as the *sale basis*, is most common and has been most widely supported in the literature.

Paton and Littleton state:

For the great majority of business enterprises the sale basis of measuring revenue clearly meets the requirements of accounting standards more effectively than any other possible basis. Revenue is the financial expression of the product of business operation and hence should be gauged in terms of the decisive stage or step in the stream of activity. Revenue, moreover, should be evidenced and supported by new and dependable assets, preferably cash or near-cash. These fundamental requirements are well met by adopting the completed sale as the test of the realization of revenue.

For most concerns engaged in making or dealing with tangible goods the sale is the most conclusive, and the most financially significant, of the chain of events making up the business process; the sale is the capstone of activity, the end toward which all efforts are directed....

If product is in the form of service, as in transportation, banking, etc., the act or process of furnishing service may be viewed as the equivalent of sale for the purpose of measuring revenue ...[4]

One of the six rules adopted by the membership of the American Institute of Certified Public Accountants (AICPA) in 1934, and reprinted in Accounting Research Bulletin (ARB) No. 43

---

[4] W. A. Paton and A. C. Littleton, *An Introduction to Corporate Accounting Standards* (AAA, Sarasota, FL, 1940), pp. 53–54.

(Chapter 1, Section A, par. 1), states: "Profit is deemed to be realized when a sale in the ordinary course of business is effected, unless the circumstances are such that the collection of the sale price is not reasonably assured." The APB reaffirmed that view in 1966 in APB Opinion No. 10 (par. 12), stating: "Revenues should ordinarily be accounted for at the time a transaction is completed, with appropriate provision for uncollectible accounts."

George O. May stated the rationale behind the widespread use of the sale basis as long ago as 1943:

> The problem of allocation of income to particular short periods obviously offers great difficulty—indeed, it is the point at which conventional treatment becomes indispensable, and it must be recognized that some conventions are scarcely in harmony with the facts. Manifestly, when a laborious process of manufacture and sale culminates in the delivery of the product at a profit, that profit is not attributable, except conventionally, to the moment when the sale or delivery occurred. The accounting convention which makes such an attribution is justified only by its demonstrated practical utility.

> It is instructive to consider how it happens that a rule which is violative of fact produces results that are practically useful and reliable. The explanation is, that in the normal business there are at any one moment transactions at every stage of the production of profit, from beginning to end. If the distribution were exactly uniform, an allocation of income according to the proportion of completion of each unit would produce the same result as the attribution of the entire profit to a single stage.

> A number of conclusions immediately suggest themselves: first, that the convention is valid for the greatest variety of purposes where the flow of product is most uniform; second, that it is likely to be more generally valid for a longer than for a shorter period; and, third, that its applicability is seriously open to question for some purposes where the final consummation is irregular in time and in amount. Thus, the rule is almost completely valid in regard to a business which is turning out a standard product in relatively small units at a reasonable stable rate of production. It is less generally valid—or, to put it otherwise, the figure of profit reached is less generally significant—in the case of a company engaged in building large units, such as battleships, or carrying out construction contracts.[5]

Objections to Using Delivery.   Using delivery as the point of revenue recognition is not without shortcomings. Paton and Paton noted the following objections that others have raised to this basis as a measure of revenue:

- Accounts receivable may become uncollectible.
- Collection expenses and other costs may be incurred subsequent to sale.
- Merchandise returns and allowances may be made.
- Accounts receivable are not the equivalent of cash and hence do not represent immediately disposable funds.
- Revenue is earned through the entire process of production and hence it is unduly conservative to postpone recognition until the time of sale.[6]

The first three objections can be overcome through periodic adjustments for uncollectible accounts, anticipated expenses, and returns and allowances. These are considered later in this chapter (see Section 19.5).

The fourth objection reflects confusion between income and cash flows. Under the accrual basis of accounting, revenue is not equated with cash receipts, as is implied by the objection.

---

[5] G. O. May, *Financial Accounting: A Distillation of Experience* (Macmillan, New York, 1943), pp. 30–31.

[6] W. A. Paton and W. A. Paton, Jr., *Corporation Accounts and Statements* (Macmillan, New York, 1955), pp. 278–279.

Moreover, that net income may not be disposable need not invalidate delivery as the point of revenue recognition. The measurement of income (results of operations) and the administration of funds generated by those operations are separate and distinct.

The fifth objection—that is, delivery is unduly conservative because revenue is earned throughout the production process—suggests that there should be no distinction between the earning and the recognition of revenue. Revenue is recognized during the entire earning process, as in the percentage-of-completion method, only when certain conditions, discussed below and in Chapter 27, are present. If those conditions are not present, a more conservative approach is appropriate.

(ii) Recognition before Delivery.   As indicated above, in certain situations the recognition of revenue may occur prior to the time of delivery. Revenue may be recognized during production, as in the construction industry, or at completion of production, as in farming.

Construction Contracts.   In the construction industry, revenue may be recognized on the completed contract or the percentage-of-completion (production) basis. (See the detailed discussion in Chapter 30) Recognizing revenue in construction projects on the basis of production often is regarded as a desirable departure from the sale basis if total revenue and cost can be reliably estimated.

Accounting for revenue by the *completed contract method*—that is, when the contract has been fully performed—is appropriate if estimates of revenue and expenses are not reliable. This method, which is the equivalent of the point of delivery, is conservative, because it eliminates the problems created when a contract is canceled after revenue and profit have been recognized. Also, the amount of profit can be more accurately determined, because the need for estimates is greatly reduced. The principal limitation of this basis in connection with long-term contracts is that periodic income statements do not reveal what is happening in the enterprise if revenue is recognized in the period of completion rather than as the work progresses. Revenue is recognized only sporadically, when contracts are completed, despite continuous performance.

For long-term contracts, as in the construction of roads, buildings, ships, and so forth, the recognition of revenue using the *percentage-of-completion method* generally results in periodic net income that is more nearly related to the earning process. The use of that basis is justified, however, only if there is reasonable assurance of the profit margin and its ultimate realization. The term *percentage of completion* ordinarily refers to the relationship between costs incurred and the total estimated cost of the completed project, although a percentage based on time or physical units of production may be used.

The percentage-of-completion method, as developed in the construction industry, has been applied, sometimes improperly, to seemingly analogous situations in other industries. The method is also widely used to recognize revenue from production-type contracts and certain service transactions.

Extractive Industries and Agriculture.   Recognizing revenue when production is complete is regarded as acceptable in certain extractive industries and agriculture when interchangeable units of the commodities are immediately salable at quoted market prices and without significant distribution costs. The mining of precious metals and growing of crops such as wheat, cotton, and oats are examples. Revenue is recognized before delivery by valuing inventory of products on hand at market value.[7]

The AICPA (ARB No. 43, "Restatement and Revision of Accounting Research Bulletins," Ch. 4, par. 16) sanctions this procedure, as follows:

> It is generally recognized that income accrues only at the time of sale, and that gains may not be anticipated by reflecting assets at their current sales prices. For certain articles, however, exceptions are permissible. Inventories of gold and silver, when there is an effective

---

[7] D. E. Kieso, J. J. Weygandt, and T. D. Warfield, *Intermediate Accounting*, Eleventh Edition (John Wiley & Sons, New York, 2004), p. 918.

government-controlled market at a fixed monetary value, are ordinarily reflected at selling prices. A similar treatment is not uncommon for inventories representing agricultural, mineral, and other products, units of which are interchangeable and have an immediate marketability at quoted prices and for which appropriate costs may be difficult to obtain. Where such inventories are stated at sales prices, they should of course be reduced by expenditures to be incurred in disposal, and the use of such basis should be fully disclosed in the financial statements.

Despite the support for recognition prior to delivery in the authoritative accounting literature, in practice revenue is generally recognized on mineral products at the time of delivery. The authoritative literature is silent on the appropriateness of recognizing revenue on agricultural products still in the growth or production stage, even if they are readily marketable at quoted prices.

Accretion.   Paton and Littleton reject considering accretion (increase in value from natural growth or aging) as revenue:

> Allied to the question of the significance of production in relation to revenue is the problem of increase resulting from growth and other natural processes.... In this situation there is no doubt that assets have increased, and the amount of the physical increase is subject to objective verification. The technical process of production, however, remains to be undertaken, followed by conversion into new liquid assets. Assuming that the final product of the enterprise is lumber, it is clearly incorrect to treat accretion as revenue.[8]

They add, however, that there is no serious objection to disclosing measurable increases from accretion as supplementary information, provided cost is not obscured and the resulting credit is clearly labeled as unrealized income. Because revenue from accretion is not recognized, the costs incurred for the purpose of encouraging accretion should, theoretically at least, be added to inventory and recognized as expenses when revenues are recognized at the time the timber, nursery stock, or other property is delivered.

Hendriksen and van Breda note that, in an economic sense, accretion gives rise to revenue. However, from a practical standpoint, the discounted value required to make the necessary comparative inventory valuations often is difficult to determine "because it depends upon expectations regarding future market prices and expectations regarding future costs of providing for growth and future costs of harvesting and getting the product ready for market."[9] Periodic recognition of accretion as revenue has not been adopted in practice.

Appreciation.   Accounting authorities for many years generally have agreed that appreciation of asset values attributable to market changes does not constitute revenue. Paton and Littleton summarize the proposition, as follows:

> Appreciation in its various forms is not income. The case for introducing estimated appreciation (or "declination") into the accounts and reports otherwise than as supplementary data is not strong....
>
> Without doubt the movement of prices has an important bearing on the economic significance of existing business assets, but there is little warrant for the view that sheer enhancement of market value, however determined, represents effective income. Appreciation, in general, does not reflect or measure the progress of operating activity; appreciation is not the result of any transaction or any act of conversion; appreciation makes available no additional liquid resources which may be used to meet obligations or make disbursements to investors; appreciation has little or no legal standing as income.[10]

---

[8] Paton and Littleton, p. 52.

[9] E. S. Hendriksen and M. F. Van Breda, *Accounting Theory*, Fifth Edition (Irwin, Homewood, IL, 1992), p. 365.

[10] Paton and Littleton, pp. 46, 62.

Several authorities have expressed approval, to varying degrees, of certain departures from historical practice and for the adoption of alternative approaches to income recognition. Statement of Financial Accounting Standards (SFAS) No. 33, "Financial Reporting and Changing Prices," provides a good example. Its requirements, however, were amended by SFAS No. 82, "Financial Reporting and Changing Prices: Elimination of Certain Disclosures," and No. 89, "Financial Reporting and Changing Prices"; the latter makes the supplementary disclosure of current cost/constant purchasing power information voluntary. Also, some financial assets are measured at fair value, and, in some cases, changes in their fair values are recognized as gains or losses (see the discussions in Chapters 18 and 26).

Cost Savings versus Revenue.   Savings resulting from efficient operation or fortunate purchases generally are classified as reductions of costs, not as revenue. Edwards and Bell define the term *cost saving* as "an increase in the current cost of assets held."[11] That usage of the term has not been widely accepted and is not adopted in this chapter.

(iii) Recognition after Delivery.   As noted earlier, in certain circumstances revenue may be recognized after delivery. Methods used include the *deposit method* (which is really a nonrecognition method), the *cost recovery method*, and the *installment method*. Both the cost recovery and installment methods are sometimes referred to as *cash bases of revenue recognition*.

The cash basis of revenue recognition should not be confused with the *cash basis of accounting*. As Paton and Littleton noted almost 60 years ago:

> Placing revenue on a cash basis when such treatment is appropriate, it is hardly necessary to say, does not imply that expense should be measured by expenditure. Revenue is the controlling element; expense is the cost of the amount of revenue acknowledged. If receipts from customers are viewed as revenue the applicable expense is the cost of producing such receipts, not the cash disbursements made during the period.[12]

The cash basis of accounting reports revenues collected, expenses paid, and the excess or deficiency of revenues collected over expenses paid, rather than revenues, expenses, and income. Revenues collected are measured by cash receipts from customers; expenses paid are measured by cash disbursements to vendors and suppliers.

It also is important to distinguish between an installment sale and the method used to recognize revenue, expense, and income from that type of sale. In installment sales, the purchaser agrees to pay for the purchase in a series of periodic payments, usually, but not always, preceded by an initial disbursement customarily termed a *down payment*. The vendor may account for installment sales in the same manner as other charge sales, that is, by recognizing income at the time of delivery, or may recognize income either proportionally as the installments are collected or after all costs have been recovered. The latter methods, known as the *installment method* and *cost recovery method*, respectively, are acceptable if certain conditions (discussed below and in Chapter 25) are present.

Installment Method and Cost Recovery Method.   When APB Opinion No. 10, "Omnibus Opinion—1966" (par. 12) expressed the view "that revenues should ordinarily be accounted for at the time a transaction is completed . . . ," it also (in a note to that paragraph) recognized that:

> [T]here are exceptional cases where receivables are collectible over an extended period of time and, because of the terms of the transactions or other conditions, there is no reasonable basis for estimating the degree of collectibility. When such circumstances exist, and as long as they exist, either the installment method or the cost recovery method of accounting may be used. (Under the cost recovery method, equal amounts of revenue and expense are recognized as collections are made until all costs have been recovered, postponing any recognition of profit until that time.)

---

[11] E. O. Edwards and P. W. Bell, *The Theory and Measurement of Business Income* (University of California Press, Berkeley and Los Angeles, 1965), p. 93.

[12] Paton and Littleton, p. 59.

Deposit Method.   In some circumstances, such as in contracts that do not qualify to be recorded as sales in retail land transactions, the *deposit method* should be used (SFAS No. 66, "Accounting for Sales of Real Estate," pars. 65–67). A liability is recognized when cash is received, and no amounts are recognized as revenue until the period has expired during which the customer may cancel and receive a full refund.

19.2 NATURE AND SIGNIFICANCE OF RECEIVABLES

(a) RECEIVABLES DEFINED.   "Receivables" is a broad designation applicable to claims for future receipt of money, goods, and services. This broad designation thus includes deposits for purchases and payments for services to be rendered in the future, such as insurance, advertising, and utilities. This chapter uses the more restrictive, but common, definition of "receivables" as a designation for claims collectible in money. Claims collectible in goods or services are termed *prepayments*.

The general classification of receivables depends on whether they are evidenced by a written statement. Thus, receivables are either:

- *Accounts receivable.* Receivables for which no written statement acknowledging the obligation has been received from the obligor.
- *Notes receivable.* Receivables for which a written statement acknowledging the obligation has been received from the obligor.

In addition, receivables may be due for purchases of goods and services charged on credit cards issued by the entity itself or by a financial institution or other organization. The types of receivables are further classified by the situation in which the receivable arose (origin), whether a security interest was obtained with the receivable, and the time of expected cash receipt.

(b) TYPES OF ACCOUNTS RECEIVABLE.   Accounts receivable are first classified by the situation giving rise to the receivable. The most frequent situation is the delivery of goods. In practice, the term *accounts receivable* is normally used to designate the recorded amounts owed by trade customers. Other terms are used to designate accounts receivable arising from revenue recognition in the normal course of business in various industries. Examples of such designations are "revenues receivable" (used by public utilities), "rents receivable" (used by real estate agencies), and "subscriptions receivable" (used by publishers).

(c) TYPES OF NOTES RECEIVABLE.   The term *notes*, used broadly, includes two types of instruments: promissory notes and drafts. (Capital leases required to be accounted for as receivables in accordance with SFAS No. 13, "Accounting for Leases," are discussed in Chapter 23.) Notes related to the issuance of stock, including stock subscriptions, are addressed in EITF Issue No. 02-1, "Balance Sheet Classification of Assets Received in Exchange for Equity Instruments"; they are discussed in Chapter 27.

Promissory notes and drafts are defined by Mallor et al. as follows:

- *A promissory note* is a promise made by one person, called the *maker*, to pay to the order of another person, called the *payee* (or to bearer), a certain sum of money on demand or at a definite future time.
- *A draft* is an instrument in which one person, called the *drawer*, orders another person, called the *drawee*, to pay a certain sum of money to another person, called the *payee* (or to bearer), on demand or at a definite future time. The drawer and drawee may be the same person. The drawer and payee may be the same person.[13]

---

[13] J. P. Mallor et al., *Business Law and the Regulatory Environment: Concepts and Cases*, Eleventh Edition (Irwin McGraw-Hill, Chicago, 2001), pp. 654–655.

To be "negotiable" within the meaning of the Uniform Commercial Code [Section 19-103:3–104], all such instruments must meet the following conditions:

- Be written
- Be signed by the maker or drawer
- Contain an unconditional promise or order to pay a certain fixed sum in money
- Be payable to order or to bearer, or otherwise qualify as a check
- Be payable on demand or at a specific time
- Not include any instructions to take any action other than paying money, except as specified in the Article

A distinctive feature of the typical commercial draft, as compared with a note, is that the former is initiated by the creditor rather than by the debtor. Bills are "orders" to pay; notes are "promises" to pay. Bills arising in domestic commerce are usually referred to as *commercial drafts*; the term *bills of exchange* is generally restricted to instruments used in foreign commerce.

(d) CREDIT CARD RECEIVABLES.   A retail business that accepts credit card drafts in payment of purchases may accept one of three types: (1) bank credit cards, (2) travel and entertainment credit cards, and (3) company credit cards (also called *in-house* credit cards). Each of these requires separate treatment by the retailer. Issuers of travel and entertainment and bank credit cards treat credit card receivables in the same fashion as a retailer treats company credit card receivables (except, of course, that the receivables are forwarded by a retailer rather than being direct sales).

For the retailer, bank and travel and entertainment credit card drafts are receivables from the issuer of the credit card. Although procedures for individual card issuers vary slightly, they generally require that the credit card drafts be accumulated and deposited with a bank, which acts as the issuer's agent. There usually is a merchant's charge (discount) for the credit card drafts, which may be recorded as cash at the time of depositing the accumulated drafts or when the payment is received from the issuer of the card. Company credit card drafts are receivables under a credit card agreement. These agreements vary, but normally they provide for a minimum payment with interest on the unpaid balance.

19.3 CRITERIA FOR RECOGNIZING REVENUE

(a) GENERAL CRITERIA.   As discussed earlier in this chapter, the general criteria for recognition traditionally have followed the realization principle stated in APB Statement No. 4, namely, that the revenue has been earned and an exchange has taken place. One of the most difficult tasks the accountant faces is applying those general criteria to specific transactions and events for the purpose of determining the most appropriate time in the earning process to recognize all or part of the revenue. For some transactions and events and for some industries, authoritative or quasi-authoritative literature provides, on an ad hoc basis, more specific criteria—and sometimes conditions—that must be met before revenue is recognized; those instances are described in Sections 19.4(a) and (b). The sections below provide guidance for selecting the appropriate method of revenue recognition in the absence of specific authoritative or quasi-authoritative pronouncements.

(b) ATTRIBUTES MEASURED BY ENTRY AND EXIT VALUES.   As noted earlier, recognizing revenue results in a shift from accounting for *entry values* to accounting for *exit values*. In theory, two attributes of assets can be measured using entry values: historical cost and current cost. Similarly, three attributes, according to SFAC No. 5 (par. 67), can be measured using exit values: current market value, net realizable value, and present value of expected cash flows.

In general, the existing accounting model measures assets at historical cost before revenues and related expenses are recognized. When revenue is recognized, the attribute measured becomes (expected) selling price in due course of business, that is, net realizable value. For example, inventory is usually accounted for at historical cost until it is sold. At that time, the cost of inventory is recognized as an expense, and the inventory disappears from the balance sheet. The inventory is replaced by a new asset, often a receivable, which is accounted for at net realizable value, and an equal amount of revenue is recognized.

Of course, other attributes of elements of financial statements besides historical cost or proceeds and the (expected) selling price in due course of business can be measured. The significant point is that when revenue is recognized, a switch is made from some entry to some exit value. Unless otherwise specified, however, this discussion assumes that the entry value is historical cost or proceeds and the exit value is net realizable value—that is, "the historical cost model."

(c) FINANCIAL ACCOUNTING STANDARDS BOARD CONCEPTUAL FRAMEWORK AND REVENUE RECOGNITION.   SFAC No. 1, "Objectives of Financial Reporting by Business Enterprises" (pars. 34 and 37), states the first two *objectives of financial reporting* by business enterprises, as follows:

> Financial reporting should provide information that is useful to present and potential investors and creditors and other users in making rational investment, credit, and similar decisions.

> Financial reporting should provide information to help present and potential investors and creditors and other users in assessing the amounts, timing, and uncertainty of prospective cash receipts from dividends or interest and the proceeds from the sale, redemption, or maturity of securities or loans. The prospects for those cash receipts are affected by an enterprise's ability to generate enough cash to meet its obligations.... Thus, financial reporting should provide information to help investors, creditors, and others assess the amounts, timing, and uncertainty of prospective net cash inflows to the related enterprise.

SFAC No. 5 (par. 6) defines recognition as "the process of formally recording or incorporating an item into the financial statements of an entity as an asset, liability, revenue, expense, or the like." Paragraph 63 specifies "fundamental recognition criteria" for recognizing a financial statement element:

> An item and information about it should meet four fundamental recognition criteria to be recognized and should be recognized when the criteria are met, subject to a cost–benefit constraint and a materiality threshold. Those criteria are:

> Definitions—The item meets the definition of an element of financial statements.

> Measurability—It has a relevant attribute measurable with sufficient reliability.

> Relevance—The information about it is capable of making a difference in user decisions.

> Reliability—The information is representationally faithful, verifiable, and neutral.

> All four criteria are subject to a pervasive cost–benefit constraint: the expected benefits from recognizing a particular item should justify perceived costs of providing and using the information.

> Recognition is also subject to a materiality threshold; an item and information about it need not be recognized in a set of financial statements if the item is not large enough to be material and the aggregate of individually immaterial items is not large enough to be material to those financial statements.

The measurability criterion states that the financial statement element "must have a relevant attribute that can be quantified in monetary units with sufficient reliability. Measurability must be considered together with both relevance and reliability" (par. 65). The qualities of relevance and reliability sometimes conflict with each other and require that trade-offs be made. Generally, the sooner that reliable information about revenue transactions can be conveyed to financial statement users, the more relevant it will be to them. By the same token, the earlier in the earning process revenue is recognized, the greater the likelihood of a divergence between the information and the underlying economic reality. Accordingly, the later in the earning process revenue is recognized, the greater the likelihood that the information presented will be reliable, but the lesser the likelihood that it will be relevant for users' decisions.

Because proper revenue recognition is critical, SFAC No. 5 (pars. 83a and 83b) specifies that two conditions must be satisfied, namely, being realized or realizable and being earned.

- Revenues are realized when products, other assets, or services are exchanged for cash or claims to cash, and revenues are realizable when assets received or held are readily convertible to known amounts of cash or claims to cash. Assets that are readily convertible have "(i) interchangeable (fungible) units and (ii) quoted prices available in an active market that can rapidly absorb the quantity held by the entity without significantly affecting the price."
- Revenues are earned "when the entity has substantially accomplished what it must do to be entitled to the benefits represented by the revenues" (par. 83b).

The FASB, however, may revise these criteria based on the results of a major project on revenue recognition that it began in mid-2002 (see Section 19.4(c)).

(d) SPECIFIC RECOGNITION CRITERIA.   The specific criteria discussed below have been suggested by various individuals or groups as being significant to the timing of revenue recognition. They address characteristics of the event or transaction that gives rise to the revenue, characteristics of the asset received in the transaction, and characteristics of the revenue recognized (see Exhibit 19.1). Despite some degree of overlap in the criteria, the classification scheme seems useful, particularly in resolving problems that are not addressed by authoritative pronouncements.

(e) CHARACTERISTICS OF THE REVENUE EVENT OR TRANSACTION.   Before revenue is recognized, the event or transaction should be nonreversible and the risks and rewards of ownership

---

Characteristics of the Revenue Event or Transaction

1. The economic substance of the transaction that precedes the recognition of revenue should be such that:
   a. Reversal of the transaction is remote—that is, the revenue recognized has permanence.
   b. If ownership of property has changed hands, the risks and rewards of ownership also should be transferred.
2. Either an event that serves as the basis of recognizing revenue should not be within the control of the entity, or it should be verifiable by external evidence.

Characteristics of the Asset Received

The asset recorded in a revenue transaction should be:

1. Liquid
2. Free from significant obligations and restrictions
3. Collectible
4. Reliably measurable

Characteristics of the Revenue Recognized

The revenue should be "earned" to the extent that it has been recognized. If the earning process is not complete or substantially complete, either the critical event in the earning process should have occurred or measurable progress should have been made toward the completion of the earning process before revenue is recognized.

Exhibit 19.1   Specific criteria for recognizing revenue.

should be transferred. Both criteria should be applied to the substance, not merely to the form, of the event or transaction. APB Statement No. 4 (par. 127) discusses substance over form as one of the basic features of financial accounting:

> **F-12. Substance over form.** Financial accounting emphasizes the economic substance of events even though the legal form may differ from the economic substance and suggest different treatment. Usually the economic substance of events to be accounted for agrees with the legal form. Sometimes, however, substance and form differ. Accountants emphasize the substance of events rather than their form so that the information provided better reflects the economic activities represented.

SAB No. 30, "Interpretation Regarding Divestitures in Connection with a Sale of a Subsidiary," states that "economic substance rather than legal form should determine the accounting and reporting of a transaction." Although the literature provides such guidance for determining the economic substance of particular transactions in specific industries, it provides little guidance for applying the substance over form notion in general. That may well be because, as noted in SFAC No. 2, "Qualitative Characteristics of Accounting Information" (par. 160), "[S]ubstance over form is, in any case, a rather vague idea that defies precise definition" (see Jaenicke for further discussion[14]).

(i) Nonreversibility. If revenue is recognized on the basis of a particular event or transaction and subsequent events or transactions reverse the effect of the earlier one, the problem is not that revenue has been recognized in the wrong accounting period—it should never have been recognized at all because the definition of revenue or asset (or both) has not been met. Thus, in addition to affecting the timing of revenue recognition, the possibility of reversal of the revenue transaction also affects the determination of whether the revenue exists. Windal states that, "for an item to be sufficiently definite [to warrant recognition], it must appear unlikely to be reversed. We might say it must appear to have permanence."[15]

In some cases, as in sales with right of return, the possibility of the transaction being permanent exists, and the likelihood of reversal may be predictable. In those cases, revenue should be recognized and appropriate allowances recorded for the estimated returns. In other cases, as in many product financing arrangements that contain repurchase agreements, the possibility of permanence is zero or extremely remote. If the economic substance of the "sale" rather than its formal designation is judged and the "sale" transaction is found to be fictitious, completion of the transaction and permanence of the revenue are absent and no revenue should be recognized. As another example, the receipt of a small down payment and small periodic payments, with a large final "balloon" payment, often suggests that an option to buy an asset has been sold, not the asset itself; the sale of the asset itself may never take place.

"Bill and hold" sales represent another type of transaction that, depending on the underlying circumstances, could be reversible. According to SEC Exchange Act Release No. 17878 (June 22, 1981), in a bill and hold transaction, "a customer agrees to purchase the goods but the seller retains physical possession until the customer requests shipment to designated locations." SAB No. 101, "Revenue Recognition," (see Section 19.3(h)) provides examples of criteria that must be met when delivery has not occurred.

(ii) Transfer of the Risks and Rewards of Ownership. The criterion that the risks and rewards of ownership should be transferred before revenue is recognized appears in several places in the accounting literature. For example, SFAS No. 13, "Accounting for Leases," (par. 60) states: "[T]he provisions of this Statement derive from the view that a lease that transfers substantially all of the benefits and risks incident to the ownership of property should be accounted for as the acquisition of an asset and the incurrence of an obligation by the lessee and as a sale or financing by the

---

[14] H. R. Jaenicke, *Survey of Present Practices in Recognizing Revenues, Expenses, Gains, and Losses* (FASB, Norwalk, CT, January 1981).

[15] F.W. Windal, "The Accounting Concept of Realization," *Accounting Review*, April 1961, p. 252.

lessor." SAB No. 30 states that in resolving the issue discussed, "[T]he principal consideration must be an assessment of whether the risks and other incidents of ownership have been transferred to the buyer with sufficient certainty." In practice, however, applying the criterion does not always yield a definitive answer because, in many transactions, the risks and rewards are divided between the two parties.[16]

Determining whether the "risks and other incidents of ownership" have been transferred to the buyer requires an examination of the underlying facts and circumstances. The following five circumstances may raise questions about whether the risks of ownership have, in substance, been transferred:

1. A continuing involvement by the seller in the transaction or in the assets transferred, such as through the exercise of managerial authority to a degree usually associated with ownership, perhaps in the form of a remarketing agreement or a commitment to operate the property

2. Absence of significant financial investment by the buyer in the asset transferred, as evidenced, for example, by a token down payment or by a concurrent loan to the buyer

3. Repayment of debt that constitutes the principal consideration in the transaction dependent on the generation of sufficient funds from the asset transferred

4. Limitations or restrictions on the buyer's use of the asset transferred or on the profits from it

5. Retention of effective control of the asset by the seller

The first three items on the list are suggested by SAB No. 30; the last two are found in Accounting Series Release (ASR) No. 95, "Accounting for Real Estate Transactions Where Circumstances Indicate That Profits Were Not Earned at the Time the Transactions Were Recorded."

Some of the circumstances above may also be useful in assessing whether other criteria noted in Exhibit 19.1 have been met. For example, a continuing involvement by the seller may affect the criteria that the asset received be free of significant obligations, that the earning process be substantially complete, and that the asset received be measurable.

(iii) Recognition Based on Events.   Revenues are sometimes recognized on the basis of events rather than transactions. For example, production that precedes revenue recognized on the percentage-of-completion basis is more properly described as an event than as a transaction because it need not involve a transfer of something of value between two or more entities.

An event occurring within the enterprise that precedes the recognition of revenue, such as production, should be verifiable by evidence external to the enterprise, such as an increase in market price or the existence of a firm contract. If revenue recognition is based on an event external to the enterprise, such as a price increase, the event should not be within the control of the enterprise.

(f) CHARACTERISTICS OF THE ASSET RECEIVED.   Paragraph 83 of SFAC No. 5 states that, before it can be recognized, revenue must be realized or realizable. This criterion is based on the presumption that, at least to some degree, the asset received is liquid, free from significant obligations or restrictions, collectible, and reliably measurable. Those tests would be relevant in addition to any characteristics of assets included in the FASB's asset definition in SFAC No. 6.

(i) Asset Liquidity.   Asset liquidity has long been suggested as a prerequisite for recognizing revenue. Canning observes that one of the usual conditions for recognizing revenue is that "the future receipt of money within one year has become highly probable."[17] Paton and Littleton note that "revenue is realized, according to the dominant view, when it is evidenced by cash receipts or receivables, or other new liquid assets."[18] The liquidity criterion also is generally interpreted as

---

[16] See Jaenicke, Ch. 2 for further discussion.

[17] J. B. Canning, *The Economics of Accounting* (Ronald Press, New York, 1929), p. 102.

[18] Paton and Littleton, p. 49.

having been met if the financial flow is in the form of a reduction of liabilities that would obviate the subsequent use of liquid assets.

Contrary to the views expressed above, however, the APB did not consider asset liquidity a significant condition for revenue recognition. APB Opinion No. 29, "Accounting for Nonmonetary Transactions" (par. 18), states:

> In general accounting for nonmonetary transactions should be based on the fair values of the assets (or services) involved, which is the same basis as that used in monetary transactions.
>
> Thus, the cost of a nonmonetary asset acquired in exchange for another nonmonetary asset is the fair value of the asset surrendered to obtain it, and a gain or loss should be recognized on the exchange.

The same Opinion (pars. 20 and 26) states, however, that illiquidity of the nonmonetary asset may prevent its fair value from being determinable (i.e., measurable) and thus prevent the recognition of gain or loss.

> Accounting for a nonmonetary transaction should not be based on the fair values of the assets transferred unless those fair values are determinable within reasonable limits.
>
> Fair value should be regarded as not determinable within reasonable limits if major uncertainties exist about the realizability of the value that would be assigned to an asset received in a nonmonetary transaction accounted for at fair value.... If neither the fair value of a nonmonetary asset transferred nor the fair value of a nonmonetary asset received in exchange is determinable within reasonable limits, the recorded amount of nonmonetary asset transferred from the enterprise may be the only available measure of the transaction.

Horngren contends that the receipt of liquid assets per se should not be a condition for recognizing revenue, but should serve as evidence that the measurability criterion has been met. (Horngren also was on the APB when Opinion No. 29 was issued.)[19]

(ii) Absence of Obligations and Restrictions.   The absence of obligations and restrictions as a criterion is expressed by Vatter as follows: "Revenue differs from other asset-increasing transactions in that the new assets are completely free of equity restrictions other than the residual equity of the fund itself." The obligations and restrictions that Vatter had in mind—repayment obligations, obligations to share income, voting rights, and dividend preferences—characterize debt and equity financing. Under this view, sales and excise taxes collected by an enterprise should be recognized as liabilities, not as revenue, because the amounts collected are earmarked for remittance to a governmental agency.[20]

There are presently no known instances of improper revenue recognition resulting from the recording of assets with obligations and restrictions attached. It is conceivable, however, for the "buyer" to impose such conditions on the asset as to suggest that the risks and rewards of the asset's ownership are not transferred to the "seller." This condition, then, would be analogous to the condition (discussed above) that the seller's risks and rewards of ownership should transfer to the buyer if revenue is to be recognized.

(iii) Asset Collectibility.   As noted above, the earliest authoritative statement of revenue recognition, ARB No. 43 (Ch. 1, par. 1), emphasized the collectibility criterion when the asset received is other than cash: "Profit is deemed to be realized when a sale in the ordinary course of business is effected, unless the circumstances are such that the collection of the sale price is not reasonably

[19] C. T. Horngren, "How Should We Interpret the Realization Concept?" *Accounting Review*, April 1965, p. 330.
[20] W. J. Vatter, *The Fund Theory of Accounting and Its Implications for Financial Reports* (University of Chicago Press, Chicago, 1947), p. 25.

assured." As discussed in subsequent authoritative and quasi-authoritative pronouncements about typical revenue recognition issues and specialized industry problems, much of the literature has been concerned with defining and refining the collectibility criterion in specific circumstances, such as for retail land sales. Little discussion of collectibility in general exists in the pronouncements of authoritative bodies; however, the collectibility criterion is rarely questioned.

From the case-by-case approach to collectibility taken by rule-making bodies, the following conditions may suggest doubtful collectibility:

- Evidence of financial weakness of the purchaser
- Uncertainty resulting from the form of consideration or method of settlement, for example, nonrecourse notes and purchaser's stock
- Small or no down payment
- Concurrent loans to purchasers, presumably to finance the down payment

This list comes from ASR No. 95. Although that release is titled "Accounting for Real Estate Transactions Where Circumstances Indicate That Profits Were Not Earned at the Time the Transactions Were Recorded," the circumstances discussed have wider applicability and appear in slightly different versions in AICPA Guides issued in the 1970s and subsequently incorporated into FASB Statements. If the conditions above are present, an event or transaction also may fail to meet other recognition criteria, particularly the "transfer of risks and rewards of ownership" test.

(iv) Asset Measurability.   This criterion is suggested by Canning as well as by a committee of the AAA. Canning notes that the measurability criterion has two aspects—first, that "the amount to be received can be estimated with a high degree of reliability," and second, that "the expenses incurred or to be incurred in the (income) cycle can be estimated with a high degree of accuracy."[21] The AAA 1964 Concepts and Standards Research Committee on the Realization Concept noted in "The Realization Concept" (pp. 314–315):

> It is difficult to be precise about what is the current prevailing practice, but it appears that presently accepted tests for realization require receipt of a current (or liquid) asset capable of objective measurement in a market transaction for services rendered .... The committee would stress measurability, and not liquidity, as the essential attribute required for recognition of realized revenue.

The measurability criterion is related to the verifiability, and hence the objectivity, of evidence supporting the amount of revenue to be recognized. Thus the FASB has stated:

> Verifiability ... generally means that independent measurers using the same methods obtain essentially the same result. Verifiability is in one sense a measure of the objectivity (freedom from bias) of financial statement measures because the more the measure reflects the characteristics of the object or event measured, the more likely that different measurers will agree.[22]

For revenue to be recognized, the asset received should be measurable with a degree of verifiability such that approximately the same amount would be used by all accountants and it would thus be free from measurer bias—that is, it would be objective. As discussed previously, measurability is one of the four recognition criteria provided in paragraph 63 of SFAC No. 5 and is defined in terms of a financial statement item having "a relevant attribute measurable with sufficient reliability."

---

[21] Canning, p. 102.

[22] FASB Discussion Memorandum, "An Analysis of Issued Related to the Conceptual Framework for Financial Accounting and Reporting: Elements of Financial Statements and Their Measurement" (FASB, Norwalk, CT, 1976), p. 158.

The measurability of the asset received, and thus of the revenue recognized, is enhanced if the asset received is liquid. Measurability also is related to the nonreversibility and collectibility criteria discussed earlier. Those criteria suggest that possible later reductions in recorded revenue should be small; the measurability criterion suggests that any such reductions be capable of reasonable estimation.

Measurability problems may arise when the assets received are a customer's common stock, preferred stock, stock warrants, stock options, or other equity instruments. (Accounting by entities issuing the instruments is addressed in EITF Issue No. 96-18, "Accounting for Equity Instruments that Are Issued to Other Than Employees for Acquiring, or in Conjunction with Selling, Goods or Services" and pars. 7–8 of SFAS No. 123 (R), "Share-Based Payment.")

Paragraph 18 of APB Opinion No. 29, "Accounting for Nonmonetary Transactions," requires revenue in these situations to be measured at the fair value of the goods or services sold or the equity instrument received, whichever is more reliably measurable. According to par. 7 of SFAS No. 121, "[q]uoted market prices in active markets are the best evidence of fair value." Several methods are available to estimate the value of equity instruments when no public market exists, such as obtaining valuations from independent experts; using valuation models, such as the Black-Scholes model for options and warrants; and using comparable arm'slength transactions with independent third parties.

Some transactions involving the receipt of equity instruments, especially those involving multiperiod arrangements or arrangements in which the terms may change after the goods or services are provided, raise more complex issues. EITF Issue No. 00-8, "Accounting by a Grantee for an Equity Instrument to Be Received in Conjunction with Providing Goods or Services," addresses two revenue-related questions when equity instruments are involved. First, the date at which fair value should be measured (i.e., the measurement date) is the earlier of the dates at which (1) ". . . the parties come to a mutual understanding of the terms of the equity-based compensation arrangement and a commitment for performance by the grantee [i.e., the seller] to earn the equity instruments (a 'performance commitment') is reached" or (2) ". . . the grantee's performance necessary to earn the equity instruments is complete (i.e., the vesting date)" (par. 4).

The second question concerns accounting for transactions in which the terms of the equity instruments may be adjusted after the measurement date based on either market conditions or future performance by the seller. The EITF concluded that if, on the measurement date, any of the terms of an equity instrument depend on achieving a market condition—for example, when the number of shares to be issued depends on the market price of the stock at some future point—total revenue should be measured as the sum of the fair value of the equity interest without regard to the market condition and the fair value of the commitment to change those terms if the market condition is met. In the second case—for example, when the life of the options originally granted to the seller will be extended if the total number of hits on a buyer's Web site exceeds a specified number—the potential fair value of the commitment to change the terms if the future performance conditions are met should not be taken into account when initially measuring the fair value of the equity instruments. Instead, subsequent changes in the fair value of the equity instrument resulting from achieving a performance condition should be recognized as additional revenue pursuant to par. 51 of SFAS Statement No. 123(R), "Share-Based Payment" ("modification accounting").

Agreements involving equity instruments issued as consideration in sales transactions also may include a seller's contingent right to receive an equity instrument after performance is completed. These arrangements are discussed in EITF Issue No. 00-18, "Accounting Recognition for Certain Transactions involving Equity Instruments Granted to Other Than Employees."

(g) CHARACTERISTICS OF THE REVENUE RECOGNIZED.   One of the most commonly suggested criteria for recognizing revenue is that it be "earned" before it is recognized. SFAC No. 5 (par. 83) states that "revenues are not recognized until earned." This criterion takes several forms.

The first form requires completion or *substantial completion* of the earning process. As noted earlier, APB Statement No. 4 (par. 150) states: "Revenue is generally recognized when both of the following conditions are met: (1) the earning process is complete or virtually complete and (2) an exchange has taken place." Paragraph 153 notes that the earning requirement

> usually causes no problems because the earning process is usually complete or nearly complete by the time of the required exchange. The requirement that revenue be earned becomes important, however, if money is received or amounts are billed in advance of the delivery of goods or rendering of services.

APB Statement No. 4 then suggests that the substantial completion test is not always followed and that revenue is sometimes recognized, as on long-term construction contracts, on the basis of *recognizable progress* toward completion of the earning process, a second form of the criterion. A third variation of the earning criterion, first suggested by Meyers, is that recognition be related to the *critical event* in the earning process.[23]

Waiting until the earning process is substantially complete may, depending on the nature of the transaction, delay the recognition of revenue more than either the "recognizable progress" or the "critical event" form of the earning criterion, thus minimizing the risk of error from incorrectly identifying the critical event or the extent of progress. Moreover, at the point of "substantial completion," the costs associated with the revenue transaction are known with more certainty than under the other two approaches because those costs have already been incurred.

The critical event form of the earning criterion permits greater flexibility in the timing of revenue, depending on the nature of the event or transaction. The recognizable progress version emphasizes that revenue is, in fact, not earned at a single point in time. Because these two forms of the earning criterion may result in revenue recognition earlier than would the substantial completion form, their use could provide information that is more relevant to the needs of users than that attainable from the substantial completion form, but at a possible sacrifice of reliability.

Determining either the point of substantial completion or the critical event may be difficult if the seller has continuing obligations after the initial transfer of the asset. Thus the criterion that the principal risks and rewards of ownership be transferred is related to the criterion that the revenue be earned. For example, special warranties by the seller, remarketing agreements, or the seller's commitment to operate the property not only may raise the question of whether the critical event or substantial completion has taken place, but also whether the risks and rewards of ownership have been transferred.

When sales of products are involved, the condition that "an exchange has taken place" is met "at the date of sale, usually interpreted to mean the date of delivery to customers" (APB Statement No. 4, par. 151). Date of delivery usually coincides with the transfer of title. The FOB (free on board) terms specify precisely when title passes: FOB destination indicates that title passes at the buyer's location; FOB shipping point indicates that title passes at the seller's location. Revenue should not be recognized when products are shipped if the terms are FOB destination.

(h) SECURITIES AND EXCHANGE COMMISSION STAFF'S VIEWS ON RECOGNIZING REVENUES. In its SAB No. 101, "Revenue Recognition," the SEC staff summarized certain of its views on applying generally accepted accounting principles (GAAP) to revenue reporting. The staff issued the Bulletin in part because of revenue reporting issues encountered by registrants that came to the Commission's attention, including issues related to earnings management (see Section 19.1).

The Bulletin (Topic 13-A.1) discusses four criteria, all of which must be met to satisfy the GAAP requirement that revenue has been realized or is realizable and has been earned and therefore should be recognized:

- There is persuasive evidence that an exchange arrangement exists.
- The product has been delivered or services have been rendered.

---

[23] J. H. Meyers, "The Critical Event and the Recognition of Net Profit," *Accounting Review*, October 1959, p. 528.

- The price is fixed or determinable.
- Collectibility is reasonably assured.

(i) Persuasive Evidence of an Arrangement.   The SEC staff intends "arrangement" here to mean the final understanding between the parties as to the specific nature and terms of the transaction. This criterion may be implied in the APB and FASB literature, but it is not made explicit there. The implication is that revenue may not be recognizable even though the product has been delivered or service has been rendered, the price is fixed or determinable, and collectibility is reasonably assured.

The staff provides two examples (Topic 13-A.2) to illustrate how the first criterion can be applied:

1. The seller, whose normal and customary business practice for this class of customer is to have a written sales agreement signed by both parties, delivers the product. The seller has signed the agreement but the buyer has not.

   The staff concludes that the seller may not recognize revenue on the sale. If the buyer had signed the agreement but its final commitment is subject to subsequent approval or execution of another agreement, the seller may not recognize revenue until the subsequent approval is obtained or the other agreement is complete.

   Other kinds of persuasive evidence of an exchange agreement could exist depending on the business practices and processes of the parties, including various forms of written or electronic evidence, such as binding purchase orders or on-line authorizations. Care must be taken to ensue that all the terms of the arrangement, including concurrent or subsequently executed side agreements, provide the needed persuasive evidence.

2. A seller delivers products to a customer on a consignment basis. Title to the products pass to the customer as the customer consumes the products in its operations. The staff concludes that the seller may not recognize revenue on the sale until the products are consumed, because until then the seller retains the risks and rewards of ownership of the products.

The staff also describes examples of circumstances in which revenue may not be recognized even though title has passed:

1. The buyer has a right to return the product and:[24]
   - The buyer neither pays at the time of the sale nor is obligated to pay at a specified date or dates.
   - The buyer does not pay at the time of sale, has to pay at a specified subsequent date or dates, and that obligation is contractually or implicitly excused until the buyer resells, consumes, or uses the product.
   - The buyer's obligation would be changed—for example, the seller would forgive the debt or grant a refund—if the product is stolen, destroyed, or damaged.
   - The seller and the buyer do not have separate economic substance.
   - The seller must subsequently perform significantly in causing the buyer to resell the product.
2. The seller must repurchase the product, a substantially identical product, or processed goods that include the product, at specified prices not subject to change except for those due to changes in finance and holding costs, and the payments by the seller will be adjusted to cover substantially all changes in costs, including interest, the buyer incurs in buying and holding the product.[25] The staff believes that each of the following is an example of indicators of the latter condition:

---

[24] See SFAS No. 48
[25] See SFAS No. 49

   ○ The seller provides financing to the buyer until the products are resold without interest or at interest significantly below market beyond the seller's customary sales terms.

   ○ The seller pays interest costs to a third party on behalf of the buyer.

   ○ The seller customarily refunds or intends to refund part of the sales price equal to interest for the period from when the buyer paid the seller until the buyer resells the product.

3. The transaction neither avoids the prohibition on reporting revenue in EITF Issue No. 95-1, "Revenue Recognition on Sales with a Guaranteed Minimum Resale Value," nor qualifies for sales-type lease accounting.

4. The product is delivered for demonstration purposes.[26]

SAB No. 104, "Revenue Recognition," contains six examples developed by the SEC staff illustrating when revenue from nonrefundable up-front fees should be deferred. The examples include initiation fees at health clubs, activation fees for cellular phone service, fees for various webs site services, and technology access fees for research and development activities.

(ii) Delivery and Performance.   The staff provides examples (Topic 13-A.3) in which questions arise as to whether delivery and performance have been accomplished:

- A seller has received a purchase order for products but the buyer is not yet ready to take delivery.
- The seller has completed manufacturing the products and has segregated them in its own warehouse or has shipped them to a third party but has retained title, and payment by the buyer depends on delivery to a site specified by the buyer.

The staff concludes that revenue may not be recognized in either of these cases. It believes that title and the risks and rewards of ownership must pass to the buyer, typically when the product is delivered to the buyer (if the terms of sale are "FOB destination") or shipped to the buyer (if the terms of sale are "FOB shipping point").

The following are examples of criteria that must be met for revenue to be recognizable when delivery has not occurred (though meeting all the criteria does not necessarily guarantee that revenue will be recognized):

- The risks of ownership must have passed to the buyer.
- The buyer must have made a fixed commitment to buy, preferably in writing.
- The buyer must have requested, preferably in writing, that the transaction be on a bill-and-hold basis and must have a substantial business reason for doing so.
- The schedule for delivery must be fixed, reasonable, and consistent with the buyer's business purpose.
- The seller must not have retained any duty to perform, making the earning process incomplete.
- The products must have been segregated and not available for shipment to other buyers.
- The product must be complete and ready for shipment.

The following circumstances also should be considered before revenue is recognized under bill-and-hold arrangements:

- The date by which payment is expected and whether the seller has modified its normal billing and credit terms
- The seller's experiences with such transactions
- Whether the buyer has the risk of loss in case the market value of the products declines

---

[26] See SOP 97-2.

- Whether the seller's risks as custodian have been insured
- Whether extended procedures are needed to make sure that the buyer's business reasons for the bill-and-hold have not introduced a contingency to the buyer's commitment

Delivery to an intermediate site should not result in revenue reporting if a substantial part of he price is payable only on delivery to a specified final site.

In addition to delivery, revenue recognition requires that the products or services have been accepted by the buyer. If the contract contains provisions concerning acceptance by the buyer, such as the right to test the product after receipt, buyer acceptance must occur or the provisions must have lapsed before revenue can be recognized.

The seller's duties under the contract must be substantially complete for delivery or performance to have occurred. Inconsequential or perfunctory actions, however, may remain incomplete if they would not result in a refund or rejection of the products delivered or services performed to date. The costs of all such actions should be accrued.

The delivery or performance of one of multiple deliverables is considered not to have occurred if undelivered deliverables are essential to the functioning of the delivered element (see Section 19.4(a)(ix)).

Revenue recognition should begin in a licensing or similar arrangement when its term begins. During the term, revenue should be recognized based on the substance of the arrangement.

The staff provides three examples (Topic 13-A.3) illustrating how these guidelines should be applied:

1. A company sells goods on layaway, setting the goods aside and collecting a cash deposit. Though a time period to finalize the sale may be set, the buyer need not enter a fixed payment commitment. The buyer receives the goods only on payment of the balance. If the buyer does not pay the balance, the deposit is forfeited. If the goods are lost, damaged, or destroyed, the deposit is refundable or substitute goods are provided.

   The staff concludes that revenue may be recognized no earlier than when the goods are delivered to the buyer. Until then, the seller has a liability for the deposit.

2. A provider of goods or services may receive a nonrefundable fee at the inception of an arrangement, such as a lifetime membership in a health club or an activation fee for telecommunications services. The buyer may agree to pay the fee to obtain a continuing right to purchase the goods or services, at or below the usual prices. Goods or services may or may not be provided at the inception of the arrangement, and, if so, they may or may not be useful to the buyer without provision of further goods or services.

   The staff concludes that revenue should be recognized only to the extent that the nonrefundable fee is for products delivered or services performed that represent the culmination of a separate earnings process, but that the rest of the fee should be deferred. Revenue should be recognized systematically as those fees are earned. Activities of the seller such as selling memberships, signing contracts, enrolling buyers, or activating telecommunications services do not constitute culmination of a separate earnings process. The earnings process is completed by performing under the terms of the arrangement.

3. A seller provides a buyer with activity tracking or similar services, such as tracking property tax payment activity or sending delinquency letters on overdue accounts, for a 10-year period. (The arrangement is not covered by SFAS No. 91.) The buyer is required to prepay for all the services to be provided during the period. The seller provides setup procedures at the outset and ongoing services in accordance with the arrangement. None of the fees is refundable if the buyer terminates the arrangement or does not use all the services to which it is entitled. The seller must refund a portion of the fee if the seller terminates the arrangement early.

   The staff concludes that the seller should report revenue on a straight-line basis over the term of the contract or the expected period of service, whichever is longer, unless there is evidence that revenue is earned in a different pattern, in which case revenue should be reported in the different pattern.

The staff believes that revenue should not be recognized as costs are incurred because the setup costs bear no direct relationship to the performance of the contracted services. Also, not all revenue should be reported at the outset with accrual of the remaining costs because the services have not been performed.

(iii) Fixed or Determinable Sales Price.   Cancellation or termination clauses, side agreements, and significant transactions with unusual terms and conditions may suggest the existence of a demonstration period, an incomplete transaction, or that the price is otherwise not fixed or determinable. For example, the sales price is not fixed or determinable if the buyer has a cancellation privilege; it becomes determinable ratably if a cancellation privilege expires ratably. Customary short-term rights of return are not cancellation privileges and should be treated in conformity with SFAS No. 48. "Revenue Recognition When Right of Return Exists" (see Section 19.4(a)(iv).

The staff provides examples to illustrate when to recognize revenue in situations where the existence of a fixed or determinable sales price is questionable (Topic 13-A.4):

1. A seller charges a membership fee at the beginning of a contract term for the buyer to have the privilege to buy goods from the seller at discount prices during the membership period. The buyer may cancel the arrangement at any time during the term and receive a full refund of the fee.

    The staff believes that revenue should not be recognized for the fee at the beginning of the term with estimated costs accrued because the seller has an unfulfilled duty to perform services; the earnings process is not complete. Further, the ability of the buyer to obtain a full refund of the fee during the membership period makes the sales price involved in the fee not fixed or determinable during the membership period. The fee should be reported as a liability, which is extinguished only on refund of the fee or expiration of the refund privilege. This conclusion holds regardless of whether there is a large population of transactions that grant buyers the same cancellation privileges and reasonable estimates can be made of the number of buyers who will cancel; service arrangements are specifically excluded from the scope of SFAS No. 48.

    Nevertheless, existing practice had developed contrary to those conclusions, and the staff believes it should not require practice to be changed without formal rule making or standard setting. The staff will therefore not object to recognizing refundable membership fees as revenue, net of estimated refunds, over the membership period, if all of the following criteria have been met:

    ○ The estimated refunds are for a large pool of homogeneous items.
    ○ Timely reliable estimates of expected refunds can be made. Such estimates cannot be made if:
        ○ There are recurring, significant differences between experience and estimated cancellation or termination rates, even if the effect of the differences is not material to the consolidated financial statements.
        ○ There are recurring variances between experience and estimated amounts of refunds that are material to revenue or net income in quarterly or annual financial statements.
        ○ The likelihood of required material adjustments to previously reported revenue is not "remote."
        ○ Buyers' termination or cancellation and refund privileges exceed one year.
    ○ Sufficient company-specific historical experience predictive of future events exists on which to estimate the refunds.
    ○ The amount of the fee is fixed other than the right to obtain a refund.

If any of those conditions are not met, revenue should not be recognized until the cancellation privileges and refund rights expire. If all of the conditions are met and revenue is recognized over the membership period:

○ The amount of the fees representing estimated refunds should be credited to a refund liability account and the rest to a nonmonetary liability account for unearned revenue.

○ At each reporting date, a footnote schedule should be provided of the beginning and ending balances of refund obligations and unearned revenue, cash received for fees, revenue recognized, refunds paid, and adjustments explained.

○ Adjustments, if any, should be based on a retrospective approach, remeasuring the refund liability and the unearned revenue at each reporting date with the offset to revenue.

The costs of vouchers issued with new memberships for discounts or other benefits should be charged to expense when issued. Other advertising costs relating to new membership offers should be reported in conformity with SOP 93-7. If revenue is deferred until the cancellation or termination privileges expire, incremental direct costs of enrolling customers, such as agents' commissions, should be (a) charged to expense when incurred if the costs are not refundable to the reporting entity when fees are refunded, or (b) reported as an asset until the earlier of termination, cancellation, or refund, if the costs are refundable to the reporting entity when fees are refunded. If revenue, net of estimated refunds, is recognized over the membership period, a like percentage of incremental direct costs should be included in earnings in the same pattern that revenue is recognized. The remainder of the incremental costs should be charged to expense when incurred if the costs are not refundable to the reporting entity when the fees are refundable. If those costs are refundable to the reporting entity when the fees are refundable, they should be reported as an asset (until the refund occurs). All costs other than incremental direct costs should be reported as expense as incurred.

2. A lessor leases retail space under an operating lease for one year for $1.2 million, payable in equal monthly installments on the first day of each month plus contingent rentals of one percent of the lessee's net sales in excess of $25 million during the year.

   The staff believes that the contingent rentals should be recognized as revenue beginning with the date the lessee's sales first exceed $25 million and continuing in subsequent periods as it becomes accruable.

3. The staff believes that the following are examples of the "other factors" referred to in paragraph 8 of SFAS No. 48 that may preclude making a reasonable estimate of product returns:

○ "Channel stuffing"—significant increases in or excess levels of inventory in a distribution channel

○ The inability to determine or observe the levels of inventory in a distribution channel and the current level of sales to end users

○ Expected introductions of new products that may cause technological obsolescence or larger-than-expected returns of current products

○ A particular distributor's significance to the reporting entity's or to its segment's business, sales, and marketing

○ The newness of the product

○ Introduction of competitor's products with superior technology and the like

(iv) Sales of Leased or Licensed Departments.   Retailers customarily recognized revenue for sales made by departments leased or licensed to others. Because of developments since the SEC issued SAB No. 1, which did not object to that treatment because of existing industry practices, SFAS No. 13, "Accounting for Leases," and a Technical Practice Aid (TIS Section 5100.16, "Rental Revenue Based on Percentage of Sales") were issued. The staff now concludes (SAB No. 101, Topic 8-A) that such sales should no longer be included in the retailer's revenue. Retailers may disclose the amounts of such sales in notes to their financial statements. Rents and fees under such arrangements should be recognized when earned.

(v) Staff Accounting Bulletin No. 104.   The SEC issued SAB No. 104, "Revenue Recognition," in December 2003 to update the guidance contained in SAB No. 101 and the related frequently asked questions (FAQ) document by applying the consensus on EITF Issue No. 00-21, "Revenue Arrangements with Multiple Deliverables," to various types of revenue transactions. For example, if the deliverables in a contractual arrangement meet the separability criteria in the EITF consensus, vendors should determine an appropriate revenue recognition policy for each deliverable and should apply that policy when accounting for each separable unit they have identified. If the deliverables in a contractual arrangement do not meet the separability criteria, an appropriate revenue recognition policy should be applied to the entire arrangement.

SAB No. 104 also clarified the accounting for contractual arrangements that do not meet the separability criteria, but for which vendors have remaining obligations, including those that are inconsequential or perfunctory as well as those that are essential to the functioning of the delivered portion of the arrangement. Although judgment must be applied in determining how consequential the remaining obligations are and the functionality of the delivered portion, the following guidance applies:

- Revenue should be recognized at the time of delivery and the cost of providing the remaining goods or services should be accrued if (a) other criteria for revenue recognition are met, (b) the undelivered element is inconsequential or perfunctory, and (c) the undelivered element is not essential for the delivered portion of the arrangement to function.
- Revenue should not be recognized at the time of delivery if (a) the undelivered element is essential to the functioning of the delivered portion of the arrangement or (b) failure to complete the undelivered portion of the arrangement would result in customers receiving refunds or rejecting the goods previously delivered or services previously performed.

Section 19.4(a)(ix) discusses EITF Issue No. 00-21 in more detail.

(vi) Revenue Recognition Criteria Used Outside the United States.   Rulemaking bodies outside the United States also have developed criteria for revenue recognition. For example, paragraphs 14–19 of International Accounting Standard (IAS) 18, "Revenue Recognition," issued in 1982 and modified in 1993, discuss five criteria for recognizing revenue from sales of products:

1. The seller has transferred to the buyer the significant risks and rewards of ownership;
2. The seller retains neither continuing managerial involvement to the degree usually associated with ownership nor effective control over the goods sold;
3. The amount of revenue can be measured reliably;
4. It is probable that the economic benefits associated with the transaction will flow to the seller; and
5. The costs incurred or to be incurred related to the transaction can be measured reliably.

For service transactions, IAS 18 (par. 20) specifies the last three of these criteria plus one additional criterion—the stage of completion at the balance sheet date can be measured reliably—that must be met in order for revenue to be recognized using a "percentage-of-completion" method. If those criteria are not met, a "cost-recovery" approach should be used. Other recognition criteria are provided for interest, royalty, and dividend revenues.

The broad recognition criteria and limited number of examples contained in IAS 18 have not, in many people's minds, provided sufficient guidance to cover the range and complexity of revenue transactions. In addition, GAAP and industry practices in many countries are not always consistent with that guidance. As a result, the International Accounting Standards Board (IASB) began a project in 2002 to replace IAS 18 and, if necessary, to revise its "Framework for the Preparation and Presentation of Financial Statements." That project, being conducted jointly with the FASB to help ensure the guidance issued by both boards converge, is described in Section 19.4(d) below.

Because of increasing inconsistencies in practice, the United Kingdom's Accounting Standards Board (ASB) began a project to develop additional guidance on accounting for revenue recognition by U.K. companies. Based on a Discussion Paper, "Revenue Recognition," published in July 2001, the ASB issued Application Note G to its Financial Reporting Standard No. 5, "Reporting the Substance of Transactions." That Note indicates that turnover (i.e., revenue) should be recognized only after companies have performed under contractual arrangements with customers. Specific guidance also is provided on recognizing revenue for various types of transactions, including long-term contracts, bill-and-hold arrangements, and sales with rights of return. Other issues addressed in the Note include reporting revenue at gross or net amounts and measuring revenue from sales with deferred payment terms and when significant risks exist about customers' ability to pay. The Application Note was issued as interim guidance because the ASB supports the joint FASB/IASB revenue recognition project (see Section 19.4(d)). The ASB intends to issue a new standard for U.K. companies after the IASB completes that project.

19.4 TYPES OF REVENUE TRANSACTIONS

(a) SPECIAL REVENUE RECOGNITION PROBLEMS.   Special revenue recognition problems are posed by events and transactions in which the source of revenue is something other than the sale of a product or the rendering of service in a transaction that is completed over a relatively short period. In some cases, authoritative or quasi-authoritative pronouncements have addressed the issue of the proper timing of revenue recognition. In other cases, such pronouncements do not exist, and the proper recognition policies can be determined only by reference to the criteria suggested earlier in this chapter. Specialized industry practices are discussed in Section 19.4(b).

(i) Revenue Recognition Problems Discussed in Other Chapters.   To avoid duplication, the special revenue recognition problems that are discussed elsewhere in this *Handbook* are listed below, with the relevant chapter numbers.

- *Contributions*. SFAS No. 116, "Accounting for Contributions Received and Contributions Made," applies to all entities that receive or make contributions. The standard is discussed in Chapter 35.
- *Installment sales*. Revenue from installment sales contracts extending over more than one accounting period may be recognized at the time of sale, on the installment basis, or on the cost recovery basis, depending on circumstances. This issue is further discussed in Chapter 25.
- *Nonmonetary exchanges of fixed assets*. APB Opinion No. 29, "Accounting for Nonmonetary Transactions," and SFAS No. 153, "Exchanges of Nonmonetary Assets," specify the conditions under which gains and losses should be recognized on the exchange of nonmonetary assets; the required accounting varies according to whether the exchange has commercial substance. Those types of exchanges are discussed in Chapter 21. Nonmonetary barter transactions are discussed in Sections 19.4(a)(vii) and (b)(vii).
- *Sale and leaseback transactions*. Recognition or deferral of gains by the seller-lessee in a sale and leaseback transaction is specified in SFAS No. 13, "Accounting for Leases," as modified by SFAS No. 98, "Accounting for Leases: Sale-Leaseback Transactions Involving Real Estate." This issue is further discussed in Chapter 23.
- *Sales-type leases*. Accounting for leases by a lessor is prescribed by SFAS No. 13. Leases that are classified in SFAS No. 13 as sales-type leases result in recognition of revenue by the lessor at the inception of the lease; Chapter 23 discusses sales-type leases. Chapter 23 also discusses EITF Issue No. 95-1, "Revenue Recognition on Sales with a Guaranteed Minimum Resale Value," and No. 95-4, "Revenue Recognition on Equipment Sold and Subsequently Repurchased Subject to an Operating Lease."

(ii) Transfers of Receivables.   SFAS No. 140, "Accounting for Transfers and Servicing of Financial Assets and Extinguishments of Liabilities," provides accounting and reporting standards for distinguishing transfers of financial assets that are sales (in which the entity derecognizes the assets transferred) from transfers that are secured borrowings (in which the entity continues to recognize the assets transferred and recognizes the liabilities it has incurred).

SFAS No. 140 is based on a "financial components" approach that focuses on control. Under that approach, a transferor accounts for a transfer of financial assets as a sale if the transferor surrenders control over the assets to the transferee, to the extent that the transferor receives consideration other than beneficial interests (i.e., rights to receive all or part of the underlying cash flows) in the transferred assets. Paragraph 9 states that the transferor is deemed to have surrendered control over the transferred assets if and only if all of the following conditions are met:

a. The transferred assets have been isolated from the transferor—put presumptively beyond the reach of the transferor and its creditors, even in bankruptcy or other receivership (paragraphs 27 and 28).

b. Each transferee (or, if the transferee is a qualifying special purpose entity (SPE) [SPE] (paragraph 35), each holder of its financial interests) has the right to pledge or exchange the assets (or beneficial interests) it received, and no condition both constrains the transferee (or holder) from taking advantage of its right to pledge or exchange and provides more than a trivial benefit to the transferor (paragraphs 29–34).

c. The transferor does not maintain effective control over the transferred assets through either (1) an agreement that both entitles and obligates the transferor to repurchase or redeem them before their maturity (paragraphs 47–49), or (2) the ability to unilaterally cause the holder to return specific assets, other than through a cleanup call (paragraphs 58 and 59).

(iii) Product Financing Arrangements.   SFAS No. 49, "Accounting for Product Financing Arrangements," establishes accounting and reporting standards for transactions in which an enterprise sells and agrees to repurchase inventory, with the repurchase price equal to the original sale price plus carrying and financing costs or other similar terms. SFAS No. 49 requires that a product financing arrangement be accounted for as a borrowing rather than as a sale.

Under SFAS No. 49 (par. 3), product financing arrangements include agreements in which an enterprise seeking to finance a product (referred to as a *sponsor*):

a. Sells the product to another entity (the enterprise through which the financing flows), and in a related transaction agrees to repurchase the product (or a substantially identical product);

b. Arranges for another entity to purchase the product on the sponsor's behalf and, in a related transaction, agrees to purchase the product from the other entity; or

c. Controls the disposition of the product that has been purchased by another entity in accordance with the arrangements described in either (a) or (b) above.

Other characteristics that are found in many, but not all, product financing arrangements are specified in paragraph 4:

a. The entity that purchases the product from the sponsor or purchases it directly from a third party on behalf of the sponsor was established expressly for that purpose or is an existing trust, nonbusiness organization, or credit grantor.

b. The product covered by the financing arrangement is to be used or sold by the sponsor, although a portion may be sold by the other entity directly to third parties.

c. The product covered by the financing arrangement is stored on the sponsor's premises.

d. The debt of the entity that purchases the product being financed is guaranteed by the sponsor.

According to paragraph 8 of SFAS No. 49, product financing arrangements that require the sponsor to repurchase the product or a substantially identical product at specified prices, adjusted to cover all costs incurred by the other entity in purchasing and holding the product, should be accounted for by the sponsor as follows:

a. If a sponsor sells a product to another entity and, in a related transaction, agrees to repurchase the product (or a substantially identical product) or processed goods of which the product is a component, the sponsor shall record a liability at the time the proceeds are received from the other entity to the extent that the product is covered by the financing arrangement. The sponsor shall not record the transaction as a sale and shall not remove the covered product from its balance sheet.

b. If the sponsor is party to an arrangement whereby another entity purchases a product on the sponsor's behalf and, in a related transaction, the sponsor agrees to purchase the product or processed goods of which the product is a component from the entity, the sponsor shall record the asset and the related liability when the product is purchased by the other entity.

(iv) Revenue Recognition When Right of Return Exists.   SFAS No. 48, "Revenue Recognition When Right of Return Exists," establishes accounting and reporting standards for sales of an enterprise's product in which the buyer has a right to return the product. Revenue from those sales transactions should be recognized at the time of sale only if all of the following six conditions are met (par. 6, footnotes omitted):

a. The seller's price to the buyer is substantially fixed or determinable at the date of sale.

b. The buyer has paid the seller, or the buyer is obligated to pay the seller and the obligation is not contingent on resale of the product.

c. The buyer's obligation to the seller would not be changed in the event of theft or physical destruction or damage of the product.

d. The buyer acquiring the product for resale has economic substance apart from that provided by the seller.

e. The seller does not have significant obligations for future performance to directly bring about resale of the product by the buyer.

f. The amount of future returns can be reasonably estimated (paragraph 8).

SFAS No. 48 (pars. 6–7) states that if revenue is recognized because the above conditions are met, provision should be made immediately for any costs or losses that may be expected in connection with any returns. Amounts of sales revenue and cost of sales reported in the income statement should exclude the portion for which returns are expected. Transactions for which revenue recognition is postponed should be recognized as revenue when the return privilege has substantially expired.

The ability to reasonably predict the amount of future returns depends on many factors. Although circumstances vary from one case to the next, the existence of the following four factors would appear to impair the ability to make a reasonable prediction, as presented in paragraph 8 of SFAS No. 48:

a. The susceptibility of the product to significant external factors, such as technological obsolescence or changes in demand.

b. Relatively long periods in which a particular product may be returned.

c. Absence of historical experience with similar types of sales of similar products, or inability to apply such experience because of changing circumstances, for example, changes in the selling enterprise's marketing policies or relationships with its customers.

d. Absence of a large volume of relatively homogeneous transactions.

(v) Service Transactions.   The FASB added a project, "Accounting for Certain Service Transactions," to its agenda in 1978 and published an "Invitation to Comment" based on a draft Statement of Position of the AICPA's Accounting Standards Division on that topic. Among the types of business mentioned that offer services rather than products are correspondence schools, health spas, retirement homes, cemetery associations, perpetual care societies, engineering firms, service and maintenance contractors, electronic security companies, advertising agencies, and computer service organizations. (The list is not intended to be all-inclusive.) The Invitation to Comment (p. 2) notes the following:

> The AICPA draft Statement of Position sets forth conclusions on (1) the guidelines to apply to transactions in which both services and products are provided, (2) the appropriate manner of revenue recognition, (3) the classification of costs as initial direct costs, direct costs, and indirect costs and the accounting for each, and (4) the accounting for initiation and installation fees. . . .

A service transaction may involve a tangible product that is sold or consumed as an incidental part of the transaction or is clearly identifiable as secondary or subordinate to the rendering of the service. The following guidelines apply to transactions in which both services and products are provided:

1. If the seller offers both a service and a product in a single transaction and if any product involved is not separately stated in such a manner that the total transaction price would vary as a result of the inclusion or exclusion of the product, the product is incidental to the rendering of the service and the transaction is a service transaction.

2. If the seller offers both a product and a service in a single transaction and any service involved is incidental and is provided or available to all purchasers, the transaction is a product transaction.

3. If the seller of a product offers a related service to purchasers of the product but separately states the service and product elements in such a manner that the total transaction price would vary as a result of the inclusion or exclusion of the service, the transaction consists of two components; a product transaction and a service transaction, and each should be accounted for separately.

Revenue from service transactions should be recognized based on performance, because performance determines the extent to which the earnings process is complete or virtually complete.

Performance is the execution of a defined act or acts or occurs with the passage of time.

Accordingly, revenue from service transactions should be recognized under one of the following methods:

1. *Specific performance method*—Performance consists of the execution of a single act and revenue should be recognized when that act takes place.

2. *Proportional performance method*—Performance consists of the execution of more than one act and revenue should be recognized based on the proportionate performance of each act. For example, if the service transaction involves a specified number of similar acts, an equal amount of revenue should be recognized for each act. If the transaction involves a specified number of defined but not similar acts, revenue recognized for each act should be based on the ratio of the seller's direct costs to perform each act to the total estimated direct costs of the transaction. If the transaction involves an unspecified number of similar acts with a fixed period for performance, revenue should be recognized on the straight-line method over the performance period.

3. *Completed performance method*—If services are performed in more than a single act, the proportion of services to be performed in the final act may be so significant in relation to the service transaction taken as a whole that performance cannot be deemed to have taken place until execution of that act. Revenue should be recognized when that act takes place.

4. *Collection method*—If there is a significant degree of uncertainty surrounding realization of service revenue (e.g., many personal services), revenue should not be recognized until collection.

The following classifications related to costs have been developed by the Division for purposes of the draft Statement of Position:

1. *Initial direct costs* are costs incurred that are directly associated with negotiating and consummating service agreements.

2. *Direct costs* are costs that have a clearly identifiable beneficial or causal relation (i) to the services performed or (ii) to the level of services performed for a group of customers.

3. *Indirect costs* are all costs other than initial direct costs and direct costs.

The principles set forth in the professional literature for recognizing costs state, in general, that costs should be charged to expense in the period in which the revenue with which they are associated is recognized as earned. Costs are not deferred, however, unless they are expected to be recoverable from future revenues.

The following is intended to provide guidance in implementing those general principles of cost recognition for service transactions:

1. *Cost recognition under the specific performance and completed performance methods*—If revenues are recognized under the specific performance or completed performance methods, all initial direct costs and direct costs should be charged to expense at the time revenues are recognized. Indirect costs should be charged to expense as incurred.

2. *Cost recognition under the proportional performance method*—Generally there is a close correlation between the amount of direct costs incurred and the extent of performance achieved. Since revenues are recognized in a manner related to performance achieved, direct costs should be charged to expense as incurred. Initial direct costs should be deferred and allocated over the term of service performance in proportion to the recognition of service revenue. Indirect costs should be charged to expense as incurred.

3. *Cost recognition under the collection method*—If the degree of uncertainty surrounding realization of service revenue is so significant that revenues are recognized only when collected, all costs (initial direct, direct, and indirect) should be charged to expense as incurred.

As of this writing, the FASB has not issued a comprehensive statement on accounting for service transactions, although parts of its "Invitation to Comment" were incorporated into SFAC No. 5. That may change as the Board continues to work on its revenue recognition project (see Section 19.4(c)).

Various standard setters, however, have used the general criteria for revenue and expense recognition of service transactions to develop specific guidance for a wide variety of service-related industries, including airlines (AICPA Industry Audit Guide, "Audits of Airlines," ch. 3); banking (see Chapter 29); broadcasting (see Section 19.4(b)(v)); brokers and dealers in securities (AICPA Accounting and Audit Guide, "Brokers and Dealers in Securities," ch. 7); cable television (see Section 19.4(b)(ii)); casinos (AICPA Accounting and Audit Guide, "Audits of Casinos," ch. 2); computer software (see Section 19.4(b)(vi)); contractors (AICPA Accounting and Audit Guides, Construction Contractors," ch. 2, and "Audits of Federal Government Contractors," ch. 3); franchising (see Section 19.4(b)(iii)); freight service (see EITF Issue No. 91–9, "Revenue and Expense Recognition for Freight Services in Process"); Internet (see Section 19.4(b)(vii)); leasing (see Chapter 21); motion picture films (see Section 19.4(b)(v)); not-for-profit organizations (see Chapter 33); record and music (see Section 19.4(b)(iv)); and regulated entities (SFAS No. 71, "Accounting for the Effects of Certain Types of Regulation"). SAB No. 101, "Revenue Recognition," and the related FAQ document address several issues related to revenue from services, including:

- *Receipt of nonrefundable up-front fees*—to be recognized as revenue over the expected period of performance (SAB No. 101, Topic 13-A, Question 5; FAQ, Topic 13-A, Question 13).

- *Receipt of refundable fees for services* — to be recognized ratably if the refund privileges expire ratably over the term of the contract; to be recognized either at expiration or ratably if they expire at the end of the term (SAB No. 101, Topic 13-A, Question 7; FAQ Topic 13-A, Questions 18–20). Revenue should be recognized ratably in the latter situation only if all of the following four criteria are met: (1) "the estimates of termination or cancellations and refunded revenues are being made for a large pool of homogenous items"; (2) "reliable estimates of the expected refunds can be made on a timely basis"; (3) "there is a sufficient company-specific historical basis upon which to estimate the refunds, and the company believes that such historical experience is predictive of future events"; and (4) "the amount of the membership fee specified in the agreement at the outset of the arrangement is fixed, other than the customer's right to request a refund" (SAB No. 101, Topic 13-A, Question 7).

- *Initial setup fees* — if all other recognition criteria are met, revenue is to be recognized, generally on a straight-line basis, over the longer of (1) the term of the arrangement or (2) the expected period during which the specific services will be performed (SAB No. 101, Topic 13-A, Question 6; FAQ, Topic 13-A, Question 10). Different accounting, however, is required in different situations, such as activation fees for basic telephone service and installation fees for additional phone jacks, in which additional services are to be provided, depending on whether they can be separated for recognition purposes from the initial services (see FAQ, Topic 13-A, Questions 11–12).

- *Licensing and similar arrangement* — revenue should not be recognized prior to the beginning of the license term (SAB No. 101, Topic 13-A, Question 3; FAQ, Topic 13-A, Question 9).

The SEC staff also notes that long-term contracts to provide services often are similar to other revenue arrangements. Assuming the general criteria for revenue recognition are satisfied, the timing of recognition should mirror the timing in which customers' obligations are satisfied.[27]

Some service providers incur incidental costs in connection with their ongoing operations that are reimbursed by their customers, either as part of the fee charged for the service or based on the actual amount of costs incurred by the service provider. Those "out-of-pocket" costs include airfare, automobile mileage, food and lodging expenditures, photocopies, and other items. The EITF consensus on Issue No. 01–14, "Income Statement Characterization of Reimbursements Received for 'Out-of-Pocket' Expenses Incurred," concludes that reimbursements received for such costs should be reported as revenue, rather than as reduction of expenses, unless specific guidance for the reimbursement transaction has been provided by higher-level GAAP, such as the guidance for insurance and reinsurance premiums, lending transactions, sales of financial assets, and broker-dealer transactions and certain other specialized industry transactions.

As of this writing, the EITF has several other projects that address various aspects of service revenue. For example:

- Issue No. 00–21, "Accounting for Revenue Arrangements with Multiple Deliverables"—This issue considers problems related to various types of sales transactions in which entities provide different goods and services to customers, where delivery of the goods and performance of the services may occur at various times, and the fees may be fixed, variable based on future performance, or a combination of both (see Section 19.4(a)(ix)).

- Issue No. 02–G, "Recognition of Revenue from Licensing Arrangements on Intellectual Property"—This project, inactive as of this writing, considers whether the accounting for these arrangements should be similar to leases of physical assets, where initial fees are recognized over the lease term (in conformity with SFAS No. 13, "Accounting for Leases," par. 19) or to software licensing or motion picture rights, where initial fees are recognized when the license has been conveyed and the seller has no further obligation (in conformity

---

[27] SEC Division of Corporate Finance, "Current Accounting and Disclosure Issues in the Division of Corporate Finance," (December 1, 2005), Section II.F.2.

with SOP 97–2, "Software Revenue Recognition," and EITF Issue No. 00–2, "Accounting by Producers or Distributors of Films").

(vi) Sales of Future Revenues.   Sales of future revenues occur when an enterprise receives cash from an investor, often a financial institution, and agrees to pay the investor a specified percentage or amount of revenue or income that the enterprise will receive from a particular product line, business segment, trademark, patent, or contractual right. The payment to the investor and the related future revenue or income may be denominated either in dollars or in a foreign currency.

Those types of transactions raise three fundamental issues, which are addressed in EITF Issue No. 88-18, "Sales of Future Revenues." These major issues are:

1. Whether the enterprise should classify the proceeds from the investor as debt or as deferred income
2. How that debt or deferred income should be amortized
3. How the foreign currency effects, if any, should be recognized

On the first issue, the Task Force agreed that classification as debt or deferred income depends on the specific facts and circumstances of the transaction. The Task Force also reached a consensus that the existence of any one of the following six factors independently makes the classification of the proceeds as debt appropriate:

1. The transaction does not purport to be a sale (i.e., the form of the transaction is debt).
2. The enterprise has significant continuing involvement in the generation of the cash flows due the investor (e.g., active involvement in the generation of the operating revenues of a product line, subsidiary, or business segment).
3. The transaction is cancellable by either the enterprise or the investor through payment of a lump sum or other transfer of assets by the enterprise.
4. The investor's rate of return is implicitly or explicitly limited by the terms of the transaction.
5. Variations in the enterprise's revenue or income underlying the transaction have only a trifling impact on the investor's rate of return.
6. The investor has any recourse to the enterprise relating to the payments due the investor.

The second factor appears to indicate that the Task Force meant to restrict deferred income accounting only to sales where the seller has no significant control over the timing and amount of cash flows. The Task Force, however, did not clarify the circumstances in which immediate income recognition might be appropriate.

Concerning the second issue, the Task Force agreed that amounts recorded as debt should be amortized under the interest method and that amounts recorded as deferred income should be amortized under the units-of-revenue method. The latter method requires calculating a ratio of the proceeds received from the investor to the total payments expected to be made to the investor over the term of the agreement, and then applying that ratio to the period's cash payment.

On the third issue, the Task Force agreed that classification of the proceeds as deferred income results in a nonmonetary liability not subject to foreign exchange gains and losses under SFAS No. 52. The Task Force also agreed that the debt would be considered a foreign currency transaction for which translation gains or losses would be recognized in accordance with SFAS No. 52, unless all of the following criteria are met:

- The debt is contractually required to be repaid only to the extent of related future revenues, if any.
- There is no recourse to the enterprise relating to the payment due the investor.
- The transaction is not cancellable by either the enterprise or the investor.

If the debt is considered a foreign currency transaction, cash flow hedge accounting specified in pars. 40–41 of SFAS No. 133, "Accounting for Derivative Instruments and Hedging Activities," as amended by par. 4 m of SFAS No. 138, "Accounting for Certain Derivative Instruments and Certain Hedging Activities," may apply.

(vii) Barter Transactions Involving Barter Credits.   In a barter transaction involving barter credits, an enterprise enters into a transaction to exchange a nonmonetary asset (e.g., inventory) for barter credits. Those transactions may occur directly between principals to the transaction or include a third party whose business is to facilitate these types of exchanges (e.g., a barter company).

The barter credits can be used to purchase goods or services, such as advertising time, from either the barter company or members of its barter exchange network. The goods and services to be purchased may be specified in a barter contract or limited to items made available by members of the exchange network. Some arrangements may require the payment of cash in addition to the barter credits to purchase goods or services. Barter credits also may have a contractual expiration date, at which time they become worthless. The issue is whether APB Opinion No. 29, "Accounting for Nonmonetary Transactions," applies to an exchange of a nonmonetary asset for barter credits and, if so, the amount of profit or loss, if any, that should be recognized.

The EITF reached a consensus in Issue No. 93-11, "Accounting for Barter Transactions Involving Barter Credits," that transactions in which nonmonetary assets are exchanged for barter credits should be accounted for under APB Opinion No. 29. An impairment of the nonmonetary asset exchanged should be recognized before recording the exchange if the fair value of that asset is less than its carrying amount. Recognition of an impairment loss also would be required in an exchange of assets or contractual rights not reported in the balance sheet (e.g., operating leases) if the transferor is not relieved of primary liability for the related obligation. (As discussed in Chapter 16, SFAS No. 144, "Accounting for the Impairment or Disposal of Long-Lived Assets," requires that certain long-lived assets be reviewed for impairment whenever events or changes in circumstances indicate that the carrying amount of an asset may not be recoverable. SFAS No. 144 establishes accounting standards for the recognition and measurement of impairment losses and sets forth an approach to determining an asset's fair value. Also, par. 34 of SFAS No. 144 requires that certain long-lived assets held for sale be reported at the lower of their carrying amounts or fair values less costs to sell.)

If an exchange involves the transfer of an operating lease, the EITF consensus also concludes that the impairment of that lease should be measured as the remaining lease costs (rental payments and unamortized leasehold improvements) in excess of the estimated fair value of probable sublease rentals for the remaining lease term.

The Task Force also reached a consensus that in reporting the exchange of a nonmonetary asset for barter credits, it should be presumed that the fair value of the nonmonetary asset exchanged is more clearly evident than the fair value of the barter credits received, so that the barter credits should be reported at the fair value of the nonmonetary asset exchanged. The Task Force noted, however, that the presumption might be overcome if an entity can convert the barter credits into cash, as evidenced by a historical practice of converting barter credits into cash, or if independent quoted market prices exist for items to be received upon exchange of the barter credits. It should also be presumed that the fair value of the nonmonetary asset does not exceed its carrying amount unless there is persuasive evidence supporting a higher value. An impairment loss on the barter credits should be recognized if it subsequently becomes apparent that (1) the fair value of any remaining barter credits is less than the carrying amount or (2) it is probable that the enterprise will not use all of the remaining barter credits.

(viii) Revenue Recognition for Separately Priced Extended Warranty and Product Maintenance Contracts.   In Issue No. 89-17, "Accounting for the Retail Sale of an Extended Warranty Contract in Connection with the Sale of a Product," the EITF addressed the question of how revenue and expense from a separately priced extended warranty or product maintenance contract should be recognized. The EITF concludes that full recognition of the revenue and the accrual of the related estimated future costs at the time of sale is inappropriate, but it did not reach a consensus on whether to account for the contracts under the full deferral or partial recognition methods, both of which were used in practice. The position of the EITF was modified and superseded by FASB Technical Bulletin No. 90-1, "Accounting for Separately Extended Warranty and Product Maintenance Contracts," which defines extended warranty and product maintenance contracts as follows:

> An extended warranty is an agreement to provide warranty protection in addition to the scope of coverage of the manufacturer's original warranty, if any, or to extend the period of coverage provided by the manufacturer's original warranty. A product maintenance contract is an agreement to perform certain agreed-upon services to maintain a product for a specified period of time.... A contract is separately priced if the customer has the option to purchase the services provided under the contract for an expressly stated amount separate from the price of the product (par. 2).

FASB Technical Bulletin No. 90-1, paragraph 3, states that revenue from separately priced extended warranty and product maintenance contracts should be deferred and recognized in income on a straight-line basis over the contract period, except in those circumstances in which sufficient historical evidence indicates that the costs of performing services under the contract are incurred on other than a straight-line basis. In those circumstances, revenue should be recognized over the contract period in proportion to the costs expected to be incurred in performing services under the contract. Costs of providing those services should be expensed as incurred.

The conclusion in Technical Bulletin No. 90-1 appears to be consistent with paragraph 13 of SFAS No. 60, "Accounting and Reporting by Insurance Enterprises," and paragraph 83 of SFAC No. 5, "Recognition and Measurement in Financial Statements of Business Enterprises." Paragraph 13 of SFAS No. 60 indicates that premiums from short-duration insurance contracts should be recognized as revenue over the period of the contract in proportion to the amount of insurance protection provided. Paragraph 83 of SFAC No. 5 states that revenue is not recognized until earned. Revenue is earned when the entity has substantially completed what it must do to be entitled to the revenue. Technical Bulletin No. 90-1 is formulated on the premise that sellers of extended warranty or product maintenance contracts have an obligation to the buyer to perform services throughout the period of the contract and, therefore, revenue should be recognized over the period in which the seller is obligated to perform.

Recognition and measurement issues related to warranties and guarantees that are not separately priced are discussed in Section 19.5(f).

(ix) Sales with Multiple Deliverables.   Sales transactions may include arrangements in which entities deliver to customers multiple products at different points in time, provide multiple services over different periods of time, or do a combination of both. Those arrangements may involve up-front fees as well as continuing payments over a period of time. For example, a cellular phone company may sign a contract with a customer to provide phone service and a "free" phone in exchange for an up-front activation fee and a monthly service fee. As another example, an entity may provide unlimited Internet access to customers for a monthly fee and, for an up-front fee, sell specific equipment necessary to access the Internet.

SFAC No. 5, "Recognition and Measurement in Financial Statements of Business Enterprises," and SAB No. 101, "Revenue Recognition in Financial Statements," include general criteria for determining when revenue for components of these arrangements should be recognized. The EITF consensus on Issue No. 00-21, "Revenue Arrangements with Multiple Deliverables," contains specific guidance concerning when vendors should identify separate units of an arrangement for revenue recognition purposes, when smaller units should be combined or excluded, how total revenue should be allocated to each unit based on its relative fair value, and how revenue recognition is affected by cancellation privileges and future vendor and customer actions. The guidance applies to all arrangements with multiple deliverables except in the following situations:

- The arrangements are the subject of higher-level guidance contained in various pronounce-ments, such as SFAS No. 13, "Accounting for Leases"; No. 45, "Accounting for Franchise Fee Revenue"; No. 66, "Accounting for Sales of Real Estate"; FASB Interpretation No. 45, "Guarantor's Accounting and Disclosure Requirements for Guarantees, Including Indirect Guarantees of Indebtedness of Others"; FASB Technical Bulletin No. 90-1, "Accounting for Separately Priced Extended Warranty and Product Maintenance Contracts"; and AICPA Statements of Position 81-1, "Accounting for Performance of Construction-Type and Certain Production-Type Contracts"; 97-2, "Software Revenue Recognition"; and 00-2, "Accounting by Producers or Distributors of Films."
- The arrangements involve vendors offering customers future consideration for achieving certain levels of sales or remaining as customers for certain time periods. Those types of arrangements are discussed in EITF Issue No. 01-9, "Accounting for Consideration Given by a Vendor to a Customer (Including a Reseller of the Vendor's Products)" (see Section 19.5(d)), and No. 02-16, "Accounting by a Customer (Including a Reseller) for Certain Consideration Received from a Vendor" (see Section 19.5(e)).

The consensus on EITF Issue No. 00-21 requires that combinations of goods, services, and rights to use assets sold to customers under single contractual arrangements should be divided by vendors into separate units of accounting at an arrangement's inception and as each item is delivered when all of the following exist:

- Delivered items can be either (a) sold separately by a vendor or (c) resold by customers on a standalone basis
- Evidence of the undelivered items' fair values is objective and reliable
- If customers have general refund rights under the arrangements, future deliveries of the items are probable and controlled by the vendors

If these three criteria are met, vendors should allocate total consideration to each of the separate accounting units based on each unit's relative fair value. When reliable and objective information about each unit's fair value is available, the allocation of total consideration should be based on those fair values. If reliable and objective information about fair value is only available for undelivered items, revenue should be allocated using the "residual method"—revenue for delivered items should be determined by subtracting the fair value of the undelivered items from the total consideration. The consensus on EITF Issue No. 00-21 notes that "[t]he best evidence of fair value is the price of a deliverable when it is regularly sold on a standalone basis" (par. 16). Such evidence often is "vendor-specific objective evidence" (VSOE), and the guidance in par. 10 of SOP 97-2, "Software Revenue Recognition," should be followed. The consensus also requires vendors to use appropriate revenue recognition criteria for each unit of accounting, but it does not include specific guidance on those criteria or on how to allocate direct costs to the units.

In December 2002, the SEC issued SAB No. 104, "Revenue Recognition," which provides additional guidance on applying the consensus on EITF No. 00-21. That guidance is described in Section 19.3(h)(v).

(x) Inventory Purchases and Sales with Same Counterparty.   Some enterprises sell inventory to customers from whom they also purchase inventory. Accounting for these types of transactions–commonly called *buy-sell arrangements* in the oil and gas industry[28]—are addressed in EITF Issue No. 04-13, "Accounting for Purchases and Sales of Inventory with the Same Counterparty." The consensus concludes that all purchases and sales of inventory with the same counterparty (except

---

[28] The SEC staff discusses accounting for "buy-sell arrangements" in letters (see *www.sec.gov/divisions/corpfin/guidance/oilgas021105.htm*) sent to various registrants in February 2005 describing recognition, measurement and disclosure requirements for these transactions. See SEC Division of Corporation Finance, "Current Accounting and Disclosure Issues" (December 1, 2005), Section II.F.1.

for transactions in the software and real estate industries which are discussed in other authoritative literature) should be combined and considered as a single arrangement if their substance suggests they were undertaken "in contemplation" of one another. Factors indicating the purchase and sale transactions were undertaken in contemplation of one another include:

- The purchase and sale transactions occur simultaneously
- The transactions do not include terms typical of market transactions
- The parties to the transactions have a legal right to offset the receivables and payables
- The reciprocal transaction is relatively certain to occur

If the substance of the transactions indicates that a single arrangement exists, the following accounting is appropriate:

- Exchanges of finished goods for raw materials or work in progress should be measured at fair value.
- Exchanges of finished goods for finished goods should be measured based on book values of those items, following the principles discussed in APB Opinion No. 29, "Accounting for Nonmonetary Transactions."

(b) SPECIALIZED INDUSTRY PROBLEMS.   Many problems concerning when to recognize revenue are specific to entire industries. For example, all franchisors face the problem of when to recognize as revenue the initial fees from the sale of franchises. As with many nonindustry-specific revenue recognition problems, the source of the difficulty is the relatively long period, often several accounting periods, over which the earning of revenue (in its broadest sense, extending through completed performance and collection) takes place. In many instances, authoritative or quasi-authoritative pronouncements have specified the appropriate timing of revenue in various circumstances. In others, the accountant must rely on judgment, but the general revenue recognition criteria suggested earlier in this chapter may be helpful.

(i) Specialized Industries Discussed in Other Chapters.   To avoid duplication the industries that are discussed elsewhere in this *Handbook* are listed below with the relevant chapter numbers:

> *Construction industry.* Revenue may be recognized when long-term construction contracts are completed (completed contract method) or as construction progresses (percentage-of-completion method), depending on the circumstances surrounding each contract. Those methods and their applicability in varying circumstances are discussed in Chapter 30.
>
> *Not-for-profit organizations.* Recognition and measurement of contributions received are addressed by SFAS No. 116, "Accounting for Contributions Received and Contributions Made," and discussed in Chapter 35 of this book.
>
> *Real estate industry.* Revenue recognition from the sale of real estate and from retail land sales depends largely on the buyer's assuming the normal risks and rewards of ownership, often evidenced by the size of the down payment, and on the seller's performance under the terms of the sales agreement. Those conditions and other related criteria for recognizing revenue are discussed in SFAS No. 66, "Accounting for Sales of Real Estate," and Chapter 30 of this book.
>
> *Banking.* Various recognition and measurement issues related to loans, leases, and other revenue generating activities of banks and other financial institutions are discussed in Chapter 31 of this book.

(ii) Cable Television Companies.   SFAS No. 51, "Financial Reporting by Cable Television Companies," discusses revenue recognition and related accounting problems. SFAS No. 51 suggests that costs incurred during construction before the first subscriber hookup and a portion of certain costs after the first subscriber hookup, but before construction of the entire system is complete, usually may be capitalized. During that period, all revenues except those from hookups should be reported as system revenues, and the portion of costs, depreciation, and amortization charged to expense, as well as specified period costs, should be included in appropriate categories of costs of services. According to SFAS No. 51 (par. 11), "[I]nitial hookup revenue shall be recognized as revenue to the extent of direct selling costs incurred. The remainder shall be deferred and amortized to income over the estimated average period that subscribers are expected to remain connected to the system."

(iii) Franchising Companies.   The major franchise accounting problem concerns the recognition of revenue from the initial franchise fee. SFAS No. 45, "Accounting for Franchise Fee Revenue," establishes accounting and reporting standards for franchisors. It requires that initial franchise fees from individual and area franchise sales be recognized as revenue only when a franchisor has satisfied all material conditions or performed substantially all material services relating to the sale. SFAS No. 45 also discusses accounting for continuing franchise fees, continuing product sales, agency sales, repossessed franchises, franchising costs, commingled revenue, and relationships between a franchisor and a franchisee.

(iv) Record and Music Industry.   SFAS No. 50, "Financial Reporting in the Record and Music Industry," requires the licensor of a record master or music copyright to recognize the licensing fee as revenue if collectibility of the full fee is reasonably assured and if the licensor:

- Has signed a noncancelable contract
- Has agreed to a fixed fee
- Has delivered the rights to the licensee, who is free to exercise them
- Has no remaining significant obligations to furnish music or records

(v) Motion Picture Films; Broadcasting Industry.   SOP 00–2, "Accounting by Producers or Distributors of Films," discusses revenue recognition for sales and licensing arrangements of feature films, television specials and series, and similar items. According to paragraph 7, a licensor should recognize revenue from a sale or licensing arrangement of a film when all of the following conditions are met:

a. Persuasive evidence of a sale or licensing agreement with a customer exists.

b. The film is complete and, in accordance with the terms of the arrangement, has been delivered or is available for immediate and unconditional delivery.

c. The license period of the arrangement has begun and the customer can begin its exploitation, exhibit, or sale.

d. The arrangement fee is fixed or determinable.

e. Collection of the arrangement fee is reasonably assured.

SFAS No. 63, "Financial Reporting by Broadcasters" (as amended by par. 5 of SFAS No. 139, "Rescission of FASB Statement No. 53 and amendments to FASB Statements No. 63, 89, and 121,"), concludes that broadcasters' accounting for television film license agreements should parallel accounting by the licensor as prescribed in SOP 00–2, and, accordingly, assets and liabilities should be recorded for the rights acquired and the obligations incurred under such agreements.

SFAS No. 63 also established standards of reporting by broadcasters for transactions in which unsold advertising time is bartered for products or services. According to paragraph 8 (footnote omitted):

All barter transactions except those involving the exchange of advertising time for network programming shall be reported at the estimated fair value of the product or service received, in accordance with the provisions of paragraph 25 of APB Opinion No. 29, "Accounting for Non-monetary Transactions." Barter revenue shall be reported when commercials are broadcast, and merchandise or services shall be reported when received or used.

(vi) Software Revenue Recognition.   SOP 97-2, "Software Revenue Recognition," provides guidance for recognizing and measuring revenues associated with licensing, selling, leasing, or otherwise marketing various computer software products, updates, enhancements, and related services, including postcontract customer support (PCS), installation, training, and consulting. SFAS No. 86, "Accounting for the Costs of Computer Software to Be Sold, Leased, or Otherwise Marketed," provides guidance for recognizing and measuring associated expenses. Costs related to computer software for an entity's own use should be accounted for in conformity with SOP 98-1, "Accounting for the Costs of Computer Software Developed or Obtained for Internal Use."

If an arrangement to deliver software requires significant production, modification, or customization of software, it should be accounted for as a construction-type or production-type contract in conformity with ARB No. 45, "Long-Term Construction-Type Contracts," and SOP 81-1, "Accounting for Performance of Construction-Type and Certain Production-Type Contracts." Otherwise, revenue should be recognized when all of the following criteria are met:

- Persuasive evidence of an arrangement exists
- Delivery has occurred
- The vendor's fee is fixed or determinable
- Collectibility is probable

O'Reilly, McDonnell, Winograd, Gerson, and Jaenicke note that "[t]he principal change in revenue recognition principles resulting from the issuance of SOP 97-2 is the requirement that revenue be allocated among all products and services specified in a software arrangement, including products that the vendor is obligated to deliver only if and when they are developed." If an arrangement includes multiple deliverables, the allocation should be based on "vendor-specific objective evidence [VSOE] of fair value," such as a price list.[29] The revenue allocated to a specific product or service should be recognized when the above criteria are met with respect to the product or service. The SOP provides guidance for determining VSOE.

Various questions have arisen about how to apply the requirements of SOP 97-2 to various types of transactions. For example, the SEC settled fraud charges against i2 Technologies, claiming that, between 1998 and 2002, the company misstated $1 billion of revenue from software license transactions. i2 accounted for much of that revenue at the time the licenses first became effective, supposedly in conformity with SOP 97-2, even though much of the software had to be modified extensively before it was functional for customers' uses.[28] The AICPA staff responded to the need for additional guidance by issuing questions and answers about the application of that SOP, published as Technical Practice Aids (TPAs) 5100.38-5100.76. In addition, the EITF consensus on Issue No. 03-5, "Applicability of AICPA SOP 97-2 to Non-Software Deliverables," concludes that when software deliverables are essential to the functioning of other deliverables, such as computer hardware or other equipment, all of the deliverables are subject to the requirements in SOP 97-2. The SOP does not apply, however, to other types of non-software deliverables.

Some entities sell software or rights to use software that have elements of film, music, or similar types of materials. Revenue from the sale of those products and services should be recognized under SOP 97–2; accounting for related costs should follow the guidance in FASB Statement No. 86, "Accounting for the Costs of Computer Software to Be Sold, Leased, or otherwise Marketed," Some of those transactions, however, involve computer files—such as mp3 and mpeg files—that

---

[29] V. M. O'Reilly, P. J. McDonnell, B. N. Winograd, J. S. Gerson, and H. R. Jaenicke, *Montgomery's Auditing*, Twelfth Edition (John Wiley & Sons, New York, 1998), p. 40–4.

are essentially films, music, or similar types of material; it is unclear whether sales of these types of software should be accounted for under FASB Statement No. 50, "Financial Reporting in the Record and Music Industry," or under SOP 97–2.

Instead of selling copies of software, some vendors provide customers with access to software over the Internet or by other electronic means; the software actually resides on a server maintained by vendors or third parties. In those situations, vendors provide customers with both the right to use software and storage of the software (a service called *hosting*). EITF Issue No. 00–3, "Application of AICPA Statement of Position 97-2, 'Software Revenue Recognition,' to Arrangements that Include the Right to Use Software Stored on Another Entity's Hardware," concludes that a hosting arrangement represents a separate software element under SOP 97-2 only if customers (1) have a contractual right to take physical possession of the software during the hosting period without significant penalty and (2) feasibly can run the software on their own computers or can contract with third parties to do do. If those criteria are met, the EITF consensus concludes that:

- Delivery of the software is presumed to occur when the customer has the ability to take immediate possession.
- The recognition criteria in SOP 97-2 must be satisfied before the vendor can recognize revenue.
- A portion of the total revenue must be allocated to each separate element of the transaction, including the hosting arrangement.
- The portion of total revenue allocated to the hosting element should be recognized as that service is provided.

The Frequently Asked Questions document that provides guidance on implementing SAB No. 101, "Revenue Recognition," indicates that entities should use a "reasoned method" when accounting for software sales and other arrangement involving multiple deliverables (Topic 13-A.3, Question 4). The SEC staff indicates it will not object to an accounting method if:

- Each deliverable represents a "separate earnings process" (i.e., the vendor does or could sell the deliverable by itself).
- Revenue is allocated to each deliverable based on reliable, verifiable, and objectively determinable fair value.
- No revenue is allocated to a delivered element until all elements necessary to ensure that the delivered element is functioning have been delivered.

The consensus to EITF Issue No. 00-21, "Revenue Arrangements with Multiple Deliverables," provides detailed guidance on accounting for sales of software and related services and similar types of arrangements (see Section 19.4(a)(ix)).

Some software vendors enter into barter transactions in which they accept, in exchange for software and related services, customers' products or services or shares of customers' stock. APB Opinion No. 29, "Accounting for Nonmonetary Transactions," as amended by SFAS No. 153, "Exchanges of Nonmonetary Assets—an amendment of APB Opinion No. 29," generally requires such exchanges of dissimilar items to be measured at the fair value of the consideration exchanged and the resulting gains or losses to be recognized. Revenue would be recognized based on the guidance in SOP 97-2, "Software Revenue Recognition." Accounting for exchanges of software between companies is discussed in AICPA Technical Practice Aid 5100.46-.47, "Nonmonetary Exchanges of Software."

Software manufacturers may offer price protection agreements, under which they refund or credit a portion of the original selling price to customers if the manufacturers subsequently reduce the price offered to other customers. Software manufacturers should set up appropriate allowances for those price concessions when they are authorized.

(vii) Internet Companies. Many accounting issues have emerged as a result of e-commerce activities and other new ways to provide products and services to customers. Those activities have also led to the formation of new types of entities that offer Internet and other services and hardware and other products. Those entities include:

- Service providers—entities that charge fees for providing Internet access
- Portal companies—entities that provide Web site content, accessible with their own or through other entities' search engines, in exchange for fees from arrangements with advertisers that may involve performance guarantees based on benchmarks, such as the number of "hits" on a Web site
- E-commerce companies—entities that sell goods or services exclusively through the Internet or that earn fees for facilitating transactions between other parties
- Internet-related companies—entities that provide hardware and software for Internet and other electronic transactions

Because of the unique nature of these companies and the goods and services they offer, it was difficult to apply existing revenue recognition criteria and measurement principles. As a result, the SEC and the EITF have issued specific revenue recognition and measurement rules covering a variety of e-commerce and related activities. Some of those issues—such as sales arrangements with separate deliverables (Section 19.4(a)(ix)), various types of sales incentives (Section 19.5(d)), and gross versus net reporting (Section 19.1(c)(i))—are discussed elsewhere in this chapter. Some types of revenue-related arrangements are unique to Internet companies; these are discussed below.

Some Internet companies receive fees from customers that include payments for providing access to, posting information on, and maintenance of customers' Web sites. SAB No. 101, "Revenue Recognition," requires those fees to be recognized as revenue over the periods in which the services are performed. The consensus to EITF Issue No. 00-21 provides additional guidance on arrangements that include separate deliverables (see Section 19.4(a)(ix)).

Internet companies also may host customers' auction sites or run their own auction sites. In those situations, the companies ordinarily do not take title to the products sold on the site. Instead, they charge up-front fees for listing products and services for sale as well as fees for facilitating transactions. The guidance provided in Questions 5–7 of SAB No. 101 and Question 10 of the related FAQ document requires the initial fees to be recognized over the performance period—the period during which customers' products and services are listed on the auction site. Nonrefundable transaction fees ordinarily should be recognized as revenue when the underlying sales transactions are completed. If those fees are refundable, or if the company hosting the auction site is substantially involved with the products or services sold on the site after the sale is completed, some or all of the refundable fees should be deferred until the earnings process is complete.

EITF Issue No. 99-17, "Accounting for Advertising Barter Transactions," concerns "banner-for-banner," "click-through for click-through," and similar types of reciprocal or co-marketing arrangements in which two entities exchange advertising on each others' Web sites without, in substance, any cash being exchanged. The consensus requires entities to recognize revenues and related expenses from those transactions at fair value when the fair value of the advertising provided can be determined from an entity's past experience involving similar cash transactions with unrelated parties. Paragraphs 5–8 of EITF No. 99-17 provide detailed guidance on how fair value should be determined. If fair value cannot be determined, barter transactions should be recorded based on the carrying value (which in most cases will be zero) of the advertising provided.

Some advertising arrangements made by Internet companies include guarantees on a minimum number of "hits" or "click-throughs" during a period. If that minimum is not achieved, the arrangements may include automatic extensions of the advertising until that number, or a larger number, of hits is achieved. Depending on the specific arrangements and the likelihood of achieving the minimum number guaranteed, revenue may be recognized when the guaranteed minimum is achieved or ratably over the period of the arrangement.

Internet companies may have periods during which, because of failures in their systems, they are unable to provide Internet and other services to customers. As a result of those "service outages," the companies incur a variety of "costs"—including refunds and credits given to customers, payments of customers' damage claims, and the costs of repairing the problems. Consistent with the consensus reached in EITF Issue No. 01-9, "Accounting for Consideration Given by a Vendor to a Customer or a Reseller of the Vendor's Products," costs incurred to repair a customer's Web site and similar costs should be treated as expenses; refunds, credit vouchers, and similar "costs" should be reported as reductions in revenue.

(c) NEED FOR ADDITIONAL GUIDANCE.   Despite the conceptual guidance and detailed, industry-specific principles described in various sections of this chapter, numerous questions continue to arise concerning when entities should recognize revenue and how it should be measured. Arriving at sound answers to those questions is critical to ensuring that an entity's financial statements present fairly the entity's operating results and financial position. Revenues typically are the largest financial statement item, and many financial statement users analyze revenue numbers and trends in those numbers when making investment, credit, and similar decisions.

Accounting problems involving revenue continue to arise frequently. In its 1999 report, "Fraudulent Financial Reporting: 1987–1997, An Analysis of U.S. Public Companies," the Treadway Commission's Committee of Sponsoring Organizations (COSO) notes that revenue recognition problems existed in about half of the financial reporting misstatement cases described in the SEC's Accounting and Auditing Enforcement Releases (AAER) issued during that period. Similar issues were identified in a study reported by the Panel on Audit Effectiveness's "Report and Recommendations" ("Panel Report"). That study of AAER cases shows that 70 percent of the problems concerned premature or fictitious revenue, including recognizing revenue before recognition criteria were met (e.g., on consignment sales and bill-and-hold transactions); in the wrong period (e.g., on products shipped after year end); or for transactions that never took place (pars. 2.126–2.142 and Appendix F).

The SEC has grown increasingly concerned about revenue recognition issues and management's ability to use aggressive recognition policies to manage earnings (see Chapter 6). In September 1999, the SEC announced charges against 68 organizations and individuals who were accused of financial reporting abuses, many of which involved revenue recognition problems similar to those cited by COSO and the Panel Report. Later that year, the SEC asked the EITF to consider 20 major Internet-related revenue problems, including recognizing revenue for services provided to customers free of charge, reporting gross instead of net revenues and recognizing revenue from barter transactions. Those problems are summarized in EITF Issue No. 99-V, "Remaining Issues from the SEC's October 18, 1999 Letter to the EITF."

As a result of the need for more detailed guidance, the SEC issued SAB No. 101, "Revenue Recognition," in December 1999 (see Section 19.3(h)). The SEC did not intend to create or change revenue recognition principles, but to provide guidelines useful for public companies, especially those involved in buying and selling over the Internet, in deciding how to apply existing GAAP. Applying the four criteria that form the foundation of SAB No. 101, however, has proven to be difficult. Part of the problem is that the criteria are drawn from the SEC's experience with Internet-related transactions, but the SAB applies to all types of revenue transactions. In addition, the guidance in the SAB is discussed in a series of questions and answers illustrating what the SEC staff considered to be sound revenue recognition practices in fact-specific situations. A small change in those facts, however, can have a major effect on how the four criteria would apply. As a result, entities and their auditors found it difficult to apply SAB No. 101 to new and increasingly more complex revenue arrangements.

Several developments improved that situation. For example, in response to numerous requests from public companies and their auditors, the SEC issued an FAQ document in October 2000 providing additional, but still very situation-specific, guidance on applying the SAB No. 101 criteria. In addition, the EITF issued consensuses on several significant revenue-related projects described previously, such as Issues No. 99-19 on gross versus net revenue reporting and No. 01-9 on sales incentives.

Despite that additional guidance, revenue recognition problems have continued to arise. For example, the SEC investigated accounting by Dynergy, Global Crossing, and Qwest Communications for "round-trip" swap transactions involving asset and service transfers whose sole purpose seemed to be inflating the companies' reported revenues. Other entities, including Xerox and ConAgra, have restated prior years' revenues following SEC investigations of their allegedly "aggressive" recognition policies.[30] The SEC also has charged members of senior management at several companies, including Homestore and L90, with inflating on-line advertising revenues through various barter transactions and misleading auditors about the nature of those transactions.[31] The Commission charged Gemstar-TV Guide International with misstating $250 million of revenue from 1999 to 2002 in a variety of ways, including front-end loading revenue from long-term and multiple-element contracts, inflating revenue from barter transactions, and shifting revenue among accounting periods. Gemstar agreed to pay $10 million to settle the SEC's civil case.[32] The SEC subsequently sanctioned the company's auditing firm, KPMG, and four of the firm's auditors for repeated failures in auditing Gemstar's revenue.[33]

More recently, the SEC:

- Charged various executives at Quest Communications International with classifying revenues from non-recurring sources as recurring Internet service revenue.
- Accused three members of senior management at IGO Corp. of recognizing revenue on consignment sales of products delivered to customers after the end of the company's fiscal period or not shipped at all.
- Filed a civil complaint accusing executives of Purchase Pro and America Online, Inc. of fraud resulting from deliberately overstating Purchase Pro's revenues from various contracts and other arrangements between the two companies.[34]

In addition, many companies—including Corinthian Colleges, Career Education Corp., and American Home Mortgage Investment Corp.—have had to restate their financial results as a result of errors in recognizing revenue. Huron Consulting Group found that almost 60 percent of the restatements made by public companies in 2004 resulted from revenue problems.[35]

The continuing problems have highlighted the need for what the Panel Report called *an authoritative statement on the broad principles of revenue recognition* (par. 2.142). The broad conceptual guidance provided by SFAC No. 5 and SAB No. 101 has not resulted in entities reporting consistent and comparable information about revenues. In addition, the more detailed guidance issued by the SEC, the EITF, and the AICPA often (1) is issued without adequate due process, (2) applies to a narrow range of problems, and, (3) at times is inconsistent with other literature.

(d) FINANCIAL ACCOUNTING STANDARDS BOARD PROJECT ON REVENUE RECOGNITION.   In mid-2002, the FASB formally recognized the need to provide additional guidance and to promote international convergence of accounting standards for revenue recognition. It initiated a joint project with the IASB to eliminate inconsistencies in the authoritative literature and provide a conceptual foundation for resolving new and emerging revenue recognition and measurement issues. The project's two components, to be completed simultaneously, are (1) a bottom-up approach to catalog existing guidance and practices and (2) a top-down approach to

---

[30] See S. Pulliam and R. Blumenstein, "SEC Broadens Investigation into Revenue-Boosting Tricks," *Wall Street Journal*, (May 16, 2002), p. A1.

[31] See SEC Accounting and Auditing Enforcement Release No. 1864 (September 18, 2003) and No. 1874 (September 26, 2003).

[32] See SEC Accounting and Auditing Enforcement Release No. 2045 (June 23, 2004).

[33] See SEC Accounting and Auditing Enforcement Release No. 2125 (October 20, 2004).

[34] See SEC Accounting and Auditing Enforcement Release No. 2165 (January 10, 2005).

[35] C. Graciano, "Revenue Recognition: A Perennial Problem," *Financial Executive Magazine* (July 14, 2005).

develop conceptual guidance that will then be tested by using it to form tentative solutions to problems identified in the bottom-up approach.

The objective of the project's first component is to develop a comprehensive, principles-based standard on revenue recognition containing clear, concise implementation guidelines for business entities. The Board's staff compiled an inventory of the authoritative literature and other sources of guidance (such as industry-specific practices) dealing with revenue recognition. The inventory includes over 180 sources of accounting principles,[36] classified under one of four "conventions":

- Mark-to-market—revenue is recognized when the fair values of assets or liabilities change
- Proportionate performance—revenue is recognized when performance occurs or with the passage of time
- Sales and delivery—revenue is recognized when performance is substantially complete
- Collection—revenue is recognized when consideration is collected following an exchange or performance

As noted in Section 19.4(c), much of the existing guidance is narrow, applying only to specific industries or types of transactions, and was issued by many different organizations—including the APB, the FASB, and various groups within the American Institute of CPAs—over a long period of time. As a result, GAAP applicable to many types of revenue and revenue-related transactions is not always clear or consistent. The FASB's goals in this first component of the project are to eliminate the inconsistencies and provide more comprehensive guidance for recognizing revenue.

The second component focuses on the need to modify existing conceptual guidance, currently contained in FASB Concepts Statements No. 5, "Recognition and Measurement in Financial Statements of Business Enterprises," and No. 6, "Elements of Financial Statements," to ensure consistency with the new revenue recognition standard. The Board has noted that the conceptual guidance on revenue recognition contained in FASB Concepts Statement No. 5, which is based on the realization and completion-of-the-earnings-process criteria discussed in Section 19.3(c) above, is inconsistent with the definition of revenue in FASB Concepts Statement No. 6, which is based on changes in assets and liabilities. As discussed in Section 19.3(h), SAB No. 101, "Revenue Recognition," and the related FAQ document were intended to help resolve those problems. SAB No. 101, however, applies only to SEC registrants, and many people are concerned that the SEC staff's conclusions may not provide suitable conceptual guidance for all types of revenue recognition issues.

The FASB's proposed standard may contain recognition and measurement principles based on recognizing changes in assets and liabilities as described in the definition of revenue contained in paragraphs 78–79 of FASB Concepts Statement No. 6. The two general criteria for recognizing revenue contained in FASB Concepts Statement No. 5 (i.e., that revenue must be both realized or realizable and earned) may no longer be used. As of this writing, the proposal calls for revenue to be measured by allocating the total amount of consideration paid by outside parties among the various performance obligations of the entity specified in the revenue arrangements.[37]

As of this writing, the FASB expects to issues a Preliminary Views document in the third quarter of 2006 that describes a new revenue recognition standard and amendments to its Concepts Statements. Among the issues to be included are:

- The criteria to be used to divide multiple-element revenue arrangements into separate units and how to measure revenue for those units based on allocating the total amount of customer consideration
- Accounting for wholly executory contracts
- Guidance for disclosing information about revenue
- Differentiating between revenue and gain transactions

---

[36] As of this writing, the FASB's inventory has not been made available to the public.
[37] FASB Project Update, "Revenue Recognition" (12/2/05), available at *www.fasb.org*.

19.5 REVENUE ADJUSTMENTS AND AFTERCOSTS

(a) NATURE OF REVENUE ADJUSTMENTS AND AFTERCOSTS. Revenue adjustments include *sales returns* and *allowances, discounts*, and *bad debts; warranties* and *guarantees* may be treated either as future revenue or as "aftercosts," depending on the circumstances; costs related to product defects should be treated as expenses.

Practice does not always clearly distinguish between events and transactions that give rise to expenses and those that are more properly treated as adjustments or valuations of revenue. Alternative definitions of revenue were presented at the beginning of this chapter; expenses are defined in paragraph 80 of SFAC No. 6 as outflows or expirations of assets sold or liabilities incurred in the process of earning revenue (as "earning" was previously defined). Hendriksen and van Breda state that:

> [S]ales returns and allowances, sales discounts, and bad debt losses are all more appropriately treated as reductions of gross revenues than as expenses. None of them represents the use of goods or services to generate revenues; each represents a reduction of the amount to be received in exchange for the product.[38]

(b) SALES RETURNS. Merchandise returned by a customer is, in effect, a cancellation of the original sales transaction, in whole or in part, and should be treated as a direct offset to gross sales rather than as a revenue adjustment. To maintain a record of sales returns as well as of the amount of gross sales, however, returns are ordinarily recorded in a contra sales account, "sales returns." A special problem arises if the returned merchandise has been used or has deteriorated to a point substantially below its original value. In those cases, the returned goods should be recorded at their net realizable value based on their present condition and estimated costs of making them ready for resale. Losses attributable to returned goods should be recognized as appropriate.

(c) SALES ALLOWANCES. Allowances to customers fall into two general classes, as follows:

1. Specific allowances on certain products, such as those for shortages in shipments, breakage, spoilage, inferior quality, failure to meet specifications, or errors in billing or handling of freight
2. Policy allowances, or allowances that the seller makes only because of the possible loss of future business it might suffer in related lines if it did not offer such allowances

Allowances falling in the first class should be treated as a direct offset to gross sales. Allowances in the second class are generally classified as revenue deductions.

(d) SALES INCENTIVES. Some vendors provide cash, credits, and other consideration to their customers in the form of discounts, coupons, rebates, and free products or services. For example, deductions from gross invoice prices, order quotations, published price lists, and other forms of discounts may be offered as:

- *Cash Discounts.* Credit terms often allow customers a cash discount for payment of invoices within a certain period. In the past, cash discounts were sometimes viewed as interest allowances to customers for prompt payment. Sales discounts taken were thus treated as financial expenses; discounts not taken were implicitly included in gross revenue. This accounting can still be found in the literature. The preferred method, however, is to regard cash discounts as revenue adjustments, either by deducting discounts taken from gross sales revenue on the income statement or by initially recording the sales at net prices and treating forfeited discounts as financing revenue. As a practical matter, the amounts involved are usually not material to the financial statements.

---

[38] Hendriksen and van Breda, p. 370.

- *Trade Discounts*. Trade discounts are deductions from list prices, allowed to customers for quantities purchased or for the purpose of establishing different price levels for different classes of customers, such as wholesalers and retailers. Trade discounts also are employed to enable vendors to change the effective prices of articles included in catalogs or similar sales publications by the relatively simple process of issuing a revised discount sheet. Revenues should be recorded after deduction of such discounts.
- *Employee Discounts*. Employees are often allowed special discounts on purchases made through the company. The discount may be limited to the company's ordinary products or merchandise, or it may extend to clothing, food, and other commodities carried in a general company store for the benefit of employees and sold to them at cost. If the sales are not recorded net of discounts initially, the total discounts should generally be treated as a revenue deduction. If a discount is in substance additional compensation, it should be treated as an operating expense.

A variety of more complex sales incentive arrangements also are used by companies in the Internet, hospitality, airline, and other industries—for example:

- Free products or services delivered when customers purchase another specified product or service (e.g., 2-for-1 offers)
- Shares of vendors' stock, stock options, or stock warrants to purchase vendors' stock
- "Points" or other credits that can be redeemed for various goods and services after customers have accumulated a specified amount ("loyalty" programs)
- Fees paid to customers to obtain space in customers' selling areas ("slotting fees")
- Reimbursements for a portion of customers' advertising costs relating to vendors' products or services ("cooperative advertising")
- Reimbursements up to specified amounts if the customers do not resell the vendors' products at greater than a specified minimum price during a specified time period (e.g., buydowns, shortfalls, factory incentives, dealer holdbacks, price protection, and factory-to-dealer incentives)

The accounting issues raised by sales incentives such as these concern how vendors should measure the costs of these arrangements and how those costs should be reported on vendors' income statements. The EITF codified its consensus on these questions in Issue No. 01-9, "Accounting for Consideration Given by a Vendor to a Customer or a Reseller of the Vendor's Product."[39] As discussed below, the appropriate accounting depends on the type of consideration offered.

(i) Cash or Equity Consideration. When cash or equity consideration is offered voluntarily and without charge by a vendor to be used in a single exchange transaction or that becomes exercisable by the customer as a result of a single exchange transaction, the cost of the incentive should be measured at the later of two dates: when the related revenue is recognized by the vendor or when the incentive is offered. The costs of these incentives generally should be reported as reductions in revenue. The costs should be reported as expenses, however, when and to the extent that vendors (1) receive, or will receive, identifiable and separable goods or services in exchange and (2) can reasonably estimate the fair value of those goods or services. Exhibits 01-9A and 01-9C of EITF Issue No. 01-9 provide examples of how this guidance applies to various types of sales incentives involving cash and equity consideration.

---

[39] That guidance summarizes and reconciles the consensuses in EITF Issue No. 00-14, "Accounting for Certain Sales Incentives," and No. 00-25, "Vendor Income Statement Characterization of Consideration Paid to a Reseller of the Vendor's Products."

(ii) Other Forms of Consideration.   Sales incentives offered to customers may involve consideration other than cash or equity instruments, such as gift certificates and offers of "free" products or services. The consensus to EITF Issue No. 01-9 considers those types of incentives to be separate deliverables and requires their cost to be reported as expenses. Although the consensus does not specify the appropriate expense classification, the SEC staff believes they should be included in cost of sales if they are delivered at the time of the sale of other goods or services. Accounting for sales incentives, such as certain loyalty programs, that offer customers free or discounted goods or services only after reaching a certain level or after being a customer for a certain period of time may be included in the FASB revenue recognition project (see Section 19.4(d)).

(iii) Customers' Accounting for Sales Incentives.   The EITF reached a consensus on Issue No. 02-16, "Accounting by a Customer (Including a Reseller) for Certain Consideration Received from a Vendor," in November 2002. That guidance applies to consideration (called *cash consideration* by the EITF) in the form of cash (such as slotting fees and cooperative advertising payments), credits against amounts due, and equity instruments of the vendor, as well as amounts payable only if customers reach a target, such as achieving a cumulative level of purchases or remaining as a vendor's customer for a specified time period. The EITF concludes that:

- There is a rebuttable presumption that cash consideration received by customers is a reduction in the price of a vendor's goods or services. Customers should not report such consideration as revenue but as reductions in their cost of sales.
- The presumption can be overcome if either of two conditions exist:
  ○ Customers provide or will provide to vendors, in exchange for cash consideration, identifiable benefits that are "sufficiently separable" from the customers' purchases. (Sufficiently separable means that customers (a) would have entered into exchange transactions with other parties to provide the benefits and (b) can reasonably estimate the fair value of the benefits provided to the vendors.) If this condition is met, customers should report the fair value of cash consideration received from vendors as revenue; consideration received in excess of the fair value of the benefits provided to vendors should be reported as a reduction in the cost of sales.
  ○ Customers receive cash consideration that reimburses them for specific incremental identifiable costs they incurred in reselling the vendor's goods or services. If this condition is met, customers should report the fair value of cash consideration as reductions in those costs; any amounts received by customers in excess of the costs being reimbursed should be reported as reductions in the cost of sales.
- Customers should not report rebates or refunds as revenue if they can reasonably estimate the probable amounts to be received under binding arrangements that specify the amount of cash consideration payable when the customer either (a) completes a specified cumulative level of purchases or (b) remains a customer for a specified period. In those situations, customers should report the cash consideration as a reduction in the cost of sales. Using a systematic, rational method, customers should allocate the total cash consideration to the transactions that demonstrate the progress the customer is making toward achieving the target level of purchases or time period. If customers cannot reasonably estimate the probable amount of future cash rebates or refunds, they should recognize the consideration as the targets are achieved. Various factors affect a customer's ability to make those estimates, such as the length of the period during which a rebate or refund offer is open and the extent of the customer's experience with similar offers. The EITF did not, however, provide guidance on when up-front nonrefundable cash consideration received by customers should be treated as liabilities or revenue.

The EITF provided additional guidance to resellers about how they should report vendor reimbursements for certain sales incentives, such as coupons and rebates, offered by manufacturers directly to consumers. The consensus to EITF Issue No. 03-10, "Application of Issue No. 02-16 by Resellers to Sales Incentives Offered to Consumers by Manufacturers," concludes that resellers should account for those reimbursements as reductions in cost of goods sold if the incentives:

- Are available to consumers to reduce the price paid to any resellers of the manufacturers' products
- Are paid directly to resellers from vendors (or vendor-authorized third parties) based on the face value of the incentives
- Are determined solely by the terms offered to consumers by manufacturers (i.e., have no terms affected by other incentive arrangements between the manufacturers and resellers) and
- Arise from express or applied agency relationships between manufacturers and vendors in connection with the sales incentive offered by the manufacturers to consumers

If a sales incentive does not meet all four of these criteria, resellers should apply the guidance in EITF Issue No. 01-9 and No. 02-16.

(e) UNCOLLECTIBLE RECEIVABLES.   According to SFAS No. 114, "Accounting by Creditors for Impairment of a Loan" (par. 8), "a loan is impaired when, based on current information and events, it is probable that a creditor will be unable to collect all amounts due according to the contractual terms of the loan agreement." (As defined in SFAS No. 114, loans include accounts receivable with terms exceeding one year and notes receivable.) SFAS No. 114 applies to all creditors; its applicability to financial institutions is discussed in Chapter 31 of this book. SFAS No. 114 does not apply to large groups of smaller-balance homogeneous loans that are collectively evaluated for impairment. Impaired loans in that category are referred to as *uncollectible receivables* in this book and are discussed in this section.

Uncollectible receivables are accounts and note receivables that probably will not be collected in the future. Providing an allowance for uncollectible receivables is required under SFAS No. 5, "Accounting for Contingencies," when a loss is probable and can be reasonably estimated. Under the *allowance method*, an allowance account is used to report the estimated uncollectible amount of receivables. The allowance account is reflected as a contra to the controlling (i.e., gross) receivables account, and the individual subsidiary accounts are left intact. When it is decided that a specific amount is uncollectible, it is charged against the allowance account. Bad debt expense is recorded when the allowance account is increased. Although not acceptable for financial statements prepared in conformity with GAAP, the *direct write-off method* is acceptable for income tax purposes. Under this method, no allowance is required; instead, uncollectible accounts are written off during the period in which they are determined to be uncollectible. The loss is charged directly to bad debt expense.

Bad debts can be classified on the income statement as (1) a financial expense or loss, (2) an operating expense (either selling or administrative), or (3) a sales adjustment. The first view assumes that all customers' claims are initially valid in the amount of their face value and that subsequent lack of collection is a financing cost that must be borne by the business as a whole. Under the second interpretation, bad debts are considered one of the costs of operating the business. The third alternative recognizes at the outset that a certain percentage of customers' claims will become uncollectible, that total credit sales are therefore tentative and subject to subsequent adjustment, and that, consequently, no expense or loss should be recognized because no asset has expired or liability been incurred.

When the allowance account is used, there are three methods for estimating its appropriate balance: (1) percentage-of-sales method, (2) percentage-of-receivables method, and (3) aging method.

(i) Percentage-of-Sales Method.   The percentage-of-sales method requires charging bad debt expense and crediting the allowance account for an amount determined by applying an estimate of uncollectibles to sales revenue for the period. It can be used with both accounts and notes receivable, either together or separately. As a practical matter, however, this method can be used advantageously with notes *only* when the notes are numerous and arise as a regular credit term granted at the time of the sale. Although the uncollectible expense percentage usually should be based on recent experience and applied to credit sales, substantially the same result often can be attained by using a smaller percentage applied to total sales (assuming the relationship of cash sales to credit sales remains fairly constant). The balance in the allowance account may become excessive or inadequate unless there are periodic reviews of probable losses and consequent adjustments of the allowance account as necessary.

(ii) Percentage-of-Receivables Method.   The percentage-of-receivables method requires a determination of collection experience. The total of estimated uncollectibles is thus ascertained by applying the loss percentage to total receivables. The allowance account is then adjusted by the amount necessary to bring the existing balance to the required amount. The percentage-of-receivables method also can be used with both accounts and notes receivable. When the notes held are relatively few in number and originate in the process of collection of accounts receivable or through loans and advances, the percentage-of-receivables method is an appropriate means of valuing notes receivable.

This method often results in a fairly accurate approximation of expected net realizable value of receivables. In terms of bad debt expense on the income statement, however, the method may be deficient in that bad debts are related to all open receivables irrespective of the period in which the claims originated, with the result that uncollectible receivable losses may not be recognized in the period in which the revenue is recorded.

(iii) Aging-of-Receivables Method.   The aging-of-receivables method is a variation of the percentage-of-receivables method. The basis for using this method is that the older the receivable, the less likely it is to be collected. The first step in aging receivables is classifying them as to time since (1) billing, (2) end of regular credit period granted, (3) payment due date, or (4) date of last payment. The amount of expected uncollectibles as determined by the aging process becomes the balance to be reflected in the allowance account. The allowance account is adjusted to bring the present balance into agreement with the required balance; the amount of the adjustment is charged to bad debt expense for the period.

If properly applied, the aging method, including use of appropriate supplemental information, provides the most accurate approximation of the expected net realizable value of receivables. Like the percentage-of-receivables method described above, the aging method may fail to recognize bad debt expenses in the period in which they arise. In the aging process, bad debts are related to impairment-of-asset values irrespective of the time of the sales activity. Receivables resulting from the most recent sales, for example, may be regarded as fully collectible in the aging process, only to prove uncollectible in the subsequent period. The aging method can be costly and time-consuming when many accounts are involved, although computerized receivables systems have greatly reduced the costs and time required.

(f) WARRANTIES AND GUARANTEES.   SFAS No. 5, "Accounting for Contingencies," (pars. 24 and 25) states:

> A warranty is an obligation incurred in connection with the sale of goods or services that may require further performance by the seller after the sale has taken place. Because of the uncertainty surrounding claims that may be made under warranties, warranty obligations fall within the definition of a contingency.... Losses from warranty obligations shall be accrued when the conditions in paragraph 8 are met. [See below.] Those conditions may be considered in relation to individual sales made with warranties or in relation to groups of similar types of sales made with warranties. If the conditions are met, accrual shall be made even though the particular parties that will make claims under warranties may not be identifiable.

> If, based on available information, it is possible that customers will make claims under warranties relating to goods or services that have been sold, the condition in paragraph 8(a) [see below] is met at the date of an enterprise's financial statements because it is probable that a liability has been incurred. Satisfaction of the condition in paragraph 8(b) [see below] will normally depend

on the experience of an enterprise or other information. In the case of an enterprise that has no experience of its own, reference to the experience of other enterprises in the same business may be appropriate. Inability to make a reasonable estimate of the amount of a warranty obligation at the time of sale because of significant uncertainty about possible claims [i.e., failure to satisfy the condition in paragraph 8(b)] precludes accrual and, if the range of possible loss is wide, may raise a question about whether a sale should be recorded prior to expiration of the warranty period or until sufficient experience has been gained to permit a reasonable estimate of the obligation.

Paragraph 8 states:

An estimated loss from a loss contingency . . . shall be accrued by a charge to income if both of the following conditions are met:

a. Information available prior to issuance of the financial statements indicates that it is probable that an asset had been impaired or a liability had been incurred at the date of the financial statements.

b. The amount of the loss can be reasonably estimated.

Accounting for separately priced extended warranty and product maintenance contracts is discussed in Section 19.4(a)(viii).

(g) OBLIGATIONS RELATED TO PRODUCT DEFECTS.   SFAS No. 5 (par. 26) states:

Obligations other than warranties may arise with respect to products or services that have been sold, for example, claims resulting from injury or damage caused by product defects. If it is probable that claims will arise with respect to products or services that have been sold, accrual for losses may be appropriate. The condition in paragraph 8(a) [see above] would be met, for instance, with respect to a drug product or toys that have been sold if a health or safety hazard related to those products is discovered and as a result it is considered probable that liabilities have been incurred. The condition in paragraph 8(b) [see above] would be met if experience or other in-formation enables the enterprise to make a reasonable estimate of the loss with respect to the drug product or the toys.

19.6 ANCILLARY REVENUE

(a) DIVIDENDS.   Generally, investors in equity securities classified as trading or available-for-sale report cash dividends and dividends paid in property of the payer corporation as "other income" unless the dividends are a major source of income to the recipient; then they are classified as operating revenue. Dividends received in property of the payer corporation are recorded as revenue in amounts equivalent to the fair market value of the property (APB Opinion No. 29, par. 18). The date an investor becomes entitled to receive a dividend is the accepted time for recognizing it as revenue. In practice, organizations often record the revenue when the cash or property is actually received.

As indicated by the AICPA (ARB No. 43, "Restatement and Revision of Accounting Research Bulletins," paragraphs 5–9), stock dividends consisting of shares received on holdings of the same class of stock do not represent income to the recipient because there is no "distribution, division, or severance of corporate assets."

Liquidating dividends do not normally result in income until their cumulative total exceeds the recipient's cost of the investment to which they apply.

(b) INTEREST.   Interest generally is classified as "other income," unless, as in financial institutions, it is a major source of income; then it is classified as operating revenue. Interest on obligations of debtors generally should be recorded as it accrues. If collectibility of interest is doubtful, the recognition of interest should be postponed until the interest is received or its collection becomes reasonably certain.

Interest income on long-term investments purchased at a premium is subject to reduction by the amount of the amortization of the premium from the date of purchase to the earliest call date or maturity. The amount of discount on investments purchased at less than face value should be similarly amortized and included in income. If collection of the principal amount of the investment is uncertain, the discount should not be amortized.

(c) PROFITS ON SALES OF MISCELLANEOUS ASSETS. Profits on sales of miscellaneous assets—those not regularly and customarily offered for sale in the normal conduct of the business—are usually classified as "other income." Such profits include gains and losses on sales of securities, real estate, machinery and equipment, automobiles and trucks, furniture and fixtures, and sundry salvaged materials. Profits on those sales are generally recorded "net"; that is, the selling price is not recorded as revenue and the carrying value of the asset sold is not shown as expense.

The EITF has completed several projects dealing with profit recognition for companies involved in trading energy contracts. EITF Issue No. 02-3, "Issues Involved in Accounting for Derivative Contracts Held for Trading Purposes and Contracts Involved in Energy Trading and Risk Management Activities," codified the guidance provided for certain derivatives traded in liquid markets that are measured at fair value. The EITF has reached consensus on the following aspects of Issue No. 02-3:

1. Initial fair value estimates should be based on transaction prices except when model values based on observable market inputs are available.[40]

2. All realized and unrealized gains and losses resulting from mark-to-market accounting should be shown net in the income statement.

3. Relevant descriptive and analytical information about energy trading activities should be disclosed in notes to the financial statements.

In the consensus on Issue No. 03-11, "Reporting Realized Gains and Losses on Derivative Instruments That Are Subject to FAS 133 and Not 'Held for Trading Purposes,' as Defined in EITF Issue No. 02-3," the EITF concluded that realized gains and loses on derivatives not held for trading can be reported either on a net or gross basis, depending on the relevant facts and circumstances facing the entity. The guidance contained in EITF Issue No. 99-19 (see Section 19.1(c)(i)) should be used to help make that determination. Entities also should disclose how all unrealized and realized gains and losses related to derivatives are reported in the financial statements.

(d) RENTS. Rents receivable should be recorded as revenue in the accounting period during which they accrue. Rents received in advance should be deferred and included in revenue in the period to which they apply.

(e) ROYALTIES. Royalties may be broadly defined as a compensation or a portion of the proceeds paid to an owner for the right to use the owner's property. The payment may be in the form of a share in kind of the product or the right that is exploited or in the form of monetary compensation at agreed rates based on units produced, used, or sold or the equivalent of their market value. The types of property for which royalties may be paid include forests, mineral and oil lands, copyrights, patents, processes, and equipment.

Royalties should be recognized as revenue as they accrue. Periodic royalty reports from the user of the property customarily form the basis for determining the amount to be accrued. Amounts collected as advance royalties or as minimum periodic royalties should be deferred to the extent that such collections may be applied in settlement of royalties accruing in a period subsequent to the period of receipt.

---

[40] This conclusion may be modified by a proposed FASB Staff Position (FSP), "Accounting for Unrealized Gains (Losses) Relating to Derivative Instruments Measured at Fair Value Under Statement 133" (*www.fasb.org*).

(f) BY-PRODUCT, JOINT PRODUCT, AND SCRAP SALES.   Horngren, Foster, and Datar state:

GAAP for recording the costs and revenues from multiple products is often affected by their classification as joint or main products, by-products, or scrap. The distinctions underlying these classifications are based on their relative sales values.

Joint products have relatively high sales values and are not separately identifiable as individual products until their splitoff point. When a single process yielding two or more products yields only one product with a relatively high sales value, that product is termed a main product.

A by-product has a low sales value compared with the sales value of the main or joint product(s). Scrap has a minimal (frequently zero) sales value . . . These distinctions are not firm in practice. The variety of terminology and accounting practice is bewildering.[41]

Joint product sales are normally recorded in the same manner as the seller's principal sources of revenue. The major accounting problem in this connection is determining the proportionate share of total product costs to be assigned to joint products. The value of by-products and scrap may be treated either as a reduction of cost or as revenue (or other income) either at the time of production or at the time of sale.

(g) SHIPPING AND HANDLING FEES.   Fees billed to customers in sales transactions for shipping and handling and related costs should be reported as revenue rather than netted against the costs incurred.[42] According to EITF Issue No. 00-10, "Accounting for Shipping and Handling Fees and Costs," that is appropriate whether amounts billed to customers equal the actual shipping and handling costs incurred or the amounts billed exceed those costs. Although the SEC staff prefers shipping and handling costs to be reported as part of cost of sales, they may be included in some other income statement classification as long as the total amount of those costs, if material, and the line item in which they are included are disclosed. The EITF did not specify what costs are to be considered "shipping and handling"; that accounting policy should be disclosed in accordance with APB Opinion No. 22, "Disclosure of Accounting Policies."

(h) LOAN GUARANTEES.   Entities may guarantee other entities' loans in order to improve those other entities' ability to borrow, or the terms under which those other entities can borrow, from third parties. EITF No. 85-20, "Recognition of Fees for Guaranteeing a Loan," requires entities to recognize fee revenue from providing those guarantees, and any direct costs associated with the guarantees, over the period during which the guarantees apply. If, however, a fee is in substance a "lending commitment" as defined in paragraph 80 of SFAS No. 91, "Accounting for Nonrefundable Fees and Costs Associated with Originating or Acquiring Loans and Initial Direct Costs of Leases," the guidance in paragraph 8 of SFAS No. 91 applies.

SAB No. 60, "Views Regarding Accounting for and Disclosure of Certain Financial Guarantees," requires entities to disclose in notes to their financial statements the following information about material financial guarantees: (1) the type of obligation guaranteed; (2) the amount of exposure related to guarantees of the debts of other parties at the date of each balance sheet presented; (3) the method used to recognize revenue; (4) the amount of unearned revenue at each balance sheet date; (5) the amount of any liabilities recognized under SFAS No. 5, "Accounting for Contingencies," and the reasons for such recognition; and (6) additional information describing the obligations that are guaranteed and the extent of risk related to those guarantees.

Financial guarantee contracts are considered derivatives under SFAS No. 133, "Accounting for Derivative Instruments and Hedging Activities," if the payment under the guarantee is based on changes in an underlying, such as the other party's creditworthiness. In conformity with SFAS

---

[41] C. T. Horngren, G. Foster, and S. M. Datar, *Cost Accounting: A Managerial Emphasis*, Fifth Edition (Prentice-Hall, Englewood Cliffs, NJ, 1994), p. 571.

[42] The only exception described in the EITF consensus is when revenue is recorded net. See the discussion of net versus gross recording of revenues in Section 19.1(c)(i).

No. 133, those contracts would be reported at fair value; accounting for changes in fair value is discussed in par. 18. SFAS No. 133 does not apply, however, if the contracts "provide payments to be made only to reimburse the guaranteed party for a loss incurred because the debtor fails to pay when payment is due, which is an identifiable insurable event" (par. 10 d).[43]

19.7 STATEMENT PRESENTATION

(a) INCOME STATEMENT AND REVENUE-RELATED DISCLOSURES.   The income statement should disclose sales for the period, usually net of discounts, returns, and allowances.

Various authoritative pronouncements contain guidance on disclosures about revenue recognition policies and the impact of events and trends on revenue. In addition to the specific disclosures described in various sections of this chapter, the following should be disclosed:

- In providing information about its accounting policies for the reporting of revenue in conformity with APB Opinion No. 22, "Disclosure of Accounting Policies," a company should disclose (SAB No. 101, Topic 13B.1):
  - Different policies for different kinds of revenue transactions, including barter sales
  - The policies for each element, such as product and service, of transactions with multiple elements
  - How each of multiple elements are determined and valued
  - Changes in estimated returns if material
  - Companies should report separately the amount of revenue from sales of merchandise, services, and other products and the related costs for each (SAB No. 101, Topic 13B.1).
  - If the chief operating decision maker reviews information about a portion of an entity, such as its Internet operations, separately from other portions, it may be considered a reportable operating segment (SFAS No. 131, "Disclosures about Segments of an Enterprise and Related Information"). Reportable segment disclosures relating to revenue include types of goods and services from which revenues are derived, total revenues from external customers and from other operating segments of the entity, interest revenue, and a reconciliation of total reportable segment revenue to total consolidated revenues. For interim periods, revenues from external customers and intersegment revenues for each reportable segment should be disclosed.
- Amounts recovered under business interruption insurance claims typically include (1) gross margin that would have been earned if normal operations had not been suspended; (2) a portion of normal fixed costs incurred during the interruption period; and (3) other out-of-pocket costs incurred as a result of the interruption of business. In Issue No. 01-13, "Income Statement Display of Business Interruption Insurance Recoveries," the EITF concluded that these recoveries could be shown in any section of the income statement as long as the classification is consistent with GAAP. For example, reporting a recovery as an extraordinary gain is acceptable only if the extraordinary item criteria in APB Opinion No. 30, "Reporting the Results of Operations, Reporting the Effects of Disposal of a Segment of a Business, and Extraordinary, Unusual and Infrequently Occurring Events and Transactions," are satisfied. A description of the event causing the loss, the total amount of the recoveries included in the income statement, and the line item or items on the income statement in which the recoveries are reported should be disclosed.
- Companies should describe the types of multiple deliverable arrangements they have with customers, including provisions related to performance, refunds, terminations, and cancellations. Companies also should disclose the recognition policies they use for such arrangements (EITF Issue No. 00-21, par. 18).

---

[43] Also see SFAS No. 133 Implementation Issue No. C7, "Certain Financial Guarantee Contracts."

The SEC staff has suggested that the following information about revenue be disclosed:

- In its management discussion and analysis (MD&A), a company should discuss unusual or infrequent transactions and known trends or uncertainties that have had or might reasonably be expected to have a favorable or unfavorable material effect on revenue, operating income, or net income and the relationship between revenue and the costs of the revenue. It should evaluate changes in revenue in terms of volume and price changes and disclose the reasons and factors contributing to the changes. The following are examples of transactions or events that should be disclosed in the MD&A (SAB No. 101, Topic 10B.1):
  - Late-period shipments that significantly reduce backlog and might reasonably be expected to result in lower shipments and revenue in the next period
  - Granting of extended payment terms and the effect on liquidity and capital resources (the fair value of trade receivables, if it does not approximate the reported amount, should be disclosed in the notes)
  - Changing trends in shipments to and sales from a sales channel or separate class of buyer that could be expected to significantly affect future sales or sales returns
  - Increasing trends toward different classes of buyer, such as to a revenue distribution channel that has a lower gross profit margin, or increasing service revenue with higher profit margins
  - Seasonal trends or variations in revenue
  - Gains or losses from the sales of assets
- Other disclosures as appropriate,[44] such as:
  - Disaggregated product and service information:
  - Product and service revenues (and costs of revenues) separately on the face of the income statement
  - Separate revenues of each major product or service within segment data
  - Description of major revenue-generating products or services
  - For major contracts or groups of similar contracts, descriptions of essential terms, including payment terms and unusual provisions or conditions
  - Details concerning when revenue is recognized, such as:
  - At delivery (indicate whether terms are customarily FOB shipping point or FOB destination)
  - At completion of service
  - At commencement of service
  - Ratably over service period
  - At satisfaction of a significant condition of sale and a description of that condition
  - After customer acceptance
  - After testing of product sold
  - After completion of all terms of contract
  - Over performance period based on progress toward completion
  - At delivery of separate elements in multielement arrangement
  - If revenue is recognized over the service period based on progress toward completion, or based on separate contract elements or milestones:
  - How the period's revenue is measured
  - How progress is measured—for example, cost to cost, time and materials, units of delivery, units of work performed
  - Types of contract payment milestones, with an explanation of how they relate to substantive performance and revenue recognition events

---

[44] SEC Division of Corporate Finance, "Current Accounting and Disclosure Issues" (December 1, 2005), Section II. F.3.

○ Description of whether contracts with a single counterparty are combined or bifurcated

○ Identification of contract elements permitting separate revenue recognition and a description of how they are distinguished

○ How contract revenue is allocated among elements

○ Whether the relative fair value or residual method is used to allocate elements

○ Whether fair values are based on vendor specific evidence or by other means

○ Material assumptions, estimates, and uncertainties, including:

○ Existing contingencies such as rights of return, conditions of acceptance, warranties, and price protection

○ How those contingencies are accounted for

○ Significant assumptions, material changes, and reasonably likely uncertainties

○ Disclosures and conditions as specified by SAB No. 101 for companies that recognize refundable revenues by analogy to SFAS No. 48, "Sales with the Right of Return"

The SEC staff has emphasized that, in order to ensure fair presentation, income statement disclosures of revenues should be classified based on the nature of the underlying events. For example, reported revenues should be reported net of consideration given to customers or resellers and should not include (1) amounts intended to offset costs incurred, (2) equity in investees' income, (3) gains or losses from fixed asset or investment sales, or (4) "other income." The staff expects companies to clarify and expand their disclosures in SEC filings regarding the accounting policies used for each material revenue-generating activity the company undertakes.[45]

(b) BALANCE SHEET DISCLOSURES. The basis for presentation of receivables in the balance sheet is the expected time of collection. Receivables expected to be collected within the next operating cycle or fiscal year, whichever is longer, are ordinarily classified as current assets. Several exceptions allowed by ARB No. 43 are discussed below. Specialized reporting requirements also are discussed below.

Kieso, Weygandt, and Warfield summarize the general rules for statement presentation in the receivables section of the balance sheet:

1. Segregate the different types of receivables that an enterprise possesses, if material;
2. Ensure that the valuation accounts are appropriately offset against the proper receivable accounts;
3. Determine that receivables classified in the current assets section will be converted into cash within the year or the operating cycle, whichever is longer;
4. Disclose any loss contingencies that exist on the receivables;
5. Disclose any receivables designated or pledged as collateral;
6. Disclose all significant concentrations of credit risk arising from receivables.[46]

(i) Presentation of Single-Payment Accounts Receivable. Ordinarily accounts receivable are classified in the balance sheet as *current assets*. Amounts that will not be collected until the next operating cycle or fiscal year, however, should be shown as noncurrent. In the interest of full disclosure, it is considered desirable to limit the "accounts receivable" designation to current claims attaching to trade customers and to identify separately other major types of receivables, such as amounts due from officers and employees, prepayments, and stock subscriptions receivable.

---

[45] *Ibid*.
[46] Kieso, Weygandt, and Warfield, p. 337.

(ii) Presentation of Installment Receivables. ARB No. 43 (Ch. 3, par. 4) specifically provides for the inclusion within *current assets* of "installment or deferred accounts and notes receivable if they conform generally to normal trade practices and terms within the business." Thus installment receivables may be classified as current regardless of the length of the collection period. Designation of annual maturity dates by separate listing of contracts receivable or by parenthetical or note disclosure is recommended to enable readers to ascertain the current position.

Conflicting opinions exist as to the proper classification of the *deferred gross profit account* related to installment receivables. The FASB concludes[47] that deferred gross profit conceptually should be treated as an asset valuation account. Because deferred gross profit is part of revenue from installment sales not yet realized, the related receivable will be overstated unless deferred gross profit is deducted. Another alternative is to report deferred gross profit as unearned revenue in the liability section. This alternative has been criticized, however, because the credit is not an obligation to an outsider.

In preparing an income statement, installment sales, cost of installment sales, and realized gross profit may be shown in the statement, or only the realized gross profit may be reported, with installment sales and cost of sales reflected in a separate supporting schedule. Paragraph 96 of SFAS No. 66, "Accounting for Sales of Real Estate," illustrates the financial statement presentation when the installment method is used for retail land sales. Also see Section 19.2(h) of this chapter.

(iii) Interest on Receivables. Notes receivable arise in many situations in which the legal form of the note specifies an interest rate (including lack of an interest rate) that varies from prevailing interest rates. APB Opinion No. 21, "Interest on Receivables and Payables," requires that, in these situations, the note receivable be recorded at its present value and that interest be imputed at an appropriate rate. The resulting discount or premium is amortized over the life of the note. APB Opinion No. 21 (par. 3) exempts the following receivables:

a. Receivables arising from transactions with customers in the normal course of business which are due in customary trade terms not exceeding approximately one year

b. Receivables from the customary cash lending activities of financial institutions

c. Receivables where interest rates are affected by the tax attributes or legal restrictions prescribed by a governmental agency

d. Receivables from a parent, subsidiary, or another firm with a common parent

19.8 SOURCES AND SUGGESTED REFERENCES

Accounting Principles Board, "Omnibus Opinion—1966," APB Opinion No. 10. AICPA, New York, 1966.

———,"Interest on Receivables and Payables," APB Opinion No. 21. AICPA, New York, 1971.

———, "Disclosure of Accounting Policies," APB Opinion No. 22. AICPA, New York, 1972.

———, "Accounting for Nonmonetary Transactions," APB Opinion No. 29. AICPA, New York, 1973.

———, "Reporting the Results of Operations—Reporting the Effects of Disposal of a Segment of a Business, and Extraordinary, Unusual and Infrequently Occurring Events and Transactions," APB Opinion No. 30. AICPA, New York, 1973.

———, "Basic Concepts and Accounting Principles Underlying Financial Statements of Business Enterprises," APB Statement No. 4. AICPA, New York, 1970. Accounting Standards Board, "Revenue Recognition," Discussion Paper. ASB, London, July 2001.

———, "Amendment to FRS 5 'Reporting the Substance of Transactions': Revenue Recognition," Application Note. ASB, London, November 2003.

American Accounting Association, Committee on Accounting Concepts and Standards, *Accounting and Reporting Standards for Corporate Financial Statements (1957 Revision).* AAA, Sarasota, FL, 1957.

---

[47] SFAC No. 6, par. 234.

————, 1964 Concepts and Standards Research Committee on the Realization Concept, "The Realization Concept," *Accounting Review,* April 1965.

American Institute of Certified Public Accountants, Accounting Standards Executive Committee, "Accounting for Performance of Construction-Type and Certain Production-Type Contracts," Statement of Position 81-1. AICPA, New York, 1981.

————, "Reporting on Advertising Costs," Statement of Position 93-7. AICPA, New York, 1993.

————, "Software Revenue Recognition," Statement of Position 97-2. AICPA, New York, 1997.

————, "Accounting for the Costs of Computer Software Developed or Obtained for Internal Use," Statement of Position 98-1. AICPA, New York, 1998.

————, "Accounting by Producers or Distributors of Films," Statement of Position 00-2. AICPA, New York, 2000.

————, "Revenue Recognition," Technical Practice Aids, Accounting and Auditing Publications Technical Questions and Answers (TIS Section 5100). AICPA, New York, 2002.

————, Auditing Revenue Steering Task Force, "Auditing Revenue in Certain Industries," Audit Guide. AICPA, New York, 2002.

————, Civil Aeronautics Subcommittee, "Audits of Airlines," Industry Audit Guide. AICPA, New York, 1981.

————, Committee on Accounting Procedure, "Restatement and Revision of Accounting Research Bulletins," Accounting Research Bulletin No. 43. AICPA, New York, 1953.

————, "Long-Term Construction Type Contracts," Accounting Research Bulletin No. 45. AICPA, New York, 1955.

————, Committee on Land Development Companies, "Accounting for Retail Land Sales," Industry Accounting Guide. AICPA, New York, 1973.

————, Construction Contractors Guide Committee, "Construction Contractors," Audit and Accounting Guide. AICPA, New York, 1981.

————, Gaming Industry Special Committee, "Audits of Casinos," Audit and Accounting Guide. AICPA, New York, 1984.

————, Government Contractors Guide Special Committee, "Audits of Federal Government Contractors," Audit and Accounting Guide. AICPA, New York, 1990.

————, Stockbrokerage and Investment Banking Committee, "Brokers and Dealers in Securities," Audit and Accounting Guide. AICPA, New York, 1997.

Canning, J. B., *The Economics of Accounting.* Ronald Press, New York, 1929.

Committee of Sponsoring Organizations of the Treadway Commission, *Fraudulent Financial Reporting: 1987–1997, An Analysis of U.S. Public Companies*. COSO, New York, March 1999.

Edwards, E. O., and Bell, P. W., The Theory and Measurement of Business Income. University of California Press, Berkeley, 1965.

Financial Accounting Standards Board, "An Analysis of Issues Related to Conceptual Framework for Financial Accounting and Reporting: Elements of Financial Statements and Their Measurement," Discussion Memorandum. FASB, Norwalk, CT, 1976.

————, "Accounting for Certain Service Transactions," Invitation to Comment. FASB, Norwalk, CT, 1978.

————, "Project Updates – Revenue Recognition." FASB, Norwalk, CT, October 13, 2005.

————, "Objectives of Financial Reporting by Business Enterprises," Statement of Financial Accounting Concepts No. 1. FASB, Norwalk, CT, 1978.

————, "Qualitative Characteristics of Accounting Information," Statement of Financial Accounting Concepts No. 2. FASB, Norwalk, CT, 1980.

————, "Recognition and Measurement in Financial Statements of Business Enterprises," Statement of Financial Accounting Concepts No. 5. FASB, Norwalk, CT, 1984.

————, "Elements of Financial Statements," Statement of Financial Accounting Concepts No. 6. FASB, Norwalk, CT, 1985.

————, "Accounting for Contingencies," Statement of Financial Accounting Standards No. 5. FASB, Norwalk, CT, 1975.

————, "Accounting for Leases," Statement of Financial Accounting Standards No. 13. FASB, Norwalk, CT, 1977.

_____, "Financial Reporting and Changing Prices," Statement of Financial Accounting Standards No. 33. FASB, Norwalk, CT, 1979.

_____, "Accounting for Franchise Fee Revenue," Statement of Financial Accounting Standards No. 45. FASB, Norwalk, CT, 1981.

_____, "Revenue Recognition When Right of Return Exists," Statement of Financial Accounting Standards No. 48. FASB, Norwalk, CT, 1981.

_____, "Accounting for Product Financing Arrangements," Statement of Financial Accounting Standards No. 49. FASB, Norwalk, CT, 1981.

_____, "Financial Reporting in the Record and Music Industry," Statement of Financial Accounting Standards No. 50. FASB, Norwalk, CT, 1981.

_____, "Financial Reporting by Cable Television Companies," Statement of Financial Accounting Standards No. 51. FASB, Norwalk, CT, 1981.

_____, "Foreign Currency Translation," Statement of Financial Accounting Standards No. 52, FASB. Norwalk, CT, 1981.

_____, "Financial Reporting by Producers and Distributors of Motion Picture Films," Statement of Financial Accounting Standards No. 53. FASB, Norwalk, CT, 1981.

_____, "Accounting and Reporting by Insurance Enterprises," Statement of Financial Accounting Standards No. 60. FASB, Norwalk, CT, 1982.

_____, "Financial Reporting by Broadcasters," Statement of Financial Accounting Standards No. 63. FASB, Norwalk, CT, 1982.

_____, "Accounting for Sales of Real Estate," Statement of Financial Accounting Standards No. 66, FASB, Norwalk, CT, 1982.

_____, "Accounting for the Effects of Certain Types of Regulation," Statement of Financial Accounting Standards No. 71. FASB, Norwalk, CT, 1982.

_____, "Financial Reporting and Changing Prices: Elimination of Certain Disclosures," Statement of Financial Accounting Standards No. 82. FASB, Norwalk, CT, 1984.

_____, "Accounting for the Costs of Computer Software to Be Sold, Leased, or Otherwise Marketed," Statement of Financial Accounting Standards No. 86. FASB, Norwalk, CT, 1985.

_____, "Financial Reporting and Changing Prices," Statement of Financial Accounting Standards No. 89. FASB, Norwalk, CT, 1986.

_____, "Accounting for Nonrefundable Fees and Costs Associated with Originating or Acquiring Loans and Initial Direct Costs of Leases," Statement of Financial Accounting Standards No. 91. FASB, Norwalk, CT, 1986.

_____, "Accounting for Leases: Sale-Leaseback Transactions Involving Real Estate," Statement of Financial Accounting Standards No. 98. FASB, Norwalk, CT, 1988.

_____, "Accounting by Creditors for Impairment of a Loan," Statement of Financial Accounting Standards No. 114. FASB, Norwalk, CT, 1993.

_____, "Accounting for Contributions Received and Contributions Made," Statement of Financial Accounting Standards No. 116. FASB, Norwalk, CT, 1993.

_____, "Accounting for the Impairment of Long-Lived Assets and for Long-Lived Assets to Be Disposed Of," Statement of Financial Accounting Standards No. 121. FASB, Norwalk, CT, 1995.

_____, "Share-Based Payment," Statement of Financial Accounting Standards No. 123 (R). FASB, Norwalk, CT, 2004.

_____, "Accounting for Transfers and Servicing of Financial Assets and Extinguishments of Liabilities," Statement of Financial Accounting Standards No. 125. FASB, Norwalk, CT, 1996.

_____, "Disclosures about Segments of an Enterprise and Related Information," Statement of Financial Accounting Standards No. 131. FASB, Norwalk, CT, 1997.

_____, "Accounting for Derivative Instruments and Hedging Activities," Statement of Financial Accounting Standards No. 133. FASB, Norwalk, CT, 1998.

_____, "Accounting for Certain Derivative Instruments and Certain Hedging Activities; An Amendment of FASB Statement No. 133," Statement of Financial Accounting Standards No. 138. FASB, Norwalk, CT, 2000.

———, "Rescission of FASB Statement No. 53 and Amendments to FASB Statements No. 63, 89, and 121," Statement of Financial Accounting Standards No. 139. FASB, Norwalk, CT, 2000.

———, "Accounting for Transfers and Servicing of Financial Assets and Extinguishments of Liabilities," Statement of Financial Accounting Standards No. 140. FASB, Norwalk, CT, 2000.

———, "Exchanges of Nonmonetary Assets—An Amendment Of APB Opinión No. 29.", FASB, Norwalk, CT, 2004.

———, "Guarantor's Accounting and Disclosure Requirements for Guarantees, Including Indirect Guarantees of Indebtedness of Others," Interpretation No. 45. FASB, Norwalk, CT, 2002.

———, "Accounting for Separately Extended Warranty and Product Maintenance Contracts," Technical Bulletin No. 90-1. FASB, Norwalk, CT, 1990.

———, Emerging Issues Task Force, "Recognition of Fees for Guaranteeing a Loan," Issue No. 85-20. FASB, Norwalk, CT, 1988.

———, "Sales of Future Revenues," Issue No. 88-18. FASB, Norwalk, CT, 1988.

———, "Accounting for the Retail Sale of an Extended Warranty Contract in Connection with the Sale of a Product," Issue No. 89-17. FASB, Norwalk, CT, 1989.

———, "Revenue and Expense Recognition for Freight Services in Process," Issue No. 91-9. FASB, Norwalk, CT, 1992.

———, "Accounting for Barter Transactions Involving Barter Credits," Issue No. 93-11. FASB, Norwalk, CT, 1993.

———, "Revenue Recognition on Sales with a Guaranteed Minimum Resale Value," Issue No. 95-1. FASB, Norwalk, CT, 1995.

———, "Revenue Recognition on Equipment Sold and Subsequently Repurchased Subject to an Operating Lease," Issue No. 95-4. FASB, Norwalk, CT, 1995.

———, "Accounting for Equity Instruments that Are Issued to Other than Employees for Acquiring, or in Conjunction with Selling, Goods or Services," Issue No. 96-18. FASB, Norwalk, CT, 2001.

———, "Accounting for Advertising Barter Transactions," Issue No. 99-17. FASB, Norwalk, CT, 2000.

———, "Reporting Revenue Gross as a Principal versus Net as an Agent," Issue No. 99-19. FASB, Norwalk, CT, 2000.

———, "Remaining Issues from the SEC's October 18, 1999 Letter to the EITF," Issue No. 99-V. FASB, Norwalk, CT, 2002.

———, "Application of AICPA Statement of Position 97-2, 'Software Revenue Recognition,' to Arrangements that Include the Right to Use Software Stored on Another Entity's Hardware," Issue No. 00-3. FASB, Norwalk, CT, 2000.

———, "Accounting by a Grantee for an Equity Instrument to Be Received in Conjunction with Providing Goods or Services," Issue No. 00-8. FASB, Norwalk, CT, 2000.

———, "Accounting for Shipping and Handling Fees and Costs," Issue No. 00-10. FASB, Norwalk, CT, 2000.

———, "Accounting for Certain Sales Incentives," Issue No. 00-14. FASB, Norwalk, CT, 2000.

———, "Accounting Recognition for Certain Transactions involving Equity Instruments Granted to Other than Employees," Issue No. 00-18. FASB, Norwalk, CT, 2002.

———, "Revenue Arrangements with Multiple Deliverables," Issue No. 00-21. FASB, Norwalk, CT, 2002.

———, "Vendor Income Statement Characterization of Consideration Paid to a Reseller of the Vendor's Products," Issue No. 00-25. FASB, Norwalk, CT, 2001.

———, "Accounting for Consideration Given by a Vendor to a Customer or a Reseller of the Vendor's Products," Issue No. 01-9. FASB, Norwalk, CT, 2001.

———, "Income Statement Display of Business Interruption Insurance Recoveries," Issue No. 01-13. FASB, Norwalk, CT, 2001.

———, "Income Statement Characterization of Reimbursements Received for 'Out-of-Pocket' Expenses Incurred," Issue No. 01-14. FASB, Norwalk, CT, 2002.

———, "Balance Sheet Classification of Assets Received in Exchange for Equity Instruments," Issue No. 02-1. FASB, Norwalk, CT, 2002.

———, "Recognition and Reporting of Gains and Losses on Energy Trading Contracts under Issues No. 98-10 and 00-17," Issue No. 02-3. FASB, Norwalk, CT, 2002.

_____ , "Recognition of Revenue from Licensing Arrangements on Intellectual Property," Issue No. 02-G. FASB, Norwalk, CT, 2002.

_____ , "Accounting by a Customer (Including a Reseller) for Certain Consideration Received from a Vendor," Issue No. 02-16. FASB, Norwalk, CT, 2003.

_____ , "Applicability of AICPA SOP 97-2 to Non-Software Deliverables," Issue No 03-05. FASB, Norwalk, CT, 2003.

_____ , "Application of EITF Issue No. 02-16, 'Accounting by a Customer (Including a Reseller) for Certain Consideration Received from a Vendor,' by Resellers to Sales Incentives Offered to Consumers by Manufacturers," Issue No. 03-10. FASB, Norwalk, CT, 2003.

_____ , "Reporting Realized Gains and Losses on Derivative Instruments That Are Subject to FAS 133 and Not 'Held for Trading Purposes,' as Defined in EITF Issue No. 02-3," Issue No. 03-11. FASB, Norwalk, CT, 2003.

_____ , "Accounting for Purchases and Sales of Inventory with the Same Counterparty," Issue No. 04-13. FASB, Norwalk, CT, 2004.

Hendriksen, E. S., and van Breda, M. F., _Accounting Theory_, Fifth Edition. Irwin, Homewood, IL, 1992.

Horngren, C. T., "How Should We Interpret the Realization Concept?" _Accounting Review,_ April 1965.

Horngren, C. T., Foster, G., and Datar, S. M., _Cost Accounting: A Managerial Emphasis,_ Fifth Edition. Prentice-Hall, Englewood Cliffs, NJ, 1994.

International Accounting Standards Board, _2003 International Financial Reporting Standards_. IASB, London, 2003.

International Accounting Standards Committee, "Revenue," International Accounting Standard 18. London, IASC, 1993.

Jaenicke, Henry R., _Survey of Present Practices in Recognizing Revenues, Expenses, Gains, and Losses_. FASB, Norwalk, CT, January 1981.

Kieso, D. E., Weygandt, J. J., and Warfield, T. D., _Intermediate Accounting_, Eleventh Edition. John Wiley & Sons, New York, 2004.

Levitt, A., "The 'Numbers Game,' " speech at NYU Center for Law and Business, September 28, 1998.

Mallor, J. P., Barnes, A. J., Bowers, T., Phillips, M. J., and Langvardt, A. W. _Business Law and the Regulatory Environment: Concepts and Cases_, Eleventh Edition. Irwin McGraw Hill, Chicago, 2001.

May, G. O., _Financial Accounting: A Distillation of Experience_. Macmillan, New York, 1943.

Meyers, J. H., "The Critical Event and the Recognition of Net Profit," _Accounting Review,_ October 1959.

O'Reilly, V. M., Hirsch, M. B., Defliese, P. L., and Jaenicke, H. R., _Montgomery's Auditing,_ Eleventh Edition. John Wiley & Sons, New York, 1990.

O'Reilly, V. M., McDonnell, P. J., Winograd, B. N., Gerson, J. S., and Jaenicke, H. R., _Montgomery's Auditing,_ Twelfth Edition. John Wiley & Sons, New York, 1998.

Paton, W. A., and Littleton, A. C., _An Introduction to Corporate Accounting Standards_. AAA, Sarasota, FL, 1940.

Paton, W. A., and Paton, W. A., Jr., _Corporation Accounts and Statements_. Macmillan, New York, 1955.

Public Oversight Board, Panel on Audit Effectiveness, _Report and Recommendations_. POB, Stamford, CT, August 31, 2000.

Pulliam, S., and Blumenstein, R. "SEC Broadens Investigation into Revenue-Boosting Tricks," _Wall Street Journal_, May 16, 2002, pp. A1 and A10.

Securities and Exchange Commission, "Accounting for Real Estate Transactions Where Circumstances Indicate That Profits Were Not Earned at the Time the Transactions Were Recorded," Accounting Series Release No. 95. SEC, Washington, DC, 1972.

_____ , "Interpretation Regarding Divestitures in Connection with a Sale of a Subsidiary," Staff Accounting Bulletin No. 30. SEC, Washington, DC, 1979.

_____ , "Views Regarding Accounting for and Disclosure of Certain Financial Guarantees," Staff Accounting Bulletin No. 60. SEC, Washington, DC, 1985.

_____ , "Revenue Recognition in Financial Statements," Staff Accounting Bulletin No. 101. SEC, Washington, DC, 1999.

_____ , "Staff Accounting Bulletin No. 101: Revenue Recognition in Financial Statements—Frequently Asked Questions and Answers." SEC, Washington, DC, October 2000.

———, "Order Instituting Proceedings and Opinion and Order Pursuant to Rule 2(e) of the Commission's Rules of Practice *In the Matter of Arthur Andersen & Co.*," Exchange Act Release No. 17878. SEC, Washington, DC, 1981.

———, Division of Corporation Finance, "Current Accounting and Disclosure Issues." SEC, Washington, DC, December 1, 2005.

———, "SEC and United States Attorney Charge Former Homestore Executives with Scheme to Inflate Advertising Revenue," Accounting and Auditing Enforcement Release No. 1864. SEC, Washington, DC, September 18, 2003.

———, "SEC and Justice Department Bring Civil and Criminal Actions Charging Former CFO of Company that Engaged in Fraudulent Barter Deals with Homestore," Accounting and Auditing Enforcement Release No. 1874. SEC, Washington, DC, September 26, 2003.

———, "Revenue Recognition," Staff Accounting Bulletin No. 104. SEC, Washington, DC, December 17, 2003.

———, "SEC Settles Securities Fraud Case with i2 Technologies, Inc. Involving Misstatement of Approximately $1 Billion in Revenues," Accounting and Auditing Enforcement Release No. 2034. SEC, Washington, DC, June 9, 2004.

———, "Gemstar-TV Guide International Agrees to Settle SEC Enforcement Action Charging the Company with Overstating Its Revenues," Accounting and Auditing Enforcement Release No. 2045. SEC, Washington, DC, June 213, 2004.

———, "Order Instituting Public Administrative Proceedings Pursuant to Rule 102(E) of the Commission's Rules of Practice, Making Findings, and Imposing Remedial Sanctions in the Matter of KPMG LLP, Bryan E. Palbaum, CPA, John M. Wong, CPA, Kenneth B. Janeski, CPA, David A. Hori, CPA," SEC Accounting and Auditing Enforcement Release No. 2125. SEC, Washington, DC, October 20, 2004.

———, "Commission Charges Three Former Purchase Pro Executives, Including Former CEO Charles Jonson, Jr., and Two Former AOL Executives in a Fraudulent Scheme to Inflate Purchase Pro's Revenues," SEC Accounting and Enforcement Release No. 2165. SEC, Washington, D.C., January 10, 2005.

Staubus, G. J., *Making Accounting Decisions*. Scholars Book Co., Houston, 1977.

Turner, L. "Revenue Recognition," speech at USC SEC and Financial Reporting Institute, May 31, 2001.

Vatter, W. J., *The Fund Theory of Accounting and Its Implications for Financial Reports*. University of Chicago Press, Chicago, 1947.

Windal, F. W., "The Accounting Concept of Realization," *Accounting Review,* April 1961.

CHAPTER 20

INVENTORY

Richard R. Jones, CPA
Ernst & Young LLP

Gary L. Smith, CPA
Ernst & Young LLP

20.1 OVERVIEW

Accounting for inventory has been guided more by practice than by pronouncement. As advances in manufacturing processes have occurred, accounting practices have evolved to identify the applicable costs to be allocated to inventory. Authoritative accounting literature related to inventory accounting and financial reporting is not extensive. The accounting profession has made it clear that examining individual facts and circumstances is important when valuing inventory and applying the established standards.

Historical cost is the normal starting point to record inventory as an asset. In determining inventory cost, a cost flow assumption must be selected. Alternate valuation methods that are exceptions to the historical cost convention are used for certain specialized types of inventory (e.g., sales price less cost of disposal for precious metals, and net realizable value for trade-in inventory). The write-down of inventory to amounts below cost may be necessary due to factors such as damage or changing market conditions.

This chapter addresses inventory costing in greater detail by identifying the pertinent guidance in the authoritative accounting literature and by citing examples that illustrate the practical application of the fundamental principles. The chapter also explains the various types of inventory and practical ways to determine inventory quantities. Finally, the chapter explores effective internal control techniques and financial statement disclosure requirements.

20.2 ESSENTIAL INVENTORY CONCEPTS

(a) INVENTORY AS AN ASSET.   Paragraph 25 of Financial Accounting Standards Board (FASB) Concepts Statement No. 6, "Elements of Financial Statements," describes assets as "probable future economic benefits obtained or controlled by a particular entity as a result of past transactions or events." Inventory generally is acquired or produced for subsequent exchange. This utility or service potential justifies the classification of inventory as an asset of the enterprise that controls it. Normally, inventory is converted into cash or other assets during the operating cycle of the business. In fact, this process is what establishes the operating cycle. As a result, inventory typically is classified as a current asset for purposes of preparing a classified balance sheet.

(b) DEFINITION OF INVENTORY.   The primary authoritative guidance addressing financial reporting for inventory is ARB No. 43, Chapter 4, "Inventory Pricing." It defines inventory of mercantile and manufacturing enterprises as:

> The aggregate of those items of tangible personal property which (1) are held for sale in the ordinary course of business, (2) are in process of production for such sale, or (3) are to be currently consumed in the production of goods or services to be available for sale.

This definition makes it clear that the trading merchandise of a retailer or wholesaler—and the finished goods, work in process, and raw materials of a manufacturer—constitute inventory. ARB No. 43 specifically excludes from inventory long-term assets subject to depreciation accounting. Fixed assets such as buildings and equipment provide benefits that generally extend beyond the operating cycle and, therefore, are classified as noncurrent assets. ARB No. 43 notes that such assets should not be classified as inventory even if they are retired and held for sale.

(c) OBJECTIVES OF ACCOUNTING FOR INVENTORY.   The sale of inventory to customers is often the most significant component of revenue for a business enterprise. Matching inventory costs with the revenues received from the sale of the goods in order to determine periodic income is the major objective of inventory accounting. Incurred inventory costs that have not been charged against operations represent the carrying amount of inventory on the balance sheet. The costs allocated to goods on hand should not, however, exceed the utility of those goods. In other words, the recorded inventory balance should not exceed the total revenues less selling costs that will result when those goods are sold.

The methods used to determine and measure the flow of inventory costs should be consistent from period to period. The methods should be objective so that comparable results are produced by similar transactions, to allow for independent verification and to prevent manipulation of results of operations. Adequate disclosure should be made regarding the nature of the inventory and the basis on which it is stated.

20.3 TYPES OF INVENTORY

(a) RETAIL–WHOLESALE.   Wholesalers and retailers typically acquire merchandise that is ready for resale to customers. Acquisition cost becomes the basis for carrying the inventory until it is sold.

(b) MANUFACTURING.   In a manufacturing operation, a production process creates goods for sale to customers or for use in other operations. Manufacturing inventories often are categorized by stage of completion.

(i) Raw Materials.   Goods to be incorporated into a product or used in the production process that have not yet entered the process are referred to as *raw materials inventory*. The output from one process can become the raw material for another process (e.g., subassemblies).

(ii) Work in Process.   Goods typically are classified as work in process inventory as soon as they are drawn from raw materials stock and enter the manufacturing process.

(iii) Finished Goods.   Products that are complete and ready for sale are considered finished goods inventory.

(iv) Supplies.   Materials necessary for the manufacturing operation but not a significant component of the final product are known as *supplies inventory*. For example, small incidental screws may be considered supplies inventory, or oil used to lubricate a grinding machine may be considered supplies inventory. The ARB No. 43 specifically mentions manufacturing supplies as a type of inventory and notes that the fact that a small portion of the supplies may be used for purposes other than production does not require separate classification.

(c) CONSIGNMENT.   Arrangements for marketing, storage, distribution, and finishing of a company's products can result in goods being held by a party other than the owner. The consignee (party holding the goods) generally is precluded from recording the inventory because legal title is retained by the consignor and no exchange has taken place. The consignment inventory balance frequently is combined with the work in process or finished goods inventory shown on the consignor's financial statements. Examples include inventories held for sale in a retail store that have been consigned by the manufacturer, and components held by an outside machine shop to be used in a larger product by the consignor.

(d) TRADE-IN.   Some companies obtain goods accepted from customers in connection with sales of other products. These goods may or may not be similar to the items sold or other products of the seller. An example is a memory board accepted in trade by a computer manufacturer when upgrading customer equipment. Trade-in inventory should be valued at net realizable value, defined as estimated selling price less costs of disposal. The discount or allowance deducted from the list price of the goods sold is not an appropriate value to assign to the trade-in inventory, because the discount often pertains to marketing strategy and other factors not related to the trade-in items.

(e) REPOSSESSED.   In connection with its collection efforts, a company may repossess its product from a customer. Companies that provide consumer financing often deal with repossessed inventory. The physical condition of the property may vary widely and will affect the company's decision regarding disposition (e.g., rework, offer for sale at a discount, scrap). Replacement cost is the primary method of valuing repossessed inventory. If replacement cost cannot realistically be determined, net realizable value should be used. Recording a repossessed item at the outstanding balance of the receivable from the customer is not appropriate, because this approach does not consider the condition and utility of the repossessed item.

(f) CONTRACT PRODUCTION.   A company may enter into a contract under which the customer provides specifications for producing goods, constructing facilities, or providing services.

(g) PRODUCTS MATURING IN MORE THAN ONE YEAR.   Certain products—such as tobacco, spirits, livestock, and forest products—are held for an extended period of time until they are mature for sale or inclusion in a finished product. Recognized trade practice is to classify such inventory items as current assets despite the required aging process.

(h) SPARE PARTS.   To service their customers, many companies (particularly equipment dealers and manufacturers) maintain a supply of spare parts for their products. Also, transportation companies hold spare parts to allow their fleets to operate continuously. Spare parts often are classified as inventory. When many small-value items are involved, companies amortize the related costs on a systematic basis. For more valuable spare parts, quantities are tracked and values are determined by the conventional inventory methods discussed in this chapter.

FINANCIAL REPORTING EXAMPLE

ABC FREIGHT CORPORATION AND SUBSIDIARIES
Consolidated Balance Sheets
(Dollars in thousands)

	December 31	
Assets	*20X1*	*20X2*
Current Assets:		
Cash	$ 35,816	$ 17,906
Trade accounts receivable, less allowance of $8,345,000 and		
$7,750,000	287,515	259,408
Spare parts and fuel inventory	34,761	33,792

Notes to Consolidated Financial Statements

Spare Parts and Fuel Inventory

Spare parts are stated at average cost and fuel inventory is stated at cost on first-in, first-out basis.

(i) Miscellaneous. Many other types of products may be classified as inventory for financial reporting purposes. Examples include by-products (secondary products that result from the manufacturing process, particularly in the chemicals and the oil and gas industries), reusable items (such as beverage containers), and extractive products.

20.4 DETERMINING PHYSICAL QUANTITIES

(a) INTRODUCTION. An important aspect of inventory accounting is to establish quantities. This section discusses the two basic methods used to determine the quantities of goods on hand, the periodic system and the perpetual system. In practice, hybrid methods often are used. Also, a company may use a periodic system for certain types of inventories and a perpetual system for others. For example, a steel company may use a perpetual system for work in process and for finished steel products but a periodic system for raw, bulk commodities such as iron ore.

A periodic system employs physical counts to determine physical quantities on hand. A perpetual system maintains detailed records to track quantities based on additions and usage. A perpetual system provides greater internal accounting control because it allows the user to identify and investigate differences between actual quantities on hand and the amounts the records indicate. The additional record-keeping requirements of a perpetual system generally are justified by the additional control given over high-value and off-site inventories. Further, perpetual systems provide improved management information for individual products that can enhance sales, marketing, and operation decisions. The greater availability and variety of automated systems have led to a proliferation of perpetual inventory systems in recent years.

Companies may use less sophisticated methods to determine inventory quantities at interim dates, compared to those used in connection with the year-end inventory valuation.

(b) PERIODIC SYSTEM. The most direct means of determining the physical quantity of inventory on hand is to count it. An inventory system that establishes quantities on the basis of recurring counts is known as a *periodic system*. After establishing quantities on hand, each unit is multiplied by its unit cost to determine its inventory value. Cost of sales is a residual amount obtained by subtracting the ending inventory amount from the cost of goods available for sale:

Beginning Inventory
+ Purchases and Costs of Production

Goods Available for Sale
− Ending Inventory

Cost of Sales

A periodic system is most likely to be used by a small company or for a department with low-value items that do not warrant more elaborate control procedures. A periodic system also is used for inventories for which reliable usage data cannot practicably be generated (e.g., certain supplies and extractive materials).

(i) Physical Count Procedures. Written instructions that describe the procedures to be performed by the individuals participating in the count are an important part of the effort and should be prepared and distributed well in advance of the physical inventory date.

The instructions should cover each phase of the procedures and address these 11 matters:

1. Names of persons drafting and approving the instructions
2. Dates and times of inventory taking
3. Names of persons responsible for supervising inventory taking

4. Plans for arranging and segregating inventory, including precautions taken to clear work in process to cutoff points

5. Provisions for control of receiving and shipping during the inventory-taking period and, if production is not shut down, the plans for handling inventory movements

6. Instructions for recording the description of inventory items and how quantities are to be determined (e.g., count, weight, or other measurement)

7. Instructions for identifying obsolete, damaged, and slow-moving items

8. Instructions for the use of inventory tags or count sheets (including their distribution, collection, and control)

9. Plans for determining quantities at outside locations

10. Instructions for review and approval of inventory by department heads or other supervisory personnel

11. Method for transcribing original counts to the final inventory sheets or summaries

Physical inventory count teams should be familiar with the inventory items. The counts should be checked, or recounts should be performed, by persons other than those making the original counts.

(ii) Cutoff.   The process to ensure that transactions are recorded in the proper accounting period is known as *cutoff*. For inventory, the general rule is that all items owned by the entity as of the inventory date should be included, regardless of location. For goods in transit, if they are shipped free on board (fob) destination, ownership does not pass from the seller to the purchaser until the purchaser receives the goods from the common carrier. For goods shipped fob shipping point, title passes from the seller to the purchaser once the seller turns the goods over to the common carrier.

In practice, purchases are recorded upon receipt, based on the date indicated on the receiving report. Inventory generally is relieved for items sold as of the date of shipment. In this manner, the accounting entries to record the purchase and sale of inventory correspond to the physical movement of the goods at the company. Assuming an accurate physical count of goods on hand is achieved, companies effectively eliminate cutoff errors by verifying that purchases have been recorded in the period of receipt and sales have been recorded in the period of shipment. This usually is accomplished by matching accounts payable invoices to receiving reports, and matching sales invoices to shipping documents. The procedure described above guarantees that both sides of the accounting entry are recorded in the same period. The inventory amount is recorded through the physical count and valuation, whereas the accounts payable/cost of sales amount is recorded through the matching procedure. This method implies all purchases are fob destination and all sales are fob shipping point. Although this is unlikely to be the case, the approach works in practice because goods in transit are typically not significant, and the procedure is applied consistently. Companies that have a significant volume of goods in transit and varying terms regarding transfer of ownership should scrutinize the inventory cutoff calculations. For example, a fob destination sale that was in transit at period end would be recorded prematurely using the method described above. As a result, pretax income would be overstated by the gross margin on the sale, accounts receivable would be overstated, and inventory would be understated. Such a situation normally is considered more of a revenue recognition issue (discussed in Chapter 17) than an inventory issue. The effect of a similar situation for a purchase would merely affect the balance sheet, because there is no margin involved for the buyer. In situations where a strict legal determination of ownership is impractical or other cutoff questions arise, the terms of the sales agreement, the intent of the parties involved, industry practices, and other factors should be considered.

Achieving an accurate cutoff is enhanced by controlling the shipping, receiving, and transfer activity during the physical count. Also, source documents (e.g., receiving reports, shipping reports, bills of lading) pertaining to goods shipped and received around the inventory date must be reviewed closely to verify that transactions have been recorded in the proper period.

(c) PERPETUAL SYSTEM. Many businesses require frequent information regarding the quantity of goods on hand or the value of their inventory. A perpetual inventory system meets this need by maintaining records that detail the physical quantity and dollar amount of current inventory items. Technological advances such as scanners and low-cost computer applications have made automated perpetual inventory systems more practical and more popular. Their ease of use and their control over inventory quantities have enhanced the productivity of users. The records are updated constantly to reflect inventory additions and usage. Physical inventory counts are performed periodically to check the accuracy of the perpetual records. Discrepancies between the physical count and the quantities shown on the perpetual records should be investigated to determine the causes. Assuming an accurate physical count was achieved, the accounting records should be adjusted to reflect the results of the count. This entry is commonly referred to as the *book to physical adjustment*. The ability to isolate the book to physical adjustment is a perpetual system control feature not present in a periodic system.

(i) Record-Keeping Procedures. In a perpetual inventory system, detailed records are maintained on an ongoing basis for each inventory item. The inventory balance is increased as items are purchased or inventoriable costs are incurred, and the balance is reduced as items are sold or transferred. Cost of sales reflects actual costs relieved from inventory. The level of sophistication of the records can vary dramatically, from manual entries posted directly to the general ledger to refined automated systems that use standard costs and detailed subsidiary records.

Cycle counting may be used with a perpetual inventory system to supplement other control procedures and to spread the physical counting effort throughout a period. A cycle count involves physically counting a portion of the inventory and comparing the quantity to that indicated by the perpetual records. Cycle counts test the reliability of the perpetual records. In connection with the ABC method of inventory control, in which higher cost items receive a greater degree of continuous control than other items, cycle counts are performed more frequently for high-cost items. Successful results from interim cycle counts can justify reliance on the perpetual records, and thereby eliminate the need to perform a companywide physical inventory at the fiscal year-end date. This approach generally is recommended in situations where unusual book to physical adjustments have not been identified during the interim cycle counts.

(ii) Cutoff. The points made above about periodic inventory system cutoff are equally applicable to a perpetual system. In fact, the detailed record-keeping procedures regularly performed in a perpetual system generally make the period-end cutoff process less burdensome.

(d) PROCEDURES TO CONTROL INVENTORY QUANTITIES. Implementation of effective accounting procedures and internal accounting controls over inventory quantities can protect the company's investment and reduce costs. A key objective is that goods or services are purchased only with proper authorization. To achieve this objective, some or all of the following 10 control procedures may be helpful:

1. Approval by designated personnel within specified dollar limits is required for requisitions and purchase orders.
2. Receiving, accounts payable, and stores personnel are denied access to purchasing records (e.g., blank purchase orders).
3. Purchasing personnel are denied access to blank receiving reports and accounts payable vouchers.
4. Purchase orders are compared to a control list or a file of approved vendors.
5. Purchase orders are issued in prenumbered order; sequence is independently checked.
6. Records of returned goods are matched to vendor credit memos.
7. Goods are compared to purchase orders or other purchase authorization before acceptance.

8. Unmatched receivers are investigated; unauthorized items are identified for return to the vendor.

9. Receipts under blanket purchase orders are monitored; quantities exceeding the authorized total are returned to the vendor.

10. Management approves overhead expense budget; variances from budgeted expenditures are analyzed and explained.

Another control objective is to prevent or detect promptly the physical loss of inventory. The following 16 controls may help to achieve this objective:

1. Responsibility for inventories is assigned to designated storekeepers; written stores requisition or shipping order is required for all inventory issues.

2. Perpetual records are regularly checked by cycle count or complete physical count.

3. Where no perpetual records are maintained, quantities are determined regularly by physical count, costing, and comparison to the inventory accounts.

4. Inventory counts and record keeping are independent of storekeepers.

5. Written instructions are distributed for inventory counts; compliance is checked.

6. Formal policies exist for scrap gathering, measuring, recording, storing, and disposal/recycling; compliance is reviewed periodically.

7. Cost of scrap, waste, and defective products is regularly reviewed and standards are adjusted.

8. Inventory adjustments are documented and require management approval.

9. Complete production is reconciled to finished goods additions.

10. Guards and/or alarm system are used.

11. Employees are identified by badge, card, and so on.

12. Employees are bonded.

13. Storage areas are secured against unauthorized admission and protected against deterioration.

14. Off-site inventories are stored in bonded warehouses.

15. Materials leaving premises are checked for appropriate shipping documents.

16. Estimation methods are used for retail inventories.

20.5 VALUATION METHODS

(a) COST. The cost principle that underlies today's financial accounting model holds that historical cost is the appropriate basis for recording and valuing assets. ARB No. 43 states:

> The primary basis of accounting for inventories is cost, which has been defined generally as the price paid or consideration given to acquire an asset. As applied to inventories, cost means in principle the sum of the applicable expenditures and charges directly or indirectly incurred in bringing an article to its existing condition and location.

Section 20.5(b) of this chapter deals with the write-down of inventory to amounts below cost by applying the lower of cost or market concept. In such circumstances, the reduced amount is considered cost for subsequent accounting periods.

ARS No. 13, "The Accounting Basis of Inventories," states that "inventories are to be priced at cost, excluding nonmanufacturing costs." Determining what costs are inventoriable is a matter of professional judgment based on the broad guidance in the authoritative literature referred to above. ARB No. 43 contains these additional comments pertaining to the determination of inventory costs:

- Selling expenses constitute no part of inventory costs.
- The exclusion of all overheads from inventory costs does not constitute an accepted accounting procedure.
- Items such as idle facility expense, excessive spoilage, double freight, and rehandling costs may be so abnormal as to require treatment as current period charges rather than as a portion of the inventory cost.
- General and administrative expenses should be included as period charges, except for the portion of such expenses that may be clearly related to production and thus constitute a part of inventory costs (product charges).

(i) Job-Order Costing. Products produced in individual units or batches, and requiring varying amounts of materials and labor (often to customer specifications) compared to other products, normally are costed using the job-order method. This technique is common in the furniture, printing, and robotics industries.

Costs of direct material and direct labor are assigned to specific jobs, based on actual usage. Usage information frequently is obtained from material requisition forms and labor time cards. Overhead typically is applied using a predetermined annual rate adjusted periodically to approximate actual costs.

(ii) Process Costing. Products produced in large quantities are normally costed using an averaging method called *process costing*. Companies in the textile, chemical, mining, and glass industries typically use process costing. Production runs are costed based on standard costs, which are the costs expected under efficient operating conditions. The total of all standard costs reported during each period is compared to actual costs incurred, based on general ledger account totals used to capture each cost category. Variances between standard costs and actual costs are analyzed and may be included in inventories or charged to expense, depending on the cause of the variance. No attempt is made to match costs of specific materials and labor to inventory units, because doing so would be highly impractical. A standard cost system can be effective in a process costing environment because of the relative predictability of unit costs. Standard costs can be developed based on each product's bill of materials and engineering specifications.

(iii) Direct Material Component. Materials contained in and traceable to a finished product are designated as direct materials. Because direct materials are a physical component of inventory items, and their cost is based on invoices from vendors, accounting for direct material costs is not difficult as long as quantities are tracked accurately. Freight and other costs of receiving materials also are inventoriable. Generally, freight-in is included as a portion of direct material, whereas receiving costs are included in the overhead pool. Paton & Paton indicate the cost of materials should be recorded net of related purchase discounts under the theory that income is not generated as a result of acquiring goods or services.[1]

For operational purposes, material price variances and usage variances are identified to highlight deviations from standard amounts. Use of the lower of cost or market criteria (described in Section 20.5(b) of this chapter) determines whether unfavorable variances or other factors such as spoilage require a write-down of the carrying amount for financial accounting purposes.

(iv) Direct Labor Component. Payroll and employee benefits costs of employees incurred in the technical operations of converting raw materials to finished product are considered direct labor. It is more difficult to associate labor costs directly with inventory than to associate material costs in that way. Labor reporting systems are often the most cumbersome part of collecting inventory costs. Labor price variances and labor efficiency variances are identified to highlight the reasons for deviations from standard costs.

---

[1] The safe harbor rule protects issuers from liability for forward-looking information, if such information has a reasonable basis and is disclosed in good faith. Otherwise, fraud actions under Rule 10b-5 may be brought against the firm.

(v) Overhead Component.   Overhead, often referred to as *factory overhead* or *indirect manufacturing costs*, consists of all costs—other than direct material and direct labor—directly related to and adding value to the manufacturing process.

ARB No. 43 states that general and administrative costs can be included in inventories only if they are clearly related to production and that selling expenses should never be included in the inventory. In addition, amounts of wasted materials (spoilage) regardless of whether it is normal or abnormal should be treated as a current period charge. For many companies, determining which costs are appropriate inventoriable costs under these criteria may be difficult. Costs typically included in the overhead pool are:

- Indirect labor and employee benefits (e.g., factory supervision and maintenance).
- Financial statement depreciation related specifically to assets utilized in the manufacturing process is an appropriate inventory cost. (Excess tax depreciation should not be included in inventory cost for financial reporting purposes.)
- Receiving department.
- Insurance costs, such as production workers' compensation and the cost of insuring the manufacturing facilities, are inventoriable. Costs related to product liability coverage and claims should not be included in inventory costs because they are related to goods that have already been sold, not those currently being produced or in inventory.
- Factory utilities.
- Other plant maintenance and repairs.

Other less obvious costs appropriate to charge to the overhead pool include (ARB No. 43 as amended by Statement of Financial Accounting Standards (SFAS) No. 151):

- Current service cost of pensions for production personnel are inventoriable. Prior service cost for production personnel may also be allocated to inventory.
- Costs of warehousing and handling finished goods may be inventoriable for financial reporting purposes if the warehousing and handling is an integral aspect of bringing the goods to a salable condition (e.g., goods received in bulk at a warehouse that must be repackaged for final sale). In some situations, warehousing and handling costs are considered costs of disposal and are not inventoriable for financial reporting purposes.
- Personnel department costs to the extent they relate to such activities as hiring and administering benefits of production personnel.
- Purchasing department costs are inventoriable to the extent they relate to the acquisition of raw materials or production supplies by manufacturers or the acquisition of goods for resale by wholesalers or retailers.
- Information systems processing costs that are specifically related to a manufacturing or cost accounting system may be included in inventory costs for financial reporting purposes. Data processing costs related to a general ledger or other financial accounting system should not be included in inventory costs.
- Legal costs incurred for labor relations or workers' compensation issues are allocable to inventory for financial reporting purposes. Costs incurred in product liability matters should not be included in inventory costs.
- Officers' salaries are inventoriable to the extent the officers' responsibilities are directly related to the production process (e.g., vice president of production or purchasing). The salary of a general officer, such as the chief operating officer, normally would not be inventoriable even though he has certain indirect responsibilities related to manufacturing operations.

SFAS No. 151 specifies that fixed overhead should be allocated to inventories based on the normal capacity of the productive facility.

Evaluating and documenting costs that may be capitalized as part of overhead cost requires judgment based on consideration of a number of factors, including a company's organizational structure and the nature of its accounting records. For example, a company that is highly decentralized may have all of its direct production costs segregated at its manufacturing facilities. The personnel, purchasing, and accounting functions related to manufacturing may all be located at the facility and their costs clearly identified. On the other hand, a highly centralized company may have all its personnel, purchasing, and accounting functions in a central location supporting sales and corporate functions as well as manufacturing. In this case, it is more difficult to establish and document a direct relationship to the production process. However, documenting a direct relationship is necessary to support including those costs in inventory under generally accepted accounting principles.

As described above, certain costs, such as selling expenses, abnormal costs, and a defined portion of general and administrative costs, are to be excluded from inventory and charged to operations as incurred. ARS No. 13 suggests relevant costs to be allocated to the overhead pool should be determined by considering a "cause-effect" relationship. "Causes are actions taken to manufacture products or to maintain the facilities and organization to manufacture products. The effects are the costs." The Research Study indicates that in conventional practice all costs associated with the selling function generally are treated as expenses of the period in which incurred, as are costs of general administration (excluding factory administration), finance, and general research. "Accounting for Research and Development Costs," FASB Statement No. 2, requires that all research and development costs encompassed by the Statement be charged to expense when incurred. FASB Statement No. 86, "Accounting for the Costs of Computer Software to Be Sold, Leased, or Otherwise Marketed," requires that all costs incurred to establish the technological feasibility of a computer software product be charged to expense as research and development. Once technological feasibility is established, software production costs are capitalized and amortized on a product-by-product basis. Capitalization of computer software costs ends when the product is available for general release to customers. Costs related to maintenance and customer support are expensed as incurred or when the related revenue is recognized, whichever occurs first. Costs incurred to duplicate the software, documentation, and training materials and to physically package the product for distribution are capitalized as inventory.

Selling costs are appropriately charged to expense as incurred, because such costs typically cannot be identified with individual sales and relate to goods previously sold rather than to inventory on hand. The question of deferring certain selling and marketing costs that relate to transactions not yet recognized for accounting purposes (i.e., in order to record the expense in the same period as the related revenue) is controversial and beyond the scope of this chapter. Nevertheless, if such costs are deferred, they should not be included with or classified as inventory. Numerous other types of costs raise questions about whether they should be included in the overhead pool or treated as a period cost. These costs include purchasing and other costs of ordering, quality control, warehousing, cost accounting, and carrying costs such as interest and insurance (on the inventory items and on the warehouse). The decision to include a cost in the overhead pool requires considerable judgment. In addition to using the "cause-effect" approach described earlier, challenging whether the cost adds value to the product is often useful. Observation of current practice indicates all of the above items except interest are included in the overhead pool by some companies and excluded by others. The FASB Statement No. 34, "Capitalization of Interest Cost," states, "Interest cost shall not be capitalized for inventories that are routinely manufactured or otherwise produced in large quantities on a repetitive basis because in the Board's judgment, the informational benefit does not justify the cost of so doing."

Including judgmental-type costs in inventory increases current assets and shareholders' equity. The effect on income of a particular period can be in either direction, depending on the relative inventory balances at the beginning and end of the period. However, for a growing company, a broadly defined overhead pool generally serves to increase income reported each period.

(vi) Overhead Allocation. Because indirect production costs cannot be directly associated with a particular inventory unit, the costs are generally assigned to various units by using allocation methods. There are several means of allocating overhead costs to inventory and cost of sales.

The traditional method has been to develop an overhead rate based on overhead cost per direct labor hour or direct labor dollar. This method allocates overhead to inventory and cost of sales in proportion to the amount of labor used. Other allocation bases may be more logical in certain circumstances. For instance, use of machine-hours may be a preferable method of overhead allocation for highly automated processes. Recording overhead costs by function and department can significantly improve the cost allocation process. Logical statistical methods can be established to allocate indirect costs. Such refinements can produce more meaningful results than use of a single plant-wide overhead rate. Increased accuracy and control results from using more specific and relevant overhead allocation methods.

Possible methods of allocating indirect costs include:

Indirect Cost	*Allocation Basis*
Materials handling	Quantity or weight of materials
Occupancy (depreciation, rent, property taxes, etc.)	Square-footage occupied
Employment-related	Number of employees, labor hours, or labor dollars

The level of sophistication in allocating indirect costs and determining overhead absorption rates can profoundly affect the inventory valuation and such other important matters as product margins and pricing.

"Accounting Changes Related to the Cost of Inventory," FASB Interpretation No. 1, indicates a change in composition of the elements of cost included in inventory is an accounting change. Reporting of such changes should conform with Accounting Principles Board (APB) Opinion No. 20, "Accounting Changes." Preference should be based on an improvement in financial reporting, not on the basis of the income tax effect alone.

(b) LOWER OF COST OR MARKET.   Generally accepted accounting principles (GAAP) require reducing the carrying amount of inventory below cost whenever the selling price less cost of disposal of the goods is less than their cost. Impairment of inventory can occur through damage, obsolescence (technological changes or new fashions have reduced or eliminated customer interest in the product), deterioration, changes in price levels, excess quantities, and other causes. In Emerging Issues Task Force (EITF) Issue No. 00-14, "Accounting for Certain Sales Incentives," and EITF Issue No. 01-9, "Accounting for Consideration Given by a Vendor to a Customer or a Reseller of the Vendor's Products," the Task Force observed, "that the offer of a sales incentive that will result in a loss on the sale of a product may indicate an impairment of existing inventory under ARB No. 43." The lower-of-cost-or-market valuation method is designed to eliminate the deferral of unrecoverable costs and to recognize the reduction in the value of inventory when it occurs.

The guidelines for calculating the lower-of-cost-or-market adjustment, as defined in ARB No. 43, state:

As used in the phrase "lower of cost or market," the term "market" means current replacement cost (by purchase or by reproduction, as the case may be) except that:

1. Market should not exceed the net realizable value (i.e., estimated selling price in the ordinary course of business less reasonably predictable costs of completion and disposal); and
2. Market should not be less than net realizable value reduced by an allowance for an approximately normal profit margin.

Use of replacement cost as the starting point for the market valuation is intended to reflect the utility of the goods based on the cost required to produce equivalent goods currently. Replacement cost also is more practical than net realizable value for establishing a market value for raw materials and component parts because these items may not be sold separately or in their existing condition.

The ceiling of the market valuation described above is related to net realizable value to ensure that replacement cost valuation does not defer costs that will not be recovered by the ultimate selling price. For example, an inventory item with a net realizable value of $10 would not be carried above that amount even if its replacement cost exceeded $10. The floor of the market valuation is intended to eliminate any write-off of costs that will be recovered from the customer even though the replacement cost of the inventory is lower. For example, an item with a normal profit margin of 20 percent to be sold to a customer for $10 would not be carried at less than $8 even if its replacement cost was less than $8.

The lower-of-cost-or-market adjustment may be recorded for each inventory item or may be aggregated for the total inventory or for major inventory categories. The choice depends on the nature of the inventory and should be the one that most clearly reflects periodic income. Once selected, the same method should be applied consistently. Any comparisons of aggregate cost and market offset unrealized gains on certain inventory items against expected losses on other items (if such loss items exist) and, therefore, reduce the amount of the inventory write-down compared to the amount calculated on an item-by-item basis. Notwithstanding the principle of conservatism, the aggregate approach may be preferable when there is only one type of inventory or when no loss is expected on the sale of all goods because price declines of certain components are offset by adequate margins on other components. Similarly, the lower-of-cost-or-market procedure should be applied on an individual item basis for unrelated items and for inventories that cannot practically be classified into categories. Profitable margins on one product line should not be used to eliminate a lower-of-cost-or-market write-down for other unrelated products. ARB No. 43 specifically requires use of the item-by-item method of applying the lower of cost or market principle to excess inventory stock (quantity of goods on hand exceeds customer demand).

ARB No. 43 also states that "if a business is expected to lose money for a sustained period, the inventory should not be written down to offset a loss inherent in the subsequent operations."

Controls that can provide reasonable assurance that obsolete, slow-moving, or overstock inventory is prevented or promptly detected and provided for include:

- Perpetual records show date of last usage; stock levels and usability are regularly reviewed.
- Physical storage methods are regularly reviewed for sources of inventory deterioration.
- Purchase requisitions are compared to preestablished reorder points and economic order quantities.
- Potential overstock is identified by regularly comparing quantities on hand with historical usage.
- Production and existing stock levels are related to forecasts of market and technological changes.
- Bill of materials and part number systems provide for identification of common parts and subassemblies; discontinued products are reviewed for reusable components.
- Work in process is periodically reviewed for old items.

Regular preparation and review of product line income statements can identify products that are losing money and may warrant a lower of cost or market write-down. Another procedure to highlight potential lower of cost or market concerns is to compare product carrying amounts to selling prices. A company can minimize lower of cost or market adjustments at year end by periodically comparing the carrying value of inventory items to net realizable value and adjusting to the lower figure.

The Task Force reached a consensus on EITF Issue No. 86-13, "Recognition of Inventory Market Declines at Interim Reporting Dates," that inventory should be written down to the lower of cost or market at an interim date unless:

- Substantial evidence exists that market prices will recover before the inventory is sold.
- In the case of last-in, first-out (LIFO) inventories, inventory levels will be restored by year end.
- The decline is due to seasonal price fluctuations.

In SAB Topic No. 100, "Restructuring and Impairment Charges" (Topic 5-BB), the Securities and Exchange Commission (SEC) staff expressed its view, based on footnote 2 of ARB No. 43, that a write-down of inventory to the lower-of-cost-or-market at the close of a fiscal period creates a new cost basis that subsequently cannot be marked up based on changes in underlying facts and circumstances.

A SEC staff announcement (EITF Issue No. 96-9, "Classification of Inventory Markdowns and Other Costs Associated with a Restructuring") on the income statement classification of inventory markdowns associated with a restructuring indicated that the SEC staff recognizes that there may be circumstances in which it can be asserted that inventory markdowns are costs directly attributable to a decision to exit or restructure an activity. However, the staff believes that it is difficult to distinguish inventory markdowns attributable to a decision to exit or restructure an activity from inventory markdowns attributable to external factors that are independent of a decision to exit or restructure an activity. Further, the staff believes that decisions about the timing, method, and pricing of dispositions of inventory generally are considered to be normal, recurring activities integral to the management of the ongoing business. Accordingly, the SEC staff believes that inventory markdowns should be classified in the income statement as a component of cost of goods sold.

(i) LIFO Considerations. In 1984, the Accounting Standards Executive Committee (AcSEC) of the American Institute of Certified Public Accountants (AICPA), in Section 6 of an issues paper, "Identification and Discussion of Certain Financial Accounting and Reporting Issues Concerning LIFO Inventories" (the AICPA Issues Paper), indicated that companies may apply the lower-of-cost-or-market provisions of ARB No. 43 to LIFO inventories on the basis of "reasonable groupings of inventory items." Further, it stated that in general a pool constitutes a reasonable grouping. Section 6 of the AICPA Issues Paper also indicates companies with more than one pool may aggregate pools for purposes of lower-of-cost-or-market determinations if the compositions of the pools are similar. The AICPA Issues Paper emphasizes the importance of "the character and composition" of the inventory in making lower-of-cost-or-market determinations. The Task Force also added the following caution: If the compositions of the pool are significantly dissimilar, they should not be aggregated.

The AICPA Issues Paper includes a discussion of the treatment of obsolete or discontinued products within the lower-of-cost-or-market review. The Task Force and AcSEC did not agree on this issue. AcSEC believes the item-by-item approach should be used for identified product obsolescence and product discontinuance, while the Task Force believes either the item-by-item approach or the aggregate-by-pool approach is appropriate. Because there was disagreement between the Task Force and AcSEC, companies can use either the item-by-item approach or the aggregate-by-pool approach for identified product obsolescence and product discontinuance. However, whatever approach used should be applied consistently.

(c) RETAIL METHOD. The retail method offers a simplified, cost-effective alternative of inventory valuation for department stores and other retailers selling many and varied goods. By using estimates of inventory cost based on the ratio of cost to selling price, it generally eliminates the procedure of referring to invoice cost to value each item. This ratio is often referred to as the *cost ratio* or *cost complement*. To avoid distortions arising from differing product mix and margins, a separate calculation is generally performed for each department. This step produces more accurate departmental costs and operating results. Also, because the types of products that constitute the inventory on hand at the balance sheet date may differ significantly from the proportion in which goods were purchased during the period, use of departmental cost ratios reduces the likelihood that these differences will improperly affect the inventory valuation.

Definitions of certain key terms used in the retail industry and important to the retail inventory method are:

- *Original retail*. The price at which merchandise is first offered for sale
- *Markon*. The difference between the retail price and the cost of merchandise sold or in inventory

- *Markup*. An addition to the original retail price
- *Markdown*. A reduction of original retail price
- *Markup cancellation*. A reduction in marked-up merchandise that does not reduce retail price below the original retail price
- *Markdown cancellation*. An addition to marked-down merchandise that does not raise retail price above the original retail price

Physical inventory counts (e.g., for year-end inventory taking) are initially priced at retail value (i.e., selling prices) and converted to cost using the cost ratio. The retail method also allows for periodic determination of inventory and cost of sales without the need for a physical count by means of a calculation similar to that shown in Exhibit 20.1. Retailers regularly use this type of calculation to value inventory at interim periods.

To perform the retail inventory calculations in a manner similar to that shown in Exhibit 20.1, a record of the cost and the retail value of the beginning inventory and of the current period purchases is kept (often referred to as the *stock ledger*). Net markups (markups less markup cancellations) are added to these amounts to determine the total goods available for sale on both the cost and retail bases. The cost ratio or cost complement calculated by dividing total cost of purchases by total selling price is used to reduce inventory at retail to cost. The markon percentage can be

	Department A Traditional Sleepwear		Department E Cosmetics	
	Cost	Retail	Cost	Retail
Beginning inventory—1/31/X2	$200,000	$ 400,000	$170,000	$ 285,000
Purchases[a]	450,000	865,000	575,000	950,000
Markups	—	5,500	—	3,500
Markup cancellations	—	(500)	—	(1,000)
Total available	650,000	1,270,000	745,000	1,237,500
Cost complement		51.18%		60.20%
Markon		48.82%		39.80%
Sales		(720,000)		(918,000)
Employee discounts		(7,500)		(5,500)
Shrinkage		(11,500)		(14,900)
Markdowns		(78,000)		(1,100)
Markdown cancellations		1,000		—
Promotional markdowns		(10,000)		—
		(826,000)		(939,500)
Ending inventory—1/31/X3				
at retail		$ 444,000		$ 298,000
at lower of cost or market	$227,239	51.18%	$179,396	60.20%

[a]The *National Retail Merchants Association Accounting Manual* states that, for department stores, markon is based on the delivered cost of merchandise and original selling price, adjusted for errors in pricing and additional markups. Markdowns and markdown cancellations do not enter into the calculation of the cost complement. Most accounting references suggest that cash purchase discounts should not be credited to purchases but should be separately accounted for, and a pro rata share of discounts should be netted against the closing inventory. As a practical matter, many retailers either run cash purchase discounts through the purchase journal or record purchases net of discount.

Exhibit 20.1   Example of retail inventory calculation. (*Source*: Wilson and Christensen, *LIFO for Retailers*, 1985.)

obtained by subtracting the cost ratio from 100 percent. The ending inventory at retail is obtained by subtracting current period sales, net markdowns (markdowns less markdown cancellations), and other reductions from the total goods available for sale on the retail basis. Finally, the ending inventory at retail is multiplied by the cost ratio to obtain the ending inventory at cost.

Note that the calculation in the exhibit excludes net markdowns from the computation of the cost ratio. Markdowns are deducted from the retail amount after the cost ratio is computed. This method values the ending inventory at an estimate of the lower-of-cost-or-market. ARB No. 43 acknowledges that this method is acceptable provided adequate markdowns are currently taken.

In contrast, the retail method is considered to approximate average costs if the calculation includes net markdowns in the computation of the cost ratio. This inclusion reduces the cost ratio denominator and thereby increases the ending inventory figure compared to the lower-of-cost-or-market methodology. To illustrate, the following calculations use the figures for Department A in the exhibit to compute the retail method variation that approximates average costs:

	Cost	*Retail*
Beginning inventory	$200,000	$ 400,000
Purchases	450,000	865,000
Markups		5,500
Markup cancellations		(500)
Markdowns		(78,000)
Markdown cancellations		1,000
Total available	650,000	1,193,000
Cost complement		54.48%
Sales		(720,000)
Employee discounts		(7,500)
Shrinkage		(11,500)
Promotional markdowns		(10,000)
		(749,000)
Ending inventory		
at retail		$ 444,000
at average cost	$241,891	54.48%

The retail LIFO valuation method is discussed in Section 20.6(c).

(d) ABOVE COST. In certain cases, inventory items possess such widely accepted value and immediate marketability that an exception is made to the normal requirement that an exchange (e.g., sale) must occur for income to be recognized. Examples of inventories often valued above cost (i.e., at sales price less costs of disposal) include precious metals, farm products, minerals, and certain other commodities. It has become standard practice in these industries to value inventories based on selling prices rather than on cost. This is a practical solution to the difficulty of determining product cost for goods that are obtained from the ground rather than from manufacture.

Financial Reporting Example

American Barrick Resources Corporation

Notes to Consolidated Financial Statements

(c) Inventories

Gold bullion inventory is valued at net realizable value.

ARB No. 43 indicates that to be valued above cost, inventory items must meet three criteria:

1. Inability to determine appropriate approximate costs
2. Immediate marketability at quoted market price
3. Unit interchangeability

Note that when inventory valuations are based on selling price, holding gains are recognized when the selling price increases and holding losses are recorded when the selling price decreases. When inventories are stated above cost, disclosure of this policy should be made in the financial statements.

Companies often hedge their exposure to commodity price fluctuations by entering into futures contracts or forward contracts. Theoretically, any gain or loss in the market value of the hedged item is directly offset by a change in the market value of the futures or forward contract. FASB Statement No. 133, "Accounting for Derivative Instruments and Hedging Activities," governs the accounting for hedge transactions and amended ARB 43, Chapter 4 (par. 526 of Statement No. 133) to require:

> If inventory has been the hedged item in a fair value hedge, the inventory's "cost" basis used in the cost-or-market-whichever-is-lower accounting shall reflect the effect of the adjustments of its carrying amount made pursuant to paragraph 22(b) of FASB Statement No. 133, "Accounting for Derivative Instruments and Hedging Activities."

Statement No. 133 requires all derivative financial instruments to be carried at fair value. If the derivative qualifies for accounting as a hedge of the fair value of inventory, then the changes in the fair value of the derivative are recorded in current earnings. In addition, changes in the fair value of the inventory that occur during the period it is hedged are also recognized in income by adjusting the inventory's carrying amount. If the derivative does not qualify as a hedge of the fair value of the inventory, changes in the fair value of the derivative would be recorded in current earnings, while the carrying amount of the inventory would not be adjusted to reflect the change in its fair value.

(e) REPLACEMENT COST. As described above, replacement cost is the starting point for determining market value under the lower of cost or market valuation method. Replacement cost also is the primary method of valuing repossessed goods.

(f) NET REALIZABLE VALUE. Certain inventory items for which cost or replacement cost is not determinable or is inappropriate for valuation purposes are valued at net realizable value, defined as estimated selling price in the ordinary course of business less reasonably predictable costs of completion and disposal. Scrap, by-products, and trade-in inventory are regularly valued at net realizable value.

FINANCIAL REPORTING EXAMPLE

AILEEN, INC.

Notes to Financial Statements

Obsolete inventory items are carried at net realizable value.

(g) GROSS MARGIN METHOD. A frequently used technique to estimate the inventory balance without performing a physical count is the gross margin method. Although the gross margin method generally is not acceptable as the inventory valuation method for financial reporting purposes because of its reliance on estimated rather than actual cost information, it is useful for a variety of purposes, including these four:

1. *Estimating the Inventory Balance at Regular Interim Periods.* This might be required to calculate operating results and to calculate borrowing limits on loans collateralized by inventory. Companies with complicated manufacturing operations may not be able to take a complete physical inventory every quarter and, therefore, might require an estimating technique such as the gross margin method.

2. *Preparing Budget Information.* Budgets usually are centered on sales forecasts. The gross margin method is useful to estimate the cost of goods sold and inventory amounts based on the sales forecast.

3. *Estimating the Value of Inventory Destroyed by a Casualty, Such as a Fire.* Such calculations may be required to support insurance claims related to the loss.

4. *Checking the Reasonableness of an Inventory Balance Determined Using a More Sophisticated Valuation Method.*

This method assumes that the gross margin percentage can be predicted with reasonable accuracy, based on results of prior periods or other calculations. This example demonstrates the estimation of an inventory balance using the gross margin method:

Cost of Goods Sold	
Sales	$100,000
× Gross margin percentage	× 25%
Gross margin	$ 25,000
Sales	$100,000
Less: Gross margin	(25,000)
Cost of goods sold	$ 75,000
Ending inventory	
Beginning inventory	$300,000
Purchases	80,000
Cost of goods available for sale	380,000
Less: Cost of goods sold	(75,000)
Ending inventory	$305,000

"Interim Financial Reporting," APB Opinion No. 28, recognizes that some companies use the gross margin method to estimate inventory and cost of goods sold for interim reporting purposes (e.g., quarterly reporting to the SEC). Such companies must disclose that this method is used and disclose any significant adjustments that result from reconciliations with the annual physical inventory.

FINANCIAL REPORTING EXAMPLE

XYZ CORPORATION AND SUBSIDIARIES

Notes to Condensed Consolidated Financial Statements (Unaudited)

Inventories

Substantially all inventories are valued using the LIFO method, which results in a better matching of current costs with current revenues. During interim periods, the valuation of inventories at LIFO and the resulting cost of sales must be based on various assumptions, including projected year-end inventory levels, anticipated gross margin percentages, and estimated inflation rates. Changes in economic events that are not presently determinable may lead to changes in the assumptions upon which the interim LIFO inventory valuation was made, which in turn could significantly affect the results of future interim quarters.

(h) IN CONNECTION WITH A PURCHASE BUSINESS COMBINATION. The following three general guidelines for assigning amounts to inventories acquired in a purchase business combination are contained in FASB Statement No. 141, "Business Combinations":

1. Finished goods and merchandise are valued at estimated selling prices less the sum of (a) costs of disposal and (b) a reasonable profit allowance for the selling effort of the acquiring enterprise.

2. Work in process is valued at estimated selling prices of finished goods less the sum of (a) costs to complete, (b) costs of disposal, and (c) a reasonable profit allowance for the completing and selling effort of the acquiring enterprise, based on profit for similar finished goods.

3. Raw materials are valued at current replacement costs.

Some business combinations accounted for as purchases are nontaxable. In those circumstances, if the acquired company accounted for inventories using the LIFO method and the acquiring company continues that LIFO election, the amounts reported as LIFO inventories for financial statement and for tax purposes will likely differ in the year of combination and in subsequent years.

FINANCIAL REPORTING EXAMPLE

LML CORPORATION

Notes to Consolidated Financial Statements

The book basis of LIFO inventories exceeded the tax basis by approximately $1,026,000 at both January 31, 20X1 and 20X0, as a result of applying the provisions of FASB Statement No. 141 to an acquisition completed in a prior year.

Some business combinations accounted for as purchases are also taxable transactions. In those instances, the portion of the purchase price allocated to inventories for financial reporting purposes may differ from that allocated to inventories for tax purposes. For example, when a "bargain purchase" is made, Statement No. 141 requires current values to be assigned to all current assets and the "bargain purchase" credit to be used to reduce the amounts otherwise assigned to noncurrent assets (except marketable securities). For income tax purposes, on the other hand, the "bargain purchase" credit usually is allocated to most of the assets acquired, including inventory.

(i) CONTROL PROCEDURES TO HELP ACHIEVE A PROPER INVENTORY VALUATION. To record inventory amounts accurately and ensure costs are assigned to inventory in accordance with the stated valuation method, controls should be implemented. These control procedures can be effective:

- Cost accounting subsidiary records are balanced regularly to the general ledger control accounts.
- Standard unit costs are compared to actual material prices, quantities used, labor rates and hours, overhead expenses, and proper absorption rate.
- Variances, including overhead, are analyzed periodically and allocated to inventory and cost of sales; results are submitted to management for review.
- Written policies exist for inventory pricing; changes are appropriately documented, quantified as to effect, and approved prior to change.

To provide assurance that goods and services are recorded correctly as to account, amount, and period, a company may select control procedures such as these eight:

1. Goods are counted, inspected, and compared to packing slips before acceptance.
2. Receiving reports are issued by the receiving/inspection department in prenumbered order; sequence is checked independently or unused receivers are otherwise controlled.
3. Services received are acknowledged in writing by a responsible employee.
4. Receiving documentation, purchase order, and invoice are matched before the liability is recorded.
5. Invoice additions, extensions, and pricing are checked.
6. Unmatched receiving reports and invoices are investigated for inclusion in the estimated liability at the close of the period.
7. Account distribution is reviewed when recording the liability or when signing the check.
8. Vendor statements are regularly reconciled.

In addition to valuing inventory properly at periodic reporting dates, an important objective is that the usage and movement of inventory be recorded correctly by account, amount (quantities and dollars), and period. To achieve this objective, these seven controls should be considered:

1. Periodic comparisons of actual quantities to perpetual records are made for raw materials, purchased parts, work in process, subassemblies, and finished goods.
2. Documentation is issued in prenumbered order for receiving, stores requisitions, production orders, and shipping (including partial shipments); sequence is checked independently.
3. Shipments of finished goods are checked for appropriate shipping documents.
4. Shipping, billing, and inventory records are reconciled on a regular basis.
5. Records are maintained for inventory on consignment (in and out), held by vendors, or in outside warehouses; these records are reconciled to reports received from outsiders.
6. Inventory accounts are adjusted for results of periodic physical counts.
7. Inventory adjustments are documented and require approval.

20.6 FLOW OF COSTS

(a) INTRODUCTION.   For cost-based inventory valuation methods, it is necessary to select an assumption of the flow of costs to value the inventory and cost of sales systematically. The reason is that the unit cost of items typically varies over time, and a consistent method must be adopted for allocating costs to inventory and cost of sales. As items are accumulated in inventory at different costs, a basis must be established to determine the cost of each item sold. The cost flow does not always match the physical movement of the inventory goods. ARB No. 43 recognizes that several cost flow assumptions are acceptable and that the major objective in selecting a method is to reflect periodic income most clearly. This emphasis on operating results rather than on financial position is contrary to the current direction of the FASB, which has, more recently, emphasized the balance sheet over the income statement in its Concepts Statements and recent pronouncements. ARB No. 43 also states that in some cases it may be "desirable to apply one of the acceptable methods of determining cost to one portion of the inventory or components thereof and another of the acceptable methods to other portions of the inventory."

Goods flow in the world outside financial reporting. Though Barden refers to ". . . the observable flow of cost, . . ."[2] *costs* do not flow in the world outside financial reporting. In that world, a cost is a sacrifice, which is incurred at a moment in time. Once costs are incurred in the world outside financial reporting, that is the end of them. They pass into history; the costs are sunk; bygones are bygones. As Thomas says, "Historical costs don't change for the same reason Napoleon doesn't change: both are dead."[3] Costs flow only in the minds of accountants, and that is not observable. Selection of a cost flow assumption is merely selection of an inventory costing method. The use of cost flow assumptions prevents reporting on inventory from complying with the FASB's qualitative characteristic of representational faithfulness, which is not intended to include representations of states of accountants' minds.

---

[2] In 1975, Statement on Auditing Standards No. 8 (AU Section 550) was issued. The statement addressed the auditor's responsibility with respect to "Other Information in Documents Containing Audited Financial Statements" and stated that while the auditor is not obligated to perform any procedures to corroborate information outside of the financial statements (such as the MD&A), such information should be read to determine whether it is consistent with the financial statements.

[3] Although the 1989 Release emphasizes prospective analysis, the historical analysis of the 1980 Release is also required. The 1989 Release interprets, but does not supersede, the 1980 release. Therefore, by continuing to require a discussion of historical changes, as well as prospective events, the SEC underscores its belief that a better understanding of the causes of past performance is necessary for investors to assess the likelihood that the past is indicative of the future.

(b) FIRST-IN, FIRST-OUT. The First-In, First-Out (FIFO) method assumes that costs flow through operations chronologically. Cost of sales reflects older unit costs whereas inventory is valued at most recent costs. In periods of rising prices, first-in, first-out can result in holding gains (also known as *inventory profits*) because older costs are matched against current sales. The ARS No. 13 concludes "that FIFO is the most logical assumed flow of costs if specific identification is not practicable." This conclusion is based on the pattern of the physical flow of goods and the valuation of inventory as close to current cost as is reasonably possible under the historical cost basis of accounting. The FIFO method is also relatively simple to apply.

In practice, the FIFO method is applied by valuing inventory items at the most recent costs of acquisition or production. For example, assume a dealer made these purchases of Item A during the year:

Date	Quantity	Unit Cost
Jan. 6	1,000	$4.00
Aug. 12	3,000	5.00
Dec. 18	2,000	6.00

If 4,000 units of Item A were held in inventory at December 31, under the FIFO method they would be valued this way:

2,000 units @ $6.00 each = $12,000
2,000 units @ $5.00 each =   10,000
                           $22,000

Note that, unlike the LIFO method, the FIFO method produces the same results whether the periodic or the perpetual inventory system is used.

(c) LAST-IN, FIRST-OUT. Last-in, first-out (LIFO) is identified in ARB No. 43, Chapter 4, as one of the accepted methods of costing inventory and is widely used in practice. The LIFO method assumes the most recent unit costs are charged to operations. This values inventory at older costs. In periods of increasing prices, LIFO produces a higher cost of sales figure than FIFO or the average cost method and, accordingly, a lower income amount. Advocates of the LIFO method point out that in periods of continuous inflation, LIFO provides a better matching of costs and revenues than other cost flow assumptions because it matches current costs with current revenues in the income statement. Because proponents of LIFO believe that the income statement is more important to users of financial statements than the balance sheet, they give less weight to the counterargument that the LIFO method "understates" the inventory balances (in periods of rising costs) in relation to current costs. In addition, LIFO often improves the company's cash flow because it results in lower income taxes. This situation is attractive to companies seeking to reduce their income tax liability, and, as a result, many companies use the LIFO method for income tax purposes. The IRS regulations contain a "conformity requirement" that companies using LIFO for tax purposes must use LIFO for external financial reporting purposes, but it is acceptable for LIFO calculations to differ for book and tax purposes. Historically, IRS regulations have had a significant effect on LIFO techniques used for financial reporting purposes.

As mentioned previously, LIFO causes the inventory amount on the balance sheet to be carried at older costs. The theory supporting this method is that because a company needs certain levels of inventory to operate its business, carrying inventories at their initial cost is consistent with the historical cost principle. Under the LIFO concept, inventory levels are carried on the balance sheet at their original LIFO cost until they are decreased. Any increases (i.e., new layers) are added to the inventory balance at the current cost in the year of acquisition and are carried forward at that amount to subsequent periods. A liquidation (or decrement) of a LIFO layer occurs when the quantity of an inventory item or pool decreases. The liquidation causes older costs to be charged to operations, failing to achieve the LIFO objective of matching current costs and revenues. To summarize, as long as inventory quantities are maintained (i.e., not decreased), the older, generally low-cost layers are preserved. If inventory quantities decrease, older layers are liquidated and charged to operations, generally increasing earnings.

Principally because of the involved calculations related to inventory pools and layers, LIFO is more complex than other inventory valuation methods. As a result, LIFO may result in higher record-keeping costs and require more management attention and planning. Certain companies, particularly publicly held companies, may be concerned with investor reaction to the lower earnings reported under LIFO when prices are rising. The IRS rules that permit companies to make supplemental disclosures of FIFO earnings may help alleviate this concern.

There are two basic methods of determining LIFO cost: specific identification and dollar value (the latter method includes the double extension technique, the link-chain technique, the retail method, and other techniques discussed below).

(i) Specific Goods Method.   The specific goods (or specific identification) method is normally the simplest LIFO approach to apply and understand. Inventory quantities and costs are measured in terms of individual units. Each item or group of similar items is treated as a separate inventory pool (e.g., a specific grade of tobacco).

The advantage of the specific goods method is that it is easy to conceptualize because LIFO costs are associated with specific items in inventory. This method has been used most frequently by companies that have basic inventory items, such as steel or commodities, and deal with a relatively low volume of transactions.

There are disadvantages, however, in using the specific goods method, especially if the inventory has a wide variety of items or if items change frequently (e.g., for technological reasons). In such circumstances, the specific goods method might become complicated, may prove costly to administer, and may produce unwanted LIFO liquidations.

(ii) Dollar-Value Method.   The dollar-value method overcomes most of the disadvantages of the specific identification method. The distinguishing feature of the dollar-value LIFO method is that it measures inventory quantities in terms of fixed dollar equivalents (base-year costs), rather than quantities and prices of individual goods. Similar items of inventory are aggregated to form inventory pools. Changes in quantities and changes in product mix within a pool are ignored. Increases or decreases in each pool are identified and measured in terms of the total base-year cost of the inventory in the pool, rather than of the physical quantities of items.

One of the most important aspects of dollar-value LIFO is selecting the pools to be used in the computations. A careful assignment of inventory items to pools will avoid most of the limitations of the specific identification method noted above. Generally, the fewer the pools, the lower the likelihood of a liquidation and the lower the resulting taxable income. Fewer pools also minimize the administrative burden associated with accounting for LIFO inventories. The AICPA Issues Paper concludes that it is not feasible to formulate detailed guidance for selecting pools that could apply to all enterprises. It advises that the objective of LIFO inventory pooling is to group inventory items to match most recently incurred costs to current revenues, after considering the manner in which the company operates its business; establishing separate pools with the principal objective of facilitating inventory liquidations would not be considered acceptable. Items that comprise a similar or identical product sold by the enterprise should be included in the same pool. The existence of separate legal entities (e.g., subsidiaries), by itself, does not justify establishing separate LIFO pools for consolidated financial reporting purposes.

For tax purposes, LIFO is applied by individual corporations rather than consolidated groups. Each subsidiary must establish its own separate pools. If an affiliated group filing a consolidated income tax return has three subsidiaries in the same line of business, a single LIFO pool encompassing the operations of all three subsidiaries cannot be adopted for tax purposes even though one of the subsidiaries does central purchasing for all three. The IRS frequently challenges the nature and number of pools selected; both must be specified when a company applies to the IRS for an accounting change to the LIFO inventory method. Once a company has established the number of pools it will use in the year LIFO is adopted, changes can be made only with permission from the

IRS. A method of pooling is considered an accounting method for tax purposes. Therefore, any change in the method of poolings requires IRS approval.

The broadest definition of a pool is the natural business unit pool. This includes, in a single pool, all inventories, including raw materials, work in process, and finished goods. This method is only available to companies—generally manufacturers and processors—whose operations consist of a single product line, or more than one if they are related. The natural business unit pool is attractive to many companies because the use of a single pool simplifies the LIFO calculations and reduces the number of layer liquidations.

Companies that do not qualify for natural business unit pooling or that wish to elect LIFO for only a portion of their inventory may elect the multiple pool method. Each of the multiple pools should consist of "substantially similar" inventory items.

Various computational techniques are used to apply the dollar-value method—the double-extension link-chain, internal indexes, the retail LIFO method (a variation of the link-chain technique) and other simplified external index techniques. These techniques have the objective of determining the base-year cost of the current-year inventory. The double-extension technique converts current-year amounts directly to base-year costs. The link-chain technique achieves the objective indirectly by developing an index based on the current-year cost increases and multiplying that index by the prior-year cumulative index. The internal index technique uses a representative sample of the entire population (e.g., 70 percent of all items in the pool or a statistical sample) that are double-extended to convert current-year amounts to base-year costs. The retail LIFO method is a dollar-value method that uses base-year retail value instead of base-year cost to compute inventory changes. The simplified external index technique applies 100 percent of the external index (e.g., price indexes published by the Bureau of Labor Statistics [BLS] to the current-year cost).

(iii) Double-Extension Technique.   The double-extension technique extends ending inventory quantities twice—once at current-year costs (unit costs for the current period, determined using another method, typically FIFO) and once at base-year costs. This double extension procedure provides the current-year index (total current-year cost divided by total base-year cost).

To determine the net inventory change for the year, the ending inventory expressed in terms of base-year costs is compared to the beginning-of-the-year inventory expressed in terms of base-year costs. If the ending inventory at base-year costs exceeds the beginning inventory at base-year costs, a new LIFO layer has been created. The new layer is valued by applying the ratio of the ending inventory at current costs (using one of the approaches described later in this chapter) to the ending inventory at base-year costs. This ratio is generally referred to as *LIFO index*. If the ending inventory at base-year costs is less than beginning inventory at base-year costs, a LIFO liquidation has occurred. When a liquidation has occurred, decrements in base-year costs are deducted from the layers of earlier years beginning with the most recent prior year.

When an item enters the inventory for the first time, a company must either use its current cost or determine its base-year cost. Under IRS regulations, current cost must be used unless the company is able to reconstruct a base-year cost. The use of manufacturing specifications or other methods may allow a company to determine what the cost of a new item would have been in the base year. This effort may be worthwhile, because it may calculate a base-year cost that is lower than the current-year cost, most likely due to inflation in the cost of materials and labor. Use of a lower base-year cost in the LIFO calculations increases the current-year index and, thereby, lowers the inventory balance and pretax income. In other words, by reconstructing a base-year cost for new items, the impact of LIFO is normally maximized.

Companies that use the double-extension technique must retain indefinitely a record of base-year unit costs of all items in inventory at the beginning of the year in which LIFO was adopted, as well as any base-year unit costs developed for new items added in subsequent years. Exhibit 20.2 is an example of the LIFO double-extension technique.

The double-extension technique can prove cumbersome, particularly when the base year extends back a number of years. Changes in product specifications and manufacturing methods are common in many industrial companies. The link-chain method eliminates the burden of reconstructing

The following example illustrates the application of the double-extension technique of dollar-value LIFO for one pool. Assume that the company's opening inventory on January 1, 20X1 (the date LIFO is adopted), totaled $150,000. Ending inventory for the next three years follows:

Item	Quantities in Ending Inventory	Base-Year Cost		Current-Year Cost		Index
		Unit Cost	Amount	Unit Cost	Amount	
Year Ended December 31, 20X1						
A	8,000	$ 1.00	$ 8,000	$ 1.15	$ 9,200	
B	7,000	4.00	28,000	4.30	30,100	
C	10,000	7.00	70,000	7.60	76,000	
D	12,000	6.00	72,000	6.35	76,200	
			$178,000		$191,500	107.58
Year Ended December 31, 20X2						
A	12,000	$ 1.00	$ 12,000	$ 1.30	$ 15,600	
B	6,000	4.00	24,000	4.75	28,500	
C	7,000	7.00	49,000	8.15	57,050	
D	15,000	6.00	90,000	6.80	102,000	
E	7,000	9.00	63,000	10.30	72,100	
			$238,000		$275,250	115.65
Year Ended December 31, 20X3						
A	18,000	$ 1.00	$ 18,000	$ 1.50	$ 27,000	
D	17,000	6.00	102,000	7.50	127,500	
E	10,000	9.00	90,000	11.20	112,000	
F	5,000	8.00	40,000	9.75	48,750	
G	3,000	10.00	30,000	12.35	37,050	
			$280,000		$352,300	125.82

Computation of LIFO Cost

	Base-Year Cost	Index	LIFO Cost
December 31, 20X1			
January 1, 20X1, base	$150,000	100.00	$150,000
December 31, 20X1, increment	28,000	107.58	30,122
	$178,000		$180,122
December 31, 20X2			
January 1, 20X1, base	$150,000	100.00	$150,000
December 31, 20X1, increment	28,000	107.58	30,122
December 31, 20X2, increment	60,000	115.65	69,390
	$238,000		$249,512
December 31, 20X3			
January 1, 20X1, base	$150,000	100.00	$150,000
December 31, 20X1, increment	28,000	107.58	30,122
December 31, 20X2, increment	60,000	115.65	69,390
December 31, 20X3, increment	42,000	125.82	52,844
	$280,000		$302,356

Exhibit 20.2   Example of LIFO double-extension technique.

base-year costs and so is a more efficient means of computing LIFO cost. In determining a LIFO index, an IRS rule of thumb holds that at least 70 percent of the total value of the pool should be matched to the prior-year costs to achieve a representative sample. If a statistical, random sampling technique is used, fewer items may be matched to obtain acceptable results.

(iv) Link-Chain Technique. Under the link-chain technique, the ending inventory is double-extended at both current-year unit costs and prior-year unit costs. The respective extensions are then totaled, and the totals are used to compute a current-year index. This current-year index is multiplied by the prior-year cumulative LIFO index to obtain a current-year cumulative index. Total current-year costs are divided by the current-year cumulative index to determine base-year costs. If ending inventory stated at base-year cost exceeds beginning inventory stated at base-year cost, a new LIFO layer has been created. The new layer is valued by applying the applicable cumulative index (using one of the approaches described later in this chapter) to the increments stated at base-year cost. If ending inventory stated at base-year cost is less than beginning inventory stated at base-year cost, a LIFO liquidation has occurred. The double extension and link-chain techniques produce identical results in the year LIFO is adopted. In subsequent years, however, changes in inventory mix and differences in the way new inventory items are handled usually create at least minor differences.

When a liquidation has occurred, decrements in base-year costs are deducted from the layers of earlier years, beginning with the most recent prior year.

If new items are included in the calculation of an index under the link-chain method, a unit cost would be reconstructed using prior-year, rather than base-year, costs. The reason is that the link-chain current-year index attempts to measure inflation for the most recent year. Exhibit 20.3 is an example of the LIFO link-chain technique and compares the results obtained to those calculated using the double-extension technique in Exhibit 20.2.

(v) Retail LIFO Method. Like the retail inventory method described earlier, the retail LIFO method is used most frequently by department stores and other retailers that sell many and varied goods. In determining the ratio of cost to retail value for the year, the retail LIFO method differs from the conventional retail inventory method (which approximates the lower of average cost or market) in two basic respects: (1) the ratio is based on transactions during the year (beginning inventories are excluded, except in the year of adoption) and (2) net markdowns during the year (exclusive of promotional markdowns—1979 IRS ruling) are reflected in determining the sales value of inventory for purposes of calculating the ratio of cost to retail. Use of retail LIFO permits these companies to match most recent costs against current revenues and, as a result, values inventory at older costs. The retail method of LIFO is an adaption of the dollar-value LIFO method. However, the retail method differs from other applications of dollar-value LIFO because in recording inventory input and output, retail sales values are used rather than cost. Items in the closing inventory are initially priced at retail value (i.e., intended sales value), and the retail value of the closing inventory in each department is converted to cost by applying a factor reflecting the relationship of those values to cost.

Most retailers that adopt LIFO continue to maintain their books for internal merchandise management and accounting purposes at the lower of non-LIFO cost or market, following the retail method described earlier in this chapter. The internal records are converted to LIFO only for external financial reporting and tax purposes.

The retail LIFO method requires that retail selling prices be adjusted for markdowns to state inventories at approximate cost rather that at the lower-of-cost-or-market, as frequently followed under the non-LIFO retail method. To state the inventory at cost, the cost complement under the retail LIFO method includes the effects of markdowns. However, temporary or promotional markdowns are not included in the cost complement calculation, because the physical inventory would never reflect such markdowns (i.e., they are applied separately at the time of sale).

Department stores using the retail LIFO method are allowed to use price indexes published by the IRS based on information furnished by the Bureau of Labor Statistics (BLS) BLS to convert the

The following example, which uses the same inventory items and unit costs as in Exhibit 20.2, is intended to illustrate the link-chain technique and to compare the results with those achieved using the double-extension technique. Because this example involves only a few items, the entire inventory has been double-extended. A representative sample also may be used with the link-chain technique. As in the double-extension example, assume that the company's opening inventory on January 1, 20X1 (the date LIFO is adopted), totals $150,000.

Item	Quantities in Ending Inventory	Prior-Year Cost		Current-Year Cost		Index	
		Unit Cost	Amount	Unit Cost	Amount	Current Year	Cumulative
Year Ended December 31, 20X1							
A	8,000	$ 1.00	$ 8,000	$ 1.15	$ 9,200		
B	7,000	4.00	28,000	4.30	30,100		
C	10,000	7.00	70,000	7.60	76,000		
D	12,000	6.00	72,000	6.35	76,200		
			$178,000		$191,500	107.58	107.58
					÷107.58		
			Base-Year Cost		$178,000		
Year Ended December 31, 20X2							
A	12,000	$ 1.15	$ 13,800	$ 1.30	$ 15,600		
B	6,000	4.30	25,800	4.75	28,500		
C	7,000	7.60	53,200	8.15	57,050		
D	15,000	6.35	95,250	6.80	102,000		
E	7,000	9.60	67,200	10.30	72,100		
			$255,250		$275,250	107.84	116.01
					÷116.01		
			Base-Year Cost		$237,264		
Year Ended December 31, 20X3							
A	18,000	$ 1.30	$ 23,400	$ 1.50	$ 27,000		
D	17,000	6.80	115,600	7.50	127,500		
E	10,000	10.30	103,000	11.20	112,000		
F	5,000	9.15	45,750	9.75	48,750		
G	3,000	11.60	34,800	12.35	37,050		
			$322,550		$352,300	109.22	126.71
					÷126.71		
			Base-Year Cost		$278,036		

(Continues)

Exhibit 20.3   Example of LIFO link-chain technique.

current-year retail value of the closing inventory to base-year retail value. In addition, other retailers that maintain a reasonably full line of inventory that comprises a representative cross-section of the inventory included in the BLS departmental groupings may use the BLS retail price indexes. Retailers that do not meet these criteria must develop their own indexes from internally generated figures, unless they make an election to use "simplified" LIFO (under which indexes are based on government-published indexes). Because price indexes are a significant element of the LIFO retail computations, internally generated indexes must be constructed on a sound basis and appropriate records must be maintained for examination by the IRS.

In a retail LIFO calculation, the current year's inventory at base-year retail value is compared with the prior year's inventory at base-year retail value to determine if there is a current-year increment or decrement. A current-year increment at base-year retail value is converted to current-year

Computation of LIFO Cost

	Base-Year Cost	Index	LIFO Cost Using Link-Chain	LIFO Cost Using Double-Extension (From Exhibit 20.2)
December 31, 20X1				
January 1, 20X1, base	$150,000	100.00	$150,000	$150,000
December 31, 20X1, increment	28,000	107.58	30,122	30,122
	$178,000		$180,122	$180,122
December 31, 20X2				
January 1, 20X1, base	$150,000	100.00	$150,000	$150,000
December 31, 20X1, increment	28,000	107.58	30,122	30,122
December 31, 20X2, increment	59,264	116.01	68,752	69,390
	$237,264		$248,874	$249,512
December 31, 20X3				
January 1, 20X1, base	$150,000	100.00	$150,000	$150,000
December 31, 20X1, increment	28,000	107.58	30,122	30,122
December 31, 20X2, increment	59,264	116.01	68,752	69,390
December 31, 20X3, increment	40,772	126.71	51,662	52,844
	$278,036		$300,536	$302,356

Exhibit 20.3   *Continued.*

retail value by use of the BLS or other computed price index and then reduced to LIFO cost by using a factor reflecting the ratio of current-year cost to retail value for the year. The LIFO cost of the increment is added to the beginning-of-year LIFO inventory cost to arrive at the end-of-year LIFO inventory.

A current-year decrement is applied against the most recent LIFO layer(s) at base-year retail value. The decrement is converted to retail value applicable to those layers by use of the index associated with such layers. The retail value so determined is reduced to LIFO cost by the factor(s) reflecting the ratio of cost to retail associated with the particular layers being liquidated. The LIFO cost of the decrement is then subtracted from the beginning-of-year LIFO inventory to arrive at the end-of-year LIFO inventory. Exhibit 20.4 is an example of the retail LIFO computation.

(vi) Valuing the Current-Year Layer.   Regardless of the technique used to compute LIFO values, an approach to price any newly created current-year LIFO layer must be selected and used consistently.

1. *Latest acquisition cost.* This approach is attractive because it frequently is the easiest to apply. Many companies on LIFO maintain their internal inventory records on FIFO because of its simplicity and because it is a logical starting point for calculating LIFO. If the latest acquisition-cost approach is used, current-year unit costs are available from FIFO inventory valuation. A disadvantage of this approach is that it results in the highest value for the new layer (and, therefore, the highest taxable income) if costs have been consistently rising throughout the year. Another disadvantage is that the company must wait until after year end to compute current-year cost.

2. *Earliest acquisition costs.* In periods of steadily increasing prices, this approach prices new layers at lower costs than the other approaches do. The result is the lowest tax liability. Another advantage is that current-year unit costs may be computed in the early part of the year. The major disadvantage of this approach is that it may require additional effort, because it generally involves a separate calculation. The separate calculation usually requires

The example below illustrates the calculation of LIFO using the retail method. (Calculation of the indexes is not shown because those principles have been discussed previously in this section.) The example illustrates the calculation for one department for the first three years the company is on LIFO.

Step No.	Item or Computation	First Year	Second Year	Third Year
1	Purchases at cost	$1,400,000	$1,600,000	$1,800,000
2	Purchases at retail, including markups	$2,900,000	$3,400,000	$3,700,000
3	Less permanent markdowns applicable to purchases	(100,000)	(150,000)	(200,000)
4	Net purchases at retail	$2,800,000	$3,250,000	$3,500,000
5	Cost complement percentage (1 4 4)	50%	49.23%	51.43%
6	Ending inventory at retail	$ 800,000	$ 900,000	$ 950,000
7	Index (computed or BLS)	104.5	109.1	112.3
8	Inventory at base-year retail (6 4 7)	765,550	824,931	845,948
9	Base-year retail, previous year	(700,000)	(765,550)	(824,931)
10	Current-year increment at base-year retail (8 − 9)	65,550	59,381	21,017
11	Valuation of current-year increment (7 × 10)	68,500	64,785	23,602
12	Current-year increment at cost (11 × 5)	34,250	31,894	12,138
13	Prior LIFO basis inventory	$ 350,000	$ 384,250	$ 416,144
14	LIFO cost of inventory (12 + 13)	$ 384,250	$ 416,144	$ 428,282

*For purposes of this example, assume the cost complement percentage for the beginning inventory also was 50% (assumed opening inventory of $700,000 × 50% = $350,000).

If there had been a decrement or liquidation in any of the years, it would have been handled in the same manner as other LIFO methods (i.e., applied to most recent layer).

LIFO Reserve

In order to disclose the LIFO reserve(i.e., the difference between the inventory amount calculated using the retail method and the inventory amount calculated using the retail LIFO method), it is necessary to calculate the cost complement percentage as though the retailer used the retail method. As mentioned earlier, however, this usually is easily derived from the internal records, because most retailers on LIFO maintain their records on the retail method. The following illustrates this calculation for the above example:

	Cost	Retail	Retail Cost Complement
First Year			
Opening inventory	$ 350,000	$ 700,000	
Purchases including markups	1,400,000	2,900,000	
Goods available	$1,750,000	$3,600,000	48.61%
Second Year			
Opening inventory	$ 388,800	$ 800,000	
Purchases including markups	1,600,000	3,400,000	
Goods available	$1,988,800	$4,200,000	47.35%
Third Year			
Opening inventory	$ 426,150	$ 900,000	
Purchases including markups	1,800,000	3,700,000	
			Continues

Exhibit 20.4   Retail LIFO method.

The retail cost method complement percentage above (48.61% in the first year, e.g.) is lower than the LIFO cost complement percentage (50% in the first year) because the retail method is a lower-of-cost-or-market method. Conversely, the LIFO method is a cost method. The LIFO reserve disclosure should represent the difference between LIFO cost and the lower of current cost or market.

	First Year	Second Year	Third Year
Summary of LIFO Reserve			
Inventory at retail	$800,000	$900,000	$950,000
Cost complement percentage	48.61%	47.35%	48.39%
Inventory at retail method	388,880	426,150	459,705
Inventory at LIFO cost above	(384,250)	(416,144)	(428,282)
LIFO reserve	$ 4,630	$ 10,006	$ 31,423

Exhibit 20.4   *Continued.*

double-extending a sample of inventory items at earliest current-year costs to obtain the earliest acquisition-cost index.

3. *Average acquisition cost*. The results obtained from this approach represent a middle ground between the other two approaches. However, this approach may require even more involved calculations than the earliest acquisition approach.

In addition, any other method that in the opinion of the IRS clearly reflects income may be used to price current-year LIFO layers.

(vii) New Items.   The treatment of new items is one of the more controversial aspects involved in using LIFO. Important considerations in this area include what constitutes a new item and how the LIFO cost of new items should be determined.

Improper designation of items as new can significantly affect reported income if base-year costs are not reconstructed. The SEC expresses its concern in this area in Financial Reporting Release (FRR) 1 (Section 205) and again in Staff Accounting Bulletin No. 58, "Last-In, First-Out (LIFO) Inventory Accounting Practices for Financial Reporting Purposes" (SAB Topic 5.L), by stating "insignificant and sometimes arbitrary" differences are not sufficient justification for new product designation, particularly when it result in a significant increase in reported income.

Section 4-21 of the AICPA Issues Paper provides the following guidance for determining if an item should be classified as a new item for financial reporting purposes:

A *new item* is a raw material, product, or cost component not previously present in significant quantities in the inventory. To be considered a new item, the material or product should not be comminged physically with other materials or products so that its identity is lost, and it should be accounted for separately. In addition, the material should have qualities (physical, chemical, or both) significantly different from those previously inventories items. Items treated as fungible with items already in the pool ordinarily should not be considered *new items*. Changes in the market value of an item or merely purchasing a virtually identical item from a different supplier does not make the item a new item [emphasis added].

The AICPA Issues Paper concludes (Section 4-27) that for financial reporting purposes, if the double extension or an index technique is used, the base-year cost of the new item should be reconstructed and the base-year cost should be estimated if it is not otherwise objectively determinable. However, if the link-chain technique is used, the AICPA Issues Paper concludes that "reconstruction of prior years' costs is unnecessary because that technique produces approximately the same results as reconstruction." To avoid the problems generally encountered in reconstructing base-year costs, companies may consider using the link-chain method if they meet IRS requirements. Some companies that frequently add new items are not able to satisfy the IRS's stringent qualifications for the use of the link-chain method. And, reconstructing base-year costs using vendor quotes or price lists is not always practical. Consequently, these companies would have added new items at current-year costs for tax purposes. Although allowable for tax purposes, adding new items to inventory using current-year costs for financial reporting would conflict with the recommendation in the AICPA Issues Paper.

(viii) Other LIFO Matters.   In the year LIFO is adopted, any market write-downs or other valuation allowances must be restored so that the opening inventory is stated at cost. Also, because the prior year's ending inventory (presumably at FIFO or average cost) becomes the opening LIFO inventory, there is no adjustment for any cumulative effect of a change in accounting principle or disclosure of pro forma amounts for prior years. APB Opinion No. 20 cites the change in inventory pricing from FIFO to LIFO as an example of a change in accounting principle for which the cumulative effect adjustment and pro forma disclosures may be omitted.

In SAB Topic 5.L, the SEC staff endorsed the AICPA Issues Paper, saying it represents an accumulation of existing acceptable LIFO accounting practices, and companies and their auditors should refer to it for guidance. The AICPA Issues Paper recommends that all companies using LIFO follow these three LIFO-related disclosures required for SEC registrants:

1. The effect on net income of LIFO quantities liquidations
2. For companies that have not fully adopted LIFO, the extent to which LIFO is used (e.g., the portion of ending inventory priced at LIFO and the portion priced under other methods)
3. For LIFO inventories, the amount and basis for determining the excess of replacement or current cost over the stated LIFO value

The AICPA Issues Paper also provides practical implementation guidance on expanded supplemental non-LIFO disclosures (such as notes to the financial statements and other supplemental information that disclose the pro forma effects of using FIFO or some other acceptable inventory method) and the use of LIFO applications for financial reporting purposes that differ from the applications used for income tax purposes.

Practice Bulletin No. 2, "Elimination of Profits Resulting from Intercompany Transfers of LIFO Inventories," issued by the AcSEC of the AICPA, which also deals with LIFO, indicates intercompany profits arising from LIFO liquidations caused by transfers between or from LIFO pools within a reporting entity should be deferred until such profits are realized by the reporting entity through dispositions outside the consolidated group.

In Accounting Series Release (ASR) No. 293, the SEC indicated LIFO accounting has been unduly influenced by IRS rules, and the amended IRS regulations that allow companies to compute LIFO differently for financial reporting and tax purposes are viewed very positively by the Commission. In this manner, companies can select for financial reporting purposes LIFO techniques (from those described above) that best reflect the company's circumstances, rather than being forced to use IRS-mandated methods that dictate the income tax return calculations. The SEC also indicated its concern that supplemental income disclosures based on non-LIFO methods may be misleading. This concern is mitigated when these three additional disclosures are made:

1. Clearly state that the use of LIFO results in a better matching of costs and revenues.
2. State the reason supplemental income disclosures are provided.
3. Provide essential information about the supplemental income calculation to enable users to appreciate the quality of the information.

As a result of the SEC release, publicly held companies that disclose supplemental income information based on non-LIFO methods also regularly make the three additional disclosures recommended by the SEC.

Written policies and procedures for performing LIFO computations and determining LIFO pools can improve the quality and consistency of the results. Because of the complexity of the calculations, a thorough detailed review by someone other than the preparer is worthwhile.

The FASB staff announced, in EITF Topic No. D-31, "Temporary Differences Related to LIFO Inventory and Tax-to-Tax Differences," its positions that FASB Statement No. 109, "Accounting for Income Taxes" (Statement 109), "requires comprehensive recognition of deferred tax liabilities and assets for temporary differences and operating loss and tax credit carryforwards." Accordingly, deferred taxes should be recognized under Statement No. 109 for LIFO inventory temporary differences (i.e., an excess of LIFO inventory for financial reporting over its tax basis requires recognition of a deferred tax liability).

(d) AVERAGE COST.   Another fairly common cost flow assumption uses an average cost per unit to determine cost of sales and the inventory value. A weighted average cost (including the cost of the beginning inventory and current period purchases and production) is used in connection with a periodic inventory system. A moving average cost typically is used with a perpetual inventory system. The average cost method is used by companies in many industries and is often viewed as producing results similar to those obtained from the FIFO method. The reason is that the inventory balance is directly influenced by current costs.

(e) SPECIFIC IDENTIFICATION.   Companies in a limited number of industries track the cost of individual items and retain costs in inventory until the related physical goods are sold using the specific identification method. This method is commonly used for large or expensive items such as automobiles or precious gems. Theoretically, this approach is preferable because it matches costs and revenues based on the actual physical flow of specific goods. However, implementing it is often difficult or impossible, because the cost of individual inventory items cannot be determined, or the expense of tracking cost by item is not justified by increased accuracy. Also, when the approach is used in situations where inventory items are not unique, manipulation of recorded amounts is possible. For example, a company having similar inventory items with different costs can record in inventory and cost of sales the item that yields the most favorable current results.

(f) OTHER ASSUMPTIONS.   Other cost flow assumptions not commonly used for external reporting but possibly useful for internal purposes include:

- Next-in, first-out
- Cost-of-last-purchase
- Base stock method (similar to LIFO in that it assumes a certain minimum level of inventory is required to operate a business. The base stock is carried at initial cost.)

These methods are not considered to be within GAAP. However, they may assist companies in identifying current product-profit margins, because they match current costs against current sales.

20.7 CONTROL OBJECTIVES AND PROCEDURES

(a) GENERAL CONTROL PROCEDURES.   For most manufacturing and merchandising companies, inventory represents a significant asset, valuable to others as well as to the company. As a result, it is important that proper internal controls are in place to protect this investment. General controls provide an environment that enhances safeguarding the inventory in a planned and systematic manner.

(i) Physical Safeguards.   The use of locks, guards, restricted access, and other physical means to secure valuable inventory items improves control and discourages theft. In addition, proper shelter and storage facilities reduce deterioration and spoilage. As with most control measures, a cost/benefit evaluation should be performed to determine the extent to implement physical safeguards.

(ii) Written Policies.   Documentation of the procedures and policies authorized by management for inventory control should exist and be updated regularly for changes. The documentation should be readily available to and understood by employees who perform these procedures. Systems documentation is particularly useful for training new employees and minimizing disruption from other changes in personnel.

(iii) Reconciliations.   Regular comparisons of physical goods to the accounting records and reconciliations of various source documents can improve control by identifying losses, problems, or other matters warranting management's timely attention. A perpetual inventory system is required to make effective use of reconciliations as a control. Reconciliations should be reviewed by the individual who supervises the person who prepares them. Many specific inventory reconciliation procedures are included in the lists of specific control procedures presented in Subsections 20.4(c) and 20.4(d).

(iv) Budgets.   In the inventory area, the use of budgets is most effective for fixed and semifixed costs. Comparison of actual costs to the budgeted amounts can identify matters for further investigation. Explanations of budget variances can assist management in determining whether to record actual costs or standard costs as the inventory amount.

(v) Use of Standard Costs and Analysis of Variances.   For variable costs, the use of regularly updated standard costs and the related variance analysis can identify differences between actual costs and standard costs, regardless of the level of volume. These differences should be examined to ascertain what caused them and what corrective action may be required.

(b) SPECIFIED CONTROL PROCEDURES.   To support the general control procedures in achieving an effective system of internal control over inventory, specific control procedures must be implemented. Several lists of potential specific control procedures related to inventory are in Subsections 20.4(c) and 20.4(d).

20.8 EFFECTS OF TAX REGULATIONS

(a) INTRODUCTION.   In many situations, governmental requirements for the treatment of inventory and related items in an entity's income tax return can influence the accounting and financial reporting. In some cases, these requirements result in two sets of accounting records. In the United States, IRS regulations have significantly affected several major aspects of inventory accounting. Subsection 20.5(b)(i) of this chapter discusses the LIFO cost flow assumption and describes the effects of IRS regulations on the LIFO computations. This section describes other areas of inventory accounting significantly affected by IRS requirements.

(b) CAPITALIZATION OF INDIRECT COSTS.   The Tax Reform Act of 1986 requires inventory for tax purposes to include a number of costs that may have been expensed under the previous IRS rules that mandated full absorption costing. The Act affects all taxpayers that account for inventories and requires the use of "uniform capitalization rules" by any producer of tangible property and by any taxpayer that acquires and holds property for resale. Because some of these costs cannot be capitalized for financial reporting purposes, many companies are required to maintain separate inventory cost records for book and tax purposes. The EITF reached a consensus on Issue No. 86-46, "Uniform Capitalization Rules for Inventory under the Tax Reform Act of 1986," concluding that the fact that a cost is capitalizable for tax purposes does not indicate that it is preferable—or even appropriate—to capitalize that cost for financial reporting purposes. The Task Force did not indicate which costs that must be capitalized for tax purposes may also be capitalized for financial reporting purposes. That determination can be made only after an analysis of the individual facts and circumstances, and it involves considerable judgment. Subsection 20.5(a) of this chapter on the overhead component provides additional guidance for making these decisions. Examples of costs that would be capitalized to inventory for tax purposes, but not for financial reporting purposes, are tax depreciation in excess of book depreciation, interest costs, and costs of disposal such as warehousing and disposal where those costs are not an integral aspect of bringing the goods to a saleable condition.

Any differences between book and tax inventories resulting from application of the uniform capitalization rules are temporary differences that generally will create deferred income taxes for financial reporting purposes under Statement No. 109.

(c) WRITE-DOWNS.   As a result of the Supreme Court decision in the case of *Thor Power Tool Co. v. IRS Commissioner* (1979), the IRS did not permit a write-down of excess inventory using a percentage or aging formula and prohibits the write-down of inventory to scrap value until the goods are disposed of. Once again, any resulting differences between inventory for book and for tax purposes are temporary differences that generally will result in a deferred tax asset or liability for financial reporting purposes. In practice, many companies check their facilities shortly before the fiscal year end to make sure all inventory to be scrapped is disposed of before the balance sheet date. In spite of such efforts, many companies record nondeductible reserves for excess inventory that has not been disposed of.

20.9 FINANCIAL STATEMENT DISCLOSURE REQUIREMENTS

(a) GENERALLY ACCEPTED ACCOUNTING PRINCIPLES REQUIREMENTS.   The primary GAAP disclosure requirements for inventory are specified in ARB No. 43 and include these four:

1. The basis of stating inventories (e.g., lower of cost or market)
2. The method of determining inventory cost (e.g., FIFO)
3. Whether inventories are stated above cost
4. Amount of net losses on firm purchase commitments

APB Opinion No. 22, "Disclosure of Accounting Policies," requires disclosure of the policies relating to inventory pricing.

The AICPA Issues Paper recommends that all companies using LIFO make several LIFO-related disclosures required for SEC registrants. These include the following three:

1. The effect on net income of LIFO quantity liquidations. The disclosure should give effect only to pools with decrements.

    FINANCIAL REPORTING EXAMPLE

    MLS COMPANY AND SUBSIDIARIES

    Notes to Financial Statements

    In millions, except for share amounts

    A reduction of certain inventories resulted in the liquidation of some quantities of LIFO inventory, which increased pretax income by $40 in 20X2, $8 in 20X1, and $16 in 20X0.

2. For companies that have not fully adopted LIFO, the extent to which LIFO is used (e.g., the portion of ending inventory priced at LIFO and under other methods). The AICPA Issues Paper concludes that the portion of the cost of sales resulting from the application of LIFO compared to total reported cost of sales is the preferred disclosure, but if it is impractical to determine that amount, companies should disclose the dollar amount of inventory priced at LIFO and under other methods. The AICPA Issues Paper indicates that disclosure of the LIFO inventory amounts is most meaningful when interrelated with disclosure of the difference between LIFO and FIFO or average cost.

Financial Reporting Example

XYZ Company

Notes to Consolidated Financial Statements

Inventories:

Inventories, net of allowances, are summarized as follows (in thousands):

	December 31	
	20X1	*20X0*
Raw materials	$ 15	$ 10
Parts and components	45	40
Work in process	20	15
Finished goods	40	35
	$120	$100
Inventories determined using the—		
LIFO basis	$ 50	$ 40
FIFO basis	70	60
	$120	$100

3. For LIFO inventories, the amount and basis for determining the excess of replacement or current cost over stated LIFO value (in most cases, the basis for determining current cost is FIFO).

In SFAS No. 86, these two disclosures are required:

1. Unamortized computer software costs included in each balance sheet presented

2. The total amount charged to expense in each income statement presented for amortization of capitalized computer software costs and for amounts written down to net realizable value

Financial Reporting Example

LNS, Inc.

Consolidated Balance Sheets

As of December 31, 20X2 and 20X1

(Dollars in thousands)

Assets	December 31	
	20X2	*20X1*
Current Assets:		
Cash and cash equivalents	$ —	$ 4,844
Short-term investments	—	2,826
Accounts receivable, net of allowances		
of $1,303 and $290	23,307	15,165
Income taxes receivable	—	229
Inventory	156	215
Prepaid expenses and other current assets	1,659	1,304
Deferred tax asset	643	445
Total current assets	25,765	25,028
Property and Equipment, net of accumulated depreciation of $5,596 and $3,875	4,805	2,968
Software Development Costs, net of accumulated amortization of $2,585 and $2,514	8,327	4,317
Purchased Software Costs, net of accumulated amortization of $1,229 and $1,176	1,079	849

Notes to Consolidated Financial Statements

Software

The cost of internally developed software which meet the criteria in SFAS No. 86, "Accounting for the Costs of Computer Software to Be Sold, Leased, or Otherwise Marketed," are capitalized. These costs are amortized on a straight-line basis over estimated economic lives ranging from three to five years.

Purchased software is capitalized at cost and amortized on a straight-line basis over estimated economic lives ranging from two to five years. Most of the contracts for purchased software require royalties to be paid based on revenues generated by the related software.

(b) SECURITIES AND EXCHANGE COMMISSION REQUIREMENTS. Rule 5-02.6 of SEC Regulation S-X indicates that inventories typically are classified as current assets and requires these five disclosures:

1. If practicable, disclose the major classes of inventories such as finished goods, inventoried cost relating to long-term contracts and programs, work in process, raw materials, and supplies.

   FINANCIAL REPORTING EXAMPLE

   CS CORPORATION AND CONSOLIDATED SUBSIDIARIES

   Consolidated Balance Sheets

	December 31	
	20X1	20X0
Current Assets:		
Cash and cash equivalents	$ 833,000	$ 744,000
Notes and accounts receivable, less allowances		
of $629,000 and $948,000, respectively	$52,914,000	$44,293,000
Inventories:		
Raw materials	$ 9,524,000	$12,037,000
Work in process	28,269,000	20,438,000
Finished goods	18,997,000	19,931,000
	$56,790,000	$52,406,000

2. The basis of determining the inventory amounts shall be stated.
3. If the cost method is used, disclose the nature of the cost elements included in inventory and the method by which amounts are removed from inventory (i.e., cost flow assumption).
4. If any general and administrative costs are charged to inventory, state in a note to the financial statements the aggregate amount of the general and administrative costs incurred in each period and the actual or estimated amount remaining in inventory at the date of each balance sheet. The most common examples of these disclosures are those made by defense and other long-term contractors in accordance with ASR No. 164.

   FINANCIAL REPORTING EXAMPLE

   LML International Corp.

   Notes to Financial Statements

   General and administrative expenses related to U.S. Government contracts incurred and charged to inventoried costs were $478.5 million, $520.1 million, and $530.7 million in 1994, 1993, and 1992, respectively. General and administrative expenses remaining in inventoried costs before consideration of progress payments were estimated at $76 million and $68 million at September 30, 1994 and 1993, respectively.

5. For LIFO inventories, disclose the amount and basis for determining the excess of replacement or current cost over stated LIFO value, if material. ASR No. 141 indicates that in determining replacement or current cost for the purpose of this disclosure, any inventory method may be used (such as FIFO or average cost) that derives a figure approximating current cost.

FINANCIAL REPORTING EXAMPLE

ABC INC.

Notes to Consolidated Financial Statements

Approximately 76 percent of total inventories at both December 31, 1996 and 1995, are stated on the last-in, first-out (LIFO) inventory valuation method. Had the average-cost method (which approximates replacement cost) been used with respect to such inventories at December 31, 1996 and 1995, total inventories would have been $124.3 million and $101.5 million higher, respectively.

SAB No. 40 requires the disclosure of the amount of income, if material, that has been recorded because a LIFO inventory liquidation took place.

20.10 SOURCES AND SUGGESTED REFERENCES

Accounting Principles Board, "Business Combinations," APB Opinion No. 16. AICPA, New York, 1970.

———, "Accounting Changes," APB Opinion No. 20. AICPA, New York, 1971.

———, "Disclosure of Accounting Policies," APB Opinion No. 22. AICPA, New York, 1972.

———, "Interim Financial Reporting," APB Opinion No. 28. AICPA, New York, 1973.

Accounting Standards Executive Committee, "Elimination of Profits Resulting from Intercompany Transfers of LIFO Inventories," Practice Bulletin No. 2. AICPA, New York, 1987.

———, "Identification and Discussion of Certain Financial Accounting and Reporting Issues Concerning LIFO Inventories." AICPA, New York, 1984.

American Institute of Certified Public Accountants, Accounting Trends and Techniques. AICPA, New York, 1996.

———, "Inventory Pricing," Accounting Research Bulletin No. 43. AICPA, New York, 1953.

———, "The Accounting Basis of Inventories," Accounting Research Study No. 13. AICPA, New York, 1973.

Financial Accounting Standards Board, "LIFO Accounting Issues," EITF Issue No. 84-24. FASB, Stamford, CT, 1984.

———, "Recognition of Inventory Market Declines at Interim Reporting Dates," EITF Issue No. 86–13. FASB, Stamford, CT, 1986.

———, "Uniform Capitalization Rules for Inventory under the Tax Reform Act of 1986," EITF Issue No. 86–46. FASB, Stamford, CT, 1996.

———, "Classification of Inventory Markdowns and Other Costs Associated with a Restructuring," EITF Issue No., 96–9. FASB, Stamford, CT, 1996.

———, "Accounting for Shipping and Handling Fees and Costs," EITF Issue No. 00–10. FASB, Stamford, CT, 2000.

———, "Accounting for Certain Sales Incentives," EITF Issue No. 00–14. FASB, Stamford, CT, 2001.

———, "Recognition by a Seller of Losses on Firmly Committed Executory Contracts," EITF Issue No. 00–26. FASB, Stamford, CT, 2001.

———, "Accounting for Consideration Given by a Vendor to a Customer or a Reseller of the Vendor's Products," EITF Issue No. 01–9. FASB, Stamford, CT, 2001.

———, "Temporary Differences Related to LIFO Inventory and Tax-to-Tax Differences," EITF Topic No. D-31, FASB, Stamford, CT, 1993.

———, "Accounting Changes Related to the Cost of Inventory," FASB Interpretation No. 1. FASB, Stamford, CT, 1974.

_____, "Elements of Financial Statements," Statement of Financial Accounting Concepts No. 6. FASB, Stamford, CT, 1985.

_____, "Accounting for Research and Development Costs," Statement of Financial Accounting Standards No. 2. FASB, Stamford, CT, 1974.

_____, "Reporting Accounting Changes in Interim Financial Statements—An Amendment of APB Opinion No. 28," Statement of Financial Accounting Standards No. 3. FASB, Stamford, CT, 1979.

_____, "Capitalization of Interest Cost," Statement of Financial Accounting Standards No. 34. FASB, Stamford, CT, 1979.

_____, "Accounting for Futures Contracts," Statement of Financial Accounting Standards No. 80. FASB, Stamford, CT, 1984.

_____, "Accounting for the Costs of Computer Software to Be Sold, Leased, or Otherwise Marketed," Statement of Financial Accounting Standards No. 86. FASB, Stamford, CT, 1985.

_____, "Accounting for Derivative Instruments and Hedging Activities," Statement of Financial Accounting Standards No. 133. FASB, Stamford, CT, 1998.

_____, "Accounting for Involuntary Conversions of Nonmonetary Assets—An Interpretation of APB Opinion No. 29," FASB Interpretation No. 30. FASB, Stamford, CT, 1979.

_____, "Inventory Costs, an Amendment of ARB No. 43, Chapter 4," Statement of Financial Accounting Standards No. 151, FASB, Norwalk, CT, 2004

International Accounting Standards Committee, "Valuation and Presentation of Inventories in the Context of the Historical Cost System," International Accounting Standard No. 2. IASC, London, 1975.

_____, "Framework for the Preparation and Presentation of Financial Statements." IASC, London, 1989.

Paton, W. A., and Paton, W. A., Jr., *Assets—Accounting and Administration*. Roberts & Roehl, Warren, MI, 1971.

Securities and Exchange Commission, "Inventories," Rule 5–02.6, Regulation S–X. SEC, Washington, DC, 1974. Updated.

_____, "LIFO Method of Accounting for Inventories," Financial Reporting Releases, §205 (ASR No. 141). SEC, Washington, DC, 1973.

_____, "Improved Disclosures Related to Defense and Other Long-Term Contract Activities," Financial Reporting Releases, §206 (ASR No. 164). SEC, Washington, DC, 1974.

_____, "LIFO Method of Accounting for Inventories," Financial Reporting Releases, §205 (ASR No. 293). SEC, Washington, DC, 1981.

_____, "Codification of SAB Nos. 1–38," Staff Accounting Bulletin No. 40. SEC, Washington, DC, 1981.

_____, "LIFO Inventory Practice," Staff Accounting Bulletin No. 58. SEC, Washington, DC, 1985.

Thor Power Tool Co. v. IRS Commissioner, 439 U.S. 522, 1979.

Wilson, P. W., and Christensen, K. E., *LIFO for Retailers*. John Wiley & Sons, New York, 1985.

CHAPTER **21**

PROPERTY, PLANT, EQUIPMENT, AND DEPRECIATION

Richard H. Moseley

American Express Tax and Business Services, Inc.

21.1 NATURE OF PROPERTY, PLANT, AND EQUIPMENT

(a) DEFINITION.   Property, plant, and equipment are presented as noncurrent assets in a classified balance sheet. The category includes such items as land, buildings, equipment, furniture, fixtures, tools, and machinery. It excludes intangibles and investments in affiliated companies.

(b) CHARACTERISTICS.   Property, plant, and equipment have several important characteristics:

- A relatively long life
- The production of income or services over its life
- Tangibility—having physical substance

(c) AUTHORITATIVE LITERATURE.   Generally accepted accounting principles (GAAP) for property, plant, and equipment have evolved without the promulgation of any Level A or B GAAP rule making on a comprehensive basis. Because of this lack of authoritative literature, many believe that diversity in practice has developed with respect to both the type of costs capitalized and the amounts. In June 2001, the Accounting Standards Executive Committee (AcSEC) of the

American Institute of Certified Public Accountants (AICPA) issued an exposure draft of a Statement of Position (SOP) titled "Accounting for Certain Costs and Activities Related to Property, Plant, and Equipment." Although a final statement has not yet been adopted, many of the concepts and practices discussed in the following pages may be significantly affected when the SOP is finalized. See Section 21.7, "Recent Developments," for a summary of this proposal.

21.2 COST

Property, plant, and equipment usually are recorded at cost, defined as the amount of consideration paid or incurred to acquire or construct an asset. Cost consists of several elements. Welsch and Zlatkovich explain:

> The capitalizable costs include the invoice price (less discounts), plus other costs such as sales tax, insurance during transit, freight, duties, ownership searching, ownership registration, installation, and break-in costs.[1]

(a) DETERMINING COST. Generally, three principles are followed for determining the cost of an asset:

1. An asset acquired by exchanging cash or other assets is recorded at cost—that is, at the amount of cash disbursed or the fair value of other assets distributed.
2. An asset acquired by incurring liabilities is recorded at cost—that is, at the present value of the future amounts to be paid.
3. An asset acquired by issuing shares of stock of the acquiring corporation is recorded at the fair value of the asset—that is, shares of stock issued are recorded at the fair value of the consideration received for the stock. That fair value is considered cost.

(i) Acquisition by Exchange. Property, plant, and equipment may be acquired by exchange, as well as by purchase. In that case, the applicable accounting requirements are set forth in Accounting Principles Board (APB) Opinion No. 29, "Accounting for Nonmonetary Transactions," which defines an exchange (par. 3c) as "a reciprocal transfer between an enterprise and another entity that results in the enterprise's acquiring assets or services or satisfying liabilities by surrendering other assets or services or incurring other obligations."

After defining nonmonetary assets (par. 3b) to include property, plant, and equipment, Opinion No. 29 further provides (par. 18) the general rule:

> Accounting for nonmonetary transactions should be based on the fair values of the assets (or services) involved.... Thus, the cost of a nonmonetary asset acquired in exchange for another nonmonetary asset is the fair value of the asset surrendered to obtain it, and a gain or loss should be recognized on the exchange. The fair value of the asset received should be used to measure the cost if it is more clearly evident than the fair value of the asset surrendered.

However, the Opinion recognizes (par. 21) an exception to its general rule if an exchange of nonmonetary assets "is not essentially the culmination of an earning process." In that case, the accounting "should be based on the recorded amount (after reduction, if appropriate, for an indicated impairment of value) of the nonmonetary asset relinquished."

Among the exchanges of nonmonetary assets that do not culminate the earning process, the Opinion includes (par. 21b) "an exchange of a productive asset [defined to include property, plant, and equipment] not held for sale in the ordinary course of business for a similar productive asset or an equivalent interest in the same or similar productive asset."

---

[1] Glenn A. Welsch and Charles T. Zlatkovich, *Intermediate Accounting*, Eighth Edition (Irwin: Homewood, IL, 1989).

However, the rule about basing exchanges of productive (nonmonetary) assets on recorded amounts has its own exception if the exchange includes monetary consideration. In that case, the Opinion (par. 22) states:

> The Board believes that the recipient of the monetary consideration has realized gain on the exchange to the extent that the amount of the monetary receipt exceeds a proportionate share of the recorded amount of the asset surrendered. The portion of the cost applicable to the realized amount should be based on the ratio of the monetary consideration to the total consideration received (monetary consideration plus the estimated fair value of the nonmonetary asset received) or, if more clearly evident, the fair value of the nonmonetary asset transferred. The Board further believes that the entity paying the monetary consideration should not recognize any gain on [an exchange not culminating the earning process] but should record the asset received at the amount of the monetary consideration paid plus the recorded amount of the nonmonetary asset surrendered. If a loss is indicated by the terms of [an exchange not culminating the earning process], the entire indicated loss on the exchange should be recognized.

The Financial Accounting Standards Board (FASB)'s Emerging Issues Task Force (EITF) later reached a consensus (EITF Issue No. 86-29) that an exchange of nonmonetary assets should be considered a monetary (rather than nonmonetary) transaction if monetary consideration is significant, and agreed that "significant" should be defined as at least 25 percent of the fair value of the exchange.

(ii) Acquisition by Issuing Debt. If property, plant, and equipment are acquired in exchange for payables or other contractual obligations to pay money (referred to collectively as *notes*), APB Opinion No. 21, "Interest on Receivables and Payables" (par. 12), and states:

> There should be a general presumption that the rate of interest stipulated by the parties to the transaction represents fair and adequate compensation to the supplier for the use of the related funds.

However, the Opinion continues:

> That presumption ... must not permit the form of the transaction to prevail over its economic substance and thus would not apply if (1) interest is not stated, or (2) the stated interest rate is unreasonable ... or (3) the stated face amount of the note is materially different from the current cash sales price for the same or similar items or from the market value of the note at the date of the transaction.

In any of these circumstances, both the assets acquired and the note should be recorded at the fair value of the assets or at the market value of the note, whichever can be more clearly determined. If the amount recorded is not the same as the face value of the note, the difference is a discount or premium, which should be accounted for as interest over the life of the note. If there is no established price for the assets acquired and no evidence of the market value of the note, the amount recorded should be determined by discounting all future payments on the note using an imputed rate of interest.

In selecting the imputed rate of interest to be used, APB Opinion No. 21 (par. 14) states that consideration should be given to:

> (a) An approximation of the prevailing market rates for the source of credit that would provide a market for sale or assignment of the note; (b) the prime or higher rate for notes which are discounted with banks, giving due weight to the credit standing of the maker; (c) published market rates for similar quality bonds; (d) current rates for debentures with substantially identical terms and risks that are traded in open markets; and (e) the current rate charged by investors for first or second mortgage loans on similar property.

(iii) Acquisition by Issuing Stock.   Assets acquired by issuing shares of stock should be recorded at either the fair value of the shares issued or the fair value of the property acquired, whichever is more clearly evident.

Smith and Skousen further explain:

> When securities do not have an established market value, appraisal of the acquired assets by an independent authority may be required to arrive at an objective determination of their fair market value. If satisfactory market values cannot be obtained for either securities issued or the assets acquired, values may have to be established by the board of directors for accounting purposes. The source of the valuation should be disclosed on the balance sheet.[2]

(iv) Mixed Acquisition for Lump Sum.   Several assets may be acquired for a lump-sum payment. This type of acquisition is often called a *basket purchase*. It is essential to allocate the joint cost carefully, because the assets may include both depreciable and nondepreciable assets, or the depreciable assets may be depreciated at different rates.

Welsch and Zlatkovich discuss the methods of allocating joint costs:

> The allocation of the purchase price should be based on some realistic indicator of the relative values of the several assets involved, such as current appraised values, tax assessment, cost savings, or the present value of estimated future earnings.[3]

(v) Donated Assets.   Property, plant, and equipment may be donated to an entity. The accounting for such donations is addressed by Statement of Financial Accounting Standards (SFAS) No. 116, "Accounting for Contributions Received and Contributions Made." Paragraph 8 of SFAS No. 116 concludes that donated property, plant, and equipment should be measured at fair value.

Paragraph 19 provides guidance for determining the fair value of donated assets and indicates that quoted market prices, if available, are the best evidence of the fair value. It further indicates that if quoted market prices are not available, fair value may be estimated based on quoted market prices for similar assets, independent appraisals, or valuation techniques, such as the present value of estimated cash flows.

(b) OVERHEAD ON SELF-CONSTRUCTED ASSETS.   Companies often construct their own buildings and equipment. Materials and labor directly identifiable with the construction are part of its cost.

As to whether overhead should be included in the cost of construction, Lamden, Gerboth, and McRae suggest:

> In the absence of compelling evidence to the contrary, overhead costs considered to have "discernible future benefits" for the purpose of determining the cost of inventory should be presumed to have "discernible future benefits" for the purpose of determining the cost of a self-constructed depreciable asset.[4]

Mosich and Larsen agree and go on to discuss two alternative views as to what overhead should be included:

> Allocate Only Incremental Overhead Costs to the Self-Constructed Asset. This approach may be defended on the grounds that incremental overhead costs represent the relevant cost that management considered in making the decision to construct the asset. Fixed overhead costs, it is argued, are period costs. Because they would have been incurred in any case, there is no relationship between the fixed overhead costs and the self-constructed project. This approach has been widely used in practice because it does not distort the cost of normal operations.

---

[2] Jay M. Smith and K. Fred Skousen, *Intermediate Accounting, Comprehensive Volume*, Ninth Edition (Southwestern Publishing: Cincinnati, OH, 1987).

[3] Welch and Zlatkovich.

[4] Charles Lamden, Dale L. Gerboth, and Thomas McRae, "Accounting for Depreciable Assets," Accounting Research Monograph, No. 1 (AICPA: New York, 1975).

Allocate a Portion of All Overhead Costs to the Self-Constructed Asset. The argument for this approach is that the proper function of cost allocation is to relate all costs incurred in an accounting period to the output of that period. If an enterprise is able to construct an asset and still carry on its regular activities, it has benefited by putting to use some of its idle capacity, and this fact should be reflected in larger income. To charge the entire overhead to only a portion of the productive activity is to disregard facts and to understate the cost of the self-constructed asset. This line of reasoning has considerable merit.[5]

(c) INTEREST CAPITALIZED.   SFAS No. 34, "Capitalization of Interest Cost," (par. 6) states:

The historical cost of acquiring an asset includes the costs necessarily incurred to bring it to the condition and location necessary for its intended use. If an asset requires a period of time in which to carry out the activities necessary to bring it to that condition and location, the interest cost incurred during that period as a result of expenditures for the asset is a part of the historical cost of acquiring the asset.

Paragraph 9 describes the assets that qualify for interest capitalization:

- Assets that are constructed or otherwise produced for an enterprise's own use (including assets constructed or produced for the enterprise by others for which deposits or progress payments have been made).
- Assets intended for sale or lease that are constructed or otherwise produced as discrete projects (e.g., ships or real estate developments).

The amount of interest capitalized is computed by applying an interest rate to the average amount of accumulated expenditures for the asset during the period. To the extent that specific borrowings are associated with the asset, the interest rate on those borrowings may be used. Otherwise, the interest rate should be the weighted average rate applicable to other borrowings outstanding during the period. In no event should the total interest capitalized exceed total interest costs incurred for the period. Imputing interest costs on equity is not permitted.

Descriptions of capitalized interest are often seen in footnotes, such as the following example from 1989 financial statements:

Delta Air Lines, Inc.

Notes to Consolidated Financial Statements

Note 1. Summary of Significant Accounting Policies

Interest Capitalized—Interest attributable to funds used to finance the acquisition of new aircraft and construction of major ground facilities is capitalized as an additional cost of the related asset. Interest is capitalized at the Company's average interest rate on long-term debt or, where applicable, the interest rate related to specific borrowings. Capitalization of interest ceases when the property or equipment is placed in service.

(d) COST OF LAND.   Determining the cost of land presents particular problems, as described by Pyle and Larson:

When land is purchased for a building site, its cost includes the amount paid for the land plus real estate commissions. It also includes escrow and legal fees, fees for examining and insuring the title, and any accrued property taxes paid by the purchaser, as well as expenditures for surveying, clearing, grading, draining, and landscaping. All are part of the cost of the land. Furthermore, any assessments incurred at the time of purchase or later for such things as the installation of streets,

---

[5] A. N. Mosich and John E. Larsen, *Intermediate Accounting*, Sixth Edition (McGraw-Hill, New York, 1986).

sewers, and sidewalks should be debited to the Land account because they add a more or less permanent value to the land.[6]

Excavation of land for building purposes, however, is chargeable to buildings rather than to land.

See Chapter 30 for a discussion of the accounting for land acquired as part of a real estate operation.

(i) Purchase Options. If a company acquires an option to purchase land and later exercises that option, the cost of the option generally becomes part of the cost of the land. Even if an option lapses without being exercised, its cost can be capitalized if the option is one of a series of options acquired as part of an integrated plan to acquire a site. In that case, if any one of the options is exercised, the cost of all may be capitalized as part of the cost of the site.

(ii) Interest. SFAS No. 34 (par. 11) describes the proper accounting for interest cost related to land:

> Land that is not undergoing activities necessary to get it ready for its intended use is not [an asset qualifying for interest capitalization]. If activities are undertaken for the purpose of developing land for a particular use, the expenditures to acquire the land qualify for interest capitalization while those activities are in progress. The interest cost capitalized on those expenditures is a cost of acquiring the asset that results from those activities. If the resulting asset is a structure, such as a plant or a shopping center, interest capitalized on the land expenditures is part of the acquisition cost of the structure. If the resulting asset is developed land, such as land that is to be sold as developed lots, interest capitalized on the land expenditures is part of the acquisition cost of the developed land.

(iii) Other Carrying Charges. SFAS No. 67, "Accounting for Costs and Initial Rental Operations of Real Estate Projects" (par. 6), states:

> Costs incurred on real estate for property taxes and insurance shall be capitalized as property cost only during periods in which activities necessary to get the property ready for its intended use are in progress. Costs incurred for such items after the property is substantially complete and ready for its intended use shall be charged to expense as incurred.

Even though the scope of the Statement excludes "real estate developed by an enterprise for use in its own operations, other than for sale or rental," this guidance is followed in capitalizing carrying charges generally.

(e) COST OF ASSETS HELD FOR RESEARCH AND DEVELOPMENT ACTIVITIES. Although SFAS No. 2, "Accounting for Research and Development Costs" (par. 12), generally requires that research and development costs be charged to expense when incurred, it makes an exception (par. 11a) for "the costs of materials (whether from the enterprise's normal inventory or acquired specially for research and development activities) and equipment or facilities that are acquired or constructed for research and development activities and that have alternate future uses (in research and development projects or otherwise)." These costs, the Statement says, "shall be capitalized as tangible assets when acquired or constructed."

21.3 IMPAIRMENT OF VALUE

(a) AUTHORITATIVE PRONOUNCEMENTS. SFAS No. 144, "Accounting for the Impairment or Disposal of Long-Lived Assets," prescribes the accounting for the impairment of long-lived

---

[6] William W. Pyle and Kermit D. Larson, *Fundamental Accounting Principles*, Tenth Edition (Irwin, Homewood, IL, 1984).

assets, including property, plant, and equipment. The SFAS applies to property, plant, and equipment that is "held and used" and to property, plant, and equipment that is held for disposal (referred to in the Statement as *assets to be disposed of*).

(b) ASSETS TO BE HELD AND USED.   SFAS No. 144 requires the following three-step approach for recognizing and measuring the impairment of assets to be held and used:

1. Consider whether indicators of impairment of property, plant, and equipment are present.
2. If indicators of impairment are present, determine whether the sum of the estimated undiscounted future cash flows attributable to the assets in question is less than their carrying amounts.
3. If less, recognize an impairment loss based on the excess of the carrying amount of the assets over their fair values.

(i) Recognition.   SFAS No. 144 requires that property, plant, and equipment that are used in operations be reviewed for impairment whenever events or changes in circumstances indicate that the carrying amount of the assets might not be recoverable—that is, information indicates that an impairment might exist. Accordingly, companies do not need to perform a periodic assessment of assets for impairment in the absence of such information. Instead, companies would assess the need for an impairment write-down only if an indicator of impairment is present. The SFAS lists the following examples of events or changes in circumstances that may indicate to management that an impairment exists:

- A significant decrease in the market value of an asset
- A significant adverse change in the extent or manner in which an asset is used or in its physical condition
- A significant adverse change in legal factors or in the business climate that affects the value of an asset or an adverse action or assessment by a regulator
- An accumulation of costs significantly in excess of the amount originally expected to acquire or construct an asset
- A current period operating or cash flow loss combined with a history of operating or cash flow losses or a projection or forecast that demonstrates continuing losses associated with an income-producing asset
- A current expectation that an asset will be sold before the end of its previously estimated useful life

The preceding list is not all-inclusive, and there may be other events or changes in circumstances, including circumstances that are peculiar to a company's business or industry, indicating that the carrying amount of a group of assets might not be recoverable and thus impaired. If indicators of impairment are present, companies must then disaggregate the assets by grouping them at the lowest level for which there are identifiable cash flows that are largely independent of the cash flows of other groups of assets. Then future cash flows expected to be generated from the use of those assets and their eventual disposal must be estimated. That estimate is comprised of the future cash inflows expected to be generated by the assets less the future cash outflows expected to be necessary to obtain those inflows. If the estimated undiscounted cash flows are less than the carrying amount of the assets, an impairment exists and an impairment loss must be calculated and recognized.

The FASB recognized that certain long-lived assets could not be readily identified with specific cash flows (e.g., a corporate headquarters building and certain property and equipment of not-for-profit organizations). In those situations, the assets should be evaluated for impairment at an entity-wide level. If management estimates that the entity as a whole will generate cash flows sufficient to recover the carrying amount of all assets used in its operations, including its corporate headquarters building, no impairment loss would be recognized.

The SFAS No. 144 provides little guidance for estimating future cash flows, even though the accounting consequences of small changes in those estimates could be significant. Accordingly, estimating future undiscounted cash flows requires a great deal of judgment. Companies must make their best estimate based on reasonable and supportable assumptions and projections that are applied on a consistent basis. SFAS No. 144 indicates that all available evidence should be considered in developing the cash flow estimates, and the weight given that evidence should be commensurate with the extent to which the evidence can be verified objectively.

(ii) Measurement. Once it is determined that an impairment exists, an impairment loss is calculated based on the excess of the carrying amount of the asset over the asset's *fair value.* Fair value is the amount at which the asset could be bought or sold in a current transaction between a willing buyer and seller. The FASB concluded that the best measure of an asset's fair value is its quoted market price in an active market. However, the FASB acknowledged that active markets for many long-lived assets often do not exist. Therefore, if a quoted market price is not available, management's best estimate of the fair value of the assets, based on the best information available under the circumstances, should be used in valuing the assets. Accordingly, in many cases, companies will have to rely on appraisals or discounted estimates of future cash flows to determine fair values for those assets.

Once management determines that an asset (or a group of assets) is impaired and the asset is written down to fair value, the reduced carrying amount represents the new cost basis of the asset. As a result, subsequent depreciation of the asset is based on the revised carrying amount, and companies are prohibited from reversing the impairment loss should facts and circumstances change or conditions improve in the future.

(c) ASSETS TO BE DISPOSED OF. SFAS No. 144 indicates that assets to be disposed of other than by sale (e.g., abandonment, exchange for another long-lived asset) shall continue to be classified as held and used until they are disposed of. An asset or asset group to be disposed of by sale should be classified as held for sale during the period in which all of the following criteria are met:

- Management commits to a plan of disposal.
- The asset is available for immediate sale.
- An active program to locate a buyer has been initiated.
- Sale of the asset within one year is probable.
- The asset is being actively marketed for sale at a reasonable price.
- Actions required to complete the plan indicate that it is unlikely the plan will be significantly modified or withdrawn.

If at any time while an asset is classified as held for sale any of the above criteria are no longer met or the entity's plans change, the asset should be reclassified to the held and used category. The asset should be reclassified at the lower of the original carrying amount immediately before the asset is transferred to held for sale (adjusted for any depreciation expense that would have been recognized had the asset been continuously classified as held and used) or fair value at the date of the change in status. An asset classified as held for sale should be measured at the lower of its carrying amount or fair value less incremental direct costs of sale. An asset classified as held for sale should not be depreciated. SFAS No. 144 requires subsequent revisions to the carrying amount of assets classified as held for sale if the estimate of fair value less cost to sale changes during the holding period. After an initial writedown of an asset to fair value less cost to sell, the carrying amount can be increased or decreased depending on changes in the fair value less cost to sell of the asset. However, an increase in carrying value cannot exceed the carrying amount of the asset immediately before its classification into the held for sale category.

SFAS No. 144 also supersedes APB Opinion No. 30 with respect to discontinued operations. The Statement indicates that the results of operations relating to assets to be disposed of comprising a component of an entity should be classified as discontinued operations if both of the following conditions are met:

1. The operations and cash flows of the component have been eliminated or will be eliminated from the ongoing operations of the entity as a result of the disposal.
2. The entity will not have any continuing involvement in the operations of the component after the disposal.

A component of an entity is defined as operations and cash flows that can be clearly distinguished from the rest of the entity both operationally and for financial reporting purposes. The definition of component of an entity under SFAS No. 144 is much broader than the APB Opinion No. 30 definition of a segment of a business. Accordingly, many more discontinued operations will be reported under SFAS No. 144 than previously. For example, if a real estate entity disposes of an individual property, that property would likely qualify as a component of an entity under SFAS No. 144 but would generally not have qualified as a disposal of a segment of a business under APB Opinion No. 30.

21.4 EXPENDITURES DURING OWNERSHIP

(a) DISTINGUISHING CAPITAL EXPENDITURES FROM OPERATING EXPENDITURES.
After property, plant, and equipment have been acquired, additional expenditures are incurred to keep the assets in satisfactory operating condition. Certain of these expenditures—capital expenditures—are added to the asset's cost. The remainder—operating expenditures (sometimes called *revenue expenditures*—are charged to expense.

Kohler defines a capital expenditure in the following two ways:

1. An expenditure intended to benefit future periods, in contrast to a revenue expenditure, which benefits a current period; an addition to a capital asset. The term is generally restricted to expenditures that add fixed-asset units or that have the effect of increasing the capacity, efficiency, life span, or economy of operation of an existing fixed asset.
2. Hence, any expenditure benefiting a future period.[7]

Although the distinction is important, immaterial capital expenditures can be charged to expense. Expenditures during ownership fall into four categories: (1) maintenance and repairs; (2) replacements, improvements, and additions; (3) rehabilitation; (4) rearrangement and reinstallation.

(b) MAINTENANCE AND REPAIRS.   The terms "maintenance" and "repairs" generally are used interchangeably. However, Kohler defines them separately, and his definitions are useful in identifying expenditures that should be accounted for as maintenance and repairs. He defines maintenance as follows:

> The keeping of property in operable condition; also, the expense involved. Maintenance costs include outlays for (a) labor and supplies; (b) the replacement of any part that constitutes less than a retirement unit; and (c) major overhauls the items of which may involve elements of the first two classes. Items falling under (a) and (b) are always regarded as operating costs, chargeable to current expense directly or through the medium of a maintenance reserve.... Costs under (c) are similarly treated unless they include the replacement of a retirement unit the outlay for which is normally capitalized.[8]

---

[7] Eric Louis Kohler, *Kohler's Dictionary for Accountants*, Sixth Edition (Prentice-Hall, Englewood Cliffs, NJ, 1983).
[8] Id., p. 315.

He defines repairs (p. 428) as follows:

> The restoration of a capital asset to its full productive capacity, or a contribution thereto, after damage, accident, or prolonged use, without increase in the asset's previously estimated service life or productive capacity. The term includes maintenance primarily "preventive" in character, and capitalizable extraordinary repairs.

(i) Accounting Alternatives. As Kohler states, except for extraordinary repairs (or major overhauls), discussed below, maintenance and repairs expenditures are accounted for in two ways:

1. Charge to expense when the cost is incurred
2. Charge to a maintenance allowance account[9]

   Charge to Expense When the Cost Is Incurred. Since ordinary maintenance and repairs expenditures are regarded as operating costs, they are usually charged directly to expense when incurred.

   Charge to a Maintenance Allowance Account. The charge to expense may be accomplished through an allowance account. In some cases, the purpose of an allowance account is to equalize monthly repair costs within a year. Total repair costs are estimated at the beginning of the year, and the total is spread evenly throughout the year. The difference between the estimated and actual amounts at the end of the year is usually spread retroactively over all months of the year rather than being absorbed entirely by the last month. In the balance sheet, this allowance account may be treated as a reduction of the related asset account.

This latter approach is supported by APB Opinion No. 28, "Interim Financial Reporting" (par. 16a):

> When a cost that is expensed for annual reporting purposes clearly benefits two or more interim periods (e.g., annual major repairs), each interim period should be charged for an appropriate portion of the annual cost by the use of accruals or deferrals.

In other cases, the purpose of a maintenance allowance account is to charge the costs of major repairs over the entire period benefited, which may be longer than one year. When airlines acquire new aircraft, for example, they begin immediately to accrue the cost of the first engine overhaul, which usually is scheduled for more than one year hence. As illustrated by the following example from 1987 financial statements, the accrual charges are credited to a maintenance allowance account, which is then charged for cost of the overhaul.

Stateswest Airlines, Inc. and Subsidiaries

Notes to Consolidated Financial Statements

Summary of Significant Accounting Policies

Engine Overhaul Reserve. For all the leased aircraft, the Company accrues maintenance expense, on the basis of hours flown, for the estimated cost of engine overhauls.

(ii) Extraordinary Repairs. Welsch, Anthony, and Short define extraordinary repairs as repairs that

> ... occur infrequently, involve relatively large amounts of money, and tend to increase the economic usefulness of the asset in the future because of either greater efficiency or longer life, or both. They are represented by major overhauls, complete reconditioning, and major replacements and betterments.[10]

---

[9] Id., p. 428.

[10] Glenn A. Welsch, Robert N. Anthony, and Daniel G. Short, *Fundamentals of Financial Accounting* (Irwin, Homewood, IL, 1984).

Because expenditures for extraordinary repairs increase the future economic usefulness of an asset, they benefit future periods and are therefore capital expenditures. Ordinarily, they are added to the related asset account, as illustrated in the following example from 1987 financial statements.

Air Midwest, Inc. and Subsidiaries

Notes to Consolidated Financial Statements

Note 1. Summary of Significant Accounting Policies

d. Maintenance and Repairs

Major renewals and betterments are capitalized and depreciated over the remaining useful life of the asset.

Some authorities recommend that the expenditures for extraordinary repairs be charged against the accumulated depreciation account. The rationale for charging accumulated depreciation is provided by Smith and Skousen:

> Often it is not possible to identify the cost related to a specific part of an asset. In these instances, by debiting accumulated depreciation, the undepreciated book value is increased without creating a build-up of the gross asset values.[11]

Other authorities argue against debiting accumulated depreciation for extraordinary repairs because the accumulated depreciation on the asset may be less than the cost of the repairs and because the practice allows the original cost of any parts replaced to remain in the asset account.

(c) REPLACEMENTS, IMPROVEMENTS, AND ADDITIONS.   Replacements, improvements, and additions are related concepts. Kohler defines a replacement as "the substitution of one fixed asset for another, particularly of a new asset for an old, or of a new part for an old part." He defines an improvement (which he calls a "betterment") as "an expenditure having the effect of extending the useful life of an existing fixed asset, increasing its normal rate of output, lowering its operating cost, increasing rather than merely maintaining efficiency or otherwise adding to the worth of benefits it can yield."[12] Improvements ordinarily do not increase the physical size of the productive facility. Such an increase is an addition.

The distinctions among replacement, improvement, and addition notwithstanding, the accounting for all three is substantially the same. Expenditures for them are capital expenditures, that is, additions to property, plant, and equipment. (In practice, immaterial amounts are often charged to expense.) The cost of existing assets that are replaced, together with their related accumulated depreciation accounts, is eliminated from the accounts.

(d) REHABILITATION.   Expenditures to rehabilitate buildings or equipment purchased in a rundown condition with the intention of rehabilitating them should be capitalized. Normally the acquisition price of a rundown asset is less than that of a comparable new asset, and the rehabilitation expenditures benefit future periods. Capitalization of the expenditures is therefore appropriate. However, the total capitalized cost of the asset should not exceed the amount recoverable through operations.

When rehabilitation takes place over an extended period, care should be taken to distinguish between the cost of rehabilitation and the cost of maintenance.

(e) REARRANGEMENT AND REINSTALLATION.   Kieso and Weygandt describe rearrangement and reinstallation costs and the accounting for them:

---

[11] Smith and Skousen.

[12] Kohler.

Rearrangement and reinstallation costs, which are expenditures intended to benefit future periods, are different from additions, replacements and improvements. An example is the rearrangement and reinstallation of a group of machines to facilitate future production. If the original installation cost and the accumulated depreciation taken to date can be determined or estimated, the rearrangement and reinstallation cost can be handled as a replacement. If not, which is generally the case, the new costs if material in amount should be capitalized as an asset to be amortized over those future periods expected to benefit. If these costs are not material, if they cannot be separated from other operating expenses, or if their future benefit is questionable, they instead should be expensed in the period in which they are incurred.[13]

(f) ASBESTOS REMOVAL OR CONTAINMENT.   Removal or containment of asbestos is regulated and required by various federal, state, and local laws. The diversity of practice in capitalizing or expensing the cost of asbestos removal or containment resulted in asbestos removal being considered by the EITF. Issue No. 89-13 asked, "whether the costs incurred to treat asbestos when a property with a known asbestos problem is acquired should be capitalized or charged to expense" and "whether the costs incurred to treat asbestos in an existing property should be capitalized or charged to expense."

The EITF reached a conclusion that the costs incurred to treat asbestos within a reasonable time period after a property with a known asbestos problem is acquired should be capitalized as part of the cost of the acquired property subject to an impairment test for that property. The consensus on existing property was not as conclusive and stated the costs "may be capitalized as a betterment subject to an impairment test for that property."

The EITF also reached a consensus that when costs are incurred in anticipation of a sale of property, they should be deferred and recognized in the period of the sale to the extent that those costs can be recovered from the estimated sales price.

The Standards Executive Committee (SEC) observer at the EITF meeting noted that regardless of whether asbestos treatment costs are capitalized or charged to expense, SEC registrants should disclose significant exposure for asbestos treatment costs in "Management's Discussion and Analysis."

The EITF in Issue No. 90-8 affirmed the Issue No. 89-13 consensus but did not provide further guidance on capitalizing or charging to expense the costs incurred on existing properties. In practice, there continues to be wide diversity of the types of costs capitalized, if any, and the accrual of costs to remove or contain asbestos in existing properties.

(g) COSTS TO TREAT ENVIRONMENTAL CONTAMINATION.   Costs to remove, contain, neutralize, or prevent existing or future environmental contamination may be incurred voluntarily or as required by federal, state, and local laws. In Issue No. 90-8, the EITF considered whether environmental contamination treatment costs should be capitalized or charged to expense.

The EITF reached a consensus that, in general, environmental contamination treatment costs should be charged to expense unless the costs are recoverable and meet one of the following three criteria:

1. The costs extend the life, increase the capacity, or improve the safety or efficiency of property owned by the company. For purposes of this criterion, the condition of that property after the costs are incurred must be improved as compared with the condition of that property when originally constructed or acquired, if later.

2. The costs mitigate or prevent environmental contamination that has yet to occur and that otherwise may result from future operations or activities. In addition, the costs improve the property compared with its condition when constructed or acquired, if later.

3. The costs are incurred in preparing for sale property currently held for sale.

---

[13] Donald E. Kieso and Jerry J. Weygandt, *Intermediate Accounting*, Fifth Edition (John Wiley & Sons, New York, 1986).

Costs to remediate environmental contamination that do not meet one of the criteria above should be expensed under the provisions of the American Institute of Certified Public Accounts (AICPA)s SOP 96-1, "Environmental Remediation Liabilities." SOP 96-1 provides authoritative guidance on the recognition, measurement, display, and disclosure of environmental remediation liabilities. The AICPA issued SOP 96-1 to improve and narrow the manner in which existing authoritative accounting literature, principally SFAS No. 5, "Accounting for Contingencies," is applied in recognizing, measuring, and disclosing environmental liabilities.

SFAS No. 5 generally requires loss contingencies to be accrued when they are both probable and estimable. According to SOP 96-1, the probability criterion of SFAS No. 5 is met for environmental liabilities if both of the following conditions have occurred on or before the date the financial statements are issued:

- Litigation, a claim, or an assessment has been asserted, or is probable of being asserted.
- It is probable that the outcome of such litigation, claim, or assessment will be unfavorable.

The AICPA concluded that there is a presumption that the outcome will be unfavorable if litigation, a claim, or an assessment has been asserted, or is probable of assertion, and if the entity is associated with the site. Assuming that both of the above conditions are met, a company would need to accrue at least the minimum amount that can reasonably be estimated as an environmental remediation liability.

Once a company has determined that it is probable that a liability has been incurred, the entity should estimate the remediation liability based on available information. In estimating its allocable share of costs, a company should include incremental direct costs of the remediation effort and postremediation monitoring costs that are expected to be incurred after the remediation is complete. An entity also should include in its estimate costs of compensation and related benefit costs for employees who are expected to devote a significant amount of their time directly to the remediation effort. The accrual of expected legal defense costs related to remediation is not required.

In cases in which joint and several liability exists and the company is one of several parties responsible for remediation, which often will be the case, the entity is required to estimate the percentage of the liability that it will be allocated. The entity also must assess the likelihood that each of the other parties will pay their allocable share of the remediation liability. An entity would accrue its estimated share of amounts related to the site that will not be paid by other parties or the government.

SOP 96-1 provides that discounting environmental liabilities is permitted, but not required, only if the aggregate amount of the obligation and the amount and timing of the cash payments are fixed or reliably determinable. Because of the nature of the remediation process and the inherent subjectivity involved in estimating remediation liabilities, most companies will find it difficult to meet the criteria for discounting.

An asset relating to recoveries only can be recognized when realization of the claim for recovery is deemed probable. If a claim for recovery is the subject of litigation, a rebuttable presumption exists that realization of the claim is not probable. An environmental liability should be evaluated independently from any potential claim for recovery. SOP 96-1 requires that probable recoveries be recorded at fair value. However, discounting a recovery claim is not required in determining the value of the recovery when the related liability is not discounted and the timing of the recovery is dependent on the timing of the payment of the liability.

The EITF provided examples of applying the consensus in Issue No. 90-8.

21.5 DISPOSALS

Asset disposals may be voluntary, through retirement, sale, or trade-in, or involuntary, from fire, storm, flood, or other casualty. In general, these terms have the same meaning for accounting purposes as they do in ordinary discourse. The one exception is retirement, which for accounting purposes means the removal of an asset from service, whether or not the asset is removed physically. This is clear from Kohler's definition (1983) of retirement as "the removal of a fixed asset from service, following its sale or the end of its productive life, accompanied by the necessary adjustment of fixed asset and depreciation-reserve accounts."

(a) RETIREMENTS, SALES, AND TRADE-INS.   Davidson, Stickney, and Weil describe the accounting for retirements, which applies also to assets that are sold or traded in:

> When an asset is retired from service, the cost of the asset and the related amount of accumulated depreciation must be removed from the books. As part of this entry, the amount received from the sale or trade-in and any difference between that amount and book value must be recorded. The difference between the proceeds received on retirement and book value is a gain (if positive) or a loss (if negative).[14]

As discussed in the following, when composite or group rate depreciation is used, no gain or loss on disposal is recognized.

When an asset is traded in, the amount that should in theory be recorded as received from the trade-in is the asset's fair market value (which is not necessarily the amount by which the cash purchase price of the replacement asset is reduced). However, in practice, a reliable market value for the old asset may not be available. In that case, the usual practice is to recognize no gain or loss on the exchange, but to record as the acquisition cost of the replacement asset the net book value of the old asset plus the cash or other consideration paid.

(b) CASUALTIES.   Casualties, the accidental loss or destruction of assets, can give rise to gain or loss, even when the assets are replaced. The FASB Interpretation No. (FIN) No. 30, "Accounting for Involuntary Conversions of Nonmonetary Assets to Monetary Assets" (par. 2), makes this clear:

> Involuntary conversions of nonmonetary assets to monetary assets are monetary transactions for which gain or loss shall be recognized even though an enterprise reinvests or is obligated to reinvest the monetary assets in replacement nonmonetary assets.

21.6 ASSET RETIREMENT OBLIGATIONS

SFAS No. 143, "Accounting for Asset Retirement Obligations," was issued in June 2001. This project was undertaken by the FASB because diversity in practice had developed in accounting for the obligations associated with the retirement of long-lived assets. Some entities were accruing the obligations over the life of the related asset either as a liability or a reduction of the carrying amount of the asset while others did not recognize the liability until the asset was retired. The Statement requires that a liability be recorded for legal obligations resulting from the acquisition, construction, or development and normal operations of a long-lived asset.

(a) INITIAL RECOGNITION AND MEASUREMENT.   If a reasonable estimate of an asset retirement obligation can be made, an entity shall recognize the fair value of the liability in the period in which it is incurred. Fair value is usually defined as the amount at which the liability could be settled in a current transaction between willing parties. (That definition is ambiguous. See Section 1.3(b)(v).) Quoted market prices in active markets are the best evidence of fair value. However, when such prices are not available, fair value should be based on the best available information, including prices for similar liabilities and the results of present value techniques. SFAS No. 143 indicates that if present value techniques are used to estimate fair value, estimates of future cash flows should be consistent with the expected cash flow approach outlined in Concepts Statement No. 7.

---

[14] Sidney Davidson, Clyde P. Stickney, and Roman L. Weil, *Financial Accounting, An Introduction to Concepts, Methods and Uses*, Fifth Edition (Dryden Press, Hinsdale, IL, 1988).

When an asset retirement obligation is initially recognized, the entity should capitalize an asset retirement cost by increasing the carrying amount of the related long-lived asset by the same amount. This cost should be charged to expense over the estimated useful life of the asset. When the asset is tested for impairment under SFAS No. 144, the asset retirement cost should be included in the carrying value tested for impairment.

(b) SUBSEQUENT RECOGNITION AND MEASUREMENT. Subsequent to initial recognition, an entity should recognize period-to-period changes in the asset retirement liability for the passage of time and revisions to either the timing or amount of the original estimate of undiscounted cash flows. Adjustments for the passage of time should use an interest method based on the credit-adjusted risk-free rate at the time of initial recognition of the liability. The adjustment should increase the amount of the liability and be charged to accretion expense. Adjustments relating to revisions in the timing or amounts of cash flows will increase or decrease the asset retirement liability and the related asset.

21.7 RECENT DEVELOPMENTS

In June 2001, AcSEC issued an exposure draft of a SOP titled "Accounting for Certain Costs and Activities Related to Property, Plant and Equipment." The proposal addresses accounting for costs related to initial acquisition, construction, improvements, betterments, additions, repairs and maintenance, planned major maintenance, turnaround, overhauls and other similar costs related to property, plant, and equipment (PP&E). Rather than try to define all of the various terms used in connection with PP&E, the proposal adopts a project stage framework consisting of four stages—preliminary, preacquisition, acquisition or construction, and in-service.

(a) PRELIMINARY STAGE. This stage occurs before the acquisition of any specific PP&E asset and before it is probable that a specific PP&E asset will be acquired or constructed. All costs, with the exception of costs related for payment of an option to acquire PP&E, should be charged to expense during the preliminary stage.

(b) PREACQUISITION STAGE. This stage is similar to the preliminary stage as no PP&E asset has yet been acquired. However, acquisition or construction of a specific PP&E asset is considered probable. All costs related to PP&E incurred during this stage should be charged to expense unless the costs are directly identifiable with the specific PP&E. Directly identifiable costs include only (a) incremental direct costs incurred in transactions with independent third parties and (b) payroll and payroll-benefit-related costs for employees who devote time to the PP&E activity. All general and administrative and overhead costs should be charged to expense and not capitalized as a cost of PP&E.

(c) ACQUISITION-OR-CONSTRUCTION STAGE. This stage begins when the entity obtains ownership of the PP&E. Only directly identifiable costs as outlined in the previous paragraph are capitalizable along with depreciation of machinery and equipment used directly in the construction of PP&E and inventory used directly in the construction or installation of PP&E. All general and administrative and overhead costs should also be charged to expense and not capitalized as a cost of PP&E.

(d) IN-SERVICE STAGE. This stage begins when a PP&E asset is substantially complete and ready for its intended use. All costs incurred in this stage are charged to expense except for costs relating to replacement of existing components of a PP&E asset or acquisition of additional components. The principles outlined under the acquisition-or-construction stage are used to determine what costs of the replacements or additional components are capitalizable. Accordingly, all costs of repairs and maintenance are charged to expense, because they cannot be considered replacements or additional components. In conjunction with the replacement of a component of PP&E, an estimate of the remaining net book value of that replaced component should be charged to expense in the period of replacement.

(e) PLANNED MAJOR MAINTENANCE ACTIVITIES. The proposed SOP prohibits the following accounting methods for planned major maintenance activities:

- Accrual of a liability before incurring the costs for a planned major maintenance activity
- Deferral and amortization of the cost of a planned major maintenance activity
- Current recognition of additional depreciation to cover future costs of a planned major maintenance activity

(f) COMPONENT ACCOUNTING. A component of a PP&E asset is defined as a tangible part or portion that can be separately identified as an asset, and it is expected to provide economic benefit for more than one year. The proposed SOP provides that if a component has an expected useful life that differs from the expected useful life of the PP&E asset to which it relates, the cost of the component should be accounted for separately and depreciated over its separate expected useful life.

(g) EFFECT ON CURRENT PRACTICE. Over 400 comment letters were received by AcSEC in response to this proposed SOP. If adopted without change, the SOP would significantly affect current practice in the following areas:

- The capitalization criteria prohibit capitalization of indirect costs, overhead, and general and administrative costs, which many entities capitalize currently as a part of their PP&E cost.
- Many entities use the methods prohibited under the section titled "Planned Major Maintenance Activities" to account for plant turnarounds and other major maintenance activities.
- Requirements to use component accounting would effectively prohibit entities from using group and composite methods of accounting for depreciation.

It is anticipated that a final SOP will be issued in early 2003 with an effective date approximately one year after final issuance.

21.8 DEPRECIATION

Property, plant, and equipment used by a business in the production of goods and services is a depreciable asset. That is, its cost is systematically reduced by charges to goods produced or to operations over the asset's estimated service life. That meaning is captured by International Accounting Standards (IAS) 4, "Depreciation Accounting," which defines depreciable assets as "assets that (a) are expected to be used during more than one accounting period, and (b) have a limited useful life, and (c) are held by an enterprise for use in the production or supply of goods and services, for rental to others, or for administrative purposes."

(a) DEPRECIATION DEFINED. Despite its widespread use, depreciation has no single, universal definition. Economists, engineers, the courts, accountants, and others have definitions that meet their particular needs. Seldom are the definitions identical.

The generally accepted accounting definition is set forth in Accounting Terminology Bulletin No. 1:

> Depreciation accounting is a system of accounting which aims to distribute the cost or other basic value of tangible capital assets, less salvage (if any), over the estimated useful life of the unit (which may be a group of assets) in a systematic and rational manner. It is a process of allocation, not of valuation. Depreciation for the year is the portion of the total charge under such a system that is allocated to the year.

As the definition says, the depreciation accounting is "a process of allocation, not of valuation." That is, its purpose is to allocate the net cost (cost less salvage) of an asset over time, not to state the asset at its current or long-term value.

Depreciation, as accountants use the term, applies only to buildings, machinery, and equipment. It is thus distinguished first from depletion, which is a process of allocating the cost of wasting resources, such as mineral deposits, and second from amortization, which is a process of allocating the cost of intangible assets.

All forms of allocation, including depreciation, depletion, and amortization, apply formulas, such as the straight-line and double-declining-balance formulas for depreciation and the compound interest formula for reporting on liabilities, selected at the beginning of the periods of allocation, supposedly to represent underlying economic events that are expected to occur in the future. Accountants cannot be that prescient about events that may occur in the future, after the formulas are selected. And events do not occur as regularly as the formulas imply.

Moreover, allocation does not even represent underlying economic events. It merely takes amounts from the world represented by financial reporting, such as costs, enters them in financial report records, and massages them there. As Hendriksen and van Breda state: ". . . annual [depreciation] is simply a fraction of the total . . . cost. . . . [and] has no necessary relation to . . . occurrences within the year. . . . [it] has no real world connotations."[15] The AICPA said the same: "Definitions are unacceptable which imply that depreciation for the year is a measurement . . . of anything that actually occurs within the year."[16] Allocation thus violates the FASB's qualitative characteristic of representational faithfulness: It represents nothing that exists or occurs in the world outside financial reporting, faithfully or otherwise. It also violates the FASB's qualitative characteristic of verifiability. As Storey and Storey stated in a study published by the FASB, "The distinguishing characteristic of accounting measures whose representational faithfulness normally cannot be verified because only the procedures used to obtain the measures are verifiable is that they result from allocations. . . ."[17]

The result of applying allocation methods is to stabilize reported income. The smooth ("systematic") formulas allocation uses have that result:

> . . . depreciation is only part of a broader scheme whose purpose is to equalize charges between different years.[18]

> The very purpose of measurement is to discover variations in empirical phenomena. By contrast, it seems that the purpose of allocation is to make the empirical phenomena appear to be smooth regardless of the actual variations.[19]

> . . . allocations [are] designed to produce smoothed income flows.[20]

As Schuetze, a Chief Accountant of the SEC, stated, allocation is used for managing earnings, for ". . . smoothing the hills and valleys of change."[21]

Further, depreciation incorporates predictions of future events, the termination of the useful lives of the depreciable assets. The amounts of depreciation for the reporting period and of the undepreciated balances at the reporting date are said to depend on events that are predicted to occur after the reporting date. Those current changes and current conditions are said to be affected by future events. Cause is thus said to follow effect in time. Because cause cannot follow effect

---

[15] Eldon S. Hendriksen and Michael F. van Breda, *Accounting Theory*, Fifth Edition (Richard D. Irwin, Inc., Boston, 1992), pp. 527, 528.

[16] AICPA, "Review and Résumé," Accounting Terminology Bulletin No. 1, p. 24.

[17] Reed K. Storey and Sylvia Storey, *The Framework of Financial Accounting Concepts and Standards* (FASB: Norwalk, 1998), p. 109.

[18] Henry Rand Hatfield, *Modern Accounting* (D. Appleton and Company: New York, 1916), p. 134.

[19] Robert R. Sterling, *Toward a Science of Accounting* (Scholars Book Co., Houston, 1979), p. 226.

[20] T. A. Lee, "The Simplicity and Complexity of Accounting," in Sterling, *Simplified*, p. 45.

[21] Walter Schuetze, "Keep It Simple," *Accounting Horizons*, June 1991, p. 113.

in time, nothing about the future should be incorporated in depreciation or any other calculations made in preparing financial statements.

The only reason accountants incorporate the future in financial statements, which are supposed to be reports, that is, recitations of history, recitations of the past up to and including the present, is to stabilize income reporting.

(b) BASIC FACTORS IN THE COMPUTATION OF DEPRECIATION. Three basic factors enter in the computation of depreciation:

1. The estimate of the service life (sometimes called the *useful life*) of the asset
2. The determination of the depreciation base
3. The choice of a depreciation method

21.9 SERVICE LIFE

(a) SERVICE LIFE AS DISTINGUISHED FROM PHYSICAL LIFE. Depreciation allocates the net cost of an asset over its service life, not its physical life. The service life of an asset represents the period of usefulness to its present owner. The physical life of an asset represents its total period of usefulness, perhaps to more than one owner. For any given asset, and any given owner, physical and service life may be identical, or service life may be shorter. For example, a company that supplies automobiles to its sales force may replace its automobiles every 50,000 miles. An automobile's physical life is usually longer than 50,000 miles. But to this particular company, the service life of an automobile is 50,000 miles, and the company's depreciation policies would seek to allocate the net cost of its automobiles over 50,000 miles.

(b) FACTORS AFFECTING SERVICE LIFE. Service life may be affected by two factors physical or functional:

1. Physical factors:
   a. Wear and tear
   b. Deterioration and decay
   c. Damage or destruction
2. Functional factors:
   a. Inadequacy
   b. Obsolescence

(i) Physical Factors. Mosich and Larsen discuss physical factors:

Physical deterioration results largely from wear and tear from use and the forces of nature. These physical forces terminate the usefulness of plant assets by rendering them incapable of performing the services for which they were intended and thus set the maximum limit on economic life.[22]

Wear and tear and deterioration and decay act gradually and are reasonably predictable. They are ordinarily taken into consideration in estimating service life. Damage or destruction, however, usually occurs suddenly, irregularly, infrequently, and unpredictably. Either one is ordinarily not taken into consideration in estimating service life. Its effects are therefore usually not recognized in the depreciation charge but as a charge to expense when the damage or destruction occurs.

(ii) Functional Factors. Asset inadequacy may result from business growth, requiring the company to replace existing assets with larger or more efficient assets. Or assets may become inadequate because of changes in the market, in plant location, in the nature or variety of products

---

[22] Mosich and Larsen.

manufactured, or in the ownership of the business. For example, a warehouse may be in good structural condition, but if more space is needed and cannot be economically provided by adding a wing or a separate building, the warehouse has become inadequate, and its remaining service life to its present owner is ended.

Obsolescence usually arises from events that are more clearly external, such as progress, invention, and technical improvement. For example, the Boeing 707 and the Douglas DC-8 jet aircraft made many propeller-driven airplanes obsolete, at least as to major airlines, because propeller-driven planes were no longer economical in long-range service.

A distinction should be made between ordinary obsolescence and extraordinary obsolescence. Ordinary obsolescence is due to normal, reasonably predictable technical progress; extraordinary obsolescence arises from unforeseen events that result in an asset being abandoned earlier than expected.

The American Accounting Association (AAA) publication, "A Statement of Basic Accounting Theory" (1966), states: "Obsolescence, to the extent it can be quantified by equipment replacement studies or similar means, should be recognized explicitly and regularly." Thus ordinary obsolescence, like wear and tear, should be considered in estimating useful life so that it can be recognized in the annual depreciation charge. But extraordinary obsolescence, like damage or destruction, is recognized outside depreciation accounting as a charge when it occurs.

(c) THE EFFECT OF MAINTENANCE.   As Welsch and Zlatkovich note, "The useful life of operational assets also is influenced by the repair and maintenance policies of the company."[23] The expected effect of a company's maintenance policy is therefore considered in estimating service lives.

(d) STATISTICAL METHODS OF ESTIMATING SERVICE LIVES.   In several industries, notably utilities, estimates of service lives have been based on historical analyses of retirement rates for specific groups of assets, such as telephone or electric wire poles. These analyses have resulted in the development of statistical techniques for predicting retirement rates and service lives. Utilities have used such techniques in defending depreciation practices, replacement needs and policies, and investment valuations for rate-making purposes. Statistical techniques are appropriate for any group of homogeneous assets where estimating individual service lives is not possible or practical (e.g., mattresses and linens in a hotel, overhead and underground cables of telephone companies, and rails and ties for railroads).

Grant and Norton mention two other statistical approaches to determining service lives:

1. Actuarial methods, which aim at determining survivor curves and frequency curves for annual retirements, as well as giving estimates of average life. These methods are generally similar to the methods developed by life insurance actuaries for the study of human mortality. They require plant records in sufficient detail so that the age of each unit of plant is known at all times.

2. Turnover methods, which aim only at estimating average life. Since turnover methods require only information about additions and retirements, they require less detail in the plant records than do actuarial methods.[24]

(e) SERVICE LIVES OF LEASEHOLD IMPROVEMENTS.   Leasehold improvements are depreciated over the shorter of the remaining term of the lease or the expected life of the asset. Lease renewal terms are usually not considered unless renewal is probable.

(f) REVISIONS OF ESTIMATED SERVICE LIVES.   Service life estimates should be reviewed periodically and revised as appropriate. The National Association of Accountants (NAA) Statement

---

[23] Welsch and Zlatkovich.

[24] E. Grant and P. Norton, *Depreciation* (Ronald Press, New York, 1955).

on Management Accounting Practices No. 7, "Fixed Asset Accounting: The Allocation of Costs," suggests that reviews of estimates involve operations, management, engineering, and accounting personnel.

A change in the estimated useful lives of depreciable assets should be accounted for as a change in an accounting estimate. As prescribed by APB Opinion No. 20, "Accounting Changes," the change is recognized in the period of change and in future periods affected. If future periods are affected, the Opinion also requires disclosure of the effect on income before extraordinary items, on net income, and on related per-share amounts of the current period. The following is an example of this disclosure from 1987 financial statements:

Crown Central Petroleum Corporation

Notes to Consolidated Financial Statements

Note N. Change in Accounting Estimate

In the second quarter of 1987, the Company increased the estimated remaining useful lives of its refinery units based on available technology and anticipated severity of service. Remaining asset lives that averaged 9 years were increased to an average of 20 years. The effects of this change in accounting estimate were to decrease 1987 depreciation expense by approximately $3,224,000 and increase net income by approximately $1,799,000, or $.25 per primary share, ($.18 per fully diluted share). ·

Note that the per-share amounts disclosed should be calculated and presented consistent with the provisions of SFAS No. 128, "Earnings per Share," which was effective for periods beginning after December 15, 1997. Accounting changes are discussed in greater detail in Chapter 11.

21.10 DEPRECIATION BASE

The cost to be depreciated, otherwise known as the *depreciation base*, is the total cost of an asset less its estimated net salvage value. When immaterial, net salvage value is commonly ignored.

(a) NET SALVAGE VALUE. *Kohler's Dictionary for Accountants* defines salvage as: "Value remaining from a fire, wreck, or other accident or from the retirement or scrapping of an asset."[25] Salvage value may be determined by reference to quoted market prices for similar items or to estimated reproduction costs, reduced by an allowance for usage. Salvage value reduced by the cost to remove the asset is net salvage value.

Net salvage value can be taken into account in either of two ways: directly, by reducing the depreciation base; or, indirectly, by adjusting the depreciation rate.

To illustrate the latter, assume an asset with a total cost of $1,000, a service life of 10 years, and an estimated net salvage value of $250. A 7.5 percent rate applied to the cost will yield the same annual depreciation charge as a 10 percent rate applied to cost less estimated net salvage value. This point should be borne in mind in interpreting stated rates of depreciation; the rates may be applied to the asset cost or to cost less net salvage value.

(b) PROPERTY UNDER CONSTRUCTION. Assets usually are not depreciated during construction, which includes any necessary pilot testing or breaking in. Such assets are not in service, and the purpose of depreciation accounting is to allocate the cost of an asset over its service life.

An exception to the general rule arises when an asset under construction is partially used in an income-producing activity. In that case, the part in use should be depreciated. An example is a building that is partially rented while still under construction.

---

[25] Kohler.

(c) IDLE AND AUXILIARY EQUIPMENT.   NAA Statement on Management Accounting Practices No. 7 recommends that depreciation be continued on idle, reserve, or standby assets. When the period of idleness is expected to be long, the assets should be set forth separately in the balance sheet, but depreciation should continue.

EITF Issue No. 84-28 raises the question of how idle facilities or facilities operating significantly below normal operating levels should be depreciated. Some EITF members stated that they were aware of a limited number of cases in which the depreciation method for such assets was changed to one of the usage methods (see below), but none expressed knowledge of cases in which depreciation of the assets was totally suspended. The EITF reached no consensus.

(d) ASSETS TO BE DISPOSED OF.   SFAS No. 144 prohibits depreciation from being recorded during the period in which the asset is being held for disposal, even if the asset is still generating revenue.

(e) USED ASSETS.   The depreciation base of a used asset is the same as for a new asset, that is, cost less net salvage value. The carrying value of a used asset in the accounts of the previous owner should not be carried over to the accounts of the new owner. See, however, Chapter 22 for the accounting for assets acquired in a business combination.

21.11 DEPRECIATION METHODS

Assets are depreciated by a variety of methods, including the following five:

1. Straight-line method
2. Usage methods:
   a. Service-hours method
   b. Productive-output method
3. Decreasing-charge methods:
   a. Sum-of-digits method
   b. Fixed-percentage-of-declining-balance method
   c. Double-declining-balance method
4. Interest methods:
   a. Annuity method
   b. Sinking-fund method
5. Other methods:
   a. Appraisal method
   b. Retirement method
   c. Replacement method
   d. Arbitrary assignment

(a) STRAIGHT-LINE METHOD.   This method recognizes equal periodic depreciation charges over the service life of an asset, thereby making depreciation a function solely of time without regard to asset productivity, efficiency, or usage. The periodic depreciation charge is computed by dividing the cost of the asset, less net salvage value, by the service life expressed in months or years:

$$\frac{\text{Cost} - \text{Net salvage value}}{\text{Service life}} = \text{Depreciation charge per period}$$

Assuming an asset cost $15,000 and has an estimated net salvage value of $750 (five percent of cost) and a service life of 10 years, the annual depreciation charge would be $1,425, calculated as follows:

$$\frac{\$15,000 - \$750}{10\,\text{years}} = \$1,425$$

When the use or productivity of an asset differs significantly over its life, the straight-line method produces what some believe is a distorted allocation of costs. For example, if an asset is more productive during its early life than later, some view an equal amount of depreciation in each year as distorted. Nevertheless, the method is widely used because of its simplicity.

A survey reported by Lamden, Gerboth, and McRae showed that the straight-line method is most frequently used for financial statement purposes by companies with the following five characteristics:

1. Relatively large investments in depreciable assets
2. Relatively high depreciation charges
3. Stock traded on one of the major stock exchanges or in the over-the-counter market
4. Managements with a high level of concern for (a) matching costs with revenues and (b) maintaining comparability with other firms in the industry
5. Managements with a low level of concern for conforming depreciation for financial statement to depreciation for tax purposes[26]

(b) USAGE METHODS. Two other methods, the service-hours method and the productive-output method, vary the periodic depreciation charge to recognize differences in asset use or productivity.

(i) Service-Hours Method. This method assumes that if an asset is used twice as much in period 1 as in period 2, the depreciation charge should differ accordingly. The depreciation rate is calculated as it is for the straight-line method, except that service life is expressed in terms of hours of use:

$$\frac{\text{Cost} - \text{Net salvage value}}{\text{Service life}} = \text{Rate per hour of use}$$

If an asset cost $15,000 and had an estimated net salvage value of $750 and an estimated service life of 38,000 hours, the calculation would be as follows:

$$\frac{\$15,000 - \$750}{38,00\,\text{hours}} = \$0.375 \text{ per hour of use}$$

If the asset is used 4,000 hours in the first year, the annual depreciation charge would be $1,500 (4,000 hours × $0.375 per hour).

Welsch and Zlatkovich state, "The service hours method usually is appropriate when obsolescence is not a primary factor in depreciation and the economic service potential of the asset is used up primarily by running time."[27]

(ii) Productive-Output Method. This method is essentially the same as the service-hours method, except that service life is expressed in terms of units of production rather than hours of use. If the asset described above had a service life of 95,000 units of production rather than 38,000 hours of use, the depreciation rate would be calculated as follows:

$$\frac{\$15,000 - \$750}{95,00\,\text{units}} = \$0.15 \text{ per unit of product}$$

---

[26] Lamden, Gerboth, and McRae.
[27] Welsch and Zlatkovich.

Depreciation by the productive-output method is illustrated by the following example from 1987 financial statements:

McDermott International, Inc.

Notes to Consolidated Financial Statements

Note 3. Change in Depreciation Method

Effective April 1, 1986, McDermott International changed the method of depreciation for major marine vessels from the straight-line method to a units-of-production method based on the utilization of each vessel. Depreciation expense calculated under the units-of-production method may be less than, equal to, or greater than depreciation expense calculated under the straight-line method in any period. McDermott International employs utilization factors as a key element in the management of marine construction operations and believes the units-of-production method, which recognizes both time and utilization factors, accomplishes a better matching of costs and revenues than the straight-line method. The cumulative effect of the change on prior years at March 31, 1986, of $25,711,000, net of income taxes of $17,362,000 ($0.70 per share), is included in the accompanying Consolidated Statement of Income (Loss) and Retained Earnings for the fiscal year ended March 31, 1987. The effect of the change on the fiscal year ended March 31, 1987, was to increase Income from Continuing Operations before Extraordinary Items and Cumulative Effect of Accounting Change and decrease Net Loss $6,556,000 ($0.18 per share). Pro forma amounts showing the effect of applying the units-of-production method of depreciation retroactively, net of related income taxes, are presented in the Consolidated Statement of Income (Loss) and Retained Earnings.

The productive-output method is sometimes used to adjust depreciation calculated by the straight-line method, when asset usage varies from normal. The adjustment may be limited to a specified range, as illustrated in the following example drawn from 1986 financial statements:

Wheeling-Pittsburgh Steel Corporation

Notes to Financial Statements

Note G. Property, Plant, and Equipment

The Corporation utilizes the modified units-of-production method of depreciation which recognizes that the depreciation of steelmaking machinery is related to the physical wear of the equipment as well as a time factor. The modified units-of-production method provides for straight-line depreciation charges modified (adjusted) by the level of production activity. On an annual basis, adjustments may not exceed a range of 60% (minimum) to 110% (maximum) of related straight-line depreciation. The adjustments are based on the ratio of actual production to a predetermined norm. Eighty-five percent of capacity is considered the norm for the Corporation's primary steelmaking facilities; 80% of capacity is considered the norm for finishing facilities. No adjustment is made when the production level is equal to norm. In 1986 depreciation under the modified units of production method exceeded straight-line depreciation by $1.5 million or 3.2%. For 1985 and 1984 aggregate straight-line depreciation exceeded that recorded under the modified units-of-production method by $10.1 million or 18.3%, $7.0 million or 12.6%, respectively.

The productive-output method recognizes that not all hours of use are equally productive. Therefore, the theory underlying the preference for a usage method would point to the productive-output method as the better of the two.

(c) DECREASING-CHARGE METHODS.   Decreasing-charge methods allocate a higher depreciation charge to the early years of an asset's service life. These methods are justified on the following grounds:

- Most equipment is more efficient (hence more productive) in its early life. Therefore, the early years of service life should bear more of the asset's cost.

- Repairs and maintenance charges generally increase as an asset gets older. Therefore, depreciation charges should decrease as the asset gets older so as to produce a more stable total charge (repairs and maintenance plus depreciation) for the use of the asset during its service life.

(i) **Sum-of-Digits Method.** This method applies a decreasing rate to a constant depreciation base (cost less net salvage value). The rate is a fraction. The denominator is the sum of the digits representing periods (years or months) of asset life. The numerator, which changes each period, is the digit assigned to the particular period. Digits are assigned in reverse order. For example, if an asset has an estimated service life of five years, the denominator would be 15, calculated as follows:

$$1 + 2 + 3 + 4 + 5 = 15$$

In the first year the rate fraction would be 5/15, in the second year 4/15, in the third year 3/15, and so on. The denominator may be calculated by means of the following formula, where n is the service life in years or months:

$$\frac{n+1}{2} \times n = \text{Denominator}$$

For example, if the service life is estimated to be 25 years:

$$\frac{25+1}{2} \times 25 = 325$$

(ii) **Fixed-Percentage-of-Declining-Balance Method.** This method produces results similar to the sum-of-digits method. However, whereas the sum-of-digits method multiplies a declining rate times a fixed balance, the fixed-percentage-of-declining-balance method multiplies a fixed rate times a declining balance. The rate is calculated by means of the following formula, where n equals the service life in years:

$$\text{Depreciation rate} = 1 - \sqrt{\frac{\text{Net salvage value}}{\text{Cost}}}$$

The rate thus determined is then applied to the cost of the asset, without regard to salvage value, reduced by depreciation previously recognized. The result is to reduce the cost of the asset to its estimated net salvage value at the end of the asset's service life. (Some salvage value must be assigned to the asset, since it is not possible to reduce an amount to zero by applying a constant rate to a successively smaller remainder. In the absence of an expected salvage value, a nominal value of $1 can be assumed.)

To illustrate, assume an asset with a cost of $10,000, an estimated salvage value of $1,296, and an estimated service life of four years:

$$\text{Depreciation rate} = 1 - \sqrt[4]{\frac{\$1,296}{\$10,000}} = 1 - \frac{6}{10} = 40\%$$

The first year's depreciation will be $4,000 ($10,000 × 40%), the second year's $2,400 [($10,000 − $4,000) × 40%], and so on, leaving at the end of the fourth year a net asset of $1,296.

(iii) **Double-Declining-Balance Method.** The double-declining-balance method was introduced into the income tax laws in 1954. Since then, it has gained increased acceptability for financial reporting as well. This method differs from the fixed-percentage-of-declining-balance method by specifying that the fixed rate should be twice the straight-line rate. Otherwise the two methods are identical: The fixed rate is applied to the undepreciated book value of the asset—a declining balance.

Year	Book Value Beginning of Period	Rate (%)	Annual Depreciation Charge	Book Value End of Period
1	$15,000	20	$3,000	$12,000
2	12,000	20	2,400	9,600
3	9,600	20	1,920	7,680
4	7,680	20	1,536	6,144

Exhibit 21.1   Depreciation using the double-declining-balance method.

To illustrate, assume an asset with a cost of $15,000, an estimated net salvage value of $750, and an estimated service life of 10 years. Twice the straight-line rate would be 20 percent. Exhibit 21.1 shows the calculation for the first four years.

Note that, as with the fixed-percentage-of-declining-balance method, the rate is applied to the cost of the asset without regard to net salvage value. This means that by the end of the asset's estimated service life, some amount of undepreciated book value will be left in the asset account. But since the depreciation rate is determined without regard to estimated net salvage value, the undepreciated amount left in the account will likely differ from net salvage value. For example, at the end of the 10-year service life of the asset illustrated in Exhibit 21.1, the asset's book value would be $1,611, which is $861 greater than estimated net salvage value. To avoid such differences, companies usually switch from the double-declining-balance method to the straight-line method sometime during an asset's service life.

To calculate the straight-line depreciation charge at the time of the switch, the net book value (cost less accumulated depreciation), less estimated net salvage value, is divided by the estimated remaining service life. For example, if an asset has a remaining depreciation base (cost less estimated net salvage value) of $4,620 and seven years of remaining service life, a straight-line charge of $660 for the next seven years will depreciate the asset to its net salvage value.

The optimal time to make a switch is when the year's depreciation computed using the straight-line method exceeds depreciation computed using the double-declining-balance method. That is usually sometime after the midpoint of the asset's life.

Exhibit 21.2 compares the annual depreciation charges computed by the straight-line method, the sum-of-digits method, and the double-declining-balance method with switch to straight-line.

Note that although all three methods charge the same total amount to expense over the same service life, the amounts charged at the midpoint of the asset's service life differ:

Year	Straight-Line	Sum-of-Digits	Double-Declining-Balance, Switch to Straight-Line
1	$ 1,425	$ 2,591	$ 3,000
2	1,425	2,322	2,400
3	1,425	2,073	1,920
4	1,425	1,814	1,536
5	1,425	1,555	1,229
6	1,425	1,295	983
7	1,425	1,036	796
8	1,425	777	796
9	1,425	518	795
10	1,425	259	795
	$14,250	$14,250	$14,250

Exhibit 21.2   Comparison of annual depreciation charges: straight-line, sum-of-digits, and declining-balance with switch to straight line.

1. Straight-line has charged 50 percent of the total.

2. Sum-of-digits has charged nearly 73 percent.

3. Double-declining-balance with switch to straight-line has charged about 71 percent.

(d) INTEREST METHODS. Two methods, the annuity method and the sinking-fund method, compute depreciation using compound interest factors. Both methods produce an increasing annual depreciation charge. Neither method is used much in practice.

(i) Annuity Method. The annuity method equalizes each year's sum of depreciation and an imputed interest charge calculated at a constant rate on the asset's undepreciated book value. Each year's sum of depreciation and imputed interest is calculated by the following formula, where n is the estimated service life of the asset in years and i is the imputed rate of interest:

$$\frac{\text{Cost of asset less present value of net salvage value}}{\text{Present value of an ordinary of annuity of } n \text{ payments of 1 at } i}$$

Assume, for example, that an asset with an economic life of five years and a net salvage value of $67,388 is acquired at a cost of $800,000. Using an imputed rate of interest of 10 percent, each year's sum of depreciation and imputed interest would be computed as follows:

$$\frac{\$800,000 - (\$67,388 \times 0.620921^*)}{3.790787}$$

$$\frac{\$800,000 - \$41,843}{3.790787}$$

$$= \$200,000$$

*Present Value of $1 for five periods at 10%.

The result is presented in Exhibit 19.3.

Imputed interest is computed only for purposes of computing depreciation; it is not charged to expense.

(ii) Sinking-Fund Method. The sinking-fund method produces a depreciation pattern that is identical to that of the annuity method but by means of a different rationale and a different formula. Under the sinking-fund method, the amount of annual depreciation is equal to the increase in a hypothetical interest-earning asset replacement fund. The increase in the fund consists of assumed equal periodic deposits to the fund plus interest at the assumed rate on the fund balance.

Each year's depreciation charge is calculated by the following formula, where n is the remaining service life of the asset in years and i is the assumed rate of interest:

$$\text{Depreciation} = \frac{\text{Cost of asset less net residual value}}{\text{Ordinary annuity of } n \text{ payments of 1 at } i}$$

Using the same facts as in Exhibit 21.3 (an asset cost of $800,000, a 5-year life, a net salvage value of $67,388, and a 10 percent interest rate), the first year's depreciation would be computed as follows:

$$\text{Depreciation} = \frac{\text{Cost of asset less net residual value}}{\text{Ordinary annuity of 5 payments of 1 at 10\%}}$$

$$\frac{\$800,000 - \$67,388}{6.1051}$$

$$= \$120,000$$

Year	Combined Depreciation and Imputed Interest	Imputed Interest (10% of Carrying Amount)	Depreciation	Accumulated Depreciation	Carrying Amount of Asset
0					$800,000
1	$ 200,000	$ 80,000	$120,000	$120,000	680,000
2	200,000	68,000	132,000	252,000	548,000
3	200,000	54,800	145,200	397,200	402,800
4	200,000	40,280	159,720	556,920	243,080
5	200,000	24,308	175,692	732,612	67,388
	$1,100,000	$267,388	$732,612		

Exhibit 21.3   Depreciation using the annuity method. (*Source:* Mosich and Larsen, *Intermediate Accounting,* McGraw-Hill, 1986, p. 627 [adapted].)

(e) OTHER METHODS.   The other methods described below attempt to distribute the net cost of an asset over its service life. But none is, properly speaking, a depreciation method.

(i) Appraisal Method.   This method reduces the asset's book value to an appraised value at the end of each year. As such, it is a method of asset valuation, not of cost allocation, and thus is not a method of depreciation accounting. It is also hard to apply in practice, since a going-concern appraisal value can seldom be determined with enough accuracy to result in an objective measurement.

(ii) Retirement and Replacement Methods.   Neither of these methods is a depreciation method, since neither distributes the cost of an asset over its estimated useful life. The retirement method writes off the entire depreciation base in the period in which the asset is retired from service. The replacement method charges depreciation for the cost of replacement assets. Under both methods, no depreciation is charged until the first retirement takes place.

Also under both methods, the property accounts on the balance sheet carry gross costs. Under the retirement method, the property accounts show the gross cost of any asset currently in use. Under the replacement method, the accounts show the gross cost of the original plant acquisitions.

Retirement and replacement methods have been used by utilities because of the practical problems encountered in depreciating large numbers of interrelated items, such as rails, ties, poles, and pipe sections, whose individual cost is small. In such situations, service life is hard to estimate, and the distinction between maintenance and replacement is often unclear.

(iii) Arbitrary Assignment.   Arbitrary assignment is not a method of depreciation, because it is not "systematic and rational." It is also highly subjective and open to abuse.

(f) DEPRECIATION FOR PARTIAL PERIODS.   Since assets are acquired and disposed of throughout the year, companies must compute depreciation for partial periods. Five computation alternatives are found in practice:

1. Depreciation is recognized to the nearest whole month. Assets acquired on or before the 15th of the month or sold after the 15th are reduced by a full month's depreciation; assets acquired after the 15th or sold on or before the 15th are excluded from the month's depreciation computation.
2. Depreciation is recognized to the nearest whole year. Assets acquired during the first six months or sold during the last six months are reduced by a full year's depreciation; assets acquired during the last six months or sold during the first six months are excluded from the year's depreciation computation.

3. One-half year's depreciation only is recognized on all assets purchased or sold during the year.

4. No depreciation is recognized on all assets purchased or sold during the year.

5. A full year's depreciation is recognized on assets acquired during the year; none is recognized on assets retired during the year.

(g) CHANGE IN DEPRECIATION METHOD. A change in depreciation method is a change in an accounting principle. In accordance with APB Opinion No. 20 (par. 18), the cumulative effect of the change is recognized in net income of the period of change. Accounting changes are discussed more fully in Chapter 9.

21.12 DEPRECIATION RATES

(a) SOURCES OF DEPRECIATION RATES. Information concerning depreciation rates for various classes of business property is available from several sources. Depreciation rates have been given attention by authors of manuals on accounting, engineering, management, rate making, and other aspects of the business process. They have been the subject of special investigation by industry through individual studies and studies conducted under the auspices of manufacturing and other trade associations.

The choice of depreciation rates has also been influenced by the requirements of tax law and regulation, discussed later in this chapter.

(b) GROUP AND COMPOSITE RATES. A group of assets may be depreciated at a single rate. Assets of electrical utilities and hotels are sometimes depreciated in this manner. The two most common methods of depreciating asset groups are the group depreciation method and the collective depreciation method.

(i) Group Depreciation. Mosich and Larsen define group depreciation as the "process of averaging the economic lives of a number of plant assets and computing depreciation on the entire class of assets as if it were an operating unit."[28] Smith and Skousen elaborate:

> Because the accumulated depreciation account under the group procedure applies to the entire group of assets, it is not related to any specific asset. Thus, no book value can be calculated for any specific asset and there are no fully depreciated assets. To arrive at the periodic depreciation charge, the depreciation rate is applied to the recorded cost of all assets remaining in service, regardless of age.[29]

To illustrate, assume that a company purchased a group of 100 similar machines having an average expected service life of five years at a total cost of $200,000. Of this group, 30 machines are expected to be retired at the end of four years, 40 at the end of five years, and the remaining 30 at the end of six years. Under the group depreciation method, depreciation is based on the average expected service life of five years, which converts to an annual depreciation rate of 20 percent. This rate is applied to those assets in service each year. Assuming the machines are retired as expected, the charges for depreciation and the changes in the group asset and accumulated depreciation accounts are summarized in Exhibit 21.4.

It should be noted that the depreciation charge per machine-year is $400—one-fifth of the unit price of $2,000. In each of the first four years, 100 machines are in use, and the annual depreciation charge is $40,000. In the fifth year, when the number of machines in use drops to 70, the charge is $28,000. In the sixth year, when only 30 units are in use, the charge is $12,000.

---

[28] Mosich and Larsen.
[29] Smith and Skousen.

End of Year	Depreciation (20% of cost)	Asset			Accumulated Depreciation			Asset Book Value
		Debit	Credit	Balance	Debit	Credit	Balance	
		$200		$200				$200
1	$ 40			200		$ 40	$ 40	160
2	40			200		40	80	120
3	40			200		40	120	80
4	40		$ 60	140	$ 60	40	100	40
5	28		80	60	80	28	48	12
6	12		60	—	60	12	—	—
	$200	$200	$200	$200	$200	$200		

Exhibit 21.4   Group depreciation (all amounts in thousands).

When an asset in the group is disposed of, no gain or loss is recognized. The asset's cost is removed from the group asset account, and the difference between the cost and the asset's actual net salvage value is removed from the accumulated depreciation account.

The advantage of group depreciation, according to Smith and Skousen, is "an annual charge that is more closely related to the quantity of productive facilities being used. Gains and losses due solely to normal variations in asset lives are not recognized, and operating results are more meaningfully stated."[30]

But what Smith and Skousen see as an advantage, Geiger sees as a weakness:

Since, for all practical purposes, the actual depreciation rate of an item is unknown and is not used, the true gain or loss at time of its sale or disposal cannot be computed. Accordingly, gain or loss on disposal of fixed assets is not recognized in the income accounts.[31]

But Smith and Skousen counter: "With normal variations in asset lives, the losses not recognized on early retirements are offset by the continued depreciation charges on those assets still in service after the average life has elapsed."[32]

(ii) Composite Depreciation.   Composite depreciation applies group depreciation procedures to groups of dissimilar assets with varying service lives.

Exhibit 21.5 illustrates the calculation of composite rates. The composite life of the assets is 9.96 years; the resulting composite depreciation rate is 9.2 percent. To determine the annual depreciation, the composite rate of 9.2 percent is applied to the asset account balance at the beginning of the year. The total acquisition cost of $30,000 is thus reduced to the estimated salvage value of $2,500 in 9.96 years.

As in group depreciation, when an asset is disposed of, no gain or loss is recognized. The asset's cost is removed from the group asset account, and the difference between cost and actual net salvage value is removed from the accumulated depreciation account.

Once a composite rate has been established, it is usually continued until a significant event indicates the need for a new rate. Such an event may be a material change in the service lives of the assets included in the group, a major asset addition, or a major asset retirement. Composite depreciation is based on the assumptions that assets are regularly retired near the end of their service lives and that the retired assets are replaced with similar assets. If replacements do not take place according to the assumptions, if the service lives of replacement assets differ substantially

---

[30] Smith and Skousen.
[31] H. Dwight Geiger, "Composite Depreciation under Depreciation Guidelines," *AAA Bulletin*, Vol. 44, No. 11, July 1963.
[32] Smith and Skousen.

Asset Item	Cost	New Salvage Value	Depreciation Base	Annual Rate	Depreciation
A	$ 2,000	$ —	$ 2,000	20.0%	$ 400
B	5,000	500	4,500	12.0	540
C	8,000	1,000	7,000	10.0	700
D	15,000	1,000	14,000	8.0	1,120
Group	$30,000	$2,500	$27,500		$2,760

Composite life: $27,500 \div \$2,760 = 9.96$ years.
Composite rate: $2,760 \div \$30,000 = 9.2\%$.

Exhibit 21.5   Composite depreciation.

from the service lives of the assets replaced, or if the cost of replacement assets differs materially from the cost of the assets replaced, continued use of the same composite rate is inappropriate.

Mosich and Larsen discuss the advantages and disadvantages of composite depreciation:

> The primary disadvantage ... is that the averaging procedure may obscure significant variations from average. The accuracy of the ... composite depreciation rate may be verified by recomputing depreciation on the straight-line basis for individual plant assets. Any significant discrepancies between the two results require a change in the composite depreciation rate.

> The advantages ... are simplicity, convenience, and a reduction in the amount of detail involved in plant asset records and depreciation computations. The availability of computers has reduced the force of this argument.[33]

(c) THE EFFECTS OF REPLACEMENTS, IMPROVEMENTS, AND ADDITIONS.   As stated in Subsection 21.4(c), major expenditures that extend the service lives of assets or otherwise benefit future years are capitalized. Such expenditures require new depreciation computations. The new periodic depreciation charge is found by dividing the asset's new book value by the new remaining service life, illustrated for straight-line depreciation, as follows:

Original asset cost (original estimated life, 10 years)	$8,000
Six years' depreciation	–4,800
Net book value before capital expenditure	3,200
Net increase in book value resulting from capital expenditure	2,400
New book value (new estimated life, eight years)	$5,600
New annual depreciation charge ($5,600 ÷ 8)	$ 700

Retroactive adjustment of previous years' depreciation is not appropriate, since the expenditures benefit future years only.

(d) TOOLS AND RELATED ASSETS.   Tools are sometimes divided into two classes: semidurable (lives of five years or more) and perishable. The cost of semidurable tools is capitalized and depreciated, usually at a group or composite rate. The rate is usually high because tools are hard to control.

Perishable tools may be handled in a variety of ways. Their cost may be charged directly to the appropriate expense or production cost account. Or the cost may be capitalized, often at some arbitrarily reduced amount, and written down when periodic inventories reveal shrinkage and deterioration. A third method is to capitalize the original cost and charge all subsequent expenditures for replacements to expense.

---

[33] Mosich and Larsen.

21.13 DEPRECIATION FOR TAX PURPOSES

Tax regulations contain their own depreciation requirements. Before 1954, the Internal Revenue Service generally allowed only the straight-line method of depreciation. Subsequently, the tax laws and regulations have been amended several times to permit accelerated depreciation methods and arbitrarily short asset lives. As a result, depreciation for financial reporting purposes and depreciation for tax purposes commonly differ. The difference between an asset's tax and accounting basis is a temporary difference that requires interperiod tax allocation under SFAS No. 109, "Accounting for Income Taxes" (see Chapter 24).

(a) CURRENT REQUIREMENTS.   Depreciation for tax purposes is currently determined under the accelerated cost recovery system (ACRS), enacted in the Economic Recovery Act of 1981, and the modified accelerated cost recovery system (MACRS), enacted in the Tax Reform Act of 1986. ACRS abandoned the term *depreciation* and replaced it with a cost recovery charge. MACRS provides for accelerated write-offs. In many cases, the asset service lives allowable for tax purposes under ACRS and MACRS are shorter than the realistic economic service lives used for financial reporting purposes.

(b) MODIFIED ACCELERATED COST RECOVERY SYSTEM.   MACRS is mandatory for most tangible depreciable property placed in service after December 31, 1986, but not if the taxpayer uses a depreciation method, such as the service-hours method, based on a service life expressed other than in years.

Under MACRS, property other than real estate is depreciated over 3, 5, 7, 10, 15, or 20 years, depending on its classification. Real estate is classified as residential rental property, which is depreciated over 27.5 years, or nonresidential real property, which is depreciated over 39 years, for purchases made after May 13, 1993. Prior to that date, nonresidential real property will be depreciated over 31.5 years.

Most property can be depreciated using an alternate method, which computes depreciation using the straight-line method with no salvage value over the applicable MACRS class life.

(c) ADDITIONAL FIRST-YEAR DEPRECIATION.   The Internal Revenue Code also allows, with certain limitations, up to $17,500 of qualified tangible personal property to be deducted as an expense in the year acquired. The additional expense must be deducted from cost to determine the asset's depreciable base for tax purposes.

21.14 FINANCIAL STATEMENT PRESENTATION AND DISCLOSURE

(a) GENERAL REQUIREMENTS.   APB Opinion No. 12, "Omnibus Opinion—1967" (par. 5), requires the following four disclosures in the financial statements or notes:

1. Depreciation expense for the period
2. Balances of major classes of depreciable assets, by nature or function, at the balance sheet date
3. Accumulated depreciation, either by major asset classes or in total, at the balance sheet date
4. A general description of the method or methods used in computing depreciation for major classes of depreciable assets

Special disclosures may include the method of accounting for fully depreciated assets and liens against property. Ordinarily, the basis of valuation is also disclosed. Chapter 3 discusses the SEC's requirements.

(b) CONSTRUCTION IN PROGRESS.   Payments to contractors for construction in progress are usually recorded as advances, since the payor does not acquire ownership until completion of the construction. Self-constructed assets are normally classified separately as construction in progress until construction is complete.

(c) GAIN OR LOSS ON RETIREMENT.   Under APB Opinion No. 30, "Reporting the Results of Operations" (par. 23), gains or losses from the sale or abandonment of property, plant, or equipment used in the business are usually not reported as extraordinary items. They are expected to recur as a consequence of customary and continuing business activities. Exceptions are recognized for gains and losses that are "a direct result of a major casualty (such as an earthquake), an expropriation, or a prohibition under a newly enacted law or regulation" and that clearly meet both criteria of unusual nature and infrequency of occurrence.

(d) FULLY DEPRECIATED AND IDLE ASSETS.   Many authorities recommend that the cost and accumulated depreciation of fully depreciated assets still in use be kept in the accounts until the assets are sold or retired. Stettler recommends disclosure not only of fully depreciated assets in use, but also of idle assets:

> Disclosure should also be made if there are material amounts of fully depreciated assets still in use or material amounts of assets still subject to depreciation that are not currently in productive use.[34]

(e) IMPAIRMENT OF ASSETS.

(i) Presentation.   The SFAS No. 144 requires that impairment losses related to assets to be held and used in operations and that impairment losses from initial adjustments (and gains and losses from subsequent adjustments) of the carrying amount of assets to be disposed of be reported as a component of income from continuing operations, before income taxes. However, it provides the following options as to how such losses may be presented within the financial statements:

- As a separate line item in the income statement
- Aggregated in an appropriate line item in the income statement (e.g., as part of "other expenses") with the amount of the loss noted parenthetically on the face of the income statement
- Aggregated in an appropriate line item in the income statement supplemented by disclosure in the notes to be financial statements of the amount of impairment loss and the income statement caption in which the loss is included

If a company presents a subtotal in its income statement (e.g., income from operations, or operating income), the impairment loss must be included in such subtotal.

(ii) Disclosures for Assets to Be Held and Used.   The SFAS No. 144 requires the following disclosures in the notes to the financial statements when an impairment loss is reported:

- A description of the assets that are impaired and the facts and circumstances leading to the impairment
- The amount of the impairment loss and how the fair value of the impaired assets was determined
- The caption in the income statement (or statement of activities for a not-for-profit organization) in which impairment gains or losses are aggregated if those gains or losses have

---

[34] Howard F. Stettler, *Auditing Principles*, Fifth Edition (Prentice-Hall, Englewood Cliffs, NJ, 1982).

not been presented in a separate caption or reported parenthetically on the face of the statement

• If applicable, the business segment(s) affected

(iii) Disclosures for Assets to Be Disposed Of.   The SFAS No. 144 requires that an entity that holds assets to be disposed of should disclose the following in financial statements that include a period during which those assets are held:

• A description of the assets to be disposed of, the facts and circumstances leading to the expected disposal, the expected disposal date, and the carrying amount of those assets, if not separately presented on the face of the balance sheet
• If applicable, the business segment(s) in which assets to be disposed of are being held
• In the period in which an initial impairment loss is recorded, the amount of the impairment loss, and in years after the initial impairment is recorded the gain or loss, if any, resulting from subsequent changes in the carrying amounts of the assets
• The caption in the income statement (or statement of activities for a not-for-profit organization) in which impairment gains or losses are aggregated if those gains or losses have not been presented in a separate caption or reported parenthetically on the face of the statement
• If applicable, amounts of revenue and pretax profit or loss reported in discontinued operations

(f) SEGMENT INFORMATION.   The SFAS No. 131, "Disclosures about Segments of an Enterprise and Related Information," requires disclosure of two items of information about property, plant, and equipment for each reportable segment:

1. Total assets, for each reportable segment
2. The aggregate amount of depreciation, depletion, and amortization expense and the amount of capital expenditures for each reportable segment

21.15 SOURCES AND SUGGESTED REFERENCES

Accounting Principles Board, "Omnibus Opinion—1967," APB Opinion No. 12. AICPA, New York, 1967.

———, "Accounting Changes," APB Opinion No. 20. AICPA, New York, 1971.

———, "Interest on Receivables and Payables," APB Opinion No. 21. AICPA, New York, 1971.

———, "Interim Financial Reporting," APB Opinion No. 28. AICPA, New York, 1973.

———, "Accounting for Nonmonetary Transactions," APB Opinion No. 29. AICPA, New York, 1973.

———, "Reporting the Results of Operations," APB Opinion No. 30. AICPA, New York, 1973.

American Accounting Association, "A Statement of Basic Accounting Theory," AAA, Sarasota, FL, 1966.

American Institute of Certified Public Accountants, "Accounting Research and Terminology Bulletins—Final Edition," AICPA, New York, 1961.

———, "Accounting for the Inability to Fully Recover the Carrying Amount of Long-Lived Assets," Issues Paper. AICPA, New York, July 15, 1980.

———, "Illustrations of Accounting for the Inability to Fully Recover the Carrying Amounts of Long-Lived Assets." AICPA, New York, April 1987.

———, "Environmental Remediation Liabilities," Statement of Position 96-1. AICPA, New York, October 1996.

———, "Accounting for Certain Costs and Activities Related to Property, Plant, and Equipment," Proposed Statement of Position. AICPA, New York, 2001.

Bendel, C. W. "Streamlining the Property Accounting Procedures," *NACA Bulletin*, Vol. 31, No. 11, 1950.

Davidson, Sidney, Stickney, Clyde P., and Weil, Roman L., *Financial Accounting, An Introduction to Concepts, Methods and Uses*, Fifth Eition Dryden Press, Hinsdale, IL, 1988.

Financial Accounting Standards Board, "Impairment of Long-Lived Assets and Depreciation of Idle Facilities," EITF Issue No. 84-28. FASB, Stamford, CT, October 18, 1984, December 19, 1985, and February 6, 1986.

———, "Nonmonetary Transactions: Magnitude of Boot and the Exceptions to the Use of Fair Value," EITF Issue No. 86-29. FASB, Stamford, CT, December 3–4, 1986, January 15, 1987, and February 26, 1987.

———, "Applicability of FASB Statement No. 2 to Business Combinations Accounted for by the Purchase Method," FASB Interpretation No. 4. FASB, Stamford, CT, 1975.

———, "Accounting for the Cost of Asbestos Removal," EITF Issue No. 89-13. FASB, Norwalk, CT, October 26, 1989.

———, "Capitalization of Costs to Treat Environmental Contamination," EITF Issue No. 90-8. FASB, Norwalk, CT, May 31, 1990, and July 12, 1990.

———, "Accounting for Involuntary Conversions of Nonmonetary Assets to Monetary Assets," FASB Interpretation No. 30. FASB, Stamford, CT, 1979.

———, "Accounting for Research and Development Costs," Statement of Financial Accounting Standards No. 2. FASB, Stamford, CT, 1974.

———, "Financial Reporting for Segments of a Business Enterprise," Statement of Financial Accounting Standards No. 14. FASB, Stamford, CT, 1976.

———, "Capitalization of Interest Cost," Statement of Financial Accounting Standards No. 34. FASB, Stamford, CT, 1979.

———, "Accounting for Costs and Initial Rental Operations of Real Estate Projects," Statement of Financial Accounting Standards No. 67. FASB, Stamford, CT, 1982.

———, "Accounting for Income Taxes," Statement of Financial Accounting Standards No. 109. FASB, Norwalk, CT, 1992.

———, "Disclosures about Segments of an Enterprise and Related Information," Statement of Financial Accounting Standards No. 131. FASB, Norwalk, CT, 1997.

———, "Accounting for Asset Retirement Obligations," Statement of Financial Accounting Standards No. 143. FASB, Norwalk, CT, 2001.

———, "Accounting for the Impairment or Disposal of Long-Lived Assets," Statement of Financial Accounting Standards No. 144. FASB, Norwalk, CT, 2001.

———, "Using Cash Flow Information and Present Value in Accounting Measurements." Statement of Financial Accounting Concepts No. 7. FASB, Norwalk, CT, 2000.

Financial Executives Institute, "Survey of Unusual Charges," Morristown, NJ, September 26, 1986.

Geiger, H. Dwight, "Composite Depreciation under Depreciation Guidelines," *NAA Bulletin*, Vol. 44, No. 11, July 1963.

Grant, E., and Norton, P., *Depreciation*. Ronald Press, New York, 1955.

International Accounting Standards Committee, "Depreciation Accounting," International Accounting Standards No. 4. IASC, London, 1977.

Kieso, Donald E., and Weygandt, Jerry J., *Intermediate Accounting*, Fifth Edition John Wiley & Sons, New York, 1986.

Kohler, Eric Louis, *Kohler's Dictionary for Accountants*, Sixth Edition Prentice-Hall, Englewood Cliffs, NJ, 1983.

Lambert, S. J., III, and Lambert, Joyce C., "Concepts and Applications in APB Opinion No. 29," *Journal of Accountancy*, March 1977, pp. 60–68.

Lamden, Charles, Gerboth, Dale L., and McRae, Thomas, "Accounting for Depreciable Assets," Accounting Research Monograph, No. 1. AICPA, New York, 1975.

Mosich, A. N., and Larsen, E. John, *Intermediate Accounting*, Sixth Edition McGraw-Hill, New York, 1986.

National Association of Accountants, Management Accounting Practices Committee, "Fixed Asset Accounting: The Capitalization of Costs," Statement on Management Accounting Practices No. 4. NAA, New York, 1973.

———, "Fixed Asset Accounting: The Allocation of Costs," Statement on Management Accounting Practices No. 7. NAA, New York, 1974.

Pyle, William W., and Larson, Kermit D., *Fundamental Accounting Principles*, Tenth Edition Irwin, Homewood, IL, 1984.

Smith, Jay M., and Skousen, K. Fred, *Intermediate Accounting, Comprehensive Volume*, Ninth Edition South-Western Publishing, Cincinnati, OH, 1987.

Stettler, Howard F., *Auditing Principles*, Fifth Edition Prentice-Hall, Englewood Cliffs, NJ, 1982.

Welsch, Glenn A., Anthony, Robert N., and Short, Daniel G., *Fundamentals of Financial Accounting*. Irwin, Homewood, IL, 1984.

Welsch, Glenn A., and Zlatkovich, Charles T., *Intermediate Accounting*, Eighth Edition Irwin, Homewood, IL, 1989.

CHAPTER 22

GOODWILL AND OTHER INTANGIBLE ASSETS*

Lailani Moody, CPA, MBA

Grant Thornton LLP

---

*This chapter was reviewed for the Eleventh Edition by Francis E. Scheuerell Jr., CPA, CMA. Mr. Scheuerell is a Partner, Financial Reporting Services with Callaway Partners, LLC in Atlanta, Georgia.

22.1 CHARACTERIZATION OF INTANGIBLE ASSETS

Intangible assets are assets, other than financial assets, that have utility and value but lack physical substance. Examples include patents, copyrights, trade names, customer lists, royalty agreements, databases, and computer software. Intangible assets can be classified as identifiable, for example, trademarks, or unidentifiable, for example, goodwill. Another way to classify intangible assets is based on how they are acquired. They can be internally developed or acquired from external sources. Intangibles acquired externally can be further categorized depending on whether they are acquired in a business combination or as a separate asset or together with other assets that do not constitute a business. Intangible assets acquired in a business combination may be recognized as assets separate from goodwill or as part of goodwill, depending on whether the intangible assets satisfy certain criteria. As discussed in this chapter, the applicable accounting pronouncements and accounting requirements differ somewhat depending on whether the intangible asset is identifiable, whether it is internally developed or acquired externally, and, if acquired externally, whether it was acquired in a business combination.

Intangible assets can also be classified by methods other than identifiability. Accounting Principles Board (APB) Opinion No. 17 (par. 10) indicates that intangible assets can be alternatively categorized three ways:

1. Manner of acquisition—acquired singly, in groups, or in business combinations or developed internally.
2. Expected period of benefit—limited by law or contract, related to human or economic factors, or indefinite or indeterminate duration.
3. Separability from an entire enterprise—rights transferable without title, salable, or inseparable from the enterprise or a substantial part of it.

22.2 ACCOUNTING OVERVIEW

Numerous pronouncements provide guidance on the accounting for intangibles. This section provides an overview of those pronouncements.

(a) INTANGIBLE ASSETS AND GOODWILL ACQUIRED IN A BUSINESS COMBINATION. Statement of Financial Accounting Standards (SFAS) No. 141, "Business Combinations," provides initial measurement and recognition guidance for intangible assets and goodwill acquired in a business combination, including guidance on whether intangible assets should be recognized as assets apart from goodwill. Subsequent accounting for the intangible assets and goodwill is provided in SFAS No. 142, "Goodwill and Other Intangible Assets." SFAS No. 142 provides that goodwill should not be amortized, mandates impairment tests of goodwill annually or, in some circumstances, more frequently, and provides guidance on recognizing impairments. It also addresses whether intangible assets other than goodwill have *indefinite* useful lives, and therefore should not be amortized but instead tested at least annually for impairment, or *finite* useful lives, and therefore should be amortized over their estimated useful life. Intangible assets with finite useful lives are tested for impairment under SFAS No. 144, "Accounting for the Impairment or Disposal of Long-Lived Assets."

(b) INTANGIBLE ASSETS ACQUIRED SEPARATELY OR WITH OTHER ASSETS. SFAS No. 142 provides initial recognition and measurement guidance for intangible assets acquired other than in a business combination, that is, intangible assets acquired individually or together with a group of other assets that do not constitute a business. SFAS No. 142 also provides subsequent accounting guidance for such intangible assets, including guidance for determining whether they have finite or indeterminate useful lives and therefore whether they should be amortized. Finally, it addresses accounting for impairments of intangible assets with indeterminate lives. SFAS No. 144 provides guidance on impairment of intangible assets with finite useful lives.

(c) INTERNALLY DEVELOPED INTANGIBLE ASSETS. SFAS No. 142 addresses the initial and subsequent accounting for internally developed intangible assets.

(d) INTANGIBLE ASSETS RECOGNIZED ON ACQUISITION OF A NONCONTROLLING INTEREST IN A SUBSIDIARY. SFAS No. 142 provides guidance on the initial and subsequent accounting for goodwill and other intangible assets recognized on acquisition of noncontrolling interests in a subsidiary.

(e) GOODWILL RECOGNIZED WHEN APPLYING THE EQUITY METHOD.   SFAS No. 142 provides that amounts recognized as goodwill in applying equity method accounting to investments should not be amortized. Equity method goodwill is tested for impairment under APB Opinion No. 18, "The Equity Method of Accounting for Investments in Common Stock."

(f) SPECIFIC GUIDANCE ON CERTAIN INTANGIBLES.   Accounting pronouncements, such as Statements of Position issued by the American Institute of Certified Public Accountants (AICPA)'s Accounting Standards Executive Committee, provide guidance on the accounting for specific intangible assets, such as start-up costs, internally developed software, and advertising. See Section 22.5.

(g) INTANGIBLE ASSETS IN SPECIALIZED INDUSTRIES.   Certain Financial Accounting Standards Board (FASB) Statements and Interpretations provide guidance on accounting for certain intangibles of specialized industries, such as airlines, financial institutions, and computer software development. See Section 22.6.

22.3 INITIAL RECOGNITION AND MEASUREMENT OF INTANGIBLE ASSETS

(a) Acquired Intangible Assets.   SFAS No. 142, "Goodwill and Other Intangible Assets," issued in June 2001, replaced APB Opinion No. 17, "Intangible Assets." It uses the term *intangible assets* to refer to intangible assets other than goodwill.

An intangible asset acquired either individually or with a group of other assets other than in a business combination is initially recognized and measured based on its fair value. The cost of a group of assets acquired in a transaction other than a business combination is allocated to the individual assets acquired based on their relative fair values and does not result in the recognition of goodwill.

Intangible assets acquired in a business combination are initially recognized and measured in conformity with SFAS No. 141. SFAS No. 141 provides that an intangible asset acquired in a business combination is recognized as an asset apart from goodwill only if one of the following applies:

- The intangible asset results from contractual or other legal rights. (It is not necessary that those rights be transferable or separable from the acquired entity or from other rights or obligations of the acquired entity.) Examples of intangible assets that meet this criterion include trademarks, newspaper mastheads, Internet domain names, order backlog, books, magazines, musical works, license agreements, construction permits, broadcast rights, mortgage servicing contracts, patented technology, and computer software.

- The intangible asset is separable from the acquired entity, that is, it can be sold, transferred, licensed, rented, or exchanged individually or in combination with a related contract, asset, or liability. It is not necessary that the acquiring entity have the intention to dispose of, sell, or rent the intangible asset. Examples of assets that meet this separability criterion include customer lists, noncontractual customer relationships, unpatented technology, and databases such as title plants.

(b) INTERNALLY DEVELOPED INTANGIBLE ASSETS.   Costs of internally developing, maintaining, or restoring intangible assets including goodwill that are not specifically identifiable, that have indeterminate lives, or that are inherent in a continuing business and related to a reporting entity as a whole, are recognized as an expense when incurred.

22.4 ACCOUNTING FOR INTANGIBLE ASSETS

(a) DETERMINING THE USEFUL LIFE OF AN INTANGIBLE ASSET. The accounting for a recognized intangible asset is based on its useful life to the reporting entity. The amount of an intangible asset with a finite useful life is amortized (but see Section 22.4(b) for a discussion of how allocation, including amortization, is an engine of earnings management); the amount of an intangible asset with an indefinite useful life is not amortized. The useful life of an intangible asset to a reporting entity is the period over which the asset is expected to contribute directly or indirectly to the future cash flows of the reporting entity. The estimate of the useful life of an intangible asset to an entity is based on an analysis of all pertinent factors, in particular the following:

- The expected use of the asset by the reporting entity
- The expected useful life of another asset or a group of assets to which the useful life of the intangible asset may relate, such as mineral rights to depleting assets
- Any legal, regulatory, or contractual provisions that may limit the useful life
- Any legal, regulatory, or contractual provisions that enable renewal or extension of the asset's legal or contractual life without substantial cost, provided that there is evidence to support renewal or extension and renewal or extension can be accomplished without material modifications of the existing terms and conditions
- The effects of obsolescence, demand, competition, and other economic factors, such as the stability of the industry, known technological advances, legislative action that results in an uncertain or changing regulatory environment, and expected changes in distribution channels
- The level of maintenance expenditures required to obtain the expected future cash flows from the asset; for example, a material level of required maintenance in relation to the carrying amount of the asset may suggest a very limited useful life
- If no legal, regulatory, contractual, competitive, economic, or other factors limit the useful life of an intangible asset to the reporting entity, that useful life is considered to be indefinite, which does not mean *infinite*.

(b) INTANGIBLE ASSETS SUBJECT TO AMORTIZATION. The amount of a recognized intangible asset is amortized over the useful of the asset to the reporting entity unless that life is determined to be indefinite. SFAS No. 142 requires the amount of an intangible asset with a finite life but without a precisely known life to be amortized over the best estimate of its useful life. The method of amortization should reflect the pattern in which the economic benefits of the intangible asset are consumed or otherwise used up. If that pattern cannot be reliably determined, a straight-line amortization method is used. An intangible asset is not written down or off in the period of acquisition unless it becomes impaired during that period.

The amount of an intangible asset to be amortized is the amount initially assigned to the asset less any residual value. The residual value of an intangible asset is assumed to be zero unless at the end of the useful life to the reporting entity the asset is expected to continue to have a useful life to another entity and (a) the reporting entity has a commitment from a third party to purchase the asset at the end of its useful life to the reporting entity or (b) the residual value can be determined by reference to an exchange transaction in an existing market for that asset and that market is expected to exist at the end of the asset's useful life.

The reporting entity is required to evaluate the remaining useful life of an intangible asset being amortized each reporting period to determine whether events and circumstances warrant a revision to the remaining period of amortization. If the estimate of an intangible asset's useful life is changed, the remaining carrying amount of the intangible asset is amortized prospectively over that revised remaining useful life. If an intangible asset being amortized is subsequently determined to have an indefinite useful life, the asset is tested for impairment, as discussed next. That intangible asset is no longer amortized and is accounted for the same way as other intangible assets not subject to amortization (see Section 22.4(c)).

An intangible asset subject to amortization is reviewed for impairment in conformity with SFAS No. 144, paragraphs 7–24. After an impairment loss is recognized, the adjusted carrying amount of the intangible asset is its new accounting basis. A previously recognized impairment loss is not subsequently reversed.

(c) INTANGIBLE ASSETS NOT SUBJECT TO AMORTIZATION.   An intangible asset determined to have an indefinite useful life is not amortized until its useful life is determined to be no longer indefinite. The reporting entity is required to evaluate the remaining useful life of an intangible asset not being amortized each reporting period to determine whether events and circumstances continue to support an indefinite useful life. An intangible asset not being amortized subsequently determined to have a finite useful life is tested for impairment, as discussed next. The asset is then amortized prospectively over its estimated remaining useful life and accounted for the same way as other intangible assets subject to amortization.

An intangible asset not subject to amortization is tested for impairment annually, or more frequently if events or changes in circumstances indicate that the asset might be impaired. The impairment test consists of a comparison of the fair value of the asset with its carrying amount. If its carrying amount exceeds its fair value, an impairment loss is recognized in amount equal to the excess. After an impairment loss is recognized, its adjusted carrying amount is the intangible assets new accounting basis. A previously recognized impairment loss is not reversed.

In EITF Issue No. 02-7, "Unit of Accounting for Testing Impairment of Indefinite-Lived Intangible Assets," the Task Force concluded that separately recorded indefinite-lived intangible assets should be combined into a single unit of accounting for testing impairment if they are operated as a single asset and are therefore essentially inseparable. An example of intangible assets that should be combined is 20 contiguous easements that a company acquires separately to support development of a single gas pipeline. Those easements would form a single unit of accounting for testing impairment of the easements under SFAS No. 142. Determining whether several intangible assets are inseparable is a matter of judgment. EITF Issue No. 02-7 includes indicators and illustrations of when intangible assets should be combined and when they should not be combined. None of the indicators is determinative.

22.5 CERTAIN IDENTIFIABLE INTANGIBLE ASSETS

(a) COPYRIGHTS.   A copyright is the exclusive right to reproduce, publish, and sell a literary product or artistic work. The term of the copyright in the United States is now the life of the author plus 50 years. Until January 1, 1978, the period was 28 years plus renewal for an additional 28 years. As in the case of a patent, the rights to a copyright may be assigned, licensed, or sold.

(i) Capitalizable Amounts for Copyrights.   The costs of developing copyrights and the costs of purchased copyrights may be substantial and should be deferred. For a copyright developed internally, costs include expenditures for government filing fees and attorneys' fees and expenses, as well as outlays for wages and materials in the preparation of the material to be copyrighted and expenditures incurred to establish the right. If a copyright is purchased, the initial valuation includes the acquisition price plus any costs incurred in establishing the right.

(ii) Amortization of Copyrights.   Copyrighted materials often do not have an active market past the first few years after the issuance of the copyright. Costs are amortized over the number of years in which sales or royalties related to the copyright can be expected. It is usually advisable to write off capitalized costs early in the copyright's legal life, if it is difficult to determine the useful life of the copyright, that is, the periods the copyright will benefit.

SFAS No. 144, "Accounting for the Impairment or Disposal of Long-Lived Assets," provides guidance on the impairment of intangible assets with finite lives, such as copyrights. Continuing review of the status of copyrights is essential to determine whether they have continuing value. If the copyrighted material will no longer be used, it should be written off.

(b) CUSTOMER AND SUPPLIER LISTS.   Customer and supplier lists can be particularly valuable to a business as they represent groups of customers or suppliers with whom business relations have been established. The value of such lists is based on the assumption of continuing business, as well as possibly reducing the marketing costs that would otherwise be necessary.

(i) Capitalizable Amounts for Customer and Supplier Lists.   Customer or supplier lists are often developed internally, and the cost specifically identified with development is generally impossible to determine. Such costs are not deferred, but when lists are purchased from others, the acquisition cost should be deferred. However, a customer or supplier list acquired in a business combination would not meet the criteria for recognition apart from goodwill if there are terms of confidentiality or other agreements that prohibit selling, leasing, or otherwise exchanging customer or supplier information.

(ii) Amortization of Customer and Supplier Lists.   The value of customer or supplier lists decreases as customers or suppliers are lost or cease to exist. The cost of the list should be written off based on these factors, but in practice it is often difficult to precisely track lost customers or suppliers. The estimate of the useful life should consider all available information and be reevaluated each reporting period.

(c) FRANCHISES.   Franchises may be granted by governmental units, individuals, or corporate entities. Public utilities are granted franchises by the communities they serve. These franchises establish the right to operate and specify the conditions under which utilities must function. Such franchises may place certain restrictions on the enterprise concerning rates and operating conditions, but they also confer certain privileges, ranging from those of a minor nature to the granting of a monopoly. Private franchises are contracts for the exclusive right to perform certain functions or to sell certain (usually branded) products or services. Such agreements involve the use by the franchisee of a trademark, trade name, patent, process, or know-how of the franchisor for the term of the franchise. For example, a manufacturer may grant a dealer a franchise to market a product within a given territory and agree not to allow other dealers to market the same product in that area.

(i) Capitalizable Amounts for Franchise and Amortization Period.   Costs of obtaining a franchise include any fees paid to the franchisor, as well as legal and other expenditures incurred in obtaining the franchise. If a franchise agreement covers a specified period of time, the cost of the franchise should be written off over that period unless the economic life is anticipated to be less. If the franchise is perpetual, the franchisee should evaluate the expected useful life of the franchise, considering the effect of obsolescence, demand, competition, and other relevant economic factors. Additional periodic payments based on revenues or other factors may be required in addition to initial fees. These period costs are expensed as incurred because they relate only to the current period and represent no future benefit. The franchise agreement may also require certain property improvements that should be capitalized and included in property, plant, and equipment.

(d) LEASES AND LEASEHOLD RIGHTS.   A favorable lease is one in which the property rights obtained under the lease could presently be obtained only at a higher rental. This concept is not to be mistaken for the issue of capitalized leases or capital additions classified as leasehold improvements. Favorable leases may be recognized when a business is purchased or when a payment is made to an existing lessee for the right to sublease.

(i) Capitalizable Amounts for Favorable Leases and Leasehold Rights.   The favorable lease is usually measured by the present value of the cost differential between the terms of the lease and the amount that could be obtained currently in an arm's-length transaction.

(ii) Amortization of Favorable Leases.   The cost assigned to a favorable lease is amortized over the lease term. A lump-sum payment at the inception of the lease should be amortized to rent expense over the life of the lease.

(e) ORGANIZATION COSTS.   Organization costs are expenditures made to promote and organize a concern, including costs of establishing the entity's existence.

Under SOP 98-5, "Reporting on the Costs of Start-Up Activities," start-up activities as defined in the SOP include organization costs. This SOP concludes that costs of start-up activities, including organization costs, should be expensed as incurred.

(f) PATENTS.   Accounting for patents is affected by the laws governing the legal rights of a patent holder. A U.S. patent is a nonrenewable right granted by the government of the United States that enables the recipient to exclude others from the manufacture, sale, or other use of an invention for a period of 17 years from the date of the grant. Enforceability of a patent begins only upon the grant of the patent, and the exclusive right of use is not retroactive. However, the filing of a patent application provides protection from the claims of a later inventor for the same item so that, in effect, the period of protection may be considered to extend from the date of the original application. Also, the effective period of competitive advantage may extend beyond the original 17-year patent term if additional patents are obtained as improvements are made. The rights to a patent may be assigned in whole or in part, as well as the right to use the patent (i.e., licenses under the patent) on a royalty or other basis.

(i) Capitalizable Amounts for Patents.   Patents may be purchased from others or developed internally as a result of research and development activities. The cost of a purchased patent includes the purchase price and any related expenditures, such as attorney's fees. If a patent is developed internally, its cost includes legal fees in connection with patent applications, patent fees, litigation fees, litigation costs, costs of sale or licensing, and filing fees. Any related research, experimental and developmental expenditures, including the cost of models and drawings not specifically required for a patent application, are research and development costs and should be expensed as incurred in accordance with SFAS No. 2.

The grant of a patent through the U.S. Patent Office is no guarantee of protection. It is often necessary to defend the patent in court tests of the patent's validity and alleged infringement of other patents, as well as infringement of the patent by others. The costs of successful court tests may be deferred.

However, if the litigation is unsuccessful, the costs of the litigation should be written off immediately.

(ii) Amortization of Patents.   A U.S. patent has a specified legal life. It provides protection for 17 years, and that is the maximum amortization period. The period used in practice is often less because of technological or market obsolescence, the issuance of new patents to competitors, improved models, substitutes, or general technological progress. These factors must be taken into account in determining the original useful life and subsequent reviews of remaining economic life. The amortization period should not extend beyond the market life of the product with which the patent is associated, unless the patent can also be used in other applications. However, if it is possible to extend a patent's economic life by obtaining additional patents, it is permissible to amortize the remaining balance of the costs of the old patent over the estimated economic lives of the new ones. The impairment accounting guidance in SFAS No. 144 is applicable to patents. Once it is determined that the monopolistic advantage offered by use and ownership of the patent no longer exists, the remaining unamortized balance should be written off. Also, any increases in deferred costs, due to such factors as an additional lawsuit establishing the validity of the patent, should be written off over the remaining estimated economic life of the patent.

(g) REGISTRATION COSTS.   The Securities and Exchange Commission (SEC) staff in Staff Accounting Bulletin (SAB) Topic 5A stated that specific incremental costs directly attributable to a proposed or actual offering of securities may properly be deferred and charged against the gross proceeds of the offering. Management salaries or other general and administrative expenses may not be allocated as costs of the offering. Costs of an aborted offering may not be deferred and charged against a subsequent offering. A postponement of up to 90 days does not represent an aborted offering.

(h) MOVING COSTS.   The EITF Issue No. 88-10, "Costs Associated with Lease Modification or Termination," dealt with the question of whether moving costs incurred by the lessee in connection with changing from one lease to another lease may be deferred and amortized over the new lease term. The Task Force did not reach a consensus, but its members agreed that the predominant practice is to charge the costs of moving to expense as incurred. The SEC observers at their meeting noted that, as a general rule, the SEC staff would object to the deferral of moving costs.

Subsequent to the EITF consideration of this issue, the FASB issued FTB No. 88-1, "Issues Relating to Accounting for Leases." Paragraph 8 states that "The lessee's immediate recognition of expenses or losses, such as moving expenses, . . . is not changed by this Technical Bulletin." Even if the costs of moving are assumed by the new lessor, the lessee should expense the relocation costs and establish a corresponding deferred credit that is written off over the term of the new lease.

In SFAS No. 146, "Accounting for Costs Associated with Exit or Disposal Activity," costs of relocating employees are accruable exit costs in the period in which the liability is incurred. However, in EITF Issue No. 95-3, "Recognition of Liabilities in Connection with a Purchase Business Combination," the costs to relocate employees of an acquired company should be recognized as liabilities assumed in a purchase business combination.

(i) RESEARCH AND DEVELOPMENT COSTS.   SFAS No. 2, "Accounting for Research and Development Costs" (par. 12), requires that research and development costs be charged to expense when incurred. SFAS No. 142 did not change that accounting. Paragraph 8 includes the following definitions of research and development:

> Research is planned search or critical investigation aimed at discovery of new knowledge with the hope that such knowledge will be useful in developing a new product or service . . . or a new process or technique . . . or in bringing about a significant improvement to an existing product or process.

> Development is the translation of research findings or other knowledge into a plan or design for a new product or process or for a significant improvement to an existing product or process whether intended for sale or use. It includes the conceptual formulation, design, and testing of product alternatives, construction of prototypes, and operation of pilot plants. It does not include routine or periodic alterations to existing products, production lines, manufacturing processes, and other on-going operations even though those alterations may represent improvements and it does not include market research or market testing activities.

The SFAS No. 2 does not apply to Research and Development (R&D) costs incurred for others under a contractual agreement or to costs incurred in activities unique to the extractive industries.

Research and development costs, according to SFAS No. 2 (par. 11), include the following elements:

> *Materials, Equipment and Facilities*. The cost of materials . . . and equipment or facilities that are acquired or constructed for research and development activities and that have alternative future uses . . . shall be capitalized as tangible assets when acquired or constructed. The cost of such materials consumed in research and development activities and the depreciation of such equipment or facilities used in those activities are research and development costs. However, the costs of materials, equipment, or facilities that are acquired or constructed for a particular research and

development project and that have no alternative future uses ... are research and development costs at the time the costs are incurred.

Personnel. Salaries, wages and other related costs of personnel engaged in research and development activities shall be included in research and development costs.

Intangibles Purchased from Others. The costs of intangibles that are purchased from others for use in research and development activities and that have alternative future uses ... shall be accounted for in accordance with FASB Statement No. 142, "Goodwill and Other Intangible Assets." ... The amortization of those intangible assets used in research and development activities is a research and development cost. However, the costs of intangibles that are purchased from others for a particular research and development project and that have no alternative future uses ... are research and development costs at the time the costs are incurred.

Contract Services. The costs of services performed by others in connection with the research and development activities of an enterprise, including research and development conducted by others in behalf of the enterprise, shall be included in research and development costs.

Indirect Costs. Research and development costs shall include a reasonable allocation of indirect costs. However, general and administrative costs that are not clearly related to research and development activities shall not be included as research and development costs.

SFAS No. 2 (par. 12) requires that all costs of activities identified as R&D be charged to expense as incurred. The only exception is that government-regulated enterprises may be required to defer certain costs for rate-making purposes. This occurs when the rate regulator reasonably assures the recovery of R&D costs by permitting the inclusion of the costs in allowable costs for rate-making purposes. SFAS No. 2 (par. 13) also requires disclosure of total R&D costs charged to expense in each period.

Subsequent accounting by the combined enterprise for the costs allocated to assets to be used in R&D activities is prescribed by SFAS No. 2, that is, costs assigned to assets to be used in particular R&D projects and having no alternative future uses are charged to expense at the date of acquisition.

The SEC staff has stated that, if a significant portion of the purchase price in a business combination is expensed as purchased R&D, the SEC staff may to raise issues such as the following:

- Purchased R&D must be valued based on appropriate assumptions and valuation techniques; it may not be determined as a residual amount similar to goodwill.
- Allocation of purchase price to purchased R&D will be questioned if differing significantly from the estimated replacement cost for the acquiring enterprise.
- Policies used for internally developed products should be used to determine if R&D is in process or complete and whether alternative future uses exist.
- If substantially all of the purchase price is allocated to purchased R&D, the staff will challenge whether some should be allocated to other identifiable intangible assets and goodwill and would object to useful lives of those intangible assets and goodwill exceeding five to seven years.

The AICPA has issued the following Practice Aid on accounting for R&D projects acquired in a business combination: "Assets Acquired in a Business Combination to Be Used in Research and Development Activities: A Focus in Software, Electronic Devices, and Pharmaceutical Industries."

(j) ROYALTY AND LICENSE AGREEMENTS.   Royalty and license agreements are contracts allowing the use of patented, copyrighted, or proprietary (trade secrets) material in return for royalty payments. An example is the licensing of a patented chemical process for use in a customer's operating system.

The costs to be assigned to royalty and license agreements include any initial payments required plus legal costs incurred in establishing the agreements. Royalty or usage fees are expensed as incurred, because they relate to services of products and not to future benefits.

The capitalized costs of royalty and license agreements should be amortized over the lesser of the life of the agreement or the expected economic life, with the useful life reassessed each reporting period. Unamortized costs of royalty and license agreements should be written off when it is determined that they have become worthless.

(k) SECRET FORMULAS AND PROCESSES. A formula or process known only to a particular producer may be a valuable asset, even if not patented. As in the case of a patent, the value of a trade secret is derived from the exclusive control that it gives. Trade secrets, like patents and copyrights, are recognized legal property and are transferable.

Costs that can be directly identified with secret formulas and processes are properly capitalized, except that costs of activities constituting research and development as defined by SFAS No. 2 must be expensed. Costs are normally assigned only to acquired secret formulas and processes. Because secret formulas and secret processes have unlimited lives in a legal sense, costs capitalized are amortized over the useful life of the secret formula or are not amortized if the secret formula is determined to have an indefinite useful life. Whether the value of the formula or process is impaired because of lack of demand for the related product, development of a substitute product or process, loss of exclusivity, or other factors should be determined as discussed in Section 22.4(b) or (c), as appropriate.

(l) START-UP ACTIVITIES. Under SOP 98-5, "Reporting on the Costs of Start-Up Activities," costs of start-up activities, including organization costs, should be expensed as incurred. For purposes of the SOP, start-up activities are defined broadly as those one-time activities related to opening a new facility, introducing a new product or service, conducting business in a new territory, conducting business with a new class of customer or beneficiary, initiating a new process in an existing facility, or commencing some new operation. Start-up activities include activities related to organizing a new entity (commonly referred to as *organization costs*). The SOP applies to all nongovernmental entities and would apply to development-stage entities as well as established operating entities.

(m) TOOLING COSTS. Initial tooling costs are sometimes treated as an intangible asset, but they are more often considered an element of property, plant, and equipment or, in the case of certain long-term contracts, inventory. SFAS No. 2 (par. 9) states that the design of tools, jigs, molds, and dies involving new technology is a research and development cost, which must be expensed as incurred. However, routine design of those items is not research and development, and the cost may be deferred and amortized over the periods expected to benefit. Deferred tooling may be written off over a period of time (generally less than five years, with shorter periods used when tooling relates to products with frequent style or design obsolescence) or anticipated production (using the unit-of-production method). Replacements of parts of tooling for reasons other than changes in the product are usually expensed.

If deferred initial tooling costs are material, the accounting policy regarding those costs should be disclosed. SEC registrants are required to state, if practicable, the amount of unamortized deferred tooling costs applicable to long-term contracts or programs [Regulation S-X, Rule 5.02-6(d)(i)].

EITF Issue No. 99-5, "Accounting for Pre-Production Costs Related to Long-Term Supply Arrangements," provides guidance on design and development and tooling costs related to new long-term supply arrangements. The Task Force concluded that:

- Design and development costs for products to be sold under long-term supply arrangements should be expensed as incurred.
- Design and development costs for molds, dies, and other tools that a supplier will own and that will be used in producing the products under the long-term supply arrangements should, in general, be capitalized as part of the cost of the molds, dies, and other tools. However, if the molds, dies, and tools involve new technology, their costs should be expensed as incurred.

- If the supplier will not own the molds, dies, and other tools, the design and development costs should be capitalized only if the supply arrangement provides the supplier the noncancelable right to use them during the supply arrangement. Otherwise, the design and development costs should be expensed as incurred, including costs incurred before the supplier receives a noncancelable right to use the molds, dies, and other tools during the supply arrangement.
- Design and development costs that would otherwise be expensed should be capitalized if the supplier has a contractual guarantee for reimbursement of those costs. A contractual guarantee means a legally enforceable agreement under which the amount of the reimbursement can be objectively measured and verified.

SEC registrants are expected to disclose their accounting policy for preproduction design and development costs and the aggregate amount of the following:

- Assets recognized pursuant to agreements that provide for contractual reimbursement of preproduction design and development costs
- Assets recognized for molds, dies, and other tools that the supplier owns
- Assets recognized for molds, dies, and other tools that the supplier does not own

Design and development costs for molds, dies, and other tools that are capitalized are subject to impairment assessment under SFAS No. 144.

(n) TRADEMARKS AND TRADE NAMES.   Broadly defined, a trademark is any distinguishing label, symbol, or design used by a concern in connection with a product or service. A trade name identifies the entity.

Trademarks can be registered with the U.S. Patent Office to provide access to the federal courts for litigation and to serve as notice of ownership. Proof of prior and continuing use of the trademark is required to obtain and retain the right to use the registered item. Protection of trademarks and trade names that cannot be registered or are not registered can also be sought through common law. These assets have an unlimited life as long as they are used continuously, although technically the term of registration at the U.S. Patent Office is 20 years with indefinite renewal for additional 20-year periods. They may also be registered under the laws of most states. It is customary to consider trademarks and trade names as being of value only as long as they are used. The value of a trademark or trade name consists of the product differentiation and identification that it provides, which theoretically contributes to revenue by enabling a business to sell such products at a higher price than unbranded products. Although closely related to goodwill, trademarks and trade names are property rights that are separately identifiable and, as such, can be assigned or sold.

(i) Capitalizable Amounts for Trademarks and Trade Names Costs.   The cost of a trademark or trade name developed internally consists of legal fees associated with successful litigation involving the trademark or trade name, registration fees, and all developmental expenditures that can be reasonably associated with trademarks, such as payments to design firms. The cost of a purchased trademark or trade name is its purchase price and any other costs required to maintain exclusive use of the mark or name. Obviously, much of the value of a trademark or trade name is established by continuing operations that create a reputation with customers. Some of that reputation, however, may have been gained through the use of advertising and other marketing techniques. The costs should be amortized over the trademark's or trade name's useful life to the entity, unless the trademark or trade name is determined to have an indefinite useful life, in which case it is not amortized, as discussed in Section 22.4(c). The useful life should be reassessed each reporting period. That these expenditures should be accounted for under SOP 93-7, which is discussed next.

(ii) Amortization of Trademarks and Trade Names.   Because of the legal status of trademarks and trade names, established trademarks and trade names have unlimited legal lives as long as they are used. There is no specified statutory life that restricts the amortization period.

(o) ADVERTISING.   Under SOP 93-7, "Reporting on Advertising Costs," the costs of advertising should be expensed either as incurred or the first time the advertising takes place, unless the advertising is direct-response advertising that meets specific criteria. Examples of first-time advertising include the first public showing of a television commercial for its intended purpose or the first appearance of a magazine advertisement for its intended purpose.

The cost of direct-response advertising is deferred as an asset, subject to amortization, if the primary purpose of the advertising is to elicit sales to customers who can be shown to have responded specifically to the advertising and if the advertising results in probable future benefits. Showing that a customer responded to specifically identifiable direct-response advertising requires documentation, including a record that can identify the name of the customer and the advertising that elicited the direct response. Such documentation could include, for example, files listing the customer names and the related direct-response advertisement, a coded order form, coupon, or response card included with the advertisement that would indicate the customer's name, or a log of customers who made phone calls responding to a number appearing in an advertisement.

Probable future benefits are probable future primary revenues resulting from the direct-response advertising, net of future costs to realize the revenues. Probable future primary revenues are limited to revenues from sales to customers receiving and responding to the direct-response advertising. To demonstrate that direct-response advertising will result in probable future benefits, an entity is required to provide persuasive evidence that the results of the advertising will be similar to the results of its past direct-response advertising activities that had future benefits. The evidence should include verifiable historical patterns of results specific to the entity. To determine if results will be similar, attributes to consider include the demographics of the audience, the method of advertising, the product, and economic conditions. Industry statistics would not provide objective evidence of probable future benefits in the absence of the entity's own operating history.

Other requirements of the SOP include:

- Costs of direct-response advertising should only include incremental direct costs incurred in transactions with independent third parties plus payroll and payroll-related costs for the activities of employees that are directly associated with the direct-response advertising project. Allocated administrative costs, rent, depreciation, and other occupancy costs are not costs of direct-response advertising activities.

- The costs of the direct-response advertising directed to all prospective customers, not just the cost related to the portion of the potential customers that is expected to respond to the advertising, should be deferred.

- Deferred direct-response advertising costs should be amortized using a cost-pool method over the period during which the future benefits are expected to be received. The amortization should be the ratio that current period revenues for a cost pool bear to the total current and estimated future period revenues for that cost pool. The amount of estimated future revenues should not be discounted, but it may be adjusted in subsequent periods. The ratio should be recalculated at each reporting date.

- The realizability of the deferred advertising should be evaluated, at each balance sheet date, by comparing, on a cost-pool by cost-pool basis, the carrying amount of the deferred advertising with the probable remaining future net revenues expected to result directly from such advertising. Only probable future primary revenues should be used to determine the probable remaining future net revenues.

- There are certain disclosures required, such as the accounting policy selected for advertising, the total amount charged to advertising, a description of the direct-response advertising reported as assets (if any), the accounting policy and amortization period of direct-response advertising, the total amount of advertising reported as assets, and the amounts, if any, written down to net realizable income.

The SEC staff has announced that it considers the requirements for deferral of direct-response advertising costs to be met only if the advertising results in a direct revenue-generating response;

for example, the respondent orders the product when placing the call to the advertised number. The staff believes capitalization is not appropriate for advertising that results not in sales, but in sales opportunities that are likely to produce results. For example, an advertisement for aluminum siding that includes a phone number to call to schedule a visit from a sales representative would not qualify for capitalization as direct-response advertising because the advertisement leads only indirectly to the revenue-generating transaction.

The SEC staff also announced that it would object to the classification of deferred advertising costs as current assets because such costs do not meet the definition of a current asset in ARB No. 43.

(p) WEB SITE DEVELOPMENT COSTS.   In EITF Issue No. 00-2, the Task Force developed the following guidance for accounting for Web site development costs:

- During the planning phase, an entity develops a project plan, determines the desired functionalities of the Web site, identifies the needed hardware and software applications, and determines whether suitable technology exists. All costs incurred in the planning stage should be expensed as incurred.

- During the Web site development phase, the entity acquires or develops hardware and software to operate its Web site and develops appropriate graphics. Costs related to software and graphics should be accounted for under SOP 98-1 as software for internal use unless the entity has or is developing a plan to market the software. Software, including graphics, to be marketed should be accounted for under SFAS No. 86, "Computer Software to Be Sold, Leased, or Otherwise Marketed." See Section 22.6(f) for a discussion of SOP 98-1 and SFAS No. 86. Costs incurred for Web site hosting should generally be expensed over the period of benefit.

22.6 INTANGIBLE ASSETS IN SPECIALIZED INDUSTRIES

Intangible assets are particularly significant or receive unique accounting treatment in certain industries.

(a) AIRLINES.   Under the AICPA Industry Audit Guide, Audits of Airlines, as amended by SOP 88-1, "Accounting for Developmental and Preoperating Costs, Purchases and Exchanges of Take-off and Landing Slots, and Airframe Modifications," and SOP 98-5, "Reporting on the Costs of Start-Up Activities," the capitalization of preoperating costs related to integration of new types of aircraft. The costs of acquiring take off and landing slots, whether by exchange of stock or through purchase, are identifiable intangible assets. Developmental costs related to preparation of new routes should not be capitalized.

(b) BANKING AND THRIFTS.   Under SFAS No. 72, "Accounting for Certain Acquisitions of Banking or Thrift Institutions," as amended by SFAS No. 147, "Acquisitions of Certain Financial Institutions," applies only to acquisitions of financial institutions that are mutual enterprises by other financial institutions that are also mutual enterprises. In such acquisitions, goodwill that is created by an excess of the fair value of liabilities assumed over the fair value of tangible and identified intangible assets acquired is to be amortized by the interest method over a period no greater than the estimated remaining life of the long-term, interest-bearing assets acquired. If the assets acquired do not include a significant amount of long-term, interest-bearing assets, such goodwill is amortized over a period not exceeding the estimated average life of the existing customer (deposit) base acquired. That accounting is unchanged under SFAS No. 141, which requires that any unidentified intangible asset recognized under paragraph 5 of SFAS No. 72 be classified as an asset apart from goodwill at the date SFAS No. 142 is adopted in its entirety. That asset continues to be amortized as required by SFAS No. 72. The FASB issued an Exposure Draft in May 2002 and plans to issue a new Statement by the end of 2002 that will require entities to reclassify to good-will the carrying amount of unidentified intangible assets recognized in past business combinations under SFAS No. 72.

(c) MORTGAGE BANKING.   Under SFAS No. 140, "Accounting for Transfers and Servicing of Financial Assets and Extinguishments of Liabilities," servicing of mortgage loans becomes a distinct asset or liability only when contractually separated from the underlying amounts by sale or securitization of the assets with servicing retained or separate purchase or assumption of the servicing rights.

An entity that undertakes a contract to service financial assets shall recognize either a servicing asset or a servicing liability, unless the transferor transfers the assets in a guaranteed mortgage secu-ritization, retains all of the resulting securities, and classifies them as debt securities held-to-maturity in accordance with SFAS No. 115, in which case the servicing asset or liability may be reported together with the asset being serviced. Each sale or securitization with servicing retained or sep-arate purchase or assumption of servicing results in a servicing contract. Each servicing contract results in a servicing asset (when the benefits of servicing are expected to be more than adequate compensation to the servicer for performing the servicing) or a servicing liability (when the benefits of servicing are not expected to compensate the servicer adequately for performing the servicing).

If the servicer is more than adequately compensated and if the servicing was retained in a sale or securitization, the servicer shall account for the contracts to service the mortgage loans separately from the loans by initially measuring the servicing assets at their allocated previous carrying amounts based on relative fair value at the date of sale or securitization. If the servicing asset is purchased or servicing liability assumed, it is measured at fair value. If the servicer is not adequately compensated, a servicing liability undertaken in a sale or securitization is measured at fair value.

Servicing assets are amortized in proportion to and over the period of estimated net servicing income—the excess of service revenues over servicing costs. Servicing liabilities are amortized in proportion to and over the period of estimated net servicing loss—the excess of servicing costs over servicing revenues, if practicable.

Impairment of servicing assets should be measured as follows: (1) stratify servicing assets based on one or more of the predominant risk characteristics of the underlying assets, (2) recognize impairment through a valuation allowance for an individual stratum for the amount by which the carrying amount of the servicing assets for the stratum exceeds their fair value, and (3) adjust the valuation allowance to reflect changes in the measurement of impairment subsequent to the initial measurement of impairment.

Rights for future income from the serviced assets that exceed contractually specified servicing fees should be accounted for separately. Those rights are not servicing assets; they are financial assets, effectively interest-only strips to be accounted for in accordance with paragraph 14 of SFAS No. 140.

In EITF No. 95-5, "Determination of What Risks and Rewards, If Any, Can Be Retained and Whether Any Unresolved Contingencies May Exist in a Sale of Mortgage Loan Servicing Rights," the EITF addressed the issue of whether the inclusion of any provision that results in the seller's retention of specified risk (1) precludes recognition of a sale at the date title passes or (2) allows recognition of the sale at that date if (a) the seller can reasonably estimate, and record a liability for, the costs related to protection provisions, or (b) the sale agreement provides for substantially all risks and rewards to irrevocably pass to the buyer, and the seller can reasonably estimate, and record a liability for, the minor protection provisions. The EITF reached a consensus that sales of rights to service mortgage loans should be recognized when the following conditions are met: (1) title has passed, (2) substantially all risks and rewards of ownership have irrevocably passed to the buyer, and (3) any protection provisions retained by the seller are minor and can be reasonably estimated. If a sale is recognized and minor protection provisions exist, a liability should be accrued for the estimated obligation associated with those provisions. The seller retains only minor protection provisions if (a) the obligation associated with those provisions is estimated to be no more than 10 percent of the sales price and (h) risk of prepayment is retained for no longer than 120 days.

Mortgage banking is covered in more detail in Chapter 29.

(d) BROADCASTING INDUSTRY.   The principal intangible assets in the broadcasting industry are Federal Communications Commission (FCC) licenses, broadcast rights (license agreement to program material), and network affiliation agreements. Television and radio stations may not operate without an FCC license, which specifies, for example, the frequency to be used. A broadcasting license is granted for a 10-year period and is renewable for additional 10-year periods if the entity provides at least an average level of service to its customers and complies with applicable FCC rules and policies. Licenses maybe renewed indefinitely at little cost. If the entity intends to renew the license indefinitely and has the ability to do so, a broadcast license would be deemed to have an indefinite useful life. It would not be amortized until its useful life was no longer deemed to be indefinite. Impairment would be tested as provided in Section 22.4(c). If the entity does not intend to renew a broadcast license indefinitely, if would amortize the license over its remaining useful life and follow the impairment guidance in SFAS No. 144.

(i) Broadcast Rights.   Broadcast rights result from a contract or license to exhibit films, programs, or other works and permit one or more exhibitions during a specified license period. Compensation is ordinarily payable in installments over a period shorter than the period of the licensing contract, but it may also take the form of a lump-sum payment at the beginning of the period. The license expires at the end of the contract period. The accounting for broadcast rights is specified in SFAS No. 63, "Financial Reporting by Broadcasters." Amounts recorded for broadcasting rights are to be segregated on the balance sheet as current and noncurrent assets based on estimated usage within one year. Rights should be amortized based on the estimated number of future showings. Items that may be used on an unlimited basis, rather than a limited number of showings, may be amortized over the period covered by the agreement. An accelerated method of amortization is required when the first showing is more valuable than reruns, as is usually the case. Straight-line amortization is allowable only when each telecast or broadcast is expected to generate approximately the same revenue. Feature programs are to be amortized on a program-by-program basis; however, amortization as a package may be appropriate if it approximates the amortization that would have been provided on a program-by-program basis.

The capitalized costs of rights to program material should be reported in the balance sheet at the lower of unamortized cost or estimated net realizable value on a program-by-program, series, package, or daypart basis, as appropriate. If management's expectations of the programming usefulness of a program, series, package, or daypart are revised downward, it may be necessary to write down unamortized cost to estimated net realizable value. Daypart is defined in SFAS No. 63 as an aggregation of programs broadcast during a particular time of day (e.g., daytime, evening, late night) or programs of a similar type (e.g., sports, news, children's shows). A write-down from unamortized cost to a lower estimated net realizable value establishes a new cost basis.

(ii) Revoked or Nonrenewed Broadcast Licenses.   When broadcasting licenses are not renewed or are revoked, unamortized balances should be written off. If a network affiliation is terminated and is not immediately replaced or under agreement to be replaced, the unamortized balance of the amount originally allocated to the network affiliation agreement should be charged to expense. If a network affiliation is terminated and immediately replaced or under agreement to be replaced, a loss is recognized to the extent that the unamortized cost of the terminated affiliation exceeds the fair value of the new affiliation. Gain is not to be recognized if the fair value of the new network affiliation exceeds the unamortized cost of the terminated affiliation.

(e) CABLE TELEVISION.   Cable television companies experience a long preoperating and development period. SFAS No. 51, "Financial Reporting by Cable Television Companies," defines the prematurity period as the period when a cable television system is partially under construction and partially in service. Costs incurred during this period that relate to both current and future operations are partially expensed and partially capitalized. In a cable system, portions or segments that are in the prematurity period and can be clearly distinguished from the remainder of the system should be accounted for separately. Costs incurred to obtain and retain subscribers and general and administrative expenses incurred during the prematurity period are to be expensed as period costs. Programming costs and other system costs that will not vary significantly regardless of the number of subscribers are allocated between current and future operations. The amount currently expensed is based on a relationship of subscribers during the current month (as prescribed in the SFAS) and the total number of subscribers expected at the end of the prematurity period. The capitalized portions decrease each month as the cable company progresses toward the end of the prematurity period. Prior to the prematurity period, system-related costs are capitalized; subsequent thereto, none of these costs is deferred. Capitalized costs should be amortized over the same period used to depreciate the main cable television plant.

Costs of successful franchise applications are capitalized and amortized in accordance with SFAS No. 142. Costs of unsuccessful applications and abandoned franchises are charged to expense.

(f) COMPUTER SOFTWARE. SFAS No. 86, "Computer Software to Be Sold, Leased, or Otherwise Marketed," prescribes the accounting for the costs of computer software purchased or internally developed as a marketable product by itself. Costs incurred to establish the technological feasibility are charged to expense when incurred. Technological feasibility is established on completion of all planning design, coding, and testing activities necessary to establish that the product can be produced. The completion of a detailed program design or completion of a working model provides evidence of the establishment of technological feasibility. Costs incurred subsequent to the establishment of technological feasibility are capitalized. Software used as an integral part of product or process is not capitalized until both technological feasibility has been established and all research and development activities for the other components have been completed. When the product is available for release to customers, capitalization ceases. Costs of maintenance and customer support are expensed when the related revenue is recognized or when the costs are incurred, whichever occurs first. Purchased software that has alternative future uses should be capitalized but subsequently accounted for according to its use.

Amortization of capitalized software costs is based on the ratio that current gross revenues bear to the total current and anticipated revenues with a minimum amortization equivalent to straight-line over the remaining estimated economic life of the product. The excess of unamortized capitalized costs over a product's net realizable value is written off (and not subsequently restored).

The unamortized computer costs included in the balance sheet, the total amortization charged to expense in each income statement presented and amounts written down to net realizable value should be disclosed.

FIN No. 6 (par. 4) states that, to the extent the acquisition, development, or improvement of a process for use in selling and administrative activities includes costs for computer software, these costs are not research and development costs. Examples given of excluded costs are the development by an airline of a computerized reservation system or the development of a general management information system. SFAS No. 86 does not cover accounting for costs of software used internally, but see the discussion of SOP 98-1 in this subsection.

In Issue No. 96-6, "Accounting for the Film and Software Cost Associated with Developing Entertainment and Educational Software Products," the EITF considered the issue of how companies should account for the film and software costs associated with developing entertainment and educational (EE) software products such as computer games, interactive videos, and other multimedia products. The SEC staff announced that EE products that are sold, leased, or otherwise marketed are subject to the accounting requirements of SFAS No. 86. The SEC staff believes that the film costs incurred in development of an EE product should be accounted for under the provisions of SFAS No. 86. In addition, exploitation costs should be expensed as incurred unless those costs include advertising costs that qualify for capitalization in accordance with SOP 93-7. Because of the SEC staff's position, the EITF was not asked to reach a consensus on this Issue.

In EITF No. 97-13, "Accounting for Costs Incurred in Connection with a Consulting Contract or an Internal Project That Combines Business Process Reengineering and Information Technology Transformation," the EITF addressed the accounting for business process reengineering costs. These costs may be included in a contract that combines business process reengineering and a project to acquire, develop, or implement internal-use software. The Issue does not address the accounting for internal-use software development costs. The EITF reached a consensus that costs of business process reengineering, whether done internally or by third parties, should be expensed as incurred. If the project is carried out by a third party and some of the costs are capitalizable, such as fixed asset costs, the EITF concluded that the total contract cost should be allocated to various activities based on the relative fair value of the separate activities. The allocation should be based on the objective evidence of the fair value of the elements in the contract, not separate prices stated within the contract. The consensus opinion identified the following as third-party or internally generated costs typically associated with business process reengineering activities that should be expensed as incurred:

- Preparation of request for proposal
- Current state assessment
- Process reengineering
- Restructuring the workforce

The cost of software used internally is accounted for under SOP 98-1, "Accounting for the Costs of Computer Software for Internal Use." The SOP divides the process of computer software development into three stages: preliminary project stage (conceptual formulation and evaluation of alternatives, determination of existence of needed technology, and final selection of alternatives), application development stage (design of chosen path, coding, installation to hardware, and testing), and postimplementation/operation stage (training and application maintenance). Computer software costs that are incurred in the preliminary project stage should be expensed as incurred. Once the capitalization criteria of the SOP have been met, external direct costs of materials and services consumed in developing or obtaining internal-use computer software, payroll costs for employees who are directly associated with and who devote time to the project, and interest costs incurred in developing the software should be capitalized. Capitalization should cease no later than the point at which a computer software project is substantially complete and ready for its intended use. Internal and external training costs and maintenance costs incurred in the postimplementation/operation stage should be expensed as incurred. General and administrative costs and overhead costs should not be capitalized as costs of internal use software.

(g) EXTRACTIVE INDUSTRIES.   Intangible assets in the extractive industries include leased or purchased rights to exploit mineral and other natural resources based on lump-sum, periodic, or production-based payments. The rights are usually included in the property section of the balance sheet. A comprehensive discussion of the accounting for these and other assets in the extractive industries is given in Chapter 29, "Oil, Gas, and Other Natural Resources."

(h) PRODUCERS OR DISTRIBUTORS OF FILMS.   SOP 00-2, "Accounting by Producers or Distributors of Films," provides guidance on the accounting for costs related to all types of films and is applicable to both producers and distributors of films. The costs of producing a film include film costs, participation costs, exploitation costs, and manufacturing costs. Marketing and other exploitation costs, other than advertising, should be expensed as incurred. Advertising costs should be accounted for under SOP 93-7, "Reporting on Advertising Costs."

Entities are required to amortize film costs using the individual-film-forecast-computation method. That method provides for amortization of costs in the same ratio that current period actual revenue bears to estimated remaining unrecognized ultimate revenue as of the beginning of the current fiscal year. Amortization begins when a film is released and the entity begins to recognize revenue from the film.

Certain events or changes in circumstances may occur, such as an adverse change in the expected performance of a film or a substantial delay in completion of the film, that indicate the fair value of the film may be less than the related unamortized film costs. If such an event occurs, an entity should assess whether the fair value of the film is less than its unamortized film costs. If the unamortized capitalized film costs exceed the film's fair value, the excess should be written off and may not be subsequently restored. See Chapter 32 for more on this topic.

(i) PUBLIC UTILITIES.   The general provisions of accounting for intangible assets of various types apply to public utilities. However, since public utilities are required by regulatory agencies to maintain their accounts in accordance with accounting practices that may vary from generally accepted accounting principles (GAAP), certain differences in treatment may result. An example is research and development costs, which certain regulatory agencies allow to be deferred.

The rate regulator may reasonably assure the existence of an asset by permitting the inclusion of a cost in allowable costs for rate-making purposes. SFAS No. 71, "Accounting for the Effects of Certain Types of Regulation" (par. 9), states the two criteria to be met in order for a utility to capitalize a cost that would otherwise be expensed:

1. It is probable that future revenue in an amount at least equal to the capitalized cost will result from inclusion of that cost in allowable costs for rate-making purposes.
2. Based on available evidence, the future revenue will be provided to permit recovery of the previously incurred cost rather than to provide for expected levels of similar future costs. If the revenue will be provided through an automatic rate-adjustment clause, this criterion requires that the regulator's intent clearly be to permit recovery of the previously incurred cost.

If at any time the capitalized cost no longer meets those two criteria, it should be expensed.

The value of an asset may be impaired by a regulator's rate actions. If a rate regulator excludes all or part of a capitalized cost from allowable costs and the cost was capitalized based on the above criteria, the asset should be reduced to the extent of the excluded cost. Whether other assets have been impaired is determined under the general rules for impairment, which are described in Section 22.4(b) and (c).

If an enterprise discontinues application of SFAS No. 71 because, for example, its operations have been deregulated, it would eliminate from its GAAP balance sheet assets consisting of costs capitalized that would not have been capitalized by unregulated entities.

Numerous state legislatures and/or regulatory commissions have approved or are considering deregulating utilities' generation (production) cost of electricity, although the portion of the kilowatt charge attributable to transmission of the electricity to the local area and the distribution cost to the customer are not being deregulated. If some, but not all, of a utility's operations are regulated, SFAS No. 71 should be applied to the portion of the operations that continue to meet the requirements of SFAS No. 71 for regulatory accounting. SFAS No. 101, "Regulated Enterprises—Accounting for the Discontinuation of Application of FASB Statement No. 71," addresses how an entity that ceases to meet the criteria for application of SFAS No. 71 to all or part of its operations should report that event in its financial statements.

An issue related to the current deregulation environment is when an entity should cease to apply the regulated enterprise accounting model prescribed by SFAS No. 71 to the generation portion of its operations if deregulation is under consideration. In Issue No. 97-4, "Deregulation of the Price of Electricity—Issues Related to the Application of FASB Statements No. 71 and 101," the EITF reached a consensus that when deregulatory legislation or a rate order is issued that contains sufficient detail to determine how the deregulatory plan will affect the portion of the business being deregulated, the entity should stop applying SFAS No. 71 to that separable portion of its business. The Task Force considered the following fact situation: If legislation is passed requiring deregulation of generation charges at the end of five years, the date the legislation is passed is the latest date that the entity can discontinue application of the SFAS No. 71 accounting model to the generation portion of its operations. The consensus does not address whether an entity should stop applying SFAS No. 71 at an earlier time. The Task Force also observed that the financial statements should segregate, either on their face or in the notes, the amounts that pertain to the separable portion.

With regard to goodwill, a regulator may permit a utility to amortize purchased goodwill over a specified period, may direct a utility not to amortize goodwill, or may direct the utility to write off goodwill. SFAS No. 71 (par. 30) requires the goodwill to be amortized for financial reporting purposes over the period during which it will be allowed for rate-making purposes. If the regulator either excludes amortization from allowable costs for rate-making purposes or directs the utility to write off goodwill, goodwill should not be amortized, and it should be accounted for under SFAS No. 142.

(j) RECORD AND MUSIC INDUSTRY.   Significant intangible assets in the record and music industry include record masters, recording artist contracts, and copyrights. Accounting for copyrights generally follows that used in other industries, but the accounting for record masters and recording artist contracts is unique.

SFAS No. 50, "Financial Reporting in the Record and Music Industry," is the primary source of accounting principles in this area. Costs of producing a record master include the costs of musical talent; technical talent for engineering, directing, and mixing; equipment to record and produce the master; and studio facility charges. When past performance of an artist provides a reasonable basis for estimating that the cost of a record master borne by the record company will be recovered from future sales, that cost should be recorded as an asset and, when material, should be separately disclosed. The cost of record masters should be amortized by a method that reasonably relates the cost to the net revenue expected to be realized. Ordinarily, amortization occurs over a very short period. Unamortized amounts should be written off when it becomes apparent that they will not be recovered through future sales. The cost of the record master recoverable from the artist's royalties is to be accounted for as an advance royalty.

A recording artist contract is a contract for personal services. A major portion of the artist's compensation consists of participation in earnings (measured by sales and license fee income, commonly referred to as a *royalty*) or of a nonrefundable advance against royalties. Advances should be recorded as an asset (as a prepaid royalty, classified as current or noncurrent depending on when amounts are expected to be realized) if it is anticipated that they will be recovered against royalties otherwise payable to the artist. When it is determined that a prepayment will not be recovered, the balance should be written off.

(k) TIMBER INDUSTRY.   Companies in the forest products industry may make lump-sum payments for timber-cutting rights, which allow them to remove trees for a specified period or in specified quantities. Lump-sum payments made at the inception of an agreement are properly deferred and amortized over the period of the agreement or on the basis of estimates of recoverable timber. Periodic or production-based payments are expensed as they do not represent future benefits. Cutting rights are ordinarily included in the Property section of the balance sheet and are stated at cost less amortization. The amortization policy should be disclosed.

22.7 ACCOUNTING FOR GOODWILL

(a) INITIAL VALUATION.   SFAS Nos. 141, "Business Combinations," and 142, "Goodwill and Other Intangible Assets," issued in June 2001, which replaced APB Opinions Nos. 16 and 17, define goodwill as:

> The excess of the cost of an acquired entity over the net of the amounts assigned to assets acquired and liabilities assumed. The amount recognized as goodwill includes acquired intangible assets that do not meet the criteria in SFAS No. 141, "Business Combinations," for recognition as an asset apart from goodwill.

Those criteria are discussed in Section 22.3(a). For accounting purposes, the cost of purchased goodwill is the residual cost remaining after all other identifiable assets and liabilities have been valued.

(b) SUBSEQUENT ACCOUNTING.   Goodwill is not amortized. It is tested for impairment at a level of reporting referred to as a *reporting unit* (see Section 22.7(b)(iv) for a definition of a reporting unit). Impairment is the condition that exists when its carrying amount is greater than its implied fair value. A two-step impairment test, discussed next, is used to identify potential goodwill impairment and measure the amount of a goodwill impairment loss to be recognized, if any.

(i) Recognition and Measurement of an Impairment Loss.   The first step of a goodwill impairment test compares the fair value of a reporting unit with its carrying amount, including goodwill, applying the guidance in Section 22.7(b)(ii). If the fair value of the reporting unit is more than its carrying amount, goodwill of the reporting unit is considered not impaired, and the second step of the impairment test is not performed. If the carrying amount of the reporting unit is more than its fair value, the second step of the goodwill impairment test, discussed next, is performed to measure the amount of impairment, if any.

The second step of the goodwill impairment test compares the implied fair value of reporting unit goodwill (explained in the next paragraph) with the carrying amount of the goodwill. If the carrying amount of reporting unit goodwill is more than the implied fair value of the goodwill, an impairment loss is recognized in an amount equal to the excess. The loss recognized cannot exceed the carrying amount of goodwill. When a goodwill impairment loss is recognized, the adjusted carrying amount of goodwill is its new accounting basis. Once the measurement of the loss is completed, previously recognized goodwill impairment loss is not reversed.

The implied fair value of goodwill is determined the same way as the amount of goodwill recognized in a business combination is determined. The reporting entity allocates the fair value of the reporting unit to all of the assets and liabilities of the unit, including any unrecognized intangible assets, the same way it would be allocated had the reporting unit been acquired in a business combination and had the fair value of the reporting unit been the price paid to acquire the reporting unit. The excess of the fair value of the reporting unit over the amounts assigned to its assets and liabilities is the *implied fair value of goodwill*. The allocation process is performed only to test goodwill for impairment; a reporting entity does not write up or down a recognized asset or liability, and it does not recognize a previously unrecognized intangible asset as a result of the allocation process.

If the second step of the goodwill impairment test is not complete before the financial statements are issued and a goodwill impairment loss is probable and can be reasonably estimated, the best estimate of the loss is recognized in those financial statement. Any adjustment to the estimated loss based on completion of the measurement of the impairment loss is recognized in the next reporting period.

(ii) Fair Value Measurements.   SFAS No. 142 defines *fair value* the way FASB Statement of Concepts No. 7, page 1, does:

> The amount at which that asset (or liability) could be bought (or incurred) or sold (settled) in a current transaction between willing parties, that is, other than in a forced or liquidation sale.

See Section 2.3(b)(v) for a discussion of the view that the definition is ambiguous.

According to that definition, the fair value of a reporting unit is the amount at which the unit as a whole could be bought or sold in a current transaction between willing parties. Quoted market prices in active markets are the best evidence of fair value and are used as the basis for measurement, if available. However, the market price of an individual equity security and thus the market capitalization of a reporting unit with publicly traded equity securities may not be representative of the fair value of the reporting unit as a whole, because of a control premium. The quoted market price of an individual equity security, therefore, need not be the sole measurement basis of the fair value of a reporting unit. SEC registrants should be aware that the SEC staff has sometimes questioned valuations not based on the market price of the equity security.

If quoted market prices are not available, the estimate of fair value is based on the best information available, including prices for similar assets and liabilities and the results of using other valuation techniques. A present value technique is often the best available technique with which to estimate the fair value of a group of net assets (such as a reporting unit). If a present value technique is used to measure fair value, estimates of future cash flows used in the technique are to be consistent with the objective of measuring fair value. The cash flow estimates should incorporate assumptions that marketplace participants would use in their estimates of fair value. If that information is not available without undue cost and effort, a reporting entity may use its own assumptions. An entity should base the cash flow estimates on reasonable and supportable assumptions after consideration of all available evidence. The weight given to the evidence should be commensurate with the extent to which the evidence can be verified objectively. If the entity estimates a range for the amount or timing of possible cash flows, it should consider the likelihood of possible outcomes. FASB Concepts Statement No. 7 gives guidance.

In estimating the fair value of a reporting unit, a valuation technique based on multiples of earnings or revenue or a similar performance measure may be used if that technique is consistent with the objective of measuring fair value. Use of such multiples may be appropriate, for example, when the fair value of an entity that has comparable operations and economic characteristics is observable and the relevant multiples of the comparable entity are known. Conversely, such multiples are not used in situations in which the operations or activities of an entity whose multiples are known are not of a comparable nature, scope, or size as the reporting unit for which fair value is being estimated.

It should be noted that in 2006, SFAS No. 157 "Fair Value Measurements" was issued. It is effective for financial Statements issued for fiscal years beginning after November 15, 2007 (including interim reports in that fiscal year). While not intended to change the guidance in various FASB statements, the document serves as a framework for discussing the FASB's views on fair value and provides a common definition in order to reduce the inconsistencies in guidance and application that have arisen over time. Fair value is defined as "the price that would be received to sell an asset or paid to transfer a liability in an orderly transaction between market participants at the measurement date." The definition of fair value retains the exchange price character in earlier definitions, and focuses on the price to sell the asset or paid to transfer the liability (an exit price), not the price to acquire the asset or received to assume the liability (an entry price).

(iii) When to Test Goodwill for Impairment.   Goodwill of a reporting unit is tested for impairment annually and between annual tests in certain circumstances, discussed below. The annual goodwill impairment test may be performed any time during the fiscal year provided the test is performed at the same time every year. Different reporting units may be tested for impairment at different times.

A detailed determination of the fair value of a reporting unit may be carried forward from one year to the next if all of the following criteria have been met:

- The assets and liabilities that make up the reporting unit have not changed significantly since the most recent fair value determination.
- The most recent fair value determination resulted in an amount that exceeded the carrying amount of the reporting unit by a substantial margin.
- Based on an analysis of events that have occurred and circumstances that have changed since the most recent fair value determination, the likelihood that a current fair value determination would be less than the current carrying amount of the reporting unit is remote.

Goodwill of a reporting unit is tested for impairment between annual tests if an event occurs or circumstances change that would more likely than not reduce the fair value of a reporting unit below its carrying amount. Examples of such events or circumstances include the following:

- A significant adverse change in legal factors or in the business climate
- An adverse action or assessment by a regulator
- Unanticipated competition
- A loss of key personnel
- A more-likely-than-not expectation that a reporting unit or a significant portion of a reporting unit will be sold or otherwise disposed of
- Testing for recoverability under SFAS No. 144 of a significant asset group within a reporting unit
- Recognition of a goodwill impairment loss in the financial statements of a subsidiary that is a component of a reporting unit

Also see Section 22.7(b)(vii) for the need to test goodwill for impairment after a portion of goodwill has been allocated to a business to be disposed of.

If goodwill and another asset or asset group of a reporting unit are tested for impairment at the same time, the other asset or asset group is tested before goodwill. If the asset or asset group is found to be impaired, the impairment loss is recognized before goodwill is tested for impairment.

(iv) Reporting Unit.   A reporting unit is an operating segment or one level below an operating segment, referred to as a *component*. An operating segment is defined in paragraph 10 of SFAS No. 131, "Disclosures about Segments of an Enterprise and Related Information." A component of an operating segment is a reporting unit if the component constitutes a business, as discussed in EITF Issue No. 98-3, for which discrete financial information is available and segment management, as defined in paragraph 14 of SFAS No. 131, regularly reviews the operating results of that component. Segment management may consist of one or more segment managers. Two or more components of an operating segment are aggregated and deemed a single reporting unit if the components have similar economic characteristics, as discussed in paragraph 17 of SFAS No. 131. An operating segment is deemed a reporting unit if all of its components are similar, if none of its components is a reporting unit, or if it comprises only a single component.

Because considerable judgment is required for entities to determine their reporting units and the guidance in SFAS No. 142 is quite limited, the FASB staff provided further clarification of that guidance in EITF Topic No. D-101. The basic guidance requires that a component of an operating segment is a reporting unit if (1) it constitutes a business, (2) discrete financial information on the component is available, and (3) segment management regularly reviews the results of the reporting unit. A fourth requirement provides that components with similar economic characteristics should be combined into one reporting unit. Topic No. D-101 provides that the first three factors are required for a component to be a reporting unit, but no one factor is determinative. The determinative factors are how an entity manages its operations and how an acquired entity is integrated with the acquiring entity. Topic No. D-101 provides the following clarification of each factor:

- *Component constitutes a business*. Judgment is required to determine whether a component constitutes a business, and entities are required to consider the guidance in EITF Issue No. 98-3 in determining that. To be a business under the guidance in EITF Issue No. 98-3, the activities and assets should include "all the inputs and processes necessary" to conduct normal operations. The fact that operating information may be available does not mean the operations constitute a business. They may be just a part of a business, such as one product line.
- *Discrete financial information*. For purposes of both SFAS No. 131 and SFAS No. 142, discrete financial information can consist of just operating information, with no balance sheet information prepared for the component. However, if the component is a reporting unit, the entity would be required to identify and allocate assets and liabilities applicable to the component to test goodwill for impairment.

- *Reviewed by segment management.* Under SFAS No. 131, segment management may be one level below the chief operating decision maker and there may be one or more segment managers. The focus of SFAS No. 142 is on how operating segments are managed rather than on how the entity as a whole is managed.
- *Similar economic characteristics.* The evaluation of whether two components have similar economic characteristics requires consideration of the factors in paragraph 17 of SFAS No. 131: similar economic characteristics, such as similar long-term average gross margins; the nature of the products and/or services; the nature of production processes; the type or class of customers; the methods used to distribute products and provide services; and the nature of any regulatory environment. Topic No. D-101 provides that not all factors have to be met for economic similarity to exist and the evaluation should be more qualitative than quantitative. Topic No. D-101 also provides additional factors to consider when evaluating whether components should be combined in a reporting unit because they are economically similar:
  - How an entity operates its business and the nature of the operations
  - Whether goodwill is recoverable from the separate operations of each component business or from the components working together because, for example, the components are economically interdependent
  - The extent to which the component businesses share assets and other resources
  - Whether the components provide support and receive benefits from the same research and development projects

Components of different operating segments for purposes of SFAS No. 131 cannot be combined into the same reporting unit, even if they have similar economic characteristics. This might occur, for example, if the entity organized its operating segments on a geographic basis.

Questions have arisen about whether one or more components of operating units aggregated into one reporting unit under SFAS No. 131 could be economically dissimilar and therefore be in separate reporting units under SFAS No. 142. Topic No. D-101 provides two explanations of why that could happen:

1. The determination of reportable segments under SFAS No. 131 requires identification of operating segments and then determination of whether economically similar operating segments should be aggregated. However, the determination of reporting units under SFAS No. 142 begins with operating segments and then requires an analysis of whether economically dissimilar components of an operating segment should be disaggregated.

2. For a component of an operating segment to be an operating segment under SFAS No. 131, its operating performance must be regularly reviewed by the chief operating decision maker. That same component, however, could be a reporting unit if a segment manager regularly reviews its operating performance.

For the purpose of testing goodwill for impairment, acquired assets and assumed liabilities are assigned to a reporting unit as of the acquisition date if both of the following criteria are met:

1. The asset will be employed in or the liability relates to the operations of a reporting unit.
2. The asset or liability will be considered in determining the fair value of the reporting unit.

Assets or liabilities that an entity considers part of its corporate assets or liabilities are also assigned to a reporting unit if both of the preceding criteria are met. Examples are environmental liabilities that relate to an existing operating facility of the reporting unit and a pension obligation that would be included in the determination of the fair value of the reporting unit.

Some assets or liabilities may be employed in or relate to the operations of multiple reporting units. The methodology used to determine the amount of those assets or liabilities to assign to a reporting unit is on a reasonable and supportable basis and applied in a consistent manner. For example, assets and liabilities not directly related to a specific reporting unit but from which the reporting unit benefits could be allocated according to the benefit received by the different reporting units or based on the relative fair values of the different reporting units. A pro rata allocation based on payroll expense might be used for pension items.

For the purpose of testing goodwill for impairment, all goodwill acquired in a business combination is assigned to one or more reporting units as of the acquisition date. Goodwill is assigned to reporting units of the acquiring entity expected to benefit from the synergies of the combination even though other assets or liabilities of the acquired entity may not be assigned to that reporting unit. The total amount of acquired goodwill may be divided among a number of reporting units. The methodology used to determine the amount of goodwill to assign to a reporting unit should be reasonable and supportable and applied in a consistent manner. Also, the methodology has to be consistent with the objectives of the process of assigning goodwill to reporting units described next.

In concept, the amount of goodwill assigned to a reporting unit would be determined in a manner similar to how the amount of goodwill recognized in a business combination is determined. The fair value of the acquired business or portion of the acquired business that will be included in a particular reporting unit is, in essence, the purchase price of that business. The entity allocates that purchase price to the assets acquired and liabilities incurred related to (the portion of) the acquired business assigned to the reporting unit. Any excess purchase price is the amount of goodwill assigned to that reporting unit. However, if the goodwill is to be assigned to a reporting unit that has not been assigned any of the assets acquired or liabilities assumed in that acquisition, the amount of goodwill to be assigned to that unit might be determined by applying a "with and without" computation. That is, the difference between the fair value of that reporting unit before the acquisition and its fair value after the acquisition represents the amount of goodwill to be assigned to that reporting unit.

When an entity reorganizes its reporting structure in a manner that changes the composition of one or more of its reporting units, the guidance given earlier in this section for assigning acquired assets and assumed liabilities to reporting units is used to reassign assets and liabilities to the reporting units affected. However, goodwill is reassigned to the reporting units affected using a relative fair value allocation approach similar to that used when a portion of a reporting unit is to be disposed of, which is discussed in Section 22.7(b)(vii). For example, if existing reporting unit A is to be integrated with reporting units B, C, and D, goodwill of reporting unit A would be assigned to units B, C, and D based on the relative fair values of the three portions of reporting unit A before those portions are integrated with reporting units B, C, and D.

(v) Goodwill Impairment Testing by a Subsidiary.   All goodwill recognized by a public or non-public subsidiary in its separate financial statements prepared in conformity with GAAP, known as *subsidiary goodwill*, is accounted for in conformity with SFAS No. 142. It is tested for impairment at the subsidiary level using the subsidiary's reporting units. If a goodwill impairment loss is recognized at the subsidiary level, goodwill of the reporting unit or units at the consolidated level in which the subsidiary's reporting unit with impaired goodwill resides is tested for impairment if the event that gave rise to the loss at the subsidiary level more likely than not would reduce the fair value of the reporting unit at the consolidated level below its carrying amount. A goodwill impairment loss is recognized at the consolidated level only if goodwill at the consolidated level is impaired.

(vi) Goodwill Impairment Testing.   When a noncontrolling interest exists. goodwill from a business combination with a minority interest is tested for impairment using an approach consistent with the approach used to measure the noncontrolling interest at the acquisition date. For example, if goodwill is first recognized based on only the controlling interest of the parent, the fair value of the reporting unit used in the impairment test is based on the controlling interest and does not reflect the portion of fair value attributable to the noncontrolling interest. Similarly, the implied fair value of goodwill determined in the second step of the impairment test used to measure the impairment loss reflects only the parent's interest in the goodwill.

(vii) Disposal of All or a Portion of a Reporting Unit.   When a reporting unit is to be disposed of in its entirety, the carrying amount of goodwill of the reporting unit is included in the carrying amount of the reporting unit in determining the gain or loss on disposal. When a portion of a reporting unit that constitutes a business is to be disposed of, the carrying amount of goodwill associated with the business is included in the carrying amount of the business in determining the gain or loss on disposal. The portion of the carrying amount of goodwill to be included in that carrying amount is based on the relative fair values of the business to be disposed of and the portion of the reporting unit to be retained. However, if the business to be disposed of was never integrated into the reporting unit after its acquisition and thus the benefits of the acquired goodwill were never realized by the rest of the reporting unit, the current carrying amount of the acquired goodwill is included in the carrying amount of business to be disposed of. When only a portion of goodwill is allocated to a business to be disposed of, the goodwill remaining in the portion of the reporting unit to be retained is tested for impairment.

(viii) Equity Method Investments.   The portion of the difference between the cost of an investment and the amount of underlying equity in net assets of an equity method investee recognized as goodwill in conformity with paragraph 19(b) of APB Opinion No. 18, "The Equity Method of Accounting for Investments in Common Stock," known as *equity method goodwill*, is not amortized. However, equity method goodwill is not tested for impairment in conformity with SFAS No. 142. Equity method investments continue to be reviewed for impairment in conformity with paragraph 19(h) of APB Opinion No. 18.

(ix) Entities Emerging from Bankruptcy.   SOP 90-7, "Financial Reporting by Entities in Reorganization Under the Bankruptcy Code," provides that when an entity applies fresh-start accounting on emerging from bankruptcy, the reorganization value should be allocated to all tangible and intangible assets following the procedures in APB Opinion No. 16, "Business Combinations." SFAS No. 142 provides that entities should report the excess reorganization value as goodwill and account for it in the same manner as other elements of goodwill.

22.8 DEFERRED INCOME TAXES

SFAS No. 142 does not change the requirements in SFAS No. 109, "Accounting for Income Taxes," paragraphs 30, 261, and 262, for recognition of deferred income taxes related to goodwill and intangible assets.

22.9 FINANCIAL STATEMENT PRESENTATION

(a) INTANGIBLE ASSETS.   All intangible assets are aggregated and presented as a separate line item in the statement of financial position. In addition, individual intangible assets or classes of intangible assets may be presented as separate line items. Amortization expense and impairment losses for intangible assets are presented in income statement line items within continuing operations as deemed appropriate for each entity. An impairment loss resulting from such an impairment test should not be recognized as a change in accounting principle.

(b) GOODWILL.   The aggregate amount of goodwill is presented as a separate line item in the statement of financial position. The aggregate amount of goodwill impairment losses are presented as a separate line item in the income statement before the subtotal *income from continuing operations*, or a similar caption, unless a goodwill impairment loss is associated with a discontinued operation. A goodwill impairment loss associated with a discontinued operation is included net of tax within the results of discontinued operations.

22.10 DISCLOSURES

The following information is disclosed in the notes to the financial statements in the period of acquisition of intangible assets acquired either individually or with a group of assets:

a. For intangible assets subject to amortization:

1. The total amount assigned and the amount assigned to any major intangible asset class

2. The amount of any significant residual value, in total and by major intangible asset class

3. The weighted-average amortization period, in total and by major intangible asset class

b. For intangible assets not subject to amortization, the total amount assigned and the amount assigned to any major intangible asset class

c. The amount of research and development assets acquired and written off in the period and the line item in the income statement in which the amounts written off are aggregated

The following information is disclosed in the financial statements or the notes to the financial statements for each period for which a statement of financial position is presented:

a. For intangible assets subject to amortization:

1. The gross carrying amount and accumulated amortization, in total and by major intangible asset class

2. The aggregate amortization expense for the period

3. The estimated aggregate amortization expense for each of the five succeeding fiscal years

b. For intangible assets not subject to amortization, the total carrying amount and the carrying amount for each major intangible asset class

c. The changes in the carrying amount of goodwill during the period, including:

1. The aggregate amount of goodwill acquired

2. The aggregate amount of impairment losses recognized on goodwill

3. The amount of goodwill included in the gain or loss on disposal of all or a portion of a reporting unit

Reporting entities that report segment information in conformity with SFAS No. 131 should provide the preceding information about goodwill in total and for each reportable segment and should disclose any significant changes in the allocation of goodwill by reportable segment. If any portion of goodwill has not yet been allocated to a reporting unit at the date the financial statements are issued, that unallocated amount and the reasons for not allocating the amount are disclosed.

For each impairment loss recognized related to an intangible asset, the following information is disclosed in the notes to the financial statements that include the period in which the impairment loss is recognized:

- A description of the impaired intangible asset and the facts and circumstances leading to the impairment
- The amount of the impairment loss and the method for determining fair value
- The caption in the income statement or the statement of activities in which the impairment loss is aggregated
- If applicable, the segment in which the impaired intangible asset is reported under SFAS No. 131

For each goodwill impairment loss recognized, the following information is disclosed in the notes to the financial statements that include the period in which the impairment loss is recognized:

- A description of the facts and circumstances leading to the impairment

- The amount of the impairment loss and the method of determining the fair value of the associated reporting unit
- If a recognized impairment loss is an estimate that has not yet been finalized, that fact and the reasons for it and, in subsequent periods, the nature and amount of any significant adjustments made to the initial estimate of the impairment loss

22.11 EFFECTIVE DATE AND TRANSITION PROVISIONS OF STATEMENT OF FINANCIAL ACCOUNTING STANDARDS NO. 142

All of the provisions of SFAS No. 142 are initially applied in fiscal years beginning after December 15, 2001, to all goodwill and other intangible assets recognized in a reporting entity's statement of financial position at the beginning of that fiscal year, regardless of when those previously recognized assets were first recognized. Early application is permitted for entities with fiscal years beginning after March 15, 2001, provided that the first interim financial statements have not been issued previously. The provisions of the Statement are first applied at the beginning of a fiscal year. They may not be applied retroactively.

The Statement is not applied to previously recognized goodwill and intangible assets acquired in a combination between two or more mutual enterprises, acquired in a combination between not-for-profit organizations, or from the acquisition of a for-profit business entity by a not-for-profit organization until interpretive guidance related to the application of the purchase method to those transactions is issued.

See Section 10.3(o) for transition provisions related to goodwill and intangible assets acquired in business combination for which the acquisition date was before July 1, 2001, that were accounted for by the purchase method.

(a) GOODWILL AND INTANGIBLE ASSETS ACQUIRED AFTER JUNE 30, 2001.   Goodwill acquired in a business combination for which the acquisition date is after June 30, 2001, is not amortized. Intangible assets other than goodwill acquired in a business combination or other transaction for which the date of acquisition is after June 30, 2001, are amortized or not amortized in conformity with the discussion in Sections 22.4(b) and (c). Goodwill and intangible assets acquired in a transaction for which the acquisition date is after June 30, 2001, but before the date that SFAS No. 142 is applied in its entirety are reviewed for impairment in conformity with APB Opinion No. 17 or SFAS No. 121 (as appropriate) until the date SFAS No. 142 is applied in its entirety. The financial statement presentation and disclosure provisions of SFAS No. 142 are not applied to those assets until SFAS No. 142 is applied in its entirety.

Goodwill and intangible assets acquired in a combination between two or more mutual enterprises, acquired in a combination between not-for-profit organizations, or from the acquisition of a for-profit business entity by a not-for-profit organization for which the acquisition date is after June 30, 2001, continue to be accounted for in conformity with APB Opinion No. 17 until the FASB issues guidance on issues related to the application of the purchase method to such transactions.

(b) PREVIOUSLY RECOGNIZED INTANGIBLE ASSETS.   To apply SFAS No. 142 to previously recognized intangible assets (those acquired in a transaction for which the acquisition date is on or before June 30, 2001), the useful lives of those assets are reassessed using the guidance in Section 22.4(a) and the remaining amortization periods adjusted accordingly. For example, the amortization period for a previously recognized intangible asset might be increased if its original useful life was estimated to be longer than the 40-year maximum amortization period allowed by APB Opinion No. 17. The reassessment is completed before the end of the first interim period of the fiscal year in which SFAS No. 142 is first applied. Previously recognized intangible assets deemed to have indefinite useful lives are tested for impairment as of the beginning of the fiscal year in which SFAS No. 142 is first applied. The transitional intangible asset impairment test is completed in the first interim period in which SFAS No. 142 is first applied, and any resulting impairment loss is recognized as the effect of a change in accounting principle. The effect of the accounting change and related income tax effects are presented in the income statement between the captions *extraordinary items* and *net income*. The per-share information presented in the income statement includes the per-share effect of the accounting change.

(c) PREVIOUSLY RECOGNIZED GOODWILL. At the date SFAS No. 142 is first applied, the reporting entity is required to establish its reporting units based on its reporting structure at that date and the guidance in Section 22.7(b)(iv). Recognized net assets and liabilities that do not relate to a reporting unit, such as an environmental liability for an operation previously disposed of, need not be assigned to a reporting unit. All goodwill recognized in a reporting entity's statement of financial position at the date SFAS No. 142 is first applied is assigned to one or more reporting units. Goodwill is assigned in a reasonable and supportable manner. The sources of previously recognized goodwill are considered in making that initial assignment as well as the reporting units to which the related acquired net assets were assigned. Section 22.7(b)(iv) provides guidance that may be useful in assigning goodwill to reporting units on initial application of SFAS No. 142.

Goodwill in each reporting unit is tested for impairment as of the beginning of the fiscal year in which SFAS No. 142 is first applied in its entirety. The first step of the test should be completed within six months from the date the reporting entity first applies SFAS No. 142. However, the amounts used in the transitional goodwill impairment test are measured as of the beginning of the year of first application. If the carrying amount of the net assets of a reporting unit (including goodwill) exceeds the fair value of the reporting unit, the second step of the transitional goodwill impairment test is completed as soon as possible, but no later than the end of the year of first application.

An impairment loss recognized as a result of a transitional goodwill impairment test is recognized as the effect of a change in accounting principle. The effect of the accounting change and related income tax effects are presented in the income statement between the captions *extraordinary items* and *net income*. The per-share information presented in the income statement should include the per-share effect of the accounting change. Though a transitional impairment loss for goodwill may be measured in other than the first interim reporting period, it is recognized in the first interim period regardless of the period in which it is measured, consistent with paragraph 10 of SFAS No. 3, "Reporting Accounting Changes in Interim Financial Statements." The financial information for the interim periods of the fiscal year that precede the period in which the transitional goodwill impairment loss is measured is restated to reflect the accounting change in those periods. The aggregate amount of the accounting change is included in restated net income of the first interim period of the year of first application (and in any year-to-date or last-12-months-to-date financial reports that include the first interim period). Whenever financial information is presented that includes the periods that precede the period in which the transitional goodwill impairment loss is measured, that financial information should be presented on the restated basis.

If events or changes in circumstances indicate that goodwill of a reporting unit might be impaired before completion of the transitional goodwill impairment test, goodwill is tested for impairment when the impairment indicator arises, as discussed in Section 22.7(b)(iii). A goodwill impairment loss that does not result from a transitional goodwill impairment test is recognized as discussed in Section 22.9(b).

A reporting entity performs the required annual goodwill impairment test in the year SFAS No. 142 is first applied in its entirety in addition to the transitional goodwill impairment test unless the reporting entity designates the beginning of its fiscal year as the date for its annual goodwill impairment test.

(d) EQUITY METHOD GOODWILL. When SFAS No. 142 is first applied, the portion of the excess of cost over the underlying equity in net assets of an investee accounted for using the equity method that has been recognized as goodwill is no longer amortized. However, equity method goodwill should not be tested for impairment under SFAS No. 142.

(e) TRANSITIONAL DISCLOSURES.   On completion of the first step of the transitional goodwill impairment test, the reportable segment or segments in which an impairment loss might have to be recognized and the period in which the potential loss will be measured is disclosed in any interim financial information.

In the period of initial application and thereafter until goodwill and all other intangible assets have been accounted for in conformity with SFAS No. 142 in all periods presented, the following information is displayed either on the face of the income statement or in the notes to the financial statements: income before extraordinary items and net income for all periods presented, adjusted to exclude amortization expense (including any related tax effects) recognized in those periods related to goodwill, intangible assets that are no longer being amortized, any deferred credit related to an excess over cost (amortized in conformity with APB Opinion No. 16), and equity method goodwill. The adjusted income before extraordinary items and net income also reflect any adjustment for changes in amortization periods for intangible assets that will continue to be amortized as a result of initially applying SFAS No. 142 (including any related tax effects). The notes to the financial statements should disclose a reconciliation of reported net income to the adjusted net income. Similarly adjusted earnings-per-share amounts for all periods presented may be presented either on the face of the income statement or in the notes to the financial statements.

22.12 SOURCES AND SUGGESTED REFERENCES

Accounting Principles Board, "Business Combinations," APB Opinion No. 16. AICPA, New York, 1970.

———, "Intangible Assets," APB Opinion No. 17. AICPA, New York, 1970.

———, "Disclosure of Accounting Policies," APB Opinion No. 22. AICPA, New York, 1973.

———, "Reporting the Results of Operations," APB Opinion No. 30. AICPA, New York, 1973.

———, "Restatement of Revision of Accounting Research Bulletins," Accounting Research Bulletin No. 43. AICPA, New York, 1968.

American Institute of Certified Public Accountants, "Push Down Accounting," Issues Paper. AICPA, New York, 1979.

———, "Financial Reporting by Entities in Reorganization Under the Bankruptcy Code," Statement of Position 90-7. AICPA, New York, November 19, 1990.

———, "Reporting on Advertising Costs," Statement of Position 93-7. AICPA, New York, December 29, 1993.

———, "Accounting for Developmental and Preoperating Costs, Purchases and Exchanges of Take-off and Landing Slots, and Airframe Modifications," Statement of Position 88-1. AICPA, New York, 1988.

———, "Accounting for the Costs of Computer Software Developed or Obtained for Internal Use," Statement of Position 98-1. AICPA, New York, 1998.

———, "Reporting on the Cost of Start-Up Activities," Statement of Position 98-5. AICPA, New York, 1998.

———, "Accounting by Producers or Distributors of Films," Statement of Position 00-2. AICPA, New York, 2000.

———, "Assets Acquired in a Business Combination to Be Used in Research and Development Activities: A Focus on Software, Electronic Devices, and Pharmaceutical Industries," AICPA Practice Aid Series. AICPA, New York, 2001.

Financial Accounting Standards Board, "Costs Associated with Lease Modifications or Termination," EITF Issue No. 87-10. FASB, Norwalk, CT, 1988.

———, "Applicability of FASB Statement No. 2 to Computer Software (An Interpretation of FASB Statement No. 2)," FASB Interpretation No. 6. FASB, Stamford, CT, 1975.

———, "Accounting for Research and Development Costs," Statement of Financial Accounting Standards No. 2. FASB, Stamford, CT, 1974.

———, "Accounting for Franchise Fee Revenue," Statement of Financial Accounting Standards No. 45. FASB, Stamford, CT, 1981.

———, "Financial Reporting in the Record and Music Industry," Statement of Financial Accounting Standards No. 50. FASB, Stamford, CT, 1981.

_____, "Financial Reporting by Cable Television Companies," Statement of Financial Accounting Standards No. 51. FASB, Stamford, CT, 1981.

_____, "Financial Reporting by Broadcasters," Statement of Financial Accounting Standards No. 63. FASB, Stamford, CT, 1982.

_____, "Accounting for the Effects of Certain Types of Regulation," Statement of Financial Accounting Standards No. 71. FASB, Stamford, CT, 1982.

_____, "Accounting for Certain Acquisitions of Banking or Thrift Institutions," Statement of Financial Accounting Standards No. 72. FASB, Stamford, CT, 1983.

_____, "Accounting for the Costs of Computer Software to Be Sold, Leased, or Otherwise Marketed," Statement of Financial Accounting Standards No. 86. FASB, Stamford, CT, 1985.

_____, "Statement of Cash Flows," Statement of Financial Accounting Standards No. 95. FASB, Stamford, CT, 1987.

_____, "Issues Relating to Accounting for Leases," FASB Technical Bulletin No. 88-1. FASB, Norwalk, CT, 1988.

_____, "Accounting for Income Taxes," Statement of Financial Accounting Standards No. 109. FASB, Norwalk, CT, February, 1992.

_____, "Recognition of Liabilities in Connection with a Purchase Business Combination," EITF Issue No. 95-3. FASB, Norwalk, CT, 1995.

_____, "Determination of What Risks and Rewards, If Any, Can Be Retained and Whether Any Unresolved Contingencies May Exist in a Sale of Mortgage Loan Servicing Rights," EITF Issue No. 95-5. FASB, Norwalk, CT, 1995.

_____, "Accounting for Contingent Consideration Paid to the Shareholders of an Acquired Enterprise in a Purchase Business Combination," EITF Issue No. 95-8. FASB, Norwalk, CT, 1995.

_____, "Accounting for the Film and Software Costs Associated with Developing Entertainment and Educational Software Products," EITF Issue No. 96-6. FASB, Norwalk, CT, 1996.

_____, "Accounting for Transfers and Servicing of Financial Assets and Extinguishments of Liabilities," Statement of Financial Accounting Standards No. 125. FASB, Norwalk, CT, 1996.

_____, "Deregulation of the Price of Electricity—Issues Related to the Application of FASB Statements 71 and 101," EITF Issue No. 97-4. FASB, Norwalk, CT, 1997.

_____, "Accounting for Contingent Consideration Issued in a Purchase Business Combination," EITF Issue No. 97-8. FASB, Norwalk, CT, 1997.

_____, "Accounting for Costs Incurred in Connection with a Consulting Contract or an Internal Project That Combines Business Process Reengineering and Information Technology Transformation," EITF Issue No. 97-13. FASB, Norwalk, CT, 1997.

_____, "Disclosures about Segments of an Enterprise and Related Information," Statement of Financial Accounting Standards No. 131. FASB, Norwalk, CT, 1997.

_____, "Business Combinations," Statement of Financial Accounting Standards No. 141. FASB, Norwalk, CT, June 2001.

_____, "Goodwill and Other Intangible Assets," Statement of Financial Accounting Standards No. 142. FASB, Norwalk, CT, June 2001.

AAA Financial Accounting Standards Committee, "Equity Valuation Models and Measuring Goodwill Impairment," *Accounting Horisons*, June 2001.

_____, "Accounting for the Impairment or Disposal of Long-Lived Assets," Statement of Financial Accounting Standards No. 144. FASB, Norwalk, CT, June 2001.

_____, "Accounting for Costs Associated with Exit or Disposal Activities," Statement of Financial Accounting Standards No. 146. FASB, Norwalk, CT, June 2002.

_____, "Acquisitions of Certain Financial Institutions," Statement of Financial Accounting Standards No. 147. FASB, Norwalk, CT, October 2002.

Securities and Exchange Commission, "Acquisitions Involving Financial Institutions," Staff Accounting Bulletin Topic 2-A3. SEC, Washington, DC, 1981.

_____, "Expenses of Offering," Staff Accounting Bulletin Topic 5A. SEC, Washington, DC, 1975.

_____, "Push Down Basic of Accounting Required in Certain Limited Circumstances," Staff Accounting Bulletin Topic 5J. SEC, Washington, DC, 1983.

CHAPTER 23

LEASES

James R. Adler, CPA, CFE, PhD

Adler Consulting, Ltd.

23.1 INTRODUCTION AND BACKGROUND INFORMATION

A lease is an agreement conveying the right to use property, plant, or equipment, usually for a stated period of time. Since World War II, the leasing industry has become a major economic force, and leasing has become a method by which to finance acquisitions of property.

The rapid growth created by the demand to lease everything from equipment to automobiles, furniture, and even people has caused a highly price-competitive environment. Lessors earn their profits by buying equipment at lower prices than ordinary buyers, charging brokerage fees, and getting tax deductions for equipment write-offs. The 1986 Tax Reform Act has wiped out tax credits, removing some of the traditional cash flow advantages that lessors could gain upon initiating a leasing transaction.

Traditionally, lessees prefer to have operating leases rather than capital leases so that the future lease payment obligations do not appear on the balance sheet as a liability.

(a) **FINANCING ADVANTAGES OF LEASING.**   The financing advantages associated with leasing include the following:

- Leasing permits 100 percent financing, whereas a normal equipment loan may require a 20 percent to 40 percent initial down payment. Leasing can thereby conserve cash and working capital.
- Longer terms than are normally available with loans can be arranged for leasing many types of capital equipment.
- Financing of initial acquisition costs is possible because these costs can be included in a lease. Such costs, for example, delivery charges, interest on advance payments, sales or use taxes, and installation costs, are not normally financed under other methods of equipment financing.
- Leasing offers greater convenience than either debt or equity financing because of the reduced documentation.
- The risk of obsolescence can be avoided by the lessee as compared with the risk he would assume on the purchase of such equipment.

(b) **FINANCING DISADVANTAGES OF LEASING.**   Some of the financing disadvantages associated with leasing are as follows:

- The effective interest rate is generally greater than if the lessee obtained a bank loan for the same term. This may not be true, however, for leveraged leases.

- The lessee suffers the loss of residual rights to the property at the termination of the lease.
- The lessee does not enjoy the tax benefits of accelerated depreciation and interest expense.

23.2 ACCOUNTING ISSUES AND PRONOUNCEMENTS

Exhibit 23.1 lists the technical accounting pronouncements concerning leases. These numerous pronouncements are an indication of the complexity and controversy surrounding the accounting for leases. The manufacturer or dealer is concerned with the issue of when a lease becomes a sale with the respective profit and loss recognition. Other lessors are perceived as either renting out their asset or providing financing for the acquisition of this asset by a lessee, depending on the circumstances. Likewise, the lessee either has an asset and a liability or is committed to an obligation to rent an asset. The accounting issues can then be summarized according to the following four questions:

1. On whose balance sheet should the leased asset appear?
2. What is the timing of financial statement recognition of lease events?
3. How are measurements made for both balance sheet and income statement effects of leases?
4. What disclosures should be made in the financial statements?

The Financial Accounting Standards Board (FASB) issued Statement of Financial Accounting Standards (SFAS) No. 13 in November 1976 to resolve the issues. The SFAS No. 13 superseded all preceding technical literature and established the primary current standard in accounting for leases. Under this pronouncement, when substantially all of the risks and rewards of ownership have passed from the lessor to the lessee, the leased property transfers from the lessor to the lessee. The questions of whose asset it is and the related income statement effect are answered by establishing where the substantial risks and rewards of ownership lie. Timing is at the inception of the lease, and measurement is usually at the fair value of the leased property to the lessor at that date.

The FASB regularly releases a codification of the authoritative pronouncements issued on lease accounting. The last codification was in 1998. Essentially, the codification is a reproduction of the lease accounting section included in the FASB Current Text. All of the FASB Statements, Interpretations, and Technical Bulletins were utilized and integrated into this publication. However, the discussion of issues by the Emerging Issues Task Force (EITF) concerning lease accounting were not included in the codification. When a consensus is reached by the Task Force, the agreement represents current thoughts where no lease accounting standards exist. Additional decisions and issues will be considered by the Task Force in the future, and any such consensus previously reached is subject to change. A summary of the proceedings of the Task Force on each lease accounting issue is published by the FASB in the EITF Abstracts.

(a) LEASE ACCOUNTING CLASSIFICATION—LESSEE.   From the standpoint of the lessee, a lease may be classified as either a capital lease or an operating lease. If the lease meets any one of the following four criteria, then the lessee should classify and account for the arrangement as a capital lease:

1. The lease transfers ownership of the property to the lessee at the end of the lease term.
2. The lease contains a bargain purchase option.
3. The lease term is equal to at least 75 percent of the estimated economic life of the property. (If the beginning of the lease term falls within the last 25 percent of the total estimated life including earlier use, this criterion should not be used.)
4. The present value of the minimum lease payments at the beginning of the lease term, excluding that portion of the payments representing executory costs, is 90 percent or more

FASB Statements

13	Accounting for Leases
22	Changes in the Provisions of Lease Agreements Resulting from Refundings of Tax-Exempt Debt
23	Inception of the Lease
27	Classification of Renewals or Extensions of Existing Sales-Type or Direct Financing Leases
28	Accounting for Sales with Leasebacks
29	Determining Contingent Rentals
91	Accounting for Nonrefundable Fees and Costs Associated with Originating or Acquiring Loans and Initial Direct Costs of Leases
94	Consolidation of All Majority-Owned Subsidiaries
98	Accounting for Leases:

- Sale-Leaseback Transactions Involving Real Estate
- Sales-Type Leases of Real Estate
- Definition of the Lease Term
- Initial Direct Costs of Direct Financing Leases

109	Accounting for Income Taxes
140	Accounting for the Transfers and Servicing of Financial Assets and Extinguishments of Liabilities
141	Business Combinations
145	Rescission of FASB Statements No. 4, 44, and 64, Amendment of FASB Statement No. 13 and Technical Corrections

FASB Interpretations

19	Lessee Guarantee of the Residual Value of Leased Property (SFAS No. 13)
21	Accounting for Leases in a Business Combination (SFAS No. 13)
23	Leases of Certain Property Owned by a Governmental Unit or Authority (SFAS No. 13)
24	Leases Involving Only Part of a Building (SFAS No. 13)
26	Accounting for Purchase of a Leased Asset by the Lessee During the Term of the Lease (SFAS No. 13)
27	Accounting for a Loss on a Sublease (SFAS No. 13 and APB Opinion No. 30)

FASB Technical Bulletins

79-10	Fiscal Funding Clauses in Lease Agreements
12	Interest Rate Used in Calculating the Present Value of Minimum Lease Payments
13	Applicability of FASB Statement No. 13 to Current Value Financial Statements
14	Upward Adjustment of Guaranteed Residual Values
15	Accounting for Loss on a Sublease Not Involving the Disposal of a Segment
16R	Effect of a Change in Income Tax Rate on the Accounting for Leveraged Leases
79-18	Transition Requirements of Certain FASB Amendments and Interpretations of FASB Statement No. 13
85-3	Accounting for Operating Leases with Scheduled Rent Increases
86-2	Accounting for an Interest in the Residual Value of a Leased Asset:

- Acquired by a Third Party or
- Retained by a Lessor That Sells the Related Minimum Rental Payments

88-1	Issues Relating to Accounting for Leases:

- Time Pattern of the Physical Use of the Property in an Operating Lease
- Lease Incentives in an Operating Lease
- Applicability of Leveraged Lease Accounting to Existing Assets of the Lessor
- Money-Over-Money Lease Transactions
- Wrap Lease Transactions

(Continues)

Exhibit 23.1   Technical pronouncements on lease accounting

Emerging Issues Task Force Issues

The EITF has discussed and published issue papers on leases as follows:

84-37 Sale-Leaseback Transaction with Repurchase Option
Status: Partially resolved by SFAS No. 98. See also Issue 97-10.

*85-16 Leveraged Leases
a. Real Estate Leases and Sale-Leaseback Leases
b. Delayed Equity Contributions by Lessors
Status: Consensus reached. Additional guidance provided by SFAS No. 98.

85-27 Recognition of Receipts from Made-Up Rental Shortfalls
Status: Consensus reached. See SFAS No. 133. As Amended

86-17 Deferred Profit on Sale-Leaseback Transaction with Lessee Guarantee of Residual Value
Status: Consensus reached. Additional guidance provided by SFAS No. 98.

86-33 Tax Indemnification in Lease Agreements
Status: Consensus reached.

86-43 Effect of a Change in Tax Law on Rates in Leveraged Leases
Status: Consensus reached. See SFAS No. 109.

86-44 Effect of a Change in Tax Law on Investments in Safe Harbor Leases
Status: Consensus reached.

87-7 Sale of an Asset Subject to a Lease on Nonrecourse Financing: Wrap Lease Transactions
Status: Consensus reached. Additional guidance provided by FTB No. 88-1.

87-8 Tax Reform Act of 1986: Issues Related to the Alternative Minimum Tax
Status: Consensus partially nullified by SFAS No. 109.

88-21 Accounting for the Sale of Property Subject to the Seller's Preexisting Lease
Status: Consensus reached.

89-16 Consideration of Executory Costs in Sale-Leaseback Transactions
Status: Consensus reached.

89-20 Accounting for Cross Border Tax Benefit Leases
Status: Consensus reached.

90-14 Unsecured Guarantee by Parent of Subsidiary's Lease Payments in a Sale-Leaseback Transaction
Status: Consensus reached.

90-20 Impact of an Uncollateralized Irrevocable Letter of Credit on a Real Estate Sale-Leaseback Transaction
Status: Consensus reached. See FASB Interpretation 45.

92-1 Allocation of Residual Value or First-Loss Guarantee to Minimum Lease Payments
Status: Consensus reached. See FASB Interpretation 45.

93-8 Accounting for the Sale and Leaseback of an Asset That Is Leased to Another Party
Status: Consensus reached.

95-1 Revenue Recognition on Sales with a Guaranteed Minimum Resale Value
Status: Consensus reached. See SFAS No. 133.

95-4 Revenue Recognition on Equipment Sold and Subsequently Repurchased Subject to an Operating Lease
Status: Consensus reached.

95–6 Accounting by a Real Estate Investment Trust for an Investment in a Service Corporation
Status: Consensus reached.

95–17 Accounting for Modifications to an Operating Lease That Do Not Change the Lease Classification
Status: Consensus reached.

96–21 Implementation Issues in Accounting for Lease Transactions, Involving Special-Purpose Entities
Status: Consensus reached.

97–1 Implementation Issues in Accounting for Lease Transactions, Including Those Involving Special-Purpose Entities
Status: Consensus reached. See Issue 97-10 for Related Issue.

97–10 The Effect of Lessee Involvement in Asset Construction
Status: Consensus reached. See FASB Interpretation 45.

Exhibit 23.1 *Continued.*

98–9	Accounting for Contingent Rent
	Status: Consensus reached.
99–13	Application of Issue No. 97-10 and FASB Interpretation No. 23 to Entities That Enter into Leases with Governmental Entities
	Status: Consensus reached.
00–11	Lessors' Evaluation of Whether Leases of Certain Integral Equipment Meet the Ownership Transfer Requirements of FASB Statement No. 13
	Status: Consensus reached.
00-13	Determining Whether Equipment Is "Integral Equipment" Subject to FASB Statements No. 66 and No. 98
	Status: Consensus reached.
01–4	Accounting for Sales of Fractional Interests in Equipment
	Status: No further discussion by EITF since project on revenue recognition will supersede and cover this issue.
01–08	Determining Whether an Arrangement Is a Lease
	Status: Consensus reached.
01–10	Accounting for the Impact of the Terrorist Attacks of September 11, 2001
	Status: Consensus reached. See FASB Statement 144.
01–12	The Impact of the Requirements of FASB Statement No. 133 on Residual Value Guarantees in Connection with a Lease
	Status: Consensus reached. See Interpretation 45.
03-12	Impact of FASB Interpretation 45 on Issue No. 95-1.
	Status: Consensus reached.

Topic No. D-8 Accruing Bad Debts Expense at the Inception of a Lease.
Topic No. D-24 Sale-Leaseback Transactions with Continuing Involvement.
Topic No. D107 Lessor Consideration of Third Party Residual Value Guarantees.}

Exhibit 23.1 *Continued.*

of the fair value of the leased property to the lessor at the inception date, less any related investment tax credit retained by and expected to be realized by the lessor. The discount rate that the lessee used in computing the present value of the lease payments is the lessee's incremental borrowing rate, defined in SFAS No. 13 as "The rate that, at the inception of the lease, the lessee would have incurred to borrow the funds necessary to buy the leased asset on a secured loan with repayment terms similar to the payment schedule called for in the lease." However, if the lessee knows the implicit rate used by the lessor and that rate is less than the lessee's borrowing rate, SFAS No. 13 requires use of the implicit rate. (If the beginning of the lease term falls within the last 25 percent of the total estimated life including earlier use, this criterion should not be used.)

Leases that do not meet any of these criteria are classified as operating leases by the lessee.

(b) LEASE ACCOUNTING CLASSIFICATION—LESSOR. SFAS No. 13 specifies the following classifications of leases for lessors:

- Direct financing
- Sales type
- Operating
- Leveraged

A lease is classified as a direct financing lease if it meets any one of the four lease classification criteria and, in addition, meets both of the following criteria:

1. Collectibility of the minimum lease payments is reasonably predictable.

2. No important uncertainties surround the amount of unreimbursable costs yet to be incurred by the lessor under the lease.

A lease is classified as a sales-type lease if it qualifies as a direct financing lease and, in addition, has a fair market value in excess of the property's carrying value. Sales-type leases are generally associated with dealers and manufacturing lessors. Leases that do not meet these criteria are classified as operating leases. Leveraged leases are covered in Subsection 23.8(a).

(c) DEFINITIONS OF LEASE TERMS.   The following 28 technical terms have been defined in accounting pronouncements on leases:

1. *Bargain Purchase Option.* A provision allowing the lessee, at the lessee's option, to purchase the leased property for a price that is sufficiently lower than the expected fair value of the property at the date the option becomes exercisable so that exercise of the option appears, at the inception of the lease, to be reasonably assured.

2. *Bargain Renewal Option.* A provision allowing the lessee, at the lessee's option, to renew the lease for a rental sufficiently lower than the fair rental of the property at the date the option becomes exercisable so that exercise of the option appears, at the inception of the lease, to be reasonably assured.

3. *Capital Lease.* A lease that must be capitalized by a lessee because it meets one of the four SFAS No. 13 lease classification criteria.

4. *Contingent Rentals.* The increases or decreases in lease payments that result from changes occurring subsequent to the inception of the lease in the factors (other than the passage of time) on which lease payments are based, except as provided in the following sentence. Any escalation of minimum lease payments relating to increases in construction or acquisition cost of the leased property or for increases in some measure of cost or value during the construction or preconstruction period shall be excluded from contingent rentals. Lease payments that depend on a factor directly related to the future use of the leased property, such as machine hours of use or sales volume during the lease term, are contingent rentals and, accordingly, are excluded from minimum lease payments in their entirety.

   However, lease payments that depend on an existing index or rate, such as the consumer price index or the prime interest rate, shall be included in minimum lease payments based on the index or rate existing at the inception of the lease; any increases or decreases in lease payments that result from subsequent changes in the index or rate are contingent rentals and thus affect the determination of income as accruable.

5. *Direct Financing Leases.* A lease that meets any one of the four SFAS No. 13 lease classification criteria for a lessor plus two additional criteria:

   a. Collectibility of minimum lease payments must be reasonably predictable.

   b. No uncertainties may surround the amount of unreimbursable costs to be incurred by the lessor under the lease.

6. *Estimated Economic Life of Leased Property.* The estimated remaining period during which the property is expected to be economically usable by one or more users, with normal repairs and maintenance, for the purpose for which it was intended at the inception of the lease, without limitation by the lease term.

7. *Estimated Residual Value of Leased Property.* The estimated fair value of the leased property at the end of the lease term.

8. *Executory Costs.* Those costs such as insurance, maintenance, and taxes incurred for leased property, whether paid by the lessor or lessee. Amounts paid by a lessee in consideration for a guarantee from an unrelated third party of the residual value are also executory costs. If executory costs are paid by a lessor, any lessor's profit on those costs is considered the same as executory costs.

9. *Fair Value of the Leased Property*. The price for which the property could be sold in an arm's-length transaction between unrelated parties. The following are examples of the determination of fair value:

   a. When the lessor is a manufacturer or dealer, the fair value of the property at the inception of the lease will ordinarily be its normal selling price, reflecting any volume or trade discounts that may be applicable. However, the determination of fair value shall be made in light of market conditions prevailing at the time, which may indicate that the fair value of the property is less than the normal selling price and, in some instances, less than the cost of the property.

   b. When the lessor is not a manufacturer or dealer, the fair value of the property at the inception of the lease will ordinarily be its cost, reflecting any volume or trade discounts that may be applicable. However, when there has been a significant lapse of time between the acquisition of the property by the lessor and the inception of the lease, the determination of fair value shall be made in light of market conditions prevailing at the inception of the lease, which may indicate that the fair value of the property is greater or less than its cost or carrying amount, if different.

10. *Finance Lease*. A financing device by which a user can acquire use of an asset for most of its useful life. Rentals are net to the lessor, and the user is responsible for maintenance, taxes, and insurance. Rent payments over the life of the lease are sufficient to enable the lessor to recover the cost of the equipment plus interest on its investment.

11. *Inception of the Lease*. The date of the lease agreement or commitment, if earlier. For purposes of this definition, a commitment shall be in writing, signed by the parties in interest to the transaction, and shall specifically set forth the principal provisions of the transaction. If any of the principal provisions is yet to be negotiated, such a preliminary agreement or commitment does not qualify for purposes of this definition.

12. *Initial Direct Costs*. Only those costs incurred by the lessor that are (a) costs to originate a lease incurred in transactions with independent third parties resulting directly from and essential to acquiring that lease and which would not have been incurred had that leasing transaction not occurred, and (b) certain costs directly related to specified activities performed by the lessor for that lease. Those activities include evaluating the prospective lessee's financial condition; evaluating and recording guarantees, collateral, and other security arrangements; negotiating lease terms; preparing and processing lease documents; and closing the transaction. The costs directly related to those activities include only that portion of the employees' total compensation and payroll-related fringe benefits directly related to time spent performing those activities for that lease and other costs related to those activities that would not have been incurred but for that lease. Initial direct costs do not include costs related to activities performed by the lessor for advertising, soliciting potential lessees, servicing existing leases, and other ancillary activities related to establishing and monitoring credit policies, supervision, and administration. They also do not include administrative costs, rent, depreciation, any other occupancy and equipment costs and employees' compensation and fringe benefits related to ancillary activities, unsuccessful origination efforts, and idle time.

13. *Interest Rate Implicit in the Lease*. The discount rate that, when applied to (a) the minimum lease payments, excluding that portion of the payments representing executory costs to be paid by the lessor, together with any profit thereon, and (b) the unguaranteed residual value accruing to the benefit of the lessor causes the aggregate present value at the beginning of the lease term to be equal to the fair value of the leased property to the lessor at the inception of the lease, minus any investment tax credit retained by the lessor at the inception of the lease and minus any investment tax credit retained by the lessor and expected to be realized by him. (This definition does not necessarily purport to include all factors that a lessor might recognize in determining his rate of return.)

14. *Lease*. An agreement conveying the right to use property, plant, or equipment (land or depreciable assets or both) usually for a stated period of time.

15. *Lease Term*. The fixed noncancelable term of the lease plus:

a. All periods, if any, covered by bargain renewal options.

b. All periods, if any, for which failure to renew the lease imposes a penalty on the lessee in such amount that a renewal appears, at the inception of the lease, to be reasonably assured.

c. All periods, if any, covered by ordinary renewal options during which a guarantee by the lessee of the lessor's debt directly or indirectly related to the leased property is expected to be in effect or a loan from the lessee to the lessor directly or indirectly related to the leased property is expected to be outstanding.

d. All periods, if any, covered by ordinary renewal options preceding the date as of which a bargain purchase option is exercisable.

e. All periods, if any, representing renewals or extensions of the lease at the lessor's option. However, in no case shall the lease term be assumed to extend beyond the date a bargain purchase option becomes exercisable. A lease that is cancelable only upon the occurrence of some remote contingency, only with the permission of the lessor, only if the lessee enters into a new lease with the same lessor, or only if the lessee incurs a penalty in such amount that continuation of the lease appears, at inception, reasonably assured shall be considered "noncancelable" for purposes of this definition.

16. *Lessee's Incremental Borrowing Rate*. The rate that, at the inception of the lease, the lessee would have incurred to borrow over a similar term the funds necessary to purchase the leased asset.

17. *Leveraged Lease*. A lease that meets the definition as a direct financing lease for a lessor and, in addition, has all the following characteristics:

a. At least three partners are involved: a lessee, a lessor, and a long-term lender.

b. The financing provided by the lender is substantial to the transaction and without recourse to the lessor.

c. The lessor's net investment declines during the early years of the lease and rises during the latter years of the lease.

18. *Minimum Lease Payments*

a. From the standpoint of the lessee: The payments that the lessee is obligated to make or can be required to make in connection with the leased property. Contingent rentals are excluded from minimum lease payments. However, a guarantee by the lessee of the lessor's debt and the lessee's obligation to pay (apart from the rental payments) executory costs in connection with the leased property shall be excluded. If the lease contains a bargain purchase option, only the minimum rental payments over the lease term and the payment called for by the bargain purchase option shall be included in the minimum lease payments. Otherwise, minimum lease payments include the following:

   i. The minimum rental payments called for in the lease over the lease term.

   ii. Any guarantee by the lessee or any party related to the lessee of the residual value at the expiration of the lease term, whether or not payment of the guarantee constitutes a purchase of the leased property. When the lessor has the right to require the lessee to purchase the property at termination of the lease for a certain or determinable amount, that amount shall be considered a lessee guarantee. When the lessee agrees to make up any deficiency below a stated amount in the lessor's realization of the residual value, the guarantee to be included in the minimum lease payments is the stated amount, rather than an estimate of the deficiency to be made up.

   iii. Any payment that the lessee must make or can be required to make upon failure to renew or extend the lease at the expiration of the lease term, whether or not the payment would constitute a purchase of the lease property. In this connection, it should be noted that the definition of lease term includes "all periods, if any, for which failure to renew the lease imposes a penalty on the lessee in an amount such that renewal appears, at the inception of the lease, to be reasonably assured." If the lease term has been extended because of that provision, the related penalty is not included in minimum lease payments.

   b. From the standpoint of the lessor: The payments described above plus any guarantee of the residual value or of rental payments beyond the lease term by a third party unrelated to either the lessee or the lessor, provided the third party is financially capable of discharging the obligations that may arise from the guarantee.

19. *Net Lease*. In a net lease, executory costs in connection with the use of the equipment are to be paid by the lessee and are not a part of the rental. For example, taxes, insurance, and maintenance are paid directly by the lessee. Most finance leases are net leases.

20. *Nonrecourse Financing*. Lending or borrowing activities in which the creditor does not have general recourse to the debtor but rather has recourse only to the property used for collateral in the transaction or other specific property.

21. *Operating Lease*. A lease that does not meet any of the lease classification criteria of a capital lease (lessee) or direct financing lease (lessor). Also describes a short-term rental agreement by which a user can acquire use of an asset for a fraction of the useful life of that asset.

22. *Penalty*. Any requirement that is imposed or can be imposed on the lessee by the lease agreement or by factors outside the lease agreement to disburse cash, incur or assume a liability, perform services, surrender or transfer an asset or rights to an asset or otherwise forgo an economic benefit, or suffer an economic detriment. Factors to consider when determining if an economic detriment may be incurred include, but are not limited to, the uniqueness of purpose or location of the property, the availability of a comparable replacement property, the relative importance or significance of the property to the continuation of the lessee's line of business or service to its customers, the existence of leasehold improvements or other assets whose value would be impaired by the lessee vacating or discontinuing use of the leased property, adverse tax consequences, and the ability or willingness of the lessee to bear the cost associated with relocation or replacement of the leased property at market rental rates or to tolerate other parties using the leased property.

23. *Related Parties*. A parent company and its subsidiaries, an owner enterprise and its joint ventures (corporate or otherwise) and partnerships, and an investor (including a natural person) and its investees, provided that the parent company, owner enterprise, or investor has the ability to exercise significant influence over operating and financial policies of the related party. In addition to the foregoing examples of significant influence, significant influence may be exercised through guarantees of indebtedness, extensions of credit, or through ownership of warrants, debt obligations, or other securities. If two or more enterprises are subject to the significant influence of a parent company, owner enterprise, investor (including a natural person), or common officers or directors, those enterprises shall be considered related parties with respect to each other.

24. *Renewal or Extension of a Lease*. The continuation of a lease agreement beyond the original lease term including a new lease under which the lessee continues to use the same property.

25. *Sale-Leaseback Accounting*. A method of accounting for a sale-leaseback transaction in which the seller-lessee records the sale, removes all property and related liabilities from its balance sheet, recognizes gain or loss from the sale, and classifies the leaseback as a financing or operating lease as appropriate.

26. *Sales Recognition*. Any method to record a transaction involving real estate, other than the deposit method, or the methods to record transactions accounted for as financing, leasing, or profit-sharing arrangements. Profit recognition methods commonly used to record transactions involving real estate include, but are not limited to, the full accrual method, the installment method, the cost recovery method, and the reduced profit method.

27. *Sales-Type Lease.* A direct financing lease that also contains a dealer or manufacturer's profit; the fair market value of the property at lease inception exceeds the related carrying value.

28. *Unguaranteed Residual Value.* The estimated residual value of the leased property exclusive of any portion guaranteed by the lessee or by a third party unrelated to the lessor.

23.3 OPERATING LEASES

(a) LESSEE ACCOUNTING FOR OPERATING LEASES.   Normally, rental on an operating lease is charged to expense over the lease term as it becomes payable. If rental payments are not made on a straight-line basis, rental expense nevertheless is recognized on a straight-line basis unless another systematic and rational basis is more representative of the time pattern in which use benefit is derived from the leased property, in which case that basis would be used (see Section 23.9).

(b) LESSEE DISCLOSURES FOR OPERATING LEASES.   The following three items of information with respect to operating leases must be disclosed in the lessee's financial statements or the notes thereto:

1. For operating leases having initial or remaining noncancelable lease terms in excess of one year:
   a. Future minimum rental payments required as of the date of the latest balance sheet presented, in the aggregate and for each of the five succeeding fiscal years.
   b. The total of minimum rentals to be received in the future under noncancelable subleases as of the date of the latest balance sheet presented.
2. For all operating leases, rental expense for each period for which an income statement is presented, with separate amounts for minimum rentals, contingent rentals, and sublease rentals. Rental payments under leases with terms of a month or less that were not renewed need not be included.
3. For all operating leases, a general description of the lessee's leasing arrangements including, but not limited to, the following:
   a. The basis on which contingent rental payments are determined
   b. The existence and terms of renewal or purchase options and escalation clauses
   c. Restrictions imposed by lease agreements, such as those concerning dividends, additional debt, and further leasing

(c) LESSOR ACCOUNTING FOR OPERATING LEASES.   Operating leases are accounted for by the lessor as follows:

- Leased property is included with or displayed near other property, plant, and equipment in the balance sheet.
- Depreciation is recorded following the lessor's normal depreciation policy for like assets, and accumulated depreciation is displayed as a reduction of the leased property.
- Rent is recorded as income over the lease terms as it becomes receivable under the provisions of the lease. However, if the rentals vary from the straight-line basis, the income is recognized on a straight-line basis unless another systematic and rational basis is more representative of the time pattern in which the benefit from the leased property is diminished, in which case that basis is used.

- Initial direct costs are deferred and allocated over the lease term in proportion to revenue recognition under the lease. However, these costs may be expensed when incurred if the effect is not materially different from that which would have resulted from the use of the method prescribed above.

(d) AN EXAMPLE OF OPERATING LEASES.   The Williams Company leases property with a cost and fair value of $5,000 and a life of 10 years to the Scotts Company for 4 years with a rental of $2,000 per year for years 1 and 2 and $1,000 per year for years 3 and 4.

WILLIAMS COMPANY

Years 1 and 2
Cash	$2,000	
Rent Income		$1,500
Deferred Rent Income		500
Depreciation Expense	500	
Accumulated Depreciation		500
$5,000/10 years = $500		

Years 3 and 4
Deferred Rent Income	500	
Cash		1,000
Rent Income		1,500
Depreciation Expense	500	
Accumulated Depreciation		500
$5,000/10 years = $500		

SCOTTS COMPANY

Years 1 and 2
Rent Expenses	$1,500	
Prepaid Rent	500	
Cash		$2,000

Years 3 and 4
Rent Expense	1,500	
Prepaid Rent		500
Cash		1,000

This example assumes that some other time pattern other than straight-line is not of benefit to the lessee and dimunition of benefit to the lessor does not exist. For simplicity, the straight-line depreciation method was used although other methods could be selected by the lessor.

23.4 CAPITAL LEASES

(a) ACCOUNTING FOR CAPITAL LEASES.   For capital leases, the lease transaction is viewed as a form of financing in which an asset is acquired and a liability is incurred. The lessee records a capital lease as an asset and a liability on the balance sheet. The amount recorded on the balance sheet is the present value of the minimum lease payments. Executory costs such as insurance, maintenance, and taxes to be paid by the lessor are excluded from the minimum payments. However, the amount recorded as an asset and liability must not exceed the fair value of the leased property.

The lessee will record depreciation expense and interest expense on capitalized leases. A capitalized asset should be depreciated by the lessee in a manner consistent with the lessee's normal depreciation policy. The depreciation period to be used is the lease term, unless there is a bargain purchase or transfer of ownership at the end of the lease term, in which case the depreciation is over the life of the assets, as if owned.

Interest expense is recognized by the lessee in proportion to the remaining balance of the capitalized lease obligation. This is accomplished by allocating each minimum lease payment between interest expense and reduction of lease obligation so as to produce a constant periodic rate of interest on the remaining lease obligation. This method is called the *effective interest method*.

(b) DISCLOSURE FOR CAPITAL LEASES. The following five areas of information on capital leases must be disclosed.

1. The gross amount of assets recorded under capital leases as of the date of each balance sheet presented by major classes according to nature or function. This information may be combined with the comparable information for owned assets.
2. Future minimum lease payments as of the date of the latest balance sheet presented, in the aggregate and for each of the five succeeding fiscal years, with separate deductions from the total for the amount representing executory costs, including any profit thereon, included in the minimum lease payments and for the amount of the imputed interest necessary to reduce the net minimum lease payments to present value.
3. The total of minimum sublease rentals to be received in the future under noncancelable subleases as of the date of the latest balance sheet presented.
4. Total contingent rentals actually incurred for each period for which an income statement is presented.
5. Assets recorded under capital leases and the accumulated amortization thereon shall be separately identified in the lessee's balance sheet or in notes thereto. Likewise, the related obligations shall be separately identified in the balance sheet as obligations under capital leases and shall be subject to the same considerations as other obligations in classifying them with current and noncurrent liabilities in classified balance sheets. Unless the charge to income resulting from amortization of assets recorded under capital leases is included with depreciation expense and the fact that it is so included is disclosed, the amortization charge shall be separately disclosed in the financial statements or notes thereto.

(c) AN EXAMPLE OF CAPITAL LEASE—LESSEE. SFAS No. 13 offers an example illustrating classification and accounting for leases. Assume that lessee and lessor sign a lease with the following provisions:

- The lease has a noncancelable term of 30 months, and payments of $135 are due at the beginning of each month.
- The equipment costs $5,000, has a 5-year economic life, and has a residual value guaranteed by lessee of $2,000.
- Lessee receives any excess of the sales price over the guaranteed amount.
- Lessee pays executory costs.
- Lessee's incremental borrowing rate is 10.5 percent.
- The interest rate implicit in the lease is unknown to the lessee because the lessor's unguaranteed residual value assumption is unknown to the lessee.
- Lessee depreciates similar equipment on a straight-line basis.
- No investment tax credit is available.

(i) Minimum Lease Payments. Minimum lease payments for both lessee and lessor are calculated as follows:

Payments $135 × 30 months	$4,050
Residual value guarantee	2,000
Total minimum lease payments	$6,050

(ii) Lease Classification.   The lease is classified by reviewing the four lease capitalization criteria presented in Section 23.3.

1. *Not Met*. The lease does not transfer ownership.
2. *Not Met*. The lease does not contain a bargain purchase option.
3. *Not Met*. The lease is not for a term equal to or greater than 75 percent of the economic life of the property.
4. *Met*. For the lessee, the present value of the minimum lease payments using the lessee's incremental borrowing rate exceeds 90 percent of the fair value of the property at the inception of the lease (calculations below). Even if the lessee knows the implicit rate, he uses his incremental borrowing rate because it is lower. Therefore lessee classifies the lease as a capital lease.

Present values using the lessee's incremental borrowing rate of 10.5 percent are as follows:

Present value:	
Rental payments (present value of $135 at 0.875 percent per month for 29 months)	$3,580
Residual guarantee (present value of $2,000 in 30 months at 0.875 percent per month)	1,540
Total	$5,120

Although the lessee's incremental borrowing rate produces a present value of $5,120 for lease classification criteria, SFAS No. 13 stipulates that the lease is not to be capitalized in excess of fair value, or $5,000 in this example. When the present value is adjusted to total $5,000, the interest rate raises to 12.036 percent or 1.003 percent per month as follows:

Present value:	
Rental payments (present value of $135 at 1.003 percent per month for 29 months)	$3,517
Residual guarantee (present value of $2,000 in 30 months at 1.003 percent per month)	$1,483
Total	$5,000

(iii) Lessee Accounting at Inception.   At the beginning of the lease, the lessee's journal entries are:

Equipment under capital lease	$5,000	
Capital lease obligation		$5,000
The first month's payment is recorded as:		
Capital lease obligation	135	
Cash		135
Interest Expense	49	
Accrued Interest		49
Then at the beginning of the second month:		
Capital lease obligation	86	
Accrued Interest	49	
Cash		135

(iv) Lessee Depreciation.   Depreciation would be taken on a straight-line basis over 30 months. Total depreciation to be taken equals the capitalized lease value of $5,000, less its estimated residual value of $2,000. Each month's depreciation would be recorded as follows:

Depreciation expense	$100	
Accumulated depreciation—		
Equipment under capital lease		$100

(v) Lease Payments.   Each lease payment contains both interest and principal, and SFAS No. 13 requires that interest be calculated on the effective interest method, as follows:

Payment Number	Lease Payment	Interest (1.003%) on Principal	Reduction of Principal	Net Lease Obligation
1	$135	0	0	$4,865
2	135	$49	$86	4,779
3	135	48	87	4,692
4	135	47	88	4,604
5	135	46	89	4,515

23.5 DIRECT FINANCING LEASES

(a) ACCOUNTING FOR DIRECT FINANCING LEASES.   In a direct financing lease, a lessor accounts for the investment in the lease as a receivable. A direct financing lease is accounted for by recording the following:

- *Gross investment*. The minimum lease payments (excluding executory costs paid by the lessor) plus any unguaranteed residual value accruing to the lessor are recorded as the gross investment in finance leases.
- *Unearned income*. The difference between the gross investment and the cost or carrying amount of the leased property is recorded as unearned income. This unearned income, reduced by an amount equal to initial direct costs, is amortized to income over the lease term, applying the effective interest method to produce a constant rate of return on the net investment in the lease.
- *Net investment*. The net investment consists of the gross investment less the unearned income.
- *Initial direct costs*. These costs are expensed as incurred.
- *Earned income*. Earned income consist of two elements: (1) An amount equal to initial direct costs, which is recorded at the inception of the lease; and (2) the remaining unearned income, which is amortized to income over the lease term using the effective interest method.

(b) AN EXAMPLE OF DIRECT FINANCING LEASES.   Assume that a lessor executes the same lease described earlier. In addition, for simplicity, assume that there were no initial direct costs. This lease does not meet the first three criteria for a direct finance lease, but it does meet the 90 percent of fair value test. Having met this test and assuming that the collectibility and uncertainty tests are also met, the lessor will classify this lease as a direct financing lease. The interest rate implicit in this lease is the internal rate of return that discounts the minimum lease payments ($135 × 30 plus $2,000 residual value) to the fair value of the property at the inception of the lease ($5,000). That rate is 12.036 percent or 1.003 percent per month.

In this case, the rate is shown by adding the present values of the components of return:

Present value of 29 payments of $135 at 1.003 percent per month	$3,382
Plus $135 for first payment	$0,135
Equals present value of rental payments	$3,517
Plus present value of $2,000 in 30 months at 1.003 percent per month	1,483
	$5,000

The lessor uses this rate to calculate the present value of the minimum lease payments in the 90 percent of fair value test, as follows:

Present value:	
Rental payments	$3,517
Residual guarantee	$1,483
Total	$5,000

Fair value of property at inception of lease	$5,000
Present value of minimum lease payments as percentage of fair value	100 percent

In all direct financing leases where an unguaranteed residual value is recorded, the fair value of property will exceed the present value of minimum lease payments. This is because the unguaranteed residual value is excluded from the lessor's present value calculation. The lessor must produce the following information to record the lease:

- Gross investment is $6,050. Payments of $135 × 30 plus $2,000 guaranteed residual value.
- Unearned income is $1,050. Gross investment less $5,000 cost of equipment.
- Net investment is $5,000. The gross investment less the unearned income.

The entries for the lessor at the inception of the lease are:

Minimum lease payments receivable	$6,050	
Equipment		$5,000
Unearned income		1,050
Monthly lease payments would be recorded as:		
Cash	135	
Minimum lease payments receivable		135

Earned income (excluding any applicable income to cover initial direct costs) for the first month would be recorded as:

Unearned income	$49	
Earned income		$49

A similar pattern is followed for the remainder of the lease term.

The following table summarizes the income recognition and net investment of the lessor over the term of the lease.

Payment Number	Payment	Interest Income on Net Investment	Principal Reduction	Net Investment Beginning of Month
1	$ 135	$ 0	$ 135	$4,865
2	135	49	86	4,779
3	135	48	87	4,692
4	135	47	88	4,604
—	—	—	—	—
—	—	—	—	—
—	—	—	—	—
30	135	21	114	1,980
	0	$ 20	$ (20)	$2,000
	$4,050	$1,050	$3,000	

23.6 SALES-TYPE LEASES

The major difference between a direct financing lease and a sales-type lease is the presence of a manufacturer's profit in a sales-type lease; for example, the fair market value of the property is greater than the carrying value of such property.

(a) ACCOUNTING FOR SALES-TYPE LEASES. A sales-type lease is accounted for by recording the following four items:

1. *Gross investment*. The minimum lease payments (excluding executory costs paid by the lessor) plus any unguaranteed residual value accruing to the lessor are recorded as the gross investment in finance leases.

2. *Unearned income*. The difference between the gross investment and the cost or carrying amount of the leased property is recorded as unearned income. This unearned income is amortized to income over the lease term, applying the effective interest method to produce a constant rate of return on the net investment in the lease.

3. *Net investment*. The net investment consists of the minimum lease gross investment less the unearned income.

4. *Cost of goods sold or cost of sales.* The cost or carrying amount of the lease property less the present value of any unguaranteed residual value accruing to the benefit of the lessor.

(b) AN EXAMPLE OF SALES-TYPE LEASES.   In the case presented in Section 23.6, assume that the lessor produces the equipment for a cost of $4,000. The information needed to record the salestype lease consists of these four items:

1. Gross investment is $6,050 ($4,050 of lease payments plus $2,000 of guaranteed residual value).

2. Unearned interest income is $1,050 (gross investment of $6,050 less $5,000).

3. Sales price is $5,000 (present value of minimum lease payments).

4. Cost of goods sold is $4,000 less the present value of any unguaranteed residual value accruing to the benefit of the lessor. Because there is no unguaranteed residual value, the cost of goods sold equals the lessor's cost to produce the equipment under lease.

The transaction is recorded by the lessor as follows:

Lease payments receivable	$6,050
Cost of goods	4,000
Sales revenue	5,000
Equipment	4,000
Unearned income	1,050

Thereafter, the accounting for lessors would follow the example of the direct financing lease.

BALANCE SHEET PRESENTATION—CAPITAL LEASE—LESSEE

Long-lived assets:	
Leased property under capital leases less accumulated amortization	$XXX
Current liabilities:	
Obligations under capital leases	$XXX
Long-term liabilities:	
Obligations under capital leases	$XXX

BALANCE SHEET PRESENTATION—CAPITAL LEASE—LESSOR

Current assets:	
Net investment in direct financing and sales-type leases—current portion	$XXX
Noncurrent assets:	
Net investment in direct financing and sales-type leases	$XXX
Long-lived assets:	
Property on operating leases and property held for leases net of accumulated depreciation	$XXX

23.7 SALE OR ASSIGNMENT OF A LEASE OR OF PROPERTY SUBJECT TO A LEASE ACCOUNTED FOR AS A SALES-TYPE OR DIRECT FINANCING LEASE

SFAS No. 135 requires the sale or assignment of a lease or of property subject to a lease that was accounted for as a sales-type lease or a direct financing lease not to negate the original accounting treatment for the lease. A transfer of minimum lease payments or guaranteed residual values subject to a sales-type lease or direct financing lease is required to be accounted in conformity with SFAS No. 140. (See Chapter 19.) Transfers of unguaranteed residual values are not subject to SFAS No. 140.

23.8 LEVERAGED LEASES

(a) LEVERAGED LEASE ACCOUNTING.   Leveraged leases derive their name from a characteristic of the transaction, namely that the lessor tends to have a small equity in the leased property and borrows or otherwise finances a large part of the cost of owning the asset. Frequently the lessor's equity is reduced by an immediate return from investment tax credits related to the leased property, which offsets income taxes otherwise payable by the lessor. The lessor (equity participant) is frequently a financial institution able to finance the leverage at a relatively low cost. This combination, together with the security of a high-quality lessee (or lease), tends to produce a comparatively low usage cost of the asset to the lessee.

The lessor's investment in a finance lease may be zero or even negative at certain times during the lease period. The concept of recognizing a profit during a period of negative investment caused some theoretical problems in determining the proper accounting for leveraged leases.

(i) Characteristics of a Leveraged Lease.   The SFAS No. 13 defines a leveraged lease to be one having all of the following four characteristics:

1. It meets the definition of a direct financing lease.
2. It involves at least three parties: a lessee, a long-term creditor, and a lessor (commonly called the *equity participant*).
3. The financing provided by the long-term creditor is nonrecourse as to the general credit of the lessor (although the creditor may have recourse to the specific property leased and the unremitted rentals relating to it), and the amount of the financing is sufficient to provide the lessor with substantial "leverage" in the transaction.
4. The lessor's net investment declines during the early years once the investment has been completed and rises during the later years of the lease before its final elimination. Provided the lease meets these requirements and the investment tax credit, if any, is not accounted for using the flow-through method, the lease is treated as a leveraged lease.

(ii) Lessee Accounting.   From the viewpoint of the lessee, leveraged leases are classified and accounted for in the same manner as nonleveraged leases.

(iii) Lessor Accounting for Investment.   The lessor records the investment in a leveraged lease net of the nonrecourse debt. The net balance of the following four accounts represents the initial and continuing investment in leveraged leases:

1. Rentals receivable, net of that portion of the rental applicable to principal and interest on the nonrecourse debt
2. A receivable for the amount of the investment tax credit to be realized on the transaction
3. The estimated residual value of the leased asset
4. Unearned income (the remaining amount of estimated pretax lease income or loss and investment tax credit to be allocated to income over the lease term, after deducting initial direct costs)

(iv) Lessor Recognition of Income. The lessor in a leveraged lease transaction recognizes income by use of the investment with separate phases method. Under this method, lease income is recognized at a level aftertax rate of return on net investment in those years in which the net investment at the beginning of the period is positive. Deferred taxes should be used to calculate the net investment for use in computing income from the lease. However, deferred taxes should not be offset against the investment in the lease for balance sheet presentation. Usually, the lessor's net investment in a leveraged lease is as follows:

- *Early period*. Positive, due to the initial investment in leased property.
- *Middle period*. Negative, due to income tax reductions provided by accelerated depreciation, interest on nonrecourse debt, and investment tax credits, the cash flows are shielded from payment of taxes. In this period, the lessor has not only recovered his initial investment but has received additional funds, which are temporarily invested in other operations.
- *Later period*. Positive, due to a transfer from a tax shelter position to a tax-paying position arising primarily from reduced depreciation and interest charges.
- *Final period*. Zero, when the residual value is realized on sale of the property.

The investment with separate phases method identifies two separate and distinct types of earnings: primary earnings and earnings from reinvestment. Primary earnings consist of three elements: pretax lease income, tax effect of pretax lease income, and investment tax credit. The income that is recognized at a level rate of return in the years in which the net investment is positive consists only of the primary earnings from the lease.

In the middle years of a leveraged lease, the net investment is typically negative. The lessor has recovered his initial investment and has the further use of cash that is shielded from tax by high depreciation and interest expense charges. The earnings from the reinvestment of excess funds are taken into income during the years when the net investment is negative and are independent of the reporting of the leveraged lease income. The result is that lease income is recognized at a level rate of return on the net investment (cost of property less nonrecourse debt and less the investment tax credit) in the years in which the net investment is positive at the beginning of the year. During the years when the net investment is negative, only the earnings from the reinvested funds are realized.

(b) LEVERAGED LEASE DISCLOSURES. When leasing activities, exclusive of leveraged leasing, are a significant part of the lessor's business activities in terms of revenue, net income, or assets, the following three items of information with respect to leases should be disclosed in the financial statements or notes:

1. For sales-type and direct financing leases:
  a. The components of the net investment in sales-type and direct financing leases as of the date of each balance sheet presented:
    i. Future minimum lease payments to be received, with separate deductions for amounts representing executory costs, including any profit thereon, included in the minimum lease payments and the accumulated allowance for uncollectible minimum lease payments receivable.
    ii. The unguaranteed residual values accruing to the benefit of the lessor.
    iii. For direct financing leases only, initial direct costs.
    iv. Unearned income.
  b. Future minimum lease payments to be received for each of the five succeeding fiscal years as of the date of the latest balance sheet presented.
  c. Total contingent rentals included in income for each period for which an income statement is presented.

2. For operating leases:

   a. The cost and carrying amount, if different, of property on lease or held for leasing by major classes of property according to nature or function, and the amount of accumulated depreciation in total as of the date of the latest balance sheet presented.

   b. Minimum future rentals on noncancelable leases as of the date of the latest balance sheet presented, in the aggregate and for each of the five succeeding fiscal years.

   c. Total contingent rentals included in income for each period for which an income statement is presented.

3. A general description of the lessor's leasing arrangements.

23.9 REAL ESTATE LEASES

Leases involving real estate can be categorized in one of the following four ways:

1. Land only leases
2. Land and building leases
3. Real estate and equipment leases
4. Leases involving part of a building

The same criteria are used to determine classification as an operating or capital lease.

(a) LEASES INVOLVING LAND ONLY. If land is the only item of property leased and the lease transfers ownership of the property or contains a bargain purchase option, the lessee should account for the lease as a capital lease; because ownership of the land is expected to pass to the lessee, the asset recorded under the lease is not normally amortizable. If the lease does not meet either of those criteria, the lease is an operating lease.

If the lease transfers ownership and meets the requirements of collectibility and uncertainty, the lessor accounts for the lease as either a sales-type or a direct financing lease, whichever is appropriate. If the lease does not meet those requirements, it is an operating lease. The lessor does not use the bargain purchase option criterion to classify the lease.

(b) LEASES INVOLVING LAND AND BUILDINGS. When the lease either transfers ownership or contains a bargain purchase option, there are two forms of accounting:

   1. *Lessee's accounting.* If the lease transfers ownership or contains a bargain purchase option, the land and the buildings are separately capitalized by the lessee. The present value of the minimum lease payments is apportioned between land and buildings in relation to their fair values at the inception of the lease. The building should be amortized under the normal accounting policies of the lessee.

   2. *Lessor's accounting.* If the lease transfers ownership and meets both the collectibility and uncertainty tests, the lessor accounts for the lease as a single unit. If there is a manufacturer or dealer profit, the lease would be a sales-type lease. Without such profit, it would be a direct financing lease or leveraged lease, as appropriate. If the lease does not meet these tests, the lessor accounts for the lease as an operating lease. The lessor does not use the bargain purchase option criterion to classify the lease.

When the lease neither transfers ownership nor contains a bargain purchase option, whether the land and the building are considered together or separately depends on the relation of the fair value of the land to the total fair value of the leased property.

If the fair value of the land is less than 25 percent of the total fair value of the leased property, both the lessee and the lessor must consider the land and the building as a single unit, the economic life of the building.

If the lease term is at least 75 percent of the property's estimated economic life or if the present value of the minimum lease payments is 90 percent or more of the fair value of the property, the lessee capitalizes the land and buildings as a single unit and amortizes it. If the lease does not meet those requirements, it is accounted for as an operating lease.

If the lease term is at least 75 percent of the property's economic life or if the present value of minimum lease payments is 90 percent or more of the fair value of the property and both the collectibility and uncertainty tests are met, the lessor accounts for the lease as a single unit, a sales-type lease, a direct financing lease, or a leveraged lease. If the lease does not meet those requirements, it is accounted for as an operating lease.

If the building in the lease meets the economic life or 90 percent fair value tests, the building is accounted for as a capital lease by the lessee. The land element of the lease is separately accounted for as an operating lease. However, if the building element in the lease meets neither the economic life nor the fair value test, both the building and the land are accounted for as a single operating lease by the lessee.

If the building in the lease meets the economic life or fair value test as well as the criteria for uncertainty and collectibility, the lessor accounts for the building elements as a sales-type lease, a direct financing lease, or a leveraged lease, as appropriate. The land is accounted for as an operating lease. As with lessees, if the building does not meet the economic life or fair value tests and does not meet the tests for collectibility, both the building and the land are accounted for collectively as a single operating lease.

(c) LEASES INVOLVING LAND AND EQUIPMENT.   If a lease involves land and equipment, the portion of the minimum lease payments applicable to the equipment is estimated by whatever means is appropriate and reasonable. The equipment is then to be treated separately for purposes of applying the criteria and accounted for separately according to its classification by both lessee and lessor.

(d) LEASES INVOLVING ONLY PART OF A BUILDING.   When the leased property is part of a larger entity, its cost and fair value may not be objectively determinable as, for example, if a floor in an office building was leased. If the cost and fair value of the leased property are objectively determinable, both the lessee and the lessor should classify and account for the lease as described above.

Unless both the cost and the fair value are objectively determinable, the lease is classified and accounted for in the following two ways:

1. *Lessee*. If the fair value of the leased property is not objectively determinable, the lessee shall classify the lease pursuant to whether it meets the 75 percent of economic life test.

2. *Lessor*. If either the cost or the fair value of the property is not objectively determinable, the lessor shall account for the lease as an operating lease.

23.10 SELECTED ISSUES IN LEASE ACCOUNTING

(a) PARTICIPATION BY THIRD PARTIES.   The sale or assignment of a lease or property subject to a lease to a third party does not change the original accounting for the lease. Any profit or loss on the sale should be recognized at the time of the transaction, unless the transaction is between related parties or is sold with recourse (see SFAS No. 140, "Accounting for the Transfers and Servicing of Financial Assets and Extinguishments of Liabilities").

(b) RELATED PARTY LEASES. In general, related party leases are classified in accordance with the same criteria as all other leases, unless it is clear that the terms of the transaction have been significantly affected by the relationship of the lessees and lessor. The economic substance of such a transaction may cause the accounting for such leases to be modified from that which would be suggested by the strict terms of the lease.

(c) SUBLEASES. If the original lease was classified as a capital lease because of transfer of title or a bargain purchase option, the sublease by the lessee should be treated as a new lease and classified according to the same criteria as any other lease. If the original lease was classified as a capital lease because of the economic life or 90 percent fair value tests, only the economic life test should be used to classify the sublease except where the lessee who is now becoming a lessor was really only an intermediary between the new lessee and original lessor. In that event, the 90 percent fair value test should also be used. If the original lease was an operating lease, the sublease must also be an operating lease.

(d) CHANGES IN THE PROVISIONS OF LEASES. From the standpoint of the lessor, three changes can take place as follows:

1. The change does not give rise to a new agreement. A new agreement is defined as a change that, if in effect at the inception of the lease, would have resulted in a different classification.
2. The change does give rise to a new agreement that would be classified as a direct financing lease.
3. The change gives rise to a new agreement classified as an operating lease.

If either (1) or (2) occur, the balance of the minimum lease payment receivable and the estimated residual value are adjusted to reflect the effect of the change. The net adjustment is to be charged (or credited) to the unearned income account, and the accounting for the lease adjusted to reflect the change.

If the new agreement is an operating lease, then the transaction should be accounted for under the sale-leaseback requirements.

(e) RENEWAL, EXTENSION, OR TERMINATION OF LEASES. A renewal or extension involves one of two circumstances that affect the accounting for an existing lease:

1. A guarantee or penalty is rendered inoperative.
2. A new agreement exists.

In both circumstances, the lessee in a capital lease adjusts the current balance of the leased asset and obligation to the present value of the future minimum lease payments based on the implicit interest rate in the original lease. If a new agreement exists and it is classified as an operating lease, then the lessee continues to account for the existing capital lease until the end of the term. The renewal or extension is an operating lease and is accounted for as such. In both circumstances, the lessor in a direct financing lease would adjust the lease receivable and estimated residual value charging or crediting unearned income for the difference. An upward revision to estimated residual value is prohibited, however. If a renewal or extension constitutes a new agreement and is an operating lease, then the lessor continues to account for the existing lease until the end of the term and accounts for the renewal/extension as an operating lease. If the new agreement is a sales-type lease, the renewal or extension is accounted for as a sales-type lease providing the renewal/extension occurred at or near the end of the existing lease term.

In a termination, the lessor eliminates the remaining net investment and records the leased asset at its lower of present fair value, current book value, or historical cost. The net difference is reflected in the income statement of the current period. The lessor in a capital lease will eliminate the asset and obligation from the financial statements recording a gain or loss on termination. In an operating lease, no adjustment is required.

(f) LEASES AND BUSINESS COMBINATIONS.   If, in connection with a business combination, the provisions of a lease are modified such that the revised lease is essentially a new agreement, this new lease should be classified as any new lease would be.

In a pooling of interests, unless the lease has been modified as above, no changes should be made in the accounting for the leases in effect.

In a purchase, unless the terms of the lease have been changed, the previous classification would remain in effect. However, the amounts assigned to the assets and liabilities arising from the accounting for leases should be determined in accordance with the guidelines under FASB No. 141, "Business Combinations."

(g) CHANGE IN RESIDUAL VALUE.   A lessor should at a minimum annually review the estimated residual values in any leasing transactions. For any decline in value that is deemed to be permanent, a loss should be recognized in the period of decline and the residual value should be revised. For any declines that are deemed to be temporary, no such action need be taken. No change in residual values is ever recognized for estimated increases in such values.

(h) SALE AND LEASEBACK.   A sale and leaseback transaction is one involving the sale of property by the owner (seller-lessee), who simultaneously leases it back from the new owner. Sale and leaseback transactions are frequently entered into as a means of raising additional cash from assets that are owned and used by a company. For example, a company may sell a building it owns and simultaneously lease it back. The facilities of the building are still available to the company. The cash received can be invested in the company's productive process or business at a relatively high rate of return. Since real estate investors, who purchase and lease the building, frequently accept lower rates of return than are available to the company from its normal operations, overall rate of return is improved. In effect, the company transfers funds invested in real estate (or similar) assets to higher yielding, more active investments. The lease in a sale and leaseback transaction is frequently a net lease, which provides that the lessee remains liable for all executory costs, taxes, maintenance, and so on.

(i) Lessee Accounting.   If the lease meets one of the criteria for treatment as a capital lease, the seller-lessee accounts for it as a capital lease. If the lease does not meet one of the criteria, then it is an operating lease. In general, any profit or loss on the sale is deferred and recognized in proportion to the amortization of the leased asset in a capital lease or to the gross rental expense in an operating lease. The three exceptions to the general rule are:

1. The seller-lessee relinquishes rights to substantially all of the property sold, retaining only a minor portion. Both the sale and leaseback are treated as separate transactions unless they require an adjustment due to the unreasonable amount of rentals called for by the leaseback compared to market conditions.

2. The seller-lessee retains more than a minor part of the property but less than substantially all. Only the profit on the sale in excess of the present value of the minimum lease payments or recorded value of the leased asset is recognized at the date of sale.

3. The fair value of the property is less than its net book value, in which case a loss should be immediately recognized.

(ii) Lessor Accounting.   If the lease meets any one of the lease classification criteria and both criteria for collectibility and uncertainty, the purchaser-lessor must record the transaction as a purchase and a direct financing lease. If the lease does not meet these criteria, the lessor records the transaction as a purchase and an operating lease.

(iii) Sale-Leaseback for Real Estate.   A sale-leaseback for real estate involves any transaction that involves real estate, including real estate with equipment or furniture and fixtures, regardless of the relative value of the equipment or furniture and fixtures and the real estate. Sale-leaseback can be used by a seller-lessee only if the agreement includes all of the following:

- A normal leaseback
- Payment terms and provisions adequately demonstrating the buyer-lessor's initial and continuing investment in the property (see SFAS No. 66, "Accounting for Sales of Real Estate," [FASB, 1982])
- Payment terms and provisions transferring all of the other risks and rewards of ownership as demonstrated by the absence of any other continuing involvement by the seller-lessee A normal leaseback involves active use of the property by the seller-lessee in exchange for the payment of rent except for minor subleasing (10 percent or less of the fair value). Terms and provisions substantially different than those that an independent lessor or lessee would normally accept are considered an exchange of unstated rights or privileges that should be considered in evaluating continuing involvement by the seller-lessee. These may include sales price or interest rate. A sale-leaseback that does not qualify for a normal leaseback because of the continuing involvement by the seller-lessee should be accounted for by the deposit method or as a financing.

Continuing involvement includes these five:

1. Sale-leaseback of property improvements or equipment without leasing the underlying land
2. Buyer-lessor shares the future appreciation of the property with the seller-lessee
3. Seller-lessee has an option or obligation to repurchase
4. Seller-lessee guarantees buyer-lessor's investment or return on investment for some period of time
5. Guarantee by the seller-lessee such as fair value of property at end of lease, providing nonrecourse financing, remaining as liable on obligation, and so on

Disclosures required include the terms of the sale-leaseback, the obligation for future minimum lease payments in the aggregate and for each of the five succeeding fiscal years, and the total of minimum sublease rentals in the aggregate and for each of the five succeeding fiscal years.

(i) GUIDANCE FOR SELECTED LEASING TRANSACTIONS.   In recent years, numerous complexities regarding leasing transactions have required the EITF to address the accompanying accounting issues:

(i) EITF Abstracts No. 84-37—Sale-Leaseback Transaction with Repurchase Option

Issue.   Certain inconsistencies have been perceived between Statement No. 13, as amended by Statement No. 28, and Statement No. 66. The four issues are:

1. In a sale-leaseback transaction with a short initial lease term and one or more renewal options, over what period profit should be recognized if the lease does not meet the criteria for classification as a capital lease.
2. In a real estate sale-leaseback transaction in which (a) the seller has an obligation to repurchase the leased property, (b) the buyer can compel the seller to repurchase the property, or (c) the seller has an option to repurchase the property, whether it is appropriate to report the transaction as a sale.
3. In a real estate sale-leaseback transaction in which the seller finances the purchaser's acquisition, whether the lease term includes the renewal periods exercisable during the term of the loan.

4. How rental shortfall agreements that would warrant accounting as an adjustment of the purchase price by the buyer-lessor (as addressed in Issue No. 85-27, "Recognition of Receipts from Made-Up Rental Shortfalls") should be distinguished from a sale-leaseback transaction (as addressed by Statement No. 13).

Emerging Issues Task Force Discussion.

Issue 1: The Task Force was unable to reach a consensus on this issue. Some Task Force members stated that the period over which the gain should be amortized is dependent on the individual facts and circumstances, such as the economic consequences of not renewing the lease, the intent to renew, and the existence of viable alternatives to renewal. Others discussed the use of an arbitrary period of time in circumstances in which the lease period does not appear to be appropriate. (*Note:* See section Status.)

Issue 2: The Task Force was unable to reach a consensus on this issue.

Issue 3: The Task Force was unable to reach a consensus on this issue.

Issue 4: The Task Force was unable to reach a consensus on this issue.

Status. In May 1988, the FASB issued Statement No. 98, which affects the above issues as summarized next.

Issue 1: Statement No. 98 revises the definition of lease term for all leasing transactions to include all periods, if any, during which a loan from the lessee to the lessor directly or indirectly related to the leased property is expected to be outstanding. Statement No. 98 also defines the term *penalty* as used in the lease terms provisions of paragraph 5(f) of Statement No. 13 and thereby may cause lease terms to be longer than previously contemplated. Those modifications of the lease term provisions of Statement No. 13 apply to all leases, not just to sale-leaseback transactions involving real estate. Thus, the period over which profit would be recognized on a sale-leaseback transaction may be affected by the guidance in Statement No. 98.

Issue 2: Statement No. 98 states that sale-leaseback accounting (as defined in Statement No. 98) shall be used by a seller-lessee only if, among other criteria, the sale-leaseback transaction includes payment terms and provisions that transfer all of the risks and rewards of ownership other than the leaseback itself as demonstrated by the absence of any continuing involvement by the seller-lessee. Paragraphs 25–39 and 41–43 of Statement No. 66 describe forms of continuing involvement by the seller-lessee with the leased property that result in the seller-lessee not transferring the risks and rewards of ownership to the buyer-lessor.

Issue 3: Statement No. 98 revises the definition of lease term for all leasing transactions to include all periods, if any, during which a loan from the lessee to the lessor directly or indirectly related to the leased property is expected to be outstanding.

Issue 4: This issue is not addressed in Statement No. 98.

(ii) EITF Abstracts No. 86-17—Deferred Profit on Sale-Leaseback Transaction with Lessee Guarantee of Residual Value

Issue. In a sale-leaseback transaction, the seller-lessee guarantees to the lessor that the residual value will be a stipulated amount. The seller-lessee retains more than a minor part but less than substantially all of the use of the property through the leaseback. The lease does not meet the criteria for classification as a capital lease.

The issue is how the residual value guarantee should affect the determination of profit to be deferred on the sale in accordance with Statement No. 28. If the residual value guarantee affects the determination of deferred profit, should the gross amount of the guarantee or its present value be used?

EITF Discussion The Task Force reached a consensus that profit equal to the present value of the periodic rent plus the gross amount of the guarantee should be deferred at the date of sale. The amount of deferred profit equal to the gross guarantee should be deferred until the guarantee is resolved at the end of the lease term. The remaining deferred profit, equal to the present value of the periodic rents, should be amortized in relation to gross rent expense over the lease term. Some Task Force members believed that this accounting is appropriate because the guaranteed amount represents a contingent gain.

Status In May 1988, the FASB issued Statement No. 98, which addresses the accounting for sale-leaseback transactions involving real estate. Statement No. 98 states that sale-leaseback accounting (as defined in Statement No. 98) shall be used by a seller-lessee only if, among other criteria, the sale-leaseback transaction includes payment terms and provisions that transfer all the risks and rewards of ownership other than the leaseback itself as demonstrated by the absence of *any* other continuing involvement by the seller-lessee.

(iii) EITF Abstracts No. 88-21—Accounting for the Sale of Property Subject to the Seller's Pre-Existing Lease

Issue. An entity owns an interest in property and also is a lessee under an operating lease for all or a portion of the property. Acquisition of an ownership interest in the property and consummation of the lease occurred at or near the same time. This owner-lessee relationship can occur when the entity has an investment in a partnership that owns the leased property. The entity sells its interest or the partnership sells the property to an independent third party and the entity continues to lease the property under the pre-existing operating lease. The four issues are:

1. Whether the transaction should be accounted for as a sale-leaseback transaction
2. Whether the amount of profit deferred, if any, should be affected by the seller-lessee's prior ownership in the property
3. Whether Statement No. 98 should be applied to transactions involving property under the scope of that Statement if pursuant to provisions in the pre-existing lease, the seller-lessee vacates and intends to sublease the property or exercises a renewal option
4. Whether Statement No. 98 should be applied to transactions involving property under the scope of that Statement if the pre-existing lease is between parties under common control of the seller

EITF Discussion. The Task Force reached a consensus on the first issue that a transaction should be considered a sale-leaseback transaction if the pre-existing lease is modified in connection with the sale, except for insignificant changes. Under this consensus, transactions with modifications to the pre-existing lease involving property within the scope of Statement No. 98 should be accounted for under that Statement. The Task Force also reached a consensus on the first issue that if the preexisting lease is not modified in conjunction with the sale, except for insignificant changes, profit should be deferred and recognized in accordance with Statement No. 28. If the transaction involves real estate, Statement No. 66 must also be applied in all cases; however, Statement No. 98 is applicable only if the lease was entered into after June 30, 1988. In applying Statement No. 77 when Statement No. 98 is not applicable, all continuing involvement included in the pre-existing lease is not considered for purposes of determining if a sale should be recognized.

The Task Force reached a consensus on the second issue that, irrespective of lease modifications, the calculation of the amount of deferred profit should not be affected by the seller-lessee's prior ownership percentage in the property.

The Task Force reached a consensus on the third issue that the exercise of a renewal option for a period that was included in the original minimum lease term [as lease term is defined in paragraph 5(f) of Statement No. 13] or a sublease provision contained in the pre-existing lease, does not affect the accounting for the transaction. Under this consensus, however, exercise of a renewal option for a period that was not included in the original lease term is a new lease, and Statement No. 98 should be applied.

The Task Force reached a consensus on the fourth issue that a lease between parties under common control should not be considered a pre-existing lease for purposes of this consensus and that Statement No. 98 should be applied to transactions that include property within its scope, except when Statement No. 71 applies. That is, if one of the parties under common control is a regulated enterprise with a lease that has been approved by the appropriate regulatory agency, that lease should be considered a pre-existing lease.

The Task Force did not address the accounting when the acquisition of the ownership interest in the property and the consummation of the lease did not occur at or near the same time.

(iv) EITF Abstracts No. 89-16—Consideration of Executory Costs in Sale-Leaseback Transactions

Issue. Executory costs (such as insurance, maintenance, and taxes) of property leased in a sale-leaseback transaction (1) may be paid by the buyer-lessor who expects to recover the costs through the monthly rentals established in the lease, (2) may be paid by the buyer-lessor and in turn billed to the seller-lessee as an addition to the rent, or (3) may be paid directly by the seller-lessee. The issue is how to consider executory costs in the calculation of profit to be deferred in a sale-leaseback transaction.

EITF Discussion. The Task Force reached a consensus that executory costs of the leaseback should be excluded from the calculation of profit to be deferred on a sale-leaseback transaction irrespective of who pays the executory costs or the classification of the leaseback.

(v) EITF Abstracts No. 89-20—Accounting for Cross-Border Tax Benefit Leases

Issue. A U.S. enterprise purchases a depreciable asset and enters into an arrangement with a foreign investor that provides the foreign investor with an ownership right in, but not necessarily title to, the asset. That ownership right enables the foreign investor to claim certain benefits of ownership of the asset for tax purposes in the foreign tax jurisdiction.

The U.S. enterprise also enters into an agreement in the form of a leaseback for the ownership right with the foreign investor. The lease agreement contains a purchase option for the U.S. enterprise to acquire the foreign investor's ownership right in the asset at the end of the lease term.

The foreign investor pays the U.S. enterprise an amount of cash based on an appraised value of the asset. The U.S. enterprise immediately transfers a portion of that cash to a third party, and that third party assumes the U.S. enterprise's obligation to make the future lease payments, including the purchase option payment. The cash retained by the U.S. enterprise is consideration for the tax benefits to be obtained by the foreign investor in the foreign tax jurisdiction. The U.S. enterprise may agree to indemnify the foreign investor against certain future events that would reduce the availability of tax benefits to the foreign investor. The U.S. enterprise also may agree to indemnify the third party trustee against certain future events.

The result of the transaction is that both the U.S. enterprise and the foreign investor have a tax basis in the same depreciable asset.

The issue is whether the cash consideration received by the U.S. enterprise from the foreign investor for tax benefits that the foreign investor will obtain in the foreign tax jurisdiction should immediately be recognized in income or deferred.

EITF Discussion. The Task Force acknowledged that practice is diverse and that in some cases the cash consideration received by the U.S. enterprise has been recognized in income immediately and in other cases has been deferred. The Task Force reached a consensus that the timing of income recognition should be determined based on individual facts and circumstances but that immediate income recognition is not appropriate if there is more than a remote possibility of loss of the cash consideration received due to indemnification or other contingencies.

(vi) EITF Abstracts No. 90-14—Unsecured Guarantee by Parent of Subsidiary's Lease Payments in a Sale-Leaseback Transaction

Issue. Subsidiary S (seller-lessee), a subsidiary of Company A, enters into a sale-leaseback transaction for a building with Company B (buyer-lessor). Company B requires Company A to provide an unsecured guarantee of the lease payments. The transaction otherwise meets all of the provisions under Statement No. 98 for Subsidiary S to use sale-leaseback accounting.

The issue is whether Company A's unsecured guarantee of Subsidiary S's lease payments is a form of continuing involvement that precludes the application of sale-leaseback accounting under Statement No. 98 in (1) Subsidiary S's separate financial statements and (2) Company A's consolidated financial statements.

EITF Discussion. The Task Force expressed the view that an entity's unsecured guarantee of its own lease payments is not a form of continuing involvement that precludes sale-leaseback accounting under Statement No. 98 because such a guarantee does not provide the buyer-lessor with additional collateral that reduces the buyer-lessor's risk of loss, except in the event of the seller-lessee's bankruptcy. The Task Force reached a consensus that an unsecured guarantee of the lease payments of one member of a consolidated group by another member of the consolidated group is not a form of continuing involvement that precludes sale-leaseback accounting under Statement No. 98 in the consolidated financial statements. However, the Task Force also reached a consensus that an unsecured guarantee of the lease payments of one member of a consolidated group by another member of the consolidated group is a form of continuing involvement that precludes sale-leaseback accounting under Statement No. 98 in the separate financial statements of the seller-lessee because such a guarantee provides the buyer-lessor with additional collateral that reduces the buyer-lessor's risk of loss.

(vii) EITF Abstracts No. 90-20—Impact of an Uncollateralized Irrevocable Letter of Credit on a Real Estate Sale-Leaseback Transaction

Issue. Company A (seller-lessee) enters into a real estate sale-leaseback transaction with unrelated Company B (buyer-lessor). Company B requires Company A to provide an irrevocable letter of credit securing all or a portion of the lease payments as required under the lease agreement. The issuer of the letter of credit does not require Company A to pledge specific assets as collateral. The transaction otherwise qualifies for sale-leaseback accounting under Statement No. 98. The issue is whether Company A's uncollateralized, irrevocable letter of credit is a form of continuing involvement that precludes sale-leaseback accounting under Statement No. 98.

EITF Discussion. The Task Force reached a consensus that an uncollateralized, irrevocable letter of credit is not a form of continuing involvement that precludes sale-leaseback accounting under Statement No. 98. The Task Force notes that the continuing involvement provisions of Statement No. 98 do not preclude a lessee from providing an independent third-party guarantee of the lease payments in a sale-leaseback transaction. However, the Task Force noted that all written contracts that exist between the seller-lessee in a sale-leaseback transaction and the issuer of a letter of credit must be considered. For example, the Task Force acknowledged that a financial institution's right of setoff of any amounts on deposit with the institution against any payments made under the letter of credit constitutes collateral and, therefore, is a form of continuing involvement that precludes sale-leaseback accounting under Statement No. 98.

(viii) EITF Abstracts No. 92-1—Allocation of Residual Value or First-Loss Guarantee to Minimum Lease Payments in Lease Involving Land and Building(s)

Issue.   Leases may include a residual value or first-loss guarantee (Guarantee) by the lessee of the leased property. Those Guarantees are used by lessors as a means of transferring some of the risks in the property to the lessee and of ensuring that the lessor receives a return on and of its investment. Statement No. 13 includes Guarantees in minimum lease payments for purposes of determining the classification of leases.

The 90 percent test in Statement No. 13 is not applicable to a lease of land only, and thus a Guarantee would not be considered in determining the classification of a lease of land only. However, for a lease of both land and building(s), applying Statement No. 13 results in a Guarantee being included in minimum lease payments for purposes of performing the 90 percent test. If the fair value of the land is 25 percent or more of the total fair value of the leased property at the inception of the lease, Statement No. 13 requires that the lease be separated into its land and building components for purposes of applying the economic life and 90 percent tests to determine the classification of the building component of the lease.

The issue is what the accounting treatment of the Guarantee should be for purposes of performing the 90 percent test.

EITF Discussion.   The Task Force reached a consensus that a literal application of Statement No. 13 is appropriate. Statement No. 13 states that the annual minimum lease payments applicable to the land are determined for both the lessee and lessor by multiplying the fair value of the land by the lessee's incremental borrowing rate. As a result, the remaining minimum lease payments, including the full amount of the Guarantee, are attributed to the building.

(ix) EITF Abstracts No. 93-8—Accounting for the Sale and Leaseback of an Asset That Is Leased to Another Party

Issue.   An enterprise enters into a sale-leaseback of personal property outside of the scope of Statement No. 98, which is either (a) subject to an operating lease or (b) subleased or intended to be subleased by the enterprise to another party under an operating lease. This transaction makes the enterprise a seller-lessee-sublessor, under an operating lease.

The issue is if substantial risks and rewards of ownership in the property are retained by the seller, whether the accounting for the personal property subject to the operating lease should be as a borrowing under third-party participations in operating leases as described in Statement No. 13 or as a sale-leaseback transaction in accordance with Statement No. 28.

EITF Discussion.   The Task Force reached a consensus that the seller-lessee-sublessor should account for the transaction as a sale-leaseback in accordance with Statement No. 28. The seller-lessee-sublessor records the sale, removes the asset from its balance sheet, and classifies the leaseback in accordance with paragraph 6 of Statement No. 13. Any gain on the transaction should be recognized or deferred and amortized in accordance with Statement No. 28.

Status.   Consensus reached. No further EITF discussion is planned.

(x) EITF Abstracts No. 95-1—Revenue Recognition on Sales with a Guaranteed Minimum

Resale Value.   In EITF Issue No. 95-1, "Revenue Recognition on Sales with a Guaranteed Minimum Resale Value," there is consideration of the situation where a manufacturer sells products to a dealer and gives a rebate to the retail purchaser. The rebate is determined for large bulk and fleet purchases by guaranteeing a minimum residual value. There continues to be discussion as to whether and the extent to which such a guaranty precludes recognition of a sale to the dealer.

(xi) EITF Abstracts No. 95-4—Revenue Recognition on Equipment Sold and Subsequently Repurchased Subject to an Operating Lease   In EITF No. 95-4, "Revenue Recognition on Equipment Sold and Subsequently Repurchased Subject to an Operating Lease," products are sold by a manufacturer to a dealer, who subsequently resells the goods. The customer pays the dealer cash or may use financing including leasing arrangements. The financing source may include the manufacturer or an affiliate of manufacturer (finance affiliate). The issue is whether revenue recognition is precluded to the extent the dealer enters into an operating lease with the manufacturer or its financing affiliate.

Status.   The consensus is that the manufacturer is not precluded from recognizing revenue if the following conditions exist: (a) The dealer is an independent enterprise transacting business separately with dealer and customer, (b) The goods have been delivered to the manufacturer who assumes risks and rewards of ownership and for insurability. There is no right of return if the customer fails to enter into a lease with the finance affiliate or manufacturer, (c) The financing affiliate or manufacturer has no legal obligation to enter into the operating lease, (d) The customer has other financing alternatives available unaffiliated with manufacturer and is in control of those choices.

(xii) EITF Abstracts No. 95-17—Accounting for Modifications to an Operating Lease That Do Not Change the Lease Classification   A lessee and lessor subject to an operating lease modify the lease by shortening the term and increasing payments such that the lease remains an operating lease. How should this modification be accounted for?

EITF Discussion.   The accounting for the increased payments depends on the facts and circumstances. If the increase is only a modification, these payments should be accounted for prospectively over the term of the lease. If they are substantively a termination penalty, these payments should be charged to income in the period of modification. The penalty should be calculated as the excess of the modified payments over the payments that would have been required over the shorter period under the original lease.

(xiii) EITF Abstracts No. 96-21—Implementation Issues in Accounting for Leasing Transactions Involving Special-Purpose Entities   A lessee is required to consolidate a special purpose entity (SPE) when certain conditions are met. (See Issue No. 90-15.) Several additional issues about SPE's have arisen that the Task Force reached a consensus on.

EITF Discussion

MULTIPLE PROPERTIES WITHIN A SINGLE SPE-LESSOR.   The use of nonrecourse debt with no cross-collateralization segregates the two leases and effectively creates two SPE's.

MULTITIERED SPE STRUCTURES.   The test for compliance with condition 1 of Issue No. 90-15 should be applied at the lowest level at which the parties to a transaction create an isolated entity.

PAYMENTS MADE BY LESSEE PRIOR TO BEGINNING OF LEASE TERM.   Payments made prior to the beginning of the lease term should be considered as part of the minimum lease payments and included in the 90 percent of fair value recovery test. Just as future payments are discounted to present value, these early payments should be included at their future value at the beginning of the lease using the same interest rate as used in the lease analysis. If an operating lease, these advanced payments are prepaid rent.

PAYMENTS TO EQUITY OWNERS OF AN SPE DURING THE LEASE TERM.   The characterization of any payments made by the SPE-lessor to its owners should be based in the SPE's-GAAP basis financial statements such that distributions of earnings are a return on capital while distributions in excess of earnings are a return of equity capital.

FEES PAID TO OWNERS OF RECORD OF AN SPE.   Fees paid by a lessee to owners of the SPE are part of the minimum lease payments for purposes of the 90 percent fair value recovery test.

SOURCE OF INITIAL MINIMUM EQUITY INVESTMENT.   If the source of funds used to make the initial equity investment is financed with nonrecourse debt, the investment would not meet the at-risk requirement of Issue No. 90-15. Similarly, if the owners purchased or obtained a guarantee of the recovery of their investment, the at-risk requirements are not met. If loans are made to finance the investment, the owners are considered at risk to the extent that they are liable for the decline in the fair value of the residual interest and other significant assets that they have.

EQUITY CAPITAL AT RISK.   An initial equity investment must represent a residual equity interest in legal form, be subordinate to all debt, and represent residual equity for the entire term of the lease to be considered at risk.

PAYMENTS TO OWNERS OF RECORD OF AN SPE PRIOR TO THE LEASE TERM.   Payments made by an SPE to its owners during the construction period are a return of control equity investment and may reduce this below the minimum amount required under Issue No. 90-15.

COSTS INCURRED BY LESSEE PRIOR TO ENTERING INTO A LEASE AGREEMENT.   A lessee who commences construction would reorganize the asset, construction in progress, on its balance sheet and apply FASB Statement No. 98 to any subsequent lease arrangement. Commencement of construction means that hard costs are incurred, ground has been broken, or soft costs that are more than 10 percent of the expected fair value of the leased property have been incurred.

INTEREST ONLY PAYMENTS.   Lessees recognize rent expenses usually by the straight-line method. Although the maximum deficiency guaranteed by the lessee is included in minimum lease payments for purposes of the 90 percent fair value recovery test, they are not considered part of the amounts to be recorded as rent expense under an operating lease until it is probable that the residual value will be less than the amount guaranteed by the lessee.

(xiv) EITF Abstracts No. 97-1—Implementation Issues in Accounting for Lease Transactions, Including Those Involving Special-Purpose Entities   For SPEs, how should shared environmental risks and nonperformance-related default covenants be utilized in lease classification? Also, how should the SPE calculate depreciation when the lessee returns the residual with the substantial risks and rewards of the leased property?

EITF Discussion.   A provision that requires the lessee to indemnify the lessor for any environmental contamination caused by the lessee during its use of the property would not affect the lessee's classification of the lease. However, for preexisting conditions, the lessee's indemnification requires them to assess, at the inception of the lease, the likelihood of loss to determine whether it should be considered the owner of the property. If the likelihood of loss is remote, the indemnity would not affect the classification. If the likelihood is at least reasonably possible, the lessee is deemed to have purchased, sold, and leased back the property and should apply FASB Statement No. 98.

Nonperformance-related default covenants do not affect lease classification when these five conditions exist:

1. Default covenant is customary in financing arrangements.
2. Occurrence of the event of default is objectively determinable.
3. Predefined criteria have been established for determination of the event of default.
4. Based on facts and circumstances, the event of default reasonably will not occur.
5. The entities will consider recent trends in the lessee's operations.

If any of these conditions do not exist, then the maximum amount the lessee could be required to pay should be included on the minimum lease payments for the 90 percent fair value recovery test. If the lease is a sale-leaseback under FASB Statement No. 98, a default provision violates the continuing involvement criteria and should be accounted for by the deposit method or as a financing.

Depreciation should be calculated for an SPE where a lessee has retained the substantive residual risks and rewards of the leased asset assuming the useful life equals the lease term and the expected salvage value is equal to the lesser of the guaranteed residual value or the expected fair value of the property at the end of the lease term.

(xv) EITF Abstracts No. 97-10—The Effect of Lessee Involvement in Asset Construction

How does a lessee that is involved with the construction of a build-to-suit real estate project that is to be leased to the lessee when completed, determine whether the transaction is a sale-leaseback within the scope of FASB Statement No. 98?

EITF Discussion.   The Task Force rejected the concept that any lessee risk in excess of agreed on fees makes them the owner of the project requiring the use of FASB Statement No. 98. Also, this applicability should not be based on a probability assessment. Further discussion is pending.

(xvi) EITF Abstracts No. 98-9—Accounting for Contingent Rent

Issue.   The issue is how both lessors and lessees should account for contingent rent based on future specified targets prior to the achievement of these targets.

EITF Discussion.   In December 1999, the Securities and Exchange Commission (SEC) issued Staff Accounting Bulletin (SAB) No. 101, which provided guidance for lessors in accounting for contingent future rent. Basically, this requires lessors to defer the recognition of such rent until the target is met. However, for lessees the Task Force reached a consensus that contingent rent expense should be recognized before the specified target is obtained, once that achievement is deemed probable.

(xvii) EITF Abstracts No. 00-11—Lessors' Evaluation of Whether Leases of Certain Integral Equipment Meet the Ownership Transfer Requirements of FASB Statement No. 13

Issue 1.   Whether integral equipment subject to a lease should be evaluated as real estate under Statement No. 13.

Issue 2.   If integral equipment subject to a lease is evaluated as real estate under Statement No. 13, how the requirement in paragraph 7(a) of Statement No. 13 for the transfer of ownership should be evaluated when no statutory title registration system exists for the leased assets.

EITF Discussion.   The Task Force reached a consensus on Issue 1 that integral equipment subject to a lease should evaluated as real estate under Statement No. 13 as amended by Statement No. 98. The Task Force reached a consensus on Issue 2 that for such equipment or property improvements for which no statutory title registration system exists, the criterion of paragraph 7a of Statement No. 13 is met if the lessor shall execute documents, such as a bill of sale, as may be required to transfer ownership to the lessee. Also, the criterion is met when the lessee pays a nominal amount for the transfer of ownership. If, however, the lease agreement specifies that ownership does not transfer unless the lessee pays the specified fee, this is a purchase option (bargain or not) and would not satisfy criterion 7A of Statement No. 13.

(xviii) EITF Abstracts No. 00-13—Determining Whether Equipment Is "Integral Equipment" Subject to FASB Statements No. 66 and No. 98

Issue.   The issue is how the determination of integral equipment should be made.

EITF Discussion.   The Task Force agreed that a determination of whether equipment is integral equipment should be based on the materiality of the cost to remove equipment from its existing location combined with the decrease in value of the equipment as a result of the removal (which is at least the cost to repair, remove, ship and install the equipment at a new site). An illustration of this application by the EITF follows.

Company A leases equipment to Company B for use in a manufacturing facility. The fair value of the production equipment (installed) at lease inception is $1,075,000. The estimated cost to remove the equipment after installation (estimate is as of the beginning of the lease term) is $80,000, which includes $30,000 to repair damage to the existing location as a result of the removal. The estimated cost to ship and reinstall the equipment at a new site (estimated as of the beginning of the lease term) is $85,000. For this example, assume that the equipment would have the same fair value (installed) to the seller and a potential buyer. Therefore, there is no diminution in fair value of the equipment beyond the discount a purchaser would presumably require to cover the cost to ship and reinstall the equipment.

In accordance with this consensus, Company A would assess whether or not the production equipment is integral equipment as follows: ($80,000 + $85,000)/$1,075,000 = 15.3 percent. Because the cost of removal combined with the diminution in value exceeds 10 percent of the fair value (installed) of the production equipment, the cost to remove the equipment and use it separately is deemed to be significant. Therefore, the production equipment is integral equipment.

(xix) EITF Abstracts No. 01-8—Determining Whether an Arrangement Contains a Lease

Issue.   How to determine whether an arrangement contains a lease within the scope of FASB 13. In applying this issue, separate contracts with the same parties that are entered into near or at the same time are presumed to be a single arrangement unless there is sufficient evidence to the contrary.

EITF Discussion.   The Task Force reached a consensus that the guidance in paragraph 8 of FASB 13 should be used to determine whether an arrangement contains a lease. Although specific property, plant and equipment may be explicitly identified in an arrangement, it is not the subject of a lease if fulfillment of the arrangement is not dependent on the use of specific property, plant and equipment. Neither a warrantee that permits or requires substitution nor a contract provision that does the same, precludes the lease treatment prior to the date of substitution.

An arrangement conveys the right to use property, plant and equipment if the arrangement conveys the right to control use of the underlying property, plant and equipment.

The Task Force reached a consensus that the assessment of whether an arrangement contains a lease should be made at the inception of the arrangement using all facts and circumstances. This is only reassessed if there is a change in the contractual terms, a renewal option is exercised or an extension is agreed upon, a change in the determination as to whether fulfillment is dependent on specified property, plant or equipment or there is a substantial physical change to the specified property, plant or equipment.

(xx) EITF Abstracts No. 01-12—The Impact of the Requirements of FASB Statement No. 133 on Residual Value Guarantees in Connection with a Lease

Issue 1.   How to resolve the scope overlap between Statement No. 13 and Statement No. 133 with respect to residual value guarantees

Issue 2.   Whether a third-party residual value guarantor should account for a residual value guarantee under the requirements of Statement No. 133

EITF Discussion.   The Task Force reached a consensus on Issue 1 that residual guarantees that are subject to the requirements of lease accounting literature (including Statement No. 13 was amended) are not subject to the requirements of Statement No. 133. This conclusion was reached because the Board did not use Statement No. 133 to amend Statement No. 13. This suggests that it did not intend to make such a change.

The Task Force also reached a consensus on Issue 2 that a third-party residual guarantor should consider the guidance in Statement No. 133 in order to consider whether the guarantees are derivatives and whether they qualify for any of the scope exceptions in that statement.

(xxi) EITF Abstracts No. 03-12—Impact of FASB Interpretation No. 45 on Issue No. 95-1

Issue.   The Task Force reached a consensus on Issue No. 95-1 "Revenue Recognition on Sales With a Guaranteed Minimum Resale Value," that a manufacturer is precluded from recognizing a sale if he guarantees the resale value of the equipment to the purchaser except if it is a sale type lease. The status section of Issue 95-1 was updated to reflect the issuance of Interpretation 45 which partially nullified it. The effect of that partial nullification is that Statement 13 will apply for transactions within the scope of Issue 95-1 and will continue to be applied in determining minimum lease payments. However, manufacturers will recognize the fair value of the guarantee in accordance with Interpretation 45 when recording a sale type lease.

EITF Discussion.   The Task Force reached a consensus that Interpretation 45 does not affect Issue 95-1 because the Interpretation does not apply to a guarantee related to an asset of the guarantor. Because the manufacturer continues to recognize the guaranteed residual value as an asset when recording a sale type lease, that guarantee is not subject to Interpretation 45. Therefore, the accounting prescribed by Issue 95-1 is unaffected by Interpretation No. 45.

(j) ARE ACTIVE LEASES EXECUTORY CONTRACTS?   A Special Report *Leases: Implementation of a New Approach* of the G4 + 1 Group of accounting standard setters, those from Australia, Canada, New Zealand, the United Kingdom, and the United States recently stated that active leases are not executory contracts:

> Leases can be distinguished from executory contracts by the fact that leases cease to be executory when the leased property is delivered or otherwise made available to the lessee.

Others have said the same:

> Where a lease contract is not cancelable by the lessor it is probable that a nonexecutory contract exists. The lessor has provided the property for the period of the lease. . . . The lessor has performed his obligations. . . . the lease contract would need to be "effectively cancelable" for an executory contract to exist.[1]

> It can be argued that a lease contract is fully executed by a lessor when possession of the leased asset is transferred to a lessee.[2]

---

[1] Scott Henderson and Graham Peirson, *Issues in Financial Accounting*, 2nd ed. (Longman Cheshire Pty Limited, Melbourne, 1980), p. 352.
[2] Harry I. Wolk, Jere R. Francis, and Michael G. Tearney, *Accounting Theory: A Conceptual and Institutional Approach*, Third Edition (South-Western Publishing Co., Cincinnati, 1992), p. 512.

NOTES TO CONSOLIDATED FINANCIAL STATEMENTS
Note L—Lease Obligations

Certain airport and other retail facilities, a cruise ship, buses and bus terminals (primarily subleased), plants, offices, and equipment are leased. The leases expire in periods ranging from 1 to 46 years, and some provide for renewal options ranging from 1 to 25 years. Also, certain leases contain purchase options. Leases that expire are generally renewed or replaced by similar leases.

Capital leases included in the cost of property and equipment aggregate $40,992,000 and $79,395,000 at December 31, 1988 and 1987, respectively, with related accumulated depreciation of $28,704,000 and $45,656,000, respectively.

At December 31, 1988, future minimum payments and related sublease rentals receivable with respect to capital leases and noncancelable operating leases with terms in excess of one year, are as follows:

| (000 omitted) | Capital Leases | Operating Leases | | | | |
		Airport Terminal Concessions	Buses	Cruise Ship	Other	Total
1989	$ 4,621	$ 42,942	$20,138	$12,949	$ 37,144	$113,173
1990	4,570	42,116	19,479	12,949	33,763	108,307
1991	4,973	46,125	19,466	12,949	30,720	109,260
1992	4,858	47,174	17,996	12,949	25,188	103,307
1993	4,641	49,354	7,048	12,949	22,078	91,429
Thereafter	41,002	93,239		23,742	133,183	250,164
Total future minimum lease payments	64,665	$320,950	$84,127	$88,487	$282,076	$775,640
Less imputed interest	$27,795					
Present value of future minimum capital lease payments	$36,870					

Rentals Receivable under Subleases
(000 omitted)

	Subleased Buses	Other (Principally Airport Concessions)	Total
1989	$21,727	$ 16,628	$ 38,355
1990	21,043	16,546	37,589
1991	21,043	17,424	38,467
1992	19,576	17,290	36,866
1993	7,325	15,632	22,957
Thereafter		39,622	39,622
	$90,714	$ 123,142	$ 213,856

Information regarding net operating lease rentals for the three years ended December 31, 1988, is as follows:

(000 omitted)	1988	1987	1986
Minimum rentals	$130,795	$88,120	$50,617
Contingent rentals	38,925	18,676	12,179
Sublease rentals	(55,753)	(32,285)	(1,112)
Total net rentals	$113,967	$74,511	$61,684

Contingent rentals on operating leases are based primarily on sales and revenues for buildings and leasehold improvements and usage for other equipment.

Exhibit 23.2   Lessee disclosure.

SUN COMPANY, INC.
NOTES TO CONSOLIDATED FINANCIAL STATEMENTS
8 (in part): Long-Term Receivables and Investments

	December 31	
	1987	**1986**
Investment in:	(millions of dollars)	
Leveraged leases	$ 85	$ 79
Direct financing and sales-type leases	276*	271
	361	350
Accounts and notes receivable	114	68
Investments in and advances to affiliated companies	27	34
Other investments, at cost	19	12
	$521	$464

*Includes $129 million used with $26 million of other assets as collateral for $87 million recourse longterm debt—leasing notes associated with sales-type leases (Note 12).

Sun, as lessor, has entered into leveraged, direct financing, and sales-type leases of a wide variety of equipment including oceangoing vessels, aircraft, mining equipment, railroad rolling stock, and various other transportation and manufacturing equipment. The components of Sun's investment in these leases at December 31, 1987 and 1986 are set forth below (in millions of dollars):

	Leveraged Leases December 31		Direct Financing and Sales-Type Leases December 31	
	1987	**1986**	**1987**	**1986**
Minimum rentals receivable	$63*	$50*	$401	$417
Estimated unguaranteed residual value of leased assets	61	61	60	55
Unearned and deferred income	(39)	(32)	(185)	(201)
Investment in leases	85	79	$276	$271
Deferred taxes arising from leveraged leases	(60)	(54)		
Net investment in leveraged leases	$25	$25		

*Net of principal of and interest on related nonrecourse financing aggregating $234 and $247 million in 1987 and 1986, respectively.

The following is a schedule of minimum rentals receivable by years at December 31, 1987 (in millions of dollars):

	Leveraged Leases	Direct Financing and Sales-Type Leases
Year ending December 31:		
1988	$ 4	$ 51
1989	5	49
1990	5	48
1991	4	46
1992	6	37
Later years	39	170
	$63	$401

Exhibit 23.3 Lessor disclosure.

The lessor. . . turned [the assets] over to the lessee. . . . The lease is fully performed on the lessor's side. . . .[3]

The FASB has stated what amounts to the same:

To have an asset, an entity must control future economic benefit to the extent that it can benefit from the asset and generally deny or regulate access to that benefit by others, for example, by permitting access only at a price. . . . Leases . . . give a lessee a right to possess and use the property.[4]

(k) SHOULD ALL ACTIVE NONCANCELABLE LEASES OF LESSEES BE REPORTED AS PROVIDING ASSETS AND CAUSING LIABILITIES? If an active noncancelable lease is not an executory contract, it provides items that satisfy the FASB's definitions of assets and liabilities. Though the FASB states what amounts to a position that such a lease is not an executory contract, it nevertheless requires that some such leases, which it terms operating leases, not be reported as providing assets and causing liabilities.

23.11 EXAMPLES OF LEASE DISCLOSURE

Exhibits 23.2 and 23.3 provide comprehensive illustrations of lease disclosure. Exhibit 23.2 presents a lessee's disclosure of capital and operating leases. Exhibit 23.3 presents a lessor's disclosure.

23.12 THE FASB ADDS LEASE ACCOUNTING BACK ON IT'S AGENDA

The FASB recently decided to reconsider the current guidance on lease accounting as identified in this chapter. The Board announced that it would do so with the International Accounting Standards Board (IASB) as part of the convergence of GAAP project.

Although it is uncertain where this project will lead, undoubtedly there will be major changes to the existing standards. Basically, lease accounting concentrates on establishing the difference between a capital lease and an operating lease through complex and complicated standards. However, the economic reality is that there is no difference between various leases. All leased property meets the definition of assets, in that the economic benefit is controlled by the lessee. Likewise, all lease obligations are unconditional obligations and are liabilities regardless of whether the lease is a capital or obligating one. In addition, from an income statement perspective, there is rarely a material difference between an operating lease and a capital lease.

Theoretically, all leases can be considered as operating leases and accounted for as such and included as such on the income statement. For balance sheet purposes, both an asset and a liability can be established at balanced sheet date at the net present value of the remaining minimum lease payments. This could clearly simplify lease accounting and remove most of the complex and arbitrary rules. At the present time, the FASB has not provided any insights into their thinking so the current standards remain in effect for the near future.

23.13 SOURCES AND SUGGESTED REFERENCES

Bisgay, Louis, "FASB Issues Statement 98," *Management Accounting*, Vol. 70, August 1988, p. 63.

Byington, J. Ralph, Moores, Charles, T., and Munter, Paul H., "How Initial Direct Costs Affect Lessors," *The CPA Journal*, Vol. 58, February 1988, pp. 67–69.

---

[3] Homer Kripke, "Reflections on the FASB's Conceptual Framework for Accounting and on Auditing," *Journal of Accounting, Auditing & Finance*, Winter 1989, p. 38.

[4] FASB, Statement of Concepts No. 6, "Elements of Financial Statement," pars. 183 and 185.

Financial Accounting Standards Board, Statement of Financial Accounting Standards No. 66, "Accounting for Sales of Real Estate." FASB, Stamford, CT, 1982.

———, Statement of Financial Accounting Standards No. 140, "Accounting for Transfers and Servicing of Financial Assets and Extinguishments of Liabilities." FASB, Norwalk, CT, 2000.

"Firms Now Lease Everything But Time," *U.S. News & World Report*, August 14, 1989, p. 45.

Johnson, James M., *Fundamentals of Finance for Equipment Lessors: A Transaction Orientation*. American Association of Equipment Lessors, Arlington, VA, 1986.

McMeen, Albert R., *Treasurer's and Controller's New Equipment Leasing Guide*. Prentice-Hall, Englewood Cliffs, NJ, 1984.

Nailor, Hans, and Lennard, Andrew, *Leases: Implementation of a New Approach*, issued by the Financial Accounting Standards Board, February 2000.

Vernor, James D., "Comparative Lease Analysis Using a Discounted Cash Flow Approach," *Appraisal Journal*, Vol. 56, July 1988, pp. 391–398.

ACCOUNTING FOR INCOME TAXES*

E. Raymond Simpson, CPA
Financial Accounting Standards Board

*The Financial Accounting Standards Board (FASB) encourages its members and staff to express their individual views. The views expressed in Chapter 24 are those of Mr. Simpson. Official positions of the FASB on accounting matters are determined only after extensive due process and deliberation.

This chapter was updated from the Ninth Edition by the editors with the assistance of Reva Steinberg of BDO Seidman LLP.

24.1 ACCOUNTING RECOGNITION OF INCOME TAXES

(a) THE BASIC PROBLEM. Accounting for income taxes is one of the most complex and controversial accounting subjects in this country. The basic problem is that transactions and events may be reported in different years for financial reporting and for income tax purposes. This may be because different accounting methods are used for each purpose, for example, accrual accounting versus cash basis accounting, straight-line depreciation versus an accelerated depreciation method, the percentage-of-completion versus the completed contract methods on long-term contracts, or revenue recognition at time of sale versus the installment method. It may also be because a different estimated useful life is elected for depreciation or amortization. These differences may occur because the income tax reporting requirements and generally accepted accounting principles (GAAP) are different for a particular event or transaction or because a taxpayer is able to elect to report differently.

The accounting procedure employed to recognize the tax effects of amounts that are reported in different years for financial reporting and for income tax reporting has been known as *interperiod income tax allocation* or *tax effect accounting*. The more neutral description of "recognition" of income taxes is used in this chapter, and the other terms are not generally used.

Several different approaches to the recognition of income taxes have been used at various times in the United States. An income statement approach known as the *deferred method* of interperiod income tax allocation was adopted in 1967 in Accounting Principles Board (APB) Opinion No. 11, "Accounting for Income Taxes." Under that method, amounts reported in different years for financial reporting and for income tax reporting are known as *timing differences*. Using accelerated depreciation on the income tax return and straight-line depreciation in the income statement, for example, causes a timing difference to originate each year during the early life of an asset; the timing difference reverses or "turns around" during the later life of the asset. Other items, known as *permanent differences*, are not considered taxable income, are not tax deductible, or are special deductions for income tax reporting purposes. Because they always differ for financial and income tax reporting purposes, there is a permanent, nonrecurring difference. For example, interest income from state and local government bonds is financial revenue that is not taxable under the federal income tax.

The *liability method* is a balance sheet approach to accounting for income taxes. That method was first adopted in the United States in Statement of Financial Accounting Standards (SFAS) No. 96, "Accounting for Income Taxes," and was continued in the replacement for that Statement in SFAS No. 109, "Accounting for Income Taxes." Under that method, differences between the amounts reported in the balance sheet for assets and liabilities and the income tax bases of those assets and liabilities are known as *temporary differences*. Thus, whereas the difference between the amount of depreciation on the tax return and in the income statement in a single year is a timing difference under APB Opinion No. 11, the cumulative difference at the balance sheet date between the tax basis of the asset and its cost (or other amount) reported in the balance sheet is a temporary difference under SFAS No. 109. Temporary differences may also result from causes other than cumulative timing differences [see Subsection 24.2(a) (i)]. Because the concepts underlying timing differences and temporary differences are so different, the term *timing difference* will be used in this chapter only in the explanation of APB Opinion No. 11 and earlier accounting requirements; elsewhere the more current term *temporary difference* in SFAS No. 109 will be used.

(b) TAX RECOGNITION CONCEPTS.   Income taxes are seldom, if ever, paid completely in the period to which they relate. Thus, the cash basis is not acceptable under GAAP. Income taxes, like other expenses, should be recognized on an accrual basis of accounting. Although there is agreement that, at a minimum, income tax expense should include income taxes paid and payable for a period as determined on the income tax return for the period, the taxes payable method ignores timing and temporary differences and is not acceptable under GAAP.

(i) Development in the United States.   There has long been general agreement in this country on the need for, at a minimum, recognition of deferred taxes for nonrecurring material differences that will reverse in a relatively short period. That partial recognition position was taken in 1944 in Accounting Research Bulletins (ARB) No. 23, "Accounting for Income Taxes," carried forward in 1953 in ARB No. 43, "Restatement and Revision of Accounting Research Bulletins," and reaffirmed in 1954 in ARB No. 44, "Declining-Balance Depreciation." In 1958 ARB No. 44 (Revised), "Declining-Balance Depreciation," further called for tax allocation even though depreciation differences were of a recurring nature, or a plant was expanding, so there would be long-term deferral of an increasing tax balance. That comprehensive recognition approach extended the applicability of the interperiod income tax allocation procedure to depreciation differences to which it had not previously been broadly applied. In 1962 APB Opinion No. 1, "New Depreciation Guidelines and Rules," further extended the applicability of that procedure to differences arising from adoption of shorter lives for income tax depreciation in relation to those used for financial reporting.

Whether the concepts in those pronouncements applied for timing differences other than depreciation was uncertain, however, and interperiod income tax allocation was not literally required for most timing differences until APB Opinion No. 11 became effective in 1968. That opinion also generally resolved the question of which method should be applied in favor of the deferred method with comprehensive allocation. Although the deferred method was preferred in earlier pronouncements mentioned previously, the liability and net-of-tax methods were also acceptable. In the research study published by the American Institute of Certified Public Accountants (AICPA) before APB Opinion No. 11 was issued, Black discussed those methods in detail.[1]   They are summarized below.

Deferred Method.   The deferred method is an income statement approach to interperiod income tax allocation that seeks to match the tax effects of revenues and expenses with those items in the period for which they are recognized for financial reporting purposes. Deferred taxes are determined on the basis of tax rates in effect when timing differences originate and are not adjusted for changes in tax rates or for new taxes. The tax effect of a timing difference that reduces income tax currently payable is reported as an increase in income tax expense in the income statement and as a deferred tax credit in the balance sheet; conversely, the tax effect of a timing difference that increases income tax currently payable is reported as a reduction in income tax expense in the income statement and as a deferred tax charge (or reduction of deferred tax credits) in the balance sheet. Because the beginning amount of income tax expense in the income statement is based on taxes currently payable, in concept the deferred method adjusts tax expense as if originating timing differences for the period were included in taxable income. The tax effects of reversing timing differences likewise adjust tax expense, but in concept at the tax rates in effect when those timing differences originated. Paragraph 57 of APB Opinion No. 11 states that "deferred charges and

---

[1] Homer A. Black, *Interperiod Allocation of Corporate Income Taxes*, Accounting Research Study No. 9 (New York: AICPA, 1966).

deferred credits relating to timing differences represent the cumulative recognition given to their tax effects and as such do not represent payables or receivables in the usual sense."

Liability Method.   The liability method is a balance sheet approach to accounting for income taxes. The method seeks to determine the liability for income taxes payable in the future or the asset for prepaid income taxes and, accordingly, measures the tax effect of a temporary difference at the tax rate or rates in effect when the difference will reverse. If tax rates change or new taxes are imposed, the balance sheet accounts are adjusted with a corresponding adjustment to income tax expense.

Net-of-Tax Method.   The net-of-tax method is a method of valuing an asset or liability and the related revenue or expense by recognizing that those amounts are worth more or less because of their tax status. Under this method, if straight-line depreciation is used for financial reporting and accelerated depreciation is used for income tax, the tax effect of the difference is an adjustment to depreciation expense and to the allowance for depreciation. Accordingly, in the early years of an asset's life, the net book value of the asset is less (in relation to what it would be under other methods) because of the increased allowance. In later years, depreciation expense and the addition to the allowance are less each year than straight-line depreciation. The theory is that an asset's *tax* depreciability is used up, it is worth less and its book value should reflect that fact. Tax effects under the net-of-tax method may be determined using either a deferred or a liability approach.

Comprehensive Recognition.   Under comprehensive recognition of deferred taxes, the tax effects of all timing and temporary differences are recognized. Thus recurring transactions will have both originating and reversing timing or temporary differences that may offset in the tax return but nevertheless leave temporary differences in the balance sheet. In this case the deferred taxes in the balance sheet "roll over" in a "revolving account," as do accounts receivable or accounts payable. Recurring timing or temporary differences of continually increasing amounts cause deferred income taxes in the balance sheet to likewise continually increase. An expanding company using various elections to defer income taxes currently payable on recurring transactions will have an increasing balance of deferred income taxes under comprehensive recognition.

Partial Recognition.   Partial recognition of deferred taxes ignores recurring timing or temporary differences and timing or temporary differences that will not reverse for long periods. Income tax expense is based on income taxes currently payable, adjusted for the tax effects of nonrecurring timing or temporary differences that will materially increase or decrease income taxes payable in a relatively short period, such as five years. Accordingly, balance sheet amounts for deferred income taxes would be considerably less for most companies under partial recognition than under comprehensive recognition of deferred taxes.

Although APB Opinion No. 11 was generally a comprehensive approach to accounting for income taxes, exceptions were made for several special areas. Although some of these exceptions continue, SFAS No. 109 eliminates some significant exceptions, and the exceptions discussed later in this section are the only items for which SFAS No. 109 allows partial recognition. Because APB Opinion No. 11 only considered the tax effects of timing differences in any single year, other tax effects of basis differences were ignored, such as an increase in the tax basis of assets in a taxable business combination accounted for as a pooling of interests when the former book values of the assets are carried forward for financial reporting. In SFAS No. 109 such differences are considered temporary differences for which deferred taxes must be recognized and eliminates those exceptions to tax allocation that existed under APB Opinion No. 11.

(ii) Move to the Liability Method.   The Financial Accounting Standards Board (FASB) issued SFAS No. 96 adopting the liability method in December 1987 as the culmination of a six-year project to reconsider the accounting for income taxes. For various reasons, preparers, auditors, users, and educators had strongly supported moving from the deferred method to the liability method when the FASB undertook the project and while it was in process. Some objected to the increasing amounts of deferred taxes reported in balance sheets under APB Opinion No. 11 even though corporate income tax rates had been declining. Others believed income tax allocation under APB Opinion No. 11 had become too complex and viewed the liability method as a simpler approach. Still others thought the results obtained from applying the deferred method could only be explained procedurally and believed the liability method would be conceptually superior.

The amounts reported as liabilities under the liability method do not conform with the FASB's definition of *liabilities*, which is the following:

> ... probable future sacrifices of economic benefits arising from present obligations of a particular entity to transfer assets or provide service to other entities in the future as a result of past transactions or events.

It therefore is an unsound method.[2] The FASB states three tests, *all* of which must be passed for an amount to conform with the definition. The third test is: "Has the transaction or other event obligating the entity already happened?" The FASB states that that test is passed because "Deferred tax liabilities result from the same past events that create taxable temporary differences."[3] The FASB does not identify the past events it alludes to in that Statement, so the reader has to infer them. They are (1) preparing a tax return one way and (2) preparing financial statements another way. The second of those events is bookkeeping. Because a reporting entity's own bookkeeping cannot be one of the events necessary to cause the reporting entity to incur a liability, a real-world detrimental relationship it has with another entity, the test is failed. Were it a liability, it could be "paid off" by restating the financial statements. Liabilities cannot be paid off by restating financial statements.

(iii) Delay and Reconsideration.   Some companies adopted SFAS No. 96 in their 1987 financial statements before they were required to do so, but others complained that the statement was too complex and difficult to apply and disagreed with some of the results of applying it. In December 1988, the FASB issued SFAS No. 100, "Accounting for Income Taxes—Deferral of the Effective Date of FASB Statement No. 96," to delay the required application of SFAS No. 96 by one year to 1990. In large part, the delay was to permit the FASB to provide implementation guidance. At the same time, the FASB began considering requests to simplify the application of SFAS No. 96, to relax its requirements for recognizing a deferred tax asset, and to modify several other specific requirements. In December 1989, the FASB issued SFAS No. 103, "Accounting for Income Taxes—Deferral of the Effective Date of FASB Statement No. 96," further delaying the required application of SFAS No. 96 until 1992 to continue consideration of those requests. In June 1991, the FASB issued an exposure draft, "Accounting for Income Taxes," of a replacement for SFAS No. 96, and in February 1992 issued SFAS No. 109 to supersede SFAS No. 96. SFAS No. 108, "Accounting for Income Taxes—Deferral of the Effective Date of FASB Statement No. 96," further delayed the required application of SFAS No. 96 so that it never became mandatory. SFAS No. 109 is required for financial statements for fiscal years beginning after December 15, 1992. The APB Opinion No. 11, "Accounting for Income Taxes," or SFAS No. 96 are permitted to be applied for financial statements for earlier periods.

Criticisms and concerns with SFAS No. 96 focused on (1) the restrictive criteria for recognition and measurement of deferred tax assets and (2) the complexity of scheduling the future reversals of temporary differences and of considering hypothetical tax-planning strategies that were, to a large degree, a consequence of those criteria for deferred tax assets. SFAS No. 109 resulted from a comprehensive reconsideration of both APB Opinion No. 11 and SFAS No. 96. SFAS

---

[2] Paul Rosenfield and William C. Dent, "No More Deferred Taxes," *Journal of Accountancy*, February 1983.

[3] FASB, Statement of Financial Accounting Standards No. 109, "Accounting for Income Taxes," par. 79.

No. 109 permits, in more instances than SFAS No. 96, recognition of deferred tax assets that are expected to be realized and reduces the complexity of scheduling and consideration of tax-planning strategies. Other changes from SFAS No. 96 in SFAS No. 109 that should reduce the cost and complexity of deferred tax accounting are the revised requirements for transfers of assets [see Subsection 24.1(c)(iv)], foreign nonmonetary assets [see Subsection 24.1(c)(v)], measurement of deferred tax liabilities and assets when graduated tax rates or the alternative minimum tax are a significant factor [see Subsection 24.2(b)(iv)], and balance sheet classification [see Subsection 24.4(b)].

(c) GENERAL APPROACH TO RECOGNITION OF INCOME TAXES AND EXCEPTIONS.
The GAAP for recognition of income taxes are specified by SFAS No. 109. The statement, however, did not change a limited number of long-standing exceptions to its recognition principles and provided some specific exceptions.

(i) General Approach to Recognition.   SFAS No. 109 requires comprehensive recognition of the effects of income taxes for temporary differences by the liability method. Under that method, the tax effect of a temporary difference is computed by multiplying the difference by the enacted tax rate(s) scheduled to be in effect for the year(s) the difference is expected to be reported in an income tax return(s). The tax effect may be either a deferred tax asset or a deferred tax liability. The statement, however, provides certain exceptions.

(ii) Valuation Allowance.   A valuation allowance is recognized to reduce a deferred tax asset if it is more likely than not that some portion or all of the deferred tax asset will not be realized. The term *more likely than not* means a level of likelihood that is more than 50 percent.

(iii) Goodwill and Leveraged Lease Exceptions.   SFAS No. 109 prohibits recognition of a deferred tax liability related to goodwill for which amortization is not deductible for tax purposes (or a deferred tax asset related to unallocated negative goodwill). This was a practical decision because recognizing a deferred tax liability would increase goodwill by a like amount since goodwill is merely the amount of the purchase price that cannot be allocated to identifiable assets in a business combination accounted for as a purchase. Not changing the accounting specified by SFAS No. 13, "Accounting for Leases," for income taxes related to leveraged leases also represented a practical decision. Although that accounting is not consistent with SFAS No. 109, the FASB concluded that changing it would require reconsidering the accounting for leveraged leases. SFAS No. 142, "Goodwill and Other Intangible Assets," terminated the amortization of goodwill for financial statement purposes. It does not change the foregoing guidance for the recognition of deferred taxes related to goodwill.

(iv) Transfers of Assets.   SFAS No. 109 does not amend ARB No. 51, "Consolidated Financial Statements," for income taxes paid on intercompany profits on assets remaining within the group. Thus, the tax paid by the seller is deferred, and recognition of a deferred tax asset for the amount the buyer's tax basis exceeds the cost of those assets as reported in the consolidated financial statements is prohibited. Otherwise, tax expense or benefit would be recognized before the assets are sold or depreciated.

(v) Foreign Nonmonetary Assets.   Under SFAS No. 52, "Foreign Currency Translation," the U.S. dollar is the functional currency for certain foreign operations, and nonmonetary assets are remeasured using historical exchange rates. Changes in exchange rates and indexing for tax purposes will create differences between the foreign currency equivalent of the U.S. dollar cost of those assets and their foreign currency tax basis. However, recognition of a deferred tax liability or asset for those differences is prohibited. Otherwise, deferred taxes would be recognized for the effect of changes in exchange rates on nonmonetary assets that are measured at historical U.S. dollar cost.

(vi) Other Special Areas.   APB Opinion No. 11 provided exceptions to recognition of deferred taxes in the areas addressed by APB Opinion No. 23, "Accounting for Income Taxes—Special Areas," and APB Opinion No. 11 did not address deposits in statutory reserve funds by U.S. steamship companies. SFAS No. 109 expands the APB Opinion No. 23 exception for foreign undistributed earnings to include the total the book basis exceeds the tax basis of an investment in a foreign subsidiary or corporate joint venture. The SFAS No. 109 requirements for the other APB Opinion No. 23 exceptions "grandfather" temporary differences that arose prior to certain dates, and require recognition of a deferred tax liability for temporary differences that arise after those dates. The grandfathered temporary differences are undistributed earnings of a domestic subsidiary or corporate joint venture and "policyholders' surplus" of a stock life insurance company that arose in fiscal years beginning on or before December 15, 1992, and "bad-debt reserves" of savings and loan associations that arose in tax years beginning before December 31, 1987. A deferred tax liability for the APB Opinion No. 23 exceptions that continue under SFAS No. 109 (as described above) is not recognized unless it becomes apparent that those temporary differences will reverse in the foreseeable future. SFAS No. 109 addresses deposits in statutory reserve funds by U.S. steamship companies. If not previously recognized, the tax effects of temporary differences that arose in fiscal years beginning on or before December 15, 1992, are recognized when those temporary differences reverse in later years. A deferred tax liability is recognized for temporary differences that arise after that cut-off date.

24.2 APPLYING STATEMENT OF FINANCIAL ACCOUNTING STANDARDS NO. 109

(a) BASIC PRINCIPLES.   The basic objective of accounting for income taxes under SFAS No. 109 is to recognize the tax consequences of all events recognized in the financial statements or income tax returns. Income tax liabilities and assets are measured by applying the enacted tax laws for each jurisdiction in which the company is subject to tax.

Most transactions and events are reported at the same time and in the same manner in the financial statements and in the tax return, and income taxes currently payable or refundable are determined from the tax return. Some items reported in the financial statements, however, are never reported in the tax return. Interest income from municipal bonds is not taxable on a U.S. federal income tax return, for example, and fines paid are not deductible.

Items that are reported partially or completely in different periods or in different amounts in the financial statements and in the tax return create temporary differences. For example, a temporary difference between the reported amount of depreciable assets and their tax basis is created when depreciation is deducted sooner in the tax return than the expense is reported in the income statement. A deferred tax liability or asset is recognized for the estimated tax effects in future years as a result of temporary differences between the reported amount of an enterprise's assets and liabilities and their tax basis. The deferred tax liability or asset is measured applying enacted tax law for the future years in which temporary differences will result in taxable or deductible amounts. Tax planning strategies are considered when determining the need for and amount of a valuation allowance for a deferred tax asset. The only exceptions to comprehensive recognition of deferred taxes are described in Subsection 24.1(c).

(i) Temporary Differences.   Tax laws and financial accounting standards differ as to when or how some items are recognized or measured. Consequently, items may be reported sooner or later or in different amounts on the tax return than in the financial statements.

Following are six examples:

1. *Revenue or gain that is recognized in income before it is taxable.* The receivable for an installment sale is a temporary difference that becomes taxable when collected.
2. *Expense or loss that is recognized in income before it is deductible for taxes.* A liability for product warranty cost is a temporary difference that becomes deductible when settled.

3. *Revenue or gain that is taxable before it is recognized in income.* Prepaid rental income is taxable when cash is received. The liability for financial reporting is a temporary difference that becomes deductible (or results in nontaxable income) when the liability is settled.

4. *Expense or loss that is deductible before it is recognized in income.* An asset may be expensed or depreciated by an accelerated method on the tax return but depreciated straight-line for financial reporting. The amount by which the undepreciated cost exceeds the tax basis is a temporary difference that becomes taxable when the undepreciated cost is recovered.

5. *Differences caused by tax credits.* Investment tax credit (ITC) or other tax credits may reduce the tax basis of an asset, and deferred ITC reduces the cost of the related asset for financial reporting. In either case, the difference between the accounting cost and tax basis is a temporary difference.

6. *Purchase business combinations.* The amounts assigned to assets and liabilities in a business combination accounted for by the purchase method may differ from their tax bases. Those differences are temporary differences.

A difference between the tax basis of an asset or liability and the amount at which it is reported in the balance sheet is a temporary difference. It will be deductible or taxable in some future year when the related asset is recovered or the related liability is settled. An assumption inherent in financial statements prepared in accordance with GAAP is that amounts reported for assets will be recovered and for liabilities will be settled. A tax liability or asset is recognized for the deferred tax consequences of temporary differences. A valuation allowance is recognized for the portion (or all) of a deferred tax asset for which it is more likely than not a tax benefit will not be realized.

A few temporary differences do not relate to a particular asset or liability on the balance sheet. For example, research and development costs are charged to expense as incurred under SFAS No. 2, "Accounting for Research and Development Costs," but may be deferred and amortized for tax reporting. Also, a contract accounted for by the percentage-of-completion method for which amounts billed have been collected but reported by the completed-contract method for tax purposes is a temporary difference for which no identifiable amount appears in the balance sheet. In those situations, there is an asset or liability for tax purposes and none for financial reporting.

Two types of differences between the tax basis of an asset and the amount at which it is reported in the balance sheet might or might not be a temporary difference depending on the manner in which the asset will be recovered. One type is cash surrender value of life insurance in excess of premiums paid. It is a temporary difference if that asset will be recovered by cashing in the policy. Recovery of the asset in that manner will result in taxable amounts in future years. There is no temporary difference if that asset will be recovered from the proceeds of the policy upon the death of the insured. Under current U.S. tax law, those proceeds are not taxable.

The other type of difference is the amount the book basis of an investment in a domestic subsidiary (more than 50 percent-owned) exceeds its tax basis. It is a temporary difference if that asset will be recovered by sale of the subsidiary because recovery of the investment in that manner will result in taxable amounts in future years. There is no temporary difference if the investment will be recovered by a tax-free liquidation or merger that is structured in accordance with certain requirements specified under current U.S. tax law.

(ii) Annual Computation.   Income taxes should be separately computed for each tax jurisdiction and for each tax-paying component in each tax jurisdiction. One reason, for example, is that a loss carryforward for a subsidiary in tax jurisdiction A does not offset taxable income for another subsidiary in tax jurisdiction B. Another reason is that different tax jurisdictions have different enacted tax laws and tax rates. This issue as it pertains to state and local tax jurisdictions is addressed by question 3 in the FASB special report on implementation of SFAS No. 109.

The first step is to determine the type and amount of all temporary differences at the date of the financial statements. Temporary differences that will result in taxable amounts in future years are referred to as *taxable temporary differences*. Temporary differences that will result in deductible amount in future years are referred to as *deductible temporary differences*. In addition, the nature and amount of each type of loss and tax credit carryforward (collectively referred to as *carryforwards*) and the remaining length of the carryforward period for each must be determined.

The next step is to measure and recognize the total deferred tax liability for all taxable temporary differences and the total deferred tax asset for all deductible temporary differences and carryforwards.

The final step is to assess whether a valuation allowance is needed for the deferred tax asset. All available evidence, both positive and negative, should be assessed. A valuation allowance is needed if the weight of that evidence indicates that some portion or all of the deferred tax asset will not be realized. The criterion for making that assessment is more likely than not. The amount of valuation allowance recognized equals the amount of deferred tax asset for which it is more likely than not that a tax benefit will not be realized.

(b) RECOGNITION AND MEASUREMENT. Deferred tax liabilities and assets are recognized and measured under SFAS No. 109 by applying enacted tax laws and rates to determine the estimated tax effects in future years as a result of temporary differences and carryforwards that exist at the date of the financial statements. Discounting is not permitted.

(i) Recognition of Deferred Tax Liabilities and Assets. Deferred tax liabilities and deferred tax assets are recognized separately. Thus, a deferred tax liability is recognized for all taxable temporary differences, and a deferred tax asset is recognized for all deductible temporary differences and carryforwards. Likewise, a valuation allowance for the deferred tax asset, if needed, is recognized separately. Some netting is permitted for balance sheet presentation, but disclosure of the total of all deferred tax liabilities, deferred tax assets, and valuation allowances is required.

To illustrate, assume that at the end of the current year an enterprise has $600 of taxable temporary differences and $500 of deductible temporary differences. The enacted tax rate for the last several years and all future years is 34 percent. The enterprise would recognize a deferred tax liability in the amount of $204 ($600 at 34 percent) and a deferred tax asset in the amount of $170 ($500 at 34 percent). All available evidence would be considered to determine whether a valuation allowance is needed for some portion or all of the $170 deferred tax asset.

(ii) Recognition of a Valuation Allowance. A deferred tax asset is realized by reducing the amount of tax paid on taxable income. A deferred tax asset might not be realized, and a valuation allowance might be needed, for any of three reasons. One obvious reason is that there might not be enough taxable income to realize the deferred tax asset. Equally important, the taxable income must occur within the right time period, that is, sometime during the carryback or carryforward years specified by the tax law. Finally, the nature or type of taxable income sometimes is important, for example, if future capital gains are the only way to realize a deferred tax asset for a capital loss carryforward.

Thus, the critical factor in determining whether a valuation allowance is needed for a deferred tax asset is taxable income—a sufficient amount of the appropriate type of taxable income that occurs during the required time period. In SFAS No. 109, the following potential four sources of taxable income are identified:

1. Future reversals of taxable temporary differences
2. Future taxable income exclusive of those reversals
3. Taxable income in the current or prior years for which loss carryback is permitted by the tax law
4. Tax-planning strategies

In the example above, the enterprise recognized a deferred tax liability in the amount of $204 for $600 of taxable temporary differences and a deferred tax asset in the amount of $170 for $500 of deductible temporary differences. Future realization of the deferred tax asset must be assessed to determine whether a valuation allowance should be recognized. Future realization could occur as a result of any one or combination of the four potential sources of taxable income. To illustrate, a tax benefit might be realized for the $500 of deductible temporary differences by offsetting one of four sources:

1. $500 of taxable income that results from reversing taxable temporary differences in future years
2. $500 of taxable income (exclusive of reversals) that results from operations in future years
3. $500 of taxable income in the current or prior years by loss carryback to those years
4. $500 of taxable income in any of the three circumstances above *and* as a result of a tax-planning strategy

The four sources of taxable income may be considered in any sequence. If one source is sufficient to eliminate the need for a valuation allowance, the other three sources do not need to be considered. Or if two sources are sufficient, the other two do not need to be considered, and so forth. Thus, it may make sense to first consider the source(s) that, potentially, is the most fertile source of taxable income. Alternatively, some people may prefer to first consider the source(s) that is easiest for them to evaluate.

Recognition of a valuation allowance when none is needed, however, is prohibited. When a valuation allowance is recognized, each of the four sources of taxable income must be considered to determine the amount of the valuation allowance. For example, recognition of a valuation allowance that is measured based on a consideration of two of the sources and without regard to taxable income from the other two sources is not permitted. The valuation allowance should reduce the deferred tax asset to the amount that is expected to be realized, and it should not reduce the deferred tax asset below that amount.

Future Reversals of Taxable Temporary Differences.   The future reversal of taxable temporary differences is a ready source of taxable income for future realization of a deferred tax asset for deductible temporary differences and carryforwards. This future taxable income is already "on hand," so to speak, at the balance sheet date.

One note of caution is appropriate. The taxable temporary differences must reverse sometime within the window of opportunity for realizing a tax benefit for deductible temporary differences and carryforwards. The U.S. federal tax jurisdiction has a very large window. The window of opportunity generally is 23 years for deductible temporary differences (the reversal year, two carryback years, and 20 carryforward years), and the window is up to 20 years for loss and tax credit carryforwards. One exception is that there is no time limit for Alternative Maximum Tax (AMT) credit carryforwards. Temporary regulations released in 2002 expand the window further. They permit five-year carryback for net operating losses for any taxable year ending in 2001 and 2002. The window of opportunity may be larger or smaller for state, local, and foreign tax jurisdictions.

A general understanding of the timing of future reversals of temporary differences is, in many cases, relevant in assessing the need for a valuation allowance. Most temporary differences reverse when the related asset is recovered or the related liability is settled. Since most enterprises know, at least approximately, when their assets and liabilities will be recovered and settled, those enterprises already have a general understanding of the timing of the future reversals of their temporary differences.

The requirements in SFAS No. 96 for "scheduling" were controversial and one of the primary reasons it was reconsidered and replaced by SFAS No. 109. SFAS No. 109 does not require the sort of scheduling that was described and illustrated in SFAS No. 96 but does require an informed decision about the need for a valuation allowance. The amount of scheduling, if any, that will be required will depend on the facts and circumstances of each situation. Additional guidance regarding the timing and reversal pattern of temporary differences is provided by questions 1–7 in the FASB special report on implementation of SFAS No. 109.

Future Taxable Income Exclusive of Reversals.   Unlike the first source, taxable temporary differences, this source of future taxable income is not already "on hand" at the balance sheet date. This source results from earning taxable income (exclusive of reversals) in future years. Thus, assessments of this source of taxable income are more subjective, and more judgment is required. The subjective nature of the assessments and the need for judgment, however, do not provide reasons either to ignore this source of potential taxable income or to arbitrarily assume, in the name of conservatism or anything else, that future taxable income will be zero.

Sometimes this source of future taxable income may be the easiest and most fruitful starting point. For example, assume that an enterprise has $500 of deductible temporary differences and that it has earned taxable income of at least $100 in each of the last three years. This enterprise is relatively free of negative evidence, and future operations are reasonably expected to be equally profitable. That level of future taxable income is more than sufficient to realize a tax benefit for $500 of deductible temporary differences during the window of opportunity in the U.S. federal tax jurisdiction. In other circumstances, however, there may be a considerable amount of negative evidence, or the relationship between the amount of deductible temporary differences and the expected level of future taxable income may be less favorable. In those circumstances, determining the need for a valuation allowance based on an assessment of future taxable income (exclusive of reversals) is more difficult.

SFAS No. 109 provides examples of negative and positive evidence. The examples of negative evidence involve losses that have occurred in the recent past or that are expected to occur in the near future, carryforwards that have expired unused, unsettled circumstances that could result in reducing profit levels on a continuing basis in future years, and tax jurisdictions with a very small window of opportunity (i.e., short or no carryback and carryforward periods). The examples of positive evidence involve existing contracts or firm sales backlog, appreciated net assets, and a nonrecurring loss that is an aberration for an otherwise profitable enterprise.

The examples of negative and positive evidence in SFAS No. 109 are truly intended to be no more than examples. They are not intended to be used as a checklist for determining when a valuation allowance is or is not required. Furthermore, the examples provided are not all-inclusive lists. All available evidence should be considered—regardless of whether a particular type of evidence is one of the examples cited in SFAS No. 109. The objective is to determine whether the weight of the available evidence indicates a valuation allowance is needed.

Judgment is required in considering the relative impact of negative and positive evidence. An accounting standard obviously cannot set forth requirements for how to apply judgment. Regarding negative evidence in the form of cumulative losses in recent years, however, paragraph 23 states that "forming a conclusion that a valuation allowance is not needed is difficult when there is negative evidence such as cumulative losses in recent years," and paragraph 103 states that "a cumulative loss in recent years is a significant piece of negative evidence that is difficult to overcome."

Under APB Opinion No. 11, a deferred tax asset was recognized for an operating loss carry-forward only if realization of the asset was *assured beyond any reasonable doubt*. Under SFAS No. 109, the accounting objective and criterion for recognition of deferred tax assets are different. The objective is to produce accounting results that come closest to the expected outcome, that is, recognition of deferred tax assets that are expected to be realized, and nonrecognition of deferred tax assets that are not expected to be realized. To accomplish that objective, a deferred tax asset is recognized for all deductible temporary differences and carryforwards, and a valuation allowance is recognized if it is *more likely than not* that the asset will not be realized. More likely than not means a level of likelihood that is more than 50 percent.

Taxable Income in the Current or Prior Years.   Taxable income in the current or prior years for which loss carryback is permitted by the tax law is another ready source of taxable income for future realization of a deferred tax asset for deductible temporary differences. Like taxable temporary differences, this taxable income is already "on hand," so to speak, at the balance sheet date.

Referring again to the example above, the enterprise needs to determine whether a valuation allowance is needed for the $170 deferred tax asset for $500 of deductible temporary differences.

Assume that the tax jurisdiction is the U.S. federal tax jurisdiction and that taxable income and the tax paid for the current year exceed $500 and $170, respectively. If the deductible temporary differences will reverse within the next three years, nothing needs to be known about future taxable income exclusive of reversals. Regardless of whatever else occurs in the future, the deferred tax asset is realizable by loss carryback to the current year.

Tax-Planning Strategies.   Tax-planning strategies are another potential source of taxable income to be considered in determining the need for a valuation allowance. For example, a strategy to switch from tax-exempt to taxable investments would result in additional future taxable income that could reduce or eliminate the need for a valuation allowance at the end of the current year.

A tax-planning strategy, as that term is used in SFAS No. 109, refers to an action that an enterprise ordinarily would not take except for the express purpose of preventing a loss or tax credit carryforward from expiring unused. The term does *not* refer to all of the various actions, assumptions, strategies, and so forth that are implicit either in the normal course of conducting a business or in estimates of expected future taxable income (exclusive of reversals); there are no detailed criteria, rules, and requirements for those types of assumptions and strategies.

The two criteria for a tax-planning strategy, as that term is used in SFAS No. 109, are that the action must be prudent and the action must be feasible. Management would not implement a strategy if that action is not prudent, and might not be able to implement a strategy unless that action is primarily within the control of management, although unilateral control is not required.

Tax-planning strategies are not "hypothetical" strategies under SFAS No. 109. Instead, they involve an action that management intends to and would implement if and when confronted with a carryforward that otherwise is about to expire unused. If future taxable income turns out to be more than expected, the enterprise ultimately may not have to actually implement the strategy, that is, if more than expected future taxable income uses up the carryforward, the need for the tax-planning strategy is obviated.

Most tax-planning strategies involve actions or elections that accelerate or delay taxable or deductible items. Three examples follow:

1. A sale and leaseback of property, plant, and equipment
2. Disposal of obsolete inventory or a sale of loans for which there is a large allowance for bad debts
3. An election to change from the installment basis to the accrual basis for measuring taxable income on future sales (in a tax jurisdiction that permits temporary deferral of gains on installment sales)

Some tax-planning strategies may involve actions that would result in incurring significant expenses (e.g., lawyers' and other fees) or recognizing significant losses (e.g., from the sale of investments carried at cost if market value is less). In those cases, the expenses or losses, net of any related and realizable tax benefits, are recognized by including them as a component of the valuation allowance.

Tax-planning strategies only pertain to the determination of a valuation allowance for deferred tax assets, and tax-planning strategies may not be considered for purposes of nonrecognition of a deferred tax liability. A deferred tax liability is recognized for all taxable temporary differences except the particular types of taxable temporary differences for which exceptions are specified in SFAS No. 109 [see Subsection 24.1(c)].

Questions 25–28 in the FASB Special Report on implementation of SFAS No. 109 provide guidance about the requirements for tax-planning strategies.

(iii) Recognition of a Change in the Valuation Allowance.   The gross amount of a deferred tax asset will change because of deductible temporary differences and carryforwards that originate or are realized during the year or that expire unused at the end of the year. The need for and, if so, the amount of a valuation allowance for a gross deferred tax asset is redetermined at least annually. A change in the net amount of a deferred tax asset (i.e., the gross asset less the valuation allowance) results in deferred tax expense or benefit. The general requirements for the allocation of tax expense or benefit among continuing operations and other items are discussed in Subsection 24.4(a).

Sometimes there will be a change in the amount of valuation allowance for particular deductible temporary differences and carryforwards that exist at both the beginning and end of the year. That ordinarily will occur because a significant change in the enterprise's facts and circumstances causes a change in judgment about the amount of taxable income (exclusive of reversals) expected in future years. In those circumstances, deferred tax expense from an increase in the valuation allowance always is allocated to continuing operations, and deferred tax benefit from a decrease in the valuation allowance also is allocated to continuing operations unless the tax benefit is one of those that are never recognized in comprehensive income [see Subsection 24.4(a)].

(iv) Measurement of Deferred Tax Liabilities and Assets.   Measurements of deferred tax liabilities for taxable temporary differences and deferred tax assets for deductible temporary differences and carryforwards are based on enacted tax laws and rates. The objective is to measure the estimated future tax effects of temporary differences and carryforwards that exist at the date of the financial statements.

In the U.S. federal tax jurisdiction, if taxable income exceeds a certain amount, all taxable income is taxed at a single tax rate. Lower levels of taxable income are taxed at graduated tax rates. Deferred tax liabilities and assets are measured using (1) the single tax rate for enterprises that ordinarily are not subject to graduated tax rates and (2) an estimated average graduated tax rate for enterprises that ordinarily are subject to graduated tax rates. The estimated average graduated tax rate is based on the estimated average annual taxable income in the future years that deferred tax liabilities and assets are estimated to be settled and realized.

Sometimes there may be a different enacted tax rate for certain types of income, such as capital gains. If, for example, the enacted tax rate for capital gains is different, that enacted tax rate is used to measure a deferred tax liability for taxable temporary differences that, when they reverse, will result in capital gains.

A zero tax rate cannot be used to measure deferred tax liabilities and assets even if losses are expected in future years. A zero tax rate is not used to measure deferred tax liabilities because the FASB decided, for practical reasons, that anticipation of the tax consequences of future losses or expenses to eliminate a deferred tax liability should not be permitted. A zero tax rate is not used to measure deferred tax assets because future losses (more precisely, the absence of future taxable income) are a factor that is considered in determining the need for a valuation allowance. Thus, in circumstances when the tax rate otherwise might be zero, deferred tax liabilities and assets are measured using the single tax rate or the lowest graduated tax rate depending on the type of enterprise (see above).

Alternative Minimum Tax.   Under SFAS No. 109, the AMT tax rate is never used to measure deferred tax liabilities and assets. Instead, the regular tax rate is used, and a deferred tax asset is recognized for any AMT credit carryforward and then assessed to determine whether a valuation allowance is needed. The window of opportunity for realization of a deferred tax asset for an AMT credit carryforward encompasses the entire life of the enterprise. That positive factor distinguishes this type of deferred tax asset from virtually every other type of deferred tax asset.

What if, however, the enterprise will always be an AMT taxpayer? A valuation allowance is needed if the AMT credit carryforward is expected to expire unused at the end of the life of the enterprise. But that future scenario might not occur as often as some people might intuitively expect. AMT credit carryforwards arise primarily because of either "timing" differences (such as depreciation) or preference items (such as certain special deductions). If an enterprise is an AMT taxpayer because of timing differences, those differences ultimately will unwind (toward the end of the life of the enterprise) and thereby provide an opportunity to realize the AMT credit carryforward. Alternatively, if an enterprise is an AMT taxpayer because of preference or other items, income earned from the investment of funds available at the end of the life of the enterprise (i.e., prior to the final distribution of those funds to sharcholders) might provide an opportunity to realize an AMT credit carryforward.

An Enacted Change in Tax Laws or Rates.   Deferred tax liabilities and assets are adjusted for the effects of changes in tax laws or rates. A change in tax laws or rates is accounted for as a discrete event that is recognized in the period that includes the enactment date. In the U.S. federal tax jurisdiction, the enactment date is the date that the change is signed into law by the president. If an enterprise prepares its annual financial statements on a calendar-year basis, a change that is enacted any time in year 2 through December 31 is recognized in the financial statements for year 2, and a change that is enacted any time in year 3 starting on January 1 is recognized in the financial statements for year 3. Disclosure of the effect of a change that is enacted after the end of the year and before issuing the financial statements for that year usually is necessary.

An understanding of the timing of future reversals of temporary differences is needed when there is a phased-in change in tax rates. For example, assume that the new enacted tax rates for future years are X percent for years 2–4, Y percent for years 5–7, and Z percent for year 8 and thereafter. Deferred tax liabilities and assets for the estimated future tax effects of temporary differences are measured as follows: (1) at X percent for temporary differences that will reverse in years 2–4, (2) at Y percent for temporary differences that will reverse in years 5–7, and (3) at Z percent for temporary differences that will reverse in year 8 and thereafter.

Different enacted tax rates for different years create another, related issue that occasionally might be encountered in practice. Sometimes an enterprise may know or expect that the deferred tax liability for taxable temporary differences reversing in a particular future year will not be settled in that year, or that the deferred tax asset for deductible temporary differences reversing in a particular future year will not be realized in that year. That would occur, for example, if there is a loss in the future reversal year, and if the reversing taxable and deductible temporary differences only serve to decrease or increase that loss. If the loss is carried back, it will decrease taxes for an earlier year, or if it is carried forward, it will decrease taxes for a later year. When there are different enacted tax rates for the reversal (loss) year and the carryback or carryforward year, the deferred tax liability and asset for temporary differences reversing in the loss year should be measured using the enacted tax rate for the carryback or carryforward year.

A Change in Tax Status.   A change in the tax status of an enterprise also is accounted for as a discrete event. A deferred tax liability or asset is recognized or eliminated in the period that the change in tax status occurs. The date of change is the approval date if the change is voluntary, and it is the enactment date of a change in tax law that changes the tax status of an enterprise. If approval of a voluntary change is not necessary, the date of change is the filing date, for example, changes to or from the taxable C corporation status or nontaxable S corporation status in the U.S. federal tax jurisdiction. Questions 11 and 12 in the FASB Special Report on implementation of SFAS No. 109 provide additional guidance.

(c) SPECIAL APPLICATIONS.   SFAS No. 109 provides for a number of special applications.

(i) Regulated Companies.   SFAS No. 71, "Accounting for the Effects of Certain Types of Regulation," provides special accounting rules for companies that are rate regulated, such as utilities. A company subject to SFAS No. 71, for example, may be required to capitalize a cost that other companies would charge to expense. If capitalization of that cost creates a temporary difference, a deferred tax liability is recognized. If it is probable that future revenue will be provided for the payment of that deferred tax liability, a new asset is recognized for that probable future revenue. That asset and the deferred tax liability are shown as an asset and liability and are not offset. Similar accounting also may result from other special accounting rules for rate-regulated companies, such as those for (1) the equity component of the allowance for funds used during construction, (2) tax benefits that are flowed through to customers when temporary differences originate, and (3) adjustments of a deferred tax liability or asset for an enacted change in tax law or rates (see Chapter 33, "Regulated Utilities").

(ii) Leveraged Leases. SFAS No. 13, "Accounting for Leases," and Financial Interpretation (FIN) No. 21, "Accounting for Leases in a Business Combination," specify special accounting for the tax benefits associated with a leveraged lease. However, SFAS No. 109 does not change that special accounting (except to substitute temporary difference for timing difference) (see Chapter 23 "Leases").

Deferred tax credits related to leveraged leases are a source of taxable income, subject to certain limitations, that are considered in determining the need for and amount of a valuation allowance for a deferred tax asset for deductible temporary differences and carryforwards not related to leveraged leases.

(iii) Business Combinations.[4] SFAS No. 109 significantly changes the accounting for the income tax effects of business combinations. Under APB Opinion No. 16, "Business Combinations," the tax effect of a difference between the fair value and the tax basis of an asset acquired or a liability assumed in a purchase business combination was recognized in the accounting cost assigned to the asset or liability, that is, it was recorded on a net-of-tax basis. Sometimes the tax effect was discounted. Also any difference between the tax basis and recorded amount of an asset or liability was not a timing difference under APB Opinion No. 11. Questions 13–17 in the FASB Special Report on implementation of SFAS No. 109 address business combinations.

Nontaxable Business Combinations. A business combination may be accomplished in a tax-free exchange so that the tax bases of assets and liabilities carry over. Differences between the amounts assigned and the tax bases of assets and liabilities are temporary differences and deferred tax liabilities and assets (and related valuation allowances, if necessary) are recognized except for temporary differences related to the portion of goodwill for which amortization is not deductible for tax purposes, negative goodwill, leveraged leases, and certain acquired APB Opinion No. 23 differences.

The following example illustrates the accounting for a nontaxable business combination. The assumptions are as follows:

- The purchase price is $30,000.
- The acquired company's only assets are depreciable assets with a pretax fair value of $28,000 and a tax basis of $20,000. The only liability is the deferred tax liability for the temporary difference related to those depreciable assets.
- The enacted tax rate is 34 percent for all years.

The amounts recorded to account for the purchase transaction would be as follows:

Depreciable assets	$28,000)
Deferred tax liability (34 percent of the $8,000 temporary difference between the assigned value and the tax basis of the depreciable assets)	(2,720)
Goodwill	4,720
Purchase price	$30,000

Taxable Business Combinations. The amounts assigned to various assets and liabilities may differ for tax and accounting in a taxable purchase business combination. Those differences are temporary differences and a deferred tax liability or asset is recognized except for temporary differences that are the exceptions identified in (i) above.

---

[4] SFAS No. 141, "Business Combinations," supersedes APB Opinion No. 16. SFAS No. 141 prohibits the use of the pooling-of-interest method for all business combinations initiated after June 30, 2001. It requires purchase accounting for all business combinations initiated after that date.

Carryforwards—Purchase Method.   If (1) the combining companies expect to file a consolidated tax return and (2) the tax law permits an operating loss or tax credit carryforward of one company to offset taxable income of the other company, a deferred tax asset (net of a valuation allowance, if necessary) is recognized for deductible temporary differences and carryforwards of either company based on an assessment of *combined* past and expected future operations as of the acquisition date. The effect is to reduce positive goodwill in the acquisition (or produce negative goodwill that reduces all acquired assets except (1) financial assets other than investments accounted for by the equity method, (2) assets to be disposed of by sales, (3) deferred tax assets, (4) prepaid assets relating to pension or other post retirement benefit plans, and (5) any other current assets).

Subsequent Recognition of Carryforwards.   Tax benefits of acquired deductible temporary differences and carryforwards that were not recognized at the date of a purchase business combination, when subsequently recognized by reducing a valuation allowance or taxes payable, are first applied to reduce any goodwill from the acquisition to zero, are next applied to reduce any other noncurrent intangible assets from the combination to zero, and any remaining tax benefits are recognized as a reduction of income tax expense.

The tax benefits of deductible temporary differences and carryforwards that arise after the combination date are recognized as a reduction of income tax expense. Whether subsequently recognized tax benefits are attributable to items existing at the combination date or arising thereafter is determined by the tax rules for the sequence in which those items are utilized for tax purposes. If not determinable by reference to the tax law, tax benefits are prorated between (1) a reduction of goodwill and other noncurrent intangible assets and (2) income tax expense.

A carryforward from a prior year may sometimes offset taxable income attributable to an originating deductible temporary difference in the current year, for example, a temporary difference related to a liability for unearned rental income or for subscriptions received in advance. In effect, the carryforward at the beginning of the year is replaced by a deductible temporary difference at the end of the year. Recognition of a tax benefit depends on whether that deductible temporary difference meets the criteria for recognition of tax benefits.

(iv) Quasi Reorganizations.   In a quasi reorganization, charges or credits go directly to contributed capital and any deficit in retained earnings is eliminated by a charge to contributed capital. Because a quasi reorganization is considered an accounting "fresh start," any unrecognized tax benefits of deductible temporary differences and carryforwards existing at the time of the quasi reorganization are credited directly to contributed capital if subsequently recognized. The only exception is for enterprises that have previously both adopted SFAS No. 96 and effected a reorganization that involved only a deficit reclassification from retained earnings; the tax benefit of carryforwards for that limited exception are reported in income normally and then are reclassified to contributed capital.

(v) Separate Financial Statements of a Subsidiary.   If separate financial statements are issued for companies that are included in a consolidated tax return, total tax expense for the group should be allocated to the individual members using a method that is systematic, rational, and consistent with the broad principles of SFAS No. 109. One example of a method that meets those criteria is the "separate return" method. Examples of unacceptable methods are methods that (1) allocate only current tax expense to a member that has taxable temporary differences, (2) are fundamentally different from the asset and liability method, and (3) allocate no current or deferred tax expense because the group has no current or deferred tax expense.

(vi) Issues Addressed by the Emerging Issues Task Force.   The FASB's Emerging Issues Task Force (EITF) has addressed a number of implementation issues on the accounting for income taxes. They are listed below in chronological order by EITF Issue number.

- Issue 91-8 addresses the combination of a state franchise tax and an income tax and concludes that the income tax portion is only the portion that will exceed the franchise tax.
- Issue 92-8 addresses the accounting for income tax when there is a change in the functional currency of a foreign operation because the foreign economy ceases to be highly inflationary.
- Issue 93-7 addresses the accounting for uncertainties related to income taxes in a purchase business combination.
- Issue 93-9 addresses the accounting for income taxes in foreign financial statements restated for general price-level changes.
- Issue 93-12 addresses the recognition and measurement of the tax benefit of excess tax-deductible goodwill resulting from a retroactive change in tax law.
- Issue 93-13 specifies that retroactive changes in enacted tax rates should be determined as of the date of enactment.
- Issue 93-16 addresses the recognition of deferred income taxes related to "inside" basis differences of foreign subsidiaries that meet the indefinite reversal criterion of APB Opinion No. 23, "Accounting for Income Taxes—Special Areas."[5]
- Issue 93-17 addresses the recognition of deferred tax assets for a parent company's excess tax basis in the stock of a subsidiary that is accounted for as a discontinued operation.
- Issue 94-1 addresses the accounting for investments subject to the affordable housing income tax credit. It specifies that investments that meet specified conditions may be accounted for by the effective yield method; other investments should be consolidated if appropriate or accounted for by the equity method unless a limited partner's investment is so minor as to have virtually no influence, in which case the cost method should be used with amortization of the investment.
- Issue 94-10 addresses the accounting for income tax effects of transactions among shareholders or between the company and its shareholders and specifies those tax effects that should be recognized in income and those that should be recognized in stockholders' equity.
- Issues 95-9 and 95-10 address the tax effects of distributions to shareholders by companies in France and Germany where different tax rates (or tax credits) apply to income distributed as dividends and income retained.
- Issue 95-20 addresses measurement of deferred taxes in the consolidated financial statements of a parent company related to the operations of a foreign subsidiary that receives tax credits related to dividend payments.
- Issue 96-7 addresses the accounting for deferred taxes on in-process research and development activities acquired in a purchase business combination.
- Issue 98-11 addresses the treatment of acquired temporary differences in purchase transactions that are not accounted for as business combinations.
- Issue 99-15 addresses the decrease in a deferred tax valuation allowance that initially was recorded in a business combination as a result of a change in tax regulations.
- Issue 00-15 addresses the classification in the statement of cash flows of income tax benefit received by a company upon exercise of a nonqualified employee stock option.
- Issue 00-16 addresses when an employer should recognize a liability and corresponding cost for employer payroll taxes on employee stock compensation.
- Issue 02-13 addresses deferred income tax considerations in applying the goodwill impairment test in FASB Statement No. 142.

---

[5] Accounting Principles Board, "Accounting for Income Taxes—Special Areas," APB Opinion No. 23 (AICPA, New York, 1972).

(vii) Other Technical Matters.   The EITF also has discussed the following technical matters that do not relate specifically to a numbered EITF issue:

- Topic No. D-31 discusses temporary differences related to LIFO inventory and tax-to-tax differences (the difference between the tax basis of the stock of an acquired company and the tax basis of the net assets of the acquired company).
- Topic No. D-32 discusses the computation of the tax effect of pretax income from continuing operations.
- Topic No. D-33 discusses the recognition of tax benefits for pre-reorganization temporary differences and carryforwards when post-reorganization net operating loss carryforwards exist.
- Topic D-56 discusses the accounting for a change in functional currency and deferred taxes when an economy becomes highly inflationary.

FASB Staff Positions.   Beginning in February 2003, the FASB staff introduced the FASB Staff Position (FSP) to issue application guidance. The staff has issued the following FSPs on the accounting for income taxes.

- FSP FAS 109.1 addresses the application of FASB Statement No. 109 to the tax deduction on qualified production activities provided by the American Jobs Creation Act of 2004
- FSP FAS 109.2 addresses accounting and disclosure guidance for the foreign earnings repatriation provision within the American Jobs Creation Act of 2004
- FSP FAS 123(R) -3 addresses the transition election related to accounting for the tax effects of share-based payment awards

24.3   ACCOUNTING FOR THE INVESTMENT TAX CREDIT

(a) BACKGROUND.   The ITC was first provided by the Revenue Act of 1962. Since then, some features of the credit have been modified, and the credit has been discontinued and reinstated and discontinued again. Some other countries have similar programs, but they have not generated nearly as much controversy over accounting treatment. The credit was introduced as an inducement to increase business investment in productive assets and thereby stimulate the economy; how to account for it immediately caused strong differences of opinion in and among the accounting profession, industry, and government agencies.

The first APB Opinion on how to account for the credit was largely ignored by industry, and the SEC effectively suspended it before the APB modified the Opinion to make either of two methods acceptable. Nearly a decade later, when the investment credit was being reinstated in the tax system, the APB again sought to establish a single method to account for the credit; Congress intervened and wrote into the Revenue Act authorizing the new credit a provision that prohibited the APB or any other such body, such as the SEC, from mandating a single method to account for the ITC.

(b) CONCEPTUAL APPROACHES AND THE RESULTING CONTROVERSY.   When the ITC was first enacted, the APB considered three approaches in APB Opinion No. 2 on how to account for the credit:

1. Contribution to capital in the form of a subsidy from the government to the taxpayer.
2. Tax reduction that reduces a company's income tax expense in the year the credit is received. This approach views the credit as a selective reduction in income tax rates.

3. Cost reduction that should be recognized in income over the productive life of the asset to which the credit relates:

   a. Through reduced depreciation, or

   b. Through reduced tax expense

The first approach, viewing the credit as a subsidy to be treated as contributed capital, was rejected by the APB and has received no serious consideration in this country since. The question, therefore, is not whether the credit should be included in income but rather when—in the year "earned" or over the life of the property.

By a narrow margin, the APB adopted the cost reduction approach in APB Opinion No. 2, "Accounting for the 'Investment Credit.'" Under the Revenue Act of 1962, the investment credit reduced the tax basis of the related asset, thus reducing the amount of depreciation a taxpayer could claim over the life of the asset. The APB favored the same approach for financial reporting—that is, reduce the carrying amount of the asset by the amount of the credit and thereby recognize the credit in income over the life of the asset through reduced depreciation—but other approaches that would achieve the same result were also acceptable. For example, an investment credit could be carried as a deferred credit that would be amortized to income over the life of the asset. Also, under Opinion No. 2, the amount of credit to be recognized was limited to the amount realized as a reduction of income taxes payable; investment credit carryforwards were not to be recognized as assets.

When Opinion No. 2 was issued in December 1962, APB opinions relied on "general acceptability" for authority, and that Opinion was not well received. To the contrary, many companies indicated they would not follow the Opinion. In January 1963, the SEC issued ASR No. 96, "Accounting for the 'Investment Credit,'" which indicated that the SEC would allow companies subject to its jurisdiction to report the investment credit in income over the productive life of the property or by the "48–52 percent" method, or in certain cases as a reduction of income tax expense in the year the credit arises.

The Revenue Act of 1964 eliminated the requirement to reduce the tax basis of the property by the amount of the investment credit. In March 1964, the APB issued Opinion No. 4, "Accounting for the 'Investment Credit'" (Amending APB No. 2), indicating that the method specified by Opinion No. 2 should be considered preferable but that the alternative of reducing income tax expense by the amount of the credit in the year the credit arises is also an acceptable method.

Because of a "booming" economy later in the 1960s, Congress suspended the investment credit in 1966, reinstated it in 1967, and eliminated it in 1969. Then, to stimulate investment in the recession that occurred in the early 1970s, Congress began considering the possibility of reinstating the investment credit. In an attempt to resolve the accounting for the credit, the APB rushed out an exposure draft of an opinion proposing to require that the credit be recognized in income over the life of the asset rather than in the year it reduces income taxes payable. In enacting the credit in the Revenue Act of 1971, however, Congress included in the Act a provision that no one could require a particular method of accounting to be followed in reports to federal agencies, including the SEC. As a result, the APB did not issue another opinion addressing the accounting for the ITC, and APB Opinions No. 2 and No. 4 continue in force.

Although not so described in Opinions No. 2 and No. 4, the two methods of accounting for the ITC allowed by those two opinions are known in practice as the *deferral method* and the *flow-through method*, respectively. (The deferred method of interperiod income tax allocation is also sometimes called the *deferral method* and should not be confused with the deferral method of accounting for the investment credit.)

(c) DEFERRAL METHOD.   Although the deferral method (APB Opinion No. 2) was deemed the preferable method of accounting for the ITC by the APB, it is less widely used in practice. The deferral method is used most widely by financial institutions, such as banks and leasing companies, to account for investment credits retained on property leased on financing leases (sales-type, direct financing, and leveraged leases under SFAS No. 13). In essence, such institutions often consider the investment credit as part of the yield on a financing lease, that is, like interest on a note receivable.

Although APB Opinion No. 2 encouraged reducing the carrying amount of the asset by the amount of the credit, Accounting Series Release (ASR) No. 96, "Accounting for the 'Investment Credit,'" prohibited that approach for companies subject to SEC jurisdiction. The usual approach in practice under the deferral method now is to carry the investment credit as a deferred credit and to amortize the credit to income on some systematic and rational basis. Amortization might be (1) in proportion to depreciation on the related asset, (2) by the interest method described in APB Opinion No. 21, "Interest on Receivables and Payables," for a financing lease, or (3) as the credit is no longer subject to recapture, for tax purposes. Opinion No. 2 also encourages including the amortization of the investment credit as a component of accounting income before income taxes, but the credit is now generally treated as a reduction of income tax expense except when it is treated as part of the yield on a financing lease.

(d) FLOW-THROUGH METHOD AND RECOGNITION OF THE CREDIT.   The flow-through method of accounting for ITCs, which is recognized as an acceptable method under APB Opinion No. 4, is widely used in practice. Under this method, the amount of the credit recognized in a year is treated as a reduction of income tax expense of that year.

Under SFAS No. 109, if ITCs have not been realized as a reduction of income taxes payable on a company's income tax return, including credits carried back and realized as a refund of income taxes previously paid, the company recognizes a deferred tax asset for the ITC carryforward and then assesses whether a valuation allowance is needed. A tax credit carryforward functions the same as an operating loss carryforward under SFAS No. 109. Any existing or enacted future limitations on realization of the credit apply, such as a limitation allowing only a percentage of the tax due for any year to be offset by the credit.

Although the ITC was eliminated by the 1986 Revenue Act, various other tax credits remain available. Those credits are treated the same as the investment credit in applying SFAS No. 109. Further, given the history of the ITC in this country, it could be reinstated the next time Congress decides to use the tax system to encourage companies to purchase new production equipment as a means of stimulating the economy.

(e) INVESTMENT CREDITS IN FINANCING LEASES.   SFAS No. 13, "Accounting for Leases," specifically addresses the accounting for the ITC only in paragraphs 42–44 concerning a lessor's accounting for leveraged leases. One condition for accounting for a lease as a leveraged lease under that statement is that the ITC be accounted for as specified by those paragraphs. In essence, an ITC to be realized on a leveraged lease transaction must be recorded as a receivable and as unearned income. The unearned income is then recognized in income over the term of the lease only in the years the lessor's net investment in the lease is positive.

However, SFAS No. 13 does not address the accounting for ITC retained by a lessor on leases of other types, and either the deferral or the flow-through method may be used for a sales-type, direct financing, or operating lease. Frequently, however, financial institutions, such as banks and leasing companies, account for the investment credit by the deferral method and consider it as part of the "yield" on the lease receivable for a financing lease.

24.4 FINANCIAL REPORTING

(a) TAX ALLOCATION WITHIN A PERIOD.   The process of allocating income taxes among income from continuing operations and other items within a period is known as *intraperiod tax allocation*. (This should not be confused with tax allocation among interim periods of a year, which is discussed later in this section.) Intraperiod income tax allocation is the apportionment of total income tax for the period among income from continuing operations, discontinued operations, extraordinary items, other comprehensive income, and direct entries to stockholders' equity.

In general, the first step in intraperiod income tax allocation under SFAS No. 109 is to determine the tax expense or benefit related to income from continuing operations. The difference between that amount and total tax expense or benefit is the tax effect to be allocated to all of the other items listed above. If there is only one other item (e.g., an extraordinary item), the remaining tax effect is allocated to it. If there is more than one item, the remaining tax effect is allocated between (or among) them as follows:

- Determine the tax benefit of all items with a loss.
- Allocate the tax benefit for all loss items pro rata among those items.
- Allocate the difference between (a) the tax expense or benefit determined earlier for income or loss from all items other than continuing operations and (b) the tax benefit determined in (1) above for all items with a loss (c) pro rata among all items with a gain.

The general approach described above is supplemented by specific requirements for allocation of the tax expense or benefit attributed to certain types of items. These specified requirements override the general approach whenever the general approach would produce a different result. Tax expense or benefit allocated to continuing operations includes the tax effects of changes in a valuation allowance because of a change in judgment about realization in future years (except for initial recognition of tax benefits that are never recognized in comprehensive income—see below), changes in tax laws or rates, changes in tax status, and tax-deductible dividends paid to stockholders (except for certain dividends paid to an Employees Stock Ownership Plan (ESOP)—see below). Tax expense or benefit allocated to stockholders' equity includes the tax effects of adjustments of the opening balance of retained earnings, items of comprehensive income excluded from net income, an increase or decrease in contributed capital, employee stock options as required by paragraph 44 of FASB Statement No. 123, "Accounting for Stock-Based Compensation," and paragraph 17 of APB Opinion No. 25, "Accounting for Stock Issued to Employees," dividends paid on unallocated shares held by an ESOP and charged to retained earnings, and a quasi-reorganization (see Subsection 24.2(c)). The tax benefits of an acquired company's deductible temporary differences and carryforwards, when initially recognized after the combination date, are applied to reduce goodwill to zero and then to reduce other acquired noncurrent intangible assets to zero before any tax benefits are applied to reduce income tax expense (see Subsection 24.2(c)).

Question 19 in the FASB Special Report on implementation of SFAS No. 109 provides guidance on intraperiod income tax allocation.

(b) FINANCIAL STATEMENT PRESENTATION AND DISCLOSURE.   The SFAS No. 109 requires deferred tax liabilities or assets to be classified as current and noncurrent in a classified balance sheet. The classification is determined for each tax jurisdiction, and offset of liabilities and assets attributable to different tax jurisdictions is not permitted. Deferred tax liabilities and assets are classified as current or noncurrent based on the classification of the nontax assets and liabilities that give rise to the underlying temporary differences. Classification of deferred tax liabilities and assets for temporary differences that are not related to an asset or liability on the balance sheet and for carryforwards are classified pursuant to FASB Statement No. 37, "Balance Sheet Classification of Deferred Taxes," as amended by SFAS No. 109. The valuation allowance for a particular deferred tax asset is classified as current or noncurrent on a pro rata basis.

Disclosure of the total of all (1) deferred tax liabilities, (2) deferred tax assets, and (3) valuation allowances is required. The net change in the total of all valuation allowances is also disclosed. Public companies disclose the approximate tax effect of each type of temporary difference or carryforward that constitutes a significant portion of deferred tax liabilities and deferred tax assets. Nonpublic companies also disclose the types of temporary differences and carryforwards but need not disclose the tax effects of each.

The income statement or notes must disclose the following eight components of income tax expense for continuing operations for each income statement presented:

1. Current tax expense or benefit
2. Deferred tax expense or benefit, not including the effects of other components below
3. ITCs
4. Government grants that reduce income tax expense
5. Benefits of operating loss carryforwards
6. Adjustments of deferred tax assets or liabilities for changes in tax laws, tax rates, or tax status (i.e., the company becomes taxable or tax exempt)
7. Adjustments of a valuation allowance because of a change in judgment about realization in future years
8. Tax expense that results from allocating certain tax benefits to stockholders' equity or to reduce goodwill and acquired intangible assets

Disclosure is also required for the amount of tax expense or benefit allocated to continuing operations and the amounts separately allocated to other items for each year whenever those items are reported.

An amount or percentage reconciliation of the income tax expense for continuing operations to the comparable tax that would result from applying domestic federal statutory tax rates is required (regular tax rates if there are alternative tax systems). Public companies must disclose the nature and estimated amount of each significant reconciling item: Nonpublic companies may omit the amount. A public company not subject to income tax because its income is taxed directly to its owners (such as a publicly held limited partnership) must disclose that fact and the net difference between its reported assets and liabilities and their tax bases.

Companies that have not recognized a deferred tax liability for any of the exceptions listed in Subsection 24.1(c) (vi) must disclose:

- The type of temporary difference involved and what would cause it to become taxable
- The cumulative amount of the temporary difference
- The amount of the unrecognized tax liability (If determination of the amount related to foreign investees is not practicable, that fact may be disclosed instead.)

Disclosure is required of the amounts and expiration dates of operating loss and tax credit carryforwards for tax purposes. If significant, the amount of carryforwards for which any recognized tax benefits will be applied to reduce goodwill and other noncurrent intangible assets or allocated directly to stockholders' equity must also be disclosed.

In separately issued financial statements, a company that is included in a consolidated tax return must disclose these two items:

1. The current and deferred tax expense for each income statement presented and any tax-related amounts due to or from affiliates for each balance sheet presented
2. How the consolidated tax expense is allocated to members of the group and the nature and effect of any change in the method of allocation or determining amounts to or from affiliates for the periods included in (1) above

Question 18 in the FASB Special Report on implementation of SFAS No. 109 provides guidance on disclosure.

The SEC's disclosure requirements in Rule 4-08(h) of Regulation S-X related to the accounting for income taxes reflect the issuance of SFAS No. 109 and require the following two disclosures that are not required by SFAS No. 109:

1. Domestic and foreign pretax accounting income if income (loss) from operations located outside the registrant's home country is five percent or more of total pretax accounting income

2. The tax related to the amounts disclosed under (1) is five percent or more of total tax expense

As does SFAS No. 109, the SEC requires a reconciliation of tax expense to what tax expense would be at federal domestic statutory tax rates. If the statutory rate used is not the U.S. federal corporate income tax rate, the rate used and the basis for using that rate must be disclosed.

(c) OTHER DISCLOSURES. APB Opinions No. 2 and 4 call for disclosure of the method used to account for the ITC and any material amounts involved.

24.5 ACCOUNTING FOR INCOME TAXES IN INTERIM PERIODS

(a) RELEVANT PRONOUNCEMENTS. APB Opinion No. 28, "Interim Financial Reporting" (pars. 19–20), specifies the general concepts for accounting for income taxes and ITCs in interim periods. Essentially, Opinion No. 28 adopted the integral approach for income taxes and credits by requiring that they be determined for interim periods by using an estimated annual effective tax rate. However, income taxes and credits associated with significant unusual or extraordinary items are reported in the interim period in which they occur. FIN No. 18, "Accounting for Income Taxes in Interim Periods—An Interpretation of APB Opinion No. 28," explains those general concepts and illustrates how to compute income taxes for an interim period in various circumstances. SFAS No. 16, "Prior Period Adjustments," addresses adjustments related to prior interim periods of the current fiscal year. The pronouncements described elsewhere in this chapter that specify how to determine the appropriate annual provision for income taxes must also be applied to determine tax expense for an interim period.

(b) ESTIMATED ANNUAL EFFECTIVE TAX RATE. For convenience, FIN No. 18 (par. 5) defines certain terms that are used in special ways for interim period income taxes as follows:

a. **"Ordinary" income (or loss)** refers to "income (or loss) from continuing operations before income taxes (or benefits) excluding significant "unusual or infrequently occurring items." Extraordinary items, discontinued operations, and cumulative effects of changes in accounting principles are also excluded from this term. The term is *not* used in the income tax context of ordinary income v. capital gain. [Footnote omitted.]

b. **Tax (or benefit)** is the total income tax expense (or benefit), including the provision (or benefit) for income taxes both currently payable and deferred. [Words in parentheses are deleted in the following discussion.]

The estimated annual effective tax rate is the estimated income tax for the year allocated to ordinary income divided by the estimated ordinary income for the year. The estimated income tax for the year includes anticipated ITCs accounted for by the flow-through method, foreign taxes and credits, the effect of items that receive special income tax treatment, such as percentage depletion and long-term capital gains, and other available tax planning alternatives.

In theory, the estimated income tax for the year is determined by forecasting what the balances of income taxes payable and deferred income taxes will be at year end and adjusting for beginning of the year balances. In practice, estimates of tax for the year may suffice. Having estimated income tax for the year, the procedures described in this section for intraperiod income tax allocation are used to allocate the estimated income tax for the year between ordinary income and the items that are treated separately (e.g., unusual, infrequently occurring, and extraordinary items and discontinued operations). A new estimate of the annual effective tax rate should be made whenever assumptions change significantly.

(c) INTERIM PERIOD TAX. The income tax for the current interim period is determined in several steps. First, the year-to-date ordinary income is multiplied by the current estimated annual effective tax rate to determine the applicable year-to-date tax. Second, the total tax applicable to ordinary income for prior interim periods of that fiscal year is subtracted to determine tax applicable to ordinary income for the current interim period. Third, income tax allocated to unusual or infrequently occurring items and similar items included in income from continuing operations but handled on a discrete basis is added. The result is the income tax applicable to income from continuing operations for the current interim period.

Procedures such as the recognition of the tax benefit of a loss or tax credit carryforward because of taxable income from the future reversal of taxable temporary differences and intraperiod tax allocation must be properly applied when application in computing the estimated annual effective tax rate to correctly determine interim period income taxes.

(d) SPECIAL INTERIM PERIOD PROBLEMS. FIN No. 18 addresses several special interim period problems.

First, it may not be possible to make a reliable estimate of the annual effective tax rate. In those situations, the actual effective tax rate for the year to date may be the best estimate of the annual effective tax rate. Also, if components of ordinary income or the related tax cannot be reliably estimated, those components may be excluded from the overall estimated annual effective tax rate and handled on an actual effective tax rate for the year to date.

Second, several estimated annual effective tax rates may have to be computed for one company. For example, a company that is subject to income tax in several jurisdictions may have losses in some jurisdictions for which no tax benefit can be recognized. Separate annual effective tax rates must be estimated for those loss jurisdictions. Another example is a U.S. company that has foreign operations and is unable to make a reliable estimate *in dollars* of the ordinary income or of the related tax for the foreign operations. Those amounts must be reported on a discrete basis.

Third, new tax legislation poses special problems for reporting income taxes in interim periods. In the past, some companies have anticipated the effect of proposed tax legislation, but SFAS No. 109 amended paragraph 20 of APB Opinion No. 28 to make it clear that the tax effects of new legislation, such as a change in tax rates, are not recognized prior to enactment.

Fourth, the tax effect of a change in a valuation allowance because of a change in judgment about realization in future years is recognized in the period that the change in judgment occurs and is not allocated to subsequent interim periods by an adjustment of the estimated annual effective tax rate for the remainder of the year.

24.6 COMPARISON OF U.S. GENERALLY ACCEPTED ACCOUNTING PRINCIPLES TO THOSE OF OTHER COUNTRIES

(a) GENERAL COMPARISON. In the United States, comprehensive recognition of deferred taxes has applied rather broadly since 1968. The United States differs from other countries in methods used, the extent to which they are used, and how long they have been used.

The results of a 1979 survey of accounting practices in 64 countries by Price Waterhouse International are shown in Exhibit 24.1, with respect to the breakdown in accounting for income taxes.[6]

A 1991 survey of the accounting practices for income taxes in eight countries (Australia, Canada, France, Germany, Italy, Japan, the Netherlands, and United Kingdom) by KPMG Peat Marwick that was published by the Big Six accounting firms found a move to comprehensive allocation by the liability method and from partial allocation by the deferred method in comparison to the

---

[6] R. D. Fitzgerald, A. D. Stickler, and T. R. Watts. *International Survey of Accounting Principles and Reporting Practices* (Scarborough, Ontario: Butterworth & Co. Ltd., 1979).

	Comprehensive Allocation	Partial Allocation	No Tax Allocation	Liability Method	Deferred Method
Required	5*	2	5	1	4*
Predominant practice	6	1	41	15	5
Minority practice	20	15	7	9	18
Rarely or not found	23	33	1	28	29
Not accepted or permitted	8	11*	8*	4*	1
Not applicable	2	2	2	7	7
Totals	64	64	64	64	64

* Includes United States and Canada.

Exhibit 24.1   Tax allocation practices in 64 countries.

1979 survey of 64 countries shown in Exhibit 24.1. The following was summarized from the 1991 survey:

	Number of Countries
Comprehensive allocation	3
Generally comprehensive allocation	1
Partial allocation	2
Comprehensive or partial allocation permitted in consolidated financial statements	2
Total	8
Liability method	5
Deferred method	1
Deferred method or liability method in consolidated financial statements	2
Total	8

(b) UNITED KINGDOM. In 1975 the Accounting Standards Committee (ASC) in the United Kingdom issued SSAP No. 11, "Accounting for Deferred Taxation," which called for comprehensive interperiod income tax allocation by the deferred method. The following year the ASC announced that it was reviewing SSAP No. 11 and implementation was deferred. In 1977 the ASC issued Exposure Draft(ED) No. 19, "Accounting for Deferred Taxation," which called for tax allocation by the liability method for short-term timing differences that normally reverse the following year and took an approach similar to APB Opinion No. 23, by not calling for tax allocation for certain kinds of timing differences for which it could be demonstrated that payment of taxes could be postponed indefinitely.

In 1978 the ASC issued SSAP No. 15, "Accounting for Deferred Taxation," which required tax allocation for short-term timing differences and for other originating timing differences unless it could be demonstrated that (1) there will be no tax liability for timing differences that would reverse within three years and (2) the situation was not likely to change. If tax allocation was required, partial allocation might be appropriate. Unlike ED No. 19, SSAP No. 15 (pars. 26–30) did not specify the liability method but rather allowed either the liability or the deferred method.

SSAP No. 15 was revised in May 1985. The revised Statement specifies the liability method and calls for timing differences to be accounted for only if based on reasonable assumptions it is probable that a liability or asset will "crystallize." Assessing whether a tax liability will "crystallize" is based on a review of financial plans or projections for three to five years for a regular pattern of timing differences and a longer period for an irregular pattern.

Amended in 1992, SSAP No. 15 permitted recognition of deferred tax benefits for pension and other postemployment costs that are not actually paid until many years after the costs are first recognized in the financial statements. A Discussion Paper, "Accounting for Tax," was issued in March 1995 as the first step in total reconsideration of accounting for income taxes in the United Kingdom.

In December 2000, SSAP No. 15 was superseded by Financial Reporting Standard (FRS) No. 19, "Deferred Tax." The general principle underlying FRS No. 19 is that deferred taxes should be recognized when there is an obligation now to pay more tax in the future or there is a right to pay less tax in the future. FRS No. 19 requires an entity to recognize deferred tax assets and liabilities that arise from timing differences between the recognition of gains and losses in the financial statements and their recognition in a tax computation. Under FRS No. 19, similar to FAS No. 109, a deferred tax asset is recognized to the extent it is more likely than not that it will be recovered. However, unlike SFAS No. 109, FRS No. 19 permits discounting deferred tax assets and liabilities. The standard is effective for years beginning after January 23, 2002, with earlier adoption encouraged.

(c) INTERNATIONAL STANDARDS. In October 1996 International Accounting Standards Committee (IAS) 12 (Revised), "Income Taxes," was issued and became effective in 1998. IAS 12 takes a similar basic approach to accounting for income taxes as SFAS No. 109. With only limited exceptions, IAS 12 requires comprehensive recognition of deferred taxes. The major exception is nonrecognition of deferred taxes for temporary differences related to investments in subsidiaries, branches and associates, and interests in joint ventures if (1) the enterprise can control the timing of the reversal of the temporary difference, (2) it is probable that the temporary difference will not reverse in the foreseeable future, and (3) in the case of associates, there is an agreement requiring that the profits of the associate will not be distributed in the foreseeable future. A deferred tax asset is recognized for deductible temporary differences and carryforwards if future realization of the tax benefit is probable. The international standard is not binding unless it is made so by the appropriate body in a country.

24.7 SOURCES AND SUGGESTED REFERENCES

Accounting Principles Board, "Accounting for the Investment Credit," APB Opinion No. 2. AICPA, New York, 1962.

———, "Accounting for the 'Investment Credit,'" APB Opinion No. 4 (Amending No. 2). AICPA, New York, 1964.

———, "Accounting for Income Taxes," APB Opinion No. 11. AICPA, New York, 1967.

———, "Business Combinations," APB Opinion No. 16. AICPA, New York, 1970.

———, "Accounting for Income Taxes—Special Areas," APB Opinion No. 23. AICPA, New York, 1972.

———, "Accounting for Stock Issued to Employees," APB Opinion No. 25. AICPA, New York, 1992.

———, "Interim Financial Reporting," APB Opinion No. 28. AICPA, New York, 1973.

Accounting Standards Board, "Accounting for Tax," Discussion Paper. The Accounting Standards Board Limited, London, 1995.

———, "Deferred Tax," Financial Reporting Standard 19. The Accounting Standards Board Limited, London, 2000.

Accounting Standards Committee, "Accounting for Deferred Taxation," Statement of Standard Accounting Practice No. 15. The Institute of Chartered Accountants in England and Wales, London, 1978, revised 1985.

American Institute of Accountants, "Accounting for Income Taxes," Accounting Research Bulletin No. 23. AIA (now AICPA), New York, 1944.

_____, "Restatement and Revision of Accounting Research Bulletins," Accounting Research Bulletin No. 43. AIA (now AICPA), New York, 1953.

on_____, "Declining-Balance Depreciation," Accounting Research Bulletin No. 44. AIA (now AICPA), New York, 1954.

_____, "Declining-Balance Depreciation," Accounting Research Bulletin No. 44 (Revised). AIA (now AICPA), New York, 1958.

American Institute of Certified Public Accountants, "New Depreciation Guidelines and Rules," APB Opinion No. 1. AICPA, New York, 1962.

Arthur Andersen & Co., Coopers & Lybrand, Deloitte & Touche, Ernst & Young, KPMG Peat Marwick, Price Waterhouse, "Survey of International Accounting Practices." Published by the authors and available from the AICPA, New York, 1991.

Black, Homer A., "Interperiod Allocation of Corporate Income Taxes," Accounting Research Study No. 9. AICPA, New York, 1966.

FASB Emerging Issues Task Force, "EITF Abstracts—A Summary of Proceedings of the FASB Emerging Issues Task Force." FASB, Norwalk, CT, 2001 (published annually).

Financial Accounting Standards Board, "Accounting for Income Taxes in Interim Periods—An Interpretation of APB Opinion No. 28," FASB Interpretation No. 18. FASB, Stamford, CT, 1977.

_____, "Accounting for Leases in a Business Combination," FASB Interpretation No. 21. FASB, Stamford, CT, 1978.

_____, "Accounting for Research and Development Costs," Statement of Financial Accounting Standards No. 2. FASB, Stamford, CT, 1974.

_____, "Accounting for Leases," Statement of Financial Accounting Standards No. 13. FASB, Stamford, CT, 1977.

_____, "Prior Period Adjustments," Statement of Financial Accounting Standards No. 16. FASB, Stamford, CT, 1977.

_____, "Balance Sheet Classification of Deferred Taxes," Statement of Financial Accounting Standards No. 37. FASB, Stamford, CT, 1980.

_____, "Foreign Currency Translation," Statement of Financial Accounting Standards No. 52. FASB, Stamford, CT, 1981.

_____, "Accounting for the Effects of Certain Types of Regulation," Statement of Financial Accounting Standards No. 71. FASB, Stamford, CT, 1982.

_____, "Accounting for Income Taxes," Statement of Financial Accounting Standards No. 96. FASB, Stamford, CT, 1987.

_____, "Accounting for Income Taxes—Deferral of the Effective Date of FASB Statement No. 96," Statement of Financial Accounting Standards No. 100. FASB, Norwalk, CT, 1988.

_____, "Accounting for Income Taxes—Deferral of the Effective Date of FASB Statement No. 96," Statement of Financial Accounting Standards No. 103. FASB, Norwalk, CT, 1989.

_____, "Accounting for Income Taxes—Deferral of the Effective Date of FASB Statement No. 96," Statement of Financial Accounting Standards No. 108. FASB, Norwalk, CT, 1991.

_____, "Accounting for Income Taxes," Statement of Financial Accounting Standards No. 109. FASB, Norwalk, CT, 1992.

_____, "Accounting for Stock-Based Compensation," Statement of Financial Accounting Standards No. 123. FASB, Norwalk, CT, 1995.

_____, "Goodwill and Other Intangible Assets," Statement of Financial Accounting Standards No. 142, FASB, Norwalk, CT, June, 2001.

_____, "Accounting for Income Taxes," Proposed Statement of Financial Accounting Standards. FASB, Norwalk, CT, June 5, 1991.

Fitzgerald, R. D., Stickler, A. D., and Watts, T. R., Editors, Price Waterhouse International, *International Survey of Accounting Principles and Reporting Practices*. Butterworth & Co. (Canada) Ltd., Scarborough, Ontario, 1979.

International Accounting Standards Committee, "Income Taxes," IAS 12 (Revised). IASC, London, 1996.

Perry, Raymond E., and Simpson, E. Raymond, "A Guide to Implementation of Statement No. 109 on Accounting for Income Taxes—Questions and Answers." FASB, Norwalk, CT, 1992.

Securities and Exchange Commission, "Accounting for the 'Investment Credit,'" Accounting Series Release No. 96. SEC, Washington, DC, 1963.

———, "Form and Content of and Requirements for Financial Statements," Regulation S-X, Part 210 of Title 17 of the Code of Federal Regulations. SEC, Washington, DC, as amended through July 1995.

Simpson, E. Raymond, Cassel, Jules M., Giles, Jill Peperone, and Jones, Gregory J., "Special Report: A Guide to Implementation of Statement 96 on Accounting for Income Taxes—Questions and Answers." FASB, Norwalk, CT, 1989.

CHAPTER 25

LIABILITIES

Frederick Gill, CPA

American Institute of Certified Public Accountants
Accounting Standards Team
Senior Technical Manager

The views of Mr. Gill, as expressed in this publication, do not necessarily reflect the views of the AICPA. Official positions are determined through certain specific committee procedures, due process, and deliberation.

25.1 NATURE OF LIABILITIES

(a) DEFINITION OF LIABILITIES. FASB Statement of Financial Accounting Concepts No. 6, "Elements of Financial Statements," defines liabilities as:

> [P]robable future sacrifices of economic benefits arising from present obligations of a particular entity to transfer assets or provide services to other entities in the future as a result of past transactions or events.

Probable is used with its usual general meaning and refers to that which can reasonably be expected on the basis of available evidence but is not certain. *Obligation* is broader than "legal obligation," referring to duties imposed legally or socially and to that which one is bound to do by contract, promise, or moral responsibility. Concepts Statement No. 6 (par. 36) elaborates that a liability has three essential characteristics:

1. [I]t embodies a present duty or responsibility to one or more other entities that entails settlement by probable future transfer or use of assets at a specified or determinable date, on occurrence of a specified event, or on demand,
2. the duty or responsibility obligates a particular entity, leaving it little or no discretion to avoid the future sacrifice, and
3. the transaction or other event obligating the entity has already happened.

(i) Executory Contracts as Liabilities. The furnishing of goods, services, or money to another party is usually a prerequisite for the recording of a liability. Agreements for the exchange of resources in the future that are at present unfulfilled commitments on both sides are not recorded until one of the parties at least partially fulfills its commitment. The effects of some executory contracts, however, are recorded, for example, losses under purchase commitments. The FASB stated the following in Concepts Statement No. 5 (par. 107):

> Several respondents urged the Board to address in this Statement certain specific recognition and measurement issues including definitive guidance for recognition of contracts that are fully

executory (i.e., contracts as to which neither party has as yet carried out any part of its obligations, which are generally not recognized in present practice) and selection of measurement attributes for particular assets and liabilities. Those issues have long been, and remain, unresolved on a general basis.

(ii) Credit Balances That Are Not Liabilities. Items such as minority interest and deferred gross profit on installment sales are sometimes found on the right side of balance sheets. On occasion, such items are confused with liabilities. Neither minority interest nor deferred gross profit on installment sales is a liability, and the presentation of those items in financial statements should be such as to clearly segregate them from any long-term liabilities.

(b) OFFSETTING OF LIABILITIES AGAINST ASSETS. APB Opinion No. 10, "Omnibus Opinion—1966," states in paragraph 7 that "It is a general principle of accounting that the offsetting of assets and liabilities in the balance sheet is improper except where a right of setoff exists." FASB Interpretation No. 39, "Offsetting of Amounts Related to Certain Contracts," clarifies that a *right of setoff* is a debtor's legal right, by contract or otherwise, to discharge all or a portion of the debt owed to another party by applying against the debt an amount that the other party owes to the debtor. The Interpretation states in paragraph 5 that a right of setoff exists when all of the following conditions are met:

- Each of *two* parties owes the other determinable amounts.
- The reporting party has the right to set off the amount owed by the other party.
- The reporting party intends to set off the amount owed by the other party.
- The right of setoff is enforceable at law.

A debtor having a valid right of setoff may offset the related asset and liability and report the net amount.

For purposes of the Interpretation, cash on deposit at a financial institution is to be considered by the depositor as cash rather than as an amount owed to the depositor. Thus, for example, an overdraft in a bank account at a particular bank may not be offset against a cash balance at the same institution because the cash balance is not considered an amount owed to the depositor.

The Interpretation addresses offsetting of amounts recognized for forward, interest-rate swap, currency swap, option, and other conditional or exchange contracts. The fair value of those contracts or an accrued receivable or payable arising from those contracts, rather than the notional amounts or the amounts to be exchanged, is recognized in the statement of financial position. The fair value of contracts in a loss position should not be offset against the fair value of contracts in a gain position unless a right of setoff exists. Similarly, amounts recognized as accrued receivables should not be offset against amounts recognized as accrued payables unless a right of setoff exists. An exception is made to permit offsetting of fair value amounts recognized for forward, swap, and other conditional or exchange contracts executed with the same counterparty under a master netting arrangement, without regard to whether the reporting party intends to set them off. A master netting arrangement exists if the reporting entity has multiple contracts, whether for the same type of conditional or exchange contract or for different types of contracts, with a single counterparty that are subject to a contractual agreement that provides for net settlement of all contracts through a single payment in a single currency in the event of default on or termination of any one contract. Offsetting the fair values recognized for forward, interest rate swap, currency swap, option, and other conditional or exchange contracts outstanding with a single counterparty results in the net fair value of the position between the two counterparties being reported as an asset or a liability in the statement of financial position.

Various accounting pronouncements specify accounting treatments in circumstances that result in offsetting or in a presentation in a statement of financial position that is similar to the effect of offsetting, for example, the accounting for pension plan assets and liabilities under FASB Statement No. 87, "Employers' Accounting for Pensions," and the accounting for advances received on construction contracts under the American Institute of Certified Public Accountants (AICPA) Audit and Accounting Guides *Construction Contractors* and *Audits of Federal Government Contractors*. Interpretation No. 39 does not modify the accounting treatment prescribed by other pronouncements.

FASB Interpretation No. 41, "Offsetting of Amounts Related to Certain Repurchase and Reverse Repurchase Agreements," modified Interpretation No. 39 to permit offsetting in the statement of financial position of payables and receivables that represent repurchase agreements, without regard to whether the reporting party intends to set them off, if conditions specified in the Interpretation are met.

(c) MEASUREMENT OF LIABILITIES. FASB Concepts Statement No. 5 (par. 67) recognized that items currently reported in financial statements are measured by different attributes, depending on the nature of the item. Liabilities that involve obligations to provide goods or services to customers are generally reported as historical proceeds, which is the amount of cash, or its equivalent, received when the obligations were incurred and may be adjusted after acquisition for amortization or other allocations. Liabilities that involve known or estimated amounts of money payable at unknown future dates, for example, trade payable or warranty obligations, generally are reported at their net settlement value, which is an undiscounted amount. Long-term payables are reported at their present value, discounted at the implicit or historical rate, which is the present value of future outflows required to settle the liability. (See Section 4.2 for a discussion of how the use of present value and discounting concepts in measuring long-term payables contributes to earnings management by the faulty design of generally accepted accounting principles (GAAP).)

Many liabilities result from financial instruments, for example, bonds and notes payable. (See "Disclosures about Fair Value of Financial Instruments" below for the definition of a financial instrument.) The FASB concluded in Statement No. 133, "Accounting for Derivative Instruments and Hedging Activities," issued in June 1998, that fair value is the most relevant measure for financial instruments and that fair value measurement is practical for most financial assets and liabilities. Paragraph 334 of Statement No. 133 states:

> The Board is committed to work diligently toward resolving, in a timely manner, the conceptual and practical issues related to determining the fair values of financial instruments and portfolios of financial instruments. Techniques for refining the measurement of the fair values of financial instruments continue to develop at a rapid pace, and the Board believes that all financial instruments should be carried in the statement of financial position at fair value when the conceptual and measurement issues are resolved.

Only certain liabilities resulting from financial instruments, such as liabilities resulting from derivative financial instruments and guarantees, are currently reported at fair value.

The fair value of a liability is commonly said to be the amount at which that liability could be settled in a current transaction between willing parties, that is, other than in a forced or liquidation transaction. (The ambiguity of that definition is discussed in Section 1.3(b)(v).) Quoted market prices in active markets are the best evidence of fair value. Thus, if a quoted market price is available for an instrument, its fair value is the product of the number of trading units of the instrument times that market price. If an instrument trades in more than one market, the price in the most active market for that instrument should be used. If quoted market prices are not available, the estimate of fair value may be based on the best information available in the circumstances, including prices for similar liabilities and the results of using other valuation techniques such as the present value technique.

In February 2000, the FASB issued Concepts Statement No. 7, "Using Cash Flow Information and Present Value in Accounting Measurements". The Board introduced in that Concepts Statement the expected cash flow approach, which focuses on explicit assumptions about the range of possible estimated cash flows and their respective probabilities. That approach differs from the traditional approach to present value applications, which have typically used a single set of estimated cash flows and treated uncertainties implicitly in the selection of a single interest rate.

The Board also concluded in that Concepts Statement that, when using present value techniques to estimate the fair value of a liability, the objective is to estimate the value of the assets required currently to (1) settle the liability with the holder or (2) transfer the liability to an entity of comparable credit standing. In either case, the measurement should reflect the credit standing of the entity obligated to pay. Thus, an improvement in a debtor's credit standing would result in the debtor's reporting a greater liability in its statement of financial position, and deterioration in the debtor's credit standing would result in the debtor reporting a smaller liability. The income statement results of that treatment have been challenged.

FASB Concepts Statements do not establish standards prescribing accounting procedures or disclosure practices for particular items or events. They do, however, guide the Board in developing accounting and reporting standards and may provide some guidance in analyzing new or emerging problems of financial accounting and reporting in the absence of applicable authoritative pronouncements.

At the time of this writing, the FASB has on its agenda a project to provide guidance for measuring and reporting essentially all financial assets and liabilities at fair value in the financial statements.

(d) DISCLOSURES ABOUT FAIR VALUES OF FINANCIAL INSTRUMENTS.   FASB Statement No. 107, "Disclosures about Fair Values of Financial Instruments" (par. 3), defines a financial instrument as—

Cash, evidence of an ownership interest in an entity, or a contract that both:

a. Imposes on one entity a contractual obligation (1) to deliver cash or another financial instrument to a second entity or (2) to exchange other financial instruments on potentially unfavorable terms with the second entity.

b. Conveys to that second entity a contractual right (1) to receive cash or another financial instrument from the first entity or (2) to exchange other financial instruments on potentially favorable terms with the first entity.

Contractual obligations encompasses both those that are conditioned on the occurrence of a specified event and those that are not. All contractual obligations that are financial instruments meet the definition of a liability set forth in FASB Concepts Statement No. 6, "Elements of Financial Statements," although some may not be recognized as liabilities in financial statements, that is, they may be "off-balance sheet," because they fail to meet some other criterion for recognition. For some financial instruments, the obligation is owed to or by a group of entities rather than a single entity.

Examples of contractual obligations that are financial instruments include loans; bonds; notes payable; trade payables; deposit liabilities of banks; interest rate swaps; foreign currency contracts; put and call options on stock, foreign currency, or interest rate contracts; commitments to extend credit; and guarantees of the indebtedness of others, regardless of whether explicit consideration was received for the guarantees.

FASB Statement No. 107 requires disclosure, either in the body of the financial statements or in the accompanying notes, of (1) the fair value of financial instruments, regardless of whether recognized in the statement of financial position, for which it is practicable to estimate that value; and (2) the method(s) and significant assumptions used to estimate the fair value of financial instruments.

Practicable, in this context, means that an estimate of fair value can be made without incurring excessive costs.[1]

---

[1] Until recently, companies relied on the practicability proviso to avoid disclosure of the fair value of guarantees of the indebtedness of others. FASB Interpretation No. 45, "Guarantor's Accounting and Disclosure Requirements for Guarantees, Including Indirect Guarantees of Indebtedness of Others," however, contains no such proviso. See Subsection 25.8(k).

If it is not practicable to estimate the fair value of a financial instrument or a class of financial instrument, Statement No. 107 requires disclosure of the following:

- Information pertinent to estimating the fair value of that financial instrument or class of financial instruments, such as the carrying amount, effective interest rate, and maturity
- The reasons why it is not practicable to estimate fair value

Quoted market prices, if available, should be used to measure fair value. If quoted market prices are not available, management's best estimate of fair value may be based on the quoted market price of a financial instrument with similar characteristics or on valuation techniques (e.g., the present value of estimated cash flows using a discount rate commensurate with the risks involved, option pricing models, or matrix pricing models). In estimating the fair value of deposit liabilities, a financial entity should not take into account the value of core deposit intangibles. For deposit liabilities without defined maturities, the fair value to be disclosed is the amount payable on demand at the date of the financial statements.

The disclosures about fair value are not required for:

- Employers' and plans' obligations for pension benefits, other postretirement benefits including health care and life insurance benefits, employee stock option and stock purchase plans, and other forms of deferred compensation arrangements
- Substantively extinguished debt
- Insurance contracts other than financial guarantees and investment contracts
- Lease contracts
- Warranty obligations
- Unconditional purchase obligations

In addition, no disclosure is required for trade payables when their carrying amount approximates fair value.

25.2 INTEREST

There is a general presumption that, if a contractual obligation to pay money on a fixed or determinable date (referred to below for convenience as a *note*) was exchanged for property, goods, or services in a bargained transaction entered into at arm's length, the rate of interest stipulated by the parties to the transaction represents fair and adequate compensation to the supplier for the use of the money. That presumption does not apply, however, if:

- Interest is not stated.
- The stated interest rate is unreasonable.
- The stated face amount of the note is materially different from the current cash sales price for the same or similar items or from the market value of the note at the date of the transaction.

In those circumstances, APB Opinion No. 21, "Interest on Receivables and Payables," requires that the note, the sales price, and the cost of the property, goods, or services exchanged for the note be recorded at the fair value of the property, goods, or services or at an amount that reasonably approximates the market value of the note, whichever is more clearly determinable. Established exchange prices may be used to determine the fair value of the property, goods, or services exchanged for the note, or, when notes are traded in an open market, the market rate of interest and market value of the notes are evidence of fair value. In other circumstances, the present value of the note should be determined by discounting all future payments on the note using an imputed interest rate.

The interest rate should be selected by reference to interest rates on similar instruments of the same or comparable issuers, with similar maturities, security, and so on. APB Opinion No. 21 notes that the objective is "to approximate the rate that would have resulted if an independent lender had negotiated a similar transaction under comparable terms and conditions with the option to pay the cash price upon purchase or to give a note for the amount of purchase which bears the prevailing rate of interest to maturity." The difference between the amount at which the note is recorded and the face amount of the note is referred to as a *premium* or *discount*.

The premium or discount is amortized[2] as interest expense or income over the life of the note using the interest method, or capitalized in accordance with FASB Statement No. 34, "Capitalization of Interest Cost." The interest method allocates the premium or discount over the life of the note in such as way as to result in a constant rate of interest when applied to the amount outstanding at the beginning of any given period.[3] The interest method is discussed further in Section 25.5.

APB Opinion No. 21 does not apply to:

- Receivables and payables arising from transactions with customers or suppliers in the normal course of business that are due in customary trade terms not exceeding approximately one year
- Amounts that will be applied to the purchase price of the property, goods, or services involved, for example, deposits or progress payments on construction contracts, advance payments for acquisition of resources and raw materials, advances to encourage exploration in the extractive industries
- Amounts intended to provide security for one party to an agreement, for example, security deposits, retainages on contracts
- The customary cash lending activities and demand or savings deposit activities of financial institutions whose primary business is lending money
- Transactions where interest rates are affected by the tax attributes or legal restrictions prescribed by a governmental agency, for example, industrial revenue bonds, tax exempt obligations, government guaranteed obligations, or income tax settlements
- Transactions between a parent and its subsidiary or between subsidiaries of a common parent

25.3 CURRENT LIABILITIES

(a) NATURE OF CURRENT LIABILITIES. Accounting Research Bulletin (ARB) No. 43, "Restatement and Revision of Accounting Research Bulletins," Chapter 3, paragraph 7, as amended by FASB Statement No. 78, "Classification of Obligations That Are Callable by the Creditor," states, in part:

---

[2] Amortization of a discount is sometimes referred to as "accumulation" or "accretion" of the discount. Those usages are incorrect, because the balance of the discount is systematically being reduced, not increased. It is correct, however, to refer to "accretion" of the carrying amount of a loan.

[3] The interest method came over time to be widely accepted as the conceptually superior method of amortizing premiums or discounts. The superiority of the interest method was challenged by Leonard Lorenson in AICPA Accounting Research Monograph No. 4, "Accounting for Liabilities," published in 1992. The FASB acknowledged in Concepts Statement No. 7, "Using Cash Flow Information and Present Value in Accounting Measurements," that "no allocation method can be demonstrated to be superior to all others in all circumstances." The Board nevertheless maintains that the interest method is generally considered more relevant than other methods when applied to assets and liabilities that exhibit one or more of the following characteristics:

a. The transaction giving rise to the asset or liability is commonly viewed as a borrowing and lending.

b. Period-to-period allocation of similar assets or liabilities employs an interest method.

c. A particular set of estimated future cash flows is closely associated with the asset or liability.

d. The measurement at initial recognition was based on present value.

The term current liabilities is used principally to designate obligations whose liquidation is reasonably expected to require the use of existing resources properly classifiable as current assets, or the creation of other current liabilities. As a balance-sheet category, the classification is intended to include obligations for items which have entered into the operating cycle, such as payables incurred in the acquisition of materials and supplies to be used in the production of goods or in providing services to be offered for sale; collections received in advance of the delivery of goods or performance of services; and debts which arise from operations directly related to the operating cycle, such as accruals for wages, salaries, commissions, rentals, royalties, and income and other taxes. Other liabilities whose regular and ordinary liquidation is expected to occur within a relatively short period of time, usually twelve months, are also intended for inclusion ... The current liability classification is also intended to include obligations that, by their terms, are due on demand or will be due on demand within one year (or operating cycle, if longer) from the balance sheet date, even though liquidation may not be expected within that period. It is also intended to include long-term obligations that are or will be callable by the creditor either because the debtor's violation of a provision of the debt agreement at the balance sheet date makes the obligation callable or because the violation, if not cured within a specified grace period, will make the obligation callable.

Under FASB Statement No. 109, "Accounting for Income Taxes," deferred tax liabilities (i.e., the deferred tax consequences attributable to taxable temporary differences) are classified as current or noncurrent based on the classification of the related asset or liability for financial reporting. A deferred tax liability that is not related to an asset or liability, including deferred tax assets related to carryforwards, is classified according to the expected reversal date of the temporary difference.

A suggestion has been made to eliminate the classification of current liabilities (and current assets). See Loyd Heath, Accounting Research Monograph No. 3, "Financial Reporting and the Evaluation of Solvency," AICPA, 1978.

(i) Long-Term Obligations Approaching Maturity. If part of a long-term liability matures or otherwise becomes payable within one year after the balance sheet date, for example, serial maturities of long-term obligations and amounts required to be expended within one year under sinking fund provisions, that part of the liability should be classified as current.

(ii) Short-Term Obligations to Be Refinanced. Under FASB Statement No. 6, "Classification of Short-Term Obligations Expected to Be Refinanced," short-term obligations other than obligations arising from transactions in the normal course of business that are due in customary terms are classified as noncurrent if:

- The enterprise intends to refinance the obligations on a long-term basis.
- The intent to refinance on a long-term basis is evidenced either by (a) an actual post-balance-sheet-date issuance of long-term debt or equity securities or (b) the enterprise having entered into a firm agreement, before the balance sheet is issued, to make an appropriate refinancing.

If short-term obligations are excluded from current liabilities pursuant to Statement No. 6, the financial statements should disclose:

- A general description of the financing arrangement
- Terms of any new obligation incurred or expected to be incurred, or equity securities issued or expected to be issued, as a result of the refinancing

Obligations that do not qualify for exclusion from current liabilities based on expected refinancing include obligations for items that have entered into the operating cycle, such as payables incurred in the acquisition of materials and supplies to be used in the production of goods or in providing services to be offered for sale; collections received in advance of the delivery of goods or performance of services; and debts that arise from operations directly related to the operating cycle, such as accruals for wages, salaries, commissions, rentals, royalties, and income and other taxes.

FASB Interpretation No. 8, "Classification of a Short-Term Obligation Repaid Prior to Being Replaced by a Long-Term Security," clarified that, if a short-term obligation is repaid after the balance sheet date and subsequently a long-term obligation or equity securities are issued whose proceeds are used to replenish current assets before the balance sheet is issued, the short-term obligation may not be excluded from current liabilities at the balance sheet date.

(iii) Classification of Obligations Callable by the Creditor.   FASB Statement No. 78, "Classification of Obligations That Are Callable by the Creditor," states that current liability classification includes obligations that are due on demand or that will be due on demand within one year (or operating cycle, if longer) from the balance sheet date, even though liquidation may not be expected within that period.

Current classification also applies to long-term obligations that are or could become callable by the creditor either because the debtor's violation of a provision of the debt agreement at the balance sheet date makes the obligation callable or because the violation, if not cured within a grace period, will make the obligation callable. However, long-term classification is appropriate if the creditor has waived or subsequently lost the right to demand repayment for more than a year, or if it is probable that the violation will be cured within a grace period. In the latter case disclosure is required of the circumstances.

(iv) Demand Notes.   Loan agreements may specify the debtor's repayment terms but may also enable the creditor, at his discretion, to demand payment at any time. The loan arrangement may have wording such as "the term *note* shall mature in monthly installments as set forth therein or on demand, whichever is earlier," or "principal and interest shall be due on demand, or if no demand is made, in quarterly installments beginning on ..." The Emerging Issues Task Force (EITF) in Issue No. 86-5 concluded that such an obligation should be considered a current liability in accordance with FASB Statement No. 78. Further, under FASB Technical Bulletin No. 79-3, "Subjective Acceleration Clauses in Long-Term Debt Agreements," the demand provision is not a subjective acceleration clause as discussed below.

(v) Subjective Acceleration Clause in Long-Term Debt Agreements.   FASB Statement No. 6 defines a subjective acceleration clause contained in a financing agreement as one that would allow the cancellation of an agreement for the violation of a provision that can be evaluated differently by the parties. The inclusion of such a clause in an agreement that would otherwise permit a short-term obligation to be refinanced on a long-term basis would preclude that short-term obligation from being classified as long term. However, Statement No. 6 does not address financing agreements related to long-term obligations. Under FASB Technical Bulletin No. 79-3, the treatment of long-term debt with a subjective acceleration clause would vary depending on the circumstances. In some situations, only disclosure of the existing clause would be required. Neither reclassification nor disclosure would be required if the likelihood of the acceleration of the due date were remote, such as when the lender historically has not accelerated due dates in similar cases, and the borrower's financial condition is strong and its prospects are good.

(b) KINDS OF CURRENT LIABILITY.   Common kinds of current liability include:

- Accounts payable and accrued expenses
- Short-term notes payable
- Dividends payable
- Deferred income or revenue
- Advances and deposits
- Withheld amounts
- Estimated liabilities

Accounts payable includes all trade payable arising from purchases of merchandise or services. In published balance sheets this classification normally also includes the liability related to non-financial expenses that are incurred continuously, that is, estimated amounts payable for wages and salaries, rent, and royalties. Accrued interest and taxes are also normally included under this caption. Federal income taxes payable are frequently shown separately. The traditional distinction between accounts payable and accrued expenses has tended to disappear, and the common practice today is to include the two items in one heading.

In most cases, notes payable, if shown as a separate category, refers to a definite borrowing of funds, as distinguished from goods purchased through the use of trade acceptances. In this latter case, relatively rare today, notes payable may be presented as part of accounts payable. Dividends payable, the liability to shareholders representing dividend declarations, has traditionally been viewed as a distinct kind of obligation. Deferred revenues appear when collection is made in whole or part prior to the actual furnishing of goods or services. A common example is found in the insurance industry, where premiums are regularly collected in advance. Tickets, service contracts, and subscriptions are other deferred revenue items.

Advances and deposits required to guarantee performance and returnable to the depositor are current liabilities. The returnable containers used in many industries are sometimes included in this category. Withheld amounts, also referred to as *agency obligations*, result from the collection or acceptance of cash or other assets for the account of a third party. By far the most common items today are federal, state, and local income taxes and payroll taxes withheld from wages.

Estimated liabilities refer to obligations whose amount may be uncertain but the existence of which is unquestioned. Examples include product and service guarantees and warranties.

(c) ACCOUNTS PAYABLE: TRADE.   In some cases, the term *accounts payable* is restricted to trade creditors' accounts, represented by unpaid invoices for the purchase of merchandise or supplies. In other cases, "accounts payable" includes all unpaid invoices, regardless of their nature. In the accounting system, of course, accounts payable will normally be limited to those transactions for which the company has received an invoice. As stated previously, for financial statement presentation purposes, it is common to include "accrued expenses" in the same balance sheet caption.

Accounts payable may be recorded at gross invoice price (i.e., without deducting discounts offered for prompt payment), or they may be shown net. Although it has been argued that the latter treatment is conceptually superior regardless of the circumstances, in practice receivables tend to be recorded gross. Accounts payable should be recorded net, however, if it is customary in an industry to permit customers to take the discount regardless of when the invoice is paid. If the discount is always allowed, it amounts to a purchase price reduction and should be accounted for as such. If it is allowed only within the discount period, it appears to be more in the nature of a financial item.

The practical difficulties of apportioning small discounts to a series of items on one invoice lead most companies to account for discounts separately from the purchase price of merchandise. Inventory is recorded at the gross price, and the credit balances resulting from the discount are normally netted against the total year's purchases. In principle, year-end adjustments should be made for that portion of the purchases that remains in inventory, but in practice that is rarely done.

Some companies consider that the rate of interest implicit in the usual trade discount is so large that substantial efforts should be devoted to assuring that it is not lost. If conditions preclude the taking of the discount, the difference between the gross price actually paid and the net price that would have been paid may be accounted for as "discount lost." The balance of this account may be interpreted as a financial expense or as evidence of inefficiency in the accounts payable operation.

(d) NOTES PAYABLE: BANK.   Bank loans evidenced by secured or unsecured notes payable to commercial banks are a common method of short-term financing. Ordinarily the notes are interest bearing, and in such cases the amount borrowed and the liability to be recorded is the face amount of the note.

In some instances, however, non-interest-bearing or "discount" paper is issued. In such transactions, the bank deducts the interest in advance from the amount given to the borrower, who subsequently repays the full amount of the note.

Assume, for example, that the X Company gives the bank a $1,000 non-interest-bearing 2-month note on a 12 percent basis. The customary entry to record the borrowing is as follows:

Cash	$980	
Prepaid interest	20	
Notes payable—bank		$1,000

Reporting of the discount as "prepaid interest" has been objected to on the ground that the company has borrowed only $980 and that, therefore, the $20 asset is in no way a prepaid item. Essentially the same problem arises on a long-term basis when bonds are issued at a discount. This matter is discussed in Subsection 25.4(f).

In some cases bank loans or notes are taken for short periods, but with the intent on the part of both borrower and lender that the note will be continuously refinanced. See "Current and Long-Term Liabilities" for a discussion of short-term obligations expected to be refinanced.

(e) NOTES PAYABLE: TRADE AND OTHERS.   Short-term notes payable often arise directly or indirectly from purchases of merchandise, materials, or equipment. If such notes arise directly from purchases, they may be classified in the financial statements with accounts payable. If, however, the notes arise indirectly, or have substantially different payment dates from the usual trade payables, they should be shown separately.

(f) ACCRUED EXPENSES.   An accounts payable figure can be determined at the balance sheet date from the control account, even though it is normally necessary to review all invoices paid for a reasonable period subsequent to the balance sheet date (search for unrecorded liabilities) to assure that all amounts actually payable at the balance sheet date are properly recorded. In contrast, although some part of the balance of accrued expenses may be determined from recurring expense accruals, in general it is necessary to make a thorough review of all the company's relevant expense accounts—rent, salaries, and so on—to determine the appropriate amount at year end. Thus accrued liabilities (expenses) arise principally only when financial statements are prepared. When preparing the accruals for the different expenses, it is well to keep in mind a sense of balance between the possibility of producing financial statements with every conceivable accrual determined precisely and the added economic value of that precision. In many cases the amount of extra work necessary to estimate certain accruals with extreme accuracy may not be justified by their value to a user of the financial statements. For such immaterial items, relatively rough estimates may suffice.

(i) Interest Payable.   Outside of financial institutions, it is usually not deemed necessary to accrue interest liabilities from day to day, but it is essential that such liabilities be fully recognized at the close of each period. Accrued interest must be calculated in terms of the various outstanding obligations that bear interest such as accounts, notes, bonds, and capitalized leases.

(ii) Accrued Payrolls.   Full recognition of the liability for wages and salaries earned, but not paid, should be made at the close of each accounting period. Accruals should include not only hourly wages and salaries up to the close of business on the last day of the period, but also estimates of bonuses accrued, commissions earned, employer share of Social Security, and so on.

The liability for unclaimed wages is a related item usually of minimal size but of some legal significance. Payroll checks that have been outstanding for a period should be restored to the bank account and credited to unclaimed wages. In many states the amount of unclaimed wages escheats to the state after a number of years and therefore should be carefully accounted for until such payment is made. In other states the balance of unclaimed wages should be credited to income after a reasonable period.

(iii) Vacation Pay.   Prior to FASB Statement No. 43, "Accounting for Compensated Absences," practice related to accruing for vacation pay varied. Most companies did not make such accruals, but a minority did. The prevalent practice was to record compensation for vacation pay as paid. Statement No. 43 requires an employer to accrue a liability for employees' right to receive compensation for future absences if all of the following conditions are met:

- The employer's obligation relating to employees' rights to receive compensation for future absences is attributable to services already rendered.
- The obligation relates to rights that vest or accumulate. "Accumulate" means that earned but unused rights to compensated absences may be carried forward to one or more periods subsequent to that in which they are earned, even though there may be a limit to the amount that may be carried forward.
- Payment of the compensation is probable.
- The amount can be reasonably estimated.

If the first three conditions are met but the employer does not accrue the cost because of an inability to reasonably estimate the amount, that fact must be disclosed.

(iv) Commissions and Fees.   All liabilities for commissions, fees, and similar items should be accrued whenever financial statements are prepared. The principal problem is the determination of the precise amount to be accrued as of a given date. In the case of salespeople's commissions, which are in no sense contingent or conditional, if all sales have been recorded, the precise amount usually is readily determinable. However, commissions are subject to reduction in the event of cancellation of sales, uncollectibility, or other contingencies, it is not possible to make an exact determination of the liability. In such circumstances, a reasonable estimate should be made, taking into consideration the maximum liability based on performance to date, reduced by the expected amount of adjustments due to cancellations and similar contingencies.

In the case of professional services, such as those furnished by accountants and lawyers, the client often finds it difficult to determine the amount due or earned as of a given date. If billing from accountants or lawyers is based on hourly or per diem rates, a statement to date can be obtained and no difficulty is involved in setting up the proper liability. If, however, the engagement has been undertaken for a lump sum, or if the fee will not be determined until the outcome is known, as is common in legal services, the accrual may be very difficult to estimate. If no reasonable estimate can be made, and the amount may be material, the matter should be disclosed in the notes to the financial statements.

(v) Federal Income Taxes.   The determination of the precise liability for federal corporate income taxes is a complex process. In the rush accompanying preparation of year-end financial statements and annual reports, it is not uncommon to obtain an automatic extension for the filing of a tax return (Form 4868) and to delay the preparation of the return, hence determination of the precise tax liability, until after the financial statements have been prepared. It is necessary, under such circumstances, to make an estimate of the income taxes payable and to record that estimate as a liability in the financial statements.

In some instances, there may be income tax items for which the appropriate tax treatment is unclear. Attitudes toward the treatment of such items vary, but many companies will tend to resolve them in their own favor and await possible disallowance by Internal Revenue Service (IRS) examining agents. The calculation of current and deferred taxes for financial reporting purposes should be based on the probable tax treatment.[4] In addition, interest may need to be accrued for expected adjustments by the taxing authorities.

---

[4] On July 14, 2005, the FASB issued a proposed Interpretation, "Accounting for Uncertain Tax Positions—An Interpretation of FASB Statement No. 109." Readers should be alert to any final pronouncement.

If the estimate of the tax liability proves to be reasonably accurate, small corrections are usually adjusted to the expense account in the following period.

The determination of the federal income tax liability in interim statements is a more difficult problem, as it requires an estimate of the year's tax burden. For a complete discussion of treatment of tax provisions in interim statements, see Chapter 15.

(vi) Property Taxes.   Tax laws, income tax regulations, and court decisions have mentioned various dates on which property taxes may be said to accrue legally. Such dates include assessment date, date on which tax becomes a lien on the property, and date or dates tax is payable, among others. The IRS holds that property taxes accrue on the assessment date, even if the amount of tax is not determined until later.

The legal liability for property taxes must be considered when title to property is transferred at some point during the taxable year in order to determine whether buyer or seller is liable for the taxes and to adjust the purchase price accordingly. For normal accounting purposes, however, the legal liability concept is held to be secondary to the general consideration that property taxes arise ratably over time. The AICPA (ARB No. 43) states the following:

> Generally, the most acceptable basis of providing for property taxes is monthly accrual on the taxpayer's books during the fiscal period of the taxing authority for which the taxes are levied. The books will then show, at any closing date, the appropriate accrual or prepayment. . . .

> An accrued liability for real or personal property taxes, whether estimated or definitely known, should be included among current liabilities. . . .

(vii) Rent Liabilities.   If property is held under a lease agreement with cash rents payable currently to the lessor and the lease is classified as an operating lease under FASB Statement No. 13, rent should be accrued ratably with occupancy as an expense and any unpaid portions shown as current liabilities. For treatment of other lease liabilities, see Chapter 23.

Rent advanced by a tenant represents deferred revenue on the books of the lessor and should also be classed as a liability. Generally, tenants' deposits and sureties should be recorded as separate items. In some jurisdictions, interest must be paid on tenants' deposits and should be accrued.

(g) ADVANCES FROM OFFICERS AND EMPLOYEES.   Advances from officers and employees are related-party transactions that may require disclosure in accordance with FASB Statement No. 57, "Related Party Disclosures," and, for Securities and Exchange Commission (SEC) registrants, Regulations S-X and S-K. Related-party disclosures are not required, however, for compensation arrangements, expense allowances, and other similar items in the ordinary course of business. The requirements for disclosure of related-party transactions are discussed in Subsection 25.8(a).

(h) DIVIDENDS PAYABLE.   The amount of cash dividends declared, but unpaid, is commonly treated as a current liability in balance sheets. See Chapter 27 for a discussion of the nature and treatment of dividends.

Stock dividends declared, constituting only a rearrangement of the equity accounts, are not recorded as a liability.

(i) Deferred Revenue.   Advances by customers or clients that are to be satisfied by the future delivery of goods or performance of services are liabilities and should be shown as such. These items are often labeled "deferred revenue" or "deferred credits." It is better disclosure to provide a title that clearly describes the nature of the item, such as "advances from customers." Commonly such accounts are payable in goods or services rather than in cash, and as a rule a margin of profit will emerge in making such payment. For a discussion of timing of the recognition of income associated with this type of transaction, see Chapter 19, "Revenues and Receivables."

(i) CONTINGENCIES. In Statement No. 5, "Accounting for Contingencies" (par. 1), the FASB defines a contingency as:

> [A]n existing condition, situation, or set of circumstances involving uncertainty as to possible gain or loss to an enterprise that will ultimately be resolved when one or more future events occur or fail to occur. Resolution of the uncertainty may confirm the acquisition of an asset or the reduction of a liability or the loss or impairment of an asset or the incurrence of a liability.

Not all the uncertainties inherent in the accounting process result in the type of contingencies foreseen by Statement No. 5. Estimates, such as those required in the determination of useful lives, do not make depreciation a contingency. Similarly, a requirement that the amount of a liability be estimated does not produce a contingency as long as there is no uncertainty that the obligation has been incurred. Thus amounts owed for services received, such as advertising and utilities, are not contingencies, although the amounts actually owed may have to be estimated at the time financial statements must be prepared.

(i) Likelihood of Contingencies. In Statement No. 5, the FASB indicates that the likelihood of contingencies occurring may vary and stipulates different accounting depending on that likelihood. The standard (par. 3) suggests three possibilities:

1. *Probable*. The future event or events are likely to occur.
2. *Reasonably Possible*. The chance of the future event or events occurring is more than remote but less than likely.
3. *Remote*. The chance of the event or future events occurring is slight.

(ii) Examples of Loss Contingencies. Among the kinds of loss contingency suggested by Statement No. 5 are the following:

- Collectibility of receivables
- Obligations related to product warranties and product defects
- Risk of loss or damage of enterprise property by fire, explosion, or other hazards
- Threat of expropriation
- Pending or threatened litigation
- Actual or possible claims or assessments
- Risk of loss from catastrophes assumed by property and casualty insurance companies.
- Guarantees of indebtedness of others
- Obligations of commercial banks under "standby letters of credit"
- Agreements to repurchase receivables (or to repurchase the related property) that have been sold

Some of those contingencies involve impairment of an asset rather than the incurrence of a liability.

Contingencies may involve either short-term obligations or long-term obligations, or both. Contingent liabilities are addressed in this section without regard to when they are expected to be settled.

(iii) Accrual of Loss Contingencies. In Statement No. 5, the FASB requires that an estimated loss from a loss contingency be accrued by a charge to income if both of the following two conditions are met:

1. Information available prior to the issuance of the financial statements indicates that it is probable that an asset had been impaired or a liability had been incurred at the date of the

financial statements. This condition implies that it must be probable that one or more future events will occur confirming the fact of the loss.

2. The amount of loss can be reasonably estimated.

Items become liabilities of an entity only as a result of transactions or other events or circumstances that have already occurred.

(iv) Estimating Amounts to Be Accrued.   As noted immediately above, Statement No. 5 requires that an estimated loss be accrued when it appears that a liability has been incurred and the amount of the loss can be reasonably estimated.

The term *reasonably estimated* is susceptible to interpretation. In many cases, particularly with litigation and claims, estimates of the amount of the loss may be difficult. Although Statement No. 5 does not define "reasonably estimated" specifically, FASB Interpretation No. 14, "Reasonable Estimation of the Amount of a Loss," attempts to define the term more clearly.

If a reasonable estimate of the loss is a range, Interpretation No. 14 indicates that the "reasonably estimated" criterion is satisfied. If no value in the range is more likely than any other, the minimum amount should be accrued. Thus if the loss from a contingency is probable and will be within a range of $4 million to $6 million, and there is no better estimate within that range, $4 million should be accrued. On the other hand, if within the $4 million to $6 million range, $5.5 million is the most likely outcome, that latter amount should be accrued.

(v) Disclosure of Loss Contingencies.   FASB Statement No. 5 states that disclosure of the nature of an accrual made pursuant to its provisions, and in some circumstances the amount accrued, may be necessary for the financial statements to be not misleading.

In many circumstances a loss contingency exists but does not satisfy the two conditions calling for accrual, or exposure to loss exists in excess of the amount accrued. In such cases, Statement No. 5 requires disclosure of the loss contingency. Disclosure is required when there is at least a reasonable possibility that a loss or additional loss may have occurred. The disclosure should indicate the nature of the contingency and should give an estimate of the possible loss or range of loss or state that such an estimate cannot be made.

FASB Statement No. 5 also requires disclosure of guarantees such as (1) guarantees of the indebtedness of others, (2) obligations of commercial banks under "standby letters of credit," and (3) guarantees to repurchase receivables (or, in some cases, to repurchase the related property) that have been sold or otherwise assigned, even though the possibility of loss may be remote. The requirement also applies to other contingencies that in substance have the characteristic of a guarantee. The disclosure must include the nature and amount of the guarantee. Consideration should also be given to disclosing, if estimable, the value of any recovery that could be expected to result, for example, from the guarantor's right to proceed against an outside party.

FASB Interpretation No. 45, "Guarantor's Accounting and Disclosure Requirements for Guarantees, Including Indirect Guarantees of Indebtedness of Others," discussed in Subsection 25.8(k), provides further guidance on accounting for and disclosure of guarantee obligations.

SEC Codification of Financial Reporting Policies Sec. 104 points out that oral guarantees, even if legally unenforceable, may have the same financial reporting significance as written guarantees.

In accordance with APB Opinion No. 28, "Interim Financial Reporting," contingencies and other uncertainties that could be expected to affect the fairness of presentation of financial data at an interim date should be disclosed in interim reports in the same manner required for annual reports. Such disclosures should be repeated in interim and annual reports until the contingencies have been removed, resolved, or become immaterial.

Financial statements sometimes contain a contingency conclusion that addresses the estimated total unrecognized exposure to one or more loss contingencies. It may state, for example, that "management believes that the outcome of these uncertainties should not have (or 'may have') a material adverse effect on the financial condition, cash flows, or operating results of the enterprise." Alternatively, the disclosure may indicate that the adverse effect could be material to a particular financial statement or to results and cash flows of a quarterly or annual reporting period. AICPA Statement of Position (SOP) 96-1, "Environmental Remediation Liabilities," states the following about contingency conclusions:

> Although potentially useful information, these conclusions are not a substitute for the required disclosures of ... FASB Statement No. 5, such as [its] requirement to disclose the amounts of material reasonably possible additional losses or to state that such an estimate cannot be made. Also, the assertion that the outcome should not have a material adverse effect must be supportable. If an entity is unable to estimate the maximum end of the range of possible outcomes, it may be difficult to support an assertion that the outcome should not have a material adverse effect.

AICPA SOP 94-6, "Disclosure of Certain Significant Risks and Uncertainties," requires disclosure about significant estimates used to determine the carrying amounts of assets or liabilities and the disclosure of gain or loss contingencies if (1) it is at least reasonably possible that the estimate of the effect on the financial statements of a set of circumstances that existed at the financial statement date will change in the near term due to one or more future confirming events and (2) the effect of the change would be material. *Near term* is a period not to exceed one year from the date of the financial statements. Disclosure requirements include the nature of the uncertainty and an indication that it is at least reasonably possible that a material change will occur in the near term. Disclosure of factors causing the uncertainty is encouraged but not required. If an uncertainty is a loss contingency under Statement No. 5, disclosure must also provide an estimate of the possible loss or range of loss. If the SOP's disclosure criteria are not met as a result of the use of risk-reduction techniques, the disclosures that would otherwise be required by the SOP and disclosure of the risk-reduction techniques are encouraged but not required.

Examples of estimates subject to change in the near term include litigation-related obligations, contingent liabilities for guarantees of other entities, and amounts reported for pensions and other benefits.

(vi) Uninsured Risks.   Enterprises may decide to insure against certain risks by specifically obtaining coverage. In other cases risks may be borne by the company either through use of deductible clauses in insurance contracts or by not purchasing insurance at all. Insurance policies purchased from a subsidiary or investee, to the extent that policies have not been reinsured with an independent insurer, are considered not to constitute insurance. Some risks, such as a decline in business, may not be insurable.

FASB Statement No. 5 states that the absence of insurance does not mean that an asset has been impaired or that a liability has been incurred at the date of the enterprise's financial statements. Therefore, exposure to uninsured risks does not constitute a contingency requiring either disclosure or accrual. However, Statement No. 5 does not discourage disclosure of noninsurance or underinsurance in appropriate circumstances, and such disclosure may be necessary, for example, because the noninsurance or underinsurance violates a debt covenant.

If an event has occurred, such as an accident, for which the enterprise is not insured and for which some liability is suggested, the proper accounting or disclosure of that event must be considered within the framework of the standard.

(vii) Litigation, Claims, and Assessments.   Accounting for and disclosure of litigation, claims, and assessments, either actual or possible, often presents problems. Those problems may involve the probability of payment, estimates of amounts, and, in a particularly sensitive area, the reluctance of companies to disclose information that may be actually or potentially adverse. Full disclosure or the accrual of a loss contingency, when litigation is threatening or pending, may well be seized on by the opposing party as evidence to support its case.

FASB Statement No. 5 does not exempt from its accounting or disclosure provisions entities that believe complying with those provisions could damage their position in litigation. If the underlying cause of the litigation, claim, or assessment is an event occurring before the date of the financial statements, the probability of an unfavorable outcome must be assessed to determine whether it is probable a liability has been incurred. Among the factors that should be considered are the nature of the litigation, claim, or assessment, the progress of the case (including progress after the date of the financial statements but before those statements are issued), the opinions or views of legal counsel and other advisers, the company's experience in similar cases, the experience of other companies in similar cases, and any decision of the company's management as to how the company intends to respond to the lawsuit, claim, or assessment (e.g., a decision to contest the case vigorously or a decision to seek an out-of-court settlement). The fact that legal counsel is unable to express an opinion that the outcome will be favorable should not necessarily be interpreted to mean that a loss is probable.

Among the most difficult issues to resolve is that of unasserted claims. An unasserted claim exists, for example, when the company knows that an event such as a product failure has occurred, but no actions have yet been brought against the company. It is conceivable that disclosure of the event, along with a discussion indicating the possibility of claims being asserted, could trigger litigation adverse to the company that might not have been brought in the absence of the company's own disclosure. FASB Statement No. 5 states that a judgment must first be made as to whether the assertion of a claim is probable. If the judgment is that assertion is not probable, no accrual or disclosure would be required. If, however, the judgment is that assertion is probable, a second judgment must be made as to the degree of probability of an unfavorable outcome.

For both asserted and unasserted litigation, claims, and assessments, if an unfavorable outcome is determined to be probable and the amount of loss is reasonably estimable, the loss should be accrued. If an unfavorable outcome is determined to be reasonably possible but not probable, or if the amount of loss cannot be reasonably estimated, a loss should not be accrued, but the disclosures required for other contingencies would be required.

Caution should be used in disclosing "contingency conclusions" (discussed in Section 25.3(j)(v)). In at least one case, a disclosure to the effect that the outcome of litigation should not have a material adverse effect on the financial condition, cash flows, or operating results of the enterprise was the basis for the awarding by a jury of punitive damages well in excess of those originally sought in a lawsuit.

(viii) General Reserves for Contingencies Not Permitted.   In the past, some companies have provided, sometimes through income, reserves for general contingencies. In other cases, such reserves have been established as appropriations of retained earnings. FASB Statement No. 5 does not permit such general contingency reserves to be charged to income. Appropriation of retained earnings is not prohibited provided that it is shown within the stockholders' equity section of the balance sheet and is clearly identified as an appropriation of retained earnings.

(ix) Warranty Obligations.   The obligation to satisfy a product warranty, incurred in connection with the sale of goods or services, is a loss contingency of the kind that requires accrual under FASB Statement No. 5. That is, future obligations under warranties should be estimated and provided for. Such estimates may be difficult, particularly if new products or changed warranty terms are involved. Still, an effort should be made to determine the liability. If necessary, reference may be made to the experiences of other companies.

If there is inadequate information to permit a reasonable estimate of the obligation for warranties, the propriety of recording a sale of the goods until the warranty period has expired should be questioned.

(x) Accounting for Environmental Liabilities.   SOP 96-1, "Environmental Remediation Liabilities," provides accounting guidance on environmental remediation liabilities that relate to pollution arising from some past act. The SOP states that such liabilities should be accrued when the criteria of FASB Statement No. 5 are met, and it includes benchmarks to aid in determining when environmental liabilities should be recognized.

The SOP establishes a presumption that, given the legal framework within which most environmental remediation liabilities arise, (1) if litigation has commenced or a claim or assessment has been asserted or if commencement of litigation or assertion of a claim or assessment is probable and (2) if the company is associated with the site—that is, if it in fact arranged for the disposal of hazardous substances found at a site or transported hazardous substances to the site or is the current or previous owner or operator of the site—the outcome of such litigation, claim, or assessment will be unfavorable.

The estimate of the liability should include (1) the entity's allocable share of the liability for a specific site and (2) the entity's share of amounts related to the site that will not be paid by other potentially responsible parties or the government.

Costs to be included in the measurement of the liability include:

- Incremental direct costs of the remediation effort
- Costs of compensation and benefits for those employees who are expected to devote a significant amount of time directly to the remediation effort, to the extent of that amount of time

The measurement of the liability should be based on enacted laws and existing regulations and policies—no changes in regulations or policies should be anticipated. The measurement of the liability should be based on the reporting entity's estimate of what it will cost to perform all elements of the remediation effort when they are expected to be performed, using remediation technology that is expected to be approved to complete the remediation effort. The measurement of the liability, or of a component of the liability, may be discounted to reflect the time value of money if the aggregate amount of the liability or component of the liability and the amount and timing of cash payments for the liability or component are fixed or reliably determinable.

The SOP provides financial statement display guidance and encourages, but does not require, a number of disclosures that are incremental to the FASB Statement No. 5 and SOP 94-6 requirements.

For SEC registrants, SEC Staff Accounting Bulletin (SAB) No. 92, "Accounting and Disclosures Relating to Loss Contingencies," provides additional accounting, display, and disclosure guidance concerning environmental liabilities. SAB No. 92 also states that the staff would not object to a registrant accruing site restoration, postclosure and monitoring, or other environmental exit costs that are expected to be incurred if that is established accounting practice in the registrant's industry. In other industries, the staff would raise no objection provided that the liability is probable and reasonably estimable. If the use of an asset in operations gives rise to growing exit costs that represent a probable liability, the accrual of the liability should be recognized as an expense in accordance with the consensus in EITF Issue No. 90-8, "Capitalization of Costs to Treat Environmental Contamination."

(xi) Vulnerability from Concentrations.   Vulnerability due to concentrations arises because of exposure to risk of loss greater than an enterprise would have had if it mitigated its risk through diversification. Although an exposure to risk from a concentration is not the same as a liability, the subject is included in this chapter because it tends to be associated with the subject of liabilities.

SOP 94-6 requires disclosure of the following kinds of concentrations:

- Concentrations in volume of business with a particular customer, supplier, lender, grantor, or contributor
- Concentrations in revenue from particular products, services, or fund-raising events
- Concentrations in available sources of supply of materials, labor or services, or licenses or other rights used in operations
- Concentrations in the market or geographic area in which the entity operates

Disclosure is required if all of the following conditions are met:

- The concentration exists at the balance sheet date.
- The enterprise is vulnerable to a near-term severe impact as a result of the concentration.

- It is at least reasonably possible that the events that could cause the severe impact will occur in the near term.

Severe impact, which is defined as a significant financially disruptive effect on the normal functioning of the entity, is a higher threshold than material, but the concept includes matters that are less than catastrophic, such as those that would result in bankruptcy.

The disclosure requirements also apply to group concentrations, which may arise if a number of counterparties or items have similar economic characteristics.

Although other kinds of concentrations may create equal, or even greater, vulnerability, they are not covered by the SOP for practical reasons. For example, a business's dependence on key management personnel might make it vulnerable to a severe impact in the event of the loss of those persons' services. However, a requirement to disclose that the occurrence of an adverse effect of that vulnerability is reasonably possible in the near term might violate accepted rights to privacy, for example, by causing information about an individual's health or marital problems to be revealed, and place an unreasonable burden on the accountant to know that information.

Disclosure should include information that is adequate to inform users of the general nature of the risk associated with the concentration. For labor subject to collective bargaining agreements meeting the disclosure requirements, the notes should include the percent of the labor force covered by collective bargaining agreements and the percent of the labor force covered by agreements that will expire within one year. For operations outside the home country, the disclosures should include the carrying amount of net assets and geographical areas in which the assets are located.

(j) EXIT OR DISPOSAL ACTIVITY OBLIGATIONS. An entity's commitment to a plan to exit an activity, by itself, does not create a present obligation to others that meets the definition of a liability. FASB Statement No. 146, "Accounting for Exit or Disposal Activities," requires recognition of a liability for costs associated with an exit or disposal activity when a liability has been incurred, and points out that a liability is not incurred until a transaction or event occurs that leaves an entity with little or no discretion to avoid the future transfer or use of assets to settle the liability.

(i) One-Time Termination Benefits. Under FASB Statement No. 146, a one-time benefit arrangement exists at the date the plan of termination meets all of the following criteria and has been communicated to employees:

- Management, having the relevant authority to approve the action, commits to a plan of termination.
- The plan identifies the number of employees to be terminated, their job classifications or functions and their locations, and the expected completion date.
- The plan establishes the terms of the benefit arrangement, including the benefits that employees will receive upon termination, in sufficient detail to enable employees to determine the kind and amount of benefits they will receive if they are involuntarily terminated.
- Actions required to complete the plan indicate that it is unlikely that significant changes to the plan will be made or that the plan will be withdrawn.

The timing of recognition of and measurement of a liability for one-time termination benefits depends on whether employees are required to render service until they are terminated in order to receive the termination benefits and, if so, whether they will be retained beyond the minimum retention period. If employees are not required to render service until they are terminated (i.e., if employees are entitled to receive the termination benefits regardless of when they leave) or if they will not be retained to render service beyond the minimum retention period, a liability is recognized and measured at fair value at the date the plan of termination has been communicated to the employees (referred to as the *communication date*).

If employees are required to render service until they are terminated in order to receive termination benefits and will be retained to render service beyond the minimum retention period, a liability for termination benefits is measured initially at the communication date based on the fair value of the liability as of the termination date. The liability should be recognized ratably over the future service period. Any change resulting from a revision to either the timing or the amount of estimated cash flows over the future service period should be measured using the credit-adjusted risk-free rate that was used to measure the liability initially, and the cumulative effect of the change should be recognized as an adjustment to the liability in the period of the change.

If a plan of termination changes and employees who were expected to be terminated within the minimum retention period are retained beyond that period, a liability previously recognized at the communication date should be adjusted to the amount that would have been recognized had the employees originally been expected to render service beyond the minimum retention period. The cumulative effect of the change should be recognized as an adjustment of the liability in the period of the change.

If a plan of termination includes both involuntary termination benefits and termination benefits offered for a short period in exchange for employees' voluntary termination of service, a liability for the involuntary termination benefits should be recognized in accordance with Statement No. 146 and a liability for the excess of the voluntary termination benefit amount over the involuntary termination benefit amount should be recognized in accordance with FASB Statement No. 88, "Employers' Accounting for Settlements and Curtailments of Defined Benefit Pension Plans and for Termination Benefits."

(ii) Contract Termination Costs.   A liability for costs to terminate, in connection with an exit activity, an operating lease or other contract before the end of its term should be recognized and measured at its fair value when the entity terminates the contract in accordance with the contract terms (e.g., by giving written notice or otherwise negotiating a termination with the lessor). No liability for contract termination costs may be recognized solely because of an entity's commitment to an exit or disposal plan. The termination of a capital lease should be accounted for in accordance with FASB Statement No. 13, "Accounting for Leases."

A liability for costs that will continue to be incurred under a contract for its remaining term without economic benefit should be recognized and measured at its fair value when the entity ceases using the right conveyed by the contract (referred to as the *cease-use date*). If the contract is an operating lease, the fair value of the liability at the cease-use date is determined based on the remaining lease rentals, reduced by estimated sublease rentals that could reasonably be obtained for the property, even if the entity does not intend to sublease. Remaining rentals may not be an amount less than zero.

(iii) Other Associated Costs.   A liability for other costs associated with an exit or disposal activity, such as costs to consolidate or close facilities and relocate employees, should be recognized and measured at its fair value in the period in which the liability is incurred, which is generally when goods or services associated with the activity are received. No liability should be recognized before it is incurred, even if the costs are incremental to other operating costs and will be incurred as a direct result of a plan.

(iv) Financial Statement Presentation.   Costs associated with an exit or disposal activity should be included either in income from continuing operations before income taxes or in results of discontinued operations, depending on whether the exit or disposal activity involves a discontinued operation. If an exit or disposal activity does not involve a discontinued operation, the costs may not be presented in the income statement net of taxes or in any manner that implies they are similar to an extraordinary item.

If an entity's responsibility to settle a liability for a cost associated with an exit or disposal activity recognized in a prior period is discharged or removed, the liability should be reversed and the costs should be reversed through the same income statement line items used when the costs were recognized initially.

(v) Disclosure.   FASB Statement No. 146 requires disclosure of the following information in the period in which an exit or disposal activity is initiated and any subsequent period until the activity is completed:

- A description of the exit or disposal activity, including the facts and circumstances leading to the expected activity and the expected completion date
- For each major kind of cost associated with the activity (e.g., one-time termination benefits, contract termination costs, and other associated costs)
  - The total amount expected to be incurred in connection with the activity, the amount incurred in the period, and the cumulative amount incurred to date
  - A reconciliation of the beginning and ending liability balances showing separately the changes during the period attributable to costs incurred and charged to expense, costs paid or otherwise settled, and any adjustments to the liability with an explanation of the reasons therefore
- The line item(s) in the income statement or the statement of activities in which the cost in the second bullet above are aggregated
- For each reportable segment, the total amount of costs expected to be incurred in connection with the activity, the amount incurred in the period, and the cumulative amount incurred to date, net of any adjustments to the liability with an explanation of the reasons therefore
- If a liability for a cost associated with an activity is not recognized because fair value cannot be reasonably estimated, that fact and the reasons therefore

(k) TRANSLATION OF LIABILITIES IN FOREIGN CURRENCIES.   When a domestic corporation consolidates a foreign branch or subsidiary or when an importer purchases goods or incurs liabilities expressed in foreign currencies, the problem arises of translating the liabilities into U.S. dollar amounts. Accounting principles in this area have undergone considerable change in recent years and are discussed in Chapter 13.

(l) STATEMENT PRESENTATION OF CURRENT LIABILITIES.   As indicated previously, obligations expected to be liquidated within the next operating cycle by the use of current assets or the creation of other current obligations should be classified as current liabilities.

(i) Balance Sheet Classification.   The SEC [Regulation S-X, Rule 5.02(19)] requires the following classification in balance sheets:

Accounts and notes payable. State separately amounts payable to:

1. Banks for borrowings
2. Factors or other financial institutions for borrowings
3. Holders of commercial paper
4. Trade creditors
5. Related parties
6. Underwriters promoters, and employees (other than related parties)
7. Others

Rule 5.02(19) also requires disclosure of the amount and terms of unused lines of credit for short-term financing.

(ii) Other Current Liabilities.   Regulation S-X, Rule 5.02(20), requires the separate statement in the balance sheet or in a note thereto of any item in excess of five percent of total current liabilities. Such items may include, but are not limited to, accrued payrolls, accrued interest, taxes, indicating the current portion of deferred income taxes, and the current portion of long-term debt. Remaining items may be shown in one amount.

NOTE 7. SHORT-TERM DEBT

The Company borrows on a short-term basis, as necessary, by the issuance of commercial paper and by obtaining short-term bank loans. The maximum and average amount of short-term borrowings during 1988 were $112 million and $56 million, respectively, at a weighted average interest rate of 7.77 percent. The Company has an agreement for a line of credit for up to $200 million through December 1991. No short-term debt was outstanding at December 31, 1988. The line of credit is on a fee basis.

Exhibit 25.1   Sample presentation of short-term liabilities as required by the SEC. (*Source:* Oklahoma Gas & Electric Co., 1988 Annual 10K Report.)

Many companies disclose arrangements for compensating balances in the note covering short-term debt, although these are covered in Regulation S-X under requirements related to cash.

An example of a note that presents the required SEC information is given in Exhibit 25.1.

In the less detailed form used in published reports to shareholders, it is common to present current liabilities as follows:

- Payable to banks
- Accounts payable and accrued expenses
- Federal income taxes payable
- Current portion of long-term debt

As a general rule, current liabilities should not be offset against related assets. For example, an overdraft at one bank should not be canceled against a debit balance at another bank; such offsetting distorts the current ratio. An exception to the general rule is indicated by APB Opinion No. 10, *Omnibus Opinion—1966*, in the instance of short-term government securities "when it is clear that a purchase of securities (acceptable for the payment of taxes) is in substance an advance payment of taxes that will be payable in the relatively near future...."

Supplemental disclosure should be used to indicate partially and fully secured current claims, overdue payments, and special conditions of future payment [see Subsection 25.1(b)].

25.4 NATURE AND ISSUE OF BONDS PAYABLE

(a) BONDS DEFINED.   Bonds are essentially long-term notes issued under a formal legal procedure and secured either by the pledge of specific properties or revenues or by the general credit of the issuer. In the last case, the bonds are considered "unsecured." The most common bonds are those issued by corporations, governments, and governmental agencies. A significant difference, from the viewpoint of the holder although not the issuer, is that most obligations of state and local governmental units are free of federal income taxes on interest and sometimes of state taxes, as well. Both state and local government bonds are usually called *municipals*. Agency bonds are obligations of government agencies and frequently carry a form of guarantee from the government unit. The typical bond contract, known as an *indenture*, calls for a series of "interest" payments semiannually and payment of principal or face amount at maturity. Bonds differ from individual notes in that they represent fractional shares of participation in a group contract, under which a trustee acts as intermediary between the corporation and holders of the bonds. The terms are set forth in the trust indenture covering the entire issue. Indentures are frequently long and complex documents and normally contain various conditions and restrictions related to the operations of the borrower.

The conditions and restrictions referred to as *covenants* may include restrictions on dividend payments and an agreement to maintain a minimum amount of working capital. Failure to comply with covenants would lead to default and acceleration of the due date of the debt. This event may trigger default on other obligations of the corporation under cross-covenant provisions.

Bonds, like stocks, are a means of providing the funds required for the long-run operation of the corporation and have been used for this purpose on a large scale, particularly in the utility field. The primary difference between the two broad classes of securities is that bonds represent a contractual liability, whereas stocks represent a residual equity. Failure to pay interest and principal as agreed under the bond indenture usually results in definite legal action to protect the rights of the bondholder. As long as the corporation meets all obligations as prescribed, the bondholder has little or no influence on the administration of the company. However, if the issuer violates one or more of the restrictive covenants in the indenture, the power of the holders may increase substantially.

Bonds are normally long-term securities and are often issued for periods of 10 years or longer. Maturities vary with industry and with general conditions at the time of issue. Intermediate-term securities, with maturities of one to five years, like bonds in every other respect, are normally called *notes*. Whereas bonds are usually issued in units of $1,000, prices are quoted in multiples of $100. Thus a bond quoted at $85 would actually be priced at $850. Alternatively, bond prices may be quoted in terms of their interest yield.

(b) BONDS CLASSIFIED. Bonds may be classified in a number of different ways. The security given in connection with the bond may range from a first or senior lien on specific physical property, such as a first mortgage bond or an equipment obligation, to securities that are a general lien, such as debentures, and finally to conditional promises with no lien, such as income bonds. The analysis of bonds is treated in detail in Chapter 18.

The traditional distinction between bonds and stocks became blurred through the increasing use of hybrid types such as convertible bonds, bonds with stock-purchase warrants attached, and redeemable preferred stocks. Similarly, the popularity of serial bonds, in which a portion of the issue matures each year, has blurred distinctions based on maturities.

For financial statement purposes, clear identification of bonds that are "secured" and similarly clear labeling of the assets involved are absolute requirements.

(i) Convertible Bonds. Bonds may have characteristics of both the typical senior security and the typical common stock. The most common form of privileged *issue* is the convertible bond, which includes a provision giving the right to the holder to exchange the bond for common stock on certain stipulated terms. Another method of introducing an equity element into a bond is the bond with warrants attached, under which holders of the bond may purchase common shares in amounts, at prices and during periods that are stipulated in advance.

Chapter 10 includes a complete discussion of the effects of warrants and conversion features on per share earnings computations.

These privileged issues have created several other problems in accounting. Aside from the accounting required upon conversion, the existence of warrants or a conversion feature provides difficulties in the determination of the amount of discount. These points are considered in Subsections 25.5(c).

(ii) Serial Bonds and Sinking Funds. Sinking funds may be established for the retirement of bonds, either as a requirement of the bond indenture or voluntarily. A disadvantage of bond sinking funds is that as a result of transferring cash to the sinking fund, a portion of the money borrowed for use in the business is not available for that purpose.

Generally, the same type of protection sought by a sinking fund can be obtained by the use of serial bonds, issues that mature in installments. For most serial bonds, coupon interest rates differ with each maturity, and the issue price is relatively similar for all maturities. In principle, a default of any issue in a serial maturity or a failure to make a sinking fund payment causes the entire issue to become due and payable. In practice, as long as the issuer continues to meet interest payments, some remedy short of total default is normally arranged.

(c) AUTHORITY TO ISSUE BONDS. The general right of a corporation to create a bonded indebtedness is found in the power to borrow funds granted by statute, and specific authorization of such action is usually included in the charter or bylaws. However, the authority of the directors to place a mortgage on corporate assets may be subject to shareholder approval. Securing such approval is often advisable, even if not required, in the event of a heavy borrowing program, in view of the effect of such a program on the shareholders' position. Under some statutes, corporate borrowing is subject to general restrictions (e.g., limitation to a certain percentage of total capital stock).

(d) OUTLINE OF ISSUING PROCEDURE. Following is an outline of 14 procedural steps when bonds are issued through investment bankers:

1. Directors authorize management to proceed with negotiations.
2. Investment bankers are interviewed by corporation's representatives.
3. Propositions of investment bankers are submitted to board of directors, and board approves a particular proposal.
4. Plan is submitted to corporation's attorneys.
5. Meeting of shareholders is called, and resolution is passed approving the bond issue.
6. Appraisers and certified public accountants, acceptable to bankers, are instructed to make an investigation and submit reports.
7. Attorneys examine titles and arrange legal details.
8. An underwriting agreement with investment bankers is drawn up.
9. Trust indenture is prepared and trustee is appointed.
10. Application for registration is made to the SEC if bonds are to be marketed outside the state of origin.
11. Application is made to state commissions of states in which bonds are to be sold.
12. Certificates are printed and prepared for delivery.
13. Bonds are signed by corporate officers and trustee.
14. Bonds are delivered to underwriter and money is received by corporation.

(e) RECORDING ISSUE OF BONDS. If the entire issue is "sold" to the underwriters, which is the most frequent procedure, and the corporation has no responsibility with respect to the process of distribution, the entries covering the issue boil down to a charge to the underwriters—or directly to "cash," if payment is made upon delivery—and a credit to "bonds payable." If the corporation disposes of the bonds through the efforts of its own organization, the accounting will be more extended and may include the recording of subscriptions.

Assume, for example, that a company authorizes debenture bonds in the par amount of $1 million and undertakes to dispose of the bonds at par through its own office. Assume, further, that subscriptions are taken at par for 700 bonds of $1,000 each. The following general entries are required:

Subscriptions to bonds	$700,000	
Debenture bonds subscribed		$700,000

Assuming cash is received in full for 500 bonds, the entries are:

Cash	$500,000	
Subscriptions to bonds		$500,000

When the bonds are issued, the account with bonds subscribed is charged and the regular liability account, "bonds payable," is credited.

When bond subscriptions are collected on the installment plan, it may be advisable to set up separate accounts for each installment receivable, as a means of controlling collections and segregating balances past due. In any event, detailed records of each subscription must be maintained.

On the balance sheet, bond subscriptions are preferably shown as a receivable, with bonds subscribed reported as a form of liability.

(i) Origin of Bond Discount and Premium.   Bond discount is defined as the excess of face or maturity value over the amount of cash or equivalent paid in by the original bondholder, and, conversely, premium is defined as the excess of cash paid in over maturity value. The explanation of this excess is the fact that in the discount case, the nominal or "coupon" rate of interest stated on the bond is less than the market rate. In this case the investor is unwilling to pay maturity value for the bond, since this price would yield only the coupon rate. Instead, the price of the bond is set at some lower point at which the yield to the buyer is the same as the market rate of interest on comparable securities. In the case of a premium, the coupon interest rate exceeds the market rate, and the price of the bond is set at a point above maturity value that will yield to the investor only the market rate of interest.

Until the 1950s, it was common for companies to issue bonds with low, even-percentage coupons (such as four percent) to demonstrate the solidity of the company. The result, frequently, was large amounts of discount, accompanied by major accounting disputes over proper treatment. It has since become common to state the nominal rate of interest on bonds in rather precise fractions. An attempt is usually made to align the nominal rate as closely as possible with the market or effective rate, and the absolute magnitude of the discount or premium tends to be small. This condition does not simplify the accounting for discount and premium, but it does suggest that in many cases theoretical arguments will be disposed of on grounds of materiality.

(ii) Issue of Bonds at Discount and Premium.   Bonds are recorded in the main liability account at par or maturity value. If issued for less than par, the difference is charged to a discount account, illustrated as follows:

Cash	$ 97,550	
Discount on bonds payable	2,450	
Bonds payable		$100,000
Or, if subscriptions are involved,		
	(1)	
Bond subscriptions	97,550	
Discount on bonds payable	2,450	
Bonds subscribed	1	100,000
To record taking of subscriptions.		
	(2)	
Cash	97,550	
Bond subscriptions		97,500
To record collection of subscriptions.		
	(3)	
Bonds subscribed	100,000	
Bonds payable		100,000

An account "discount on bond subscriptions" may be used to reflect the discount until the bond subscriptions are collected in full, at which time the account will be transferred to "discount on bonds payable."

If bonds are issued for cash in excess of the face amount of the bonds, the excess is credited to a premium account as follows:

Cash	$102,700	
Bonds payable		$100,000
Premium on bonds payable		2,700

The entries for bond subscriptions at a premium would correspond with the discount illustration shown above.

The practice of recording the face amount of the bonds and discount (or premium) in separate accounts is thoroughly established, in spite of the fact that on the investors' books it is good practice to record the purchase of the bond at cost without regard to face or maturity value. It is theoretically correct to credit "bonds payable" with the proceeds of the bond issue, but the practice illustrated above is not objectionable, provided it is properly interpreted and reported.

(iii) Segregation of Bond Issue Costs.   Charges connected with the issue of new bonds—such as legal expenses in preparing the bond contract and mortgage, cost of printing certificates, registration costs, and commission to underwriters—are costs of the use of capital obtained for the whole life of the issue and should be capitalized and written off over that period.

It is common practice to lump these costs with actual discount (or net them against premium, as the case may be). Good accounting requires careful distinction between these costs and bond discount, which is properly an offset to the maturity value of the bonds. Issue costs should likewise not be offset against the premium liability.

Occasionally the amount of bond issue costs is difficult to determine. That is particularly true where bonds are sold through underwriters who share expenses. As a general rule, the difference between the amount paid in by the first bona fide bondholders and maturity value represents premium or discount. The difference between this amount paid in and net proceeds to the issuer represents bond issue cost.

For example, if bonds with a face value of $1 million are issued through underwriters to original holders at a price of 1001/2, and if the net proceeds to the issuer are 981/4, out of which bond issue costs amounting to $15,000 are paid, the entries are:

	(1)		
Cash		$982,500	
Bond issue costs		22,500	
Bonds payable			$1,000,000
Premium on bonds payable			5,000
To record receipt of bond proceeds from underwriters.			
	(2)		
Bond issue costs		15,000	
Cash			15,000

Bond issue costs of $37,500 are classified on the balance sheet as an intangible asset and amortized over the life of the bond issue on a straight-line basis.

(iv) Allocation of Debt–Issue Costs in a Business Combination.   In SAB No. 77, the SEC's staff took the position that fees paid to an investment banker for advisory services, including financing services, must be allocated between direct costs of the acquisition and debt issue costs. This position is consistent with APB Opinion No. 16, "Business Combinations," which states that debt issue costs are an element of the effective interest cost of the debt, and neither the source of the debt financing nor the use of the debt proceeds changes the nature of such costs. The allocation would apply whether the services were billed as a single amount or separately. Tests of reasonableness should consider such factors as fees charged by investment bankers in connection with other recent bridge financings and fees charged for advisory services when obtained separately. The allocation should result in an effective debt service cost and interest and amortization of debt issue costs that are comparable to the effective cost of other recent debt issues of similar investment risk and maturity.

The bridge financing costs should be amortized over the estimated interim period preceding the placement of the permanent financing; any unamortized amounts should be charged to expense if the bridge loan is repaid prior to the expiration of the estimated interim period.

(v) Bonds Issued between Interest Dates.   When a bond is sold after the stated issue date, the price paid by the purchaser will include interest accrued at the coupon rate from the issue date on the bond. At the outset this accrued interest represents a liability to the issuer covering the amount of interest advanced by the investor, in view of the date of purchase, and payable at the next interest date.

For example, 10 percent bonds in maturity amount of $100,000 and dated January 1 are marketed at par and accrued interest one month after the stated date. The entries to record the sale and the initial payment of interest are:

	February 1		
Cash		$100,833.34	
Bonds payable			$100,000.00
Bond interest payable			833.34
	July 1		
Bond interest payable		833.34	
Bond interest charges		4,066.66	
Cash			5,000.00

When a bond is finally sold after one or more interest coupons have matured, the matured coupons are detached by the issuing company and the buyer is charged only with interest accrued since the last interest payment date.

Cases involving discount and premium are discussed below.

(f) DETERMINATION OF BOND ISSUE PRICE. When an investor buys a bond, he acquires two rights: (1) the right to receive periodic interest payments from the date of purchase to maturity and (2) the right to receive face value at maturity date. It follows that the current price of the bond is the sum of (1), the present value of the interest payments, plus (2), the present value of the face amount.

For example, a corporation plans to issue $1 million face value, 20-year bonds. The bonds bear interest (coupon rate) of nine percent, payable semiannually. If the market yield (rate of interest) on securities of this quality is 10 percent at the date of issue, the sale price of the bond is the sum of the following two:

1. The present value of 40 semiannual payments of $45,000 each
2. The present value, 40 periods hence, of $1,000,000

Here both present values are calculated to yield 10 percent per annum (or, more precisely, 5 percent each six months, since interest is compounded semiannually).

The present value of item 1, an annuity of $45,000 for 40 periods at 5 percent, is $772,158.89. The present value of the maturity payment of $1,000,000, payable in 20 years at 10 percent, is $142,045.68. Thus we can compute the value of the bond and the discount as:

Present value of interest payments	$ 772,158.89
Present value of principal	+ 142,045.68
Value of the bond	914,204.57
Less face value of bond	−(1,000,000.00)
Discount on issue	$ 85,795.43

The effect of various yield rates on the issue price of this bond issue can be shown by calculating the bond issue price at various yields, as shown in the following table:

(1) Assumed Semiannual Yield Rate	*(2)* Present Value of Interest Payments	*(3)* Present Value of Payment at Maturity	*(4)* Present Issue Price *(col. 2 + col. 3)*
7%	$599,926.90	$66,780.38	$666,707.28
6	677,083.36	97,222.19	774,305.55
5	772,158.89	142,045.68	914,204.57
4.5	828,071.30	171,928.70	1,000,000.00
4	890,674.82	208,289.04	1,098,963.86

As shown in the 4.5 percent line of the table above, when the yield rate is the same as the coupon rate, the investor pays face value for the bonds.

In some cases, the issue price of the bonds is determined first; then the problem arises of estimating the effective rate established by that price. More sophisticated financial calculators are capable of determining the yield under such conditions.

(g) BOND DISCOUNT AND PREMIUM IN THE BALANCE SHEET.   It was standard practice for many years to show bond discount on the balance sheet as a deferred charge and bond premium as a deferred credit, with the bond liability account remaining at face value throughout the life of the bonds.

A debate over this accounting practice raged for decades. However, it was ended by APB Opinion No. 21, which states: "[D]iscount or premium resulting from the determination of present value in cash or non-cash transactions is not an asset or liability separable from the note which gives rise to it."

Also APB Opinion No. 21 calls for the presentation in the balance sheet of discount or premium as direct deduction or addition to the face amount of the note. Such an amount should not be classified as a deferred charge or credit.

Examples in APB Opinion No. 21 show discount presented either in parenthetical form in the caption for a note or as a separate statement amount deducted from the outstanding balance of the note. The Opinion notwithstanding, some companies apparently classify discount or premium in some other account when the amount is inconsequential. As noted earlier, this is frequently the case when coupon values are almost identical to market interest rates.

25.5 BOND INTEREST PAYMENTS, PREMIUM, AND DISCOUNT AMORTIZATION

(a) ACCRUAL OF BOND INTEREST.   Interest payment dates may not coincide with accounting period dates. In such circumstances, it is necessary to accrue interest on outstanding bonds. And even when the stated date of payment and the end of the accounting period are the same, systematic accrual of interest expense and liability is good procedure, especially since interest money may be deposited prior to the interest date and payment of all coupons may not be effected on that date. A regular monthly accrual is usually desirable.

For example, if 12 percent bonds in the par amount of $1,000,000 are issued at par on June 1, the issuing company may well make entries at the end of each month throughout the life of the bonds as follows:

Bond interest charges	$10,000.00	
Bond interest payables		$10,000.00

(b) PAYMENT OF INTEREST.   Bond interest is ordinarily paid semiannually. Thus the regular cash requirement for interest on an issue of $1,000,000 of 12 percent bonds is 6 percent or $60,000 every six months. Interest may be paid directly by the issuer or through the trustee. In the former case, the issuer mails checks to all registered holders and makes a deposit in some specified bank sufficient to cover all outstanding coupons (or, in some instances, makes payments by check or in actual cash to parties presenting coupons). In the latter case, the issuer deposits the required interest money with the trustee and depends on the trustee to carry out the actual process of paying the individual bondholders. Assuming that deposit with the trustee is tantamount to payment, the entries covering such deposit are, for example:

Bond interest payable	$60,000	
Cash		$60,000

However, a more complete and satisfactory treatment is to charge the trustee with the money deposit and cancel the liability when payment of coupons has been reported (or coupons have been returned). Thus:

	(1)		
Interest fund—Blank Trust Co.		$60,000	
Cash			$60,000
	(2)		
Bond interest payable		60,000	
Interest fund—Blank Trust Co.			60,000

The amount of unredeemed coupons due at any time is represented by the balance of "bond interest payable," and the amount available for payment is the balance of the interest fund. If desired, the amount of past-due coupons may be transferred to a distinct account.

Paid or canceled coupons should be filed systematically either by the issuing company or by the trustee.

(i) Interest on Treasury Bonds.   Any matured coupons attached to Treasury bonds (either unissued or reacquired) should be removed, canceled, and filed. The interest entries should be confined to bonds actually outstanding. When payment is made by the trustee, coupons on bonds in the Treasury may be forwarded with the check for interest on outstanding bonds, or they may be filed by the company with notice to the trustee that the bonds are in the Treasury.

(ii) Interest on Bonds Held by Trustee.   Bonds of the company's own issue in the hands of the trustee are not truly outstanding, and any "interest" payments on such bonds required by the trust agreement should not be permitted to affect the interest accounts of the issuer. A requirement that "interest" be deposited on bonds already held by the trustee is simply a means of accelerating the accumulation of the sinking fund.

Assume, for example, that 10 percent of an issue on which the total semiannual interest is $20,000 is in the hands of the trustee and that the agreement calls for deposit of the entire amount. The appropriate entries are:

	(1)		
Bond interest charges		$18,000	
Bond interest payable			$18,000
To record accrual of interest on outstanding bonds.			
	(2)		
Interest and sinking fund—Blank Trust Co.		20,000	
Cash			20,000
To record periodic payment to trustee.			
	(3)		
Bond interest payable		18,000	
Interest and sinking fund—Blank Trust Co.			18,000
To record payment of coupons by trustee.			

(c) PREMIUM AND DISCOUNT AMORTIZATION.   APB Opinion No. 21 requires that bond discount or premium be charged systematically to income as interest expense or income over the life of the bond issue using the interest method. The effect on the income statement of systematic amortization of premium or discount is to show interest expense at the effective amount.

As an illustration of the interest method, assume a $1 million issue of five-year bonds with 8 percent annual interest (payable semiannually), priced to yield 10 percent to investors, for a market price of $922,782.65.

The interest method is a procedure for absorbing the discount or premium in accord with the ordinary mathematical interpretation of the composition of the issue price; it provides for spreading of the total interest charge in terms of the effective or market rate of interest. Under the interest method, the periodic amortization is the difference between the interest due and effective rates of interest applied to the carrying amount of bonds outstanding at the interest date. For the illustrative issue, the entry to record interest and the amortization of discount for the first period is:

Bond interest expense (5% × $922,782.65)	$46,139.13	
Discount on bonds payable		$ 6,139.13
Bond interest payable (4% × $1,000,000)		40,000.00

In each subsequent period, bond interest expense will be charged with the effective rate of interest times the carrying amount of the bonds, and the periodic amortization will be the difference between that amount and the bond interest liability. The amortization of premium is given similar treatment.

An accumulation table for the bonds above for the first three years under the interest method is as follows:

Half-Year Period	Carrying Amount of Bonds	Interest Expense	Interest Payments	Amortization of Discount
1	$922,782.65	$46,139.13	$40,000.00	$6,139.13
2	928,921.78	46,446.09	40,000.00	6,446.09
3	935,367.87	46,768.39	40,000.00	6,768.39
4	942,136.26	47,106.81	40,000.00	7,106.81
5	949,243.07	47,462.15	40,000.00	7,462.15
6	956,705.22	47,835.26	40,000.00	7,835.26

In practice, it is common to develop such tables when bonds are first issued, to provide a basis for subsequent accounting. As interest dates are not likely to coincide with financial reporting dates, tables are frequently developed on a monthly or daily basis to permit correct entries whenever financial statements are prepared. Similar entries and tables result for the amortization of bond premium.

(d) DISCOUNT ON CONVERTIBLE BONDS AND BONDS WITH WARRANTS. Bonds that may eventually be converted into a certain number of shares of common stock and bonds that have warrants attached, permitting the purchase of common stock at a fixed price, have achieved considerable popularity. The attraction to the buyer of such issues is obvious—they provide the fixed income of bonds along with the opportunity to participate in an equity increase. An attraction of such issues to the issuing corporation is that they are typically sold at interest rates below those that would be required for similar securities in the absence of the equity privileges. In some cases, the corporation's credit may be such that debt could not be issued at all without the conversion privilege or warrants.

APB Opinion No. 14, "Accounting for Convertible Debt and Debt Issued with Stock Purchase Warrants," states that no portion of the proceeds from the issuance of convertible debt or debt with nondetachable stock purchase warrants should be accounted for as attributable to the conversion feature. Such securities include debt securities that are convertible into common stock of the issuer or an affiliated company at a specified price at the option of the holder and that are sold at a price or have a value at issuance not significantly in excess of face amount. The terms of such securities generally include:

- An interest rate that is lower than the issuer could obtain for nonconvertible debt
- An initial conversion price that is greater than the market value of the common stock at the time of issuance
- A conversion price that does not decrease except pursuant to antidilution provisions

If convertible debt is issued at a substantial premium, there is a presumption that the premium represents paid-in capital.

Opinion No. 14 requires that the proceeds of debt securities with detachable stock purchase warrants be allocated between the debt and paid in capital, based on the relative fair values of the two securities at the time of issuance. Any resulting discount or premium on the debt securities should be accounted for as such. The same accounting treatment applies to issues of debt securities (issued with detachable warrants) that may be surrendered in settlement of the exercise price of the warrant.

EITF Issue No. 98-5, "Accounting for Convertible Securities with Beneficial Conversion Features or Contingently Adjustable Conversion Ratios," addressed the accounting for a convertible security with a nondetachable conversion feature that is in-the-money at the commitment date. That issue also addressed certain convertible securities that have a conversion price that is variable based on future events. A number of practical issues regarding the application of the guidance in Issue No. 98-5 were raised subsequent to the final consensus. The EITF addressed those issues in Issue No. 00-27, "Application of Issue No. 98-5 to Certain Convertible Instruments." At the date of this writing, EITF Issue No. 00-27 continues to be on the Task Force's agenda.

(e) BLOCKS ISSUED AT DIFFERENT RATES. In some cases bonds of a particular class and series are marketed at different times and at different prices. Assume, for example, that of an issue with a maturity amount of $1 million, the first $600,000 is sold at 102 and the second $400,000 at 105. Under such conditions two alternative procedures are available. The two blocks of the issue may be accounted for separately, and the premium on each block may be amortized at the effective rate involved. The alternative is to combine both blocks in the accounts and to apply an overall approximate rate, determined in the light of the conditions under which the two blocks were issued. Separate computations are generally advisable where considerable time elapses between issue dates and there is a substantial difference between the effective rates involved.

(f) TREATMENT OF SERIAL BONDS. In the rare case of various maturities of serial bonds being issued at the same yield rate, that rate can be applied to the net book value of the entire issue to determine amortization as in the interest method illustrations above.

In the much more common case of serial bonds that are issued with different yields on each maturity, the interest method of amortization of discount or premium should be applied to each maturity, treating it as if it were a separate issue. Formerly, such treatment was considered "too complex," but the development of sophisticated financial calculators obviates that argument.

25.6 BOND REDEMPTION, REFUNDING, AND CONVERSION

(a) PAYMENT AT MATURITY. No special accounting problems arise when bonds are paid as agreed at maturity, assuming that items of bond issue cost and of discount or premium have been disposed of systematically.

The amount of any matured bonds not presented for redemption by the holder at maturity date should be segregated in a special account. That balance should be carried as a current liability except where a special fund—not reported in current assets—is maintained to redeem the bonds when they are presented. No interest accrues on matured bonds not in default.

(b) SETTLEMENT AFTER MATURITY. If default occurs at maturity, no special entries are required prior to the settlement made through reorganization procedure, although the fact that the liability has matured but remains unpaid should be indicated in the balance sheet. Occasionally, creditors consent to a postponement of payment provided the corporation continues to pay interest at a specified rate. Where a special settlement following default at maturity provides for issue of new securities to replace the defaulted bonds, the book value assigned to such securities will presumably equal the maturity amount of the bonds (plus any unpaid interest accruing since maturity), except as conditions clearly warrant some other treatment.

(c) DEFAULTED BONDS.   Default of bonds prior to maturity creates a situation similar to that of default at maturity. Generally, no entries are called for, but the condition of default should be clearly described in the statements. Interest continues to accrue on defaulted bonds under conditions prescribed in the contract and should be recorded.

(d) CLASSIFICATION OF OBLIGATIONS BY THE CREDITOR.   In Issue No. 86-30 the EITF considered whether the waiver of a lender's rights resulting from the violation of a covenant with retention of the periodic covenant test represents, in substance, a grace period. If viewed as a grace period, the borrower must classify the debt as current under FASB Statement No. 78, unless it is probable that the borrower can cure the violation (comply with the covenant) within the grace period. The Task Force's consensus was that unless the facts and circumstances would indicate otherwise, the borrower should classify the obligation as noncurrent unless (1) a covenant violation has occurred at the balance sheet date or would have occurred absent a loan modification and (2) it is probable that the borrower will not be able to cure the default at measurement dates that are within the next 12 months.

(e) COMPOSITIONS WITH CREDITORS.   Compositions with creditors in the event of financial weakness often involve a scaling down of acknowledged liabilities, either through actual cancellation of the claims or through issue of stock to cover some element of the total debt. Chapter 11 of the Bankruptcy Act is designed to facilitate such agreements, to eliminate losses due to forced sale of property, and to prevent cash payments to dissenting minorities when a revision in the debt structure is agreed to by a substantial majority of claimants of the same class. These procedures tend to encourage continued operations under the same management when this seems desirable (see Chapter 45).

(f) REDEMPTION BEFORE MATURITY.   Many bond contracts provide for the calling of any portion, usually selected by random draw, or all of the issue at the option of the company at a stated price, usually above par, to allow the corporation to reduce its debt before maturity as the occasion arises. When interest rates decline, debtors may consider transactions that would use the leverage of an existing call provision to reduce the higher interest rate on an older debt issue. For example, the debtor may exchange new noncallable debt with a lower interest rate for old callable debt or have the creditor pay a fee in return for an agreement not to exercise the call provision for the life of the debt or for a shorter period. In periods of high interest rates, buyers of new bonds prefer indentures that restrict the call privilege. Also, bonds are often retired piecemeal through sinking fund operations, or acquired by the issuer on the open market.

FASB Statement No. 140, *Accounting for Transfers and Servicing of Financial Assets and Extinguishment of Liabilities*, provides guidance as to when debt should be considered to be extinguished for financial reporting. See Subsection 25.9(b) for a discussion of Statement of Financial Accounting Standards (SFAS) No. 140.

As interest rates rose in the 1970s, some corporations retired older, low-interest bonds (and, in some cases, low-yielding convertible bonds), to increase earnings by passing the gain on retirement through income. In many cases, these retirements appeared to be uneconomic, suggesting that earnings creation was the principal reason. See below, under "Gains and Losses from Extinguishment of Debt," for a more complete discussion.

Outstanding bonds acquired by the issuer may be permanently retired or—if the conditions of acquisition permit—they may be held in the corporate treasury for reissue at some later date. If the bonds were issued at par and are redeemed at par, the only special problem is the absorption of any bond issue costs remaining on the books. Additional problems arise when there is unabsorbed discount or premium on the books at the time of redemption, or where the redemption price differs from the maturity value.

Assuming outright redemption, all balances relating to the bonds redeemed should be eliminated.

The M Co., for example, has outstanding a bond issue of $100,000 maturity amount. On the books related to this issue are unamortized bond issue costs of $2,000 and unamortized discount of $3,000. At this point the entire issue is called at 105, and costs are incurred in the carrying out of this transaction of $1,500. The summarized entries are:

Bonds payable	$100,000	
Loss on redemption of bonds	11,500	
Bond issue costs		$ 2,000
Discount on bonds payable		3,000
Cash		106,500

When bonds are redeemed by purchase on the market, a book profit may result.

Assume conditions as in the preceding example except that instead of calling the entire issue, the M Co. bought bonds in par amount of $20,000 on the market at a total expenditure, including all charges, of $15,000. The summarized entries are:

Bonds payable	$20,000	
Bond issue costs		$ 400
Discount on bonds payable		600
Cash		15,000
Gain on redemption of bonds		4,000

In this case, with 20 percent of the issue retired, the write-off of issue costs and discount is restricted to 20 percent.

(i) Gains and Losses from Extinguishment of Debt.   Losses resulting from unamortized bond issue costs, unamortized discount, call premium, or a combination of these factors and gains or losses resulting from market conditions, upon retirement, should be recognized currently as income of the period in which the debt extinguishment takes place.

Previously, all gains and losses on extinguishment of debt were classified as extraordinary. FASB Statement No. 140, *Rescission of FASB Statements No. 4, 44, and 64, Amendment of FASB Statement No. 13, and Technical Corrections*, changed that. Currently, only gains and losses that meet both the *unusual nature* and *infrequency of occurrence* criteria of APB Opinion No. 30, *Reporting the Results of Operations—Reporting the Effects of Disposal of a Segment of a Business, and Extraordinary, Unusual and Infrequently Occurring Events and Transactions*, are classified as extraordinary.

The SEC in SAB No. 94 stated that disclosures as to a planned extinguishment and its likely effects would be required in notes to financial statements and in the management discussion and analysis. The staff also indicated that announcement of a plan to extinguish debt in the future does not in itself result in a requirement to recognize a loss, nor does an irrevocable offer to repurchase a debt obligation. A debt holder's acceptance of that offer prior to the balance sheet date by tendering the security and surrendering all rights is considered an extinguishment. When debt is called, extinguishment does not occur until interest ceases to accrue or accrete under the obligation as a result of the call.

(ii) Noncash Extinguishments.   FASB Technical Bulletin No. 80-1, *Early Extinguishment of Debt through Exchange for Common or Preferred Stock*, indicates that APB Opinion No. 26 applies to all extinguishments of debt effected by issuance of common or preferred stock, including redeemable and fixed maturity preferred stock, unless the extinguishment is a troubled debt restructuring or a conversion (a) pursuant to conversion privileges provided in the terms of the debt at issuance or (b) when conversion privileges provided in the terms of the debt at issuance are changed to induce conversion as described in FASB Statement No. 84. The reacquisition price is determined by the value of the common or preferred stock issued or the value of the debt, whichever is more clearly evident.

In EITF Issue No. 96-19, "Debtor's Accounting for Modification or Exchange of Debt Instruments," the Task Force reached a consensus that an exchange of debt instruments with substantially different terms is a debt extinguishment and should be accounted for in accordance with FASB Statement No. 125. (Statement No. 125 has since been superseded by FASB Statement No. 140.

Statement No. 140 revises the standards for accounting for securitizations and other transfers of financial assets and collateral and requires certain disclosures, but it carries over most of Statement No. 125's provisions without reconsideration.) The guidance in EITF Issue No. 96-19 is discussed in more detail in Subsection 25.10(b).

(g) TREATMENT AND REISSUE OF TREASURY BONDS. Bonds acquired by the corporation as a result of call or purchase may be canceled by formal action, or they may be held in substantially the same category as authorized bonds that have never been issued. The most common modern form of presentation is to show only the net amount of bonds outstanding on the balance sheet and to indicate the existence of treasury bonds in a note to the statements.

It follows from this that the acquisition by a corporation of its own bonds amounts to redemption of those bonds, and disposition of any balances of unamortized premium or discount, or bond issue costs, should follow the recommendations presented above under "Gains and Losses from Extinguishment of Debt," permitting recognition of book gain or loss.

Where the recommendations above for accounting for acquisition of treasury bonds have been followed, accounting for reissue is essentially the same as for bonds that have never before been outstanding. If the par amount of the treasury bonds is carried in a special account, that account is credited at par when the bonds are issued.

(h) USE OF SINKING FUNDS. Retirement of bonds through the operation of a special fund is familiar financial practice. The fund procedure may be a plan adopted by the issuing corporation and entirely within its control, or it may be an arrangement provided by contract, involving a trustee.

Most commonly, the sinking fund is an arrangement rather than an actual fund. That is, the bond indenture requires the borrowing corporation to make specific, periodic payments to the trustee, who then acquires the necessary bonds. Whether the sinking fund actually holds the bonds or arranges for their retirement is actually a moot question, since when held by the sinking fund, the bonds are effectively retired. In the past, sinking funds might actually consist of a fund, holding assets other than the debt in question. Because the purpose of the sinking fund arrangement is to provide gradual retirement of the debt, there is no reason for the fund to undertake the risk of holding securities of another issuer. In another common arrangement the company may acquire bonds in the open market or through calls, hold them as treasury bonds, then deposit them in satisfaction of sinking fund requirements at appropriate dates. In the case of some convertible debt, the conversion of enough bonds may satisfy the sinking fund requirements.

When the trustee has used the funds to acquire the corporation's bonds, either at or before maturity, the bonds so acquired are in effect retired and should be reported as such on the balance sheet of the corporation. Accounting for corporation bonds acquired by a sinking fund trustee should follow the same procedures described in Subsection 25.6(f). This treatment is proper even when the bonds are kept "alive" by the trustee for the purpose of accumulating "interest" from the corporation issuer. "Interest" payments by the corporation to the trustee on the corporation's own bonds held in the fund should be treated simply as additional deposits.

(i) Payment by Refunding. In the utility field, in particular, the funded debt is often viewed as a permanent part of the capital structure. This means that corporate policy is not always directed toward the permanent retirement of long-term liabilities; instead, the usual procedure is to secure the funds to meet maturing obligations by floating new loans.

A distinction should be drawn between retirement of bonds through an exchange and payment by refunding or refinancing. In the typical refunding operation a new bond issue, with new terms, is floated through investment channels, and the funds so provided are specifically employed to retire the preceding bond issue. However, in some cases the holders of the old issue are given the opportunity to exchange their bonds directly for bonds of the new issue. To the extent that direct exchange can be arranged by the issuing corporation, the cost of refinancing is minimized.

No additional accounting problems are encountered when bonds are refunded at maturity. The retirement of the old bonds and the issue of the new bonds are separate transactions.

(i) DETERMINING WHEN TO REFUND. Ignoring effect on taxes and other special factors, there is no object in refunding prior to maturity except when more favorable terms can be secured, particularly with respect to interest rate. However, the bare fact that the market rate has fallen does not justify refunding. To retire a complete issue of outstanding bonds prior to maturity ordinarily necessitates exercise of right of call, and this means payment of a redemption premium, usually substantial. Moreover, the costs of refunding must be considered. When the old issue is called before maturity, the trustee will require a fee for additional services. There will be legal and accounting fees, taxes, and printing costs. More serious are the added costs of registration and marketing the issue. Another factor that may be important is the additional interest charge required by the overlapping of the two issues.

There has been considerable discussion in financial circles as to the proper method of computing the saving—if any—to be realized by refunding under a specified set of conditions. Probably the most significant approach is that which compares the present values at the prevailing effective rate of the cash requirements of the two programs, considering the new issue to run for only the remaining life of the old. (It is pure speculation to make the comparison for a longer term.)

For example, the M Co. has outstanding $1 million, maturity amount, of six percent bonds, with 10 years yet to run. These bonds are callable at any interest date at 105. Assume that the effective market rate of interest for this class of security is currently only four percent, for loans of 10 years or longer. The service costs of various kinds required to call the old bonds and float the new loan are estimated at $30,000. The present cash value of the obligations under the old contract is found as follows:

Present value of amount due in 20 periods (10 years) at 2% per period	$ 672,971.33
Present value of annuity of $30,000 per period for 20 periods at 2%	490,543.00
	$1,163,514.33

The amount of cash required to meet these claims through the medium of a new loan is $1,080,000 (including redemption premium of $50,000 and costs of $30,000). By comparison, it appears that an advantage is realized by refunding.

It is important to note that the question of book loss realized on redemption has no bearing on the determination of the financial advantage of a refunding program over continuation of the existing contract.

However, as noted above in connection with early retirement of bonds and notes, some companies have undertaken early retirement to produce reported earnings, even though the transactions are inherently uneconomical.

The desire to realize a book loss for tax purposes in the form of unamortized discount and expense may be an important or even a decisive factor in bringing about a decision to refund. It is even possible for a situation to develop in which a refunding might seem to be advantageous, in view of the tax angle, although no saving in interest charges results.

(j) BOND CONVERSION. When convertible bonds issued at par are converted into stock at par, dollar for dollar, the conversion is ordinarily assumed to be the equivalent of the payment of the liability and the issue of additional stock at par. The entries necessary to recognize conversion under these conditions, accordingly, consist essentially of a charge to bonds outstanding and a corresponding credit to capital stock. In the case of the conversion of bonds issued at a premium into stock on a par-for-par basis, the unamortized premium on the date of conversion is preferably treated as a form of stock premium. Similarly, an unaccumulated discount attaching to bonds converted into stock on a par-for-par basis should be set up as a type of stock discount, although that discount would presumably not represent an amount that might be collected from shareholders by assessment. The schedule of accumulation of discount or amortization of premium set up for convertible bonds should disregard the possibility of conversion and should be adhered to until conversion takes place.

When bonds are convertible into stock at some specified price other than par or stated value, the book value of the bonds converted is generally made the basis of the credit to capital stock.

Assume, for example, that a company has outstanding an issue of debenture bonds in the par amount of $1 million, with applicable unamortized discount of $50,000, and that those bonds are convertible into the common stock of the company on any interest date at a price of $25 per share, or on the basis of 40 shares of stock for each bond in the maturity amount of $1,000. The shares of this class of stock have a stated value of $10 each. At this point 10 percent of the bond issue is presented for conversion, and shares are issued in accordance with the exchange ratio. The summarized entries are:

Debenture bonds—Maturity amount	$100,000	
Discount on debenture bonds		$ 5,000
Capital stock—Stated value		40,000
Capital stock—Contributions in excess of stated value		55,000

In some cases the specified conversion price of the stock increases in terms of stated periods. The contract may also provide for termination of the conversion privilege at a specified date. A minor complication arises when the exchange ratio is such that conversion calls for issue of fractional shares. In that situation the converting bondholder may pay—in sufficient cash to entitle him to a whole number of shares, the corporation may make an appropriate cash payment, or the corporation may actually issue the fractional shares.

The treatment of unamortized bond issue cost on conversion date is something of a problem. As a matter of convenience, such cost may be absorbed in the conversion entries in the same manner as bond discount. However, a better treatment would be to retain the balance of issue cost as in effect a cost of stock financing. A convertible bond is potential capital stock and may become actual stock at any time the bondholder elects. As long as the bonds are outstanding, the schedule of amortization of issue costs based on the total life of the bonds should be maintained, as conversion is not assured and is beyond the control of the issuer. Upon conversion, nevertheless, the contingency becomes controlling, and the balance of bond issue cost becomes a cost of issuing stock.

(k) INDUCED CONVERSION. FASB Statement No. 84, "Induced Conversions of Convertible Debt," which amends APB Opinion No. 26, "Early Extinguishment of Debt," specifies that when a convertible debt is converted to equity securities of the debtor pursuant to an inducement offer, the debtor should recognize an expense (not extraordinary) equal to the fair value of all securities and other consideration transferred in excess of the fair value of securities issuable pursuant to the original conversion terms.

Measurement of the fair value of the securities should be as of the date the inducement is accepted. Usually that is when conversion takes place or a binding agreement is signed.

Inducement includes changes made by the debtor to the conversion privileges for purposes of inducing conversion. The Statement applies only to conversions occurring pursuant to changed conversion privileges that are exercisable for a limited period and include the issuance of all of the equity securities issuable pursuant to conversion privileges included in the terms of the debt at issuance for each debt instrument that is converted. Inducements include reducing the original conversion price, issuing warrants or other securities not included in the original terms, or payment of cash.

(l) ACCRUED INTEREST UPON CONVERSION OF CONVERTIBLE DEBT. In Issue No. 85-17, the EITF concluded that when accrued but unpaid interest is forfeited at the date of conversion of convertible debt, either because the conversion date falls between interest payment dates or because there are no interest payment dates (a zero coupon convertible instrument), interest should be accrued or imputed to the date of conversion of the debt instrument. Accrued interest from the last interest payment date, if applicable, to the date of conversion, net of unrelated income tax effects, if any, should be charged to expense and credited to capital as part of the cost of the securities issued. Thus, accrued interest is accounted for in the same way as the principal amount of the debt and any unamortized issue or premium discount.

(m) SUBSCRIPTION RIGHTS AND WARRANTS SOLD WITH BONDS.   Bonds are sometimes sold with warrants or subscription rights attached. The rights or warrants permit their holder to purchase other securities, normally common shares, at some fixed or determinable price in a future period or at a certain future date. The warrants are essentially calls or options on the common stock. The theory, of course, is that the combination of the warrant and the bond enables the company to market the bond at a lower interest rate.

As mentioned previously, Opinion No. 14 requires that the proceeds of debt securities with detachable stock purchase warrants be allocated between the debt and paid-in capital, based on the relative fair values of the two securities at the time of issuance. Any resulting discount or premium on the debt securities should be accounted for as such. The same accounting treatment applies to issues of debt securities (issued with detachable warrants) that may be surrendered in settlement of the exercise price of the warrant.

As an illustration of the accounting for a bond with warrants, consider the following example. A company issues a bond at par with an 8.75 percent yield. Each bond has a warrant attached that permits the holder of the warrant to purchase a share of the company's stock for $20, within five years. The common shares are currently selling for $50. It is determined that the company's bond, without the warrant attached (a straight bond), could have been sold for 95, that is, $950 per bond.

The underwriter handling the issue estimates that the warrant will be worth about $75 when issued. Note that APB Opinion No. 14 calls for this valuation (and that of the comparable straight bond) to be made "at the time of issuance," which it defines as "the date when agreement as to terms has been reached and announced." That is not the actual date of issue of the securities, when relative market values for the two securities could be determined. The date given in APB Opinion No. 14 is earlier. Thus the fair value will be approximated or estimated by someone, probably the underwriter.

The allocation required under APB Opinion No. 14 is as follows:

$$\frac{\text{Value of bonds}}{\substack{\text{Value of bonds without warrants} \\ + \text{ Value of warrants}}} \times \text{Purchase price} = \text{Value assigned to bonds}$$

$$\frac{\$950}{\$950 + \$75} \times \$1,000 = \$927.00$$

$$\frac{\text{Value of warrants}}{\substack{\text{Value of bonds without warrants} \\ + \text{ Value of warrants}}} \times \text{Purchase price} = \text{Value assigned to warrants}$$

$$\frac{\$75}{\$950 + \$75} \times \$1,000 = \$73.00$$

The entries, for the issuance assuming one bond, would be:

Cash	$927	
Discount on bonds	73	
Bonds payable		$1,000
Cash	73	
Paid-in capital		73

This accounting applies to warrants that are "separable" from the bonds, which is the most common situation. If the warrants were required to trade with the bond, the issue would be almost identical to a convertible bond and should be accounted for as a convertible.

25.7 STATEMENT PRESENTATION OF LONG-TERM DEBT

There is general agreement about the nature of information that should be presented on the balance sheet or in the notes to the financial statements concerning long-term debt. That information includes the major categories of debt (e.g., notes payable to banks, mortgages notes payable, notes to related parties); maturity dates; interest rates; methods of liquidation; conversion features; assets pledged as collateral; covenants to reduce debt, maintain working capital, or restrict dividends; and other significant matters (e.g., subordinated features).

FASB Statement No. 5, "Accounting for Contingencies" (par. 18), requires disclosure of unused letters of credit, assets pledged as security for loans, and commitments such as those for plant acquisition or an obligation to reduce debts, maintain working capital, restrict dividends.

FASB Statement No. 47, "Disclosure of Long-Term Obligations," requires disclosure of the maturities and sinking fund requirements, if any, for all long-term borrowings for each of the five years following the balance sheet date.

FASB Statement No. 129, "Disclosure of Information about Capital Structure," requires disclosure of the following information concerning debt that is a security:

> An entity shall explain, in summary form within its financial statements, the pertinent rights and privileges of the various securities outstanding. Examples of information that shall be disclosed are . . . liquidation preferences . . . call prices and dates, conversion or exercise prices or rates and pertinent dates, sinking fund requirements, and significant terms of contracts to issue additional shares.

FASB Statement No. 107, "Disclosures about Fair Value of Financial Instruments," as amended by FASB Statement No. 126, "Exemption from Certain Required Disclosure about Financial Instruments for Certain Nonpublic Entities," and FASB Statement No. 133, "Accounting for Derivative Instruments and Hedging," require public entities with total assets equal to at least $100 million to disclose both the fair value and the bases for estimating the fair value of long-term debt unless it is not practicable to estimate that value.

SOP 94-6, "Disclosure of Certain Significant Risks and Uncertainties," requires disclosure of current vulnerability due to a concentration in the volume of business transacted with a particular lender if the concentration makes the borrower vulnerable to the risk of a near-term severe impact and it is at least reasonably possible that the events that could cause the severe impact will occur in the near term.

General requirements of the SEC for disclosure of long-term debt are stated in Regulation S-X [5-02(22)]:

> Bonds, mortgages and other long-term debt . . . (a) State separately in the balance sheet or in a note thereto, each issue or type of obligation and such information as will indicate (1) the general character of each type of debt including the interest rate; (2) the date of maturity, or if maturing serially, a brief indication of the serial maturities . . . ; (3) if the payment or principal or interest is contingent, an appropriate indication of such contingency; (4) a brief indication of priority; (5) if convertible, the basis.

Other disclosures called for by the SEC in Regulation S-X include:

- Rule 4.08(b). Security
- Rule 4.08(c). Defaults
- Rule 4.08(f). Significant changes in bonds, mortgages, and similar debt
- Rule 5.02(23). Indebtedness to related parties
- Rule 12.29. Scheduled mortgage loans on real estate

Exhibit 25.2 provides a sample presentation on long-term debt.

25.8 OTHER LONG-TERM LIABILITIES

(a) MORTGAGES AND LONG-TERM NOTES.   A mortgage is essentially a pledge of title to physical property as security for repayment of a loan. A mortgage refers to the security for a debt, not the debt itself. A promissory note usually accompanies the granting of a mortgage. On the balance sheet the liability should appear as "Mortgage Notes Payable" or "Notes Payable—Secured"

R. Debt	2001	2000
Short-term debt (1)		
Commercial paper		$ 56
U.S. dollar bank loans/overdrafts	$416	55
Other currency bank loans/overdrafts	48	121
Total short-term debt	$464	$ 232
Long-term debt		
U.S. dollars:		
Credit facility borrowings (2)	$1,402	$1,962
Private placements		
7.54% due 2005	105	105
Senior notes and debentures:		
7.13% due 2002	350	350
6.75% due 2003 (3)	400	400
6.75% due 2003	200	200
8.38% due 2005	300	300
7.00% due 2006 (3)	300	300
8.00% due 2023	200	200
7.38% due 2026	350	350
7.50% due 2096	150	150
Other indebtedness:		
rates in 2001 ranging from 2.00% to 10.77%, due 2002 through 2015	60	106
	3,817	4,423
Other currencies:		
Credit facility borrowings (2)	741	353
6.00% Euro Bond due 2004	266	281
Other indebtedness in various currencies		
(average rates in 2001 ranging from 3.54% to		
14.3%), due 2003 through 2010	13	35
Capital lease obligations in		
various currencies	19	25
Total long-term debt (3)	4,856	5,117
Less: current maturities	(381)	(68)
Long-term debt, less current maturities	$4,475	$5,049

(1) The weighted average interest rates for commercial paper outstanding during 2000 and 1999 were 5.9% and 4.9% respectively. The weighted average interest rates for bank loans and overdrafts outstanding during 2001, 2000, and 1999 were 5.7%, 7.0% and 5.5% respectively.

(2) A committed $2,500 multicurrency revolving credit facility was in place at both December 31, 2001 and December 31, 2000. At December 31, 2001, $257 was available under the credit facility.

(3) On December 12, 1996, two wholly owned finance subsidiaries located in the United Kingdom and France sold public debt securities that were fully guaranteed by the Company. The face value of the notes bear interest ranging from 6.75% to 7.0%. The offerings by the subsidiaries, amounting to $700, were simultaneously converted into fixed rate, 8.28% Sterling and 5.75% Euro obligations through cross-currency swaps with various counterparties. In May 2000, the cross-currency swap on the Euro obligation was converted to a floating rate instrument with a coupon rate of EURIBOR less .89%. At December 31, 2001, the equivalent rate was 2.46%.

(Continues)

Exhibit 25.2   Sample presentation of long-term debt. (Source: Crown Cork & Seal, 2001 Annual Report.)

Aggregate maturities of long-term debt for the five years subsequent to December 31, 2001, are $381, $2,777, $272, $407, and $305, respectively. Cash payments for interest during 2001, 2000 and 1999 were $469, $385, and $377, respectively (including amounts capitalized of $1 in each of the three years).

The estimated fair value of the Company's long-term borrowings, based on quoted market prices for the same or similar issues, was $3,612 at December 31, 2001.

On March 2, 2001, the Company amended and restated its $2,500 multicurrency revolving credit facility and obtained a new $400 term loan. The amended and restated credit facility bears interest at LIBOR plus 2.5%, and the maturity date was extended from February 4, 2002 to December 8, 2003. The term loan bears interest at LIBOR plus 3.5%, with a maturity date of February 4, 2002. In connection with the new facility and the term loan, the Company pledged as collateral the stock of certain of the Company's subsidiaries and substantially all of the assets of the borrowing companies and the Company's domestic subsidiaries, except for those assets which are already pledged, are precluded from being pledged under existing or anticipated agreements, or are impractical to pledge under local law. The credit facility and term loan contain covenants which include (i) interest coverage and leverage ratios, (ii) restrictions on the repayment of notes, debentures, and private placements, (iii) restrictions on the assumption of indebtedness and payment of dividends, and (iv) restrictions on the use of proceeds from asset sales. Any credit facility or term loan repayments made using proceeds from the sale of assets will permanently reduce the funds available under the agreement. At December 31, 2001, there were outstanding letters of credit of $115 including $100 which reduced the borrowings available under the credit facility.

On January 30, 2002, the maturity date for $225 of the term loan was extended to August 4, 2002, and the remaining $175 was subsequently repaid on its original due date using net proceeds of $100 from asset sales and $75 of availability under the credit facility. The term loan balance was further reduced to $201 during the first quarter of 2002 using additional asset sale proceeds. The amended term loan bears an interest rate of LIBOR plus 4.5%.

Exhibit 25.2   *Continued.*

with brief reference to the property pledged. The term *mortgage payable* as a liability caption is, nevertheless, occasionally found in financial statements.

If mortgages are payable on the installment plan, the liability account is charged each payment date with the amount of principal paid. When the periodic installments are fixed amounts covering both payment on principal and accrued interest, the payments must be apportioned between principal and interest (see "Installment Purchase Contracts").

With respect to individual mortgages and accompanying notes, the borrower usually receives cash in the face amount of the note, in which case the face amount is the true liability and discount or premium is not involved. However, when the consideration for the note is in the form of property, as is the case when a mortgage is given on the property purchased or when "points" are given, the liability may be more or less than the face of the note. Points are the analogue, in mortgage financing, of original issue discount for bonds. They raise the effective interest rate above that specified in the note. A point is one percent of the face of the note. For example, if a 20-year mortgage note for $100,000 face were signed, but the banker demanded four points, the borrower would receive four percent less than $100,000, or $96,000. If the note carried an interest rate of 10.75 percent, for example, the borrower would still be obligated to make the monthly payments on $100,000, that is, $1,015 per month. Since he received only $96,000, the borrower's effective interest rate is increased to about 12.3 percent on the money he received. Accounting for this transaction would follow the reasoning outlined in Subsection 25.4(d).

In some mortgage loan arrangements, the lender is entitled to participate in appreciation in the market value of the mortgaged real estate project or the results of operations of the mortgaged real estate project, or in both. Accounting for such arrangements is discussed in Chapter 13.

(i) Related-Party Transactions.   Companies sometimes borrow from related parties such as principal owners, management, or members of their immediate family, or from other subsidiaries of a common parent. FASB Statement No. 57, "Related Party Disclosures," requires disclosure of material transactions with related parties unless those transactions are eliminated in the preparation of consolidated or combined financial statements. The disclosures must include:

- The nature of the relationship(s) involved
- A description of the transactions, including transactions to which no amounts or nominal amounts were ascribed, for each of the periods for which income statements are presented, and such other information deemed necessary to an understanding of the effects of the transactions on the financial statements
- The dollar amounts of transactions for each of the period for which income statements are presented and the effects of any change in the method of establishing the terms from that used in the preceding period
- Amounts due from or to related parties as of the date of each balance sheet presented and, if not otherwise apparent, the terms and manner of settlement

If necessary to the understanding of the relationship, the name of the related party should be disclosed.

Transactions involving related parties cannot be presumed to be carried out on an arm's-length basis, as the requisite conditions of competitive, free-market dealings may not exist. Representations about transactions with related parties, if made, may not imply that the related party transactions were consummated on terms equivalent to those that prevail in arm's-length transactions unless those representations can be substantiated.

For SEC registrants, SEC regulation S-X, rules 4-08(k)(1) and (2) set forth the following additional requirements:

(k) Related party transactions which affect the financial statements. (1) Related party transactions should be identified and the amounts stated on the face of the balance sheet, income statement, or statement of cash flows.

(2) In cases where separate financial statements are presented for the registrant, certain investees, or subsidiaries, separate disclosure shall be made in such statements of the amounts in the related consolidated financial statements which are (i) eliminated and (ii) not eliminated. Also, any intercompany profits or losses resulting from transactions with related parties and not eliminated and the effects thereof shall be disclosed.

In addition, SEC Regulation S-K (Reg. § 229.404) sets forth nonfinancial statement disclosure requirements concerning certain relationships and related transactions.

(ii) Debtor's Accounting for Forfeiture of Real Estate Subject to a Nonrecourse Mortgage.
EITF Issue No. 91-2 deals with a situation where a borrower under a nonrecourse loan purchases real property. The only security for the loan is the real property and the lender accepts that limitation. After repaying a portion of the loan, the borrower transfers the property, which by then has a reduced fair value, in satisfaction of the loan balance, which exceeds the value of the property. For example, assume the purchased property cost of $1000, which was totally financed. After repaying $200, the borrower transfers the property, which now has a fair value of $600, to the lender in full satisfaction of the balance due. The issue is whether FASB Statement No. 15 applies in this case.

If Statement No. 15 on troubled debt restructuring applies, the borrower would record a loss on the asset of $400, and a gain of $200 on the extinguishment of the debt. The FASB staff and the SEC observer agree that Statement No. 15 applies in this case and calls for the two-step approach illustrated above.

An alternative one-step approach would be for the borrower to record a loss of $200, the difference between the asset carrying amount of $1000 and the $800 balance of the loan.

The Task Force did not reach a consensus on this issue.

(b) INSTALLMENT PURCHASE CONTRACTS.   Installment purchase contracts are a popular means of financing asset acquisitions. In the typical case, the buyer secures possession upon making a down payment and agrees to pay the balance in a series of installments, usually with interest, over an extended period. In some cases, buyers with excellent credit ratings are not required to provide down payments. Transfer of title is often deferred until payment of the final installment. Proper accounting requires showing the asset at full cost and the balance of the contract payable as a liability.

Purchase contracts are commonly payable in equal periodic installments. The regular installment may include both interest on the contract balance and a payment on the principal, or it may apply entirely to principal, with interest paid separately.

To illustrate the first plan, assume a contract covering the purchase of equipment for $5,000, with interest at 12 percent, which provides for semiannual payments of $500 each until the entire obligation has been discharged. The division of these payments between interest and retirement of principal, at an interest rate of 12 percent, compounded semiannually, is shown in the accompanying table.

The entries in this case for the first semiannual payment (assuming no interim accrual of interest) are:

Purchase contract payable	$200	
Interest on purchase contract	300	
Cash		$500

Half-Year Period	Balance of Debt	Interest 6% per Period	Payment	Amortization of Debt
1	$5,000.00	$ 300.00	$ 500.00	$ 200.00
2	4,800.00	288.00	500.00	212.00
3	4,588.00	275.28	500.00	224.72
4	4,363.28	261.80	500.00	238.20
5	4,125.08	247.50	500.00	252.50
6	3,872.58	232.36	500.00	267.64
7	3,604.94	216.30	500.00	283.70
8	3,324.24	199.27	500.00	300.73
9	3,020.51	181.23	500.00	318.77
10	2,701.74	162.10	500.00	337.90
11	2,363.84	141.83	500.00	358.17
12	2,005.67	120.34	500.00	379.66
13	1,626.01	97.56	500.00	402.44
14	1,223.57	73.41	500.00	426.59
15	796.98	47.82	500.00	452.18
16	$ 344.80	$ 20.69	$ 365.49	$ 344.80
		$2,865.49	$7,865.49	$5,000.00

In this example, the fair value of the property is assumed to be the full contract price of $5,000, because interest is provided at a presumably adequate rate. If no interest were provided, the provisions of APB Opinion No. 21 would apply.

(c) LONG-TERM LEASES.   Leasing, as a means of financing the acquisition of long-term assets, has seen a rapid expansion in the United States and other countries since World War II. It was not until the 1960s, however, that authoritative accounting pronouncements began to significantly affect lease accounting. There now exist several major pronouncements and many interpretations. The related accounting is complex. Chapter 23 is devoted entirely to lease accounting, from both the lessee and lessor points of view.

(d) DEFERRED REVENUE OBLIGATIONS.   *Deferred revenue* is the term often applied to liabilities that arise from the receipt of payment in advance of furnishing the service for which the funds are received. Usually deferred revenues are current, in that the service will be rendered in the next accounting period and the obligation discharged. A more complete discussion of accounting for deferred revenue is given above in connection with current liabilities. In some cases, however, payments are received covering a period of years, and here it is necessary to reduce the obligation each period by an appropriate amount, with a concurrent credit to revenue. Such long-term collections in advance should be shown as long-term liabilities in the balance sheet, under an appropriate title. The amount to be discharged in the following accounting period should be classed as current, with only the balance shown as a long-term liability.

Casualty insurance premiums are frequently collected three to five years in advance, and the long-term portions of such premiums represent long-term liabilities on the books of the insurer.

(e) LONG-TERM EXPENSE ACCRUALS.   Although most accruals of expenses are properly classified as current liabilities, there are some commitments such as three-to-five-year product and service warranties, self-insurance programs, and pension plans that deserve classification as long-term obligations. The amount of the obligation is estimated in the light of a company's past experience and is established by an expense charge. That the amount is estimated and the identity of the specific obligee may be unknown at the time the obligation is recognized do not affect the propriety of the entry. Subsequently, when payment or service is made, the long-term liability account is eliminated.

The extent to which inflation should be recognized in long-term expense accruals is unclear. If, for example, a company gives a five-year repair warranty on a product, it is reasonable to assume that the labor cost of repair work performed in five years will be considerably higher than it is today. It is not clear whether the accrual of the liability for the warranty work should be made at current prices or at estimated future prices.

SOP 96-1, "Environmental Remediation Liabilities" (par. 6.12), states:

> The measurement of environmental remediation liabilities should be based on the reporting entity's estimate of what it will cost to perform each of the elements of the remediation effort . . . when those elements are expected to be performed. Although this approach is sometimes referred to as "considering inflation," it does not simply rely on an index and should take into account factors such as productivity improvements due to learning from experience with similar sites and similar remedial action plans. In situations in which it is not practicable to estimate inflation and such other factors because of uncertainty about the timing of expenditures, a current-cost estimate would be the minimum in the range of the liability to be recorded until such time as these cost effects can be reasonably estimated.

That guidance may be applicable to other kinds of liabilities by analogy.

In the past it was common to refer to such long-term expense accruals as operating or liability reserves, which, on occasion, were located ambiguously between the liability and equity sections of the balance sheets. These amounts are clearly liabilities and should be presented as such. The use of the term *reserve* in this context is not good practice.

(f) BORROWINGS ON OPEN ACCOUNT.   Long-term borrowings on open account from affiliated corporations or other parties are a kind of long-term liability and should normally be shown separately. Long-term advances received for future use of property or merchandise, or for service to be rendered, represent a liability on the books of the party obligated to furnish property or render the service. Classification of this type of item as a "deferred credit" is not recommended.

(g) ASSET RETIREMENT OBLIGATIONS.   FASB Statement No. 143, "Accounting for Assets Retirement Obligations," sets forth accounting and disclosure requirements for legal obligations associated with the retirement of a tangible long-lived asset that result from the acquisition, construction, or development and (or) the normal operation of a long-lived asset. Accounting for asset retirement obligations is discussed in Chapter 21.

(h) PENSION PLANS AND DEFERRED COMPENSATION CONTRACTS.   Plans for payment of employee pensions and other retirement allowances involve assumption of obligations that are deferred until employee retirement dates. Accounting for retirement plans is the subject of Chapter 38. Deferred compensation is covered in Chapter 39.

(i) FUTURE INCOME TAXES.   The objectives of accounting for income taxes, as set forth in FASB Statement No. 109, *Accounting for Income Taxes*, are:

> . . . to recognize (a) the amount of taxes payable or refundable for the current year and (b) deferred tax liabilities and assets for the future tax consequences of events that have been recognized in an enterprise's financial statements or tax returns.

The following four basic principles are applied in accounting for income taxes at the date of the financial statements:

1. A current tax liability or asset is recognized for the estimated taxes payable or refundable on tax returns for the current year.
2. A deferred tax liability or asset is recognized for the estimated future tax effects attributable to temporary differences and carryforwards.
3. The measurement of current and deferred tax liabilities and assets is based on provisions of the enacted tax law; the effects of future changes in tax laws or rates are not anticipated.
4. The measurement of deferred tax assets is reduced, if necessary, by the amount of any tax benefits that, based on available evidence, are not expected to be realized.

A complete discussion of this subject is in Chapter 24 of this *Handbook*.

(j) DISCLOSURE OF UNCONDITIONAL PURCHASE AND OTHER LONG-TERM OBLIGATIONS.   FASB Statement No. 47, *Disclosure of Long-Term Obligations*, requires that an enterprise disclose its commitments under unconditional purchase obligations, such as take-or-pay contracts or through-put contracts that are associated with suppliers' financing arrangements. Such arrangements result in obligations to transfer funds in the future for fixed or minimum amounts or quantities of goods or services at fixed or minimum prices.

Disclosure is required of an unconditional purchase obligation that (par. 6):

a. Is noncancelable, or cancelable only
   1. Upon the occurrence of some remote contingency or
   2. With the permission of the other party or
   3. If a replacement agreement is signed between the same parties or
   4. Upon payment of a penalty in an amount such that continuation of the agreement appears reasonably assured
b. Was negotiated as part of arranging financing for the facilities that will provide the contracted goods or services or for costs related to those goods or services
c. Has a remaining term in excess of one year

If the obligation is not recognized on the purchaser's balance sheet, the required disclosures, which may be combined for similar or related obligations, include (par. 7):

a. The nature and the term of the obligation(s)
b. The amount of the fixed and determinable portion of the obligation(s) as of the date of the latest balance sheet presented in the aggregate and, if determinable, for each of the five succeeding fiscal years
c. The nature of any variable components of the obligation(s)

d. The amounts purchased under the obligation(s) for each period for which an income statement is presented

Disclosure of the amount of imputed interest necessary to reduce the unconditional purchase obligation(s) to present value is encouraged but not required. The discount rate to determine the present value of the obligation(s) should be the interest rate of the borrowings that financed the facilities that will provide the goods or services, if known by the purchaser. If not, the rate should be the purchasers' incremental borrowing rate at the date the obligation is entered into.

For obligations that are recognized on the balance sheet, Statement No. 47 requires as the following disclosures for each of the five years following the latest balance sheet date (par. 10):

1. The aggregate amount of payments for unconditional purchase obligations
2. The combined aggregate amount of maturities and sinking fund requirements for all long-term borrowings

(k) GUARANTEE OBLIGATIONS. FASB Interpretation No. 45, *Guarantor's Accounting and Disclosure Requirements for Guarantees, Including Indirect Guarantees of Indebtedness of Others*, issued in November 2002, changed dramatically the accounting for guarantees within its scope by creating the concept of a noncontingent obligation to "stand ready" to perform over the term of the guarantee in the event that specified triggering events or conditions occur.

Guarantors are now required to recognize, at the inception of a guarantee, a liability for the fair value of the obligations they have undertaken in issuing the guarantee. The liability consists of two elements:

1. Any contingent liability that meets the recognition criteria of FASB Statement No. 5.
2. A liability for the guarantor's ongoing obligation to stand ready to perform over the term of the guarantee in the event that the specified triggering events or conditions occur. This element is considered to be noncontingent, thus the liability is recognized even if it is not probable that the specified triggering events or conditions will occur. Furthermore, the liability is recognized regardless of whether any explicit premium or other compensation was received for the guarantee.

(i) Scope of Interpretation 45. Interpretation No. 45 applies only to direct and indirect guarantees with any of the following contract characteristics:

1. Contracts and indemnification agreements that contingently require the guarantor to make payments (either in cash, financial instruments, other assets, shares of its stock, or provision of services) to the guaranteed party based on changes in an underlying that is related to an asset, a liability, or an equity security of the guaranteed party. An "underlying" is a variable such as a specified interest rate or commodity price. An underlying also includes the occurrence or nonoccurrence of a specified event, such as a scheduled payment under a contract or an adverse judgment in a lawsuit.
2. Indirect guarantees of the indebtedness of others (meaning the creditor's claim against the guarantor is based solely on the right to enforce the debtor's claim against the guarantor), even though the payment to the guaranteed party may not be based on changes in an underlying that is related to an asset, a liability, or an equity security of the guaranteed party.
3. Contracts that contingently require the guarantor to make payments (either in cash, financial instruments, other assets, shares of its stock, or provision of services) to the guaranteed party based on another entity's failure to perform under an obligating agreement (performance guarantees).

Following are examples of guarantees that meet the characteristic-based scope provisions of the Interpretation:

- A financial standby letter of credit, which is an irrevocable undertaking (typically by a financial institution) to guarantee payment of a specified financial obligation
- A guarantee to repurchase receivables that have been sold or otherwise assigned
- A market value guarantee on either a financial asset (such as a security) or a nonfinancial asset owned by the guaranteed party
- A guarantee of the market price of the common stock of the guaranteed party
- A guarantee of the collection of the scheduled contractual cash flows from individual financial assets held by a special-purpose entity (SPE)
- An indemnification against an adverse judgment in a lawsuit
- An indemnification against the imposition of additional taxes due to either a change in the tax law or an adverse interpretation of the tax law.
- A performance standby letter of credit, which is an irrevocable undertaking by a guarantor to make payments in the event a specified third party fails to perform under a nonfinancial contractual obligation

Following are examples of arrangements that do not meet the characteristic-based scope provisions of the Interpretation:

- Guarantees of an entity's *own* performance
- Guarantees of funding, such as commercial letters of credit and other loan commitments
- Subordination agreements, wherein one class of investors agrees not to receive any cash until investors in a priority class are paid

Interpretation No. 45 also provides numerous specific scope exclusions—some from the entire Interpretation, others solely from the initial recognition and measurement provisions. Those exclusions are summarized below.

Excluded from the entire Interpretation	*Excluded from the initial recognition requirements (disclosure only)*
Guarantees that are excluded from the scope of FASB Statement No. 5 under paragraph 7 of that Statement, for example, pensions and stock options	Contracts that guarantee the functionality of nonfinancial assets that are owned by the guaranteed party, e.g., product warranties
Residual value guarantees issued by a lessee that accounted for a lease as a capital lease	Guarantees that are accounted for under FASB Statement No. 133 as a derivative instrument at fair value
Guarantees that require payments due to changes in an underlying that belongs to the guaranteed party, but that are accounted for as contingent rents.	Guarantees issued in a business combination that represent contingent consideration Guarantees for which the guarantor's obligation would be reported as an equity item (rather than a liability) under GAAP
Guarantees issued by either an insurance or a reinsurance company and accounted for under specified FASB Statements	Guarantees issued by an original lessee that has become secondarily liable under a new lease that relieved the original lessee of the primary obligation under the original lease
Guarantees that require payments due to changes in an underlying that belongs to the guaranteed party, but provide vendor rebates by the guarantor based on either the sales revenues of, or the number of units sold by, the guaranteed party	Guarantees issued either between parents and their subsidiaries or corporations under common control Guarantees by a parent of its subsidiary's debts to third parties
Guarantees that prevent the guarantor from accounting for a transaction as a sale or recognizing the profit from that sale transaction in earnings	Guarantees by a subsidiary of debts owed to third parties by either its parent or other subsidiaries of that parent

(ii) Initial Recognition.   If a guarantee is issued in a standalone arm's-length transaction with an unrelated party, the liability should be recognized initially at the amount of the premium received or receivable by the guarantor. If a guarantee is issued as part of a transaction with multiple elements with an unrelated party, the liability should be recognized initially at its estimated fair value. If a guarantee is issued as a contribution to an unrelated party, the liability should be recognized initially at its fair value.

If, at the inception of the guarantee, the guarantor is required to recognize a liability under FASB Statement No. 5 for a contingent loss, the liability to be initially recognized for that liability is the greater of (a) the amount that satisfies the fair value objective described in the preceding paragraph or (b) the contingent liability amount required to be recognized by Statement No. 5. It would be unusual, however, for the contingent liability amount required to be recognized by Statement No. 5 to be greater than the amount that satisfies the fair value objective.

The Interpretation does not prescribe a specific account for the guarantor's offsetting entry when it recognizes the liability at the inception of the guarantee. The offsetting entry depends on the circumstances in which the guarantee was issued. For example,

- If a guarantee is issued in connection with the sale of assets or a business, the overall proceeds received from the transaction would be allocated between consideration for the guarantee and proceeds from the sale.
- If a guarantee is issued in connection with the formation of a joint venture, the offsetting entry would probably be to the investment in the joint venture.
- If a guarantee is issued by a lessee when entering into an operating lease, the offsetting entry would be to prepaid rent.

(iii) Subsequent Accounting.   Subsequent to initial recognition, the noncontingent liability would typically be reduced by a credit to income as the guarantor is released from risk under the guarantee. Depending on the nature of the guarantee, the release from risk is typically recognized over the term of the guarantee (a) only upon either expiration or settlement of the guarantee, (b) by a systematic and rational amortization method, or (c) as the fair value of the guarantee changes. Some view the selection of methods for subsequent reduction of the noncontingent liability as an accounting policy election. Any contingent liability required to be recognized under Statement No. 5 should be adjusted accordingly.

(iv) Disclosure.   Interpretation No. 45 requires disclosures about guarantees within its scope in addition to those required by FASB Statement No. 5, FASB Statement No. 57, and FASB Statement No. 107:

- The nature and approximate term of the guarantee, the circumstances that gave rise to the guarantee, and the conditions that require the guarantor to make payments under the guarantee.
- Except for product warranties, the maximum potential amount of future payments (undiscounted and not reduced for possible recoveries) under the guarantee. If the guarantor cannot estimate the amount, the reason should be disclosed.
- The carrying amount of the guarantor's contingent and noncontingent obligation under the guarantee.
- The nature and extent of recourse provisions and collateral related to the guarantee and, if estimable, the extent to which the maximum potential loss under the guarantee would be covered.
- The fair value of financial guarantees.
- For product warranties, (a) the accounting policy and methodology used in determining the guarantor's liability (including any liability associated with extended warranties) and (b) a tabular reconciliation of the changes in the guarantor's aggregate product warranty liability for the period. The reconciliation should present the beginning balance of the aggregate

product warranty liability, aggregate reductions in the liability for payments made (in cash or in kind), aggregate changes in the liability for accruals related to warranties issued during the period, aggregate changes in the liability for accruals related to preexisting warranties (including changes in estimates), and the ending balance of the aggregate product warranty liability.

25.9 FINANCIAL INSTRUMENTS WITH CHARACTERISTICS OF BOTH LIABILITIES AND EQUITY

(a) FINANCIAL INSTRUMENTS CLASSIFIED AS LIABILITIES. The dividing line between equity and liabilities seems clear in concept. FASB Concepts Statement No. 6, *Elements of Financial Statements*, defines equity as net assets, that is, the residual interest that remains in the assets of an entity after deducting its liabilities. In practice, however, the difference may be obscured. Certain securities issued by business enterprises seem to have characteristics of both liabilities and equity in varying degrees, or the name given to some securities may not accurately describe their essential characteristics.

FASB Statement No. 150, *Accounting for Certain Financial Instruments with Characteristics of Both Liabilities and Equity*, provides guidance on accounting for *freestanding* financial instruments that have both liability and residual-interest characteristics, including those that comprise more than one option or forward contract. Financial instruments are freestanding if they are entered into separately from other interests or transactions or are legally detachable and separately exercisable. At the time of this writing, the FASB has on its agenda a project to develop a comprehensive standard on financial instruments with characteristics of equity, liabilities, or both. That project is also expected to produce amendments to the definition of a liability in Concepts Statement No. 6, aspects of which are already reflected in Statement No. 150.

Three classes of freestanding financial instruments are required to be classified as a liability (or an asset in some cases):

1. mandatorily redeemable financial instruments
2. obligations to repurchase the issuer's equity shares by transferring assets
3. certain obligations to issue a variable number of shares

(i) Mandatorily Redeemable Financial Instruments. A mandatorily redeemable financial instrument is one that embodies an unconditional obligation requiring the issuer to redeem it by transferring its assets at a specified or determinable date (or dates) or upon an event that is certain to occur. Mandatorily redeemable financial instruments must be classified as liabilities unless redemption is required to occur only upon the liquidation or termination of the reporting entity. An example of a common mandatorily redeemable financial instrument is mandatorily redeemable preferred stock, which, prior to the effective date of Statement No. 150, typically was classified in the "mezzanine" between liabilities and equity. Another example is stock of a privately held company that must be sold back to the company upon the holder's termination of employment by the company or upon the holder's death.[5]

Contingently redeemable financial instruments become mandatorily redeemable—and, therefore, liabilities—when the contingency is satisfied.

(ii) Obligations to Repurchase the Issuer's Equity Shares. A financial instrument, other than an outstanding share, that, at inception, embodies or is indexed to an obligation to repurchase the issuer's equity shares and that requires or may require the issuer to settle the obligation by transferring assets. Common examples are a forward purchase contract that is to be physically

---

[5] An insurance contract covering the cost of redemption does not affect the classification of the stock as a liability.

settled or net cash settled and a written put option on the issuer's equity shares that is to be physically settled or net cash settled.

(iii) Certain Obligations to Issue a Variable Number of Shares. A financial instrument that embodies an unconditional obligation, or a financial instrument other than an outstanding share that embodies a conditional obligation, that the issuer must or could settle by issuing a variable number of its equity shares, if, at inception, the monetary value of the obligation is based solely or predominantly on any of the following:

  a. A fixed monetary amount known at inception, for example, a payable settleable with a variable number of the issuer's equity shares

  b. Variations in something other than the fair value of the issuer's equity shares, for example, a financial instrument whose value is based on a stock market index and that is settleable with a variable number of the issuer's equity shares

  c. Variations inversely related to changes in the fair value of the issuer's equity shares, for example, a written put option that could be settled by one party delivering stock equal to the fair value of the counterparty's gain (net share settled).

(b) MEASUREMENT. With one exception, all instruments within the scope of Statement No. 150 are initially measured at their fair value. The exception is that, for freestanding "physically settled" forward purchase contracts that obligate the issuer to purchase a fixed number of its own shares for cash, fair value is adjusted for any consideration or unstated rights or privileges that may have affected the terms of the transaction. For example, if the underlying shares are expected to pay dividends before the repurchase date, the dividends should be reflected in the implicit interest rate used in determining the fair value of the instrument. For another example, if a physically settled forward purchase contract on the issuer's own shares is issued to a customer to whom the issuer simultaneously sold a product at a discount, that discount would be taken into account in arriving at an appropriate implied discount rate.

With two exceptions, all instruments within the scope of Statement No. 150 are subsequently measured at fair value, with changes in fair value recognized in earnings. The two exceptions are the physically settled forward purchase contracts discussed above and mandatorily redeemable instruments. If both the amount to be paid under a physically settled forward purchase contract or a mandatorily redeemable instrument and the settlement date are fixed, the liability is measured subsequently at the present value of the amount to be paid at settlement, accruing interest cost at the rate implicit at inception. If either the amount to be paid or the settlement date varies based on specified conditions, the liability is measured subsequently at the amount of cash that would be paid under the conditions specified in the contract if settlement occurred at the reporting date, and the difference between the amount so determined and the amount reported for the liability at the previous reporting date would be reflected in interest cost.

(c) PRESENTATION AND DISCLOSURE. Entities that have only one class of "equity" instruments, all of which are mandatorily redeemable financial instruments required to be classified as liabilities, must describe those instruments in the balance sheet as "shares subject to mandatory redemption" to distinguish them from other liabilities. Similarly, payments to holders of such instruments and related accruals must be presented separately from payments to and interest due to other creditors in the statement of cash flows and in the income statement. In addition, such entities must disclose the related par value and paid-in capital amounts separately from retained earnings or accumulated deficit.

FASB Statement No. 150 requires disclosure of detailed information about each financial instrument within its scope. In addition, FASB Statement No. 129, *Disclosure of Information about Capital Structure*, requires entities that issue redeemable stock to disclose the amount of redemption requirements, separately by issue or combined, for all issues of capital stock that are redeemable at fixed or determinable prices on fixed or determinable dates in each of the five years following the date of the latest statement of financial position presented.

25.10 RESTRUCTURING AND EXTINGUISHMENT OF LIABILITIES

(a) TROUBLED DEBT RESTRUCTURINGS. If a debtor has difficulty making scheduled payments on a debt, a restructuring of the debt may be arranged. That is, the creditor may agree to alter the payments of principal, interest, or both in such a manner as to make it more likely that the debtor can make the payments. For example, the creditor may agree to a reduction in the original interest rate, deferral of interest payments, extension of the time for payment of principal, a reduction in the absolute value of the principal amount, or some combination thereof. Creditors may also accept cash, other assets, or an equity interest in the debtor in satisfaction of the debt even though the value received is less than the amount of the debt.

FASB Statement No. 15, "Accounting by Debtors and Creditors for Troubled Debt Restructurings," governs the accounting for the restructuring of a "contractual ... obligation to pay money on demand or on fixed or determinable dates that is already included as ... [a] liability in the ... debtor's balance sheet at the time of the restructuring." Examples of such obligations are accounts payable, debentures and bonds, and related accrued interest. Statement No. 15 does not apply, however, to lease agreements; employment-related agreements; or debtors' failure to pay trade payables according to their terms, or creditors' delays in taking legal action to collect overdue amounts of interest and principal, unless they involve an agreement between the debtor and creditor to restructure.

Under FASB Statement No. 15, if the debtor transfers its receivables from third parties, real estate, or other assets to a creditor to settle fully a debt, the debtor should recognize a gain on "restructuring" of the debt equal to the excess of (1) the carrying amount of the debt settled (including accrued interest and unamortized premium or discount, finance charges, and issue costs, as applicable) over (2) the fair value of the assets transferred. Fair value of assets is measured by (in order of preference): (1) their market value in an active market, (2) the selling prices of similar assets for which there is an active market, or (3) a forecast of expected cash flows, discounted at a rate commensurate with the risk involved.

If only the terms of the debt are modified (i.e., no assets or equity interest are transferred), the carrying amount of the payable at the time of the restructuring is not changed unless it exceeds the total future cash payments (undiscounted) specified by the new terms. If the total future cash payments specified by the new terms are less than the carrying amount of the payable:

- The carrying amount of the payable is reduced to the amount of the total future cash payments specified by the new terms.
- Unless indeterminate future cash payments are involved (discussed below), a gain is recognized on restructuring equal to the amount of the reduction.

If the debtor may be required to pay additional amounts based on a contingency such as its financial condition improving, the debtor must assume that the contingent future payments will have to be paid and include them in the "total future cash payments specified by the new terms" to the extent necessary to prevent recognition of a gain on restructuring that may be offset in future periods. The same principle applies if the amount of future payments is uncertain, for example, if the number of future interest payments is uncertain because the principal and accrued interest are payable on demand.

If a troubled debt restructuring involves a partial settlement by transferring assets or granting an equity interest and a modification of terms of the remaining payable, the carrying amount of the payable should first be reduced by the fair value of the assets transferred or equity interest granted. The difference between the carrying amount and the fair value of the assets transferred is recognized as a gain or loss. The reduced carrying amount of the debt is then compared with the total future cash payments specified by the new terms in accounting for the portion of the restructuring that is a modification of terms of the remaining debt.

Interest expense is recorded by the debtor subsequent to the restructuring so that a constant effective interest rate is applied to the carrying amount of the payable at the beginning of the period between the restructuring and the maturity. That is, in substance, the interest method prescribed by APB Opinion No. 21 and described elsewhere in this chapter (Sections 25.2 and 25.5). If a gain is recognized on a troubled debt restructuring, no interest expense is recognized on the debt going forward, other than for any contingent interest payments.

Also, Statement No. 15 requires disclosure of the principal features of a restructuring, of any gain or loss, and of the per share effects.

FASB Technical Bulletin No. 81-6, "Applicability of FASB Statement 15 to Debtors in Bankruptcy Situations," indicates that the principles of troubled debt restructuring of Statement No. 15 do not apply if a company is involved in a Chapter 19 bankruptcy proceeding that will result in a restatement of all of its indebtedness, say at 50 cents on the dollar. However, Statement No. 15 would apply to an isolated troubled debt restructuring by a debtor involved in a bankruptcy proceeding as long as it did not result in a general restatement of the debtor's liabilities.

The following conditions would indicate that a debt restructuring may not be a troubled debt restructuring for purposes of Statement No. 15:

- The fair value of cash, other assets, or an equity interest accepted by a creditor from a debtor in full satisfaction of its receivable at least equals the creditor's recorded investment in the receivable.
- The fair value of cash, other assets, or an equity interest transferred by a debtor to a creditor in full settlement of its payable at least equals the debtor's carrying amount of the payable.
- The creditor reduces the effective interest rate on debt primarily to reflect a decrease in market interest rates in general or a decrease in the risk so as to maintain a relationship with the debtor that can readily obtain funds from other sources at the current market interest rate.
- The debtor issues in exchange for its debt new marketable debt having an effective interest rate based on its market price that is at or near the current market interest rates of debt with similar maturity dates and stated interest rates issued by nontroubled debtors.

Statement No. 15 notes that, in general, a debtor that can obtain funds from sources other than the existing creditor at market interest rates at or near those for nontroubled debt is not involved in a troubled debt restructuring.

EITF Issue No. 02-4, "Determining Whether a Debtor's Modification or Exchange of Debt Instruments Is within the Scope of FASB Statement No. 15," provides further guidance for determining whether an event is a troubled debt restructuring for purposes of Statement No. 15. If a modification or exchange of debt instruments is not within the scope of Statement No. 15, the provisions of EITF No. 96-19, "Debtor's Accounting for a Modification or Exchange of Debt Instruments" (see below), should be applied.

(b) EXTINGUISHMENT OF LIABILITIES. FASB Statement No. 140, "Accounting for Transfers and Servicing of Financial Assets and Extinguishments of Liabilities," provides guidance to debtors as to when debt should be considered to be extinguished for financial reporting purposes:

- The debtor pays the creditor and is relieved of its obligations with respect to the debt. This includes the debtor's reacquisition of its outstanding debt securities in the public securities markets, regardless of whether the securities are canceled or held as so-called treasury bonds.
- The debtor is legally released from being the primary obligor under the debt either judicially or by the creditor.

Previously under FASB Statement No. 76, "Extinguishment of Debt," a debtor considered debt to be extinguished if it irrevocably placed cash or other assets in a trust to be used solely for satisfying scheduled payments of both interest and principal of a specific obligation and the possibility that the debtor would be required to make future payments with respect to the debt was remote. An in-substance defeasance transaction does not meet Statement No. 140's criteria for derecognizing a liability. For debt that was considered defeased under the provisions of FASB

Statement No. 76, there should continue to be a general description of the defeasance transaction and the amount of the debt that is considered extinguished at the end of the period so long as that debt remains outstanding.

If a creditor releases a debtor from primary obligation on the condition that a third party assumes the obligation and the original debtor becomes secondarily liable as guarantor, the original debtor treats the release as an extinguishment. However, as a guarantor, the original debtor must recognize a guarantee obligation in the same manner as had he never been primarily liable to that creditor, with due regard for the likelihood that the third party will perform on its obligation. The guarantee obligation is initially measured at its fair value and that amount reduces the gain or increases the loss recognized on extinguishment.

In EITF Issue No. 96-19, the Task Force reached a consensus that an exchange of debt instruments with substantially different terms is debt extinguishment and should be accounted for in accordance with paragraph 16 of Statement 125 (par. 16 of Statement No. 125 is now included in FASB Statement No. 140). Thus, a substantial modification of terms should be accounted for like, and reported in the same manner as, an extinguishment.

EITF No. 96-19 concluded that, from the debtor's perspective, an exchange of debt instruments between or a modification of a debt instrument by a debtor and a creditor in a nontroubled debt situation is deemed to have been accomplished with debt instruments that are *substantially different* if present value of the cash flows under the terms of the new debt instrument is at least *10 percent* different from the present value of the remaining cash flows under the terms of the original instrument.

Cash flows can be affected by changes in principal amounts, interest rates, or maturity. They can also affected by fees exchanged between the debtor and creditor to change:

- Recourse or nonrecourse features
- Priority of the obligation
- Collateralized (including changes in collateral) or noncollateralized features
- Debt covenants, waivers, or both
- The guarantor (or elimination of the guarantor)
- Option features

If the terms of a debt instrument are changed or modified in any of the ways described above and the cash flow effect on a present value basis is less than 10 percent, the debt instruments are not considered to be substantially different.

The following guidelines are to be used to calculate the present value of the cash flows for purposes of applying the 10 percent test:

1. The cash flows of the new debt instrument include all cash flows specified by the terms of the new debt instrument plus any amounts paid by the debtor to the creditor less any amounts received by the debtor from the creditor as part of the exchange or modification.

2. If the original debt instrument, the new debt instrument, or both have a floating interest rate, the variable rate in effect at the date of the exchange or modification is to be used to calculate the cash flows of the variable-rate instrument.

3. If either the new debt instrument or the original debt instrument is callable or puttable, separate cash flow analyses are to be performed assuming exercise and nonexercise of the call or put. The cash flow assumptions that generate the smaller change would be the basis for determining whether the 10 percent threshold is met.

4. If the debt instruments contain contingent payment terms or unusual interest rate terms, judgment should used to determine the appropriate cash flows.

5. The discount rate to be used to calculate the present value of the cash flows is the effective interest rate, for accounting purposes. of the original debt instrument.

6. If within a year of the current transaction the debt has been exchanged or modified without being deemed to be substantially different, the debt terms that existed a year ago should be used to determine whether the current exchange or modification is substantially different.

If it is determined that the original and new debt instruments are substantially different, the calculation of the cash flows related to the new debt instrument at the effective interest rate of the original debt instrument is *not* used to determine the initial amount recorded for the new debt instrument or to determine the debt extinguishment gain or loss to be recognized. The new debt instrument should be initially recorded at fair value, and that amount should be used to determine the debt extinguishment gain or loss to be recognized and the effective rate of the new instrument

If it is determined that the original and new debt instruments are not substantially different, a new effective rate must be determined based on the carrying amount of the original debt instrument and the revised cash flows.

Fees paid by the debtor to the creditor or received by the debtor from the creditor (fees may be received by the debtor from the creditor to cancel a call option held by the debtor or to extend a no-call period) as part of the exchange or modification are to be accounted for as follows:

- If the exchange or modification is to be accounted for in the same manner as a debt extinguishment and the new debt instrument is initially recorded at fair value, the fees paid or received are to be associated with the extinguishment of the old debt instrument and included in determining the debt extinguishment gain or loss to be recognized.
- If the exchange or modification is not to be accounted for in the same manner as a debt extinguishment, the fees are to be associated with the replacement or modified debt instrument and, along with any existing unamortized premium or discount, amortized as an adjustment of interest expense over the remaining term of the replacement or modified debt instrument using the interest method.

Costs incurred with third parties directly related to the exchange or modification (such as legal fees) are to be accounted for as follows:

- If the exchange or modification is to be accounted for in the same manner as a debt extinguishment and the new debt instrument is initially recorded at fair value, the costs are to be associated with the new debt instrument and amortized over the term of the new debt instrument using the interest method in a manner similar to debt issue costs.
- If the exchange or modification is not to be accounted for in the same manner as a debt extinguishment, the costs should be expensed as incurred.

EITF Issue No. 96-19 also carried over the consensus from EITF Issue No. 86-18, which it superseded, that a borrower should not account for the original debt securities as extinguished and that those securities should not be offset against the receivable from the third party in the borrower's financial statements in the following situation:

- A borrower, instead of acquiring debt securities directly, loans funds to a third party, who in turn acquires the borrower's original debt securities.
- The borrower and third party agree that they may settle their respective receivables and obligation by right of setoff as payments become due, contingent on the third party's continued retention of the borrower's original debt.

25.11 ACCOUNTING FOR SELECTED FINANCING INSTRUMENTS

(a) INTRODUCTION. In recent years numerous modifications to traditional debt instruments have required the EITF to address the accompanying accounting issues. In one instance, a traditional convertible debt instrument was modified by giving the buyer the option to put (sell) the issue back to the issuer at a premium. Other modifications to traditional debt have included debt issuances that have altered the traditional way in which interest rates are set. There have been issuances of debt with increasing interest rates and deferral of the setting of interest rates as well as issuances of debt instruments that provide not only for principal repayment, but also contingent payments. Companies have also sold their marketable securities granting the buyer the right to sell those assets back to the issuer. Those modifications have led to such fundamental questions as whether the transaction is a sale or a borrowing, the amount of liability to be accrued, the amount of interest expense and pattern of interest recognition, and the method of accounting for possible impairments. The following section summarizes both the accounting issues that have arisen from these financial instrument modifications and the EITF consensus agreements on acceptable accounting.

(i) EITF Issue No. 85-29—Convertible Bonds with a Premium Put. The EITF considered convertible bonds issued at par value with a put allowing the bondholder to require that the corporation redeem the bonds at a future date for cash at a premium to the bond's par value. At the date of issue, the carrying amount of the bonds exceeds the market value of the common stock into which they are convertible.

The questions addressed in Issue No. 85-29 are as follows:

- Should a liability be accrued for the put premium and, if so, over what period?
- Should the liability continue to be accrued if the value of debt or equity changes, making exercise of the put unlikely?
- If the put expires unexercised, should the put be recognized as income or paid-in capital, amortized as a yield adjustment, or continue to be carried as part of debt?

The EITF reached the following consensus:

- The issuer should accrue the put premium over the period from the date of issuance to the first put date. The accrual should continue even if changes in market value of the bond or underlying common stock indicate the put will not be exercised.
- If the put expires unexercised, the amount accrued should be credited to additional paid-in capital if the market value of the common stock exceeds the put price. Otherwise, if the put price exceeds the market value of the common stock, the put premium should be amortized as a yield adjustment over the remaining life of the bonds.

FASB Statement No. 133 partially nullified this consensus. Under Statement No. 133, the embedded feature warrants separate accounting as a derivative. However, because Statement No. 133 permits entities not to account separately for certain derivatives embedded in pre-1998 or pre-1999 hybrid instruments, the consensus on this issue continues to apply to those convertible bonds for which the embedded derivative is not accounted for separately.

(ii) EITF Issue No. 86-15—Increasing-Rate Debt. The EITF dealt with debt that matures three months from date of issuance but may be extended at the discretion of the issuer for an additional period at each maturity date until final maturity. The rate of interest increases each time the note's maturity is extended.

Issue No. 86-15 addressed the following:

- How should the borrower's interest expense be determined and what maturity date should be used in establishing the interest rate?
- How should the debt be classified?
- What period is to be used for amortization?
- If debt is paid at an earlier date than that assumed in arriving at the interest rate, how should the excess accrual be accounted for?

The EITF reached the following consensus:

- The borrower's periodic interest cost should be based on the estimated outstanding term of the borrowing. Plans, intent, and ability to service debt should be considered in estimating the term of the debt.
- Classification of debt as current or noncurrent should reflect the borrower's anticipated source of repayment and is not necessarily identical to the time period used to establish periodic interest rate. That is, if short-term debt is expected to be used to refinance the debt, then the original debt is current. If FASB Statement No. 6 requirements are met, the debt is noncurrent.
- Debt issuance costs should be amortized over the same period used in interest cost determination.
- If debt is redeemed at par value before estimated maturity, the excess interest expense accrual is an adjustment to interest expense and is not an extraordinary item.

The first point above was affected, however, by FASB Statement No. 133, as amended. Under Statement No. 133, the term-extending provisions of the debt instrument should be analyzed to determine whether those provisions constitute an embedded derivative that warrants separate accounting as a derivative.

(iii) EITF Issue No. 86-28—Accounting Implications of Indexed Debt Instruments.   The Task Force considered debt instruments with both contingent and guaranteed payments. The contingent payments were linked to the price of specific commodities or a specific index. In some instances, the right to the contingent payment is separable from the debt instrument.

The issues are:

- Should the proceeds be allocated between the debt liability and the investor's right to receive the contingent payment?
- How should the issuer account for changes in the underlying commodity or index values?

The EITF reached the following consensus:

If the investor's right to a contingent payment is separable, the issuer should allocate the proceeds between the debt instrument and the right. The premium or discount on the debt instrument should be accounted for in accordance with APB Opinion No. 21. No consensus was reached on situations where the contingent payments are not separable.

Whether or not there is any initial allocation of proceeds to the contingent payment, if the index changes so that the issuer would have to pay the investor a contingent payment at maturity, the issuer must recognize a liability. The amount recognized is measured by the extent to which the contingent payment exceeds the amount, if any, originally allocated to that feature. When no proceeds are originally allocated to the contingent payment, the additional liability is an adjustment to the carrying amount of the debt.

This EITF Issue was effectively nullified prospectively by FASB Statement No. 133. The consensus would not apply to debt instruments that contain an embedded derivative that is accounted for under Statement No. 133. However, Statement No. 133 permits entities not to account separately for certain derivatives embedded in pre-1998 or pre-1999 hybrid instruments, including indexed debt instruments.

(iv) EITF Issue No. 00-19—Accounting for Derivative Financial Instruments Indexed to, and Potentially Settled in, a Company's Own Stock.   EITF Issue No. 00-19 codified a consensus reached in earlier EITF Issues concerning a situation in which notes are issued with detachable warrants that include a put. The notes mature in about seven years. The detachable warrants give the holder the right to purchase 6,250 shares of stock for $75 per share and also the right to sell back (put) these warrants to the firm for $2,010 per share at a date several months after the notes mature.

The issues are:

- Should the proceeds received at date of issuance be allocated between the debt and warrant?
- Should the carrying amount of the warrants be accrued to the put price?
- If there is an accrual, should the charge be to interest expense or immediately to retained earnings associated with the equity instrument?

The EITF's consensus is:

The proceeds should be allocated between warrants and debt based on their relative fair values, and the discount should be amortized using the effective interest rate approach in APB Opinion No. 21.

(v) EITF Issue No. 90-19—Convertible Bonds with Issuer Option to Settle for Cash upon Conversion. The EITF considered a situation in which a company issues a debt instrument convertible into a fixed number of shares of stock. Upon conversion, the issuer is either required or has the option to satisfy part or all of the obligation in cash. If the instrument is not converted, cash is paid by the issuer at maturity. Three variants of this transaction are:

1. Upon conversion, the issuer is required to satisfy the entire obligation in cash.
2. Upon conversion, the issuer may satisfy the entire obligation in either cash or stock.
3. Upon conversion, the issuer must satisfy the accreted value in cash and may satisfy the conversion spread in either cash or stock.

The Task Force addressed whether under these three variants the issuer should separately account for the debt obligation and the conversion feature. It also addressed the accounting for the conversion spread (excess of conversion value over accreted amount).

This Issue was subsequently affected by FASB Statement No. 133, which would require the embedded derivative in transaction 1 above to be separated from the debt host contract and accounted for separately as a derivative instrument. Transactions 2 and 3 above should continue to be accounted for in accordance with the consensus, which was that:

- Combined accounting for the conversion feature and debt obligation is appropriate.
- Instrument 2 should be accounted for as conventional convertible debt.
- Instrument 3 should be accounted for similar to indexed debt obligations. The issuer should adjust the carrying amount of the instrument in each reporting period to reflect the current stock price, but not below the accreted value of the instrument. Adjustments to the carrying amount are included currently in income and not spread over future periods.

(b) ASSET-SECURITIZATION TRANSACTIONS. Under FASB Statement No. 140, "Accounting for Transfers and Servicing of Financial Assets and Extinguishments of Liabilities," a transfer of financial assets (or all or a portion of a financial asset) in which the transferor surrenders control over those financial assets is accounted for as a sale to the extent that consideration other than beneficial interests in the transferred assets is received in exchange. The transferor has surrendered control over transferred assets if and only if all of the following conditions are met:

- The transferred assets have been isolated from the transferor—put presumptively beyond the reach of the transferor and its creditors, even in bankruptcy or other receivership.
- Each transferee (or, if the transferee is a qualifying special-purpose entity, each holder of its beneficial interests) has the right to pledge or exchange the assets (or beneficial interests) it received, and no condition both constrains the transferee (or holder) from taking advantage of its right to pledge or exchange and provides more than a trivial benefit to the transferor.

- The transferor does not maintain effective control over the transferred assets through (1) an agreement that both entitles and obligates the transferor to repurchase or redeem them before their maturity or (2) the ability to unilaterally cause the holder to return specific assets, other than through a "cleanup call."

If a transfer of financial assets does not meet criteria for sales recognition, the transferor accounts for the transaction as a secured borrowing with a pledge of collateral.

25.12 SOURCES AND SUGGESTED REFERENCES

Accounting Principles Board, "Omnibus Opinion–1966," APB Opinion No. 10. AICPA, New York, 1966.

———, "Accounting for Convertible Debt and Debt Issued with Stock Purchase Warrants," APB Opinion No. 14. AICPA, New York, 1969.

———, "Interest on Receivables and Payables," APB Opinion No. 21. AICPA, New York, 1971.

———, "Early Extinguishment of Debt," APB Opinion No. 26. AICPA, New York, 1972.

Accounting Standards Executive Committee "Disclosure of Certain Significant Risks and Uncertainties," Statement of Position No. 94-6. AICPA, New York, 1994.

Committee on Accounting Procedure, "Working Capital," Accounting Research Bulletin No. 43, Chapter 3. AICPA, New York, 1953.

Financial Accounting Standards Board, "Sale of Marketable Securities with a Put Option," EITF Issue No. 84-5. FASB, Stamford, CT, 1984.

———, "Convertible Bonds with a Premium Put," EITF Issue No. 85-29. FASB, Stamford, CT, 1985.

———, "Sale of Marketable Securities at a Gain with a Put Option," EITF Issue No. 85-30. FASB, Stamford, CT, 1985.

———, "Comprehensive Review of Sales of Marketable Securities with Put Arrangements," EITF Issue No. 85-40. FASB, Stamford, CT, 1985.

———, "Increasing-Rate Debt," EITF Issue No. 86-15. FASB, Stamford, CT, 1986.

———, "Accounting Implications of Indexed Debt Instruments," EITF Issue No. 86-28. FASB, Stamford, CT, 1986.

———, "Classification of Obligations When a Violation Is Waived by the Creditor," EITF Issue No. 86-30. FASB, Stamford, CT, 1986.

———, "Allocation of Recorded Investment When a Loan or Part of a Loan Is Sold," EITF Issue No. 88-11. FASB, Norwalk, CT, 1988.

———, "Maximum Guarantees on Transfers of Receivables with Recourse." EITF Issue No. 89-2. FASB, Norwalk, CT, 1989.

———, "Convertible Bonds with Issuer Option to Settle for Cash Upon Conversion." EITF Issue No. 90-19. FASB, Norwalk, CT, 1991.

———, "Debtors Accounting for Forfeiture of Real Estate Subject to a Nonrecourse Mortgage," EITF Issue No. 91-2. FASB, Norwalk, CT, 1991.

———, "Measuring Loss Accruals by Transferors for Transfers of Receivables With Recourse." EITF Issue No. 92-2. FASB, Norwalk, CT, 1992.

———, "Debtor's Accounting for a Modification or Exchange of Debt Instruments." EITF Issue No. 96-19. FASB, Norwalk, CT, 1997.

———, "Liability Recognition for Certain Employee Termination Benefits and Other Costs to Exit an Activity (including Certain Costs Incurred in a Restructuring)." EITF Issue No. 94-3. FASB, Norwalk, CT, 1994.

———, "Classification of a Short-Term Obligation Repaid Prior to Being Replaced by a Long-Term Security." FASB Interpretation No. 8. FASB, Stamford, CT, 1976.

———, "Reasonable Estimation of the Amount of a Loss," FASB Interpretation No. 14. FASB, Stamford, CT, 1976.

———, "Offsetting of Amounts Related to Certain Contracts (an Interpretation of APB Opinion No. 10 and FASB Statement No. 105)," FASB Interpretation No. 39. FASB, Norwalk, CT, 1993.

_____, "Offsetting of Amounts Related to Certain Repurchase and Reverse Repurchase Agreements (an Interpretation of APB Opinion No. 10 and a Modification of FASB Interpretation No. 39)," FASB Interpretation No. 41. FASB, Norwalk, CT, 1994.

_____, "Elements of Financial Statements," Statement of Financial Accounting Concepts No. 6. FASB, Stamford, CT, 1985.

_____, "Accounting for Contingencies," Statement of Financial Accounting Standards No. 5. FASB, Stamford, CT, 1975.

_____, "Classification of Short-Term Obligations Expected to Be Refinanced," Statement of Financial Accounting Standards No. 6. FASB, Stamford, CT, 1975.

_____, "Accounting for Leases," Statement of Financial Accounting Standards No. 13. FASB, Stamford, CT, 1976.

_____, "Accounting by Debtors and Creditors for Troubled Debt Restructurings," Statement of Financial Accounting Standards No. 15. FASB, Stamford, CT, 1977.

_____, "Balance Sheet Classification of Deferred Income Taxes," Statement of Financial Accounting Standards No. 37. FASB, Stamford, CT, 1980.

_____, "Accounting for Compensated Absences," Statement of Financial Accounting Standards No. 43. FASB, Stamford, CT, 1980.

_____, "Disclosure of Long-Term Obligations," Statement of Financial Accounting Standards No. 47. FASB, Stamford, CT, 1981.

_____, "Accounting for Product Financing Arrangements," Statement of Financial Accounting Standards No. 49. FASB, Stamford, CT, 1981.

_____, "Classification of Obligations That Are Callable by the Creditor," Statement of Financial Accounting Standards No. 78. FASB, Stamford, CT, 1983.

_____, "Accounting for Income Taxes," Statement of Financial Accounting Standards No. 109. FASB, Stamford, CT, 1991.

_____, "Accounting for Transfers and Servicing of Financial Assets and Extinguishments of Liabilities," Statement of Financial Accounting Standards No. 140. FASB, Norwalk, 2000.

_____, "Disclosure of Information about Capital Structure," Statement of Financial Accounting Standards No. 129. FASB, Norwalk, 1997.

_____, "Early Extinguishment of Debt through Exchange for Common or Preferred Stock," Technical Bulletin No. 80-1. FASB, Stamford, CT, 1980.

_____, "Classification of Debt Restructurings by Debtors and Creditors," Technical Bulletin No. 80-2. FASB, Stamford, CT, 1980.

_____, "Applicability of FASB Statement 15 to Debtors in Bankruptcy Situations," Technical Bulletin No. 81-6. FASB, Stamford, CT, 1981.

Heath, Loyd, "Financial Reporting and the Evaluation of Solvency," Accounting Research Monograph No. 3. AICPA, 1978.

Securities and Exchange Commission, "Form and Content of and Requirements for Financial Statements," Regulation S-X. SEC, Washington DC, Updated.

_____, "Allocation of Debt Issue Costs in a Business Combination," Staff Accounting Bulletin No. 77. SEC, Washington DC, 1988.

_____, "Accounting and Disclosures Relating to Loss Contingencies," Staff Accounting Bulletin 92. SEC, Washington, DC, 1993.

_____, "Recognition of a Gain or Loss on Early Extinguishment of Debt," Staff Accounting Bulletin 94. SEC, Washington, DC, 1995.

Lorenson, Leonard, "Accounting for Liabilities," Accounting Research Monograph No. 4. AICPA, New York, 1992.

Storey, Reed, and Storey, Sylvia, "The Framework of Financial Accounting Concepts and Standards," Special Report. FASB, Norwalk, CT, 1998.

Schroeder, Alice D., and Upton, Wayne S., "A Fresh Look at Statement 5," FASB Status Report. No. 244. pp. 4–12. FASB, Norwalk, CT.

Financial Accounting Standards Board, "Using Cash Flow Information and Present Value in Accounting Measurements," Statement of Financial Accounting Concepts No. 7. FASB, Norwalk, CT, 2000.

———, "Accounting for Convertible Securities with Beneficial Conversion Features or Contingently Adjustable Conversion Ratios," EITF Issue No. 98-5. FASB, Norwalk, CT, 1998.

———, "Accounting for Derivative Financial Instruments Indexed to, and Potentially Settled in, a Company's Own Stock," EITF Issue No. 00-19. FASB, Norwalk, CT, 2000.

———, "Application of Issue No. 98-5 to Certain Convertible Instruments," EITF Issue 00-27. FASB, Norwalk, CT, 2000.

———, "Disclosures about Fair Value of Financial Instruments," Statement of Financial Accounting Standards No. 107. FASB, Norwalk, CT, 1991.

———, "Exemption from Certain Required Disclosures about Financial Instruments for Certain Nonpublic Entities," Statement of Financial Accounting Standards No. 126. FASB, Norwalk, CT, 1996.

———, "Distinguishing between Liability and Equity Instruments and Accounting for Instruments with Characteristics of Both," Discussion Memorandum. FASB, Norwalk, CT, 1990.

Financial Accounting Standards Board, "Rescission of FASB Statements No. 4, 44, and 64, Amendment of FASB Statement No. 13, and Technical Corrections," Statement of Financial Accounting Standards No. 145. FASB, Norwalk, CT, 2002.

———, "Guarantor's Accounting and Disclosure Requirements for Guarantees, Including Indirect Guarantees of Indebtedness of Others—an interpretation of FASB Statements No. 5, 57, and 107 and rescission of FASB Interpretation No. 34." FASB Interpretation No. 45. FASB, Norwalk, CT, 2002.

———, "Accounting for Certain Financial Instruments with Characteristics of both Liabilities and Equity." Statement of Financial Accounting Standards No. 150. FASB, Norwalk, CT, 2003.

———, "Application of FASB Interpretation No. 45 to Minimum Revenue Guarantees Granted to a Business or Its Owners." FASB Staff Position No. FIN 45-3. FASB, Norwalk, CT, 2005.

———, "Accounting for Costs Associated with Exit or Disposal Activities." Statement of Financial Accounting Standards No. 146. FASB, Norwalk, CT, 2002.

———, "Accounting for Conditional Asset Retirement Obligations." FASB Interpretation No. 47. FASB, Norwalk, CT, 2005.

———, "Disclosure Requirements under FASB Statement No. 129, *Disclosure of Information about Capital Structure*, Relating to Contingently Convertible Securities." FASB Staff Position No. FAS 129-1, FASB, Norwalk, CT, 2004.

———, "Determining Whether a One-Time Termination Benefit Offered in Connection with an Exit or Disposal Activity Is, in Substance, an Enhancement to an Ongoing Benefit Arrangement." FASB Staff Position No. FAS 146-1. FASB, Norwalk, CT, 2003.

———, "Accounting for Mandatorily Redeemable Shares Requiring Redemption by Payment of an Amount that Differs from the Book Value of Those Shares, under FASB Statement No. 150, *Accounting for Certain Financial Instruments with Characteristics of both Liabilities and Equity*." FASB Staff Position No. FAS 150-2. FASB, Norwalk, CT, 2003.

———, "Effective Date, Disclosures, and Transition for Mandatorily Redeemable Financial Instruments of Certain Nonpublic Entities and Certain Mandatorily Redeemable Noncontrolling Interests under FASB Statement No. 150, *Accounting for Certain Financial Instruments with Characteristics of both Liabilities and Equity*." FASB Staff Position No. FAS 150-3. FASB, Norwalk, CT, 2003.

———, "Issuers' Accounting for Employee Stock Ownership Plans under FASB Statement No. 150, *Accounting for Certain Financial Instruments with Characteristics of both Liabilities and Equity*." FASB Staff Position No. FAS 150-4. FASB, Norwalk, CT, 2003.

———, "Issuers' Accounting under Statement 150 for Freestanding Warrants and Other Similar Instruments on Shares That Are Redeemable." FASB Staff Position No. FAS 150-5. FASB, Norwalk, CT, 2005.

———, "Accounting for Intellectual Property Infringement Indemnifications under FASB Interpretation No. 45, *Guarantor's Accounting and Disclosure Requirements for Guarantees, Including Indirect Guarantees of Indebtedness of Others*." FASB Staff Position No. FIN 45-1. FASB, Norwalk, CT, 2003.

———, "Whether FASB Interpretation No. 45, *Guarantor's Accounting and Disclosure Requirements for Guarantees, Including Indirect Guarantees of Indebtedness of Others*, Provides Support for Subsequently Accounting for a Guarantor's Liability at Fair Value. FASB Staff Position No. FIN 45-2. FASB, Norwalk, CT, 2003.

———, "Application of FASB Interpretation No. 45 to Minimum Revenue Guarantees Granted to a Business or Its Owners." FASB Staff Position No. FIN 45-3. FASB, Norwalk, CT, 2005.

———, "Application of EITF Issue No. 00-19 to Freestanding Financial Instruments Originally Issued as Employee Compensation." FASB Staff Position No. EITF 00-19-1. FASB, Norwalk, CT, 2005.

———, "Determining Whether a Debtor's Modification or Exchange of Debt Instruments is within the Scope of FASB Statement No. 15." EITF Issue No. 02-4. FASB, Norwalk, CT, 2002.   International Accounting Standards Committee, "Framework for the Preparation and Presentation of Financial Statements." IASC, London, 1989.

Accounting Standards Executive Committee, "Environmental Remediation Liabilities," Statement of Position 96–1. AICPA, New York, 1996.

Securities and Exchange Commission, "Codification of Financial Reporting Policies." SEC, Washington, DC, Updated.

Accounting Standards Executive Committee, "Accounting by Participating Mortgage Loan Borrowers," Statement of Position 97-1. AICPA, New York, 1997.

CHAPTER 26

DERIVATIVES AND HEDGE ACCOUNTING

Robert L. Royall II, CPA, CFA, MBA
Ernst & Young LLP

Francine Mellors, CPA
Ernst & Young LLP

The editors wish to acknowledge the previous contributions to this chapter by Norman Strauss, CPA, of the Stan Ross Department of Accountancy, Zicklen School of Business.

26.1 INTRODUCTION

In January 1992, the Financial Accounting Standards Board (FASB) began deliberating issues related to derivatives and hedging transactions. After much controversy, the FASB issued Statement No. 133, "Accounting for Derivative Instruments and Hedging Activities," in June 1998. It was discussed at over 100 FASB meetings, was exposed for comments twice, and was the subject of two different congressional hearings. Legislation had even been proposed in an attempt to override the Statement.

Statement No. 133 was effective for financial statements for fiscal years beginning after June 15, 2000, and calendar-year companies were required to apply the new standard on January 1, 2001. The transition adjustments resulting from adoption were required to be recognized in income and other comprehensive income (stockholders' equity), as appropriate, as a cumulative effect of an accounting change. The Statement superseded Statement No. 80, "Accounting for Futures Contracts," Statement No. 105, "Disclosure of Information about Financial Instruments with Off-Balance-Sheet Risk and Financial Instruments with Concentrations of Credit Risk," and Statement No. 119, "Disclosures about Derivative Financial Instruments and Fair Value of Financial Instruments," and amends the hedging sections of Statement No. 52, "Foreign Currency Translation." It amended Statement No. 107, "Disclosures about Fair Value of Financial Instruments," to include in Statement No. 107 the disclosure provisions about concentrations of credit risk from Statement No. 105.

(a) THE FUNDAMENTAL CONCEPTS. The FASB considered various approaches to reconcile and extend the existing hedge accounting guidelines in Statements Nos. 52 and 80. However, the Board decided that such an approach was not practical and instead decided to pursue a new approach to applying hedge accounting. The four basic underlying premises of the new approach are:

1. Derivatives represent rights or obligations that meet the definitions of assets (future cash inflows due from another party) or liabilities (future cash outflows owed to another party) and should be reported in the financial statements.
2. Fair value is the most relevant measure for financial instruments and the only relevant measure for derivatives. Derivatives should be measured at fair value, and adjustments to the carrying amount of hedged items should reflect changes in their fair value (i.e., gains and losses) attributable to the risk being hedged arising while the hedge is in effect.
3. Only items that are assets or liabilities should be reported as such in the financial statements. (The Board believes gains and losses from hedging activities are not assets or liabilities and, therefore, should not be deferred.)

4. Special accounting for items designated as being hedged should be provided only for qualifying transactions, and one aspect of qualification should be an assessment of the expectation of the effectiveness of the hedge (i.e., offsetting changes in fair values or cash flows).

The Board has announced that Statement No. 133 on derivatives and hedging is simply an interim step on the road to accomplish its "vision" of having all financial instruments measured at fair value.

The key changes are:

- All derivatives are carried at fair value.
- Hedge accounting continues, but the accounting varies based on the type of hedge: fair value, cash flow, or net investments in foreign operations.
- Specific criteria to be able to use hedge accounting are established.
- The ineffective portion of a hedge is recognized in income and not deferred, thus creating potential volatility in income.
- Cash flow hedges are recognized in other comprehensive income, thus creating potential volatility in equity.
- Hedging certain foreign currency transactions is easier under the new rules. The definition of a derivative is now broader.
- New disclosures are required.

(b) SCOPE OF STATEMENT NO. 133

(i) General Scope Provisions. Statement No. 133 applies to all entities. However, special provisions govern not-for-profit entities and other entities (e.g., employee benefit plans) that do not report earnings as a separate caption in a statement of financial performance.

(ii) What Is a Derivative? An understanding of the FASB's complex definition of a derivative is essential to be able to apply the new Statement. While Statement No. 133 takes several paragraphs to define a derivative, it reflects the following key concepts:

- A derivative's cash flows or fair value must fluctuate and vary based on the changes in one or more underlying variables.
- The contract must be based on one or more notional amounts or payment provisions or both, even though title to that amount never changes hands. The underlying and notional amount determine the amount of settlement, even regardless of whether a settlement is required.
- The contract requires no initial net investment, or an insignificant initial net investment.
- The contract can readily be settled by a net cash payment, or with an asset that is readily convertible to cash.

Examples of derivatives include swaps, options, futures, some forward contracts, swaptions, caps, collars, and floors. In a significant change from prior practice, certain items such as convertible debt held as an investment, some commodity purchase agreements, some structured notes, and some insurance contracts also are derivatives or contain embedded derivatives.

(iii) What Is an "underlying"?. An "underlying" is a variable or index whose market movements cause the fair market value or cash flows of a derivative to fluctuate. An underlying may be a price or rate of an asset or liability but is not the asset or liability itself. Examples of underlyings include London Interbank Offered Rate (LIBOR) in an interest rate swap, the price of crude oil in a forward crude oil contract, or the spot exchange rate of a foreign currency in a foreign currency option. When the underlying fluctuates, the market value of the derivative and the amount of cash projected to be exchanged between the parties change. Some derivatives have multiple underlyings.

(iv) Notional Amount.   While the underlying is the variable in a derivative, the notional amount is the fixed amount or quantity that determines the size of the change caused by the movement of the underlying. Examples include the stated principal amount in an interest rate swap, the stated number of bushels in a wheat futures contract, the number of barrels in a crude oil swap contract, and the contracted amount of Euros in a foreign currency forward.

(v) Initial Net Investment.   Derivatives are unique in that the parties do not have to initially invest in or exchange the notional amount. Though some contracts can settle through physical delivery (e.g., futures and forwards), a derivative really represents an investment in the change in value caused by the underlying, and not an actual investment in the notional amount or quantity of the underlying. The notional amount is just a factor in determining the size of the potential changes in fair value of the derivative. For example, in a typical receive fixed and pay floating interest rate swap with a notional amount of $10 million, no one pays or receives $10 million. The $10 million notional amount is only multiplied by the difference in the fixed interest rate and the floating rate to determine how much cash must be paid between the parties and by whom. As the notional amount gets larger, the greater the effect that changes in the underlying will have on the amount exchanged between the parties.

Some derivatives will require an initial net investment as compensation for time value (such as an option premium) or for "off-market" terms (such as a premium on an interest rate swap which pays the holder a higher fixed rate than current market rates would indicate). Such contracts are still considered "derivatives" in the scope of Statement No. 133.

(vi) Net Settlement.   Typically, a derivative can be settled in cash rather than by the delivery of the underlying item. However, Statement No. 133 will extend this concept to include contracts that can be settled in assets that are readily convertible into cash (e.g., Treasury securities, marketable equity securities, commodities) or for which a market mechanism exists to facilitate liquidation of the contract for a net cash payment even though the contract itself does not contemplate a net cash settlement (e.g., futures contracts).

To meet the criterion of an asset that puts the recipient in a position not substantially different from net settlement, the asset must be readily convertible to cash. (By cash, the FASB generally means the functional currency of the reporting entity.) The FASB believes that to be readily convertible into cash, the asset must have interchangeable (fungible) units and quoted prices available in an active market that can rapidly absorb the quantity held by the entity without significantly affecting the price. Thus, the asset being received must be actively traded. Under this concept, a forward contract entered into by a rental car company to buy automobiles would not be a derivative; but a forward contract to buy unleaded gasoline may (see specific exclusions, which follow) be a derivative, because unleaded gasoline is actively traded.

Additional examples will be helpful in understanding the types of instruments that will be included in the definition. Consider first a contract for the purchase of a U.S. Treasury security that provides for a settlement date at a date that would be later than normal for the purchase of such an investment. Because a Treasury security can be readily converted to cash, this contract would be considered a derivative even though the only means of settlement is by delivery of the security. Similarly, a foreign currency forward contract for a highly liquid currency (e.g., Japanese yen) also would be considered a derivative, even if it is required to be settled by delivery of the currency. However, a foreign currency forward contract that requires the delivery of an illiquid currency (e.g., Venezuelan bolivars) would not be considered a derivative under Statement No. 133. (Delivery of a foreign currency is not delivery of "cash" unless that currency is the functional currency of the reporting entity.) Making these distinctions will require considerable judgment.

(vii) "Surprise" Derivatives.   The effect of defining a derivative by characteristics rather than by contract types has often surprising implications. Companies may hold stock purchase warrants, participating in alliances with Internet start-ups. These warrants meet the definition of a derivative if they can be settled by delivery of shares in a publicly traded company, and those shares once delivered are not restricted from trading for the first 31 days. Typically, warrants to purchase shares in an Internet start-up company satisfy the definition of a derivative after that company undergoes an initial public offering (IPO). Ordinary commodity contracts, in addition to commodity futures contracts, also satisfy the definition of a derivative if the commodity has interchangeable (fungible) units and quoted prices available in an active market. Therefore, contracts to purchase or sell crude oil, natural gas, corn, cotton, gold, aluminum, and a host of other commodities will likely satisfy the definition, and the fair value of such contracts will fluctuate if the transaction price is fixed or partially fixed. As the next section explains, such commodity contracts may be able to be exempted from the provisions of Statement No. 133 if they are deemed to be "normal."

(viii) Items the Financial Accounting Standards Board Specifically Excluded from the Definition of a Derivative. The FASB believed that certain contracts that otherwise meet the literal definition of a derivative should not be accounted for as derivatives. Accordingly, Statement No. 133 specifically excludes several types of contracts from the scope and, therefore, the methods of accounting for these contracts will not be affected. These include:

- "Regular-way" (normal) securities trades (e.g., purchases or sales of securities that settle in the normal course for the particular security).
- Normal purchases and sales of assets other than financial instruments (i.e., commodities) for which net settlement is not intended and physical delivery is probable (and so documented) that are in quantities expected to be used or sold over a reasonable period in the normal course of business (e.g., the forward purchase of unleaded gasoline by a rental car company for the quantity it expects to use in the next month). Evaluating what is "normal" will be unique to each entity and may be influenced by industry customs for acquiring and storing commodities, an entity's operating locations, past trends, expected future demand, and other contracts for delivery of similar items.
- Certain insurance contracts[1] that compensate the holder only as a result of an identifiable insurable event (generally, traditional life insurance and property and casualty contracts).
- Certain financial guarantee contracts that provide for payments to reimburse the guaranteed party for a loss because the debtor fails to pay. Other financial guarantee contracts could be derivatives under the new Statement if they provide for payments to be made in response to a change in an underlying, such as a decrease in a referenced entity's credit rating (i.e., credit derivatives).
- Contracts issued by an entity in connection with stock compensation arrangements (e.g., performance-based stock option plans). (These contracts could be derivatives to the recipient.)
- Contracts indexed to the entity's own stock and classified in stockholders' equity (e.g., rights, warrants, and options). (These contracts may be derivatives to the counterparty.)
- Contracts issued by an entity as contingent consideration in a business combination. (These contracts could be derivatives to the recipient.)
- Nonexchange-traded contracts with underlyings based on the following:
  - Climatic, geological, or other physical variables (e.g., heating degree days, level of snowfall, seismic readings).
  - The price or value of a nonfinancial asset or liability of one of the parties that is not readily convertible to cash or does not require delivery of an asset that is readily convertible to cash (e.g., an option to purchase or sell real estate that one of the parties own, or a firm commitment to purchase or sell machinery). This exception applies only to nonfinancial assets that are unique and only if a nonfinancial asset related to the underlying is owned by the party that would not benefit under the contract from an increase in the price or value

---

[1] Contracts issued by insurance enterprises that differ from the "traditional" type contracts may meet the definition of a derivative (e.g., equity indexed annuities and variable life contracts).

of the nonfinancial asset. For example, an option to buy real estate at a fixed price is not a derivative because the owner (i.e., prospective seller) would not benefit from the contract if the price of the real estate increases above the option price.

   ◦ Specified volumes of sales or service revenues of one of the parties (e.g., royalty agreements).

• Derivatives that serve as impediments to sales accounting (e.g., a residual value guarantee of a leased asset by the lessor that prevents the lease from being a sales-type lease or a call option that enables a transferor of financial instruments to repurchase the transferred assets and prevents sales accounting for the transfer).

(ix) Embedded Derivatives.   Occasionally, derivatives are embedded in other instruments, such as a debt instrument where the interest payments fluctuate with changes in the Standard and Poor's (S&P) 500 index or where the principal amount is affected by the price of gold. Generally, if the economic characteristics and risks of the embedded derivative are clearly and closely related to the economic characteristics and risks of the host contract, it is outside the scope of the new Statement, and the accounting for the derivative is based on the accounting for the host instrument. When the economic characteristics and risks of the embedded derivative are not clearly and closely related to the economic characteristics and risks of the host instrument, however, the embedded derivative should be separated and accounted for as a derivative instrument under Statement No. 133.[2] (The bifurcation provisions do not extend to a derivative embedded in another derivative, such as a cancelable swap.)

In the case of an equity indexed note (e.g., principal indexed to the S&P's 500 index), changes in the stock indices are not clearly and closely related to the interest rate based economic characteristics of debt, so the derivative would have to be bifurcated and separately accounted for using the new rules. However, a note with interest payments tied to changes in the debtor's credit rating (which could not result in a negative yield) would meet the "clearly and closely related" test and would not have to be accounted for as a derivative, because interest rates are closely aligned with the credit rating of the debtor. Similarly, typical callable and putable bonds also are not subject to Statement No. 133 because the changes in value of the call and put features are clearly and closely related to market interest rate changes, like the bond itself.

Statement No. 133 does not necessarily treat the issuer and recipient of certain contracts in the same way. In several instances, the recipient of a contract will be considered to have a derivative contract, while the issuer of the same contract will not. For example, an investor in convertible debt that includes an embedded equity call option which is not clearly and closely related to a debt instrument will be required to bifurcate the option and separately account for it as a derivative. Issuers of convertible debt, however, will not be considered to have issued a derivative because the option can be settled only by issuance of the issuer's own equity securities.

Statement No. 133 includes numerous examples illustrating the "clearly and closely related" criterion to help preparers determine if bifurcation is necessary.

(c) GENERAL REQUIREMENTS.   The Statement requires all derivatives to be recorded on the balance sheet at fair value. The guidance in Statement No. 107 is to be applied in determining fair values.

Fair value represents the amount at which an asset (liability) could be bought (incurred) or sold (settled) in a current transaction between willing parties; that is, other than in a forced or liquidation

---

[2] As a "boundary" to the "clearly and closely related" concept, the Statement also contains the following additional guidance: If the host contract is a debt instrument and the embedded derivative's underlying is interest rate related, the embedded derivative meets the clearly and closely related criteria unless (1) the hybrid instrument could be settled in such a way that the investor would not recover substantially all of its initial recorded investment or (2) the embedded derivative could at least double the investor's initial rate of return on the host contract and could also result in a rate of return that is at least twice what otherwise would be the market return for a similar contract.

sale. (The ambiguity of that definition is discussed in Section 1.3(b)(v).) The requirement to obtain fair values for all derivatives on a regular (at least quarterly) basis is a significant change from prior practice.

Statement No. 133 allows "special accounting" for the following three categories of hedge transactions:

1. Hedges of changes in the fair value of assets, liabilities, or firm commitments (referred to as *fair value hedges*)
2. Hedges of variable cash flows of recognized assets or liabilities, or of forecasted transactions (cash flow hedges)
3. Hedges of foreign currency exposures of net investments in foreign operations

Changes in the fair value of derivatives not meeting the criteria to use one of these three hedging categories must be recognized in income. For those that meet the criteria, Statement No. 133 provides an approach to hedge accounting that differs from prior practice. The three hedge types, the criteria, and the special accounting provisions for derivatives that meet the criteria are discussed in further detail in the following sections. However, for background purposes, the following is a brief overview of the special accounting within Statement No. 133:

- To even be considered as a hedge, in addition to other criteria, a derivative instrument must be "highly effective" in offsetting exposure due to changes in fair value or cash flows of the hedged item.
- In a fair value hedge, changes in the fair value of both the derivative and the hedged item attributable to the risk being hedged are recognized in earnings. Thus, to the extent the hedge is perfectly effective, the change in the fair value of the hedged item will be offset in income with only the net effect of the hedge impacting earnings.
- In a cash flow hedge, to the extent the hedge is effective, changes in the fair value of the derivative are recognized as a component of other comprehensive income in stockholders' equity until the hedged transaction affects earnings. The accounting for the hedged transaction is unaffected by the placement of the hedge.
- In a hedge of foreign currency exposures in a net investment in a foreign operation, to the extent the hedge is effective, the change in the fair value of the derivative is treated as a translation gain/loss and recognized in other comprehensive income offsetting other translation gains/losses arising in consolidation. Thus, for this hedge type, the new rules are similar to prior practice.
- If a derivative is highly effective but not perfectly effective and does not exactly offset the changes in fair value or cash flows of the hedged item or transaction, the ineffective portion must be recognized in income when the change in fair value of the derivative is recognized on the balance sheet.

Statement No. 133 clarifies that a hedging instrument generally can be only a derivative, as defined by the new Statement. A nonderivative instrument (e.g., a Treasury note) cannot be designated as a hedging instrument except when it results in a foreign currency transaction gain or loss and is designated as hedging the foreign currency exposure of a net investment in a foreign operation or of changes in the fair value of a foreign currency-denominated firm commitment.

(d) HEDGE EFFECTIVENESS AND OTHER CRITERIA FOR SPECIAL ACCOUNTING

(i) Hedge Effectiveness. One of the most difficult aspects of the Statement is determining when the special accounting for hedges is allowed. The basic premise for all three types of hedges is that a derivative must be expected to be highly effective in achieving offsetting changes in fair value attributable to the risk being hedged. In other words, the change in the value of the hedging instrument must offset the change in the value of the hedged item. The FASB has been purposefully vague in providing guidance as to how much ineffectiveness is permitted before a hedge relationship can no longer be deemed highly effective. The Statement refers to prior guidance on correlation (i.e., Statement No. 80), in which an 80 percent effective hedge is considered to be highly effective, but anything less effective is considered "ineffective." Further, the Statement requires a company to define how it will measure the effectiveness of a hedge relationship, at both the inception of the hedge and over the entire life of the relationship.

Under Statement No. 133, hedge effectiveness affects more than just whether the derivative qualifies for hedge accounting. In a change from prior practice, hedge ineffectiveness, the amount by which the change in the value of the hedge does not exactly offset the change in the value of the hedged item, will often be recorded in income immediately, even for highly effective derivatives that qualify for hedge accounting. For example, if a hedged item's fair value increases by $10, but the derivative only offsets the change by $8, there is $2 of hedge ineffectiveness. Likewise, if the derivative's fair value changes by $10, but the hedged item's fair value changes by only $8, there also is $2 of hedge ineffectiveness. The extent to which the ineffectiveness is recognized in earnings differs depending on whether a hedge is a fair value or cash flow hedge.[3]

(ii) Derivatives with Inherent Ineffectiveness.   Statement No. 133 permits the exclusion of a portion of a change in value of a derivative from the effectiveness assessment. The change in value of the excluded component of the fair value of the derivative is considered to be inherently ineffective and recognized in earnings immediately. For example, companies may exclude the time value of options and differences between forward and spot rates that exist at the inception of a hedge with a forward contract from their assessment of hedge effectiveness, because there is no offsetting change in the value of the hedged item for this element of the hedge. These costs can be viewed as the cost of entering into the hedge, similar to an insurance premium when obtaining insurance. As a result, these costs are effectively excluded from the special accounting for the hedge. However, unlike prior practice in which such costs could be recorded in income ratably over the life of a hedge, as one might account for an actual insurance premium, the Statement requires that they be recognized in income based on changes in their fair value because these costs are components of the overall fair value of the derivative. The result is a much more volatile earnings recognition process for these hedging costs, even though the amounts of such costs are known at the outset of a hedge.

To illustrate this concept, assume in order to hedge an anticipated transaction six months from now, a company enters into a six-month Euro forward foreign currency contract when the forward exchange rate is Euro 1.1:$1 but the spot rate is Euro 1.0:$1. The anticipated transaction will actually be consummated at the spot rate on the date of the transaction, and as it gets closer to the date of the transaction, the forward rate and the spot rate will converge. If at the date of the hedged transaction, the spot rate is still Euro 1.0:$1, the fair value of the derivative will have changed due to the passage of time by the Euro 0.1 change in the forward rate. However, the present value of expected cash flows of the hedged transaction will have changed only due to the passage of time and not because the spot rate has changed. Thus, the change in value of the derivative due to the initial difference between the forward rate and the spot rate is inherently ineffective at hedging the anticipated transaction. As a result, the Statement allows companies to exclude this difference from their assessment of hedge effectiveness. However, the derivative itself, the forward contract, must always be carried at fair value on the balance sheet. Therefore, the difference in the forward and the spot rates at inception, commonly referred to as the *premium* or *discount*, is effectively part of the cost of the hedge that is recognized in income over the life of the contract as the contracts change in fair value and the forward and spot rates converge.[4]

---

[3] For cash flow hedges, when the change in fair value of the derivative is less than the change in the expected future cash flows on the hedged transaction, the hedge is not considered to have ineffectiveness that must be recorded in the income statement.

[4] Statement No. 133, in the case of foreign currency forwards, does not allow an entity to base its assessment of effectiveness o changes in the forward rates, rather than changes in the spot rates, which

A similar effect occurs with the time value of options. At inception, the value of an option consists of time value and perhaps intrinsic value, if the option is already in-the-money. This time value decays as an option approaches its expiration date, while intrinsic value may increase or decrease depending on movements of the fair value of the underlying item. As the intrinsic value increases, the holder of the option will desire to exercise it. If exercised, the value of an option is based primarily on its intrinsic value. Thus, when exercised, a derivative has changed in value because the time value component of the option has decreased from its original fair value, but the hedged item will not have experienced an offsetting change in value that can be related to the time value decay. Therefore, the time value of the option is inherently ineffective in most common hedge designs. Again, the Statement allows companies to exclude the time value of the option from their assessment of hedge effectiveness, but the option must always be carried at its fair value including any time value that may exist. This results in changes in the fair value of the time value of the option being recognized in income over the life of the option. This recognition pattern will be different from the straight-line amortization method that has generally been previously used. Most bothersome for many companies is that time value can actually increase in certain periods leading to an even greater future decay, particularly when the underlying experiences highly volatile movements or the fair value of the underlying moves closer to the exercise price of the option.

(iii) Derivatives with Ineffective Designs.   In contrast to the concept of derivatives with inherent ineffectiveness, hedge ineffectiveness can also result when there is a less than perfect matching of the derivative and the hedged item. A derivative that has a similar, but not identical, underlying basis with the hedged item illustrates this condition. For example, using a Dutch guilder-based forward to hedge a Belgian currency exposure, or using a LIBOR-based swap to hedge debt tied to commercial paper rates, results in some hedge ineffectiveness. Ineffectiveness also arises when differences in the terms of the derivative and the hedged item exist, even when the underlying bases are the same. Such differences might include the notional amounts, rate reset dates, maturity, cash flow receipt/payment dates, or, in the case of commodity hedges, delivery location differences. For example, foreign currency swaps that call for quarterly settlements will not perfectly hedge anticipated royalty payments that occur monthly. Likewise, fixed rate debt that pays interest on February 1 and August 1 cannot be perfectly hedged with a swap with cash flow dates set to be April 1 and October 1.

(iv) The Shortcut Method.   In an effort to relieve companies from having to constantly assess whether their derivatives are perfectly effective, Statement No. 133 outlines certain criteria for derivatives that, if met, permit an assumption that the hedge is perfectly effective. These criteria are sometimes referred to as the *shortcut method*, because when these criteria are met, the hedge is considered perfectly effective and the accounting is significantly simplified. However, the ability to use the shortcut method is limited, because the Statement only provides for the shortcut method with respect to interest rate swaps and commodity forward contracts.

An entity may assume that a hedge of a forecasted purchase of a commodity with a forward contract will be highly effective and that there will be no ineffectiveness if:

- The forward contract is for purchase of the same quantity of the same commodity at the same time and location as the hedged forecasted purchase.
- The fair value of the forward contract at inception is zero.
- Either the change in the discount or premium on the forward contract is excluded from the assessment of effectiveness or the change in expected cash flows on the forecasted transaction is based on the forward price for the commodity.

---

effectively allows the time value to be considered part of the hedge itself instead of being recognized currently in income.

Statement No. 133 also provides specific guidelines as to when an interest rate swap can be assumed to be perfectly effective. All of the following conditions must be met:

- The notional amount of the swap matches the principal amount of the interest bearing asset or liability.
- The fair value of the swap at the inception of the hedge is zero. The formula for computing net settlements under the swap is the same for each net settlement (i.e., the fixed rate is the same throughout the term, and the variable rate is based on the same index and includes the same constant adjustment or no adjustment).
- The interest-bearing asset or liability is not prepayable at other than its fair value.[5]
- The index on which the variable leg of the swap is based matches the benchmark interest rate designated as the interest rate risk being hedged for that hedging relationship.
- Any other terms in the interest-bearing instrument or swap are typical of those instruments and do not invalidate the assumption of no ineffectiveness.

In addition, if the hedge is a fair value hedge, the swap must have the following:

- The expiration date of the swap must match the maturity date of the interest-bearing asset or liability.
- There can be no floor or ceiling on the variable interest rate of the swap.
- The interval between repricings of the variable leg of the swap must be frequent enough to justify an assumption that the variable payment or receipt is at a market rate (generally, three to six months or less).

The short-cut method is available only for cash flow hedges of variable rate assets and liabilities. It is not available for hedges of forecasted transactions that result from the maturity and reissuance of short-term fixed-rate assets and liabilities, such as commercial paper programs. In a cash flow hedge, the swap must have the following:

- All interest receipts or payments on the variable-rate asset or liability during the term of the swap must be designated as hedged, and no interest payments beyond the term of the swap are designated as hedged.
- There can be no floor or cap on the variable interest rate of the swap unless the variable-rate asset or liability has a floor or cap. In that case, the swap must have a floor or cap on the variable interest rate that is comparable to the floor or cap on the variable-rate asset or liability. The Statement indicates that "comparable" does not mean equal. However, by illustrating comparability, the FASB has indicated that a strict algebraic relationship should exist between the barriers. The Statement indicates that if a swap's variable rate is LIBOR and an asset's variable rate is LIBOR plus 2 percent, a 10 percent cap on the swap would be comparable to a 12 percent cap on the asset.
- The repricing dates must match those of the variable-rate asset or liability.

Through the Derivatives Implementation Group (DIG) interpretations, the FASB has insisted that the use of the term *match* — in the criteria required to apply the shortcut method-means "exactly match." A company cannot use the shortcut method if it merely comes close to matching some of these criteria. In addition, the shortcut method cannot be analogized to any other types of derivative instruments.

---

[5] This criterion does not apply to an interest-bearing asset or liability that is prepayable solely due to an embedded call or put option, provided that the hedging interest rate swap contains an embedded mirror-image call or put option.

Another key benefit, in addition to not having to periodically evaluate effectiveness, is the accounting simplicity of the shortcut method. As always, the derivative is recorded at fair value as either an asset or a liability. But with the shortcut method, a company can assume that the hedged item changes exactly as much as the derivative's fair value changes. In a fair value hedge, the hedged item is adjusted exactly the same amount as the derivative, with no impact on earnings. In a cash flow hedge, other comprehensive income is adjusted exactly the same amount as the derivative, with no impact on earnings. With respect to interest rate swaps, each periodic cash settlement is accrued in the income statement as an adjustment to interest income or expense, as typically was done prior to Statement No. 133. In many ways, the shortcut method mirrors the prior "synthetic instrument" accounting in the income statement, but the balance sheet is grossed up as a necessary consequence of reflecting the derivative at fair value.

(e) CRITERIA FOR HEDGING.   The following criteria apply to all derivatives and hedged items, as indicated below:

(i) Hedge Criteria (All Hedges)

- *At inception*, there must be formal documentation (designation) of the hedging relationship and the entity's risk management objective and strategy for undertaking the hedge, including identification of the derivative, the related hedged item, the nature of the particular risk being hedged, and how the hedging instrument's effectiveness will be assessed (including any decision to exclude certain components of a specific derivative's change in fair value, such as time value, from the assessment of hedge effectiveness). Note that because designation is required at inception, the use of hedge accounting is, in essence, optional (i.e., management could elect not to designate a derivative as a hedge). However, this determination must be made at inception and cannot be retroactively applied after the changes in fair value of the derivative are known.
- *At inception and on an ongoing basis*, the hedge must be expected to be highly effective as a hedge of the identified item. The effectiveness in achieving offsetting changes to the risk being hedged must be assessed, consistent with the originally documented risk management strategy.
- If the derivative provides only a one-sided offset against the hedged risk (i.e., an option contract), the increases (or decreases) in the fair value or cash flows of the derivative must be expected to be highly effective in offsetting decreases (or increases) in the fair value or cash flows of the hedged item.
- For a written option designated as a hedge, the combination of the hedged item and the written option must provide at least as much potential for gains as a result of favorable changes as exposure to losses from unfavorable changes. In other words, a percentage favorable change in the fair value of the combined instruments provides at least as much gain as would the loss incurred from an unfavorable change of the same percentage. (The impact of this requirement is that most written options will not qualify for hedge accounting.)

(ii) Hedged Item Criteria (Fair Value Hedges and Cash Flow Hedges)

- If similar assets, liabilities, firm commitments, or transactions are aggregated and hedged as a portfolio, the individual items that make up the portfolio must share the risk exposure designated as being hedged in approximately the same magnitude.
- The hedged item presents an exposure that could affect reported earnings.
- The hedged item cannot be related to an asset or liability that is, or will be, remeasured with the changes in fair value reported currently in earnings (e.g., a debt security classified as trading or its interest cash flows).

- The hedged item cannot be related to a business combination or the acquisition or disposition of subsidiaries, minority interests, or equity method investees, or to an entity's own equity instruments classified in stockholders' equity.

- Interest rate risk cannot be hedged for a held-to-maturity debt security or for its cash flows; however, changes in fair value attributable to an option component of the security, credit risk, or foreign exchange risk can be hedged.

- For a *nonfinancial* asset or liability or its cash flows, the designated risk being hedged must be the risk of changes in fair value or cash flows for the entire hedged asset or liability and not the price risk of a similar asset in a different location or of a major ingredient.[6]

- If the hedged item is a financial asset or liability, a recognized loan servicing right, or the financial component of a nonfinancial firm commitment, or the cash flows of such an item, the designated risk being hedged must be (1) the risk of changes in the overall fair value or cash flows for the hedged asset or liability, (2) the risk of changes in fair value or cash flows attributable to changes in the designated benchmark interest rate (referred to as *interest rate risk*), (3) the risk of changes in fair value or cash flows attributable to changes in the related foreign currency exchange rates, (4) the risk of changes in fair value or cash flows attributable to both changes in the obligor's creditworthiness and changes in the spread over the benchmark interest rate with respect to the hedged item's credit sector at inception of the hedge (referred to as *credit risk*), or (5) some combination of the risks enumerated in (2) through (4).

- A nonderivative instrument, such as a Treasury note, generally cannot be designated as a hedging instrument.[7]

As described above, one of the hedgeable risks permitted under Statement No. 133 is the risk of changes in the designated benchmark interest rate. Statement No. 133 as amended currently permits two benchmark interest rates to be hedged, and they must be specifically designated and documented at the inception of the hedge:

- Interest rate swap rates based on the LIBOR, a rate considered by international financial markets as inherently liquid, stable, and reliable, and therefore commonly used in many swaps and other hedging instruments, and

- The risk-free rate, which in the United States is considered to be the interest rate on direct Treasury obligations of the U.S. government. (In foreign markets, the rate of interest on sovereign debt may be considered the benchmark interest rate.)

While companies may wish to designate other benchmark interest rates, such as prime, Fed Funds, or commercial paper indices, the Statement does not permit it. Rather, companies may use derivatives based on nonauthorized benchmarks and designate the derivative as a hedge of the risk of changes in the *overall* fair value or cash flows of the hedged item.

A derivative can hedge a portion or percentage of a hedged item, even though it cannot hedge ingredients or components of nonfinancial items. For example, a company seeking to hedge its exposure to changing gasoline prices can hedge 50 percent of its gasoline on hand or a specific

---

[6] To illustrate, in hedging the price exposure for gasoline, a company cannot designate the risk of changes in the crude oil component of gasoline as the risk being hedged. However, crude oil instruments can still be used to hedge gasoline, but only to the extent that changes in the fair value or cash flows of the crude oil instrument are effective in hedging against the risk of changes in the entire fair value or cash flows of the hedged gasoline. Because crude oil prices do not correlate precisely with gasoline prices, some degree of hedge ineffectiveness will result and will be reflected in income.

[7] A nonderivative financial instrument that may give rise to a foreign currency transaction gain or loss under Statement No. 52 can be designated as hedging either the changes in fair value of an unrecognized firm commitment related to the foreign currency exposure or the foreign currency exposure of a net investment in a foreign operation.

volume of expected sales in the month of June, even if it cannot hedge the risk of price fluctuations of the crude oil component of gasoline.[8] Similarly, a proportion of the total or a portion of the life of a hedged financial asset or liability can also be designated as a hedged item, including one or more selected contractual cash flows. For example, a company will be able to designate either 50 percent of its 10-year debt or the first five years' cash flows as the hedged item in a hedging relationship. However, only the designated cash flows are considered in the effectiveness assessment, rendering most previous partial-term hedging strategies to fail to qualify as hedges under Statement No. 133.

The process of documenting and identifying the hedging relationship, the derivative, the hedged item, the nature of the particular risk being hedged, and how the hedging instrument's effectiveness will be assessed is a much more extensive requirement than the prior hedge accounting requirements, which merely contemplated "designating" the hedge.

How a hedge is designated at inception can significantly affect the presentation of the hedge in the financial statements and its effect on earnings. In some cases, designating a specific derivative as a fair value hedge or as a cash flow hedge will be optional, but because the accounting for each type of hedge is different, the designation decisions are important. For example, a company that keeps a portfolio of short-term investments and has long-term fixed rate debt outstanding would be able to designate an interest rate swap entitling it to receive a fixed interest rate and to pay a variable interest rate as either a cash flow hedge of the future interest income from its short-term investments or as a fair value hedge of its long-term debt obligation. In either case, the derivative would protect the company from the effects of declining interest rates. Hedge documentation must be performed at the inception of the special accounting. Management cannot wait to see whether it is more advantageous to designate the hedge one way or another.

In addition to the highly effective criteria, the Statement includes specific criteria for both the derivative and the hedged item. The three hedge types share some common criteria, while other criteria are specific to the type of hedge (i.e., fair value, cash flow, or net investment). Unless the hedge and the hedged item meet all of the applicable criteria, the hedge fails to qualify for the "special accounting," and the change in fair value of the derivative must be recognized in income as it occurs without consideration of the change in value of any related exposure. Similarly, the "special accounting" will only be able to be applied while the criteria are met. As a result, if the criteria, even the elective criteria such as designation, cease to be met during the life of a derivative or hedged item, the "special accounting" permitted by Statement No. 133 will cease. In addition, if the criteria fail to be met because the hedged forecasted transaction is probable of not occurring, any gains or losses from the derivative that have not yet been included in earnings are immediately charged or credited to income.

In addition to the criteria discussed above, each of the three hedge types also has additional criteria. The additional criteria, as well as the approach to the financial reporting for each type of hedge, are discussed in the following sections.

26.2 FAIR VALUE HEDGES

(a) WHAT IS A FAIR VALUE HEDGE?   Fair value hedges protect against the changes in value caused by fixed terms, rates, or prices. As an example, a company with fixed rate debt enters into an interest rate swap to receive a fixed rate of interest and pay a variable rate to protect against paying higher than market interest rates if interest rates decline. As a result, if rates decline, the company will be able to refinance its debt at the lower interest rates without incurring a loss from the extinguishment of the debt (because it will be offset by an increase in the value of the swap). Alternatively, the company may view the swap, when coupled with the debt, as effectively providing the company with an obligation to make interest payments at a variable rate.

---

[8] Unlike the volume of gasoline on hand, the designation for future sales cannot be for a percentage of future volumes, because the exact volume cannot be computed.

As another example, a refinery, concerned that crude prices may fall while it is contracted to buy 1 million barrels of crude oil at a fixed price, enters into a short crude oil futures contract. If prices decrease, the company pays an above market price under its purchase contract, but realizes a gain in value of its futures contract that compensates the company as if it had effectively sold the crude at the prior, now above market, price.

In both of the above examples, the company's future cash flows for interest and crude, respectively, were fixed. The derivative protected the company from subsequent changes in value of the hedged item attributable to changes in market prices.

(b) THE ACCOUNTING TREATMENT FOR A FAIR VALUE HEDGE.   In a significant change to the conventional "deferral" approach for hedging transactions, Statement No. 133 requires companies to recognize in income, in the period that a change in value occurs, gains or losses from a derivative designated as a fair value hedge. In addition, changes in the fair value of the hedged item (i.e., the asset, liability, or firm commitment), *to the extent they are attributable to the risk designated as being hedged*, would also be simultaneously recognized in income and as an adjustment to the carrying amount of that item. In theory, perfectly effective hedges will produce perfectly offsetting income statement entries, so that only the desired effect of the hedge impacts net income. However, any aspect of a fair value hedging relationship that is ineffective will be immediately reflected in income. An unrealized gain or loss on a hedged asset, liability, or firm commitment that existed prior to the establishment of the hedge would not be recognized, nor would changes in value of a hedged item during the life of a hedge that are not attributable to the risk being hedged. A hedge can be entered into or removed by undesignating the derivative as a hedge at any time for an asset, liability, or firm commitment.

For hedged items that absent the hedge would be measured at fair value with changes in fair value reported in other comprehensive income (e.g., available-for-sale debt securities), the adjustment of the hedged item's carrying amount (attributable to the risk being hedged) should be recognized in income rather than other comprehensive income while the hedge exists.

Adjustments to the carrying amounts of hedged items that are recorded as a result of a fair value hedging relationship must be subsequently accounted for as any other adjustment of the basis of the asset or liability. For example, if the hedged item is a commodity that will be used in a manufacturing process, the adjustments to the carrying amount of the raw material inventory as a result of the fair value hedge relationship will be included in inventory as would any other component of the cost of the commodity. If the hedged item is a fixed income financial instrument, such adjustments to its carrying amount will be treated as adjustments to the contractual interest rate provisions and amortized as a yield adjustment of the hedged item. To simplify the mechanics of the special hedge accounting, the Statement indicates that amortization of the resulting adjustments of hedged financial instruments is not required to begin until the hedge is removed.

The new accounting treatment represents an even more radical change for hedges of firm commitments than it does for hedges of existing assets or liabilities. Fair value hedges of an asset or liability result in fair value adjustments to amounts that already exist on the balance sheet. Fair value hedges of firm commitments, however, cause an asset or liability to be recorded that had previously not been recognized under generally accepted accounting principles (GAAP). Under the Statement, in addition to recognizing the change in fair value of the derivative, entities also recognize, as assets or liabilities, changes in the fair value of the firm commitment that arise while a hedge of the firm commitment exists and that are attributable to the risk being hedged. The new rules create this asset or liability for only the period the commitment is hedged. Thus, if the hedge is entered into subsequent to entering into the firm commitment, the recorded asset or liability for the firm commitment may not equal the actual fair value of the commitment.

An example will help put the unique accounting for firm commitments into perspective. Consider a company that has a commitment to purchase a piece of machinery in six months from a German manufacturer at a contractually determined amount of Euros. The company decides to hedge its foreign currency obligation by entering into a foreign currency forward contract to purchase the required Euros at the date they will be needed at a predetermined exchange rate. During the life of this fair value hedge, the change in value of the foreign currency forward contract will be recorded in income. In addition, the change in value of the foreign currency component of the firm commitment will also be recorded in income. To the extent the hedge is effective, the amounts recorded in income will offset, resulting in no income statement effect. However, the firm commitment will be carried on the balance sheet at an amount representing the change in value of its foreign currency component during the periods the hedge is in place. Upon delivery of the machine, the carrying amount of the firm commitment will become a part of the carrying amount of the machine and will be included in future depreciation of the cost of the machinery. This aspect, namely how the gain or loss on the hedged firm commitment is recognized in earnings, must be anticipated and formally documented at the inception of the hedge.

(i) What Is a Firm Commitment? Statement No. 133 defines a firm commitment as an agreement with an unrelated party, binding on both parties, and usually legally enforceable, under which performance is probable because of a sufficiently large disincentive for nonperformance. It further indicates that all significant terms of the transaction should be specified in the agreement, including the quantity to be exchanged, the fixed price, and the timing of the transaction. The definition is similar to that included in Statement No. 80 for futures contracts and has been applied in prior practice to foreign currency hedges of firm commitments.

Examples of contractual commitments satisfying the definition of a firm commitment include:

- A commodity purchase agreement that provides for both the quantity to be delivered and the price to be paid at a specific date
- Contract for the purchase of a fixed asset at a specified delivery date and price denominated in a foreign currency (In this case, the exchange rate is not fixed, but the amount of foreign currency is.)
- License or royalty agreement that provides for fixed periodic payments at specific time intervals. (A license or royalty agreement that specifies a unit price, but does not include a minimum quantity would not meet the definition even though future sales that will result in the royalty are probable.)

Intercompany contracts generally would not qualify under the definition as a firm commitment because they are with related parties. However, many intercompany contracts could still be hedged as an anticipated or forecasted transaction as a cash flow hedge.

(ii) Hedge Ineffectiveness. The recognition of hedge ineffectiveness in a fair value hedge is relatively straightforward. The ineffectiveness is recognized in the income statement as a result of the requirement to recognize both the change in fair value of the derivative and the change in fair value *related to the hedged risk* of the hedged item. If the offsetting changes in fair value do not equal, the difference must be recognized in earnings. Note that if the difference is significant, the transaction may not meet the hedging criteria ("highly effective") at all, and thus the derivative would be marked to market through income with no offset for changes in the fair value of the hedged item.

This fair value hedge accounting approach has been described by the FASB as achieving a result similar to the prior practice of deferring hedging gains and losses. However, the result will only be the same when changes in the value of the hedged item equal or exceed the offsetting gain or loss from the derivative. In addition, the similarity will generally end at a comparison of the income statement results. The balance sheet will differ significantly as a result of the recognition of derivatives at fair value and the recognition of related changes in value of the hedged items.

(c) FAIR VALUE HEDGES OF FOREIGN CURRENCY EXPOSURE. Statement No. 133 allows the foreign currency exposure relating to the following to be hedged in fair value hedge relationships:

- An unrecognized firm commitment
- A recognized asset or liability (including an available-for-sale security)

The FASB decided to specifically prohibit hedge accounting if the related asset or liability is or will be measured at fair value, with changes in fair value reported in earnings when they occur, such as securities classified as "trading" under Statement No. 115. Any asset or liability that is denominated in a foreign currency and remeasured into the functional currency under Statement No. 52 is permitted to be hedged as either a fair value hedge or a cash flow hedge, because such accounting is not deemed equivalent to measuring such assets or liabilities at fair value through earnings. However, foreign currency-denominated assets and liabilities must still be accounted for in accordance with Statement No. 52 (i.e., remeasured at spot rates with the changes in the carrying amount reported currently in earnings even when they are the hedged item in a fair value hedge).

Unrecognized firm commitments would qualify for fair value hedge accounting, because firm commitments are not recognized on the balance sheet and accordingly are not measured at fair value that would affect earnings. Similarly, available-for-sale securities also would qualify for fair value hedge accounting, because in accordance with Statement No.115, changes in the fair value of available-for-sale securities are not accounted for currently in earnings, but in other comprehensive income.

(d) EXAMPLES OF FAIR VALUE HEDGES.   The following examples illustrate the accounting for fair value hedges for a company that has adopted Statement No. 133 on January 1, 2000:

> Example 1—No Ineffectiveness. On July 15, 2000, the Company issues a $10 million, 9% fixed rate note due on July 15, 2004, with semiannual interest payments on the anniversary dates of the issue. On the same day, it also enters into a $10 million notional amount receive fixed and pay floating interest rate swap. The swap calls for semiannual settlement between January 15, 2001, and July 15, 2003. The Company receives payments based on 8% and pays LIBOR. There is no exchange of a premium at the initial date of the swap. The documentation of the hedge relationship would be as follows:
>
> Date of Designation—July 15, 2000.
>
> Hedge Instrument—$10 million notional amount, receive fixed (8%) and pay floating (LIBOR) interest rate swap, dated July 15, 2000, payable semiannually through July 15, 2003.
>
> Hedged Item—$10 million, 9% note payable due July 15, 2003 (comprised of a benchmark LIBOR rate of 8% plus a 1% credit spread).
>
> Strategy and Nature of Risk Being Hedged—Changes in the fair value of the interest rate swap are expected to perfectly offset changes in the fair value of the fixed rate debt due to changes in the benchmark LIBOR swap interest rate.
>
> How Hedge Effectiveness Will Be Assessed—Because the terms of the debt and the fixed rate payments to be received on the swap coincide (notional amount, payment dates, term, and rates), the hedge will be considered perfectly effective against changes in the fair value of the debt over its term. The hedge is structured to qualify for use of the shortcut method, and by definition there is no hedge ineffectiveness or a need to periodically reassess the effectiveness. The hedge meets the criteria for a fair value hedge.

On January 15, 2001, the benchmark LIBOR swap rate falls to seven percent. Due to the decrease in rates, the fair value of the swap increases to $226,000, and the carrying value of the debt should be increased to $10,226,000, such that the gain in value of the swap has offset the loss in value of the debt due to changes in the benchmark LIBOR swap rate. Thus, on January 15, 2001, the following entries are necessary:

Interest rate swap (asset)	$226,000	
Other income/expense		$226,000
To recognize the change in the fair value of the swap.		
Other income/expense	$226,000	
9% Note payable		$226,000

To recognize the change in the fair value of the debt attributable to the hedged risk.

During the six months ended January 15, 2001, the Company also would have paid interest on its debt of $450,000, received a fixed rate payment from the swap counterparty of $400,000, and made a payment based on LIBOR to the swap counterparty. These payments would all be netted in the interest expense account, resulting in interest expense at the variable rate of LIBOR plus the spread between the LIBOR swap rate and the actual rate on the debt. Note that while the hedge is in effect, the adjustment to the carrying amount of the debt does not have to be amortized.

On July 15, 2001, assume that the benchmark LIBOR rate has remained the same. Due to the additional payments that have been made and the passage of time, the fair value of the debt attributable to the benchmark LIBOR swap rate would decrease to $10,184,000 and the positive fair value of the swap would decline to $184,000. Accordingly, the following entry would be required to adjust the carrying amount of the swap to its fair value and record the change in the fair value of the debt attributable to interest rate changes:

9% Note payable	$42,000	
Other income/expense		$42,000

To recognize the change in the fair value of the debt attributable to the hedged risk.

Other income/expense	$42,000	
Interest rate swap (asset)		$42,000

To recognize the change in the fair value of the swap.

As during the prior semiannual period, the Company will have offsetting fixed interest rate payments and receipts and make a payment of a LIBOR rate of interest on the notional amount of the swap. These amounts will be netted in interest expense to result in a variable rate of interest expense.

The Company will follow the same procedure of constantly adjusting the carrying amount of the swap to its fair value and adjusting the carrying amount of the debt by the same amount, to reflect its change in its fair value attributable to the hedged risk. Because the hedge was designed to be perfectly effective, the periodic adjustments to the carrying amount of the debt and the swap will be for the same amounts. The Company's net interest expense will be equal to the LIBOR payments made to the swap counterparty plus the spread between the fixed rates paid and received. Thus, the effect on income is the same as prior practice for swaps, but the balance sheet effect is different. Had the swap been partially ineffective, then the effect on income also could have differed from prior practice.

The accounting can become more complex when ineffectiveness is present. This will occur whenever the hedging relationship cannot be considered perfectly effective; that is, when differences between the hedging instrument and the hedged item exist. The following example illustrates the accounting under the Statement in this situation:

Example 2—Ineffectiveness Present. On January 1, 2000, a gold mining operation enters into a fixed price contract (i.e., a firm commitment) to deliver 100 troy ounces of gold on June 30, 2000, to a customer in London at a price of $310/troy ounce, the published June 30, 2000, forward price of gold on January 1, 2000, in London. The firm commitment is not accounted for as a derivative contract because it qualifies for the "normal sales" exception of Statement No. 133. The Company would have preferred for the sales contract to have been at the market price on the date of delivery, but as a concession to its customer offered it a fixed price contract. To hedge against the potential increase in gold prices, on January 1, 2000, the Company buys a NYMEX (New York Mercantile Exchange) futures contract (100 troy ounces) at a futures price of $300/troy ounce for delivery in June. The NYMEX contract requires delivery in New York. Assume that the forward curve is flat and that the six months' futures price equals the spot price in New York on January 1, 2000. The $10/troy ounce price difference relates to the London versus New York delivery locations.

The Company's strategy is that, because it is concerned that prices will go up between now and delivery in June, the long futures contract effectively eliminates the risk of being locked into a sales price over the next six months at the January 1 price. Through the hedge, the Company has effectively unlocked the sales price. If prices do go up over the next six months, the Company will benefit from the hedge, but the fair value of the firm sales commitment will decline because it will then be at a below market price. However, the Company is accepting some "basis" risk in that it is assuming that the NYMEX price will fluctuate consistently with the London price over the next six months. To the extent that the two markets do not fluctuate consistently, hedge ineffectiveness will result. The Company's designation would be as follows:

Date of Designation—January 1, 2000.

Hedge Instrument—NYMEX long futures contract for 100 troy ounces at $300/troy ounce for June 2000 delivery.

Hedged Item—Firm commitment to deliver 100 troy ounces of gold in London at a price of $310/troy ounce on June 30, 2000.

Strategy and Nature of Risk Being Hedged—Changes in the fair value of the gold futures contract should substantially offset changes in the fair value of the firm commitment caused by changes in the London spot price of gold.

How Hedge Effectiveness Will Be Assessed—The use of a six-month NYMEX futures contract to hedge against changes in the London spot price would have been highly effective over the last six months of 1999 as the London spot price has increased $50, while the New York futures price also increased $50.[9] Going forward, the difference between the change in the London spot price, as determined by reference to the quoted price in The Wall Street Journal for the London Fixing Spot and the change in the June NYMEX futures price will be used to measure ineffectiveness. The hedge meets the criteria of a fair value hedge of a firm commitment-the sales contract.

At March 31, 2000, the London spot price is $350 and the June NYMEX futures price is $345. The fair value of the futures contract is $4,500 ($45 increase in NYMEX futures price ∞ 100 ounces). However, the firm commitment has decreased in value because the London spot price has risen $40/troy ounce, causing an unrealized loss of $4,000. Through the first quarter of 2001, the Company would have made entries (ignoring margin requirements) totaling the following:

NY gold futures contract	$4,500	
Other income/Expense		$4,500

To recognize change in the fair value of futures contract.

Other income/Expense	$4,000	
Change in fair value of firm commitment (liability)		$4,000

To recognize the change in the fair value of the firm contract to sell gold at a price of $310 when the current price is $350/troy ounce.

The hedge ineffectiveness can be calculated as follows:

Change in NY futures price	$ 45
Change in London spot price	$ 40
Difference	$ 5
	$\times \dfrac{\times 100 \text{ ounces}}{\$ 500}$
Total Ineffectiveness	$ 500

If there were no further changes in the London spot price or NYMEX futures price, the entries would unwind on June 30 as follows:

Cash	$ 4,500	
NY gold futures contract		$ 4,500
To recognize settlement of futures contract.		

---

[9] As a practical matter, for nonperfect hedges companies should justify why they expect the derivative to be highly effective based on prior history as well as how they will assess effectiveness in the future.

Cash	$31,000	
Changes in fair value of firm commitment	4,000	
Sales		35,000

To recognize sale of gold contracted at $310/troy ounce but hedged to spot price of $350/troy ounce.

At the conclusion of the transaction and after the effect of the hedge, the Company has effectively sold the gold at the June spot price even though the contract was at a price fixed in January and recognized a $500 gain from the ineffectiveness caused by using the change in the NYMEX futures to hedge the change in London spot prices. The change in fair value of sales contract that occurred ($4,000) is recognized in sales because it is considered part of the hedged transaction, the sale of gold. The $500 is recorded in other income, not sales, because this portion of the change in value of the derivative does not qualify for the special hedge accounting.

26.3 CASH FLOW HEDGES

(a) WHAT IS A CASH FLOW HEDGE?   Cash flow hedges protect against the risk caused by variable prices, costs, rates, or terms that cause future cash flows to be uncertain. A cash flow hedge is a hedge of an anticipated or forecasted transaction that is probable of occurring in the future, but the amount of the transaction has not been fixed. In some circumstances, the anticipated or forecasted transaction is related to a contractual requirement (e.g., percentage of sales royalty arrangement payable in a foreign currency) or an existing balance (e.g., variable rate term debt). This contrasts with fair value hedges that protect against the risk created by fixed prices, costs, rates, or terms (e.g., contracted quantities and prices, fixed rate debt).

A typical example of a cash flow hedge would be the expected purchase of Swiss watches by a U.S. importer. Prior to signing any firm contracts, the importer's budget reflects the purchase of 12,000 watches spread ratably over the next calendar year. The importer typically pays for its Swiss watch purchases in Swiss francs. At the current spot exchange rate, the anticipated purchases over the next year will cost $12 million. The company, concerned that the Swiss franc may appreciate over the next year compared to the dollar, enters into a series of foreign currency forward contracts to buy Swiss francs each month over the next year at today's forward exchange rate. If the Swiss franc strengthens compared to the dollar, the importer will pay more, in dollar terms, for the watches; however, gains on the forward contracts will offset the higher purchase prices. If the Swiss franc weakens, the Company will pay less for the watches, but will incur losses on the forwards. In either case, provided the 12,000 watches are purchased, the exchange rate on the $12,000,000 has been effectively fixed. In this example, the price (both in U.S. dollar and Swiss franc terms) and the exchange rate are variable, and the purchases represent forecasted transactions. Thus, the importer could classify the forward contracts as a cash flow hedge.

(i) Difference between a Forecasted Transaction and a Firm Commitment.   Forecasted transactions are eligible for cash flow hedge accounting, while firm commitments are eligible for fair value hedge accounting. Forecasted transactions are broadly defined as probable future transactions that do not meet the definition of a firm commitment. They can be contractually established or merely probable because of a company's past or expected business practices. As discussed previously, to meet the definition of a firm commitment, all of the relevant terms must be fixed (e.g., price, quantity, timing, interest rate). To qualify as a forecasted transaction, some element of the transaction (other than the currency) must be variable. Therefore, the distinguishing characteristic between a forecasted transaction and a firm commitment is the certainty and enforceability of the terms of the transaction. Using the example above, the purchase of the watches would change from a forecasted transaction to a firm commitment if the importer contracts with a Swiss vendor for a specified quantity of watches at a specified price at a specified date.

Examples of forecasted transactions include:

- Issuance of long-term debt three months from now (i.e., the interest rate is not known)
- Budgeted sales of products at market terms for the upcoming year
- Royalty or license payments denominated in a foreign currency based on future sales volume
- Contracts requiring delivery of specified quantities of a commodity at market (variable) prices in the future
- Expected interest obligations on renewal of short-term commercial paper obligations
- Contractually required interest payments on a floating rate long-term borrowing arrangement
- Variable rate cash flows from a long-term investment

In each of the above cases, the amount of cash to be paid or received is variable, and hedging could be used to lock in the amount.

A firm commitment that is denominated in a foreign currency can be treated as either a fair value exposure or a cash flow exposure under Statement No. 133. The designation determines whether the effects of the hedge will be recognized in income or in equity. For example, if a company contracts to buy a piece of machinery at a specified date and price denominated in a foreign currency, the terms of the purchase are fixed and represent a firm commitment. However, the exchange rate is not fixed and represents a variable exposure. Accordingly, the Statement permits the hedge to be structured as either a fair value hedge or a cash flow hedge.

Sometimes the same derivative can be paired up with a forecasted transaction in a cash flow hedge and then redesignated as a fair value hedge if the forecasted transaction later becomes a firm commitment. Consider a U.S. company that on January 1 anticipates an inventory purchase denominated in a foreign currency on July 1. The U.S. company enters into a foreign currency forward maturing on July 1 and initially designates the forward as a cash flow hedge of the anticipated purchase. On May 1, the company contracts with a vendor for the purchase, and the contract represents a firm commitment. At that time, the company chooses to redesignate the derivative as a fair value hedge. Gains or losses on the forward from January 1 to April 30 would remain in other comprehensive income, while gains or losses from May 1 to July 1 would be recognized in earnings, offsetting remeasurement gains or losses on the firm commitment. On July 1, when the purchase is complete, the firm commitment balance becomes part of the basis of the inventory and the forward transaction is closed out. When the inventory is sold in August, the company recognizes the gains and losses deferred in other comprehensive income in earnings. The firm commitment balance that became part of the basis in the inventory also is recognized in cost of sales. ("The Accounting Treatment for Cash Flow Hedges" section below provides further insight and background into this treatment.)

(ii) Criteria Specific to Cash Flow Hedges.   To qualify for the "special accounting" applicable to cash flow hedges, both the derivative and the hedged cash flows must meet the general criteria previously discussed as well as certain criteria specific to cash flow hedges. The specific criteria are:

- The forecasted transaction being hedged must be explicitly preidentified and formally documented with sufficient specificity so that when a transaction occurs, it is clear whether that transaction is or is not the hedged transaction. The nature of the asset or liability involved and the expected currency amount or quantity of the forecasted transaction must be specified.
- The forecasted transaction must be probable of occurring.
- Except for forecasted intercompany transactions denominated in a foreign currency, the forecasted transaction must be a transaction with a third party, external to the reporting entity. (Forecasted foreign currency transactions with affiliates may be accounted for as cash flow hedges—see below.)

In addition, Statement No. 133 contains special provisions for basis swaps. Basis swaps are most commonly interest rate swaps that require the exchange of one variable rate of interest for another. They are used by entities that seek to modify variable cash flows from one variable index (e.g., bank debt tied to the prime rate) to another variable index (e.g., LIBOR). The Statement only permits basis swaps to be accounted for as hedges when they are designated as hedges at inception and an entity has assets with one variable rate to which one leg of the swap can be linked and liabilities with the other variable rate to which the other leg of the swap can be linked. For example, an entity with variable rate debt tied to changes in the prime rate can use a swap to modify the interest payments to a six-month LIBOR base only if the entity also owns investments with interest income tied to the six-month LIBOR rate. As a result of this provision, commercial companies that borrow from a bank at the prime rate may not be able to use a basis swap to convert the interest characteristics of the debt to a more variable rate, such as LIBOR, and treat the swap as a hedge for financial reporting purposes.

(b) THE ACCOUNTING TREATMENT FOR CASH FLOW HEDGES.   Derivatives designated as hedges of forecasted transactions are carried at fair value with the effective portion of a derivative's gain or loss recorded in other comprehensive income (i.e., a separate component of shareholders' equity) and subsequently recognized in earnings in the same period or periods the hedged forecasted transaction affects earnings.[10] The change in the present value of the expected future cash flows (which represents the fair value) of the hedged transaction is not recognized in the financial statements. For example, a hedge of the commodity price risk of anticipated inventory purchases is marked to market through comprehensive income and subsequently recognized in income at the date the inventory is sold rather than the inventory purchase date. Similarly, the gain/loss of a cash flow hedge related to a fixed asset purchase, initially deferred in other comprehensive income, is maintained in other comprehensive income and amortized as an adjustment to depreciation expense over the depreciable life of the fixed asset.

(i) Hedge Ineffectiveness.   As with all hedges, the hedge must be highly effective to even qualify as a hedge under the Statement's criteria. However, after qualifying as a cash flow hedge, the treatment of hedge ineffectiveness is more complicated compared to a fair value hedge where both the derivative and the hedged item are marked to market (with respect to the hedged risk) through earnings. The cash flow model essentially records any overeffectiveness (i.e., overhedge) in earnings, while not permitting any recognition of an undereffective (i.e., underhedge) portion of a hedge. For cash flow hedges under Statement No. 133, accumulated other comprehensive income associated with the hedged transaction shall at all times reflect the lesser of the following:

- The cumulative gain or loss on the derivative from the inception of the hedge (less any component of the derivative excluded from the effectiveness assessment and any amount previously reclassified from other comprehensive income to earnings)
- The portion of the cumulative gain or loss on the derivative necessary to offset the cumulative change in expected future cash flows on the hedged transaction from inception of the hedge (less the derivative's gains or losses previously reclassified from accumulated other comprehensive income to earnings)

Keeping in mind that the derivative must always be carried at fair value, any difference between the change in fair value of the derivative and the amount that may be recorded in other comprehensive income must be recorded in earnings as the ineffective element of the hedge (i.e., the cumulative "mismatch").

To illustrate, if a derivative changes in fair value by $10, but the present value of expected cash flows of the hedged transaction only changes by an offsetting $8, there is $2 of hedge

---

[10] Our Accounting Release (SCORE Retrieval No. BB4094) explains the requirements of FASB Statement No. 130, "Reporting Comprehensive Income."

ineffectiveness included in the change in fair value of the derivative. Thus, the entry to other comprehensive income is limited to $8 with the $2 difference immediately recognized in earnings. If, instead, the present value of expected cash flows of the hedged transaction changes by $12, the adjustment to comprehensive income is $10 because the entire change in the value of the derivative is effective. In the latter case, no entry is required for the $2 difference.

This provision is further complicated by the fact that the comparison is on the *cumulative* change in the value of the derivative and the present value of the expected cash flows, requiring that cumulative calculations be made throughout the life of the hedge. As stated above, if at the end of one month the fair value of the derivative has changed by $10, but the present value of the expected cash flows of the hedged transaction have only changed by an offsetting $8, the adjustment to other comprehensive income is limited to $8. If at the end of the next month, the fair value of the derivative has increased to $15, or an additional $5, and the offsetting present value of the expected cash flows has changed to $15 (an additional $7), then the entire $15 is included in other comprehensive income and the $2 difference from the previous month is "caught up" in the current month, resulting in $2 being reversed through income.

As previously discussed, firm commitments and forecasted transactions are similar in that they both represent probable future transactions. Thus, the differences in the treatment of hedge ineffectiveness for cash flow hedges and fair value hedges are significant. For instance, in the previous example, when the present value of expected cash flows of an anticipated transaction changed by $12, but the derivative only offsets the change by $10, only the $10 was recognized in other comprehensive income and no entry was recognized for the $2 difference. However, had the forecasted transaction been a firm commitment, the entire change in fair value of the derivative ($10) and the change in fair value of the firm commitment attributable to the risk being hedged ($12) would have been recognized in income, thereby impacting income by $2.

Exhibit 26.1 highlights the significant differences between the treatment of fair value and cash flow hedges.

(c) HEDGING FOREIGN CURRENCY CASH FLOWS.   If the hedged item is denominated in a foreign currency, an entity may designate a cash flow hedge of the foreign currency exposure of the following:

- A forecasted transaction with either an external party (i.e., an export sale to an unaffiliated foreign entity) or an intercompany party (i.e., a sale to a foreign subsidiary or a forecasted royalty from a foreign subsidiary)
- An unrecognized firm commitment (because even though the price is fixed, the ultimate cash flow varies based on foreign exchange rate movements)
- The forecasted functional currency-equivalent cash flows associated with a recognized asset or liability.

In most cases, the entity with the foreign currency exposure must be a party to the hedging instrument.

In a cash flow hedge of the variability of the functional currency-equivalent cash flows for a recognized foreign-denominated asset or liability that is remeasured at spot rates under Statement No. 52, the effective portion of the change in value of the derivative is initially recorded in other comprehensive income. An amount that will offset the related transaction gain or loss arising from the remeasurement will be reclassified each period from other comprehensive income to earnings. For cash flow hedges, this provision of Statement No. 133, as amended, helps to minimize volatility in earnings caused by the FASB's insistence that Statement No. 52 continue to govern the accounting for foreign-denominated monetary assets and liabilities.

Although Statement No. 133 requires that a specific entity in a consolidated group that has the foreign currency exposure also enter into the hedge, the Statement accommodates the fact that many companies enter into derivatives through centralized Treasury operations. Therefore, the Statement allows a derivative contract with another member of a consolidated group (e.g., a central Treasury

Situation	Fair Value Hedge	Cash Flow Hedge
To the extent the hedge is effective the change in the fair value of the derivative is recognized in:	• Income, but it is offset by the change in the fair value (attributable to the hedged risk) of the hedged item.	• Other comprehensive income (equity) until the forecasted transaction affects income. At that time, the amounts previously recognized in other comprehensive income are reclassified to income.
When the cumulative change in the fair value of the derivative exceeds the cumulative change in the fair value of the hedged item for the risk being hedged, the ineffective portion of the derivative's change is:-	• Recognized in income, as changes in fair value of both the derivative and the hedged item are recognized in earnings.	• Recognized in income. The derivative must always be carried at fair value, but in this case, the amount recognized in other comprehensive income is limited to the cumulative changes in expected cash flows of the anticipated transaction. Thus, the difference must be recognized in income.
When the cumulative change in the fair value of the derivative is less than the cumulative change in the fair value of the hedged item for the risk being hedged, the ineffective portion of the hedge relationship is:	• Recognized in income, as changes in fair value of both the derivative and the hedged item are recognized in earnings.	• Not recognized. In this case, the fair value of the derivative is deferred in other comprehensive income. The ineffectiveness will not be recognized until either the cumulative change in the hedged item is less than the cumulative change in the derivative or when the hedged transaction affects income.

Exhibit 26.1   Differences between the treatment of fair value and cash flow hedges.

operation) to be designated as a hedge provided the internal derivative meets the requirements of the Statement to be treated as a foreign currency cash flow hedge and the other member (e.g., the central Treasury operation) enters into an offsetting contract with an unrelated third party. However, this offsetting requirement will restrict the operations of many centralized hedging operations that, in the past, have aggregated internally offsetting exposures and accordingly, managed the net exposure on an overall, rather than specific, basis, because such central hedgers must abide by the following:

- Within three business days of initiating the internal derivatives as hedges, the central hedger must enter into an external third-party derivative that offsets, on a net basis for each currency, the foreign exchange risk arising from multiple internal derivative contracts. The external third-party derivative must generate equal or closely approximating gains and losses when compared with the aggregate or net losses and gains generated by the internal derivatives.
- The central hedger must track the exposure from each hedging affiliate and maintain documentation of the linkage of each internal derivative with the net external derivative.

- The single net external derivative and all the internal derivatives must involve the same currency exposure and all mature within the same 31-day period.

- The central hedger cannot consider any internal derivatives not designated and linked to the single net external derivative, or that do not qualify as cash flow hedges by the affiliate, or any nonderivative contracts in evaluating the effectiveness of the hedge.

- The central hedger cannot alter the external derivative unless the hedging affiliate initiates that action. Otherwise, any alteration or termination by the central hedger causes the cessation of hedge accounting for all internal derivatives.

- This arrangement is not permitted for cash flow exposure relating to recognized foreign currency-denominated assets or liabilities.

The central treasury provisions are only available for certain foreign currency cash flow hedges. They are not available for interest rate, commodity, or other hedge relationships.

In the past under Statement No. 52, forward contracts could hedge firm commitments, but not anticipated transactions. Further, even if a contract with specified terms existed between members of a consolidated group, they often were not considered "firm." Thus, to achieve hedge accounting results for anticipated transactions or intercompany commitments, companies had to use more expensive option contracts rather than forwards.

Statement No. 133 offers companies more latitude in hedging foreign currency risks. The new Statement amends Statement No. 52, so that anticipated transactions can be hedged using forward contracts as cash flow hedges. In combination with the ability to designate intercompany transactions as the hedged transaction, Statement No. 133 significantly increases the flexibility that will be provided to many multinational companies. Forward contracts can be used to hedge intercompany transactions, and as a result, the cost of hedging many typical anticipated foreign currency transactions that are not firm commitments generally should decrease under Statement No. 133.

(i) Examples of Cash Flow Hedges.   The following examples illustrate the accounting for cash flow hedges:

Example 1—No ineffectiveness. On January 1, 2000, Company A enters into a $20 million, 10-year variable rate note due 2010, that will require interest payments at the risk-free rate (the 10-year U.S. Treasury bond rate) plus 1%. Interest is payable on January 1, April 1, July 1, and October 1 until maturity. The principal is due at maturity. Also on January 1, 2000, the Company enters into a 10 year, receive variable and pay fixed interest rate swap on a notional amount of $10,000,000 with settlement every January 1, April 1, July 1, and October 1. The Company pays 9% and receives the 10-year constant maturity Treasury (CMT) rate on the notional amount. On January 1, 2000, the CMT rate is 8%. This position locks the interest rate for $10,000,000 of the note at 10% (the 9% pay rate of the swap plus the 1% differential between the variable rate of the debt (CMT plus 1%) and the variable rate of the swap (CMT)). There is no payment due or received at inception of the swap. The documentation for the hedge relationship is as follows:

Date of Designation—January 1, 2000.

Hedge Instrument—Notional amount $10,000,000, receive variable (CMT) and pay fixed (9%), interest rate swap through January 1, 2010, with settlement every January, April, July, and October 1. (Company A makes certain that the variable leg of its hedging instrument is based on one of the permitted benchmarks—such as the risk-free rate—in order to be eligible to use the shortcut method. Use of a derivative with a variable leg tied to the prime rate, for example, would be ineligible.)

Hedged Transaction—Each of the quarterly variable-rate interest payments on $10 million of the $20 million CMT-based note payable due January 1, 2010.

Strategy and Nature of Risk Being Hedged—Changes in the cash flows of the interest rate swap should offset changes in the interest rate payments on the debt, eliminating the Company's exposure to fluctuations in the benchmark risk-free interest rate on one-half of the outstanding amount. The hedge locks the interest rate at 10% for one-half of the note.

How Hedge Effectiveness Will Be Assessed—Because the terms of $10 million of the $20,000,000 note coincide (notional amount, payment dates, term, and underlying index), the hedge will be effective against changes in the benchmark risk-free rate over the term of the debt. The hedge is structured to qualify for the shortcut method. The hedge qualifies as a cash flow hedge.

During the first six months of 2000, the CMT rate is 8%. Therefore, the Company pays interest of 9% or $900,000 ($450,000 on the hedged amount). In addition, it receives CMT-based payments on the swap totaling $400,000 and pays the fixed rate payments on the swap totaling $450,000. These payments are all recorded as interest expense on the debt and total $950,000. Of this total, $500,000 is on the hedged amount ($450,000 – $400,000 + $450,000), which represents an effective 10% fixed rate of interest on the portion of the debt hedged.

On June 30, 2000, the 10-year market interest rate on which the swap was originally based increases from 9% to 11%. In addition, the 10-year CMT rate increases from 8% to 10%. Due to the increase in interest rates, assume that the fair value of the swap increases from zero to $1,165,000.

The Company would make the following entry:

Interest rate swap (asset)	$1,165,000	
Other comprehensive income		$1,165,000

To recognize the fair value of the interest rate swap. (This journal entry has the effect of increasing stockholders' equity. In contrast, if the Company had borrowed $10 million on a fixed rate basis at 10%, equity would not be affected.)

On July 31, 2000 (assuming no further changes in the benchmark risk-free rate), the Company makes the following entries:

Interest expense	$183,333	
Accrued interest		$183,333

To accrue interest expense for one month on $20,000,000 note payable (11% or CMT plus 1%).

Accrued swap payment receivable	$8,333	
Interest expense		$8,333

To accrue expected receipt from interest rate swap [$10 million @ 1% (10% receive rate less 9% pay rate) for one month].

Proof of interest expense:

Nonhedged portion—$10,000,000 @ 11% for one month	$91,667
Hedged portion—$10,000,000 @ 10% for one month	83,333
Net interest expense from entries above	$175,000

At July 31, 2000, and throughout the remaining term of the debt and swap, the Company would continually adjust the swap to its fair value with an offsetting adjustment to other comprehensive income. Presuming that interest rates for 10-year debt do not change any more, the entries would decrease both the swap asset and other comprehensive income as interest and swap payments are made. The net effect of the swap causes the Company to recognize interest on the $10 million hedged portion of the debt at the fixed rate of 10% even though prime plus 1% will fluctuate.

The Statement does not require that the amount in other comprehensive income be amortized to income unless the swap is terminated. In addition, at the maturity of the swap its value will be zero, just as it was at the inception date. Therefore, provided that the swap is perfectly effective and remains in place until its maturity, there is no need to amortize the amount included in other comprehensive income. Rather, accounting for the cash flows of the swap as adjustments to interest expense each period accomplishes the objectives of the Statement.

Example 2—Foreign Currency. On December 1, 2000, a calendar year-end U.S. manufacturer has budgeted a $1 million (10 million pesos or NP) sale to a customer in Mexico in June 2001. The sales invoice will be denominated in NP. If the NP deteriorates, the Company does not believe it could increase the sales price in NP due to intense Mexican competition. However, the Company is incurring significant costs in dollars to manufacture the goods. To protect itself against a devaluation of the NP, the Company enters into a forward contract to sell 10,000,000 NP in June at the December 1, 2000 forward rate of NP11:$1 (or $909,090 in total). The spot rate on December 1, 2000, is NP10:$1.

The Statement permits a company to assess effectiveness in this situation based either on changes in the forward value of the forecasted sale or changes in its spot value. A forward-based assessment will eliminate the ineffectiveness that will be recorded based on a spot-based assessment. The Company must document how it will assess effectiveness at the initiation of the hedge. The Company's strategy is to base its effectiveness assessment on changes in spot rates. Therefore, it believes it is incurring an expense (the ineffective portion of the hedge) of $90,910 ($1,000,000 less $909,090—the difference between the spot rate and the forward rate) to lock in the spot exchange rate to protect itself against any deterioration in the spot exchange rate. The fair value of the forward contract will fluctuate over the life of the contract due to the convergence of the forward and spot rates as well as changes in the spot rate and dollar and peso interest rates. However, because of the Company's designation, the anticipated transaction only will change in value due to changes in the spot rate. Thus, because the transaction will be executed at the spot rate in June 2002, the $90,910 (the built-in difference at inception between the forward and the spot rates) will be inherently ineffective with no offsetting change in value of the hedged sale. The $90,910 will be recognized in income as the cost of the hedge over the life of the forward as the fair value of the forward fluctuates. A straight-line approach to recording this expense is inconsistent with the Statement's requirements.

The documentation of the hedge would be as follows:

Date of Designation—December 1, 2000.

Hedge Instrument—December 1, 2000, forward contract to sell 10 million NPs in June 2001.

Hedged Item—The Company has a probable NP10,000,000 sale to customer X for June delivery.

Strategy and Nature of Risk Being Hedged—The change in the cash flow, determined in USD, of the forward contract should offset any change in the expected NP sales revenues after exchange into USD.

How Hedge Effectiveness Will Be Assessed—The Company views the premium on the forward contract (i.e., the difference between the contracted forward rate and the spot rate at inception) as the cost of "insurance" to lock in the exchange rate. It will be excluded from the assessment of effectiveness of the contract. Because the change in the spot exchange rate will be the same in both the forecasted revenues and the forward contract, the hedge (excluding the premium) will be considered perfectly effective. However, the premium must be recognized based on the change in the fair value of the forward contract in a manner similar to the ineffective portion of a hedge. (The premium is an inherently ineffective portion of the derivative.)

Exhibit 26.2 outlines the key assumed facts by relevant date over the life of the forward:

1. The fair value of the forward can be estimated by taking the change in the U.S. dollar value due to the change in forward rates and discounting that value for the remaining term of the forward. At March 31, the calculation is as follows: (NP10,000,000/11) – (NP10,000,000/12) less a discount of $1,500 (assumed) until settlement of the forward in one quarter.

2. (NP10,000,000/10) – (NP10,000,000/11.5) or the U.S. dollar change due to the change in spot rates from inception to March 31.

3. At May 31, the fair value of the forward is computed as follows: (NP10,000,000/11) – (NP10,000,000/11.5) less a discount of $325 (assumed) until settlement of the forward in one month.

4. Same as item 3 above, except that there is no longer any discount because the forward contract is at maturity at June 30, 2001.

Date	Forward Rate	Spot Rate	Fair Value of Forward	Change in Fair Value due to Changes in the Spot Rate
12/01/00	NP11:$1	NP10:$1	$0	$0
12/31/00	NP11:$1	NP10:$1	$0	$0
03/31/01	NP12:$1	NP11.5:$1	$74,300[1]	$130,435[2]
5/31/01	NP11.5:$1	NP11.5:$1	$39,200[3]	$0
6/30/01	NP11.5:$1	NP11.5:$1	$39,525[4]	$0

Exhibit 26.2   Key assumed facts by relevant date over the life of the forward.

At inception, the fair value of the forward contract is zero, thus no entries are required.

Spot and forward rates remain unchanged at December 31, 2001. Therefore, the forward continues to have a fair value of zero. No entries are required.

On March 31, 2001, the spot rate has changed to NP11.5:$1 and the June 2002 forward rate is NP12:$1. As a result, the fair value of the forward contract is a positive $74,300. The Company would make the following entry (income statement accounts designated by *):

To record change in value of NP forward.

The change in the fair value of the forward contract can be thought of as arising from two components: the effect of the change in spot rates and the effect of the change in forward rates. However, the Company assesses effectiveness based on changes in the spot rate and not the forward rate. Therefore, the effect of changes in the forward rate are excluded from the special accounting for the hedge. Gains/losses due to changes in the forward rates are recognized separately from the hedge as the fair value of the forward contract changes. In other words, any changes in the fair value of the forward that are due to changes in the forward rate are excluded from the effectiveness comparison of the cumulative change in fair value of the derivative to the cumulative change in present value of expected cash flows of the forecasted transaction.

Because the Company has decided to assess effectiveness in this way, the hedge will be perfectly effective (i.e., changes in the spot rate will have the same effect on both the derivative and the anticipated transaction). Thus, under the Statement, the cumulative change in the fair value of the derivative due to changes in the spot rate is equal to the cumulative change in the present value of expected cash flows of the hedged sale, so other comprehensive income is credited for the change in value attributable to changes in the spot rate ($130,435).

Though the effect of changes in the forward rate is excluded from the accounting for the hedge, under the Statement, the derivative still must be marked to market in its entirety, including the change in the forward rates. As a result, a loss must be recognized. The loss occurs because of the difference between the change in the spot rate and the change in the forward rate. The loss also can be viewed as the portion of the locked-in "cost of hedging" (difference between the forward and spot rates at inception) that should be recognized for this period based on the convergence of the spot and forward rate that has occurred this period.

On May 31, 2001, the spot rate and the June forward rate are both NP11.5:$1 and the fair value of the forward has changed by $35,100 and is now $39,200. The following entries are made to the items that were recorded at March 31, 2001:

To adjust derivative to fair value.

The spot rate did not change; therefore, none of the change in the derivative was taken to other comprehensive income.

In June 2001, the exchange rate remains at NP11.5:$1. The forward contract has increased in value to $39,525 due merely to the passage of time (the discount included in the value of the forward has been eliminated). The hedged sale occurs and the forward contract is settled with the counterparty. The following entries are made:

To recognize the increase in the fair value of the forward prior to maturity.

To record sales of NP10,000,000 at the spot exchange rate of NP11.5:1.

To record settlement of forward contract.

To recognize in income amounts previously deferred in other comprehensive income related to June to a Mexican customer. (Note that as a result of the hedge, the Company has recorded a total of $1,000,000 in sales, which had been the stated goal on December 1, 2000.)

Reconciliation of earnings:	
Sale price at inception	$1,000,000
Less cost of hedging[11]	90,910
Sum of P&L entries (accounts designated by*	$ 909,090

(d) BUSINESS IMPLICATIONS OF CASH FLOW HEDGES.   The fact that cash flow hedges affect total equity could cause some companies concerns as a result of debt covenants tied to equity and the effect on other key financial ratios (e.g., debt to equity, return on equity). Many commercial companies will need to consider modifying debt arrangements and disclosing in the footnotes to the financial statements the nature of the hedged forecasted transactions to ensure that the offsetting impacts of the amounts in other comprehensive income are clearly understood. However, because Statement No. 133 is more flexible in the use of foreign currency forwards to hedge foreign currency transactions, including anticipated and intercompany foreign currency transactions, cash flow hedges will be extensively utilized.

26.4 FOREIGN CURRENCY NET INVESTMENT HEDGES

(a) HEDGES OF THE FOREIGN CURRENCY EXPOSURE OF A NET INVESTMENT IN A FOREIGN OPERATION.   Consistent with Statement No. 52, "Foreign Currency Translation," Statement No. 133 allows hedging the foreign currency risk of an investment in a subsidiary or equity method investee and permits a foreign currency-denominated nonderivative financial instrument (e.g., foreign currency denominated debt) to be treated as a hedge of a net investment in a foreign operation (net investment hedges). The FASB decided not to change practice in allowing nonderivatives to be used for net investment hedges. As required by Statement No. 52, the instrument must be designated and effective as an economic hedge of the net investment.

Statement No. 52 previously required that translation gains or losses when consolidating foreign subsidiaries (and their related hedge gains or losses) be recognized as a component of other comprehensive income. Cumulative translation gains and losses, created in consolidation when foreign subsidiaries' financial statements are translated from foreign functional currencies into U.S. dollars, are reported in other comprehensive income and not in income. Similarly, under Statement No. 52, the effect of hedging the translation adjustment is generally not recognized in income either. Statement No. 133 essentially preserves this accounting.

---

[11] At the inception of the hedge, the cost of hedging is the difference between the spot rate and the forward rate calculated as [(NP10,000,000 / 10) − (NP10,000,000 / 11)].

(i) Criteria Specific to Net Investment Hedges. There are no hedged item criteria that are specific to hedges of net investments. Therefore, only the general hedge criteria discussed earlier need to be complied with in order to obtain the special accounting treatment for net investment hedges.

(b) THE ACCOUNTING TREATMENT FOR NET INVESTMENT HEDGES. Statement No. 133 requires that the change in value of a derivative designated as a net investment hedge be included in other comprehensive income (i.e., currency translation adjustment) to the extent of the offsetting translation gain or loss recorded in other comprehensive income. However, any ineffective portion of a derivative gain or loss may not be included in the cumulative translation adjustment account in other comprehensive income.

(i) Hedge Ineffectiveness. The FASB has indicated that the "perfect" hedge of a net investment would consist of (1) a forward currency contract with a single cash flow exchange at its maturity in the identical currency and matched notionally with the designated net investment amount, or (2) a nonderivative financial instrument in the identical currency that is matched notionally with the designated net investment amount. For hedge relationships involving these two hedging instruments, all changes in fair value of such instruments are recorded in other comprehensive income. Any hedging instruments with characteristics *other than* those described above would result in ineffectiveness, which would have to be reflected in earnings. Ineffectiveness would be measured by comparing the actual hedging instrument in use to a hypothetical hedging instrument with the "perfect" characteristics described above. Ineffectiveness from both "overhedging" and "under-hedging" must be reflected in earnings. Generally, compound derivatives, such as cross currency interest rate swaps (instruments with embedded interest rate swaps), cannot be used to hedge net investments, because they are not solely focused on hedging foreign currency risk.

(c) EXAMPLE OF A NET INVESTMENT HEDGE. The following example illustrates the accounting for a net investment hedge:

Company A has a Canadian subsidiary that uses the Canadian dollar as its functional currency. Its cumulative translation loss at December 31, 2001, is $5,000,000, while its equity in the subsidiary is $20,000,000 (CD40,000,000). The spot exchange rate on December 31, 2001, is CD2:$1. On January 1, 2002, Company A (the parent) issues a debt instrument for CD20,000,000 due December 31, 2010 (one-half of the net investment). It designates the CD denominated debt as a hedge of a portion of its net investment in the Canadian subsidiary. The documentation of the debt as a hedge would be as follows:

Date of Designation—January 1, 2002.

Hedge Instrument—CD20,000,000 debt due 2010.

Hedged Item—$10,000,000 of the net investment in the Canadian subsidiary.

Strategy and Nature of Risk Being Hedged—Change in the fair value of the foreign currency debt attributable to foreign exchange risk should offset any translation gain/loss on one-half ($10,000,000 or CD20,000,000) of the Company's net investment in its Canadian subsidiary.

How Hedge Ineffectiveness Will Be Assessed—The change in the carrying amount of the CD20,000,000 debt on the parent's books, attributable to changes in the spot foreign exchange rate, is nationally matched with CD20,000,000 or $10,000,000 of the net investment in the Canadian subsidiary. There should be no hedge ineffectiveness. The hedge qualifies as a net investment hedge.

How Hedge Ineffectiveness Will Be Measured—Technically, the hypothetical hedging instrument method will be used. In this case, the actual hedging instrument coincides with the hypothetically perfect hedging instrument, so there should be no hedge ineffectiveness to measure.

On December 31, 2002, the Canadian subsidiary has paid a dividend equal to its earnings for the year. Therefore, its equity and Company A's net investment is still CD40,000,000. However, as a result of the CD strengthening against the dollar, the spot exchange rate has changed to CD1.8:$1. The following entry would be reflected:

Investment in subsidiary	$2,222,222	
Cumulative translation adjustment (equity)		$2,222,222

To record translation gain on the net investment in Canadian subsidiary. (Calculated as CD40,000,000/$1.8 = $22,222,222 less CD40,000,000/$2 = $20,000,000.)

Cumulative Translation Adjustment (equity)	$1,111,1111	
CD Denominated Debt		$1,111,1111

To treat the transaction loss on the CD denominated debt as a hedge of the net investment in Canadian subsidiary. (Calculated as CD20,000,000/$1.8 = $11,111,111 less CD20,000,000/$2 = $10,000,000.)

At December 31, 2002, the cumulative translation loss is $3,888,889 ($5,000,000 − $2,222,222 + $1,111,111). Had a different hedge instrument been used (e.g., an option strategy), it is likely the change in the derivative would have been either greater than or less than the translation gain on CD20,000,000 of the investment in the Canadian subsidiary ($1,111,111, or one-half the translation gain) for the period. Ineffectiveness would have been assessed by comparison to the hypothetically "perfect" net investment hedge.

26.5 DISCLOSURES

Statement No. 133 contains disclosure requirements based on the type of hedge (i.e., fair value, cash flow, or net investment in a foreign operation). In addition, the Securities and Exchange Commission (SEC) requires disclosures based on the type of market risk that is being hedged (i.e., interest rate, foreign currency, commodity).

(a) GENERAL DISCLOSURE REQUIREMENTS.   The disclosures that are required by Statement No. 133 for all hedging activities, including the use of nonderivative instruments when permitted, include:

- The entity's objectives and strategies for holding or issuing derivatives
- A description of the entity's risk management policy for each type of hedge, including a description of the items or transactions for which risks are hedged
- The net gain or loss recognized in earnings during the reporting period representing (1) the amount of the hedges' ineffectiveness and (2) the component of the derivatives' gain or loss, if any, excluded from the assessment of hedge effectiveness (e.g., time value component of an option or the discount or premium on a forward), and a description of where the net gain or loss is reported in the income statement or other statement of financial performance (e.g., not-for-profit entities)

Though the above requirements apply to all hedging activities, the disclosures must be segregated among fair value, cash flow, and net investment in foreign operation hedges.

(b) ADDITIONAL DISCLOSURE SPECIFIC TO FAIR VALUE HEDGES.   Statement No. 133 has one specific disclosure requirement for a fair value hedge of a firm commitment: The amount of net gain or loss recognized in earnings at the time the hedge of a firm commitment no longer qualifies as a fair value hedge. For example, if a hedged contract to purchase a piece of machinery in a foreign currency is canceled, any amount previously recorded as a result of adjusting the foreign currency component of the firm commitment to its fair value would be required to be written off immediately to income. The amounts of such adjustments are required to be disclosed.

(c) ADDITIONAL DISCLOSURES SPECIFIC TO CASH FLOW HEDGES.   The following specific disclosures must be made for cash flow hedges:

- A description of the transactions or other events that will result in the reclassification into earnings of gains and losses that are reported in accumulated other comprehensive income, and the estimated amount of the existing gains and losses at the reporting date that are expected to be reclassified into earnings within the next 12 months.
- The amount of gains and losses reclassified into earnings as a result of the discontinuance of cash flow hedges because it is probable that the original forecasted transaction will not occur.
- The maximum period of time over which the entity is hedging its exposure to the variability in future cash flows for forecasted transactions (i.e., the expected period of time until no more gains and losses are being recorded in other comprehensive income). However, this disclosure is not required for hedges of variable interest rates (because the maturity of the debt is already required to be disclosed).

(d) ADDITIONAL DISCLOSURE SPECIFIC TO HEDGES OF THE NET INVESTMENT IN A FOREIGN OPERATION.   For derivatives and foreign currency-denominated nonderivative instruments that qualify as net investment hedges, the following must also be disclosed:

- The net amount of gains or losses on the hedging instrument included in the cumulative translation adjustment during the reporting period

Disclosures required by Statement No. 130, "Reporting Other Comprehensive Income," will apply to entities using cash flow hedges and hedges of net investments in foreign operations. Further, an entity must display as a separate classification within other comprehensive income the net gain or loss on derivative instruments designated and qualifying as cash flow hedges. Beginning accumulated derivative gains and losses are rolled forward to ending accumulated derivative gains and losses, identifying current period changes including net amounts reclassified into earnings.

The Statement does not require disclosures of gains and losses on derivatives that are not accounted for as hedges but does require that the purpose for holding these derivatives be disclosed.

(e) ACCOUNTING POLICY DISCLOSURES.   Statement No. 133 does not have any specific accounting policy disclosure requirements. However, the SEC regulations continue to specify seven specific areas that registrants should include in their accounting policy disclosures about derivatives. Hopefully, now that the FASB has eliminated the diversity in the financial reporting treatment of derivatives, the SEC will follow through with its stated intentions and streamline or eliminate its required disclosures in the near future.

Statement No. 119, "Disclosure about Derivative Financial Instruments and Fair Value of Financial Instruments," is superseded by Statement No. 133. The Statement does not continue the Statement No. 119 requirement to disclose the nature and terms of derivatives transactions and positions. However, under Statement No. 107, companies are required to disclose the fair value of all financial instruments, including derivatives. The carrying amount of derivatives under the Statement and the amounts required to be disclosed by Statement No. 107 should be the same.

26.6 EFFECTIVE DATE AND TRANSITION

(a) EFFECTIVE DATE.   Statement No. 133, as amended by Statement No. 138, is required to be adopted for fiscal years beginning after June 15, 2000.[12] As a result, calendar year-end companies

---

[12] In June 1999, the FASB issued Statement No. 137, "Accounting for Derivative Instruments and Hedging Activities—Deferral of the Effective Date of FASB Statement No. 133." This Statement deferred the effective date of Statement No. 133 to become effective for all fiscal quarters of all fiscal years beginning after June 15, 2000.

had until January 1, 2001, to adopt. Early application is encouraged, but permitted only as of the beginning of any fiscal quarter. Retroactive application to previous periods, even previous quarters within the same fiscal year, is not permitted. A calendar year-end company was first able to adopt Statement No. 133 as of July 1, 1998, and Statement No. 138 as of July 1, 2000.

Upon adoption, Statement No. 133 must be applied to all derivatives and hedging activities. That is, it cannot be selectively applied, for example, to currency hedging activities, without also being applied to other hedging activities (e.g., interest rate or commodity risk).

(b) TRANSITION REQUIREMENTS.   Statement No. 133's transition provisions are intended to result in all derivatives that exist at the date of adoption becoming subject to the new requirements immediately. The transition provisions therefore address the financial reporting of unrealized changes in value of both derivatives and hedged items that exist at the date of adoption and any separately recognized deferred gains or losses from derivatives that had been treated as hedges under prior rules. Under Statement No. 133:

- Hedging relationships will be designated anew and documented as of the date of adoption of Statement No. 133 in accordance with its requirements. In most cases, after considering the new criteria, such designations were expected to be consistent with the hedging purpose previously in place as well as any prior documentation thereof. However, there was no requirement that a prior hedge designation continue after the date of initial adoption. Derivatives that were not previously designated as hedges cannot retroactively be designated as hedges. However, such derivatives could be designated as hedges on a prospective basis as of the date of adoption.
- The nature of the historical hedge designations prior to adoption will dictate the classification of the derivative (i.e., fair value hedge, cash flow hedge, net investment in a foreign operation hedge, or no hedging relationship) for purposes of computing the transition adjustments discussed below.
- At the date of adoption, an entity will recognize all derivatives as either assets or liabilities and measure them at fair value.
- For derivatives that, based on their historical designations, would be considered fair value-type hedges, the entity will adjust the carrying amount of the derivative to its fair value. In addition, the entity had to record unrealized differences between the carrying amount and fair value of hedged assets, liabilities, and firm commitments, but only to the extent of the required adjustment to recognize the fair value of the designated hedging instrument (derivative). This adjustment is without regard to whether the change in value of the hedged item occurred during the period the hedge was in place. For fair value hedges, both the adjustment required to recognize derivatives at fair value and the adjustment of the hedged items are recorded in income as a cumulative effect of an accounting change.
- For derivatives that, based on their historical designations, would be considered cash flow-type hedges, the entity will record the adjustment of the carrying amount of the derivative to its fair value to other comprehensive income at the date of adoption.
- Previous derivative gains/losses that were recognized as basis adjustments to existing assets or liabilities are not adjusted. We believe that this transition provision relates to the nature of the deferred amount rather than the general ledger accounts that are used to record them. For example, if a company had previously used an interest rate swap to hedge a fixed rate debt obligation to a variable rate, the termination gain or loss from the derivative may be recorded in a separate general ledger account and amortized as an adjustment of the fixed interest obligation on the continuing debt obligation. However, for financial reporting purposes, the unamortized deferred termination gain or loss would be considered to be a component of the basis of the debt obligation and would continue to be amortized as a yield adjustment.
- Separately deferred derivatives gains or losses from past hedging relationships that would have been considered cash flow hedges under the Statement would be reclassified as a part of the transition adjustment in other comprehensive income.

- Other separately deferred gains or losses from derivatives must be written off as transition adjustments in net income as part of the cumulative effect of adoption.

- In some cases, at different times over its life, a derivative may have been used as both a cash flow-type hedge and a fair value-type hedge. In these cases, adjustments must be allocated to the cumulative effect in other comprehensive income and net income. Though the Statement does not specify the method of allocation, we believe that the allocation should be based on the historical changes in fair value or cash flows that arose while the derivative was used in each respective manner.

- In the year of initial application, the amount of gains and losses reported in accumulated other comprehensive income and associated with the transition adjustment that are being reclassified into earnings during the 12 months following the date of initial application must be disclosed.

Statement No. 133 includes several special transition provisions in order to alleviate certain inequities that might otherwise have resulted from adoption. Since most of these provisions are favorable, companies will want to be aware of the following options:

- At the adoption date, held-to-maturity securities may be reclassified to the available-for-sale or trading portfolios without tainting the remaining securities in the held-to-maturity portfolio. Reclassifications may be made even if such held-to-maturity securities were not previously hedged. The unrealized holding gain or loss of the formerly held-to-maturity security would be recorded in other comprehensive income (if reclassified to available-for-sale) or net income (if reclassified to trading) as part of the overall cumulative effect adjustment(s). This provision was deemed necessary because the Statement no longer allows an enterprise to hedge interest rate risk of a held-to-maturity security.[13]

- Additionally, available-for-sale securities may be reclassified to trading upon adoption of the Statement. Normally transfers of previously owned securities to the trading category are considered to be "rare." When an available-for-sale security is transferred to trading under this provision, the unrealized gain or loss previously recorded in equity is recognized through the income statement. However, the Statement does not allow this reclassification to be part of the cumulative effect adjustment. This restriction is intended to prevent companies from reclassifying securities with unrealized losses to trading at the date of adoption and avoid having to ultimately recognize the loss through income from operations. Likewise, if a derivative instrument had been hedging an available-for-sale security that is transferred into the trading category and the entity had reported an unrealized gain or loss on that security and an offsetting unrealized gain or loss on the derivative in other comprehensive income in accordance with Statement No. 115, the entity would reclassify the security's and the derivative's offsetting gains or losses into earnings as part of the cumulative effect adjustment. However, any additional unrealized gain or loss on the security that was not offset by the derivative would be directly reclassified into earnings separate from the cumulative effect adjustment.

- As of the date of adoption, companies may have on-balance sheet financial instruments that contain embedded derivatives that would have to be bifurcated and accounted for separately as a derivative under the Statement. However, an entity can choose to exclude financial instruments with embedded derivatives that were recorded as of December 31, 1997 or 1998.[14] This exemption cannot be applied selectively to individual embedded derivatives. If

---

[13] The SEC has indicated that for any security reclassified from held-to-maturity to available-for-sale at adoption and subsequently sold in the same quarter, the reclassification adjustment should be as if the held-to-maturity security had been reclassified to trading at adoption with the unrealized gains or losses recorded in net income as part of the overall cumulative effect adjustment.

[14] Statement No. 137, which delayed the effective date of Statement No. 133, also provided an extension of the "grandfather" provision of Statement No. 133 to allow companies a choice of transition grandfather dates. Companies could now apply the transition grandfather provision as of December 31, 1997, or

the exemption is utilized, it must be utilized for all embedded derivatives on hand at December 31, 1997 or 1998, and must be applied consistently for all embedded derivatives identified. For embedded derivatives arising after December 31, 1997 or 1998, but prior to adoption, the bifurcation provisions of the Statement must be applied, and the initial recognition of the fair value of the embedded derivative must be included in the cumulative effect of adoption.

In applying the bifurcation provisions, the new carrying amounts as of the application date should be the fair value of the embedded derivative as of the date of adoption and the fair value of the host instrument at the original acquisition date adjusted for subsequent activity, such as receipts, payments, or amortization. Embedded, bifurcated derivatives cannot be designated as hedges upon adoption of the new Statement unless they were previously designated as hedges, which would have been extremely rare. Thus, in virtually all cases, the resulting transition adjustments (i.e., the difference between the previous carrying amounts and the new carrying amounts as of the date of adoption) for bifurcated derivatives and the host contracts will be recognized in the cumulative effect of adoption in income.

- Generally, the Statement does not allow the bifurcation of compound derivatives (e.g., a cancelable interest rate swap). As a result, the FASB believes it will be rare that compound derivatives will qualify for hedge accounting, because the entire derivative must be shown to be part of a highly effective hedge relationship. However, at transition the Statement makes a special accommodation for compound derivatives where at least one of the components is a foreign currency derivative. A foreign currency derivative and the remaining derivative can be bifurcated at adoption and each then accounted for separately. Therefore, in the case of a cross-currency interest rate swap hedging a net investment, the fixed currency swap portion can be eligible for hedge accounting even if the interest rate swap probably will not be (because net investments have no interest rate risk).

- Similar to the discussion of held-to-maturity securities above, mortgage bankers and other servicers of financial assets may restratify their servicing rights in a manner that would enable the strata to constitute "a portfolio of similar assets or liabilities" under Statement No. 133 that can be hedged as a group. The effect of that change in application of an accounting principle should be included as part of the cumulative effect on income and other comprehensive income. This provision was deemed necessary because previous stratifications may have been based on other risk characteristics, such as date of origination or geographic location, which have no relevance for hedging purposes under the Statement.

(c) DISCLOSURES UPON ADOPTION.   Statement No. 133 states that the transition adjustments resulting from adoption of the new Statement will be reported in net income and other comprehensive income as the effect of a change in accounting principle "in a manner similar to the cumulative effect of a change in accounting principle as described in paragraph 20 of APB Opinion No. 20, "Accounting Changes." The pro forma effects of retroactive application on the previous periods presented and the effect on income before the cumulative effect in the year of adoption are not required to be disclosed.

(d) EXAMPLE OF ADOPTION DISCLOSURE.   The following example illustrates the disclosure in the period of adoption. The disclosure would need to be modified slightly if the new Statement were adopted at the beginning of a quarter that was not the beginning of a fiscal year due to the presentation of the year-to-date statement of earnings.

Example—Disclosure at Adoption

Summary of Significant Accounting Policies

Derivatives and Hedging Activities

December 31, 1998. However, all contracts had to be evaluated at the same date and companies had to apply the provision on an all-or-nothing basis.

In June 1998, the FASB issued Statement No. 133, "Accounting for Derivative Instruments and Hedging Activities," and its amendments Statement No. 137 and 138, in June 1999 and June 2000, respectively. The Statement requires the Company to recognize all derivatives on the balance sheet at fair value. Derivatives that are not hedges must be adjusted to fair value through income. If the derivative is a hedge, depending on the nature of the hedge, changes in the fair value of derivatives are either offset against the change in fair value of assets, liabilities, or firm commitments through earnings or recognized in other comprehensive income until the hedged item is recognized in earnings. The ineffective portion of a derivative's change in fair value will be immediately recognized in earnings. The adoption of Statement No. 133, as amended on—1, XXXX, resulted in the cumulative effect of an accounting change of $XXXX being recognized as income in the statement of net income and a charge of $XXXX in other comprehensive income.

Under the Statement, the cumulative effect on income and the cumulative effect on accumulated other comprehensive income are required to be disclosed in the applicable financial statements. These amounts would appear on the face of the income statement and the statement that includes other comprehensive income. They are not required to be disclosed in a footnote, but we believe that including the amounts in the footnote is helpful to the reader of the financial statements. Further, the basic and diluted per share amounts of the cumulative effect of adoption reported in net income are required to be disclosed either on the face of the income statement or in the notes to the financial statements. This presentation assumes that the earnings per share (EPS) amounts have been disclosed on the face of the income statement. In addition, the tax effect should be disclosed.

Because prior period financial statements that are presented are based on the previously followed accounting policies, disclosure of those policies should be continued. In addition, companies should consider making disclosures to facilitate comparability.

(e) COMPARISON OF OLD RULES TO STATEMENT NO. 133.   Exhibit 26.3 contrasts how hedging generally was treated under the old rules compared to FASB Statement No. 133.

Situation	Old Treatment	Statement No 133
Interest Rate Swap	• Swap generally was treated off-balance sheet, and interest rate of hedged item was adjusted to "synthetic" rate for the effect of the swap. • When swap was used as hedge of available-for-sale security or other item carried at fair value, swap was also carried at fair value with gain or loss treated in the same manner as gain or loss on the hedged item. • Little attention was paid to the degree of correlation between changes in fair values or cash flows of swap and hedged item.	• Fair value of swap is recognized in all instances. • If hedging fixed rate instrument, changes in fair value of the swap and the hedged item with respect to interest rate risk (i.e., the risk of changes of the benchmark rate) are simultaneously marked to market and recognized in earnings. Differentials in the changes in fair value between the swap and the hedged item flow through earnings. • If hedging variable rate instrument, change in fair value of swap is recorded in other comprehensive income. Ineffectiveness from overhedging the variable-rate instrument flows through earnings. • The differential in amounts paid and received on the swap results in an adjustment to interest income or expense, as in prior practice.

(Continues)

Exhibit 26.3   Comparison of old rules to Statement No. 133.

Situation	Old Treatment	Statement No 133
Foreign Currency Forward to Hedge Transaction Gains or Losses	• Although often used as economic hedges, forward contracts could not be treated as accounting hedges of anticipated transactions or intercompany transactions not backed by third-party firm commitments. The forward was marked to market, and gains and losses could not be deferred to match the timing of these types of transactions. • When hedging a firm, third-party foreign currency commitment, the gain or loss on the forward, as measured by the change in spot rates, was deferred until the hedged transaction was completed. The initial difference between the spot rate at inception of the hedge and the forward rate (i.e., the discount or premium) was either amortized to earnings while the forward was outstanding or was also deferred until the hedged transaction was completed.	• Forward contracts can be used as hedges of anticipated transactions, forecasted intercompany foreign-denominated transactions, and third-party firm commitments. • When hedging a firm, third-party foreign currency commitment, both the forward and the firm commitment are simultaneously marked to market and recognized in earnings. • When hedging variable cash flows of anticipated transactions and forecasted intercompany foreign-denominated transactions, the effective portion of the change in the fair value of the forward is recognized in other comprehensive income until the related transaction affects income. The discount/premium on the forward is the portion that may be excluded from the hedge effectiveness assessment. The change in value of the discount/premium (i.e., the change in the difference between the spot rate and the forward rate), if considered ineffective, is therefore reported directly in earnings.
Hedge of Net Investment in Foreign Subsidiary	• The hedge instrument's gain/loss attributable to changes in the spot exchange rate was treated as translation gain/loss in other comprehensive income. The initial difference between the spot and forward rates (discount on premium) was amortized to either earnings or other comprehensive income. There was typically no other impact on earnings. • Companies with foreign subsidiaries typically issued domestic debt and swapped it into synthetic foreign-denominated debt, designating the synthetic debt as a net investment hedge. The currency translation account in other comprehensive income absorbed any exchange rate fluctuations, while the interest rate differential was recorded in interest expense.	• Generally same as prior practice, although any change in the derivative's fair value due to ineffectiveness must be reflected in earnings. The forward discount or premium of the hypothetical perfect derivative (a currency forward contract with a single cash flow exchange at maturity) is included in other comprehensive income. • Companies that have issued domestic currency debt have no foreign currency risk associated with that debt. The foreign currency derivative can be designated as a hedge of the net investment, but there will be ineffectiveness recorded in income based on a comparison of the change in value to the hypothetical perfect forward contract. There will be no adjustment to "interest expense."

Exhibit 26.3   *Continued.*

Situation	Old Treatment	Statement No 133
Commodity Futures Transaction	• If hedging an existing asset or liability, the change in fair value of the futures contract was treated as an adjustment to the basis of the related asset or liability. • If hedging a firm commitment or anticipated transaction, the gain or loss on the futures contract was deferred and included in the measurement of the hedged transaction.	• If hedging the fair value of an existing asset, liability, or firm commitment, the change in fair value of the futures contract and the change in fair value of the hedged item, to the extent attributable to the hedged risk, are simultaneously marked to market and recognized in earnings. • If hedging future cash flows, the change in the fair value of the derivative is recognized in other comprehensive income (to the extent effective) and then income when the hedged transaction affects earnings.
Purchased Options	• Purchased options were eligible for hedge accounting, including hedges of net investments in a foreign subsidiary. Premiums paid were segregated between purchased intrinsic value and time value at the time of purchase. Purchased time value could either be amortized to expense ratably over life of the option or included in the carrying amount of the hedged transaction • Changes in the intrinsic value of the option were treated as an adjustment of the basis of the hedged asset or liability. • If the option hedged an anticipated transaction, the gain or loss from changes in the entire value of the option or only the intrinsic value were included in the measurement of the hedged transaction.	• Purchased options are eligible for hedge accounting, but the fair value of the option is recognized in all instances. Separate treatment of the time value and intrinsic value are determined by risk management strategy and management's approach to determining effectiveness. If the time value portion is excluded from the hedge effectiveness assessment, its change in fair value is reflected currently in earnings, rather than amortized ratably. • If hedging the fair value of an asset, liability, or firm commitment, the change in value of the option and the hedged item are marked to market and simultaneously recognized in earnings. • If hedging cash flows, the effective portion of the change in value of the option is recognized in other comprehensive income until the hedged transaction affects earnings. • If hedging a net investment in a foreign subsidiary, the effective portion of the change in value of the option is treated as a translation gain/loss in other comprehensive income.
Written Options	• Generally, written options were marked to market through earnings in all situations, unless part of a combination of options, such as a collar, which also includes a purchased option of equal or greater fair value	• Written options continue to be marked to market through earnings. However, in certain situations, written options may be designated as fair value hedges of purchased options embedded in other instruments. *(Continues)*

Exhibit 26.3   *Continued.*

Situation	Old Treatment	Statement No 133
Written Options *(Continued)*	• Option combinations in which a net premium was received were treated as written options in their entirety while combinations with a net premium paid were treated as purchased options in their entirety.	• The characterization of option combinations as net purchased or net written options is consistent with prior practice.
Investment in Convertible Securities (investor accounting only)	• The conversion feature was not separated from the investment in the security unless conversion option was detachable.	• The conversion feature is bifurcated because it generally fails the clearly and closely related criterion applicable to embedded derivatives and is accounted for separately from the host. • The bifurcated conversion option is eligible for hedge accounting if the criteria are met.
Structured Note	• Derivative feature was generally not bifurcated or separated from host security.	• Derivative feature is bifurcated if it fails the clearly and closely related criterion and is accounted for separately from the host security at fair value. • The bifurcated derivative is eligible for hedge accounting if the criteria are met.
Hedges of Firm Commitments	• Generally, gain or loss on hedging instrument was not recognized until the hedged transaction was recognized, and then it was included in the measurement of the hedged transaction.	• Both the hedging instrument and the change in the fair value of the firm commitment to the extent of the hedged risk are recognized on the balance sheet as part of a fair value hedge relationship. The cumulative change in fair value of the firm commitment is included in the measurement of the hedged transaction.
Hedge Ineffectiveness	• High correlation between hedge instrument and hedged item generally had to exist to qualify for hedge treatment. • Hedge ineffectiveness was not segregated and treated separately from the effective portion of the change in the fair value of the derivative. Rather, if the derivative was considered highly effective, the entire gain or loss on the derivative was included as an adjustment of the carrying amount of the hedged item.	• Hedging instrument must be highly effective in offsetting changes in fair value or expected cash flows attributable to the hedged risk to qualify for hedge accounting. • The ineffective portion of the change in fair value of the derivative must be immediately recognized in earnings.

Exhibit 26.3   *Continued.*

CHAPTER 27

SHAREHOLDERS' EQUITY

Martin Benis, PhD, CPA

The Stan Ross Department of Accountancy
Zicklin School of Business
Bernard M. Baruch College, CUNY

This chapter was updated from the Ninth Edition by the editors.

27.1 THE CORPORATION

(a) DEFINITION.   A corporation is a statutory form of organization created under rules promulgated by the legislature of the state in which it is incorporated. It is "an artificial being, invisible, intangible, and existing only in contemplation of law. Being the mere creature of law, it possesses only those properties which the charter of its creation confers upon it."[1]   Thus, a corporation is a distinct and unique entity, separate from the personal affairs and other interests of its owners.

(b) ADVANTAGES OF CORPORATE FORM.   The important advantages of doing business as a corporation are the following:

- Continuity of life
- Limited liability for owners
- Ease of transferability of ownership

The combination of these three advantages provides the corporation with the ability to raise large sums of capital. It is the sources of this capital and the claims on it that are of concern to the accountant.

(c) OWNERS' INTERESTS.   Since the corporation is separate and distinct from its owners, owners merely have claims against its net assets. These claims and their nature and origin are presented in the shareholders' equity section of the corporate balance sheet. Shareholders' equity generally comprises three broad categories:

1. Capital stock or legal capital
2. Additional paid-in capital
3. Retained earnings (deficit)

The reporting of transactions affecting these classifications is influenced by legal as well as by accounting principles.

(d) CERTIFICATE OF INCORPORATION.   In order to form a corporation, incorporators—usually at least three—file articles of incorporation with the secretary of state in the state of incorporation. The Model Business Corporation Act (MBCA), prepared by the American Bar Association and adopted in a majority of states, lists in Section 54 the required provisions of the articles. Those of relevance to this section are the following:

- The aggregate number of shares which the corporation shall have authority to issue; if such shares are to consist of one class only, the par value of each of such shares, or a statement that all of such shares are without par value; or, if such shares are to be divided into classes, the number of shares of each class, and a statement of the par value of the shares of each such class or that such shares are to be without par value.
- If the shares are to be divided into classes, the designation of each class and a statement of the preferences, limitations and relative rights in respect of the shares of each class.
- If the corporation is to issue the shares of any preferred or special class in a series, then the designation of each series and a statement of the variations in the relative rights and preferences as between series. . . .

When the secretary of state determines that the articles of incorporation conform to law, he or she issues a certificate of incorporation, after which corporate life commences.

---

[1] *The Trustees of Dartmouth College v. Woodward*, 4 Wheaton 518; 4 L. Ed. 629 (1819).

27.2 SHARES OF STOCK

(a) CERTIFICATES REPRESENTING SHARES.   Shares of a corporation are represented by stock certificates that include the following ten items:

1. State in which the corporation was organized
2. Date of issuance of the stock
3. Name of the person to whom issued
4. Certificate number
5. Class of shares, and the designation of the series, if any, which the certificate represents
6. Par value of each share represented by the certificate, or a statement that the shares are without par value
7. Name of the issuing corporation
8. Number of shares represented by the certificate
9. Number and classes of shares authorized
10. Rights of each class of stock

Certificates for shares may not be issued until the full amount of consideration has been received; however, New York and other states provide an exception to this rule for shares purchased under employee stock option plans.[2] Neither promissory notes nor future services constitute payment or part payment for shares of a corporation.

Shares of stock are classified as either preferred or common with subclassifications within each of these two major classifications.

(b) COMMON STOCK.   A corporation has the power to create and issue the number of shares for the various classes of stock stated in its certificate of incorporation. Holders of shares have the right to vote, the right to share in profits through dividend distributions, and the right to share in assets distributed in full or partial liquidation. Traditionally, common shareholders had *preemptive* rights, such as the right to maintain their proportionate interest when more shares are issued. More recently, however, the cost of satisfying this requirement has led many corporations to eliminate it. The certificate of incorporation may limit these rights; however, limitation of the rights of any class is precluded unless one class has no such limitations.

Preferred stock generally contains limitations of all of the above rights. Because of these limitations, the holders are given various preferences as to dividends and in liquidation. Common stock contains no limitations as to voting, dividend distributions, or liquidation distributions. However, the shares represent residual interests; preferred shares must receive dividends first, and in liquidation all obligations, including those to preferred shareholders, must be satisfied before the common shareholders receive anything.

Generally, a corporation has only one class of common stock. However, some corporations, such as Ford Motor Co., have two or more classes of common stock with each class reflecting different voting or dividend rights.

(c) PREFERRED STOCK.   Preferred stock is given preference over common stock as to distributions of corporate earnings and distributions of assets in the event of corporate liquidations. Sometimes, in involuntary liquidations, the preference is in excess of the par or stated value of the shares. Accounting Principles Board (APB) Opinion No. 10, "Omnibus Opinion—1986" (par. 10), recommends that in these situations, "the liquidation preference of the stock be disclosed in the equity section of the balance sheet in the aggregate, either parenthetically or in short, rather than on a per share basis or by disclosure in notes." In exchange for these preferences, preferred shareholders usually relinquish certain rights, such as the right to vote.

---

[2] New York Business Corporation Law, § 505(e).

Preferred stock generally has a fixed dividend rate and usually has a par value of $100. In some aspects it is similar to a bond; however, dividends on preferred stock are not deductible for income tax purposes, whereas interest on bonds is tax deductible. Therefore, capital obtained through the issuance of preferred stock is expensive. Nevertheless, corporations may use this method at times because of the following three circumstances:

1. A high debt-to-equity ratio may adversely affect bond ratings.
2. Investors, such as pension funds, prefer this type of investment.
3. Banks and insurance companies that desire to minimize the risks inherent in equity securities favor preferred stock. Although an investment in bonds minimizes risks even further, interest is fully taxable to most corporate investors, whereas 70 percent of preferred dividends are excluded from corporate taxable income.

In recent years, preferred stock has acquired even more of the characteristics of bonds because of mandatory redemption provisions.

(i) Preferred Stock Subject to Mandatory Redemption. A corporation, at its option, may redeem its stock at the market price or at a price stated in the stock certificate. However, recently corporations have issued preferred stock with mandatory redemption provisions. The Financial Accounting Standards Board (FASB) has not provided guidance as to how the issuing corporation should classify this type of stock. It has, however, in Statement of Financial Accounting Standards (SFAS) No. 129, stated that for each of the five years following the date of the balance sheet presented, "an entity that issues redeemable stock shall disclose the amount of redemption requirements, separately by issue or combined, for all issues of capital stock that are redeemable at fixed or determinable prices on fixed or determinable dates."

(ii) Classification Requirements for Mandatory Redeemable Preferred Stock. The FASB has been silent about classification requirements of the issues of mandatory redeemable preferred stock. It did state, however, in SFAS No. 115, "Accounting for Certain Investments in Debt and Equity Securities," that an equity security "does not include . . . preferred stock that by its terms either must be redeemed by the issuing enterprise or is redeemable at the option of the investor" (Appendix C).

The Securities Exchange Commission (SEC), on the other hand, has been rigorous in its requirements for issuers of mandatory redeemable preferred stock. In 1979, the Commission amended Regulation S-X to modify the financial statement presentation of preferred stocks subject to mandatory redemption requirements or whose redemption is outside the control of the issuers. Companies having these types of securities outstanding are required to present separately in their balance sheets amounts applicable to the following three general classes of securities:

1. Preferred stocks subject to mandatory redemption requirements or whose redemption is outside the control of the issuer
2. Preferred stocks that are not redeemable or are redeemable solely at the option of the issuer
3. Common stocks

A general heading, "Stockholders' Equity," is prohibited as is presentation of a combined total for equity securities, inclusive of mandatorily redeemable preferred stock.

Companies have been reporting mandatory redeemable preferred stock on their balance sheets between the last liability account and the equity section. The SEC suggests that in these circumstances, the equity section be captioned "Non-Redeemable Preferred Stocks, Common Stocks, and Other Stockholders' Equity."

In addition to the above, the SEC requires disclosure in the notes to financial statements. The note should be captioned "Redeemable Preferred Stocks" and should include (1) terms of redemption, (2) five-year maturity date, and (3) changes in these securities. Aggregate redemption amounts are required to be presented on the face of the balance sheet.

(iii) Dividends on Mandatory Redeemable Preferred Stock. The SEC has not established whether this type of preferred stock is, in fact, debt, therefore, there is no change in the calculation of debt equity ratios. In addition, dividends paid on these securities are accounted for in the same manner as dividends paid on other equity securities—a reduction of retained earnings.

(iv) Carrying Amount of Mandatory Redeemable Preferred Stock. When mandatory redeemable preferred stock is issued, it should be recorded at its fair value at date of issue. If the fair value of the security at date of issue is less than the mandatory redemption amount, its carrying amount should be increased by periodic accretions, using the interest method, so that the carrying amount will equal the redemption amount at the mandatory redemption date. The corresponding entry for the periodic accretion is a reduction of retained earnings.

(v) Callable Preferred Stock. Since preferred stock is a burden of which corporations want to be relieved, many preferred issues contain a callable feature. This feature gives the corporation the right to call in the preferred stock at a stated redemption price, generally in excess of the par value or issue price of the stock. This excess is to compensate the owner for his involuntary loss. When preferred stock is called, all dividend arrearages must be satisfied.

The APB Opinion No. 10 (par. 11) requires financial statements to disclose either on the face of the balance sheet or in the notes to financial statements "the aggregate or per share amounts at which preferred shares may be called or are subject to redemption through sinking fund operations or otherwise; . . . ."

(vi) Cumulative Preferred Stock. Generally, preferred stock contains a cumulative provision whereby dividends omitted in previous years must be paid before dividends on other outstanding shares may be paid. Inasmuch as dividends do not become a corporate liability until declared, dividend arrearages should be disclosed.

(vii) Fully Participating Preferred Stock. Participating preferred stock is entitled to dividends in excess of its specified rate after the common stock has received the same rate. Preferred stock may be fully or partially participating. If it is fully participating with a five percent dividend rate, then, after the common stockholders receive five percent dividends, both the common and the preferred shareholders receive additional dividends on a pro rata basis. The dividend rate is based on the par values of the stocks, and the allocation of excess dividends between common and preferred stockholders is based on the total par values of the classes of stock involved.

(viii) Partially Participating Preferred Stock. If preferred stock is partially participating, it shares with common stock dividends in excess of its specified rate, limited by its participation percentage. If five percent preferred stock is partially participating up to a maximum of an additional 10 percent, it and the common stock may receive up to 15 percent on par value; after which, the common shareholders receive all additional dividends.

Participating preferred stock is not common today; the overwhelming majority of preferred stock currently issued is nonparticipating.

(ix) Convertible Preferred Stock. Convertible preferred stock may be converted into common shares at a specified ratio at the option of the shareholder. It is issued in order to make the preferred stock more attractive to investors while at the same time reducing the dividend rate. Under certain conditions, convertible preferred is considered to be a common stock equivalent for the computation of earnings per share (see Chapter 10).

When conversion occurs, a realignment of the components of stockholders' equity takes place. This realignment may result in an increase in additional paid-in capital or a decrease in retained earnings; it may not result in an increase in retained earnings.

At the time of conversion, the company must reduce its preferred stock and additional paid-in capital-preferred stock accounts for the amount originally received for the stock. This amount is then credited to the common stock and additional paid-in capital-common stock accounts. For example, if a $100 par value preferred share, convertible into six shares of $1 par value common, was issued at $103, the journal entry to record the conversion is as follows:

Preferred stock—$100 par value	$100	
Capital in excess of par value—preferred stock	3	
Common stock—$1 par value		$ 6
Capital in excess of par value—common stock		97

If, however, the par value of the common stock was $20, the journal entry to record the conversion would be as follows:

Preferred stock—$100 par value	$100	
Capital in excess of par value—preferred stock	3	
Retained earnings	17	
Common stock—$20 par value		$120

(x) Increasing-Rate Preferred Stock—Staff Accounting Bulletin (SAB) No. 68. Published in May 1987, SAB No. 68 expresses the staff's views regarding accounting for increasing-rate preferred stock. Essentially, increasing-rate preferred stock is cumulative preferred and carries either a zero dividend rate in the early years after issuance or a low dividend rate, which increases over time to a higher "permanent" rate. The higher dividend rate is usually a market rate for dividend yield given the preferred's characteristics, other than scheduled cash dividend entitlements (voting rights, liquidation preference, etc.), as well as the registrant's financial condition and future prospects. Therefore, the issue price is well below the amount that could be expected, based on the future permanent dividend.

Balance Sheet Treatment. The staff's view is that the increasing-rate preferred stock should be recorded initially at its fair value at the date of issuance. Thereafter, the carrying amount should be increased periodically.

Amortization of Discount. It is unacceptable to recognize the dividend costs according to their stated schedules. Any discount due to the absence of dividends, or gradually increasing dividends, for an initial period represents prepaid, unstated dividend cost. The discount is based on the price the stock would have sold for had the permanent dividend been in effect from the date of issuance. The discount should be amortized over the periods preceding commencement of the perpetual dividend by charging imputed dividend cost against retained earnings and increasing the carrying amount of the preferred stock by a corresponding amount.

Computation of Discount and Amortization. The discount at the time of issuance should be computed as the present value of the difference between (1) any dividends that will be payable in the periods preceding commencement of the perpetual dividend and (2) the perpetual dividend amount for a corresponding number of periods, discounted at a market rate for dividend yield on preferred stocks that are comparable (other than with respect to dividend payment schedules) from an investment standpoint.

The amortization in each period should be the amount that, together with any stated dividend for the period, results in a constant rate of effective cost relative to the carrying amount of the preferred stock (the market rate that was used to compute the discount). The staff believes that this approach is consistent with APB Opinion No. 21, "Interest on Receivables and Payables."

The imputed dividends would be considered an adjustment of net income in the computation of earnings per common share during the amortization period.

If stated dividends on an increasing-rate preferred stock are variable, computations of the initial discount and subsequent amortization should be based on the value of the applicable index at the date of issuance and should not be affected by subsequent changes in the index.

(xi) Voting Rights of Preferred Stock. Each share of stock, regardless of classification, is entitled to one vote. The corporation may, however, in its articles of incorporation, deny voting rights to any class of stock. This usually is done with preferred stock.

The denial of voting rights to preferred stock is generally contingent on the maintenance of dividends. The New York Stock Exchange (NYSE) will deny listing to any preferred issue that does not give holders the right to elect at least two members of the board of directors if six quarterly dividends are passed. Some companies will make the following disclosure in the financial statements:

> Holders of the series of preferred stock will not have voting rights, except that if six quarterly dividends shall be in arrears in part or in full, . . . , holders of preferred stock voting separately as a class . . . will be entitled to elect two directors of the Company until such time as all such dividends . . . in arrears on all outstanding shares of preferred stock have been satisfied.

(d) PAR AND NO PAR VALUE STOCK. Prior to 1912, all shares of corporate stock contained a par value—an arbitrarily assigned amount below which the stock could not be issued. The function of the par value was to provide an upper limit to the shareholder's liability, while at the same time indicating to creditors the minimum amount of permanent capital of the corporation.

In the late 1800s and early 1900s, corporations generally issued stock with high par values. However, as corporations split their stock, par values declined so that today the par value of the common stock of IBM is $1.25 and that of General Motors is $1.67. In addition, many states assess corporate taxes based on the par value of a company's stock, thereby providing an incentive for low par value stock.

In 1912, New York State enacted a law permitting corporations to issue no par value stock. Most states quickly followed New York and enacted similar laws. When no par value stock is issued, the board of directors may give it a stated value after which, for accounting purposes, it is reported in a manner similar to par value stock.

(e) RECORDING THE ISSUANCE OF STOCK. When par value stock is issued at par value, the stock account is increased by the amount of the proceeds. When par value stock is issued at a price in excess of par value, the excess is included in the additional paid-in capital of that class of stock. Section 18 of the MBCA states that shares may be issued for not less than their par values; however, in states where this is not mandated, shares may be issued for a price below par value and the difference, the *discount*, is reported as a deduction in the stockholders' equity section of the balance sheet. The discount is the amount the stockholders who paid less than par value for the stock may be forced to ultimately pay to the corporation.

When no par value stock with a stated value is issued, the consideration in excess of the stated value increases the additional paid-in capital for that class of stock. When no par value stock without a stated value is issued, the entire proceeds are included in the account of that class of stock.

(f) STATED CAPITAL. Section 2(j) of the MBCA defines stated capital as the sum of the following three items:

1. The par value of all shares of the corporation having a par value that have been issued
2. The amount of the consideration received by the corporation for all shares of the corporation without par value that have been issued, except such part of the consideration therefrom as may have been allocated to capital surplus in a manner permitted by law
3. Such amounts not included (above) . . . as have been transferred to stated capital of the corporation, whether upon the issue of shares as a share dividend or otherwise, minus all reductions from such sum as have been effected in a manner permitted by law

Thus the stated or legal capital of the corporation represents the permanent investment of the shareholders; it is that portion of the net assets that cannot be distributed legally to stockholders prior to partial or total liquidation.

(g) BALANCE SHEET PRESENTATION.   Below is the shareowners' equity section of Eastman Kodak Company, a company with one class of par value stock outstanding, as presented in its December 27, 1987, balance sheet.

(dollars in thousands)	*1987*	*1986*
Shareowners' equity:		
Common stock, par value $2.50 per share	$ 933	$ 622
500,000,000 shares authorized; issued		
at December 27, 1987—373,379,570		
at December 28, 1986—248,705,111		
Additional capital paid or transferred from retained earnings	—	314
Retained earnings	7,139	6,533
	8,072	7,469
Less Treasury stock at cost	2,059	1,081
at December 27, 1987—49,008,666 shares		
at December 28, 1986—34,007,309 shares		
Total shareowners' equity	$6,013	$6,388

The stockholders' equity section of a company with no par value common stock and authorized but unissued preferred stock is presented in the balance sheet as follows:

	19X1	*19X0*
Stockholders' equity:		
Preferred stock, no par value authorized		
1,000,000 shares, none issued	$ —	$ —
Common stock, no par value, authorized		
8,000,000 shares, shares issued and outstanding of		
2,688,198 in 19X1 and 2,347,074 in 19X0	10,320,000	5,673,000
Retained earnings	19,726,000	17,014,000
Total stockholders' equity	$30,046,000	$22,687,000

Although no preferred stock has been issued, it is reported on the balance sheet. Rule 5-02 of Regulation S-X requires the disclosure of all classes of stock and the number of shares authorized and issued or outstanding, as appropriate. The stockholders' equity section also indicates that the no par value stock does not have a stated value since there is no additional paid-in capital.

The stockholders' equity section of a company with both preferred stock and common stock outstanding is presented in the balance sheet as follows:

	19X1	*19X0*
Stockholders' equity:		
Senior preferred stock, without par or stated value		
Authorized 3,000,000 shares, issued and outstanding		
1,600,000 shares, preference in liquidation—$40,000	$40,000	
Preferred stock, without par or stated value		
Authorized 1,000,000 shares, issued and outstanding		
204,000 shares, preference in liquidation—$10,200	7,132	$7,132
Common stock, par value $1 per share		
Authorized 20,000,000 shares, issued and outstanding		
9,908,000 and 6,024,000 shares respectively	9,908	6,024
Additional paid-in capital	71,370	53,438
Retained earnings	38,925	7,966
Total stockholders' equity	$167,335	$74,560

As required by APB Opinion No. 10 (par. 10), the liquidation preference of each class of preferred stock is disclosed in the equity section of the balance sheet in the aggregate, rather than on a per share basis or by disclosure in notes.

27.3 ISSUANCE OF STOCK

(a) AUTHORIZED CAPITAL STOCK.   The maximum number of shares of stock a corporation is authorized to issue is specified in its articles of incorporation. However, a corporation may, with stockholder approval, amend its articles to increase the number of its authorized shares.

Rule 5-02 of Regulation S-X of the SEC requires the corporate balance sheet to state, for each class of stock, the following four items:

1. The title of the issue
2. The number of shares authorized
3. The number of shares issued or outstanding, as appropriate
4. The dollar amount of the shares issued or outstanding

A company may issue its shares immediately for full consideration, or it may receive payments in installments and not issue its shares until all installments have been collected.

(b) COST OF ISSUING STOCK.   When a corporation issues stock, it incurs certain costs, such as printing of certificates; security registration and listing fees; legal and accounting fees; and commissions, fees, and expenses of its investment bankers and underwriters. SAB Topic 5A states that specific incremental costs directly attributable to a proposed or actual offering of securities may properly be deferred and charged against the gross proceeds of the offering [see Section 17.3(h)].

Section 507 of the New York Business Corporation Law states:

> The reasonable charges and expenses of formation or reorganization of a corporation, and the reasonable expenses of and compensation for the sale of underwriting of its shares may be paid or allowed by the corporation out of consideration received by it in payment for the shares without thereby impairing the fully paid and nonassessable status of such shares.

If a corporation withdraws shares it intended to issue, the costs incurred for the contemplated sale are charged to income in the year of withdrawal. The charge is *not* an extraordinary item.

(c) ISSUANCE OF SHARES FOR CASH.   From an accounting perspective, the par value or stated value of capital serves one purpose only: That amount, and only that amount, appears in the stock account of the corporate records. The excess is included in an appropriate additional paid-in capital account. Thus, if common stock with a par value of $10 is issued for $12 and the consideration is cash, the entry is as follows:

Cash	$12	
Common stock		$10
Capital in excess of par value—common stock		2

The consideration for the issuance of shares may be paid, in whole or in part, in other than cash.

(d) ISSUANCE OF SHARES FOR PROPERTY OR SERVICES.   Under the MBCA, in the absence of fraud, the judgment of the board of directors or the shareholders as to the value of consideration received for shares shall be conclusive. APB Statement No. 4, "Basic Concepts and Accounting Principles Underlying Financial Statements of Business Enterprises" (par. 182), states:

Measurements of owners' investments are generally based on the fair value of the assets or the discounted present value of liabilities that are transferred. The market value of stock issued may be used to establish an amount at which to record owners' investments but this amount is only an approximation when the fair value of the assets transferred cannot be measured directly.

Thus, when a publicly held corporation issues its stock for property or services, the market value of the stock issued may be used to approximate the fair value of the consideration received. However, a closely held corporation will have to rely on its board of directors to determine the fair value of consideration other than cash received for its stock.

(e) SUBSCRIPTION FOR SHARES.   Sale of stock on a subscription basis generally occurs when a closely held corporation sells stock either to outsiders or to employees or when a publicly held corporation offers stock to its employees. When stock is sold on a subscription basis, the full price of the stock is not received and the stock generally is not issued until full payment is made.

(i) Recording Subscription.   When stock is sold on a subscription basis, two accounts are set up: Subscriptions Receivable and Capital Stock Subscribed. For example, if common stock with a par value of $10 is subscribed to for $12, the entry would be:

Subscription receivable	$12	
Common stock subscribed		$10
Additional paid-in capital		2

The common stock subscribed account is similar to the common stock account in that only the par value or stated value of the stock is entered in this account. As cash is collected on the subscription, the receivable is reduced, and when the final payment is made, the common stock subscribed account is reduced and the common stock account is increased by a similar amount.

(ii) Balance Sheet Presentation.   If common stock subscribed has not been issued, it is still reported on the balance sheet as part of stockholders' equity, either as a separate caption or as part of the common stock with appropriate disclosure.

Subscriptions receivable may be presented in the balance sheet as an asset or as a deduction from stockholders' equity. However, Rule 5-02 of Regulation S-X requires a company to show the total dollar amount of capital shares subscribed but unissued, reduced by subscriptions receivable in the capital shares section of stockholders' equity. Below is the shareholders' equity section of the balance sheet of a company that has stock subscriptions receivable.

Shareholders' equity:	
Common stock, $.10 per value, authorized	
5,000,000 shares; outstanding 1,769,500 shares subscribed 57,000 shares	$ 182,650
Capital surplus	4,612,598
	4,795,248
Less—Common stock subscriptions receivable	(114,000)
	$4,681,248

The total shares of 1,769,500 outstanding plus 57,000 subscribed equal 1,826,500 shares. This number multiplied by the par value of 10 cents equals the common stock amount of $182,650.

(iii) Defaulted Subscriptions.   The disposition of the cash received before default is determined by state law. Under the New York Business Corporation Law, if the subscriber paid at least 50 percent of the subscription price, the shares subscribed for must be offered for sale for cash. The offering price must be sufficient to pay the full balance owed by the subscriber plus all expenses incidental to the sale. Excess proceeds realized must be remitted to the delinquent subscriber.

If less than 50 percent of the subscription price has been paid, or if there is no cash offer sufficient to pay expenses plus the full balance owed by a delinquent subscriber who paid at least 50 percent of the subscription price, the shares subscribed for must be canceled. Under these conditions, payments previously made by the subscriber are forfeited to the corporation and credited to an additional paid-in capital account.

(f) STOCK PREMIUM AND STOCK DISCOUNT. The accounting treatment for stock issued at a premium is covered in ATB No. 1, "Review and Resume." Paragraph 66 states:

These [stockholder] interests include the entire proprietary capital of the enterprise, frequently divided further, largely on the basis of source, as follows:

1. Capital stock, representing the par or stated value of the shares.
2. Capital surplus, representing (a) capital contributed for shares in excess of their par or stated value or (b) capital contributed other than for shares.

In a subsequent paragraph, however, the Bulletin states that the use of the term *surplus* should be discontinued and in its place should be the term *capital contributed for*, or *assigned to*, *shares in excess of such par on stated value*.

Rule 5-02 of Regulation S-X requires separate captions in the stockholders' equity section for paid-in additional capital and other additional capital.

It is rare today for stock to be issued at a discount; however, if it is, the discount is reported in the balance sheet as a deduction from capital contributed. The discount is a liability of the shareholder to the creditors of the corporation, not to the corporation. Below is the stockholders' equity section of the balance sheet of a company that has issued stock in excess of par value and below par value.

	19X1	*19X0*
Stockholders' equity		
Capital stock:		
Preferred—$100 par value, authorized		
260,000 shares, issued 99,817 shares, less discount		
of $1,500,000	$ 8,482,000	$ 8,482,000
Common—$.625 par value, authorized		
7,500,000 shares, issued 5,795,061 shares	3,622,000	3,622,000
Capital in excess of par value	6,246,000	6,246,000
Retained earnings	40,892,000	33,812,000
Less—common stock in treasury,		
311,503 and 328,753 shares respectively	(2,090,000)	(2,206,000)
Total stockholders' equity	$57,152,000	$49,956,000

27.4 COMMON STOCK ADJUSTMENTS

(a) STOCK SPLITS. Corporations can achieve wider distribution of shares or maintain the market price of shares within a specified range by means of stock splits. Chapter 7B of Accounting Research Bulletins (ARB) No. 43, "Restatement and Revision of Accounting Research Bulletins," defines a split as the issuance "... by a corporation of its own common shares to its common shareholders without consideration and under conditions indicating that such action is prompted mainly by a desire to increase the number of outstanding shares for the purpose of effecting a reduction in their unit market price and thereby, of obtaining wider distribution and improved marketability of the shares."

(i) Split with Change in Par Value. Generally, a stock split is executed by changing the par value of the stock. In the early part of 1979, the stock of IBM was selling for approximately $300 a share. The stockholders approved a 4 for 1 split of its stock when the par value of the shares was $5. After the split, the shares traded at approximately $75 and the par value was reduced to $1.25

a share. This type of stock split requires no monetary entry on the corporation's books; however, a memorandum entry should be made to note the change in the number of shares outstanding and the change in the par value.

(ii) Split with No Change in Par Value.   A corporation may execute a stock split without changing the par value of its stock; it may transfer from additional paid-in capital to common stock an amount equal to the additional shares issued multiplied by the par value. For example, if 1 million shares of common stock with a par value of $10 are split 2 for 1 without adjusting the par value, $10 million will be transferred from additional paid-in capital to common stock. A corporation may also increase the number of its shares outstanding by means of a stock dividend. This adjustment is explained in the discussion of dividends.

(iii) Reverse Splits.   At times, a corporation may wish to raise the market price of its shares and reduce the number of shares outstanding. This may be accomplished by means of a reverse split, in which the number of shares outstanding is reduced and the par value is increased proportionately. For example, if a company with 1 million shares of its $5 par value stock outstanding desires to reduce the number of outstanding shares, it may execute a 1 for 2 reverse split. The outstanding shares would be reduced to 500,000 and the par value would be increased to $10.

27.5 REACQUISITION AND RETIREMENT OF CAPITAL STOCK

(a) TREASURY STOCK.   Treasury shares are shares that were issued by a corporation and subsequently reacquired that have not been canceled or restored to the status of authorized but unissued shares. Treasury shares are issued but not outstanding and may be resold below par value without liability attaching to their purchase.

A corporation may purchase its own shares unless restricted by its certificate of incorporation or the corporation law of its state of incorporation. Section 513 of the New York Business Corporation Law applies to the purchase or redemption by a corporation of its own shares. It states the following:

1. A corporation may purchase its own shares or redeem its redeemable shares out of surplus except when the corporation is insolvent or would be made insolvent by the purchase.
2. A corporation may redeem or purchase its redeemable shares out of stated capital except when the corporation is insolvent or would be made insolvent by the transaction.

Actually, a reporting entity never purchases its own shares. A purchase is an exchange, a reciprocal transfer as defined by APB Statement No. 4, a two-way transaction in which the reporting entity obtains something of value to it and sacrifices something of value to it. In a reacquisition of its own shares, the reporting entity gives up something of value to it, money, but does not receive anything of value to it (its own shares are not an asset to it). A reacquisition of shares is, as to the reporting entity, simply a partial nonproportional liquidating dividend.

(i) Restrictions on Retained Earnings.   The corporation laws of most states provide that distributions from retained earnings—in some states, retained earnings plus additional paid-in capital—are restricted to the extent of the cost of treasury shares until the shares are either disposed of or canceled. The APB Opinion No. 6, "Status of Accounting Research Bulletins" (par. 13), requires the disclosure of these restrictions.

(ii) Agreements to Purchase.   Several states allow a corporation to contract to purchase its own shares, even though at the time of the agreement it is unable to pay for them because of the insolvency provisions of the law. Section 514 of the New York Business Corporation Law permits such an agreement if, at the time of partial or full payment, the corporation is solvent and the payment will not render it insolvent.

(b) BALANCE SHEET PRESENTATION OF TREASURY STOCK.   Under paragraph 12(b) of APB Opinion No. 6, a corporation may report its treasury stock in the following three ways:

1. The cost of acquired stock may be shown separately as a deduction from the total capital stock, additional paid-in capital, and retained earnings.
2. The stock may be accorded the treatment appropriate for retired stock.
3. In some circumstances, treasury shares may be shown as an asset.

Generally, treasury shares are reported as described in (1) and (2) above. Treasury stock is rarely reported as an asset because it is difficult to justify classifying what is essentially equivalent to unissued stock as an asset. However, occasionally corporations acquire their own stock to satisfy a specific obligation and classify these reacquired shares as assets. The SEC staff has indicated that asset classification of treasury stock is appropriate only if the shares repurchased are expected to be reissued promptly (within one year) under existing stock plans.

In SFAS No. 135, the FASB provided that it is no longer acceptable to show stock of a corporation held in its own treasury as an asset.

Reporting the cost of reacquired shares as a deduction from the total stockholders' equity is commonly known as the *cost method* or the *single-transaction* and *unallocated deduction method*. Treating reacquired shares as retired stock is commonly known as the *par value method* or the *two-transaction* and *contraction of capital method*.

(c) REPORTING TREASURY STOCK TRANSACTIONS—COST METHOD.   The cost method is more frequently used than the par value method in reporting Treasury stock transactions. Seiden and Rikert noted that in 1994, of the 600 annual reports reviewed, 373 disclosed treasury stock. Of these, 342 reported treasury shares under the cost method, 23 under the par value method, and 8 under other methods.[3]

Under the cost method, the acquisition of treasury shares is treated as the initial step of a financing operation that will culminate in the resale of these shares, that is, the purchase and sale are viewed as one continuous transaction. As a result, treasury stock assumes the status of a capital element in suspense, and the ultimate disposition of the shares marks the time for recognizing any adjustment among the various capital elements. A treasury stock account is debited for the cost of the shares purchased, and on resale the account is credited for the cost. If possible, the cost of each acquisition should be accounted for separately. When the treasury stock is resold, it should be reissued on the basis of specific identification. If specific identification is not possible, the stock may be assigned a cost on the basis of first-in, first-out (FIFO) or, as a last resort, average cost.

(i) Disposition of Treasury Stock.   When treasury stock is sold for less than its cost, the charge for the loss depends on the laws of the state of incorporation and the status of shareholders' equity accounts in excess of legal or stated capital. It is customary to assign losses on treasury stock transactions to the following accounts in the order given: capital in excess of par value from previous treasury stock transactions of the same class of shares, capital in excess of par value from original sale of the same class of shares, pro rata, and retained earnings.

When treasury stock is sold for more than its cost, the gain is credited to additional paid-in capital, treasury stock transactions for that class of stock.

(ii) Treasury Stock Retired.   When reacquired stock is retired, the stock account is debited for the amount credited when the stock was issued originally, the treasury stock account is credited at cost, and if the difference is a gain, it is credited to Capital in Excess of Par Value—Retired Stock. If the retirement results in a loss, it is debited to the following three accounts in the order given:

---

[3] Neil Seiden and Richard Rikert, eds., *Accounting Trends and Techniques*, 49th Edition (New York: AICPA, 1995).

1. Capital in Excess of Par Value to the extent of the credit when the stock was issued
2. Capital in Excess of Par Value from previous treasury stock transactions of the same class of stock
3. Retained Earnings

APB Opinion No. 9, "Reporting the Results of Operations" (par. 28), reaffirmed the provisions of Chapter 1B of ARB No. 43 and stated:

> . . . the following should be excluded from the determination of net income or the results of operations under all circumstances: (a) adjustments or charges or credits resulting from transactions in the company's own stock. . . .

Under both generally accepted accounting principles (GAAP) and provisions of the Internal Revenue Code (IRC), gains and losses on treasury stock transactions are not included in determining income and, therefore, do not affect provisions for income taxes.

(d) REPORTING TREASURY STOCK TRANSACTIONS—PAR VALUE METHOD. Under the par value method for treasury stock, the reacquisition is viewed as the termination of the contract between the corporation and the shareholder, requiring the elimination of all capital elements identified with these shares. As a result, any adjustment between the retiring and remaining equityholders is made at the time of acquisition. The subsequent disposition of the treasury shares is regarded as a completely independent transaction. The purchase and resale of stock constitutes two transactions. Although accounting practitioners have turned increasingly to the cost method, the par value method has received more theoretical support.

Under the par value method, the acquisition of treasury shares has essentially the same effect on paid-in capital as the purchase and retirement of the stock. The treasury stock account is debited for the par (or stated) value of the stock acquired. The related capital in excess of par (or stated) value accounts is debited for the same amount as was identified with the stock when originally sold. If the reacquisition cost exceeds the original sales proceeds, the excess is charged to retained earnings. When the original sales proceeds exceed the reacquisition price, the difference is credited to Capital in Excess of Par (or Stated) Value—Treasury Stock. If the company cancels the reacquired stock, proper accounting requires that the balance in the treasury stock account be transferred to the account credited when the stock was originally sold.

The subsequent resale of acquired stock is accounted for in a manner similar to that for the sale of unissued stock. The treasury stock account is credited for par (or stated) value. Any proceeds from the sale in excess of the par (or stated) value should be credited to Capital in Excess of Par (or Stated) Value—Treasury Stock. Should the proceeds be less than par (or stated) value, the difference is debited to retained earnings because no discount liability attaches to the sale of treasury stock.

(e) DONATED TREASURY STOCK. In situations not so common today, shareholders may donate shares of company stock to the company. Whatever the reasons for the donation, it does not affect either total assets or total stockholders' equity. Kieso and Weygandt discuss the following three methods of accounting for donated stock when it is received:

1. Treasury Stock is debited and Donated Capital is credited for the current market value of the donated shares. When the donated treasury shares are received, they are accounted for in the same manner as other treasury stock applying the cost method.
2. Treasury Stock is debited for the par or stated value (or if it is true no-par stock, the average price paid in may be used), Paid-in Capital in Excess of Par or Stated Value is debited for the original premium paid in at the time of issuance, and Donated Capital is credited for the sum of the two debits. When the donated shares are reissued, they are accounted for in the same manner as other treasury stock applying the par value method, that is, as newly issued shares.

3. The donated shares are assumed to have no cost. Only a memorandum record is made indicating the number of shares received. The entire proceeds from reissuance of the donated treasury shares would be credited for Donated Capital.[4]

(f) CONTRAST IN ACCOUNTING FOR TREASURY STOCK TRANSACTIONS UNDER THE COST AND PAR VALUE METHODS.

The cost and par value methods of accounting for treasury stock transactions are illustrated below. Assume the following facts:

Common stock, $10 par value; issued and outstanding 1,000 shares	$10,000
Capital contributed in excess of par value	1,000
Retained earnings	9,000
Total Stockholders' Equity	$20,000

Furthermore, assume the following:

1. Company acquired 200 shares of its stock, 100 at $12 and 100 at $9.

2. (a) Sold the 200 shares for $13.
  (b) Sold the 200 shares for $7.

The journal entries are as follows:

	Cost Method		Par Value Method	
1. To record purchase of shares at $12 and $9				
Treasury stock	$1,200		$1,000	
Capital contributed in excess of par value			100	
Retained earnings			100	
Cash		$1,200		$1,200
Treasury stock	$ 900		$1,000	
Capital contributed in excess of par value				
Treasury stock transactions			$ 100	
Cash		$ 900		900
2(a). To record sales of shares at $13				
Cash	$2,600		$2,600	
Contributed capital, Treasury stock transactions		$ 500		$ 600
Treasury stock		2,100		2,000
2(b). To record sale of shares at $7				
Cash	$1,400		$1,400	
Capital contributed in excess of par value	200		100	
Capital in excess of par value, Treasury stock transactions			100	
Retained earnings	500		400	
Treasury stock		$2,100		$2,000

---

[4] Donald E. Kieso and Jerry J. Weygandt, *Intermediate Accounting*, Sixth Edition (John Wiley & Sons, New York, 1989).

(g) PRESENTATION OF TREASURY STOCK IN SHAREHOLDERS' EQUITY.   Below are the shareholders' equity sections of the balance sheets of two companies showing the usual manner of reporting treasury stock under both methods.

COST METHOD
Shareholders' equity (dollars in thousands):

Preference stock	$	248
Common stock, par value $2.50 per share; authorized 100,000,000 shares;		
issued 28,988,757 shares		72,472
Additional paid-in capital		206,316
Retained earnings		734,020
		1,013,056
Less common stock in treasury, at cost; 1,249,110 shares		68,440
Total shareholders' equity	$	944,616

PAR VALUE METHOD
Shareholders' equity:

Capital stock	
Common stock; authorized 10,000,000 shares of $2.50 par value each;	
issued 4,316,045 shares	$ 10,790,000
Less: treasury stock—157,611 shares	394,000
Outstanding—4,158,434 shares	$ 10,396,000
Capital in excess of par value	35,487,000
Retained earnings	108,297,000
Total shareholders' equity	$154,180,000

In its notes to the consolidated financial statements, this company indicated that its capital in excess of par value is increased for the proceeds of the sale of treasury stock in excess of par value and decreased by the cost in excess of par value of treasury stock purchased.

Other companies using the par value method for reporting treasury stock merely report the number of shares outstanding and parenthetically state the number of shares held in the treasury.

(h) PURCHASE OF TREASURY SHARES AT A PRICE SIGNIFICANTLY IN EXCESS OF CURRENT MARKET PRICE.   Recently, companies that have been targets of unfriendly takeover attempts have paid prices in excess of market for their stock to persons holding the stock and attempting the takeover. These payments have been called *greenmail*. FTB No. 85-6 requires the company to allocate the cost of the reacquired stock to treasury stock for the market price of the stock and to other elements of the transaction for the balance. The other elements should be accounted for according to their substance.

The FTB No. 85-6 requires disclosure of the allocation of the cost of the reacquired stock and the accounting treatment of the allocated costs.

27.6 STOCK EQUIVALENTS

(a) USE OF STOCK EQUIVALENTS.   Corporations attempt to make debt more appealing but less costly, stock more desirable, and employees more committed. Stock equivalents are used to achieve these goals. Tax incentives also have served to enhance the use of stock equivalents. For purposes of this section, stock equivalents comprise the following three:

1. Stock warrants and stock rights
2. Employee stock options
3. Employee stock ownership plans (ESOPs)

(b) STOCK WARRANTS AND STOCK RIGHTS.   Stock warrants are issued in conjunction with and attached to debt securities, are sold separately, or are given to investment bankers, stockbrokers, and attorneys as compensation for services rendered in the issuance of the company's stock. Stock warrants entitle the holder to purchase the company shares, generally its common stock, at a specified price, either within a given period or for an indefinite period.

(i) Issued with Debt.   When stock warrants are issued with debt or any other security, they may be either detachable or nondetachable. The APB Opinion No. 14, "Accounting for Convertible Debt and Debt Issued with Stock Purchase Warrants" (par. 16), states that "the portion of the proceeds of debt securities issued with detachable stock purchase warrants which is allocable to the warrants should be accounted for as paid-in capital." The allocation is based on the relative fair values of the two securities at time of issuance, and the amount allocated to the warrant either increases the bond discount or reduces the bond premium. If, however, the warrant is not detachable, no allocation is made and the proceeds are attributed entirely to the debt.

Fair values may not be readily determinable when the company's securities are not publicly traded. In these circumstances, the company should estimate what the interest rate on the debt would be without the accompanying warrant. This rate would naturally be higher than the rate on the debt and warrant. The future cash flows from the payment of the debt and the interest payments should be discounted to the present. The difference between this amount and the amount received for the debt and the warrant is attributable to the warrant.

(ii) Sale of Warrants.   When stock warrants are sold, the transaction is reported in a manner similar to the sale of stock; that is, the proceeds are credited to a paid-in capital account, generally Stock Warrants Outstanding.

(iii) Issued for Services.   When stock warrants are issued for services, the fair market value of the services or the warrants, whichever is more clearly determinable, should be credited to paid-in capital.

(iv) Exercise of Warrants.   When the stock warrant is exercised, part of the cost of the stock is considered to be the value allocated to the warrant. Therefore, this amount is removed from the stock warrants outstanding account and, together with the cash received, credited to the stock account for the par or stated value. Any excess is credited to the capital in excess of par value account.

(v) Stock Rights.   Stock rights and stock warrants are, for all practical purposes, the same. The differences are essentially mechanical. Stock warrants may be sold alone, whereas stock rights are usually sold in conjunction with a debt or equity security. Generally, one warrant, but more than one right, is required to acquire one share of stock. Whatever the esoteric differences may be between stock rights and stock warrants, they are reported in a similar manner for accounting purposes.

(vi) Lapsed Warrants and Rights.   When stock warrants and stock rights lapse, the accounts should be closed and a paid-in capital account should be credited. The following stockholders' investment section of a company's comparative balance sheets shows the results of a lapse of warrants.

	1989	1988
Stockholders' Investment:		
Common stock—$.10 per value,		
5,000,000 shares authorized, 1,816,318		
shares issued and outstanding	$ 181,632	$ 181,632
Warrants outstanding	—	15,000
Paid-in capital	982,833	967,833
Retained earnings (deficit)	693,834	(676,867)
	$1,858,299	$ 487,598

In 1988, the warrants expired and the $15,000 was added to paid-in capital.

(vii) Tax Consequence of Lapsed Warrants.   A company may have taxable income when its warrants lapse. In these circumstances, the company could avoid adverse tax consequences by extending the expiration date of the warrants. Before any action is taken, however, the company should consult with its tax adviser.

(viii) Reacquisition of Warrants.   When stock warrants are reacquired, the amount paid in excess of the amount assigned to the warrants at issuance is charged to retained earnings. If the warrants are reacquired at a price less than the amount originally assigned to them, the difference is credited to additional paid-in capital.

(ix) Contingent Warrants.   Occasionally, a company will issue warrants to certain of its customers to purchase its stock at a specified price. These warrants become exercisable only if those customers purchase specified amounts of the company's product. These warrants are contingent warrants. The SEC in SAB No. 57 stated that the warrants should not be valued or recorded until the customer had made the specified amount of sales and any other uncertainties were resolved. However, the company should periodically determine whether it is probable, as defined in SFAS No. 5, "Accounting for Contingencies," that the customers will make purchases sufficient to earn the warrants. Sales made subsequent to the date that a probable cost will occur should be charged with a pro rata amount of the estimated ultimate cost of the warrants.

(c) EMPLOYEE STOCK OPTIONS.   Stock options are nontransferable rights granted by a corporation to its employees to purchase shares of the corporation at a stated price, either at a specified date or during a specified period. Stock options may be either compensatory or noncompensatory. Chapter 13B of ARB No. 43 states that "to the extent that such options and rights involve a measurable amount of compensation, this cost of services received should be accounted for as such..."

(i) Compensatory Stock Options.   Stock options involving an element of compensation generally arise when the employee has the right to purchase the company's stock at a price below market value at the measurement date. Paragraph 10(b) of APB Opinion No. 25, "Accounting for Stock Issued to Employees," states:

> The measurement date for determining compensation cost in stock option, purchase, and award plans is the first date on which are known both (1) the number of shares that an individual employee is entitled to receive and (2) the option or purchase price, if any. That date for many or most plans is the date an option is granted.

Compensation is the difference between the market price of the stock at the measurement date and the amount, if any, that the employee is required to pay. The amount allocated to compensation costs is credited to a paid-in capital account. Kieso and Weygandt illustrate the accounting and reporting of a compensatory stock option plan with the following example.

On January 1, 1989, a company grants options to its officers for 10,000 shares of its $1 par value common stock. The options may be exercised at any time within the next 10 years, commencing two years after the date of the grant. At the time of the grant, the market price of the stock is $70 a share and the option price for the stock is $60; therefore, there is an element of compensation in this option to the extent of $100,000 ($10 × 10,000). The company will record the following entries in 1989:

```
January 1, 1989
    Deferred compensation expense        $100,000
        Paid-in capital-stock options                   $100,000
December 31, 1989
    Compensation expense                 $ 50,000
        Deferred compensation expense                   $ 50,000
```

At December 31, 1989, the Stockholders' Equity section of the company's balance sheet is as follows:

Stockholders' equity:		
Common stock, $50 par, 20,000 shares issued and outstanding		$1,000,000
Paid-in capital-stock options	$100,000	
Less deferred compensation	50,000	50,000
Total stockholders' equity		$1,050,000

At December 31, 1990, the remaining $50,000 to the deferred compensation account is written off and charged to income. If 20 percent or 2000 of the 10,000 options were exercised on June 1, 1992, the following entry would be recorded:

Cash (2000 × $60)	$120,000	
Paid-in capital-stock option		
(20% × $100,000)	20,000	
Common Stock (2,000 × $1)		$ 2,000
Paid-in Capital in Excess of Par		138,000

If the remaining stock options lapse, the balance in the "Paid-in Capital—Stock Option" account is transferred to a new account, "Paid-in Capital—Expired Stock Options."[5]

(ii) Disclosure Requirements.   The SFAS No. 123, "Accounting for Stock-Based Compensation" (pars. 46–48; see also *FASB Accounting Standards—Current Text—General Standards* [pars. C74.145–147]) states the disclosure requirements for stock options.

(d) EMPLOYEE STOCK OWNERSHIP PLANS (ESOP); REPORTING THE ESOP.   An Employee Stock Ownership Plan (ESOP) is a plan under which employees acquire stock of their employer. It is also a means by which the corporation can obtain additional capital. Generally, the ESOP borrows from the bank and uses the proceeds to buy the company's shares, either from the corporation or from shareholders with significant holdings. The corporation guarantees the loan made to the ESOP, and the ESOP repays the loans from tax-deductible contributions made to it by the corporation.

Therefore, under the ESOP and variations of it, such as a Tax Reduction Act Stock Ownership Plan (TRASOP), the stockholders' equity section of the company reports a deduction to the extent of the ESOP outstanding debt that it guaranteed.

Financial reporting by the corporation of its ESOP is determined by the provisions of SOP 93-6, "Employers' Accounting for Employee Stock Ownership Plans." The Stock Ownership Plan (SOP) was adopted on November 22, 1993, and superseded SOP 76-3, "Accounting Practices for Certain Employee Stock Ownership Plans." The financial reporting requirements of SOP 93-6 are described in the following paragraphs.

(i) Reporting the Purchase of Shares by Employee Stock Ownership Plans.   The employers should do the following:

- For a leveraged ESOP, report the issuance of shares or the sale of shares when they occur. The corresponding charge should be to unearned ESOP shares, a contra account to be reported separately in the stockholders' equity section.
- If a leveraged ESOP buys outstanding employers' shares in the market, the employer should charge unearned ESOP shares and credit either cash or debt, depending on whether the ESOP is internally or externally leveraged.

---

[5] Id.

(ii) Reporting the Release of Employee Stock Ownership Plan Shares. When ESOP shares are committed to be released by a leveraged ESOP, unearned ESOP shares should be credited and either compensation cost, dividends payable, or compensation liabilities should be charged depending on the purpose for which the shares are released.

The difference between the fair value of the shares committed to be released and the cost of those shares to the ESOP should be charged or credited to additional paid-in capital.

(iii) Reporting Dividends on Employee Stock Ownership Plan Shares. Dividends should be reported in the following two ways:

1. For a leveraged ESOP:
   a. Dividends on unallocated shares used to pay debt service should be reported as reduction of either debt on accrued interest payable.
   b. Dividends on unallocated shares paid to participants or added to participant accounts should be reported as compensation expense.
   c. Dividends on allocated shares should be charged to retained earnings.
2. For a nonleveraged ESOP, dividends on shares held by the ESOP should be charged to retained earnings.

(iv) Reporting Redemptions of Employee Stock Ownership Plan Shares. Employers should report their purchase of shares held by ESOP participants as the purchase of treasury stock.

(e) OTHER STOCK COMPENSATION PLANS. The extent of stock compensation plans is limited only by the imagination and ingenuity of company management. Because of the proliferation of these plans, the FASB has been studying the subject of employee stock compensation plans and the method of accounting for them. In its 1984 *Invitation to Comment*, "Accounting for Compensation Plans Involving Certain Rights Granted to Employees," the FASB classified three plans as follows:

1. *Market performance plans*. These are plans in which the amounts involved are solely a function of the market price of the company's stock. Examples of these plans are the following:
   a. Incentive stock options
   b. Nonqualified stock options
   c. Stock appreciation rights
   d. Phantom stock units
   e. Restricted stock awards
   f. Restricted stock purchase rights
   g. Qualified employee stock purchases
2. *Enterprise performance plans*. These are plans in which the amounts involved are solely a function of enterprise performance based on established criteria, such as earnings per share, but not based on the market price of the company's stock. Examples of these plans are the following:
   a. Performance units
   b. Book value units
   c. Book value purchase rights
3. *Market/enterprise performance plans (combination plans)*. These are plans in which the amounts involved are a function of both market performance and enterprise performance. Examples of these plans are the following:
   a. Performance share units

    b. Stock appreciation rights with performance requirements

    c. Stock options with performance requirements

Accounting for these plans is explained in Chapter 39 of this *Handbook*. Authoritative pronouncements that provide guidance are found in the following four sources:

1. APB Opinion No. 25, "Accounting for Stock Issued to Employees."
2. FIN No. 28, "Accounting for Stock Appreciation Rights and Other Variable Stock Option or Award Plans."
3. FIN No. 31, "Treatment of Stock Compensation Plans in EPS Computations."
4. SFAS No. 123, "Accounting for Stock-Based Compensation."

27.7 RETAINED EARNINGS

(a) DEFINITION.　The MBCA states that the retained earnings of a corporation is

> equal to its net profits, income, gains and losses from the date of incorporation or from the latest date when a deficit was eliminated by an application of its capital surplus or stated capital or otherwise, after deducting subsequent distributions to shareholders and transfers to stated capital and capital surplus. . . .

    A corporation is an entity separate and distinct from its shareholders, and legally it cannot make a distribution to shareholders from permanent capital. Therefore, a credit balance in the retained earnings account represents the maximum potential claim that the shareholders have against the net assets of the corporation. The claim is no longer potential when, and to the extent that, the company's board of directors declares a dividend.

    The board of directors may declare a dividend except when the corporation is insolvent or when the dividend payment would render the corporation insolvent. Dividends may be declared only out of the unreserved and unrestricted retained earnings of the corporation; however, in some states, dividends may also be declared out of additional paid-in capital.

(b) EVENTS AFFECTING RETAINED EARNINGS.　The balance in the retained earnings account is increased by net income and reduced by net loss. In addition, the balance is affected by the following five things:

1. Prior period adjustments
2. Dividends
3. Recapitalizations and reorganizations
4. Treasury stock transactions
5. Stock redemptions

Treasury stock transactions and stock redemptions were discussed earlier in this section. The first three items are discussed below.

(c) PRIOR PERIOD ADJUSTMENTS.　The theoretical undesirability of prior period adjustments has been acknowledged for many years:

> . . . it is plainly desirable that all costs, expenses, and losses, and all profits of a business, . . . be included in the determination of income. If this principle could in practice be carried out perfectly, there would be no charges or credits to earned surplus [retained earnings] except those relating to distributions and appropriations of final net income. This is an ideal upon which all may agree, but because of conditions impossible to foresee it often fails of attainment. (ARB No. 43, ch. 2B, par. 3)

Although Chapter 2B has been superseded, the undesirability of prior period adjustments is still recognized. Conditions under which prior period adjustments may be recorded have been narrowed so that except for items specifically noted in authoritative pronouncements, only one item may be accounted for as a prior period adjustment and recorded directly in the retained earnings account.

(i) Correction of an Error in Prior Period Financial Statements. SFAS No. 16, "Prior Period Adjustments," as amended, states that "an item of profit and loss related to the correction of an error in the financial statements of a prior period ... shall be accounted for and reported as a prior period adjustment and excluded from the determination of net income for the current period."

"Errors in financial statements result from mathematical mistakes, mistakes in the application of accounting principles, or oversight or misuse of facts that existed at the time the financial statements were prepared," according to APB Opinion No. 20, "Accounting Changes" (par. 13).

(ii) Reporting Prior Period Adjustments. SFAS No. 16 (par. 16a) states that "those items that are reported as prior period adjustments shall, in single period statements, be reflected as adjustments of the opening balance of retained earnings." When comparative income statements are presented, the previously issued statements, if affected by the adjustment, shall be restated. If the prior period adjustment affects years prior to those being presented, the opening retained earnings of the earliest year must be adjusted.

(d) OTHER PRIOR PERIOD ADJUSTMENTS. In addition to the adjustment of retained earnings required by SFAS No. 16, other events require an adjustment of retained earnings.

The FASB has made many of its pronouncements effective on a retroactive basis. This requires restatements of all prior years' statements presented and, if applicable, an adjustment of the opening retained earnings of the earliest year presented.

In addition to FASB requirements for retained earnings adjustments, APB Opinion No. 20 (pars. 27 and 29) provides examples of changes in accounting principle requiring retroactive application. In those situations, balances in retained earnings must be adjusted.

(e) DIVIDENDS. Dividends are pro rata distributions of company assets to its shareholders, limited by business considerations, availability of resources, and, in most states, the amount of retained earnings. They represent the portion of the accumulated earnings that the board decides it can distribute without adversely affecting the operations of the company.

Although shareholders have the right to share in the earnings of the company, they are not entitled to receive the earnings or any part thereof without action by the board of directors. The declaration by the board and the distribution by the corporation of dividends involve three dates:

1. The declaration date
2. The record date
3. The payment date

Dividends are of the following five types:

1. Cash
2. Stock
3. Property
4. Scrip or liability
5. Liquidating

(f) DIVIDEND DATES.   For dividends other than stock dividends, the corporation incurs a liability at the time of declaration. This is the date when the board of directors meets and votes the dividend. At this meeting, the board also establishes the record date and the payment date for the dividend. When a stock dividend is declared, the board may rescind it prior to distribution.

At declaration date for other than a stock dividend, the company reduces its retained earnings by the amount of the dividend and records a liability. The record date does not affect the corporation. It must pay dividends on the number of shares outstanding; the record date merely establishes who will receive the dividend. For stocks that are publicly traded, generally the stock is traded ex-dividend—without the dividend—four or five days prior to the record date.

On the record date, the person responsible for distributing the dividend determines the individuals who will receive the dividend, and on the payment date the dividend is remitted to the stockholder. On the record date, no entry is required on the corporate books; on the payment date, the corporation eliminates its liability by distributing the assets necessary to satisfy the liability.

(g) CASH DIVIDENDS.   Declaration of a cash dividend is the usual manner in which the board initiates a distribution to the shareholders. The declaration is usually quarterly and may be stated as either a percentage of the par value of the shares or a dollar amount per share. However stated, at the date of declaration the corporation has assumed a liability and must therefore record it with a corresponding reduction of retained earnings.

As noted earlier, the company makes no entry in recognition of the record date of the dividend. On the payment date, the corporation satisfies its liability by distributing the cash.

(h) STOCK DIVIDENDS.   ARB No. 43 (ch. 7B, par. 1) defines a stock dividend as follows:

> An issuance by a corporation of its own common shares to its common shareholders without consideration and under conditions indicating that such action is prompted mainly by a desire to give the recipient shareholders some ostensibly separate evidence of a part of their respective interests in accumulated corporate earnings without distribution of cash or other property which the board of directors deems necessary or desirable to retain in the business.

A stock dividend is the second most common type of dividend, and it is the only one that, when declared, does not create a legally enforceable corporate liability. The declaration of a stock dividend is not a commitment to distribute corporate assets; it merely indicates an intent to realign the accounts constituting stockholders' equity by issuing additional stock to current shareholders.

(i) Small Stock Dividend.   ARB No. 43 (ch. 7B) indicates that a distribution less than 20 percent to 25 percent of the shares previously outstanding would be considered a small stock dividend. Recipients of small stock dividends view them as distributions of corporate earnings, usually in an amount equal to the fair value of the shares received. ARB No. 43 (ch. 7B, par. 10) states:

> [I]t is to be presumed that such views of recipients are materially strengthened in those instances, which are by far the most numerous, when the issuances are so small in comparison with the shares previously outstanding that they do not have any apparent effect upon the share market prices and, consequently, the market value of the shares previously held remains substantially unchanged. The committee therefore believes that when these circumstances exist the corporation should in the public interest account for the transaction by transferring from earned surplus to the category of permanent capitalization (represented by the capital stock and capital surplus accounts) an amount equal to the fair value of the additional shares issued.

Therefore, when a small stock dividend is declared or distributed (see below for time of recording), the corporation must do the following:

- Reduce retained earnings by the fair value of the shares
- Increase the common stock account by the par or stated value of the shares

- Increase capital paid in excess of par or stated value by the difference between such value and the amount determined in the first bullet above

If no par value stock is distributed, its total market value should be credited to the common stock account.

(ii) Large Stock Dividend. A distribution of 20 percent to 25 percent or more of the shares previously outstanding is considered a large stock dividend; therefore, it is reasonable to assume a reduction in the market value of outstanding shares. Under these circumstances, the retained earnings account is reduced and the stock account increased by the par or stated value of the shares. If no par value stock is distributed, the amount is computed by multiplying the number of shares distributed by the average amount per share paid in.

(iii) Closely Held Corporation. For closely held corporations, market value is not a factor in determining the amount of the stock dividend. Under these circumstances, "there is no need to capitalize earned surplus other than to meet legal requirements" (ARB No. 43, ch. 7B, par. 12). Therefore, the par or stated value of the shares distributed determines the amount of the reduction of retained earnings.

(iv) Record Date. Since there is no legally enforceable obligation at the declaration date to issue the stock, the dividend should be recorded at the market value on the date the stock is distributed. However, many accountants prefer to record the dividend at the date of declaration. When this is done, the corporation establishes a new account, Stock Dividend Distributable, which, at the date of declaration, is credited for the par or stated value of the shares to be distributed.

(v) Reasons for Stock Dividends. Stock dividends usually are declared for the following four reasons:

1. To permanently retain earnings in the business by capitalizing a portion of accumulated earnings
2. To maintain a record of paying dividends without affecting corporate assets
3. To increase the number of shares outstanding without affecting the market price significantly
4. To take advantage of the nontaxability of stock dividends

The last reason is significant since not only are stock dividends not taxable on receipt, but also the stock is assumed to have the same holding period as the shares on which the dividend was declared.

(i) PROPERTY DIVIDENDS. Occasionally, a corporation will pay a dividend in kind, that is, it will pay the dividend in property, inventory, real estate, marketable securities of other corporations. Prior to the adoption of APB Opinion No. 29, "Accounting for Nonmonetary Transactions," dividends of this nature were accounted for at book value.

APB Opinion No. 29 (par. 18) states:

> A transfer of a nonmonetary asset to a stockholder or to another entity in a nonreciprocal transfer should be recorded at the fair value of the asset transferred, and a gain or loss should be recognized on the disposition of the asset.

However, if the transfer is a spinoff or other form of reorganization or liquidation, it should be recorded at book value, not market value.

The recording of a property dividend is explained in the following example. Assume that a corporation owns 1,000 shares of "X" Corp. stock, which it acquired at $10 a share and which now has a market value of $25. If it declares a property dividend of 600 shares, it must record a gain on the disposal of the 600 shares. Therefore, at the declaration date, it increases its investment by \$9,000 (600 shares × \$15) and credits an account, Gain on Disposal of Investment. It then reduces retained earnings by \$15,000 (600 shares × \$25) and records its liability. The \$9,000 gain is reported in the income statement; however, for income tax purposes, this gain is not taxable. Since this item does not have tax consequences, it is not considered when computing income taxes under the provisions of SFAS No. 109, "Accounting for Income Taxes."

(j) SCRIP OR LIABILITY DIVIDENDS.   Although it is rarely done, a corporation may pay a dividend in scrip—a note. The accounting and reporting is the same as for a cash dividend, except that the corporation records notes payable rather than dividends payable as the liability. Notes payable for dividends bear interest that, when accrued, is charged to the interest expense account.

One reason for scrip dividends is that the shareholders may want a cash dividend; however, at the time of declaration, the corporation wishes to conserve its cash. After the shareholders receive the notes for the dividend, they can discount them and thereby obtain the desired cash.

(k) LIQUIDATING DIVIDENDS.   A liquiding dividend is any dividend not based on profits; therefore, it must be recorded as a reduction of paid-in capital. Dividends of this nature are common in industries involved in natural resources. Section 45(b) of the MBCA recognizes the possibility of this kind of dividend. It states:

> If the articles of incorporation of a corporation engaged in the business of exploiting natural resources so provide, dividends may be declared and paid in cash out of the depletion reserves, but each such dividend shall be identified as a distribution of such reserves and the amount per share paid from such reserves shall be disclosed to the shareholders receiving the same concurrently with the distribution thereof.

Liquidating dividends also may be declared as a result of contraction of a corporation's operations. For example, a corporation may dispose of a division or a subsidiary and decide not to reinvest the proceeds.

When a liquidating dividend is declared and stock is not redeemed, accounts other than the retained earnings and capital stock accounts must be reduced. These accounts are capital in excess of par value, donated capital, capital arising from treasury stock transactions, or some similar capital account.

(l) QUASI REORGANIZATION.   In the early years of a corporation's existence, it is not unusual for the corporation to be unprofitable and build up an accumulated deficit. When the corporation becomes profitable, it will not be able to pay dividends until this deficit is eliminated. One way of eliminating the deficit is a reorganization—an adjustment of the financial structure of the company.

Reorganizations may be formal and be subject to the provisions of the Federal Bankruptcy Law and the jurisdiction of the bankruptcy courts, or they may be informal. Informal reorganizations, generally called *quasi reorganizations*, adjust the corporate capital structure without recourse to the courts. In addition to speeding up the reorganization process, a quasi reorganization is less costly than the more formal court-supervised reorganization.

The GAAP state that "capital surplus, however created, should not be used to relieve the income account of the current or future years of charges which would otherwise . . . be made . . . according to ARB No. 43, Ch. 1A (par. 2)." However, exceptions to this rule are provided for in the case of a quasi reorganization.

(i) Procedures in a Quasi Reorganization.   Chapter 7A of ARB No. 43 explains the procedures used in a quasi reorganization. Assets are revalued downward to fair value at the date of adjustment; however, upward adjustments of items within the same asset classification are permitted so long as the net effect of the adjustments does not result in a write-up of the net assets (see SAB No. 78). The net reduction in assets is a charge to the accumulated deficit of the corporation. After all asset adjustments are completed, the accumulated deficit is written off against any additional paid-in capital accounts. If the total in these accounts is not sufficient to absorb the accumulated deficit, additional paid-in capital should be created by means of a reduction in the par or stated value of the stock.

(ii) Retained Earnings After Readjustment. ARB No. 43 states: "When the readjustment has been completed, the company's accounting should be substantially similar to that appropriate for a new company" (par. 9). Therefore, retained earnings must be zero, and thereafter, whenever a balance sheet is prepared, the retained earnings should be dated to indicate from which date these earnings have been accumulated. ARB No. 46 indicates that generally this dating should continue over a period of 10 years, although there may be exceptional circumstances where dating may cease before 10 years.

Dating of retained earnings may be done either on the face of the balance sheet or in the notes to financial statements. In its 1988 balance sheet, Genentech, Inc., reported the following:

	1988	1987
Shareholders' Equity:		
Preferred stock, $.02 par value; authorized 100,000,000 shares; none issued	$ —	$ —
Common stock, $.02 par value; authorized 297,00,000 shares; outstanding; 1988—82,924,439; 1987—78,739,896	1,658	1,575
Earnings convertible restricted stock $.02 par value; authorized 3,000,000 shares; outstanding: 1988—none; 1987—2,927,260	—	59
Additional paid-in capital	366,518	336,267
Notes receivable from sale of stock	—	(320)
Retained earnings (since October 1, 1987, quasi reorganization in which a deficit of $329,457 was eliminated)	31,119	17,831
Total stockholders' equity	399,295	355,412
Total liabilities and stockholders' equity	$668,755	$618,973

In its notes to financial statements explaining its reorganization, the Company stated:

> On February 18, 1988 the Company's Board of Directors approved the elimination of the Company's accumulated deficit through an accounting reorganization of its stockholders' equity accounts (quasi-reorganization) effective October 1, 1987. The quasi-reorganization did not involve any revaluation of assets or liabilities. The effective date of the quasi-reorganization (October 1, 1987) reflects the beginning of the quarter in which the Company received approval for and commenced marketing of its second major product, and as such, marks a turning point in the Company's operations. The accumulated deficit was eliminated by a transfer from additional paid-in capital in an amount equal to the accumulated deficit. The Company's stockholders' equity accounts at October 1, 1987 before and after the quasi-reorganization, are reflected in the consolidated statements of stockholders' equity. The tax benefits recognized subsequent to the quasi-reorganization that relate to items occurring prior to the quasi-reorganization have been reclassified from retained earnings to additional paid-in capital.

(iii) Tax Loss Carryforwards. A corporation that undertakes a quasi reorganization probably has operating loss or tax credit carryforwards that have not been recognized as assets. When the benefits of these carryforwards are realized subsequent to the quasi reorganization, they should be reported as a direct addition to contributed capital. If, however, the quasi reorganization involved only the elimination of the accumulated deficit by a reduction in contributed capital, subsequent recognition of prior operating loss or tax credit carryforwards should be accounted for as if the quasi reorganization had not occurred. That is, it should be recognized in the income statement. However, after this recognition, the tax benefit should be reclassified from retained earnings to contributed capital, according to SFAS No. 109.

(m) RESTRICTIONS OF RETAINED EARNINGS.   Although retained earnings indicates the maximum that may be distributed to shareholders, this amount may be subject to certain constraints and restrictions. Paragraph 199 of APB Statement No. 4 states that information about restrictions on assets and of owners' equity should be disclosed.

Restrictions of retained earnings are classified as legal, contractual, or voluntary.

(i) Legal Restrictions.   A legal restriction on retained earnings was noted in Subsection 27.5(a), which discussed treasury stock. Under Section 6 of the MBCA, a corporation has the right to acquire its stock but only to the extent of unreserved or unrestricted retained earnings. The section further states:

> To the extent that earned surplus or capital surplus is used as the measure of the Corporation's right to purchase its own shares, such surplus shall be restricted so long as such shares are held as treasury shares. . . .

(ii) Contractual Restrictions.   Bond indentures and loan agreements with banks usually contain restrictions on retained earnings. Typical of these restrictions and the related disclosure is the note in the 1987 financial statements of Occidental Petroleum Corporation:

> At December 31, 1987, under the most restrictive covenants of certain financing agreements, the capacity for the payment of all cash dividends and other distributions on, and for acquisitions of, capital stock was approximately $2.2 billion, assuming that such dividends, distributions or acquisitions were made without incurring additional borrowing. The net assets of certain subsidiaries of Occidental are restricted from being advanced, loaned, or dividended to Occidental and its affiliates by certain financing agreements. At December 31, 1987, net assets of consolidated subsidiaries so restricted were approximately $1.1 billion.

(iii) Voluntary Restrictions.   Occasionally, a corporation will voluntarily restrict the distribution of dividends because of some loss contingency that does not qualify for deduction on the income statement or because of future plans for major construction or renovation. In these situations, the corporation is merely informing the user of its financial statements that it has voluntarily restricted the payment of dividends.

(iv) Liquidating Value of Preferred Stock.   The question of whether the excess of the liquidating value of preferred stock over its par value is a restriction on retained earnings is a legal determination. When state law is unclear, the uncertainty should be disclosed.

(n) APPROPRIATIONS OF RETAINED EARNINGS.   Usually, restrictions of retained earnings are disclosed in the notes to financial statements and recorded on the books by means of a memorandum entry. Sometimes, by action of the board of directors, retained earnings may be appropriated; that is, total retained earnings is reduced and a new account, Appropriated Retained Earnings, is established. However, the total retained earnings remains the same. Rarely is appropriated retained earnings reported on the balance sheet.

(o) LOSS CONTINGENCIES.   Appropriated retained earnings may not relieve the income statement of an expense. SFAS No. 5 (par. 15) states:

> Some enterprises have classified a portion of retained earnings as "appropriated" for loss contingencies. . . . Appropriation of retained earnings is not prohibited by this Statement provided that it is shown within the stockholders' equity section of the balance sheet and is clearly identified as an appropriation of retained earnings. Costs or losses shall not be charged to an appropriation of retained earnings, and no part of the appropriation shall be transferred to income.

When the event for which the appropriation was established has passed, the appropriated retained earnings account is reduced by the amount originally established and the retained earnings account increased by a similar amount.

27.8 OTHER ITEMS AFFECTING STOCKHOLDERS' EQUITY

(a) MINORITY INTERESTS.   When consolidated financial statements are prepared in situations where the parent company does not own 100 percent of the stock of its subsidiary, the minority interest in the subsidiary usually is presented between long-term debt and stockholders' equity. The presentation represents essentially a proprietary theory approach and implies that the minority interest is a liability. However, minority interests do not represent liabilities any more than the interests of the majority shareholders do. Under the entity theory of consolidated statements, controlling shareholder and minority interests should be accorded the same reporting treatment.

Griffin, Williams, and Larson state:

> The acceptance of the entity notion for consolidated statements carries with it the obligation to regard all shareholders equal per share claimants to the combined resources of the affiliated companies. The presentation of shareholders' interests should be made in such a manner as to clearly indicate the values attributable to controlling and noncontrolling interests, but without reference to legal preference or implications as to hierarchical status. Clearly, according to this view, an identification of minority interests as liabilities in consolidated statements is inappropriate; it may also be argued that the compromise consolidated position between the liabilities and the controlling stockholders' equity divisions violates the spirit of the entity theory.[6]

General Telephone & Electronics Corporation has always recognized the entity theory of consolidated financial statements. Its 1987 balance sheet reported the following:

(thousands of dollars)	1987	1986
Shareholders' equity:		
GTE Corporation—		
Preferred stock	$ 544,030	$ 22,153
Common stock—shares issued 340,549,668 and		
331,464,120	34,055	33,146
Amounts paid in, in excess of par value	4,769,391	4,457,642
Foreign currency translation adjustment	(83,685)	(141,069)
Reinvested earnings	3,637,926	3,372,738
Common stock held in treasury—15,000,000 and		
1,506,000 shares, at cost	(598,428)	(59,336)
	8,303,289	7,885,274
Minority interests in equity of subsidiaries	780,583	732,865
Total shareholders' equity	$9,083,872	$8,618,139

(b) COMBINED FINANCIAL STATEMENTS.   Consolidated financial statements are required when one company owns more than 50 percent of the outstanding voting shares of another company. However, a group of independent companies may have common controlling shareholders. For example, an individual may have controlling interest in two or more corporations or a parent company may have more than one subsidiary. When these commonly controlled companies present financial information, "combined financial statements ... are more meaningful than ... separate statements," according to ARB No. 51, "Consolidated Financial Statements."

---

[6] Charles H. Griffin, Thomas H. Williams, and Kermit D. Larson, *Advanced Accounting*, Fourth Edition (Irwin, Homewood, IL, 1980).

When combined financial statements are presented, intercompany transactions and profits or losses must be eliminated. When combining balance sheets, all components are combined except for the outstanding stock of the separate entities, which is presented separately. The shareholders' equity section of the 1983 combined balance sheet of AMP Incorporated and Pamcor, Inc. and their subsidiaries was presented as follows:

	1983	1982
Shareholders' equity:		
AMP Incorporated		
Common stock, without par value—		
Authorized 50,000,000 shares, issued 37,440,000 shares	$ 12,480	$ 12,480
Pamcor, Inc.		
Common stock, par value $1.00 per share—		
Authorized and issued, 20,000 shares	20	20
Other capital	27,235	26,262
Cumulative translation adjustments	(39,439)	(24,665)
Retained earnings	853,845	748,085
	854,141	762,182
Less—Treasury stock, at cost	53,288	47,685
Total shareholders' equity	$800,853	$714,497

In the notes to combined financial statements, the principles of combination were explained as follows:

> The financial statements of AMP and Pamcor and their subsidiaries (all wholly owned with one exception) are combined, as each company is owned beneficially by identical shareholders. Intercompany and affiliated company accounts are eliminated in the combination.

(c) INVESTOR AND INVESTEE TRANSACTIONS.   There are situations where a parent– subsidiary relationship exists and the subsidiary issues additional shares to someone other than its parent. In these circumstances, the parent's percentage interest in the subsidiary decreases, and the book balance of its investment may change, depending on the price at which the new stock is sold.

Assume that on January 2, 1989, Company P owns a 90 percent interest in Company S whose balance sheet on that date is as follows:

Assets	$10,000
Liabilities	$ 1,000
Stockholders' equity	9,000
Total	$10,000

Company S has outstanding 1,000 shares of which Company P owns 900 shares; each share has a book value of $9 ($9,000 4 1,000). Further assume that, when Company P acquired its shares, there was no goodwill; therefore, at January 2, 1989, its investment account has a balance of $8,100 (90% × $9,000).

(i) Investee Sale at Book Value.   Assume Company S sells 500 shares to the public on January 2, 1989, at its book value of $9 a share or $4,500. The outstanding shares therefore increase to 1,500 and the balance sheet of Company S is as follows:

Assets	$14,500
Liabilities	$ 1,000
Stockholders' equity	$13,500
Total	$14,500

Company P's ownership dropped to 60 percent (900 shares of 1,500 outstanding), but 60 percent of $13,500 still equals $8,100, and the transaction does not affect the carrying value of the investor's investment.

(ii) Investee Sale in Excess of Book Value.   If Company S sells the 500 shares for $10 a share ($1 over book value) or $5,000, the result is different. After the sale, the balance sheet of Company S is as follows:

Assets	$15,000
Liabilities	$ 1,000
Stockholders' equity	14,000
Total	$15,000

Under these circumstances, Company P's investment account should reflect a balance of 60 percent of $14,000 or $8,400. The increase represents 60 percent of $500 (the amount paid in excess of book value). This increase is not an item of income nor is it an item to be credited to retained earnings. It is a capital transaction; the investment account must be increased by $300 and the corresponding credit is to an additional paid-in capital account.

(iii) Investee Sale Below Book Value.   If Company S sells the 500 shares below book value—$7 a share or $3,500—a different situation exists. After the sale, the balance sheet of Company S is as follows:

Assets	$13,500
Liabilities	$ 1,000
Stockholders' equity	12,500
Total	$13,500

Under these circumstances, Company P's investment account should reflect a balance of 60 percent of $12,500 or $7,500. The decrease represents 60 percent of $1,000 (the amount paid below book value). Company P therefore must reduce its investment account by $600 and reduce additional paid-in capital by a similar amount. If there is not a sufficient balance in the additional paid-in capital account of Company P, the excess must be applied to a reduction of retained earnings.

(iv) Staff Accounting Bulletin (SAB) No. 51.   The SEC, in this Bulletin, stated that where the investee sales are not part of a planned reorganization, it would permit the investor to recognize the gain or loss in its income statement as a separate line item.

(v) No Parent Subsidiary Relationship.   If the investor company owns more than 20 percent but 50 percent or less of the outstanding voting stock of the investee, the same treatment must be accorded investee transactions in its own stock. However, if the investor's interest falls below 20 percent, no adjustment is made to the investment account as stated in APB Opinion No. 18, "The Equity Method of Accounting for Investments in Common Stock."

If an investor company initially owns less than 20 percent of the voting stock of the investee and in a subsequent period increases its percentage ownership to 20 percent or more, either by its actions or by the actions of the investee, "the investment, results of operations (current and prior periods presented), and retained earnings of the investor should be adjusted retroactively in a manner consistent with the accounting for a step-by-step acquisition of a subsidiary," as explained in APB Opinion No. 18. The mechanics of a step-by-step acquisition of a subsidiary are explained in ARB No. 51 (par. 10) and reported in Chapter 10 of this *Handbook*.

Enterprise
Statement of Changes in Equity
Year Ended December 31, 20X9

	Total[a]	Comprehensive Income	Retained Earnings	Accumulated Other Comprehensive Income	Common Stock	Paid-in Capital
Beginning balance	$563,500		$ 88,500	$25,000	$150,000	$300,000
Comprehensive income						
Net income	63,250	[63,250]	63,250			
Other comprehensive income, net of tax						
Unrealized gains on securities, net of reclassification adjustment (see disclosure)	11,500	11,500				
Foreign currency translation adjustments	8,000	8,000				
Minimum pension liability adjustment	(2,500)	(2,500)				
Other comprehensive income		17,000		17,000		
Comprehensive income		[$80,250]				
Common stock issued	150,000				50,000	100,000
Dividends declared on common stock	(10,000)		(10,000)			
Ending balance	$783,750		$141,750	$42,000	$200,000	$400,000
Disclosure of reclassification amount:[b]						
Unrealized holding gains arising during period		$13,000				
Less: reclassification adjustment for gains included in net income		(1,500)				
Net unrealized gains on securities		$11,500				

[a]Alternatively, an enterprise can omit the separate column labeled "Comprehensive Income" by displaying an aggregate amount for comprehensive income ($80,250) in the "Total" column.

[b]It is assumed that there was no sale or liquidation of an investment in a foreign entity. Therefore, there is no reclassification adjustment for this period.

(Continues)

Exhibit 27.1   Statement of changes in equity approach.

Enterprise
Notes to Financial Statements
Year Ended December 31, 20X9

	Foreign Currency Items	Unrealized Gains on Securities	Minimum Pension Liability Adjustment	Accumulated Other Comprehensive Income
Beginning balance	$ (500)	$25,500	$ 0	$25,000
Current-period change	8,000	11,500	(2,500)	17,000
Ending balance	$7,500	$37,000	$(2,500)	$42,000

Alternatively, the balances of each classification within accumulated other comprehensive income can be displayed in a statement of changes in equity or in a statement of financial position.

Exhibit 27.1   *Continued.*

(d) REPORTING COMPREHENSIVE INCOME.   Paragraph 8 of SFAS No. 130, "Reporting Comprehensive Income," refers to FASB Concepts Statement No. 6, which defines comprehensive income as "the change in equity of a business enterprise during a period from transactions and other events and circumstances from nonowner sources." Paragraph 10 states:

> This Statement uses the term comprehensive income to describe the total of all components of comprehensive income, including net income. This Statement uses the term other comprehensive income to refer to revenues, expenses, gains, and losses that under generally accepted accounting principles are included in comprehensive income but excluded from net income.

Paragraph 26 of SFAS No. 130 states:

> The total of other comprehensive income for a period shall be transferred to a component of equity that is disclosed separately from retained earnings and additional paid-in capital in a statement of financial position at the end of an accounting period. ... An enterprise shall disclose accumulated balances for each classification in that separate component of equity on the face of a statement of financial position, in a statement of changes in equity, or in notes to the financial statements.

The provisions of SFAS No. 130 are effective for fiscal years beginning after December 15, 1997. Earlier application is permitted. If comparative financial statements are provided for earlier periods, those financial statements shall be reclassified to reflect application of the provisions of the Statement. Exhibit 27.1 illustrates a statement of changes in equity and related disclosures as required by SFAS No. 130.

27.9 DISCLOSURE OF INFORMATION ABOUT CAPITAL STRUCTURE

SFAS No. 129, "Disclosure of Information about Capital Structure," essentially consolidated disclosure requirements found in other authoritative pronouncements. Disclosures concerning a company's stock are as follows:

- Dividend and liquidation preferences
- Participation rights
- Call prices and dates
- Conversion or exercise prices or rates and pertinent rates
- Sinking fund requirements

- Unusual voting rights
- Significant terms of contracts to issue additional shares
- The number of shares issued upon conversion, exercise, or satisfaction of required conditions during at least the most recent annual fiscal period and any subsequent interim period presented

(a) PREFERRED STOCK.   A company that issues preferred stock or other senior stock with a preference in involuntary liquidation considerably in excess of par or stated value should disclose the relationship between the liquidation preference and the par or stated value. This disclosure should be made in the equity section of the balance sheet in the aggregate.

The company should also disclose (a) the aggregate or per-share amounts at which preferred stock may be called or is subject to redemption, and (b) the aggregate and per-share amounts of arrearages in cumulative preferred stock.

27.10 SOURCES AND SUGGESTED REFERENCES

Accounting Principles Board, "Status of Accounting Research Bulletins," APB Opinion No. 6. AICPA, New York, 1965.

———, "Reporting the Results of Operations," APB Opinion No. 9. AICPA, New York, 1966.

———, "Accounting for Convertible Debt and Debt Issued with Stock Purchase Warrants," APB Opinion No. 14. AICPA, New York, 1969.

———, "The Equity Method of Accounting for Investments in Common Stock," APB Opinion No. 18. AICPA, New York, 1971.

———, "Accounting Changes," APB Opinion No. 20. AICPA, New York, 1971.

———, "Interest on Receivables and Payables," APB Opinion No. 21. AICPA, New York, 1971.

———, "Accounting for Stock Issued to Employees," APB Opinion No. 25. AICPA, New York, 1972.

———, "Accounting for Nonmonetary Transactions," APB Opinion No. 29. AICPA, New York, 1973.

———, "Basic Concepts and Accounting Principles Underlying Financial Statements of Business Enterprises," APB Statement No. 4. AICPA, New York, 1970.

American Bar Association, Committee on Corporate Laws of Section of Corporation, Banking and Business Law: Model Business Corporation Act. American Law Institute—American Bar Association Committee on Continuing Professional Education, Philadelphia, PA, 1975.

American Institute of Certified Public Accountants, "Restatement and Revision of Accounting Research Bulletins," Accounting Research Bulletin No. 43. AICPA, New York, 1953.

———, "Review and Resume," Accounting Terminology Bulletin No. 1. AICPA, New York, 1953.

———, "Discontinuance of Dating Earned Surplus," Accounting Research Bulletin No. 46. AICPA, New York, 1956.

———, "Consolidated Financial Statements," Accounting Research Bulletin No. 51. AICPA, New York, 1959.

———, "Employers' Accounting for Employee Stock Ownership Plans," Statement of Position 93-6. AICPA, New York, 1993.

Financial Accounting Standards Board, "Accounting for Stock Appreciation Rights and Other Variable Stock Option or Award Plans," FASB Interpretation No. 28. FASB, Stamford, CT, 1978.

———, "Treatment of Stock Compensation Plans in EPS Computations," FASB Interpretation No. 31. FASB, Stamford, CT, 1980.

———, "Determining the Measurement Date for Stock Option, Purchase, and Award Plans Involving Junior Stock," FASB Interpretation No. 38. FASB, Stamford, CT, 1984.

———, "Accounting for Compensation Plans Involving Certain Rights Granted to Employees," Invitation to Comment. FASB, Stamford, CT, 1984.

———, "Objectives of Financial Reporting by Business Enterprises," Statement of Financial Accounting Concepts No. 1. FASB, Stamford, CT, 1978.

———, "Qualitative Characteristics of Accounting Information," Statement of Financial Accounting Concepts No. 2. FASB, Stamford, CT, 1980.

_____, "Recognition and Measurement in Financial Statements of Business Enterprises," Statement of Financial Accounting Concepts No. 5. FASB, Stamford, CT, 1984.

_____, "Elements of Financial Statements," Statement of Financial Accounting Concepts No. 6. FASB, Stamford, CT, 1985.

_____, "Accounting for Contingencies," Statement of Financial Accounting Standards No. 5. FASB, Stamford, CT, 1975.

_____, "Prior Period Adjustments," Statement of Financial Accounting Standards No. 16. FASB, Stamford, CT, 1977.

_____, "Accounting for Income Taxes," Statement of Financial Accounting Standards No. 109. FASB, Stamford, CT, 1992.

_____, "Accounting for Stock-Based Compensation," Statement of Financial Accounting Standards No. 123. FASB, Stamford, CT, 1995.

_____, "Disclosure of Information about Capital Structure," Statement of Financial Accounting Standards No. 129. FASB, Stamford, CT, 1997.

_____, "Reporting Comprehensive Income," Statement of Financial Accounting Standards No. 130. FASB, Stamford, CT, 1997.

_____, "Accounting for the Conversion of Stock Options into Incentive Stock Options as a Result of the Economic Recovery Tax Act of 1981," FASB Technical Bulletin No. 82-2. FASB, Stamford, CT, 1982.

_____, "Accounting for a Purchase of Treasury Shares at a Price Significantly in Excess of the Current Market Price of the Shares and the Income Statement Classification of Costs Incurred in Defending against a Takeover Attempt," FASB Technical Bulletin No. 85-6. FASB, Stamford, CT, 1985.

Griffin, Charles H., Williams, Thomas H., and Larson, Kermit D., *Advanced Accounting*, Fourth Edition Irwin, Homewood, IL, 1980.

Kieso, Donald E., and Weygandt, Jerry J., *Intermediate Accounting*, Sixth Edition John Wiley & Sons, New York, 1989.

Melcher, Beatrice, "Stockholders' Equity," Accounting Research Study No. 15. AICPA, New York, 1973.

Securities and Exchange Commission, "Accounting Rules," Regulation S-X. SEC, Washington, DC.

_____, "Accounting for Sales of Stock by Subsidiary," Staff Accounting Bulletin No. 51. SEC, Washington, DC, 1983.

_____, "Views Concerning Accounting for Contingent Warrants in Connection with Sales Agreements with Certain Major Customers," Staff Accounting Bulletin No. 57. SEC, Washington, DC, 1984.

_____, "Increasing Role of Preferred Stock," Staff Accounting Bulletin No. 68. SEC, Washington, DC, 1987.

_____, "Views Regarding Certain Matters Relating to Quasi Reorganizations, Including Deficit Eliminations," Staff Accounting Bulletin No. 78. SEC, Washington, DC, 1988.

Seiden, Neil, and Rikert, Richard, eds., *Accounting Trends and Techniques*, 49th Edition AICPA, New York, 1995.

CHAPTER 28

AUDITING STANDARDS AND AUDIT REPORTS FOR NONPUBLIC COMPANIES

Dan M. Guy, PhD, CPA
Clemson University

Alan J. Winters, PhD, CPA
Clemson University

28.1 SERVICES OFFERED BY INDEPENDENT ACCOUNTANTS

(a) CLASSIFICATION OF SERVICES.   The term *independent accountant* is used interchangeably with "independent auditor" and "independent public accountant." Generally, the term is limited to either certified public accountants (CPAs) or public accountants licensed to perform audits and express opinions on financial statements under applicable state accountancy laws.

Because they are knowledgeable about accounting principles and accounting systems, tax matters, and the like, independent accountants provide a wide range of services in addition to audits. These include accounting and review services, tax services, consulting services, personal financial planning, and other types of special service. The range of their services has recently become contentious.

(b) AUDITING SERVICES.   An audit involves the application of a variety of procedures and techniques to obtain evidential matter sufficient for the independent accountant to express an informed opinion about whether the financial statements conform with generally accepted accounting principles (GAAP). When serving as an auditor, the independent accountant is guided by a Code of

Professional Conduct and a variety of standards promulgated by professional bodies established for that purpose.

Rule of Conduct 202 of the American Institute of Certified Public Accountants' (AICPA's) Code of Professional Conduct provides:

> A member who performs auditing, review, compilation, management consulting, tax or other professional services shall comply with standards promulgated by bodies designated by … [the AICPA].

(i) Generally Accepted Auditing Standards.   Ten generally accepted auditing standards (GAAS) are cited by *AICPA Professional Standards* (AU 150):

GENERAL STANDARDS

1. *Training and proficiency*. The audit is to be performed by a person or persons having adequate technical training and proficiency as an auditor.
2. *Independence*. In all matters relating to the assignment, an independence in mental attitude is to be maintained by the auditor or auditors.
3. *Due care*. Due professional care is to be exercised in the planning and performance of the audit and the preparation of the report.

STANDARDS OF FIELD WORK

4. *Planning and supervision*. The work is to be adequately planned and assistants, if any, are to be properly supervised.
5. *Understanding of entity and its environment*. The auditor must obtain a sufficient understanding of the entity, and its environment, including its internal control, to assess the risk of material misstatement of the financial statements whether due to error or fraud, and to design the nature, timing, and extent of further audit procedures.
6. *Evidence*. The auditor must obtain sufficient appropriate audit evidence by performing audit procedures to afford a reasonable basis for an opinion regarding the financial statements under audit.

STANDARDS OF REPORTING

7. *Generally accepted accounting principles*. The report shall state whether the financial statements are presented in accordance with GAAP.
8. *Consistency*. The report shall identify those circumstances in which such principles have been consistently observed in the current period in relation to the preceding period.
9. *Disclosure*. Informative disclosures in the financial statements are to be regarded as reasonably adequate unless otherwise stated in the report.
10. *Expression of opinion*. The report shall either contain an expression of opinion regarding the financial statements, taken as a whole, or an assertion to the effect that an opinion cannot be expressed. When an overall opinion cannot be expressed, the reasons therefore should be stated. In all cases where an auditor's name is associated with financial statements, the report should contain a clear-cut indication of the character of the auditor's work, if any, and the degree of responsibility the auditor is taking.

(ii) Statements on Auditing Standards.   Statements on Auditing Standards (SASs) are pronouncements issued by the Auditing Standards Board (ASB) of the AICPA to guide auditing practice. As Rule 202 indicates, SASs are enforceable under the Code; but perhaps of equal importance, courts generally view adherence to SASs as the standard for assessing an auditor's liability.

For audits of nonpublic companies, the SASs specify required auditing procedures, provide guidance on important areas of judgment often encountered in audits, and establish the form and content of the auditor's report. They are issued individually in a numbered series and are codified in a loose-leaf service. Bound versions of the loose-leaf service are issued annually and provide the most convenient form for use in practice.

(iii) Interpretive Publications.   Interpretive publications consist of auditing interpretations of the SASs, auditing guidance included in AICPA Audit and Accounting Guides, and AICPA Auditing Statements of Position. They deal with the application of SASs to particular circumstances, thus are usually more limited and specific in coverage. These publications are issued under the authority of the AICPA's ASB after review and comment by ASB members. Although they are not auditing standards, the auditor should be aware of and consider interpretive publications applicable to the audit. If the auditor decides not to apply the auditing guidance in these publications, the auditor should be prepared to explain how he complied with the SAS provisions addressed by the publications.

(iv) Other Auditing Publications.   Other auditing publications include AICPA publications not referred to in Sections (ii) or (iii). Examples include articles in professional journals, auditing articles in the AICPA CPA Letter, continuing education programs, and other instruction materials, textbooks, guide books, and other auditing publications from state CPA societies, other organizations, and individuals. These publications have no authoritative status, but they may help the auditor understand and apply SASs.

(c) ACCOUNTING SERVICES.   Accounting services include all forms of involvement with financial statements or financial information other than an audit, such as bookkeeping, compilation of financial statements from a trial balance, and review of financial statements. The accountant's responsibilities for the unaudited financial statements of a nonpublic company are set forth in Statements on Standards for Accounting and Review Services (SSARS), a numbered series of pronouncements issued by the Accounting and Review Services Committee of the AICPA. Technically, an accountant is not "associated" with the unaudited financial statements of a nonpublic company under SSARS No. 1, "Compilation and Review of Financial Statements" (AR 100), but has a similar reporting obligation:

> An accountant should not consent to the use of his name in a document or written communication containing unaudited financial statements of a nonpublic entity unless (a) he has compiled or reviewed the financial statements and his report accompanies them, or (b) the financial statements are accompanied by an indication that the accountant has not compiled or reviewed the financial statements and he assumes no responsibility for them. If an accountant becomes aware that his name has been used improperly in any client-prepared document containing unaudited financial statements, he should advise his client that the use of his name is inappropriate and should consider what other actions might be appropriate, including consultation with his attorney.

The accountant should not submit unaudited financial statements of a nonpublic entity to his client or others unless, as a minimum, he complies with the provisions of this statement applicable to a compilation engagement.

Thus, the only types of report an accountant may issue in connection with the unaudited financial statements of a nonpublic company are for the accounting services of a compilation or review. These services are defined as follows in SSARS No. 1 (AR 100):

- *Compilation*. Presenting in the form of financial statements information that is the representation of management (owners) without undertaking to express any assurance on the statements.
- *Review*. Performing inquiry and analytical procedures that provide the accountant with a reasonable basis for expressing limited assurance that there are no material modifications that

should be made to the statements in order for them to be in conformity with GAAP or, if applicable, with another comprehensive basis of accounting.

An accountant may provide a variety of other accounting services to a nonpublic client, such as preparing a trial balance, assisting in adjusting books, or providing various manual, automated, or electronic bookkeeping services. However, if the accountant submits financial statements as a result of these services, he must issue a communication under SSARS No. 1, as amended by SSARS No. 8. Submission of financial statements is defined in paragraph 4 of SSARS No. 1, as amended by SSARS No. 8. The type of communication should be either (1) a compilation report on the financial statements or (2) an engagement letter to the entity's management. The accountant's decision as to the specific type of communication is based on expected third-party use of the financial statements (see Section 28.5).

(d) RELATED SERVICES.   In addition to the typical accounting and auditing services related to financial statements, the training and the experience of independent public accountants qualify them to provide a wide variety of tax services, consulting services, personal financial planning, and other special services. In carrying out such engagements, a member of the AICPA complies with the general standards for professional competence, due care, planning and supervision, and sufficient relevant data as set forth in Rule 201 of the AICPA's Code of Professional Conduct. Other, more specific standards may apply for particular types of engagements, such as those involving prospective information.

(i) Tax Services.   The accountant may be called on to deal with a variety of tax problems, including those involving federal and state income taxes, estate and inheritance taxes, sales and use taxes, payroll taxes, and property taxes. The field of *income taxes* is especially important. The services rendered by the accountant in this area include determination of taxable income, preparation of tax returns and claims for refunds, representation of clients before taxing authorities, and cooperation with lawyers in the settlement of tax suits by litigation. The AICPA publishes Statements on Responsibilities in Tax Practice for the guidance of its members.

(ii) Consulting Services.   The AICPA's Management Consulting Services Executive Committee issues pronouncements related to the conduct of a variety of consulting services. Statement on Standards for Consulting Services No. 1, *Consulting Services: Definitions and Standards*, describes the consulting process as "activities relating to the determination of client objectives, fact-finding, definition of the problems or opportunities, evaluation of alternatives, formulation of proposed action, communication of results, implementation, and follow-up." The process includes:

- Counseling management in its analysis, planning, organizing, operating, and controlling functions
- Conducting special studies, preparing recommendations, proposing plans and programs, and providing advice and technical assistance in their implementation
- Reviewing and suggesting improvement of policies, procedures, systems, methods, and organizational relationships
- Introducing new ideas, concepts, and methods to management

(iii) Other Special Services.   The independent public accountant may be called on to make special investigations or to report in connection with the special requirements of a government agency. Those services may require aspects of tax, consulting, and accounting and auditing skills.

Special services often involve services other than an audit of one or more financial statements. Examples of these services include reviews or compilations of financial statements, examinations or reviews of nonfinancial information, such as compliance with laws and regulations, circulation statistics for advertising media, and labor contract negotiation data. These services also include application of agreed-on procedures to specified elements, accounts, or items of a financial statement or to nonfinancial information.

28.2 THE AUDIT PROCESS FOR NONPUBLIC AUDITS

(a) OBJECTIVE OF THE AUDIT. *AICPA Professional Standards* (AU110) states that "the objective of the ordinary audit of financial statements by the independent auditor is the expression of an opinion on the fairness with which they present, in all material respects, financial position, results of operations, and cash flows in conformity with GAAP." The process designed to achieve that objective is complex. It involves the application of numerous procedures and the coordination of many activities. Although those procedures and activities overlap, the audit process encompasses:

- Plan the audit
- Gather and evaluate information about the entity and its environment, including internal control
- Assess risks of material misstatement
- Design an audit response and further audit procedures
- Perform further audit procedures
- Evaluate audit findings

(b) PLAN THE AUDIT. Audit planning begins with determining the requirements for the engagement. It involves developing an overall strategy for the expected conduct of the audit. The nature, extent, and timing of planning vary with the size and complexity of the entity, experience with the entity, and knowledge of the entity and its environment. Proper planning is essential to efficient and effective auditing. Consequently, seasoned auditors ordinarily are involved in the planning process.

The auditor should establish an understanding with entity regarding the nature of the services to be provided. This understanding should include the objectives of the engagement, management's responsibilities, the auditor's responsibilities, and limitations of the engagement. An engagement letter reduces to writing the understanding of the arrangements concerning the services to be provided and helps eliminate potential misunderstandings that otherwise may arise. Exhibit 28.1 illustrates an audit engagement letter.

(c) GATHER AND EVALUATE INFORMATION ABOUT THE ENTITY AND ITS ENVIRONMENT, INCLUDING INTERNAL CONTROL. The auditor must gather sufficient background information to assess the risks of material misstatement of the financial statements and to design the nature, timing, and extent of further audit procedures. This information also allows the auditor to make judgments about matters such as materiality, the appropriateness of accounting principles, and areas requiring special audit consideration.

Risk assessment procedures are used to gather the information about the entity and its environment. These procedures include inquires of management, analytical procedures, observation, inspection, and other information gathering procedures. The auditor is attempting to obtain an overall understanding of the entity's industry; the entity's operations, ownership, governance, methods of financing, objectives, strategies, and business risks; the manner in which management measures and reviews financial performance; and the entity's internal control. This understanding allows the auditor to identify account balances, classes of transactions, and disclosures with a high risk of material misstatement.

Knowledge obtained about the entity's industry encompasses an understanding of the accounting and auditing practices common to that industry and other unique aspects of the industry. Pertinent information about the industry includes trends and growth patterns; government regulation; unusual accounting, tax, or financing practices; and areas requiring special audit considerations.

The auditor should be aware of the general state of the economy and its impact on the entity and its industry. Such matters as credit availability, environmental efforts, and the impact on the industry of changes in consumer disposable income can have a significant effect on the entity's operations. For example, corporate liquidity may be affected by the level of business activity, high interest rates, and the availability of money.

Good, Better, & Best   Certified Public Accountants

[*Date*]
Mr. Thomas Tofias, President
Anonymous Company, Inc.
Route
Nowhere, New York 10000

Dear Mr. Tofias:

This will confirm our understanding of the arrangements for our audit of the financial statements of Anonymous Company, Inc., for the year ending [*date*].

We will audit the Company's balance sheet at [*date*], and the related statements of income, retained earnings, and cash flows for the year then ended, for the purpose of expressing an opinion on them. The financial statements are the responsibility of the Company's management. Our responsibility is to express an opinion on the financial statements based on our audit.

We will conduct our audit in accordance with U.S. generally accepted auditing standards. Those standards require that we plan and perform the audit to obtain reasonable assurance about whether the financial statements are free of material misstatement. An audit includes examining, on a test basis, evidence supporting the amounts and disclosures in the financial statements. An audit also includes assessing the accounting principles used and significant estimates made by management, as well as evaluating the overall financial statement presentation. We believe that our audit will provide a reasonable basis for our opinion.

Our procedures will include tests of documentary evidence supporting the transactions recorded in the accounts, tests of the physical existence of inventories, and direct confirmation of receivables and certain other assets and liabilities by correspondence with selected customers, creditors, legal counsel, and banks. At the conclusion of our audit, we will request certain written representations from you about the financial statements and matters related thereto.

Our audit is subject to the risk that material errors and irregularities, including fraud or defalcations, if they exist, will not be detected. However, we will inform you of irregularities that come to our attention, unless they are inconsequential.

If you intend to publish or otherwise reproduce the financial statements and make reference to our firm, you agree to provide us with printers' proofs or masters for our review and approval before printing. You also agree to provide us with a copy of the final reproduced material for our approval before it is distributed.

We will review the Company's federal and state [*identify states*] income tax returns for the fiscal year ended [*date*]. These returns, we understand, will be prepared by your controller.

Further, we will be available during the year to consult with you on the tax effects of any proposed transactions or contemplated changes in business policies.

Our fee for these services will be at our regular per diem rates, plus travel, and other out-of-pocket costs. Invoices will be rendered every two weeks and are payable on presentation.

We are pleased to have this opportunity to serve you.

If this letter correctly expresses your understanding, please sign the enclosed copy where indicated and return it to us.

Very truly yours,

Good, Better, & Best

_____
     Partner
APPROVED:
By _____
Date _____

Exhibit 28.1   Illustrative audit engagement letter.

(i) Internal Control Considerations.   Not all of the entity's internal controls are relevant to an audit. Controls that are relevant to a financial statement audit are those that could affect the entity's ability to prepare financial statements that are in accordance with GAAP.

Internal control is defined as a process—effected by an entity's board of directors, management, and other personnel—to provide reasonable assurance regarding the achievement of objectives in the following categories: (1) reliability of financial reporting, (2) effectiveness and efficiency of operations, and (3) compliance with applicable laws and regulations.

Components of Internal Control.   For purposes of an audit, an entity's internal control consists of five interrelated components which are:

1. *Control environment.* The control environment sets the tone of an organization, influencing the control consciousness of its people. It is the foundation for all other components of internal control, providing discipline and structure.
2. *Risk assessment.* Risk assessment is the entity's identification and analysis of relevant risks to achievement of its objectives, forming a basis for determining how the risks should be managed.
3. *Control activities.* Control activities are the policies and procedures that help ensure management directives are carried out.
4. *Information and communication.* Information and communication systems support the identification, capture, and exchange of information in a form and time frame that enable people to carry out their responsibilities.
5. *Monitoring.* Monitoring is a process that assesses the quality of internal control performance over time.

Exhibit 28.2 contains the complete definitions.

Understanding Internal Control.   Because this knowledge is so critical to the audit process, the auditor is required to obtain an understanding of each of the five components of internal control sufficient to assess the risk of material misstatements and design further audit procedures. The auditor's understanding of internal control should sufficient to allow the auditor to:

a. Evaluate control design, and
b. Determine whether the control has been implemented.

As discussed above, the auditor obtains the understanding of internal control by performing risk assessment procedures, including, inquires of management, analytical procedures, observation, and inspection.

(ii) Evaluate the Information about the Entity and its Environment.   Once the auditor has gathered the information about the entity and its environment, the auditor must assimilate and synthesize the information to determine how it might affect the audit. As an example, information about business risks may allow the auditor to identify financial reporting risks that will affect the way in which the auditor designs audit procedures.

(d) ASSESS RISKS OF MATERIAL MISSTATEMENT.   As described in Exhibit 28.3, financial statements consist of a series of assertions or representations by management about accounts, transactions, and disclosures. The auditor uses the understanding of the entity and its environment to assess the risks of material misstatement both at the relevant assertion level and at the financial statement level. Financial statement level risks relate pervasively to the financial statements as a whole and potentially affect many financial statement assertions.

For a financial statement audit, an entity's internal control consists of five interrelated components:

Control Environment

The control environment sets the tone of an organization, influencing the control consciousness of its people. It is the foundation for all other components of internal control, providing discipline and structure. Control environment factors include:

- Integrity and ethical values
- Commitment to competence
- Board of directors or audit committee participation
- Management's philosophy and operating style
- Organizational structure

Risk Assessment

An entity's risk assessment for financial reporting purposes is its identification, analysis, and management of risks relevant to the preparation of financial statements that are fairly presented in conformity with GAAP. Risks relevant to financial reporting include external and internal events and circumstances that may occur and adversely affect an entity's ability to initiate, process, and report financial data consistent with the assertions of management in the financial statements.

Risks can arise or change due to circumstances such as the following:

- Changes in operating environment
- New personnel
- New or revamped information systems
- Rapid growth
- New technology
- New business models, products, or activities
- Corporate restructurings
- Expanded foreign operations
- New accounting pronouncements

Control Activities

Control activities are the policies and procedures that help ensure that management directives are carried out. They help ensure that necessary actions are taken to address risks to achievement of the entity's objectives. Control activities, whether automated or manual, have various objectives and are applied at various organizational and functional levels. Generally, control activities that may be relevant to an audit may be categorized as policies and procedures that pertain to—

Performance reviews
Information processing
Physical controls
Segregation of duties

Information and Communication

The information system relevant to financial reporting objectives, which includes the accounting system, consists of the procedures, whether automated or manual, and records established to initiate, process, and report entity transactions (as well as events and conditions) and to maintain accountability for the related assets, liabilities, and equity. The quality of system-generated information affects management's ability to make appropriate decisions in controlling the entity's activities and to prepare reliable financial reports.

(Continues)

Exhibit 28.2   Components of internal control.

Communication involves providing an understanding of individual roles and responsibilities pertaining to internal control over financial reporting.

Monitoring

An important management responsibility is to establish and maintain internal control. Management monitors controls to consider whether they are operating as intended and that they are modified as appropriate for changes in conditions.

Monitoring is a process that assesses the quality of internal control performance over time. It involves assessing the design and operation of controls on a timely basis and taking necessary corrective actions. This process is accomplished through ongoing activities, separate evaluations, or a combination of the two. In many entities, internal auditors or personnel performing similar functions contribute to the monitoring of an entity's activities. Monitoring activities may include using information from communications from external parties such as customer complaints and regulator comments that may indicate problems or highlight areas in need of improvement. In many entities, much of the information used in monitoring may be produced by the entity's information system. If management assumes that data used for monitoring are accurate without having a basis for that assumption, errors may exist in the information, potentially leading management to incorrect conclusions from its monitoring activities.

Exhibit 28.2   *Continued.*

The auditor's ultimate objective is to identify assertions about accounts, transactions, and disclosures that are more likely to be materially misstated. For each significant assertion, the auditor considers:

- What could go wrong?
- How likely is it that it will go wrong?
- What are the likely amounts involved?

As a part of the risk assessment process, the audit team should have a discussion of the susceptibility of the entity's financial statements to material misstatement. This discussion is designed to allow team members to gain a better understanding of the risks of material misstatement of the financial statements, and the audit procedures that might effectively address those risks. For efficiency purposes this discussion is often held in conjunction with the discussion among the audit team related to fraud as required by SAS No. 99, "Consideration of Fraud in a Financial Statement Audit."

The risk of material misstatement of a particular assertion is a function of both inherent and control risks. Inherent risk is the risk of material misstatement of an assertion without considering internal control, and control risk is the risk that the entity's internal control will fail to prevent or detect and correct material misstatements. Many inherent risks arise because of business risks faced by management, including the risk of fraud. Auditing standards allow the auditor to make a separate assessment of inherent risk and control risk, or to make a combined assessment of the risk of material misstatement for each significant assertion.

The auditor's assessment of control risk involves analyzing the design and implementation of internal control to decide whether internal control appears adequate to prevent or detect and correct material misstatements in the assertions. Individual controls often do not address a risk completely by themselves. Often, only several control activities, together with other components of internal control, for example aspects of the control environment, will be sufficient to address a risk.

(i) Significant Risks.   Another part of the risk assessment process involves the identification of significant risks, which are risks that require special audit consideration. For example, because of the nature of the entity or its industry, the auditor may decide that revenue recognition requires special audit consideration. The special audit consideration means that the auditor should evaluate the design of controls that address the risk, and perform substantive procedures that are linked

	Description of Assertions		
	Classes of Transactions and Events During the Periods	Account Balances at the End of the Period	Presentation and Disclosure
Occurrence/Existence	Transactions and events that have been recorded have occurred and pertain to the entity.	Assets, liabilities, and equity interests exist.	Disclosed events and transactions have occurred and pertain to the entity.
Rights and Obligations	—	The entity holds or controls the rights to assets, and liabilities are the obligations of the entity.	—
Completeness	All transactions and events that should have been recorded have been recorded.	All assets, liabilites, and equity interests that should have been recorded have been recorded.	All disclosures that should have been included in the financial statements have been included.
Accuracy/Valuation and Allocation	Amounts and other data relating to recorded transactions and events have been recorded appropriately.	Assets, liabilities, and equity interests are included in the financial statements at appropriate amounts and any resulting valuation or allocation adjustments are recorded appropriately.	Financial and other information is disclosed fairly and at appropriate amounts.
Cut-off	Transactions and events have been recorded in the correct accounting period.	—	—
Classification and Understandability	Transactions and events have been recorded in the proper accounts.	—	Financial information is appropriately presented and described and information in disclosures is expressed clearly.

Exhibit 28.3   Financial statement assertions.

clearly to the risk. When the auditor's approach to the audit of the significant risk consists only of substantive procedures, he or she should perform either tests of details, or a combination of tests of details and substantive analytical procedures. In other words, the auditor cannot rely solely on substantive analytical procedures to obtain evidence about misstatement of the assertion. Also, if the auditor is relying on the effectiveness of internal controls to mitigate the significant risk, the controls must be tested in the current period. The auditor cannot rely upon tests of controls performed in prior periods.

(ii) Other Factors That Affect the Auditor's Risk Assessment.   When assessing risks, the auditor considers other factors that might require the extension or modification of audit tests, such as the possibility of fraud or the existence of related party transactions. The auditor also has responsibility for certain illegal acts that may have occurred and for assessing the entity's ability to continue as a going concern.

Fraud. SAS No. 99 provides guidance on the auditor's consideration of fraud in a financial statement audit. It is the auditor's responsibility to plan and perform the audit to obtain reasonable assurance about whether the financial statements are free from material misstatement, whether caused by error or fraud. SAS No. 99 describes two types of fraud, fraudulent financial reporting and misappropriation of assets that are relevant to the auditor's consideration of fraud in a financial statement audit. The auditor is required by SAS No. 99 to:

- Have a discussion among the audit team members about fraud risk. Specifically, the discussion should be designed to allow the more experienced team members to share insights and exchange ideas about how and where the entity's financial statements might be susceptible to material misstatement due to fraud and to emphasize the importance of maintaining the proper degree of professional skepticism regarding the possibility of fraud. As indicated previously, it is generally efficient to coordinate this discussion with the required generally team discussion of the risks of material misstatement.
- Make inquiries of management and other personnel to identify fraud risks.
- Perform analytical procedures to identify fraud risks.
- Consider risk factors that may be indicative of fraud. SAS No. 99 provides lists of such factors organized around the three fundamental conditions necessary for the commission of fraud: (1) some type of incentive or pressure, (2) an opportunity to commit fraud, and (3) an attitude that allows the individual to rationalize the act.
- Identify fraud risks that may require an audit response. Since material misstatements due to fraudulent financial reporting often involve management override of internal controls resulting in overstatement of revenue, the auditor ordinarily should determine that there is a fraud risk related to revenue recognition.
- Address this risk of override of internal control by management regardless of whether the auditor identifies other fraud risks.
- Respond to fraud risks by (1) modifying the approach to the overall audit, (2) altering the nature, timing, or extent of procedures performed, or (3) performing procedures to further address the risk of management override of internal control. Procedures to address the risk of management override include examining journal entries and other adjustments for evidence of fraud, reviewing accounting estimates for evidence of biases, and evaluating the business rationale for significant unusual transactions.
- Evaluate the results of audit tests for evidence of fraud.
- Evaluate the implications of any fraud discovered and communicate information about fraud to the appropriate level of management.

Related Party Transactions. SAS No. 45, "Related Parties" (AU 334), provides the independent auditor with guidance on procedures to be considered to identify related parties and transactions with such parties. The statement also illustrates procedures for examining identified related party transactions and provides guidance for adequate disclosure. Parties are related when one party has the ability to influence the other(s) to the extent that the other party(s) does not fully pursue its (their) own separate interest (e.g., a parent company and its subsidiary; an entity and its principal shareholders).

Many of the procedures specified in SAS No. 45 are carried out in the ordinary course of an audit. Such procedures may indicate the possible existence of related party transactions, in which case, additional procedures would be required. Other procedures are directed specifically to related party transactions.

Illegal Acts. The auditor's responsibility for illegal acts is discussed in SAS No. 54, "Illegal Acts by Clients" (AU 317). Although an auditor is not expected to possess the legal background necessary to recognize all possible violations of laws or regulations, he or she should be familiar with those laws or regulations that directly affect the financial statements. For example, if a client violates the Internal Revenue Code, the income tax provision in its financial statements might be inadequate, which could cause the financial statements to be materially misstated. Therefore, the auditor's responsibility to detect illegal acts that have a direct and material effect on the financial statements is the same as the auditor's responsibility for detection of misstatements due to error or fraud—to design the audit to provide reasonable assurance that the financial statements are free of material misstatement.

Many other laws and regulations (e.g., regulations of the Environmental Protection Agency and the Federal Trade Commission) are highly specialized and complex. The auditor does not ordinarily have a sufficient legal knowledge to always recognize violations of these laws or regulations. Therefore, according to SAS No. 54, the auditor is responsible for these "indirect effect" illegal acts only when information comes to the auditor's attention that suggests an illegal act might have taken place. If information about an illegal act that could have a material effect on the financial statements through a contingent liability comes to the auditor's attention, the auditor must perform procedures to ascertain whether the illegal act has occurred.

SAS No. 54 also requires the auditor to make sure that the audit committee or its equivalent is informed about illegal acts unless they are clearly inconsequential. Further, in certain circumstances (e.g., in response to a subpoena or in response to inquiries of a successor auditor), the auditor might have to notify persons not associated with the client about illegal acts.

Going Concern. Financial statements are ordinarily prepared on the assumption that the entity will continue in business; an auditor does not search for evidence to support this assumption. However, SAS No. 59, "The Auditor's Consideration of an Entity's Ability to Continue as a Going Concern" (AU 341), requires the auditor to consider whether the aggregate results of all audit procedures performed indicate that there could be substantial doubt about the entity's ability to continue as a going concern for a reasonable period of time (not to exceed one year from the date of the audited financial statements). Conditions and events such as recurring operating losses, working capital deficiencies, defaults on loans, or the loss of a principal customer or supplier might indicate that there is a going concern problem.

If substantial doubt exists, SAS No. 59 directs the auditor to consider management's plans for dealing with the adverse condition. In considering management's plans, the auditor should obtain evidence about whether the adverse condition or event will be mitigated within a reasonable period of time. If, after considering management's plans, the auditor still concludes that there is substantial doubt, he or she should include an explanatory paragraph in the audit report that describes that doubt [see Subsection 28.3(d)(iii)]. The auditor should note that SAS No. 64, "Omnibus Statement on Auditing Standards—1990," amended SAS No. 59 to require the auditor to use the phrase "substantial doubt about its (the entity's) ability to continue as a going concern" or similar wording that includes the term *substantial doubt* and *going concern* when the auditor decides an explanatory paragraph is necessary.

SAS No. 59 recognizes that the auditor is not responsible for predicting the future, and the absence of a reference to substantial doubt in an auditor's report should not be construed as providing assurances about the entity's continued existence.

Substantive tests may be accomplished through inspection, observation, inquiry, confirmation, and computation. The selection of evidence to be obtained and evaluated—hence the audit procedures to be applied—depends on a variety of factors including the appropriateness, sufficiency, and availability of evidence. The reliability of evidence varies. Evidence obtained from independent sources outside the organization generally is reliable. The degree of reliability of evidence obtained from within the organization generally depends on the system developed by management to produce information. Furthermore, evidence obtained by the auditor through physical examination observation, computation, and inspection is more persuasive than information obtained indirectly (e.g., from internal control matters). Evidence also must be sufficient to form a reasonable basis for the auditor's opinion.

The auditor selects the most readily available audit evidence, provided it is appropriate and sufficient for audit purposes. In some circumstances, appropriate and sufficient evidence may be difficult to obtain. Nevertheless, the independent auditor cannot substitute inappropriate evidence merely because such evidence happens to be readily available.

Judgment is necessary in choosing the evidence to obtain and evaluate. However, judgment cannot be applied without a thorough knowledge of the entity being audited and the relative importance (materiality) of the specific assertions under study.

(e) DESIGN AN AUDIT RESPONSE AND FURTHER AUDIT PROCEDURES.   The results of the auditor's risk assessment provide a basis for designing further audit procedures. Further audit procedures are performed to obtain the audit evidence necessary to support the audit opinion. Such procedures include tests of controls and substantive tests. Tests of controls must be designed when the auditor's strategy includes an assumption that the controls are operating effectively, and when substantive procedures alone cannot provide sufficient audit evidence about a particular assertion.

(f) PERFORM FURTHER AUDIT PROCEDURES.   After the auditor has designed the further audit procedures he or she performs the tests of controls and substantive procedures.

(i) Tests of Controls.   Tests of controls provide evidence about the design and operating effectiveness of internal controls in preventing or detecting material misstatements. Tests of controls include inquiries of appropriate management, supervisory and other personnel, inspection of documents, observation of the entity's operations, and reperformance.

The assessed level of control risk or the risk of material misstatement relates directly to the substantive tests the auditor performs. The more effective the entity's internal control, the lower the risk of material misstatement in the financial statements. Lower the risk of misstatement, the less evidence the auditor needs from substantive audit procedures to form an opinion on the financial statements.

(ii) Analytical Procedures.   SAS No. 56, "Analytical Procedures" (AU 329), defines analytical procedures as comparisons of recorded amounts, or ratios developed from recorded amounts, to expectations developed by the auditor. It requires the auditor to use analytical procedures in the planning and overall review stages of all audits. The nature and extent of procedures performed, however, are up to the auditor.

In the planning stage, an auditor uses analytical procedures to gain an understanding of the client's business and the events and transactions that have occurred since the prior audit. They also help him or her identify areas in which the risk of material misstatement is high. In the overall review stage, auditors use analytical procedures to ensure that they have obtained explanations for all significant fluctuations in financial statement amounts, that all amounts make sense based on the audit results, and that they are satisfied with the sufficiency of the audit procedures performed.

SAS No. 56 also encourages, but does not require, auditors to use analytical procedures as substantive tests. For some accounts, analytical procedures can be more effective than tests of details in detecting material misstatements in the financial statements. For example, an analytical procedure comparing salaries paid to the total number of employees in a division might indicate unauthorized payments; a test of details might not have uncovered this. In deciding whether to perform analytical procedures or tests of details, the auditor considers factors such as the nature of the assertion and the reliability of and availability of information used to develop the expectation.

(iii) Accounting Estimates.   Although many users typically see accounting as exact and precise, the truth is accounting estimates are pervasive in a set of financial statements. Because of the fundamental importance of these estimates and the risks associated with their preparation and evaluation, SAS No. 57, "Auditing Accounting Estimates" (AU 342), requires the auditor to obtain sufficient evidence to provide reasonable assurance that all accounting estimates that could be material to the financial statements have been developed, that those estimates are reasonable, and that the estimates conform to GAAP.

(iv) Other Required Auditing Procedures. Although the nature, timing, and extent of auditing procedures are matters of judgment, certain procedures are required to be applied on all audit engagements. They include communication with predecessor auditors, confirmation of receivables, observation of inventories, obtaining management's written representations, and inquiry of a client's lawyer concerning litigation, claims, and assessments. Independent auditors who do not employ these procedures have the burden of justifying the opinion expressed.

(v) Communication with Predecessor Auditors. SAS No. 84, "Communications Between Predecessor and Successor Auditors" (AU 315), explains, "[I]nquiry of the predecessor auditor is a necessary procedure because the predecessor auditor may be able to provide information that will assist the successor auditor in determining whether to accept the engagement." Those inquiries, which should be made with the prospective client's authorization, should address (1) matters that may bear on the integrity of management, (2) disagreements with management about accounting principles, auditing procedures, or other similarly significant matters, and (3) communications to audit committees or others with equivalent authority and responsibility regarding fraud, illegal acts by clients, and internal control–related matters and on the predecessor auditor's understanding of why a change of auditors is being made. If a prospective client refuses to permit such communication, the reasons should be determined and consideration should be given to whether acceptance of the engagement is appropriate. Other communications, although not required, may be made to facilitate the current audit.

(vi) Confirmation of Receivables. SAS No. 67, "The Confirmation Process" (AU 330), states:

> Confirmation of accounts receivable is a generally accepted auditing procedure.... [It] is generally presumed that evidence obtained from third parties will provide the auditor with higher-quality audit evidence than is typically available from within the entity. Thus, there is a presumption that the auditor will request the confirmation of accounts receivable during an audit unless one of the following is true:

- Accounts receivable are immaterial to the financial statements.
- The use of confirmations would be ineffective.
- The auditor's combined assessed level of inherent and control risk is low, and the assessed level, in conjunction with the evidence expected to be provided by analytical procedures or other substantive tests of details is sufficient to reduce audit risk to an acceptably low level for the applicable financial statement assertions.

An auditor who has not requested confirmations in the examination of accounts receivable should document how he or she overcame this presumption.

SAS No. 67 defines accounts receivable as (1) the entity's claims against customers that have arisen from the sale of goods or services in the normal course of business, and (2) a financial institution's loans.

Two forms of confirmations are used in practice: positive (i.e., the debtor is asked to respond in all cases) and negative (i.e., a response is requested only if there is disagreement). If no response is received to a positive reply, the auditor ordinarily applies alternative procedures such as examining evidence of subsequent cash receipts and sales and shipping records.

SAS No. 67 establishes three specific conditions that must exist before the auditor may use negative confirmation requests. These conditions are

- The combined assessed level of inherent and control risk (risk of material misstatement) is low.

- A large number of small balances is involved.
- The auditor has no reason to believe that the recipients of the requests are unlikely to give them consideration.

(vii) Observation of Inventories.   *AICPA Professional Standards* (AU 331) states:

> When inventory quantities are determined solely by means of a physical count, and all counts are made as of the balance-sheet date or as of a single date within a reasonable time before or after the balance-sheet date, it is ordinarily necessary for the independent auditor to be present at the time of count and, by suitable observation, tests, and inquiries, satisfy himself or herself respecting the effectiveness of the methods of inventory-taking and the measure of reliance which may be placed upon the client's representations about the quantities and physical condition of the inventories.
>
> When the well-kept perpetual inventory records are checked by the client periodically by comparisons with physical counts, the auditor's observation procedures usually can be performed either during or after the end of the period under audit.

Auditors may become satisfied as to inventory quantities when statistical sampling methods are used to determine those quantities. Except when inventories are held in public warehouses or by other outside custodians (in which case direct confirmation in writing may be acceptable), it will always be necessary for the auditor to make or observe some physical inventory counts.

(viii) Management's Written Representations.   SAS No. 85, "Management Representations" (AU 333), requires that the auditor obtain written representations from management. Management's refusal to furnish a written representation constitutes a limitation on the scope of his or her audit sufficient to preclude an unqualified opinion and is ordinarily sufficient to cause an auditor to disclaim an opinion or withdraw from the engagement. Exhibit 28.4 illustrates a management representation letter.

(ix) Inquiry of a Client's Lawyer.   With respect to litigation, claims, and assessments, auditors obtain evidential matter relevant to the existence of uncertainties that may result in a loss, the period involved, the degree of probability of unfavorable outcome, and the amount or range of potential loss. Gain contingencies also are addressed. Such information is obtained from management and corroborated through a written response by the client's lawyer to the auditor's letter of audit inquiry. SAS No. 12, "Inquiry of a Client's Lawyer Concerning Litigation, Claims, and Assessments" (AU 337), provides auditors with detailed guidance related to these matters.

(g) REVIEW OF AUDIT WORK.   Auditing Standards require the review of work performed by assistants. This review is a critical evaluation of the work carried out on the engagement. In general, it should include a review of work papers to see that they clearly indicate work performed and that they support conclusions to be expressed in the auditor's report.

(h) REQUIRED AUDITOR COMMUNICATIONS.   As a by-product of an audit, the auditor is required to communicate certain matters to an audit committee or others with equivalent authority. SAS No. 60, "Communication of Internal Control Related Matters Noted in an Audit" (AU 325), requires the auditor to communicate significant deficiencies. Significant deficiencies are matters coming to the auditor's attention that, in his or her judgment, should be communicated (to the audit committee or others, including the board of directors, owners in owner-managed entities, etc.) because they could adversely affect the entity's ability to prepare financial statements. Such deficiencies can occur in any of the five components of internal control: the control environment, risk assessment, control activities, information and communication, and monitoring.

[Date]

To *[Independent Auditor]*

We are providing this letter in connection with your audit(s) of the *[identification of financial statements]* of *[name of entity]* as of *[dates]* and for the *[periods]* for the purpose of expressing an opinion as to whether the *[consolidated]* financial statements present fairly, in all material respects, the financial position, results of operations, and cash flows of *[name of entity]* in conformity with generally accepted accounting principles. We confirm that we are responsible for the fair presentation in the *[consolidated]* financial statements of financial position, results of operations, and cash flows in conformity with generally accepted accounting principles.

Certain representations in this letter are described as being limited to matters that are material. Items are considered material, regardless of size, if they involve an omission or misstatement of accounting information that, in the light of surrounding circumstances, makes it probable that the judgment of a reasonable person relying on the information would be changed or influenced by the omission or misstatement.

We confirm, to the best of our knowledge and belief, *[as of (date of auditor's report),]* the following representations made to you during your audit(s).

1. The financial statements referred to above are fairly presented in conformity with generally accepted accounting principles.

2. We have made available to you all—

    a. Financial records and related data

    b. Minutes of the meetings of stockholders, directors, and committees of directors, or summaries of actions of recent meetings for which minutes have not yet been prepared.

3. There have been no communications from regulatory agencies concerning noncompliance with or deficiencies in financial reporting practices.

4. There are no material transactions that have not been properly recorded in the accounting records underlying the financial statements.

5. There has been no—

    a. Fraud involving management or employees who have significant roles in internal control.

    b. Fraud involving others that could have a material effect on the financial statements.

6. The company has no plans or intentions that may materially affect the carrying value or classification of assets and liabilities.

7. The following have been properly recorded or disclosed in the financial statements:

    a. Related-party transactions, including sales, purchases, loans, transfers, leasing arrangements, and guarantees, and amounts receivable from or payable to related parties.

    b. Guarantees, whether written or oral, under which the company is contingently liable.

    c. Significant estimates and material concentrations known to management that are required to be disclosed in accordance with the AICPA's Statement of Position 94-6, "Disclosure of Significant Risks and Uncertainties."

8. There are no—

    a. Violations or possible violations of laws or regulations whose effects should be considered for disclosure in the financial statements or as a basis for recording a loss contingency.

    b. Unasserted claims or assessments that our lawyer has advised us are probable of assertion and must be disclosed in accordance with Financial Accounting Standards Board (FASB) Statement No. 5, "Accounting for Contingencies."

    c. Other liabilities or gain or loss contingencies that are required to be accrued or disclosed by FASB Statement No. 5.

9. The company has satisfactory title to all owned assets, and there are no liens or encumbrances on such assets nor has any asset been pledged as collateral.

(Continues)

Exhibit 28.4   Illustrative management representation letter.

10. The company has complied with all aspects of contractual agreements that would have a material effect on the financial statements in the event of noncompliance.

To the best of our knowledge and belief, no events have occurred subsequent to the balance-sheet date and through the date of this letter that would require adjustment to or disclosure in the aforementioned financial statements.

[*Name of Chief Executive Officer and Title*]

[*Name of Chief Financial Officer and Title*]

Exhibit 28.4   *Continued.*

Under SAS No. 60, the auditor can communicate significant deficiencies either orally or in writing, although a written communication is preferable. If the auditor communicates in a written report, that report should:

- State that the purpose of the audit is to report on the financial statements and not to provide assurance on internal control
- Include the definition of a significant deficiency
- Include a statement that restricts the distribution of the report to the audit committee, board of directors, or owner-manager

The auditor is not required to search for significant deficiencies; rather, he or she is obligated to report those that come to his or her attention during the audit.

SAS No. 61, "Communication with Audit Committees" (AU 380), requires an auditor to ensure that the audit committee (or its equivalent) is informed about the following matters:

- The scope of the audit and the level of assurance (reasonable, not absolute) that the auditor provides in an audit of financial statements
- The auditor's responsibility for internal control matters
- Management's initial selection of accounting policies and changes in significant accounting policies or their application
- The process management uses to formulate sensitive accounting estimates and the basis for the auditor's conclusions about the reasonableness of those estimates
- Any audit adjustments that could have a significant effect on the entity's financial reporting process
- Any uncorrected misstatements aggregated by the auditor that pertain to the latest period presented and were determined by management to be immaterial
- The auditor's judgments about the quality, not just the acceptability, of the company's accounting principles, including such matters as the consistency of application of the entity's accounting policies and their application and the clarity and completeness of the entity's financial statements, which include related disclosures as well as certain items that have a significant impact on the representational faithfulness, verifiability, neutrality, and consistency of the accounting information included in the financial statements
- The auditor's responsibility for other information in documents containing audited financial statements

- Disagreements with management about matters that could be significant to the entity's financial statements
- The auditor's views on significant matters about which management consulted with other accountants
- Major issues discussed by the auditor with management in connection with his or her retention
- Serious difficulties encountered with management in performing the audit (e.g., management setting unreasonable timetables or not providing information required by the auditor)

Unlike SAS No. 60, however, the auditor is only required to make these communications to a public company (as defined in the statement) or to entities that either have an audit committee or have formally designated oversight of the financial reporting process to a group equivalent to an audit committee. This means that, in audits of most smaller companies that only have a board of directors, the auditor may, but is not required to, make these communications.

28.3 THE INDEPENDENT AUDITOR'S REPORT

(a) **FORMAT OF REPORT DOCUMENT.**   The ordinary report document consists of the *basic financial statements* and the *independent auditor's report*. Also, it may include additional information and the independent auditor's report on that supplementary information.

Basic financial statements include the balance sheet, statement of income, statement of retained earnings, statement of cash flows, and related notes. Disclosure of changes in other categories of stockholders' equity presented in financial statement format also are considered basic financial statements.

Although independent auditors may assist in the preparation of the basic financial statements or draft them based on management's accounts and records, the auditor's responsibility is limited to an opinion on the basic financial statements. Management is responsible for the fair presentation of financial position, results of operations, and cash flows in conformity with GAAP.

Notes to financial statements are used to present information considered necessary for informative disclosure concerning the financial statements that generally is not shown on the face of the statements. A notation may be included on the basic financial statements to draw the reader's attention to the notes (e.g., "The accompanying notes are an integral part of these financial statements"). Notes to the financial statements are often captioned with a short, but descriptive title of the matter discussed. Often the caption is the same as a balance sheet or income statement caption (e.g., "investments," "property, plant, and equipment"). Notes may be numbered or lettered. When both audited and unaudited information is presented, the note information relating to unaudited information is appropriately identified.

Supplementary information, like the basic financial statements, is the responsibility of management. Supplemental information consists of data presented beyond those necessary for presentation of the basic financial statements. Supplemental information may include statistical data, explanatory comments, and other information, some of which may be of a nonaccounting nature. For example, it may include schedules of selling, general, and administrative expenses; statistical data relating to results of operations such as key ratios; analyses of property accounts; or consolidating schedules representing the financial statements of components of the consolidated group. Some supplementary information is required by pronouncements of the FASB and Government Accounting Standards Board (GASB). (The auditor's responsibility for reporting on supplemental information is discussed in Section 28.5.)

(b) **THE AUDITOR'S STANDARD REPORT.**   The auditor's usual objective in an audit of an entity's financial statements is to express an unqualified or "clean" opinion on those statements. An unqualified opinion states that the financial statements present fairly, in all material respects, the entity's financial position, results of operation, and cash flows in conformity with GAAP. An auditor may give an unqualified opinion only when both of the following conditions are met:

- The audit has been conducted in accordance with GAAS.
- The financial statements are in all material respects in conformity with GAAP.

An unqualified opinion is most frequently expressed by issuing a standard report. The term *standard report* is used because it consists of three paragraphs containing standardized words and phrases having a specific meaning. The use of standardized wording serves two purposes: It helps avoid confusion among report readers, and it helps identify situations in which the auditor has modified the standard report to bring specific circumstances to the reader's attention.

(c) CONTENT OF THE AUDITOR'S STANDARD REPORT. SAS No. 58, "Reports on Audited Financial Statements" (AU 508), prescribes the form of the auditor's standard report on the basic financial statements, which includes the following seven items:

1. Title
2. Addressee
3. Introductory paragraph
4. Scope paragraph
5. Opinion paragraph
6. Signature
7. Date

A typical example of the auditor's standard report is shown in Exhibit 28.5.

(i) Title. According to SAS No. 58, the title of an auditor's report must include the word "independent." This informs financial statement users that the report is from an unbiased CPA. It also distinguishes the report from those of others, such as management or internal auditors.

INDEPENDENT AUDITOR'S REPORT
Stockholders and Board of Directors
AUD Company

We have audited the accompanying balance sheet of AUD Company as of December 31, 20X2, and the related statements of income, retained earnings, and cash flows for the year then ended. These financial statements are the responsibility of the Company's management. Our responsibility is to express an opinion on these financial statements based on our audit.

We conducted our audits in accordance with auditing standards generally accepted in the United States. Those standards require that we plan and perform the audit to obtain reasonable assurance about whether the financial statements are free of material misstatement. An audit includes examining, on a test basis, evidence supporting the amounts and disclosures in the financial statements. An audit also includes assessing the accounting principles used and significant estimates made by management, as well as evaluating the overall financial statement presentation. We believe that our audit provides a reasonable basis for our opinion.

In our opinion, the financial statements referred to above present fairly, in all material respects, the financial position of AUD Company as of December 31, 20X2, and the results of its operations and its cash flows for the year then ended in conformity with principles generally accepted in the United States.

Good, Better, & Best CPAs
February 15, 20X3

Exhibit 28.5   Auditor's standard report.

(ii) Addressee.   The auditor's report may be addressed to the entity whose financial statements were audited or to its board of directors or stockholders. A report on the financial statements of an unincorporated entity will be addressed as circumstances dictate. For example, such a report might be addressed to the partners, the general partner, or the proprietor. Occasionally, an auditor is retained to audit the financial statements of an entity that is not his or her client. In such circumstances, the report is customarily addressed to the client and not to the directors or stockholders of the entity whose financial statements are being audited.

(iii) Introductory Paragraph.   The introductory paragraph identifies the financial statements that were audited and contrasts management's responsibility for the financial statements with the auditor's responsibility to express an opinion on those statements.

(iv) Scope Paragraph.   The scope paragraph makes several important points. First, it states that the auditor performed the audit in accordance with GAAS. The scope paragraph should identify the country of origin of the auditing standards the auditor followed in performing the audit, for example, auditing standards generally accepted in the United States. Second, it describes the objective of an audit—to obtain reasonable, but not absolute, assurance that the financial statements are free of material misstatements due to errors or fraud and that those statements are in conformity with GAAP. Third, the scope paragraph provides a brief description of what an audit includes by detailing several factors inherent in the audit process that affect the assurance the auditor provides on the financial statements. Last, it clarifies that the procedures performed by the auditor are, in his or her opinion, sufficient to enable expression of an opinion on the financial statements.

(v) Opinion Paragraph.   In the opinion paragraph, the auditor communicates the results of the audit. This paragraph expresses an informed, expert opinion about whether the financial statements are presented fairly, in all material respects, in conformity with GAAP.[1] The paragraph should identify the country of origin of the accounting principles used to prepare the financial statements, for example, accounting principles generally accepted in the United States. The auditor's opinion is not an absolute statement because the auditor cannot guarantee that the financial statements are totally accurate.

If an opinion cannot be expressed or if the independent auditor has reservations concerning the expression of an overall opinion, the reasons must be set forth in a separate paragraph and the opinion appropriately modified or disclaimed.

(vi) Signature.   The independent auditor generally signs the firm's name on the report manually. In published annual reports, the accountant's name may be printed or the signature reproduced. In filings with the Services Executive Committee (SEC), a manual signature may be required.

(vii) Date.   The date of the independent auditor's report ordinarily represents the date of completion of all substantive auditing procedures performed at the client's business locations. Usually that date also is the date of the client's written representation as well as the date on which letters from attorney are requested.

Occasionally, an event requiring disclosure occurs after the report date (i.e., after completion of field work, but before issuance of the report). In such circumstances, SAS No. 1 (AU 530) provides two methods for dating the audit report. The auditor: "... may use 'dual dating,' for example, 'February 16, 19X1, except for Note X as to which the date is March 1, 19X1,' or he or she may date the report as of the later date."

If the later date is used, the auditor's responsibility for the review of events subsequent to the date of the financial statements extends to that later date. If the report is dual dated, the

---

[1] In addition to being informative, the phrase "in conformity with generally accepted accounting principles" is limiting. The limiting message is that the financial statements fairly present only to the extent that current GAAP is not defective. See Section 2.2(a)(iii).

auditor's responsibility for events subsequent to the date of the audit report is limited to specific data disclosed as of the later date.

When an independent auditor's report is reissued (e.g., in a report to a regulatory agency, or to satisfy a request for additional copies), use of the original report date generally is appropriate. However, if an event occurring subsequent to the original report date requiring disclosure in or adjustment of the financial statements comes to the auditor's attention, other dating may be required. Depending on the circumstances, the auditor's report may be one of these three:

1. Dual dated.

2. Dated as of the date of a subsequent event disclosed in the notes, in which case the auditor's responsibility for the review of subsequent events is extended to that later date.

3. Dated as of the date of the original report. When this alternative is appropriate, SAS No. 1 (AU 530) provides: "[T]he event may be disclosed in a separate note to the financial statements captioned somewhat as follows: 'Event (Unaudited) Subsequent to the Date of the Report of Independent Auditor.'"

(d) DEPARTURES FROM THE AUDITOR'S STANDARD REPORT.   Although the auditor's standard report is synonymous with an unqualified opinion, an important distinction exists between an audit report and an audit opinion. An *audit report* represents the entire communication from the auditor about what he or she did and what he or she concluded. The audit opinion is only one part of the report—the conclusions reached. In certain circumstances, the auditor can modify the wording of the standard report but still express an unqualified opinion. Under other circumstances, the auditor will not be able to express an unqualified opinion; therefore, he or she will have to modify the wording of the standard report, including the opinion.

(i) Types of Audit Opinions.   As mentioned earlier, two conditions must be met before an auditor can issue an unqualified opinion. If one of these conditions is not met, the auditor will have to issue one of the following opinions.

- *Qualified opinion.* This type of opinion excludes a specific item from the auditor's opinion. Thus, the auditor expresses an opinion that the financial statements as a whole present fairly in conformity with GAAP, excluding the item or items specified in the report.
- *Adverse opinion.* This type of opinion states that the financial statements as a whole do *not* present fairly in conformity with GAAP. The auditor expresses this opinion when he or she believes that the financial statements taken as a whole are misleading.
- *Disclaimer of opinion.* This is not an opinion but rather a statement by the auditor that an opinion cannot be expressed. That is, the auditor has no opinion on the financial statements taken as a whole.

The specific circumstances encountered in the audit and its materiality generally determine the type of opinion necessary. To avoid obscuring the basic message, the audit report should give a brief explanation of the circumstance in a separate paragraph (preceding the opinion paragraph).

(ii) Modification of Both Wording and Opinion.   Three circumstances prevent the auditor from expressing an unqualified opinion:

1. *Scope limitation.* Circumstances may arise in the audit that prevent application of one or more audit procedures the auditor considers necessary.

2. *GAAP departure.* A departure from GAAP, including adequate disclosures, may have a material effect on the financial statements.

3. *Lack of independence.* If the auditor is not independent, he or she must disclaim an opinion on the financial statements. (If the entity is a nonpublic entity, a compilation report is required.)

The first two circumstances, when material, preclude the auditor from issuing an unqualified opinion and require the auditor to modify the report wording not only to express a different type of opinion but also to describe the circumstance causing the change in opinion. These circumstances are discussed below, along with their effect on the type of opinion to be expressed and the modification of report wording. Lack of independence is a condition that requires a specially worded disclaimer, and the cause of lack of independence should not be disclosed.

Scope Limitation.   Circumstances sometimes arise that make it impossible or impracticable to apply certain audit procedures the auditor believes necessary. Such restrictions on the scope of the audit may be imposed by the client, such as refusal to permit confirmation of accounts receivable or refusal to permit inquiry of outside legal counsel. *Scope limitations* may also arise because the client's records are not adequate to permit an audit of the financial statements or because of the timing of the auditor's work, such as when the auditor is appointed too late to observe physical inventory.

Because auditors cannot express an unqualified opinion unless they have been able to apply all of the audit procedures considered necessary, scope limitations require auditors either to express a qualified opinion or to disclaim an opinion. An adverse opinion is inappropriate for scope limitations because such an opinion relates to a deficiency in the financial statements rather than to a deficiency in the scope of the audit.

Once the auditor has decided that an unqualified opinion is not appropriate, a choice must be made between a qualified opinion and a disclaimer of opinion. This choice is based on the importance of the omitted procedures to the auditor's ability to form an opinion on the financial statements taken as a whole. If the potential effects of the scope limitation are not so material as to preclude the auditor from forming an opinion on the financial statements taken as a whole, the auditor should issue a qualified opinion. Exhibit 28.6 illustrates a qualified opinion for a scope limitation.

If the potential effects of the scope limitation relate to many financial statement items, they may be so material as to preclude the auditor from forming an opinion on the financial statements taken as a whole. Also, if the client imposes the scope limitation, the auditor usually does not express an opinion. Under these circumstances, a disclaimer of opinion is appropriate.

Departure from Generally Accepted Accounting Principles.   When a departure from GAAP has a material effect on the financial statements, the auditor cannot express an unqualified opinion. Departures from GAAP include using inappropriate accounting principles, such as valuing property, plant, and equipment in a manufacturing company at current value rather than historical cost; improperly applying accounting methods, such as incorrect application of the last-in first-out (LIFO) costing method to inventory; and inadequate disclosure, such as failing to disclose the pledging of material amounts of inventory as collateral for a loan.

SAS No. 69, "The Meaning of Present Fairly in Conformity with Generally Accepted Accounting Principles," as amended by SAS No. 91, "Federal GAAP Hierarchy" (AU 411), establishes the relative authority of the various sources of GAAP. The SAS creates three separate but parallel hierarchies: one for nongovernmental entities, one for state and local governmental entities, and one for federal governmental entities.

Each successive category in the hierarchy has a different level of authority. Categories A through D rank the authority of sources of established accounting principles. If an accounting treatment for a transaction or event is not specified by a category (a) pronouncement, the auditor should consider whether the accounting treatment is specified by a source in categories (b), (c), or (d). If a conflict exists between accounting principles from one or more sources in category (b), (c), or (d), the auditor should follow the treatment specified by the higher category. When an accounting treatment is not specified by categories (a), (b), (c), or (d), the auditor may consider the guidance provided by other accounting literature in category (e).

This GAAP hierarchy applies not only to financial statements that are audited, but also to those that are compiled or reviewed.

Opening Paragraph

We have audited the accompanying balance sheet of AUD Company as of December 31, 20X2, and the related statements of income, retained earnings, and cash flows for the year then ended. The financial statements are the responsibility of the Company's management. Our responsibility is to express an opinion on these financial statements based on our audit.

Opening paragraph is the same as in the standard report.

Scope Paragraph

Except as discussed in the following paragraph, we conducted our audits in accordance with auditing standards generally accepted in the United States. Those standards require that we plan and perform the audit to obtain reasonable assurance about whether the financial statements are free of material misstatement. An audit includes examining, on a test basis, evidence supporting the amounts and disclosures in the financial statements. An audit also includes assessing the accounting principles used and significant estimates made by management, as well as evaluating the overall financial statement presentation. We believe that our audit provides a reasonable basis for our opinion.

Wording of the scope paragraph is modified to include a restriction affecting the scope of the audit.

Explanatory Paragraph

We were unable to obtain audited financial statements supporting the Company's investment in a foreign affiliate stated at $2,500,000 at December 31, 20X2, or its equity in earnings of that affiliate of $300,000, which is included in net income for the year then ended as described in Note X to the financial statements; nor were we able to satisfy ourselves as to the carrying value of the investment in the foreign affiliate or the equity in its earnings by other auditing procedures.

Separate paragraph is added to explain the nature of the scope limitation.

Opinion Paragraph

In our opinion, *except for the effects of such adjustments, if any, as might have been determined to be necessary had we been able to examine evidence regarding the foreign affiliate investment and earnings,* the financial statements referred to above present fairly, in all material respects, the financial position of AUD Company as of December 31, 20X2, and the results of its operations and its cash flows for the year then ended in conformity with principles generally accepted in the United States.

Opinion is qualified "except for" any adjustments the auditor might have found necessary had he or she been able to examine the records supporting AUD Company's investment in the foreign affiliate.

Exhibit 28.6   Report with a qualified "except for" opinion due to a limitation on the scope of the engagement. Annotations appear to the right.

When the financial statements contain a material departure from GAAP, the auditor should express either a qualified or an adverse opinion if an audit in accordance with GAAP has been performed. A disclaimer of opinion is inappropriate if the auditor is in a position to express an opinion. The auditor cannot avoid disclosing a known departure from GAAP by denying an opinion on the financial statements.

The auditor's choice between a qualified or adverse opinion is based on the materiality of the departure from GAAP. Materiality is evaluated by considering (1) the dollar magnitude of the effects, (2) the significance of the item to the client, (3) the number of financial statement items affected, and (4) the effect of the departure on the financial statements taken as a whole.

If the departure from GAAP is not so material as to cause the financial statement taken as a whole to be misleading, the auditor will express a qualified opinion, as illustrated in Exhibit 28.6.

Opening Paragraph

We have audited the accompanying balance sheet of AUD Company as of December 31, 20X2, and the related statements of income, retained earnings, and cash flows for the year then ended. These financial statements are the responsibility of the Company's management. Our responsibility is to express an opinion on these financial statements based on our audit.

Opening paragraph is the same as in the standard report.

Scope Paragraph

We conducted our audits in accordance with auditing standards generally accepted in the United States. Those standards require that we plan and perform the audit to obtain reasonable assurance about whether the financial statements are free of material misstatement. An audit includes examining, on a test basis, evidence supporting the amounts and disclosures in the financial statements. An audit also includes assessing the accounting principles used and significant estimates made by management, as well as evaluating the overall financial statement presentation. We believe that our audit provides a reasonable basis for our opinion.

Scope paragraph is the same as in the standard report because no limitations have been placed on the scope of the audit.

Explanatory Paragraph

The Company has excluded, from property and debt in the accompanying balance sheets, certain lease obligations which in our opinion, should be capitalized in order to conform with generally accepted accounting principles. If these lease obligations were capitalized, property would be increased by $5,500,000, long-term debt by $7,200,000, and retained earnings would be decreased by $1,700,000 as of December 31, 20X2. Additionally, net income would be decreased by $500,000 and earnings per share would be decreased by $.50 for the year then ended.

Separate paragraph has been added to explain the departure from GAAP and its effect on the financial statements.

Opinion Paragraph

In our opinion, *except for the effects of not capitalizing certain lease obligations, as discussed in the preceding paragraph,* the financial statements referred to above present fairly, in all material respects, the financial position of AUD Company as of December 31, 20X2, and the results of its operations and its cash flows for the year then ended, in conformity with principles generally accepted in the United States.

Opinion paragraph is qualified "except for" due to the departure from GAAP regarding lease capitalization.

Exhibit 28.7   Report with a qualified "except for" opinion due to a departure from GAAP. Annotations appear to the right.

If the effects of the departure from GAAP are so material that they cause the financial statements as a whole to be misleading, the auditor will express an adverse opinion, as illustrated in Exhibit 28.7.

Consideration of Exhibits 28.8 and 28.9 helps clarify the effect of materiality on the auditor's decision to issue a qualified or adverse opinion. The qualified opinion in Exhibit 28.6 was issued because the client failed to capitalize leased assets and the related obligation that met the requirements for capitalization under GAAP. The effects of this departure caused both the property and the long-term debt accounts to be materially misstated. The misstatements in these accounts, however, when considered in relation to the financial statements as a whole, were not considered

Opening Paragraph

We have audited the accompanying balance sheet of AUD Company as of December 31, 20X2, and the related statements of income, retained earnings, and cash flows for the year then ended. These financial statements are the responsibility of the Company's management. Our responsibility is to express an opinion on these financial statements based on our audit.

Opening paragraph is the same as in the standard report.

Scope Paragraph

We conducted our audits in accordance with auditing standards generally accepted in the United States. Those standards require that we plan and perform the audit to obtain reasonable assurance about whether the financial statements are free of material misstatement. An audit includes examining, on a test basis, evidence supporting the amounts and disclosures in the financial statements. An audit also includes assessing the accounting principles used and significant estimates made by management, as well as evaluating the overall financial statement presentation. We believe that our audit provides a reasonable basis for our opinion.

Scope paragraph is the same as in the standard report because no limitations have been placed on the scope of the audit.

Explanatory Paragraph 1

As discussed in Note X to the financial statements, the Company carries its property, plant, and equipment accounts at appraisal values, and provides depreciation on the basis of such values. Further, the Company does not provide for income taxes with respect to differences between financial income and taxable income arising because of the use, for income tax purposes, of the installment method of reporting gross profit from certain types of sales. Principles generally accepted in the United States. Require that property, plant, and equipment be stated at an amount not in excess of cost, reduced by depreciation based on such amount, and that deferred income taxes be provided.

Separate paragraphs have been added to explain the departures from GAAP and their effects on the financial statements.

Explanatory Paragraph 2

Because of the departures from principles generally accepted in the United States, identified above, as of December 31, 20X2, inventories have been increased $450,000 by inclusion in manufacturing overhead of depreciation in excess of that based on cost; property, plant, and equipment, less accumulated depreciation, is carried at $12,500,000 in excess of an amount based on the cost to the Company; and deferred income taxes of $2,500,000 have not been recorded, resulting in an increase of $2,950,000 in retained earnings and in appraisal surplus of $12,500,000. For the year ended December 31, 20X2, cost of goods sold has been increased $350,000 because of the effects of the depreciation accounting referred to above, and deferred income taxes of $1,000,000 have not been provided, resulting in an increase in net income of $650,000.

Opinion Paragraph

In our opinion, *because of the effects of the matters discussed in the preceding paragraphs, the financial statements referred to above do not present fairly,* in conformity with principles generally accepted in the United States, the financial position of AUD Company as of December 31, 20X2, or the results of its operations or its cash flows for the year then ended.

Opinion expressed is adverse—the departures from GAAP are so material that the financial statements as a whole are misleading.

Exhibit 28.8   Report with an adverse opinion due to departures from GAAP. Annotations appear to the right.

We are not independent with respect to AUD Company, and the accompanying balance sheet as of December 31, 20X2, and the related statements of income, retained earnings, and cash flows for the year then ended were not audited by us and accordingly, we do not express an opinion on them.	Reason for the lack of independence and any procedures performed should not be described.

Exhibit 28.9   Disclaimer of opinion when not independent (public entity). Annotations appear to the right.

Opening Paragraph

We have audited the accompanying *balance sheets* of AUD Company as of December 31, 20X2 and 20X1 and the related statements of income, retained earnings, and cash flows for the *years* then ended. These financial statements are the responsibility of the Company's management. Our responsibility is to express an opinion on these financial statements based on our *audits.*	Opening paragraph is modified to refer to "balance sheets", to cover two (or more) years presented, and to refer to "audits" as plural.

Scope Paragraph

We conducted our audits in accordance with auditing standards generally accepted in the United States. Those standards require that we plan and perform the audit to obtain reasonable assurance about whether the financial statements are free of material misstatement. An audit includes examining, on a test basis, evidence supporting the amounts and disclosures in the financial statements. An audit also includes assessing the accounting principles used and significant estimates made by management, as well as evaluating the overall financial statement presentation. We believe that our *audits* provide a reasonable basis for our opinion.	Except for the reference to "audits," the scope paragraph is the same as in the standard report.

Opinion Paragraph

In our opinion, the financial statements referred to above present fairly, in all material respects, the financial position of AUD Company as of December 31, 20X2 and 20X1, and the results of its operations and its cash flows *for the years* then ended in conformity with principles generally accepted in the United States.	Opinion paragraph is modified to cover two (or more) years.

Exhibit 28.10   Report on comparative financial statements: Previous opinion reexpressed. Annotations appear to the right.

---

to be material enough to cause the statements taken as a whole to be misleading. Therefore, the auditor did not consider an adverse opinion appropriate.

The adverse opinion in Exhibit 28.9 was issued because property, plant, and equipment was stated at appraisal value rather than historical cost and because the client did not provide for deferred income taxes. These departures affected numerous accounts and, in the auditor's judgment, caused the financial statements taken as a whole to be misleading. Thus, the auditor considered an adverse opinion necessary.

Lack of Independence.   When an accountant is not independent, any procedure performed would not be in accordance with GAAS. Thus, SAS No. 26 (AU 504) requires the accountant who is not independent to issue a special disclaimer of opinion. Exhibit 28.10 illustrates the nonindependent disclaimer for financial statements of a public entity.

(iii) Modification of Wording Only.   Circumstances may require modification of the wording of the standard report but not modification of the auditor's opinion on the financial statements. There are five such situations:

1. Part of the audit was performed by another independent auditor.
2. A departure from a promulgated accounting principle is necessary to keep the financial statements from being misleading.
3. The auditor has substantial doubt about the entity's ability to continue as a going concern.
4. A material change in accounting principles causes the financial statements to be inconsistent with those of the prior period.
5. The auditor wishes to emphasize a matter regarding the financial statements but still express an unqualified opinion.

Part of Audit Performed by Another Independent Auditor.   More than one audit firm may participate in an audit, particularly when the entity being audited is widespread geographically. For example, an entity may have its major operations in the Southeast audited by a local CPA firm while having its western subsidiary audited by a different auditor on the West Coast.

When involved in an audit in which part of the audit has been performed by other auditors, the auditor must first decide whether he or she can serve as *principal auditor* and report on the financial statements even though he or she has not audited all of the subsidiaries, divisions, branches, or components that will be included in the financial statements. According to *AICPA Professional Standards* (AU 543), "Part of Audit Performed by Other Independent Auditors," in making this decision the auditor should consider:

- The materiality of the portion of the financial statements audited in comparison with the portion audited by other auditors
- Knowledge of the overall financial statements
- The importance of the components audited in relation to the entity as a whole

The auditor must decide first if it is appropriate to serve as the principal auditor and then, if so, whether to assume responsibility for the work of the other auditor. The principal auditor is never required to assume responsibility for the other auditor's work. However, if the principal auditor does assume responsibility, he or she must be satisfied as to (1) the independence of the other auditor, (2) the professional reputation of the other auditor, and (3) the other auditor's work.

If a principal auditor decides to accept responsibility for the other auditor's work, the standard report is issued without modification. In such a case, the report expresses an opinion on the financial statements as if the principal auditor had conducted the entire audit; no reference is made to the other auditors or their work in the audit report.

If the principal auditor decides not to assume responsibility for the other auditor's work, the responsibility is shared. Sharing responsibility in no way raises questions about the quality of the other auditor's work, nor does it imply less assurance about the reliability of the financial statements. It means simply that the principal auditor is not in a position to assume responsibility for the other auditor's work as if the principal auditor had done the work.

The indication of shared responsibility is communicated to audit report readers by a modification of the wording of the standard report. The opinion on the financial statements is not affected by the participation of more than one audit firm in the audit. Thus, only the report wording—not the opinion—is modified as follows:

- *Opening paragraph*. The subsidiaries that the principal auditor has not audited are identified, preferably by name, and the magnitude of the portion of the financial statements audited by the other auditor is disclosed by indicating dollar amounts or percentages of appropriate criteria, such as assets or revenues. In addition, the principal auditor specifies that part of the audit was made by other auditors. (The other auditor need not be, and usually is not, identified. The other auditor's permission must be obtained, and his or her report also must be presented, if he or she is identified in the principal auditor's report.)

- *Scope paragraph.* The principal auditor indicates that he or she believes that his or her audit *and the report of the other auditors* provide a reasonable basis for the opinion on the consolidated financial statements.

- *Opinion paragraph.* The principal auditor indicates that the opinion is based in part on the other auditor's audit. The opinion itself is not modified simply because of shared responsibility.

Departure from a Promulgated Principle. Rule 203 of the *AICPA Code of Professional Conduct* precludes the auditor from expressing an unqualified opinion on financial statements that contain a material departure from a promulgated accounting principle. A promulgated accounting principle is one issued by the bodies designated by the AICPA to establish accounting principles.

There is, however, an exception in Rule 203 that permits the auditor to issue an unqualified opinion, despite a departure from a promulgated accounting principle, when the auditor believes that, due to unusual circumstances, the departure is necessary to keep the financial statements from being misleading. When this rare situation exists, the auditor modifies the wording of the report by adding a separate explanatory paragraph, usually between the scope and opinion paragraphs. This paragraph describes the departure, the approximate effects, if practicable, and the reasons compliance with the pronouncement would result in misleading financial statements. The opening, scope, and opinion paragraphs, however, are identical to those in the standard report. The opinion on the financial statements is unqualified because the departure from the pronouncement is necessary to conform with GAAP.

Going Concern Matters. As discussed earlier, SAS No. 59, "The Auditor's Consideration of an Entity's Ability to Continue as a Going Concern" (AU 341), states that the auditor has a responsibility to evaluate whether there is substantial doubt about the entity's ability to continue as a going concern for a reasonable period of time.

An auditor might add an explanatory paragraph such as the one below to the report after the opinion paragraph because of an uncertainty about a going concern. The three paragraphs in the auditor's standard report are unchanged.

The accompanying financial statements have been prepared assuming that the Company will continue as a going concern. As discussed in Note X to the financial statements, the Company has suffered recurring losses from operations and has a net capital deficiency that raise substantial doubt about its ability to continue as a going concern. Management's plans in regard to these matters are also described in Note X. The financial statements do not include any adjustments that might result from the outcome of this uncertainty.

Lack of Consistency. The second standard of reporting (the consistency standard) is concerned with financial statement comparability among accounting periods. This standard requires the auditor to identify changes in accounting principles that have a material effect on the comparability of the financial statements between the current and prior periods.

Although a change in accounting principle is not the only accounting change that can affect financial statement comparability, it is the only accounting change that requires a report wording modification under the consistency standard. Thus, the factor that determines whether the auditor's report must be modified because of a lack of consistency is whether the accounting change involves a change in accounting principle (including a change in the method of applying a principle) that causes a material lack of comparability. Changes in accounting principle may take the following forms:

- Change from one GAAP to another GAAP, such as changing from the straight-line method to the declining balance method for plant assets

- Change in the reporting entity covered by the financial statements, such as when consolidated financial statements are presented in place of the statements of individual entities
- Correction of an error in an accounting principle by changing from a principle that is not generally accepted to one that is, such as changing from an appraisal value basis for property, plant, and equipment to a historical cost basis

When there is a change in an accounting principle that has a material effect on the financial statements, the auditor should not modify the unqualified opinion on the financial statements. That is, the change in accounting principle, if properly accounted for and disclosed in the financial statement, requires modification of the auditor's standard report, but not qualification or modification of the opinion paragraph.

When a lack of consistency exists, report wording generally is modified by adding an explanatory paragraph to the audit report following the opinion paragraph, identifying the nature of the change and referring the reader to the note in the financial statement that discusses the change in detail. The opening, scope, and opinion paragraphs are not changed. An example of an explanatory paragraph an auditor might add to the report because of a change in accounting follows:

As discussed in Note X to financial statements, the company changed its method of computing depreciation in 19X1.

Two other sets of circumstances relating to the consistency standard occur frequently enough in audit engagements to warrant brief discussion.

1. *First audit of a client.* When an auditor has not audited the financial statements of a client for the preceding year, scope limitations may prevent the auditor from forming an opinion on the consistency of the current year with the prior year. The auditor's report should be modified for a scope limitation and the explanatory separate paragraph, which should precede the opinion paragraph, should indicate that an opinion on consistency could not be formed. The opinion is qualified "except for" or disclaimed.

2. *Change in accounting principle not in conformity with GAAP.* A change in accounting principle must meet the three conditions specified in Accounting Principles Board (APB) Opinion No. 20, "Accounting Changes," to be in conformity with GAAP: (1) the new principle must be a GAAP, (2) the method of accounting for the change must conform with GAAP, and (3) the change must be justified by management as being preferable. If one or more of these conditions are not met, the auditor's report on the year of change should be modified because of a departure from GAAP. In this situation, the paragraph explaining the GAAP departure should precede the opinion paragraph, and the opinion is qualified "except for" or is adverse.

Emphasis of a Matter.   Under certain circumstances, the auditor may wish to emphasize a specific matter regarding the financial statements even though an unqualified opinion has been expressed. Examples of such matters include important events occurring after the balance sheet date or identification of the entity as a subsidiary of a larger enterprise.

These matters are not deficiencies in the financial statements. They represent matters, properly treated in the financial statements, that are, in the auditor's judgment, sufficiently important to be accentuated in the report. To emphasize matters in the report, the auditor includes a separate explanatory paragraph, usually between the scope and opinion paragraphs of the standard report.

(e) COMPARATIVE FINANCIAL STATEMENTS.   When financial statements of one or more prior periods are presented on a comparative basis with those of the current period, the fourth reporting standard requires a report on those comparative statements. The type of report, its content, and who issues it depend on whether the current auditor is a continuing auditor or is following a predecessor auditor. In addition, the report is affected by (1) whether the opinion(s) on the prior-period statement(s) is the same as or different from the opinion on the current-period statements, (2) whether the opinion on the prior-period statements should be revised in light of new circumstances, and (3) whether the comparative statements are audited or unaudited. SAS No. 58 provides guidance to the auditor on comparative financial statements.

(i) Continuing Auditor. A *continuing auditor* is one who has audited the financial statements of the current period and of one or more consecutive periods immediately preceding the current period. Basically, this means that the auditor must have audited the current period and at least the immediately preceding period to be a continuing auditor.

The reporting responsibilities for a continuing auditor differ from those for one who is not. A continuing auditor has the responsibility to update the report on prior-period financial statements that have been audited and that are presented for comparative purposes. *Updating* requires the auditor to consider whether, based on information obtained in the audit of the current-period statements, the auditor should reexpress the same opinion on prior statements shown on the comparative statements or express a revised opinion on them.

After considering the information obtained during the current audit, an auditor may conclude that the opinion originally expressed on the comparative statements is still appropriate. Exhibit 28.10 illustrates an updated auditor's report when the opinion expressed in the previous period is re-expressed in the updated report. This report is essentially the standard report for a single period expressed in plural form because it both expresses an opinion on the current-period statements and repeats the opinion originally expressed on the prior-period statements. Because the report is updated, the report date for the comparative statements is, in effect, changed to the report date for the current-period statements—the date of the completion of the audit of the most recent financial statements.

In Exhibit 28.11, the opinion expressed on the prior-period statements (20X1) was the same type of opinion expressed on the current-period statements: Both were unqualified opinions. In some audit engagements, the opinion expressed on the prior-period statements might not be the same type of opinion as that expressed on the current-period statements.

During the current engagement, the auditor might become aware of circumstances that would cause a change in the type of opinion previously expressed on the prior-period statements. For example, when departures from GAAP in prior-period statements are corrected in the current year by restating those statements, a qualified or adverse opinion on the prior-period statements is no longer appropriate.

The wording of an updated report that expresses a revised opinion on prior-period statements is modified by adding a separate explanatory paragraph, preceding the opinion paragraph, that discloses the following information:

- Date of the auditor's previous report
- Type of opinion previously expressed
- Circumstances that caused the revised opinion
- Statement that the updated opinion differs from the prior opinion

An example of this explanatory paragraph follows:

In our report dated March 1, 20X2, we expressed an opinion that the 20X1 financial statements did not fairly present financial position, results of operations, and cash flows in conformity with generally accepted accounting principles because of two departures from such principles: (1) the Company carried its property, plant, and equipment at appraisal values, and provided for depreciation on the basis of such values, and (2) the Company did not provide for deferred income taxes with respect to differences between income for financial reporting purposes and taxable income. As described in Note X, the Company has changed its method of accounting for these items and restated its 20X1 financial statements to conform with generally accepted accounting principles. Accordingly, our present opinion on the 20X1 financial statements, as presented herein, is different from that expressed in our previous report.

Board of Directors
Diamond Partnership

We have audited the accompanying statements of assets, liabilities, and capital—income tax basis of Diamond Partnership as of December 31, 20X2 and 20X1, and the related statements of revenue and expenses—income tax basis and of changes in partners' capital accounts—income tax basis for the years then ended. These financial statements are the responsibility of the Partnership's management. Our responsibility is to express an opinion on these financial statements based on our audits.

The first paragraph identifies the financial statements audited. The auditor also emphasizes that the financial statements are management's responsibility.

We conducted our audits in accordance with auditing standards generally accepted in the United States. Those standards require that we plan and perform the audit to obtain reasonable assurance about whether the financial statements are free of material misstatement. An audit includes examining, on a test basis, evidence supporting the amounts and disclosures in the financial statements. An audit also includes assessing the accounting principles used and significant estimates made by management, as well as evaluating the overall financial statement presentation. We believe that our audits provide a reasonable basis for our opinion.

The scope paragraph states that the audit was conducted in accordance with GAAS.

As described in Note X, these financial statements were prepared on the accounting basis used for income tax purposes, which is a comprehensive basis of accounting other than generally accepted accounting principles.

The third paragraph refers to the note in the financial statements that states the basis of presentation upon which the statements were prepared.

In our opinion, the financial statements referred to above present fairly, in all material respects, the assets, liabilities, and capital of Diamond Partnership as of December 31, 20X2 and 20X1, and its revenue and expenses and changes in partners' capital accounts for the years then ended, on the basis of accounting described in Note X.

The opinion paragraph expresses the auditor's opinion on whether the financial statements are presented fairly, in all material respects, in conformity with the basis described.

Exhibit 28.11   Financial statements prepared on the entity's income tax basis. Annotations appear to the right.

(ii) Predecessor Auditor.   When the current auditor is not a continuing auditor and the client presents comparative statements, two situations can exist: (1) the prior-period statements were reported on by a predecessor auditor, or (2) the prior-period statements have not been reported on by any auditor.

If one or more prior periods included in the comparative statements have been audited by a predecessor auditor, either of the following reporting approaches may be taken:

- The current (successor) auditor may refer to the predecessor auditor's report in the report on the current-period financial statements.
- The predecessor auditor may reissue his or her report on the prior-period statements.

Most frequently, the successor auditor refers to the predecessor auditor's report. In that circumstance, the successor auditor adds a sentence such as the following to the opening paragraph of the current-period report: "The financial statements of AUD Company as of December 31, 20X1, were audited by other auditors whose report dated March 1, 20X2, expressed an unqualified opinion on those statements."

If a predecessor auditor is asked to reissue the report and agrees to accept that request, the predecessor auditor must perform procedures to determine if the original report is still appropriate: If the predecessor auditor decides that the opinion on the prior-period statements is still appropriate, the previous report should be reissued. The date of the reissued report should be the same as the date of the original report to avoid any implication that any records, transactions, or events after that date have been examined.

If the predecessor auditor believes transactions or events have occurred that may affect the previous opinion on the financial statements, he or she should perform whatever procedures are believed necessary to determine whether the opinion needs to be revised. If the predecessor auditor concludes that a revised report should be issued, the same reporting guidelines that apply to a continuing auditor's updated report also apply to the predecessor. However, the predecessor's updated report is normally dual dated rather than redated to the report date on the current financial statements.

(iii) Prior Period Unaudited.   When the financial statements of the prior period have not been audited, the report on the current period should contain a separate paragraph that includes:

- A statement of the service performed in the prior period
- The date of the report on that service
- A description of any material modifications noted in that report
- A statement that the service was less in scope than an audit and does not provide a reasonable basis for the expression of an opinion on the financial statements taken as a whole

When the financial statements are those of a public entity, the separate paragraph should include a disclaimer of opinion as discussed in SAS No. 26, "Association with Financial Statements" or a description of a review of the financial statements under SAS No. 71, "Interim Financial Information" (AU 722) [discussed in Subsection 28.4(d)].

When the financial statements are those of a nonpublic entity and the financial statements were compiled or reviewed, the separate paragraph should contain a description of the compilation or review. These engagements are discussed later in this chapter.

28.4 OTHER REPORTS

Subsections 28.3(b) to 28.3(e) are concerned with audit reports issued by the auditor after an audit of financial statements prepared in accordance with GAAP. However, auditing and attestation standards also cover other situations, in which the auditor issues other kinds of reports. These other types of reports include:

- Special reports
- Reports on internal control over financial reporting
- Involvement with other information
- Review of interim financial information
- Reports on financial forecasts and projections
- Reports on financial statements prepared for use in other countries
- Reports on the application of accounting principles
- Reports on compliance with laws and regulations

(a) SPECIAL REPORTS.   SAS No. 62, "Special Reports" (AU 623), identifies the following five types of special reports:

1. Reports on financial statements prepared on comprehensive bases of accounting other than GAAP

2. Reports on specified elements, accounts, or items of a financial statement

3. Reports on compliance with aspects of contractual agreements or regulatory requirements related to audited financial statements

4. Reports on financial presentations to comply with contractual agreements or regulatory provisions

5. Reports on financial information presented in prescribed forms or schedules that require a prescribed form of auditor's report

(i) Other Comprehensive Bases of Accounting.   Auditors frequently examine financial statements that are prepared on a basis of accounting that differs from GAAP. SAS No. 62 recognizes this and provides reporting guidance to the auditor when financial statements are prepared on "other comprehensive bases of accounting" (OCBOA). The auditor's report should provide reasonable assurance that the financial statements conform with OCBOA.

According to SAS No. 62, a measurement basis must meet one of four criteria to be classified as an OCBOA. The measurement must be:

1. A basis of accounting that the reporting entity uses to comply with the reporting provisions of a government regulatory agency to whose jurisdiction the entity is subject. For example, insurance companies use bases of accounting pursuant to the rules of state insurance commissions.

2. A basis of accounting that the reporting entity uses or expects to use to file its federal income tax return for the period covered by the financial statements.

3. The cash receipts and disbursements basis of accounting, and modifications of the cash basis having substantial support, such as recording depreciation on fixed assets or accruing income taxes.

4. A definite set of criteria having substantial support that is applied to all material items appearing in the financial statements, such as the price level basis of accounting.

Exhibit 28.12 indicates a sample auditor's report on financial statements prepared on the entity's income tax basis.

(ii) Opinions on Specified Elements, Accounts, or Items of a Financial Statement.   Sometimes auditors are requested to issue a report on certain aspects of the financial statements. For example,

---

We have audited, in accordance with auditing standards generally accepted in the United States, the balance sheets of Lex Company as of December 31, 20X2 and 20X1, and the related statements of income, retained earnings, and cash flows for the years then ended, and have issued our report thereon dated February 16, 20X3.

> The first paragraph identifies the financial statements audited and states that they were audited in accordance with GAAS.

In connection with our audits, nothing came to our attention that caused us to believe that the Company failed to comply with the terms, covenants, provisions, or conditions of Sections 10 to 15, inclusive, of the Indenture dated July 21, 20X0, with XYZ Bank insofar as they relate to accounting matters. It should be noted, however, that our audits were not directed primarily toward obtaining knowledge of such noncompliance.

> The middle paragraph provides negative assurance about contract violations. The auditor notes that the audit was not directed toward obtaining such knowledge.

This report is intended solely for the information and use of the board of directors and management of Lex Company and XYZ Bank and should not be used for any other purpose.

> The last paragraph indicates that distribution of the report is limited to the parties to the contract.

Exhibit 28.12   Report on compliance with contractual provisions. Annotations appear to the right.

We have audited the accompanying schedule of gross sales (as defined in the lease agreement dated March 4, 20X0, between XYZ Company, as lessor, and Stony Stores Corporation, as lessee) of Stony Stores Corporation at its East Street store, Brewster, New York, for the year ended December 31, 20X2. This schedule is the responsibility of the Stony Stores Corp. management. Our responsibility is to express an opinion on this schedule based on our audit.	The first paragraph identifies the sales schedule, the lease agreement, and the parties to the agreement. The auditor also indicates that the schedule is management's responsibility.
We conducted our audits in accordance with auditing standards generally accepted in the United States. Those standards require that we plan and perform the audit to obtain reasonable assurance about whether the schedule of gross sales is free of material misstatement. An audit includes examining, on a test basis, evidence supporting the amounts and disclosures in the schedule of gross sales. An audit also includes assessing the accounting principles used and significant estimates made by management, as well as evaluating the overall schedule presentation. We believe that our audit provides a reasonable basis for our opinion.	The scope paragraph states that the audit was conducted in accordance with GAAS.
In our opinion, the schedule of gross sales referred to above presents fairly, in all material respects, the gross sales of Stony Stores Corporation at its East Street store, Brewster, New York, for the year ended December 31, 20X2, as defined in the lease agreement referred to in the first paragraph.	The opinion paragraph expresses the auditor's opinion on whether the schedule presents fairly, in all material respects, the gross sales as defined in the lease agreement.
This report is intended solely for the information and use of the board of directors and management of Stony Stores Corp. and XYZ Company and should not be used for any other purpose.	The final paragraph indicates that distribution of the report is limited to the parties identified.

Exhibit 28.13   Report relating to amount of sales for the purpose of computing rental charges. Annotations appear to the right.

a shopping mall may charge rent to its tenants based on a percentage of the tenants' sales. In this situation, the mall may require a report by the auditor that the sales reported by the tenants are fairly presented in conformity with GAAP. Other examples include reports on royalties and profit participations.

The audit of specified elements, accounts, or items may be undertaken as a separate engagement or in conjunction with an audit of financial statements. In such an engagement, the auditor expresses an opinion on each of the specified elements, accounts, or items encompassed by the report; therefore, the measurement of materiality must be related to each individual element, account, or item audited rather than to the aggregate thereof or to the financial statements taken as a whole. Consequently, the audit is usually more extensive than if the same information were being considered in conjunction with an audit of the financial statements taken as a whole.

An example of a report related to the amount of sales for the purpose of computing rental charges is shown in Exhibit 28.13.

(iii) Applying Agreed-Upon Procedures.   An accountant may undertake an engagement to apply agreed-upon procedures to specified elements, accounts, or items of a financial statement or to nonfinancial statement subject matter, such as circulation statistics for advertising media and labor contract negotiation data. Statements on Standards for Attestation Engagements (SSAE) No. 10, "Attestation Standards: Revision and Recodification," Chapter 2, "Agreed-Upon Procedures" (AT 201), applies to these engagements. The general, fieldwork, and reporting standards in SSAE No. 10, Chapter 1, "Attest Engagements" (AT 101), also should be followed by the practitioner in agreed-upon procedures engagements.

An agreed-upon procedures engagement is one in which the practitioner is engaged to issue a report of findings to specified parties based on specific procedures performed on financial or nonfinancial information (subject matter). The practitioner and specified parties agree on the procedures and the specified parties accept responsibility for the sufficiency of the procedures in meeting their needs.

In an agreed-upon procedures engagement, the practitioner does not perform an examination and thus does not express an opinion on the subject matter. Instead, the practitioner's report is expressed in the form of procedures and findings. AT 201 prohibits the practitioner from expressing negative assurance on the fair presentation of the subject matter.

The practitioner's report in an engagement performed under AT 201 should contain the following 17 elements:

1. A title that includes the word "independent"
2. Identification of the specified parties
3. Identification of the subject matter (or written assertion related thereto) and the character of the engagement
4. Identification of the responsible party
5. A statement that the subject matter is the responsibility of the responsible party
6. A statement that the procedures performed were those agreed to by the specified parties identified in the report
7. A statement that the agreed-upon procedures engagement was conducted in accordance with attestation standards established by the AICPA
8. A statement that the sufficiency of the procedures is solely the responsibility of the specified parties and a disclaimer of practitioner's responsibility for the sufficiency of those procedures
9. A list of the procedures performed (or reference thereto) and related findings
10. Where applicable, a description of any agreed-upon materiality limits
11. A statement that the practitioner was not engaged to and did not conduct an examination (or audit) of the subject matter, the objective of which would be the expression of an opinion, a disclaimer of opinion on the subject matter, and a statement that if the practitioner had performed additional procedures, other matters might have come to his or her attention that would have been reported
12. A statement of restrictions on the use of the report because it is intended to be used solely by the specified parties
13. Where applicable, reservations or restrictions concerning procedures or findings
14. For an agreed-upon procedures engagement on prospective financial information, all items included in AT 301.55
15. Where applicable, a description of the nature of the assistance provided by a specialist
16. The manual or printed signature of the practitioner's firm
17. The date of the report

(iv) Compliance Reports Related to Audited Financial Statements. Companies may be required by contractual agreements or by regulatory agencies to furnish *compliance reports* by independent auditors. For example, loan agreements usually impose on borrowers a variety of covenants involving matters such as payments into sinking funds, payments of interest, maintenance of current ratio, restriction of dividends payments, and use of the proceeds of sales of property.

Under SAS No. 62, the auditor is allowed to give a negative assurance report on compliance with contractual agreements provided that:

- He or she has audited the financial statements to which the contractual agreement or regulatory provision relates.
- He or she has not issued an adverse opinion or disclaimer of opinion on such financial statements.
- He or she only reports on matters that audit procedures were applied to during the audit of the financial statements.

A report on compliance with contractual provisions is shown in Exhibit 28.11.

(v) Financial Presentations to Comply with Contractual Agreements or Regulatory Provisions. Auditors are sometimes requested to report on special-purpose financial statements prepared to comply with a contractual agreement or regulatory provisions. Generally, these types of reports are intended solely for the use of the parties to the agreement, regulatory bodies, or other specified parties. According to SAS No. 62, "Special Reports" (AU 623), these types of presentations fall into two categories:

1. Those that do not constitute complete presentation of the entity's assets, liabilities, revenues, and expenses (an incomplete presentation) but are otherwise prepared in conformity with GAAP or an OCBOA
2. Those prepared on a basis of accounting prescribed in an agreement that result in presentations not in conformity with GAAP or an OCBOA

An auditor may be requested to report on a financial presentation to meet the special purposes of regulatory agencies or parties to an agreement. For example, the SEC may require a schedule of gross income and certain expenses of an entity's real estate operation in which income and expenses are measured in conformity with GAAP, but expenses are defined to exclude certain items such as interest, depreciation, and income taxes. Also, a buy-sell agreement may specify a schedule of gross assets and liabilities of the entity measured in conformity with GAAP but limited to the assets to be sold and liabilities to be transferred pursuant to the agreement. Such financial presentations are regarded as financial statements even though certain items may be excluded. The presentations differ from complete financial statements only to the extent necessary to meet the special purposes for which they are prepared. An example of a special report on such financial presentations is shown in Exhibit 28.14.

An auditor also might be asked to report on a financial presentation prepared to comply with the provisions of a contract or regulatory agreement that results in a presentation not in conformity with GAAP or OCBOA. For example, a loan agreement might call for financial statements prepared in conformity with GAAP except for certain assets, such as inventories and property, plant, and equipment, for which the valuation basis is specified in the agreement. These financial statements are not prepared in conformity with GAAP or OCBOA since they do not meet the requirements of being a measurement basis "having substantial support." When reporting on a non-GAAP, non-OCBOA presentation, the auditor would modify the end of the third paragraph in Exhibit 28.14 to read "... and are not intended to be a presentation in conformity with GAAP."

(vi) Prescribed Forms.   Auditors are sometimes requested to complete prescribed forms or schedules designed by bodies with which they are to be filed. These forms sometimes also prescribe the wording of the auditor's report. For example, state licensing boards for construction contractors often require the auditor both to complete a prescribed form that presents financial information and to sign a prescribed auditor's report.

Sometimes, these prescribed report forms cannot be signed by the auditor because the report does not conform to the standards of reporting. For example, a report may include a statement that is not consistent with the auditor's responsibility. Sometimes the report can be made acceptable by inserting appropriate additional wording. In other situations, however, the auditor may have to completely reword the form or attach a separate report. In no circumstances should the auditor sign a report that violates professional reporting standards.

We have audited the accompanying statement of net assets sold of Bender Company as of June 8, 20X1. This statement of net assets sold is the responsibility of Bender Company's management. Our responsibility is to express an opinion on the statement of net assets sold based on our audit.	The first paragraph identifies the audited statement of net assets sold. The auditor emphasizes that the statement is management's responsibility.
We conducted our audits in accordance with auditing standards generally accepted in the United States. Those standards require that we plan and perform the audit to obtain reasonable assurance about whether the statement of net assets sold is free of material misstatement. An audit includes examining, on a test basis, evidence supporting the amounts and disclosures in the statements. An audit also includes assessing the accounting principles used and significant estimates made by management, as well as evaluating the overall presentation of the statement of net assets sold. We believe that our audit provides a reasonable basis for our opinion.	The second paragraph states that the audit was conducted in accordance with GAAS.
The accompanying statement was prepared to present the net assets of Bender Company sold to XYZ Corporation pursuant to the purchase agreement described in Note X, and is not intended to be a complete presentation of Bender Company's assets and liabilities.	The third paragraph identifies the note in the statement that describes the basis of presentation as defined in the purchase agreement.
In our opinion, the accompanying statement of net assets sold presents fairly, in all material respects, the net assets sold of Bender Company as of June 8, 20X1, pursuant to the purchase agreement referred to in Note X, in conformity with principles generally accepted in the United States.	The opinion paragraph states whether the statement is fairly presented in all material respects, pursuant to the agreement in conformity with GAAP.
This report is intended solely for the information and use of the board of directors and management of Bender Company and XYZ Corporation and should not be used for any other purpose.	This paragraph indicates that distribution of the report is limited to the parties to the contract.

Exhibit 28.14   Report on a statement of assets sold and liabilities transferred to comply with a contractual agreement. Annotations appear to the right.

(b) REPORTS ON AN ENTITY'S INTERNAL CONTROL OVER FINANCIAL REPORTING.
SSAE No. 10, "Attestation Standards: Revision and Recodification," Chapter 5, "Reporting on an Entity's Internal Control Over Financial Reporting" (AT 501), provides guidance to practitioners who are engaged to examine and report on the effectiveness of an entity's internal control over financial reporting as of a point in time or on an assertion thereon. The Statement does not change the auditor's responsibility for considering the entity's internal control in an audit of financial statements.

A practitioner may accept an engagement under SSAE No. 10 (AT 501) when management presents its written assertion about the effectiveness of internal control over financial reporting. Such assertion may be in a separate report that accompanies the accountant's report or in a representation letter to the accountant. When no written assertion is expressed, the accountant cannot provide any assurance about the entity's internal control. An accountant may accept the engagement when management is sufficiently knowledgeable about the entity's internal control and is able to evaluate internal control using reasonable criteria established by a recognized body. Sufficient evidential matter must exist to support management's assertion.

In performing an engagement under SSAE No. 10 (AT 501), the practitioner should obtain an understanding of internal control. He or she should also evaluate the design effectiveness of the internal control policies and procedures and test and evaluate the operating effectiveness of such policies and procedures.

The practitioner may examine and report directly on an entity's effectiveness of internal control over financial reporting, or he or she may examine and report on the responsible party's written assertion thereon. The choice of report depends on whether management makes an assertion about internal control effectiveness in a separate report or only in a representation letter to the practitioner. When management's assertion is made only in the representation letter, the practitioner will use direct reporting. When management makes a separate assertion, the practitioner may report on the assertion. The choice of report format does not affect the acceptance, planning, or performance of the examination, only the report wording in the introductory and opinion paragraphs.

(c) INVOLVEMENT WITH OTHER INFORMATION.   Various SASs address information that is presented in addition to the basic financial statements. These include SAS No. 8, "Other Information in Documents Containing Audited Financial Statements" (AU 550); SAS No. 52, "Omnibus SAS-1987 (Required Supplementary Information)" (AU 558); and SAS No. 29, "Reporting on Information Accompanying the Basic Financial Statements in Auditor-Submitted Documents."

The auditor has different reporting responsibilities for information appearing in an auditor-submitted document than for information appearing in a client-prepared document.

(i) Client-Prepared Documents.   Client-prepared documents are the responsibility of the client. In such documents, the reader would generally expect the auditor's report to cover only the information identified in the report. Other information in the document usually can be clearly identified as furnished by management. For this reason, SAS No. 8 provides that the auditor's responsibility for other information in a client-prepared document containing audited financial statements does not extend beyond the financial information identified in the audit report.

An auditor is not required to perform any audit procedures to substantiate the other information in a client-prepared document. However, SAS No. 8 does require the auditor to read the other information and consider the manner in which it is presented to assess whether it is materially inconsistent with the financial statements. For example, in reading a president's letter in the annual report, the auditor should assess whether the president's comments about operating income are consistent with the income statement. If the auditor does not identify any material inconsistencies, no comment whatsoever is made about the other information. However, if the other information is not consistent with the financial statements, and the financial statements are correct, the auditor would consider taking one of the following steps:

- Requesting the client to revise the information to eliminate the inconsistency
- Revising the audit report to include an explanatory paragraph describing the inconsistency
- Withholding the audit report in the document
- Withdrawing from the engagement

While reading the other information to determine whether there is a material inconsistency, the auditor may become aware of information that he or she believes is a material misstatement of fact even though it is not inconsistent with the financial statements. For example, the auditor may note that the president incorrectly states in the annual report that the client is the largest company in its industry. Even though this statement does not contradict the financial statements, the auditor may be aware that the statement is incorrect. SAS No. 8 notes that the auditor may not have the expertise to evaluate the statement, that standards may not exist to assess the statement, and that valid differences of judgment or opinion may exist. However, if the auditor has a valid basis of concern, he or she should discuss the matter with the client, consider notifying the client in writing, and consider consulting legal counsel.

(ii) Auditor-Submitted Documents.   Auditor-submitted documents are bound in the CPA firm's report cover and are sometimes printed on paper bearing the auditor's logo or watermark. The appearance of these documents often leads readers to assume that the auditor is taking some degree of responsibility for all the information in the document. As a result, SAS No. 29 (AU 551) requires the auditor to report on all the information in an auditor-submitted document.

The auditor's report on additional information may be presented separately in the document or may be included as a separate paragraph of the auditor's report on the financial statements. Regardless of the method selected, the report must state that the audit was made for the purpose of forming an opinion on the financial statements taken as a whole, identify the additional information, and indicate that it is presented for purposes of additional analysis and is not a required part of the basic financial statements.

The auditor must either express an opinion on whether the additional information is fairly stated in all material respects to the financial statements as a whole or disclaim an opinion. Expression of an opinion is appropriate only when the information has been subjected to the auditing procedures applied to the financial statements. An auditor has no obligation to apply any auditing procedures to the additional information, and if the additional information in an auditor-submitted document has not been subjected to the auditing procedures applied to the basic financial statements, the auditor should disclaim an opinion on that information.

(iii) Supplementary Information Required by the FASB or GASB.   The FASB and the GASB require certain entities to present information supplementary to the financial statements. Currently, these requirements include FASB standards regarding information about oil and gas reserves and a GASB standard on pension disclosures. Required supplementary information is not necessary for the fair presentation of financial statements in conformity with GAAP. However, the information is an essential part of the broader concept of financial reporting in general. For this reason, SAS No. 52 requires an auditor to apply certain limited procedures to this information. These procedures are principally inquiries of management regarding methods of measuring and presenting the supplementary information.

The auditor's reporting responsibility on required supplementary information again depends on whether the information is contained in an auditor-submitted or a client-prepared document. When an auditor-submitted document contains required supplementary information, the auditor should disclaim an opinion on that information unless the auditor has been specifically engaged to audit and express an opinion on the information. The disclaimer is required even though limited procedures must be applied to the information. The following is an illustration of a disclaimer:

> The supplementary oil and gas reserve information is not a required part of the basic financial statements of Horn Company for 20X1, but is supplementary information required by the Financial Accounting Standards Board. We have applied certain limited procedures that consisted principally of inquiries of management regarding the methods of measurement and presentation (or disclosure) of the supplementary information. However, we did not audit the information and we express no opinion on it.

In a client-prepared document, the exception reporting principle applies. SAS No. 52 requires the auditor to report on the required supplementary information only if:

- The required supplementary information is not presented.
- The auditor concludes that the data are not prepared or presented in accordance with FASB or GASB requirements.
- The auditor is unable to perform the limited procedures.
- The auditor has unresolved doubts about the required supplementary information.

When one of the above circumstances causes the auditor to report on the supplementary information in a client-prepared document, the auditor's opinion on the financial statements would not be affected. This is because the required supplementary information is not considered by the FASB or GASB to be part of GAAP and, therefore, does not affect the financial statements.

(d) PROSPECTIVE FINANCIAL STATEMENTS. CPAs are sometimes involved with financial information that is future oriented. For example, a client may want a forecast of its earnings for the next year. Or a client may be considering whether to make an investment and therefore may want a projection of future cash flows. Such information that is future oriented is termed *prospective financial information*.

SSAE No. 10, "Attestation Standards: Revision and Recodification," Chapter 3, "Financial Forecasts and Projections" (AT 301), provides guidance for practitioner services on prospective financial statements.

The statement establishes standards for the three types of services that can be provided on prospective financial statements expected to be used by third parties: compilation, application of agreed-upon procedures, and examination. The statement also prohibits the accountant from providing services on prospective financial statements for third-party use if the statements do not disclose the underlying assumptions or if projections (as defined below) appropriate only for limited use are to be distributed to *passive users*—that is, persons who are not negotiating directly with the user.

In addition, in 1993 the Auditing Standards Division updated the *Guide for Prospective Financial Statements*, which establishes preparation and presentation guidelines (analogous to GAAP) for prospective financial statements.

(i) Financial Forecasts and Financial Projections. The statement (AT 301) defines *financial forecasts* as "prospective financial statements that present, to the best of the responsible party's knowledge and belief, an entity's expected financial position, results of operations, and changes in financial position." Financial forecasts are based on the responsible party's assumptions, reflecting conditions it expects to exist and the course of action it expects to take.

Alternatively, the statement defines *financial projections* as "prospective financial statements that present, to the best of the responsible party's knowledge and belief, given one or more hypothetical assumptions, an entity's expected financial position, results of operations, and changes in financial position." A financial projection is sometimes prepared to present one or more hypothetical courses of action for evaluation, as in response to a question such as "What would happen if. . .?" A financial projection is based on the responsible party's assumptions reflecting conditions it expects would exist and the course of action it expects would be taken, given one or more hypothetical assumptions.

In a *forecast*, all assumptions are expected to occur. In a *projection*, one or more (hypothetical) assumptions are not necessarily expected to occur (although they may if management chooses a certain course of action). For example, a company may project the construction of a new building without having made the decision to construct the building. All the other assumptions would be expected to occur if the hypothetical assumption occurs.

Prospective financial statements (forecasts or projections) may be presented as complete statements of financial position, results of operations, and cash flows, or may be presented in a summarized or condensed form. Certain items are required for a presentation to qualify as a prospective financial statement, including revenues, gross profit or cost of sales, unusual or infrequent items, income taxes, discontinued operations or extraordinary items, income from continuing operations, net income, earnings per share, and significant changes in financial position. Presentations that omit one or more of these minimum items are called *partial presentations*.

(ii) Levels of Service. As noted previously, the statement provides three levels of service on prospective financial statements expected to be used by third parties:

1. *Compilation engagement*. A compilation engagement involves assembling prospective financial statements based on the responsible party's assumptions and considering whether the presentation appears to be presented in conformity with AICPA presentation guidelines and whether it is or is not obviously inappropriate.

2. *Agreed-upon procedures engagement.* An agreed-upon procedures engagement is generally an engagement that involves (1) applying to prospective financial statements procedures that have been agreed to or established by specified users of the data (e.g., a specific bank) and (2) issuing a report that enumerates the procedures performed, states the accountant's findings, and restricts report distribution to specified parties.

3. *Examination.* Examination is generally an audit that involves (1) evaluating the preparation, the support underlying the assumptions, and the presentation of the prospective financial statements for conformity with AICPA presentation guidelines, and (2) issuing an examination report. The examination report expresses a positive opinion on whether the assumptions provide a reasonable basis for the prospective financial statements. An example of a standard report on forecasted financial statements is shown in Exhibit 28.15.

The logic underlying the examination procedures for prospective financial statements is basically the same as that underlying the audit of historical financial statements. However, the literature does contain some distinctive reporting requirements for examinations. If a prospective presentation fails to disclose one or more significant assumptions or if one or more significant assumptions do not have a reasonable basis, an adverse opinion is required. Similarly, if a scope limitation exists—that is, the inability to apply a necessary procedure because of circumstances or client restrictions—a disclaimer is required.

(e) REPORTING ON FINANCIAL STATEMENTS PREPARED FOR USE IN OTHER COUNTRIES. Most U.S. companies prepare financial statements for use in the United States in conformity with GAAP accepted in the United States. However, some U.S. companies have valid reasons for presenting their financial statements in conformity with accounting principles generally accepted in another country (non-U.S. GAAP). For example, a U.S. company may be a subsidiary of a foreign company or may wish to raise capital abroad.

SAS No. 51, "Reporting on Financial Statements Prepared for Use in Other Countries" (AU 534), provides guidance to a U.S. auditor who expresses an opinion on a U.S. entity's financial statements prepared in conformity with non-U.S. GAAP. The auditor should be familiar with the

---

We have examined the accompanying forecasted balance sheet, statements of income, retained earnings, and cash flows of ABC Company as of December 31, 20XX, and for the year then ending. ABC Company's management is responsible for the forecast. Our responsibility is to express an opinion on the forecast based on our examination.

Our examination was conducted in accordance with attestation standards established by the AICPA and, accordingly, included such procedures as we considered necessary to evaluate both the assumptions used by management and the preparation and presentation of the forecast. We believe that our examination provides a reasonable basis for our opinion.

In our opinion, the accompanying forecast is presented in conformity with guidelines for presentation of a forecast established by the AICPA, and the underlying assumptions provide a reasonable basis for management's forecast. However, there will usually be differences between the forecasted and actual results, because events and circumstances frequently do not occur as expected, and those differences may be material. We have no responsibility to update this report for events and circumstances occurring after the date of this report.

The first paragraph identifies the forecasted statements examined and explains that they were examined in accordance with guidelines established by the AICPA.

The second paragraph expresses an opinion as to whether the forecast is presented in conformity with guidelines set up by the AICPA. It also notes that there are usually differences between actual and forecasted results, and that there is no responsibility to update the report.

Exhibit 28.15   Accountant's standard report on an examination of a forecast. Annotations appear to the right.

non-U.S. GAAP used in order to report on the financial statements and should consider consulting with accountants having expertise in such principles. The auditor should also understand and obtain management's written representations about the purpose and use of non-U.S. GAAP financial statements. The auditor should comply with U.S. GAAS but might need to modify certain procedures for assertions embodied in the non-U.S. GAAP financial statements that differ from those in U.S. GAAP financial statements. (e.g., some countries require inflation adjustments in financial statements, in which case the U.S. auditor would need to perform procedures to test the inflation restatement)

According to SAS No. 51, if the non-U.S. GAAP financial statements are prepared for use only outside the United States, the auditor may report using either: (1) a U.S.-style report modified to report on the accounting principles of another country or, if appropriate, (2) the report form of another country. When the U.S. auditor uses the report form of another country, he or she should determine that the report would be used by non-U.S. auditors in similar circumstances and that the attestations contained in the report are appropriate. Non-U.S. GAAP financial statements are ordinarily not useful to U.S. users. Accordingly, if a company's financial statements are needed for use in both another country and the United States, the auditor may report on two sets of financial statements, one prepared using non-U.S. GAAP and the other prepared using U.S. GAAP.

(f) REPORTS ON THE APPLICATION OF ACCOUNTING PRINCIPLES. Accountants are sometimes engaged by entities, for whom they are not the continuing auditor (that is, the entity is audited by another CPA), to provide consultations regarding a proposed or completed transaction. This type of consultation is often referred to as *opinion shopping* because some infer that the entity will shop around until it finds an accountant who will agree with its position and then hire that accountant as the auditor. There are public perceptions that opinion shopping is not in the public interest because it may compromise the accountant's objectivity.

As a result of these concerns, the ASB issued SAS No. 50, "Reports on the Application of Accounting Principles" (AU 625). SAS No. 50 applies to accountants who provide reports, written or oral, on the accounting treatments of proposed or completed specific transactions to persons or entities other than continuing clients.

Before providing advice, the accountant should consider the identity of the requestor, the circumstances and purpose of the request, and the use of the resulting report. SAS No. 50 also requires the reporting accountant to exercise due professional care, have adequate technical training and proficiency, properly plan and supervise the engagement, and accumulate sufficient information to provide a reasonable basis for the professional judgment described in the report.

In forming a judgment, the accountant should:

- Understand the form and substance of the transaction
- Review applicable accounting principles
- Consult with other professionals or experts, as appropriate
- Perform research and consider precedents and analogies, as appropriate

Finally, and most important, the reporting accountant is required to consult with the entity's continuing auditor to ascertain all the relevant facts. The continuing auditor can often provide information not otherwise available to the reporting accountant, such as the form and substance of the transaction, how management has applied accounting principles to similar transactions, and whether the method of accounting recommended by the continuing auditor is disputed by management.

(g) REPORTS ON COMPLIANCE WITH LAWS AND REGULATIONS. Statement on Standards for Attestation Engagements No. 10, "Attestation Standards: Revision and Recodification," Chapter 6 (AT 601), provides guidance for practitioners who are engaged to report on an entity's compliance with laws, regulations, rules, contracts, or grants ("specified requirements") or on the effectiveness of internal control over such specified requirements. The standard primarily affects reports on compliance required by the 1991 FDIC Improvement Act.

SSAE No. 10 is concerned with management's written assertion concerning (a) compliance with specified laws, regulations, rules, contracts, or grants, or (b) the effectiveness of internal control over such compliance matters.

For either type of assertion, compliance, or internal control effectiveness, a practitioner may be engaged to perform an agreed-upon procedures engagement or an examination (although examinations of either type of assertion are frequently less desirable). An examination of the effectiveness of internal control over compliance is discouraged because specific suitable criteria for such controls often are not well developed. If such an engagement is accepted, the practitioner should perform the engagement in accordance with AT 101, with supplemental guidance from AT 501. A review engagement is specifically prohibited.

"Special Reports," SAS No. 62 (AU 623), is still the relevant literature if, in conjunction with the audit, the practitioner is engaged to report on compliance with a contractual agreement (such as loan covenants contained in a debt agreement). SSAE No. 3 applies only if the practitioner is engaged to report separately on (or apply agreed-upon procedures to) management's assertion concerning compliance.

Under SSAE No. 10 (AT 601), a practitioner may examine and report directly on an entity's compliance or on the responsible party's written assertion regarding compliance. The choice of report depends on whether management makes an assertion about internal control effectiveness in a separate report or only in a representation letter to the practitioner. When management's assertion is made only in the representation letter, the practitioner will use direct reporting. When management makes a separate assertion, the practitioner may report on the assertion. The choice of report format does not affect the acceptance, planning, or performance of the examination, only the report wording in the introductory and opinion paragraphs.

As discussed in Section 28.1(c), whenever an accountant submits unaudited financial statements of a nonpublic entity to his or her client or others, the accountant must issue either a compilation or review report. Standards for these services are established in SSARS No. 1, "Compilation and Review of Financial Statements," as amended by SSARS No. 8, "Amendment to Statement on Standards for Accounting and Review Services No. 1, Compilation and Review of Financial Statements" (AR 100). These standards apply to financial statements prepared in conformity with GAAP or another comprehensive basis of accounting.

AR 100.04 defines submission of financial statements as "presenting to a client or third parties financial statements that the accountant has prepared either manually or through the use of computer software." This definition creates two conditions that must be satisfied before the accountant is deemed to have submitted financial statements: (1) prepare the statements and (2) present them. The term *prepared* is not defined in AT 100, thus the accountant must use judgment in determining whether he or she has prepared financial statements. When the accountant decides that he or she has prepared the financial statements and then presents those statements to the client or third parties, the accountant must either compile or review the statements.

AT 100 establishes standards for performing and reporting on a compilation engagement. The performance standards require the accountant to:

- Establish an understanding with the entity regarding the services to be performed.
- Have or obtain knowledge of the accounting principles and practices of the entity's industry sufficient to compile the financial statements.
- Have knowledge of the entity's business transactions, form of its accounting records, qualifications of accounting personnel, and the basis of accounting used to prepare the financial statements sufficient to compile the financial statements.
- Consider whether it will be necessary to perform other accounting services to compile the financial statements.
- Obtain additional or revised information when he or she becomes aware that information supplied by the entity is incorrect, incomplete, or otherwise unsatisfactory.

- Read the compiled financial statements and consider whether they appear to be appropriate in form and free from obvious material errors.

SSARS No. 1, as amended by SAARS No. 8, establishes two types of accountant communications for compilation engagements. One is the standard compilation report shown in Section 28.5(a). This report is required if the compiled financial statements are expected to be used by third parties. The other type of communication is a written engagement letter submitted to management. This is an option to the standard compilation report and may be used only if the financial statements are not expected to be used by third parties. Since this is an option, the accountant is not precluded from issuing the standard compilation report even if third party use is not expected.

SSARS No. 1, as amended by SSARS No. 8, defines third parties as "all parties except for members of management who are knowledgeable about the nature of the procedures applied and the basis of accounting and assumptions used in the preparation of the financial statements." Thus, to qualify for the engagement letter option, the financial statements should not be distributed to members of management who are not familiar with their limitations.

When compiled financial statements are not expected to be used by third parties and the accountant elects the engagement letter communication option, SSARS No. 1, as amended by SSARS No. 8, requires the letter to contain a description of or statement about each of the following:

- The nature and limitations of the services to be performed.
- A compilation is limited to presenting in the form of financial statements information that is the representation of management.
- The financial statements will not be audited or reviewed.
- No opinion or any other form of assurance on the financial statements will be provided.
- Management has knowledge about the nature of the Procedures applied and the basis of accounting and assumptions used in the preparation of the financial statements.
- Acknowledgment of management's representation and agreement that the financial statements are not to be used by third parties.
- The engagement cannot be relied on to disclose errors, fraud, or illegal acts.

The documentation of the understanding (engagement letter) should also address the following additional matters if applicable:

- Material departures from GAAP or OCBOA may exist and the effects of those departures, if any, on the financial statements may not be disclosed.
- Substantially all disclosures (and statement of cash flows, if applicable) required by GAAP or OCBOA may be omitted.
- Lack of independence.
- Refer to supplementary information.

28.5 COMPILATION AND REVIEW SERVICES

(a) STANDARD COMPILATION REPORT.   Compiled financial statements are accompanied by a report that indicates that a compilation has been performed and that such a service is limited to presenting, in financial statement format, information that is the representation of management or owners. The report also states that the financial statements have not been audited or reviewed, thus no opinion or any other form of assurance is expressed on them. No reference is made to any other procedures performed before or during the compilation engagement. The following form of report is appropriate when reporting on a compilation.

We have compiled the accompanying balance sheets of ABC Co. as of December 31, 20x2 and 20x1, and the related statements of income, retained earnings, and cash flows in accordance with

Statements on Standards for Accounting and Review Services issued by the American Institute of Certified Public Accountants.

A compilation is limited to presenting in the form of financial statements information that is the representation of management (owners). We have not audited or reviewed the accompanying financial statements and, accordingly, do not express an opinion or any other form of assurance on them.

The report should be dated as of the date the compilation service is completed. Each page of the compiled financial statements should include a reference such as "See accountant's compilation report." On the basic financial statements that notation may be stated somewhat as follows: "See accompanying notes to the unaudited financial statements and accountant's compilation report."

(b) STANDARD REVIEW REPORT.   Reviewed financial statements are accompanied by a report that indicates that a review was performed in accordance with AICPA standards. The report describes a review engagement, states that the information in the financial statements is the representation of management (or owners), and disclaims an opinion on the financial statements taken as a whole. Nevertheless, SSARS No. 1 (AR 100) provides the report also should state that: "The accountant is not aware of any material modifications that should be made to the financial statements in order for them to be in conformity with GAAP, other than those modifications, if any, indicated in his report." No reference is made to any other procedures performed before or during the review engagement.

The following form of report is appropriate when reporting on reviewed financial statements. Such a report cannot be issued when the independent accountant is unable to complete inquiry and analytical procedures considered necessary to express the limited assurances described above or when the client does not provide the accountant with a representation letter. Obtaining a client representation letter is a required procedure when performing a review engagement under SSARS.

We have reviewed the accompanying balance sheets of ABC Co. as of December 31, 20X2 and 20X1, and the related statements of income, retained earnings, and cash flows for the years then ended, in accordance with Statements on Standards for Accounting and Review Services issued by the American Institute of Certified Public Accountants. All information included in these financial statements is the representation of the management (Owners) of ABC Co.

A review consists principally of inquiries of company personnel and analytical procedures applied to financial data. It is substantially less in scope than an audit in accordance with generally accepted auditing standards, the objective of which is the expression of an opinion regarding the financial statements taken as a whole. Accordingly, we do not express such an opinion.

Based on our reviews, we are not aware of any material modifications that should be made to the accompanying financial statements in order for them to be in conformity with generally accepted accounting principles.

The report is dated as of the date inquiry and analytical procedures are completed. Each page of the reviewed financial statements should include a reference such as "See accountant's review report." On the basic financial statements, that notation may be stated somewhat as follows: "See accompanying notes to the unaudited financial statements and accountant's review report."

(c) GENERALLY ACCEPTED ACCOUNTING PRINCIPLES DEPARTURES.   If the independent accountant becomes aware of a departure from GAAP (or, if applicable, a comprehensive basis of accounting other than GAAP) that appears to be material to the financial statements being compiled or reviewed, and the financial statements are not revised, the standard compilation or review report should be modified by including a separate paragraph that discloses the following:

• The nature of the departure.

- The effects of the departure on the financial statements if they have been determined by management or are known as a *result of the accountant's procedures*; or the fact that the effects of the departure have not been determined by management. The accountant is not required to determine the effects of a departure.

An example of a review report modified to disclose a departure from GAAP follows:

(Standard First Paragraph)

(Standard Second Paragraph)

(Modified Third Paragraph)

Based on our review(s), with the exception of the matter(s) described in the following paragraph(s), we are not aware of any material modifications that should be made to the accompanying financial statements in order for them to be in conformity with generally accepted accounting principles.

(Explanatory Paragraph)

As disclosed in Note X to the financial statements, generally accepted accounting principles require that inventory cost consist of material, labor, and overhead. Management has informed us that the inventory of finished goods and work in process is stated in the accompanying financial statements at material and labor cost only, and that the effects of this departure from generally accepted accounting principles on the financial position, results of operations, and cash flows have not been determined.

The independent accountant should consider whether modification of the standard review or compilation report is adequate to disclose departures from GAAP. If modification of the standard report does not appear adequate to indicate the deficiencies in the financial statements taken as a whole (e.g., numerous exceptions, or an exception of the type that would lead to an adverse opinion in an audit), the accountant should consider whether to withdraw from the engagement and provide no further services on the financial statements.

(i) Omission of a Statement of Cash Flows.   Presentation of a statement of cash flows is required when both a balance sheet and a statement of income and retained earnings are presented. If the statement of cash flows has been omitted, reference to the statement of cash flows should be eliminated from the first paragraph of the accountant's report and a reservation as to presentation should be set forth in a separate paragraph. The reporting for the omission of a statement of cash flows is different if substantially all disclosures are omitted from compiled financial statements. An example of such reporting is provided below.

(ii) Omission of Disclosure.   The independent accountant may be requested to compile financial statements that omit substantially all disclosures required by GAAP (e.g., notes and the disclosures appearing in the body of the financial statements). Independent accountants may compile and report on such financial statements if the omission of substantially all disclosures is not, to their knowledge, undertaken with the intention of misleading users of the compiled statements. For example, it may be misleading for a company to present financial statements without disclosure in the face of a major new uncertainty that has not previously been disclosed in the company's financial statements. The special reporting requirements permitted by SSARS No. 1 apply to the omission of substantially all disclosures. They do not apply to the omission of selected disclosures, in which case a departure from GAAP exists. Further, they do not apply to review engagements. Omission of a required disclosure from reviewed financial statements would result in a GAAP departure.

When compiled financial statements omit substantially all disclosures, the standard report should be modified to indicate that omission. For example, the following paragraph may be added to the standard compilation report when substantially all disclosures have been omitted and the client also omits a statement of cash flows.

Management has elected to omit substantially all the disclosures and the statement of cash flows required by generally accepted accounting principles. If the omitted disclosures and the statement of cash flows were included in the financial statements, they might influence the user's conclusions about the company's financial position, results of operations, and cash flows. Accordingly, these financial statements are not designed for those who are not informed about such matters.

If financial statements compiled in conformity with a comprehensive basis of accounting other than GAAP fail to disclose the basis of accounting used, the basis should be disclosed in the independent accountant's report. If a company wishes to include disclosures concerning only a few matters in the form of notes to the financial statements, such disclosures should be appropriately labeled: for example, "Selected information—Substantially all disclosures required by GAAP are not included."

(iii) Uncertainties and Inconsistent Application of Generally Accepted Accounting Principles. SSARS No. 1 (AR 100) states:

Normally, neither an uncertainty, about an entity's ability to continue as a concern, nor an inconsistency in the application of accounting principles would cause the accountant to modify the report provided the financial statements appropriately disclose such matters. Nothing in this statement, however, is intended to preclude an accountant from emphasizing in a separate paragraph of his report a matter regarding the financial statements.

(iv) Lack of Independence.   The lack of independence does not preclude an accountant from issuing a compilation report. In such circumstances, the following should be included as the last paragraph of the report: "We are not independent with respect to ABC Co." The reasons for lack of independence should not be given. On the other hand, the accountant cannot issue a review report if independence is lacking.

(v) Change in Engagement from Audit to Review or Compilation.   An independent accountant originally engaged to perform an audit of the financial statements of a *nonpublic* entity may be requested to change the engagement to a review or compilation of the financial statements. Before agreeing to change the engagement, consideration should be given to the surrounding circumstances, including these three:

1. The reason given by the client for changing the engagement, particularly the implications of a restriction on the scope of the audit.
2. The additional audit effort required to complete the audit.
3. The estimated cost to complete the audit. (If auditing procedures are substantially complete or the cost to complete them is relatively insignificant, a change may not be appropriate.)

The reason for the change may result from a change in circumstances (e.g., a decision by the company's banker to accept a review report rather than an audit report). When such situations are present, the request for a change in engagement ordinarily would be considered reasonable. The same considerations are applicable when an accountant receives a request to change the engagement from a review to a compilation.

28.6 SOURCES AND SUGGESTED REFERENCES

AICPA, *AICPA Professional Standards: Vol. 1, U.S. Auditing Standards, Attestation Standards;* and *Vol. 2. Accounting and Review Services, Code of Professional Conduct, Bylaws, International Accounting and Auditing, Consulting Services, Quality Control, Quality Review, Tax Practice, and Personal Financial Planning.* American Institute of Certified Public Accountants, New York, 2005. A loose-leaf service that includes the currently effective pronouncements on professional standards issued by the American Institute of Certified Public Accountants as well as the International Accounting Standards of the International Accounting Standards Committee and the International Auditing Guidelines of the International Auditing Practices Committee.

_____, *AICPA Audit and Accounting Manual*. American Institute of Certified Public Accountants, New York, 2005, paperbound annual update. A loose-leaf service of nonauthoritative audit tools and illustrations prepared by the AICPA's Technical Information Division, geared primarily to the needs of local practitioners.

_____, *AICPA Technical Practice Aids*. American Institute of Certified Public Accountants, New York, 2002, paperbound annual update. A loose-leaf-service that includes selected Technical Information Service Inquiries and Replies, Statements of Position of the Auditing and Accounting Standards Divisions of the AICPA, Practice Bulletins by the AcSEC, and a list of issues papers of the Accounting Standards Division of the AICPA.

_____, *Public Accountants, How to Choose and Use a CPA*. American Institute of Certified Public Accountants, New York. Booklet answering such questions as: Who needs a CPA? How do you find a CPA? What qualifications should you look for? What do CPAs charge? How can you get the most value from a CPA's services?

_____, *Understanding Audits and the Auditor's Report: A Guide for Financial Statement Users*. American Institute of Certified Public Accountants, New York. Forty-page booklet containing a description of the nature of an audit, illustrative examples of the auditor's standard report, and discussion of the responsibilities of management, the auditor, and users.

_____, *What Does a CPA Do? A Guide to CPA Services*. American Institute of Certified Public Accountants, New York. Fifteen-page booklet explaining the various roles of the CPA—as auditor; as small business, management, and tax adviser; and as personal financial planner. The CPA's role in business and industry, education, government, and nonprofit organizations is also explained.

Ramos, Michael, *Wiley's Practitioner's Guide to GAAS 2006: Covering All SASs, SSAEs, SSARSs, and Interpretations*. John Wiley & Sons, New York, 2006.

Whittington, R. and Pany, K., *Principles of Auditing and Other Assurance Services*. McGraw-Hill/Irwin, New York, 2005.

INDEX